W9-DEI-275

Developmental Psychology

CHILDHOOD AND ADOLESCENCE

Fifth Edition

I dedicate this book to the memory of Dewboise Herbert "Herb" Shaffer (1921–1996), a humble electrician and a terrific father, whose insatiable curiosity and immense respect for scientists persuaded me to become one.

David R. Shaffer *is a professor of psychology, chair of the Social Psychology program, and past chair of the Life-Span Developmental Psychology program at the University of Georgia, where he has taught courses in human development to graduate and undergraduate students for the past 25 years. His many research articles have concerned such topics as altruism, attitudes and persuasion, moral development, sex roles and social behavior, self-disclosure, and social psychology and the law. He has also served as associate editor for the* Journal of Personality and Social Psychology, Personality and Social Psychology Bulletin, *and* Journal of Personality. *In 1990 Dr. Shaffer received the Josiah Meigs award for Excellence in Instruction, the University of Georgia's highest instructional honor.*

Developmental Psychology

CHILDHOOD AND ADOLESCENCE

Fifth Edition

David R. Shaffer

UNIVERSITY OF GEORGIA

Brooks/Cole Publishing Company

I(T)P® *An International Thomson Publishing Company*

Pacific Grove • Albany • Belmont • Bonn • Boston • Cincinnati • Detroit • Johannesburg • London • Madrid • Melbourne • Mexico City • New York • Paris • Singapore • Tokyo • Toronto • Washington

Sponsoring Editor: *Jim Brace-Thompson*
Project Development Editor: *Jim Strandberg*
Marketing Team: *Lauren Harp, Jean Thompson*
Editorial Assistant: *Bryon Granmo*
Production Coordination: *Keith Faivre*
Production Service: *Katy Spining, GTS Graphics, Inc.*
Manuscript Editor: *Sheila Pulver*
Permissions Editor: *Fiorella Ljunggren*
Interior Design: *Gary Head*
Interior Illustration: *Cyndie C. H. Wooley and GTS Graphics, Inc.*
Cartoons: *Ryan Cooper and Wayne Clark*
Cover Design: *Vernon T. Boes*
Cover Photo: *Daniel Pangbourne / FPG International*
Photo Research: *Judy Mason*
Typesetting: *GTS Graphics, Inc.*
Cover Printing: *Phoenix Color Corporation*
Printing and Binding: *World Color Versailles*
(Credits continue on page C-1)

For more information, contact:

BROOKS/COLE PUBLISHING COMPANY
511 Forest Lodge Road
Pacific Grove, CA 93950
USA

International Thomson Publishing Europe
Berkshire House 168-173
High Holborn
London WC1V 7AA
England

Thomson Nelson Australia
102 Dodds Street
South Melbourne, 3205
Victoria, Australia

Nelson Canada
1120 Birchmount Road
Scarborough, Ontario
Canada, M1K 5G4

International Thomson Editores
Seneca 53
Col. Polanco
11560 México, D. F., México

International Thomson Publishing GmbH
Königswinterer Strasse 418
53227 Bonn
Germany

International Thomson Publishing Asia
60 Albert Street
#15-01 Albert Complex
Singapore 189969

International Thompson Publishing Japan
Hirakawacho Kyowa Building, 3F
2-2-1 Hirakawacho
Chiyoda-ku, Tokyo 102
Japan

Printed in the United States of America

10 9 8 7 6 5 4 3 2

Library of Congress Cataloging-in-Publication Data

Shaffer, David R. (David Reed), [date]
Developmental psychology : childhood and adolescence / David R. Shaffer. — 5th ed.
p. cm.
Includes bibliographical references and indexes.
ISBN 0-534-35592-7
1. Child psychology. 2. Adolescent psychology. I. Title.
BF721.S4688 1999
155.4-dc21 98-23000
CIP

Brief Contents

Contents

Part I Theory and Research in the Developmental Sciences

Part III Language, Learning, and Cognitive Development

Chapter 6 Early Cognitive Foundations: Sensation, Perception, and Learning 189

Chapter 7 Cognitive Development: Piaget's Theory and Vygotsky's Sociocultural Viewpoint 228

By David Shaffer and David Bjorklund

Part IV Social and Personality Development

Chapter 11 Emotional Development and the Establishment of Intimate Relationships 391

Chapter 12 Development of the Self and Social Cognition 433

Part V The Ecology of Development

Chapter 15 The Family 557

Chapter 16 Extrafamilial Influences: Television, Computers, Schools, and Peers 597

Preface

My purpose in writing this book has been to produce a current and comprehensive overview of child and adolescent development that reflects the best theories, research, and practical advice that developmentalists have to offer. Throughout my many years of teaching, I had longed for a substantive developmental text that is also interesting, accurate, up to date, and written in clear, concise language that an introductory student could easily understand. At this level, a good text should talk "to" rather than "at" its readers, anticipating their interests, questions, and concerns and treating them as active participants in the learning process. In the field of human development, a good text should also stress the processes that underlie developmental change, so that students come away from the course with a firm understanding of the causes and complexities of development. Last but not least, a good text is a relevant text—one that shows how the theory and research that students are asked to digest can be applied to a number of real-life settings.

The present volume represents my attempt to accomplish all of these objectives. I have tried to write a book that is both rigorous and applied, one that challenges students to think about the fascinating process of human development, to share in the excitement of our young and dynamic discipline, and to acquire a knowledge of developmental principles that will serve them well in their roles as parents, teachers, nurses, day-care workers, pediatricians, psychologists, or in any other capacity by which they may one day influence the lives of developing persons.

PHILOSOPHY

Certain philosophical views underlie any systematic treatment of a field as broad as human development. My philosophy can be summarized as follows:

I Believe in Theoretical Eclecticism. There are many theories that have contributed to what we know about developing persons, and this theoretical diversity is a strength rather than a weakness. Although some theories may do a better job than others of explaining particular aspects of development, we will see—time and time again—*that different theories emphasize different aspects of development* and that knowledge of many theories is necessary to explain the course and complexities of human development. So this book will not attempt to convince its readers that any one theoretical viewpoint is "best." The psychoanalytic, behavioristic, cognitive-developmental, ecological, sociocultural, information-processing, ethological, and behavioral genetic viewpoints (as well as several less-encompassing theories that address selected aspects of development) are all treated with respect.

The Best Information about Human Development Comes from Systematic Research. To teach this course effectively, I believe that one must convince students of the value of theory and systematic research. Although there are many ways to achieve these objectives, I have chosen to contrast the modern developmental sciences with their "prescientific" origins and then to discuss and illustrate the many methodological approaches that researchers use to test their theories and answer important questions about developing children and adolescents. I've taken care to explain why there is no one "best method" for studying developing persons, and I've repeatedly stressed that our most reliable findings are those that can be replicated using a variety of methods.

I Favor a Strong "Process" Orientation. A major complaint with many developmental texts (including some best sellers) is that they describe human development without adequately explaining why it occurs. In recent years, investigators have become increasingly concerned about identifying and understanding developmental processes—the biological and environmental factors that cause us to change—and this book clearly reflects this emphasis. My own process orientation is based on the belief that students are more likely to remember what develops and when if they know and understand the reasons *why* these developments take place.

I Favor a Strong "Contextual" Orientation. One of the more important lessons that developmentalists have learned is that children and adolescents live in historical eras and sociocultural contexts that affect each and every aspect of their development. I have chosen to highlight these contextual influences in three major ways. First, *cross-cultural comparisons* are discussed throughout the text. Not only do students enjoy learning about the development of people in other cultures and ethnically diverse subcultures, but cross-cultural research also helps them to see how human beings can be so much alike and, at the same time, so different from one another. In addition, the impacts of such immediate contextual influences as our families, neighborhoods, schools, and peer groups are considered (1) throughout the first 14 chapters as we discuss each aspect of human development, and (2) again in the final two chapters, as important topics in their own right.

Human Development Is a Holistic Process. Although individual researchers may concentrate on particular topics such as physical development, cognitive development, or the development of moral reasoning, development is not piecemeal but *holistic:* human beings are at once physical, cognitive, social, and emotional creatures, and each of these components of "self" depends, in part, on the changes that are taking place in other areas of development. This holistic perspective is a central theme in the modern developmental sciences—and one that is emphasized throughout the text.

A Developmental Text Should Be a Resource Book for Students—One That Reflects Current Knowledge. I have chosen to cite more than 1000 new studies and reviews (most of which were published since the fourth edition) to ensure that my coverage (and any outside readings that students may undertake) will represent our current understanding of a topic or topics. However, I have avoided the tendency, common in textbooks, to ignore older research simply because it is older. In fact, many of the "classics" of our discipline are prominently displayed throughout the text to illustrate important breakthroughs and to show how our knowledge about developing persons gradually builds on these earlier findings and insights.

ORGANIZATION

There are two traditional ways of presenting human development. In the *chronological,* or "ages and stages," approach, the coverage begins at conception and proceeds through the life span, using ages or chronological periods as the organizing principle. By contrast, the *topical* approach is organized around areas of development and follows each from its origins to its mature forms. Each of these presentations has its advantages and disadvantages. On the one hand, a chronological focus highlights the holistic character of development but may obscure the links between early and later events within each developmental domain. On the other hand, a topical approach highlights developmental sequences and processes, but at the risk of failing to convey that development is a holistic enterprise.

I've chosen to organize this book topically to focus intently on developmental processes and to provide the student with an uninterrupted view of the sequences of change that children and adolescents experience within each developmental domain. In my opinion, this topical approach best allows the reader to appreciate the flow of development—the systematic, and often truly dramatic, transformations that take place over the course of childhood and adolescence, as well as the developmental continuities that make each individual a reflection of his or her past self. At the same time, I consider it essential to paint a holistic portrait of the developing person. To accomplish this aim, I've stressed the fundamental interplay among biological, cognitive, social, and cultural influences in my coverage of *each and every aspect of development.* So even though this text is topically organized, students will not lose sight of the whole person and the holistic character of human development.

CONTENT

I made an effort to retain in this edition the major qualities that students and professors have said that they like. One such quality is a division of the book into five parts and 16 chapters.

- **Part I: Theory and Research in the Developmental Sciences.** This first part presents an orientation to the discipline and the tools of the trade, including a thorough discussion and illustration of *research methodologies* in **Chapter 1,** and a succinct review of the *major theories of human development* in **Chapter 2.** These chapters illustrate why research methods and theories are so important for understanding human development. The coverage also analyzes the contributions and the limitations of each research method and each major theory.
- **Part II: Foundations of Development.** Chapters 3–5 address foundations of development heavily influenced by biological factors. **Chapter 3** focuses on *hereditary contributions* to human development and illustrates how genes and environments interact to influence most human characteristics. **Chapter 4** focuses on *prenatal development* and on the many prenatal and perinatal environmental factors that influence a newborn's health and readiness for adapting to the world outside the womb. **Chapter 5** is devoted to *physical growth,* including the *development of the brain* and *motor skills.* Connections between physical growth and psychological development (particularly in adolescence) are emphasized.
- **Part III: Language, Learning, and Cognitive Development.** The five chapters of Part III address the many theories and voluminous research pertaining to the development of language, learning capabilities, and intellectual development. **Chapter 6** begins exploring the growth of *perceptual* and *learning* capabilities: two crucial cognitive foundations for many other aspects of development. **Chapter 7** is devoted to two major viewpoints of intellectual growth: Piaget's *cognitive-developmental theory* and Vygotsky's *sociocultural theory.* These two theories are covered in detail, for each is important to understanding the social, emotional, and language developments that are covered in later chapters. **Chapter 8** explores perhaps the dominant model of intellect and development today—the

information-processing viewpoint. Highlighted in this chapter are the many contributions information-processing researchers have made in assisting children to master academic lessons. **Chapter 9** focuses on individual differences in intellectual performance. Here we review the *intelligence testing* movement, the many factors that influence children's IQ scores, and the merits of compensatory interventions designed to improve intellectual performance. The chapter then concludes with a discussion of *creative abilities* and their development. Finally, **Chapter 10** explores the fascinating topic of *language development,* addressing such intriguing issues as: Can apes acquire language?; Do children acquire language easier than adults?; Is sign language a true language?; and Does bilingualism promote or inhibit linguistic proficiency and cognitive development?

- **Part IV: Social and Personality Development.** The next four chapters focus on crucial aspects of social and personality development. **Chapter 11** examines the process of *emotional development,* the developmental significance of individual differences in *temperament,* and the growth and implications for later development of the *emotional attachments* that children form with their close companions. **Chapter 12,** on the *self,* traces the development of the *self-concept* and children's emerging sense of *self-esteem,* the establishment of an *interpersonal identity* (including a sense of ethnic identity) in adolescence, and the growth of *social cognition* and *interpersonal understanding.* **Chapter 13** focuses on *sex differences* and on how biological factors, social forces, and intellectual growth interact to steer males and females toward different gender roles. The chapter also examines the utility (or lack thereof) of traditional gender roles and discusses ways in which we might be more successful at *combating unfounded gender stereotypes.* **Chapter 14** examines three interrelated aspects of social development that people often consider when making judgments about one's character: *aggression, altruism, and moral development.*
- **Part V: The Ecology of Development.** The final section of the text concentrates on the settings or contexts in which people develop, or the "ecology" of development. **Chapter 15** is devoted to *family influences,* focusing on the functions that families serve, patterns of child rearing that foster adaptive or maladaptive outcomes, the impacts of siblings on developing children, and the effects of family diversities and family transitions on child and adolescent development. **Chapter 16** concludes the text with an in-depth examination of four extrafamilial influences on developing children and adolescents: *television, computers, schools, and the society of one's peers.*

NEW TO THIS EDITION

This fifth edition contains many important changes in the treatment of theoretical, empirical, and practical issues, reinforcing themes that are at the forefront of research today. At the most general level, these changes include: (1) increased attention throughout to cultural/subcultural/historical influences, with a special emphasis on the impacts of economic deprivation on child development; (2) an even stronger focus on the intricate interplays among biological and environmental forces in shaping development; (3) clearer illustrations that developmental outcomes depend very crucially on the "goodness of fit" between persons and their socializing environments; (4) greater emphasis on the importance of peer relations (and on the interplays between families and peers as socializing agents); and (5) expanded coverage of adolescent development. The empirical literature has been extensively updated, with the result that nearly 70 percent of the references date from 1990 through early 1998, when this book went into production.

Each chapter has been thoroughly revised and updated to add the new topics that reflect current trends in our discipline. To make way for these additions, I have condensed or otherwise reorganized other topics or, in some cases, have eliminated coverage that the newer evidence has rendered obsolete. Here is a sampling of these changes:

- Incorporation of psychophysiological methods, ethnography, and updated examples of most other research strategies (Chapter 1).
- Expanded coverage of information-processing theory and current versions of Bronfenbrenner's ecological systems theory, with research citations illustrating the impact of each ecological system (Chapter 2).
- New advances in genetics such as genetic imprinting and germline gene therapy (Chapter 3).
- Controversies surrounding the use of new genetic technologies, and the issue of whether "good parenting" is all that important in light of our genetic dispositions, are raised and discussed (Chapter 3).
- New evidence on the impacts of maternal nutrition, maternal stress, and sexually transmitted diseases on prenatal development (Chapter 4).
- New findings on the prevention of spina bifida and sudden infant death syndrome (SIDS) (Chapter 4).
- Expanded coverage of brain development, including synaptic pruning, the changes that occur in adolescence, and their implications for intellectual development (Chapter 5).
- New data on adolescent sexuality and an applied section on preventing teenage pregnancies through methods other than traditional sex education (Chapter 5).

Many changes in chapters 6–9 resulted from my collaboration with renowned cognitive-developmentalist David F. Bjorklund, who coauthored chapters 7 and 8. Some of the major changes are the following:

- Chapter 6 has been reorganized to focus on two early cognitive foundations that influence so many aspects of later development: perceptual growth and early learning capabilities.
- Addition of expert opinion on the many contributions Piaget made to our field (Chapter 7).
- Expanded coverage of Vygotsky's sociocultural theory, Rogoff's theory of guided participation, and explicit comparisons of the Vygotsky/Rogoff perspective with Piaget's theory (Chapter 7).
- New theories addressing the role of inhibitory processes on cognitive development (cognitive clutter model) and the growth of processing strategies (Sieglar's strategy choice model) (Chapter 8).
- New sections on fuzzy-trace theory, the growth of event and autobiographical memory, and the implications of these lines of research for children's credibility as eyewitnesses in court proceedings (Chapter 8).
- New section on applications of information-processing theory, focusing heavily on mathematical reasoning and on cultural variations in the development of arithmetic strategies (Chapter 8).
- Inclusion of Steele's exciting work on stereotype threat as a contributor to racial differences in intellectual performance (Chapter 9).
- Thoroughly revised section of the development of creative potential which emphasizes Sternberg and Lubart's new Investment (or confluence) Theory of creativity (Chapter 9).
- Coverage of language development is extensively revised to focus more on contemporary interactionist theories of language development (Chapter 10).
- Expanded coverage of cultural variations in emotional development and on the goodness of fit of temperamental attributes to socializing environments (Chapter 11).

- New research to illustrate that parenting attributes other than sensitivity contribute to attachment security (Chapter 11).
- Updated coverage of the maternal employment/day care controversy which highlights the important conclusions of the recent NICHD Early Child Care Research Network report (Chapter 11).
- Updated research illustrating that children's theory of mind is subject to cultural influences (Chapter 12).
- New research on the factors that contribute most heavily to adolescent self-esteem (Chapter 12).
- Addition of research on the origins, development, and strategies for reducing racial discrimination/prejudice (Chapter 12).
- Updated and expanded coverage of ethnic identity formation (Chapter 12).
- New evidence on the long-term impacts of gender reassignment (Chapter 13).
- Addition of Halpern's psychobiosocial viewpoint on sex differences and gender-role development.
- Expanded coverage of cognitive and social interventions to reduce gender-stereotyping, including those appropriate for elementary school instructors (Chapter 13).
- New findings on sex differences in aggression (Chapter 14).
- New research distinguishing proactive and reactive aggression and their linkage to bullying and victimization (Chapter 14).
- Expanded coverage of Kochanska's exciting research on the early origins of conscience and the "goodness-of-fit" between temperament and moral socialization (Chapter 14).
- A new section on ethnic variations in child rearing (Chapter 15).
- A new look at the impacts of part-time employment on adolescent development (Chapter 15).
- Expanded coverage of diversity in family life including new sections on adoptive families and gay/lesbian families (Chapter 15).
- New evidence on the dynamics, correlates, and treatment of childhood sexual abuse (Chapter 15).
- New information on the prevalence of TV violence and on strategies for reducing its potentially harmful effects (Chapter 16).
- Expanded coverage of the positive effects of and concerns about children's computer use (Chapter 16).
- Dramatic new data on the benefits of participating in after-school extracurricular activities (Chapter 16).
- New evidence on the effectiveness of cooperative learning methods as strategies for educating students with special needs (Chapter 16).
- Increased attention to the influence of friends and on how the quality of these ties affect child and adolescent development (Chapter 16).

WRITING STYLE

My goal has been to write a book that speaks directly to its readers and treats them as active participants in an ongoing discussion. I have tried to be relatively informal and down to earth in my writing style and to rely heavily on questions, thought problems, concept checks, and a number of other exercises to stimulate students' interest and involvement. Most of the chapters were "pretested" on my own students, who red-penciled whatever wasn't clear to them and suggested several of the concrete examples, analogies, and occasional anecdotes that I've used when introducing and explaining complex ideas. So, with the valuable assistance of my student-critics, I have attempted to prepare a manuscript that is substantive and challenging but that reads more like a dialogue or a story than like an encyclopedia.

SPECIAL FEATURES

The pedagogical features of the text have been greatly expanded in this fifth edition. Among the more important features that are included to encourage student interest and involvement and make the material easier to learn are the following:

- **Four-color design.** An attractive four-color design brightens the book and makes photographs, drawings, and other illustrations come alive.
- **Outlines and chapter summaries.** An outline and brief introductory section at the beginning of each chapter provide the student with a preview of what will be covered. Each chapter concludes with a comprehensive summary, organized according to the major subdivisions of each chapter and highlighting key terms, that allows one to quickly review the chapter's major themes.
- **Subheadings.** Subheadings are employed very frequently to keep the material well organized and to divide the coverage into manageable bites.
- **Vocabulary/key terms.** More than 700 key terms appear in boldface type to alert the student that these are important concepts to learn.
- **Running glossary, key term lists, and comprehensive end-of-the-book glossary.** A running glossary provides on-the-spot definitions of boldfaced key terms as they appear in the text. At the end of each chapter is a list of key terms that appeared in the narrative, as well as the page number on which each term is defined. A complete glossary of key terms for the entire text appears at the end of the book.
- **Boxes.** Each chapter contains three to five boxes that call attention to important ideas, processes, issues, or applications. The aim of these boxes is to permit a closer or more personal examination of selected topics while stimulating the reader to think about the questions, controversies, practices, and policies under scrutiny. Twenty-one of these boxes are new to this edition, and another 18 have been substantially updated. The boxes fall into five categories: **Cultural Influences,** which examine the impacts of culture, subcultures, or other social contexts on selected aspects of child/adolescent development ("Is Shyness a Disadvantage? It Depends on One's Culture"); **Focus on Research,** which discuss a classic study or set of studies that have been highly influential in illuminating the causes of development ("How Girls Are More Aggressive Than Boys"); **Current Controversies,** which address hotly debated issues today ("Must Parenting Be 'Good' or Simply 'Good Enough'?"; "Should Preschoolers Attend School?"); **Developmental Issues,** which permit a detailed examination of a variety of developmentally significant topics or processes ("Sudden Infant Death Syndrome (SIDS)"; "Temperament, Discipline, and Moral Internalization"); and **Applying Developmental Research,** which focuses on applying what we know to optimize developmental outcomes ("Combating Gender Stereotypes with Cognitive Interventions"). All of these boxes are carefully woven into the chapter narrative and were selected to reinforce central themes in the text.
- **Illustrations.** Photographs, tables, and figures are used extensively and one noteworthy addition is the expanded use of chronological tables to review important developmental milestones. Although the illustrations are designed, in part, to provide visual relief and to maintain student interest, they are not merely decorations. All visual aids, including the occasional cartoons, were selected to illustrate important principles and concepts and thereby enhance the educational goals of the text.

- **Concept checks.** The concept checks, introduced in the fourth edition, became an immediate hit. Many, many student comment cards indicated that these brief exercises (three per chapter) were having the intended effects of being engaging, challenging, and permitting an *active* assessment of one's mastery of important concepts and developmental processes. Several students explicitly stated that concept checks helped them far more than the typical "brief summary" sections appearing in their other texts (which were perceived as too brief and too general to be of much use). Thirty-seven of the 48 concept checks have been totally rewritten or substantially revised to incorporate the kinds of questions students found most useful, and to reflect the new concepts and new understandings included in this edition. Answers to all concept checks can be found in the Appendix at the back of the book.
- **Critical thought questions.** New to this edition is the "What Do You Think?" feature—three thought questions per chapter that are designed to encourage students to think about current controversies and/or to apply what they have learned in formulating their own reasoned position on developmentally significant issues. Some of these questions address issues too new to have generated anything other than anecdotal evidence, and I have occasionally mentioned citations so that students can research the issue further before formulating an opinion. Any and all of these questions may serve as excellent springboards for class discussion; in fact, that is where many of them came from, having been raised in class by students as we discussed topics pertaining in some way to these issues.

SUPPLEMENTARY AIDS

The supplemental support materials for the fifth edition have been thoroughly updated and enhanced. These supplements have been coordinated carefully, with learning objectives for each chapter made clear and consistent throughout.

Instructor's Resource Manual

The Instructor's Manual, prepared by a new author, Linda Marshall, for this edition, contains web links, chapter outlines, summaries and objectives, key terms, suggestions for class lectures and activities, transparency masters, and lists of particularly effective media materials.

Transparency Acetates

75 full-color acetate transparencies illustrating concepts from the text are available to professors who adopt the fifth edition for their course.

Test Items

The Test Bank for this edition was prepared by Shirley-Anne Hensch, of the University of Wisconsin Center-Marshfield/Wood County. Over 100 multiple-choice questions are provided for each chapter, and all questions are classified as being factual, definition, applied, or conceptual. Each question is cross-referenced to the learning objectives for each chapter and to its page location in the text.

Electronic Test Items

All questions from the printed Test Items are available (Windows or Macintosh) in Thomson World Class Testing Tools format. World Class Testing Tools allows instructors not only to create the exact assessment tools that are needed, but also allows you to choose how to deliver those tools—via print, disk or hard drive, LAN, or Internet.

Student Study Guide

The Study Guide, written by Shirley-Anne Hensch, highlights the learning objectives for each chapter (which are consistent with the learning ovjectives in the Test Bank and the Instructor's Manual), and includes the following: a chapter outline with a summary of key points, a two-part vocabulary self-test, a set of short-answer study questions related to the learning objectives for each chapter, a 10–15 question multiple-choice self-test, and a set of activities and projects related to class material. Annotated answers are provided for the multiple-choice self-test, to explain why the indicated answer is correct and why the distracters are incorrect.

CNN Video on Child Development Issues
Available to adopters of the text is a videotape of CNN stories on child development issues. Focusing on a range of topics from prenatal testing to adolescent concerns, these video segments have been selected to address important areas covered in the developmental psychology course.

Visit the Brooks/Cole Psychology Study Center on the World Wide Web
More information on development issues and a host of links to related websites are available when you visit the Brooks/Cole Psychology Study Center at the following address: **http://psychstudy.brookscole.com**

ACKNOWLEDGMENTS

As is always the case with projects as large and as long-lasting as this one, there are many, many individuals whose assistance was invaluable in the planning and production of the book. The quality of any volume in human development depends to a large extent on the quality of the prepublication reviews from developmentalists around the world. Many colleagues (including several dozen or so interested and unpaid volunteers) have influenced this book by contributing constructive criticisms, as well as useful suggestions, references, and a whole lot of encouragement. Each of those experts has helped to make the final product a better one, and I thank them all.

The reviewers of the first edition were Martin Banks, University of California at Berkeley; Don Baucum, Birmingham-Southern College; Jay Belsky, Pennsylvania State University; Keith Berg, University of Florida; Marvin Berkowitz, Marquette University; Dana Birnbaum, University of Maine at Orono; Kathryn Black, Purdue University; Robert Bohlander, Wilkes College; Cathryn Booth, University of Washington; Yvonne Brackbill, University of Florida; Cheryl Bradley, Central Virginia Community College; John Condry, Cornell University; David Crowell, University of Hawaii; Connie Hamm Duncanson, Northern Michigan University; Mary Ellen Durrett, University of Texas at Austin; Beverly Eubank, Lansing Community College; Beverly Fagot, University of Oregon; Larry Fenson, San Diego State University; Harold Goldsmith, University of Oregon; Charles Halverson, University of Georgia; Lillian Hix, Houston Community College; Patricia Leonhard, University of Illinois at Champaign-Urbana; Frank Laycock, Oberlin College; Mark Lepper, Stanford University; John Ludeman, Stephens College; Phillip J. Mohan, University of Idaho; Robert Plomin, Pennsylvania State University; Judith Powell, University of Wyoming; Daniel Richards, Houston Community College; Peter Scharf, University of Seattle; and Rob Woodson, University of Texas.

The reviewers of the second edition were Kathryn Black, Purdue University; Thomas J. Brendt, Purdue University; Mary Courage, Memorial University of Newfoundland; Donald N. Cousins, Rhode Island College; Mark L. Howe, Memorial University of Newfoundland; Gerald L. Larson, Kent State University; Sharon Nelson-Le Gall, University of Pittsburgh; David Liberman, University of Houston; Richard Newman, University of California at Riverside; Scott Paris, University of Michigan; Thomas S. Parish, Kansas State University; Frederick M. Schwantes, Northern Illinois University; Renuka R. Sethi, California State College at Bakersfield; Faye B. Steuer, College of Charleston; Donald Tyrell, Franklin and Marshall College; and Joachim K. Wohlwill, Pennsylvania State University.

The reviewers of the third edition were David K. Carson, University of Wyoming; Marcia Z. Lippman, Western Washington University; Philip J. Mohan, University of Idaho; Gary Novak, California State University, Stanislaus; Elizabeth Rider, Elizabethtown College; James O. Rust, Middle Tennessee State University; Mark Shatz, Ohio University; and Linda K. Swindell, University of Mississippi.

The reviewers of the fourth edition were M. Kay Alderman, University of Akron; Peggy A. DeCooke, Purchase College, State University of New York; David Dodd, University of Utah; Beverly Fagot, University of Oregon; Rebecca Glover, University of Arkansas; Paul A. Miller, Arizona State University; Amy Needam, Duke University; Spencer Thompson, University of Texas of the Permian Basin; and Albert Yonas, University of Minnesota.

The reviewers of this edition were Mark Alcorn, University of Northern Colorado; AnnJanette Alejano-Steele, Metropolitan State College of Denver; Cynthia Berg, University of Utah; Kathleen Brown, California State University, Fullerton; Gary Creasey, Illinois State University; Teresa Davis, Middle Tennessee State University; K. Laurie Dickson, Northern Arizona University; Daniel Fasko, Morehead State University; John Felton, University of Evansville; Cynthia Frosch, University of North Carolina; John Gaa, University of Houston; Judith Hudson, Rutgers University; Kimberly Kinsler, Hunter College; Lacy Barnes-Mileham, Reedley College; Sandra Pipp-Siegel, University of Colorado at Boulder; Robert Russell, University of Michigan-Flint; and Frank Sinkavich.

Dr. Stephen Black of Bishop's University deserves a special note of thanks for making many useful suggestions for revision that were incorporated into the 5th edition. I am also heavily indebted to Carol K. Sigelman of George Washington University, a most talented writer with whom I have collaborated on another Brooks/Cole project (*Lifespan Human Development,* 1st and 2nd editions) and who has influenced this book. About every four to six weeks, Carol provided me with new references and many, many useful suggestions for supplementing or clarifying my presentation. It is clearly an understatement to say that Dr. Sigelman has had a meaningful and salutary effect on every section of this book, for she is directly or indirectly responsible for many of its positive qualities. Thank you, Carol, for your invaluable support and assistance.

David F. Bjorklund, of Florida Atlantic University, provided experience and expertise that was simply invaluable in revising portions of the book dealing with cognitive development. Many developmentalists are familiar with Dave's empirical research and his excellent text, *Children's thinking: Developmental function and individual differences.* I am also indeed fortunate to have had a scientist and a writer of Dave's caliber to coauthor chapters 7 and 8 and to endorse a reviewer's very reasonable suggestion that I combine the topics of perceptual development and basic learning processes into a new chapter entitled Basic Cognitive Foundations.

Special thanks and bouquets go to Michele Carter, whose eyesight has unfortunately deteriorated, I fear, as she squinted to turn my many tiny handwritten insertions into presentable, error-free manuscript. I also benefited immensely from Michele's editorial and copyediting skills at many points in this project, and I cannot conceive of trying to produce a volume of this sort without the assistance of a wonderful associate such as herself.

Many other people have contributed their professionalism and skills to the production of the fifth edition of this text. I am especially grateful to Keith Faivre, who served as production editor for this volume, and to my friend Fiorella Ljunggren, past production services manager at Brooks/Cole, for her dedication to my past volumes over the past 21 years (not to mention her coming out of retirement to play a supporting role by obtaining permissions for the present volume). I also wish to express my gratitude to Gary Head for listening carefully to my design requests and implementing them to create a most attractive volume; to Vernon T. Boes, Brooks/Cole's art director, for creating once again a stunning cover for the book; to Sheila Pulver, the manuscript editor, for her attention to detail in copyediting; to Katy Spining of GTS Graphics for carrying out the production of this book with skill and efficiency; and to Judy Mason, the photo researcher, for her diligence and patience in finding images to illustrate my points.

Last, but not least, I owe especially important debts of gratitude to my past and present sponsoring editors. C. Deborah Laughton conceived this project many years ago, and was always there throughout the first and most of the second editions, answering questions, solving problems, and finding ways to get more work out of me than I believed was possible. Vicki Knight came on board for the third edition, and her dedication to the project would make one think that she had conceived it herself. Jim Brace-Thompson has skillfully shepherded me through the fourth and fifth editions and is responsible for many of the improvements in the book's design and content. And last but not least, developmental editor Jim Strandberg made many useful suggestions for streamlining coverage and improving pedagogy while also interjecting the kind of humor into our interactions that reminded me that it was the project (rather than myself or my gripes) that should be taken seriously. Though different in their "styles," each of these persons is a splendid editor who has taught me so much about the preparation of effective educational materials. I am indeed fortunate to have had their counsel over the years, and I wish to thank them sincerely for their many, many efforts on my behalf.

David R. Shaffer

Introduction to Developmental Psychology and Its Research Strategies

Let's begin this book with a question: Why did *you* choose to enroll in a course on human development? For many of you majoring in psychology, home economics, elementary education, or nursing, this class is required. Expectant parents may take the course in order to learn more about their babies. Occasionally, people elect the course seeking to answer specific questions about their own behavior or that of a friend or a family member. For example, a college roommate of mine, who happened to be a fisheries major, studied child development hoping to discover why he and his identical twin often seemed to have the same thoughts in similar situations.

Whatever your reasons for taking this course, at one time or another you have probably been curious about one or more aspects of human development. For example:

- What does the world look like to newborn infants? Can they make any sense of their new surroundings?
- When do infants first recognize their mothers? their fathers? themselves (in a mirror)?
- Why do many 1-year-olds seem so attached to their mothers and wary of strangers?
- Foreign languages are difficult to understand from listening to conversations, yet infants and toddlers acquire their native language by constant exposure to such conversations rather than from formal instruction. How is this possible? Is language learning easier for children than for adults? Is a child in a bilingual home at a disadvantage?
- Why do many young children say that objects like the sun and clouds are alive?
- Why do you remember so little about the first 2 or 3 years of your life?
- Why are some people friendly and outgoing while others are shy and reserved? Does the home environment influence one's personality? If so, then why are children from the same family often so different from one another?
- What are the impacts on children of losing a parent (due to death or divorce) or gaining a stepparent?
- What roles do close friends play in a child's or an adolescent's development?
- Why is it that all humans turn out to be so similar in many ways and, at the same time, so different from one another?

Simply stated, the aim of this book is to seek answers for these and many other fascinating questions about developing persons by reviewing the theories, methods, discoveries, and many practical achievements of the modern developmental sciences. This introductory chapter lays the groundwork for the remainder of the book by addressing important issues concerning the nature of human development and how knowledge about development is gained. What does it mean to say that people "develop" over time? How is your experience of development different from that of developing persons in past eras or in other cultures? When were scientific studies of human development first conducted and why are they necessary? And what strategies or research methods do scientists use to study the development of children and adolescents? Let us begin by considering the nature of development.

WHAT IS DEVELOPMENT?

Simply stated, **development** refers to systematic continuities and changes in the individual that occur between conception (when the father's sperm penetrates the mother's ovum, creating a new organism) and death. By describing *changes* as "systematic," we imply that they are orderly, patterned, and relatively enduring, so that temporary mood swings and other transitory changes in our appearances, thoughts, and behaviors are

development
systematic continuities and changes in the individual over the course of life.

therefore excluded. We are also interested in **continuities** in development, or ways in which we remain the same or continue to reflect our past.

If development represents the continuities and changes that an individual experiences from "womb to tomb," the science of development is the study of these phenomena. Actually, we might well speak of the sciences of development, for this area of study is truly a multidisciplinary enterprise. Although **developmental psychology** is the largest of these disciplines, many biologists, sociologists, anthropologists, educators, physicians, home economists, and even historians share an interest in developmental continuity and change and have contributed in important ways to our understanding of both human and animal development. Because the science of development is multidisciplinary, we use the term *developmentalist* to refer to any scholar—regardless of discipline—who seeks to understand the developmental process.

What Causes Us to Develop?

To grasp the meaning of development more fully, we must understand two important processes that underlie developmental change. One of these processes, **maturation,** refers to the biological development according to a plan contained in the *genes*—the hereditary material passed from parents to their child at conception. Just as seeds become mature plants, assuming that they receive adequate moisture and nourishment, human beings grow within the womb. The human maturational program also calls for us to walk and to utter our first meaningful words at about 1 year of age, to reach sexual maturity at about age 11 to 15, and then to age and die on similar schedules. Since the brain undergoes many maturational changes, maturation is partly responsible for psychological changes such as our increasing ability to concentrate, solve problems, and understand another person's thoughts or feelings. So one reason that we humans are similar in so many important respects is that our common "species heredity," or maturational blueprints, guides all of us through many of the same developmental changes at about the same points in our lives.

Despite the common assumption that superstars are natural athletes, the special skills they display require an enormous amount of practice. Indeed, Michael Jordan, the world's best basketball player, struggled just to become a promising professional baseball player.

A second critical developmental process is **learning**—the process through which our *experiences* produce relatively permanent changes in our feelings, thoughts, and behaviors. Let's consider a very simple example. Although a certain degree of physical maturation is necessary before a grade-school child can become reasonably proficient at dribbling a basketball, careful instruction and many, many hours of practice are essential if this youngster is ever to approximate the ball-handling skills of such wizards as Michael Jordan. Most of our abilities and habits do not simply unfold as part of nature's grand plan; we often learn to feel, think, and behave in new ways from our observations of and interactions with parents, teachers, and other important people in our lives, as well as from events that we experience. Stated another way, we change in response to our *environments,* particularly in response to the actions and reactions of the people around us. Of course, most developmental changes are the product of *both* maturation and learning. And as we will see throughout this book, some of the more lively debates about human development are arguments about which of these processes contributes most to particular developmental changes.

developmental continuities
ways in which we remain stable over time or continue to reflect our past.

developmental psychology
branch of psychology devoted to identifying and explaining the continuities and changes that individuals display over time.

maturation
developmental changes in the body or behavior that result from the aging process rather than from learning, injury, illness, or some other life experience.

learning
a relatively permanent change in behavior (or behavioral potential) that results from one's experiences or practice.

What Goals Do Developmentalists Pursue?

Just what objectives have developmentalists set for themselves? Three major goals stand out: to describe, to explain, and to optimize development (Baltes, Reese, & Lipsitt, 1980). In pursuing the goal of *description,* human developmentalists carefully observe the behavior of people of different ages, seeking to specify how human beings change over time. Though there are typical pathways of development that virtually all people follow, researchers have discovered that no two persons are exactly alike. Even when raised in the same home, children often display very different interests, values, abilities, and behavior. Thus, to adequately describe development, it is necessary to focus both on typical patterns of change (or **normative development**) and on individual variations (or **ideographic development**), seeking to identify the important ways that developing humans resemble each other and how they are likely to differ as they proceed through life.

Adequate description provides us with the "facts" about development, but it is only the starting point. Ultimately, developmentalists seek to explain the changes they have observed. In pursuing this goal of *explanation,* researchers hope to determine *why* humans develop as they typically do and *why* some individuals turn out differently than others. Stated another way, explanation centers both on normative changes *within* individuals and variations in development *between* individuals. As we will see throughout the text, it is often easier to describe development than to conclusively establish (explain) why it occurs.

Finally, many researchers and practitioners hope to optimize development by applying what they have learned in attempts to help human beings develop in positive directions. This is clearly a practical side to the study of human development that has led to such breakthroughs as ways to:

- Promote strong affectional ties between fussy, unresponsive infants and their frustrated parents.
- Assist children with learning difficulties to succeed at school.
- Help socially unskilled children and adolescents avoid the emotional difficulties that could result from having few friends and being rejected by peers.

Of course, such *optimization* goals often cannot be achieved until researchers have adequately described normal and abnormal pathways of development and their causes.

Some Basic Observations about the Character of Development

Now that we have defined development and talked very briefly about the goals that developmentalists pursue, let's consider some of the conclusions they have drawn about the character of development.

A Continual and Cumulative Process

In his famous poem *Paradise Lost,* John Milton wrote: "Childhood shows the man as morning shows the day." This interesting analogy can be interpreted in at least two ways. It could be translated to mean that the events of childhood have little or no real impact on one's adult life, just as a sunny summer morning often fails to forecast an impending afternoon thundershower. Yet most people do not interpret Milton's statement that way. Instead, they take it to mean that the events of childhood play a very meaningful role in forecasting the future. Human developmentalists clearly favor this latter interpretation.

Although no one can specify precisely what adulthood holds in store from even the most meticulous examination of a person's childhood, developmentalists have learned that the first 12 years are an extremely important part of the life span that sets the stage for adolescence and adulthood. And yet, how we perform on that stage also depends on the experiences we have later in life. Obviously, you are not the same person now that you were at age 10 or even at age 15. You have probably grown somewhat, acquired new academic skills, and developed very different interests and aspirations from those you had as a fifth-grader or a high school sophomore. And the path of such developmental change stretches through middle age and beyond, culminating in the final change that occurs when we die. In sum, human development is

normative development
developmental changes that characterize most or all members of a species; typical patterns of development.

ideographic development
individual variations in the rate, extent, or direction of development.

Table 1.1 A Chronological Overview of Human Development

Period of life	Approximate age range
1. Prenatal period	Conception to birth
2. Infancy and toddler period[a]	First 2 years of life
3. Preschool period	2 to 6 years of age
4. Middle childhood	6 to 12 or so years of age (until the onset of puberty)
5. Adolescence	12 or so to 20 years of age (many developmentalists define the end of adolescence as the point at which the individual begins to work and is reasonably independent of parental sanctions)
6. Young adulthood	20 to 40 years of age
7. Middle age	40 to 65 years of age
8. Old age	65 years of age or older

[a]Some prefer to describe as "toddlers" children who have begun to walk and are approximately 1 to 2 years of age.
Note: The age ranges listed here are approximate and may not apply to any particular individual. For example, a few 10-year-olds have experienced puberty and are properly classified as adolescents. Some teenagers are fully self-supporting, with children of their own, and are best classified as young adults.

best described as a *continual* and cumulative process. The one constant is change, and the changes that occur at each major phase of life can have important implications for the future.

Table 1.1 presents a chronological overview of the life span as developmentalists see it. Our focus in this text is on development during the first five periods of life—the epochs known as childhood and adolescence. By examining how children develop from the moment they are conceived until they reach young adulthood, we will learn more about ourselves and the determinants of our behavior. Our survey will also provide some insight as to why no two individuals are ever exactly alike, even when raised together in the same home. I won't promise that you will find answers to every important question you may have about developing children and adolescents. The study of human development is still a relatively young discipline with many unresolved issues. But as we proceed, it should become quite clear that developmentalists of the past half-century have provided an enormous amount of very practical information about younger people that can help us to become better educators, child/adolescent practitioners, and parents.

A Holistic Process

It was once fashionable to divide developmentalists into three camps: (1) those who studied *physical growth* and development, including bodily changes and the sequencing of motor skills, (2) those who studied *cognitive* aspects of development, including perception, language, learning, and thinking, and (3) those who concentrated on *psychosocial* aspects of development, including emotions, personality, and the growth of interpersonal relationships. Today we know that this classification is somewhat misleading, for researchers who work in any of these areas have found that changes in one aspect of development have important implications for other aspects. Let's consider an example.

What determines a person's popularity with peers? If you were to say that social skills are important, you would be right. Social skills such as warmth, friendliness, and willingness to cooperate are characteristics that popular children typically display. Yet there is much more to popularity than meets the eye. We now have some indication that the age at which a child reaches puberty, an important milestone in physical development, has a very real effect on social life. For example, boys who reach puberty early enjoy better relations with their peers than do boys who reach puberty later (Livson & Peskin, 1980). Children who do well in school also tend to be more popular with their peers than do children of average intelligence or below who perform somewhat less admirably in the classroom.

We see, then, that popularity depends not only on the growth of social skills but also on various aspects of both cognitive and physical development. As this example illustrates, development is not piecemeal but **holistic;** humans are physical, cognitive, and social beings, and each of these components of self depends, in part, on changes taking place in other areas of development. This holistic perspective is perhaps the dominant theme of human development today, around which this book is organized.

Plasticity

Plasticity refers to a capacity for change in response to positive or negative life experiences. Although we have described development as a continual and cumulative process and noted that past events often have implications for the future, developmentalists have known for some time that the course of development can change abruptly if important aspects of a person's life change. For example, somber babies living in barren, understaffed orphanages often become quite cheerful and affectionate when placed in socially stimulating adoptive homes (Rutter, 1981). Highly aggressive children who are intensely disliked by peers often improve their social status after learning and practicing social skills that popular children display (Mize & Ladd, 1990; Shure, 1989). It is indeed fortunate that human development is so plastic, for children who have horrible starts can often be helped to overcome their deficiencies.

Historical/Cultural Context

No single portrait of development is accurate for all cultures, social classes, or racial and ethnic groups. Each culture, subculture, and social class transmits a particular pattern of beliefs, values, customs, and skills to its younger generations, and the content of this cultural socialization has a strong influence on the attributes and competencies that individuals display. Development is also influenced by societal changes: historical events such as wars, technological breakthroughs such as the development of personal computers, and social causes such as the women's movement. Each generation develops in its own way, and each generation changes the world for succeeding generations. So we should not automatically assume that developmental sequences observed in samples of North American or European children (the most heavily studied populations) are optimal, or even that they characterize persons developing in other eras or cultural settings (Laboratory for Comparative Human Cognition, 1983). Only by adopting a historical/cultural perspective can we fully appreciate the richness and diversity of human development.

HUMAN DEVELOPMENT IN HISTORICAL PERSPECTIVE

Contemporary Western societies can be described as "child-centered": People often think of births as "blessed events," spend a great deal of money to care for and educate their young, and excuse children from shouldering the full responsibilities of adulthood until attaining the legal age of 14 to 21 (depending on the society), when they have presumably gained the wisdom and skills to "pull their own weight." Yet, childhood and adolescence were not always regarded as the very special, sensitive periods that we regard them as today. To understand how developmentalists think about and approach the study of children, it is necessary to see how the concept of childhood "developed" over time. You may be surprised just how recent our modern viewpoint really is. Of course, it was only after people came to view childhood as a special period that they began to study children and the developmental process.

holistic perspective
a unified view of the developmental process that emphasizes the important interrelationships among the physical, mental, social, and emotional aspects of human development.

plasticity
capacity for change; a developmental state that has the potential to be shaped by experience.

Childhood in Premodern Times

In the early days of recorded history, children had few if any rights, and their lives were not always valued by their elders. Archeological research, for example, has shown that the ancient Carthaginians often killed children as religious sacrifices and embedded them in the walls of buildings to "strengthen" these structures (Bjorklund & Bjorklund, 1992). Until the fourth century A.D., Roman parents were legally entitled to kill their deformed, illegitimate, or otherwise unwanted infants. After this active infanticide was outlawed, unwanted babies were often left to die in the wilderness, or were sold as servants or for sexual exploitation upon reaching middle childhood (deMause, 1974). Even "wanted" children were often treated rather harshly by today's standards. For example, male children in the city-state of Sparta were exposed to a strict regimen designed to train them for the grim task of serving a military state. As infants, they were given cold baths to "toughen" them. At age 7, when children in modern society are entering second grade, Spartan boys were taken from their homes and housed in public barracks, where they were often beaten or underfed to instill the discipline they would need to become able warriors (deMause, 1974; Despert, 1965).

Not all early societies treated their children as harshly as the citizens of Carthage, Rome, and Sparta. Yet, for several centuries after the birth of Christ, children were viewed as family "possessions" who had no rights (Hart, 1991) and whom parents were free to exploit as they saw fit. In fact, it wasn't until the 12th century A.D. in Christian Europe that secular legislation equated infanticide with murder (deMause, 1974)!

Currently, there is some debate about what childhood was like during the medieval era. Historian Philippe Aries (1962) has analyzed documents and paintings from medieval Europe and concluded that European societies had *no* concept of childhood as we know it before 1600. Medieval children were not coddled or indulged to the extent that today's children are. They were often dressed in miniature versions of adult clothing and were depicted in artwork working alongside adults (usually close relatives) in the shop or the field or drinking and carousing with adults at parties. And except for exempting *infants* from criminal culpability for their wrongdoing, medieval law generally made no distinctions between childhood and adult offenses (Borstelmann, 1983; Kean, 1937). But were medieval children really considered to be miniature adults?

Probably not. More recent and extensive examinations of medieval history reveal that childhood was generally recognized as a distinct phase of life and that children were thought to have certain needs above and beyond those of adults (see Borstelmann, 1983; Kroll, 1977). Clearly, the experiences of children were different during medieval times than they are today, for many medieval children routinely performed economic functions that closely resemble adult work by today's standards. But it is almost certainly an overstatement to conclude that medieval societies had absolutely no concept of childhood and merely treated their young as miniature adults.

Although medieval children dressed like their elders and often worked alongside them, it is doubtful that they were considered miniature adults.

Toward Modern-Day Views on Childhood

During the 17th and 18th centuries, attitudes toward children and child-rearing began to change. Religious leaders of that era stressed that children were innocent and helpless souls who should be shielded from the wild and reckless behavior of adults. One method of accomplishing this objective was to send young people to school. Although the primary purpose of schooling was to provide a proper moral and religious education, it was now recognized that teaching important subsidiary skills such as reading and writing would transform the innocents into "servants and workers" who would provide society "with a good labor force" (Aries, 1962, p. 10; see also Box 1.1). Although children were still considered family possessions, parents were now discouraged from abusing their sons and daughters and were urged to treat them with more warmth and affection (Aries, 1962; Despert, 1965).

Early Philosophical Perspectives on Childhood

Why did attitudes toward children change so drastically in the 17th and 18th centuries? Although the historical record is not very clear on this point, it is likely that the thinking of influential social philosophers contributed in a meaningful way to the new perspective on children and child care. Lively speculation about human nature led these philosophers to consider each of the following issues:

1. Are children inherently good or bad?
2. Are children driven by inborn motives and instincts, or, rather, are they products of their environments?
3. Are children actively involved in shaping their characters, or are they passive creatures molded by parents, teachers, and other agents of society?

Debates about these philosophical questions produced quite different perspectives on children and child-rearing. For example, Thomas Hobbes's (1651/1904) doctrine of **original sin** held that children are inherently selfish egoists who must be restrained by society, whereas Jean Jacques Rousseau's (1762/1955) doctrine of **innate purity** maintained that children are born with an intuitive sense of right and wrong that society often corrupts. These two viewpoints clearly differ in their implications for child-rearing. Proponents of original sin argued that parents must actively control their egoistic offspring, while innate purists viewed children as "noble savages" who should be given freedom to follow their inherently positive inclinations.

Another influential view on children and child-rearing was suggested by John Locke (1690/1913), who believed that the mind of an infant is a **tabula rasa,** or "blank slate," and that children have no inborn tendencies. In other words, children are neither inherently good nor inherently bad, and how they turn out depends entirely on their worldly experiences. Like Hobbes, Locke argued in favor of disciplined child-rearing to ensure that children develop good habits and acquire few if any bad ones.

These philosophers also differed on the question of children's participation in their own development. Hobbes maintained that children must learn to rechannel their naturally selfish interests into socially acceptable outlets; in this sense, they are passive subjects to be molded by the more powerful elements of society—namely, parents. Locke, too, believed that the child's role is passive, since the mind of an infant is a blank slate on which experience writes its lessons. But a strikingly different view was proposed by Rousseau, who believed that children are actively involved in the shaping of their own intellects and personalities. In Rousseau's words, the child is not a "passive recipient of the tutor's instruction" but a "busy, testing, motivated explorer. The active searching child, setting his own problems, stands in marked contrast to the receptive one . . . on whom society fixes its stamp" (quoted in Kessen, 1965, p. 75).

Clearly, these philosophers had some interesting ideas about children and how they should be raised. But how could anyone decide whether their views were correct? Unfor-

original sin
the idea that children are inherently negative creatures who must be taught to rechannel their selfish interests into socially acceptable outlets.

innate purity
the idea that infants are born with an intuitive sense of right and wrong that is often misdirected by the demands and restrictions of society.

tabula rasa
the idea that the mind of an infant is a "blank slate" and that all knowledge, abilities, behaviors, and motives are acquired through experience.

1.1

CULTURAL INFLUENCES

On the "Invention" of Adolescence

Although modern-day concepts of childhood date to the 1700s, formal recognition of *adolescence* as a distinct phase of life came even later, during the early years of this century (Hall, 1904). Ironically, the spread of industry in Western societies is probably the event most responsible for the "invention" of adolescence. As immigrants poured into industrialized nations and took jobs that had formerly been filled by children and teenagers, young people became economic liabilities rather than assets (or, as one person put it, "economically worthless but emotionally priceless" (Zelizer, cited in Remley, 1988). Moreover, the increasingly complex technology of industrial operations placed a premium on obtaining an educated labor force. So laws were passed in the late 19th century to restrict child labor and make schooling compulsory (Kett, 1977). Suddenly teens were spending much of their time surrounded by agemates and separated from adults. As they hung out with friends and developed their own colorful "peer cultures," teenagers came to be viewed as a distinct class of individuals who had clearly emerged from the innocence of childhood but who were not yet ready to assume adult responsibilities (Hall, 1904).

After World War II, the adolescent experience broadened as increasing numbers of high school graduates postponed marriages and careers to pursue college (and postgraduate) educations. Today, it is not at all unusual for young people to delay their entry into the workaday adult world until their mid to late 20s (Hartung & Sweeney, 1991; Vobejda, 1991). And we might add that society condones this "extended adolescence" by requiring workers to obtain increasingly specialized training to pursue their chosen careers (Elder, Liker, & Cross, 1984).

Interestingly, many of the world's cultures have no concept of adolescence as a distinct phase of life. The St. Lawrence Eskimos, for example, simply distinguish boys from men (or girls from women), following the tradition of many preliterate societies that passage to adulthood occurs at puberty (Keith, 1985). And yet, other cultures' depictions of the life span are much more intricate than our own. The Arasha of East Africa, for example, have at least six meaningful age strata for males: youths, junior warriors, senior warriors, junior elders, senior elders, and retired elders.

In some cultures, passage to adulthood occurs at puberty, and adolescents are expected to assume adult responsibilities.

The fact that age does not have the same meaning in all eras or cultures reflects a basic truth that we have already touched on and will emphasize repeatedly throughout this book: The course of human development in one historical or cultural context is apt to differ, and to differ substantially, from that observed in other eras and cultural settings. Aside from our biological link to the human race, we are largely products of the times and places in which we live!

tunately, the philosophers collected no objective data to back their pronouncements, and the few observations they did make were limited and unsystematic. Can you anticipate the next step in the evolution of developmental sciences?

Children as Subjects: The Baby Biographies

The first glimmering of a systematic study of children can be traced to the late 19th century. This was a period in which investigators from a variety of academic backgrounds began to observe the development of their own children and to publish these data in works known as **baby biographies.**

baby biography
a detailed record of an infant's growth and development over a period of time.

Perhaps the most influential of the baby biographers was Charles Darwin, who made daily records of the early development of his son (Darwin, 1877; and see Charlesworth, 1992). Darwin's curiosity about child development stemmed from his earlier theory of evolution. Quite simply, he believed that young, untrained infants share many characteristics with their nonhuman ancestors, and he advanced the (now discredited) idea that the development of the individual child retraces the entire evolutionary history of the species, thereby illustrating the "descent of man." So Darwin and many of his contemporaries viewed the baby biography as a means of answering questions about our evolutionary past.

Baby biographies left much to be desired as works of science. Different baby biographers emphasized very different aspects of their children's behavior, so that different baby biographies were difficult to compare. Then, too, parents are not entirely objective about their own children, and baby biographers like Charles Darwin may also have let their assumptions about the nature of development bias their observations so that they "found" what they were looking for. Finally, each baby biography was based on a single child—and often the child of a distinguished individual, at that. Conclusions based on a single case may not hold true for other children.

Despite these shortcomings, baby biographies were a step in the right direction. The fact that eminent scientists such as Charles Darwin were now writing about developing children implied that human development was a topic worthy of scientific scrutiny.

American psychologist G. Stanley Hall (1846–1924) is recognized as one of the founders of developmental psychology.

Origins of a Science of Development

Introductory textbooks in virtually all academic areas typically credit someone as the "founder" of the discipline. In developmental psychology there were several influential pioneers who might merit consideration for this honor. Still, the person who is most often cited as the founder of developmental psychology is G. Stanley Hall.

Well aware of the shortcomings of baby biographies, Hall set out in the late 19th century to collect more objective data on larger samples. Specifically, he was interested in children's thinking, and he developed a now familiar research tool—the *questionnaire*—to explore "the contents of children's minds" (Hall, 1891). By asking children questions about a range of topics, Hall discovered that children's understanding of the world grows rapidly during childhood and that the "logic" of young children is not very logical at all. Hall later wrote an influential book titled *Adolescence* (1904) that was the first work to call attention to adolescence as a unique phase of the life span. His work was the first large-scale scientific investigation of developing youth, and it is on this basis that G. Stanley Hall merits consideration as the founder of developmental psychology (White, 1992).

At about the time Hall was using questionnaires to study children's minds, a young European neurologist was trying a different method of probing the mind and revealing its contents. The neurologist's approach was very fruitful, providing information that led him to propose a theory that revolutionized thinking about children and childhood. The neurologist was Sigmund Freud. His ideas came to be known as *psychoanalytic theory.*

In many areas of science, new theories are often revisions or modifications of old theories. But in Freud's day, there were few "old" theories of human development to modify. Freud was truly a pioneer, formulating his psychoanalytic theory from the thousands of notes and observations he made while treating patients for various kinds of emotional disturbances.

Freud's highly creative and unorthodox theorizing soon attracted a lot of attention. Shortly after the publication of Freud's earliest theoretical monographs, the *International Journal of Psychoanalysis* was founded, and other researchers began to report their tests of Freud's thinking. By the mid-1930s much of Freud's work had been translated into other languages, and the impact of psychoanalytic theory was felt around the world. Over the years, Freud's theory proved to be quite *heuristic,* meaning that it continued to generate new research and to prompt other researchers to revise and extend Freud's

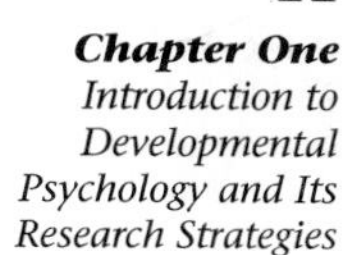

thinking. Clearly, the field of developmental psychology was thriving by the time Freud died in 1939.

Freud's work—and other scientists' reactions to it—aptly illustrates the role that theories play in the scientific study of human development. Although the word *theory* is an imposing term, theories are something that everybody has. If I were to ask you why males and females appear so very different as adults when they seem so very similar as infants, you would undoubtedly have some opinions on the issue. Your answer would state or at least reflect your own underlying theory of sex differences. So a **theory** is really nothing more than a set of concepts and propositions that allow the theorist to describe and explain some aspect of experience. In the field of psychology, theories help us to describe and explain various patterns of behavior.

Good theories have another important feature: the ability to predict future events. These theoretical predictions, or **hypotheses,** are then tested by collecting additional data. The information we obtain when testing hypotheses not only provides some clues about the theory's ability to explain new observations but may also lead to new theoretical insights that extend our knowledge even further.

Today there are many theories that have contributed to our understanding of child and adolescent development, and in Chapter 2 we will examine several of the more influential of these viewpoints. Although it is quite natural for people reading about various theories to favor one, the scientist uses a rather stringent yardstick to evaluate theories: He or she will formulate hypotheses and conduct research to determine whether the theory can adequately predict and explain new observations. Thus, there is no room for subjective bias when evaluating a theory. Theories in the developmental sciences are only as good as their ability to predict and explain important aspects of human development.

In the next section of the chapter, we will focus on the "tools of the trade"—that is, the research methods that investigators use to test their theories and gain a better understanding of child and adolescent development.

RESEARCH METHODS IN DEVELOPMENTAL PSYCHOLOGY

When detectives are assigned cases to solve, they first gather the facts, formulate hunches, and then sift through the clues or collect additional information until one of their hunches proves correct. Unraveling the mysteries of development is in many ways a similar endeavor. Investigators must carefully observe their subjects, study the information they collect, and use these data to draw conclusions about the ways people develop.

Our focus in this section is on the methods that researchers use to gather information about developing children and adolescents. Our first task is to understand why developmentalists consider it absolutely essential to collect all these facts. We will then discuss the advantages and disadvantages of five basic fact-finding strategies: self-report methodologies, systematic observation, case studies, ethnography, and psychophysiological methods. Finally, we will consider the ways developmentalists might design their research to detect and explain age-related changes in children's feelings, thoughts, abilities, and behaviors.

The Scientific Method

Modern developmental psychology is appropriately labeled a scientific enterprise because those who study developing organisms have adopted a value system we call the **scientific method** that guides their attempts at understanding. There is nothing

theory
a set of concepts and propositions designed to organize, describe, and explain an existing set of observations.

hypothesis
a theoretical prediction about some aspect of experience.

scientific method
an attitude or value about the pursuit of knowledge that dictates that investigators must be objective and allow their data to determine the merits of their theorizing.

mysterious about the scientific method. It is really more of an *attitude* or *value* than a method; one which dictates that, above all, investigators must be *objective* and must allow their observations (or data) to decide the merits of their thinking.

In earlier eras, when social philosophers such as Hobbes, Locke, and Rousseau were presenting their views on children and child-rearing, their largely unsubstantiated claims were often accepted as fact. People assumed that great minds always had great insights. Very few individuals questioned the word of these well-known scholars because the scientific method was not yet a widely accepted criterion for evaluating knowledge.

The intent here is not to criticize the early social philosophers. In fact, today's developmentalists (and children) are deeply indebted to these thinkers for helping to modify the ways in which society regarded and treated its young. However, great minds may on occasion produce miserable ideas that can do a great deal of harm if their errors in thinking are uncritically accepted and influence the way human beings are treated. The scientific method, then, is a valuable safeguard that helps to protect the scientific community and society at large against flawed reasoning. Protection is provided by the practice of evaluating the merits of various theoretical pronouncements against the objective record, rather than simply relying on the academic, political, or social credibility of the theorist. Of course, this also means that the theorist whose ideas are being evaluated must be equally objective and, thus, willing to discard pet notions when there is evidence against them.

? **WHAT DO YOU THINK?**

What might you say to a person who rejects an established finding by saying "It didn't happen that way for my child"? If this parent's recollection is accurate, does this invalidate the finding?

Gathering Data: Basic Fact-Finding Strategies

No matter what aspect of development we hope to study—be it the perceptual capabilities of newborn infants, the growth of friendships among grade-school children, or the reasons some adolescents use drugs—we must find ways to measure what interests us. Today researchers are fortunate in having many tried-and-true procedures that they can use to measure behavior and test their hypotheses about human development. But regardless of the technique used, scientific measures must always display two important qualities: **reliability** and **validity.**

A measure is *reliable* if it yields consistent information over time and across observers. Suppose you go into a classroom and record the number of times each child behaves aggressively toward others, but your research assistant, using the same scheme to observe the same children, does not agree with your measurements. Or you measure each child's aggressiveness one week but come up with very different aggressiveness scores while applying the same measure to the same children a week later. Clearly, your observational measure of aggression is unreliable because it yields highly inconsistent information. To be reliable and thus useful for scientific purposes, your measure would have to produce comparable estimates of children's aggression from independent observers *(interrater reliability),* and would yield similar scores for individual children from one testing to another shortly thereafter *(temporal stability).*

A measure is *valid* if it measures what it is supposed to measure. Obviously, an instrument must be reliable and measure consistently before it can possibly be valid. Yet reliability, by itself, does not guarantee validity (Miller, 1997). For example, a highly reliable observational scheme that is intended as a measure of children's aggression may provide grossly overinflated estimates of aggressive behavior if the investigator simply classifies all acts of physical force as examples of aggression. What the researcher has failed to recognize is that much high-intensity behavior may simply represent enjoyable forms of rough-and-tumble play without harmful or aggressive intent. Clearly, researchers must demonstrate that they are measuring the attribute they say they are measuring before we can have much faith in the data they collect or the conclusions they reach.

reliability
the extent to which a measuring instrument yields consistent results, both over time and across observers.

validity
the extent to which a measuring instrument accurately reflects what the researchers intended to measure.

Keeping in mind the importance of establishing the reliability and validity of measures, let us consider some of the different ways that aspects of human development might be measured.

Self-report Methodologies

Three common procedures that developmentalists use to gather information and test hypotheses are interviews, questionnaires (including psychological tests), and the clinical method. Although these approaches are similar in that each asks participants to answer questions posed by the investigator, they differ in the extent to which the investigator treats individual participants alike.

Interviews and Questionnaires. Researchers who opt for interview or questionnaire techniques will ask the child (or the child's parents) a series of questions pertaining to such aspects of development as the child's perceptions, feelings, beliefs, or characteristic methods of thinking. Collecting data via a questionnaire (and most psychological tests) simply involves putting questions on paper and asking participants to respond to them in writing, whereas interviews require participants to respond orally to the investigator's queries. If the procedure is a **structured interview** or **structured questionnaire,** all who participate in the study are asked the same questions in the same order. The purpose of this standardized or structured format is to treat each person alike so that the responses of different participants can be compared.

One interesting use of the interview technique is a project in which kindergarten, second-grade, and fourth-grade children responded to 24 questions designed to assess their knowledge of social stereotypes about males and females (Williams, Bennett, & Best, 1975). Each question came in response to a different short story in which the central character was described by either stereotypically masculine adjectives (for example, *aggressive, forceful, tough*) or stereotypically feminine adjectives (for example, *emotional, excitable*). The child's task was to indicate whether the character in each story was male or female. Williams and his associates found that even kindergartners could usually tell whether the stories referred to boys or girls. In other words, these 5-year-olds were quite knowledgeable about gender stereotypes, although children's thinking became much more stereotyped between kindergarten and second grade. One implication of these results is that stereotyping of the sexes must begin very early if kindergartners are already thinking along stereotyped lines.

Interviews and questionnaires have some very real shortcomings. First, neither approach can be used with very young children who cannot read or comprehend speech very well. Investigators must also hope that the answers they receive are honest and accurate and are not merely attempts by respondents to present themselves in a favorable or socially desirable way. Many adolescents, for example, might be reluctant to admit that they regularly masturbate, or that they sniff glue, or enjoy the risks of shoplifting. Clearly, inaccurate or untruthful responses lead to erroneous conclusions. Investigators must also be careful to ensure that participants of all ages interpret questions in the same way; otherwise, the age trends observed in the study may reflect differences in children's ability to comprehend and communicate rather than real underlying changes in their feelings, thoughts, or behaviors. Finally, researchers who interview both developing children and their parents (or teachers) may have trouble determining which set of reports is more accurate should the children's descriptions of their own behaviors differ from those of the other informants.

Despite these potential shortcomings, structured interviews and questionnaires can be excellent methods of obtaining large amounts of useful information in a short period of time. Both approaches are particularly useful when the investigator emphasizes to participants that their responses will be confidential and/or challenges them to report exactly what they know about an issue, thereby maximizing the likelihood of a truthful or accurate answer. In the gender stereotyping study, for example, the young participants probably considered each question a personal challenge or a puzzle to be solved and were thus motivated to answer accurately and to display exactly what they knew about males and females. Under the circumstances, then, the structured interview was an excellent method of assessing children's perceptions of the sexes.

structured interview or structured questionnaire
a technique in which all participants are asked the same questions in precisely the same order so that the responses of different participants can be compared.

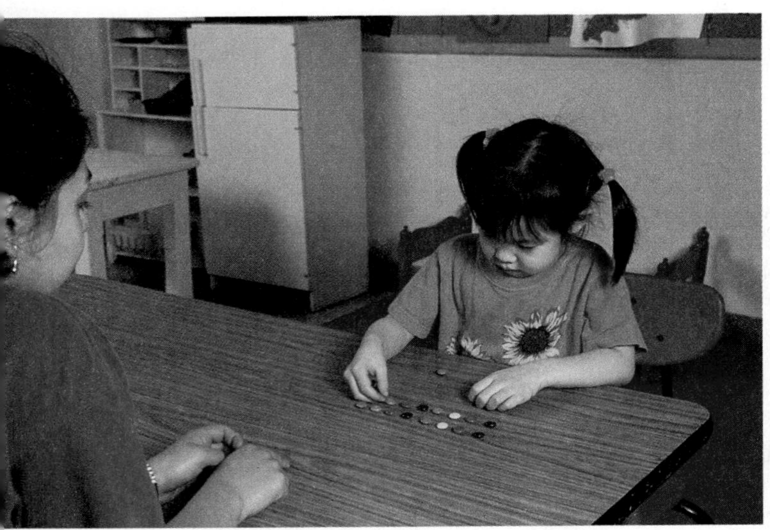

Investigator using the clinical method. All participants are asked the same questions at first, but each participant's answers to these initial questions determine what the researcher will ask next.

The Clinical Method. The **clinical method** is a very close relative of the interview technique. The investigator is usually interested in testing a hypothesis by presenting the research participant with a task or stimulus of some sort and then inviting a response. After the participant responds, the investigator typically asks a second question or introduces a new task to clarify the participant's original answer. Although subjects are often asked the same questions initially, each participant's answer determines what he or she is asked next. Thus, the clinical method is not standardized; it considers each subject to be unique.

Jean Piaget, a famous Swiss psychologist, relied extensively on the clinical method to study children's moral reasoning and intellectual development. The data from Piaget's research are largely protocol records of his interactions with individual children. Here is a small sample from Piaget's work (1932/1965, p. 140) on the development of moral reasoning, which shows that this young child thinks about lying in a very different way than adults do:

> Do you know what a lie is?—*It's when you say what isn't true.*—Is 2 + 2 = 5 a lie?—*Yes, it's a lie.*—Why?—*Because it isn't right.*—Did the boy who said 2 + 2 = 5 know it wasn't right or did he make a mistake?—*He made a mistake.*—Then if he made a mistake, did he tell a lie or not?— *Yes, he told a lie.*

Like structured interviews, clinical methods are often useful for gathering large amounts of information in relatively brief periods. Proponents of this approach also cite its flexibility as an advantage: By asking follow-up questions that are tailored to the participant's original answers (as Piaget did in the above example), it is often possible to obtain a rich understanding of the meaning of those answers. However, the flexibility of the clinical method is also a potential shortcoming. Consider that it may be difficult, if not impossible, to directly compare the answers of participants who are asked different questions. Furthermore, this nonstandardized treatment of participants raises the possibility that the examiner's preexisting theoretical biases may affect the particular follow-up questions asked and the interpretations provided. Since conclusions drawn from the clinical method depend, in part, on the investigator's *subjective* interpretations, it is always desirable to verify these insights using other research techniques.

Observational Methodologies

Often researchers prefer to observe people's behavior directly rather than asking them questions about it. One method that many developmentalists favor is **naturalistic observation**—observing people in their common, everyday (that is, natural) surroundings. To observe children, this usually means going into homes, schools, or public parks and playgrounds and carefully recording their behavior. Rarely do investigators try to record every event that occurs; they are usually testing a specific hypothesis about one type of behavior, such as cooperation or aggression, and will focus exclusively on acts of this kind. One strength of naturalistic observation is the ease with which it can be applied to infants and toddlers, who often cannot be studied through methods that demand verbal skills. But perhaps the greatest advantage of the naturalistic observation is that it illustrates how people actually behave in everyday life (Willems & Alexander, 1982).

However, naturalistic observation also has its limitations. First, some behaviors occur so infrequently (for example, heroic rescues) or are so socially undesirable (for example, overt sex play or thievery) that they are unlikely to be witnessed by an unknown observer in the natural environment. Second, many events are usually happening at the same time in a natural setting, and any (or some combination) of them may affect people's behavior. This makes it difficult to pinpoint the causes of partici-

clinical method
a type of interview in which a participant's response to each successive question (or problem) determines what the investigator will ask next.

naturalistic observation
a method in which the scientist tests hypotheses by observing people as they engage in everyday activities in their natural habitats (for example, at home, at school, or on the playground).

pants' actions or of any developmental trends in behavior. Finally, the mere presence of an observer sometimes makes people behave differently than they otherwise would. Children may "ham it up" when they have an audience, whereas parents may be on their best behavior, showing a strong reluctance, for example, to spank a misbehaving child as they normally might. For these reasons, researchers often attempt to minimize **observer influence** by (1) videotaping their participants from a concealed location or (2) spending time in the setting before collecting their "real" data so that the individuals they are observing grow accustomed to their presence and behave more naturally.

Several years ago, Mary Haskett and Janet Kistner (1991) conducted an excellent piece of naturalistic observation to compare the social behaviors of nonabused preschoolers with those of day-care classmates identified by child protection agencies as having been physically abused by their parents. The investigators first defined examples of the behaviors they wished to record—both *desirable* behaviors such as appropriate social initiations and positive play, and *undesirable* behaviors such as aggression and negative verbalizations. They then monitored 14 abused and 14 nonabused preschool children as they mingled with peers in a play area of a day-care facility. Each child was observed during three 10-minute play sessions on three different days. To minimize their influence on the play activities, observers stood outside the play area while making their observations.

Children's tendency to perform for an observer is one of the problems that researchers must overcome when using the method of naturalistic observation.

The results were disturbing. As shown in Figure 1.1, abused children initiated fewer social interactions than their nonabused classmates and were somewhat socially withdrawn. And when they did interact with playmates, the abused youngsters displayed many more aggressive acts and other negative behaviors than did their nonabused companions. Indeed, nonabused children often blatantly ignored the positive social initiations of an abused child, as if they did not want to get involved with him or her.

In sum, Haskett and Kistner's observational study shows that abused children are unattractive playmates who are likely to be disliked and even rejected by peers. But as is almost always the case in naturalistic observational research, it is difficult to pinpoint the exact cause of these findings. Did the negative behaviors of abused children cause their peers to reject them? Or did peer rejection cause the abused children to display negative behaviors? Either possibility can account for Haskett and Kistner's results.

How might observational researchers study unusual or undesirable behaviors that they are unlikely to observe in the natural environment? One method is to conduct **structured observations** in the laboratory. In a structured observational study, each participant is exposed to a setting that might cue the behavior in question, and is then surreptitiously observed (via a hidden camera or through a one-way mirror) to see if he or she performs the behavior. For example, Leon Kuczynski (1983) asked children to promise to help him with a boring task and then left them alone to work in a room where attractive toys were present. This procedure enabled Kuczynski to determine whether youngsters would break a promise to work (an undesirable act that many children displayed) when they thought there was no one present to observe their transgression.

Aside from being a most feasible way of studying behaviors that occur infrequently or are not openly displayed in the natural environment, structured observations also ensure that every participant in the sample is exposed to the *same* eliciting stimuli and has an *equal opportunity* to perform the target behavior—circumstances that are not

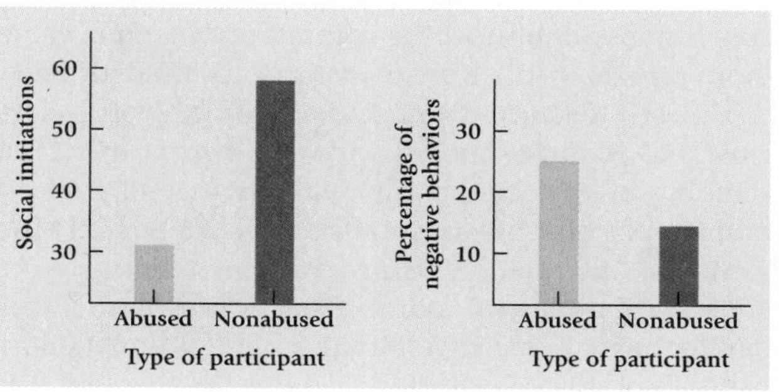

Figure 1.1 *Social initiations and negative behaviors of abused and nonabused preschool children. Compared with their nonabused companions, abused youngsters initiate far fewer social interactions with peers and behave much more negatively toward them.*

observer influence
tendency of participants to react to an observer's presence by behaving in unusual ways.

structured observation
an observational method in which the investigator cues the behavior of interest and observes participants' responses in a laboratory.

always true in the natural setting. Of course, the major disadvantage of structured observations is that participants may not always respond in a contrived laboratory setting as they would in everyday life.

Case Studies

Any or all of the data collection methods we have discussed—structured interviews, questionnaires, clinical methods, and behavioral observations—can be used to compile a detailed portrait of a single individual's development through the **case study** method. In preparing an individualized record, or "case," the investigator typically seeks many kinds of information about the participant, such as his or her family background, socioeconomic status, health records, academic or work history, and performance on psychological tests. Much of the information included in any case history comes from interviews with and observations of the individual, although the questions asked and observations made are typically not standardized and may vary considerably from case to case.

The baby biographies of the 19th and early 20th centuries are examples of case studies, and Sigmund Freud conducted many fascinating case studies of his clinical patients. In analyzing his cases, Freud noticed that different patients often described very similar events and experiences that had been noteworthy to them as they were growing up. He inferred from the observations that there must be important milestones in human development that all people share. As he continued to observe his patients and to listen to accounts of their lives, Freud concluded that each milestone in the life history of a patient was meaningfully related to earlier events. He then inferred that he had the data to construct a comprehensive explanation of human development—the account we know today as *psychoanalytic theory.*

Although Freud and many other developmentalists have used case studies to great advantage, there are major drawbacks to this approach. For example, it is often difficult to directly compare cases who have been asked different questions, taken different tests, and been observed under different circumstances. Case studies may also lack *generalizability*; that is, conclusions drawn from the experiences of the small number of individuals studied may simply not apply to most people. In fact, one recurring criticism of Freud's psychoanalytic theory is that it was formulated from the life histories of *emotionally disturbed patients* who are hardly typical of the general population. For these reasons, any conclusions drawn from case studies should always be verified through the use of other research techniques.

Ethnography

Ethnography—a form of participant observation often used in the field of anthropology—is becoming increasingly popular among researchers who hope to understand the impact of culture on developing children and adolescents. To collect their data, ethnographers often live within the cultural or subcultural community they are studying for periods of months or even years. The data they collect is typically diverse and extensive, consisting largely of naturalistic observations, notes made from conversations with members of the culture, and initial interpretations of these events. These data are eventually used to compile a detailed portrait of the cultural community and to draw conclusions about how the community's unique values and traditions influence one or more aspects of the development of its children and adolescents.

Clearly detailed ethnographic portraits of a culture or subculture that arise from close and enduring contact with members of the community can lead to a richer understanding of that community's traditions and values than is possible through a small number of visits, in which outsiders make limited observations and conduct a few interviews (LeVine et al., 1994). In fact, these extensive cultural or subcultural descriptions are particularly useful to investigators hoping to understand cultural conflicts and other developmental challenges faced by minority children and adolescents in diverse multicultural societies (Segal, 1991; see also Patel, Power, & Bhavnagri, 1996). But despite these

case study
a research method in which the investigator gathers extensive information about the life of an individual and then tests developmental hypotheses by analyzing the events of the person's life history.

ethnography
method in which the researcher seeks to understand the unique values, traditions, and social processes of a culture or subculture by living with its members and making extensive observations and notes.

clear strengths, ethnography is a highly subjective method because researchers' own cultural values and theoretical biases can cause them to misinterpret what they have experienced. In addition, ethnographic conclusions pertain only to the culture or subculture studied and cannot be assumed to generalize to other contexts or social groups.

Ethnographic researchers attempt to understand cultural influences by living within the community and partcipating in all aspects of community life.

Psychophysiological Methods

In recent years, developmentalists have turned to **psychophysiological methods**—techniques that measure the relationship between physiological responses and behavior—to explore the biological underpinnings of children's perceptual, cognitive, and emotional responses. Psychophysiological methods are particularly useful for interpreting the mental and emotional experiences of infants and toddlers who are unable to report such events (Bornstein, 1992).

Heart rate is an involuntary physiological response that is highly sensitive to one's psychological experiences. Compared with their normal resting, or *baseline,* levels, infants who are carefully attending to an interesting stimulus may show a *decrease* in heart rate, whereas those who are uninterested in it may show no heart rate change, and others, who are wary of or angered by the stimulus, may show a heart rate *increase* (Campos, Bertenthal, & Kermoian, 1992; Fox & Fitzgerald, 1990). Measures of brain function are also very useful for assessing psychological state. For example, electroencephalogram (EEG) recordings of brain wave activity can be obtained by attaching electrodes to the scalp. Since different patterns of EEG activity characterize different arousal states, such as sleep, drowsiness, and alertness, investigators can track these patterns and determine how sleep cycles and other states of arousal change with age. Novel stimuli or events also produce short-term changes in EEG activity. So an investigator who hopes to test the limits of infant sensory capabilities can present novel sights and sounds and look for changes in brain waves (called *event-related potentials,* or *ERPs*) to determine whether these stimuli have been detected, or even discriminated, since two stimuli sensed as "different" will produce different patterns of brain activity (Bornstein, 1992).

Though very useful, psychophysiological responses are far from perfect indicators of psychological states. Even though an infant's heart rate or brain wave activity may indicate that he or she is attending to a stimulus, it is often difficult to determine exactly which aspect of that stimulus (shape, color, etc.) has captured attention. Furthermore, changes in physiological responses often reflect mood swings, fatigue, hunger, or even negative reactions to the physiological recording equipment, rather than a change in the infant's attention to a stimulus or emotional reactions to it. For these reasons, physiological responses are more likely to be valid indications of psychological experiences when participants (particularly very young ones) are initially calm, alert, and contented.

psychophysiological methods methods that measure the relationships between physiological processes and aspects of children's physical, cognitive, or emotional behavior/development.

Concept Check 1.1
Matching Research Methods to Research Questions

Check your understanding of the uses and strengths of various research methods by determining which method is best suited for investigating each of the following questions. Choose from the following methods: (a) structured interview, (b) ethnography, (c) naturalistic observation, (d) structured observation, (e) psychophysiological methods. Answers appear in the Appendix in the back of the book.

_____ 1. Will young elementary school children break a solemn promise to watch a sick puppy when no one is observing them?

_____ 2. Do 6-year-olds know any negative stereotypes about minority group members?

_____ 3. Can 6-month-old infants discriminate the colors red, green, blue, and yellow?

_____ 4. Are the aggressive actions that boy playmates display toward each other different from those that occur in girls' play groups?

_____ 5. How does life change for boys from the Sambia tribe once they have experienced tribal rites of puberty?

Table 1.2 Strengths and Limitations of Seven Common Research Methods

Method	Strengths	Limitations
Self-reports		
Interviews and questionnaires	Relatively quick way to gather much information; standardized format allows the investigator to make direct comparisons between data provided by different participants.	Data collected may be inaccurate or less than completely honest, or may reflect variations in respondents' verbal skills and ability to understand questions.
Clinical methods	Flexible methodology that treats subjects as unique individuals; freedom to probe can be an aid in ensuring that the participant understands the meaning of the questions asked.	Conclusions drawn may be unreliable in that participants are not all treated alike; flexible probes depend, in part, on the investigator's subjective interpretations of the participant's responses; can be used only with highly verbal participants.
Systematic observations		
Naturalistic observation	Allows study of behavior as it actually occurs in the natural environment.	Observed behaviors may be influenced by observer's presence; unusual or undesirable behaviors are unlikely to be observed during the periods when observations are made.
Structured observation	Offers a standardized environment that provides every child an opportunity to perform target behavior. Excellent way to observe infrequent or socially undesirable acts.	Contrived observations may not always capture the ways children behave in the natural environment.
Case Studies	Very broad method that considers many sources of data when drawing inferences and conclusions about individual participants.	Kind of data collected often differs from case to case and may be inaccurate or less than honest; conclusions drawn from individual cases are subjective and may not apply to other people.
Ethnography	Provides a richer description of cultural beliefs, values, and traditions than is possible in brief observational or interview studies.	Conclusions may be biased by the investigator's values and theoretical viewpoints; results cannot be generalized beyond the groups and settings that were studied.
Psychophysiological methods	Useful for assessing biological underpinnings of development and identifying the perceptions, thoughts, and emotions of infants and toddlers who cannot report them verbally.	Cannot indicate with certainty what participants sense or feel; many factors other than the one being studied can produce a similar physiological response.

Table 1.2 provides a brief review of the data-gathering methods that we have examined thus far. In the sections that follow, we will consider how investigators might design their research to test hypotheses and detect developmental continuities and changes.

DETECTING RELATIONSHIPS: CORRELATIONAL AND EXPERIMENTAL DESIGNS

Once researchers have decided what they want to study, they must then devise a research plan, or design, that permits them to identify relationships among events and behaviors and to specify the causes of these relationships. Here we consider the two general research designs that investigators might employ: correlational and experimental.

The Correlational Design

In a **correlational design,** the investigator gathers information to determine whether two or more variables of interest are meaningfully related. If the researcher is testing a specific hypothesis (rather than conducting preliminary descriptive or exploratory research), he or she will be checking to see whether these variables are related as the hypothesis specifies they should be. No attempts are made to structure or to manipulate the participants' environment in any way. Instead, correlational researchers take people as they find them—already "manipulated" by natural life experiences—and try to determine whether variations in people's life experiences are associated with differences in their behaviors or patterns of development.

To illustrate the correlational approach to hypothesis testing, let's work with a simple theory specifying that youngsters learn a lot from watching television and are apt to imitate the actions of the characters they observe. One hypothesis we might derive from this theory is that the more frequently children observe TV characters who display violent and aggressive acts, the more inclined they will be to behave aggressively toward their own playmates. After selecting a sample of children to study, our next step in testing our hypothesis is to measure the two variables that we think are related. To assess children's exposure to violent themes on television, we might use the interview or naturalistic observational methods to determine what each child watches, and then count the number of aggressive acts that occur in this programming. To measure the frequency of the children's own aggressive behavior toward peers, we could observe our sample on a playground and record how often each child behaves in a hostile, aggressive manner toward playmates. Having now gathered the data, it is time to evaluate our hypothesis.

The presence (or absence) of a relationship between variables can be determined by subjecting the data to a statistical procedure that yields a **correlation coefficient,** (symbolized by an r). This statistic provides a numerical estimate of the strength and the direction of the relationship between two variables. It can range in value from +1.00 to −1.00. The absolute value of r (disregarding its sign) tells us the *strength* of the relationship. Thus, correlation coefficients of −.70 and +.70 are of equal strength, and both are stronger than a moderate correlation of .50. An r of .00 indicates that the two variables are unrelated. The sign of the correlation coefficient indicates the *direction* of the relationship. If the sign is positive, this means that as the variable increases, the other variable also increases. For example, height and weight are positively correlated: As children grow taller, they tend to get heavier (Tanner, 1990). Negative correlations, however, indicate inverse relationships; as one variable increases, the other *decreases.* Among grade-school students, for example, aggression and popularity are negatively correlated: Children who behave more aggressively tend to be *less* popular with their peers (Crick, 1996).

Now let's return to our hypothesized positive relationship between televised violence and children's aggressive behavior. A number of investigators have conducted correlational studies similar to the one we have designed, and the results (reviewed in Liebert & Sprafkin, 1988) suggest a moderate positive correlation (between +.30 and +.50) between the two variables of interest: Children who watch a lot of violent programming are more likely to behave aggressively toward playmates than are those who watch little violent programming (see Figure 1.2 on page 20 for a visual display).

Do these correlational studies establish that exposure to violent TV programming *causes* children to behave more aggressively? *No, they do not!* Although we have detected a relationship between exposure to televised violence and children's aggressive behavior, the causal direction of the relationship is not at all clear. An equally plausible alternative explanation is that relatively aggressive children are more inclined to prefer violent programming. Another possibility is that the association between TV viewing and aggressive behavior is actually caused by a third variable we have not measured. For example, perhaps parents who fight a lot at home (an unmeasured variable) cause their children to become more aggressive *and* to favor violent TV programming. If this were true, the

correlational design
a type of research design that indicates the strength of associations among variables; though correlated variables are systematically related, these relationships are not necessarily causal.

correlation coefficient
a numerical index, ranging from −1.00 to +1.00, of the strength and direction of the relationship between two variables.

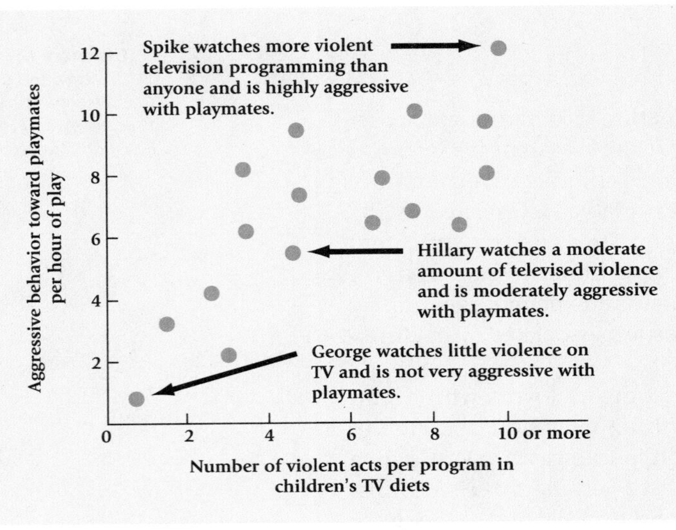
Spike watches more violent television programming than anyone and is highly aggressive with playmates.
Hillary watches a moderate amount of televised violence and is moderately aggressive with playmates.
George watches little violence on TV and is not very aggressive with playmates.
Aggressive behavior toward playmates per hour of play
12
10
8
6
4
2
0
2
4
6
8
10 or more
Number of violent acts per program in children's TV diets

Figure 1.2 *Plot of a hypothetical positive correlation between the amount of violence that children see on television and the number of aggressive responses they display. Each dot represents a specific child who views a particular level of televised violence (shown on the horizontal axis) and commits a particular number of aggressive acts (shown on the vertical axis). Although the correlation is less than perfect, we see that the more acts of violence a child watches on TV, the more inclined he or she is to behave aggressively toward peers.*

latter two variables may be correlated, even though their relationship to each other is not one of cause and effect.

In sum, the correlational design is a versatile approach that can detect systematic relationships between any two or more variables that we might be interested in and capable of measuring. However, its major limitation is that *it cannot unambiguously indicate that one thing causes another.* How, then, might a researcher establish the underlying causes of various behaviors or other aspects of human development? One solution is to conduct experiments.

The Experimental Design

In contrast to correlational studies, **experimental designs** permit a precise assessment of the cause-and-effect relationship that may exist between two variables. Let's return to the issue of whether viewing violent television programming *causes* children to become more aggressively inclined. In conducting a laboratory experiment to test this (or any) hypothesis, we would bring participants to the lab, expose them to different treatments, and record their responses to these treatments as data.

The different treatments to which we expose our participants represent the **independent variable** of our experiment. To test the hypothesis we have proposed, our independent variable (or treatments) would be the type of television program that our participants observe. Half the children might view a program in which characters behave in a violent or otherwise aggressive manner toward others, whereas the other half would watch a program that contains little if any violence.

Children's reactions to the television shows would become the data, or **dependent variable,** in our experiment. Since our hypothesis centers on children's aggression, we would want to measure (as our dependent variable) how aggressively children behave after watching each type of television show. A dependent variable is called "dependent" because its value presumably depends on the independent variable. In the present case, we are hypothesizing that future aggression (our dependent variable) will be greater for children who watch violent programs (one level of the independent variable) than for those who watch nonviolent programs (the second level of the independent variable). If we are careful experimenters and exercise precise control over *all* other factors that may affect children's aggression, then the pattern of results that we have anticipated will allow us to draw a strong conclusion: Watching violent television programs *causes* children to behave more aggressively.

An experiment similar to the one we have proposed was actually conducted (Liebert & Baron, 1972). Half the 5- to 9-year-olds in this study watched a violent 3½-minute clip from the *Untouchables* that contained two fistfights, two shootings, and a stabbing. The remaining children watched a 3½-minute film of a nonviolent but exciting track meet. So the *independent variable* was the type of program watched. Then each child was taken into another room and seated before a panel that had wires leading into an adjoining room. On the panel was a green button labeled HELP, a red button labeled HURT, and a white light between the buttons. An experimenter then told the child that another child in an adjoining room would soon be playing a handle-turning game that

experimental design
a research design in which the investigator introduces some change in the participant's environment and then measures the effect of that change on the participant's behavior.

independent variable
the aspect of the environment that an experimenter modifies or manipulates in order to measure its impact on behavior.

dependent variable
the aspect of behavior that is measured in an experiment and assumed to be under the control of the independent variable.

would illuminate the white light. The participant was told that by pushing the buttons when the light was lit, he or she could either *help* the other child by making the handle easy to turn or *hurt* the child by making the handle become very hot. When it was clear that the participant understood the instructions, the experimenter left the room, and the light came on 20 times over the next several minutes. So each participant had 20 opportunities to help or hurt another child. The total amount of time each participant spent pushing the hurt button served as a measure of his or her aggression—the *dependent variable* in this study.

The results were clear: Despite the availability of an alternative, helping response, *both boys and girls were much more likely to press the HURT button if they had watched the violent television program.* So it appears that a mere 3½-minute exposure to televised violence can *cause* children to behave more aggressively toward a peer, even though the aggressive acts they witnessed on television bore no resemblance to those they committed themselves.

WHAT DO YOU THINK?

Short of ridding all homes of televisions, what steps might concerned parents take to lessen the potentially harmful impacts of televised violence on young children? After formulating your plan, compare it with suggestions offered by the experts in Table 16.1 on page 602.

When students discuss this experiment in class, someone invariably challenges this interpretation of the results. For example, one student recently proposed an alternative explanation that "maybe the kids who watched the violent film were naturally more aggressive than those who saw the track meet." In other words, he was suggesting that a **confounding variable**—children's preexisting levels of aggression—had determined their willingness to hurt a peer and that the independent variable (type of television program) had had no effect at all! Could he have been correct? How do we know that the children in the two experimental conditions really didn't differ in some important way that may have affected their willingness to hurt a peer?

This question brings us to the crucial issue of **experimental control.** In order to conclude that the independent variable is causally related to the dependent variable, the experimenter must ensure that all other confounding variables that could affect the dependent variable are *controlled*—that is, equivalent in each experimental condition. One way to equalize these extraneous factors is to do what Liebert and Baron (1972) did: randomly assign children to their experimental treatments. The concept of *randomization,* or **random assignment,** means that each research participant has an equal probability of being exposed to each experimental treatment or condition. Assignment of individual participants to a particular treatment is accomplished by an unbiased procedure such as the flip of a coin. If the assignment is truly random, there is only a very slim chance that participants in the two (or more) experimental conditions will differ on any characteristic that might affect their performance on the dependent variable; all these confounding variables will have been randomly distributed within each condition and equalized across the different conditions. Because Liebert and Baron randomly assigned subjects to experimental conditions, they could be reasonably certain that children who watched the violent TV program were not naturally more aggressive than those who watched the nonviolent TV program. So it was reasonable for them to conclude that the former group of children was more aggressive *because* they had watched a TV program in which violence and aggression were central.

The greatest strength of the experimental method is its ability to establish unambiguously that one thing causes another. Yet, critics of laboratory experimentation have argued that the tightly controlled laboratory environment is often contrived and artificial and that children are likely to behave differently in these surroundings than they would in a natural setting. Urie Bronfenbrenner (1977) has charged that a heavy reliance on laboratory experiments has made developmental psychology "the science of the strange behavior of children in strange situations with strange adults" (p. 19). Similarly, Robert McCall (1977) notes that experiments tell us what *can* cause a developmental change but do not necessarily pinpoint the factors that *actually do* cause such changes in natural settings. Consequently, it is quite possible that conclusions drawn from laboratory experiments do not always apply to the real world. In Box 1.2, we consider a step that experimentalists can take to counter this criticism and assess the **ecological validity** of their laboratory findings.

confounding variable
some factor other than the independent variable that, if not controlled by the experimenter, could explain any differences across treatment conditions in participants' performance on the dependent variable.

experimental control
steps taken by an experimenter to ensure that all extraneous factors that could influence the dependent variable are roughly equivalent in each experimental condition; these precautions must be taken before an experimenter can be reasonably certain that observed changes in the dependent variable were caused by manipulation of the independent variable.

random assignment
a control technique in which participants are assigned to experimental conditions through an unbiased procedure so that the members of the groups are not systematically different from one another.

ecological validity
state of affairs in which the findings of one's research are an accurate representation of processes that occur in the natural environment.

FOCUS ON RESEARCH

1.2

Assessing Causal Relationships in the Real World: The Field Experiment

How can we be more certain that a conclusion drawn from a laboratory experiment also applies in the real world? One way is to seek converging evidence for that conclusion by conducting a similar experiment *in a natural setting*—that is, a **field experiment.** This approach combines all the advantages of naturalistic observation with the more rigorous control that experimentation allows. In addition, subjects are typically not apprehensive about participating in a "strange" experiment because all the activities they undertake are everyday activities. Indeed, they may not even be aware that they are being observed or participating in an experiment.

Let's consider a field experiment (Leyens et al., 1975) that sought to test the hypothesis that heavy exposure to media violence can cause viewers to become more aggressive. The subjects were Belgian delinquents who lived together in cottages at a minimum-security institution for adolescent boys. Before the experiment began, the experimenters observed each boy in their research sample to measure his characteristic level of aggression. These initial assessments served as a *baseline* against which future increases in aggression could be measured. The baseline observations suggested that the institution's four cottages could be divided into two subgroups consisting of two cottages populated by relatively aggressive inmates and two cottages populated by less aggressive peers. Then the experiment began. For a period of one week, *violent* movies (such as *Bonnie and Clyde* and *The Dirty Dozen*) were shown each evening to one of the two cottages in each subgroup, and *neutral* films (such as *Daddy's Fiancée* and *La Belle Américaine*) were shown to the other cottages. Instances of physical and verbal aggression among residents of each cottage were recorded twice daily (at lunchtime and in the evenings after the movie) during the movie week and once daily (at lunchtime) during a posttreatment week.

The most striking result of this field experiment was the significant increase in *physical* aggression that occurred in the evenings among residents of both cottages assigned to the violent-film condition. Since the violent movies contained a large number of physically aggressive incidents, it appears that they evoked similar responses from the boys who watched them. But as shown in the figure, violent movies prompted larger increases in aggression among boys who were already relatively high in aggression. Furthermore, exposure to the violent movies caused the highly aggressive boys to become more *verbally aggressive* as well—an effect that these boys continued to display through the movie week *and* the posttreatment week.

Clearly, the results of the Belgian field experiment are consistent with Liebert and Baron's (1972) laboratory study in suggesting that exposure to media violence does indeed instigate aggressive behavior. Yet it also qualifies the laboratory findings by implying that the instigating effects of media violence *in the natural environment* are likely to be stronger and more enduring for the more aggressive members of the audience (and see Friedrich & Stein, 1973 for similar results with nursery-school children).

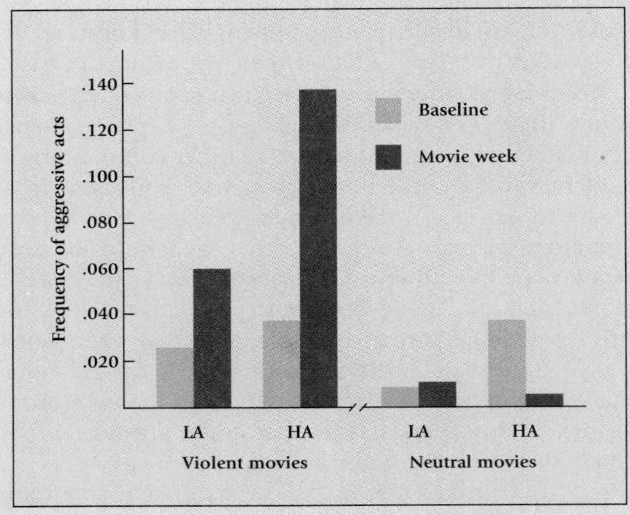

Mean physical aggression scores in the evening for highly aggressive (HA) and less aggressive (LA) boys under baseline conditions and after watching violent or neutral movies. ADAPTED FROM LEYENS ET AL., 1975.

The Natural (or Quasi-) Experiment

field experiment
an experiment that takes place in a naturalistic setting such as home, school, or a playground.

There are many issues to which an experimental design either cannot be applied or should not be used for ethical reasons. Suppose, for example, that we wish to study the effects of social deprivation in infancy on children's intellectual development. Clearly, we cannot ask one group of parents to lock their infants in an attic for 2 years so that we can collect the data we need. It is simply unethical to subject children to any experimental treatment that would adversely affect their physical or psychological well-being.

However, we might be able to accomplish our research objectives through a **natural** (or **quasi-**) **experiment** in which we observe the consequences of a natural event that subjects have experienced. So if we were able to locate a group of children who had been raised in impoverished institutions with very limited contact with caregivers over the first 2 years, we could compare their intellectual development with that of children raised at home with their families. This comparison would provide valuable information about the likely impact of early social deprivation on children's intellectual development. (Indeed, precisely this kind of natural experiment is described in detail in Chapter 11.) The independent variable in a natural experiment is the "event" that subjects experience (in our example, the social deprivation experienced by institutionalized infants). The dependent variable is whatever outcome measure one chooses to study (in our example, intellectual development).

Let's note, however, that researchers conducting natural experiments do not control the independent variable, nor do they randomly assign participants to experimental conditions; instead, they merely observe and record the apparent outcomes of a natural happening or event. And in the absence of tight experimental control, it is often hard to determine precisely what factor is responsible for any group differences that are found. Suppose, for example, that our socially deprived institution children showed a poorer pattern of intellectual outcomes than children raised at home. Is the *social deprivation* that institutionalized children experienced the factor that accounts for this difference? Or is it that institutionalized children differed in other ways from family-reared children (for example, were more sickly as infants or more poorly nourished, or simply had less intellectual potential) that might explain their poorer outcomes? Without randomly assigning participants to treatments and controlling other factors that may vary across treatments (for example, nutrition received), we simply cannot be certain that *social deprivation* is the factor responsible for the poor intellectual outcomes that institutionalized children display.

Despite its inability to make precise statements about cause and effect, the natural experiment is useful nonetheless. Why? Because it can tell us whether a natural event could *possibly* have influenced those who experienced it and, thus, can provide some meaningful clues about cause and effect.

Table 1.3, on page 24, summarizes the strengths and limitations of each of the general research designs we have discussed. Now let's consider designs that focus more specifically on detecting developmental continuities and changes.

natural (or quasi-) experiment
a study in which the investigator measures the impact of some naturally occurring event that is assumed to affect people's lives.

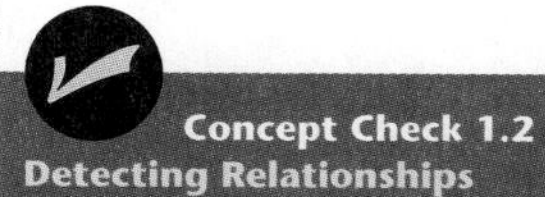

Concept Check 1.2
Detecting Relationships

Check your understanding of the meaning of various relationships that developmentalists might detect as described in items 1 and 2. Answers appear in the Appendix.

1. Jo Brown finds that the better children feel about themselves (that is, the higher their *self-esteem* as reported in an interview), the higher their grades at school. Check any *acceptable* conclusions based on these data.
   ______a. Low grades cause low self-esteem.
   ______b. Self-esteem and grades earned are positively correlated.
   ______c. Having high self-esteem causes children to earn good grades.

2. Ike Chang assigns ten boys to a condition in which they receive positive feedback about their academic abilities, a manipulation that increases their self-esteem. Ten girls in the same class receive no such feedback. Chang then finds that the ten boys earn higher grades over the course of the next year than the ten girls do. He might conclude that:
   ______a. Increases in self-esteem cause children to earn higher grades.
   ______b. Increases in self-esteem cause boys, but not girls, to earn higher grades.
   ______c. Neither of the above; Chang's experiment has failed to control for confounding variables (name one if you choose this answer).

Table 1.3 Strengths and Limitations of General Research Designs

Design	Procedure	Strengths	Limitations
Correlational	Gathers information about two or more variables without researcher intervention.	Estimates the strength and direction of relationships among variables in the natural environment.	Does not permit determination of cause-and-effect relationships among variables.
Laboratory experiment	Manipulates some aspect of participants' environment (independent variable) and measures its impact on participants' behavior (dependent variable).	Permits determination of cause-and-effect relationships among variables.	Data obtained in artificial laboratory environment may lack generalizability to the real world.
Field experiment	Manipulates independent variable and measures its impact on the dependent variable in a natural setting.	Permits determination of cause-and-effect relationships and generalization of findings to the real world.	Experimental treatments may be less potent and harder to control when presented in the natural environment.
Natural (quasi-) experiment	Gathers information about the behavior of people who experience a real-world (natural) manipulation of their environment.	Permits a study of the impact of natural events that would be difficult or impossible to simulate in an experiment; provides strong clues about cause-and-effect relationships.	Lack of precise control over natural events or the participants exposed to them prevents the investigator from establishing definitive cause-and-effect relationships.

DESIGNS FOR STUDYING DEVELOPMENT

Developmentalists are not merely interested in examining people's progress at one particular phase of life; instead, they hope to determine how people's feelings, thoughts, abilities, and behaviors *develop* or *change* over time. How might we design research to chart these developmental trends? Let's briefly consider three approaches: the cross-sectional design, the longitudinal design, and the sequential design.

The Cross-Sectional Design

In a **cross-sectional design** people who *differ in age* are studied at *the same point in time.* By comparing the responses of participants in different age groups, investigators can often identify age-related changes in whatever aspect of development they happen to be studying.

An experiment by Brian Coates and Willard Hartup (1969) is an excellent example of a cross-sectional comparison. Coates and Hartup were interested in determining why preschool children are less proficient than first- or second-graders at learning new responses displayed by an adult model. Their hypothesis was that younger children do not spontaneously *describe* what they are observing, whereas older children produce verbal descriptions of the modeled sequence. When asked to perform the actions they have witnessed, the preschoolers are at a distinct disadvantage because they have no verbal "learning aids" that would help them to recall the model's behavior.

To test these hypotheses, Coates and Hartup designed an interesting cross-sectional experiment. Children from two age groups—4- to 5-year-olds and 7- to 8-year-olds—watched a short film in which an adult model displayed 20 novel responses, such as throwing a beanbag between his legs, lassoing an inflatable toy with a Hula Hoop, and so on. Some of the children from each age group were instructed to describe the model's

cross-sectional design
a research design in which subjects from different age groups are studied at the same point in time.

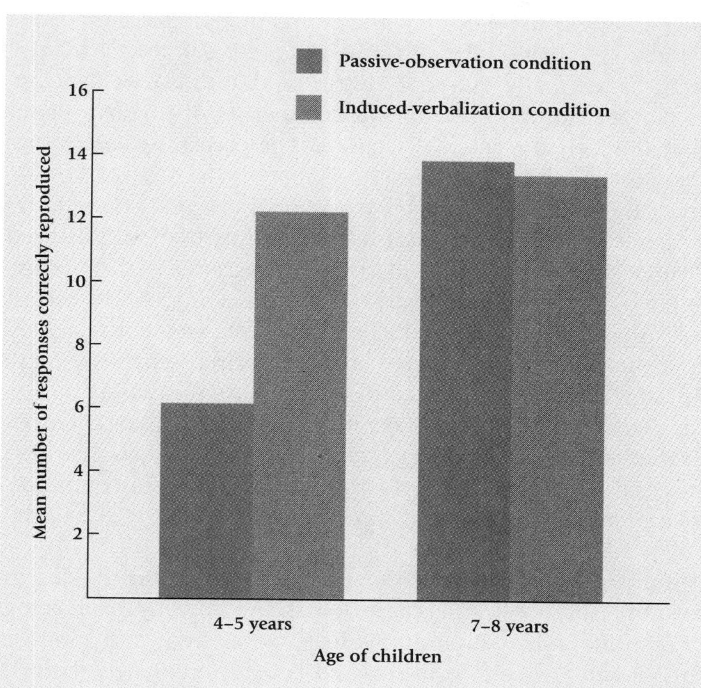

Figure 1.3 *Children's ability to reproduce the behavior of a social model as a function of age and verbalization instructions.* *Adapted from Coates & Hartup, 1969.*

actions, and they did so as they watched the film (induced-verbalization condition). Other children were not required to describe the model's actions as they observed them (passive-observation condition). When the show ended, each child was taken to a room that contained the same toys seen in the film and was asked to demonstrate what the model had done with these toys.

Figure 1.3 illustrates three interesting findings that emerged from this experiment. First, the 4- to 5-year-olds who were *not* told to describe what they had seen (that is, the passive observers) reproduced *fewer* of the model's responses than the 4- to 5-year-olds who described the model's behavior (the induced verbalizers) or the 7- to 8-year-olds in either experimental condition. This finding suggests that 4- to 5-year-old children may not produce the verbal descriptions that would help them to learn unless they are explicitly instructed to do so. Second, the performance of younger and older children in the induced-verbalization condition was comparable. So younger children can learn just as much as older children by observing a social model *if the younger children are told to describe what they are observing.* Finally, 7- to 8-year-olds in the passive-observation condition reproduced about the same number of behaviors as 7- to 8-year-olds in the induced-verbalization condition. This finding suggests that instructions to describe the model's actions had little effect on 7- to 8-year-olds, who apparently describe what they have seen, even when not told to. Taken together, the results imply that 4- to 5-year-olds may often learn less from social models because they, unlike older children, do not spontaneously produce the verbal descriptions that would help them to remember what they have observed.

An important advantage of the cross-sectional design is that the investigator can collect data from children of different ages over a short time. For example, Coates and Hartup did not have to wait 3 years for their 4- to 5-year-olds to become 7- to 8-year-olds in order to test their developmental hypotheses. They merely sampled from two age groups and tested both samples simultaneously. Yet there are two important limitations of cross-sectional research.

Cohort Effects

Notice that in cross-sectional research, participants at each age level are *different* people. That is, they come from different cohorts, where a *cohort* is defined as a group of people of the same age who are exposed to similar cultural environments and historical events as they are growing up. The fact that cross-sectional comparisons always involve different cohorts presents us with a thorny interpretive problem, for any age differences that are found in the study may not always be due to age or development but, rather, may reflect other cultural or historical factors that distinguish members of different cohorts. Stated another way, cross-sectional comparisons *confound age and cohort effects.*

An example should clarify the issue. For years, cross-sectional research consistently indicated that young adults score slightly higher on intelligence tests than middle-aged adults, who, in turn, score much higher than the elderly. But does intelligence decline with age, as these findings would seem to indicate? Not necessarily! More recent research (Schaie, 1990) reveals that individuals' intelligence test scores remain relatively stable over the years and that the earlier studies were really measuring something quite different: age differences in education. The older adults in the cross-sectional studies had had less schooling and, therefore, scored lower on intelligence tests than the middle-aged and young adult samples. Their test scores had not declined but, rather, had always been lower than those of the younger adults with whom they were compared. So the earlier cross-sectional research had discovered a **cohort effect,** not a true developmental change.

Despite this important limitation, the cross-sectional comparison is still the design that developmentalists use most often. Why? Because it has the advantage of being quick and easy; we can go out this year, sample individuals of different ages, and be done with it. Moreover, this design is likely to yield valid conclusions when there is little reason to believe that the cohorts being studied have had widely different experiences while growing up. So if we compared 4- to 5-year-olds with 7- to 8-year-olds, as Coates and Hartup did, we might feel reasonably confident that history or the prevailing culture had not changed in any major way in the 3 years that separate these two cohorts. It is mainly in studies that attempt to make inferences about development over a span of many years that cohort effects present a serious problem.

Data on Individual Development

There is a second noteworthy limitation of the cross-sectional design: It tells us nothing about the development of *individuals* because each person is observed *at only one point in time.* So cross-sectional comparisons cannot provide answers to questions such as "When will *my* child become more independent?" or "Will aggressive 2-year-olds become aggressive 5-year-olds?" To address issues like these, investigators often turn to a second kind of developmental comparison, the longitudinal design.

The Longitudinal Design

In a **longitudinal design,** the same participants are observed repeatedly over a period of time. The time period may be relatively brief—six months to a year—or it may be very long, spanning a lifetime. Researchers may be studying one particular aspect of development, such as intelligence, or many. By repeatedly testing the same participants, investigators can assess the *stability* (continuity) of various attributes for each person in the sample. They can also identify normative developmental trends and processes by looking for commonalities, such as the point(s) at which most children undergo various changes and the experiences, if any, that children seem to share prior to reaching these milestones. Finally, the tracking of several participants over time helps investigators to understand *individual differences* in development, particularly if they are able to establish that different kinds of earlier experiences lead to very different outcomes.

Several very noteworthy longitudinal projects have followed children for decades and have assessed many aspects of development (see, for example, Kagan & Moss, 1962; Newman et al., 1997). However, most longitudinal studies are much more modest in direction and scope. For example, Carolee Howes and Catherine Matheson (1992) con-

cohort effect
age-related difference among cohorts that is attributable to cultural/historical differences in cohorts' growing-up experiences rather than to true developmental change.

longitudinal design
a research design in which one group of subjects is studied repeatedly over a period of months or years.

Leisure activities of the 1930s (left) and the 1990s (right). As these photos illustrate, the kinds of experiences that children growing up in the 1930s had were very different from those of today's youth. Many believe that cross-generational changes in the environment may limit the results of a longitudinal study to the youngsters who were growing up while the research was in progress.

ducted a study in which the pretend play activities of a group of 1- to 2-year-olds were repeatedly observed at 6-month intervals over the next 3 years. Using a classification scheme that assessed the cognitive complexity of play, Howes and Matheson sought to determine (1) whether play did reliably become more complex with age, (2) whether children reliably differed in the complexity of their play, and (3) whether the complexity of a child's play reliably forecasted his or her social competencies with peers. Not surprisingly, all children displayed increases in the complexity of their play over the 3-year period, although there were reliable individual differences in play complexity at each observation point. In addition, there was a clear relationship between the complexity of a child's play and social competence with peers: Children who engaged in more complex forms of play at any given age were the ones who were rated as most outgoing and least aggressive at the next observation period 6 months later. So this longitudinal study shows that complexity of pretend play not only increases with age but is also a reliable predictor of children's future social competencies with peers.

Although we have portrayed the longitudinal design in a very favorable manner, this approach has several potential drawbacks as well. For example, longitudinal projects can be very *costly* and *time-consuming*. These points are especially important in that the focus of theory and research in the developmental sciences is constantly changing, and longitudinal questions that seem exciting at the beginning of a 10- or 20-year project may seem rather trivial by the time the project ends. **Practice effects** can also threaten the validity of longitudinal studies: Participants who are repeatedly interviewed or tested may become test-wise or increasingly familiar with the content of the test itself, showing performance improvements that are unrelated to normal patterns of development. Longitudinal researchers may also have a problem with **selective attrition**; children may move away or become bored with participating, or they may have parents who, for one reason or another, will not allow them to continue in the study. The result is a smaller and potentially **nonrepresentative sample** that not only provides less information about the developmental issues in question but also may limit the conclusions of the study to those children who do not move away and who remain cooperative over the long run.

There is another shortcoming of long-term longitudinal studies that students often see right away—the **cross-generational problem.** Children in a longitudinal project are typically drawn from one cohort and are likely to have very different kinds of experiences than youngsters from other eras. Consider, for example, how the times have changed since the 1930s and 1940s, when children in some of the early long-term longitudinal studies were growing up. In this age of dual-career families, more youngsters

practice effect
changes in participants' natural responses as a result of repeated testing.

selective attrition
nonrandom loss of participants during a study which results in a nonrepresentative sample.

nonrepresentative sample
a subgroup that differs in important ways from the larger group (or population) to which it belongs.

cross-generational problem
the fact that long-term changes in the environment may limit conclusions of a longitudinal project to that generation of children who were growing up while the study was in progress.

are attending day-care centers and nursery schools than ever before. Modern families are smaller than those of years past, meaning that children now have fewer brothers and sisters. Families also move more frequently than they did in the 1930s and 1940s, so that many children from the modern era are exposed to a wider variety of people and places than was typical in years gone by. And no matter where they may be living, today's youngsters grow up in front of television sets and computers, influences that were not available during the 1930s and 1940s. So children of earlier eras lived in a very different world, and we cannot be certain that these youngsters developed in precisely the same way as today's children. Stated another way, cross-generational changes in the environment may limit the conclusions of a longitudinal project to those participants who were growing up while the study was in progress.

We have seen that the cross-sectional and the longitudinal designs each have distinct advantages and disadvantages. Might it be possible to combine the best features of both approaches? A third kind of developmental comparison—the sequential design—tries to do just that.

The Sequential Design

Sequential designs combine the best features of cross-sectional and longitudinal studies by selecting participants of different ages and following each of these cohorts over time. To illustrate, imagine that we wished to study the development of children's logical reasoning abilities between the ages of 6 and 12. We might begin in 1999 by testing the logical reasoning of a sample of 6-year-olds (the 1993 birth cohort) and a sample of 8-year-olds (the 1991 birth cohort). We could then retest the reasoning abilities of both those groups in 2001 and 2003. Notice that the design calls for us to follow the 1993 cohort from ages 6 through 10 and the 1991 cohort from ages 8 through 12. A graphic representation of this research plan appears in Figure 1.4.

sequential design
a research design in which subjects from different age groups are studied repeatedly over a period of months or years.

There are three major strengths of this sequential design. First, it allows us to determine whether cohort effects are influencing our results by comparing the logical reasoning of same-aged children who were born in different years. As shown in the figure, cohort effects are assessed by comparing the logical reasoning of the two samples at ages 8 and 10. If the samples do not differ, we can assume that cohort effects are not operating. Figure 1.4 also illustrates a second major advantage of our sequential design: It allows us to make both longitudinal and cross-sectional comparisons in the same study. If the age trends in logical reasoning are similar in both the longitudinal and the cross-sectional comparisons, we can be quite confident that they represent true developmental changes in logical reasoning abilities. Finally, sequential designs are often more efficient than standard longitudinal designs. In our example, we could trace

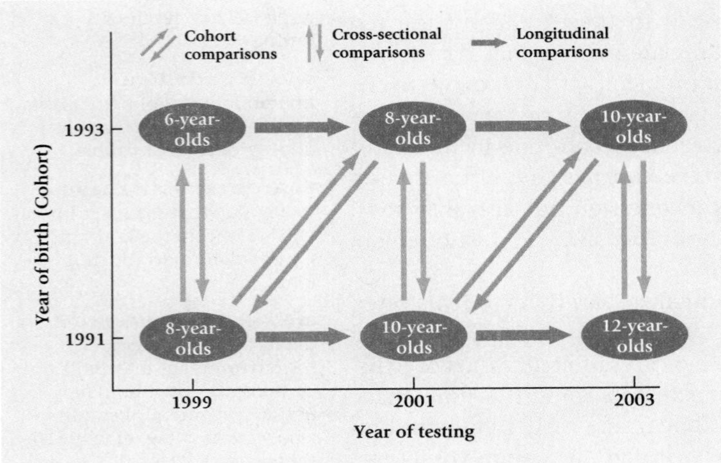

Figure 1.4 *Example of a sequential design. Two samples of children, one born in 1991 and one born in 1993, are observed longitudinally between the ages of 6 and 12. The design permits the investigator to assess cohort effects by comparing children of the same age who were born in different years. In the absence of cohort effects, the longitudinal and cross-sectional comparisons in this design also permit the researcher to make strong statements about the strength and direction of any developmental changes.*

Table 1.4 Strengths and Limitations of Three Developmental Designs

Design	Procedure	Strengths	Limitations
Cross-sectional	Observes people of different ages (or cohorts) at one point in time.	Demonstrates age differences, hints at developmental trends; relatively inexpensive; takes little time to conduct.	Age trends may reflect extraneous differences between cohorts rather than true developmental change; provides no data on the development of individuals because each participant is observed at only one point in time.
Longitudinal	Observes people of one cohort repeatedly over time.	Provides data on the development of individuals; can reveal links between early experiences and later outcomes; indicates how individuals are alike and how they are different in the ways they change over time.	Relatively time-consuming and expensive; selective attrition may yield nonrepresentative sample that limits the generalizability of one's conclusions; cross-generational changes may limit one's conclusions to the cohort that was studied.
Sequential	Combines the cross-sectional and the longitudinal approaches by observing different cohorts repeatedly over time.	Discriminates true developmental trends from cohort effects; indicates whether developmental changes experienced by one cohort are similar to those experienced by other cohorts; often less costly and time-consuming than the longitudinal approach.	More costly and time-consuming than cross-sectional research; despite being the strongest design, may still leave questions about whether a developmental change is generalizable beyond the cohorts studied.

the development of logical reasoning over a 6-year age range, even though our study would take only 4 years to conduct. A standard longitudinal comparison that initially sampled 6-year-old participants would take 6 years to provide similar information. Clearly, this combination of the cross-sectional and longitudinal designs is a rather versatile alternative to either of these approaches.

WHAT DO YOU THINK?

Suppose that you hoped to study the effects of famine on developing children. What research methods and designs would you choose to conduct your study?

To help you review and compare the three major developmental designs, Table 1.4 provides a brief description of each, along with its major strengths and weaknesses.

CROSS-CULTURAL COMPARISONS

Developmentalists are often hesitant to publish a new finding or conclusion until they have studied enough people to determine that their "discovery" is reliable. However, their conclusions are frequently based on participants living at one point in time within one particular culture or subculture, and it is difficult to know whether these conclusions will apply to future generations or even to youngsters currently growing up in other societies or subcultures (Lerner, 1991). Today, the generalizability of findings across samples and settings has become an important issue, for many theorists have implied that there are "universals" in human development—events and outcomes that all children share as they progress from infancy to adulthood.

Cross-cultural studies are those in which participants from different cultural or subcultural backgrounds are observed, tested, and compared on one or more aspects of development. Studies of this kind serve many purposes. For example, they allow the investigator to determine whether conclusions drawn about the development of children from one social context (such as middle-class, white youngsters in the United States) also characterize children growing up in other societies or even those from different ethnic or socioeconomic backgrounds within the same society (for example, American children of Hispanic ancestry or those from economically disadvantaged homes). So the **cross-cultural comparison** guards against the overgeneralization of research findings and, indeed, is the only way to determine whether there are truly "universals" in human development.

However, many investigators who favor the cross-cultural approach are looking for *differences* rather than similarities. They recognize that human beings develop in societies that have very different ideas about issues such as the proper times and procedures for disciplining children, the activities that are most appropriate for boys and for girls, the time at which childhood ends and adulthood begins, the treatment of the aged, and countless other aspects of life. They have also learned that people from various cultures differ in the ways they perceive the world, express their emotions, think, and solve problems. So apart from its focus on universals in development, the cross-cultural approach also illustrates that human development is heavily influenced by the cultural context in which it occurs (see Box 1.3 for a dramatic illustration of cultural diversity in gender roles).

Isn't it remarkable how many methods and designs that developmentalists have at their disposal? This diversity of available procedures is a definite strength because findings gained through one procedure can then be checked and perhaps confirmed through other procedures. Indeed, providing such *converging evidence* serves a most important function by demonstrating that the conclusion a researcher draws is truly a "discovery" and not merely an artifact of the method or the design used to collect the original data. So there is no "best method" for studying children and adolescents; each of the approaches we have considered has contributed substantially to our understanding of human development.

ETHICAL CONSIDERATIONS IN DEVELOPMENTAL RESEARCH

When designing and conducting research with humans, researchers may face thorny issues centering on *research ethics*—the standards of conduct that investigators are ethically bound to honor in order to protect their research participants from physical or psychological harm. Some ethical issues are easily resolved: One simply does *not* conduct experiments that will almost certainly cause physical or psychological damage, such as physical abuse, starvation, isolation for long periods, and the like. However, most ethical issues are far more subtle. Here are some of the dilemmas that developmentalists may have to resolve during their careers as researchers:

cross-cultural comparison
a study that compares the behavior and/or development of people from different cultural or subcultural backgrounds.

Concept Check 1.3
Selecting a Design

Check your understanding of the uses and strengths of various developmental designs by selecting a design that seems most appropriate for each of the following research questions. Choose from the following designs: (a) cross-sectional, (b) longitudinal, (c) sequential, (d) cross-cultural. Answers appear in the Appendix.

_____ 1. A researcher wants to quickly assess whether 4-, 6-, and 8-year-olds differ in their willingness to donate part of their allowance to children less fortunate than themselves.

_____ 2. A researcher who has money for a 6-week summer preschool education program wants to know whether the program will have greater long-term benefits for 2-year-olds than for 3- or 4-year-olds.

_____ 3. A developmentalist hopes to determine whether all children go through the same stages of intellectual development between infancy and adolescence.

_____ 4. A specialist in early childhood education hopes to learn whether especially bright 2-year-olds are likely to remain smarter than most peers by the time they are 6 years old.

1.3

CULTURAL INFLUENCES

A Cross-Cultural Comparison of Gender Roles

One of the greatest values of cross-cultural comparisons is that they can tell us whether a developmental phenomenon is or is not universal. Consider the roles that males and females play in our society. In our culture, playing the masculine role has traditionally required traits such as independence, assertiveness, and dominance. By contrast, females are expected to be more nurturant and sensitive to other people. Are these masculine and feminine roles universal? Could biological differences between the sexes lead inevitably to sex differences in behavior?

Some years ago, anthropologist Margaret Mead (1935) compared the gender roles adopted by people in three tribal societies on the island of New Guinea, and her observations are certainly thought provoking. In the Arapesh tribe, both men and women were taught to play what we would regard as a feminine role: They were cooperative, nonaggressive, and sensitive to the needs of others. By contrast, both men and women of the Mundugumor tribe were brought up to be aggressive and emotionally unresponsive to other people—a masculine pattern of behavior by Western standards. Finally, the Tchambuli displayed a pattern of gender-role development that was the direct opposite of the Western pattern: Males were passive, emotionally dependent, and socially sensitive, whereas females were dominant, independent, and assertive!

Mead's cross-cultural comparison suggests that cultural learning may have far more to do with the characteristic behavior patterns of men and women than biological differences do. So we very much need cross-cultural comparisons such as Mead's. Without them, we might easily make the mistake of assuming that whatever holds true in our society holds true everywhere; with their help, we can begin to understand the contributions of biology and environment to human development.

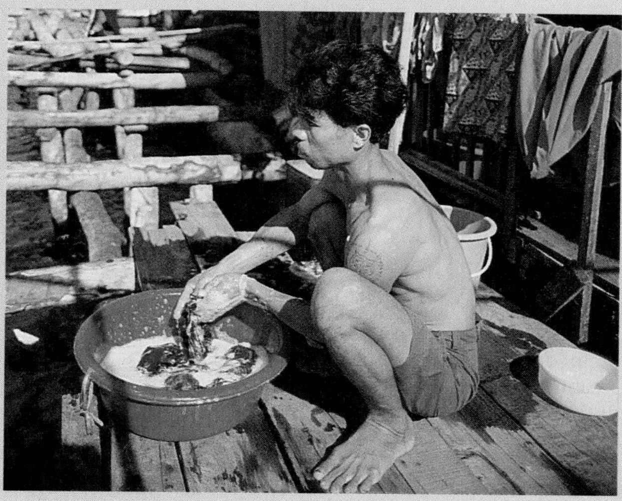

The roles assumed by men and women may vary dramatically from culture to culture.

- Can children or adolescents be exposed to temptations that virtually guarantee that they will cheat or break other rules?
- Am I ever justified in deceiving participants, either by misinforming them about the purpose of my study or by telling them something untrue about themselves (for example, "You did poorly on this test")?
- Can I observe my participants in the natural setting without informing them that they are the subjects of a scientific investigation?
- Is it acceptable to tell children that their classmates think that an obviously incorrect answer is "correct" to see whether participants will conform to the judgments of their peers?
- Am I justified in using verbal disapproval as part of my research procedure?

Before reading further, you may wish to think about these issues and formulate your own opinions. Then read Table 1.5 on page 32 and reconsider your viewpoints.

Have any of your opinions changed? It would not be terribly surprising if they hadn't. As you can see, the table guidelines are very general; they do not explicitly permit or prohibit specific operations or practices such as those described in the preceding dilemmas. In fact, any of these dilemmas can be resolved in ways that permit an investigator to use the procedures in question and still remain well within current ethical guidelines. For example, it is generally considered permissible to observe young children in natural settings (for example, at school or in a park) without informing them that they are being studied if the investigator has previously obtained the

Table 1.5 **Major Rights of Children and Responsibilities of Investigators Involved in Psychological Research**

Ethical considerations are especially complex when children participate in psychological research. Children are more vulnerable than adolescents and adults to physical and psychological harm. Moreover, young children may not always fully understand what they are committing themselves to when they agree to participate in a study. In order to protect children who participate in psychological research and to clarify the responsibilities of researchers who work with children, the American Psychological Association (1992) and the Society for Research in Child Development (1993) have endorsed special ethical guidelines, the more important of which are as follows:

Protection from Harm[a]
The investigator may use no research operation that may harm the child either physically or psychologically. Psychological harm is difficult to define; nevertheless, its definition remains the responsibility of the investigator. When an investigator is in doubt about the possible harmful effects of the research operations, he or she must seek consultation from others. When harm seems possible, he or she is obligated to find other means of obtaining the information or abandon the research.

Informed Consent
The informed consent of parents as well as others who act in the child's behalf—teachers, superintendents of institutions—should be obtained, preferably in writing. Informed consent requires that the parent or other responsible adult be told all features of the research that may affect his or her willingness to allow the child to participate. Moreover, federal guidelines in the United States specify that all children 7 years of age and older have the right to have explained to them, in understandable language, all aspects of the research that could affect their willingness to participate. Of course, children of any age always have the right to choose not to participate or to discontinue participation in research at any time. This provision is a tricky one, however: Even if they are told that they can stop participating in a study at any time, young children may not really grasp how to do so or may not really believe that they can stop without incurring a penalty of some kind. However, children are much more likely to understand their rights of assent and to exercise them if the researcher carefully explains that he or she would not be upset if the child chose not to participate or to stop participating (Abramovitch et al., 1995).

Confidentiality
Researchers must keep in confidence all information obtained from research participants. Children have the right to concealment of their identity on all data collected and reported, either in writing or informally. The one exception is most states have laws that prohibit an investigator from withholding the names of suspected victims of child abuse or neglect (Liss, 1994).

Deception/Debriefing/Knowledge of Results
Although children have the right to know the purposes of a study in advance, a particular project may necessitate concealment of information, or deception. Whenever concealment or deception is thought to be essential to the conduct of research, the investigator must satisfy a committee of peers that this judgment is correct. If deception or concealment is used, participants must later be *debriefed*—that is, told, in language they can understand, the true purpose of the study and why it was necessary to deceive them. Children also have the right to be informed, in language they can understand, of the results of the research in which they have participated.

[a]Ross Thompson (1990) has published an excellent essay on this topic that I would recommend to anyone who conducts (or plans to conduct) research with children.

informed consent (see Table 1.5) of the adults responsible for the children's care and safety in these settings. Ethical guidelines are just that: guidelines. The ultimate responsibility for treating children fairly and protecting them from harm falls squarely on the shoulders of the investigator.

How, then, do investigators decide whether to use a procedure that some may consider questionable on ethical grounds? They generally weigh the advantages and disadvantages of the research by carefully calculating its possible *benefits* (to humanity or to the participants) and comparing them with the potential *risks* that participants may face. If the **benefits-to-risks ratio** is favorable, and if there are no other less-risky procedures that could be used to produce these same benefits, the investigator will generally proceed. However, there are safeguards against overzealous researchers who underestimate the riskiness of their procedures. In the United States and Canada, for example, universities, research foundations, and government agencies that fund research with children have set up human-subjects review committees to provide second (and sometimes third) opinions on the ethical ramifications of all proposed research. The function of these review committees is to reconsider the potential risks and benefits of the proposed research and, more important, to help ensure that all possible steps are taken to protect the welfare of those who may choose to participate in the project.

Interestingly, clashes between the ethical provisions of **confidentiality** and **protection from harm** can pose serious ethical dilemmas for researchers who learn that the well-being of one or more participants (or their associates) may be seriously jeopardized by such life-threatening events as suicidal tendencies and untreated sexually transmitted diseases. These are risks that many investigators may feel ethically bound

informed consent
the right of research participants to receive an explanation, in language they can understand, all aspects of research that may affect their willingness to participate.

benefits-to-risks ratio
a comparison of the possible benefits of a study for advancing knowledge and optimizing life conditions versus its costs to participants in terms of inconvenience and possible harm.

confidentiality
the right of participants to concealment of their identity with respect to the data that they provide.

protection from harm
the right of research participants to be protected from physical or psychological harm.

to report or to help the participant to self-report to the appropriate medical, social, or psychological services. Indeed, adolescents view reporting of these very serious risks (or, alternatively, helping the participant to self-report) in a very favorable way; and they may perceive inaction on the investigator's part as an indication that the problem is considered unimportant, that no services are available to assist them, or that knowledgeable adults cannot be depended upon to help youngsters in need. (See Fisher et al., 1996 for an excellent discussion of the confidentiality dilemmas researchers may face and adolescents' views about appropriate courses of action for researchers to take.)

Ethical considerations may force an investigator to abandon procedures that cause harm or pose unforeseen risks to research participants.

Of course, final approval of all one's safeguards and reporting procedures by a review committee does not absolve investigators of the need to reevaluate the benefits and costs of their projects, even while the research is in progress (Thompson, 1990). Suppose, for example, that a researcher studying children's aggression in a playground setting came to the conclusion that his subjects had (1) discovered his own fascination with aggressive behavior and (2) begun to beat on one another in order to attract his attention. At that point, the risks to participants would have escalated far beyond the researcher's initial estimates, and he would be ethically bound (in my opinion) to stop the research immediately.

In the final analysis, guidelines and review committees do not guarantee that research participants will be treated responsibly; only investigators can do that by constantly reevaluating the consequences of their operations and by modifying or abandoning any procedure that may compromise the welfare or the dignity of those who have volunteered to participate.

POSTSCRIPT: ON BECOMING A WISE CONSUMER OF DEVELOPMENTAL RESEARCH

At this point, you may be wondering "Why do I need to know so much about the methods that developmentalists use to conduct research?" This is a reasonable question given that the vast majority of students who take this course will pursue other careers and will never conduct a scientific study of developing children or adolescents.

My answer is straightforward: Although survey courses such as this one are designed to provide a solid overview of theory and research in the discipline to which they pertain, they should also strive to help you evaluate the relevant information you may encounter in the years ahead. Even if you don't read academic journals in your role as a teacher, school administrator, nurse, probation officer, social worker, or other professional who works with developing persons, then certainly you will be exposed to such information through the popular media—television, newspapers, magazines, and the like. How can you know whether that seemingly dramatic and important new finding you've just read or heard about should be taken seriously?

This is an important issue, for new information about human development is often chronicled in the popular media several months or even years before the data on which the media reports are based finally make their appearance in professional journals. What's more, less than 30% of the findings that developmentalists submit are judged worthy of publication by reputable journals in our discipline. Many media reports of "dramatic" new findings are based on research that other scientists do not regard as very dramatic or even worth publishing.

Even if a media report is based on a published article, coverage of the research and its conclusions is often misleading. For example, one recent TV news story reported on a published article, saying that there was clear evidence that "alcoholism is inherited." As we will see in Chapter 3, this is a far more dramatic conclusion than the authors actually drew. Another metropolitan newspaper report summarized a recent article from the prestigious journal *Developmental Psychology* with the headline "Day care harmful for children." What was never made clear in the newspaper article was the researcher's (Howes, 1990) conclusion that *very-low-quality* day care may be harmful to the social and intellectual development of *some* preschool children but that most youngsters receiving good day care suffer no adverse effects. (The issue of day care and its effects on developing children is explored in depth in Chapter 11.)

I don't mean to imply that you can never trust what you read; rather, I'd caution you to be skeptical and to evaluate media (and journal) reports, using the methodological information presented in this chapter. You might start by asking: How were the data gathered, and how was the study designed? Were appropriate conclusions drawn given the limitations of the method of data collection and the design (correlational vs. experimental; cross-sectional vs. longitudinal) that the investigators used? Were there proper control groups? Have the results of the study been reviewed by other experts in the field and published in a reputable academic journal? Don't assume that published articles are beyond criticism. Many theses and dissertations in the developmental sciences are based on problems and shortcomings that students have identified in previously published research. So take the time to read and evaluate published reports that seem especially relevant to your profession or to your role as a parent. Not only will you have a better understanding of the research and its conclusions, but any lingering questions and doubts you may have can often be addressed through a letter, an e-mail message, or a phone call to the author of the article.

In sum, one must become a knowledgeable consumer in order to get the most out of what the field of human development has to offer. Our discussion of research methodology was undertaken with these objectives in mind, and a solid understanding of these methodological lessons should help you to properly evaluate the research you will encounter, not only throughout this text but from many other sources in the years to come.

SUMMARY

What Is Development?

♦ **Developmental psychology** is the largest of many disciplines that study **development**—the systematic continuities and changes that individuals display over the course of their lives that reflect the influence of biological **maturation** and **learning. Normative developments** are typical developments characterizing all members of a species, whereas **ideographic developments** describe those that may vary across individuals. Developmentalists' goals are to describe, explain, and to optimize development. Human development is a continual and cumulative process that is **holistic,** highly **plastic,** and heavily influenced by the historical and cultural contexts in which it occurs.

Human Development in Historical Perspective

♦ In medieval times, children were afforded few of the rights and protections of today's youth. The 17th and 18th century philosophies of **original sin, innate purity,** and **tabula**

rasa contributed to a more humane outlook on children, and some parents began to record the development of their infant sons and daughters in **baby biographies.** The scientific study of development did not emerge until nearly 1900 when G. Stanley Hall and Sigmund Freud began to collect data and formulate **theories** about human development. Soon, other researchers were deriving **hypotheses** and conducting research to evaluate and extend early theories.

Research Methods in Developmental Psychology

♦ Today's developmentalists, guided by the **scientific method,** use objective data to determine the viability of their theories. Acceptable research methods possess both **reliability** and **validity.** A method is reliable if it produces consistent, replicable results; it is valid if it accurately reflects what it was intended to measure.

♦ The most common methods of data collection in child and adolescent development are self-reports, observational methodologies, case studies, ethnography, and psychophysiological methods. Self-reports include standardized procedures, such as **structured interviews** or **structured questionnaires,** that allow direct comparisons among research participants, and flexible approaches like the **clinical method,** which yields an individualized portrait of each participant's feelings, thoughts, and behaviors.

♦ **Naturalistic observations** are obtained in the natural environments of children or adolescents, whereas **structured observations** take place in laboratories where the investigator cues the behavior of interest.

♦ **Case studies** allow investigators to obtain an in-depth understanding of individual children or adolescents by collecting data based on interviews, observations, and test scores, as well as information from such knowledgeable sources as teachers and parents.

♦ **Ethnography,** used originally by anthropologists, is a descriptive procedure in which the researcher becomes a participant observer within a cultural or subcultural context. He or she carefully observes community members, makes notes from conversations, and compiles information into a detailed portrait of the group's values and traditions and their impacts on developing children and adolescents.

♦ **Psychophysiological methods** measure the relationship between physiological responses and behavior. They are often used to reveal the biological underpinnings of development and to interpret children's perceptual, cognitive, or emotional responses.

Detecting Relationships: Correlational and Experimental Designs

♦ Two general research designs permit researchers to identify relationships among variables that interest them. **Correlational designs** examine relationships as they naturally occur, without any intervention. The **correlation coefficient** is used to estimate the strength and magnitude of the association between variables. However, correlational studies cannot specify whether correlated variables are causally related.

♦ The **experimental design** points to cause-and-effect relationships. The experimenter manipulates one (or more) **independent variables,** exercises **experimental control** over all other **confounding variables** (often by **random assignment** of participants to treatments), and observes the effect(s) of the manipulation(s) on the **dependent variable.** Experiments may be performed in the laboratory or in the natural environment (that is, a **field experiment**), thereby increasing the **ecological validity** of the results. The impact of events that researchers cannot manipulate or control can be studied in **natural (quasi-) experiments.** However, lack of control over natural events prevents the quasi-experimenter from drawing definitive conclusions about cause and effect.

Designs for Studying Development

♦ Cross-sectional, longitudinal, and sequential designs are employed to detect developmental change. The **cross-sectional design,** which compares different age groups at a single point in time, is easy to conduct, but it cannot tell us how individuals develop, and its results may be misleading if the age trends observed are actually due to **cohort effects** rather than true developmental change.

♦ The **longitudinal design** detects developmental change by repeatedly examining the same participants as they grow older. Though it identifies developmental continuities and changes and individual differences in development, the longitudinal design is subject to such problems as **practice effects** and **selective attrition,** which results in **nonrepresentative samples.** Moreover, the **cross-generational** problem of long-term longitudinal studies implies that results may be limited to the particular cohort studied.

♦ The **sequential design,** a combination of the cross-sectional and longitudinal designs, offers researchers the advantages of both approaches and allows them to discriminate true developmental trends from troublesome cohort effects.

Cross-cultural Comparisons

♦ **Cross-cultural studies,** in which participants from different cultures and subcultures are compared on one or more aspects of development, are becoming increasingly important. Only by comparing people from many cultures can we identify universal patterns of development and, at the same time, demonstrate that other aspects of development are heavily influenced by social contexts.

Ethical Considerations in Developmental Research

♦ Research conducted with children and adolescents raises some challenging ethical issues. The benefits to be gained from the research should always exceed the risks to participants. But no matter how positive this **benefits-to-risks ratio,** participants have the rights to expect **protection from harm,** give **informed consent** to participate (or to stop participating), have their data treated with **confidentiality,** and receive explanations for any deception that may have been necessary to collect their data.

Researchers investigating human development employ a variety of research techniques. They utilize different research methodologies, including experimentation, correlation studies, case studies, and clinical interviews. In addition, the time frames for developmental research may be very short, using cross-sectional samples, or much longer, using longitudinal or sequential samples. You can learn more about the "research road" by visiting: **http://trochim.human.cornell.edu/kb/content1.htm** At this web site you can access an online research methods text.

KEY TERMS

development, 2
developmental continuities, 3
developmental psychology, 3
maturation, 3
learning, 3
normative development, 4
ideographic development, 4
holistic perspective, 6
plasticity, 6
original sin, 8
innate purity, 8
tabula rasa, 8
baby biography, 9
theory, 11
hypothesis, 11
scientific method, 11
reliability, 12
validity, 12
structured interview or structured questionnaire, 13
clinical method, 14
naturalistic observation, 14
observer influence, 15
structured observation, 15
case study, 16
ethnography, 16
psychophysiological methods, 17
correlational design, 19
correlation coefficient, 19
experimental design, 20
independent variable, 20
dependent variable, 20
confounding variable, 21
experimental control, 21
random assignment, 21
ecological validity, 21
field experiment, 22
natural (or quasi) experiment, 23
cross-sectional design, 24
cohort effects, 26
longitudinal design, 26
practice effect, 27
selective attrition, 27
nonrepresentative sample, 27
cross-generational problem, 27
sequential design, 28
cross-cultural comparison, 30
informed consent, 32
benefits-to-risks ratio, 32
confidentiality, 32
protection from harm, 32

2

Theories of Human Development

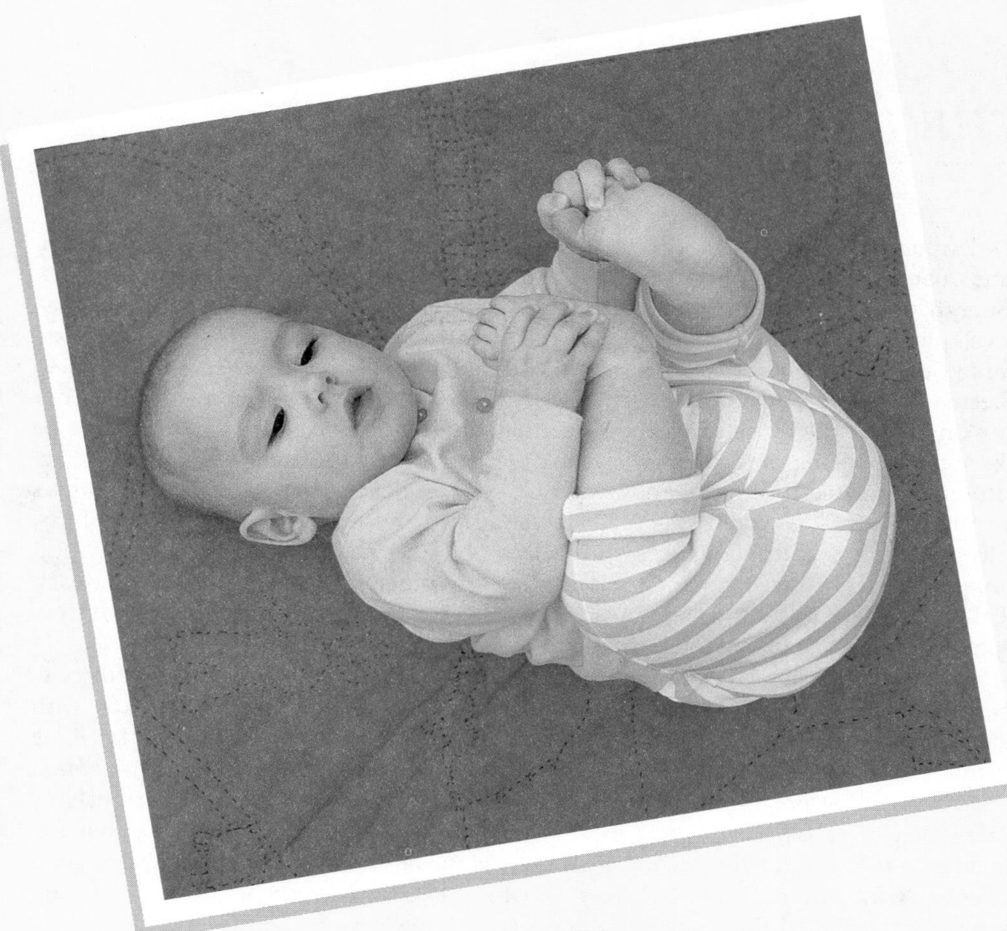

That's only true in theory, not in practice!

ANONYMOUS

There is nothing as practical as a good theory.

KURT LEWIN

Recently, a first-year graduate student expressed her opinion that participating in sports contributed strongly to young women's self-esteem. When I asked her why she thought this, she jokingly replied "It worked for me!" I laughed and said, "I think you'll need more of a conceptual framework than that to guide your proposed research," and sent her off to think about the issue. Several days later, having read what limited research was available, she returned with a *theory:* Allegedly, sports participation for teenage girls promotes positive body images, perceptions of physical competence, and more flexible outlooks on what it means to be a woman, all of which should contribute positively to a young woman's sense of self-worth. This student had now not only specified a relationship that she believed to be true (that is, sports participation promotes women's self-esteem) but had also indicated *why* she believed that relationship to be true. Within weeks, she had refined her theory to the point of formulating a research design and selecting measures to assess all the important variables, and she is now writing a thesis on her work in this area.

THE NATURE OF SCIENTIFIC THEORIES

A scientific **theory** is nothing more than a set of concepts and propositions that indicate what a scientist believes to be true about his or her specific area of investigation. Some theories in the developmental sciences are broad in scope, seeking to explain the development of global domains, such as personality or cognition, whereas others are limited to a specific issue, such as the impact of sports participation on women's self-esteem. But the beauty of all scientific theories is that they help us to organize our thinking about the aspects of experience that interest us. Imagine what life might be like for a researcher who plugs away at collecting data and cataloging fact after fact without organizing this information around a set of concepts and propositions. Chances are that this person would eventually be swamped by seemingly unconnected facts, thus qualifying as a trivia expert who lacks a "big picture." So theories are of critical importance to the developmental sciences (or any other scientific discipline), for each of them provides us with a "lens" through which we can interpret any number of specific observations about developing individuals.

What are the characteristics of a good theory? Ideally, it should be concise, or **parsimonious,** and yet be able to explain a broad range of phenomena. A theory with few principles that accounts for a large number of empirical observations is far more useful than a second theory that requires many principles and assumptions to explain the same number of (or fewer of) observations. In addition, good theories are **falsifiable**—that is, capable of making explicit predictions about future events so that the theory can be supported or disconfirmed. And as the falsifiability criterion implies, good theories do not limit themselves to that which is already known. Instead, they are **heuristic**—meaning that they build on existing knowledge by continuing to generate testable hypotheses that, if confirmed by future research, will lead to a much richer understanding of the phenomena of interest (see Figure 2.1).

Clearly, a theory that simply "explains" a set of observations without making any new predictions is neither falsifiable nor heuristic and is of limited scientific value. And even if a theory is parsimonious, falsifiable, and sufficiently heuristic to formulate a hypothesis, it may still be inaccurate or *invalid,* and may have to be discarded altogether if its predictions are consistently disconfirmed. So it may seem at times that some theoretical pronouncements *are* true only in theory, not in practice. However, there is clearly another side to this issue. Even "bad" theories that are later disconfirmed may have served a useful purpose by stimulating the new knowledge that led to their demise. We might also note that good theories survive because they continue to generate new knowledge, much of which may have practical implications that truly

theory
a set of concepts and propositions that describe, organize, and explain a set of observations.

parsimony
a criterion for evaluating the scientific merit of theories, a parsimonious theory is one that uses relatively few explanatory principles to explain a broad set of observations.

falsifiability
a criterion for evaluating the scientific merit of theories. A theory is falsifiable when it is capable of generating predictions that could be disconfirmed.

heuristic value
a criterion for evaluating the scientific merit of theories. An heuristic theory is one that continues to stimulate new research and discoveries.

Figure 2.1 *The role of theory in scientific investigation.*

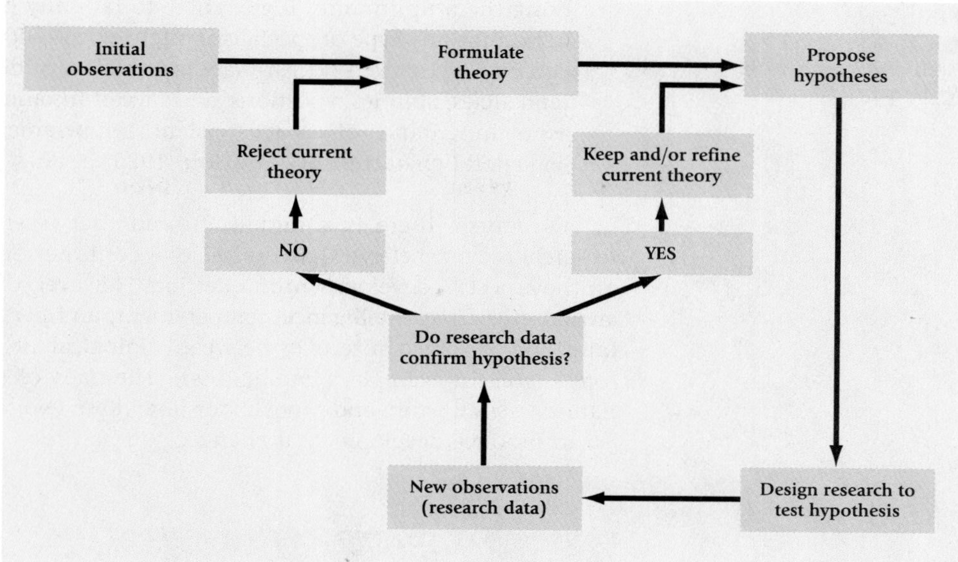

benefit humanity. In this sense, there is nothing quite so practical as a *good* theory.

In this chapter, we will examine the basic premises of six broad theoretical perspectives that have each had a major impact on the science of human development: the *psychoanalytic* viewpoint, the *learning* viewpoint, the *cognitive-developmental* viewpoint, the *information-processing* viewpoint, the *evolutionary* viewpoint, and the *ecological systems* viewpoint. Although these theories are central to our discipline and could be characterized as the conceptual bedrock of developmental psychology, there are many other recent viewpoints that have emerged as extensions of or complements to "the grand theories," and we consider the strengths and weaknesses of these alternative approaches. For example, exciting new theories of *behavioral genetics* are introduced in Chapter 3, where we concentrate on hereditary influences on human development.

As we will see in our upcoming review, different theories emphasize different areas or aspects of development. In addition, each theory makes a particular set of assumptions about human nature and the causes of development. So before reviewing the content of our "grand theories," it may be helpful to consider some of the more basic issues on which they differ.

QUESTIONS AND CONTROVERSIES ABOUT HUMAN DEVELOPMENT

What are developing humans like? What causes development? What courses does it follow? Let us look at three major issues on which developmental theories often disagree.

The Nature/Nurture Issue

Is human development primarily the result of nature (biological forces) or nurture (environmental forces)? Perhaps no theoretical controversy has been any more heated than this **nature/nurture issue.** Here are two opposing viewpoints:

> Heredity and not environment is the chief maker of man. . . . Nearly all of the misery and nearly all of the happiness in the world are due not to environment. . . . The differences among men are due to differences in germ cells with which they were born (Wiggam, 1923, p. 42).

> Give me a dozen healthy infants, well formed, and my own specified world to

nature/nurture issue
the debate among developmental theorists about the relative importance of biological predispositions (nature) and environmental influences (nurture) as determinants of human development.

> bring them up in and I'll guarantee to take any one at random and train him to become any type of specialist I might select—doctor, lawyer, artist, merchant, chief, and yes, even beggar-man and thief, regardless of his talents, penchants, tendencies, abilities, vocations, and race of his ancestors. There is no such thing as an inheritance of capacity, talent, temperament, mental constitution, and behavioral characteristics (Watson, 1925, p. 82).

Of course, there is a middle ground that is endorsed by many contemporary researchers who believe that the relative contributions of nature and nurture depend on the aspect of development in question. However, they stress that all complex human attributes such as intelligence, temperament, and personality are the end products of a long and involved interplay between biological predispositions and environmental forces (see, for example, Plomin, 1990). Their advice to us, then, is to think less about nature *versus* nurture and more about how these two sets of influences combine or *interact* to produce developmental change.

The Active/Passive Issue

Another topic of theoretical debate is the **active/passive issue.** Are children curious, active creatures who largely determine how agents of society treat them? Or are they passive souls on whom society fixes its stamp? Consider the implications of these opposing viewpoints. If we could show that children are extremely malleable—literally at the mercy of those who raise them—then perhaps individuals who turned out to be less than productive would be justified in suing their overseers for malfeasance. Indeed, one troubled young man in the United States used this logic to bring a malfeasance suit against his parents. Perhaps you can anticipate the defense that the parents' lawyer offered. Counsel argued that the parents had tried many strategies in an attempt to raise their child right but that he responded favorably to none of them. The implication is that this young man played an *active* role in determining how his parents treated him and is largely responsible for creating the climate in which he was raised.

Which of these perspectives do you consider more reasonable? Think about it, for very soon, you will have an opportunity to state your views on this and other topics of theoretical debate.

activity/passivity issue
a debate among developmental theorists about whether children are active contributors to their own development or passive recipients of environmental influence.

continuity/discontinuity issue
a debate among theorists about whether developmental changes are quantitative and continuous or qualitative and discontinuous (i.e., stagelike).

quantitative change
incremental change in degree without sudden transformations; for example, some view the small yearly increases in height and weight that 2- to 11-year-olds display as quantitative developmental changes.

qualitative change
changes in kind that make individuals fundamentally different than they were before. The transformation of a prelinguistic infant into a language user is viewed by many as a qualitative change in communication skills.

The Continuity/Discontinuity Issue

Think for a moment about developmental change. Do you think that the changes we experience occur very gradually? Or would you say that these changes are rather abrupt?

On one side of this **continuity/discontinuity issue** are continuity theorists who view human development as an additive process that occurs gradually and continuously, without sudden changes. They might represent the course of developmental change with a smooth growth curve like the one in Figure 2.2(a). By contrast, discontinuity theorists describe the road to maturity as a series of abrupt changes, each of which elevates the child to a new and presumably more advanced level of functioning. These levels, or stages, are represented by the steps of the discontinuous growth curve in Figure 2.2(b).

A second aspect of the continuity/discontinuity issue centers on whether developmental changes are quantitative or qualitative in nature. **Quantitative changes** are changes in *degree*. For example, children grow taller and run a little faster with each passing year, and they acquire more and more knowledge about the world around them. By contrast, **qualitative changes** are changes in *kind* that make the individual fundamentally different in some way than he or she was earlier. The transformation of a

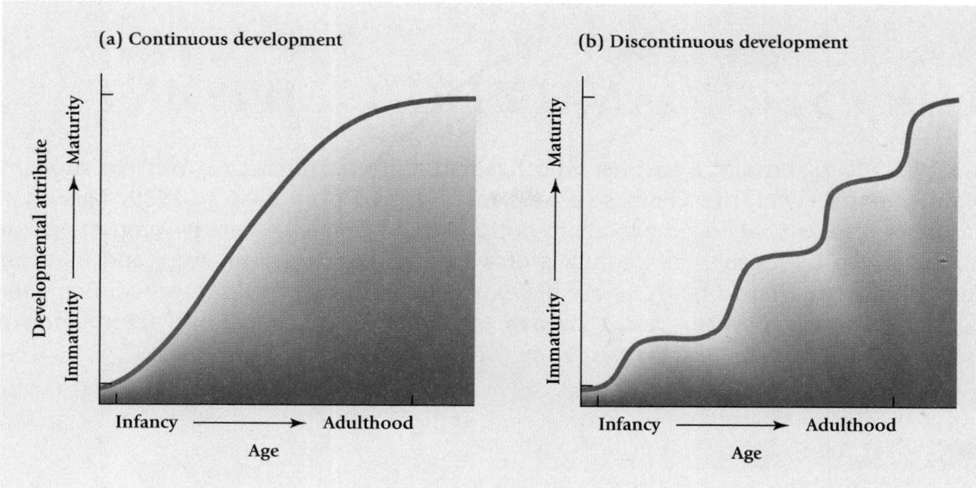

Figure 2.2 *The course of development as described by continuity and discontinuity (stage) theorists.*

tadpole into a frog is a qualitative change. Similarly, an infant who lacks language may be qualitatively different from a preschooler who speaks well, and an adolescent who is sexually mature may be fundamentally different from a classmate who has yet to reach puberty. Continuity theorists generally think that developmental changes are basically quantitative in nature, whereas discontinuity theorists tend to portray development as a sequence of qualitative changes. Indeed, discontinuity theorists claim that we progress through **developmental stages,** each of which is a distinct phase of life characterized by a particular set of abilities, emotions, motives, or behaviors that form a coherent pattern.

Interestingly, societies may take different positions on the continuity/discontinuity issue. Some Pacific and Far Eastern cultures, for example, have words for infant qualities that are never used to describe adults, and adult terms such as *intelligent* or *angry* are never used to characterize infants (Kagan, 1991). People in these cultures view personality development as discontinuous, and infants are regarded as so fundamentally different from adults that they cannot be judged on the same personality dimensions. By contrast, North Americans and Northern Europeans are more inclined to assume that personality development is a continuous process and to search for the seeds of adult personality in babies' temperaments.

These, then, are the major developmental controversies that theories resolve in different ways. You may wish to clarify your own stand on these issues by completing the brief questionnaire in Box 2.1. At the end of the chapter, Table 2.4 indicates how the major developmental theories address these questions so you can compare their assumptions about human development with your own.

Now let's begin our survey of the theories, starting with Freud's psychoanalytic approach.

developmental stage
a distinct phase within a larger sequence of devleopment; a period characterized by a particular set of abilities, motives, behaviors, or emotions that occur together and form a coherent pattern.

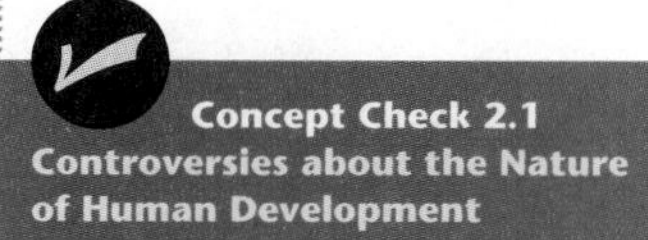

Concept Check 2.1
Controversies about the Nature of Human Development

Check your understanding of conceptual controversies about the nature of human development by identifying the following spokesperson's position on the nature/nurture issue, the active/passive issue, and the continuity/discontinuity issue:

> Children the world over go through the same distinct phases of intellectual development. Yet, there are clear individual differences. Very bright parents have the brightest youngsters; even when these children are cared for by undereducated nannies, their brightness will show through as long as they have many puzzles to solve and other challenges to master on their own.

THE PSYCHOANALYTIC VIEWPOINT

It is difficult to think of a theorist who has had a greater impact on Western thought than Sigmund Freud, the Viennese physician who lived from 1856 to 1939. This revolutionary thinker challenged prevailing notions about human nature by proposing that we are driven by motives and conflicts of which we are largely unaware and that our personalities are shaped by our early life experiences. In this section, we will first consider Freud's early **psychosexual theory** of human development and then compare Freud's theory with that of his best-known follower, Erik Erikson.

The psychoanalytic theory of Sigmund Freud (1856–1939) changed our thinking about developing children.

Freud's Psychosexual Theory

Freud was a practicing neurologist who formulated his theory of human development from his analyses of his emotionally disturbed patients' life histories. Seeking to relieve their nervous symptoms and anxieties, he relied heavily on such methods as hypnosis, free association (a quick spelling out of one's immediate thoughts), and dream analysis because they gave some indication of **unconscious motives** that patients had **repressed** (that is, forced out of their conscious awareness). By analyzing these motives and the events that caused their suppression, Freud concluded that human development is a conflictual process: As biological creatures, we have basic sexual and aggressive **instincts** that *must* be served, yet society dictates that many of these drives are undesirable and *must* be restrained. According to Freud, the ways in which parents manage these sexual and aggressive urges in the first few years of life play a major role in shaping their children's conduct and character.

DEVELOPMENTAL ISSUES

2.1

Where Do You Stand on Major Developmental Issues?

1. Biological influences (heredity, maturational forces) and environmental influences (culture, neighborhoods, parenting styles, educational experiences) both contribute to development. Overall:
   a. biological factors contribute more than environmental factors.
   b. biological and environmental factors are equally important.
   c. environmental factors contribute more than biological factors.
2. Children and adolescents are:
   a. active beings who play a major role in determining their own developmental outcomes.
   b. passive beings whose developmental outcomes largely reflect the influences of other people and circumstances beyond their control.
3. Development proceeds:
   a. through distinct stages, so that the individual changes abruptly into a quite different kind of person than he or she was in an earlier stage.
   b. continuously, in small increments without abrupt changes.
4. A good analogy for a developing human being might be:
   a. a complex machine that becomes ever more complex as its parts (behaviors, emotions, abilities) grow more numerous and sophisticated.
   b. an entity that cannot be likened to a collection of parts and that blossoms with age, much as a simple seed evolves into a blooming rose.

	Questions			
	1	2	3	4
Your Answers	_____	_____	_____	_____

Three Components of Personality

Freud's psychosexual theory specifies that three components of personality—the id, ego, and superego—develop and gradually become integrated in a series of five psychosexual stages. The **id** is all that is present at birth. Its sole function is to satisfy inborn biological instincts, and it will try to do so immediately. If you think about it, young infants do seem to be "all id." When hungry or wet, they simply fuss and cry until their needs are met, and they are not known for their patience.

The **ego** is the conscious, rational component of the personality that reflects the child's emerging abilities to perceive, learn, remember, and reason. Its function is to find realistic means of gratifying instincts, as when a hungry toddler, remembering how she gets food, seeks out mom and says "cookie." As their egos mature, children become better at controlling their irrational ids and finding realistic ways to gratify needs on their own.

However, realistic solutions to needs are not always acceptable, as a hungry 3-year-old who is caught snitching cookies between meals may soon discover. The final component of personality, or **superego,** is the seat of the conscience. It arises between the ages of 3 and 6 as children *internalize* (take on as their own) the moral values and standards of their parents (Freud, 1933). Once the superego emerges, children do not need an adult to tell them they have been good or bad; they are now aware of their own transgressions and feel guilty or ashamed about their unethical conduct. So the superego is truly an internal censor. It insists that the ego find socially acceptable outlets for the id's undesirable impulses.

Obviously, these three components of personality inevitably conflict (Freud, 1940/1964). In the mature, healthy personality, a dynamic balance operates: The id communicates basic needs, the ego restrains the impulsive id long enough to find realistic methods of satisfying these needs, and the superego decides whether the ego's problem-solving strategies are morally acceptable. The ego is clearly "in the middle"; it must serve two harsh masters by striking a balance between the opposing demands of the id and the superego, all the while accommodating to the realities of the external world.

Stages of Psychological Development

Freud thought that sex was the most important instinct because his patients' mental disturbances often revolved around childhood sexual conflicts that they had repressed. But are young children really sexual beings? Yes, said Freud (1940/1964), whose view of sex was very broad, encompassing such activities as thumbsucking and urinating. Freud believed that, as the sex instinct matured, its focus shifted from one part of the body to another, and that each shift brought on a new stage of psychosexual development. Table 2.1 briefly describes each of Freud's five stages of psychosexual development.

Freud believed that parents must walk a fine line with their children at each psychosexual stage. He thought that permitting either too much or too little gratification of sexual needs caused a child to become obsessed with whatever activity was strongly encouraged or discouraged. The child might then **fixate** on that activity (that is, display arrested development) and retain some aspect of it throughout life. For example, an infant who was strongly punished for and thus conflicted about sucking her thumb might express this oral fixation through such substitute activities as chain smoking or oral sex as an adult. In sum, Freud claimed that early childhood experiences and conflicts may influence adult interests, activities, and personalities.

Contributions and Criticisms of Freud's Theory

How plausible do you think Freud's ideas are? Do you think that we are relentlessly driven by sexual and aggressive instincts? Or might the sexual conflicts that Freud thought

psychosexual theory
Freud's theory that states that maturation of the sex instinct underlies stages of personality development, and that the manner in which parents manage children's instinctual impulses determines the traits that children display.

unconscious motives
Freud's term for feelings, experiences, and conflicts that influence a person's thinking and behavior, but lie outside the person's awareness.

repression
a type of motivated forgetting in which anxiety-provoking thoughts and conflicts are forced out of conscious awareness.

instinct
an inborn biological force that motivates a particular response or class of responses.

id
psychoanalytic term for the inborn component of the personality that is driven by the instincts.

ego
psychoanalytic term for the rational component of the personality.

superego
psychoanalytic term for the component of the personality that consists of one's internalized moral standards.

fixation
arrested development at a particular psychosexual stage which can prevent movement to higher stages.

TABLE 2.1 Freud's Stages of Psychosexual Development

Psychosexual stage	Age	Description
Oral	Birth–1 year	The sex instinct centers on the mouth, as infants derive pleasure from such oral activities as sucking, chewing, and biting. Feeding activities are particularly important. For example, an infant weaned too early or abruptly may later crave close contact and become overdependent on a spouse.
Anal	1–3 years	Voluntary urination and defecation become the primary methods of gratifying the sex instinct. Toilet-training produces major conflicts between children and parents. The emotional climate that parents create can have lasting effects. For example, children who are punished for toileting "accidents" may become inhibited, messy, or wasteful.
Phallic	3–6 years	Pleasure is now derived from genital stimulation. Children develop an incestuous desire for the opposite-sex parent (called the *Oedipus complex* for boys and *Electra complex* for girls). Anxiety stemming from this conflict causes children to internalize the sex-role characteristics and moral standards of their same-sex parental rival.
Latency	6–11 years	Traumas of the phallic stage cause sexual conflicts to be repressed and sexual urges to be rechanneled into school work and vigorous play. The ego and superego continue to develop as the child gains more problem-solving abilities at school and internalizes societal values.
Genital	age 12 onward	Puberty triggers a reawakening of sexual urges. Adolescents must now learn how to express these urges in socially acceptable ways. If development has been healthy, the mature sex instinct is satisfied by marriage and raising children.

so important merely have been reflections of the sexually repressive Victorian era in which he and his patients lived?

Few developmentalists today are strong proponents of Freud's theory. There is not much evidence that any of the early oral, anal, and genital conflicts that Freud stressed reliably predict adult personality (see, for example, Bem, 1989; Crews, 1996). One reason for this may be that Freud's account of human development was based on the recollections of a relatively small number of emotionally disturbed adults whose experiences may not apply to most people.

Yet, we should not reject all Freud's ideas simply because some of them may now seem a bit outlandish. Perhaps Freud's greatest contribution was his concept of *unconscious motivation.* When psychology came into being in the mid-19th century, investigators were concerned with understanding isolated aspects of *conscious* experience, such as sensory processes and perceptual illusions. It was Freud who first proclaimed that the vast majority of psychic experience lay below the level of conscious awareness. Freud also deserves considerable credit for focusing attention on the influence of early experience on later development. Debates continue about exactly how critical early experiences are, but few developmentalists today doubt that some early experiences *can* have lasting effects. Finally, we might thank Freud for studying the emotional side of human development—the loves, fears, anxieties, and other powerful emotions that play important roles in our lives. These aspects of life have often been overlooked by developmentalists who have tended to concentrate on observable behaviors or rational thought processes. In sum, Freud was truly a great pioneer who dared to navigate murky, uncharted waters that his predecessors had not even thought to explore. In the process, he changed our views of humankind.

Erik Erikson (1902–1994) emphasized the sociocultural determinants of personality in his theory of psychosocial development.

Erikson's Theory of Psychosocial Development

As Freud became widely read, he attracted many followers. However, Freud's pupils did not always agree with him, and eventually they began to modify some of his ideas and became important theorists in their own right. Among the best known of these *neo-Freudian* scholars was Erik Erikson.

Comparing Erikson with Freud

Although Erikson (1963; 1982) accepted many of Freud's ideas, he differed from Freud in two important respects. First, Erikson (1963) stressed that children are *active,* curious explorers who seek to adapt to their environments, rather than passive slaves to biological urges who are molded by their parents. Erikson has been labeled an "ego" psychologist because he believed that, at each stage of life, people must cope with social *realities* (in ego function) in order to adapt successfully and display a normal pattern of development. So in Erikson's theory, the ego is far more than a simple arbiter of the opposing demands of the id and superego.

A second critical difference between Erikson and Freud is that Erikson places much less emphasis on sexual urges and far more emphasis on cultural influences than Freud did. Clearly, Erikson's thinking was shaped by his own varied experiences. He was born in Denmark and raised in Germany, and spent much of his adolescence wandering throughout Europe. After receiving his professional training, Erikson came to the United States, where he studied college students, combat soldiers, civil rights workers in the South, and Native Americans. Having observed many similarities and differences in development across these diverse social groups, it is hardly surprising that Erikson emphasized *social* and *cultural* aspects of development in his own **psychosocial theory.**

WHAT DO YOU THINK? ?

The id, ego, and superego have been compared with the three branches of a democratic government. Which component of the Freudian personality seems to serve an executive function? A judicial function? A legislative function?

Eight Life Crises

Erikson believed that human beings face eight major crises or conflicts during the course of their lives. Each conflict emerges at a distinct time dictated by both biological maturation and social demands that developing people experience at particular points in life. Each crisis must be resolved successfully in order to prepare for a satisfactory resolution of the next life crisis. Table 2.2, on page 46, briefly describes each of Erikson's eight crises (or psychosocial stages) and lists the Freudian psychosexual stage to which it corresponds. Notice that Erikson's developmental stages do not end at adolescence or young adulthood as Freud's do. Erikson believed that the problems of adolescents and young adults are very different from those faced by parents who are raising children or by the elderly who may be grappling with retirement, a sense of uselessness, and impending death. Most contemporary developmentalists agree.

Contributions and Criticisms of Erikson's Theory

Many people prefer Erikson's theory to Freud's because they simply refuse to believe that human beings are dominated by sexual instincts. An analyst like Erikson, who stresses our rational, adaptive nature, is much easier to accept. In addition, Erikson emphasizes many of the social conflicts and personal dilemmas that people may remember, are currently experiencing, or can easily anticipate or observe in people they know.

Erikson seems to have captured many of the central issues of life in his eight psychosocial stages. Indeed, we will discuss his ideas on such topics as the emotional development of infants in Chapter 11, the growth of the self-concept in childhood and the identity issues facing adolescents in Chapter 12, and the influence of friends and playmates on social development in Chapter 16. (See also Sigelman & Shaffer, 1995, for a discussion of Erikson's contributions to the field of adult development.) On the other hand, Erikson's theory can be criticized for being vague about the *causes* of development. What kinds of experiences must people have to cope with and successfully resolve various psychosocial conflicts? How exactly does the outcome of one psychosocial stage influence personality at a later stage? Unfortunately, Erikson is not very explicit about

psychosocial theory
Erikson's revision of Freud's theory that emphasizes sociocultural (rather than sexual) determinants of development and posits a series of eight psychosocial conflicts that people must resolve successfully to display healthy psychological adjustment.

Table 2.2 Erikson's and Freud's Stages of Development

Approximate age	Erikson's stage or "psychosocial" crisis	Erikson's viewpoint: Significant events and social influences	Corresponding Freudian stage
Birth to 1 year	Basic trust versus mistrust	Infants must learn to trust others to care for their basic needs. If caregivers are rejecting or inconsistent, the infant may view the world as a dangerous place filled with untrustworthy or unreliable people. The primary caregiver is the key social agent.	Oral
1 to 3 years	Autonomy versus shame and doubt	Children must learn to be "autonomous"—to feed and dress themselves, to look after their own hygiene, and so on. Failure to achieve this independence may force the child to doubt his or her own abilities and feel shameful. Parents are the key social agents.	Anal
3 to 6 years	Initiative versus guilt	Children attempt to act grown up and will try to accept responsibilities that are beyond their capacity to handle. They sometimes undertake goals or activities that conflict with those of parents and other family members, and these conflicts may make them feel guilty. Successful resolution of this crisis requires a balance: The child must retain a sense of initiative and yet learn not to impinge on the rights, privileges, or goals of others. The family is the key social agent.	Phallic
6 to 12 years	Industry versus inferiority	Children must master important social and academic skills. This is a period when the child compares him- or herself with peers. If sufficiently industrious, children acquire the social and academic skills to feel self-assured. Failure to acquire these important attributes leads to feelings of inferiority. Significant social agents are teachers and peers.	Latency
12 to 20 years	Identity versus role confusion	This is the crossroad between childhood and maturity. The adolescent grapples with the question "Who am I?" Adolescents must establish basic social and occupational identities, or they will remain confused about the roles they should play as adults. The key social agent is the society of peers.	Early genital (adolescence)
20 to 40 years (young adulthood)	Intimacy versus isolation	The primary task at this stage is to form strong friendships and to achieve a sense of love and companionship (or a shared identity) with another person. Feelings of loneliness or isolation are likely to result from an inability to form friendships or an intimate relationship. Key social agents are lovers, spouses, and close friends (of both sexes).	Genital
40 to 65 years (middle adulthood)	Generativity versus stagnation	At this stage, adults face the tasks of becoming productive in their work and raising their families or otherwise looking after the needs of young people. These standards of "generativity" are defined by one's culture. Those who are unable or unwilling to assume these responsibilities become stagnant and/or self-centered. Significant social agents are the spouse, children, and cultural norms.	Genital
Old age	Ego integrity versus despair	The older adult looks back at life, viewing it as either a meaningful, productive, and happy experience or a major disappointment full of unfulfilled promises and unrealized goals. One's life experiences, particularly social experiences, determine the outcome of this final life crisis.	Genital

these important issues. So his theory is really a *descriptive* overview of human social and emotional development that does not adequately *explain* how or why this development takes place.

Psychoanalytic Theory Today

Freud and Erikson are only two of many psychoanalysts who have had a meaningful influence on the study of human development (Tyson & Tyson, 1990). For example, Karen Horney (1967) has challenged Freud's ideas about sex differences in development and is now widely credited as a founder of the discipline we know today as the psychology of women. Alfred Adler (1929/1964), a contemporary of Freud's, was among the first to suggest that *siblings* (and sibling rivalries) are important contributors to social and personality development, a proposition we will explore in detail in Chapter 15. And American psychoanalyst Harry Stack Sullivan (1953) wrote extensively about how close, same-sex friendships during middle childhood set the stage for intimate love relationships later in life (see Chapter 16 for a discussion of this and other contributions that friends make to social and personality development). Although their theories differ in focus, all these *neo-Freudians* place much more emphasis on *social* influences on development and less emphasis on the role of sexual instincts than Freud did.

Despite the important contributions that Freud and the neo-Freudians have made, many contemporary developmentalists have largely rejected the psychoanalytic perspective because its propositions are very difficult to either falsify or confirm. Suppose, for example, that we wanted to test a basic Freudian hypothesis that the "healthy" personality is one in which the id, ego, and superego are roughly equal in strength. How could we do it? There are objective tests that we could use to select "mentally healthy" persons, but we have no instrument that measures the relative strengths of the id, ego, and superego. The point is that many psychoanalytic hypotheses are untestable by any method other than the interview or a clinical approach, and unfortunately, these techniques are time-consuming, expensive, and among the least objective of all methods used to study human development.

However, the main reason that so many developmentalists have abandoned the psychoanalytic perspective is that other theories seem more compelling. One perspective favored by many is the learning approach, to which we now turn.

John B. Watson (1878–1958) was the father of behaviorism and the first social-learning theorist.

THE LEARNING VIEWPOINT

Earlier, we encountered a developmentalist who claimed that he could take a dozen healthy infants and train them to be whatever he chose—doctor, lawyer, beggar, and so on—regardless of their backgrounds or ancestry. What a bold statement! It implies that nurture is everything and that nature, or hereditary endowment, counts for nothing. The statement was made by John B. Watson, a strong proponent of the importance of learning in human development and the father of a school of thought known as **behaviorism** (Horowitz, 1992).

Watson's Behaviorism

A basic premise of Watson's (1913) behaviorism is that conclusions about human development should be based on observations of overt behavior rather than on speculations about unconscious motives or cognitive processes that are unobservable. Moreover, Watson believed that well-*learned* associations between external stimuli and observable responses (called **habits**) are the building blocks of human development. Like John Locke, Watson viewed the infant as a *tabula rasa* to be written on by experience. Children have no inborn tendencies; how they turn out depends entirely on their rearing environments and the ways in which their parents and other significant people in their lives treat them. According to a behavioral perspective, then, it is a mistake to assume that children progress through a series of distinct stages, dictated by biological maturation, as Freud (and others) have argued. Instead, development is viewed as a continuous process of behavioral change that is shaped by a person's unique environment and may differ dramatically from person to person.

To prove just how malleable children are, Watson set out to demonstrate that

behaviorism
a school of thinking in psychology that holds that conclusions about human development should be based on controlled observations of overt behavior rather than speculation about unconscious motives or other unobservable phenomena; the philosophical underpinning for the early theories of learning.

habits
well-learned associations between stimuli and responses that represent the stable aspects of one's personality.

infantile fears and other emotional reactions are acquired rather than inborn. In one demonstration, for example, Watson and Rosalie Raynor (1920) presented a gentle white rat to a 9-month-old named Albert. Albert's initial reactions were positive; he crawled toward the rat and played with it as he had previously with a dog and a rabbit. Then, two months later, Watson attempted to instill a fear response. Every time Albert reached for the white rat, Watson slipped behind him and banged a steel rod with a hammer. Albert eventually associated the white rat with the loud noise and came to fear his furry playmate, thus illustrating that fears are easily learned.

Watson's belief that children are shaped by their environments carried a stern message for parents: They were largely responsible for what their children would become. Watson (1928) cautioned parents that they should begin to train their children at birth and cut back on the coddling if they hoped to instill good habits. Treat them, he said

> . . . as though they were young adults. . . . Let your behavior always be objective and kindly firm. Never hug and kiss them, never let them sit on your lap. . . . Shake hands with them in the morning. Give them a pat on the head if they have made an extraordinarily good job of a difficult task. . . . In a week's time, you will find how easy it is to be perfectly objective . . . [yet] kindly. You will be utterly ashamed at the mawkish, sentimental way you have been handling [your child] (pp. 81–82).

Since Watson's day, several theories have been proposed to explain how we learn from our social experiences and form the habits that Watson viewed as "bricks in the edifice of human development." Perhaps the one theorist who did more than anyone to advance the behaviorist approach was B. F. Skinner.

B. F. Skinner (1904–1990) proposed a learning theory that emphasized the role of external stimuli in controlling human behavior.

Skinner's Operant-Learning Theory (Radical Behaviorism)

Through his research with animals, Skinner (1953) came to understand a very important form of learning that he believed is the basis for most habits. Quite simply, Skinner proposed that both animals and humans repeat acts that lead to favorable outcomes and suppress those that produce unfavorable outcomes. So a rat that presses a bar and receives a tasty food pellet is apt to perform that response again. In the language of Skinner's theory, the freely emitted bar-pressing response is called an *operant,* and the food pellet that strengthens this response (by making it more probable in the future) is called a **reinforcer.** Similarly, a young girl may form a long-term habit of showing compassion toward distressed playmates if her parents consistently reinforce her kindly behavior with praise, or a teenage boy may become more studious if his work is rewarded by higher grades. **Punishers,** on the other hand, are consequences that suppress a response and decrease the likelihood that it will occur in the future. If the rat who had been reinforced for bar pressing were suddenly given a painful shock each time it pressed the bar, the "bar-pressing" habit would begin to disappear. Similarly, a teenage girl who is grounded every time she stays out beyond her curfew usually becomes more careful about being home on time.

reinforcer
any consequence of an act that increases the probability that the act will recur.

punisher
any consequence of an act that suppresses that act and/or decreases the probability that it will recur.

operant learning
a form of learning in which voluntary acts (or operants) become either more or less probable, depending on the consequences they produce.

Like Watson, then, Skinner believed that habits develop as a result of unique **operant learning** experiences. One boy's aggressive behavior may be reinforced over time because his playmates "give in" to (reinforce) his forceful tactics. Another boy may become relatively nonaggressive because his peers actively suppress (punish) aggressive conduct by fighting back. The two boys may develop in entirely different directions based on their different histories of reinforcement and punishment. According to Skinner, there is no "aggressive stage" in child development nor an "aggressive instinct" in human beings. Instead, he claims that the majority of habits that children acquire—the very responses that comprise their unique "personalities"—are freely emitted operants that have been shaped by their consequences. So Skinner's *operant learning theory* claims that the directions in which we develop depend on *external* stimuli (reinforcers and punishers) rather than on internal forces such as instincts, drives, or biological maturation.

Today's developmentalists appreciate that human behavior can take many forms and that habits can emerge and disappear over a lifetime, depending on whether they have positive or negative consequences (Gewirtz & Pelaez-Nogueras, 1992). Yet many believe that Skinner placed far too much emphasis on operant behaviors shaped by *external* stimuli (reinforcers and punishers), while ignoring important *cognitive* contributors to social learning. One such critic is Albert Bandura, who has proposed a cognitive social learning theory of human development that is widely respected today.

Bandura's Cognitive Social Learning Theory

Can human social learning be explained on the basis of research with animals? Bandura (1977, 1986, 1992) doesn't think so. He agrees with Skinner that operant conditioning is an important type of learning, particularly for animals; however, Bandura stresses that humans are *cognitive* beings—active information processors—who, unlike animals, are likely to think about the relationships between their behavior and its consequences. Therefore, they are often more affected by what they *believe* will happen than by the events they actually experience. Consider your own situation as a student. Your education is expensive and time-consuming and may impose many stressful demands. Yet, you tolerate the cost and toil because you may *anticipate* greater rewards after you obtain your degree. Your behavior is not shaped by immediate consequences; if it were, few students would ever make it through the trials and turmoils of college. Instead, you persist as a student because you have *thought about* the long-term benefits of obtaining an education and have decided that they outweigh the short-term costs you must endure.

Albert Bandura (1925–   ) has emphasized the cognitive aspects of learning in his social-learning theory.

Nowhere is Bandura's cognitive emphasis clearer than in his decision to highlight **observational learning** as a central developmental process. Observational learning is simply learning that results from observing the behavior of other people (called *models*). A 2-year-old may learn how to approach and pet the family dog by simply watching his older sister do it. An 8-year-old may acquire a very negative attitude toward a minority after hearing her parents talk about this group in a disparaging way. Observational learning simply could not occur unless cognitive processes were at work. We must *attend* carefully to a model's behavior, actively digest, or *encode,* what we observe, and then *store* this information in memory (as an image or a verbal label) in order to imitate what we have observed at a later time. Indeed, as we will see in Box 2.2, children need not even be reinforced in order to learn this way.

Why does Bandura stress observational learning in his cognitive social learning theory? Simply because this active, cognitive form of learning permits young children to quickly acquire literally thousands of new responses in a variety of settings where their "models" are simply pursuing their own interests and are not trying to teach them anything. In fact, many of the behaviors that children observe, remember, and imitate are actions that models display but actually want to discourage such as swearing, smoking, or eating between meals. So Bandura claims children are continually learning both desirable and undesirable responses by "keeping their eyes (and ears) open," and he is not at all surprised that human development proceeds so very rapidly along so many different paths.

Social Learning as Reciprocal Determinism

Early versions of learning theory were largely tributes to Watson's doctrine of **environmental determinism**: Young, unknowing children were viewed as passive recipients of environmental influence, becoming whatever parents, teachers, and other

observational learning
learning that results from observing the behavior of others.

environmental determinism
the notion that children are passive creatures who are molded by their environments.

FOCUS ON RESEARCH

2.2

An Example of No-Trial (Observational) Learning without Reinforcement

In 1965, Bandura made what was then considered a radical statement: Children can learn by merely observing the behavior of a social model, *even without first performing the responses themselves or receiving any reinforcement for performing them.* Clearly, this "no-trial" learning is inconsistent with Skinner's theory, which claims that one must perform a response and then be reinforced in order to have learned that response.

Bandura (1965) then conducted a now-classic experiment to prove his point. Nursery-school children each watched a short film in which an adult model directed an unusual sequence of aggressive responses toward an inflatable Bobo doll, hitting the doll with a mallet while shouting "sockeroo," throwing rubber balls while shouting "bang, bang," and so on. There were three experimental conditions:

1. Children in the *model-rewarded* condition saw a second adult give the aggressive model candy and soda for a "championship performance."

2. Children in the *model-punished* condition saw a second adult scold and spank the model for beating up Bobo.

3. Children in the *no-consequence* condition simply saw the model behave aggressively.

When the film ended, each child was left alone in a playroom that contained a Bobo doll and the props that the model had used to beat up Bobo. Hidden observers then recorded all instances in which the child imitated one or more of the model's aggressive acts. These observations revealed how willing children were to *perform* the responses they had witnessed. The results of this "performance" test appear on the left-hand side of the figure. Notice that children in the model-rewarded and no-consequences conditions imitated more of the model's aggressive acts than those who had seen the model punished for aggressive behavior. Clearly, this looks very much like the kind of no-trial observational learning that Bandura had proposed.

But an important question remained. Had children in the first two conditions actually learned more from observing the model than those who had seen the model punished? To find out, Bandura devised a test to see just how much they had learned. Each child was now offered trinkets and fruit juice for reproducing all the model's behaviors that he or she could recall. As we see in the right-hand side of the figure, this "learning test" revealed that children in each of the three conditions had learned about the same amount by observing the model. Apparently, children in the model-punished condition had imitated fewer of the model's responses on the initial performance test because they felt that they too might be punished for striking Bobo. But when offered a reward, they showed that they had learned much more than their initial performances had implied.

In sum, it is important to distinguish what children *learn* by observation from their willingness to *perform* these responses. Clearly, reinforcement is not necessary for observational learning—that is, for the formation of images or verbal descriptions that would enable the observer to imitate the model's acts. However, the reinforcing or punishing consequences that the model received may well affect the observer's tendency to *perform* what he or she has already learned by observation.

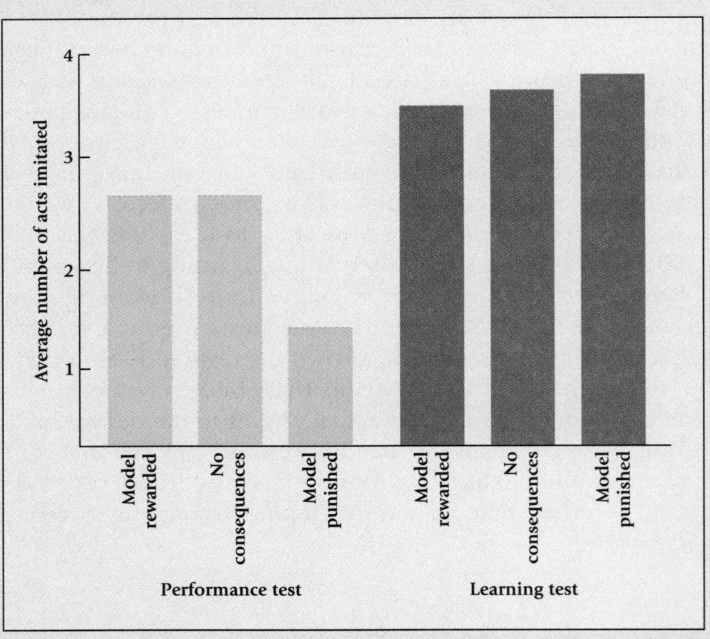

Average number of aggressive responses imitated during the performance test and the learning test for children who had seen a model rewarded, punished, or receive no consequences for his actions. ADAPTED FROM BANDURA, 1965.

agents of society groomed them to be. Bandura (1986; 1989) takes strong exception to this point of view, stressing that children and adolescents are active, thinking beings who contribute in many ways to their own development. Observational learning, for example, requires the observer to *actively* attend to, encode, and retain the behaviors

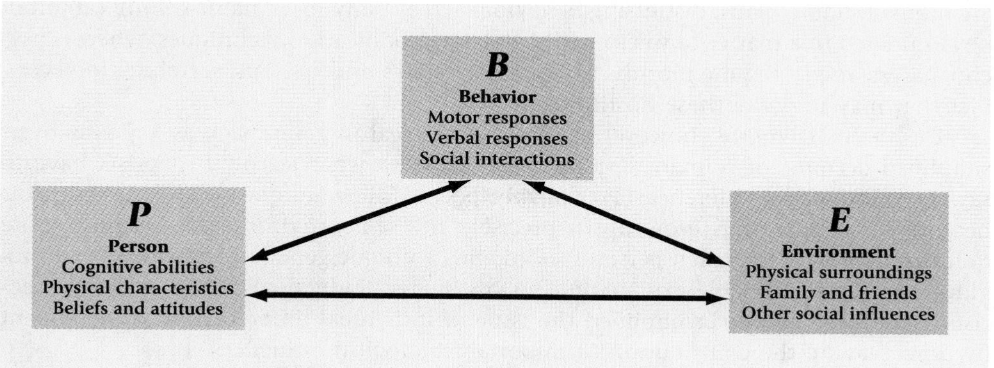

Figure 2.3 *Bandura's model of reciprocal determinism.* ADAPTED FROM BANDURA, *1978.*

displayed by social models. And children are often free to choose the models to whom they will attend, so they have some say about *what* they will learn from others.

Bandura (1986) has proposed the concept of **reciprocal determinism** to describe his view that human development reflects an interaction among an "active" person (P), the person's behavior (B), and the environment (E) (see Figure 2.3). Unlike Watson and Skinner, who maintained that the environment (E) shaped a child's personality and her behavior, Bandura and others (most notably Richard Bell, 1979) propose that links among persons, behaviors, and environments are *bidirectional.* Thus, a child can influence his environment by virtue of his own conduct. Consider an example.

Suppose that a 4-year-old discovers that he can gain control over desirable toys by assaulting his playmates. In this case, control over the desired toy is a favorable outcome that reinforces the child's aggressive behavior. But note that the reinforcer here is produced by the child himself through his aggressive actions. Not only has bullying behavior been reinforced (by obtaining the toy), but *the character of the play environment has changed.* Playmates who were victimized may be more inclined to "give in" to the bully which, in turn, may make him more likely to pick on these same children in the future (Patterson, Littman, & Bricker, 1967).

In sum, cognitive learning theorists believe that human development is best described as a continuous *reciprocal interaction* between children and their environments. The situation or "environment" that a child experiences surely affects her, but her behavior is thought to affect the environment as well. The implication is that children are actively involved in shaping the very environments that influence their growth and development.

Contributions and Criticisms of Learning Theories

Perhaps the major contribution of the learning viewpoint is the wealth of information it has provided about developing children and adolescents. Learning theories are very precise and testable (Horowitz, 1992). And by conducting tightly controlled experiments to determine how their participants react to various environmental influences, learning theorists have begun to understand how and why developing persons form emotional attachments, adopt gender roles, make friends, learn to abide by moral rules, and change in countless other ways over the course of childhood and adolescence. As we will see throughout the text, the learning perspective has contributed substantially to our knowledge of many aspects of human development (see also Gewirtz & Pelaez-Nogueras, 1992; Grusec, 1992).

Learning theory's emphasis on the immediate causes of overt behaviors has also produced important clinical insights and practical applications. For example, many problem behaviors can now be quickly eliminated by behavioral modification techniques in which the therapist (1) identifies the reinforcers that sustain unacceptable habits and eliminates them while (2) modeling or reinforcing alternative behaviors that

reciprocal determinism
the notion that the flow of influence between children and their environments is a two-way street; the environment may affect the child, but the child's behavior also influences the environment.

are more desirable. Thus, distressing behavior such as bullying or name-calling can often be eliminated in a matter of weeks with behavior-modification techniques, whereas psychoanalysts might require months to probe the child's unconscious, searching for a conflict that may underlie these hostilities.

Despite its strengths, however, many view the learning approach as a grossly oversimplified account of human development. Consider what learning theorists have to say about individual differences. Presumably, people follow unique developmental paths because no two persons grow up in precisely the same environment. Yet, critics are quick to point out that each person is born with a unique genetic endowment that provides an equally plausible explanation for his or her "individuality." So learning theorists may have badly oversimplified the issue of individual differences in development by downplaying the contribution of important biological influences.

Yet another group of critics, whose viewpoint we will soon examine, can agree with the behaviorists that development depends very heavily on the contexts in which it occurs. However, these *ecological systems theorists* argue that the "environment" that so powerfully influences development is really a series of social systems (for example, families, communities, and cultures) that interact with each other and with the individual in complex ways that are impossible to simulate in a laboratory. Only by studying children and adolescents in their natural settings are we likely to understand how environments truly influence development.

One final point: Despite the popularity of recent cognitively oriented learning theories that stress the child's active role in the developmental process, some critics maintain that learning theorists give too little attention to *cognitive* influences on development. Proponents of this "cognitive-developmental" viewpoint believe that a child's mental abilities undergo a series of qualitative changes (or stages) that behaviorists completely ignore. Further, they argue that a child's impressions of and reactions to the environment depend largely on his or her level of **cognitive development.** Let's now turn to this viewpoint and see what it has to offer.

THE COGNITIVE-DEVELOPMENTAL VIEWPOINT

No theorist has contributed more to our understanding of children's thinking than Jean Piaget (1896–1980), a Swiss scholar who began to study intellectual development during the 1920s. Piaget was truly a remarkable individual. At age 10, he published his first

Concept Check 2.2
Understanding the Positions of Four Major Theorists: Freud, Erikson, Skinner, and Bandura

Check your understanding of the implications of work by four of the major theorists reviewed in this chapter by indicating who is likely to have made each statement quoted below. Choose from the following: (a) Sigmund Freud, (b) Erik Erikson, (c) B.F. Skinner, (d) Albert Bandura. Answers appear in the Appendix at the end of the book.

_____ 1. "Growing is . . . differentiation during a sequence of critical periods. In personality growth, it is a task of the ego and of the social processes together (so that) at all times a human being is an ego and a member of society."

_____ 2. "Cognition has causal influence on behavior. A theory that denies that thoughts can regulate actions does not lend itself . . . to the explanation of complex human behavior."

_____ 3. "In the traditional view, a person is free. . . . He can therefore be held responsible for what he does and justly punished if he offends. That view must be reexamined when a scientific analysis reveals unsuspected controlling relations between behavior and environment."

_____ 4. "The task of making conscious the most hidden recesses of the mind is one which . . . is quite possible to accomplish."

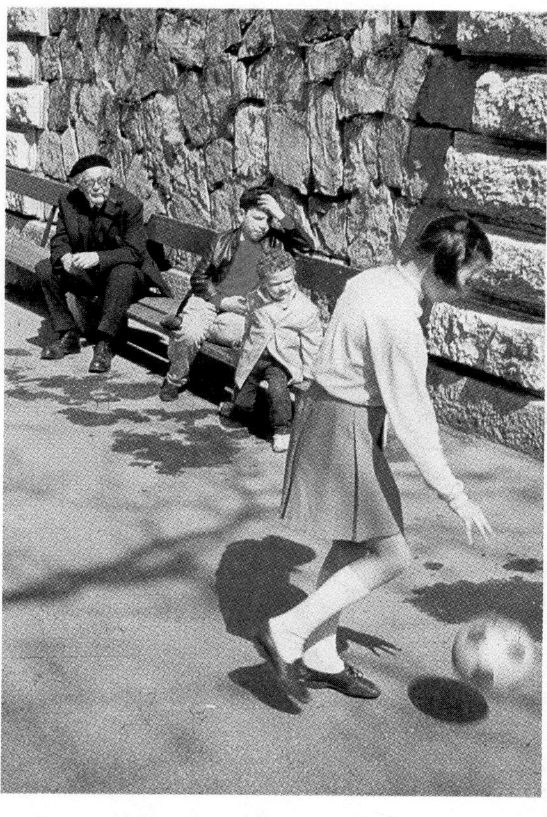

In his cognitive-developmental theory, Swiss scholar Jean Piaget (1896–1980) focused on the growth of children's knowledge and reasoning skills.

scientific article about the behavior of a rare albino sparrow. His early interest in the ways that animals adapt to their environments eventually led him to pursue a doctoral degree in zoology, which he completed in 1918. Piaget's secondary interest was *epistemology* (the branch of philosophy concerned with the origins of knowledge), and he hoped to be able to integrate his two interests. Thinking that psychology was the answer, Piaget journeyed to Paris, where he accepted a position at the Alfred Binet laboratories, working on the first standardized intelligence test. His experiences in this position had a profound influence on his career.

In testing mental ability, an estimate is made of the person's intelligence based on the number and kinds of questions that he or she answers correctly. However, Piaget soon found that he was more interested in children's *incorrect* answers than their correct ones. He first noticed that children of about the same age produced the same kinds of wrong answers. But why? As he questioned children about their misconceptions, using the clinical method he had learned while working in a psychiatric clinic, he began to realize that young children are not simply less intelligent than older children; rather, their thought processes are completely different. Piaget then set up his own laboratory and spent 60 years charting the course of intellectual growth and attempting to determine how children progress from one mode (or stage) of thinking to another.

Piaget's View of Intelligence and Intellectual Growth

Influenced by his background in biology, Piaget (1950) defined intelligence as a basic life process that helps an organism to *adapt* to its environment. By adapting, Piaget means that the organism is able to cope with the demands of its immediate situation. For example, the hungry infant who grasps a bottle and brings it to her mouth is behaving adaptively, as is the adolescent who successfully interprets a road map while traveling. As children mature, they acquire ever more complex "cognitive structures" that aid them in adapting to their environments.

A cognitive structure—or what Piaget called a **scheme**—is an organized pattern of thought or action that is used to cope with or explain some aspect of experience. For example, many 3-year-olds insist that the sun is alive because it comes up in the morning and goes down at night. According to Piaget, these children are operating on the basis of a simple cognitive scheme that things that move are alive. The earliest *schemes,* formed in infancy, are motor habits such as rocking, grasping, and lifting that prove to be adaptive. For example, a curious infant who combines the responses of extending an arm (reaching) and grasping with the hand is suddenly capable of satisfying her

cognitive development
age-related changes that occur in mental activities such as attending, perceiving, learning, thinking, and remembering.

scheme
an organized pattern of thought or action that a child constructs to make sense of some aspect of his or her experience; Piaget sometimes uses the term *cognitive structures* as a synonym for schemes.

curiosity by exploring almost any interesting object that is no more than an arm's length away. Simple as these behavioral schemes may be, they permit infants to operate toys, to turn dials, to open cabinets, and to otherwise master their environments. Later in childhood, cognitive schemes take the form of "actions of the head" (for example, mental addition or subtraction) that allow children to manipulate information and think logically about the issues and problems they encounter in everyday life. At any age, children rely on their current cognitive structures to understand the world around them. And because cognitive structures take different forms at different ages, younger and older children may often interpret and respond to the same objects and events in very different ways.

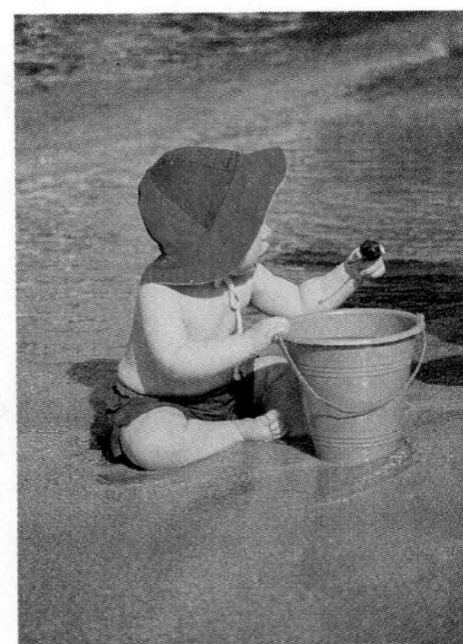
Piaget believed that children are naturally curious explorers who are constantly trying to make sense of their surroundings.

How do children grow intellectually? Piaget claimed that infants have no inborn knowledge or ideas about reality, as some philosophers have claimed. Nor are children simply given information or taught how to think by adults. Instead, they *actively construct* new understandings of the world based on their own experiences. Children watch what goes on around them; they experiment with objects they encounter; they make connections or associations between events; and they are puzzled when their current understandings (or schemes) fail to explain what they have experienced.

To illustrate, let's return for a moment to the 3-year-old who believes that the sun is alive. Surely this idea is not something the child learned from an adult; it was apparently constructed by the child on the basis of her own worldly experiences. After all, many things that move *are* alive. So long as the child clings to this understanding, she may regard any new moving object as alive; that is, new experiences will be interpreted in terms of her current cognitive structures, a process Piaget called **assimilation.** Eventually, however, this child will encounter moving objects that almost certainly couldn't be alive, such as a paper airplane that was nothing more than a sheet of newsprint before dad folded it, or a wind-up toy that invariably stops moving until she winds it again. Now here are contradictions (or what Piaget termed **disequilibriums**) between the child's understanding and the facts. It becomes clear to the child that her "objects-that-move-are-alive" scheme needs to be revised. She is prompted by these disconfirming experiences to **accommodate**—that is, to alter her existing schemes so that they provide a better explanation of the distinction between animate and inanimate objects (perhaps by concluding that only things that move under their own power are alive).

So it goes through life; Piaget believed that we continually rely on the complementary processes of assimilation and accommodation to adapt to our environments. Initially, we attempt to understand new experiences or solve problems using our current cognitive schemes (assimilation). But we often find that our existing schemes are inadequate for these tasks, which then prompts us to revise them (through accommodation) so that they provide a better "fit" with reality (Piaget, 1952). Biological maturation also plays an important role: As the brain and nervous system mature, children become capable of increasingly complex cognitive activities that help them to construct better understandings of what they have experienced (Piaget, 1970). Eventually, curious, active children, who are always forming new schemes and reorganizing their knowledge, progress enough to think about old issues in entirely new ways; that is, they pass from one stage of cognitive development to the next higher stage.

assimilation
Piaget's term for the process by which children interpret new experiences by incorporating them into their existing schemes.

disequilibriums
imbalances or contradictions between one's thought processes and environmental events. By contrast, **equilibrium** refers to a balanced, harmonious relationship between one's cognitive structures and the environment.

accommodation
Piaget's term for the process by which children modify their existing schemes in order to incorporate or adapt to new experiences.

invariant developmental sequence
a series of developments that occur in one particular order because each development in the sequence is a prerequisite for the next.

Four Stages of Cognitive Development

Piaget proposed four major periods (or stages) of cognitive development: the *sensorimotor* stage (birth to age 2), the *preoperational* stage (ages 2 to 7), the *concrete-operational* stage (ages 7 to 11 or 12), and the *formal-operational* stage (ages 11 to 12 and beyond). These stages form what Piaget called an **invariant developmental sequence**—that is, all children progress through the stages in exactly the order in which they are listed. They cannot skip stages because each successive stage builds on the previous stage and represents a more complex way of thinking.

Table 2.3 summarizes the key features of Piaget's four cognitive stages. Each of these periods of intellectual growth will be discussed in much greater detail when we return to the topic of cognitive development in Chapter 7.

TABLE 2.3 Piaget's Stages of Cognitive Development

Approximate age	Stage	Primary schemes or methods of representing experience	Major developments
Birth to 2 years	Sensorimotor	Infants use sensory and motor capabilities to explore and gain a basic understanding of the environment. At birth, they have only innate reflexes with which to engage the world. By the end of the sensorimotor period, they are capable of complex sensorimotor coordinations.	Infants acquire a primitive sense of "self" and "others," learn that objects continue to exist when they are out of sight (object permanence), and begin to internalize behavioral schemes to produce images or mental schemes.
2 to 7 years	Preoperational	Children use symbolism (images and language) to represent and understand various aspects of the environment. They respond to objects and events according to the way things appear to be. Thought is egocentric, meaning that children think everyone sees the world in much the same way that they do.	Children become imaginative in their play activities. They gradually begin to recognize that other people may not always perceive the world as they do.
7 to 11 years	Concrete operations	Children acquire and use cognitive operations (mental activities that are components of logical thought).	Children are no longer fooled by appearances. By relying on cognitive operations, they understand the basic properties of and relations among objects and events in the everyday world. They are becoming much more proficient at inferring motives by observing others' behavior and the circumstances in which it occurs.
11 years and beyond	Formal operations	Adolescents' cognitive operations are reorganized in a way that permits them to operate on operations (think about thinking). Thought is now systematic and abstract.	Logical thinking is no longer limited to the concrete or the observable. Adolescents enjoy pondering hypothetical issues and, as a result, may become rather idealistic. They are capable of systematic, deductive reasoning that permits them to consider many possible solutions to a problem and to pick the correct answer.

Contributions and Criticisms of Piaget's Viewpoint

Like Freud and Watson, Piaget was an innovative renegade. He was unpopular with psychometricians because he claimed that their intelligence tests only measure what children know and tell us nothing about the most important aspect of intellect—how children think. In addition, Piaget dared to study an unobservable, mentalistic concept, "cognition," that had fallen from favor among psychologists from the behaviorist tradition (Beilin, 1992).

By the 1960s, the times had clearly changed. Not only had Piaget's early theorizing and research legitimized the study of children's thinking, but his early work linking moral development to cognitive development (see Chapter 14 for an extended discussion) contributed immensely to a whole new area of developmental research—*social cognition.* Recent social-cognitive theorists such as Lawrence Kohlberg and Robert Selman have found that the same mind that gradually constructs increasingly sophisticated understandings of the physical world also comes, with age, to form more complex ideas about sex differences, moral values, the significance of human emotions, the meaning and obligations of friendship, and countless other aspects of social life. The development of social cognition is a primary focus of Chapter 12, and the links between one's social-cognitive abilities and various aspects of social and personality development are discussed throughout the text.

Piaget's theory has also had a strong impact on education. For example, popular *discovery-based* educational programs are based on the premise that young children do not think like adults and learn best by having "hands-on" educational experiences with familiar aspects of their environment. So a preschool teacher in a Piagetian classroom might introduce the difficult concept of number by presenting her pupils with different numbers of objects to stack, color, or arrange. Presumably, new concepts like number are best transmitted by methods in which curious, active children can apply their existing schemes and make the critical "discoveries" for themselves.

Although Piaget's pioneering efforts have left a deep and lasting imprint on our thinking about human development (see Beilin, 1992), many of his ideas have now been challenged. It now appears that Piaget regularly underestimated the intellectual capabilities of infants, preschoolers, and grade-school children, all of whom show much greater problem-solving skills when presented with simplified tasks that are more familiar and thereby allow them to display their competencies (Bjorklund, 1995). Other investigators have noted that performance on Piagetian problems can be improved dramatically through training programs, which would seem to challenge Piaget's assumption that individualized discovery learning, rather than direct instruction, is the best way to promote intellectual growth.

Piaget's notion that cognitive growth proceeds through a universal and invariant sequence of stages has also been challenged, both in theory and in research (Bjorklund, 1995). In his own **sociocultural theory,** Russian developmentalist Lev Vygotsky (1934/1962) focused on how *culture*—the beliefs, values, traditions, and skills of a social group—is transmitted from generation to generation. Rather than depicting children as independent explorers who make critical discoveries on their own, Vygotsky viewed cognitive growth as a *socially mediated activity*—one in which children gradually acquire new ways of thinking and behaving through cooperative dialogues with more knowledgeable members of society. Vygotsky also rejected the notion that all children progress through the same stages of cognitive growth. New skills that children master through their interactions with more competent associates are often specific to their culture rather than universal cognitive structures. So from Vygotsky's perspective (which we will explore in more depth in Chapter 7), Piaget largely ignores important social and cultural influences on human development.

Today, several influential developmentalists continue to believe that cognitive growth *is* stagelike but that Piaget's description of these stages is simply too broad (Case & Okamoto, 1996). However, *information-processing* theorists take a dramatically different point of view. Let's examine the most important assumptions of this interesting and influential perspective.

The Information-Processing Viewpoint

By 1990, many developmentalists, disenchanted by the narrow, antimentalistic bias of behaviorism and the problems they saw in Piaget's theory, turned to such fields as cognitive psychology and computer science, seeking new insights about children's thinking. Digital computers, which rely on mathematically specified programs to operate on input (information) and generate solutions to problems, provided the framework for a new **information-processing perspective** on cognitive growth. According to information-processing theory, the human mind is like a computer into which information flows, is operated on, and converted to output—that is, answers, inferences, or solutions to problems (Klahr, 1992; Siegler, 1996). Continuing to use the computer analogy, information-processing theorists view cognitive development as age-related changes that occur in the mind's *hardware* (that is, the brain and central nervous system) and *software* (mental processes such as attention, perception, memory, and problem-solving strategies).

Like Piaget, information-processing theorists acknowledge that biological maturation is an important contributor to cognitive growth. But unlike Piaget, who was vague

sociocultural theory
Vygotsky's perspective on development, in which children acquire their culture's values, beliefs, and problem-solving strategies through collaborative dialogues with more knowledgeable members of society.

information-processing theory
a perspective that views the human mind as a continuously developing, symbol-manipulating system, similar to a computer, into which information flows, is operated on, and is converted to output (answers, inferences, and solutions to problems).

about the connections between biological and cognitive development, information-processing theorists contend that maturation of the brain and nervous system enables children and adolescents to process information faster (Kail, 1992). As a result, developing persons become better at sustaining attention, recognizing and storing task-relevant information, and executing mental programs that allow them to operate on what they have stored so as to answer questions and solve problems. Yet, information-processing theorists are also keenly aware that the strategies that children develop for attending to and processing information are greatly influenced by their *experiences*—that is, by the kinds of problems presented to them, by the kinds of instruction they receive at home and at school, and even by the skills that their culture or subculture specifies that they must master.

In what is perhaps their biggest break with Piaget, information-processing theorists insist that cognitive development is a *continuous* process that is not at all stagelike. Presumably, the strategies we use to gather, store, retrieve, and operate on information evolve gradually over the course of childhood and adolescence. So cognitive development from an information-processing perspective involves small *quantitative* rather than large qualitative, changes.

Contributions and Criticisms of the Information-Processing Viewpoint

Clearly, this new perspective on cognitive development is changing the ways that developmentalists (and educators) view children's thinking. As we will see in Chapter 8, information-processing theorists have provided a host of new insights on the growth of many cognitive abilities that Piaget did not emphasize, and their research has also filled in many of the gaps in Piaget's earlier theory. Furthermore, the rigorous and intensive research methods favored by information-processing researchers have enabled them to identify how children and adolescents approach various problems and why they may make logical errors (see Box 2.3 on page 57). Educators have seen the practical utility of this research: If teachers understand exactly *why* children are having difficulties with their reading, math, or science lessons, it becomes easier to suggest alternative strategies to improve student performances (Siegler & Munakata, 1993).

Despite its many strengths, information-processing theory is subject to criticism. Some question the utility of a theory based on the thinking that children display in artificial laboratory studies, arguing it may not accurately reflect their thinking in everyday life. Others contend that the computer model on which information-processing theory is based seriously underestimates the richness and diversity of human cognition. After all, humans (but not computers) can dream, create, and reflect on their own and other's states of consciousness, and information-processing theory does not adequately explain these cognitive activities. Although there is some merit to both criticisms, information-processing researchers are beginning to address them by studying children's memories for everyday events and activities, as well as the reasoning they display in conversations with parents and peers, and the strategies they use in processing social information to form impressions of themselves and other people in their natural environments (see, for example, Hayden, Haine, & Fivush, 1997; Waldman, 1996).

You may have noticed that both Piaget and the information-processing theorists contend that intellectual development is heavily influenced by the forces of nature (biological maturation) *and* nurture (that is, the environments that children and adolescents experience, which provide the input that they operate on to construct knowledge and develop problem-solving strategies). We will examine two additional theoretical perspectives, both of which concede that nature *and* nurture make important contributions to human development. However, one of these theories, *ethology,* emphasizes the biological side of development, whereas the other, *ecological systems theory,* stresses the crucial role that *contexts* play in influencing developmental outcomes. Let's first consider the ethological viewpoint.

APPLYING DEVELOPMENTAL RESEARCH

2.3

Helping Children to Correct Their Mistakes: An Information-Processing Approach

At any age, children and adolescents may make logical errors if they don't attend to or utilize all the information that would help them to solve the problems they face. Imagine that 6-year-old John and 10-year-old Jorge are presented with the balance-scale problem illustrated in the figure and are asked to predict what will happen (will the arms remain balanced? will the left arm go up? down?) when a brake that holds the arms motionless is released. Clearly, two aspects of balance-scale problems are important: the number of weights on each arm and the distance of the weights from the fulcrum. For us, the problem shown in the figure is easy. We recognize that, although each arm has the same number of weights, the left arm will still drop because the weights are further from the fulcrum. Although Jorge correctly answers that the left arm will drop, John says the arms will remain balanced. As shown in the figure, John and Jorge rely on difficult strategies to derive their answers. John is using a simple *weight-only* rule: If one arm has more weight on it than the other, it will drop; otherwise the arms remain balanced. He does not consider distance information and may not even encode it. By contrast, Jorge considers both the number of weights on each arm and their distances from the fulcrum. He then concludes that, because weight is equalized, the arm with weights farthest from the fulcrum will drop.

How might we help John to solve similar balance-scale problems? According to Robert Siegler (1976), the answer depends on whether John had attended to and encoded the distance information. This might be assessed by memory tests that indicate whether John can remember the numbers and locations of weights he had seen on a balance scale when the scale is no longer visible. If John accurately recalls both the weight and distance information, then a few demonstrations with different balance-scale problems should be sufficient to illustrate that the distance information *he had encoded* is important and should be considered when formulating answers. But if John has only encoded the number-of-weights information, simple demonstrations may not be enough to convince him to attend to, encode, retain, and use the distance information that he routinely ignores (Siegler, 1976). Under the circumstances, we would first have to persuade John to pay attention to distance information before he is likely to discover its relevance to solving balance-scale problems.

Perhaps you can see the practical benefits of this approach. By carefully examining the information-processing strategies that children and adolescents use to attack scientific reasoning tasks, math problems, and even reading comprehension exercises, educators can often pinpoint the reasons that their pupils are failing and devise effective interventions to improve their performances (Siegler & Crowley, 1992; Siegler & Munakata, 1993).

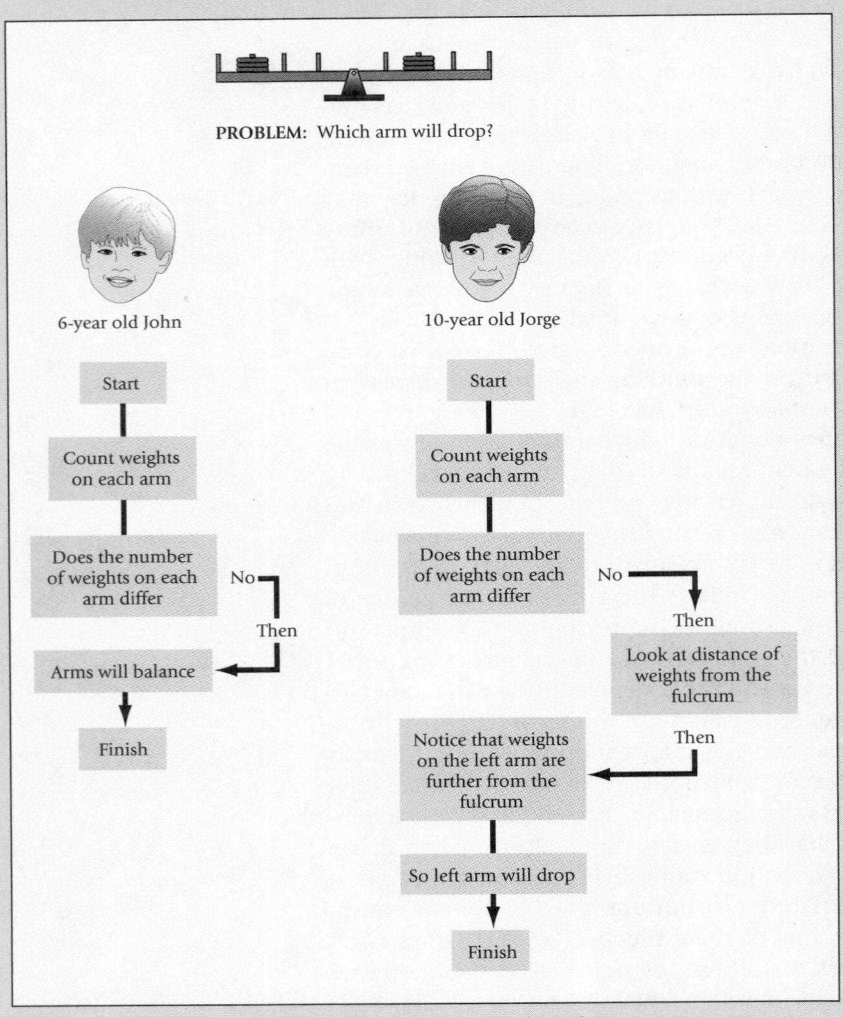

PROBLEM: Which arm will drop?

6-year old John

Start → Count weights on each arm → Does the number of weights on each arm differ → No → Then → Arms will balance → Finish

10-year old Jorge

Start → Count weights on each arm → Does the number of weights on each arm differ → No → Then → Look at distance of weights from the fulcrum → Then → Notice that weights on the left arm are further from the fulcrum → So left arm will drop → Finish

Information-processing flow chart showing the steps that a 6-year-old and a 10-year-old might take to answer a simple physics problem. Jorge's solution is correct, whereas John's leads to an incorrect answer.

THE ETHOLOGICAL (OR EVOLUTIONARY) VIEWPOINT

Behaviorist John Watson may have taken the extreme environmental stand he did partly because other prominent theorists of his era, most notably Arnold Gesell (1880–1961), took an equally extreme but opposing position that human development is largely a matter of biological maturation. Gesell (1933) believed that children, like plants, simply "bloomed," following a pattern and timetable laid out in their genes; the way that parents raised their young he thought to be of little importance.

Although today's developmentalists have largely rejected Gesell's radical claims, the notion that biological influences play a significant role in human development is alive and well in **ethology**—the scientific study of the evolutionary basis of behavior and the contributions of evolved responses to a species's survival and development (Archer, 1992). The origins of this discipline can be traced to Charles Darwin; however, modern ethology arose from the work of Konrad Lorenz and Niko Tinbergen, two European zoologists whose animal research highlighted some important links between evolutionary processes and adaptive behaviors (Dewsbury, 1992). Let's now examine the central assumptions of classical ethology and their implications for human development.

Assumptions of Classical Ethology

The most basic assumption ethologists make is that members of all animal species are born with a number of "biologically programmed" behaviors that are (1) products of evolution and (2) adaptive in that they contribute to survival. Many species of birds, for example, seem to be biologically prepared to engage in such instinctual behaviors as following their mothers (a response called *imprinting* that helps to protect the young from predators and to ensure that they find food), building nests, and singing. These biologically programmed characteristics are thought to have evolved as a result of the Darwinian process of **natural selection;** that is, over the course of evolution, birds with genes responsible for these adaptive behaviors were more likely to survive and to pass their genes on to offspring than were birds lacking these adaptive characteristics. Over many generations, the genes underlying the most adaptive behaviors became widespread in the species, characterizing nearly all individuals.

So ethologists focus on inborn or instinctual responses that (1) are shared by members of a species and (2) may steer individuals along similar developmental paths. Where might one search for these adaptive behaviors and study their developmental implications? Ethologists have always preferred to study their subjects in the natural environment. Why? Simply because they believe that the inborn behaviors that shape human (or animal) development are most easily identified and understood if observed in the settings where they evolved and have proven to be adaptive (Hinde, 1989).

Ethology and Human Development

Instinctual responses that seem to promote survival are relatively easy to spot in animals. But do humans really display such behaviors? And if they do, how might these preprogrammed responses influence their development?

Human ethologists such as John Bowlby (1969; 1973) not only believe that children display a wide variety of preprogrammed behaviors, but they also claim that each of these responses promotes a particular kind of experience that will help the individual to survive and develop normally. For example, the cry of a human infant is thought

ethology
the study of the bioevolutionary bases of behavior and development.

natural selection
an evolutionary process, proposed by Charles Darwin, stating that individuals with characteristics that promote adaptation to the environment will survive, reproduce, and pass these adaptive characteristics to offspring; those lacking these adaptive characteristics will eventually die out.

The cry is a distress signal that attracts the attention of caregivers.

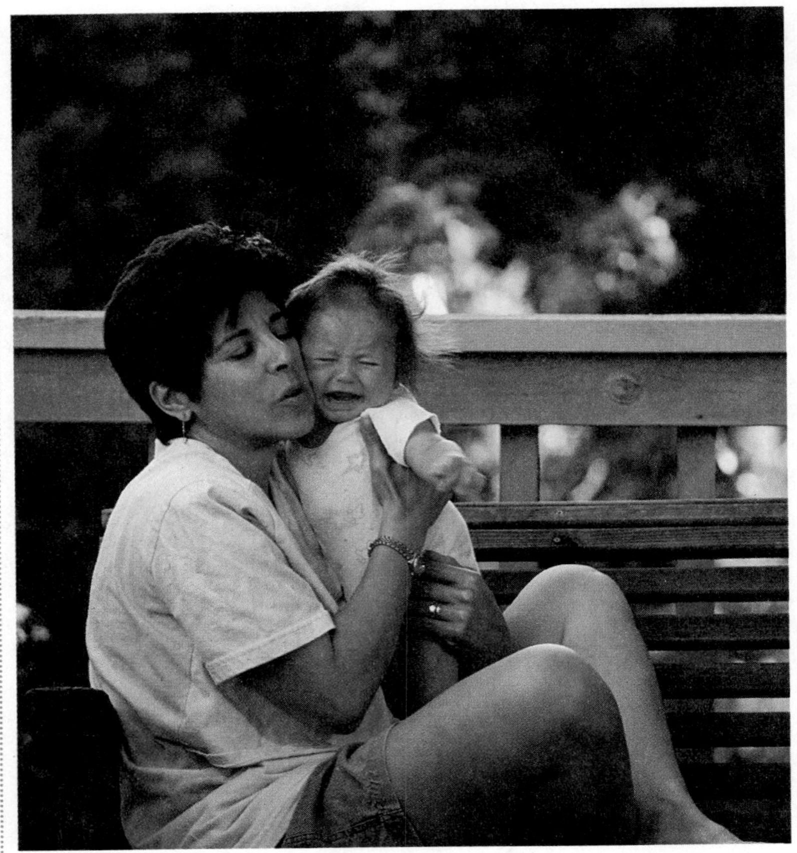

to be a biologically programmed "distress signal" that attracts the attention of caregivers. Not only are infants said to be biologically programmed to convey their distress with loud, lusty cries, but ethologists also believe that caregivers are biologically predisposed to respond to such signals. The adaptive significance of an infant's crying is to ensure that (1) the infant's basic needs (for example, hunger, thirst, safety) are met and (2) the infant has sufficient contact with other human beings to form primary emotional attachments (Bowlby, 1973).

Although ethologists are especially critical of learning theorists for largely ignoring the biological bases of human development, they are well aware that development could not progress very far without learning. For example, an infant's cry may be an innate signal that promotes the human contact from which emotional attachments emerge. However, these emotional attachments do not happen automatically. The infant must first *learn* to discriminate familiar faces from those of strangers before showing any evidence of being emotionally attached to a regular companion. Presumably, the adaptive significance of this discriminatory learning goes back to a period in evolutionary history when humans traveled in nomadic tribes and lived outdoors. In those days, it was crucial that an infant become attached to familiar companions and wary of strangers, for failure to stay close to caregivers and to cry in response to a strange face might make the infant an easy prey for a predatory animal.

Now consider the opposite side of the argument. Some caregivers who suffer from various life stresses of their own (for example, prolonged illnesses, depression, an unhappy marriage) may be routinely inattentive or neglectful, so that an infant's cries rarely promote any contact with them. Such an infant will probably not form secure emotional attachments to her caregivers and may become rather shy and emotionally unresponsive to other people for years to come (Ainsworth, 1979; 1989). What this infant has learned from her early experiences is that her closest companions are undependable and are not to be trusted. Consequently, she may become ambivalent or wary around her caregivers and may later assume that other regular associates, such as teachers and peers, are equally untrustworthy individuals who should be avoided whenever possible.

How important are an individual's early experiences? Like Freud, ethologists believe that early experiences are *very* important. In fact, they have argued that there may be "critical periods" for the development of many attributes. A *critical period* is a limited time span during which developing organisms are biologically prepared to display adaptive patterns of development, provided they receive the appropriate input; outside this period, the same environmental events or influences are thought to have no lasting effects. Although this concept of critical period does seem to explain certain aspects of animal development, such as imprinting in young fowl, many human ethologists think that the term *sensitive period* is a more accurate description of human development. A **sensitive period** refers to a time that is optimal for the emergence of particular competencies or behaviors and in which the individual is particularly sensitive to environmental influences. The time frames of sensitive periods are less rigid or well-defined than those of critical periods. It is possible for development to occur outside of a sensitive period, but is much more difficult to foster.

To illustrate, some ethologists believe that the first 3 years of life are a sensitive period for the development of social and emotional responsiveness in human beings (Bowlby, 1973). Presumably, people are most susceptible to forming close emotional ties during the first 3 years; should they have little or no opportunity to do so during this period, they will find it much more difficult to make close friends or to enter into intimate emotional relationships with others later in life. Clearly, this is a most interesting and provocative claim about the emotional lives of human beings, which we will examine carefully when we discuss early social and emotional development in Chapter 11.

In sum, ethologists clearly acknowledge that we are heavily influenced by our experiences (Gottlieb, 1996). Yet they emphasize that humans are inherently biological creatures whose inborn characteristics affect the kinds of learning experiences they are likely to have.

Contributions and Criticisms of the Ethological Viewpoint

If this text had been written 30 years ago, it would not have included a section on ethological theory. Although ethology came into its own in the 1960s, the early ethologists studied animal behavior. Only within the past 20 years have ethologists made a serious attempt to specify evolutionary contributors to human development, and many of their hypotheses may still be considered speculative (Lerner & von Eye, 1992). Nevertheless, human ethologists have already made important contributions to our discipline by reminding us that every child is a biological creature who comes equipped with a number of adaptive, genetically programmed characteristics—attributes that influence other people's reactions to the child and, thus, the course that his development is likely to take. In addition, ethologists have made a major methodological contribution by showing us the value of (1) studying human development in normal, everyday settings and (2) comparing human development with that of other species.

One intriguing ethological notion that we will discuss in detail in Chapter 11 is that infants are inherently sociable creatures who are quite capable of promoting and sustaining social interactions from the day they are born. This viewpoint contrasts sharply with that of behaviorists, who portray the newborn as a *tabula rasa,* and with Piaget's "asocial" infant, who enters the world equipped only with a few basic reflexes. Ethologists also believe that humans have evolved in ways that predispose us to develop and display prosocial motives such as **altruism** that contribute to the common good, permitting us to live and work together in harmony. Box 2.4 describes some observations suggesting that there may be a biological basis for certain aspects of altruism.

By way of criticism, evolutionary approaches are like psychoanalytic theory in being very hard to test. How does one prove that various motives, mannerisms, and behaviors are inborn, adaptive, or products of

sensitive period
period of time that is optimal for the development of particular capacities or behaviors and in which the individual is particularly sensitive to environmental influences that would foster these attributes.

altruism
concern for the welfare of others that is expressed through such prosocial acts as sharing, cooperating, and helping.

WHAT DO YOU THINK? ?

What human attributes and behaviors would you say are part of the human genetic code through natural selection? Does your list include language, morality, love, and aggression, as some have claimed? Why or why not?

FOCUS ON RESEARCH

2.4

Is Altruism Part of Human Nature?

Darwin's notion of survival of the fittest seems to argue against altruism as an inborn motive. Many have interpreted Darwin's idea to mean that powerful, self-serving individuals who place their own needs ahead of others' are the ones who are most likely to survive. If this were so, evolution would favor the development of selfishness and egoism—not altruism—as basic components of human nature.

Martin Hoffman (1981) has challenged this point of view, listing several reasons why the concept of survival of the fittest actually implies altruism. His arguments hinge on the assumption that human beings are more likely to receive protection from natural enemies, satisfy all their basic needs, and successfully reproduce if they live together in cooperative social units. If this assumption is correct, cooperative, altruistic individuals would be the ones who are most likely to survive long enough to pass along their "altruistic genes" to their offspring; individualists who go it alone would probably succumb to famine, predators, or some other natural disaster that they could not cope with by themselves. So, over thousands of generations, natural selection would favor the development of innate social motives such as altruism. Presumably, the tremendous survival value of being "social" makes altruism, cooperation, and other social motives much more plausible as components of human nature than competition, selfishness, and the like.

It is obviously absurd to argue that infants routinely help other people. However, Hoffman believes that even newborn babies are capable of recognizing and experiencing the emotion of others. This ability, known as **empathy**, is thought to be an important contributor to altruism, for a person must recognize that others are distressed in some way before he or she is likely to help. So Hoffman is suggesting that at least one aspect of altruism—empathy—is present at birth.

Hoffman's claim is based on an experiment (Sagi & Hoffman, 1976) in which infants less than 36 hours old listened to (1) another infant's cries, (2) an equally loud computer simulation of a crying infant, or (3) no sounds at all (silence). The infants who heard a real infant crying soon began to cry themselves, to display physical signs of agitation such as kicking, and to grimace. Infants exposed to the simulated cry or to silence cried much less and seemed not to be very discomforted. (A second study by Martin & Clark, 1982, has confirmed these observations.)

Hoffman argues that there is something quite distinctive about the human cry. His contention is that infants listen to and experience the distress of another crying infant and become distressed themselves. Of course, this finding does not conclusively demonstrate that humans are altruistic by nature. But it does imply that the capacity for empathy may be present at birth and thus may serve as a biological basis for the eventual development of altruistic behavior.

evolutionary history? Such claims are often difficult to confirm. Ethological theory has also been criticized as a *retrospective,* or "post-hoc," explanation of development. One can easily apply evolutionary concepts to explain what has already happened, but can the theory *predict* what is likely to happen in the future? Many developmentalists believe that it cannot.

Finally, proponents of other viewpoints (most notably, learning theory) have argued that, even if there is a biological basis for certain human motives or behaviors, these predispositions will soon become so modified by learning that it may not be helpful to spend much time wondering about their prior evolutionary significance. Even strong, genetically influenced attributes can be modified by experience. Consider, for example, that young mallard ducklings clearly prefer their mothers' vocal calls to those of other birds—a behavior that ethologists claim is innate and adaptive as a product of mallard evolution. Yet Gilbert Gottlieb (1991a) found that duckling embryos that were prevented from vocalizing and exposed to chicken calls before hatching preferred the call of a chicken to that of a mallard mother! In this case, the ducklings' *prenatal experiences* overrode a genetic predisposition. Of course, human beings have a much greater capacity for learning than ducklings do, leading many critics to argue that cultural learning experiences quickly overshadow innate evolutionary mechanisms in shaping human conduct and character.

Despite these criticisms, the evolutionary perspective remains a valuable addition to the developmental sciences. Not only has it provided a healthy balance to the heavy environmental emphasis of learning theories by identifying important biological contributions to human development, but it has also reinforced a crucial premise of our final theory: There is much to be learned about the process of development by studying children and adolescents in their everyday environments.

empathy
the ability to experience the same emotions that someone else is experiencing.

THE ECOLOGICAL SYSTEMS VIEWPOINT

American psychologist Urie Bronfenbrenner offers an exciting new perspective on child and adolescent development that addresses many of the shortcomings of earlier "environmentalist" approaches. Behaviorists John Watson and B.F. Skinner had defined *environment* as any and all external focuses that shape the individual's development. Although modern learning theorists such as Bandura (1986, 1989) have backed away from this extremely mechanistic view by acknowledging that environments both influence and *are influenced by* developing individuals, they continue to provide only vague descriptions of the environmental contexts in which development takes place.

By contrast, Bronfenbrenner's **ecological systems theory** (1979; 1989; 1993) provides a detailed analysis of environmental influences. And since it also concedes that a person's biologically influenced characteristics interact with environmental forces to shape development, it is probably more accurate to describe this perspective as a *bio-ecological* theory (Bronfenbrenner, 1995).

In his ecological systems theory, Urie Bronfenbrenner (1917–) describes how multiple levels of the surrounding environment influence child and adolescent development.

Bronfenbrenner (1979) begins by assuming that *natural* environments are the major source of influence on developing persons—and one that is often overlooked (or simply ignored) by researchers who choose to study development in the highly artificial context of the laboratory. He proceeds to define environment (or the natural ecology) as "a set of nested structures, each inside the next, like a set of Russian dolls" (p. 22). In other words, the developing person is said to be at the center of and embedded in several environmental systems, ranging from immediate settings such as the family to more remote contexts such as the broader culture (see Figure 2.4 on page 64). Each of these systems is thought to interact with the others and with the individual to influence development in important ways. Let's take a closer look.

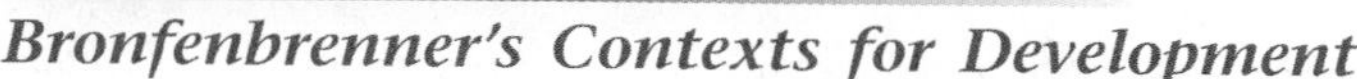

Bronfenbrenner's Contexts for Development

The Microsystem

Bronfenbrenner's innermost environmental layer, or **microsystem,** refers to the activities and interactions that occur in the person's immediate surroundings. For most young infants, the microsystem may be limited to the family. Yet, this system eventually becomes much more complex as children are exposed to day care, preschool classes, youth groups, and neighborhood playmates. Not only are children influenced by the people in their microsystems, but their own biologically and socially influenced characteristics—their habits, temperaments, physical characteristics, and capabilities—influence the behavior of companions as well. For example, a temperamentally difficult infant can alienate her parents or even create friction between them that may be sufficient to impair their marital relationship (Belsky, Rosenberger, & Crnic, 1995). And interactions between any two individuals in microsystems are likely to be influenced by third parties. Fathers, for example, clearly influence mother–infant interactions; happily married mothers who have close supportive relationships with their husbands tend to interact much more patiently and sensitively with their infants than do mothers who experience marital tension, little support from their spouses, and feel that they are raising their children on their own (Cox et al., 1989; 1992). So microsystems are truly dynamic contexts for development in which each person influences and is influenced by all other persons in the system.

ecological systems theory
Bronfenbrenner's model emphasizing that the developing person is embedded in a series of environmental systems that interact with one another and with the person to influence development.

microsystem
the immediate settings (including role relationships and activities) that the person actually encounters; the innermost of Bronfenbrenner's environmental layers or contexts.

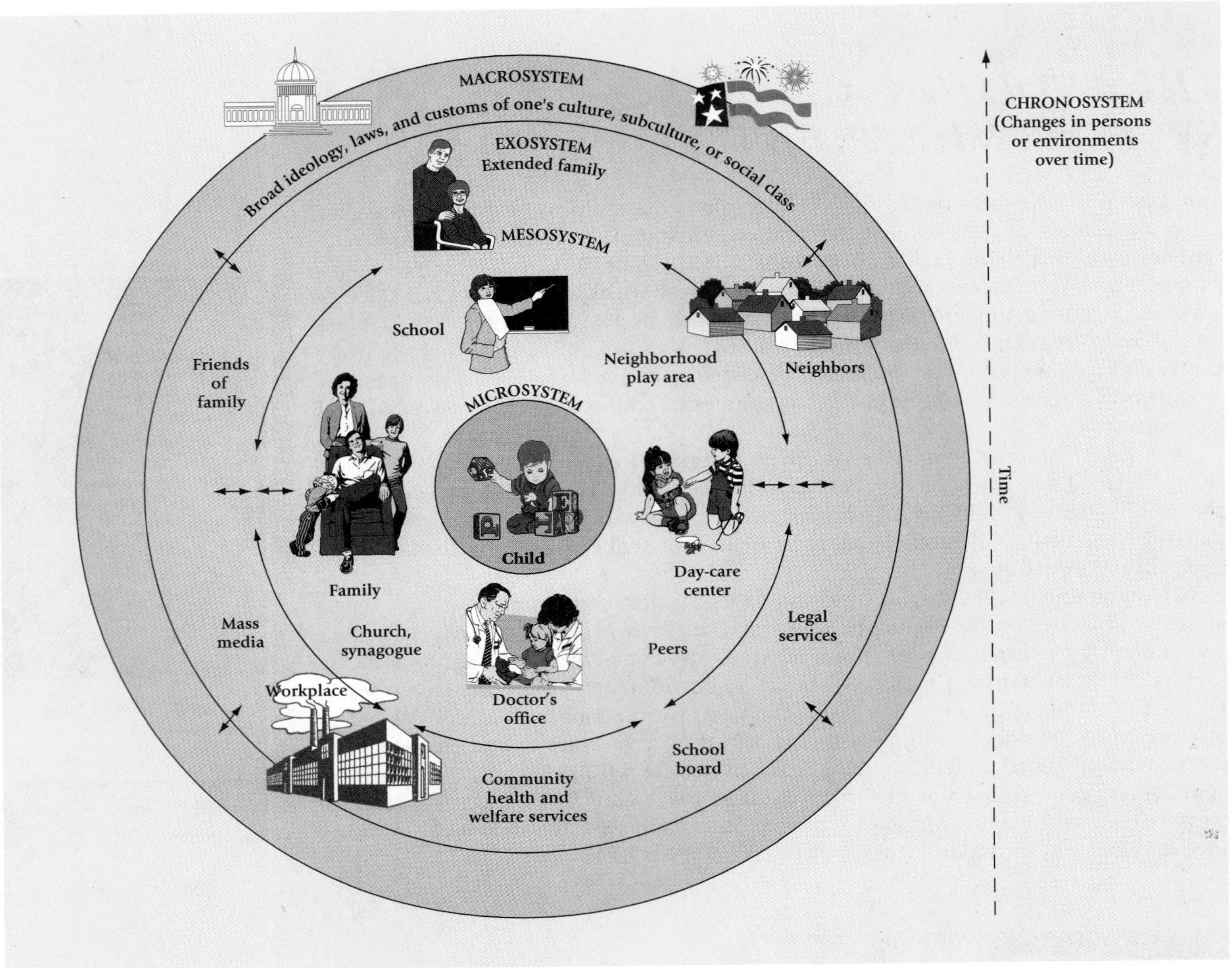

Figure 2.4 *Bronfenbrenner's ecological model of the environment as a series of nested structures. The microsystem refers to relations between the child and the immediate environment, the mesosystem to connections among the child's immediate settings, the exosystem to social settings that affect but do not contain the child, and the macrosystem to the overarching ideology of the culture.* Based on Bronfenbrenner, *1979.*

The Mesosystem

The second of Bronfenbrenner's environmental layers, or **mesosystem,** refers to the connections or interrelationships among such microsystems as homes, schools, and peer groups. Bronfenbrenner believes that development is likely to be optimized by strong, supportive links between microsystems. For example, youngsters who have established secure and harmonious relationships with parents are especially inclined to be accepted by peers and to enjoy close, supportive friendships during childhood and adolescence (Gavin & Furman, 1996; Kerns, Klepec, & Cole, 1996; Shulman, Elicker, & Sroufe, 1994). A child's ability to master lessons at school depends not only on the quality of instruction that his teachers provide, but also on the extent to which parents value these scholastic activities and consult or cooperate with teachers (Luster & McAdoo, 1996; Stevenson, Chen, & Lee, 1993). On the other hand, nonsupportive links between microsystems can spell trouble. For example, when peer groups devalue academic achievement, they often undermine an adolescent's scholastic performance, despite the encouragement of parents and teachers to study (Steinberg, Dornbusch, & Brown, 1992).

mesosystem
the interconnections among an individual's immediate settings or microsystems. The second of Bronfenbrenner's environmental layers or contexts.

The Exosystem

Bronfenbrenner's third environmental layer, or **exosystem,** consists of contexts that children and adolescents are not a part of but which may nevertheless influence their development. For example, parents' work environments are an exosystem influence, and children's emotional relationships at home may be influenced considerably by whether or not their parents enjoy their work (Greenberger, O'Neil, & Nagel, 1994). Similarly, children's experiences in school may also be affected by their exosystem—by a social integration plan adopted by the school board, or by a factory closing in the community that results in a decline in the school's revenue.

The Macrosystem

Bronfenbrenner also stresses that development occurs in a **macrosystem**—that is, a cultural, or subcultural, or social class context in which microsystems, mesosystems, and exosystems are imbedded. The macrosystem is really a broad, overarching ideology that dictates (among other things) how children should be treated, what they should be taught, and the goals for which they should strive. Of course, these values differ across cultures (and subcultures and social classes) and can greatly influence the kinds of experiences children have in their homes, neighborhoods, schools, and all other contexts that affect them, directly or indirectly. To cite one example, the incidence of child abuse in families (a microsystem experience) is much lower in those cultures (or macrosystems) that discourage physical punishment of children and advocate nonviolent ways of resolving interpersonal conflict (Belsky, 1993; Levinson, 1989).

Finally, Bronfenbrenner's model includes a temporal dimension, or **chronosystem,** which emphasizes that changes *in the child* or in any of the ecological contexts of development can affect the direction that development is likely to take. Cognitive and biological changes that occur at puberty, for example, seem to contribute to increased conflict between young adolescents and their parents (Paikoff & Brooks-Gunn, 1991; Steinberg, 1988). And the impacts of environmental changes also depend upon another chronological variable—the age of the child. For example, even though a parents' divorce may hit hard at youngsters of all ages, adolescents are less likely than younger children to experience the guilty sense that *they* were the cause of the breakup (Hetherington & Clingempeel, 1992).

Contributions and Criticisms of the Ecological Systems Theory

Though we have touched briefly on the ecological perspective here and will explore its propositions through the text, perhaps you can already see that it provides a much richer description of environment (and environmental influences) than anything offered by learning theorists. Each of us functions in particular microsystems that are linked by a mesosystem and embedded in the larger contexts of an exosystem and a macrosystem. It makes little sense to an ecological theorist to try to study environmental influences in contrived laboratory contexts. Instead, they argue that only by observing transactions between developing persons and their ever-changing *natural* settings will we understand how individuals influence and are influenced by their environments.

Bronfenbrenner's detailed analyses of environmental influences has suggested many ways in which the development of children and adolescents might be optimized. To illustrate, imagine a working mother who is having a tough time establishing a pleasant relationship with her temperamentally difficult infant. At the level of the microsystem, a successful intervention might assist the father to become a more sensitive companion who assumes some of the drudgery of child care and encourages the mother to be more responsive to and patient with their baby (Howes & Markman, 1989). At the level of the exosystem, mothers (and fathers) can often be helped to improve their relationships with

exosystem
social systems that children and adolescents do not directly experience but that may nonetheless influence their development; the third of Bronfenbrenner's environmental layers or contexts.

macrosystem
the larger cultural or subcultural context in which development occurs; Bronfenbrenner's outermost environmental layer or context.

chronosystem
in ecological systems theory, changes in the individual or the environment that occur over time and influence the direction of development.

Parenting classes are an "exosystem" influence that can help parents establish more harmonious relationships with their children.

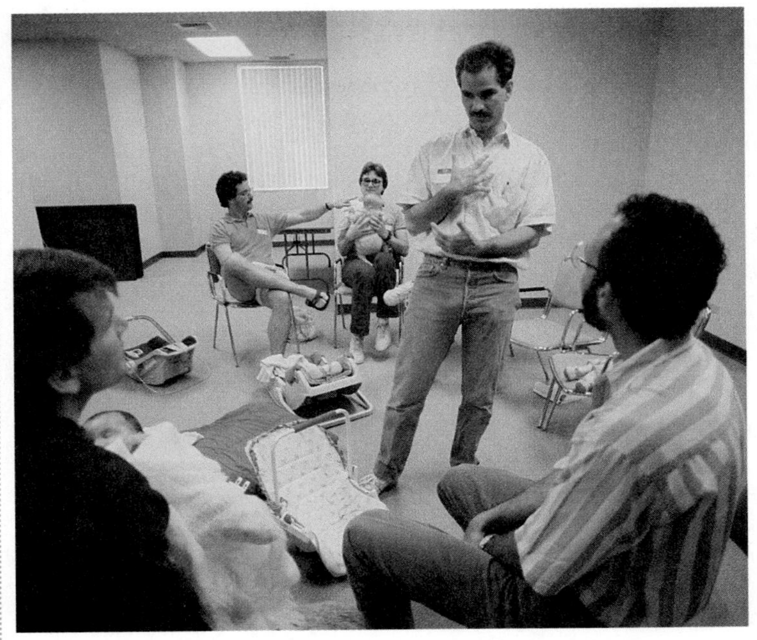

their children if their community has parenting classes or groups where parents can express their concerns, enlist others' emotional support, and learn from each other how to elicit more favorable reactions from their children (Lyons-Ruth et al., 1990). And at the level of the macrosystem, a social policy guaranteeing parents the right to take paid or unpaid leave from their jobs to attend to family matters may be an especially important intervention indeed, allowing distressed parents more time to resolve difficulties that arise with their children, and conveying the attitude that resolution of family problems is important to society's well-being (Bronfenbrenner & Neville, 1995).

Yet, despite its strengths, ecological systems theory falls far short of being a complete account of human development. Though Bronfenbrenner characterizes the theory as a bioecological model, it really has very little to say about specific biological contributors to development. And even though developmentalists are indebted to the ecological systems perspective for describing the complexities of the natural environments that influence and are influenced by developing persons, we must still understand how children and adolescents process environmental information and learn from their experiences before we can fully comprehend how environments influence human development. So while the ecological systems approach is an important addition to the field, it is a complement to rather than a replacement for other developmental theories.

THEORIES AND WORLD VIEWS

Now that we have completed our survey of the major theories of human development, how might we compare them? One way is to group the theories into even grander categories, for each is grounded in a broader set of philosophical assumptions or *world view.* By examining the fundamental assumptions that underlie different theories, we can perhaps better appreciate just how deeply some of their disagreements run.

Early developmental theories adopted either of two broad world views (Overton, 1984). The **mechanistic model** likens human beings to machines by viewing them as (1) a collection of parts (behaviors) that can be decomposed, much as machines can be taken apart piece by piece, (2) passive, changing mostly in response to outside influences (much as machines depend on external energy sources to operate), and (3) changing gradually or continuously as their parts (specific behavior patterns) are added or

mechanistic model
view of children as passive entities whose developmental paths are primarily determined by external (environmental) influences.

subtracted. By contrast, the **organismic model** compares humans to other living organisms by viewing them as (1) whole beings who cannot be understood as a simple collection of parts, (2) active in the developmental process, changing under the guidance of internal forces (such as instincts or maturation), and (3) evolving through distinct (discontinuous) stages as they mature.

Which theorists have adopted which model? Clearly, learning theorists such as Watson and Skinner favor the mechanistic world view, for they see human beings as passively shaped by environmental events and they analyze human behavior response by response. Bandura's social learning theory is primarily mechanistic, yet it reflects the important organismic assumption that human beings are active creatures who both influence and are influenced by their environments. By contrast, psychoanalytic theorists such as Freud and Erikson and cognitive-developmentalists from the Piagetian tradition all base theories primarily on the organismic model: Given some nourishment from their surroundings, human beings will progress through discontinuous steps or stages, directed by forces lying within themselves, much as seeds evolve into blooming plants.

Another broad world view, the **contextual model,** has recently emerged as the perspective that many developmentalists favor (Lerner, 1996). The contextual model views development as the product of a dynamic interplay between person and environment. People are assumed to be active in the developmental process (as in the organismic model), *and* the environment is active as well (as in the mechanistic model). Development may have both universal aspects *and* aspects peculiar to certain cultures, times, or individuals. The potential exists for both qualitative and quantitative change, and development may proceed along many different paths depending on the intricate interplay between internal forces (nature) and external influences (environment).

Although none of the theories we've reviewed provides a pure example of the contextual world view, three come reasonably close. Information-processing theorists describe children and adolescents as active processors of environmental input whose capabilities are heavily influenced by maturation *and* by the kinds of social and cultured experiences they encounter. (Note that Vygotsky's sociocultural theory that we touched on briefly makes the same assumption.) Although they view development as basically continuous rather than stagelike, many information-processing theorists concede that changes that occur within particular intellectual domains may be uneven and that qualitative leaps in one's intellectual performances are possible.

Ethologists also seem to favor a contextual world view. They clearly make the organismic assumptions that humans are active beings who are born genetically equipped to display certain behaviors that promote adaptive developmental outcomes. However, they recognize that biological predispositions by themselves do not guarantee healthy development and that a child's outcomes depend critically on the environment he experiences. In addition, ethologists claim that we are *continuously* developing adaptive behaviors over the course of our lives (a mechanistic premise), although they stress that change can be abrupt, or *discontinuous,* as when a new, adaptive response emerges during its sensitive period for development.

organismic model
view of children as active entities whose developmental paths are primarily determined by forces from within themselves.

contextual model
view of children as active entities whose developmental paths represent a continuous, dynamic interplay between internal forces (nature) and external influences (nurture).

Concept Check 2.3
Understanding Theoretical Propositions

Check your understanding of four major theories by noting which best exemplifies each proposition below. Choose from the following options: (a) Piaget's cognitive-developmental theory, (b) information-processing theory, (c) ethology, or (d) ecological systems theory. Answers appear in the Appendix at the end of the book.

_____ 1. Children are prepared to display adaptive patterns of development, provided that they receive appropriate kinds of environmental inputs at the most appropriate times.

_____ 2. Children actively construct knowledge, making important discoveries for themselves.

_____ 3. The natural environment that influences a developing child is a complex interlocking set of contexts that influence and are influenced by the child.

_____ 4. The developing human mind is a system that operates on stimulus input to convert it to such output as inferences, solutions, etc.

_____ 5. Children are active agents who influence the character of their own developmental outcomes. (Note all theories that apply.)

Table 2.4 **A Summary of the Philosophies Underlying Six Major Developmental Perspectives**

Theory	Active vs. passive person	Continuous vs. discontinuous development	Nature vs. nurture	World view
Psychoanalytic perspective	*Active:* Children are driven by inborn instincts which are channeled (with the assistance of others) into socially desirable outlets.	*Discontinuous:* Emphasis is on stages of psychosexual development (Freud) or psychosocial development (Erikson).	*Both nature and nurture:* Biological forces (instincts, maturation) precipitate psychosexual stages and psychosocial crises; parental child-rearing practices influence the outcomes of these stages.	Organismic
Learning perspective	*Passive:* Children are molded by their environments (although Bandura claims that developing persons also influence these environments).	*Continuous:* Emphasizes the gradual addition of learned responses (habits) which make up one's personality.	*Nurture most important:* Environmental input, rather than biological influences, is what determines the course of development.	Mechanistic
Piaget's cognitive-developmental theory	*Active:* Children actively construct more sophisticated understandings of the self, others, and the environment to which they adapt.	*Discontinuous:* Emphasizes an invariant sequence of qualitatively distinct cognitive stages.	*Both nature and nurture:* Children have an inborn need to adapt to the environment, which is in turn nurtured by a stimulating environment that provides many adaptive challenges.	Organismic
Information-processing perspective	*Active:* Children actively process environmental information to answer questions, solve problems, or otherwise master challenges.	*Continuous:* Emphasizes gradual quantitative changes in attention, perception, memory, and problem-solving skills.	*Both nature and nurture:* Active processing capabilities that develop are heavily influenced by maturation and by social/cultural/educational influences.	Contextual
Ethological perspective	*Active:* Humans are born with biologically programmed behaviors that promote adaptive developmental outcomes.	*Both:* Emphasizes that adaptive behaviors are added continuously, but adds that some adaptive capabilities emerge abruptly (or fail to emerge) during sensitive periods for their development.	*Nature:* Biologically programmed adaptive behaviors are stressed, although an appropriate environment is necessary for successful adaptation.	Contextual
Ecological systems perspective	*Both:* Humans actively influence the environmental contexts that influence their development.	*Both:* Emphasizes that transactions between ever-changing individuals and ever-changing environments lead to quantitative developmental changes. However, discontinuous personal or environmental events (for example, reaching puberty, parents' divorce) can produce abrupt qualitative changes.	*Nurture:* Impacts of environmental contexts on development are most clearly emphasized, although children's biologically influenced attributes can affect their environments.	Contextual
My viewpoint: (Review Box 2.1)	____________	____________	____________	______

Finally, Bronfenbrenner's ecological systems theory makes the mechanistic assumption that humans are heavily influenced by many environmental contexts, ranging from home settings to the wider society in which they live. Yet, Bronfenbrenner is clearly aware that children and adolescents are active biological beings who change as they mature, and whose behaviors and biologically influenced attributes influence the very environments that are influencing their development. So development is viewed as the product of a truly dynamic interplay between an active person and an ever-changing active environment, and it is on this basis that the ecological systems approach qualifies as a contextual theory.

Table 2.4 summarizes the philosophical assumptions and world views underlying each of the broad theoretical perspectives that we have reviewed. As you compare the viewpoints you expressed in Box 2.1 with those of the theorists, see if you can clearly determine your own world views on human nature and the character of human development.

In case you are wondering, we don't expect you to choose one of these theories as a favorite and reject the others. Indeed, because different theories emphasize different aspects of development, one may be more relevant to a particular issue or to a particular age group than another. Today, many developmentalists are theoretical **eclectics:** individuals who rely on many theories, recognizing that no one theory can explain all aspects of development, but that each makes an important contribution to our understanding. For the remainder of this book, we will borrow from many theories to integrate their contributions into a unified, holistic portrait of the developing person. Yet, we will also continue to explore theoretical controversies which often produce some of the most exciting breakthroughs in the field. So please join me now in examining not just the specific facts about human development, but also the broader theoretical insights that have helped to generate these facts and give them a larger meaning.

eclectics
those who borrow from many theories in their attempts to predict and explain human development.

WHAT DO YOU THINK? ?

After a divorce, children fare much better if their divorced parents can agree on how their children should be raised and support each other's parenting efforts. Which developmental theory seems best suited to explaining this finding, and how might it do so?

SUMMARY

The Nature of Scientific Theories

♦ A **theory** is a set of concepts and propositions that describe and explain observations. Theories are particularly useful if they are concise, or **parsimonious,** and yet applicable to a wide range of phenomena. Good theories are also **falsifiable** and have **heuristic value,** which means that they build on existing knowledge by continuing to generate testable hypotheses leading to new discoveries and important practical applications.

Questions and Controversies about Human Development

♦ Theories of human development differ with respect to three fundamental issues: (1) Is development primarily determined by **nature** or **nurture**?; (2) Are humans **actively** or **passively** involved in their development?; and (3) Is development a quantitative and **continuous** process, or does it proceed in a **discontinuous** fashion through a series of qualitatively distinct **developmental stages**? Some theories take an intermediate position on one or more of these issues.

The Psychoanalytic Viewpoint

♦ The psychoanalytic perspective originated with Sigmund Freud's **psychosexual theory** that claimed that humans are driven by inborn sexual and aggressive instincts that must be controlled. Much of human behavior was said to reflect **unconscious motives** that people **repress.** Freud proposed five stages of psychosexual development—oral, anal, phallic, latency, and genital—in which three components of personality, the **id, ego,** and **superego,** emerge and become closely integrated.

♦ Eric Erikson's **psychosocial theory** revises and extends Freud's theory by concentrating less on the sex instinct and more on important sociocultural determinants of human development. According to Erikson, people progress through a series of eight psychosocial conflicts beginning with trust versus mistrust in infancy and concluding with integrity versus despair in old age. Each conflict must be resolved in favor of the positive trait (trust, for example) if development is to be healthy.

The Learning Viewpoint

♦ The learning viewpoint, or **behaviorism,** originated with John B. Watson, who argued that infants are **tabula rasae** who develop **habits** as a result of their learning experiences. Development was viewed as a continuous process that could proceed in many different directions, depending on the kinds of environments to which a person is exposed. B.F. Skinner, who extended Watson's theory, claimed that development reflects the **operant** conditioning of children who are **passively** shaped by the **reinforcers** and **punishments** that accompany their behaviors. By contrast, Albert Bandura's cognitive social-learning theory views children as *active* information processors who quickly develop many new habits through **observational learning.** Bandura rejects Watson's **environmental determinism,** proposing instead that children have a hand in creating the environments that influence their development (**reciprocal determinism**).

The Cognitive-Developmental Viewpoint

♦ The cognitive-developmental viewpoint of Jean Piaget depicts children as active explorers who construct cognitive **schemes,** through the processes of **assimilation** and **accommodation,** that enable them to resolve **disequilibriums** and adapt successfully to their environments. Piaget described **cognitive development** as an **invariant sequence** of four stages: sensorimotor, preoperational, concrete-operational, and formal-operational. According to Piaget, the person's stage of cognitive development determines how she will interpret various events and, thus, what she can learn from her experiences. By contrast, Lev Vygotsky's **sociocultural theory** argues that cognitive growth is largely a *socially mediated* activity, heavily influenced by culture.

♦ **Information-processing theory** views the mind as a complex symbol-manipulating system into which information flows, and is operated on and converted to output (answers, inferences, and solutions). Cognitive development is said to be continuous rather than stagelike, as children and adolescents gradually become better at attending to information, remembering and retrieving it, and formulating strategies to solve the problems they face.

The Ethological (or Evolutionary) Viewpoint

♦ The evolutionary viewpoint, as expressed in **ethology,** is that humans are born with a number of adaptive attributes that have evolved through **natural selection** and channel development in ways that promote survival. Ethologists recognize that humans are influenced by their experiences and even claim that certain adaptive characteristics are most likely to develop during **sensitive periods,** provided that the environment fosters this development. However, they remind us that humans' biologically influenced attributes affect the kind of learning experiences they are likely to have.

The Ecological Systems Viewpoint

♦ Urie Bronfenbrenner's **ecological systems theory** views development as the product of transactions between an ever-changing person and an ever-changing environment. Bronfenbrenner proposes that the natural environment actually consists of interacting contexts or systems—**microsystem, mesosystem, exosystem,** and **macrosystem**—each of which is also influenced by the **chronosystem,** that is, by changes that occur over time in the individual or in other environmental contexts. This detailed analysis of person–environment interactions has stimulated many new interventions to optimize development.

Theories and World Views

♦ Theories can be grouped according to the world views that underlie them. As developmentalists have come to appreciate the incredible complexity and diversity of human development, more of them favor a **contextual model** over the **mechanistic model** that guides learning theories or the **organismic model** that underlies stage theories. In addition, most contemporary developmentalists are theoretically **eclectic,** recognizing that no single theory offers a totally adequate account of human development but that each contributes importantly to our understanding of developing persons.

Sigmund Freud's psychoanalytic theory revolutionized thinking about children and childhood. Freud suggested that biosocial conflicts emerge at various points during childhood, and these conflicts shape our personalities and character. You can learn more about the details of Freud's theory by visiting: http://www.utm.edu/research/iep/f/freud.htm At this web site you will find a brief biography of Sigmund Freud as well as links to other sites dealing with the concepts he outlined in his psychoanalytic theory.

KEY TERMS

theory, 38
parsimony, 38
falsifiability, 38
heuristic value, 38
nature/nurture issue, 39
activity/passivity issue, 40
continuity/discontinuity issue, 40
quantitative change, 40
qualitative change, 40
developmental stage, 41
psychosexual theory, 43
unconscious motives, 42
repression, 42
instinct, 42
id, 43
ego, 43
superego, 43
fixation, 43
psychosocial theory, 45
behaviorism, 47
habits, 47
reinforcer, 48
punisher, 48
operant learning, 48
observational learning, 49
environmental determinism, 49
reciprocal determinism, 51
cognitive development, 53
scheme, 53
assimilation, 54
disequilibriums, 54
accommodation, 54
invariant developmental sequence, 54
sociocultural theory, 56
information-processing theory, 56
ethology, 59
natural selection, 59
sensitive period, 61
altruism, 61
empathy, 62
ecological systems theory, 63
microsystem, 63
mesosystgem, 63
exosystem, 65
macrosystem, 65
chronosystem, 65
mechanistic model, 66
organismic model, 67
contextual model, 67
eclectics, 69

Hereditary Influences on Development

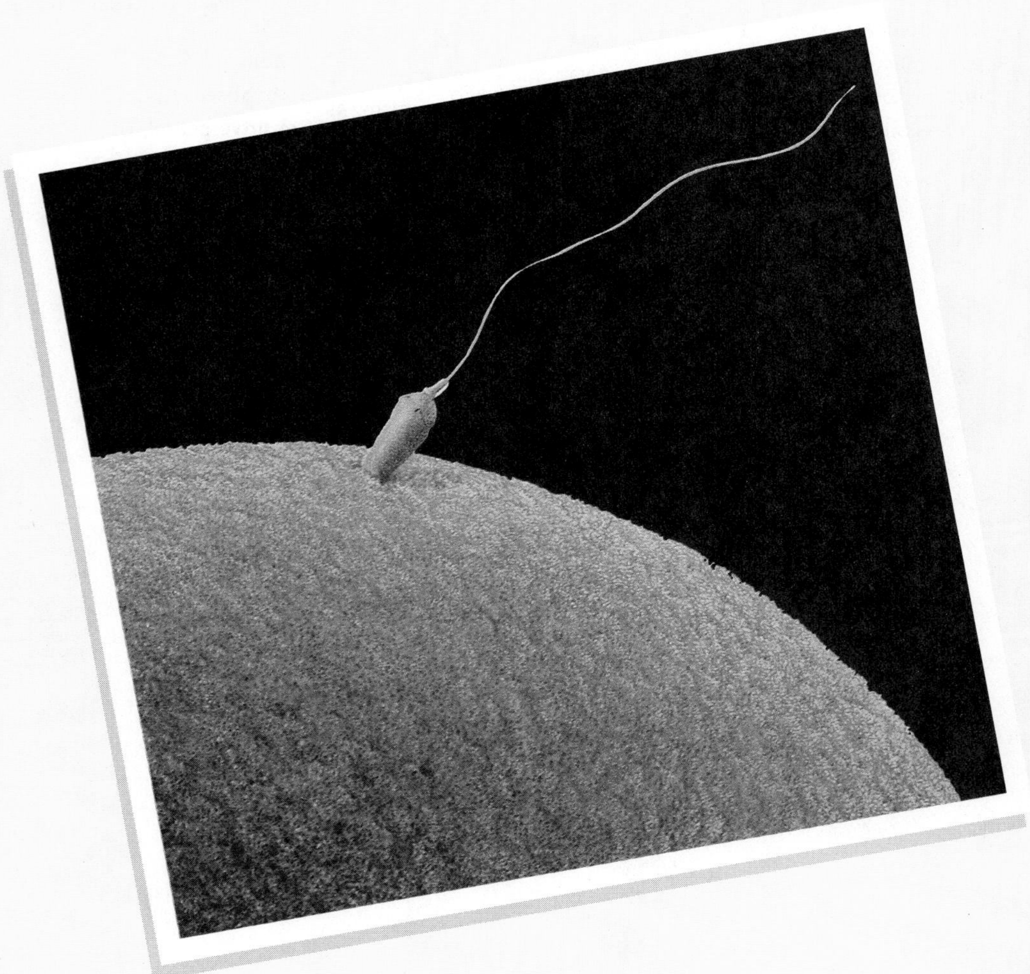

Can you remember when you were first introduced to the concept of heredity? Consider the experience of one first-grader at a parent–teacher conference. The teacher asked the boy whether he knew in which country his ancestors had lived before coming to the United States. He proudly proclaimed "the Old West" because he was "half cowboy and half black." The adults had a good laugh and then tried to convince the boy that he couldn't be of African-American ancestry because his parents were not, that he could only become what mom and dad already were. Evidently, the constraints of heredity did not go over too well with the child. He became rather distressed and asked "You mean I can't be a fireman?"

This chapter approaches human development from a hereditary perspective, seeking to determine how one's **genotype** (the **genes** that one inherits) is expressed as a **phenotype** (one's observable or measurable characteristics). We will first explore how hereditary information is transmitted from parents to their offspring and why the workings of heredity conspire to make us unique individuals. We will then review the evidence for hereditary contributions to such important psychological attributes as intelligence, personality, and even our inclinations toward displaying mentally healthy (or unhealthy) patterns of behavior. Indeed, this evidence implies that many (and some would say all) of our most noteworthy phenotypic characteristics are influenced by the genes passed to us by our parents. And yet, the biggest lesson we might take from this chapter is that genes, by themselves, determine less than you might imagine and that the expression "hereditary constraint" is something of a misnomer. As we will see, most complex human attributes are the result of a long and involved interplay between the forces of nature (heredity) and nurture (environment) (Plomin, 1994).

PRINCIPLES OF HEREDITARY TRANSMISSION

To understand the workings of heredity, we must start at **conception,** the moment when an ovum released by a woman's ovary and on its way to the uterus via the fallopian tube is fertilized by a man's sperm. Once we establish what is inherited at conception, we can examine the mechanisms by which genes influence the characteristics we display.

The Genetic Code

The very first development that occurs after conception is protective: When a sperm cell penetrates the lining of the ovum, a biochemical reaction repels other sperm, thus preventing them from repeating the fertilization process. Within a few hours, the sperm cell begins to disintegrate, releasing its genetic material. The ovum also releases its genetic material, and a new cell nucleus forms around the hereditary information provided by the father's sperm and the mother's ovum. This new cell, called a **zygote,** is only 1/20th the size of the head of a pin. Yet this tiny cell contains the code, or biochemical recipe, for the zygote's development from a single cell into a recognizable human being.

What hereditary material is present in a human zygote? The new cell nucleus contains 46 elongated, threadlike bodies called **chromosomes,** each of which consists of thousands of chemical segments, or *genes*—the basic units of heredity. With one exception, which we will soon discuss, chromosomes come in matching pairs. Each member of a pair corresponds to the other in size, shape, and the hereditary functions it serves. One member of each chromosome pair comes from the mother's ovum and the

genotype
the genetic endowment that an individual inherits.

genes
hereditary blueprints for development that are transmitted unchanged from generation to generation.

phenotype
the ways in which a person's genotype is expressed in observable or measurable characteristics.

conception
the moment of fertilization, when a sperm penetrates an ovum, forming a zygote.

zygote
a single cell formed at conception from the union of a sperm and an ovum.

chromosome
a threadlike structure made up of genes; in humans there are 46 chromosomes in the nucleus of each body cell.

other from the father's sperm cell. Thus, each parent contributes 23 chromosomes to each of their offspring.

The genes on each chromosome also function as pairs, the two members of each gene pair being located at the same sites on their corresponding chromosomes. Genes are actually stretches of **deoxyribonucleic acid (DNA),** a complex "double-helix" molecule that resembles a twisted ladder and provides the chemical "code" for development. A unique feature of DNA is that it can duplicate itself. The rungs of this ladderlike molecule split in the middle, opening somewhat like a zipper. Then each remaining half of the molecule guides the replication of its missing parts. This special ability of DNA to replicate itself is what makes it possible for a one-celled zygote to develop into a marvelously complex human being.

Growth of the Zygote and Production of Body Cells

As the zygote moves through the fallopian tube toward its prenatal home in the uterus, it begins to reproduce itself through the process of **mitosis.** At first, the zygote divides into two cells, but the two soon become four, four become eight, eight become sixteen, and so on. Just before each division, the cell duplicates its 46 chromosomes, and these duplicate sets move in opposite directions. The division of the cell then proceeds, resulting in two "daughter" cells, each of which has the identical 23 pairs of chromosomes (46 in all) and thus the same genetic code as the original parent cell. This remarkable process is illustrated in Figure 3.1.

By the time a child is born, he or she consists of billions of cells, created through mitosis, that make up muscles, bones, organs, and other bodily structures. Mitosis continues throughout life, generating new cells that enable us to grow and replacing old ones that are damaged. With each division, the hereditary blueprint is duplicated, so that every new cell contains an exact copy of the 46 chromosomes we inherited at conception.

Figure 3.1 *Mitosis: the way that cells reproduce themselves.*

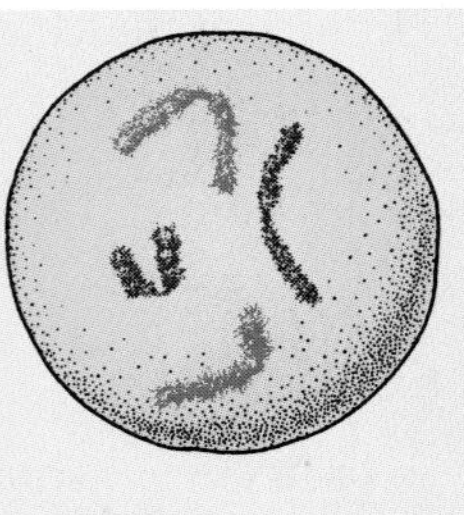

Step 1
Original parent cell (for illustrative purposes this cell contains but four chromosomes).

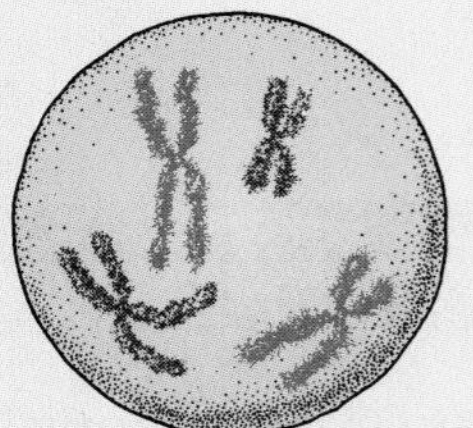

Step 2
Each chromosome splits lengthwise, producing a duplicate.

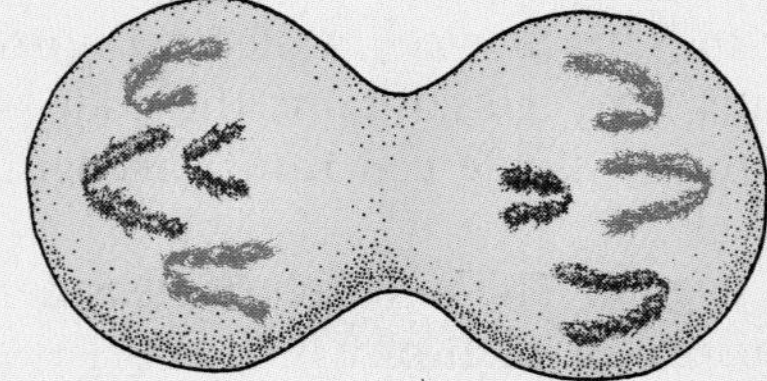

Step 3
The duplicate sets of chromosomes move to opposite ends of the parent cell, which then begins to divide.

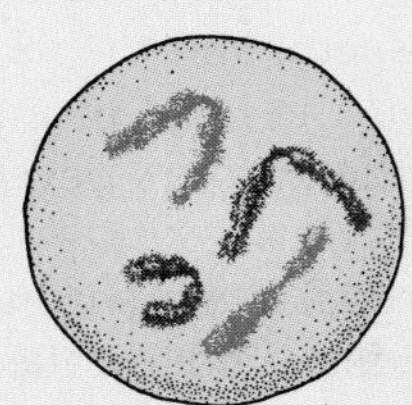

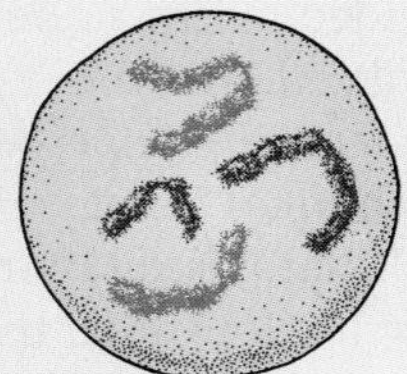

Step 4
The cell completes its division, producing two daughter cells that have identical sets of chromosomes.

deoxyribonucleic acid (DNA)
long, double-stranded molecules that make up chromosomes.

mitosis
the process in which a cell duplicates its chromosomes and then divides into two genetically identical daughter cells.

The Germ (or Sex) Cells

We have learned that sperm and egg combine to form a zygote that has 46 chromosomes (23 from each parent). But if cells normally contain 46 chromosomes apiece, why don't we start life with 92 chromosomes, 46 coming from the father's sperm cell and 46 from the mother's ovum? The answer is relatively simple.

Production of Gametes through Meiosis

In addition to body cells, human beings have *germ* cells that serve one special hereditary function—to produce *gametes* (sperm in males and ova in females). When male germ cells in the testes and female germ cells in the ovaries produce sperm and ova, they do so through a process called **meiosis** that is illustrated in Figure 3.2. The germ cell first duplicates its 46 chromosomes. Then an event called **crossing-over** often takes place: Adjacent chromosomes cross and break at one or more points along their length, exchanging segments of genetic material, much as if you were to exchange a couple of fingers with a friend after a handshake. Notice, then, that this transfer of genes during crossing-over creates new and unique hereditary combinations. Next, pairs of duplicated chromosomes (some of which have been altered by crossing-over) segregate into two parent cells that each contain 46 chromosomes. Finally, the parent cells divide so that each of their daughter cells (or gametes) contains 23 single, or *unpaired,* chromosomes. At conception, then, a sperm with 23 chromosomes unites with an ovum with 23 chromosomes, producing a zygote with a full complement of 46 chromosomes.

Brothers and sisters who have the same mother and father inherit 23 chromosomes from each of these parents. Why is it, then, that offspring of the same parents sometimes barely resemble each other? The reason is that meiosis conspires to make us genetically unique.

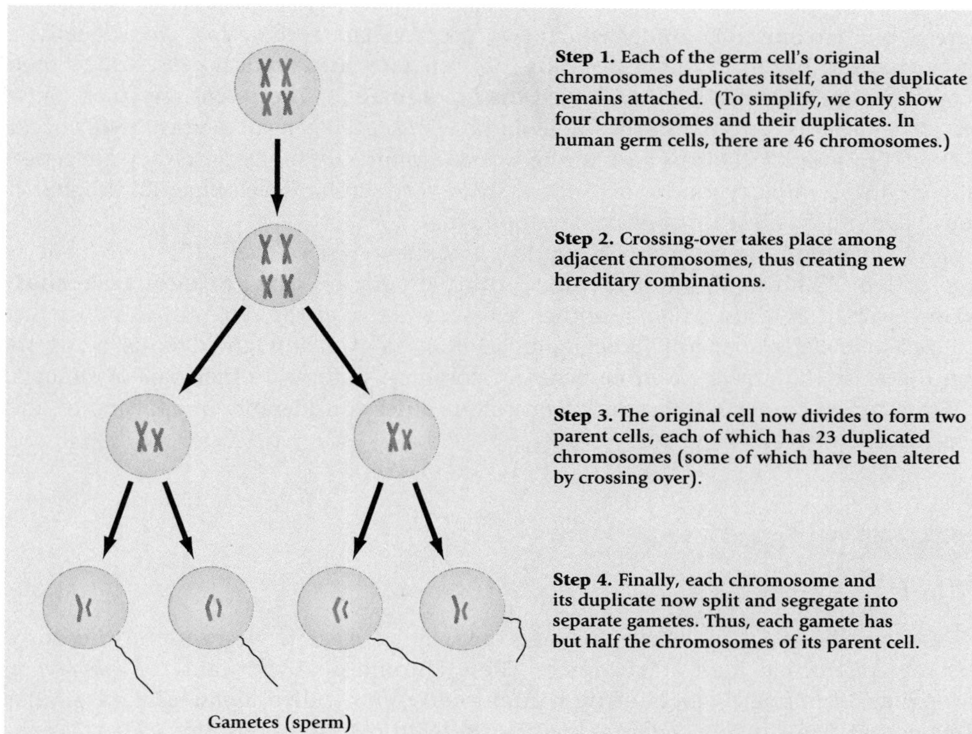

Step 1. Each of the germ cell's original chromosomes duplicates itself, and the duplicate remains attached. (To simplify, we only show four chromosomes and their duplicates. In human germ cells, there are 46 chromosomes.)
Step 2. Crossing-over takes place among adjacent chromosomes, thus creating new hereditary combinations.
Step 3. The original cell now divides to form two parent cells, each of which has 23 duplicated chromosomes (some of which have been altered by crossing over).
Step 4. Finally, each chromosome and its duplicate now split and segregate into separate gametes. Thus, each gamete has but half the chromosomes of its parent cell.
Gametes (sperm)

Figure 3.2 *Diagram of the meiosis of a male germ cell.*

meiosis
the process in which a germ cell divides, producing gametes (sperm or ova) that each contain half of the parent cell's original complement of chromosomes; in humans, the products of meiosis contain 23 chromosomes.

crossing-over
a process in which genetic material is exchanged between pairs of chromosomes during meiosis.

Hereditary Uniqueness

When a pair of chromosomes segregates during meiosis, it is a matter of chance which of the two chromosomes will end up in a particular parent cell. And because each chromosome pair segregates independently of all other pairs according to the principle of **independent assortment,** there are many different combinations of chromosomes that could result from the meiosis of a single germ cell. Since human germ cells contain 23 chromosome pairs, each of which is segregating independently of the others, the laws of probability tell us that each parent can produce 2^{23}—more than 8 million—different genetic combinations in their sperm or ova. If a father can produce 8 million combinations of 23 chromosomes and a mother can produce 8 million, any couple could theoretically have 64 *trillion* babies without producing two children who inherited precisely the same set of genes! In fact, the odds of exact genetic replication in two siblings are even smaller than 1 in 64 trillion. Why? Because the *crossing-over* process, which occurs during the earlier phases of meiosis, actually alters the genetic composition of chromosomes and thereby increases the number of possible variations in an individual's gametes far beyond the 8 million that could occur if chromosomes segregated cleanly, without exchanging genetic information.

Of course, brothers and sisters resemble one another to some extent because their genes are drawn from a gene pool provided by the same two parents. Each brother or sister inherits half of each parent's genes, although two siblings never inherit the same half, owing to the random process by which parental chromosomes (and genes) segregate into the sperm and ovum that combine to produce each offspring. Thus, each individual is genetically unique. From an evolutionary perspective, the genetic variability produced by meiosis is highly adaptive because it increases the likelihood that some members of each species would survive any catastrophic changes in the environment (Strachan & Read, 1996).

Multiple Births

There is one circumstance under which two people share a genotype. Occasionally, a zygote that has begun to duplicate splits into separate but identical cells, which then become two individuals. These are called **monozygotic** (or **identical**) **twins** because they have developed from a *single* zygote and have *identical* genes. Identical twins occur in about 1 of every 250 births around the world (Plomin, 1990). Because they are genetically identical, monozygotic twins should show very similar developmental progress if genes have much effect on human development.

More common, however (occurring in approximately 1 of every 125 births and as often as 1 in 20 births to mothers using fertility drugs), are **dizygotic** (or **fraternal**) **twins**—pairs that result when a mother releases *two* ova at the same time and each is fertilized by a *different* sperm (Brockington, 1996). So even though fraternal twins are born together, they have no more genes in common than any other pair of siblings. As illustrated in Figure 3.3, fraternal twins often differ considerably in appearance and need not even be the same sex.

Male or Female?

A hereditary basis for sex differences becomes quite clear if we examine the chromosomes of normal men and women. These chromosomal portraits, or *karyotypes,* reveal that 22 of the 23 pairs of human chromosomes (called *autosomes*) are similar in males and females. Sex is determined by the 23rd pair. In males, the 23rd pair consists of one elongated body known as an **X chromosome** and a short, stubby com-

independent assortment
the principle stating that each pair of chromosomes segregates independently of all other chromosome pairs during meiosis.

monozygotic (or identical) twins
twins that result when a single zygote divides into two separate but identical cells that each develop independently. As a result, each member of a monozygotic twin pair inherits exactly the same set of genes.

dizygotic (or fraternal) twins
twins that result when a mother releases two ova at roughly the same time and each is fertilized by a different sperm, producing two zygotes that are genetically different.

X chromosome
the longer of the two sex chromosomes; normal females have two X chromosomes, whereas normal males have but one.

Figure 3.3 ***Identical, or monozygotic, twins (left) develop from a single zygote. Because they have inherited identical sets of genes, they look alike, are the same sex, and share all other inherited characteristics. Fraternal, or dizygotic, twins (right) develop from separate zygotes and have no more genes in common than siblings born at different times. Consequently, they may not look alike (as we see in this photo) and may not even be the same sex.***

panion called a **Y chromosome.** In females, both these sex chromosomes are Xs (see Figure 3.4).

Throughout history, mothers have often been belittled, tortured, divorced and even beheaded for failing to bear their husbands a male heir! This is both a social and a biological injustice in that fathers determine the sex of their offspring. When the sex chromosomes of a genetic (XY) male segregate into gametes during meiosis, half of the sperm produced will contain an X chromosome and half will contain a Y chromosome. By contrast, the ova produced by a genetic (XX) female all carry an X chromosome. So a child's sex is determined by whether an X-bearing or a Y-bearing *sperm* fertilizes the ovum. Located on the Y chromosome is a single "sex gene" that is responsible for male sexual development (Milunsky, 1992). If this gene is absent, the individual that develops is a female.

So far, so good: We have a genetically unique boy or girl who has inherited about 100,000 genes in all on his or her 46 chromosomes (Jonsen, 1996). Now an important question: How do genes regulate development and influence a person's phenotypic characteristics?

Y chromosome
the shorter of the two sex chromosomes; normal males have one Y chromosome, whereas females have none.

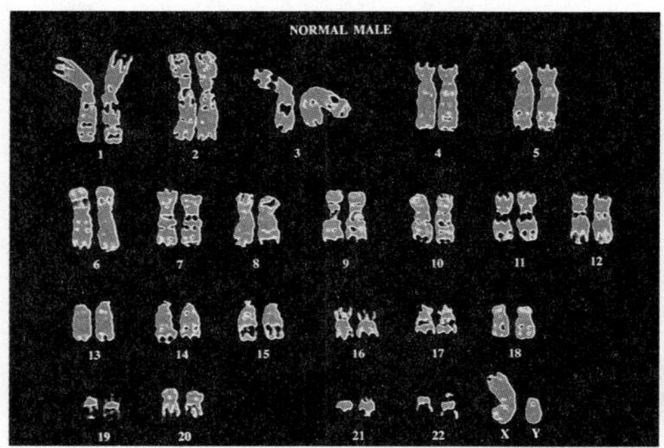

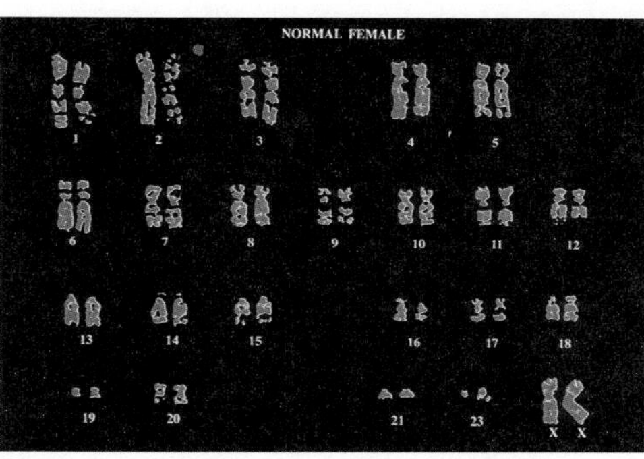

Figure 3.4 *These karotypes of a male (left) and a female (right) have been arranged so that the chromosomes could be displayed in pairs. Note that the 23rd pair of chromosomes for the male consists of one elongated X chromosome and a Y chromosome that is noticeably smaller, whereas the 23rd pair for the female consists of two X chromosomes.*

What Do Genes Do?

How do genes promote development? At the most basic, biochemical level, they call for the production of enzymes and other proteins that are necessary for the formation and functioning of new cells (Aldridge, 1996). Genes, for example, regulate the production of a pigment called melanin in the iris of the eye. People with brown eyes have genes that call for much of this pigment, whereas people with lighter (blue or green) eyes have genes that call for less pigmentation. Genes also guide cell differentiation, thereby insuring that some cells become the brain and central nervous system, whereas others become the circulatory system, bones, skin, and so on. Genes influence and are influenced by the biochemical environment surrounding them during development. For example, a particular cell might become part of an eyeball or part of an elbow depending on what cells surround it during early embryonic development. However, no one completely understands the remarkable process that transforms a single-celled zygote into a remarkably complex, living, breathing human being.

Some genes are responsible for *regulating* the pace and timing of development. That is, specific genes with specific developmental blueprints are "turned on" or "turned off" by other regulatory genes at different points in a person's life span (Plomin et al., 1997). Regulatory genes, for example, might "turn on" the genes responsible for the growth spurt we experience as adolescents, and then shut these growth genes down in adulthood.

Finally, an important point: *Environmental factors clearly influence how messages coded in the genes are carried out* (Gottlieb, 1996). Consider, for example, that a child who inherits genes for tall stature may or may not be tall as an adult. Should he experience very poor nutrition for a prolonged period early in life, he could end up being only average or even below average in height, despite having the genetic potential for exceptional stature. So environmental influences combine with genetic influences to determine how a genotype is translated into a particular phenotype—the way one looks, feels, thinks, and behaves.

Another way to approach the riddle of how genes influence development is to consider the major patterns of genetic inheritance: the ways in which parents' genes are expressed in their children's phenotypes.

How Are Genes Expressed?

There are five main patterns of genetic expression: simple dominant-recessive inheritance, codominance, sex-linked inheritance, genetic imprinting, and polygenic (or multiple gene) inheritance.

Simple Dominant-Recessive Inheritance

Many human characteristics are influenced by only one pair of genes (called **alleles**): one from the mother, one from the father. Although he knew nothing of genes, a 19th-century monk named Gregor Mendel contributed greatly to our knowledge of single gene-pair inheritance by cross-breeding different strains of peas and observing the outcomes. His major discovery was a predictable pattern to the way in which two alternative characteristics (for example, smooth seeds versus wrinkled seeds; green pods versus yellow pods) appeared in the offspring of cross-breedings. He called some characteristics (for example, smooth seeds) "dominant" because they appeared more often in later generations than their opposite traits, which he called "recessive" traits. Among peas and among humans, an offspring's phenotype often is not simply a "blend" of

alleles
alternative forms of a gene that can appear at a particular site on a chromosome.

the characteristics of mother and father. Instead, one of the parental genes often dominates the other, and the child resembles the parent who contributed the dominant gene.

To illustrate the principles of **simple dominant-recessive inheritance,** consider the fact that about three-fourths of us have the ability to see distant objects clearly (that is, normal vision), whereas the remaining one-fourth of us cannot and are myopic (nearsighted). It happens that the gene associated with normal vision is a **dominant allele.** A weaker gene calling for nearsightedness is said to be a **recessive allele.** So a person who inherits one allele for normal vision and one allele for myopia would display a phenotype of normal vision because the normal-vision gene overpowers (that is, dominates) the nearsightedness gene.

Since a normal-vision allele dominates a nearsightedness allele, we represent the normal vision gene with a capital *N* and the nearsightedness gene with a lower-case *n*. Perhaps you can see (no pun intended) that there are three possible genotypes for this visual characteristic: (1) two normal-vision alleles *(NN),* (2) two nearsightedness alleles (*nn*), and (3) one of each (*Nn*). People whose genotype for an attribute consists of two alleles of the same kind are said to be **homozygous** for that attribute. Thus, an *NN* individual is homozygous for normal vision and will pass only genes for normal vision to his or her offspring. An *nn* individual is homozygous nearsighted (the only way one can actually be nearsighted is to inherit two of these recessive alleles) and will pass nearsightedness genes to his or her offspring. Finally, an *Nn* individual is said to be **heterozygous** for this visual trait because he or she has inherited alternative forms of the allele. This person will have normal vision, because the *N* allele is dominant. And what kind of allele will the heterozygous person pass along to offspring? Either a normal-vision gene or a nearsightedness gene! Even though a heterozygous person has normal vision, exactly half the gametes produced by this individual will carry a gene for normal vision, and half will carry a gene for nearsightedness.

Can two individuals with normal vision ever produce a nearsighted child? The answer is yes—if each parent is heterozygous for normal vision and is a **carrier** of the recessive allele for nearsightedness. In Figure 3.5, the genotype of a carrier father appears at the head of the columns, and that of a carrier mother appears at the left of the rows. What kind of vision will their children have? The various possibilities appear in the four quadrants of the chart. If a sperm bearing a normal-vision *(N)* allele unites with an ovum carrying a normal vision *(N)* allele, the result is an *NN,* or a child that is homozygous for normal vision. If a sperm bearing an *N* gene fertilizes

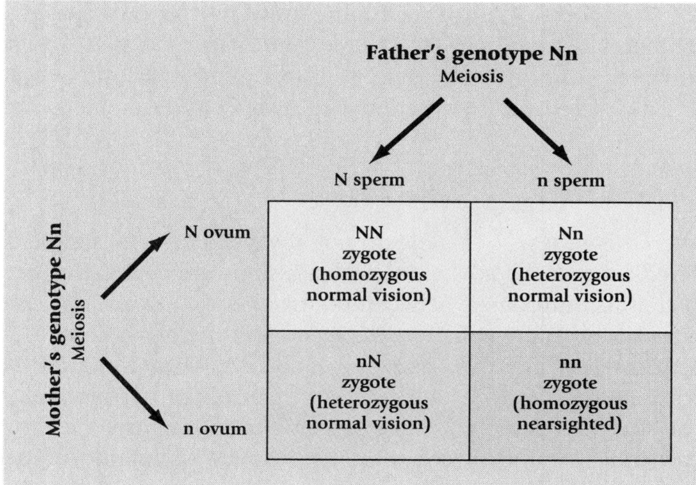

Figure 3.5 *Possible genotypes and phenotypes resulting from a mating of two heterozygotes for normal vision.*

simple dominant-recessive inheritance
a pattern of inheritance in which one allele dominates another so that only its phenotype is expressed.

dominant allele
a relatively powerful gene that is expressed phenotypically and masks the effect of a less powerful gene.

recessive allele
a less powerful gene that is not expressed phenotypically when paired with a dominant allele.

homozygous
having inherited two alleles for an attribute that are identical in their effects.

heterozygous
having inherited two alleles for an attribute that have different effects.

carrier
a heterozygous individual who displays no sign of a recessive allele in his or her own phenotype but can pass this gene to offspring.

DEVELOPMENTAL ISSUES

3.1

Examples of Dominant and Recessive Traits in Human Heredity

Our discussion of dominant and recessive genes has centered on two particular alleles, a gene for normal vision and a gene for nearsightedness. Listed here are a number of other dominant and recessive characteristics in human heredity (Connor, 1995; McKusick, 1995).

A quick glance through the list reveals that most of the undesirable or maladaptive attributes are recessive. For this we can be thankful. Otherwise genetically linked diseases and defects might become widespread and eventually decimate the species.

One important genetic disease produced by a *dominant* gene is Huntington's disease, a condition that causes a gradual deterioration of the nervous system, leading to a progressive decline in physical and mental abilities and ultimately to death. Although some victims of Huntington's disease die in young adulthood, the disease normally appears much later, usually after age 40. Fortunately, the dominant allele that is responsible for this lethal condition is very rare.

Dominant Traits	*Recessive Traits*
Dark hair	Blond hair
Full head of hair	Pattern baldness
Curly hair	Straight hair
Facial dimples	No dimples
Farsightedness	Normal vision
Normal vision	Color blindness[a]
Extra digits	Five digits
Pigmented skin	Albinism
Type A blood	Type O blood
Type B blood	Type O blood
Normal blood clotting	Hemophilia[a]
Huntington's disease	Congenital deafness
Normal blood cells	Sickle-cell anemia[a]
Normal physiology	Cystic fibrosis[a]
Normal physiology	Phenylketonuria[a]
Normal physiology	Tay-Sachs disease[a]

[a]These conditions are discussed elsewhere in the chapter.

an ovum carrying an *n* gene, or if an *n* sperm fertilizes an *N* ovum, the result is a heterozygous child with normal vision. Finally, if both sperm and ovum carry an *n* gene, the child will be nearsighted. Since each of these four combinations is equally likely in any given mating, the odds are 1 in 4 that a child of two *Nn* parents will be nearsighted.

The normal vision/nearsightedness trait is but one of more than 5,000 human attributes determined by a single gene pair in which one particular allele dominates another (Connor, 1995). Box 3.1 lists a number of other common dominant and recessive characteristics that people can display.

Codominance

Alternative forms of a gene do not always follow the simple dominant-recessive pattern described by Gregor Mendel. Instead, some are **codominant:** The phenotype they produce is a compromise between the two genes. For example, the alleles for human blood types A and B are equally expressive, and neither dominates the other. A heterozygous person who inherits an allele for blood type A and one for blood type B has equal proportions of A-antigens and B-antigens in his or her blood. So if your blood type is AB, you illustrate this principle of genetic codominance.

codominance
condition in which two heterozygous but equally powerful alleles produce a phenotype in which genes are both fully and equally expressed.

Another type of codominance occurs when one of two heterozygous alleles is stronger than the other but fails to mask all of its effects. The *sickle-cell* trait is a noteworthy example of this "incomplete dominance." About 9% of African Americans (and relatively few whites or Asian Americans) are heterozygous for this attribute, carrying a recessive "sickle-cell" allele (Schulman & Black, 1993). The presence of this one sickle-cell gene causes some of the person's red blood cells to assume an unusual crescent, or sickle, shape (see Figure 3.6). Sickled cells can be a problem because they tend to cluster together, distributing less oxygen throughout the circulatory system. Yet overt symptoms of circulatory distress, such as painful swelling of the joints and fatigue, are rarely experienced by these sickle-cell "carriers" unless they experience oxygen deprivation as they might at high altitudes, after heavy physical exertion, or while under anesthesia (Strachan & Read, 1996).

The consequences are much more severe for those individuals who inherit *two* recessive sickle-cell genes. They will develop a severe blood disorder, called **sickle-cell anemia,** that causes massive sickling of red blood cells and inefficient distribution of oxygen at all times. Many who suffer from this painful disease die from heart and/or kidney failure during childhood, and they are particularly vulnerable to pneumonia and other respiratory diseases (Schulman & Black, 1993).

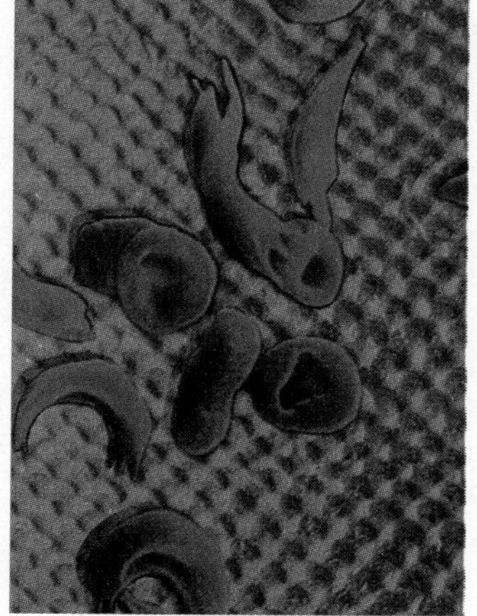

Figure 3.6 *Normal (round) and "sickled" (elongated) red blood cells from a person with sickle-cell anemia.*

Sex-linked Inheritance

Some traits are called **sex-linked characteristics** because they are determined by genes located on the sex chromosomes. In fact, the vast majority of these sex-linked attributes are produced by recessive genes that are found only on X chromosomes. Who do you suppose is more likely to inherit these recessive X-linked traits, males or females?

The answer is males, a point we can easily illustrate with a common sex-linked characteristic, *red/green color blindness*. Many people cannot distinguish red from green, an inability caused by a recessive gene that appears only on X chromosomes. Now recall that a normal (XY) male has but one X chromosome—the one he inherited from his mother. If this X chromosome carries a recessive gene for color blindness, the male will be color-blind. Why? Because there is no corresponding gene on his Y chromosome that might counteract the effect of this "color-blind" allele. By contrast, a genetic female who inherits but one gene for color blindness will not be color-blind, for the color-normal gene on her second X chromosome will dominate the color-blind gene, enabling her to distinguish red from green (see Figure 3.7). So, a female cannot be color-blind unless *both* of her X chromosomes contain a recessive gene for color blindness.

sickle-cell anemia
a genetic blood disease that causes red blood cells to assume an unusual sickled shape and to become inefficient at distributing oxygen.

sex-linked characteristic
an attribute determined by a recessive gene that appears on the X chromosome; more likely to characterize males.

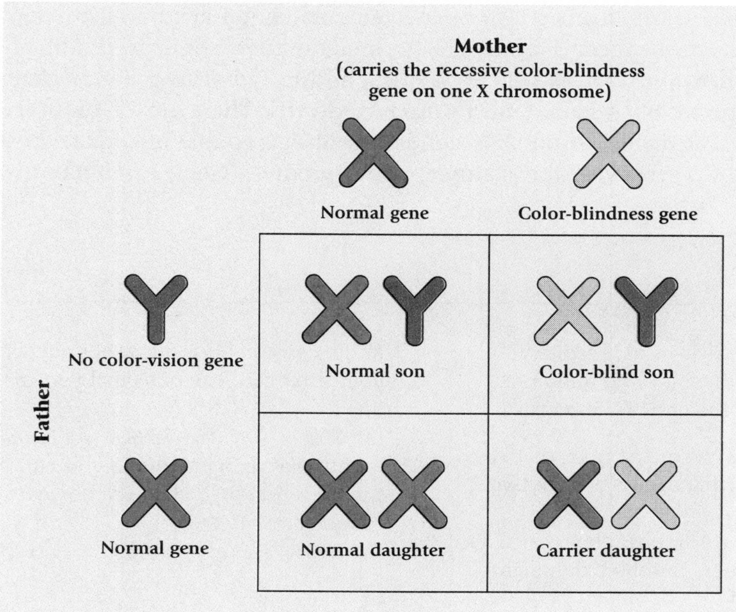

Figure 3.7 *Sex-linked inheritance of red/green color blindness. In the example here, the mother can distinguish reds from greens but is a carrier because one of her X chromosomes contains a color-blind allele. Notice that her sons have a 50% chance of inheriting the color-blind allele and being color-blind, whereas none of her daughters would display the trait. A girl can be color-blind only if her father is and her mother is at least a carrier of the color-blindness gene.*

Immediately, we have reason to suspect that more males than females will be color-blind. Indeed, roughly 8 males in 100 cannot distinguish red from green. This finding suggests that the ratio of color-blind to color-normal genes in the gene pool is approximately 1:12. Since the odds are only 1 in 12 that any single X chromosome will contain a gene for color blindness, the likelihood that a female will inherit two of these genes (and be color-blind) is $\frac{1}{12} \times \frac{1}{12}$, or only 1 in 144 (Burns & Bottino, 1989).

There are many sex-linked characteristics other than color blindness, and most of them are disabling. These include hemophilia (a disease in which the blood does not clot), two kinds of muscular dystrophy, degeneration of the optic nerve, and certain forms of deafness and night blindness (Schulman & Black, 1993). Because these disorders are determined by recessive genes on X chromosomes, males are much more likely than females to suffer their harmful effects.

Genetic Imprinting

Until recently, geneticists were confused about the distribution of certain traits that were known to be influenced by a single pair of alleles but followed none of the patterns of inheritance we have discussed. For example, children are more likely to develop diabetes if their fathers rather than their mothers have this disease, whereas *Angelman syndrome,* a disorder characterized by jerky movements, inappropriate laughter, and severe mental retardation, is typically transmitted by a person's mother rather than a person's father (Strachan & Read, 1996). Today, we know that these "parent-specific" patterns of inheritance are due to **genetic imprinting**—a process in which particular gene pairs are biochemically marked so that only one parent's allele (either the mother's or the father's) is expressed, regardless of its composition. There are only a small number of alleles that are subject to genetic imprinting, and it apparently does not occur in all individuals (Strachan & Read, 1996). At present, the causes of genetic imprinting are poorly understood, and its evolutionary significance, if any, is unknown.

Polygenic Inheritance

To this point, we have considered only those traits that are influenced by a single pair of alleles. However, most important human characteristics are influenced by many pairs of alleles and are called **polygenic traits.** Examples of polygenic traits include height, weight, intelligence, skin color, temperamental attributes, susceptibility to cancer, and a host of others (Plomin, 1990). Imagine that height were influenced by three pairs of genes, and that the alleles AA, BB, and CC tend to produce giants, whereas the genotype aa, bb, and cc tend to produce dwarfs. There are 27 genotypes that could result if we calculated all possible children that one couple of average height (each with an Aa Bb Cc genotype, for example) could produce. Gene combinations that call for average

genetic imprinting
pattern of inheritance in which a pair of alleles is biochemically marked so that only one parent's allele is expressed, regardless of its composition.

polygenic trait
a characteristic that is influenced by the action of many genes rather than a single pair.

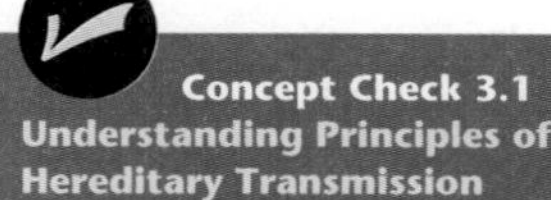

Concept Check 3.1
Understanding Principles of Hereditary Transmission

Check your understanding of the principles of hereditary transmission by answering each of the following questions. Answers appear in the Appendix at the end of the book.

1. You are a monozygotic (identical) twin. The odds that you and your twin are the same sex (that is, two boys or two girls) are:
   (a) 100% (b) 50% (c) impossible to calculate
2. Most people can curl their tongues—a simple dominant-recessive trait that is determined by a dominant gene. Your father can curl his tongue, but neither your mother nor your sister can. The odds that you can curl your tongue are:
   (a) 100% (b) 75% (c) 50% (d) 25%
3. If both *biological* parents cannot curl their tongues, then the odds that their child will be *unable* to curl his (her) tongue are:
   (a) 100% (b) 50% (c) 0%

height would be more likely than combinations calling for very tall or very short stature. When a trait is influenced by multiple genes, we therefore expect many phenotypes to appear in the population, and we expect many people to be near the average and few to be extreme. This is exactly the way height and most other measurable human traits are distributed in large populations.

To date, nobody knows exactly how many pairs of alleles influence physical stature (height), intelligence, or other polygenic traits. All we can say is that unknown numbers of genes, interacting with environmental influences, create a wide range of individual differences in most important human attributes.

CHROMOSOMAL AND GENETIC ABNORMALITIES

Although the vast majority of newborn infants are pronounced healthy at birth, approximately 5 of every 100 have a congenital problem of some kind (Schulman & Black, 1993). By definition, **congenital defects** are those that are present at birth, although many of these conditions are not detectable when the child is born. For example, the gene that produces **Huntington's disease** is present from the moment of conception. But as we learned in Box 3.1, the gradual deterioration of the nervous system associated with this condition is not apparent at birth and does not ordinarily appear until much later—usually after age 40.

In Chapter 4, we will consider a variety of congenital defects that are likely to result from abnormalities in the birth process or from harmful conditions to which children are exposed while developing within the womb. Here we will look only at those problems that are caused by abnormal genes and chromosomes.

Chromosomal Abnormalities

When a germ cell divides during meiosis, the distribution of its 46 chromosomes into sperm or ova is sometimes uneven. In other words, one of the resulting gametes may have too many chromosomes, while the other has too few. The vast majority of these chromosomal abnormalities are *lethal,* meaning that a zygote formed from the union of an abnormal and a normal gamete will fail to develop or will be spontaneously aborted. However, some chromosomal abnormalities are not lethal, as illustrated by the finding that approximately 1 child in 200 is born with either one chromosome too many or one too few (Plomin, 1986).

Abnormalities of the Sex Chromosomes

Many chromosomal abnormalities involve the 23rd pair—the sex chromosomes. Occasionally, males are born with an extra X or Y chromosome, producing the genotype XXY or XYY, and females will often survive if they inherit a single X chromosome (XO) or even three (XXX), four (XXXX), or five (XXXXX) X chromosomes. Each of these conditions has somewhat different developmental implications, as we will see in examining four of the more common sex chromosome abnormalities in Table 3.1.

In addition to the abnormalities described in Table 3.1, about 1 individual in 1000 has an X chromosome that is brittle in places and may even have separated into two or more pieces—a condition known as the **Fragile-X syndrome** (Hagerman & Cronister, 1996). This condition is second only to Down syndrome (which we will soon discuss) as a genetic cause of mental retardation, and recent research suggests that it

congenital defect
a problem that is present (though not necessarily apparent) at birth; such defects may stem from genetic and prenatal influences or from complications of the birth process.

Huntington's disease
a genetic disease caused by a dominant allele that typically appears later in life and causes the nervous system to degenerate (see Box 3.1).

Fragile-X syndrome
abnormality of the X chromosome caused by a defective gene and associated with mild to severe mental retardation, particularly when the defective gene is passed from mother to child.

Table 3.1	Four Common Sex Chromosome Abnormalities	
Name/genotype(s)	**Incidence**	**Developmental implications**
Female abnormalities		
Turner's syndrome; XO	1 in 2,500 female births	*Appearance:* Phenotypically female but small in stature with stubby fingers and toes, a webbed neck, a broad chest, and small, underdeveloped breasts. Normal sexual development lacking at puberty, although Turner females can assume a more "womanly" appearance by taking the female hormone estrogen. *Fertility:* Sterile. *Intellectual characteristics:* Normal verbal intelligence but frequently score below average on tests of spatial abilities such as puzzle assembly or the mental rotation of figures.
Poly-X or "superfemale" syndrome; XXX, XXXX, or XXXXX	1 in 1,000 female births	*Appearance:* Phenotypically female and normal in appearance. *Fertility:* Fertile; produce children with the usual number of sex chromosomes. *Intellectual characteristics:* Score somewhat below average in intelligence, with greatest deficits on tests of verbal reasoning. Intellectual deficits are detectable as early as age 2 by delays in reaching developmental milestones such as walking and talking. Developmental delays and intellectual deficits become more pronounced with an increase in the number of extra X chromosomes inherited.
Male abnormalities		
Klinefelter's syndrome; XXY or XXXY	1 in 500 male births	*Appearance:* Phenotypically male, with the emergence of some female secondary sex characteristics (enlargement of the hips and breasts) at puberty. Significantly taller than normal (XY) males. In the past, Klinefelter males from Eastern-bloc countries may have competed as females in athletic events, leading to the current practice of administering sex tests to all female Olympic athletes. *Fertility:* Have underdeveloped testes and are sterile. *Intellectual characteristics:* About 20 to 30% of Klinefelter males are deficient in verbal intelligence, and their deficiencies become more pronounced with an increase in the number of extra X chromosomes inherited.
Supermale syndrome; XYY, XYYY, or XYYYY	1 in 1,000 male births	*Appearance:* Phenotypic males who are significantly taller than normal (XY) males, have large teeth, and often develop severe acne during adolescence. *Fertility:* Typically fertile, although many of these men have abnormally low sperm counts. *Intellectual characteristics:* Although once thought to be subnormal intellectually and prone to violence and aggression, both these assumptions have been proved wrong by research. IQs of supermales span the full range of those observed in normal (XY) males. Moreover, careful studies of large numbers of XYYs indicate that they are no more violent or aggressive than normal males, and are sometimes shy and retiring.

Sources: Robinson et al., 1992; Shafer & Kuller, 1996; Tolmie, 1995.

may contribute to some cases of *infantile autism,* a serious emotional disorder of early childhood characterized by extreme self-involvement, repetitive self-stimulating behaviors, and delayed (or absent) language and social skills. About 75 percent of Fragile-X males show some degree of mental retardation (ranging from mild to severe), whereas the clear majority of females with a Fragile-X chromosome are either intellectually normal or display only mild cognitive impairments (Hagerman, 1996). Investigators have located the gene responsible for this chromosomal abnormality—an abnormal gene on the X chromosome. And recent research indicates that the defective allele at the fragile site is much more likely to produce mental retardation in daughters when the gene is passed from mother to child (Hagerman, 1996; Sherman, 1996).

Autosomal Abnormalities

Several hereditary abnormalities are attributable to the **autosomes**—that is, the 22 pairs of chromosomes that are similar in males and females. The most common type of autosomal abnormality occurs when an abnormal sperm or ovum carrying an extra autosome combines with a normal gamete to form a zygote that has 47 chromosomes

autosomes
the 22 pairs of human chromosomes that are identical in males and females.

(2 sex chromosomes and 45 autosomes). In these cases, the extra chromosome appears along with one of the 22 pairs of autosomes to yield three chromosomes of that type, or a *trisomy.*

By far the most frequent of all autosomal abnormalities (occurring once in every 800 births) is **Down syndrome,** or *trisomy-21,* a condition in which the child inherits all or part of an extra 21st chromosome. Children with Down syndrome are mentally retarded, with IQs that average 50 (the average IQ among normal children is 100). They may also have congenital eye, ear, and heart defects and are usually characterized by a number of distinctive physical features, including a sloping forehead, protruding tongue, short stubby limbs, slightly flattened nose, and almond-shaped eyes (see Figure 3.8). Although intellectually impaired, these youngsters reach many of the same developmental milestones as normal children, but at a slower pace (Kopp, 1983; Thompson et al., 1985). Most of these youngsters learn to care for their basic needs, and some have even learned to read and write (Gibson & Harris, 1988; Kopp, 1983). Their developmental progress appears to be best when parents and other regular companions are successful at coping with the children's limitations and are persistent in their attempts to stimulate them while providing ample emotional support (Atkinson et al., 1995; Mundy et al., 1988). However, they often spend many of their adult years in institutions because their developmental handicaps usually prevent them from becoming economically self-sufficient.

Figure 3.8 *Children with Down syndrome can lead happy lives if they receive affection and encouragement from their companions.*

Causes of Chromosomal Abnormalities

Clearly, most chromosomal abnormalities result from the *uneven segregation of chromosomes* during the meiosis of male and female germ cells. However, errors of meiosis are not the only contributors to chromosomal abnormalities.

As shown in Table 3.2, the likelihood of Down syndrome and other chromosomal abnormalities increases dramatically for offspring of older mothers. Notice also that mothers who have already given birth to a child with Down syndrome are much more likely to have another child with Down syndrome, should they give birth again, than are other women of the same age.

Why are older mothers at higher risk for bearing children with chromosomal abnormalities? One common explanation is the **"aging-ova hypothesis."** Although sexually mature males produce sperm throughout life, a female is born with all her ova already present in her ovaries. So a 45-year-old woman's ova are more than 45 years old and may simply have deteriorated, either because of aging or because of increased exposure to environmental hazards, such as radiation and toxic chemicals.

Interestingly, the risk of chromosomal abnormalities is not related to paternal age (Shafer & Kuller, 1996), although fathers can contribute to abnormal outcomes in other ways. Even though most cases of Down syndrome can be traced to mothers' abnormal ova, about one-fourth of these children receive their extra 21st chromosome from

Table 3.2 Risk of Down Syndrome and Other Chromosomal Abnormalities as a Function of Mother's Age

	Probability that child will have Down syndrome		
Age of mother	**At any pregnancy**	**After birth of a child with Down syndrome**	**Probability of any chromosomal abnormality at birth**
<29	<1 in 1,000	1 in 100	1 in 450
30–34	1 in 700	1 in 100	1 in 350
35–39	1 in 220	1 in 100	1 in 125
40–44	1 in 65	1 in 25	1 in 40
45–49	1 in 25	1 in 15	1 in 12

SOURCE: Adapted from Shafer & Kuller, 1996.

Down syndrome
a chromosomal abnormality (also known as trisomy-21) caused by the presence of an extra 21st chromosome; people with this syndrome have a distinctive physical appearance and are moderately to severely retarded.

aging-ova hypothesis
the hypothesis that an older mother is more likely to have children with chromosomal abnormalities because her ova are degenerating as she nears the end of her reproductive years.

their fathers rather than their mothers (Magenis et al., 1977). The risk of chromosomal abnormalities is also greater if a father has been exposed to such environmental hazards as repeated abdominal X-rays (radiation) that can damage his chromosomes (Strigini et al., 1990). And it now appears that perhaps 80 percent of girls with Turner's syndrome (see Table 3.1) originate from a normal (X) ovum that has been fertilized by an abnormal *sperm*—one that contains neither an X nor a Y chromosome (Tolmie, 1995). Only the XYY (or supermale) syndrome is always attributable to one parent—in this case, the father—because mothers have no Y chromosomes to transmit to their offspring.

Genetic Abnormalities

Parents who are themselves healthy are often amazed to learn that their child could have a hereditary defect. Their surprise is certainly understandable, for most genetic problems are recessive traits that few if any close relatives may have had. In addition, these problems simply will not appear unless *both* parents carry the harmful allele *and* the child inherits this particular gene from each parent. The exceptions to this rule are sex-linked defects that a *male* child will display if the recessive alleles for these traits appear on his X chromosome that he inherited from his mother.

Earlier in the chapter, we discussed two recessive hereditary defects, one that is sex-linked (color-blindness) and one that is not (sickle-cell anemia). Table 3.3 describes a number of additional debilitating or fatal diseases that are attributable to a single pair of recessive alleles.

Genetic abnormalities may also result from **mutations**—that is, changes in the chemical structure of one or more genes that produce a new phenotype. Many mutations occur spontaneously and are harmful or even fatal. Mutations can also be induced by environmental hazards such as toxic industrial waste, radiation, agricultural chemicals that enter the food supply, and possibly even some of the additives and preservatives in processed foods (Burns & Bottino, 1989).

Might mutations ever be beneficial? Evolutionary theorists think so. Presumably, any mutation that is induced by stressors present in the natural environment may provide an "adaptive" advantage to those who inherit the mutant genes, thus enabling these individuals to survive. The sickle-cell gene, for example, is a mutation that originated in Africa, Southeast Asia, and other tropical areas where malaria is widespread. Heterozygous children who inherit a single sickle-cell allele are well adapted to these environments because the mutant gene makes them more resistant to malarial infection and thus more likely to survive. Of course, the mutant sickle-cell gene is not advantageous in environments where malaria is not a problem.

APPLICATIONS: GENETIC COUNSELING, PRENATAL DETECTION, AND TREATMENT OF HEREDITARY DISORDERS

In years gone by, many couples whose relatives were affected by hereditary disorders were reluctant to have children, fearing that they too would bear an abnormal child. Today, services such as genetic counseling, prenatal diagnosis, and even treatments to correct some hereditary defects before a baby is born allow these parents to make reasoned decisions about conceiving a child or carrying a pregnancy to term.

mutation
a change in the chemical structure or arrangement of one or more genes that has the effect of producing a new phenotype.

TABLE 3.3	Brief Descriptions of Major Recessive Hereditary Diseases			
Disease	**Description**	**Incidence**	**Treatment**	**Prenatal detection**
Cystic fibrosis (CF)	Child lacks enzyme that prevents mucus from obstructing the lungs and digestive tract. Many who have CF die in childhood or adolescence, although advances in treatment have enabled some to live well into adulthood.	1 in 2,500 Caucasian births; 1 in 15,000 African-American births	Bronchial drainage; dietary control; gene replacement therapy	Yes
Diabetes	Individual lacks a hormone that would enable him or her to metabolize sugar properly. Produces symptoms such as excessive thirst and urination. Can be fatal if untreated.	1 in 2,500 births	Dietary control; insulin therapy	Yes
Duchenne type muscular dystrophy	Sex-linked disorder that attacks the muscles and eventually produces such symptoms as slurred speech and loss of motor capabilities.	1 in 3,500 male births; rare in females	None. Death from weakening of heart muscle or respiratory infection often occurs between ages 7 and 14	Yes
Hemophilia	A sex-linked condition sometimes called "bleeder's disease." Child lacks a substance that causes the blood to clot. Could bleed to death if scraped or cut.	1 in 3,000 male births; rare in females	Blood transfusions; precautions to prevent cuts and scrapes	Yes
Phenylketonuria (PKU)	Child lacks an enzyme to digest foods (including milk) containing the amino acid phenylalanine. Disease attacks nervous system, producing hyperactivity and severe mental retardation.	1 in 10,000 Caucasian births; rare in children of African or Asian ancestry	Dietary control	Yes
Sickle-cell anemia	Abnormal sickling of red blood cells causes inefficient distribution of oxygen, pain, swelling, organ damage, and susceptibility to respiratory diseases.	1 in 600 African-American births; even higher incidence in Africa and Southeast Asia	Blood transfusions; painkillers; drug to treat respiratory infections; bone marrow transplantation (if suitable donor is found)	Yes
Tay-Sachs disease	Causes degeneration of the central nervous system starting in the first year. Victims usually die by age 4.	1 in 3,600 births to Jews of European descent and French Canadians	None	Yes

SOURCES: Kuller, Cheschier, & Cefalo, 1996; Strachan & Read, 1996.

Genetic Counseling

Genetic counseling is a service that helps prospective parents to assess the likelihood that their children will be free of hereditary defects. Genetic counselors are trained in genetics, the interpretation of family histories, and counseling procedures. They may be geneticists, medical researchers, or practitioners, such as pediatricians. Although any couple who hopes to have children might wish to talk with a genetic counselor about the hereditary risks their children may face, genetic counseling is particularly helpful for couples who either have relatives with hereditary disorders or have already borne an abnormal child.

genetic counseling
a service designed to inform prospective parents about genetic diseases and to help them determine the likelihood that they would transmit such disorders to their children.

Genetic counselors normally begin by obtaining a complete family history, or *pedigree,* from each prospective parent to identify relatives affected by hereditary disorders. These pedigrees are used to estimate the likelihood that the couple would bear a child with a genetic disorder; in fact, pedigrees are the only basis for determining whether children are likely to be affected by certain disorders (one type of diabetes and some forms of muscular dystrophy, for example). Yet, a pedigree analysis *cannot* guarantee that a child will be healthy, even when no genetic disorders are found among blood relatives. Fortunately, blood tests and DNA analyses can now determine whether *parents* carry genes for many serious hereditary disorders, including all those listed in Table 3.3, as well as Huntington's disease and the Fragile-X syndrome (Strachan & Read, 1996).

Once all the information and tests results are in, the genetic counselor helps the couple consider the options available to them. For example, one couple I know went through genetic counseling and learned that they were both carriers for *Tay-Sachs disease,* a condition that normally kills an affected child within the first 3 years of life (see Table 3.3). The genetic counselor explained to this couple that there was one chance in four that *any* child they conceived would inherit a recessive allele from each of them and have Tay-Sachs disease. However, there was also one chance in four that the child would inherit the dominant gene from each parent, and there were two chances in four that the child would be just like its parents—phenotypically normal but a carrier of the recessive Tay-Sachs allele. After receiving this information, the young woman expressed strong reservations about having children, feeling that the odds were just too high to risk having a baby with a fatal disease.

At this point, the counselor informed the couple that before they made a firm decision against having children, they ought to be aware of procedures that can detect many genetic abnormalities, including Tay-Sachs disease, early in a pregnancy. These screening procedures cannot reverse any defects that are found, but they allow expectant parents to decide whether to terminate a pregnancy rather than give birth to an abnormal child.

Prenatal Detection of Hereditary Abnormalities

Since the overall rate of chromosomal abnormalities dramatically increases after age 35, older mothers often undergo a prenatal screening known as **amniocentesis.** A large, hollow needle is inserted into the mother's abdomen to withdraw a sample of the amniotic fluid that surrounds the fetus. Fetal cells in this fluid can then be tested to determine the sex of the fetus and the presence of chromosomal abnormalities such as Down syndrome. In addition, more than 100 genetic disorders—including Tay-Sachs disease, cystic fibrosis, one type of diabetes, Duchenne type muscular dystrophy, sickle-cell anemia, and hemophilia—can now be diagnosed by analyzing fetal cells in amniotic fluid (Whittle & Connor, 1995). Although amniocentesis is considered a very safe procedure, it triggers a miscarriage in a very small percentage of cases. In fact, the risk of miscarriage (currently about 1 chance in 150) is thought to be greater than the risk of a birth defect if the mother is under age 35 (Cabaniss, 1996).

A major disadvantage of amniocentesis is that it is not easily performed before the 11th to 14th week of pregnancy, when amniotic fluid becomes sufficiently plentiful to withdraw for analysis (Kuller, 1996). Since the results of the tests will not come back for another two weeks, parents have little time to consider a second-trimester abortion if the fetus has a serious defect and abortion is their choice. However, an alternative procedure known as **chorionic villus sampling (CVS)** collects tissue for the same tests as amniocentesis does and can be performed during the 8th or 9th week of pregnancy (Kuller, 1996). As shown in Figure 3.9, there are two approaches to CVS. Either a catheter is inserted through the mother's vagina and cervix, or a needle through her abdomen, into a membrane called the *chorion* that surrounds the fetus. Fetal cells are then extracted and tested for hereditary abnormalities, with the results typically available within 24 hours. So CVS often allows parents to know whether their fetus bears a

amniocentesis
a method of extracting amniotic fluid from a pregnant woman so that fetal body cells within the fluid can be tested for chromosomal abnormalities and other genetic defects.

chorionic villus sampling (CVS)
an alternative to amniocentesis in which fetal cells are extracted from the chorion for prenatal tests. CVS can be performed earlier in pregnancy than is possible with amniocentesis.

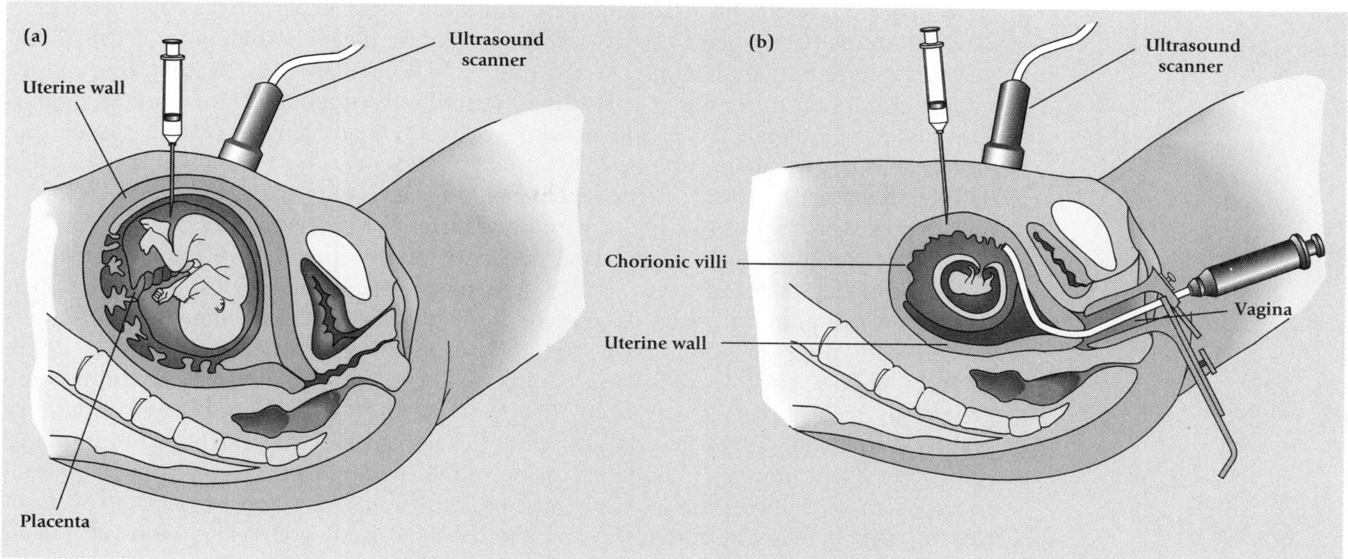

Figure 3.9 *Amniocentesis and chorionic villus sampling. (a) In amniocentesis, a needle is inserted through the abdominal wall into the uterus. Fluid is withdrawn and fetal cells are cultured, a process that takes about three weeks. (b) Chorionic villus sampling can be performed much earlier in pregnancy, and results are available within 24 hours. Two approaches to obtaining a sample of chorionic villi are shown here: inserting a thin tube through the vagina into the uterus or a needle through the abdominal wall. In either of these methods, ultrasound is used for guidance.* ADAPTED FROM MOORE & PERSAUD, 1993.

suspected abnormality very early on, giving them more time to carefully consider the pros and cons of continuing the pregnancy in the event that the fetus is abnormal. But despite its advantages, CVS is currently recommended only to parents at very high risk of conceiving an abnormal child, for it entails a greater chance of miscarriage (about one chance in 50) than does amniocentesis, and its use has, in rare instances, been linked to limb deformities in the fetus (Kuller, 1996).

Another very common and very safe prenatal diagnostic technique is **ultrasound** (sonar), a method of scanning the womb with sound waves that is most useful after the 14th week of pregnancy (Cheschier, 1996). Ultrasound provides the attending physician with an outline of the fetus in much the same way that sonar reveals outlines of fish beneath a fishing boat. It is particularly helpful for detecting multiple pregnancies and gross physical defects as well as the age and sex of the fetus. It is also used to guide practitioners as they perform amniocentesis and CVS (see Figure 3.9). Ultrasound is even a pleasant experience for many parents who seem to enjoy "meeting" their baby.

Treating Hereditary Disorders

Prenatal detection of a hereditary disorder leaves many couples in a quandary, particularly if their religious background or personal beliefs are opposed to abortion. If the disease in question is invariably fatal, like Tay-Sachs, the couple must decide either to violate their moral principles and terminate the pregnancy or to have a baby who will appear normal and healthy but rapidly decline and die young.

Might this quandary someday become a thing of the past? Very possibly. Less than 40 years ago, medical science could do little for children with another degenerative disease of the nervous system—**phenylketonuria (PKU),** Like Tay-Sachs disease, PKU is a metabolic disorder. Affected children lack a critical enzyme that would allow them to metabolize phenylalanine, a component of many foods, including milk. As phenylalanine accumulates in the body, it is converted to a harmful substance, phenylpyruvic acid, that attacks the nervous system. In years gone by, the majority of children who inherited this disorder soon became hyperactive and severely retarded.

The major breakthroughs came in the mid-1950s when scientists developed a diet low in phenylalanine, and in 1961, when they developed a simple blood test that could determine within a few days after birth if a

ultrasound
method of detecting gross physical abnormalities by scanning the womb with sound waves, thereby producing a visual outline of the fetus.

phenylketonuria (PKU)
a genetic disease in which the child is unable to metabolize phenylalanine; if left untreated, it soon causes hyperactivity and mental retardation.

WHAT DO YOU THINK?

Since Huntington's disease is caused by a dominant gene, chances are 1 in 2 (or 50%) that a child of a parent with Huntington's disease will eventually suffer this disorder. A test to detect the gene that causes this disease is now available. Would you take this test to learn your fate if your mother or father had Huntington's disease? Why or why not?

child had PKU. Newborn infants are now routinely screened for PKU, and affected children are immediately placed on a low-phenylalanine diet. The outcome of this therapeutic intervention is a happy one: Children who remain on the diet throughout middle childhood suffer few if any of the harmful consequences of this formerly incurable disease. Outcomes are best when affected individuals remain on the special diet *for life*. This is particularly true of PKU women who hope to have children of their own; if they abandon the diet and their phenylalanine levels are high, they face great risk of either miscarrying or bearing a mentally deficient child (Verp, 1993).

Today, the potentially devastating effects of many other hereditary abnormalities can be minimized or controlled. For example, new medical and surgical techniques, performed on *fetuses in the uterus,* have made it possible to treat some hereditary disorders by delivering drugs or hormones to the unborn organism (Hunter & Yankowitz, 1996), performing bone marrow transplants (Golbus & Fries, 1993), or surgically repairing some genetically transmitted defects of the heart, neural tube, urinary tract, and respiratory system (Yankowitz, 1996). In addition, children born with either Turner's syndrome or Klinefelter's syndrome can be placed on hormone therapy to make them more normal in appearance. Diabetes can be controlled by a low-sugar diet and by periodic doses of insulin, which help the patient to metabolize sugar. And youngsters who have such blood disorders as hemophilia or sickle-cell anemia may now receive periodic transfusions to provide them with the clotting agents or the normal red blood cells they lack.

Advances in the treatment of *cystic fibrosis* (CF) illustrate the remarkable rate at which researchers are gaining the knowledge to combat genetic diseases. Only 10 years ago, about all that could be done for CF patients was to administer antibiotics to lessen the discomfort of their chronic lung obstructions and infections. But in 1989, researchers located the CF gene, and only one year later, two research teams succeeded at neutralizing the damaging effects of this gene in the laboratory (Denning et al., 1991). Soon after came the development and testing of a *gene replacement therapy* that involves inserting normal genes, carried by genetically engineered cold viruses, into the noses and lungs of patients with cystic fibrosis in the hope that these imported genes would override the effects of the CF genes. A similar genetic therapy has been attempted for *adenosine deaminese deficiency,* an inherited disorder of the immune system. Although both approaches have had some limited success, they produce their benefits by lessening the patients' symptoms rather than by curing the disorders (Strachan & Read, 1996).

Finally, advances in *genetic engineering* are raising the specter of **germline gene therapy**—a process by which harmful genes are altered or replaced with healthy ones in the early embryonic stage, thereby permanently correcting a genetic defect. This approach has been used successfully to correct certain genetic disorders in animals (Strachan & Read, 1996), but the kinds of ethical issues raised in Box 3.2 may keep it from being sanctioned for use with humans for some time to come.

germline gene therapy
a procedure, not yet perfected or approved for use with humans, in which harmful genes would be repaired or replaced with healthy ones, thereby permanently correcting a genetic defect.

In sum, many abnormal children can lead near-normal lives if their hereditary disorders are detected and treated before serious harm has been done. And inspired by recent successes in fetal medicine, genetic mapping, and gene replacement therapy, geneticists and medical practitioners are hopeful that many untreatable genetic defects will become treatable, or even curable, in the near future (Khoury and the Genetics Working Group, 1996).

Concept Check 3.2
Understanding Hereditary Abnormalities

Check your understanding of hereditary abnormalities (and their detection and treatment) by matching each statement below with one of the following terms: (a) mutation; (b) supermale syndrome; (c) chorionic villus sampling (CVS); (d) phenylketonuria (PKU); (e) Down syndrome (f) Tay-Sachs disease; (g) ultrasound.

_____ 1. chromosomal abnormality transmitted by either the mother or the father
_____ 2. incurable and fatal genetic disease
_____ 3. generally safe diagnostic technique that often detects gross physical defects
_____ 4. change in the chemical structure of genes that produces a new phenotype
_____ 5. chromosomal abnormality always transmitted by the father
_____ 6. genetic disease treated with a special diet
_____ 7. riskier diagnostic procedure that permits early detection of some hereditary disorders

3.2

CURRENT CONTROVERSIES

Ethical Issues Surrounding Treatments for Hereditary Disorders

Although many children and adolescents with hereditary disorders have clearly benefitted from new treatments only recently introduced, scientists and society at large are now grappling with thorny ethical issues that have arisen from the rapid progress being made. Here is a small sampling of these concerns.

Issues surrounding fetal surgery

Most fetal surgical procedures are still experimental and often induce miscarriages and other harmful consequences. Consider that the risk of fetal death in urinary tract surgery is about 5 to 10 percent from the surgery itself, with another 20 to 30 percent suffering serious complications from the operation; and urinary tract surgery is safer than most other surgical procedures preformed on fetuses (Yankowitz, 1996). Is it really in a fetus's best interests to undergo an operation that may end its life or produce birth defects? Should parents be held legally responsible if they choose to continue a pregnancy while refusing a fetal surgical procedure that might prevent their child from suffering from a serious handicap? Think about these questions, for they are some of the very issues that medical and legal practitioners are now debating.

Issues surrounding gene replacement therapy

All current gene replacement therapies for humans involve insertion of normal genes into patients' somatic (body) tissues to relieve the *symptoms* of genetic disorders. Are there major ethical problems here? Most observers think not (Strachan & Read, 1996). Clearly, investigators and practitioners are ethically bound to ensure the safety of their patients, especially since the techniques of somatic gene therapies are experimental and can have side effects. Yet, by limiting treatment to the patient's body cells, any consequences of the procedure are confined to the patient, who is usually suffering from a debilitating and even life-threatening disease for which no other effective therapy is available (Strachan & Read, 1996). Thus, the benefits of somatic gene therapy are likely to greatly outweigh its costs. Many view this kind of treatment as analogous to (and at least as acceptable as) other medical procedures such as organ transplants. Some would even consider it *unethical* were parents to withhold somatic gene therapy from a seriously ill child who might benefit from the procedure.

Issues surrounding germline gene therapy

The hottest debates about new genetic technologies center around the prospect of *germline gene therapy,* in which attempts would be made to repair or replace abnormal genes at the early embryonic stage and thereby "cure" genetic defects. Once perfected, this technology would bring us to the edge of a slippery slope where human beings will be capable of altering their own genotypes. This prospect seems perfectly acceptable to many observers, provided it is limited to correcting diagnosed genetic defects. However, others point out that permanent modification of a patient's genotype has consequences not only for the patient, but also for all individuals who inherit the modified gene in the future. Germline gene therapy would therefore deny the rights of these descendants to have any choice about whether their genetic makeup should have been modified in the first place, a state of affairs that some view as ethically unacceptable (see Strachan & Read, 1996).

Other critics have argued that approval of germline gene therapy for use with humans will inevitably place us on the path toward *positive eugenics*—that is, toward genetic enhancement programs that could involve artificial selection for genes thought to confer advantageous traits. This possibility is frightening to many. *Who* would decide *which traits* are advantageous and should be selected? And even if these decision makers had motives that were beyond reproach, would they really be any better at engineering a hardy human race than nature already has through the process of natural selection? Of course, the biggest concern that many people have about germline genetic engineering is its potential for political and social abuse. In the words of two molecular geneticists (Strachan & Read, 1996, p. 586):

> The horrifying nature of *negative eugenics* programs (most recently in Nazi Germany and in many states in the USA where compulsory sterilization of [feeble-minded] individuals was practiced well into the present century) serves as a reminder . . . of the potential Pandora's box of ills that could be released if ever human germline gene therapy were to be attempted.

HEREDITARY INFLUENCES ON BEHAVIOR

We have seen that genes play a major role in determining our physical appearance and many of our metabolic characteristics. But to what extent does heredity affect such characteristics as intelligence? Can a strong case be made for genetic contributions to personality or mental health?

In recent years, investigators from the fields of genetics, zoology, population biology, and psychology have asked the question, "Are there certain abilities, traits, and patterns of behavior that depend very heavily on the particular combination of genes that an individual inherits, and if so, are these attributes likely to be modified by one's experiences?" Those who focus on these issues in their research are known as *behavioral geneticists.*

Before we take a closer look at the field of **behavioral genetics,** it is necessary to dispel a common myth. Although behavioral geneticists view development as the process through which one's *genotype* (the set of genes one inherits) is expressed in one's *phenotype* (observable characteristics and behaviors), they are not strict hereditarians. They recognize, for example, that even physical characteristics such as height depend to some extent on environmental variables, such as the adequacy of one's diet (Plomin, 1990). They acknowledge that the long-term effects of inherited metabolic disorders such as PKU and diabetes also depend on one's environment—namely, the availability of medical facilities to detect and to treat these conditions. In other words, the behavioral geneticist is well aware that even attributes that have a strong hereditary component are often modified in important ways by environmental influences.

How, then, do behavioral geneticists differ from ethologists, who are also interested in the biological bases of development? The answer is relatively simple. Ethologists study inherited attributes that characterize *all* members of a species and conspire to make them *alike* (that is, attributes that contribute to *common* developmental outcomes). By contrast, behavioral geneticists focus on the biological bases for *variation* among members of a species. They are concerned with determining how the unique combination of genes that each of us inherit might be implicated in making us *different* from one another. Let's now consider the methods they use to approach this task.

Methods of Studying Hereditary Influences

There are two major strategies that behavioral geneticists use to assess hereditary contributions to behavior: *selective breeding* and *family studies.* Each of these approaches attempts to specify the **heritability** of various attributes—that is, the amount of variation in a trait or a class of behavior that is attributable to hereditary factors.

Selective Breeding

Deliberately manipulating the genetic makeup of animals to study hereditary influences on behavior is much like what Gregor Mendel did to discover the workings of heredity in plants. A classic example of such a **selective breeding experiment** is R. C. Tryon's (1940) attempt to show that maze-learning ability is a heritable attribute in rats. Tryon first tested a large number of rats for the ability to run a complex maze. Rats that made few errors were labeled "maze-bright;" those that made many errors were termed "maze-dull." Then, across several generations, Tryon mated bright rats with other bright rats and dull rats with dull rats. He also controlled the environments to which the rats were exposed to rule out their contribution to differences in maze-learning performance. As we see in Figure 3.10, differences across generations in the maze-learning performances of the maze-bright and maze-dull groups became progressively greater. Clearly, Tryon showed that maze-learning ability in rats is influenced by their genetic makeup. Other investigators have used this same selective breeding technique to show that genes contribute to such attributes as activity level, emotionality, aggressiveness, and sex drive in rats, mice, and chickens (Plomin et al., 1997).

behavioral genetics
the scientific study of how genotype interacts with environment to determine behavioral attributes such as intelligence, personality, and mental health.

heritability
the amount of variability in a trait that is attributable to hereditary factors.

selective breeding experiment
a method of studying genetic influences by determining whether traits can be bred in animals through selective mating.

Family Studies

Because people don't take kindly to the idea of being selectively bred by experimenters, human behavioral genetics relies on an alternative methodology known as the family study. In a typical family study, persons who live together are compared to see how

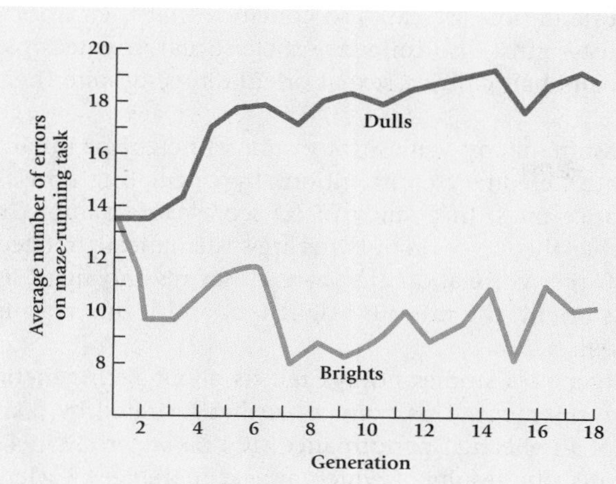

Figure 3.10 *Maze-running performance by inbred maze-bright and maze-dull rats over 18 generations.* FROM PLOMIN, DEFRIES, MCCLEARN, & RUTTER, 1997.

similar they are on one or more attributes. If the attributes in question are heritable, then the similarity between any two pairs of individuals who live in the same environment should increase as a function of their **kinship**—the extent to which they have the same genes.

Two kinds of family (or kinship) studies are common today. The first is the **twin design,** or **twin study,** which asks the question "Are pairs of identical twins reared together more similar to each other on various attributes than pairs of fraternal twins reared together?" If genes affect the attribute(s) in question, then identical twins should be more similar, for they have 100% of their genes in common (kinship = 1.00) while fraternal twins share only 50% (kinship = .50).

The second common family study, or **adoption design,** focuses on adoptees who are genetically unrelated to other members of their adoptive families. A researcher searching for hereditary influences would ask "Are adopted children similar to their biological parents, whose *genes* they share (kinship = .50), or are they similar to their adoptive parents, whose *environment* they share?" If adoptees resemble their biological parents in intelligence or personality, even though these parents did not raise them, then genes must be influential in determining these attributes.

Family studies can also help us to estimate the extent to which various abilities and behaviors are influenced by the environment. To illustrate, consider a case in which two genetically unrelated adopted children are raised in the same home. Their degree of kinship with each other and with their adoptive parents is .00. Consequently, there is no reason to suspect that these children will resemble each other or their adoptive parents unless their common environment plays some part in determining their standing on the attribute in question. Another way the effects of environment can be inferred is to compare identical twins raised in the same environment with identical twins raised in different environments. The kinship of all pairs of identical twins, reared together or apart, is 1.00. So if identical twins reared together are more alike on an attribute than identical twins reared apart, we can infer that the environment plays a role in determining that attribute.

kinship
the extent to which two individuals have genes in common.

twin design
study in which sets of twins that differ in zygosity (kinship) are compared to determine the heritability of an attribute.

adoption design
study in which adoptees are compared with their biological relatives and their adoptive relatives to estimate the heritability of an attribute.

concordance rate
the percentage of cases in which a particular attribute is present for one member of a twin pair if it is present for the other.

Estimating the Contribution of Genes and Environment

Behavioral geneticists rely on mathematical calculations to determine (a) whether or not a trait is genetically influenced and (b) the degree to which heredity *and* environment account for individual differences in that trait. When studying traits that a person either does or does not display (for example, a drug habit or clinical depression), researchers calculate and compare **concordance rates**—the percentages of pairs of people (for example, identical twins, fraternal twins, parents and their adoptive children) in which *both* members of the pair display the trait if one member has it. Suppose that you are interested in determining whether homosexuality in men is genetically influenced. You might locate gay men who have twins, either identical or fraternal, and then track down their twin siblings to determine whether they too are gay. As shown in Figure 3.11, the concordance rate for identical twins in one such study was much higher (29 of the 56 co-twins of gay men were also gay) than the concordance rate for fraternal twins (12 of the 54 co-twins were also gay). This suggests that genotype does contribute to a man's sexual orientation. But because identical twins are

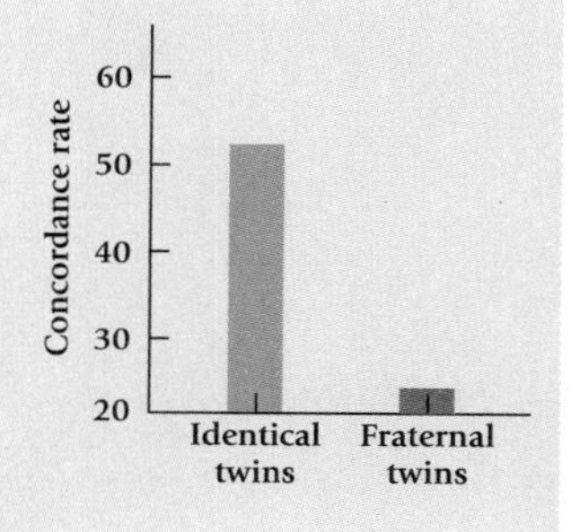

Figure 3.11 *Concordance rates for homosexuality in 110 male twin pairs. From the higher concordance for identical twin pairs, we can infer that genes influence one's sexual orientation.* BASED ON BAILEY & PILLARD, 1991.

not perfectly concordant for sexual orientation, we can also conclude that their *experiences* (that is, environmental influences) must also influence their sexual orientations. After all, 48% of the identical twin pairs had *different* sexual orientations, despite their identical genes.

For continuous traits that can assume many values (for example, height or intelligence), behavioral geneticists estimate hereditary contributions by calculating *correlation coefficients* rather than concordance rates. In a study of IQ scores, for example, a correlation coefficient indicates whether the IQ scores of twins are systematically related to the IQ scores of their co-twins. Larger correlations indicate closer resemblances in IQ, thus implying that if one twin is bright, the other is bright too, and if one twin is dull, the other is probably dull as well.

As we noted earlier, behavioral genetics studies always tell us about *both* genetic and environmental influences on development. This point is easily illustrated by considering a review of family studies of intellectual performance (IQ) based on 113,942 pairs of children, adolescents, or adults, the results of which appear in Table 3.4. Here we will focus on the twin correlations (identical and fraternal) to show how behavioral geneticists can estimate the contributions of three factors to individual differences in intellectual performance (IQ).

Gene Influences

Genetic influences on IQ are clearly evident in Table 3.4. The correlations become higher when pairs of people are more closely related genetically and are highest when the pairs are identical twins. But just how strong is the hereditary influence?

Behavioral geneticists use statistical techniques to estimate the amount of variation in a trait that is attributable to hereditary factors. This index, called a **heritability coefficient,** is calculated as follows from twin data.

$$H = (r \text{ identical twins} - r \text{ fraternal twins}) \times 2$$

In words, the equation reads: Heritability of an attribute equals the correlation between identical twins minus the correlation between fraternal twins, all multiplied by a factor of 2 (Plomin, 1990).

Now we can estimate the contribution that genes make to individual differences in intellectual performance. If we focus on sets of twins raised together from Table 3.4, our estimate becomes:

$$H = (.86 - .60) \times 2 = .52$$

heritability coefficient
a numerical estimate, ranging from .00 to +1.00, of the amount of variation in an attribute that is due to hereditary factors.

TABLE 3.4 Average Correlation Coefficients for Intelligence-Test Scores from Family Studies Involving Persons at Four Levels of Kinship

Genetic relationship (kinship)	Reared together (in same home)	Reared apart (in different homes)
Unrelated siblings (kinship = .00)	+.34	−.01[a]
Adoptive parent/adoptive offspring (kinship = .00)	+.19	—
Half-siblings (kinship = .25)	+.31	—
Biological parent/child (kinship = .50)	+.42	+.22
Siblings (kinship = .50)	+.47	+.24
Twins		
Fraternal (kinship = .50)	+.60	+.52
Identical (kinship = 1.00)	+.86	+.72

[a]This is the correlation obtained from random pairings of unrelated people living apart.
SOURCE: Bouchard & McGue, 1981.

The resulting heritability estimate for IQ is .52, which, on a scale ranging from 0 (not at all heritable) to 1.00 (totally heritable) is moderate at best. We might conclude that, within the populations from which our twins reared together came, IQ is influenced to a moderate extent by hereditary factors. However, it appears that much of the variability among people on this trait is attributable to nonhereditary factors—that is, to environmental influences and to errors we may have made in measuring the trait (no measure is perfect).

Interestingly, the data in Table 3.4 also allows us to estimate the contributions of *two* sources of environmental influence:

Nonshared Environmental Influences

Nonshared environmental influences (NSE) are unique to the individual—experiences that are *not* shared by other members of the family and, thus, make family members *different* from each other (Rowe & Plomin, 1981; Rowe, 1994). Where is evidence of nonshared environmental influence in Table 3.4? Notice that identical twins raised together are not perfectly similar in IQ, even though they share 100% of their genes and the same family environment: A correlation of +.86, though substantial, is less than a perfect correlation of +1.00. Because identical twins share the same genes and family environment, any *differences* between twins raised together must necessarily be due to differences in their *experiences*. Perhaps they were treated differently by friends, or perhaps one twin favors puzzles and other intellectual games more than the other twin does. Since the only factor that can make identical twins raised together any *different* from each other are experiences they do *not* share, we can estimate the influence of nonshared environmental influences by the following formula (Rowe & Plomin, 1981):

$$\text{NSE} = 1 - r \text{ (identical twins reared together)}$$

So, the contribution of nonshared environmental influences to individual differences in IQ performance (that is, 1 − .86 = .14) is small, but detectable nevertheless. As we will see, nonshared environmental influences make a greater contribution to other attributes, most notably personality traits.

Shared Environmental Influences

Shared environmental experiences (SE) are experiences that individuals living in the same home environment share and that conspire to make them *similar* to each other. As you can see in Table 3.4, both identical and fraternal twins (and, indeed, biological siblings and pairs of unrelated individuals) show a greater intellectual resemblance if they live together than if they live apart. One reason that growing up in the same home may increase children's degree of intellectual similarity is that parents model similar interests for *all* their children and tend to rely on similar strategies to foster their intellectual growth (Hoffman, 1991; Lewin et al., 1993).

How do we estimate the contribution of shared environmental influence (SE) to a trait? One rough estimate can be made as follows:

$$\text{SE} = 1 - (H + \text{NSE})$$

Translated to words, the equation reads: Shared environmental influences on a trait equal 1 (the total variation for that trait) minus the variation attributable to genes (H) *and* nonshared environmental influences (NSE). Previously, we found that the heritability of IQ in our twins-reared-together sample was .52, and the contribution of nonshared environment was .14. So, the contribution of shared environmental influences to individual differences in IQ (that is, SE = 1 − [.52 + .14] = .34) is moderate and meaningful.

One final note: While heritability coefficients are useful for estimating whether genes make any meaningful contribution to various human attributes, these statistics are poorly understood and often misinterpreted. In Box 3.3, we will take a closer look at what heritability estimates *can* and *cannot* tell us.

nonshared environmental influence (NSE)
an environmental influence that people living together do not share which should make these individuals different from one another.

shared environmental influence (SE)
an environmental influence that people living together share which should make these individuals similar to one another.

CURRENT CONTROVERSIES

3.3

Some Common Misconceptions about Heritability Estimates

Heritability coefficients are controversial statistics that are poorly understood and frequently misapplied. One of the biggest misconceptions that people hold is the notion that heritability coefficients can tell us whether we have inherited a trait. *This idea is simply incorrect.* When we talk about the heritability of an attribute, we are referring to the extent to which *differences* among individuals on that attribute are related to differences in the genes that they have inherited (Plomin, 1994). To illustrate that *heritable* means something other than *inherited,* consider that everyone inherits two eyes. Agreed? Yet the heritability of eyes is .00, simply because everyone has two and there are no individual differences in "eyeness" (except for those attributable to environmental events such as accidents).

In interpreting heritability coefficients, it is important to recognize that these estimates apply only to populations and *never to individuals.* So if you studied the heights of many pairs of 5-year-old twins and estimated the heritability of height to be .70, you could infer that a major reason that 5-year-olds *differ* in height is that they have different genes. But since heritability estimates say nothing about individuals, it is clearly inappropriate to conclude from an *H* of .70 that 70% of Freddie Jones's height is inherited, while the remaining 30% reflects the contribution of environment.

Let's also note that heritability estimates refer only to the particular trait in question as displayed by members of a *particular population* under *particular environmental circumstances.* Indeed, heritability coefficients may differ substantially for different research populations raised in different environments. Suppose, for example, that we located a large number of identical and fraternal twin infants, each of whom was raised in an impoverished orphanage in which his or her crib was lined with sheets that prevented much visual or social contact with other infants or with adult caregivers. Previous research (which we will examine in Chapter 11) suggests that, if we measured how sociable these infants are, we would find that they vary somewhat in sociability, but that virtually all of them are much less sociable than babies raised at home—a finding that we could reasonably attribute to their socially depriving early environment. But because all these twins experienced *the same depriving environment,* the only reason that they might show any *differences* in sociability is due to differences in their genetic predispositions. The heritability coefficient for sociability would actually approach 1.0 in this population—a far cry from the *H*s of .25 to .40 found in studies of other infants raised at home with parents (Plomin, 1994).

Finally, people have assumed that clearly heritable traits cannot be modified by environmental influences. *This, too, is a false assumption!* In Chapter 11, we will see that the depressed sociability of institutionalized infants can be improved substantially by placing them in socially responsive adoptive homes. Similarly, in Chapter 9, we will see that children who score low on the heritable attribute of IQ can dramatically improve their intellectual and academic performances when exposed to intellectually stimulating home and school environments. To assume that *heritable* means *unchangeable* (as some critics of compensatory education have done) is to commit a potentially grievous error based on a common misconception about the meaning of heritability coefficients.

In sum, the term *heritable* is not a synonym for *inherited,* and heritability estimates, which may vary widely across populations and environments, can tell us nothing about the development of individuals. And though heritability estimates are useful for helping us to determine whether there is any hereditary basis for the *differences* people display on any attribute we might care to study, they say nothing about children's capacity for change and should not be used to make public policy decisions that could constrain children's development or adversely affect their welfare.

Hereditary Influences on Intellectual Performance

As we have just seen from data presented in Table 3.4, IQ is a moderately heritable attribute; genes account for about half the total variation in people's IQ scores. But because the correlations presented in Table 3.4 are based on studies of children *and* adults, they do not tell us whether the contributions of genes and environment to individual differences in intellectual performance might change over time. Might genes be more important early in life, whereas differences in our home and school experiences increasingly account for the variations we show in intellectual performance as we get older? Sensible as this idea may sound, it seems to be wrong. As children mature, genes actually seem to contribute *more* (rather than less) to individual differences in their IQs (Plomin et al., 1997).

Consider a longitudinal study of the intellectual development of twins reported by Ronald Wilson (1978; 1983). Wilson found that identical twins were no more similar than fraternal twins on tests of infant mental development during the first year of life. By age 18 months, however, genetic influences were already detectable. Not only did identical twins show a greater resemblance in test performance than fraternal twins did, but *changes* in test scores from one testing to the next also became more similar for identical twins than for fraternal twins. If one identical twin had a big spurt in mental development between 18 and 24 months of age, the other twin was likely to show a similar spurt at the same time. So it seemed as if genes were now influencing both the *course* and the *extent* of infants' mental development.

Figure 3.12 shows what happened as these twins continued to develop. Identical twins remained highly similar in their intellectual performance (average $r = +.85$) from age 3 through age 15. By contrast, fraternal twins were most similar intellectually at age 3 ($r = +.79$) and gradually became less similar over time. By age 15, they showed no greater intellectual resemblance ($r = +.54$) than pairs of nontwin siblings. Notice, then, that if we calculated heritability coefficients at each age shown in the figure, the heritability of IQ for these twin samples would actually increase from infancy to adolescence.

Adoption studies paint a similar picture. The IQS of adopted *children* are correlated with the intellectual performances of both their biological parents (suggesting a genetic influence) and their adoptive parents (indicating effects of shared family environment). By adolescence, the resemblance to biological parents is still apparent, but adoptees no longer resemble their adoptive parents intellectually (Scarr & Weinberg, 1978). What seems to be happening, both in the twin and the adoption studies, is that the influence of shared environment on intellectual performance declines with age, whereas the influence of both genes and nonshared environment become increasingly stronger. There is a very influential theory that accounts for these changing patterns of influence on IQ scores and on personality traits as well. But before we examine this theory, let's briefly review the evidence that suggests that our personalities are influenced by the genes we have inherited.

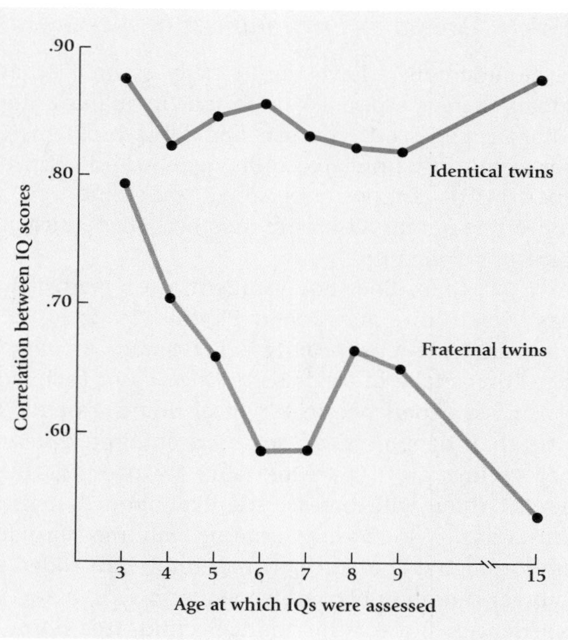

Figure 3.12 *Changes in the correlation between the IQ scores of identical and fraternal twins over childhood.* DATA FROM WILSON, 1983.

Hereditary Contributions to Personality

Although psychologists have typically assumed that the relatively stable habits and traits that make up our personalities are shaped by our environments, family studies and other longitudinal projects reveal that many core dimensions of personality are genetically influenced (Loehlin, 1992; Plomin, 1994). For example, **introversion-extroversion**—the extent to which a person is shy, retiring, and uncomfortable around others versus outgoing and socially oriented—shows about the same moderate level of heritability as IQ does (Martin & Jardine, 1986). Another important attribute that is genetically influenced is **empathic concern.** A person high in empathy recognizes the needs of others and is concerned about their welfare. In Box 2.4, we saw that newborn infants react to the distress of another infant by becoming distressed themselves—a

introversion-extroversion the opposite poles of a personality dimension: Introverts are shy, anxious around others, and tend to withdraw from social situations; extroverts are highly sociable and enjoy being with others.

empathic concern a measure of the extent to which an individual recognizes the needs of others and is concerned about their welfare.

finding that implies to some investigators that the capacity for empathy may be innate. But are there any biological bases for *individual differences* in empathic concern?

Indeed there are. As early as 14 to 20 months of age, identical twin infants are already more similar in their levels of concern for distressed companions than fraternal twin infants are (Zahn-Waxler, Robinson, & Emde, 1992). And by middle age, identical twins who have lived apart for many years since leaving home still resemble each other on measures of empathic concern ($r = +.41$), whereas fraternal twins do not ($r = +.05$), thus suggesting that this attribute is a reasonably heritable trait (Matthews et al., 1981). In fact, the authors of this adult twin study noted that "If empathic concern . . . leads to altruistic motivation, [our] study provides evidence for a genetic basis for individual differences in altruism" (p. 246).

How Much Genetic Influence?

To what extent are our personalities influenced by the genes we have inherited? We get some idea by looking at personality resemblances among family members, as shown in Table 3.5. Note that identical twins are more similar to each other on this composite measure of personality than fraternal twins are. Were we to use the twin data to estimate the genetic contribution to personality, we might conclude that many personality traits are moderately heritable (i.e., $H = +.40$). Of course, one implication of a moderate heritability coefficient is that personality is heavily influenced by environmental factors.

Which Aspects of Environment Influence Personality?

Developmentalists have traditionally assumed that the home environment that individuals *share* is especially important in shaping their personalities. Now examine Table 3.5 again and see if you can find some problems with this logic. Notice, for example, that genetically unrelated individuals who live in the same home barely resemble each other on the composite personality measure ($r = .07$). Therefore, aspects of the home environment that all family members *share* must not contribute much to the development of personality.

How, then, does environment affect personality? According to behavioral geneticists David Rowe and Robert Plomin (1981; Rowe, 1994), the aspects of environment that contribute most heavily to personality are *nonshared environmental influences*—influences that make individuals *different* from each other. And there are many sources of nonshared experience in a typical home. Parents, for example, often treat sons differently than daughters, or first-born children differently than later-borns. To the extent that siblings are not treated alike by parents, they will experience different environments, which will increase the likelihood that their personalities will differ in important ways. Interactions among siblings provide another source of nonshared environmental influence. For example, an older sibling who habitually dominates a younger one may become generally assertive and dominant as a result of these home experiences. But for the younger child, this home environment is a dominating envi-

TABLE 3.5 Personality Resemblances among Family Members at Three Levels of Kinship

	Kinship			
	1.00 (identical twins)	**.50 (fraternal twins)**	**.50 (nontwin siblings)**	**.00 (unrelated children raised in the same household)**
Personality attributes (average correlations across several personality traits)	.50	.30	.20	.07

SOURCES: Loehlin, 1985; Loehlin & Nichols, 1976.

ronment that may foster the development of such personality traits as passivity, tolerance, and cooperation.

Measuring the Effects of Nonshared Environments. How could we ever measure the impact of something as broad as nonshared environments? One strategy used by Denise Daniels and her associates (Daniels, 1986; Daniels & Plomin, 1985) is simply to ask pairs of adolescent siblings whether they have been treated differently by parents and teachers or have experienced other important differences in their lives (for example, differences in their popularity with peers). Daniels finds that siblings do report such differences, and, more important, the greater the *differences* in parental treatment and other experiences that siblings report, the more dissimilar siblings are in their personalities. Although correlational studies of this sort do not conclusively establish that differences in experiences *cause* differences in personality, they do suggest that some of the most important environmental influences on development may be nonshared experiences unique to each member of the family (Dunn & Plomin, 1990).

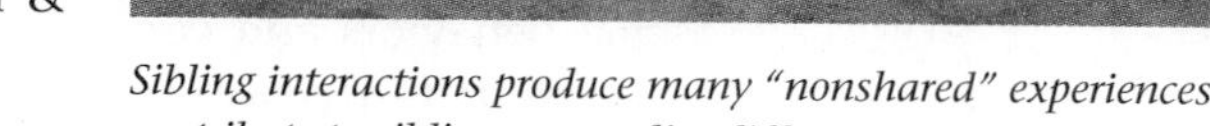

Sibling interactions produce many "nonshared" experiences that contribute to sibling personality differences.

Do Siblings Have Different Experiences Because They Have Different Genes? Stated another way, isn't it possible that a child's genetically influenced attributes might affect how other people respond to her, so that a physically attractive youngster, for example, is apt to be treated very differently by parents and peers than a less attractive sibling would be? Although genes do contribute to some extent to the different experiences that siblings have (Baker & Daniels, 1990; Pike et al., 1996; Plomin et al., 1994), there is ample reason to believe that our highly individualized, unique environments are not entirely due to our having inherited different genes. How do we know this?

WHAT DO YOU THINK? **?**

If a new and valuable mental ability was discovered and found to be totally heritable (that is, all variation among individuals was due to genetic influences), would it be folly to try to boost the performance of people who score low in that ability? Why or why not?

The most important clue comes from studies of identical twins. Since identical twins are perfectly matched from a genetic standpoint, any *differences* between them must necessarily reflect the contribution of environmental influences that they do *not* share. Clearly, these nonshared environmental influences cannot be attributed to the twins' different genes, because identical twins have identical genotypes! This is why the formula for estimating the contribution of nonshared environmental influences (that is $1 - r$ [identical twins raised together]) makes sense, because the estimate it provides is based on environmental influences that are *not* in any way influenced by genes.

With these facts in mind, let's return to Table 3.5. Here we see that the average correlation for identical twins across many personality traits is only +.50, which implies that identical twins are alike in some respects and different in others. Applying the formula for estimating NSE ($1 - .50 = .50$) tells us that nonshared environmental influences are very important contributors to personality—at least as important as genes are.

In sum, the family environment does contribute importantly to personality, but not simply because it has a standard effect on all family members that makes them alike. True, there are some important areas of socialization for which parents do treat all their children alike and foster similarities among them (Hoffman, 1991). For example, parents often model and encourage the same moral, religious, and political interests and values in all their children. For these and many other psychological characteristics, *shared environmental influences* are often as important or even more important than genes are in creating likenesses between brothers and sisters (Hoffman, 1991, 1994; Plomin, 1990). But when it comes to the shaping of many other basic personality traits, it is the *nonshared* experiences people have—in concert with genetic influences—that contribute most to their phenotypes (Plomin et al., 1997; McGue, Sharma, & Benson, 1996; Pike et al., 1996).

Hereditary Contributions to Behavior Disorders and Mental Illness

Is there a hereditary basis for mental illness? Might some people be genetically predisposed to commit deviant or antisocial acts? Although these ideas seemed absurd 30 years ago, it now appears that the answer to both questions is a qualified yes.

Consider the evidence for **schizophrenia**—a serious mental illness characterized by severe disturbances in logical thinking, emotional expression, and social behavior, which typically emerges in late adolescence or early adulthood. A survey of several twin studies of schizophrenia suggests an average concordance rate of .46 for identical twins but only .14 for fraternal twins (Gottesman & Shields, 1982). In addition, children who have a biological parent who is schizophrenic are at increased risk of becoming schizophrenic themselves, even if they are adopted by another family early in life (Loehlin, 1992). These are strong indications that schizophrenia is genetically influenced. In fact, investigators have recently found *genetic markers* for schizophrenia (that is, parts of genes that are suspected of being linked to the illness) on 2 of the 23 pairs of human chromosomes (DeAngelis, 1997).

In recent years, it has also become quite clear that heredity contributes to abnormal behaviors and conditions such as alcoholism, criminality, depression, hyperactivity, **manic-depressive** psychosis and a number of **neurotic disorders** (Baker et al., 1989; Plomin et al., 1997; Rowe, 1994). Now, you may have close relatives who were diagnosed as alcoholic, neurotic, manic depressive, or schizophrenic. Rest assured that this does *not* mean that you or your children will develop these problems. Only 5 to 10% of children who have one schizophrenic parent ever develop any symptoms that might be labeled "schizophrenic" (DeAngelis, 1997). Even if you are an identical twin whose co-twin has a serious psychiatric disorder, the odds are only between 1 in 2 (for schizophrenia) and 1 in 20 (for most other disorders) that you would ever experience anything that even approaches the problem that affects your twin.

Since identical twins are usually *discordant* (that is, not alike) with respect to mental illnesses and behavior disorders, environment must be a very important contributor to these conditions. In other words, people do not inherit behavioral disorders; instead they inherit *predispositions* to develop certain illnesses or deviant patterns of behavior. And even when a child's family history suggests that such a genetic predisposition may exist, it usually takes a number of very stressful experiences (for example, rejecting parents, a failure or series of failures at school, or a family break-up due to divorce) to trigger a mental illness (Plomin & Rende, 1991; Rutter, 1979). Clearly, these findings provide some basis for optimism, for it may be possible someday to prevent the onset of most genetically influenced disorders should we (1) learn more about the environmental triggers that precipitate these disturbances while (2) striving to develop interventions or therapeutic techniques that will help high-risk individuals to maintain their emotional stability in the face of environmental stress.

schizophrenia
a serious form of mental illness characterized by disturbances in logical thinking, emotional expression, and interpersonal behavior.

manic depression
a psychotic disorder characterized by extreme fluctuations in mood.

neurotic disorder
an irrational pattern of thinking or behavior that a person may use to contend with stress or to avoid anxiety.

Concept Check 3.3
Estimating Hereditary and Environmental Influences

A behavioral geneticist conducts a twin study to try to determine whether heredity contributes in any meaningful way to the personality trait of creativity. She finds that the correlation between identical twins on this attribute is +.61, whereas the correlation between fraternal twins is +.50 (data from Plomin, 1990). Check your answers in the Appendix.

_____ 1. The hereditary contribution to creativity is best described as:
(a) substantial (b) moderate (c) low

_____ 2. Do either shared environmental influences (SE) or nonshared environmental influences (NSE) contribute more than heredity does to individual differences in creativity?
(a) Both SE and NSE contribute more than heredity does.
(b) Only NSE contributes more than heredity does.
(c) Only SE contributes more than heredity does.
(d) Neither SE nor NSE contributes more than heredity does.

HEREDITY AND ENVIRONMENT AS DEVELOPMENTAL CO-CONSPIRATORS

Only 30 years ago, developmentalists were embroiled in the nature/nurture controversy: Was heredity or environment the primary determinant of human potential? Although this chapter has focused on biological influences, it should now be clear that *both* heredity and environment contribute importantly to development and that the often extreme positions taken by the hereditarians and environmentalists in the past are grossly oversimplified. Today, behavioral geneticists no longer think in terms of nature *versus* nurture; instead, they try to determine how these two important influences might combine or interact to promote developmental change.

The Canalization Principle

Although both heredity and environment contribute to most human traits, our genes influence some attributes more than others. Many years ago, Conrad Waddington (1966) used the term **canalization** to refer to cases where genes limit or restrict development to a small number of outcomes. One example of a highly canalized human attribute is babbling in infancy. All infants, even deaf ones, babble in pretty much the same way over the first 8 to 10 months of life. The environment has little if any effect on this highly canalized attribute, which simply unfolds according to the maturational program in our genes. By contrast, less canalized attributes such as intelligence, temperament, and personality can be deflected away from their genetic pathways in any of several directions by a variety of life experiences.

Interestingly, we now know that potent *environmental* influences can also limit, or canalize, development. In Chapter 2, for example, we discussed Gilbert Gottlieb's (1991a) intriguing finding that duckling embryos exposed to chicken calls before hatching come to prefer the calls of chickens to those of their own mothers. In this case, the ducklings' prenatal *experiences* (environment) overrode the presumably canalized genetic predisposition to favor the vocalization of their own species. Environments may also canalize human development. For example, we will see in Chapters 5 and 9 that early environments in which nutrition and social stimulation are inadequate can permanently stunt children's growth and impair their intellectual development.

In sum, the canalization principle is a simple idea, and yet, a very useful one that illustrates that (1) there are multiple pathways along which an individual might develop, (2) nature and nurture combine to determine these pathways, and (3) either genes or environment may limit the extent to which the other factor can influence development. Irving Gottesman makes the same points about gene influences in a slightly different way in his own theory of genotype/environment interactions.

canalization
genetic restriction of phenotype to a small number of developmental outcomes; a highly canalized attribute is one for which genes channel development along predetermined pathways, so that the environment has little effect on the phenotype that emerges.

The Range-of-Reaction Principle

According to Gottesman (1963), genes typically do not rigidly canalize behavior. Instead, an individual genotype establishes a range of possible responses to different kinds of life experiences: the so-called **range of reaction.** In other words, Gottesman claims that genotype sets boundaries on the range of possible phenotypes that one might display to different environments. An important corollary, is that because people differ genetically, no two individuals respond in precisely the same way to any particular environment.

range-of-reaction principle
the idea that genotype sets limits on the range of possible phenotypes that a person might display in response to different environments.

The concept of reaction range, as applied to intellectual performance, is illustrated in Figure 3.13. Here we see the effects of varying degrees of environmental enrichment on the IQs of three children: Juan, who has high genetic potential for intellectual development, Tony, whose genetic endowment for intelligence is average, and Freddie, whose potential for intellectual growth is far below average. Notice that, under similar environmental conditions, Juan always outperforms the other two children. Juan also has the widest reaction range, in that his IQ might vary from well below average in a restricted environment to far above average in an enriched environment. By contrast, Freddie has a very limited reaction range; his potential for intellectual development is low and, as a result, he shows smaller variation in IQ across environments than do the other two children.

In sum, the range-of-reaction principle is a clear statement about the interplay between heredity and environment. Presumably, a person's genotype sets a range of possible outcomes for any particular attribute, and the environment largely influences where, within that range, he or she will fall.

Genotype/Environment Correlations

Up until now, we have talked as if heredity and environment were *independent* sources of influence that somehow combine to determine our observable characteristics, or phenotypes. This view is probably much too simple. Many behavioral geneticists now believe that our genes may actually influence the kinds of environments that we are likely to experience (Plomin, DeFries, & Loehlin, 1977; Scarr & McCartney, 1983). How? In at least three ways.

Passive Genotype/Environment Correlations

According to Scarr and McCartney (1983), the kind of home environment that parents provide for their children is influenced, in part, by the parents' own genotypes. And since parents also provide their children with genes, it so happens that the rearing environments to which children are exposed are correlated with (and are likely to suit) their own genotypes.

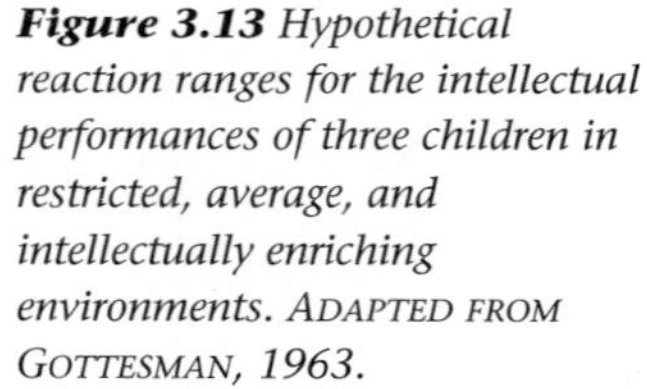

Figure 3.13 *Hypothetical reaction ranges for the intellectual performances of three children in restricted, average, and intellectually enriching environments.* ADAPTED FROM GOTTESMAN, 1963.

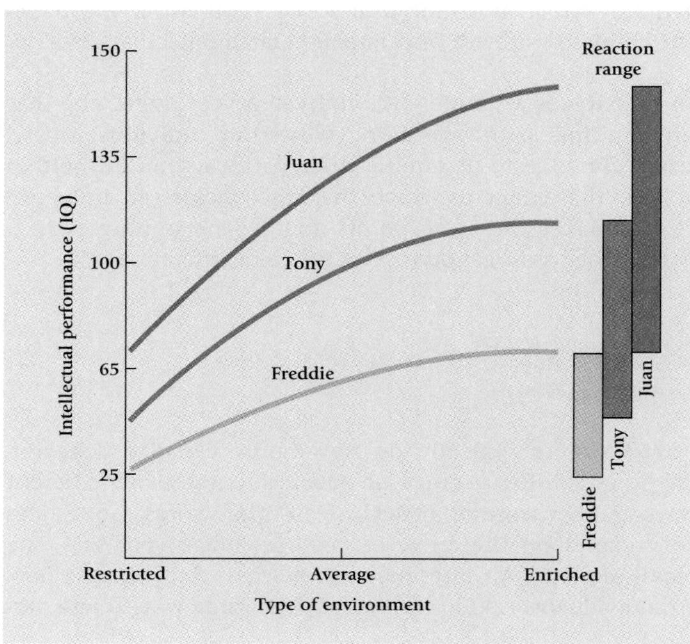

The following example illustrates a developmental implication of these **passive genotype/environment correlations.** Parents who are genetically predisposed to be athletic may create a very athletic home environment by encouraging their children to play vigorously and to take an interest in sports. Besides being exposed to an athletic environment, the children may have inherited their parents' athletic genes, which might make them particularly responsive to that environment. So children of athletic parents may come to enjoy athletic pursuits for *both* hereditary and environmental reasons, and the influences of heredity and environment are tightly intertwined.

Evocative Genotype/Environment Correlations

Earlier, we noted that the environmental influences that contribute most heavily to many aspects of personality are nonshared experiences that make individuals *different* from one another. Might the differences in environments that children experience be partly due to the fact that they have inherited different genes and may elicit different reactions from their companions?

Scarr and McCartney (1983) think so. Their notion of **evocative genotype/environment correlations** assumes that a child's genetically influenced attributes affect the behavior of others toward him or her. For example, smiley, active babies may receive more attention and social stimulation than moody and passive ones. Teachers may respond more favorably to physically attractive students than to their less attractive classmates. Clearly, these *reactions* of other people to the child (and the child's genetically influenced attributes) are environmental influences that play an important role in shaping that child's personality. So once again, we see an intermingling of hereditary and environmental influences: Heredity affects the character of the social environment in which the personality develops.

Active Genotype/Environment Correlations

Finally, Scarr and McCartney (1983) propose that the environments that children prefer and seek out will be those that are most compatible with their genetic predispositions. For example, a child genetically predisposed to be extroverted is likely to invite friends to the house, to be an avid party-goer, and to generally prefer activities that are socially stimulating. By contrast, a child who is genetically predisposed to be shy and introverted may actively avoid large social gatherings and choose instead to pursue activities such as coin collecting that can be done alone. So one implication of these **active genotype/environment correlations** is that people with different genotypes *select* different environmental niches for themselves—niches that may then have a powerful effect on their future social, emotional, and intellectual development.

How Do Genotype/Environment Correlations Influence Development?

According to Scarr and McCartney (1983), the relative importance of active, passive, and evocative gene influences changes over the course of childhood. During the first few years, infants and toddlers are not free to roam the neighborhood, choosing friends and building environmental niches. Most of their time is spent at home in an environment that parents structure for them, so that passive genotype/environment correlations are particularly important early in life. But once children reach school age and venture away from home on a daily basis, they suddenly become much freer to select their own interests, activities, friends, and hangouts. So active, niche-building correlations should exert greater influence on development as the child matures (see Figure 3.14). Finally, evocative genotype/environment correlations are always important; that is, a person's genetically influenced attributes and patterns of behavior may influence the ways other people react to him or her throughout life.

passive genotype/environment correlations
the notion that the rearing environments that biological parents provide are influenced by the parents' own genes, and hence are correlated with the child's own genotype.

evocative genotype/environment correlations
the notion that our heritable attributes affect others' behavior toward us and thus influence the social environment in which development takes place.

active genotype/environment correlations
the notion that our genotypes affect the types of environments that we prefer and seek out.

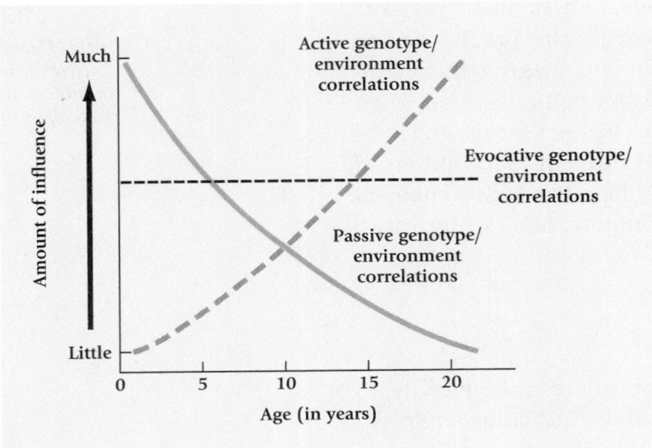

Figure 3.14 *Relative influence of passive, evocative, and active (niche-picking) genotype/ environment correlations as a function of age.*

If Scarr and McCartney's theory has any merit, then virtually all siblings other than identical twins should become less similar over time as they emerge from the relatively similar rearing environments that parents impose during the early years and begin to actively select different environmental niches for themselves. Indeed, there is ample support for this idea. Pairs of genetically unrelated adoptees who live in the same home do show some definite similarities in conduct and in intellectual performance during early and middle childhood (Scarr & Weinberg, 1978). Since these adoptees share no genes with each other or with their adoptive parents, their resemblances must be due to their common rearing environments. Yet, by late adolescence, genetically unrelated siblings barely resemble each other in intelligence, personality, or any other aspect of behavior, presumably because they have selected very different environmental niches which, in turn, have steered them along different developmental paths (Scarr, 1992; Scarr & McCartney, 1983). Even fraternal twins, who have 50% of their genes in common, are much less alike as adolescents or adults than they were as children (McCartney, Harris, & Bernieri, 1990; and recall the declining resemblance in fraternal twins' IQs over time as shown in Figure 3.12). Apparently, the genes that fraternal twins do *not* share cause these individuals to select different environmental niches, which, in turn, contribute to their declining resemblance over time.

By contrast, pairs of identical twins bear a close behavioral resemblance throughout childhood and adolescence. Not only do identical twins evoke similar reactions from other people, but their identical genotypes predispose them to prefer and select very *similar* environments (that is, friends, interests, and activities) which exert comparable influences on these twin pairs and virtually guarantee that they will continue to resemble one another. Even identical twins raised apart should be similar in some respects since their identical genes cause them to seek out and to prefer similar activities and experiences. Let's take a closer look.

Separated Identical Twins. Thomas Bouchard and his associates (Bouchard et al., 1990; Farber, 1981) have studied more than 30 pairs of *separated identical twins* who were raised in different home environments. One such pair was Oscar Stohr and Jack Yufe. Oscar was raised as a Catholic by his mother in Nazi-dominated Europe. He became involved in the Hitler Youth Movement during World War II and is now employed as a factory supervisor in Germany. Jack, a store owner, was raised as a Jew and came to loathe Nazis while growing up in a Caribbean country halfway around the world. Today, Jack is a political liberal, whereas Oscar is very conservative.

Like every pair of separated identical twins that Bouchard has studied, Oscar and Jack are different in some very noteworthy respects. One twin is usually more self-assured, outgoing, or aggressive than the other, or perhaps has a different religious or political philosophy (as Jack and Oscar do). Yet, perhaps the more remarkable finding is that all these twin pairs also show a number of striking similarities as well. As young men, for example, Oscar and Jack both excelled at sports and had difficulty with math. They have similar mannerisms, and both tend to be absent-minded. And then there are the little things, such as their common tastes for spicy foods and sweet liqueurs, their habit of storing rubber bands on their wrists, and their preference for flushing the toilet *before* and after using it.

Jack Yufe (left) and Oscar Stohr (right).

How can separated identical twins be so different and, at the same time, so similar to each other? The concept of *active gene influences* helps to explain the uncanny resemblances. When we learn that twins grow up in different environments, we tend to think of these settings as more dissimilar than they really are. In fact, identical twins raised apart are members of the same life cohort who are likely to be exposed to many of the same kinds of objects, activities, educational experiences, and historical events as they are growing up. So, if identical twins are genetically predisposed to select comparable aspects of the environment for special attention, and if their "different" environments provide them with reasonably similar sets of experiences from which to build their environmental niches, then these individuals should resemble each other in many of their habits, mannerisms, abilities, and interests.

Why, then, do separated identical twins often differ? According to Scarr and McCartney (1983), twins could be expected to differ on any attribute for which their rearing environments are so dissimilar as to prevent them from ever establishing comparable niches. Oscar Stohr and Jack Yufe are a prime example. They are alike in many ways because their separate rearing environments permitted them access to many of the same kinds of experiences (for example, sports, math classes, spicy foods, rubber bands), thereby enabling those genetically identical individuals to develop several similar habits, mannerisms, and interests. However, it was almost inevitable that they would differ in their political ideologies because their sociopolitical environments (Nazi-dominated Europe vs. the laid-back Caribbean) were so *dissimilar* as to prevent them from ever building the kinds of niches that would make them staunch political allies.

CONTRIBUTIONS AND CRITICISMS OF THE BEHAVIORAL GENETICS APPROACH

Behavioral genetics is a relatively new discipline that is having a strong influence on the way scientists look at human development. We now know, for example, that many attributes previously thought to be shaped by environment are influenced, in part, by genes. As Scarr and McCartney put it, we are products of "cooperative efforts of the nature/nurture team, directed by the genetic quarterback" (1983, p. 433). In effect, genes may exert many of their influences on human development by affecting the experiences we have, which in turn influence our behavior. And one very important implication of their viewpoint is that many of the "environmental" influences on development that have previously been identified may reflect, in part, the workings of heredity (Plomin, 1990; Plomin et al., 1997).

Of course, not all developmentalists would agree that genetic endowment is the "quarterback" of the "nature/nurture team" (Gottlieb, 1996; Wachs, 1992, and see the debate about parenting in Box 3.4). Students often object to Scarr and McCartney's theory because they sometimes read it to mean that genes *determine* environments. But this is not what the theory implies. What Scarr and McCartney are saying is this:

1. People with different genotypes are likely to evoke different responses from others and to select different environmental niches for themselves.
2. Yet, the responses they evoke and the niches they select depend to no small extent on the particular individuals, settings, and circumstances they encounter. Although a child must be genetically predisposed to be outgoing and extroverted, for example, it would be difficult to act on this predisposition if she lived in the wilds of Alaska with a reclusive father. In fact, this youngster could well become rather shy and reserved when raised in such an asocial environment.

WHAT DO YOU THINK? ?

Suppose you hear someone say "People differ in aggression only because of the way they are raised." As a budding behavioral geneticist, how would you react to this statement, and what kind of study might you design to evaluate this person's pronouncement?

CURRENT CONTROVERSIES

3.4

Need Parenting Be "Good" or Simply "Good Enough"?

True or False? Within typical families, parenting practices have a major influence on children's development.

In Chapter 2, we saw that John Watson (1928) advised parents to take their role very seriously, for he believed that parents had the power to shape their children's destiny. Sandra Scarr (1992) disagrees with Watson, arguing that parents do not have the power to mold children in any way they see fit. Yet, in some ways, Scarr's viewpoint is every bit as controversial as Watson's. She believes that human beings have evolved in ways that make them responsive to a wide range of environments and that:

1. Within the broad range of home environments that are typical of the human species, children display normal, adaptive patterns of development.

2. Particular child-rearing practices do not influence developmental outcomes to any great extent.

3. Only those home environments that fall far outside the normal range (for example, those in which parents are violent, abusive, or neglectful) are likely to seriously constrain development and produce maladaptive outcomes.

Of course, Scarr assumes that different children respond in somewhat different ways to the typical (or "average expectable") home environment due, in large part, to the fact that they have different genes. However, Scarr also believes that a child's or an adolescent's development is so influenced by the reactions he or she evokes from people other than parents and by the environmental niches he or she constructs that parental child-rearing practices have little effect on development, provided that these practices are "good enough" (that is, within the range of what might be considered normal for human beings). So, in contrast to Watson, who advocated super parenting, Scarr states that parents need only to provide an "average expectable environment" in order to foster healthy development and fulfill their own role as effective guardians. She states that:

> Children's outcomes do not depend on whether parents take (them) to a ball game or a museum so much as they depend on genetic transmission, on plentiful opportunities, and on having a *good enough* environment that supports children's development to become themselves (Scarr, 1992; p. 15, emphasis added).

What do you think about Scarr's propositions? Many developmentalists were quick to criticize them. Diana Baumrind (1993), for example, points out that different child-rearing practices that fall well within what Scarr considers the range of "good enough" parenting produce *very large differences* in children's and adolescents' developmental outcomes. In her own research, Baumrind consistently finds that "highly demanding–highly responsive" parents have children and adolescents who perform better academically and who show better social adjustment than do parents who are only moderately demanding or responsive but well within the "normal range" on these parenting dimensions. Baumrind also argues that just because children are active agents who, in part, shape their own environments in no way implies that parents are powerless to influence those environments in ways that might promote (or inhibit) adaptive outcomes. Finally, Baumrind worries that telling parents they need only be "good enough" may cause them to become less invested in promoting children's competencies and quicker to absolve themselves of responsibility should their children founder. This would be unfortunate, in her view, because research consistently indicates that parents who feel personally responsible for fostering adaptive development typically have competent, well-adjusted sons and daughters, whereas those who are less personally involved tend to have offspring whose outcomes are less adaptive. For all those reasons, Baumrind concludes that Scarr's "good enough" parenting is simply *not* good enough.

Other critics (for example, Jackson, 1993) are concerned about the possible implications of Scarr's views for public policy were they to be accepted by those in power. Specifically, if we endorse Scarr's ideas that the "average expectable environment" is all children need to approximate their genetically influenced developmental potentials, then there would be little reason to intervene in an attempt to optimize the development of economically disadvantaged children from homes that fall within the normal range of family environments. Yet, Jackson (1993) notes that many such interventions to promote the cognitive and emotional development of African-American (and other) populations have had impressive results (see Chapter 9 for a review of this research). If we assume that these interventions are unnecessary, as Scarr's theory implies to Jackson, then we would hardly be serving the best interests of perhaps 25 to 30% of America's children (not to mention the majority of children in many other countries around the world; see Baumrind, 1993).

Clearly, this debate about the influence of parenting practices illustrates the very different perspectives on development taken by behavioral geneticists (Scarr) and environmentalists (Baumrind, Jackson). At this point, the debate is far from resolved, although we will see throughout the text that parenting does seem to have a meaningful effect on the developmental outcomes of children and adolescents and that many developmentalists would advise parents to strive to be much better than "good enough."

In sum, genotypes and environments *interact* to produce developmental change and variations in developmental outcomes. True, genes exert some influence on those aspects of the environment that we are likely to experience. But the particular environments available to us limit the possible phenotypes that are likely to emerge from a particular genotype (Gottlieb, 1991b; 1996). Perhaps Donald Hebb (1980) was not too far off when he said that behavior is determined 100% by heredity and 100% by the environment, for it seems that these two sets of influences are complexly intertwined.

Interesting as these new ideas may be, critics argue that the behavioral genetics approach is merely a descriptive overview of how development might proceed rather than a well-articulated *explanation* of development. One reason for this sentiment is that we know so little about how genes exert their effects. Genes are coded to manufacture proteins and enzymes, not to produce such attributes as intelligence or sociability. Though we now suspect that genes affect behavior *indirectly* by influencing the experiences we evoke from others or create for ourselves, we are still a long way from understanding how or why genes might impel us to prefer particular kinds of stimulation or to find certain activities especially satisfying. In addition, behavioral geneticists apply the term *environment* in a very global way, making few if any attempts to measure environmental influences directly or to specify *how* environments act on individuals to influence their behavior. Perhaps you can see the problem: The critics contend that one has not *explained* development by merely postulating that *unspecified* environmental forces influenced in *unknown* ways by our genes *somehow* shape our abilities, conduct, and character (Bronfenbrenner & Ceci, 1994; Gottlieb, 1996).

How exactly do environments influence people's abilities, conduct, and character? What environmental influences, at what ages, are particularly important? These are questions that we will be seeking to answer throughout the remainder of this text. We begin in our next chapter by examining how environmental events that occur even before a child is born combine with nature's scheme to influence the course of prenatal development and the characteristics of newborn infants.

SUMMARY

Principles of Hereditary Transmission

♦ Development begins at **conception,** when a sperm cell from the father penetrates an ovum from the mother, forming a **zygote.** A normal human zygote contains 46 **chromosomes,** (23 from each parent), each of which consists of several thousand strands of **deoxyribonucleicacid** (or **DNA**) known as **genes.** Genes are the biological blueprint for the development of the zygote into a recognizable human being.

♦ Development of the zygote occurs through **mitosis,** a process by which new body cells are created as the 23 paired chromosomes in each cell duplicate themselves and separate into identical daughter cells. Specialized germ cells, which also have 23 pairs of chromosomes, divide by a process known as **meiosis** to produce gametes (sperm or ova) that each contain 23 unpaired chromosomes. **Crossing-over** and the **independent assortment** of chromosomes ensure that each gamete receives a unique set of genes from each parent.

♦ **Monozygotic** (or **identical**) **twins** result when a single zygote divides to create two cells that develop independently. **Dizygotic** (or **fraternal**) twins result when two different ova are each fertilized by a different sperm cell.

♦ Human ova normally contain an unpaired **X chromosome.** Fathers determine the sex of their children. If the sperm that fertilizes an ovum bears a **Y chromosome,** the child will be a boy; if the sperm bears an X chromosome, the child will be a girl.

♦ Among the developmental functions served by genes are the production of enzymes and other proteins that are necessary for the creation and functioning of new cells, and the regulation of the timing and pace of development. However, environmental factors influence how messages coded in genes are carried out.

♦ There are many ways in which one's **genotype** may affect **phenotype**—the way one looks, feels, thinks, or behaves. Some characteristics are determined by a single pair of **alleles,** one of which is inherited from each parent. In simple **dominant/recessive** traits, the individual displays the phenotype of the **dominant allele.** If a gene pair is **codominant,** the individual displays a phenotype in between those produced by the dominant and the **recessive alleles** (the **sickle-cell** trait is one example of such a trait). **Sex-linked**

characteristics are those caused by recessive genes on the X chromosome; they are more common in males, who have but one X chromosome and need only inherit one recessive gene to display these traits. Some traits arise because of **genetic imprinting** in which only one parent's allele is activated. Most complex human attributes, such as intelligence and personality traits, are **polygenic,** or influenced by many genes rather than a single pair.

Chromosomal and Genetic Abnormalities

◆ Occasionally, children inherit **congenital defects** (for example, **Huntington's disease**) that are caused by abnormal genes and chromosomes. In most cases of chromosomal abnormalities, the individual inherits too many or too few sex chromosomes. The **Fragile-X syndrome,** a leading cause of mental retardation, is caused by an abnormal gene on the X chromosome that is more likely to be expressed when passed from mother to child.

◆ A major **autosomal** disorder is **Down syndrome,** in which the child inherits an extra 21st chromosome, displays a number of distinctive physical features, and is mentally retarded. Older mothers are at higher risk for bearing children with chromosomal abnormalities, but fathers contribute to many such abnormalities as well.

◆ There are many genetic diseases that may be passed to children by parents who are not affected but are **carriers** of the abnormal gene. Genetic abnormalities may also result from **mutations**—changes in the structure of one or more genes that can occur spontaneously or result from such environmental hazards as radiation or toxic chemicals.

Applications: Genetic Counseling, Prenatal Detection, and Treatment of Hereditary Disorders

◆ **Genetic counseling** is a service that informs prospective parents who are at risk of giving birth to a child with a hereditary defect about the odds of that happening from their family histories and from medical tests to determine if they carry abnormal genes.

◆ A number of prenatal diagnostic methods, including **amniocentesis, chorionic villus sampling,** and **ultrasound,** make possible the early detection of many genetic and chromosomal abnormalities in offspring.

◆ Harmful effects of many heredity disorders (for example, **phenylketonuria,** or **PKU**) can now be minimized by such medical interventions as special diets, fetal surgery, drugs and hormones, and gene replacement therapy. **Germline gene therapy,** in which abnormal genes may be repaired or replaced to "cure" hereditary defects, is on the horizon; however, it raises many ethical issues that will have to be resolved before it is likely to be approved.

Hereditary Influences on Behavior

◆ **Behavioral genetics** is the study of how genes and environment contribute to individual variations in development. Although animals can be studied in **selective breeding** experiments, human behavioral geneticists must conduct family studies (often **twin designs** or **adoption designs**), estimating the **heritability** of various attributes from similarities and differences among family members who differ in **kinship.** Hereditary contributions to various attributes are estimated by evaluating **concordance rates** and **heritability coefficients.** Behavioral geneticists can also determine the amount of variability in a trait that is attributable to **nonshared environmental influences** and **shared environmental influences.**

◆ Family studies reveal that the genes people inherit influence their intellectual performances, such core dimensions of personality as **introversion-extroversion** and **empathic concern,** and even their predispositions to display such abnormalities as **schizophrenia, manic-depressive psychosis, neurotic disorders,** alcoholism, and criminality. However, none of these complex attributes is genetically "determined"; all are heavily influenced by environment.

Heredity and Environment as Developmental Co-Conspirators

◆ Several theories have been proposed to explain how heredity and environment combine to produce developmental change. For example, the **canalization** principle implies that genes channel development along predetermined pathways that are sometimes difficult for the environment to alter. The **range-of-reaction** principle states that, for most human attributes, heredity sets a range of developmental potentials and the environment influences where in that range the individual will fall. A more recent theory proposes three avenues by which genes influence the environments we are likely to experience: through **passive genotype/environment correlations,** through **evocative genotype/environment correlations,** and through **active** (or **niche-building**) **genotype/environment correlations.**

Contributions and Criticisms of the Behavioral Genetics Approach

◆ Behavioral genetics has had a strong influence on our outlook on human development by showing that many attributes previously thought to be environmentally determined are influenced, in part, by genes. It has also helped to defuse the nature versus nurture debate by illustrating that these two sources of influence are complexly intertwined.

◆ Behavioral genetics has been criticized as an incomplete theory of development that describes, but fails to *explain,* how either genes or environment influence our abilities, conduct, and character.

To fully understand patterns of genetic transmission, it is necessary to have a basic understanding of single gene-pair inheritance. You can learn the basics of dominant and recessive patterns of genetic transmission by visiting: **http://www.biology.arizona.edu/mendelian_genetics/problem_sets/monohybrid_cross/monohybrid_cross.html** At this web site, you will find an interactive tutorial that allows you to work through a series of problems that illustrates the basic principles that govern inheritance.

KEY TERMS

genotype, 73
genes, 73
phenotype, 73
conception, 73
zygote, 73
chromosome, 73
deoxyribonucleic acid (DNA), 74
mitosis, 74
meiosis, 75
crossing-over, 75
independent assortment, 75
monozygotic (or identical) twins, 76
dizygotic (or fraternal twins), 76
X chromosome, 76
Y chromosome, 76
alleles, 78
simple dominant-recessive inheritance, 79
dominant allele, 79
recessive allele, 79
homozygous, 79
heterozygous, 79
carrier, 79
codominance, 80
sickle-cell anemia, 81
sex-linked characteristic, 81
genetic imprinting, 82
polygenic trait, 82
congenital defect, 83
Huntington's disease, 83
Fragile-X syndrome, 83
autosomes, 84
Down syndrome, 85
aging-ova hypothesis, 85
mutation, 86
genetic counseling, 87
amniocentesis, 88
chorionic villus sampling (CVS), 88
ultrasound, 89
phenylketonuria (PKU), 89
germline gene therapy, 90
behavioral genetics, 92
heritability, 92
selective breeding experiment, 92
kinship, 93
twin design, 93
adoption design, 93
concordance rate, 93
heritability coefficient, 94
nonshared environmental influence (NSE), 95
shared environmental influence (SE), 95
introversion-extroversion, 97
empathic concern, 97
schizophrenia, 100
manic depression, 100
neurotic disorder, 100
canalization, 101
range-of-reaction principle, 101
passive genotype/environment correlations, 103
evocative genotype/environmental correlations, 103
active genotype/environment correlations, 103

Prenatal Development, Birth, and Newborns' Readiness for Life

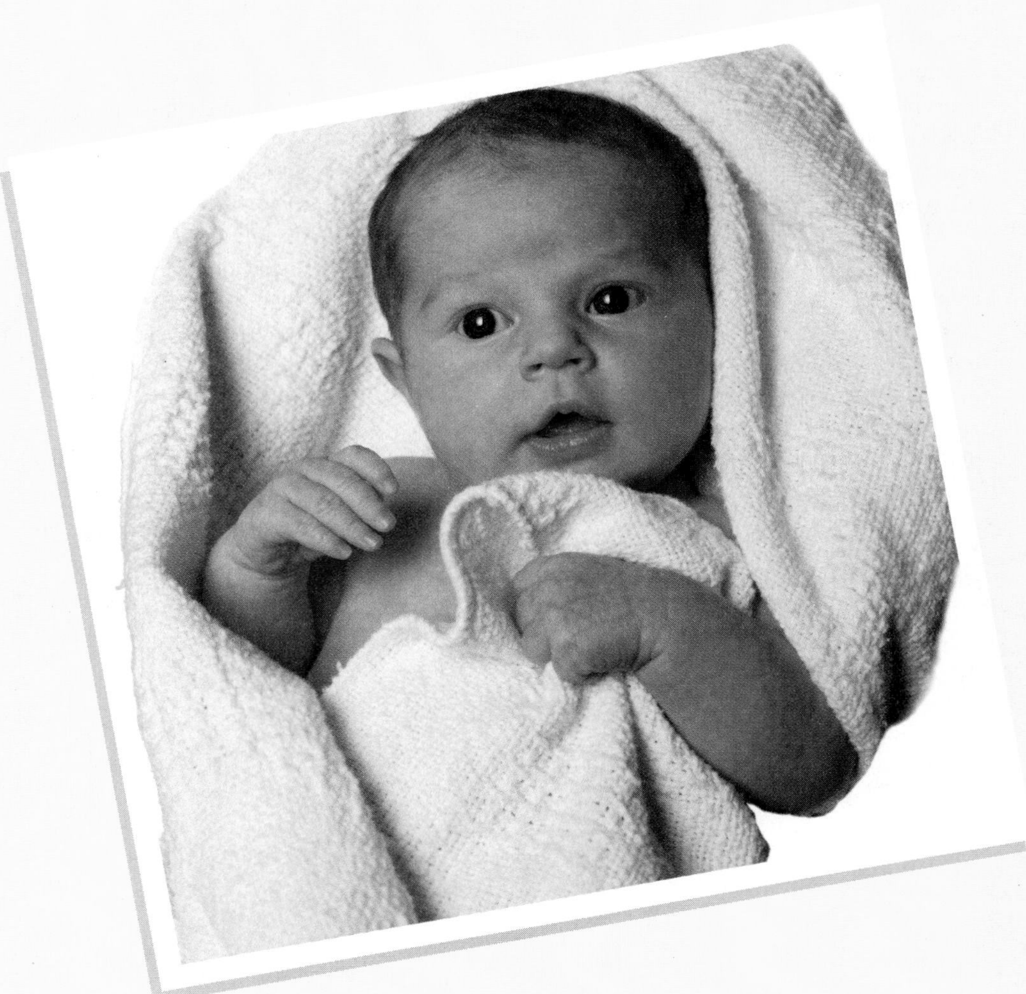

When I was a junior in college, a professor of mine gave the quiz at the right as part of the introduction to a unit entitled "The Beginnings of Life." And I didn't do very well on it, having never thought very much about any of these issues. As our class began to discuss them, a Native-American woman who had given birth to two children at home (on a reservation) claimed that few Hoopa Indian babies are born in hospitals and that birth complications among the women of her tribe were actually lower than those among hospital births in the United States. She also knew that **prenatal development**—the development that occurs between the moment of conception and birth—occurs in an "environment," the mother's uterus, and that the degree of safety or protection it affords depends upon a variety of factors, including the mother's age, health, the food she eats, the drugs she takes, and the chemicals to which she is exposed. Finally, this young woman said that, based on her many experiences with newborn infants (including her own), it seemed to her as if babies are quite sociable and well-adapted for life, as long as they receive love and good care from their companions. As our professor agreed with her on all counts, I suddenly realized that I should have answered "False" to each of the first four quiz items. Actually, many students in that class (including me) missed the fifth question as well, for as our professor began to trace the miraculous evolution of a one-celled zygote into a recognizable human being, it became quite clear to all of us that human growth and development occurs most rapidly during the *prenatal period,* months before a child is born.

True or False?

1. A mother's womb is a protective haven that shields an unborn child from such external hazards as pollution or disease.
2. The environment first affects human development the moment a baby is born.
3. Birth proceeds more smoothly with fewer complications when attended by a physician in a hospital.
4. Newborn human infants are asocial creatures who are poorly adapted for life.
5. Human beings develop most rapidly between birth and 2 years of age.

FROM CONCEPTION TO BIRTH

In Chapter 3, we learned that development begins in the fallopian tube when a sperm penetrates the wall of an ovum, forming a zygote. From the moment of conception, it will take approximately 266 days for this tiny, one-celled zygote to become a fetus of some 200 billion cells that is ready to be born.

Prenatal development is often divided into three major phases. The first phase, called the **germinal period,** (or the *period of the zygote*), lasts from conception through implantation, when the developing zygote becomes firmly attached to the wall of the uterus. The germinal period normally lasts about 14 days. The second phase of prenatal development, the **period of the embryo,** lasts from the beginning of the third week through the end of the eighth. This is the time when virtually all the major organs are formed and the heart begins to beat. The third phase, the **period of the fetus,** lasts from the ninth week of pregnancy until the child is born. During this phase, all the major organ systems begin to function, and the developing organism grows rapidly.

prenatal development
development that occurs between the moment of conception and the beginning of the birth process.

germinal period
first phase of prenatal development, lasting from conception until the developing organism becomes firmly attached to the wall of the uterus (also called period of the zygote).

period of the embryo
second phase of prenatal development, lasting from the third through the eighth prenatal week, during which the major organs and anatomical structures take shape.

period of the fetus
third phase of prenatal development, lasting from the ninth prenatal week until birth; during this period, all major organ systems begin to function and the fetus grows rapidly.

The Germinal Period

As the fertilized ovum, or zygote, moves down the fallopian tube toward the uterus, it divides by mitosis into two cells. These two cells and all their daughter cells continue to divide, forming a ball-shaped structure, or *blastocyst,* that will contain 60 to 80 cells within 4 days of conception (see Figure 4.1). Cell differentiation has already begun. The inner layer of the blastocyst, or *embryonic disk,* becomes the **embryo,** whereas the outer layer of cells develops into tissues that protect and nourish the embryo.

embryo
name given to the prenatal organism from the third through the eighth week after conception.

Implantation

As the blastocyst approaches the uterus 6 to 10 days after conception, small, burrlike tendrils emerge from its outer surface. Upon reaching the uterine wall, these tendrils burrow inward, tapping the mother's blood supply. This is **implantation.** Once the

implantation
the burrowing of the blastocyst into the lining of the uterus.

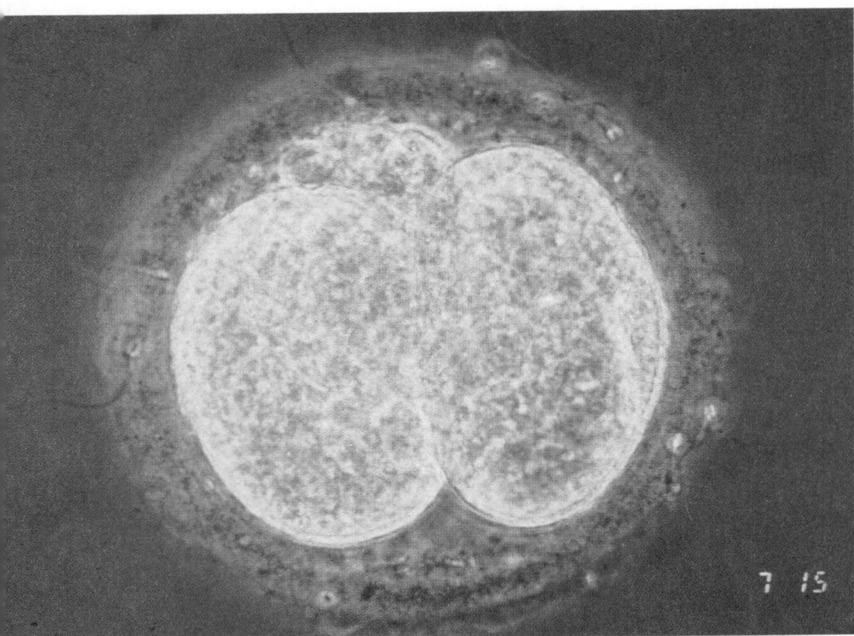

Within hours of conception, the fertilized ovum (zygote) divides, beginning a continuous process of cell differentiation.

blastocyst is implanted at 10 to 14 days after conception, it looks like a small translucent blister on the wall of the uterus (see Figure 4.1).

Implantation is quite a development in itself. Only about half of all fertilized ova are firmly implanted; perhaps as many as half of all such implants are either genetically abnormal and fail to develop, or burrow into a site incapable of sustaining them and are miscarried (Moore & Persaud, 1993; Simpson, 1993). So it appears that nearly three zygotes out of four, including most of the abnormal ones, fail to survive the initial phase of prenatal development.

Development of Support Systems

Once implanted, the blastocyst's outer layer rapidly forms four major support structures that protect and nourish the developing organism (Sadler, 1996). One membrane, the **amnion,** is a watertight sac that fills with fluid from the mother's tissues. The purposes of this sac and its *amniotic fluid* are to cushion the developing organism against blows, regulate its temperature, and provide a weightless environment that will make it easier for the embryo to move. Floating in this watery environment is a balloon-shaped *yolk sac* that produces blood cells until the embryo is capable of producing its own. This yolk sac is attached to a third membrane, the **chorion,** which surrounds the amnion and eventually becomes the lining of the **placenta**—a multipurpose organ that we will discuss in detail. A fourth membrane, the *allantois,* forms the embryo's **umbilical cord.**

Figure 4.1 *The germinal period.*

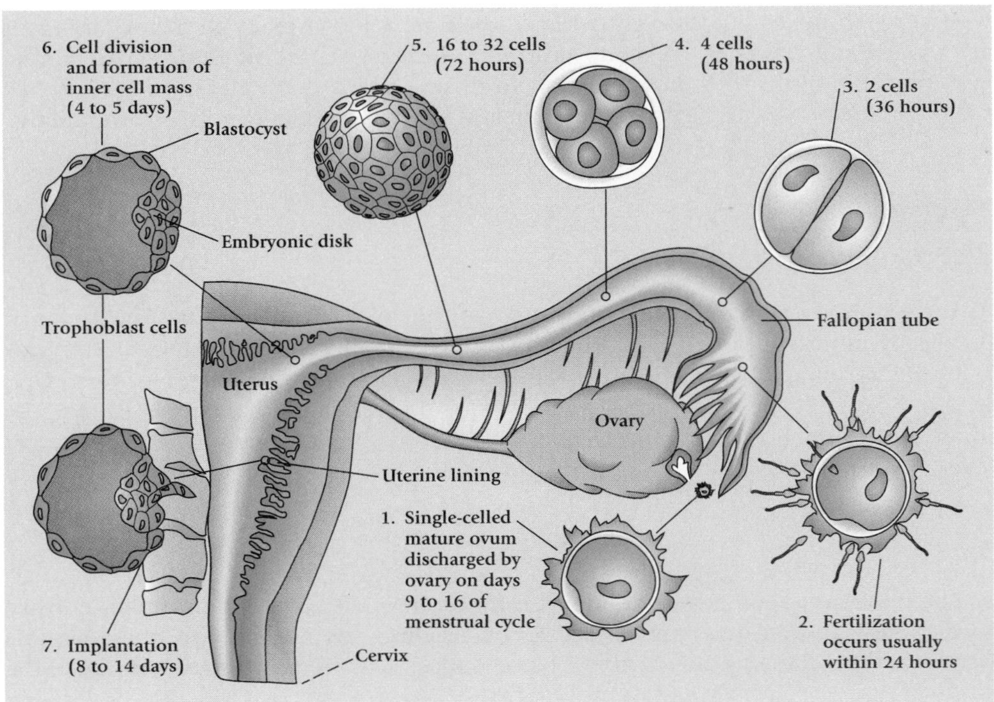

Purpose of the Placenta

Once developed, the placenta is fed by blood vessels from the mother and the embryo, although its hairlike villi act as a barrier that prevents these two bloodstreams from mixing. This placental barrier is semipermeable, meaning that it allows some substances to pass through, but not others. Gases such as oxygen and carbon dioxide, salts, and various nutrients such as sugars, proteins, and fats are small enough to cross the placental barrier. However, blood cells are too large.

Maternal blood flowing into the placenta delivers oxygen and nutrients into the embryo's bloodstream by means of the umbilical cord, which connects the embryo to the placenta. The umbilical cord also transports carbon dioxide and metabolic wastes from the embryo. These waste products then cross the placental barrier, enter the mother's bloodstream, and are eventually expelled from the mother's body along with her own metabolic wastes. Clearly, the placenta plays a crucial role in prenatal development, because this remarkable organ is the site of all metabolic transactions that sustain the embryo.

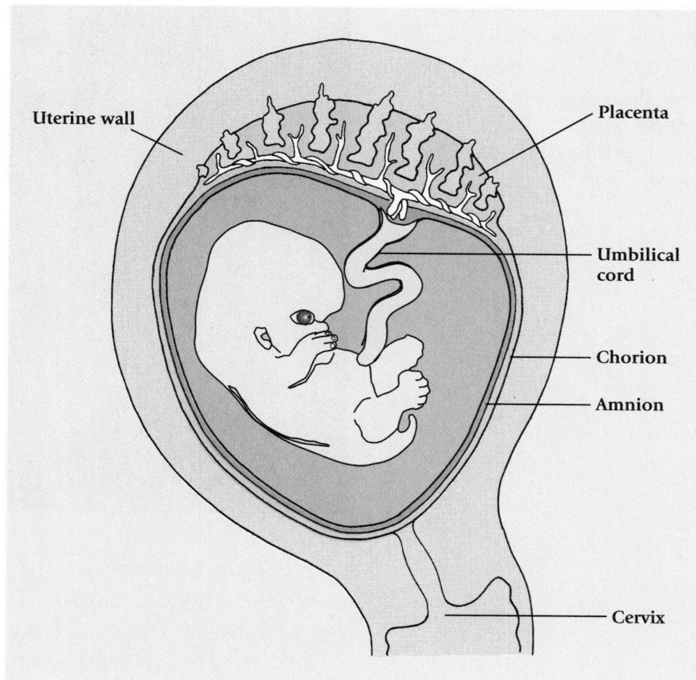

Figure 4.2 *The embryo and its prenatal environment.*

The Period of the Embryo

The period of the embryo lasts from the third through the eighth week of pregnancy. By the third week, the embryonic disk is rapidly differentiating into three cell layers. The outer layer, or *ectoderm,* becomes the nervous system, skin, and hair. The middle layer, or *mesoderm,* becomes the muscles, bones, and circulatory system. From the inner layer, or *endoderm,* come the digestive system, lungs, urinary tract, and other vital organs, such as the pancreas and liver.

Development proceeds at a breathtaking pace during the period of the embryo. In the third week after conception, a portion of the ectoderm folds into a **neural tube** that soon becomes the brain and spinal cord. By the end of the fourth week, the heart has not only formed but has already begun to beat. The eyes, ears, nose, and mouth are also beginning to form, and buds that will become arms and legs suddenly appear. Thirty days after conception, the embryo is only about 1/4 of an inch long, but already 10,000 times the size of the zygote from which it developed. At no time in the future will this organism ever grow as rapidly or change as much as it has during the first prenatal month.

The Second Month

During the second month, the embryo becomes much more human in appearance as it grows about 1/30 of an inch per day. A primitive tail appears (see Figure 4.2), but it is soon enclosed by protective tissue and becomes the tip of the backbone, the coccyx. By the middle of the fifth week, the eyes have corneas and lenses. By the seventh week, the ears are well formed, and the embryo has a rudimentary skeleton. Limbs are now developing from the body outward; that is, the upper arms appear first, followed by the forearms, hands, and then fingers. The legs follow a similar pattern a few days later. The brain develops rapidly during the second month, and it directs the organism's first muscular contractions by the end of the embryonic period.

During the seventh and eighth prenatal weeks, the embryo's sexual development begins with the appearance of a genital ridge called the *indifferent gonad.* If the embryo is a male, a gene on its Y chromosome triggers a biochemical reaction that instructs the indifferent gonad to produce testes. If the embryo is a female, the indifferent gonad

amnion
a watertight membrane that develops from the trophoblast and surrounds the developing embryo, serving to regulate its temperature and to cushion it against injuries.

chorion
a membrane that develops from the trophoblast and becomes attached to the uterine tissues to gather nourishment for the embryo.

placenta
an organ, formed from the lining of the uterus and the chorion, that provides for respiration and nourishment of the unborn child and the elimination of its metabolic wastes.

umbilical cord
a soft tube containing blood vessels that connects the embryo to the placenta.

neural tube
the primitive spinal cord that develops from the ectoderm and becomes the central nervous system.

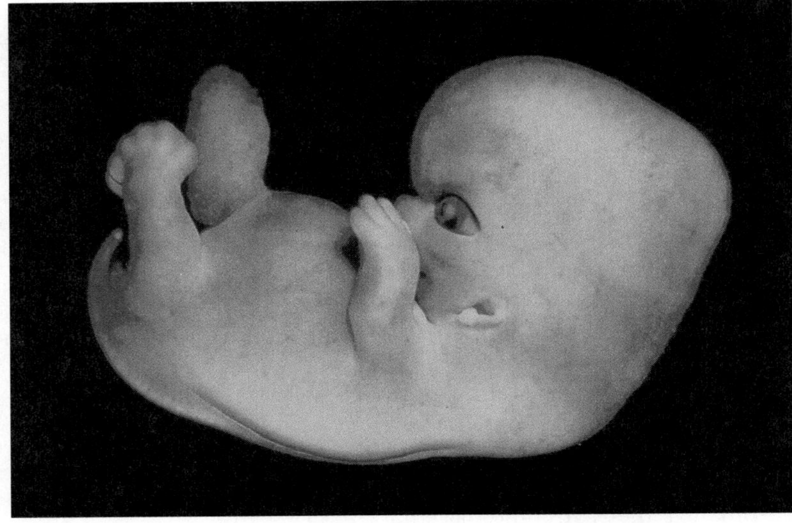

Figure 4.3 A human embryo at 40 days. The heart is now beating and the limbs are rapidly forming. Note the primitive tail (soon to become the tip of the backbone) in the far left-hand portion of the photo.

receives no such instructions and will produce ovaries. The embryo's circulatory system now functions on its own, for the liver and spleen have assumed the task of producing blood cells from the now-defunct yolk sac.

By the end of the second month, the embryo is slightly more than an inch long and weighs less than 1/4 of an ounce. Yet, it is already a marvelously complex being:

> All of the structures which will be present when the baby is born in seven more months have already formed, at least in beginning stages. . . . Medically, the unborn [organism] is no longer an embryo, but a *fetus;* not an it, but a he or she; not an indistinct cluster of cells, but an increasingly recognizable, unique human being in the making (Apgar & Beck, 1974, p. 57).

The Period of the Fetus

The last seven months of pregnancy, or period of the **fetus,** is a period of rapid growth (see Figure 4.4) and refinement of all organ systems.

The Third Month

During the third prenatal month, organ systems that were formed earlier continue their rapid growth and become interconnected. For example, coordination between the nervous and muscular systems allows the fetus to perform many interesting maneuvers in its watery environment—kicking its legs, making fists, twisting its body—although these activities are far too subtle to be felt by the mother. The digestive and excretory systems are also working together, allowing the fetus to swallow, digest nutrients, and urinate. Sexual differentiation is progressing rapidly as the male testes secrete *testosterone*—the male sex hormone responsible for the development of a penis and scrotum; in the absence of testosterone, female genitalia form. By the end of the third month, the sex of a fetus can be detected by ultrasound, and its reproductive system already contains immature ova or sperm cells. All these detailed developments are present after 12 weeks even though the fetus is a mere 3 inches long and still weighs less than an ounce.

The Second Trimester

fetus
name given to the prenatal organism from the ninth week of pregnancy until birth.

Development continues at a rapid pace during the fourth, fifth, and sixth months of pregnancy, a period called the *second trimester.* At age 16 weeks, the fetus is 8 to 10 inches long and weighs about 6 ounces. Its motor activity may include refined actions

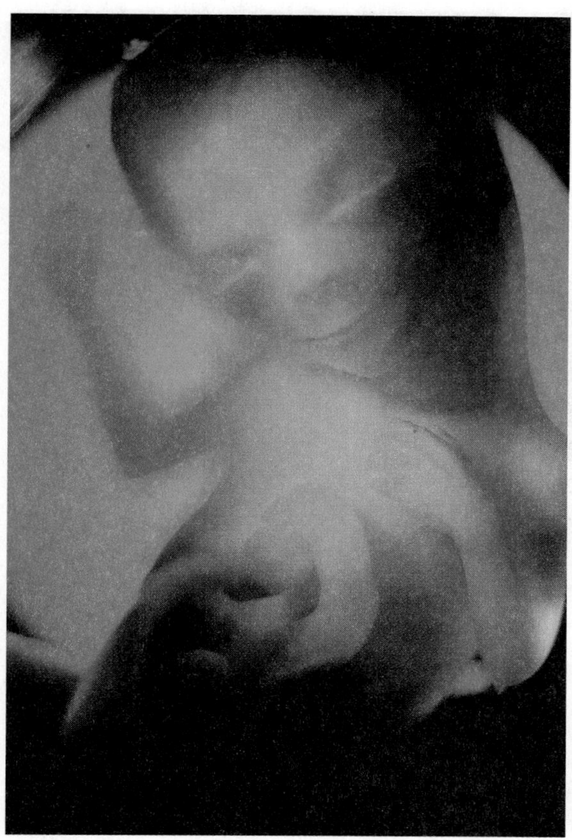

At 12 weeks after conception, the fetus is about three inches long and weighs almost one ounce. All major organ systems have formed and several are already functioning.

such as thumb sucking, as well as kicking that may be strong enough to be felt by the mother. The fetal heartbeat can easily be heard with a stethoscope, and the hardening skeleton can be detected by ultrasound. By the end of the fourth month, the fetus has assumed a distinctly human appearance, even though it stands virtually no chance of surviving outside the womb.

During the fifth and sixth months, the nails harden, the skin thickens, and eyebrows, eyelashes, and scalp hair suddenly appear. At 20 weeks, the sweat glands are functioning, and the fetal heartbeat is often strong enough to be heard by placing an ear on the mother's abdomen. The fetus is now covered by a white cheesy substance called **vernix** and a fine layer of body hair, called **lanugo.** Vernix protects fetal skin against chapping during its long exposure to amniotic fluid, and lanugo helps vernix stick to the skin.

vernix
white cheesy substance that covers the fetus to protect the skin from chapping.

lanugo
fine hair covering the fetus's body which helps vernix stick to the skin.

By the end of the second trimester, the fetus's visual and auditory senses are clearly functional. We know this because preterm infants born only 25 weeks after conception become alert at the sound of a loud bell and blink in response to a bright light (Allen & Capute, 1986). Six months after conception, the fetus is approximately 14 to 15 inches long and weighs about 2 pounds.

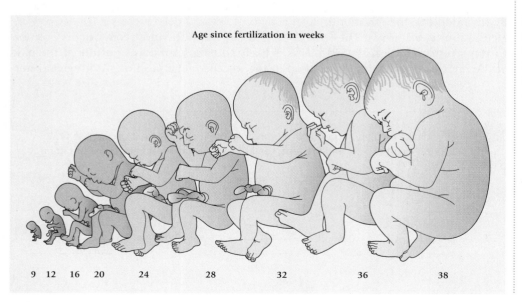

Age since fertilization in weeks

9 12 16 20 24 28 32 36 38

Figure 4.4 *Rate of body growth during the fetal period. Increase in size is especially dramatic from the 9th to the 20th week.*
Adapted from Moore & Persaud, 1993.

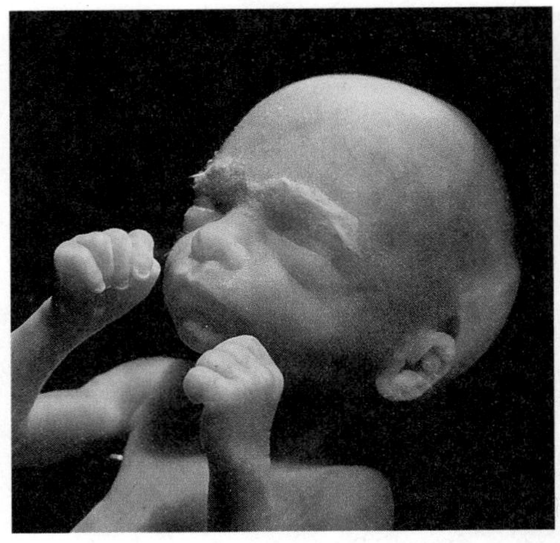

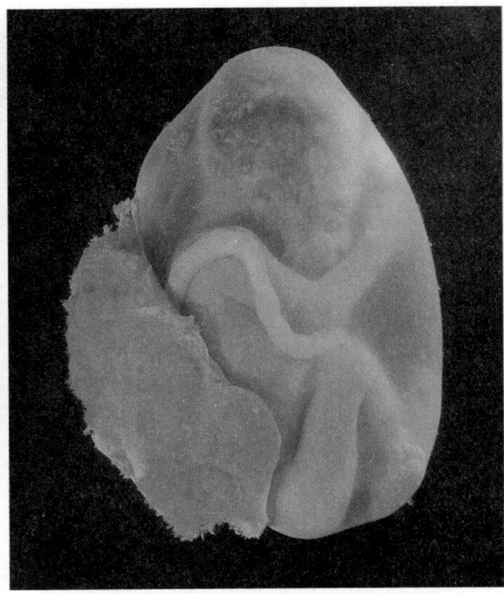

Left: This 24-week-old fetus has reached the age of viability and stands a slim chance of surviving outside the womb. From this point on, odds of survival in the event of a premature birth will increase with each day that passes.

Right: This 36-week-old fetus, covered with the cheese-like vernix that protects the skin against chapping, completely fills the uterus and is ready to be born within the next two weeks.

The Third Trimester

The last 3 months of pregnancy, or *third trimester,* is a "finishing phase" during which all organ systems mature rapidly, preparing the fetus for birth. Indeed, somewhere between 22 and 28 weeks after conception (usually in the 7th month), fetuses reach the **age of viability,** the point at which survival outside the uterus is possible (Moore & Persaud, 1993). Recent research using sophisticated fetal monitoring techniques reveals that the 28- to 32-week-old fetuses suddenly begin to show better organized and more predictable cycles of heart rate activity, gross motor activity, and sleepiness/waking activity, findings that seem to indicate that their developing nervous systems are now sufficiently well organized to allow them to survive should their birth be premature (DiPietro et al., 1996; see also Groome et al., 1997). Nevertheless, many fetuses born this young still require oxygen assistance because the tiny *pulmonary alveoli* (air sacs) in their lungs are too immature to inflate and exchange oxygen for carbon dioxide on their own (Moore & Persaud, 1993).

age of viability
a point between the 22nd and 28th prenatal weeks when survival outside the uterus is possible.

By the end of the 7th month, the fetus weighs nearly 4 pounds and is about 16 to 17 inches long. One month later, it has grown to 18 inches and put on another 1 to 2½ pounds. Much of this weight comes from a padding of fat, deposited just beneath the skin, that later helps to insulate the newborn child from changes in temperature. By the middle of the 9th month, fetal activity slows and sleep increases (DiPietro et al., 1996; Sahni et al., 1995). The fetus is now so large that the most comfortable position within a restricted, pear-shaped uterus is likely to be a head-down posture at the base of the uterus, with the limbs curled up in the so-called fetal position. At irregular inter-

Concept Check 4.1
Understanding the Timing of Prenatal Milestones

For each of the following prenatal milestones, indicate the period (germinal, embryonic, or fetal) in which it occurs, the time span (in days, weeks, or months) during which the event occurs, and the term used to refer to the developing organism during this period. The answers appear in the Appendix.

Event	*Period*	*Time span*	*Term for Organism*
Implantation	_____	_______	____________
Age of viability	_____	_______	____________
First heartbeats	_____	_______	____________
Kicks first felt by mother	_____	_______	____________
Organs form	_____	_______	____________
Sexual differentiation (external genitalia)	_____	_______	____________

vals over the last month of pregnancy, the mother's uterus contracts and then relaxes—a process that tones the uterine muscles, dilates the cervix, and helps to position the head of the fetus into the gap between the pelvic bones through which it will soon be pushed. As the uterine contractions become stronger, more frequent, and regular, the prenatal period draws to a close. The mother is now in the first stage of labor, and within a matter of hours she will give birth.

ENVIRONMENTAL INFLUENCES ON PRENATAL DEVELOPMENT

Although the vast majority of newborn infants have followed the "normal" pattern of prenatal development just described, some encounter environmental obstacles that may channel their development along an abnormal path. In the following sections, we will consider a number of environmental factors that can harm developing embryos and fetuses as well as interventions to prevent abnormal outcomes.

Teratogens

The term **teratogen** refers to any disease, drug, or other environmental agent that can harm a developing embryo or fetus by causing physical deformities, severely retarded growth, blindness, brain damage, and even death. The list of known and suspected teratogens has grown frighteningly long over the years, making many of today's parents quite concerned about the hazards their unborn children could face (Friedman & Polifka, 1996; Verp, 1993). Before considering the effects of some of the major teratogens, let's emphasize that about 95% of newborn babies are perfectly normal and that many of those born with defects have mild, temporary, or reversible problems (Gosden, Nicolaides, & Whitling, 1994; Heinonen, Slone, & Shapiro, 1977). Let's also lay out a few generalizations about the effects of teratogens that will aid us in interpreting the research that follows:

1. The effects of a teratogen on a body part or organ system are worst during the period when that structure is forming and growing most rapidly.
2. Not all embryos or fetuses are equally affected by a teratogen; susceptibility to harm is influenced by the unborn child's and the mother's genetic makeup and the quality of the prenatal environment.
3. The same defect can be caused by different teratogens.
4. A variety of defects can result from a single teratogen.
5. The longer the exposure to or higher the "dose" of a teratogen, the more likely it is that serious harm will be done.
6. Embryos and fetuses can be affected by *fathers'* as well as by mothers' exposure to some teratogens.
7. The long-term effects of a teratogen often depend on the quality of the *postnatal* environment.

Let's look more closely at the first generalization, for it is very important. Each major organ system or body part has a **sensitive period** when it is most susceptible to teratogenic agents, namely, the time when the particular part of the body is evolving and taking shape. Recall that most organs and body parts are rapidly forming during the period of the embryo (weeks 3 through 8 of prenatal development).

teratogens
external agents such as viruses, drugs, chemicals, and radiation that can harm a developing embryo or fetus.

sensitive period
a period during which an organism is quite susceptible to certain environmental influences; outside this period, the same environmental influences must be much stronger to produce comparable effects.

As we see in Figure 4.5, this is precisely the time—before a woman may even know that she is pregnant—that most organ systems are most vulnerable to damage. The most crucial period for gross physical defects of the head and central nervous system is the 3rd through the 5th prenatal weeks. The heart is particularly vulnerable from the middle of the 3rd through the middle of the 6th prenatal week; the most vulnerable period for many other organs and body parts is the 2nd prenatal month. Is it any wonder, then, that the period of the embryo is often called the critical phase of pregnancy?

Once an organ or body part is fully formed, it becomes somewhat less susceptible to damage. However, as Figure 4.5 also illustrates, some organ systems (particularly the eyes, genitals, and nervous system) can be damaged throughout pregnancy. Several years ago, Olli Heinonen and his associates (Heinonen et al., 1977) concluded that many of the birth defects found among the 50,282 children in their sample were *anytime malformations*—problems that could have been caused by teratogens at any point during the 9-month prenatal period. So it seems that the entire prenatal epoch could be considered a *sensitive period* for human development.

Finally, teratogens can have subtle effects on babies' behavior that are not obvious at birth but nevertheless influence their psychological development. For example, we

Table 4.1 A Brief Overview of Prenatal Development

Trimester	Period	Weeks	Size	Major developments
First	Zygote	1		One-celled zygote divides and becomes a blastocyst.
		2		Blastocyst implants into uterine wall; structures that nourish and protect the organism—amnion, chorion, yolk sac, placenta, umbilical cord—begin to form.
	Embryo	3–4	1/4 in.	Brain, spinal cord, and heart form, as do the rudimentary structures that will become the eyes, ears, nose, mouth, and limbs.
		5–8	1 in. 1/4 oz.	External body structures (eyes, ears, limbs) and internal organs form. Embryo produces its own blood and can now move.
	Fetus	9–12	3 in. 1 oz.	Rapid growth and interconnections of all organ systems permit such new competencies as body and limb movements, swallowing, digestion of nutrients, urination. External genitalia form.
Second	Fetus	13–24	14–15 in. 2 lb.	Fetus grows rapidly. Fetal movements are felt by the mother, and fetal heartbeat can be heard. Fetus is covered by vernix to prevent chapping; it also reacts to bright lights and loud sounds.
Third	Fetus	25–38	19–21 in. 7–8 lb.	Growth continues and all organ systems mature in preparation for birth. Fetus reaches the age of viability and becomes more regular and predictable in its sleep cycles and motor activity. Layer of fat develops under the skin. Activity becomes less frequent and sleep more frequent during last 2 weeks before birth.

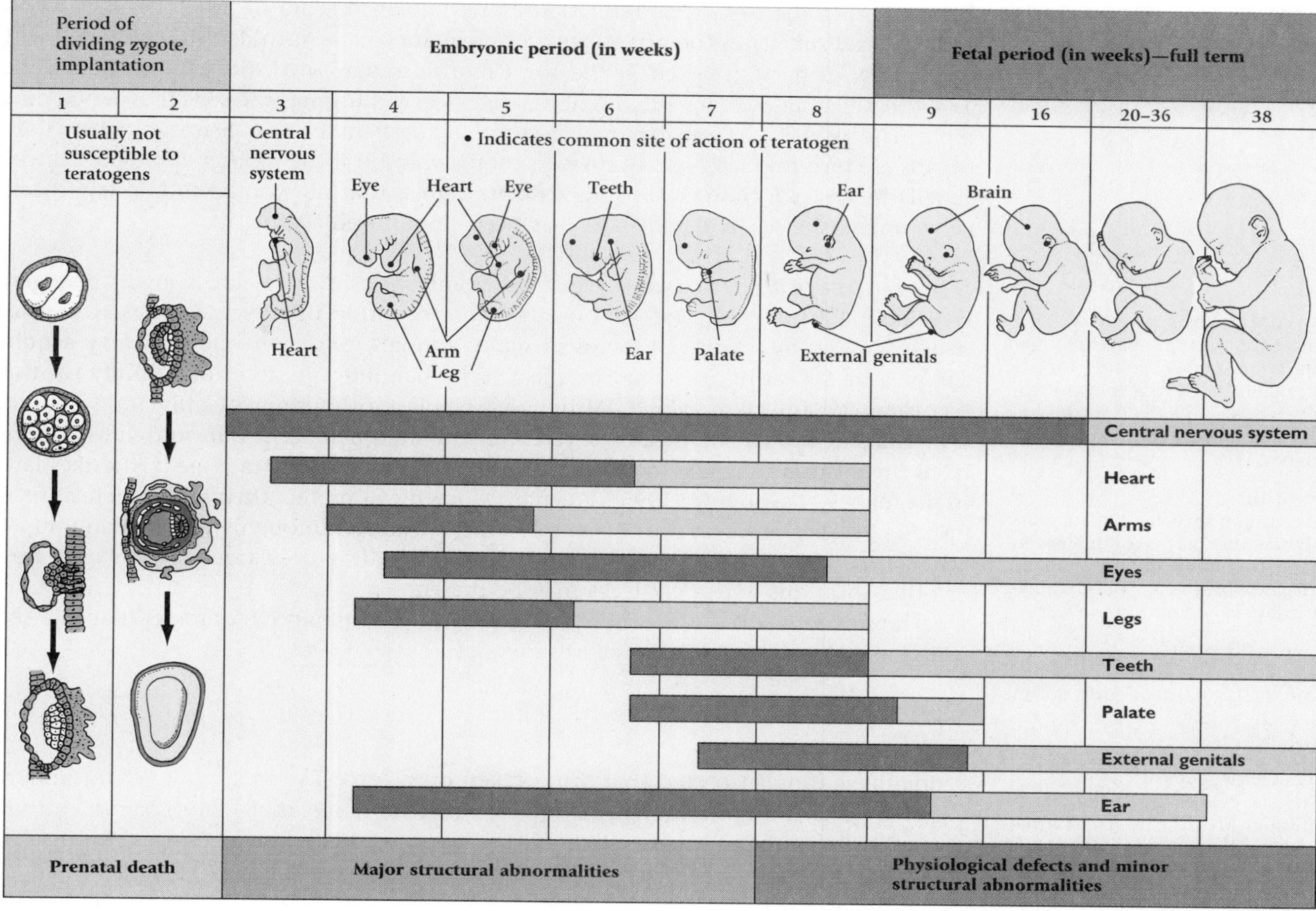

Figure 4.5 *The critical periods of prenatal development. Each organ or structure has a critical period when it is most sensitive to damage from teratogens. Dark band indicates the most sensitive periods. Light band indicates times that each organ or structure is somewhat less sensitive to teratogens, although damage may still occur.* ADAPTED FROM MOORE & PERSAUD, 1993.

will see that babies whose mothers consumed as little as half an ounce of alcohol a day while pregnant usually display no obvious physical deformities; however, they are often slower to process information and may score lower on IQ tests later in childhood than children whose mothers did not drink (Jacobson & Jacobson, 1996). These results may reflect subtle effects of alcohol on the development of the fetal brain. But there is another possibility: Caregivers may have been less inclined to stimulate a sluggish baby who was slow to respond to their bids for attention. And over time, those depressed levels of stimulation (rather than any effect of alcohol on the brain) may have stunted the child's intellectual development.

With these principles in mind, let's now consider some of the diseases, drugs, chemicals, and other environmental hazards that can adversely affect prenatal development or have other harmful consequences.

Maternal Diseases

Some disease agents are capable of crossing the placental barrier and doing much more damage to a developing embryo or fetus than to the mother herself. This makes sense when we remember that an unborn child has an immature immune system that cannot produce enough antibodies to combat infections effectively.

RUBELLA. The medical community became aware of the teratogenic effect of diseases in 1941 when an Australian physician, McAllister Gregg, noticed that many mothers who had had **rubella (German measles)** early in pregnancy delivered babies who were blind. After Gregg alerted the medical community, doctors began to notice that pregnant rubella patients regularly bore children with a variety of defects, including blindness, deafness, cardiac abnormalities, and mental retardation. Rubella is most dan-

rubella (German measles) a disease that has little effect on a mother but may cause a number of serious birth defects in unborn children who are exposed in the first 3 to 4 months of pregnancy.

toxoplasmosis
disease caused by a parasite found in raw meat and cat feces; can cause birth defects if transmitted to an embryo in the first trimester and miscarriage later in pregnancy.

syphilis
a common sexually transmitted disease that may cross the placental barrier in the middle and later stages of pregnancy, causing miscarriage or serious birth defects.

genital herpes
a sexually transmitted disease that can infect infants at birth, causing blindness, brain damage, or even death.

cesarean section
surgical delivery of a baby through an incision made in the mother's abdomen and uterus.

gerous during the first trimester. Studies have shown that 60 to 85% of babies whose mothers had rubella in the first 8 weeks of pregnancy have birth defects, compared with about 50% of those infected in the third month and 16% of those infected in weeks 13—20 (Kelley-Buchanan, 1988). This disease clearly illustrates the sensitive period principle. The risk of eye and heart defects are greatest in the first 8 weeks (when these organs are forming), whereas deafness is more common if the mother comes down with rubella in weeks 6 though 13. Today, doctors stress that no woman should try to conceive unless she has had rubella or has been immunized against it.

Other Infectious Diseases. Several other infectious diseases are known teratogens (see Table 4.2 for examples). Among the more common of these agents is **toxoplasmosis,** caused by a parasite found in many animals. Expectant mothers may acquire the parasite by eating undercooked meat or by handling the feces of a family cat that has eaten an infected animal. Although toxoplasmosis produces only mild coldlike symptoms in adults, it can cause severe eye and brain damage if transmitted to the prenatal organism during the first trimester, and can induce a miscarriage if it strikes later in pregnancy (Carrington, 1995). Pregnant women can protect themselves against infection by cooking all meat until it is well-done, washing thoroughly any cooking implements that came in contact with raw meat, and avoiding the garden, a pet's litter box, or other locations where cat feces may be present.

Finally, no infections are more common and few are more hazardous than the *sexually transmitted diseases* examined in Box 4.1.

Drugs

People have long suspected that drugs taken by pregnant women could harm unborn children. Even Aristotle thought as much when he noted that many drunken mothers had feeble-minded babies (Abel, 1981). Today, we know that these suspicions were

Table 4.2 Common Diseases That May Affect an Embryo, Fetus, or Newborn

	Effects			
Disease	**Miscarriage**	**Physical malformations**	**Mental impairment**	**Low birth weight/ premature delivery**
Sexually transmitted diseases (STDs)				
Acquired immune deficiency syndrome (AIDS)	?	?	?	+
Herpes simplex (genital herpes)	+	+	+	+
Syphilis	+	+	+	+
Other maternal diseases/conditions				
Chicken pox	0	+	+	+
Cholera	+	0	?	+
Cytomegalovirus	+	+	+	+
Diabetes	+	+	+	0
Influenza	+	+	?	?
Malaria	+	0	0	+
Mumps	+	0	0	0
Rubella	+	+	+	+
Toxemia	+	0	+	?
Toxoplasmosis	+	+	+	+
Tuberculosis	+	+	+	+
Urinary tract infection (bacterial)	+	0	0	+

Note: + = established finding; 0 = no clear evidence; ? = possible effect.
Sources: Carrington, 1995; Cates, 1995; Faden & Kass, 1996; Kelley-Buchanan, 1988.

4.1

DEVELOPMENTAL ISSUES

Teratogenic Effects of Sexually Transmitted Diseases

According to one recent estimate, as many as 32 *million* adolescents and adults in the United States either have or have had a sexually transmitted disease (STD) that is capable of producing serious birth defects or otherwise compromising their children's developmental outcomes (Cates, 1995). Three of these diseases—*syphilis, genital herpes,* and *acquired immune deficiency syndrome (AIDS)*—are especially hazardous.

Syphilis is most harmful in the middle and later stages of pregnancy, since syphilitic spirochetes (the microscopic organisms that transmit the disease) cannot cross the placental barrier until the 18th prenatal week. This is fortunate, for the disease is usually diagnosed with a blood test and treated with antibiotics long before it could harm a fetus. However, the mother who receives no treatment runs the risk of miscarrying or of giving birth to a child who has serious eye, ear, bone, heart, or brain damage (Carrington, 1995; Kelley-Buchanan, 1988).

The virus causing **genital herpes** (herpes simplex) can also cross the placental barrier, although most infections occur at birth as the newborn comes in contact with lesions on the mother's genitals (Gosden et al., 1994). Unfortunately, there is no cure for genital herpes, so mothers cannot be treated. And the consequences of a herpes infection can be severe: This incurable disease will kill about one-third of all infected newborns and cause such disabilities as blindness, brain damage, and other serious neurological disorders in another 25 to 30% (Ismail, 1993). For these reasons, mothers with active herpes infections are now routinely advised to undergo a **Cesarean delivery** (a surgical birth in which the baby is delivered through an incision in the mother's abdomen) to avoid infecting their babies.

The STD of greatest concern today is **acquired immune deficiency syndrome (AIDS),** a relatively new and incurable disease, caused by the HIV virus, which attacks the immune system and makes victims susceptible to a host of other opportunistic infections will eventually kill them. Transfer of bodily fluids is necessary to spread the HIV virus; consequently, people are normally infected during sexual intercourse or by sharing needles while injecting illegal drugs. Worldwide, more than *4 million* women of childbearing age carry the HIV virus and could transmit it to their offspring (Faden & Kass, 1996). Infected mothers may pass the virus (1) prenatally, through the placenta; (2) while giving birth, when there may be an exchange of blood between mother and child as the umbilical cord separates from the placenta; and (3) after birth, if the virus is passed through the mother's milk during breast feeding (Eldred & Chaisson, 1996). Despite all these possibilities, it appears that fewer than 30% of babies born to HIV-infected mothers are infected themselves. Prenatal transmission of the HIV virus is reduced by nearly 70% among mothers taking the antiviral drug AZT, without any indication that this drug (or the HIV virus) causes birth defects (Anderson, 1996; Friedman & Polifka, 1996).

What are the prospects for babies born infected with HIV? Early reports were extremely depressing, claiming that the virus would devastate immature immune systems during the first year, causing most HIV-infected infants to develop full-blown AIDS and die by age 3 (Jones et al., 1992). However, several recent studies (reviewed in Hutton, 1996) find that more than half of all HIV-infected infants are living beyond age 6, with a fair percentage surviving well into adolescence. The antiviral drug AZT, which interferes with HIV's ability to infect new cells, is now used to treat HIV-infected children, many of whom improve or remain stable for years if treatment is started early (Hutton, 1996). However, virtually all HIV-infected youngsters will eventually die from complications of their infection, while a much larger group of children who escaped HIV infection from their mothers will have to deal with the grief of losing their mothers to AIDS (Hutton, 1996; Wissow, Hutton, & McGraw, 1996).

Mother-to child transmission of HIV in the United States is most common among inner-city, poverty-stricken women who take drugs intravenously or have sexual partners who do (Eldred & Chaisson, 1996). Many experts believe that interventions aimed at modifying unsafe sexual practices and unsafe drug use may be about the only effective means to combat the HIV epidemic, for it may be many years before a cure for AIDS is found (Faden & Kass, 1996).

often correct and that even mild drugs that have few if any lasting effects on a mother may prove extremely hazardous to a developing embryo or fetus. Unfortunately, the medical community learned this lesson the hard way.

The Thalidomide Tragedy. In 1960, a West German drug company began to market a mild tranquilizer, sold over the counter, that was said to alleviate the periodic nausea (morning sickness) that many women experience during the first trimester of pregnancy. Presumably, the drug was perfectly safe; in tests on pregnant rats, it had had no ill effects on mother or offspring. The drug was **thalidomide.**

What came to pass quickly illustrated that drugs that are harmless in tests with laboratory animals may turn out to be violent teratogens for human beings. Thousands of

acquired immune deficiency syndrome (AIDS)
a viral disease that can be transmitted from a mother to her fetus or neonate and that results in a weakening of the body's immune system and, ultimately, death.

thalidomide
a mild tranquilizer that, taken early in pregnancy, can produce a variety of malformations of the limbs, eyes, ears, and heart.

This boy has no arms or hands—two of the birth defects that may be produced by thalidomide.

women who had used thalidomide during the first 2 months of pregnancy were suddenly giving birth to babies with horrible birth defects. Thalidomide babies often had badly deformed eyes, ears, noses, and hearts, and many displayed phocomelia—a structural abnormality in which all or parts of limbs are missing and the feet or hands may be attached directly to the torso like flippers.

The kinds of birth defects produced by thalidomide depended on when the drug was taken. Babies of mothers who had taken the drug on or around the 21st day after conception were likely to be born without ears. Those whose mothers had used thalidomide on the 25th through the 27th day of pregnancy often had grossly deformed arms or no arms. If a mother had taken the drug between the 28th and 36th day, her child might have deformed legs or no legs. But if she had waited until the 40th day before using thalidomide, her baby was usually not affected (Apgar & Beck, 1974). However, most mothers who took thalidomide delivered babies with no apparent birth defects—a finding that illustrates the dramatic differences that individuals display in response to teratogens.

Other Common Drugs. Despite the lessons learned from the thalidomide tragedy, about 60% of pregnant women take at least one prescription or over-the-counter drug. Unfortunately, some of the most commonly used drugs are suspect. Heavy use of aspirin, for example, has been linked to fetal growth retardation, poor motor control, and even infant death (Barr et al., 1990; Kelley-Buchanan, 1988), although further research has failed to confirm these findings (Friedman & Polifka, 1996). Some studies have linked heavy use of caffeine (that is, more than four soft drinks or cups of coffee per day) to such complications as miscarriage and low birth weight (Larroque, Kaminski, & Lelong, 1993; Leviton, 1993). However, the harmful outcomes attributed to caffeine may well have been caused by other drugs these mothers had used (Friedman & Polifka, 1996)—most notably alcohol and nicotine, which we will soon discuss.

Several other prescription drugs pose a slight risk to developing embryos and fetuses. For example, antidepressants containing lithium can produce heart defects when taken in the first trimester (Friedman & Polifka, 1996). Medications containing sex hormones (or their active biochemical ingredients) can also affect a developing embryo or fetus. For example, oral contraceptives contain female sex hormones, and, if a woman takes the pill, not knowing that she is pregnant, her unborn child faces a slightly increased risk of heart defects and other minor malformations (Gosden et al., 1994; Heinonen et al., 1977).

One synthetic sex hormone that can have serious long-term effects is **diethylstilbestrol (DES)**—the active ingredient of a drug that was widely prescribed for the prevention of miscarriages between the mid-1940s and 1965. The drug seemed safe enough; newborns whose mothers had used DES appeared to be normal in every way. But in 1971 physicians clearly established that 17- to 21-year-old females whose mothers had used DES were at risk for developing abnormalities of the reproductive organs, including a rare form of cervical cancer. Clearly, the risk of cancer is not very great; fewer than 1 in 1,000 DES daughters has developed the disease thus far (Friedman & Polifka, 1996). However, there are other complications. For example, DES daughters who themselves become pregnant are more likely than nonexposed women to miscarry or to deliver prematurely. What about DES sons? Although there is no conclusive evidence that prenatal exposure to DES causes cancer in sons, a small number of men who were exposed to DES before birth have developed minor genital trait abnormalities that do not affect their fertility (Wilcox et al., 1995).

Clearly, the vast majority of pregnant women who take aspirin, caffeine, oral contraceptives, or DES deliver perfectly normal babies. And under proper medical supervision, use of medications to treat a mother's ailments is usually safe for mother and fetus (McMahon & Katz, 1996). Nevertheless, the fact that seemingly harmless drugs can produce congenital defects has convinced many mothers to restrict or eliminate their intake of all drugs during pregnancy.

diethylstilbestrol (DES)
a synthetic hormone, formerly prescribed to prevent miscarriage, that can produce cervical cancer in adolescent female offspring and genital-tract abnormalities in males.

ALCOHOL. Should a no-drug policy be extended to alcohol? Most contemporary researchers think so. In 1973, Kenneth Jones and his colleagues (1973) described a **fetal alcohol syndrome (FAS)** that affects many children of alcoholic mothers. The most noticeable characteristics of fetal alcohol syndrome are defects such as microcephaly (small head) and malformations of the heart, limbs, joints, and face. FAS babies are likely to display excessive irritability, hyperactivity, seizures, and tremors. They are also smaller and lighter than normal, and their physical growth lags behind that of normal age-mates. Finally, the majority of the 3 in 1,000 babies born with FAS score well below average in intelligence throughout childhood and adolescence, and over 90% of them display major adjustment problems as adolescents and young adults (Colburn, 1996; Stratton, Howe, & Battaglia, 1996).

How much can a mother drink without harming her baby? Perhaps a lot less than you might imagine. In keeping with the dosage principle of teratology, the symptoms of FAS are most severe when the "dose" of alcohol is highest—that is, when the mother is clearly an alcoholic. Yet, even moderate "social drinking" (1 to 3 ounces a day) can lead to less serious problems, called **fetal alcohol effects (FAE),** in some babies. These effects include retarded physical growth and minor physical abnormalities, as well as such problems as poor motor skills, difficulty paying attention, and subnormal intellectual performance (Jacobson et al., 1993; Streissguth et al., 1993). Even a mother who drinks less than an ounce of alcohol a day is more likely than a nondrinker to have an infant whose mental development is slightly below average (Jacobson & Jacobson, 1996). And there is no well-defined sensitive period for fetal alcohol effects; drinking late in pregnancy can be just as risky as drinking soon after conception (Jacobson et al., 1993). In 1981, the U.S. Surgeon General concluded that *no amount* of alcohol consumption is entirely safe and has since advised pregnant women not to drink at all.

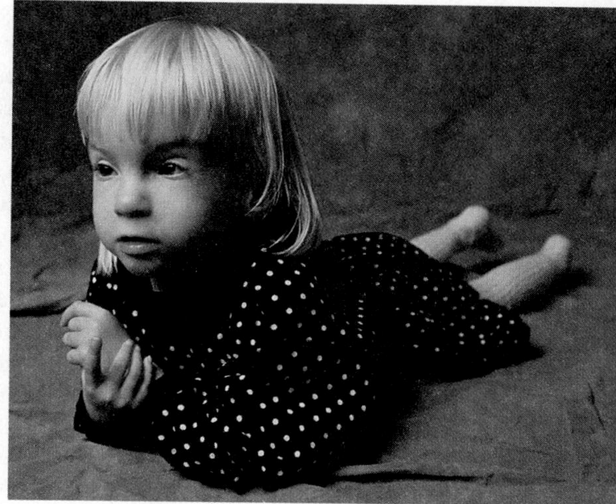

This girl's widely spaced eyes, flattened nose, and underdeveloped upper lip are three of the common physical symptoms of fetal alcohol syndrome.

CIGARETTE SMOKING. Thirty-five years ago, neither doctors nor pregnant women had any reason to suspect that cigarette smoking might affect an unborn child. Now we know otherwise. Although there is little evidence that smoking causes physical defects (Friedman & Polifka, 1996; Verp, 1993), one review of more than 200 studies concluded that smoking clearly retards the rate of fetal growth and increases the risk of spontaneous abortion or death shortly after birth in otherwise normal infants (U.S. Department of Health, Education, and Welfare, 1979). Smoking introduces nicotine and carbon monoxide into both the mother's and fetus's bloodstreams, which impairs the functioning of the placenta, especially the exchange of oxygen and nutrients to the fetus. And all these events are clearly related in that the more cigarettes mothers smoke per day, the greater their risk of spontaneous abortion or of delivering a low-birth-weight baby who may struggle to survive (Carson, 1993). Newborn infants of fathers who smoke are also likely to be smaller than normal. Why? Because mothers who live with smokers become "passive smokers," who inhale nicotine and carbon monoxide that can dampen fetal growth (Friedman & Polifka, 1996).

The long-term effects of exposure to tobacco products are less clear. Some research has found that children whose mothers smoked during pregnancy or whose parents continue to smoke after they are born tend to be smaller on average and more susceptible to respiratory infections, and show slightly poorer cognitive performances early in childhood than do children of nonsmokers (Diaz, 1997; Chavkin, 1995). Yet, differences between children of smokers and nonsmokers in these longer-term studies are typically very small, and studies that have controlled for mothers' use of alcohol and other drugs often fail to find any differences at all (see, for example, Chavkin, 1995; Lefkowitz, 1981). Nevertheless, evidence is overwhelming that smoking during pregnancy can harm fetuses (not to mention, of course, the harmful long-term effects that this habit can have on parents). For these reasons, physicians today routinely advise pregnant women and their partners to stop smoking, if not forever, at least during pregnancy.

fetal alcohol syndrome (FAS)
a group of serious congenital problems commonly observed in the offspring of mothers who abuse alcohol during pregnancy.

fetal alcohol effects (FAE)
a group of mild congenital problems that are sometimes observed in children of mothers who drink sparingly to moderately during pregnancy.

Illicit Drugs. In the United States, use of recreational drugs, such as marijuana, cocaine, and heroin, has become so widespread that as many as 700,000 infants are born each year having been exposed to one or more of these substances in the womb (Chavkin, 1995; Shearer, 1994). Marijuana, the most widely used of these drugs, produces few if any physical defects. However, mothers who report using the drug two or more times per week often deliver babies who display tremors, sleep disturbances, and a lack of interest in their surroundings over the first week or two of life (Brockington, 1996; Fried, 1993). These behavioral disturbances could place infants at risk for adverse outcomes later in childhood, although no such long-term effects have been identified.

Although heroin, methadone, and other addicting narcotic agents do not appear to produce gross physical abnormalities, women who use these drugs are more likely than nonusers to miscarry, deliver prematurely, or have babies who die soon after birth (Brockington, 1996). The first month is often difficult for the 60 to 80% of these babies who are born addicted to the narcotic their mother has taken. When deprived of the drug after birth, addicted infants experience withdrawal symptoms such as vomiting, dehydration, convulsions, extreme irritability, weak sucking, and high-pitched crying. Symptoms such as restlessness, tremors, and sleep disturbances may persist for as long as 3 to 4 months. However, longer-term studies reveal that most heroin- or methadone-addicted infants show normal developmental progress by age 2, and that indifferent parenting, rather than early drug exposure, is the most likely contributor to the poor progress that some of these children display (Brockington, 1996).

Today, much concern centers on the risks associated with cocaine use, particularly the use of "crack" cocaine, a cheap form of the drug that delivers high doses through the lungs. Cocaine use has been linked to a variety of physical defects; yet, it is difficult to tell whether cocaine itself is responsible because cocaine-using mothers are often malnourished and prone to use other teratogens such as alcohol (Friedman & Polifka, 1996). However, cocaine is known to constrict the blood vessels of both mother and fetus, thereby elevating fetal blood pressure and hampering the flow of nutrients and oxygen across the placenta (Chavkin, 1995; MacGregor & Chasnoff, 1993). As a result, babies of cocaine-using mothers, particularly mothers who use crack cocaine, are often miscarried or born prematurely; and like the babies of heroin or methadone users, they often display tremors, sleep disturbances, a sluggish inattention to the environment, and a tendency to become extremely irritable when aroused (Brockington, 1996; Lester et al., 1991).

Some investigators have suspected that the unpleasant demeanor that many cocaine babies display interferes with the emotional bonding that normally occurs between infants and their caregivers. Indeed, one study found that a majority of cocaine-exposed infants failed to establish secure emotional ties to their primary caregivers in the first year (Rodning, Beckwith, & Howard, 1991). Another study found that cocaine babies seem to derive less joy from learning than normal infants do, while showing much less concern (that is, anger or sadness) when their attempts to achieve a goal prove unsuccessful (Alessandri et al., 1993). These poor outcomes may stem from the babies' prior exposure to cocaine and their resulting negative emotional demeanor, their exposure to other teratogens (for example, alcohol and tobacco) commonly used by substance-abusing parents, or the less-than-adequate stimulation and care these babies may receive from drug-using parents. Further research is necessary to clarify this issue and properly assess the long-term impact of cocaine (and other narcotic agents) on *all* aspects of development.

Table 4.3 catalogs a number of other drugs and their known or suspected effects on unborn children. What should we make of these findings? Assuming that our first priority is the welfare of unborn children, then perhaps Virginia Apgar has summarized it best: "A woman who is pregnant, or who thinks she could possibly be pregnant should not take any drugs whatsoever unless absolutely essential—and then only when [approved] by a physician who is aware of the pregnancy" (Apgar & Beck, 1974, p. 445).

? **WHAT DO YOU THINK?**

Some people have argued that mothers who abuse alcohol or other teratogenic drugs while pregnant should be charged, if not with attempted murder, at least with child abuse. What is your view on this issue and why? If you agree, is that also a basis for charging drug-abusing fathers?

TABLE 4.3 **Partial List of Drugs and Treatments Used by the Mother That Affect (or Are Thought to Affect) the Fetus or the Newborn**

Maternal drug use	Effect on fetus/newborn
Alcohol	Small head, facial abnormalities, heart defects, low birth weight, and mental retardation (see text).
Amphetamines Dextroamphetamine Methamphetamine	Premature delivery, stillbirth, irritability, and poor feeding among newborns.
Antibiotics Streptomycin Terramycin Tetracycline	Heavy use of streptomycin by mothers can produce hearing loss in fetuses. Terramycin and tetracycline may be associated with premature delivery, retarded skeletal growth, cataracts, and staining of the baby's teeth.
Aspirin	See text. (In clinical doses, ibuprofen and acetaminophen are very safe alternatives to aspirin.)
Barbiturates	All barbiturates taken by the mother cross the placental barrier. In clinical doses, they cause the fetus or newborn to be lethargic. In large doses, they may cause anoxia (oxygen starvation) and depress fetal growth. One barbiturate, primidone, is associated with malformations of the heart, face, and limbs.
Hallucinogens LSD	Lysergic and diethylamide (LSD) slightly increases the likelihood of limb deformities.
Marijuana	Heavy marijuana use during pregnancy is linked to behavioral abnormalities in newborns (see text).
Lithium	Heart defects, lethargic behavior in newborns.
Narcotics Cocaine Heroin Methadone	Maternal addiction increases the risk of premature delivery. Moreover, the fetus is often addicted to the narcotic agent, which results in a number of complications. Heavy cocaine use can seriously elevate fetal blood pressure and even induce strokes (see text).
Sex hormones Androgens Progestogens Estrogens DES (diethylstilbestrol)	Sex hormones contained in birth control pills and drugs to prevent miscarriages taken by pregnant women can have a number of harmful effects on babies, including minor heart malformations, cervical cancer (in female offspring), and other anomalies (see text).
Tranquilizers (other than thalidomide) Chlorpromazine Reserpine Valium	May produce respiratory distress in newborns. Valium may also produce poor muscle tone and lethargy.
Tobacco	Maternal cigarette smoking is known to retard fetal growth and to increase the risk of spontaneous abortion, stillbirth, and infant mortality (see text).
Vitamins	Excessive amounts of vitamin A taken by pregnant women can cause cleft palate, heart malformations, and other serious birth defects. The popular antiacne drug Accutane, derived from vitamin A, is one of he most powerful teratogens, causing malformations of the eyes, limbs, heart, and central nervous system. Although teratogenic to animals (rabbits), vitamin D poses virtually no risk to humans, even if the mother takes 200 times the recommended daily dose.

SOURCES: Chavkin, 1995; Friedman & Polifka, 1996; Kelley-Buchanan, 1988.

Environmental Hazards

RADIATION. Soon after the atomic blasts of 1945 in Japan, scientists became painfully aware of the teratogenic effects of radiation. Not one pregnant woman who was within one-half mile of these explosions gave birth to a live child. In addition, 75% of the pregnant women who were within a mile and a quarter of the blasts had seriously handicapped children who soon died, and the infants who did survive were often mentally retarded (Apgar & Beck, 1974; Vorhees & Mollnow, 1987).

Unfortunately, no one knows exactly how much radiation it takes to harm an embryo or fetus; and even if an exposed child appears normal at birth, the possibility of developing complications later in life cannot be dismissed. For these reasons, pregnant women are routinely advised to avoid X-rays, particularly of the pelvis and abdomen, unless they are crucial for their own survival.

Chemicals and Pollutants. Pregnant women routinely come in contact with potentially toxic substances in their everyday environments, including organic dyes and coloring agents, food additives, artificial sweeteners, pesticides, and cosmetic products, some of which are known to have teratogenic effects in animals (Verp, 1993). Unfortunately, the risks associated with a large number of these common chemical additives and treatments remain to be determined.

There are also pollutants in the air we breathe and the water we drink. For example, pregnant women may be exposed to concentrations of lead, zinc, mercury, or antimony discharged into the air or water by industrial operations or present in house paint and water pipes. These heavy metals are known to impair the physical health and mental abilities of adults and children and to have teratogenic effects (producing physical deformities and mental retardation) on developing embryos and fetuses. Polluting chemicals called *PCBs (polychlorinated biphenyls)*, now outlawed but once widely used in plastics and carbon paper, represent another hazard. Joseph Jacobson and his colleagues (1984; 1985) found that even low-level exposure to PCBs, resulting from mothers eating contaminated fish from Lake Michigan, was enough to make newborns smaller on average and less responsive and neurologically mature than babies whose mothers did not eat polluted fish. At age 4, these children still performed poorly on tests of short-term memory and verbal reasoning ability, with the extent of their deficits corresponding to the "dose" of PCBs they received before birth (Jacobson, Jacobson, & Humphrey, 1990; Jacobson et al., 1992).

Even a father's exposure to environmental toxins can affect a couple's children. Studies of male doctors and dentists reveal that prolonged exposure to radiation, anesthetic gases, and other toxic substances can damage a father's chromosomes, increasing the likelihood of his child's being miscarried or having genetic defects (Gunderson & Sackett, 1982; Stone, 1992; Strigini et al., 1990). And even when expectant mothers do *not* drink alcohol or use drugs, they are much more likely to deliver a low-birth-weight baby if the father is a heavy drinker or drug user (Toner, 1991). Why? Possibly because certain substances (for example, cocaine and maybe even alcohol, PCBs, and other toxins) can apparently bind directly to live sperm and, thus, alter prenatal development from the moment of conception (Yazigi, Odem, & Polakoski, 1991). Taken together, these findings imply that (1) environmental toxins can affect the reproductive system of either parent so that (2) both mothers *and* fathers should limit their exposure to substances known to be teratogenic.

Maternal Characteristics

In addition to teratogens, a mother's nutrition, her emotional well-being, and even her age can affect the outcome of her pregnancy.

The Mother's Diet

Fifty years ago, doctors routinely advised mothers to gain no more than two pounds a month while pregnant and believed that a total gain of 15 to 18 pounds was quite sufficient to ensure healthy prenatal development. Today, mothers are more often advised to eat a healthy, high-protein, high-calorie diet on which they gain 2 to 5 pounds during the first 3 months of pregnancy and about a pound a week thereafter, for a total increase of 25 to 30 pounds (Ratcliffe, Byrd, & Sakornbut, 1996). Why has the advice changed? We now know that inadequate prenatal nutrition can be harmful.

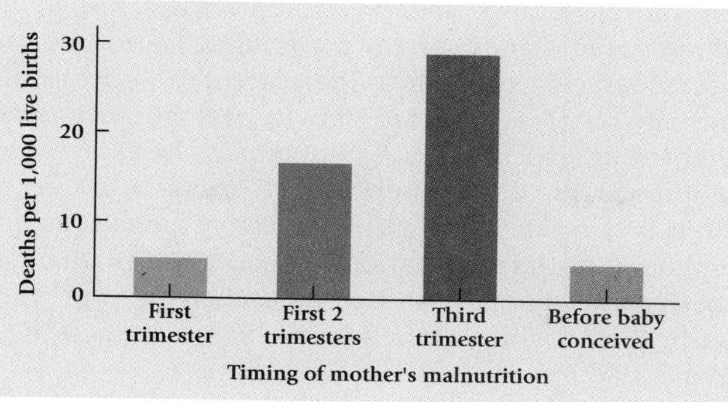

Figure 4.6 *Incidence of infant mortality in the first 12 months for babies born to Dutch mothers who had experienced famine during World War II.* ADAPTED FROM STEIN & SUSSER, *1976.*

Severe malnutrition, as often occurs during periods of famine, stunts prenatal growth and produces small, underweight babies (Susser & Stein, 1994). The precise effects of malnutrition depend on when it occurs. During the first trimester, malnutrition can disrupt the formation of the spinal cord and induce miscarriages. During the third trimester, malnutrition is more likely to result in low-birth-weight babies with small heads who may fail to survive the first year of life (Susser & Stein, 1994; and see Figure 4.6). Indeed, autopsies of stillborn infants whose mothers were malnourished during the third trimester reveal fewer brain cells and lower brain weights than is typical among babies born to well-nourished mothers (Goldenberg, 1995; Winick, 1976).

Not surprisingly, then, babies born to malnourished mothers sometimes show cognitive deficits later in childhood and a heightened risk of developing problems such as hypertension, heart disease, and diabetes as adults (Barker, 1994; Goldberg & Prentice, 1994). One contributor to these long-term problems is the babies' own behavior. Malnourished babies whose diets *remain* inadequate after birth are often apathetic and quick to become irritated when aroused—qualities that can alienate their parents, who may fail to provide the kinds of playful stimulation and emotional support that would foster their social and intellectual development (Grantham-McGregor et al., 1995). Fortunately, dietary supplements, especially when combined with stimulating day-care and programs that help parents to become more sensitive, responsive caregivers, can significantly reduce or even eliminate the potentially damaging long-term effects of prenatal malnutrition (Grantham-McGregor et al., 1995; Super, Herrera, & Mora, 1990; Zeskind & Ramey, 1981).

Finally, it is important to note that expectant mothers who have plenty to eat may still fail to obtain all of the vitamins and minerals that help to ensure a healthy pregnancy. Adding small amounts of magnesium and zinc to a mother's diet improves the functioning of the placenta and reduces the incidence of many birth complications (Friedman & Polifka, 1996). And researchers around the world have recently discovered that diets rich in **folic acid,** a B-complex vitamin found in fresh fruits, liver, and green vegetables, help to prevent **spina bifida** and other defects of the neural tube (Cefalo, 1996; Czeizel, 1995; Rose & Mennuti, 1994). Most women consume less than half the recommended daily allowance of folic acid, and intensive campaigns are now underway to persuade all women of childbearing age to take vitamin-mineral supplements that provide them with at least .4 mg (but not more than 1.0 mg) of folic acid a day (Cefalo, 1996). Folic acid enrichment is particularly important from the time of conception through the first 8 weeks of pregnancy, when the neural tube is forming (Friedman & Polifka, 1996). However, these supplementation campaigns are controversial. Many fear that some women encouraged to take vitamin-mineral supplements may assume that "more is better" and end up ingesting too much vitamin A, which in very high doses can produce birth defects (see Table 4.3). Yet, under proper medical supervision, use of vitamin-mineral supplements is considered quite safe (Friedman & Polifka, 1996).

folic acid
B-complex vitamin that helps to prevent defects of the central nervous system.

spina bifida
a bulging of the spinal cord through a gap in the spinal column.

The Mother's Emotional Well-being

Although most women are happy about conceiving a child, many pregnancies are unplanned and unintended. Does it matter how a mother feels about being pregnant or about her life while she is pregnant?

Indeed it may, at least in some cases. When a mother becomes emotionally aroused, her glands secrete powerful activating hormones such as adrenaline. These hormones may then cross the placental barrier, enter the fetus's bloodstream, and increase the fetus's motor activity. Temporarily stressful episodes such as a fall, a frightening experience, or an argument have few if any harmful consequences for a mother or her fetus (Brockington, 1996). However, *prolonged* and *severe* emotional stress is associated with stunted prenatal growth, premature delivery, low birth weight, and other birth complications (Lobel, 1994; Paarlberg et al., 1995). Others have found that babies of highly stressed mothers tend to be highly active, irritable, and irregular in their feeding, sleeping, and bowel habits (Sameroff & Chandler, 1975; Vaughn et al., 1987).

How might emotional stress stunt fetal growth and contribute to birth complications and newborn behavioral irregularities? A link between prolonged stress and growth retardation or low birth weight may reflect the influence of stress hormones, which divert blood flow to the large muscles and impede the flow of oxygen and nutrients to the fetus. Stress may also weaken the mother's immune system, making her (and her fetus) more susceptible to infectious diseases (Cohen & Williamson, 1991). Finally, emotionally stressed mothers may be inclined to eat poorly, smoke, or use alcohol and drugs, all of which are known to promote fetal growth retardation and low birth weight (Paarlberg et al., 1995). Of course, a mother whose source of stress *continues* after her baby is born may not make the most sensitive caregiver which, coupled with a baby who is already irritable and unresponsive, can perpetuate the infant's difficult behavioral profile (Brockington, 1996; Vaughn et al., 1987).

Interestingly, not all highly stressed mothers experience the complications we have discussed. Why? Because it seems that the presence of objective stressors in a woman's life is far less important than her ability to manage such stress (McCubbin et al., 1996). Stress-related complications are much more likely when mothers (1) are ambivalent or negative about their marriages or their pregnancies and (2) have no friends or other bases of social support to turn to for comfort (Brockington, 1996). Counseling aimed at managing and reducing stress may help these mothers immensely. In one study, babies of stressed mothers who received such counseling weighed significantly more at birth than babies of stressed mothers who received no help (Rothberg & Lits, 1991).

The Mother's Age

Are some ages safer than others for women to become pregnant and bear children? The answer is a qualified "yes." As shown in Figure 4.7, there is a relationship between a mother's age and the risk of death for her fetus or **neonate** (newborn). Compared with mothers in their 20s, teenage mothers experience more birth complications and are more likely to deliver prematurely and have low-birth-weight babies (Scholl, Hediger, & Belsky, 1994). Why are younger mothers and their offspring at risk? The major reason is simply that pregnant teenagers are often from economically impoverished family backgrounds characterized by poor nutrition, high levels of stress, and little access to supervised prenatal care (Abma & Mott, 1991). Indeed, teenage mothers and their babies are usually *not* at risk when they receive good prenatal care and competent medical supervision during the birth process (Baker & Mednick, 1984; see also Seitz & Apfel, 1994a).

What risks do women face should they delay childbearing until after age 35? As Figures 4.7 indicates, there is an increased incidence of spontaneous abortion, due largely to the older woman's greater likelihood of conceiving children with chromosomal abnormalities (Verp, 1993; See Chapter 3). The risks of other complications during pregnancy and delivery are also greater for older women, partly because they, like adolescents, are less likely than women in their 20s and early 30s to seek adequate prenatal care early in their pregnancies (Brown, 1988). Even so, it is important to emphasize that the *vast majority* of older women—particularly those who are healthy, well-nourished, and who receive adequate prenatal care—have normal pregnancies and healthy babies (Brockington, 1996).

neonate
a newborn infant from birth to approximately 1 month of age.

Prevention of Birth Defects

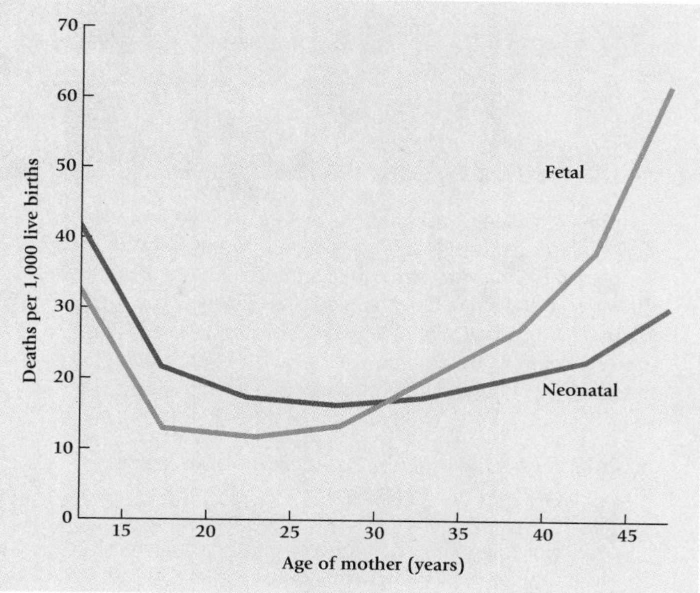

Figure 4.7 *Relationship between mother's age and risk of death for the fetus or neonate.* FROM KESSNER, 1973.

Reading a chapter such as this one can be frightening to anyone who hopes to have a child. It is easy to come away with the impression that "life before birth" is a veritable minefield. After all, so many hereditary accidents are possible, and even a genetically normal embryo or fetus may encounter a large number of potential hazards while developing in the womb.

But clearly there is another side to this story. Recall that the majority of genetically abnormal embryos do not develop to term. And it appears that the prenatal environment is not so hazardous when we note that more than 95% of newborn babies are perfectly normal and that many of the remaining 5% have minor congenital problems that are only temporary or easily correctable (Gosden et al., 1994). Although there *is* reason for concern, parents can significantly reduce the odds that their babies will be abnormal if they follow the simple recommendations in Box 4.2 on page 130. Failure to abide by one or more of the guidelines will not necessarily mean that your child will be abnormal. Nor will exact compliance guarantee that a child will be healthy; accidents do happen. Following these recommendations may seem unnecessary to parents who have already given birth to healthy children. However, Apgar and Beck (1974, p. 452) remind us that "Each pregnancy is different. Each unborn child has a unique genetic make-up. The prenatal environment a mother provides is never quite the same for another baby. Thus, we believe no amount of effort is too great to increase the chances that a baby will be born normal, healthy, and without a handicapping birth defect."

CHILDBIRTH AND THE PERINATAL ENVIRONMENT

The *perinatal environment* is the environment surrounding birth; it includes influences such as drugs given to the mother during delivery, delivery practices, and the social environment shortly after the baby is born. As we will see, this perinatal environment is an important one that can affect a baby's well-being and the course of her future development.

Concept Check 4.2
Understanding the Prenatal Environment

Check your understanding of environmental influences on prenatal development by matching each of the following influences with one of the statements below: (a) severe malnutrition, (b) toxoplasmosis, (c) diethylstilbestrol (DES), (d) rubella, (e) folic acid, (f) alcohol, and (g) syphilis.

_____ 1. disease that is most harmful to fetuses in the latter half of pregnancy
_____ 2. linked to cervical cancer in girls
_____ 3. teratogen for which father's use has been linked to low birth weight
_____ 4. disease that is a strong teratogen, even though mothers experience few symptoms
_____ 5. protects against spina bifida and defects of the neural tube
_____ 6. teratogenic effects of this disease are strongest during the first trimester
_____ 7. associated with stunted brain development if it occurs in the third trimester

4.2

APPLYING DEVELOPMENTAL RESEARCH

Preventing Birth Defects—A Checklist for Prospective Parents

In their excellent book *Is My Baby All Right?* (1974), Dr. Virginia Apgar and Joan Beck suggest several ways that prospective parents can significantly reduce the likelihood of bearing a defective child. As you read through the list, see whether you can recall why each recommendation makes good sense. In so doing, you will have reviewed much of the material on congenital defects presented in this chapter (as well as Chapter 3).

1. *If you think a close relative has a disorder that might be hereditary, you should take advantage of genetic counseling.* Do you remember what kinds of services a genetic counselor may offer or suggest? If not, you may wish to review the section on genetic counseling in Chapter 3.
2. *The ideal age for a woman to have children is between 18 and 35.* What complications might older and younger mothers face?
3. *Every pregnant woman needs good prenatal care supervised by a practitioner who keeps current on medical research in the field of teratology and who will help her deliver her baby in a reputable, modern hospital.* We have not yet examined the birth process and its complications. When we review the pros and cons of "home births," we will see that not everyone agrees that a woman should always give birth in a hospital.
4. *No woman should become pregnant unless she is sure that she has either had rubella or been effectively immunized against it.* What defects can rubella cause? When during pregnancy is the disease particularly dangerous?
5. *From the very beginning of pregnancy, a woman should do everything possible to avoid exposure to contagious diseases.* Do you remember the teratogenic effect of congenital syphilis, herpes, and other infectious agents? If not, you may wish to review Table 4.2 and the section of this chapter entitled "Maternal Diseases."
6. *Pregnant women should avoid eating undercooked red meat or having contact with any cat (or cat feces) that may carry toxoplasmosis infection.* What are the possible consequences of toxoplasmosis for the mother? For her unborn child?
7. *A pregnant woman should not take any drugs unless absolutely essential—and then only when approved by a physician who is aware of the pregnancy.* Do you remember the effects of DES, alcohol, cocaine, and other commonly used substances? If not, you may wish to review Table 4.3 and the section of this chapter entitled "Drugs."
8. *Unless it is absolutely essential for her own well-being, a pregnant woman should avoid radiation treatments and X-ray examinations.* What are the possible consequences of radiation exposure for the unborn child? How did scientists become aware of the teratogenic effects of radiation?
9. *Cigarettes should not be smoked during pregnancy.* Why not? Does a mother's cigarette smoking during pregnancy have long-term effects on her children?
10. *A nourishing diet, rich in proteins and adequate in vitamins, minerals, and total calories, is essential during pregnancy.* What are the possible effects of maternal malnutrition on the developing child? Should a pregnant woman take large amounts of extra vitamins in order to ensure that her baby will be healthy?

The Birth Process

first stage of labor
the period of the birth process lasting from the first regular uterine contractions until the cervix is fully dilated.

second stage of labor
the period of the birth process during which the fetus moves through the birth canal and emerges from the mother's body (also called *delivery*).

third stage of labor
expulsion of the placenta (afterbirth).

Childbirth is a three-stage process (see Figure 4.8). The **first stage of labor** begins as the mother experiences uterine contractions spaced at 10- to 15-minute intervals, and it ends when her cervix has fully dilated so that the fetus's head can pass through. This phase lasts an average of 8 to 14 hours for firstborn children and 3 to 8 for later-borns. As labor proceeds, the uterus contracts more frequently and intensely. When the head of the fetus is positioned at the cervical opening, the second phase of labor is about to begin.

The **second stage of labor,** or *delivery,* begins as the fetus's head passes through the cervix into the vagina and ends when the baby emerges from the mother's body. This is the time when the mother may be told to bear down (push) with each contraction to assist her child through the birth canal. A quick delivery may take a half-hour, whereas a long one may last more than an hour and a half.

The **third stage of labor,** or *afterbirth,* takes only 5 to 10 minutes as the uterus once again contracts and expels the placenta from the mother's body.

The Baby's Experience

It was once thought that birth was an extremely hazardous and torturous ordeal for a contented fetus who is suddenly expelled from a soft, warm uterus into a cold, bright world where, for the first time, it may experience chills, pain, hunger, and the startling rush of air into its lungs. Yet, few people today would describe birth and birthing practices as the "torture of the innocents" as French obstetrician Frederick LeBoyer (1975) has. Fetuses *are* stressed by birth, but their own production of activating stress hormones is adaptive, helping them to withstand oxygen deprivation by increasing their heart rate and the flow of oxygenated blood to the brain (Nelson, 1995). Birth stress also helps to ensure that babies are born wide awake and ready to breathe. Aiden MacFarlane (1977) has carefully observed many newborn babies, noting that most of them quiet down and begin to adapt to their new surroundings within minutes of that first loud cry. So birth is a stressful ordeal, but hardly a torturous one.

The Baby's Appearance

To a casual observer, many newborns may not look especially attractive. Often born bluish in color from oxygen deprivation during the birth process, babies' passage through the narrow cervix and birth canal may also leave them with flattened noses, misshapen foreheads, and an assortment of bumps and bruises. As the baby is weighed and measured, parents are likely to see a wrinkled, red-skinned little creature, about 20 inches long and weighing about 7 to 7½ pounds, who is covered with a sticky substance. But even though newborns may hardly resemble the smiley bouncing infants who appear in baby food commercials, most parents think that *their* baby is beautiful nevertheless and are usually eager to become acquainted with this new member of the family.

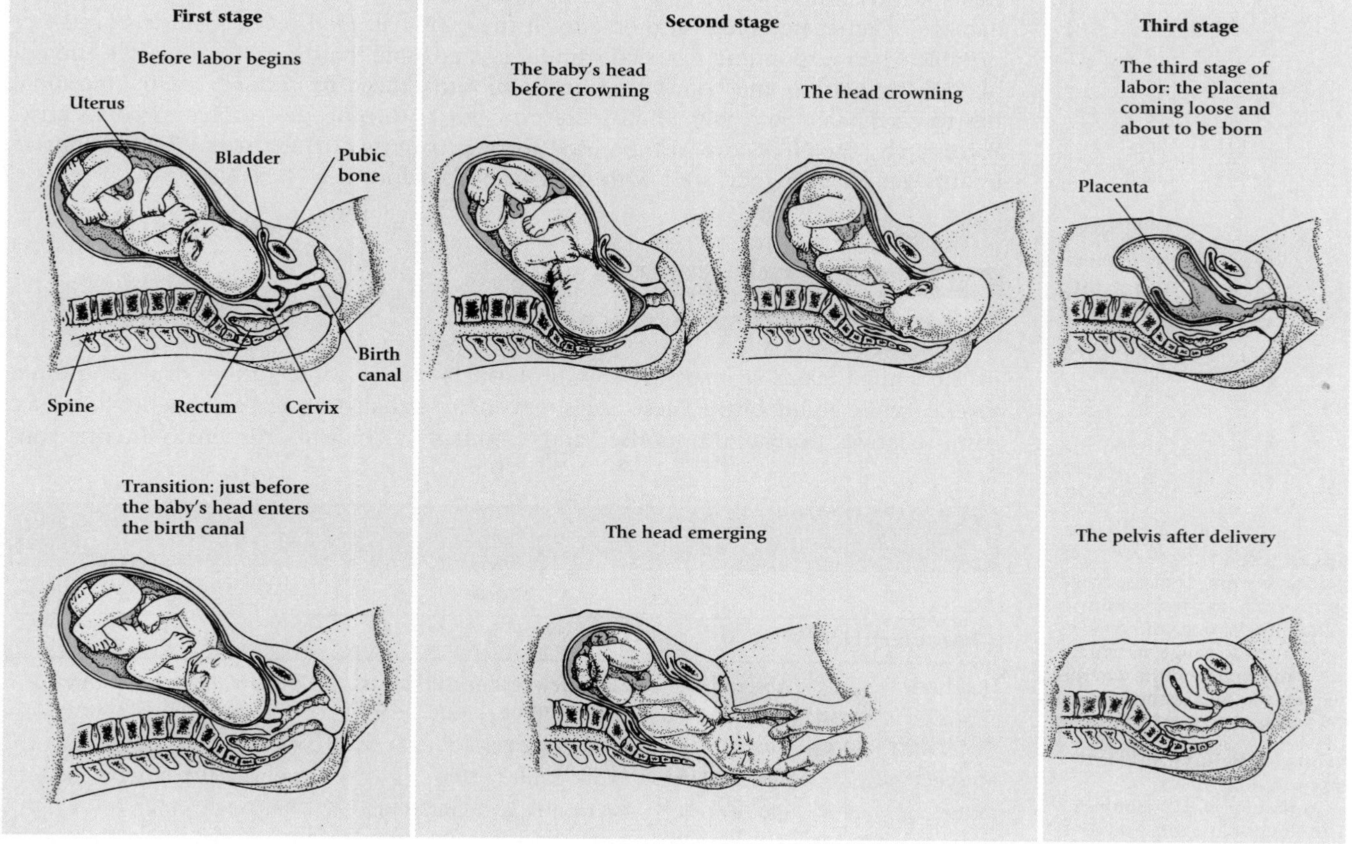

Figure 4.8 *The three stages of childbirth.*

Immediately after birth, babies are not particularly attractive, but their appearance improves dramatically over the first few weeks of life.

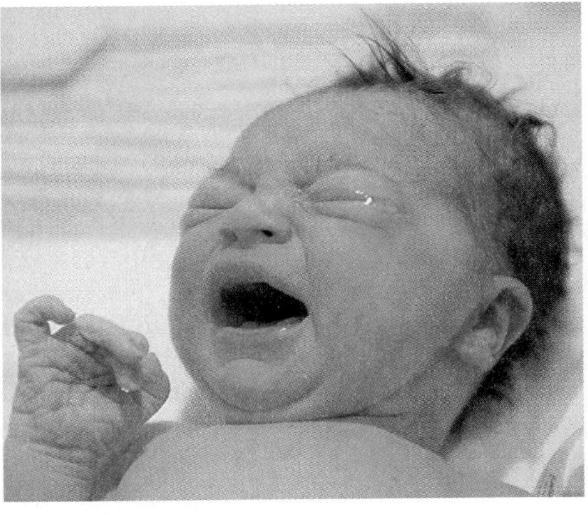

Assessing the Baby's Condition

In the very first minutes of life, a baby takes his or her first test. A nurse or a doctor checks the infant's physical condition by looking at five standard characteristics which are rated from 0 to 2, recorded on a chart, and totaled (see Table 4.4). A baby's score on this **Apgar test** (named for its developer, Dr. Virginia Apgar) can range from 0 to 10, with higher scores indicating a better condition. The test is often repeated 5 minutes later to measure improvements in the baby's condition. Infants who score 7 or higher on this second assessment are in good physical condition, whereas those who score 4 or lower are in trouble and often require immediate medical attention in order to survive.

Although useful as a quick method of detecting *severe* physical or neurological irregularities that require immediate attention, the Apgar test may miss less obvious complications. A second test, T. Berry Brazelton's **Neonatal Behavioral Assessment Scale (NBAS),** is a more subtle measure of a baby's behavioral repertoire and neurological well-being (Brazelton, 1979). Typically administered a few days after birth, the NBAS assesses the strength of 20 inborn reflexes, as well as changes in the infant's state, and reactions to comforting and other social stimuli. One important value of this test is its early identification of babies who are slow to react to a variety of everyday experiences. If the infant is extremely unresponsive, the low NBAS score may indicate brain damage or other neurological problems. If the baby has good reflexes but is sluggish or irritable when responding to social stimuli, it is possible that he will not receive enough playful stimulation and comforting in the months ahead to develop secure emotional ties to caregivers. So a low NBAS score provides a warning that problems could arise. Fortunately, the NBAS can also be used to help parents of these socially unresponsive infants get off to a good start with their babies, as shown in Box 4.3.

Labor and Delivery Medication

In the United States, as many as 95% of mothers receive some kind of drug (and often several) while giving birth. These drugs may include analgesics and anesthetics to reduce pain, sedatives to relax the mother, and stimulants to induce or intensify uterine con-

Table 4.4 The Apgar Test

	Score		
Characteristic	**0**	**1**	**2**
Heart rate	Absent	Slow (fewer than 100 beats per minute)	Over 100 beats per minute
Respiratory effort	Absent	Slow or irregular	Good; baby is crying
Muscle tone	Flaccid, limp	Weak, some flexion	Strong, active motion
Color	Blue or pale	Body pink, extremities blue	Completely pink
Reflex irritability	No response	Frown, grimace, or weak cry	Vigorous cries, coughs, sneezes

Apgar test
a quick assessment of the newborn's heart rate, respiration, color, muscle tone, and reflexes that is used to gauge perinatal stress and to determine whether a neonate requires immediate medical assistance.

Neonatal Behavior Assessment Scale (NBAS)
a test that assesses a neonate's neurological integrity and responsiveness to environmental stimuli.

APPLYING DEVELOPMENTAL RESEARCH

Helping Parents and Newborns to Get to Know Each Other

Babies who are extremely irritable or are unresponsive and apathetic can be very unpleasant companions who fail to elicit enough attention and comforting to foster the development of a warm, loving emotional bond with their parents. However, T. Berry Brazelton (1979) believes that many such adverse emotional outcomes can be prevented if parents of these "high-risk" newborns are shown how to stimulate and comfort their babies properly.

One simple method of teaching parents how to interact with their babies is to have them either watch or take part as the NBAS is administered to their child. The NBAS is well-suited as a teaching device because it is designed to elicit many of the infant's most pleasing characteristics, such as smiling, vocalizing, and gazing. As the test proceeds, parents will see that their baby can respond positively to other people, and they will also learn how to elicit these pleasant interactions.

NBAS training has proved to be an effective strategy indeed. Mothers of high-risk children who have observed the NBAS become more responsive in face-to-face interactions with their babies. In addition, their infants score higher on the NBAS 1 month later than do high-risk infants whose mothers were not trained (Widmayer & Field, 1980).

Other research (see Myers, 1982; Worobey, 1985) indicates that NBAS training even has positive effects on the parents of healthy, responsive infants. In Barbara Myer's (1982) study, parents in a treatment group were taught to give the NBAS to their neonates, whereas parents in a control group received no such training. When tested 4 weeks later, parents who had received the NBAS training were more knowledgeable about infant behavior, more confident in their caregiving abilities, and more satisfied with their infants than were control parents. In addition, fathers who had been trained were much more involved in caring for their infants at home than were the fathers who had received no training.

Although many hospitals provide brief instructions on how to diaper and bathe a baby, parents are seldom told anything about the newborn's basic behavioral abilities, such as whether she can see, hear, or carry on meaningful social dialogues with other people. NBAS training clearly illustrates what a new baby is capable of doing, and it appears to have a number of positive effects on both parents and their infants. This brief intervention does not always accomplish wonders (see Belsky, 1985); more intensive and longer-term interventions may be necessary for families experiencing a lot of stress (Britt & Myers, 1994). Nevertheless, NBAS training appears to be a good way to help start parents and babies on the right foot. As Barbara Myers (1982) points out, "the treatment is relatively inexpensive, it only takes about an hour, and the parents reported enjoying it. This type of intervention needs to be tested (further) on other populations . . . for possible consideration as a routine portion of a hospital's postpartum care" (p. 470).

tractions. Obviously, these agents are administered in the hope of making the birth process easier for the mother, and their use is often essential to save a baby's life in a complicated delivery. However, a strong dose of birth medications can have some undesirable consequences.

Mothers who receive large amounts of anesthesia, for example, are often less sensitive to uterine contractions and do not push effectively during the delivery. As a result, their babies may have to be pulled from the birth canal with *obstetrical forceps* (a device that resembles a pair of salad tongs) or a *vacuum extractor* (a plastic suction cup attached to the baby's head). Unfortunately, in a small number of cases, application of these devices to a baby's soft skull can cause cranial bleeding and brain damage (Brockington, 1996).

Labor and delivery medications also cross the placenta and, in heavy doses, can make babies lethargic and inattentive. Infants of heavily medicated mothers smile infrequently, become irritable when aroused, and are difficult to feed or cuddle in the first weeks of life (Brackbill, McManus, & Woodward, 1985). Some researchers fear that parents could fail to become very involved with or attached to such a sluggish, irritable, and inattentive baby (Murray et al., 1981). Others have even claimed that some babies of heavily medicated mothers continue to show deficits in physical and mental development for at least a year after birth (Brackbill et al., 1985), although other researchers have not been able to replicate these long-term effects (Friedman & Polifka, 1996).

So are mothers best advised to avoid all labor and delivery medications? Probably not. Some women are at risk of birth complications because they are small or are delivering large fetuses, and drugs given in appropriate doses can ease their discomfort

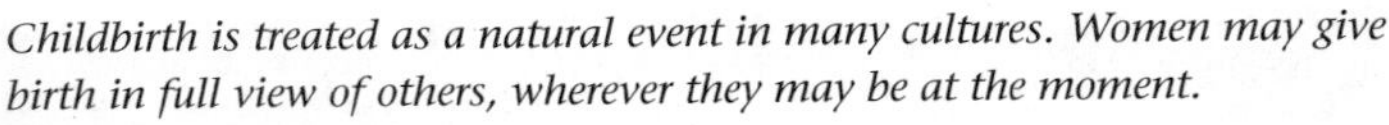

Childbirth is treated as a natural event in many cultures. Women may give birth in full view of others, wherever they may be at the moment.

without disrupting the delivery. In addition, doctors today are more likely than those of the past to use less toxic drugs in smaller doses at the safest times, so that taking medications is not as risky as it once was (Simpson & Creehan, 1996). Yet, in light of the uncertainties about the long-term consequences of obstetric medications for newborns, women and their doctors should still carefully weigh the pros and cons of their use and limit them whenever possible.

Alternative Approaches to Childbirth

Although nearly 99% of all babies in the United States are born in a hospital to a mother in bed, the majority of infants in many cultures are still born at home, often with the mother in a vertical or squatting position, surrounded by family members and assisted by other women (Philpott, 1995; Mead & Newton, 1967). And cultures clearly differ in the rituals surrounding birth (Steinberg, 1996). Among the Pokot people of Kenya, cultural rituals help to ensure strong social support of the birth mother (O'Dempsey, 1988). The whole community celebrates the coming birth, and the father-to-be must stop hunting and be available to support his wife. A midwife, assisted by female relatives, delivers the baby. The placenta is then ceremoniously buried in the goat enclosure, and the baby is given a tribal potion for its health. Mothers are secluded for a month to recover and are given 3 months, free of other chores, to devote themselves to their babies (Jeffery & Jeffery, 1993). By contrast, childbirth is viewed as shameful in Uttar Predesh in Northern India. Babies are delivered by poorly paid attendants, who discourage a mother's cries of pain and offer little social support. The mother is isolated for days after a birth, and her "dirty" baby's head is shaved to avoid "polluting" others.

Interestingly, hospital birthing is a relatively recent practice; before 1900, only 5 to 10% of U.S. babies were born in a hospital to a heavily medicated mother who was flat on her back with her legs in stirrups. Today, many parents favor a return to the practice of viewing birth as a natural family event rather than a medical crisis to be managed with high technology (Brockington, 1996). And women today have considerably more freedom to give birth as they choose.

Natural or Prepared Childbirth

The **natural,** or **prepared, childbirth** movement is a philosophy based on the idea that childbirth is a normal and natural part of life rather than a painful ordeal that women should fear. The natural childbirth movement arose from the work of Grantly Dick-Read, in England, and Fernand Lamaze in France. These two obstetricians claimed that most women could give birth quite comfortably, without medication, if they had been taught to associate childbirth with pleasant feelings and to ready themselves for the process by learning exercises, breathing methods, and relaxation techniques that make childbirth easier (Dick-Read, 1933/1972; Lamaze, 1958).

natural, or prepared, childbirth
a delivery in which physical and psychological preparations for the birth are stressed and medical assistance is minimized.

Parents who decide on a prepared childbirth usually attend classes for 6 to 8 weeks before the delivery. They learn what to expect during labor and may even visit a delivery room and become familiar with procedures used there as part of their preparation. They are also given a prescribed set of exercises and relaxation techniques to master. Typically, the father (or another companion) acts as a coach to assist the mother in toning her muscles and perfecting her breathing for labor. The birthing partner is also encouraged to support the mother during the delivery.

Research reveals that there are many benefits to natural childbirth, not least of which is the important social support mothers receive from their spouses and other close companions. When mothers attend childbirth classes regularly and have a companion present in the delivery room to assist and encourage them, they experience less pain during delivery, use less medication, and have more positive attitudes toward themselves, their babies, and the whole birth experience (Brockington, 1996; Wilcock, Kobayashi, & Murray, 1997). As a result, many more physicians now routinely recommend natural childbirth to their patients.

Home Births

A small but growing number of families are largely rejecting the medical model of childbirth, opting instead to deliver their babies at home with the aid of a certified nurse–midwife trained in nonsurgical obstetrics. They believe that home deliveries will reduce the mother's fear and offer maximum social support by encouraging friends and family to be there, rather than a host of unfamiliar nurses, aides, and physicians. They are also hoping to reduce their reliance on labor and delivery medications and other unnecessary and potentially harmful medical interventions. Indeed, it appears that the relaxed atmosphere and the social support available at a home delivery does have a calming effect on many mothers. Women who deliver at home have shorter labors and use less medication than those who deliver in hospitals (Beard & Chapple, 1995; Brackbill et al., 1985).

alternative birth center
a hospital birthing room or other independent facility that provides a homelike atmosphere for childbirth but still makes medical technology available.

Are home births as safe as hospital deliveries? Childbirth statistics from many countries suggest that they are, as long as the mother is healthy, the pregnancy has gone smoothly, and the birth is attended by a well-trained midwife (Ackermann-Liebrich et al., 1996). And there are other options for couples who seek a more comfortable homelike birth environment. Many hospitals have created birthing rooms, or **alternative birth centers,** that provide a homelike atmosphere but still make medical technology available. Yet other free-standing birth centers operate independently of hospitals and employ certified nurse-midwives (Beard & Chappell, 1995). In either case, spouses, friends, and often even the couple's children can be present during labor, and healthy infants can remain in the same room with their mothers (rooming-in) rather than spending their first days in the hospital nursery. So far, the evidence suggests that giving birth in well-run alternative birth centers is no more risky to healthy mothers and their babies than hospital deliveries are (Fullerton & Severino, 1992; Harvey et al., 1996). However, mothers at risk for birth complications are always best advised to deliver in a hospital, where life-saving technologies are immediately available should they be needed.

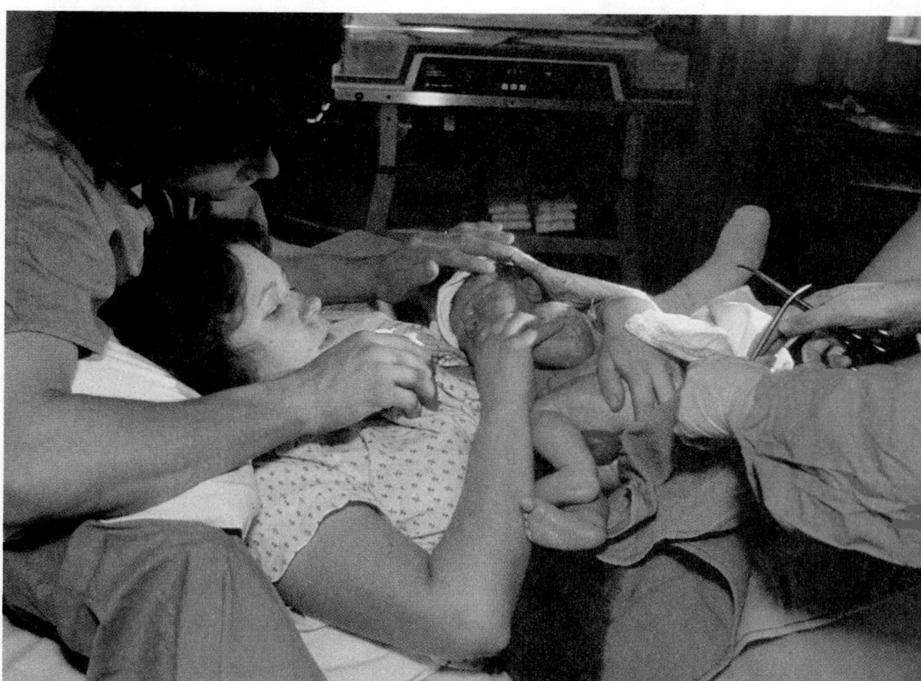

More women today are choosing to give birth at home or in alternative birth centers to share the joy of childbirth with family members. When assisted by a well-trained midwife, healthy women can give birth safely at home.

The Social Environment Surrounding Birth

Only 20 years ago, most hospitals barred fathers from delivery rooms and whisked babies away from their mothers to nurseries within minutes of a delivery. However, times have changed so that a birth today is much more likely to be a dramatic experience for both parents.

The Mother's Experience

The first few minutes after birth can be a special time for a mother to thoroughly enjoy her baby, provided she is given the opportunity. Marshall Klaus and John Kennell believe that the first 6 to 12 hours after birth are a *sensitive period* for **emotional bonding** when the mother is especially ready to respond to and develop a strong sense of affection for her baby (Kennell, Voos, & Klaus, 1979). In a study testing this hypothesis, Klaus and Kennell (1976) had half of a group of new mothers follow then-traditional hospital routine: They saw their babies briefly after delivery, visited with them 6 to 12 hours later, and had half-hour feeding sessions every 4 hours thereafter for the remainder of a 3-day hospital stay. By contrast, mothers in an "extended-contact" group were permitted 5 extra hours a day to cuddle their babies, including an hour of skin-to-skin contact that took place within 3 hours of birth.

In a follow-up 1 month later, mothers who had had early extended contact with their babies appeared to be more involved with them and held them closer during feeding sessions than did mothers who had followed the traditional hospital routine. One year later, the extended-contact mothers were still the more highly involved group of caregivers, and their 1-year-olds outperformed those in the traditional-routine group on tests of physical and mental development. Apparently, extended early contact in the hospital fostered mothers' affection for their newborns which, in turn, may have motivated those mothers to continue to interact in highly stimulating ways with their babies. In response to this and other similar studies, many hospitals have altered their routines to allow the kinds of early contact that can promote emotional bonding.

Does this mean that mothers who have no early contact with their newborns miss out on forming the strongest possible emotional ties to them? No, it does not! Later research has shown that early-contact effects are nowhere near as significant or long-lasting as Klaus and Kennell presumed (Eyer, 1992; Goldberg, 1983). Other research reveals that most adoptive parents, who rarely have any early contact with their infants, nevertheless develop strong emotional bonds with their adoptees that are just as secure, on average, as those seen in nonadoptive homes (Levy-Shiff, Goldschmidt, & Har-Even, 1991; Singer et al., 1985). So even though early contact can be a very pleasant experience that can help a mother *begin* to form an emotional bond to her child, she need not fear that problems will arise should something prevent her from having this experience.

Postpartum Depression. Unfortunately, there is a downside to the birth experience for some mothers, who may find themselves depressed, tearful, irritable, and even resentful of their babies shortly after birth. Milder forms of this condition, called the *maternity blues,* may characterize as many as 40 to 60% of all new mothers (Kessel, 1995). This mild depression, which usually passes within a matter of a week or two, is probably linked to hormonal changes following childbirth and to stresses associated with the new responsibilities of parenthood (Brockington, 1996).

By contrast, slightly more than 10% of new mothers don't bounce back so quickly, experiencing instead a more serious depressive reaction, called **postpartum depression,** that can last for months. Most victims of postpartum depression have a history of depressive episodes and are experiencing other life stresses beyond those associated with becoming a new mother (Brockington, 1996; Whiffen, 1992). Lack of social support—particularly a poor relationship with the father—dramatically increases the odds of postpartum depression (Field et al., 1985; Gotlib et al., 1991). Susan Campbell and her associates (1992) find

emotional bonding
term used to describe the strong affectionate ties that parents may feel toward their infant; some theorists believe that the strongest bonding occurs shortly after birth, during a sensitive period.

postpartum depression
strong feelings of sadness, resentment, and despair that may affect the mother shortly after childbirth and that can linger for months.

that many of these depressed women did not want their infants in the first place and perceived them as difficult babies. They also interacted less positively with their infants and in some cases seemed downright hostile toward them. Other studies suggest that, when a mother remains chronically depressed, withdrawn, and unresponsive, the attachment that develops between her and her infant is likely to be insecure, and infants may develop depressive symptoms and behavior problems of their own (Campbell, Cohn, & Myers, 1995; Murray, Fiori-Cowley, & Hooper, 1996). For their own sake and for the sake of their infants, then, mothers experiencing more than a mild case of the maternity blues should seek professional help.

This father displays a fascination with his newborn that is known as engrossment.

The Father's Experience

Fathers, like mothers, experience the birth process as a significant life event that involves a mix of positive and negative emotions. New fathers interviewed in one recent study admitted that their fears mounted during labor, but said that they tried hard to appear calm nonetheless. Although they described childbirth as an agonizing and stressful ordeal, their negative emotions usually gave way to relief, pride, and joy when the baby finally arrived (Chandler & Field, 1997).

Like new mothers, new fathers often display a sense of **engrossment** with the baby—an intense fascination with and a strong desire to touch, hold, and caress this newest member of the family (Greenberg & Morris, 1974; Peterson, Mehl, & Liederman, 1979). One young father put it this way: "When I came up to see (my) wife . . . I go look at the kid and then I pick her up and put her down. . . . I keep going back to the kid. It's like a magnet. That's what I can't get over, the fact that I feel like that" (Greenberg & Morris, 1974, p. 524). Some studies find that fathers who have handled and helped care for their babies in the hospital spend more time with them at home than fathers who have not had these early contacts with their newborns (Greenberg & Morris, 1974). Other studies have failed to find these long-term effects on father–infant interactions but suggest that early contact with a newborn can make fathers feel closer to their partners and more a part of the family (Palkovitz, 1985). So a father who is present at birth not only plays an important supportive role for the mother, but is just as likely as the mother to enjoy close contact with their newborn.

WHAT DO YOU THINK? ?

Design the perfect birth experience for you and your baby, Where would you be? Who would be there? What would be done to make things as pleasant as possible for all participants in the process?

BIRTH COMPLICATIONS

Childbirth does not always proceed as smoothly as indicated in our earlier account of the "normal" delivery. Three birth complications that can adversely influence a baby's development are anoxia (oxygen deprivation), a premature delivery, and low birth weight.

Anoxia

Nearly 1% of babies are born showing signs of **anoxia,** or oxygen deprivation. In many cases, the child's supply of oxygen is interrupted because the umbilical cord has become tangled or squeezed during childbirth, as can easily happen when infants are lying in

engrossment
paternal analogue of maternal emotional bonding; term used to describe fathers' fascination with their neonates, including their desire to touch, hold, caress, and talk to the newborn baby.

anoxia
a lack of sufficient oxygen to the brain; may result in neurological damage or death.

the **breech position** and are born feet or buttocks first. In fact, breech babies are often delivered by cesarean section to protect against anoxia (Lin, 1993a). Other cases of anoxia occur when the placenta separates prematurely, interrupting the supply of food and oxygen to the fetus. Anoxia can also happen after birth if sedatives given to the mother cross the placental barrier and interfere with the baby's breathing or if mucus ingested during childbirth becomes lodged in the baby's throat. Although newborns can tolerate oxygen deprivation far longer than older children and adults can, permanent brain damage can result if breathing is delayed for more than 3 to 4 minutes (Nelson, 1995).

Another potential cause of anoxia is a genetic incompatibility between an RH-positive fetus, who has a protein called **RH factor** in its blood, and an RH-negative mother, who lacks this substance. During labor and delivery when the placenta is deteriorating, RH-negative mothers are often exposed to the blood of their RH-positive fetuses, and they begin to produce RH antibodies. If these antibodies enter a fetus's bloodstream, they can attack red blood cells, depleting oxygen and possibly producing brain damage and other birth defects. Firstborns are usually not affected because an RH-negative mother has no RH antibodies until she gives birth to an RH-positive child. Fortunately, problems stemming from an RH incompatibility can now be prevented by administering *rhogam* after the delivery, a vaccine that prevents the RH-negative mother from forming the RH antibodies that could harm her next RH-positive baby.

Children who experience mild anoxia are often irritable at birth and may score below average on tests of motor and mental development throughout the first 3 years (Sameroff & Chandler, 1975). However, these differences between mildly anoxic and normal children become smaller and smaller and are usually not detectible by age 7 (Corah et al., 1965). So even though *prolonged* oxygen deprivation can cause neurological damage and permanent disabilities, there is no compelling evidence that *mild* anoxia has any lasting effects on children's motor skills or intellectual development (Vaughn et al., 1984).

Complications of Low Birth Weight

More than 90% of babies in the United States are born between the 37th and 42nd weeks of pregnancy and are considered "timely." The average full-term, or "timely," infant is 19 to 21 inches long and weighs about 3500 grams (7½ pounds).

The remaining 7 to 8% of babies weigh less than 2,500 grams (5½ pounds) at birth (Austin & Moawad, 1993) and, until recently, were simply labeled "premature." Yet there are actually two kinds of low-birth-weight babies. Most are born more than 3 weeks before their due dates and are called **preterm infants.** Although small in size, the body weights of these babies are often appropriate for the amount of time they spent in the womb. Other low-birth-weight babies, called **small for date,** have experienced slow growth as fetuses and are seriously underweight, even when born close to their normal due dates. Although both kinds of low-birth-weight babies are vulnerable and may have to struggle to survive, small-for-date infants are at greater risk of serious complications. For example, they are more likely to die during the first year or to show signs of brain damage. They are also more likely than preterm infants to remain small in stature throughout childhood, to experience learning difficulties and behavior problems at school, and to perform poorly on IQ tests (Goldenberg, 1995; Lin, 1993b).

What are the causes of low birth weight? We have already seen that mothers who smoke and drink heavily or use drugs or who are malnourished are likely to deliver undersized babies. Indeed, low-income women from ethnic minority groups are particularly at risk, largely because their diets and the prenatal care they receive are often inadequate (Kopp & Kaler, 1989; Lin, 1993b). Moreover, illnesses or accidents that impair the functioning of the placenta can retard fetal growth and result in a baby who is preterm or small for date. Yet another frequent contributor to undersized babies is multiple births. Multiple fetuses generally gain much less weight than a singleton after the

breech birth
a delivery in which the fetus emerges feet or buttocks first rather than head first.

RH factor
a blood protein that, when present in a fetus but not the mother, can cause the mother to produce antibodies. These antibodies may then attack the red blood cells of subsequent fetuses who have the protein in their blood.

preterm babies
infants born more than 3 weeks before their normal due dates.

small-for-date babies
infants whose birth weight is far below normal, even when born close to their normal due dates.

29th week of pregnancy. And in addition to being small for date, triplets and quadruplets rarely develop to term in the uterus; in fact, they are often born 5 to 8 weeks early (Papiernik, 1995).

Short-term Consequences of Low Birth Weight

The most trying task for a low-birth-weight baby is simply surviving the first few days of life. Although more of these infants are surviving each year, at least half of those who weigh less than 1,000 grams (2.2 pounds) die at birth or shortly thereafter, even in the best hospitals (see Table 4.5). Small-for-date babies are often malformed, undernourished, or genetically abnormal—factors that will hinder them as they struggle to survive. Moreover, preterm infants are likely to experience a number of additional problems as a consequence of their general immaturity. Their most serious difficulty is breathing. A preterm infant often has very little *surfactin,* a substance that normally coats the lungs during the last 3 to 4 weeks of pregnancy to prevent them from collapsing. A deficiency of surfactin may result in **respiratory distress syndrome,** a serious respiratory ailment in which the affected child breathes very irregularly and may stop breathing altogether.

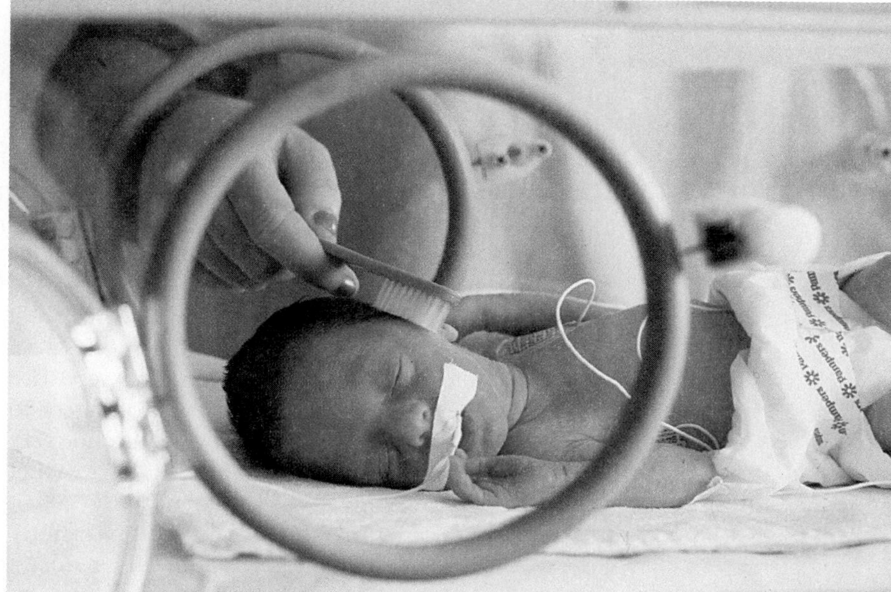

Isolettes do isolate. The holes in the apparatus allow parents and hospital staff to care for, talk to, and touch the baby, but close, tender cuddling is nearly impossible.

Preterm infants often spend their first few weeks of life in heated *isolettes* that maintain their body temperature and protect them from infection. Isolettes are aptly named because they do isolate; the infant is fed, cleaned, and changed through a hole in the device that is much too small to allow visiting parents to cuddle and love their baby in the usual way. Furthermore, preterm infants can try the patience of caregivers. Compared with full-term infants, they are slow to initiate social interactions and often respond to a parent's bids for attention by looking away or actively resisting such overtures (Lester, Hoffman, & Brazelton, 1985; Malatesta et al., 1986). Mothers of preterm infants often remark that their babies are "hard to read," and they are likely to become rather frustrated as their persistent attempts to carry on a social dialogue are apparently rebuffed by an aloof, fussy, squirming little companion (Lester et al., 1985). Indeed preterm infants are at risk of forming less secure emotional ties to their caregivers than

Table 4.5 Infant Mortality as a Function of Birth Weight

	Birth weight: Grams	Birth weight: Pounds	Percentage of babies who die
Very low birth weight	500–749	1 lb, 9 oz or less	67
	750–999	1 lb, 10 oz–2 lb, 3 oz	33
	1,000–1,249	2 lb, 4 oz–2 lb, 12 oz	16
Low birth weight	1,249–1,499	2 lb, 13 oz–3 lb, 4 oz	9
	1,500–2,500	3 lb, 5 oz–5 lb, 8 oz	6
Average birth weight	2,500–3,000	5 lb, 9 oz–6 lb, 9 oz	2
	3,001–4,500	6 lb, 10 oz–9 lb, 14 oz	1

Source: Based on Lin, 1993b.

respiratory distress syndrome
a serious condition in which a preterm infant breathes very irregularly and is at risk of dying (also called *hyaline membrane disease*).

other babies do (Mangelsdorf et al., 1996; Wille, 1991); and although the vast majority of them are never mistreated, they are more likely than full-term infants to become targets of child abuse (Brockington, 1996).

Interventions for Preterm Infants

Twenty years ago, hospitals permitted parents little if any contact with preterm infants for fear of harming these fragile little creatures. Today, parents are encouraged to visit their child often in the hospital and to become actively involved during their visits by touching, caressing, and talking to their baby. The objective of these early-acquaintance programs is to allow parents to get to know their child and to foster the development of positive emotional ties. But there may be important additional benefits, for babies in intensive care often become less irritable and more responsive and show quicker neurological and mental development if they are periodically rocked, stroked, massaged, or soothed by the sound of a mother's voice (Barnard & Bee, 1983; Scafidi et al., 1986, 1990; Schaefer, Hatcher, & Barglow, 1980).

Preterm and other low-birth-weight babies can also benefit from programs that teach their parents how to provide them with sensitive and responsive care at home. In one study, a pediatric nurse visited periodically with mothers and taught them how to read and respond appropriately to the atypical behaviors their preterm infants displayed. Although the intervention lasted only 3 months, the low-birth-weight infants whose mothers participated had caught up intellectually with normal-birth-weight peers by the age of 4 (Achenbach et al., 1990). And when combined with stimulating daycare programs, parental interventions not only foster the cognitive growth of low-birth-weight children, but can reduce the likelihood of their displaying behavioral disturbances as well (Brooks-Gunn et al., 1993; Spiker, Ferguson, & Brooks-Gunn, 1993). These interventions are most effective when they continue into the grade-school years (Bradley et al., 1994; McCarton et al., 1997).

Of course, not all low-birth-weight infants (or their parents) have opportunities to participate in successful interventions. What happens to them?

Long-term Consequences of Low Birth Weight

Before 1975, many researchers had reported that preterm and other low-birth-weight infants were likely to experience more learning difficulties later in childhood, score lower on IQ tests, and suffer more emotional problems than normal-birth-weight infants (Caputo & Mandell, 1970; Drillien, 1969). Today, we know that these conclusions are overstated and that the long-term prognosis for low-birth-weight children depends largely on the environment in which they are raised. Outcomes are likely to be especially good when mothers are knowledgeable about the factors that promote healthy development. These mothers are likely to be highly involved with their children and to create a stimulating home environment that fosters cognitive and emotional growth (Benasich & Brooks-Gunn, 1996; Caughy, 1996). By contrast, low-birth-weight children from less stable or economically disadvantaged families are likely to remain smaller in stature than full-term children, experience more emotional problems, and show some long-term deficits in intellectual performance and academic achievement (Baker & Mednik, 1994; Kopp & Kaler, 1989; Rose & Feldman, 1996).

Consider what Ronald Wilson (1985) found in his study of developing twins. Although twins are generally small for date and are often preterm, Wilson focused closely on twins who were especially small at birth (weighing under 1,750 grams, or less than 3¾ pounds). In Figure 4.9, we see that these preterm, low-birth-weight babies were indeed below average in mental performance throughout the first 3 years of life (a score of 100 on the test reflects average intellectual performance). Yet, the figure also shows that low-birth-weight twins from middle-class (high SES) homes eventually made up their intellectual deficits, scoring average (or slightly above) on the tests by age 6, whereas their counterparts from low-income (low SES) backgrounds remained substan-

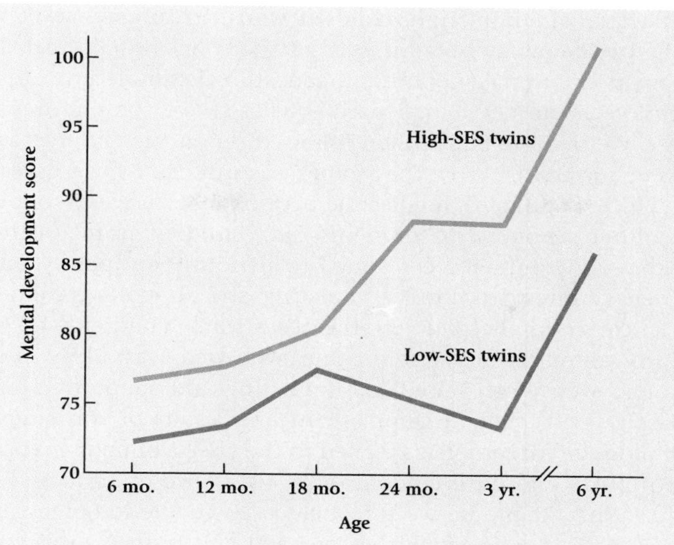

Figure 4.9 *Age trends in intellectual development for low-birth-weight twins from middle-class (high-SES) and lower socioeconomic (low-SES) backgrounds.* ADAPTED FROM WILSON, *1985.*

tially below average in their intellectual performance. So the long-term prognosis for preterm and small-for-date children seems to depend very critically on the *postnatal environment* in which they are raised.

Reproductive Risk and Capacity for Recovery

We have now discussed many examples of what can go wrong during the prenatal and perinatal periods, as well as some steps that expectant parents can take to try to prevent such outcomes (see, for example, Box 4.3). Once they occur, some of these damaging effects are irreversible; a baby blinded by rubella, for example, will never regain its sight, and a child who is mentally retarded from fetal alcohol syndrome or severe anoxia will always be mentally retarded. And yet, there are many adults who turned out perfectly normal even though their mothers smoked, drank, or contracted harmful diseases while pregnant or received heavy doses of medication while in labor and childbirth. Why is this? As we have already emphasized, not all embryos, fetuses, and newborns who are exposed to teratogens and other early hazards are affected by them. But what about those who are affected? Is it possible that many of these infants will eventually overcome their early handicaps later in life?

Indeed it is, and we now have some excellent longitudinal studies to tell us so. In 1955, Emmy Werner and Ruth Smith began to follow the development of all 670 babies born that year on the Hawaiian island of Kauai. At birth, 16% of these infants showed moderate to severe complications, another 31% showed mild complications, and 53% appeared normal and healthy. When the babies were reexamined at age 2, there was a clear relationship between severity of birth complications and developmental progress: The more severe their birth complications, the more likely children were to be lagging in their social and intellectual development. However, effects of the postnatal environment were already apparent. In homes rated high in emotional support and

Concept Check 4.3
Perinatal Influences

Check your understanding of some potentially important perinatal influences by matching the events listed below with the following *possible* consequences: (a) cranial bleeding, (b) emotional bonding/engrossment, (c) respiratory distress syndrome, (d) NBAS training, (e) RH incompatibility, (f) natural (or prepared) childbirth.

_____ 1. improvements in parent–infant interactions
_____ 2. delivery by obstetrical forceps
_____ 3. preterm delivery
_____ 4. anoxia in later-born children
_____ 5. can make the birth process easier
_____ 6. close contact with newborn

educational stimulation, children who had suffered severe birth complications scored slightly below average on tests of social and intellectual development. But in homes low in emotional support and educational stimulation, the intellectual performance of children who had experienced equally severe complications was *far* below average.

Werner and Smith then followed up on the children at ages 10 and 18, and again as young adults. What they found was striking. By age 10, early complications no longer predicted children's intellectual performance very well, but certain characteristics of the children's home environments did. Children from unstimulating and unresponsive home environments continued to perform very poorly on intelligence tests, whereas their counterparts from stimulating and supportive homes showed no marked deficiencies in intellectual performance. Clearly, children who had suffered the most severe early complications were the ones who were least likely to overcome their initial handicaps, even when raised in stimulating and supportive homes (see also Bendersky & Lewis, 1994). But in summarizing the results of this study, Werner and Smith noted that long-term problems related to the effects of poor environments outnumbered those attributable to birth complications by a ratio of 10 to 1.

What, then, are we to conclude about the long-term implications of reproductive risk? First, we do know that prenatal and birth complications can leave lasting scars, particularly if these insults are severe. Yet, the longitudinal data we have reviewed suggest ample reason for optimism should you ever give birth to a frail, irritable, unresponsive baby that is abnormal in its appearance or behavior. Given a supportive and stimulating home environment in which to grow, and the unconditional love of at least one caregiver, a majority of these children will display a strong "self-righting" tendency and eventually overcome their initial handicaps (Werner & Smith, 1992).

THE NEWBORN'S READINESS FOR LIFE

In the past, newborns were often characterized as fragile and helpless little organisms who were simply not very well-prepared for life outside the womb. This view may once have been highly adaptive, helping to ease parents' grief in earlier eras when medical procedures were rather primitive and a fair percentage of newborns did die. Even today, "many cultures in which the [newborn] death rate is high still institutionalize such practices as not speaking of the newborn as a [human] . . . or not naming him until he is 3 months old and more likely to survive" (Brazelton, 1979, p. 35).

Today, we know that newborns are much better prepared for life than many doctors, parents, and developmentalists had initially assumed. In Chapter 6, for example, we will see that all of a newborn's senses are in good working order and that she sees and hears well enough to detect what is happening around her and respond adaptively to many of these sensations. Very young infants are also quite capable of learning and can even remember some of the particularly vivid experiences they have had.

Two other indications that neonates are "organized" creatures who are quite well-adapted for life are their repertoire of inborn reflexes and their predictable patterns, or cycles, of daily activity.

Newborn Reflexes

reflex
an unlearned and automatic response to a stimulus or class of stimuli.

survival reflexes
inborn responses such as breathing, sucking, and swallowing that enable the newborn to adapt to the environment.

One of the neonate's greatest strengths is a full set of useful reflexes. A **reflex** is an involuntary and automatic response to a stimulus, as when the eye automatically blinks in response to a puff of air. Table 4.6 describes some reflexes that healthy newborns display. Some of these graceful and complex patterns of behavior are called **survival**

Table 4.6	Major Reflexes Present in Full-Term Neonates		
Name	**Response**	**Development and course**	**Significance**
Survival reflexes			
Breathing reflex	Repetitive inhalation and expiration.	Permanent	Provides oxygen and expels carbon dioxide.
Eye-blink reflex	Closing or blinking the eyes.	Permanent	Protects the eyes from bright light or foreign objects.
Pupillary reflex	Constriction of pupils to bright light; dilation to dark or dimly lit surroundings.	Permanent	Protects against bright lights; adapts the visual system to low illumination.
Rooting reflex	Turning the head in the direction of a tactile (touch) stimulus to the cheek.	Disappears over the first few weeks of life and is replaced by voluntary head turning.	Orients baby to the breast or bottle.
Sucking reflex	Sucking on objects placed (or taken) into the mouth.	Permanent	Allows baby to take in nutrients.
Swallowing reflex	Swallowing	Permanent	Allows baby to take in nutrients.
Primitive reflexes			
Babinski reflex	Fanning and then curling the toes when the bottom of the foot is stroked.	Usually disappears within the first 8 months–1 year of life.	Its presence at birth and disappearance in the first year are an indication of normal neurological development.
Palmar grasping reflex	Curling of the fingers around objects (such as a finger) that touch the baby's palm.	Disappears in first 3–4 months and is then replaced by a voluntary grasp.	Its presence at birth and later disappearance are an indication of normal neurological development.
Moro reflex	A loud noise or sudden change in the position of the baby's head will cause the baby to throw his or her arms outward, arch the back, and then bring the arms toward each other as if to hold onto something.	The arm movements and arching of the back disappear over the first 4–6 months; however, the child continues to react to unexpected noises or a loss of bodily support by showing a startle reflex (which does not disappear).	Its presence at birth and later disappearance are indications of normal neurological development.
Swimming reflex	An infant immersed in water will display active movements of the arms and legs and involuntarily hold his or her breath (thus giving the body buoyancy); this swimming reflex will keep an infant afloat for some time, allowing easy rescue.	Disappears in the first 4–6 months.	Its presence at birth and later disappearance are an indication of normal neurological development.
Stepping reflex	Infants held upright so that their feet touch a flat surface will step as if to walk.	Disappears in the first 8 weeks unless the infant has regular opportunities to practice this response.	Its presence at birth and later disappearance are an indication of normal neurological development.

Note: Preterm infants may show little or no evidence of primitive reflexes at birth, and their survival reflexes are likely to be weak. However, the missing primitive reflexes typically appear soon after birth and disappear a little later than they do among full-term infants.

reflexes because they have clear adaptive value. Examples include the breathing reflex, the eye-blink reflex (which protects the eyes against bright lights or foreign particles), and the sucking and swallowing reflexes, by which the infant takes in food. Also implicated in feeding is the *rooting* reflex: An infant who is touched on the cheek will turn in that direction and search for something to suck.

Not only do survival reflexes offer some protection against aversive stimulation and enable an infant to satisfy very basic needs, but they may also have a very positive impact on caregivers. Mothers, for example, may feel quite gratified and competent as

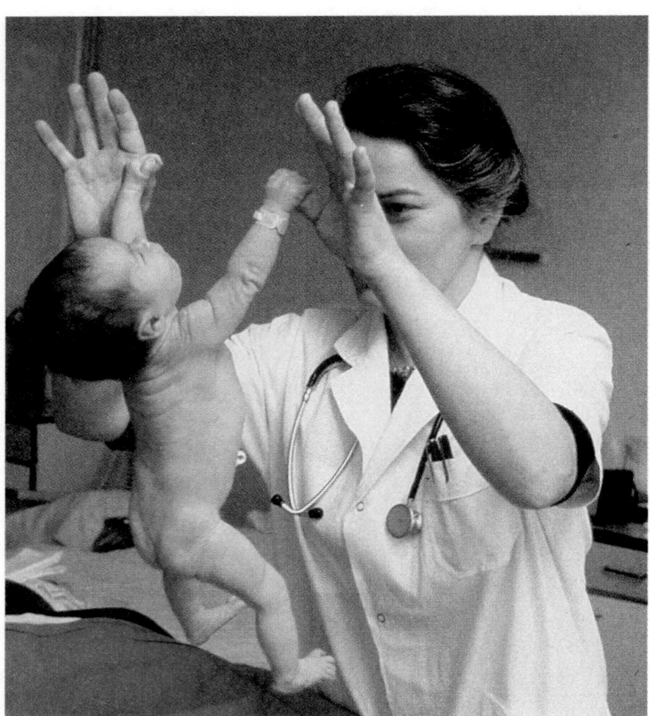

The newborn's grasping reflex is quite strong, often allowing them to support their own weight.

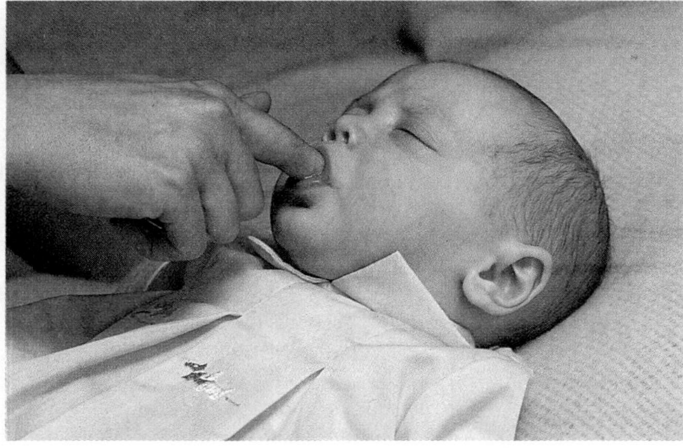

This infant illustrates the rhythmical sucking, or sucking reflex, *that neonates display when objects are placed into their mouths.*

caregivers when their hungry babies immediately stop fussing and suck easily and rhythmically at the nipple. And few parents can resist the feeling that their baby enjoys being close when he grasps their fingers tightly as his palm is touched. So if these survival reflexes help to endear infants to older companions, who can protect them and attend to their needs (Bowlby, 1969; 1988).

Other so-called **primitive reflexes** in the table are not nearly as useful; in fact, many are believed to be remnants of our evolutionary history that have outlived their original purpose. The *Babinski reflex* is a good example. Why would it be adaptive for infants to fan their toes when the bottoms of their feet are stroked? We don't know. Other primitive reflexes may still have some adaptive value, at least in some cultures (Bowlby, 1969; Fentress & McLeod, 1986). The *swimming reflex,* for example, may help keep afloat an infant who is accidentally immersed in a pond or a river. And the *grasping reflex* may help infants who are carried in slings or on their mothers' hips to hang on. Finally, other responses, such as the *stepping reflex,* may be forerunners of useful voluntary behaviors that develop later in infancy (Thelen, 1984).

Primitive reflexes normally disappear during the first few months of life. Why? Because they are controlled by the lower "subcortical" areas of the brain and are lost once the higher centers of the cerebral cortex mature and begin to guide voluntary behaviors. But even if many primitive reflexes are not very useful to infants, they are important diagnostic indicators to developmentalists. If these reflexes are *not* present at birth—or if they last too long in infancy—we have reason to suspect that something is wrong with a baby's nervous system.

In sum, a full complement of infant reflexes tells us that newborns are quite prepared to respond adaptively to a variety of life's challenges. And the timely disappearance of certain reflexes is one important sign that a baby's nervous system is developing normally.

Infant States

Newborns also display organized patterns of daily activity that are predictable and foster healthy developmental outcomes. In a typical day (or night), a neonate moves in and out of six **infant states,** or levels of arousal, that are described in Table 4.7. During the first month, a baby may move rapidly from one state to another, as mothers will testify when their wide-awake babies suddenly nod off to sleep in the middle of a feeding. Neonates spend about 70% of their time (16 to 18 hours a day) sleeping and only 2 to 3 hours in the alert, inactive (attentive) state, when they are most receptive to external stimulation (Berg & Berg, 1987; Thoman, 1990). Sleep cycles are typically

primitive reflexes
reflexes controlled by subcortical areas of the brain that gradually disappear over the first year of life.

infant states
levels of sleep and wakefulness that young infants display.

brief, lasting from 45 minutes to 2 hours. These frequent "naps" are separated by periods of drowsiness, alert or inalert activity, and crying, any of which may occur (as red-eyed parents well know) at all hours of the day and night.

The fact that neonates pass through a predictable pattern of states during a typical day suggests that their internal regulatory mechanisms are well-organized. Yet, research on infant states also makes it clear that newborns show a great deal of individuality (Brown, 1964; Thoman & Whitney, 1989). For example, one newborn in one study was alert for only about 15 minutes a day, on average, whereas another was alert for more than 8 hours daily (Brown, 1964). Similarly, one infant cried about 17% of the time, but another spent 39% of its time crying. These differences have some obvious implications for parents, who may find it far more pleasant to be with a bright-eyed baby who rarely cries than with one who is often fussy and inattentive (Columbo & Horowitz, 1987).

Developmental Changes in Infant States

Two of the states in Table 4.7—sleep and crying—show regular patterns of change over the first year and provide important information about the progress a baby is making.

Changes in Sleep

As infants develop, they spend less time sleeping and more time awake, alert, and attending to their surroundings. By age 2 to 6 weeks, babies are sleeping only 14 to 16 hours a day; and somewhere between 3 and 7 months of age, many infants reach a milestone that parents truly appreciate—they begin to sleep through the night and require but two or three shorter naps during the day (Berg & Berg, 1987; St. James-Roberts & Plewis, 1996).

From at least 2 weeks before they are born throughout the first month or two of life, babies spend at least half their sleeping hours in **REM sleep,** a state of active irregular sleep characterized by rapid eye movements (REMs) under their closed eyelids and brain-wave activity more typical of wakefulness than of regular (non-REM) sleep (Groome et al., 1997). However, REM sleep declines steadily after birth and accounts for only 25 to 30% of total sleep for a 6-month-old.

REM sleep
a state of active or irregular sleep in which the eyes move rapidly beneath the eyelids and brain-wave activity is similar to the pattern displayed when awake.

Why do fetuses and newborns spend so much time in REM sleep and why does it decline so dramatically over the first few months? The most widely accepted theory is that this active REM sleep early in life provides fetuses and very young infants, who

Table 4.7 Infant States of Arousal

State	Description	Daily duration in newborn (hours)
Regular sleep	Baby is still, with eyes closed and unmoving. Breathing is slow and regular.	8–9
Irregular sleep	Baby's eyes are closed but can be observed to move under the closed eyelids (a phenomenon known as *rapid eye movements,* or *REMs*). Baby may jerk or grimace in response to stimulation. Breathing may be irregular.	8–9
Drowsiness	Baby is falling asleep or waking up. Eyes open and close and have a glazed appearance when open. Breathing is regular but more rapid than in regular sleep.	1/2–3
Alert inactivity	Baby's eyes are wide open and bright, exploring some aspect of the environment. Breathing is even, and the body is relatively inactive.	2–3
Alert activity	Baby's eyes are open and breathing is irregular. May become fussy and display various bursts of diffuse motor activity.	1–3
Crying	Intense crying that may be difficult to stop and is accompanied by high levels of motor activity.	1–3

SOURCE: Wolff, 1966.

4.4

DEVELOPMENTAL ISSUES

Sudden Infant Death Syndrome

Each year in the United States as many as 8,000 seemingly healthy infants suddenly stop breathing and die in their sleep (Natural Center for Health Statistics, 1992). These deaths are unexpected, unexplained, and classified as examples of Sudden infant death syndrome (SIDS). In industrialized societies, SIDS is the leading cause of infant mortality in the first year of life, accounting for more than one-third of all such deaths (Wise, 1995).

Although the exact cause of SIDS is not known, we do know that preterm and other low-birth-weight babies who had poor Apgar scores and experienced respiratory distress as newborns are most susceptible (Brockington, 1996; Wise, 1995). We have also learned that mothers of SIDS victims are more likely to smoke, to have used such drugs as heroin, methadone, and cocaine, and to have received poor prenatal care (MacGregor & Chasnoff, 1993). Risks associated with smoking are much higher than those associated with maternal drug use. Babies whose caregivers smoke even moderately (that is 9 to 12 cigarettes a day) are two to six times more likely to die of SIDS than infants whose parents do not smoke (Wise, 1995). Even though few babies of smokers succumb to SIDS, the incidence of those tragic crib deaths can still be reduced significantly by simply convincing parents and other caregivers not to smoke around their babies.

SIDS is most likely to occur during the winter months among infants who are 2 to 4 months of age and who have a respiratory infection such as a cold. SIDS victims are also more likely to be sleeping on their stomachs than on their backs, and they are often wrapped tightly in clothing and blankets at the time of their death (Brockington, 1996; Dwyer et al., 1991). Clearly, all these factors can contribute to SIDS. According to Lewis Lipsitt (1979), risk of SIDS is highest at 2 to 4 months of age because this is the time when subcortical reflexes are diminishing in strength and voluntary cortical responses are not yet well-established. So if mucus blocks the nasal passages, as it easily might for a 2- to 4-month-old baby with a cold who is sleeping face down on her stomach, she may not be able to turn over and struggle for a breath because her inborn survival reflexes are waning and her voluntary protective responses to discomfort are weak or nonexistent. In addition to encouraging caregivers not to smoke around babies, intervention programs in Tasmania and England have found that SIDS rates can be reduced dramatically by simply instructing parents not to tightly bundle their babies or place them on their stomachs to sleep (Brockington, 1996).

When SIDS does occur, it has a devastating impact on most families. Parents often feel bitter or extremely guilty over their loss, and siblings may also grieve deeply over the death of a baby brother or sister and begin to display problem behaviors (Brockington, 1996). These families need social support, and, fortunately, parent support groups often help them to cope with their loss. Also available for parents who fear losing another baby is an excellent pamphlet entitled "The Subsequent Child" (available from the National Foundation for Sudden Infant Death, 1501 Broadway, New York, New York 10036) that provides information on the risks involved and helps to allay their concerns.

sleep *so* much, with enough internal stimulation to allow their nervous systems to develop properly. Consistent with this **autostimulation theory** is the finding that babies who are given lots of interesting visual stimuli to explore while awake spend less time in REM sleep than control infants who are denied these experiences (Boismier, 1977). Perhaps the reason REM sleep declines sharply over the first 6 months is that the infant's brain is rapidly maturing, she is becoming more alert, and there is simply less need for the stimulation provided by REM activity.

Few babies have problems establishing regular sleep cycles unless their nervous system is abnormal in some way. Yet one of the major causes of infant mortality is a very perplexing sleep-related disorder called crib death, or **sudden infant death syndrome (SIDS),** which we will examine more carefully in Box 4.4.

The Functions and Course of Crying

A baby's earliest cries are unlearned and involuntary responses to discomfort—distress signals by which he makes caregivers aware of his needs. Most of a newborn's early cries are provoked by such physical discomforts as hunger, pain, or a wet diaper, although chills, loud noises, and even sudden changes in illumination (as when the light over a crib goes off) are often enough to make a baby cry.

An infant's cry is a complex vocal signal that may vary from a soft whimper to piercing shrieks and wails. Although it was once thought that neonates produced

autostimulation theory
a theory proposing that REM sleep in infancy is a form of self-stimulation that helps the central nervous system to develop.

sudden infant death syndrome (SIDS)
the unexplained death of a sleeping infant who suddenly stops breathing (also called *crib death*).

distinctive cries to communicate different needs and that "pain" cries were perceived by parents as the most serious and urgent (Wolff, 1969), later research has challenged this point of view. Experience clearly plays a role in helping adults to determine why an infant may be crying, for parents are better than nonparents at this kind of problem solving, and mothers (who have more contact with infants) are better than fathers are (Holden, 1988). Yet, Philip Zeskind and his associates (1985) found that adults perceive the intense cries of hungry babies as just as arousing and urgent as equally intense "pain" cries. So crying probably conveys only one very general message—"Hey, I'm distressed"—and the effectiveness of this signal at eliciting attention depends more on the *amount* of distress it implies than on the *kind* of distress that the baby is experiencing (Gustafson & Harris, 1990; Zeskind et al., 1992).

Developmental Changes in Crying. Babies around the world cry most often during the first 3 months of life (St. James-Roberts & Plewis, 1996). In fact, the declines we see early in life in both crying and REM sleep suggest that both these changes are meaningfully related to the maturation of a baby's brain and central nervous system (Halpern, MacLean, & Baumeister, 1995). And what role do parents play? Will those who are especially responsive to their infant's cries produce a spoiled baby who enslaves them with incessant demands for attention?

Although this issue is by no means resolved, Mary Ainsworth and her associates (1972) found that the babies of mothers who are relatively quick to respond to their cries come to cry *very little!* The reason may be that caregivers who are generally sensitive to an infant's cries also tend to be responsive to other social signals, such as the smiles, babbles, and bright-eyed expressions that distressed infants are likely to display once they calm down. So responsive companions are readily available to elicit and *reinforce* alternative modes of communication, which may gradually replace crying as methods of attracting attention.

Pediatricians and nurses are trained to listen carefully to the vocalizations of a newborn infant, for congenital problems are sometimes detectable by the way an infant cries. Preterm babies, for example, and those who are malnourished, brain-damaged, or born addicted to narcotics often emit shrill, nonrhythmic cries that are perceived as much more "sickly" and aversive than those of healthy full-term infants (Frodi, 1985; Zeskind, 1980). In fact, Barry Lester (1984) reports that it is even possible to discriminate preterm infants who will develop normally from those who are likely to experience later deficiencies in cognitive development by analyzing their crying in the first few days and weeks of life. So the infant cry is not only an important communicative prompt for parents but is a meaningful diagnostic tool as well.

Methods of Soothing a Fussy Baby

Although babies can be delightful companions when alert and attentive, they may irritate the most patient of caregivers when they fuss, cry, and are difficult to pacify. Many people think that a crying baby is either hungry, wet, or in pain, and if the infant has not eaten in some time, feeding may be a very effective method of pacification. Presentation of a mild sucrose solution is particularly effective at calming distressed newborns (Smith & Blass, 1996), although even a nipplelike pacifier is often sufficient to quiet a fussy baby (Campos, 1989). Of course, the soothing effect of a pacifier may be short-lived if the baby really is hungry.

Other Soothing Techniques. When feeding or diaper changing doesn't work, rocking, humming, stroking, and other forms of continuous, rhythmic stimulation will often quiet restless babies. Swaddling (wrapping the infant snugly in a blanket) is also comforting because the wraps provide continuous tactile sensation all over the baby's body. Perhaps the infant's nervous system is programmed to respond to soft, rhythmic stimulation, for studies have repeatedly shown that rocking, swaddling, and continuous rhythmic sounds have the effect of decreasing a baby's muscular activity and lowering heart and respiratory rates (Brackbill, 1975; Campos, 1989).

One particularly effective method of soothing crying infants is simply to pick them up. Whereas soft, rhythmic stimulation may put babies to sleep, lifting is likely to have

In many cultures, babies are kept quite contented through swaddling and having ample close contact with their mothers, who stand ready to nurse at the baby's first whimper.

the opposite effect (Korner, 1972), causing them to become visually alert, particularly if their caregivers place them against their shoulder—an excellent vantage point for visual scanning. Anneliese Korner (1972) believes that parents who often soothe their infants by picking them up may be doing them a favor, for the visual exploration that this technique allows helps babies to learn more about their environment.

Individual and Cultural Differences in Soothability. Just as infants differ in their sleeping patterns and daily rhythms, they also differ in their irritability and their ability to be soothed (Korner, 1996). Even in the first few days of life, some infants are easily distressed and difficult to soothe, whereas others are rarely perturbed and calm easily should they become overstimulated. There are also cultural differences in infant soothability: Caucasian babies tend to be much more restless and more difficult to calm than Chinese-American, Native American, or Japanese infants (Freedman, 1979; Nugent, Lester, & Brazelton, 1989). These differential reactions to stress and soothing are present at birth and may be genetically influenced. Yet it is also clear that child-rearing practices can affect a baby's demeanor. Many Asian, South American, and Native American mothers, for example, are often successful at improving the dispositions of even their most irritable babies by swaddling them, carrying them around (in slings or pouches) as they do their chores, and nursing at the baby's first whimper (Nugent et al., 1989; Tronick, Thomas, & Daltabuit, 1994).

A baby who is not easily soothed can make a parent feel anxious, frustrated, or downright incompetent—reactions that may contribute to a poor parent–child relationship. For this reason, parents of difficult infants need to cast aside their preconceptions about the typical or "perfect" baby and learn how to adjust to the characteristics of their *own* child. Indeed, the NBAS training described in Box 4.3 was designed with just this objective in mind by (1) showing parents that even an irritable or unresponsive baby can react positively to them and (2) teaching the parents how to elicit these favorable responses.

Now that we have completed this chapter, please take a moment to reflect on just how much has happened since conception. A single-celled zygote evolves into a marvelously complex, organized human being who is ready to begin meeting life's demands and is usually strong enough to overcome many hazards and complications that he or she may encounter. So rather than thinking of newborns as "helpless babes," it is probably much more accurate to portray them as hardy and adaptive beings who are already hard at work writing a fascinating developmental story.

? **WHAT DO YOU THINK?**

What purposes might be served by each of the following stimuli in a newborn baby's environment: a rocker or a white noise machine; a mobile or other visual targets suspended over the crib; a caregiver who is responsive to the baby's cries?

SUMMARY

From Conception to Birth

♦ **Prenatal development** is divided into three phases. The **germinal period** (or *period of the zygote*) lasts about 2 weeks, from conception until the *blastocyst* is firmly **implanted** in the wall of the uterus. The inner layer of the blastocyst will become the **embryo;** the outer layer forms the **amnion, chorion, placenta,** and **umbilical cord**—support structures that help to sustain the developing prenatal organism.

♦ The **period of the embryo** lasts from the beginning of the third through the eighth week of pregnancy. This is the period when all major organs are formed and some have begun to function.

♦ The **period of the fetus** lasts from the ninth prenatal week until birth. All organ systems become integrated in preparation for birth. Fetuses attain the **age of viability** at the beginning of the third trimester, usually between 22 to 28 weeks after conception.

Environmental Influences on Prenatal Development

♦ Many environmental agents can complicate prenatal development and the birth process. **Teratogens**—that is, diseases such as **rubella, toxoplasmosis, syphilis, herpes,** and **AIDS,** drugs such as **thalidomide, diethylstilbestrol (DES), alcohol,** and **tobacco,** and environmental hazards such as *radiation* and *toxic chemicals*—can attack a developing embryo or fetus, interfering with growth and causing birth defects. Teratogens are dangerous throughout pregnancy, but especially so during the first 8 weeks when major organs and body parts are forming.

◆ Maternal characteristics can also influence prenatal development and birth outcomes. If a mother is malnourished, particularly during the third trimester, she runs the risk of delivering a preterm baby who may fail to survive. Supplementation of an otherwise normal diet with vitamins such as **folic acid** can help to prevent **spina bifida** and other birth defects. Malnourished babies are often irritable and unresponsive, which can contribute to poor social and intellectual development. Mothers under severe emotional stress are at increased risk of experiencing pregnancy complications. Complications are also more likely among mothers over 35 and younger teenage mothers who fail to obtain adequate prenatal care.

Childbirth and the Perinatal Environment

◆ Childbirth is a three-step process that begins with contractions that dilate the cervix (**first stage of labor**) so that the baby can be delivered (**second stage of labor**) and the afterbirth expelled (**third stage of labor**). The **Apgar test** is used to assess the newborn's condition immediately after birth, whereas the **Neonatal Behavioral Assessment Scale (NBAS),** which is typically administered a few days later, is a more extensive measure of the baby's health and well-being. Labor and delivery medication given to mothers to ease pain can, in large doses, make babies lethargic and inattentive, which may interfere with the parent-infant relationship.

◆ Childbirth practices vary widely across cultures. **Natural (or prepared) childbirth,** now common in Western societies, can reduce maternal stress and medication. Home births, or those that take place in **alternative birth centers,** are just as safe as hospital deliveries, provided that the mother is healthy and is attended by a competent doctor or midwife.

◆ Many mothers feel exhilarated shortly after birth if they have close contact with their babies and begin the process of **emotional bonding.** Fathers, too, are often **engrossed** with their newborns, and the support of fathers during pregnancy and childbirth can make the birth experience easier and more pleasant for mothers. However, a lack of support from one's partner is a major contributor to **postpartum depression** and a poor mother-infant relationship.

Birth Complications

◆ **Anoxia** is a potentially serious birth complication that can cause brain damage and other defects. Mild anoxia, however, usually has no long-term effects.

◆ Women who abuse alcohol and drugs, smoke heavily, or receive poor prenatal care are at risk for delivering preterm or low-birth-weight babies. **Small-for-date** babies usually have more severe and longer lasting problems than do **preterm** infants. Interventions to stimulate these infants and to teach their parents how to respond appropriately to their sluggish or irritable demeanor can help to normalize their developmental progress.

◆ Fortunately, the problems stemming from both prenatal and birth complications are often overcome in time, provided that the child is not permanently brain damaged and has a stable and supportive postnatal environment in which to grow.

The Newborn's Readiness for Life

◆ Newborns are remarkably capable organisms who emerge from the womb prepared to begin life. Perhaps their greatest strength is their repertoire of **survival reflexes** that helps them adapt to their new surroundings and to satisfy basic needs. Other **primitive reflexes,** thought to be remnants of evolution, are not as useful; however, their disappearance in the first year is a sign that development is proceeding normally.

◆ Newborns also have a sleep–waking cycle that becomes better organized over the first year. Although, babies move into and out of six **infant states** in a typical day, they spend up to 70% of their time sleeping. One state, **REM sleep**, is characterized by twitches, jerks, and rapid eye movements. Proponents of **autostimulation theory** believe that its function is to provide very young infants with stimulation necessary for the development of the central nervous system. Unfortunately, **sudden infant death syndrome** is a leading cause of infant mortality.

◆ Crying is the state by which infants communicate distress. If a baby's cries are very shrill and nonrhythmic, he may be brain damaged. Crying normally diminishes over the first 6 months as the brain matures, caregivers become better at soothing, and infants learn to use other methods to communicate.

At the time of conception a zygote is formed when an egg cell is fertilized by a sperm cell. Four short weeks later, development has already progressed to the point where the neural tube has formed and a tiny heart has already begun to beat. You can trace this fascinating time of development by visiting: http://visembryo.ucsf.edu At this web site you can see actual footage of development during the first four weeks of the prenatal period, and then take a self-test to assess your understanding of the very start of human growth and development.

KEY TERMS

prenatal development, 111
germinal period, 111
period of the embryo, 111
period of the fetus, 111
embryo, 111
implantation, 111
amnion, 112
chorion, 112
placenta, 112
umbilical cord, 112
neural tube, 113
fetus, 114
vernix, 115
lanugo, 115
age of viability, 116
teratogens, 117
sensitive period, 117
rubella (German measles), 119
toxoplasmosis, 120
syphilis, 120
genital herpes, 120
cesarean section, 120
acquired immune deficiency syndrome (AIDS), 121
thalidomide, 121
diethylstilbestrol (DES), 122
fetal alcohol syndrome (FAS), 123
fetal alcohol effects (FAE), 123
folic acid, 127
spina bifida, 127
neonate, 128
first stage of labor, 130
second stage of labor, 130
third stage of labor, 130
Apgar test, 132
Neonatal Behavior Assessment Scale (NBAS), 132
natural, or prepared, childbirth, 134
alternative birth center, 135
emotional bonding, 136
postpartum depression, 136
engrossment, 137
anoxia, 137
breech birth, 138
RH factor, 138
preterm babies, 138
small-for-date babies, 138
respiratory distress syndrome, 139
reflex, 142
survival reflexes, 142
primitive reflexes, 144
infant states, 144
REM sleep, 145
autostimulation theory, 146
sudden infant death syndrome (SIDS), 146

The Physical Self: Development of the Brain, the Body, and Motor Skills

My, my, she is already walking! What a smart little girl!

Look at you go. Oops, fall down, go boom!

Get your rest, little guy, it will help you grow big and strong.

He's growing like a weed—and his arms are too long!

Only 11 and she's got her period! What's the world coming to!

All that girl thinks about is boys!

Have you ever heard adults make these kinds of statements about developing children and adolescents? Few aspects of development are more interesting to the casual observer than the rapid transformation of a seemingly dependent and immobile little baby into a running, jumping bundle of energy who grows and changes at what may seem to be an astounding pace, and who may one day surpass the physical stature of his or her parents. Those physical changes that many find so fascinating are the subject of this chapter.

We will begin by focusing on the changes that occur in the body, the brain, and motor skills throughout childhood. Then we will consider the impact of *puberty*—both the dramatic physical changes that adolescents experience and their social and psychological impacts. Finally, we will close by discussing the factors that influence physical growth and development throughout the first 20 years of life.

Having experienced most (if not all) of the changes covered in this chapter, you may assume that you know quite a bit about physical development. Yet, students often discover that there is much they *don't* know. To check your own knowledge, take a minute to decide whether the following statements are true or false.

True or False

1. Babies who walk early are inclined to be especially bright.
2. The average 2-year-old is already about half of his/her adult height.
3. Half the nerve cells (neurons) in the average baby's brain die (and are not replaced) over the first few years of life.
4. Most children walk when they are ready, and no amount of encouragement will enable a 6-month-old to walk alone.
5. Hormones have little effect on human growth and development until puberty.
6. Emotional trauma can seriously impair the growth of young children, even those who are adequately nourished and free from illness, and who are not physically abused.

Jot down your responses and we will see how you have fared on this "pretest" as we discuss these issues throughout the chapter. (If you would like immediate feedback, the correct answers appear at the bottom of the page.)

AN OVERVIEW OF MATURATION AND GROWTH

Adults are often amazed at how quickly children grow. Even tiny babies don't remain tiny for long. In the first few months of life, they gain nearly an ounce each day and an inch each month. Yet, the dramatic increases in height and weight that we see are accompanied by a number of important *internal* developments in the muscles, bones, and central nervous system that will largely determine the physical feats that children are capable of performing at different ages. In this section, we will briefly chart the course of physical development from birth through adolescence and see that there is a clear relationship between the external aspects of growth that are so noticeable and the internal changes that are much harder to detect.

cephalocaudal development
a sequence of physical maturation and growth that proceeds from the head (cephalic region) to the tail (or caudal region).

proximodistal development
a sequence of physical maturation and growth that proceeds from the center of the body (the proximal region) to the extremities (distal regions).

Changes in Height and Weight

Babies grow very rapidly during the first 2 years, often doubling their birth weight by 4 to 6 months of age and tripling it (to about 21 to 22 pounds) by the end of the first year. By age 2, infants are already half their eventual adult height and have quadrupled

Answers to True/False statements: 1 F, 2 T, 3 T, 4 T, 5 F, 6 T.

their birth weight to 27 to 30 pounds. If children continued to grow at this rapid pace until age 18, they would stand about 12 feet, 3 inches and weigh several tons!

A child's growth is slow and steady from age 2 until puberty, averaging 2 to 3 inches in height and 6 to 7 pounds in weight each year. During middle childhood (ages 6 to 11), children may seem to grow very little; over the course of an entire year, 2 inches and 6 pounds gained are hard to detect on a child who stands 4 to 4½ feet tall and weighs 60 to 80 pounds (Eichorn, 1979). But as shown in Figure 5.1, physical growth and development are once again obvious at puberty, when adolescents enter a 2- to 3-year "growth spurt," during which they may post an annual gain of 10 to 15 pounds and 2 to 4 inches in height. After this growth spurt, there are typically small increases in height until full adult stature is attained in the mid to late teens (Tanner, 1990).

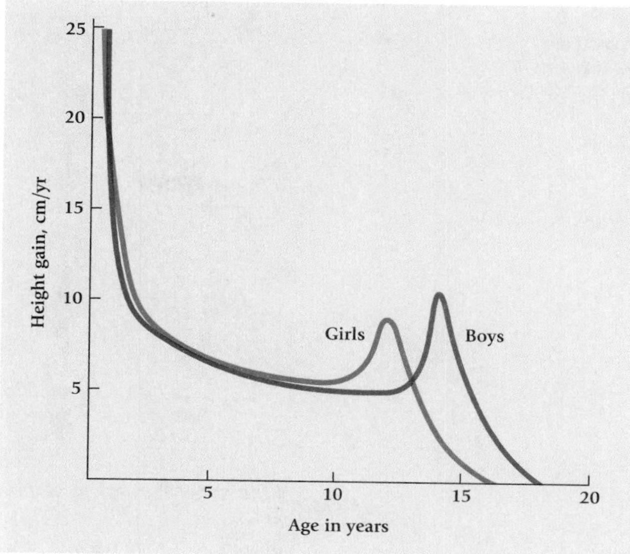

Figure 5.1 *Gain in height per year by males and females from birth through adolescence. At about age 10½, girls begin their growth spurt. Boys follow some 2½ years later and grow faster than girls once their growth begins.* Based on Tanner, Whithouse, & Takaishi, 1966.

Changes in Body Proportions

To a casual observer, neonates may appear to be "all head"—and for good reason. The newborn's head is already 70% of its eventual adult size and represents one-quarter of total body length, the same fraction as the legs.

As a child grows, body shape rapidly changes (see Figure 5.2). Development proceeds in a **cephalocaudal** (head downward) direction, and it is the trunk that grows fastest during the first year. At 1 year of age, a child's head now accounts for only 20% of total body length. From the child's first birthday until the adolescent growth spurt, the legs grow rapidly, accounting for more than 60% of the increase in height (Eichorn, 1979). During adolescence the trunk once again becomes the fastest-growing segment of the body, although the legs are also growing rapidly at this time. When we reach our eventual adult stature, our legs will account for 50% of total height and our heads only 12%.

While children grow upward, they are also growing outward according to a **proximodistal** (center outward) formula. During prenatal development, for example, the chest and internal organs form first, followed by the arms and legs, and then the hands and feet. Throughout infancy and childhood, the arms and legs continue to grow faster than the hands and feet. However, this center-outward growth pattern reverses just before puberty, when the hands and feet begin to grow rapidly and become the first body parts to reach adult proportions, followed by the arms and legs and finally the trunk. One reason teenagers often appear so clumsy or awkward is that their hands and feet (and later their arms and legs) may suddenly seem much too large for the rest of their bodies (Tanner, 1990).

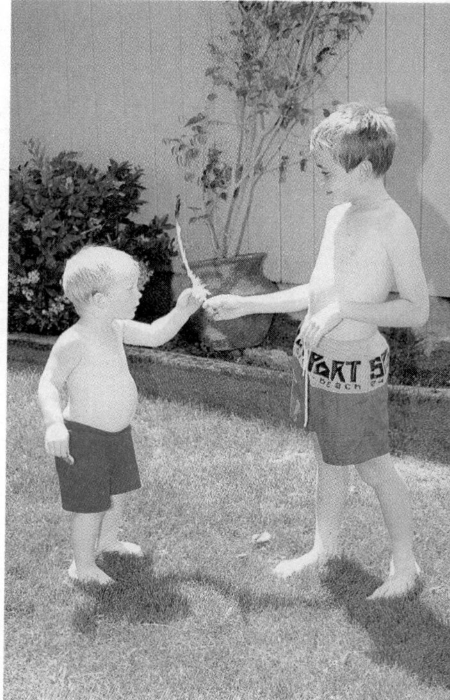

Body proportions change rapidly over the first few years as chubby toddlers become linear, long-legged, children.

Skeletal Development

The skeletal structures that form during the prenatal period are initially soft cartilage that will gradually ossify (harden) into bony material. At birth, most of the infant's bones are soft, pliable, and difficult to break. One reason that neonates cannot sit up or balance themselves when pulled to a standing position is that their bones are too small and too flexible.

Fortunately for both a mother and her baby, the neonate's skull consists of several soft bones that can be compressed to allow the child to pass through the cervix and the birth canal. These skull bones are separated by six soft spots, or *fontanelles,* that are

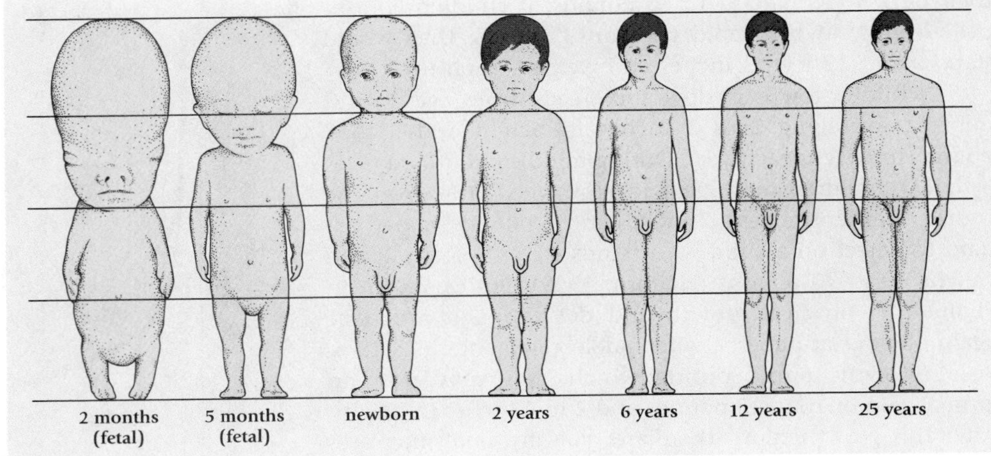

Figure 5.2 *Proportions of the human body from the fetal period through adulthood. The head represents 50% of body length at 2 months after conception but only 12–13% of adult stature. In contrast, the legs constitute about 12–13% of the total length of a 2-month-old fetus, but 50% of the height of a 25-year-old adult.*

gradually filled in by minerals to form a single skull by age 2, with pliable seams at the points where skull bones join. These seams, or sutures, allow the skull to expand as the brain grows larger.

Other parts of the body—namely, the ankles and feet and the wrists and hands—develop *more* (rather than fewer) bones as the child matures. In Figure 5.3, we see that the wrist and hand bones of a 1-year-old are both fewer and less well interconnected than the corresponding skeletal equipment of an adolescent.

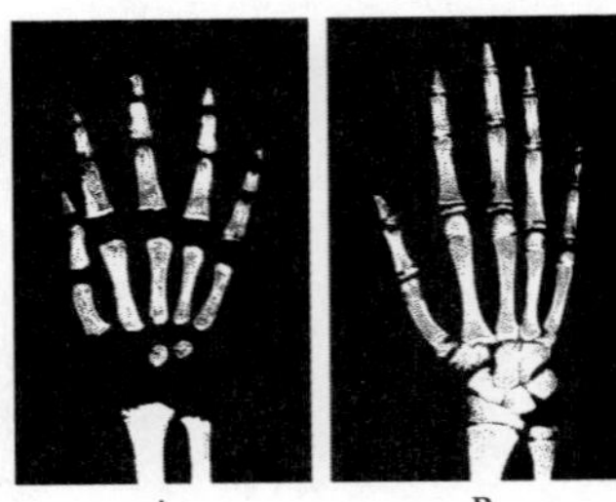

Figure 5.3 *X-rays showing the amount of skeletal development seen in (a) the hand of an average male infant at 12 months or an average female infant at 10 months and (b) the hand of an average 13-year-old male or an average 10½-year-old female.*

One method of estimating a child's level of physical maturation is to X-ray the wrist and hand (as in Figure 5.3). The X-ray shows the number of bones and the extent of their ossification, which is then interpretable as a **skeletal age.** Using this technique, researchers have found that girls mature faster than boys. At birth, girls are only 4 to 6 weeks ahead of boys in their level of skeletal maturity; but by age 12, the gender "maturation gap" has widened to 2 full years (Tanner, 1990).

Not all parts of the skeleton grow and harden at the same rate. The skull and hands mature first, whereas the leg bones continue to develop until the mid to late teens. For all practical purposes, skeletal development is complete by age 18, although the widths (or thicknesses) of the skull, leg bones, and hands increases slightly throughout life (Tanner, 1990).

Muscular Development

Although one might think otherwise after listening to the claims of body builders, neonates are born with all the muscle fibers they will ever have (Tanner, 1990). At birth, muscle tissue is 35% water, and it accounts for no more than 18 to 24% of a baby's body weight (Marshall, 1977). However, muscle fibers soon begin to grow as the cellular fluid in muscle tissue is bolstered by the addition of protein and salts.

Muscular development proceeds in cephalocaudal and proximodistal directions, with muscles in the head and neck maturing before those in the trunk and limbs. Like many other aspects of physical development, the maturation of muscle tissue occurs very gradually over childhood and then accelerates during early adolescence. One consequence of this muscular growth spurt is that members of both sexes become noticeably stronger, although increases in both muscle mass and physical strength (as measured in tests of large-muscle activity) are more dramatic for boys than for girls (Malina, 1990). By the mid-20s, skeletal muscle accounts for 40% of the body weight of an average male, compared with 24% for the average female.

skeletal age
a measure of physical maturation based on the child's level of skeletal development.

Figure 5.4 *Growth curves for different body systems. Each curve plots the size of a group of organs or body parts as a percentage of their size at age 20 (which is the 100% level on the vertical scale). The "general" curve describes changes in the body's size as well as the growth of respiratory and digestive organs and musculature. The brain and head grow more rapidly than the body in general, and the reproductive organs are the slowest to reach adult size. (The lymph nodes and other parts of the lymphoid system, which function as part of the immune system, also grow rapidly and actually exceed adult size during late childhood and adolescence.)* FROM TANNER, 1962.

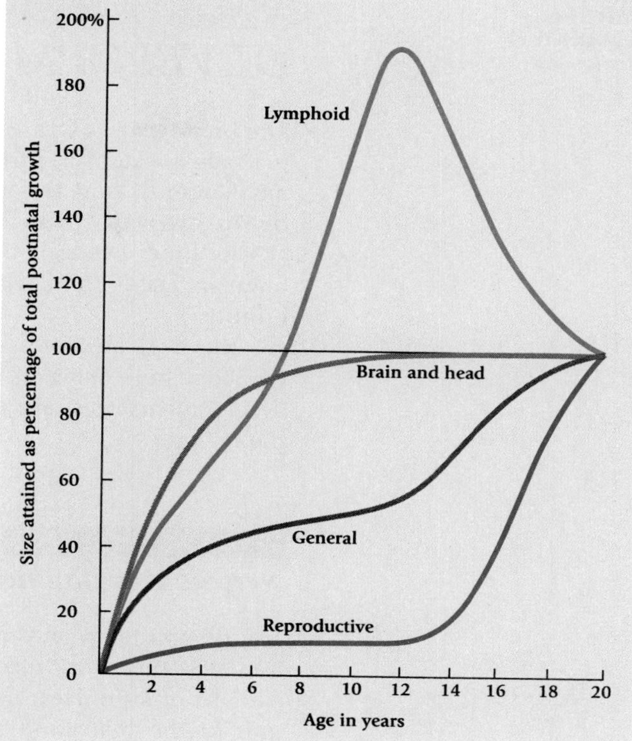

Variations in Physical Development

To this point, we have been discussing *sequences* of physical growth that all humans display. However, physical development is a very uneven process in which different bodily systems display unique growth patterns. As we see in Figure 5.4, the brain and head actually grow much faster and are quicker to reach adult proportions than the rest of the body is, whereas the genitals and other reproductive organs grow very slowly throughout childhood and develop rapidly in adolescence. Notice also that growth of the lymph tissues—which make up part of the immune system and help children to fight off infections—actually overshoots adult levels late in childhood, before *declining* rapidly in adolescence.

Individual Variations

Not only is the development of body systems an uneven or asynchronous process, but there are sizable individual variations in the rates at which individuals grow. Look carefully at the photo here. These two boys are the same age, although one has already reached puberty and looks much older. As we will see later in the chapter, two grade-school chums might begin the pubertal transition from child to adult as much as 5 years apart!

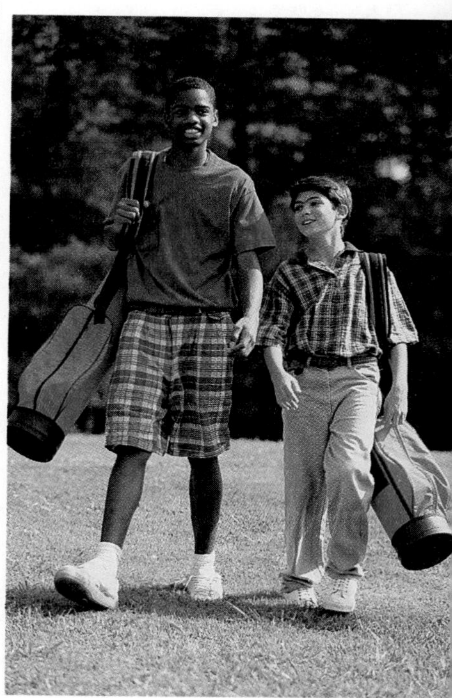

There are large individual variations in the timing of the adolescent growth spurt as we see in comparing the stature of these two boys of the same age.

Cultural Variations

Finally, there are meaningful cultural and subcultural variations in physical growth and development. As a rule, people from Asia, South America, and Africa tend to be smaller than North Americans, Northern Europeans, and Australians. In addition, there are cultural differences in the *rate* of physical growth. Asian- and African-American children, for example, tend to mature faster than European-American and European children (Berkey et al., 1994; Herman-Giddens et al., 1997).

What accounts for all these variations in growth? Current thinking is that asynchronies in the maturation of different body systems are built in to our species heredity—that is, the common maturational program that all humans share (Tanner, 1990). And later in the chapter, we will see that heredity, in concert with such environmental factors as the food people eat, the diseases they may encounter, and even the emotional climate in which they live, can produce significant variations in the rates at which they grow and the statures they attain.

DEVELOPMENT OF THE BRAIN

The brain grows at an astounding rate early in life, increasing from 25% of its eventual adult weight at birth to 75% of adult weight by age 2. Indeed, the last 3 prenatal months and the first 2 years after birth have been termed the period of the **brain growth spurt** because more than half of one's adult brain weight is added at this time. Between the seventh prenatal month and a child's first birthday, the brain increases in weight by about 1.7 grams a day, or more than a milligram per minute.

However, an increase in brain weight is a rather gross index that tells us very little about how or when various parts of the brain mature and affect other aspects of development. Let's take a closer look at the internal organization and development of the brain.

Neural Development and Plasticity

The human brain and nervous system consists of more than a trillion highly specialized cells that work together to transmit electrical and chemical signals across many trillions of **synapses,** or connective spaces between the cells. **Neurons** are the basic unit of the brain and nervous system—the cells that receive and transmit neural impulses. Neurons are produced in the neural tube of the developing embryo. From there, they migrate along pathways laid down by a network of *guiding cells* to form the major parts of the brain. Interestingly, all the neurons a person will ever have—some 100 to 200 billion of them—have already formed by the end of the second trimester of pregnancy, before the brain growth spurt has even begun (Kolb & Fantie, 1989; Rakic, 1991).

What, then, accounts for the brain growth spurt? One major contributor is the development of a second type of nerve cell, called **glia,** which nourish the neurons and eventually encase them in insulating sheaths of a waxy substance called *myelin.* Glia are far more numerous than neurons are, and they continue to form throughout life (Tanner, 1990).

Cell Differentiation and Synaptogenesis

Influenced by the sites to which they migrate, neurons assume specialized functions—as cells of the visual or auditory areas of the brain, for example. If a neuron that would normally migrate to the visual area of the brain is transplanted to the area that controls hearing, it will differentiate to become an auditory neuron instead of a visual neuron (Johnson, 1997). So individual neurons have the potential to serve any neural function, and the functions each serves depend on where it ends up.

Meanwhile, the process of **synaptogenesis**—the formation of synaptic connections among neurons—proceeds rapidly during the brain growth spurt. This brings us to one of the more interesting facts about the developing nervous system: The average infant has far more neurons and neural connections than adults do. The reason is that neurons that successfully interconnect with other neurons crowd out those that don't, so that about half the neurons produced early in life also die early in life (Janowsky & Finlay, 1986). Meanwhile, surviving neurons form hundreds of synapses, many of which also disappear if the neuron is not properly stimulated (Huttenlocher, 1994). If we likened the developing brain to a house under construction, we might imagine a builder who merrily constructs many more rooms and hallways than he needs, and then later goes back and knocks about half of them out!

brain growth spurt
the period between the seventh prenatal month and 2 years of age when more than half of the child's eventual brain weight is added.

synapse
the connective space (juncture) between one nerve cell (neuron) and another.

neurons
nerve cells that receive and transmit neural impulses.

glia
nerve cells that nourish neurons and encase them in insulating sheaths of myelin.

synaptogenesis
formation of connections (synapses) among neurons.

What is happening here reflects the remarkable **plasticity** of the young infant's brain—the fact that its cells are highly responsive to the effects of experience. As William Greenough and his colleagues (1987) explain, the brain has evolved so that it produces an excess of neurons and synapses in preparation for receiving any and all kinds of sensory and motor stimulation that a human being could conceivably experience. Of course, no human being has this broad a range of experiences, so much of one's neural circuitry remains unused. Presumably, then, neurons and synapses that are most often stimulated continue to function. Other surviving neurons that are stimulated less often lose their synapses (a process called *synaptic pruning*) and stand in reserve to compensate for brain injuries or to support new skills (Huttenlocher, 1994). Note the implication then: The development of the brain early in life is not due entirely to the unfolding of a maturational program. It is the result of both a biological program and early experience (Johnson, 1997; Greenough et al., 1987).

The Role of Experience

How do we know that early experience plays such a dramatic role in the development of the brain and central nervous system? The first clue came from research by Austin Riesen and his associates (Riesen, 1947; Riesen et al., 1951). Riesen's subjects were infant chimpanzees that were reared in the dark for periods ranging up to 16 months. His results were striking. Dark-reared chimps experienced atrophy of the retina and the neurons that make up the optic nerve. This atrophy was reversible if the animal's visual deprivation did not exceed 7 months, but was irreversible and often led to total blindness if the deprivation lasted longer than a year. So neurons that are not properly stimulated degenerate—a dramatic illustration of the "use it or lose it" principle.

Might we then foster the neural development of an immature, plastic brain by exposing participants to enriched environments that provide a wide variety of stimulation? Yes, indeed. Animals raised with lots of companions and many toys to play with have brains that are heavier and display more extensive networks of neural connections than those of litter-mates raised under standard laboratory conditions (Greenough & Black, 1992; Rosenzweig, 1984). Conversely, the brains of animals raised in stimulating environments lose some of their complexity if the animals are moved to less stimulating quarters (Thompson, 1993). Thus, even though genes may provide rough guidelines as to how the brain should be configured, early experience largely determines the brain's specific architecture.

Brain Differentiation and Growth

Not all parts of the brain develop at the same rate. At birth, the most highly developed areas are the *brain stem* and the *midbrain,* which control states of consciousness, inborn reflexes, and vital biological functions such as digestion, respiration, and elimination. Surrounding the midbrain are the *cerebrum* and *cerebral cortex,* the areas most directly implicated in voluntary bodily movements, perception, and higher intellectual activities such as learning, thinking, and production of language. The first areas of the cerebrum to mature are the *primary motor areas* (which control simple motor activities such as waving the arms) and the *primary sensory areas* (which control sensory processes such as vision, hearing, smelling, and tasting). Thus, human neonates are reflexive, "sensory-motor" beings because only the sensory and motor areas of the cortex are functioning well at birth. By 6 months of age, the primary motor areas of the cerebral cortex have developed to the point that they now direct most of the infant's movements. Inborn responses such as the palmar grasp and the Babinski reflex should have disappeared by now, thus indicating that the higher cortical centers are assuming proper control over the more primitive "subcortical" areas of the brain.

plasticity
capacity for change; a developmental state that has the potential to be shaped by experience.

Myelinization

As brain cells proliferate and grow, some of the glia begin to produce a waxy substance called *myelin,* which forms a sheath around individual neurons. This myelin sheath acts like an insulator to speed the transmission of neural impulses, thus allowing the brain to communicate more efficiently with different parts of the body.

Myelinization follows a definite chronological sequence that parallels the maturation of the nervous system. At birth or shortly thereafter, the pathways between the sense organs and the brain are reasonably well-myelinated. As a result, the neonate's sensory equipment is in good working order. As neural pathways between the brain and the skeletal muscles myelinate (in a cephalocaudal and proximodistal pattern), the child becomes capable of increasingly complex motor activities such as lifting the head and chest, reaching with the arms and hands, rolling over, sitting, standing, and eventually walking and running. Although myelinization proceeds very rapidly over the first few years of life, some areas of the brain are not completely myelinated until the mid to late teens or early adulthood (Fischer & Rose, 1995). For example, the *reticular formation* and the *frontal cortex*—parts of the brain that allow us to concentrate on a subject for lengthy periods—are not fully myelinated at puberty (Tanner, 1990). This may be one reason that the attention spans of infants, toddlers, and school-age children are much shorter than those of adolescents and adults.

Cerebral Lateralization

The highest brain center, the **cerebrum,** consists of two halves (or *hemispheres*) connected by a band of fibers called the **corpus callosum.** Each of the hemispheres is covered by a **cerebral cortex**—an outer layer of gray matter that controls sensory and motor processes, perception, and intellectual functioning. Although identical in appearance, the left and the right cerebral hemispheres serve different functions and control different areas of the body. The left cerebral hemisphere controls the right side of the body, and, as illustrated in Figure 5.5, it contains centers for speech, hearing, verbal memory, decision making, language processing, and expression of positive emotions. By contrast, the right cerebral hemisphere controls the left side of the body and contains centers for processing visual–spatial information, nonlinguistic sounds such as music, tactile (touch) sensations, and expressing negative emotions (Fox et al., 1995). Thus, the brain is a *lateralized* organ. **Cerebral lateralization** also involves a preference for using one hand or one side of the body more than the other. About 90% of adults rely on their right hands (or left hemispheres) to write, eat, and perform other motor functions, whereas these same activities are under the control of the right hemisphere among most people who are left-handed. However, the fact that the brain is a lateralized organ does not mean that each hemisphere is totally independent of the other; the corpus callosum, which connects the hemispheres, plays an important role in integrating their respective functions.

When do the two cerebral hemispheres begin to "divide the work" and become lateralized? It was once thought that lateralization took place gradually throughout childhood and was not complete until adolescence (Lenneberg, 1967). Now, however, it is thought that brain lateralization may originate during the prenatal period and be well underway at birth (Kinsbourne, 1989). For example, about two-thirds of all fetuses end up positioned in the womb with their right ears facing outward, and it is thought that this gives them a right-ear advantage and illustrates the left hemisphere's specialization in language processing (Previc, 1991). From the first day of life, speech sounds stimulate more electrical activity in the left side of the cerebral cortex than in the right (Molfese, 1977). In addition, most newborns turn to the right rather than to the left when they lie on their backs, and these same babies later tend to reach for objects with their right hands (Kinsbourne, 1989). So it seems that the two cerebral hemispheres may be biologically programmed to assume different functions and have already begun to "divide the labor" by the time a baby is born (Kinsbourne, 1989; Witelson, 1987).

However, the brain is not completely specialized at birth; throughout childhood, we come to rely more and more on one particular hemisphere or the other to serve

myelinization
the process by which neurons are enclosed in waxy myelin sheaths that will facilitate the transmission of neural impulses.

cerebrum
the highest brain center; includes both hemispheres of the brain and the fibers that connect them.

corpus callosum
the bundle of neural fibers that connects the two hemispheres of the brain and transmits information from one hemisphere to the other.

cerebral cortex
the outer layer of the brain's cerebrum that is involved in voluntary body movements, perception, and higher intellectual functions such as learning, thinking, and speaking.

cerebral lateralization
the specialization of brain functions in the left and the right cerebral hemispheres.

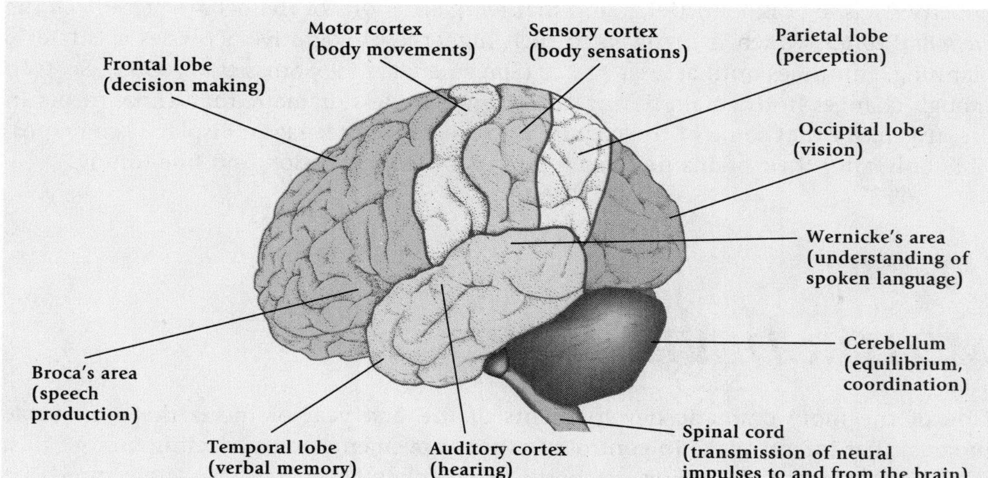

Figure 5.5 *Lateral view of the left cerebral cortex and some of the functions that it controls. Although the cerebellum and spinal cord are not part of the cerebral cortex, they serve important functions of their own.*

particular functions. Consider, for example, than even though left- or right-handedness is apparent early and is reasonably well-established by age 2, lateral preferences become stronger with age. In one experiment, preschoolers and adolescents were asked to pick up a crayon, kick a ball, look into a small, opaque bottle, and place an ear to a box to hear a sound. Only 32% of the preschoolers, but more than half of the adolescents, showed a consistent lateral preference by relying exclusively on one side of the body to perform all four tasks (Coren, Porac, & Duncan, 1981).

Because the immature brain is not completely specialized, young children often show a remarkable ability to bounce back from traumatic brain injuries as neural circuits that might otherwise have been lost assume the functions of those that have died (Kolb & Fantie, 1989; Rakic, 1991). Although adolescents and adults who suffer brain damage often regain a substantial portion of the functions they have lost, especially with the proper therapy, their recoveries are rarely as rapid or as complete as those of younger children (Kolb & Fantie, 1989). So the remarkable recuperative power of the human brain (that is, plasticity) is greatest early in life, before cerebral lateralization is complete.

Development of the Brain During Adolescence

Through the ages, adults have noticed that teenagers suddenly begin to ask hypothetical "What if" questions and to ponder weighty abstractions such as truth and justice. Are these changes in thinking tied to late developments in the brain?

Many researchers now believe that they are (Case, 1992; Somsen et al., 1997). For example, myelinization of the higher brain centers, which continues well into adolescence, may not only increase adolescents' attention spans, but also explains why they process information much faster than grade-school children do (Kail, 1991). Furthermore, we now know that the brain retains at least some of its plasticity well beyond

Concept Check 5.1
The Developing Brain

Check your understanding of the developing brain and nervous system by matching each *development* listed below with an apparent consequence, or outcome, of that development. Select your answers from the following options: (a) decline in brain plasticity, (b) increases in attention span, (c) lateral preferences, (d) loss of inborn reflexes, (e) neural degeneration, (f) brain growth spurt. The answers appear in the Appendix at the back of the book.

_____ 1. cerebral lateralization
_____ 2. maturation of higher cortical centers
_____ 3. proliferation of glia and synaptogenesis
_____ 4. loss of neurons and synapses over the course of childhood
_____ 5. myelinization
_____ 6. exposure to a depriving early environment

puberty (Nelson & Bloom, 1997), and that reorganizations of the neural circuitry of the *prefrontal cortex,* which is involved in such higher-level cognitive activities as strategic planning, continues until at least age 20 (Spreen et al., 1995; Stuss et al., 1992). So even though changes in the brain during adolescence are less dramatic than those earlier in life, it is likely that some of the cognitive advances that teenagers display become possible only after their brains undergo a process of reorganization and fine-tuning.

MOTOR DEVELOPMENT

One of the more dramatic developments of the first year of life is the remarkable progress that infants make in controlling their movements and perfecting motor skills. Writers are fond of describing newborns as "helpless babes"—a characterization that largely stems from the neonate's inability to move about on her own. Clearly, human infants are disadvantaged when compared with the young of many species, who can follow their mothers to food (and then feed themselves) very soon after birth.

However, babies do not remain immobile for long. By the end of the first month, the brain and neck muscles have matured enough to permit most infants to reach the first milestone in locomotor development—lifting their chins while lying flat on their stomachs. Soon thereafter, children lift their chests as well, reaching for objects, rolling over, and sitting up if someone supports them. Investigators who have charted motor development over the first 2 years of life find that motor skills evolve in a definite sequence, which appears in Table 5.1. Although the ages at which these skills first appear vary considerably from child to child, infants who are quick to proceed through this motor sequence are not necessarily any brighter or otherwise advantaged, compared with those whose rates of motor development are average or slightly below average. So even though the age norms in Table 5.1 are a useful standard for gauging an infant's progress as he or she begins to sit, stand, and take those first tentative steps, that rate of motor development really tells us very little about *future* developmental outcomes.

TABLE 5.1 Age Norms (in Months) for Important Motor Developments (Based on Anglo-American, Latino, and African-American Children in the United States)

Skill	Month when 50% of infants have mastered the skill	Month when 90% of infants have mastered the skill
Lifts head 90° while lying on stomach	2.2	3.2
Rolls over	2.8	4.7
Sits propped up	2.9	4.2
Sits without support	5.5	7.8
Stands holding on	5.8	10.0
Crawls	7.0	9.0
Walks holding on	9.2	12.7
Plays pat-a-cake	9.3	15.0
Stands alone momentarily	9.8	13.0
Stands well alone	11.5	13.9
Walks well	12.1	14.3
Builds tower of two cubes	13.8	19.0
Walks up steps	17.0	22.0
Kicks ball forward	20.0	24.0

SOURCES: Bayley, 1969; Frankenberg & Dodds, 1967.

Basic Trends in Locomotor Development

The two fundamental "laws" that describe muscular development and myelinization also hold true for motor development during the first few years. Motor development proceeds in a *cephalocaudal* (head-downward) direction, with activities involving the head, neck, and upper extremities preceding those involving the legs and lower extremities. At the same time, development is *proximodistal,* (center-outward) with activities involving the trunk and shoulders appearing before those involving the hands and fingers.

How do we explain the sequencing and timing of early motor development? Let's briefly consider three possibilities: the *maturational viewpoint,* the *experiential* (or practice) *hypothesis,* and a newer *dynamical systems theory* that views motor development as a product of a complex transaction among the child's physical capabilities, goals, and the experiences she has had (Thelen, 1995).

The Maturational Viewpoint

The maturational viewpoint (Shirley, 1933) describes motor development as the unfolding of a genetically programmed sequence of events which the nerves and muscles mature in a *downward* and *outward* direction. As a result, children gradually gain more control over the lower and peripheral parts of their bodies, displaying motor skills in the sequence shown in Table 5.1.

One clue that maturation plays a prominent role in motor development comes from cross-cultural research. Despite their very different early experiences, infants from around the world progress through roughly the same *sequence* of motor milestones. In addition, early studies in which one identical twin was allowed to practice motor skills (such as climbing stairs or stacking blocks) while the co-twin was denied these experiences suggested that practice had little effect on motor development. When finally allowed to perform, the unpracticed twin soon matched the skills of the co-twin who had had many opportunities to practice (Gesell & Thompson, 1929; McGraw, 1935). Taken together, these findings seemed to imply that maturation underlies motor development and that practice merely allows a child to perfect those skills that maturation has made possible.

The Experiential (or Practice) Hypothesis

Although no one denies that maturation contributes to motor development, proponents of the experiential viewpoint believe that opportunities to practice motor skills are also important. Consider what Wayne Dennis (1960) found when he studied two groups of institutionalized orphans in Iran who had spent most of their first 2 years lying flat on their backs in their cribs. These infants were never placed in a sitting position, were rarely played with, and were even fed in their cribs with their bottles propped on pillows. Was their motor development affected by these depriving early experiences? Indeed it was! None of the 1- to 2-year-olds could walk and less than half of them could even sit unaided. In fact, only 15% of the 3- to 4-year-olds could walk well alone! So Dennis concluded that maturation is *necessary but not sufficient* for the development of motor skills. In other words, infants who are physically capable of sitting, crawling, or walking will not be very proficient at these activities unless they have opportunities to practice them.

Not only does a lack of practice inhibit motor development but the cross-cultural research in Box 5.1 illustrates that a variety of enriching experiences can accelerate the process.

Motor Skills as Dynamic, Goal-Directed Systems

Although they would certainly agree that both maturation and experience contribute to motor development, proponents of an exciting new perspective—**dynamical systems theory**—differ from earlier theorists in two important ways. First, they do not

dynamical systems theory
a theory that views motor skills as active reorganizations of previously mastered capabilities that are undertaken to find more effective ways of exploring the environment or satisfying other objectives.

5.1

CULTURAL INFLUENCES

Cultural Variations in Motor Development

Cross-cultural studies tell us that the ages at which infants attain major motor milestones are heavily influenced by parenting practices. The Kipsigis of Kenya, for example, work to promote motor skills. By their eighth week, infants are already practicing their "walking" as parents grasp them by the armpits and propel them forward. And throughout the first few months, infants are seated in shallow holes, dug so that the sides support their backs and maintain an upright posture. Given these experiences, it is perhaps not surprising that Kipsigi infants sit unassisted about 5 weeks earlier and walk unaided about a month earlier than Western infants do.

Similarly, Brian Hopkins (1991) has compared the motor development of white infants in England with that of black infants whose families emigrated to England from Jamaica. As in several other comparisons of black and white infants, the black infants displayed such important motor skills as sitting, crawling, and walking at earlier ages. Do these findings reflect genetic differences between blacks and whites? Probably not, because black babies were likely to acquire motor skills early *only* if their mothers had followed traditional Jamaican routines for handling infants and nurturing motor development. These routines include massaging infants, stretching their limbs, and holding them by the arms while gently shaking them up and down. Jamaican mothers expect early motor development, work to promote it, and get it.

Dovetailing nicely with the cross-cultural work are experiments conducted by Philip Zelazo and his associates (1972; 1993) with North American infants. Zelazo found that 2- to 8-week-old babies who were regularly held in an upright posture and encouraged to practice their *stepping reflex* showed a strengthening of this response (which usually disappears early in life). They also walked at an earlier age than did infants in a control group who did not receive this training.

Why might having one's limbs stretched or being held (or sat) in an upright posture hasten motor development? Esther Thelen's (1986; Thelen & Fisher, 1982) view is that babies who are often placed in an upright position develop strength in the neck, trunk, and legs (an acceleration of muscular growth) which, in turn, promotes the early development of such motor skills as standing and walking. So it seems that both maturation and experience are important contributors to motor development. Maturation does place some limits on the age at which the child will first be capable of sitting, standing, and walking. Yet experiences such as upright posturing and various forms of practice may influence the age at which important maturational capabilities are achieved and translated into action.

Young infant displaying the stepping reflex.

view motor skills as genetically programmed responses that simply "unfold" as dictated by maturation and opportunities to practice. Instead, they view each new skill as a *construction* that emerges as infants *actively* reorganize existing motor capabilities into a new and more complex action system. At first, these new motor configurations are likely to be tentative, inefficient, and uncoordinated. New walkers, for example, spend a fair amount of time on their backsides and are not called "toddlers" for nothing. But over a period of time, these new motor patterns are modified and refined until all components mesh and become smooth, coordinated actions such as bouncing, crawling, walking, running, and jumping (Thelen, 1995; Whitall & Getchell, 1995).

But why would infants work so hard to acquire new motor skills? Unlike earlier theories that did not address this issue, dynamical systems theory offers a straightforward answer: Infants hope to acquire and perfect new motor skills that will help them to get to interesting objects they hope to explore or to accomplish other goals they may have in mind (Thelen, 1995). Consider what Eugene Goldfield (1989) learned in studying infants' emerging ability to crawl. Goldfield found that 7- to 8-month-old infants began to crawl only after they (1) regularly turned and raised their heads toward interesting sights and sounds in the environment, (2) had developed a distinct hand/arm preference when reaching for such stimuli, and (3) had begun to thrust (kick) with the leg opposite to the outstretched arm. Apparently, visual orientation *motivates* the infant to approach interesting stimuli she can't reach; reaching steers the body in the right direction; and kicking with the opposite leg propels the body forward. So far from being a preprogrammed skill that simply unfolds according to a maturational plan, crawling (and virtually all other motor skills) actually represents an active and intricate *reorganization* of *several existing capabilities* that is undertaken by a curious, active infant who has a particular *goal* in mind.

Why, then, do all infants proceed through the same sequence of locomotor milestones? Partly because of their human maturational programming, which sets the stage for various accomplishments, and partly because each successive motor skill must necessarily build on specific component activities that have developed earlier. How does experience fit in? According to the dynamical systems theory, a world of interesting objects and events provides infants with many reasons to want to reach out or to sit up, crawl, walk, and run—that is, with *purposes* and *motives* that might be served by actively reorganizing their existing skills into new and more complex action systems. Of course, no two infants have exactly the same set of experiences (or goals), which may help to explain why each infant coordinates the component activities of an emerging motor skill in a slightly different way (Thelen et al., 1993).

In sum, the development of motor skills is far more interesting and complex than earlier theories assumed. Though maturation plays a very important role, the basic motor skills of the first 2 years do not simply unfold as part of nature's grand plan. Rather, they emerge largely because goal-driven infants are constantly recombining actions they can perform into new and more complex action systems that will help them to achieve their objectives.

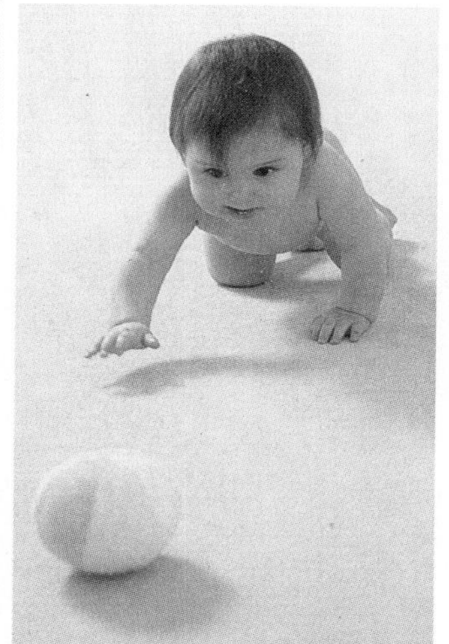

According to dynamical systems theory, new motor skills emerge as curious infants reorganize their existing capabilities in order to achieve important objectives.

Fine Motor Development

Two other aspects of motor development play especially important roles in helping infants to explore and adapt to their surroundings: *voluntary reaching* and *manipulatory* (or hand) *skills*.

Development of Voluntary Reaching

An infant's ability to reach out and manipulate objects changes dramatically over the first year. Recall that newborns come equipped with a grasping reflex. They are also inclined to reach for things, although these primitive thrusts (or *prereaches*) are really little more than uncoordinated swipes at objects in the visual field. Prereaching is truly a hit-or-miss proposition (Bower, 1982). By 2 months of age, infants' reaching and grasping skills may even seem to deteriorate. The reflexive palmar grasp disappears and prereaching occurs much less often (Bower, 1982). However, these apparent regressions set the stage for the appearance of *voluntary* reaching. Babies 3 months of age and older display this new competency as they extend their arms and make in-flight corrections, gradually improving in accuracy until they can reliably grasp their objectives (Hofsten, 1984; Thelen et al., 1993). Infants clearly differ in how they reach for objects. Some infants flap their arms at first and must learn to dampen their enthusiasm, whereas others reach tentatively and soon learn that they must supply more power to grasp their objectives (Thelen et al., 1993). So, here again, we see that reaching is a motor skill that does not simply "unfold"; instead, babies reach in different ways and take their own unique pathways to refining this important skill.

It was once thought that early reaching required visual guidance of the hand and arm for infants to locate their target. Yet recent research indicates that infants only 3 months old are just as successful at reaching for and grasping objects they can only hear (in the dark) as they are at grabbing those they can see (Clifton et al., 1993). And by age 5 months, infants are becoming proficient at reaching for and touching glowing objects that *move* in the dark, even though they cannot see what their hands are doing (Robin, Berthier, & Clifton, 1996). So early reaching seems to be guided not by vision, but by **proprioceptive information** from the arm muscles and joints. What vision may do is to help infants decide whether to reach for objects. If an object is moved further away, for example, 5-month-olds can see that it is likely to elude their grasp and will reach for it less often (Yonas & Hartman, 1993).

The pincer grasp is a crucial motor milestone that underlies the development of many coordinated manual activities.

Development of Manipulatory Skills

Once an infant is able to sit well and to reach inward, across her body midline at about age 4 to 5 months, she begins to grasp interesting objects with *both* hands and her exploratory activities forever change. Rather than merely batting or palming objects, she is now apt to transfer them from hand to hand or to hold them with one hand and finger them with the other (Rochat, 1989; Rochat & Goubet, 1995). Indeed, this fingering activity may be the primary method by which 4- to 6-month-olds gain information about objects, for their unimanual (one-handed) grasping skills are poorly developed. The reflexive palmar grasp has already disappeared by this age, and the **ulnar grasp** that replaces it is itself a rather clumsy, clawlike grip that permits little tactile exploration of objects by touch.

During the latter half of the first year, fingering skills improve and infants become much more proficient at tailoring all their exploratory activities to the properties of objects they are investigating (Palmer, 1989). Now, wheeled toys are likely to be scooted rather than banged, spongy objects are squeezed rather than scooted, and so on. The next major step in the growth of hand skills occurs near the end of the first year as infants use their thumbs and forefingers to lift and explore objects (Halverson, 1931). This **pincer grasp** transforms the child from a little fumbler into a skillful manipulator who may soon begin to capture crawling bugs and to turn knobs, dials, and rheostats, thereby discovering that he can use his newly acquired hand skills to produce any number of interesting results.

Throughout the second year, infants are becoming much more proficient with their hands. At 16 months of age, they can scribble with a crayon, and by the end of the second year, they can copy a simple horizontal or vertical line and even build towers of five or more blocks. What is happening is quite consistent with dynamical systems theory: Infants are gaining control over simple movements and then integrating these skills into increasingly complex, coordinated systems (Fentress & McLeod, 1986). Building a tower, for example, requires the child to first gain control over the thumb and the forefinger and then use the pincer grip as part of a larger action sequence that involves reaching for a block, snatching it, laying it squarely on top of another block, and then delicately releasing it. But despite their ability to combine simple motor activities into increasingly complex sequences, even 2- to 3-year-olds are not very good at catching and throwing a ball, cutting food with utensils, or drawing within the lines of their coloring books. These skills will emerge later in childhood as the muscles mature and children become more proficient at using visual information to help them coordinate their actions.

> **?** **WHAT DO YOU THINK?**
>
> Can you identify a common thread between recent changes in thinking about how (1) the brain's normal circuitry is fine-tuned and (2) the emergence of motor skills? What are the implications of these new viewpoints for the nature versus nurture debate?

Psychological Implications of Early Motor Development

Life changes dramatically for both parents and infants once a baby is able to reach out and grasp interesting objects, especially after he can crawl or walk to explore these treasures. Suddenly, parents find they have to child-proof their homes, or limit access to certain areas, or else run the risk of experiencing a seemingly endless string of disasters, including torn books, overturned vases, unraveled rolls of toilet paper, and irritable pets whose tails the little explorer has pulled. Placing limits on explorations often precipitates conflicts and a "testing of the wills" between infants and their mothers (Biringen et al., 1995). Nevertheless, parents are often thrilled by their infant's emerging motor skills, which not only provide clear evidence that development is proceeding normally, but also permit such pleasurable forms of social interaction as pat-a-cake, chase, and hide-and-seek.

Life becomes more challenging for parents as infants perfect their motor skills.

Aside from the entertainment value it provides, an infant's increasing control over bodily movements has other important cognitive and social consequences. Mobile infants may feel much more bold, for example, about meeting people and seeking challenges if they know that they can retreat to their caregivers for comfort should they feel insecure (Ainsworth, 1979). Achieving various motor milestones may also foster perceptual development. For example, crawlers (as well as noncrawlers who are made mobile with the aid of special walkers) are better able to search for and find hidden objects than infants of the same age who are not mobile (Kermoian & Campos, 1988). The self-produced movement of crawling and walking also makes infants more aware of *optical flow* (sensations that objects move as the infant does) which, in turn, helps them to orient themselves in space, improve their postures, and crawl or walk more efficiently (Higgins, Campos, & Kermoian, 1996). And as we will see in Chapter 6, crawling and walking both contribute to an understanding of distance relationships and a healthy fear of heights (Adolph, Eppler, & Gibson, 1993; Campos, Bertenthal, & Kermoian, 1992). So once again, we see that human development is a *holistic* enterprise; changes in motor skills have clear implications for other aspects of development.

Beyond Infancy: Motor Development in Childhood and Adolescence

The term *toddler* aptly describes most 1- to 2-year-olds, who often fall down or trip over stationary objects when they try to get somewhere in a hurry. But as children mature, their locomotor skills increase by leaps and bounds. By age 3, children can walk or run in a straight line and leap off the floor with both feet, although they can clear only very small (8- to 10-inch) objects in a single bound and cannot easily turn or stop while running. Four-year-olds can skip, hop on one foot, catch a large ball with both hands, and run much farther and faster than they could 1 year earlier (Corbin, 1973). By age 5, children are becoming rather graceful: like adults, they pump their arms when they run, and their balance has improved to the point that some of them can learn to ride a bicycle. Despite (or perhaps because of) the rapid progress they are making, young children often overestimate the physical feats they can perform, and the bolder ones may end up with bruises, burns, cuts, scrapes, and an assortment of other injuries (Plumert, 1995).

proprioceptive information
sensory information from the muscles, tendons, and joints that help one to locate the position of one's body (or body parts) in space.

ulnar grasp
an early manipulatory skill in which an infant grasps objects by pressing the fingers against the palm.

pincer grasp
a grasp in which the thumb is used in opposition to the fingers, enabling an infant to become more dexterous at lifting and fondling objects.

Top-heavy toddlers often lose their balance when they try to move very quickly.

With each passing year, school-age children can run a little faster, jump a little higher, and throw a ball a little further (Herkowitz, 1978; Keough & Sugden, 1985). Part of the reason that children are improving at these large-muscle activities is that they are growing larger and stronger. But they are also fine-tuning their motor skills. As shown in Figure 5.6, young children throw only with the arm, whereas adolescents are usually able to coordinate shoulder, arm, and leg movements to put the force of their bodies behind their throws. So older children and adolescents can throw farther than younger children can, not solely because they are bigger and stronger, but because they also use more refined and efficient techniques of movement (Gallahue, 1989).

At the same time, eye–hand coordination and control of the small muscles are improving rapidly so that children can make more sophisticated use of their hands. Three-year-olds find it difficult to button their shirts, tie their shoes, or copy simple designs. By age 5, children can accomplish all of these feats and can even cut a straight line with scissors or copy letters and numbers with a crayon. By age 8 or 9, they can use household tools such as screwdrivers and have become skilled performers at games such as jacks and Nintendo that require eye–hand coordination. Finally, older children display quicker *reaction times* than younger children do (Wilkinson & Allison, 1989), which helps to explain why they usually beat younger playmates at "action" games such as dodge ball or table tennis.

Boys and girls are nearly equal in physical abilities until puberty, when boys continue to post gains on tests of large-muscle activities, whereas girls level off or decline (Thomas & French, 1985; see Figure 5.7). These sex differences are, in part, attributable to biology: Adolescent boys have more muscle and less fat than adolescent girls and might be expected to outperform them on tests of physical strength (Tanner, 1990). Yet biological developments do not account for all the difference in large-muscle performance between boys and girls (Smoll & Schutz, 1990); nor do they adequately explain the *declining* performance of girls, who continue to grow taller and heavier, between ages 12 and 17. Jacqueline Herkowitz (1978) believes that the apparent physical decline of adolescent girls is a product of gender-role socialization: With their widening hips and developing breasts, girls are often encouraged to become less tomboyish and more interested in traditionally feminine (and less athletic) activities.

There is clearly an element of truth to this notion in that female *athletes* show no apparent decline in large-muscle performance over time. Furthermore, as gender roles

Figure 5.6 *As these initial tosses and mature throws illustrate large-muscle activities become more refined and efficient with age.*

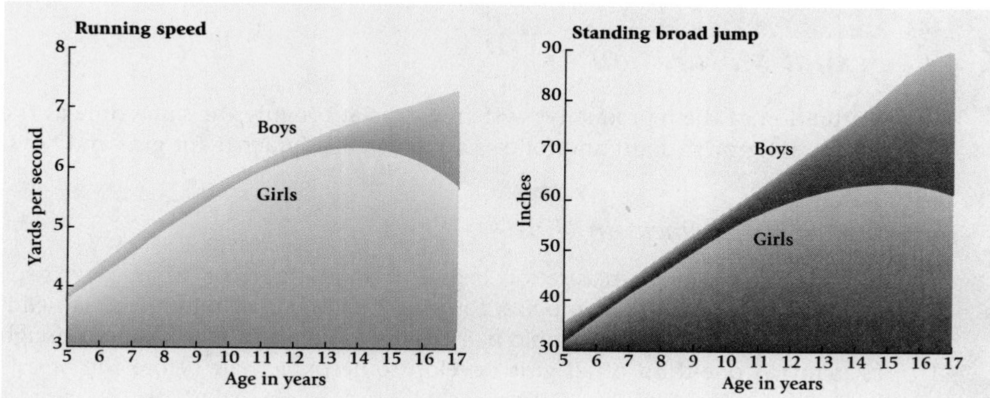

Figure 5.7 *Age and sex differences on two tests of large-muscle activity.* FROM JOHNSON & BUSKIRK, 1974.

have changed in the past few decades, female athletes have been steadily improving their performances, and the male/female gap in physical performance has narrowed dramatically (Dyer, 1977; Whipp & Ward, 1992). So it seems that adolescent girls would almost certainly continue to improve on tests of large-muscle activity if they chose to remain physically active. And they may experience other benefits as well, for high school girls who regularly participate in sports feel more physically competent, enjoy a higher sense of self-worth, and report feeling depressed less often than do female classmates who are not physically active (Richman, 1997).

PUBERTY: THE PHYSICAL TRANSITION FROM CHILD TO ADULT

The onset of adolescence is heralded by two significant changes in physical development. First, children change dramatically in size and shape as they enter the **adolescent growth spurt.** They also reach **puberty** (from the Latin word *pubertas,* meaning "to grow hairy"), the point in life when an individual reaches sexual maturity and becomes capable of producing a child.

The Adolescent Growth Spurt

The term *growth spurt* describes the rapid acceleration in height and weight that marks the beginning of adolescence. Girls typically enter the growth spurt by age 10½, reach a peak growth rate by age 12, and return to a slower rate of growth by age 13 to 13½ (Tanner, 1981). Boys lag behind girls by 2 to 3 years. They typically begin their growth spurt by age 13, peak at age 14, and return to a more gradual rate of growth by age 16. Because girls mature much earlier than boys, it is not at all uncommon for females to be the tallest two or three students in a junior high school classroom.

In addition to growing taller and heavier, the body assumes an adultlike appearance during the adolescent growth spurt. Perhaps the most noticeable changes are a widening of the hips for girls and a broadening of the shoulders for boys. Facial features also assume adult proportions as the forehead protrudes, the nose and jaw become more prominent, and the lips enlarge.

adolescent growth spurt
the rapid increase in physical growth that marks the beginning of adolescence.

puberty
the point at which a person reaches sexual maturity and is physically capable of fathering or conceiving a child.

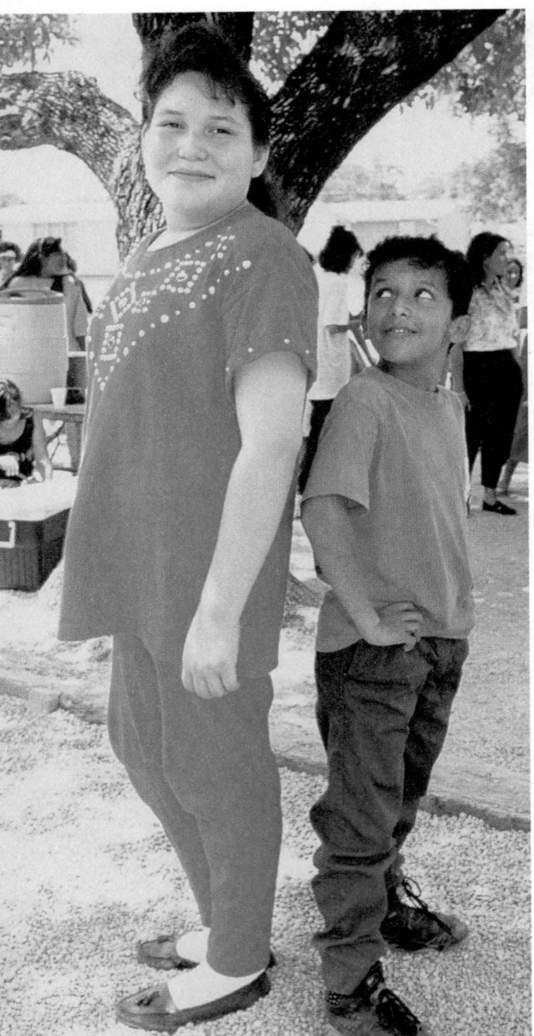

In early adolescence, girls are maturing more rapidly than boys.

Sexual Maturation

Maturation of the reproductive system occurs at roughly the same time as the adolescent growth spurt and follows a predictable sequence for girls and boys.

Sexual Development in Girls

For most girls, sexual maturation begins at about age 9 or 10 as fatty tissue accumulates around their nipples, forming small "breast buds" (Herman-Giddens et al., 1997). Usually pubic hair begins to appear a little later, although as many as one-third of all girls develop some pubic hair before the breasts begin to develop (Tanner, 1990).

As a girl enters her height spurt, the breasts grow rapidly and the sex organs begin to mature. Internally, the vagina becomes larger, and the walls of the uterus develop a powerful set of muscles that may one day be used to accommodate a fetus during pregnancy and to push it through the cervix and vagina during the birth process. Externally, the mons pubis (the soft tissue covering the pubic bone), the labia (the fleshy lips surrounding the vaginal opening), and the clitoris all increase in size and become more sensitive to touch (Tanner, 1990).

At about age 12½, the average girl in Western societies reaches **menarche**—the time of her first menstruation. Though it is generally assumed that a girl becomes fertile at menarche, young girls often menstruate without ovulating and *may* remain unable to reproduce for 12 to 18 months after menarche (Tanner, 1978). In the year following menarche, female sexual development concludes as the breasts complete their development and axillary (underarm) hair appears.

Sexual Development in Boys

For boys, sexual maturation begins at about 11 to 12 with an enlargement of the testes. The growth of the testes is often accompanied or soon followed by the appearance of unpigmented pubic hair. By the time the penis is fully developed at age 14½ to 15, most boys will have reached puberty and are now capable of fathering a child (Tanner, 1990).

Somewhat later, boys begin to sprout facial hair, first at the corners of the upper lip and finally on the chin and jawline. Body hair also grows on the arms and legs, although signs of a hairy chest may not appear until the late teens or early twenties, if at all. Another hallmark of male sexual maturity is a lowering of the voice as the larynx grows and the vocal cords lengthen. In fact, many men may laugh (years later) about their voices "cracking" up and down between a squeaky soprano and a deep baritone, sometimes within a single sentence.

Individual Differences in Physical and Sexual Maturation

So far, we have been describing developmental norms, or the average ages when adolescent changes take place. But as Figure 5.8 indicates, there are great individual differences in the timing of physical and sexual maturation. An early-maturing girl who develops breast buds at age 8, starts her growth spurt at age 9½, and reaches menarche at age 10½ may nearly complete her growth and pubertal development before the late-developing girls in her class have even begun. Individual differences among boys are at least as great. Some boys reach sexual maturity by age 12½ and are as tall as they will ever be by age 13, whereas others begin growing later than that and do not reach puberty until their late teens. This perfectly normal biological variation may be observed in any junior high classroom, where one will find a wide assortment of bodies, ranging from those that are entirely childlike to those that are very adultlike.

menarche
the first occurrence of menstruation.

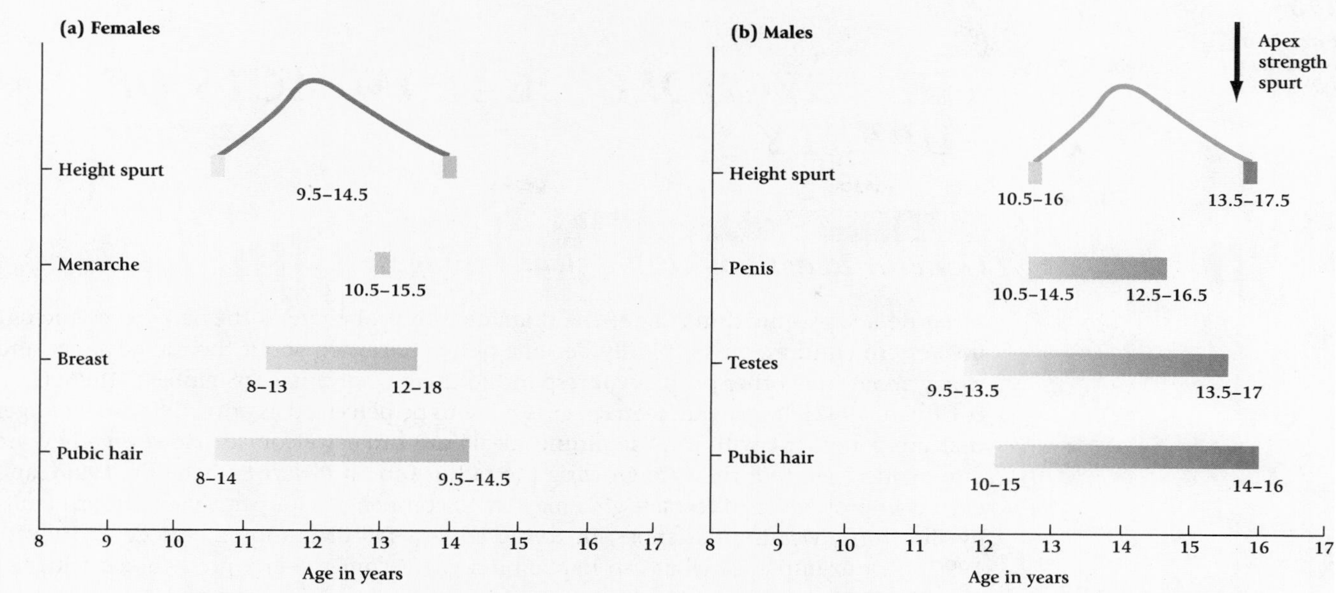

Figure 5.8 *Milestones in the sexual maturation of girls (a) and boys (b). The numbers represent the variation among individuals in the ages at which each aspect of sexual maturation begins or ends. For example, we see that the growth of the penis may begin as early as age 10½ or as late as 14½.* FROM TANNER, 1990.

Secular Trends: Are We Maturing Earlier?

About 15 years ago, women in one family were surprised when a 6th-grader began to menstruate shortly after her 12th birthday. The inevitable comparisons soon began, as the girl learned that neither of her great-grandmothers had reached this milestone until age 15 and that her grandmother had been nearly 14 and her mother 13. At this point, the girl casually replied "Big deal! Lots of girls in my class have got their periods."

As it turns out, this young woman was simply "telling it like it is." In 1900, when her great-grandmother was born, the average age of first menstruation was 14 to 15. By 1950, most girls were reaching menarche between 13½ and 14, and today's norms have dropped even further, to age 12½ (Tanner, 1990). This **secular trend** toward earlier maturation started more than 100 years ago in the industrialized nations of the world, where it has recently leveled off, and it is now happening in the more prosperous nonindustrialized countries as well. In addition, people in industrialized nations have been growing taller and heavier over the past century.

What explains these secular trends? Better nutrition and advances in medical care seem to be most responsible (Tanner, 1990). Today's children are more likely than their parents or grandparents to reach their genetic potentials for maturation and growth because they are better fed and less likely to experience growth-retarding illnesses. Even within our own relatively affluent society, poorly nourished adolescents mature later than well-nourished ones do. Girls who are tall and overweight as children tend to mature early (Graber et al, 1994), whereas many dancers, gymnasts, and other girls who engage regularly in strenuous physical activity may begin menstruating very late or stop menstruating after they have begun (Hopwood et al., 1990). Here, then, are strong clues that nature and nurture interact to influence the timing of pubertal events.

secular trend
a trend in industrialized societies toward earlier maturation and greater body size now than in the past.

WHAT DO YOU THINK? ?

Recent research (Herman-Giddens et al., 1997) reveals that nearly half of African-American girls have begun to develop breasts, pubic hair, or both by age 8, whereas only 15% of European-American girls show such early signs of pubertal change. How would you account for this race difference in female sexual maturation?

THE PSYCHOLOGICAL IMPACTS OF PUBERTY

General Reactions to Physical Changes

What do adolescents think about the dramatic physical changes they are experiencing? In Western cultures, girls typically become quite concerned about their appearance and worry about how other people will respond to them (Cauffman & Steinberg, 1996; Greif & Ulman, 1982). In general, teenage girls hope to be perceived as attractive, and changes that are congruent with the "feminine ideal" are often welcomed. However, they are often concerned that they are growing too tall or too fat (Swarr & Richards, 1996), and even well-proportioned teenage girls may try to compensate for perceived physical faults by slouching, wearing flat shoes, or trying endless fad diets (Rosen, Tracey, & Howell, 1990). (For examples of what can happen if a girl becomes overly preoccupied with her weight, see Box 5.2.)

Girls' reactions to menarche are mixed (Greif & Ulman, 1982). They are often excited but somewhat confused as well, especially if they mature very early or have not been told what to expect (Brooks-Gunn, 1988). Few girls today are traumatized by menarche, but at the same time, few are overjoyed about becoming a woman (Koff & Rierden, 1995; Moore, 1995).

Boys' body images are more positive than those of girls, and they are much more likely than girls are to welcome their weight gains (Richards et al., 1990). Teenage boys also hope to be tall, hairy, and handsome, and they may become preoccupied with the aspects of body image that center on physical and athletic prowess (Simmons & Blyth, 1987). Whereas menarche is a memorable event for girls, boys are often only dimly aware of the physical changes they are experiencing (Zani, 1991). They rarely tell anyone about their first ejaculation, often were not prepared for it, and like girls, express mixed reactions to becoming sexually mature (Gaddis & Brooks-Gunn, 1985; Stein & Reiser, 1994).

Social Impacts of Pubertal Changes

Adolescents who are maturing physically and sexually not only come to feel differently about themselves but come to be viewed and treated differently by other people. In many nonindustrialized societies, rituals called **rites of passage** inform the whole community that a child has become an adult (Schlegel & Barry, 1991). Among the Kaguru of eastern Africa, for example, pubertal boys are led into the bush, stripped, and shaved of all hair, which symbolizes losing their status as children (Beidelman, 1971). They then undergo the painful experience of circumcision without anesthesia, learn about tribal sexual practices, and are taught ritual songs and riddles that instruct them in the ways of manhood. Finally, they are "anointed" with red earth to mark their new status and led back to the village for celebrations and feasts. The Kaguru girl is initiated by herself whenever she experiences her first menstruation. Her genital area is cut as a mark of her new status, and she is instructed in the ways of womanhood, usually by her grandmother, before being welcomed back into society as an adult.

Although our society has no universal rites of passage to mark the transition from childhood to adolescence, or from adolescence to adulthood, pubertal changes may nonetheless have social consequences. Lawrence Steinberg (1981; 1988) reports that around age 11 to 13, when pubertal changes are peaking, European-American adolescents become more independent and feel less close to their parents, with whom they often argue (see also Paikoff & Brooks-Gunn, 1991). These standoffs usually involve

rites of passage
rituals that signify the passage from one period of life to another (for example, puberty rites).

5.2

DEVELOPMENTAL ISSUES

Two Serious Eating Disorders of Adolescence

Thirty years ago, a young British model nicknamed Twiggy defined the height of fashion. As her name implied, Twiggy was very thin. And the attention she received from the popular media sent a none-too-subtle message to women around the Western world: Skinny is beautiful, and fat is ugly.

Unfortunately, some adolescents carry this maxim to a life-threatening extreme. **Anorexia nervosa** (or "nervous loss of appetite") is a potentially fatal eating disorder without any known organic cause that may affect as many as 1 of every 200 adolescent girls (as compared with 1 in 2,000 adolescent boys or adult women). Anorexics have a morbid fear of becoming obese and will do whatever they can to purge their bodies of fat. The typical anorexic is a quiet, obedient teenage girl from a middle-class or affluent family who has reached puberty earlier than her peers and who suddenly begins to starve herself (Graber et al., 1994; Hsu, 1990). The process seems harmless at first as the young woman sets a modest goal and diets to the desired weight. But once she reaches her target, the anorexic simply continues to diet, eating less and less until she is little more than skin and bones. After she loses 20 to 30% of her body weight, secondary sex characteristics (breasts and hips) may be scarcely noticeable, and menstruation often stops. And even though she may resemble a walking skeleton, the 60- to 70-pound anorexic often insists that she is well-nourished and feels that she could stand to lose a few more pounds (Hsu, 1990).

Why do relatively few girls become anorexic, even though nearly all of them experience social pressure to be thin? Genetic factors may predispose some individuals to develop the disorder, for anorexia runs in families (Hsu, 1990). Yet eating disorders rarely emerge unless a susceptible girl also experiences disturbed family relationships (Swarr & Richards, 1996). According to Salvador Minuchin and his associates (1978), most anorexics have trouble making decisions and forming a personal identity. Why? Because their parents tend to be firm, overprotective guardians who tolerate little dissent or negative emotionality (see also Pike & Rodin, 1991). The result may be a young woman who can't seem to break free of her parents and who desperately hopes to establish some sense of control over her life, which she thinks she can do by rigidly controlling her diet and body image (Smolak & Levine, 1993).

Family therapy seems to be the most effective treatment for anorexia nervosa. Treatment may begin by hospitalizing the patient to tube-feed her (if her life is in danger) or to apply behavioral modification techniques (for example, rewarding her with praise and privileges for gaining weight) to change her eating habits. Once the patient begins to eat, family therapy begins. The purpose of the therapy is to persuade parents to exert less control over the adolescent's activities while convincing the anorexic that she can achieve autonomy and higher self-esteem through means other than self-starvation. Unfortunately, fewer than half of treated anorexics make a complete recovery (Zerbe, 1993), with the prognosis being best for younger patients who have been ill less than 3 years (Russell et al., 1987). By contrast, only 25 to 30% of *untreated* anorexics show any improvement, and as many as 5 to 10% of them end up committing suicide or starving themselves to death (Hsu, 1990).

Bulimia is another serious eating disorder that is much more common than anorexia. Bulimics are binge eaters who may consume several times their normal daily caloric intake in a single sitting and then purge themselves of this feast by vomiting or taking laxatives. Although anorexics are often bulimics, most who suffer from bulimia are of normal weight or are slightly overweight. Like anorexics, bulimic individuals tend to have poor body images and are overly concerned about getting fat. However, bulimics differ from anorexics in that they are often extroverted and impulsive rather than quiet and reserved, and they are far more likely than anorexics to experience open conflict and a lack of affection in their homes (Smolak & Levine, 1993). Bulimia is most common among college-age populations, where as many as 5% of women (and less than 1% of men) regularly partake in this binge/purge syndrome (Hsu, 1990).

Like anorexia, bulimia can have any number of very serious side effects. Laxatives and diuretics used as purging agents can deplete the body of potassium and induce cardiac arrhythmia and heart attacks. Regular induction of vomiting can produce hernias, and bulimics have even drowned in their own vomit. Finally, binge eating is hardly a constructive approach to most problems, particularly for someone who is concerned about getting fat. So it is perhaps understandable that many bulimics are depressed and that some turn to suicide as a solution for their problems.

Treatment for bulimia includes individual and family psychotherapy designed to help the patient understand the causes and control of binging and antidepressant medication for those with clinical depression (Seabrook, 1997). Although most bulimics respond favorably to treatment (see Hsu, 1990 for a literature review), it has been estimated that the majority of affected individuals never recognize that they have a potentially serious problem and may continue to binge without ever seeking help.

World Class gymnast Christy Henrich was only 22 years old when she died in 1994 as a result of anorexia nervosa and bulimia.

squabbles about unmade beds, late hours, and loud music rather than arguments about core values, but they can be unpleasant nonetheless. Hormonal changes in early adolescence may contribute to these conflicts, as well as to moodiness, bouts of depression, and restlessness (Buchanan, Eccles, & Becker, 1992; Udry, 1990). However, none of these experiences is inevitable. In fact, Mexican-American boys and their parents appear to become *closer* rather than more distant as puberty arrives, suggesting that cultural beliefs about the family or about the significance of becoming more adultlike can influence parent-child relations during adolescence (Molina & Chassin, 1996).

Even when parent–child relations are disrupted early in adolescence, they typically become warmer again later in adolescence, once the pubertal transition is over (Greenberger & Chen, 1996; Larson et al., 1996). Parents can help their children adjust successfully to puberty by maintaining close relationships, being patient, and helping adolescents to accept themselves and all the physical and social changes they are experiencing (Swarr & Richards, 1996). Clearly, the early teenage years are a period when biological changes interact with changes in the social environment to influence the adolescence experience (Magnusson, 1995; Paikoff & Brooks-Gunn, 1991).

Does Timing of Puberty Matter?

Think back for a moment to your own adolescence when you first realized that you were rapidly becoming a man or a woman. Did this happen to you earlier than to your friends, or later? Do you think that the timing of these events could have influenced your personality or social life?

Timing of puberty does have some meaningful implications, although its impact differs somewhat for boys and girls.

anorexia nervosa
a life-threatening eating disorder characterized by self- starvation and a compulsive fear of getting fat.

bulimia
a life-threatening eating disorder characterized by recurrent eating binges followed by such purging activities as heavy use of laxatives or vomiting.

Possible Impacts on Boys

Longitudinal research conducted at the University of California suggests that boys who mature early enjoy a number of social advantages over boys who mature late. One study followed the development of 16 early-maturing and 16 late-maturing male adolescents over a 6-year period and found late maturers to be more eager, anxious, and attention-seeking (and also rated by teachers as less masculine and less physically attractive) than early maturers (Jones & Bayley, 1950). Early maturers tended to be poised and confident in social settings and were more likely to win athletic honors and election to student offices. Although this study was based on only 32 boys in California, other researchers have found that late-maturing males do tend to feel somewhat socially inadequate and inferior (Duke et al., 1982; Livson & Peskin, 1980). Late-maturing boys also have lower educational aspirations than early maturers do, and they even score lower on school achievement tests early in adolescence (Dubas, Graber, & Petersen, 1991).

Early-maturing males tend to be poised and confident in social settings and popular with their peers.

Why is the early-maturing boy so advantaged? One reason may be that his greater size and strength often make him a more capable athlete, which in turn is apt to bring social recognition from adults and peers (Simmons & Blyth, 1987). The early maturer's adultlike appearance may also prompt others to overestimate his competencies and to grant him privileges and responsibilities normally reserved for older individuals. Indeed, parents hold higher educational and achievement aspirations for early-maturing than for late-maturing sons (Duke et al., 1982), and they have fewer conflicts with early maturers about issues such as acceptable curfews and the boy's choice of friends (Savin-Williams & Small, 1986). Perhaps you can see how this generally positive, harmonious atmosphere might promote the poise or self-confidence that enables early maturers to become popular and to assume positions of leadership within the peer group.

Do these differences between early and late maturers persist into adulthood? In general, they fade over time. By 12th grade, for example, differences in academic performance between early and late maturers have already disappeared (Dubas et al., 1991). But there are some interesting twists in the plot. Jones (1965), for example, found that early-maturing boys from the University of California study were still somewhat more sociable, confident, and responsible in their 30s than their peers who had matured later (Jones, 1965). So some of the advantages of early maturation may carry over into adulthood. Yet these early maturers were also more rigid and conforming than the late maturers, who as men seemed more innovative and better able to cope with stressful situations. Possibly their having to struggle with the problems of being "late" helped late-maturing boys to be flexible and develop effective coping skills.

Possible Impacts on Girls

For girls, maturing early may be somewhat of a *disadvantage.* Although early breast development is associated with a favorable body image and increased *self-confidence* (Brooks-Gunn & Warren, 1988), several studies find that early-maturing girls are somewhat *less* outgoing and *less* popular than their prepubertal classmates (Aro & Taipale, 1987; Clausen, 1975; Faust, 1960) and are likely to report more symptoms of anxiety and depression as well (Ge, Conger, & Elder, 1996; Hayward et al., 1997). Intuitively, these findings make some sense. A girl who matures very early may look very different from female classmates, who may tease her. She will look older than boys in the class, who will not mature for 2 to 3 years and are not yet all that enthused about an early maturer's more womanly attributes (Caspi et al., 1993). As a result, early-maturing girls often seek (or are sought out by) older companions, particularly boys, who often steer them away from academic pursuits and into more adultlike, undesirable activities, such as smoking, drinking, drug use, and sex, that they are not yet prepared to handle (Caspi et al., 1993; Stattin & Magnusson, 1990). Indeed, risks of psychological distress among early-maturing girls are much higher when they attend coed schools and have lots of boys as friends (Caspi et al., 1993; Ge et al., 1996).

Some of the curses of early maturity can be long-lasting. One Swedish study, for example, found that early-maturing girls continued to perform less well at school and were more likely to drop out than their late-maturing or on-time classmates (Stattin &

Concept Check 5.2
Psychological Aspects of Physical and Motor Development

Check your understanding of some of the psychological aspects of physical and motor development by matching one or more of the following developments with its psychological correlates as listed in items 1–8. The developments are: (a) early maturation, (b) late maturation, (c) on-time maturation, (d) peak of pubertal changes, (e) locomotor skills, (f) sex-role socialization, (g) menarche/ejaculation. Answers appear in the Appendix at the back of the book.

_____ 1. decline in girl's large muscle strength
_____ 2. increase in parent–child conflict
_____ 3. improves likelihood of good social adjustment in boys
_____ 4. presents risk of adjustment difficulties for girls early in adolescence
_____ 5. likely to be met with mixed feelings by adolescents of each sex
_____ 6. may increase one's boldness and willingness to seek new challenges
_____ 7. presents risk of promoting low self-confidence and lower social status in boys
_____ 8. often associated with favorable peer status for girls early in adolescence

Magnusson, 1990). Yet, most early-maturing girls fare better over time. Not only are they often admired later in junior high, once the female peer group discovers that early-maturing girls tend to be popular with boys (Faust, 1960), but as young adults, women who matured early are no less well-adjusted than their late-maturing peers (Stattin & Magnusson, 1990).

Overall, then, both the advantages of maturing early and the disadvantages of maturing late are greater for boys than for girls. But even though late-maturing boys and early-maturing girls are more likely to be distressed, the psychological differences between early and late maturers become smaller and more mixed in nature by adulthood. Finally, let's note that the differences between early and late maturers are not large and that many factors other than timing of puberty influence whether this period of life goes smoothly or not.

Adolescent Sexuality

The biological upheaval of puberty brings about major hormonal changes, one of which is increased production of androgens in both boys and girls, which dramatically increases one's sex drive (Udry, 1990). Although grade-school children often play kiss-and-chase games that prepare them for heterosexual relationships later in life (Thorne, 1993), the new urges they feel make adolescents increasingly aware of their own **sexuality**—an aspect of development that greatly influences their self-concepts. One major hurdle adolescents face is figuring out how to properly manage and express their sexual feelings, an issue that is heavily influenced by the social and cultural contexts in which they live.

Cultural Influences on Sexuality

Societies clearly differ in the education they provide children about sexual matters and in their attempts to prepare them for their roles as mature sexual beings (Ford & Beach, 1951). On the island of Ponape, for example, 4- and 5-year-olds receive a thorough "sex education" from adults and are encouraged to experiment with one another. Among the Chewa of Africa, parents believe that practice makes perfect; so, with the blessings of their parents, older boys and girls build huts and play at being husbands and wives in trial marriages. By contrast, *restrictive cultures* view sexuality as a taboo subject and vigorously suppress its expression. In New Guinea, for example, Kwoma children are punished for sex play and are not allowed to touch themselves. In fact, a Kwoma boy caught with an erection is likely to have his penis beaten with a stick!

Where do the United States and other Western societies fall on this continuum of sexual permissiveness–restrictiveness? Most can be classified as relatively restrictive. If you are like many Western children and adolescents, the "facts of life" may have come as a shock to you, having been related not by your parents, but by an older sibling or peer. In fact, you may have had trouble imagining your parents ever having done what it takes to conceive you (Walters, 1997). American parents generally discourage overt sex play and often find ways to elude the sexually explicit questions their children may ask (Thorne, 1993). Mainly, adults leave the task of preparing for sexual relations up to children themselves, and children and adolescents end up learning from their peers how they should relate to members of the other sex.

Sexual Attitudes and Behavior

How, then, do Western adolescents, who receive so little guidance from adults, ever learn to manage sexual urges and to incorporate their sexuality into their self-concepts? These tasks have never been easy and, as we see in Box 5.3, can be especially trying for teenagers who find themselves attracted to members of their own sex. Judging from letters to advice columns, adults seem to think that modern adolescents, driven by

sexuality
aspect of self referring to erotic thoughts, actions, and orientation.

5.3

CURRENT CONTROVERSIES

On Sexual Orientation and the Origins of Homosexuality

Part of the task of establishing one's sexual identity is becoming aware of one's *sexual orientation*—one's preference for sexual partners of the same or other sex. Sexual orientation exists on a continuum, and not all cultures categorize sexual preferences as ours does (Paul, 1993), but we commonly describe people as having primarily heterosexual, homosexual, or bisexual orientations. Most adolescents establish a heterosexual orientation without much soul-searching. For the 3 to 6% of youths who are attracted to members of their own sex, the process of accepting that they have a homosexual orientation and establishing a positive identity in the face of negative societal attitudes can be a long and torturous one (Hershberger & D'Augelli, 1995; Patterson, 1995). It is not that homosexual youths are especially critical of themselves, for their levels of general self-esteem are quite comparable with those of heterosexual peers (Savin-Williams, 1995). Yet, they may be anxious or even depressed about their gay or lesbian orientation, often because they fear rejection from family members or physical and verbal abuse from peers were their orientation to become known (Baumrind, 1995; Hershberger & D'Augelli, 1995). Consequently, many gay or lesbian youth do not gather the courage to "come out" until their mid-20s, if they come out at all (Garnets & Kimmel, 1991; Miller, 1995).

How do adolescents become homosexual or heterosexual? In addressing this issue, John Money (1988) emphasizes that sexual orientation is *not* a choice we make but, rather, something that happens to us. In other words, we do not *prefer* to be gay or straight; we simply turn out that way. Yet not everyone agrees with this viewpoint. As Diana Baumrind (1995) has noted, many bisexual individuals may actively *choose* to adopt a heterosexual identity, even though they have been sexually attracted to members of both sexes. Similarly, Celia Kitzinger and Sue Wilkinson (1995) find that many women with more than 10 years of heterosexual experience, who had always viewed themselves as heterosexuals, make a transition to lesbianism later in adulthood. Clearly, these findings imply that at least *some* homosexual individuals were not predestined to be homosexual and had at least *some* say in the matter.

How, then, might individuals become homosexual? Part of the answer lies in the genetic code, it seems. Michael Bailey and his colleagues (Bailey & Pillard, 1991; Bailey et al., 1993) find that identical twins are more alike in sexual orientation than fraternal twins are. But as we see in the table, only about half of identical twin pairs share the same sexual orientation. This means that *environment contributes at least as much as genes* to the development of sexual orientation.

	Identical Twins	**Fraternal Twins**
Both male twins are gay/bisexual if one is	52%	22%
Both female twins are gay/bisexual if one is	48%	16%

Sources: Male figures, from Bailey & Pillard, 1991; female figures, from Bailey et al., 1993.

What environmental factors might help to determine whether a person with a genetic predisposition toward homosexuality comes to be attracted to same-sex companions? We really don't know as yet. The old psychoanalytic view that male homosexuality stems from having a domineering mother and a weak father has received little support (LeVay, 1996). Nor is there any compelling evidence for the long-standing "seduction hypothesis"—the idea that homosexuals have been lured into the lifestyle by an older same-sex companion. Even the once-popular notion that fathers who reject their sons will make them effeminate and push them toward homosexuality has failed to gain much support (Bell et al., 1981; Green, 1987). And growing up with a gay or lesbian parent also seems to have little impact on later sexual orientation (Bailey et al., 1995; Golombok & Tasker, 1996). A more promising hypothesis is that hormonal influences during the prenatal period may be important. For example, women exposed before birth to diethylstilbestoral (DES) or to heightened levels of androgen are more likely than other women to express a bisexual or lesbian orientation, a finding that suggests that high prenatal doses of sex hormones may dispose at least some females to homosexuality (Dittman et al., 1992; Meyer-Bahlberg et al., 1995). However, the fact is that no one yet knows exactly which factors in the prenatal or postnatal environment contribute, along with genes, to a homosexual orientation (Berenbaum & Snyder, 1995; Paul, 1993).

raging hormones, are almost obsessed with sex and feel quite free to express their sexuality. How accurate is this portrayal?

Sexual Attitudes. Adolescents have become increasingly liberal in their thinking about sex throughout the 20th century, with recent attitudes reverting only slightly in a more conservative direction due to fears of contracting AIDS (Carroll, 1988; McKenna, 1997). Yet, it is clear that today's youth have changed some of their attitudes about sex while retaining many of the same views held by their parents and grandparents.

Some kind of sexual involvement is now part of the average adolescent's experience.

What has changed? For one thing, adolescents now firmly believe that premarital *sex with affection* is acceptable, although, like teens of earlier eras, they think that casual or exploitative sex is wrong (even if they have had such experiences). Still, only a small percentage of sexually active adolescents in one national survey (6% of the males and 11% of the females) mentioned *love* as the major reason they first had intercourse. Instead, nearly 75% of the girls and 80% of the boys attributed their loss of virginity to strong social pressures to initiate sexual relations, while also citing curiosity and sexual desire as important reasons for becoming sexually active (Harris & Associates, 1986).

A second major change in teenage attitudes about sex is the decline of the **double standard**—the idea that many sexual practices viewed as appropriate for males (for example, premarital sex, promiscuity) are less appropriate for females. The double standard hasn't completely disappeared, for college students of the early 1990s still believed that a woman who has many sexual partners is more immoral than an equally promiscuous man (Robinson et al., 1991). But Western societies are rapidly moving toward a single standard of sexual behavior for both males and females.

Finally, sexual attitudes today are highly variable and seem to reflect an *increased confusion about sexual norms.* As Philip Dreyer (1982) notes, the "sex with affection" idea is very ambiguous: Must one truly be in love, or is mere liking enough to justify sexual intercourse? It is now up to the individual(s) to decide. Yet these decisions are tough because adolescents receive mixed messages from many sources. On the one hand, they are often told by parents, clergy, and advice columnists to value virginity and to avoid such consequences as pregnancy and sexually transmitted diseases. On the other hand, adolescents are strongly encouraged to be popular and attractive, and the more than 9,000 glamorous sexual innuendos and behaviors that they see annually on television (most of which occur between *unmarried* couples) may convince them that sexual activity is one means to these ends (American Academy of Pediatrics, 1986). Apparently, the behavior of older siblings adds to the confusion, for younger brothers and sisters of a sexually active sibling tend to be sexually active themselves, often at an earlier age than the older siblings were (East, 1996; Rodgers & Rowe, 1988). One young adolescent, lamenting the strong social pressures she faced to become sexually active, offered this amusing definition of a virgin: "An awfully ugly third grader" (Gullota, Adams, & Alexander, 1986, p. 109). In years gone by, the norms of appropriate behavior were much simpler: Sex was fine if you were married (or perhaps engaged), but it should otherwise be avoided. This is not to say that your parents or grandparents always resisted the temptations they faced, but they probably had a lot less difficulty than today's adolescents in deciding whether what they were doing was acceptable or unacceptable.

Sexual Behavior. Not only have sexual attitudes changed over the years, but so have patterns of sexual behavior. Generally, today's adolescents are involved in more intimate forms of sexual activity (masturbation, petting, and intercourse) at earlier ages than adolescents of earlier eras were (Bingham & Crockett, 1996; Forrest & Singh, 1990). Figure 5.9 shows the percentages of high school students from different historical periods who reported ever having experienced premarital intercourse. Notice that the long-term increase in sexual activity at the high school level may have peaked, for the most recent data available (for 1995) indicate that about half of high school girls (down from 55% in 1990) and 55% of high school boys (down from 60% in 1990) have ever had intercourse (McKenna, 1997). (By comparison, some 70 to 80% of college students have had sexual intercourse). Notice also from the figure that the sexual behavior of girls has changed more than that of boys so that sex differences in adolescent sexual activity have all but disappeared. Finally, it is clearly a myth to assume that today's youth are having sex as early and as often as circumstances permit. Only about 30% of U.S. adolescents have had sex by age 15, and their experiences are usually limited to one partner (Hendrick, 1994). Girls are more likely than boys to insist that sex and love—physical and emotional intimacy—go together, and they are more likely than boys to have been in a steady relationship with their first sexual partner (Darling, Davidson, & Passarello, 1992). This attitudinal gap between the sexes can sometimes create misunderstandings and hurt feelings, and it may partially explain why girls are less

double standard
the view that sexual behavior that is appropriate for members of one gender is less appropriate for the other.

likely than boys to describe their first sexual experience as satisfying (Darling et al., 1992; de Gaston, Jensen, & Weed, 1995).

In sum, both the sexual attitudes and the sexual behaviors of adolescents have changed dramatically in this century—so much so that some kind of sexual involvement is now part of the average adolescent's experience (McKenna, 1997). This is true of all major ethnic groups and social classes, and differences in sexual activity among social groups are shrinking dramatically (Forrest & Singh, 1990; Hendrick, 1994).

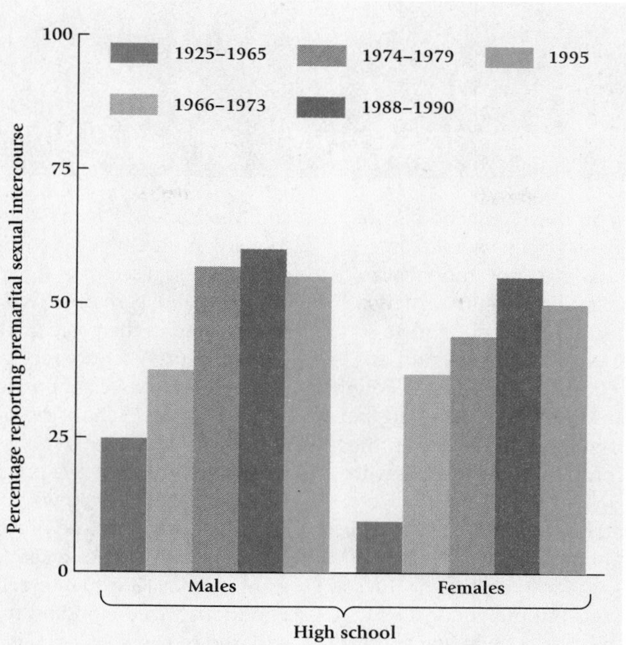

Figure 5.9 *Historical changes in the percentages of high school students reporting premarital sexual intercourse.* DATA FOR FIRST THREE TIME PERIODS ADAPTED FROM DREYER, *1982;* DATA FOR MORE RECENT PERIODS FROM BAIER, ROSENZWEIG, & WHIPPLE, *1991;* CENTERS FOR DISEASE CONTROL, *1992;* REINISCH ET AL., *1992;* MCKENNA, *1997.*

Personal and Social Consequences of Adolescent Sexual Activity

Who is most inclined to become sexually active early in adolescence and how risky is this activity? Research has identified a number of factors that contribute to early sexual involvement. Teenagers who have intercourse very early tend to be early maturers from low-income families, who are having difficulties at school, whose friends are sexually active, and who are already involved in such delinquent activities as alcohol or substance abuse (Bingham & Crockett, 1996; Capaldi, Crosby, & Stoolmiller, 1996; Tubman, Windle, & Windle, 1996). Indeed, the finding that African-American, Native American, and Hispanic-American adolescents are more likely than adolescents of other ethnicities to be sexually involved at earlier ages probably reflects the fact that more teenagers from those social groups are living in poverty and having difficulties at school, and have friends or older siblings who are sexually active (East, 1996; Sullivan, 1993).

Sadly, large numbers of sexually active adolescents fail to use contraception, largely because they are (1) uninformed about reproductive issues, (2) too cognitively immature to take seriously the possibility that their behavior could have serious long-term consequences, and (3) concerned that other people (including their partners) will think negatively of them if they appear prepared and thus "ready" to have sex (Brooks-Gunn & Furstenberg, 1989; Walters, 1997). Of course, such unsafe sex places them at risk of experiencing two serious consequences: sexually transmitted diseases and teenage pregnancy.

Sexually Transmitted Disease

In the United States, approximately one in five sexually active adolescents contracts a sexually transmitted disease (STD)—syphilis, gonorrhea, chlamydia, genital herpes, or AIDS—that, left untreated, can cause problems ranging from sterility to death in the infected individual and, as we noted in Chapter 4, birth defects and other complications for his or her children (Cates, 1995). Clearly, risk of STD is highest for teenagers who fail to use condoms regularly and for those who have sex with multiple partners.

As the number of cases of AIDS has grown, so too have efforts to educate children and adolescents about how to prevent this deadly disease. The incidence of AIDS in the

CULTURAL INFLUENCES

5.4

Educating Mexican-American Preadolescents about AIDS

Although the immediate threat of HIV infection is not as great for children as for sexually active adolescents, AIDS education aimed at grade-school students can serve many important functions. For example, information specifying how AIDS is transmitted can help students to avoid such high-risk behaviors as unprotected sex and promiscuity as they grow older. Efforts to debunk AIDS myths should also correct the anxiety-arousing misconception that this disease can be transmitted through casual contact, thus reducing fears of and fostering compassion for people with AIDS.

Recently, Carol Sigelman and her associates (1996) conducted an ambitious AIDS education program aimed at lower-income (mostly) Mexican-American children in Tucson, Arizona. The program sought to teach these youngsters that AIDS is a blood-borne disease transmitted by sexual contact, sharing needles, or other exchanges of blood between infected and noninfected individuals. They also tried to help students see that the HIV virus *cannot* be transmitted by sneezing, saliva exchange, or other forms of casual contact like colds and flu viruses can be.

Drawing on the wisdom that education is most effective when it builds on beliefs and cultural traditions of the students (see Chapter 16 for a review), Sigelman and associates carefully tailored their curriculum to their predominantly Mexican-American students. Focus groups were undertaken with Hispanic parents to assess their AIDS knowledge and their impressions of what kinds of instructions were needed. Surveys were undertaken to determine the attitudes and misconceptions that Mexican-American children had about AIDS. The curriculum was reviewed carefully by Mexican-American members of the staff, who pretested all materials on both Anglo- and Mexican-American children. Finally, attempts were made to increase the relevance of the curriculum for Mexican-American children by (1) using both Anglo- and Mexican-American names in the teaching script, (2) showing multiethnic video clips of HIV-positive teenagers discussing their disease, and (3) showing multiethnic cartoons debunking AIDS myths. Two lower-income parochial schools participated in the project. Third, 5th, and 7th grades in the "experimental" school received the AIDS education program in two 50-minute class periods on separate days. Age-mates in the "control" school did not receive the program.

The results of this study were impressive. When first tested 3 weeks after the program ended, students exposed to it not only knew significantly more about the ways AIDS is transmitted and can be prevented than control participants did, but they also endorsed fewer myths about AIDS and were more willing to interact with persons with AIDS. Equally important was the finding that, *nearly 1 year later,* students exposed to the AIDS education program still knew more about AIDS transmission and risk factors and still held more compassionate attitudes toward people with AIDS than control participants did.

In sum, early AIDS education programs can produce *long-term* gains in knowledge that may help grade-school children to avoid behaviors that would place them at risk of contracting AIDS later in adolescence. Let's also note that despite their greater likelihood of being affected by AIDS, Mexican-Americans are generally less knowledgeable about this disease and are more susceptible to AIDS myths than Anglos are (Aruffo, Coverdale, & Vallbona, 1991). Yet, the Mexican-American youth in Sigelman's study gained just as much from the AIDS education program as Anglo-American students did. So when educational programs are carefully tailored to the beliefs and values of high-risk minority populations, as Sigelman's was, there is every reason to believe that these "culturally sensitive" interventions can be *very* effective indeed.

United States is growing fastest among 13- to 19-year-olds, particularly African-American and Hispanic adolescents from urban backgrounds (Centers for Disease Control and Prevention, 1994; Faden & Kass, 1996). Most states now require some form of AIDS education in public schools, and there is evidence that these programs can increase grade-school children's knowledge about this disease and its prevention (Gill & Beazley, 1993; Osborne, Kistner, & Helgemo, 1993). As Box 5.4 indicates, AIDS education programs are particularly effective when they are tailored to the cultural traditions, beliefs, and values of the children one hopes to reach.

Teenage Pregnancy and Childbearing

Adolescents who are sexually active face another important consequence: Each year in the United States, more than *one million* unmarried teenage girls become pregnant. And although as many as 50% of these pregnancies end in miscarriage or abortion, over the next 4 years, *2 million* U.S. babies will be born to adolescent mothers (Miller et al.,

1996). The incidence of teenage pregnancy is about twice as high in the United States as in Canada and most European nations, ranging from a high of 16 pregnancies per 100 teenage girls in California to 6 pregnancies per 100 girls in North Dakota (Allan Guttmacher Foundation, as cited by McKenna, 1997). Out-of-wedlock births are more common among such economically disadvantaged groups as African-Americans, Hispanics, and Native Americans, and about two-thirds of these adolescent mothers choose to keep their babies rather than place them for adoption.

Consequences for Adolescent Mothers. Unfortunately for the adolescent who gives birth, the consequences are likely to include an interrupted education, loss of contact with her social network, and if she is one of the 50% who drop out of school, a future of low-paying (or no) jobs that perpetuates her economic disadvantage (Furstenberg, Brooks-Gunn, & Chase-Lansdale, 1989). In addition, many adolescent girls, particularly younger ones, are not prepared psychologically to become parents, a fact that can greatly affect their babies' developmental outcomes.

Consequences for Babies of Adolescent Mothers. As we noted in Chapter 4, teenage mothers, particularly those from economically disadvantaged backgrounds, are more likely than older mothers to be poorly nourished, to use alcohol and drugs while pregnant, and to fail to obtain adequate prenatal care. Consequently, many adolescent mothers experience more prenatal and birth complications than older mothers do and are more likely to deliver premature or small-for-date babies (Seitz & Apfel, 1994a).

Not only are their babies at risk for getting off to a rocky start, but so are many adolescent mothers, who are ill prepared intellectually for the responsibilities of motherhood and who rarely receive adequate financial or social support from a teenage father. Compared with older mothers, adolescent mothers know less about child development, view their infants as more difficult, experience greater parenting stress, and respond to their babies with less sensitivity and affection (Miller et al., 1996; Sommer et al., 1993). Unfortunately, this pattern of parenting can have long-term consequences, for children born to teenagers often show sizable intellectual deficits and emotional disturbances during the preschool years, and poor academic achievement, poor peer relations, and delinquent behaviors later in childhood (Furstenberg et al., 1989; Miller et al., 1996). A teenage mother's life situation and her child's developmental progress may improve later on, especially if she returns to school and avoids having more children; nevertheless, she (and her children) are likely to remain economically disadvantaged compared with peers who postpone parenthood until their 20s (Furstenberg et al., 1989).

Dealing with the Problem. How might we reduce the incidence of teenage pregnancy? One very promising approach is the privately funded Teen Outreach program now underway at nearly 50 locales around the United States. Adolescents in Teen Outreach perform volunteer service activities (for example, peer tutoring, hospital work) and take part in regular classroom discussions centering on such topics as their volunteer work, future career options, and current and future relationship decisions. A recent evaluation of Teen Outreach at 25 sites nationwide revealed that the incidence of pregnancy among female participants was less than half that of girls from similar social and family backgrounds who had not participated in the program (Allen et al., 1997). Apparently, productively engaged adolescents who have reason to be optimistic about their futures and their abilities to manage personal relationships are much less likely to become pregnant.

In addition, sex education that goes beyond the biological facts of reproduction, addressing such topics as contraception and the decision-making skills that teenagers need to resist pressures to have sex, can be very effective—especially if presented in junior high school *before* adolescents become sexually active (Pollack, 1997; St. Lawrence et al., 1995). And in light of evidence from Western Europe that free distribution of condoms does *not* encourage sexually inactive teenagers to become sexually active, many educators in this country are calling for similar contraceptive programs in the United States (Pollack, 1997). Those who favor earlier and more extensive sex

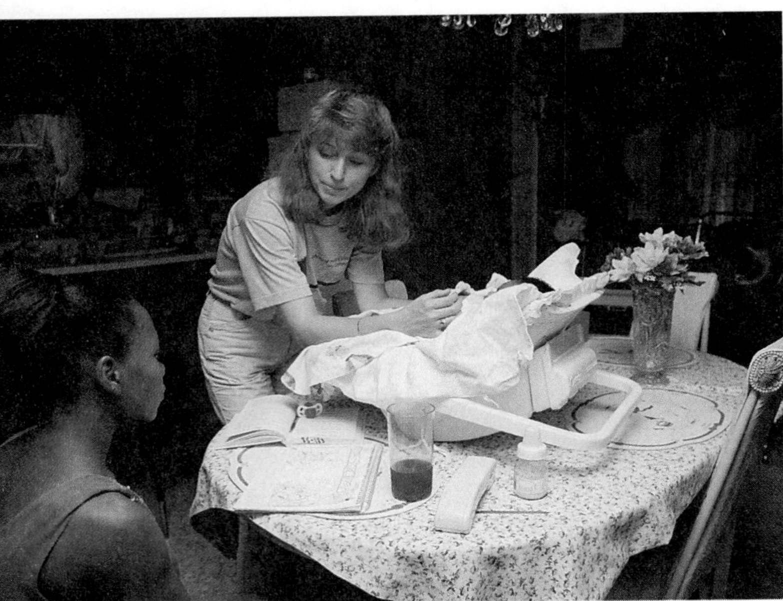

Adolescent mothers can benefit greatly from interventions that provide good prenatal care, encourage them to remain in school, and assist them to become sensitive, responsive parents.

education and free access to contraception believe that there is little chance of preventing the harmful consequences of teenage sexuality unless more adolescents either postpone sex or practice safer sex.

Finally, adolescent mothers and their babies need lots of help: good prenatal care, day-care (to allow mothers to return to school or to work), job training, and assistance in becoming a more sensitive and responsive parent. Victoria Seitz and Nancy Apfel (1994a) studied pregnant adolescents who had participated in a prenatal intervention where they received good prenatal care, lessons in parenting skills, and counseling to encourage them to complete high school and delay future pregnancies. Compared with other teenage mothers, girls who participated in the intervention had fewer low-birth-weight babies, performed better in school after giving birth, and were less likely to become pregnant again. Unfortunately, funds for these interventions are limited, and the vast majority of teenage parents do not receive the support that they need.

WHAT DO YOU THINK? ?

Suppose that interventions such as *Teen Outreach* or Seitz and Apfel's prenatal interventions for pregnant adolescents were to cost $3,000 per participant per year. Some have argued that it is "penny wise and pound foolish" for governments not to fund such programs for all at-risk teens who are likely to benefit from them. What is your position on this issue and why?

CAUSES AND CORRELATES OF PHYSICAL DEVELOPMENT

Although we have now charted the course of physical development from birth through adolescence, we've touched only briefly on the factors that influence growth. What *really* causes children to grow in the first place? And why do their bodies change so dramatically at adolescence, when growth accelerates? As we will see in the pages that follow, physical development results from a complex and continuous interplay between the forces of nature and nurture.

Biological Mechanisms

Clearly, biological factors play a major role in the growth process. Although children do not all grow at the same rate, we have seen that the *sequencing* of both physical maturation and motor development is reasonably consistent from child to child. Apparently, these regular maturational sequences that all humans share are species-specific attributes—products of our common genetic heritage.

Effects of Individual Genotypes

Aside from our common genetic ties to the human race, we have each inherited a unique combination of genes that influence our physical growth and development. For example, family studies clearly indicate that stature is a heritable attribute: Identical twins are much more similar in height than fraternal twins, whether the measurements are taken during the first year of life, at 4 years of age, or in early adulthood (Tanner, 1990). *Rate of maturation* is also genetically influenced. James Tanner (1990) reports that female identical twins reach menarche within 2 to 3 months of each other, whereas fraternal twin sisters are typically about 10 months apart. Similar genetic influences hold for milestones in skeletal growth and even for the appearance of teeth in infants.

How does genotype influence growth? We are not completely certain, although it appears that our genes regulate the production of hormones, which have major effects on physical growth and development.

Hormonal Influences—The Endocrinology of Growth

Hormones begin to influence development long before a child is born. As we learned in Chapter 4, a male fetus assumes a malelike appearance because (1) a gene on his Y chromosome triggers the development of testes, which (2) secrete a male hormone (testosterone) that is necessary for the development of a male reproductive system. By the fourth prenatal month, the thyroid gland has formed and begins to produce **thyroxine,** a hormone that is essential if the brain and nervous system are to develop properly. Babies born with a thyroid deficiency soon become mentally handicapped if this condition goes undiagnosed and untreated (Tanner, 1990). Those who develop a thyroid deficiency later in childhood will not suffer brain damage, because their brain growth spurt is over. However, they will begin to grow very slowly, a finding that indicates that a certain level of thyroxine is necessary for normal growth and development.

The most critical of the *endocrine* (hormone-secreting) glands is the **pituitary,** a "master gland" located at the base of the brain that triggers the release of hormones from all other endocrine glands. In addition to regulating the endocrine system, the pituitary produces a **growth hormone (GH)** that stimulates the rapid growth and development of body cells. Growth hormone is released in small amounts several times a day. When parents tell their children that lots of sleep will help them to grow big and strong, they are right: GH is normally secreted into the bloodstream about 60 to 90 minutes after a child falls asleep (Tanner, 1990). And GH is essential for *normal* growth and development. Children who lack this hormone do grow, and they are usually well-proportioned as adults. However, they will stand only about 130 cm tall or a little over 4 feet (Tanner, 1990).

During infancy and childhood, physical growth seems to be regulated by thyroxine and the pituitary growth hormone. What, then, triggers the adolescent growth spurt and other pubertal changes?

Research (reviewed in Tanner, 1990) has clarified the endocrinology of adolescence far beyond what we knew only 10 to 15 years ago. Long before any noticeable physical changes occur, pituitary secretions stimulate a girl's ovaries to produce more **estrogen** and a boy's testes to produce more **testosterone.** Once these sex hormones reach a critical level, the hypothalamus (a part of the brain) instructs the pituitary to secrete more growth hormone (GH). This increase in GH seems to be wholly responsible for the adolescent growth spurt in girls and is primarily responsible for boys' growth spurt. As for sexual maturation, the female hormone estrogen triggers the growth of a girl's breasts, uterus, vagina, pubic and underarm hair, and the widening of her hips. In boys, testosterone is responsible for growth of the penis and prostate, voice changes, and the development of facial and body hair. And although GH may be the primary contributor to the male growth spurt, testosterone exerts its own independent effects on the growth of a boy's muscles, the broadening of his shoulders, and the extension of his backbone. So it seems that adolescent boys experience larger growth spurts than adolescent girls do simply because testosterone promotes muscular and bone growth in ways that estrogen does not. Finally, androgen secreted by *adrenal glands* plays a secondary role in promoting the maturation of muscles and bones in both sexes (Tanner, 1990).

What causes the pituitary to activate the endocrine glands and precipitate the dramatic physical changes of adolescence? No one can say for sure. We know that skeletal

thyroxine
a hormone produced by the thyroid gland; essential for normal growth of the brain and the body.

pituitary
a "master gland" located at the base of the brain that regulates the endocrine glands and produces growth hormone.

growth hormone (GH)
the pituitary hormone that stimulates the rapid growth and development of body cells; primarily responsible for the adolescent growth spurt.

estrogen
female sex hormone, produced by the ovaries, that is responsible for female sexual maturation.

testosterone
male sex hormone, produced by the testes, that is responsible for male sexual maturation.

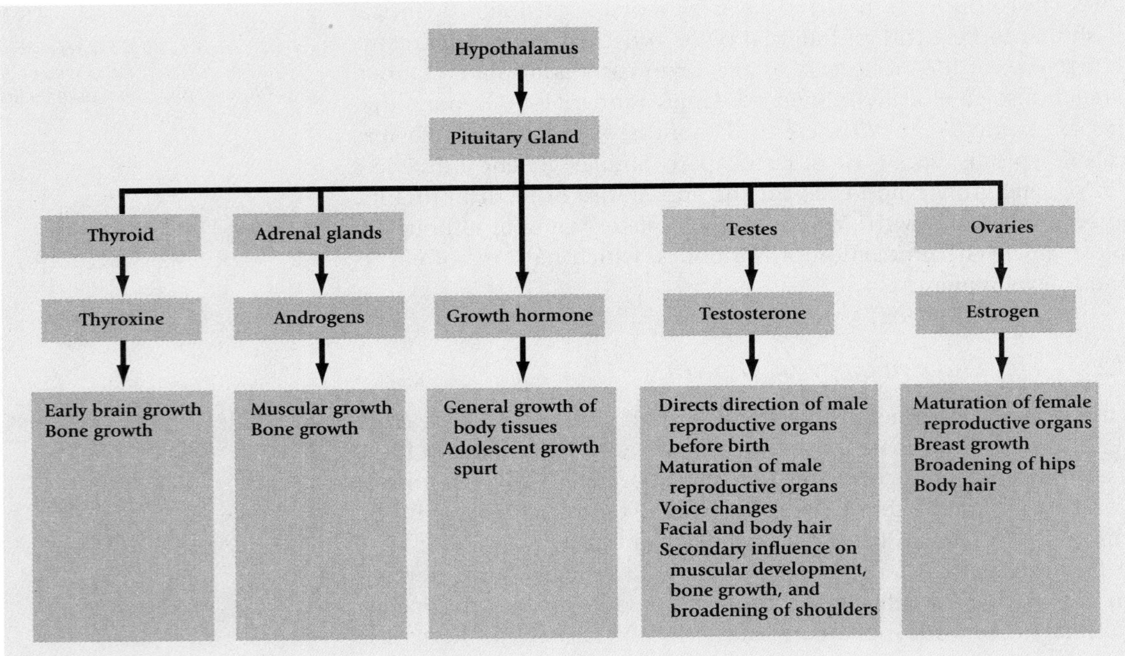

Figure 5.10 *Hormonal influences on physical development.*

maturity, which seems to be genetically controlled, is an excellent predictor of when menarche will occur (Tanner, 1990). Yet, any simple "genetic clock" theory that focuses on a singular precipitating factor is probably oversimplified, for the timing of breast growth, testicular development, and many other pubertal events are not closely synchronized with skeletal age (or with each other). So we have learned a great deal about *how* hormones affect human growth and development (see Figure 5.10 for a brief review). However, the events responsible for the timing and regulation of these hormonal influences remain unclear.

Environmental Influences

Three kinds of environmental influence can have a major effect on physical growth and development: nutrition, illnesses, and the quality of care that children receive.

Nutrition

Diet is perhaps the most potent environmental influence on human growth and development. As you might expect, children who are inadequately nourished grow very slowly, if at all. The dramatic effect of malnutrition on physical development can be seen by comparing the heights of children before and during wartime periods when food is scarce. In Figure 5.11, we see that the average heights of schoolchildren in Oslo, Norway, increased between 1920 and 1940—the period between the two world wars. However, this secular trend was clearly reversed during World War II, when it was not always possible to satisfy children's nutritional needs.

catch-up growth
a period of accelerated growth in which children who have experienced growth deficits grow very rapidly to "catch up" to the growth trajectory that they are genetically programmed to follow.

Problems of Undernutrition. If undernutrition is neither prolonged nor especially severe, children will usually recover from any growth deficits by growing much faster than normal once their diet becomes adequate. James Tanner (1990) views this **catch-up growth** as a basic principle of physical development. Presumably, children who have experienced short-term growth deficits because of malnutrition grow very rapidly in order to regain (or catch up to) their genetically programmed growth trajectory.

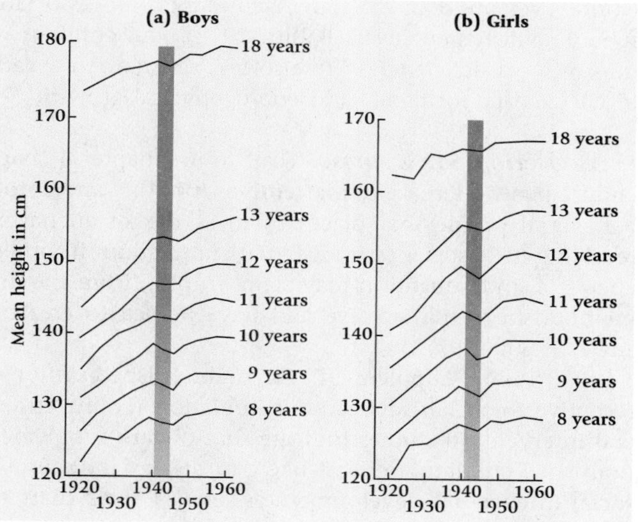

***Figure 5.11** The effect of malnutrition on growth. These graphs show the average heights of Oslo schoolchildren aged 8–18 between 1920 and 1960. Notice the trend toward increasing height (in all age groups) between 1920 and 1940, the period between the two world wars. This secular trend was dramatically reversed during World War II (the shaded section of the graphs), when nutrition was often inadequate.* FROM TANNER, *1990.*

However, prolonged undernutrition has a more serious impact, especially during the first 5 years of life: Brain growth may be seriously retarded, and children may remain relatively small in stature (Barrett & Frank, 1987; Tanner, 1990). These findings make sense when we recall that the first 5 years is a period when the brain normally gains about 65% of its eventual adult weight and the body grows to nearly two-thirds of its adult height.

In many of the developing countries of Africa, Asia, and Latin American, as many as 85% of all children under age 5 experience some form of undernutrition (Barrett & Frank, 1987). When children are severely undernourished, they are likely to suffer from either of two nutritional diseases—marasmus and kwashiorkor—each of which has a slightly different cause. **Marasmus** affects babies who get insufficient protein and too few calories, as can easily occur if a mother is malnourished and does not have the resources to provide her child with a nutritious commercial substitute for mother's milk. A victim of marasmus becomes very frail and wrinkled in appearance as growth stops and body tissues begin to waste away. Even if these children survive, they remain small in stature and often suffer impaired social and intellectual development (Barrett & Frank, 1987).

marasmus
a growth-retarding disease affecting infants who receive insufficient protein and too few calories.

kwashiorkor
a growth-retarding disease affecting children who receive enough calories but little if any protein.

Kwashiorkor affects children who get enough calories but little if any protein. As the disease progresses, the child's hair thins, the face, legs, and abdomen swell with water, and severe skin lesions may develop. In many poor countries of the world, about the only high-quality source of protein readily available to children is mother's milk. So breast-fed infants do not ordinarily suffer from marasmus unless their mothers are severely malnourished; however, they may develop kwashiorkor when they are weaned from the breast and denied their primary source of protein.

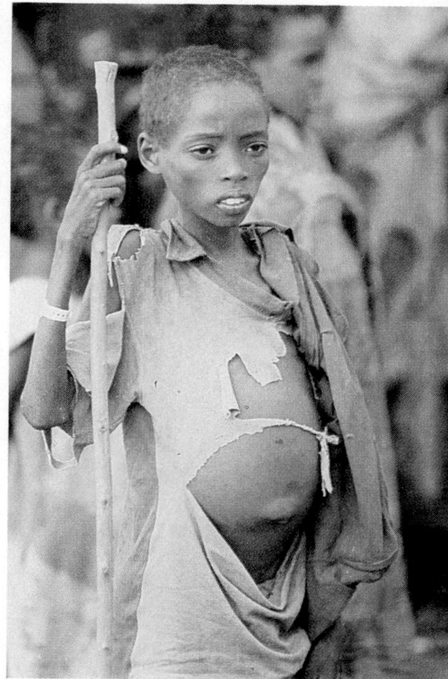

This child's swollen stomach and otherwise emaciated appearance are symptoms of kwashiorkor. Without adequate protein in the diet, children with kwashiorkor are more susceptible to many diseases and may die from illnesses that well-nourished children can easily overcome.

In Western industrialized countries, the preschool children who do experience protein/calorie deficiencies are rarely so malnourished as to develop marasmus or kwashiorkor. However, **vitamin and mineral deficiencies** affect large numbers of children in the United States, particularly African-American and Hispanic children from lower socioeconomic backgrounds (Pollitt, 1994). Especially common among infants and toddlers are iron and zinc deficiencies that occur because rapid growth early in life requires more of these minerals than a young child's diet normally provides. Thus, children whose diets are deficient in zinc grow very slowly (Pollitt et al., 1996). And prolonged iron deficiency causes **iron deficiency anemia,** which not only makes children inattentive and listless, but also retards their growth rates and is associated with poor performances on tests of motor skills and intellectual development. Unfortunately, these motor and intellectual deficiencies are hard to completely overcome, even after the anemia is corrected by supplementing the child's diet (Lozoff, 1989; Pollitt et al., 1996). So iron deficiencies are a major health problem in the United States and around the world. Even mild cases later in childhood are associated with poor performances on school achievement tests (Pollitt, 1994), and children who experience prolonged vitamin/mineral deficiencies are also less resistant to a variety of illnesses that can affect intellectual performance and retard physical growth.

Intervention Strategies. Recall from Chapter 4 that malnutrition can cause young children to be lethargic, inattentive, irritable, and intolerant of stressful situations—a behavioral profile that places them at risk of alienating their caregivers and thereby receiving little social or intellectual stimulation. In other words, many of the long-term effects of undernutrition may stem, in part, from the unstimulating environments that malnourished children live and have helped to create (Barrett & Frank, 1987; Valenzuela, 1990; 1997).

Nutritional supplements for malnourished children can make them much more receptive to social/intellectual stimulation (Pollitt et al., 1996). Yet, the results of several intervention studies indicate that dietary supplements alone are not enough. Malnourished children are least likely to display long-term deficits in physical growth and social/intellectual development when (1) their diets are supplemented *and* (2) they receive ample social and intellectual stimulation, either through high-quality day-care (Zeskind & Ramey, 1981) or through a home visitation program that teaches caregivers about the importance of such stimulation and shows them how to provide it (Grantham-McGregor et al., 1994; Super, Herrera, & Mora, 1990).

Problems of Overnutrition. Dietary excess (eating too much) is yet another form of poor nutrition that is increasing in Western societies and can have several long-term consequences (Galuska et al., 1996). The most immediate effect of overnutrition is that children may become **obese** and face added risk of diabetes, high blood pressure, and heart, liver, or kidney disease. Obese children may also find it difficult to make friends with age-mates, who are apt to tease them about their size and shape. Indeed, obese youngsters are often among the least popular students in grade school classrooms (Sigelman, Miller, & Whitworth, 1986; Staffieri, 1967).

Is a plump baby likely to become an obese adolescent or adult? Not necessarily, for there is only a slight correlation between chubbiness in infancy and obesity later in life (Roche, 1981). However, obese 4- to 6-year-olds are much more likely than their thinner peers to be obese later in adolescence and adulthood. Heredity definitely contributes to these trends, for identical twins—even those raised apart—have very similar body weights, whereas the body weights of same-sex fraternal twins may differ dramatically (Stunkard et al., 1990). Yet, a genetic predisposition does not guarantee obesity. Highest levels of obesity are found among children who eat a high-fat diet and who do not get sufficient exercise to burn the calories they've consumed (Fischer & Birch, 1995; Smith, 1997).

Bad eating habits that can lead to obesity are often established early in life (Birch, 1990). Some parents overfeed infants because they almost always infer that a fussy baby must be hungry. Other parents use food to reinforce desirable behaviors (for example, "clean your room and you can have some ice cream"), or they bribe their children to eat foods they do not want (for example, "No dessert until you eat your peas") (Olvera-Ezzell, Power, & Cousins, 1990; Smith, 1997). Unfortunately, children may attach a special significance to eating that extends far beyond its role in reducing hunger if they are encouraged to view food as a reward. Moreover, use of high-fat desserts or snacks as a reward may convince young children that the healthier foods that they are being "bribed" to eat must really be yucky stuff after all (Birch, Marlin, & Rotter, 1984).

In addition to their poor eating habits, obese children are less active than normal-weight peers. Of course, their inactivity may both contribute to obesity (obese children burn fewer calories) and be a consequence of their overweight condition. One strong clue that activity restriction contributes to obesity is that the amount of time children spend in the sedentary activity of watching television is one of the best predictors of *future* obesity (Kolata, 1986). Television viewing may also promote poor eating habits. Not only do children tend to snack while passively watching TV, but the foods they

vitamin/mineral deficiency
a form of malnutrition in which the diet provides sufficient protein and calories but is lacking in one or more substances that promote normal growth.

iron deficiency anemia
a listlessness caused by too little iron in the diet that makes children inattentive and may retard physical and intellectual development.

obese
a medical term describing individuals who are at least 20% above the ideal weight for their height, age, and sex.

see advertised are mostly high-calorie products containing lots of fat and sugar and few beneficial nutrients (Tinsley, 1992).

Crash diets for obese children are often counterproductive. Severe dietary restrictions can interfere with the development of the brain, muscles, and bones early in life, and older children on restrictive diets may feel deprived, rejected, and inclined to partake in binge eating should the opportunity arise (Kolata, 1986). To date, the most effective treatments for childhood obesity have been behavioral approaches that involve obese youngsters *and* their parents. In one particularly effective program (Epstein et al., 1987; 1990), parents and their obese children were taught to revise their eating and exercise habits, carefully monitor their own behavior to ensure compliance with the regimen, and encourage other family members to exercise more and eat healthier foods. In addition, children entered into contracts with their parents whereby they could earn rewards for losing weight. As shown in Figure 5.12, obese children who received this intensive family therapy not only lost weight, but had kept it off when observed during a follow-up 5 years later. By contrast, obese youngsters who had participated in the same program without their parents were unable to maintain the weight loss they had initially achieved. Here, then, is a strong indication that childhood obesity is a *family* problem that is most likely to be overcome when family members *work together* to change a home environment that has permitted children to become obese.

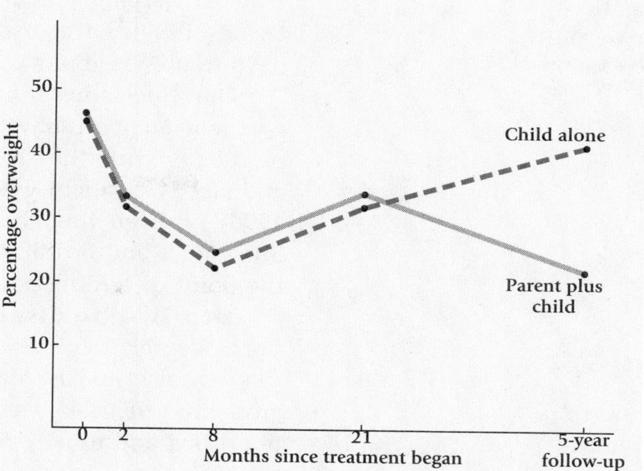

Figure 5.12 *Average percentage of excess body weight for obese children who participated in a weight-loss program with and without a parent.* ADAPTED FROM EPSTEIN ET AL., 1987.

Illnesses

Among children who are adequately nourished, common childhood illnesses such as measles, chicken pox, or even pneumonia have little if any effect on physical growth and development. Major illnesses that keep a child in bed for weeks may temporarily retard growth; but after recovering, the child ordinarily shows a growth spurt (catch-up growth) that makes up for the progress lost while he or she was sick (Tanner, 1990).

Yet, diseases are likely to permanently stunt the growth of children who are moderately to severely undernourished. A poor diet weakens the immune system, so that childhood diseases strike an undernourished child sooner and harder (Pollitt et al., 1996). Not only does malnutrition increase one's susceptibility to disease, but diseases contribute to malnutrition by suppressing a child's appetite and limiting the body's ability to absorb and utilize nutrients (Pollitt, 1994). In developing countries where gastrointestinal infections and upper respiratory illnesses are common, young school-age children who have been relatively disease-free are already 1 to 2 inches taller and 3 to 5 pounds heavier on average than their more "sickly" peers (Martorell, 1980; Roland, Cole, & Whitehead, 1977) and are outperforming them on a variety of cognitive tests as well (Pollitt, 1994).

Emotional Stress and Lack of Affection

Finally, otherwise healthy children who experience too much stress and too little affection are likely to lag far behind their age-mates in physical growth and motor development. This *failure-to-thrive* syndrome may characterize as many as 6% of preschool children in the United States and up to 5% of all patients admitted to pediatric hospitals (Lozoff, 1989).

Nonorganic failure to thrive is a growth disorder that appears early, usually by 18 months of age. Babies who display it stop growing and appear to be wasting away, in much the same way that malnourished infants with marasmus do. These infants do not have an obvious illness, and no other biological cause for their condition is apparent. Affected babies often have trouble feeding and, in many cases, their

nonorganic failure to thrive an infant growth disorder, caused by lack of attention and affection, that causes growth to slow dramatically or stop.

growth retardation is undoubtedly attributable to poor nutrition (Brockington, 1996; Lozoff, 1989). Of course, a major question is why would an otherwise healthy baby have trouble feeding?

One clue comes from these babies' behaviors around caregivers. They are generally apathetic and withdrawn, often watch their caregivers closely, but are unlikely to smile or cuddle when they are picked up. Why? Because their caregivers are typically cool and aloof, impatient with them, and sometimes even physically abusive (Brockington, 1996). So even though caregivers offer enough food for those babies to thrive, their impatience and hostility causes babies to withdraw and to become aloof themselves to the point of feeding poorly and displaying few, if any, positive social responses.

Deprivation dwarfism is a second growth-related disorder that stems from emotional deprivation and a lack of affection. It appears later, usually between 2 and 15 years of age, and is characterized by small stature and dramatically reduced rates of growth, even though children who display this disorder do not look especially malnourished and usually receive adequate nutrition and physical care. What seems to be lacking in their lives is a positive involvement with another person, namely with their primary caregivers, who themselves are likely to be depressed by an unhappy marriage, economic hardships, or some other personal problem (Brockington, 1996; Roithmaier et al., 1988). It appears that deprivation dwarfs grow very slowly because their emotional deprivation depresses the endocrine system and inhibits the production of growth hormone. Indeed, when these youngsters are removed from their homes and begin to receive attention and affection, secretion of GH quickly resumes, and they display catch-up growth on the *same diet* on which they formerly failed to thrive (Brockington, 1996; Gardner, 1972).

The prognoses for children affected by nonorganic failure to thrive and deprivation dwarfism is very good if the caregiving problems responsible for these disorders are corrected by individual or family therapy, or if the affected child is placed with caring foster parents (Brockington, 1996). However, if nonorganic failure to thrive is not identified and corrected in the first 2 years, or if the emotional neglect that underlies deprivation dwarfism persists for several years, affected children may remain smaller than normal and display long-term emotional problems and intellectual deficiencies as well (Drotar, 1992; Lozoff, 1989).

In sum, failure to thrive provides yet another indication that children require love and responsive caregiving if they are to develop normally. Fortunately, there is hope for *preventing* these deprivation-related disorders if parents whose children are at risk can be identified early. And often they can be. Even before giving birth, women whose children may fail to thrive are more likely than other mothers to feel unloved by their parents, to reject their own mothers as a model, and to say their own childhoods were unhappy. Within days of giving birth, these mothers are already having more problems feeding and soothing their babies than other mothers are (Lozoff, 1989). Clearly, these families need help and would almost certainly benefit from early interventions that teach parents how to be more sensitive and responsive caregivers.

deprivation dwarfism
a childhood growth disorder that is triggered by emotional deprivation and characterized by decreased production of GH, slow growth, and small stature.

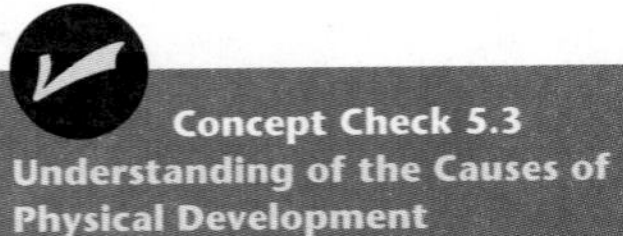

Concept Check 5.3
Understanding of the Causes of Physical Development

Check your understanding of some of the causes of physical development by matching each of the consequences listed below with one or more of the following *causes/correlates* of that condition: (a) increases in GH production during adolescence, (b) malnutrition, (c) increase in testosterone/estrogen production during adolescence, (d) stress-induced inhibition of GH, (e) insensitive or abusive caregiving, (f) sedentary lifestyle. Answers appear in the Appendix at the back of the book.

_____ 1. lethargic, inattentive, irritable demeanor
_____ 2. adolescent growth spurt
_____ 3. deprivation dwarfism
_____ 4. obesity
_____ 5. sexual maturation at puberty
_____ 6. failure to thrive

SUMMARY

An Overview of Maturation and Growth

♦ The body is constantly changing between infancy and adulthood. Height and weight increase rapidly during the first 2 years. Growth then becomes more gradual until early adolescence when there is a rapid "growth spurt."

♦ The shape of the body and body proportions also change because various body parts grow at different rates. Physical development follows a **cephalocaudal** (head-downward) and a **proximodistal** (center-onward) formula in which structures in the upper and central regions of the body mature before those in the lower and peripheral regions.

♦ Skeletal and muscular development parallel the changes occurring in height and weight. The bones become longer and thicker and gradually harden, completing their growth and development by the late teens. **Skeletal age** is an excellent measure of physical maturation. Muscles increase in density and size, particularly during the growth spurt of early adolescence.

♦ Physical growth is quite uneven, or asynchronous, because the brain, the reproductive system, and the lymph tissues mature at different rates. There are also sizable individual and cultural variations in physical growth and development.

Development of the Brain

♦ A **brain growth spurt** occurs during the last 3 months of the prenatal period and the first 2 years of life. **Neurons** form **synapses** with other neurons; **glia** form to nourish the neurons and encase them in myelin—a waxy material that speeds the transmission of neural impulses. Many more neurons and synapses are formed than are needed, and those that are used often survive. Other neurons that are stimulated less often either die or lose their synapses and stand in reserve to compensate for brain injuries. Up until puberty, the brain shows a great deal of **plasticity,** which allows it to change in response to experience and to recover from many injuries.

♦ The highest brain center, or **cerebrum,** consists of two hemispheres connected by the **corpus callosum.** Each hemisphere is covered by a **cerebral cortex.** Although the brain may be **lateralized** at birth so that the two hemispheres assume different functions, children come to rely increasingly on one particular hemisphere or the other to perform each function. **Myelinization** and reorganization of the neural circuitry of the cerebral cortex continue throughout adolescence.

Motor Development

♦ Like the physical structures of the body, motor development proceeds in a cephalocaudal and proximodistal direction. As a result, motor skills evolve in a definite sequence: Infants gain control over their heads, necks, and upper arms before they become proficient with their legs, feet, and hands. Yet, the increasingly complex motor skills that infants display do not simply unfold according to a maturational timetable. Experience plays a crucial role, as shown by the retarded motor development of institutionalized children who have few opportunities to practice motor skills, and by cross-cultural research showing that motor development can be accelerated. According to **dynamical systems theory,** each new motor skill represents an active and intricate reorganization of several existing capabilities that infants undertake to achieve important objectives.

♦ Fine motor skills improve dramatically in the first year. Prereaching is replaced by voluntary reaching, and the claw-like **ulnar grasp** is replaced by the **pincer grasp.** These reaching and grasping skills transform infants into skillful manipulators who soon are reorganizing their existing capabilities to copy lines and build towers of blocks.

♦ Emerging motor skills often thrill parents and allow new forms of play. They also support other aspects of perceptual, cognitive, and social development.

♦ With each passing year, children's motor skills improve. Boys become notably stronger than girls early in adolescence, owing to their greater muscular development and the fact that girls are less encouraged by society to remain physically active.

Puberty: The Physical Transition from Child to Adult

♦ At about age 10½ for females and age 13 for males, the **adolescent growth spurt** begins. In addition to growing taller and heavier, the body assumes a more adultlike appearance.

♦ Sexual maturation begins about the same time as the adolescent growth spurt and follows a predictable sequence. For girls, **puberty** begins with the onset of breast and pubic-hair development and follows with a widening of the hips, enlarging of the uterus and vagina, **menarche** (first menstruation), and completion of breast and pubic-hair growth. For boys, development of the testes and scrotum is followed by the emergence of pubic hair, the growth of the penis, the ability to ejaculate, the appearance of facial hair, and a lowering of the voice. Because of improved nutrition and health care, people in industrialized societies have shown a **secular trend** to grow taller and heavier, and they are reaching sexual maturity earlier than was true in the past. Yet, there are wide individual variations in the timing of sexual maturation and growth.

The Psychological Impacts of Puberty

♦ Girls react to their changing body images by hoping to be attractive and worrying about their weight. Their reactions to menarche are mixed. Boys have better body images than girls do and are somewhat more positive about their first ejaculation than girls are about menarche.

♦ Many nonindustrialized societies take pubertal changes as a sign that a child has become an adult, marking this transition with formal **rites of passage.** In other societies, parent–child conflicts often heighten at puberty and usually decline later in adolescence.

◆ Timing of puberty can have personal and social consequences. Early-maturing boys and on-time and late-maturing girls have better body images, feel more self-confident, and display better social adjustment than late-maturing boys and early-maturing girls. However, these effects do not hold for all individuals and tend to fade over time.

◆ The hormonal changes of puberty bring about an increase in sex drive and the responsibility of managing **sexuality**—a task that may be particularly difficult for teenagers who are sexually attracted to same-sex peers. Sexual attitudes have become increasingly liberal over the years, as a majority of adolescents now think that sex with affection is acceptable and reject the **double standard** for gender differences in sexual behavior. Teenage sexual activity has also increased, although the sexual behavior of girls has changed more than that of boys.

◆ Large numbers of sexually active teenagers fail to use contraception regularly, thus placing themselves at risk of contracting sexually transmitted diseases (STDs) or becoming pregnant. Efforts to educate elementary school children about AIDS have been quite successful.

◆ Adolescent pregnancy and childbearing represent a major social problem in the United States. Teenage mothers, most of whom are poor and ill-prepared psychologically to be parents, often drop out of school and perpetuate their economic disadvantage. And their poor parenting contributes to the emotional problems and cognitive deficiencies that their children often display. Improved sex education and contraceptive services, coupled with programs such as Teen Outreach and interventions for teenage mothers, can help to reduce the rate of teenage pregnancy and its undesirable consequences.

Causes and Correlates of Physical Development

◆ Physical development results from a complex interplay between biological and environmental forces. Individual genotypes set limits for stature, shape, and schedule of growth. Growth is also heavily influenced by hormones released by the endocrine glands as regulated by the **pituitary. Growth hormone (GH)** and **thyroxine** regulate growth throughout childhood. At adolescence, other endocrine glands secrete hormones, most notably **estrogen** from the ovaries, which triggers sexual development in girls, and **testosterone** from the testes, which instigates sexual development in boys.

◆ Adequate nutrition, in the form of total calories, protein, and vitamins and minerals, is necessary for children to reach their growth potentials. **Marasmus, kwashiorkor,** and **iron deficiency anemia** are three growth-retarding diseases that stem from undernutrition. In industrialized countries, **obesity** is a nutritional problem, with many physical and psychological consequences.

◆ Chronic infectious diseases can combine with poor nutrition to stunt physical and intellectual growth. **Nonorganic failure to thrive** and **deprivation dwarfism** illustrate that affection and sensitive, responsive caregiving are important to ensure normal growth.

During infancy, toddlerhood, the preschool years, and middle childhood children's brains and bodies are constantly changing. As these physical changes occur, the types of toys that promote optimal development also change. You can track basic child development in a wide variety of areas by visiting: http://www.etoys.com/shopping/etoys/html/dmain.shtml At this web site you can select a specific area of development and browse for toys suited to children's abilities at any age.

KEY TERMS

cephalocaudal, 153
proximodistal, 153
skeletal age, 154
brain growth spurt, 156
synapses, 156
neurons, 156
glia, 156
synaptogenesis, 156
plasticity, 157
myelinization, 158
cerebrum, 158
corpus callosum, 158
cerebral cortex, 158
cerebral lateralization, 158
dynamical systems theory, 161
proprioceptive information, 164
ulnar grasp, 164
pincer grasp, 164
adolescent growth spurt, 167
puberty, 167
menarche, 168
secular trend, 169
rites of passage, 170
anorexia nervosa, 171
bulimia, 171
sexuality, 174
double standard, 176
thyroxine, 181
pituitary, 181
growth hormone (GH), 181
estrogen, 181
testosterone, 181
catch-up growth, 182
marasmus, 183
kwashiorkor, 183
vitamin and mineral deficiencies, 183
iron deficiency anemia, 183
obese, 184
nonorganic failure to thrive, 185
deprivation dwarfism, 186

6

Early Cognitive Foundations: Sensation, Perception, and Learning

Imagine that you are a neonate, only 5 to 10 minutes old, who has just been sponged, swaddled, and handed to your mother. As your eyes meet hers, she smiles and says "Hi there, sweetie" in a high-pitched voice as she moves her head closer and gently strokes your cheek. What would you make of all this sensory input? How would you interpret these experiences?

Developmentalists are careful to distinguish between sensation and perception. **Sensation** is the process by which sensory receptor neurons detect information and transmit it to the brain. Clearly, neonates "sense" the environment. They gaze at interesting sights, react to sounds, tastes, and odors, and are likely to cry up a storm when poked by a needle for a blood test. But do they "make sense" of these sensations? **Perception** is the interpretation of sensory input: recognizing what you see, understanding what is said to you, or knowing that the odor you've detected is fresh-baked bread. Are newborns capable of drawing any such inferences? Do they perceive the world, or merely sense it?

We might also wonder whether very young infants can associate their sensations with particular outcomes. When, for example, might a baby first associate her mother's breast with milk and come to view mom as a valuable commodity who eliminates hunger and other kinds of distress? Are infants capable of modifying their behavior as to persuade mom to attend to them? These are questions of *learning*—the process by which our behaviors change as a result of experience.

Perhaps we should start with a more practical question: Why should we concern ourselves with the development of sensation, perception, and learning? Perhaps because these three processes are at the heart of human functioning. Virtually everything we do depends on our interpretations of and reactions to sensory input—the things we experience. So the study of early sensory, perceptual, and learning capabilities can provide some fundamental clues about how we gain knowledge of reality.

EARLY CONTROVERSIES ABOUT SENSORY AND PERCEPTUAL DEVELOPMENT

Nature vs. Nurture

Long before anyone conducted any experiments to decide the issue, philosophers were already debating what newborns might sense and perceive. *Empiricist* philosophers believed that an infant was a *tabula rasa* (blank slate) who must learn to interpret sensations. In fact, William James (1890) argued that all senses are integrated at birth, so that sights, sounds, and other sensory inputs combine to present the newborn with a "blooming, buzzing confusion."

By contrast, *nativist* philosophers such as Rene Descartes (1638/1965) and Immanuel Kant (1781/1958) took the nature side of the nature/nurture issue, arguing that many basic perceptual abilities are innate. For example, they believed that we are born with an understanding of spatial relations. Presumably, infants do not need to learn that receding objects appear smaller or that approaching objects seem to increase in size; these were said to be adaptive perceptual understandings that were built into the human nervous system over the course of evolution.

Today's developmentalists take less extreme stands on this nature/nurture issue. Although most would concede that babies see some order to their surroundings from day 1, they recognize that the perceptual world of a human neonate is rather limited

sensation
detection of stimuli by the sensory receptors and transmission of this information to the brain.

perception
the process by which we categorize and interpret sensory input.

and that *both* maturational processes and experience contribute to the growth of perceptual awareness (Smith & Katz, 1996).

Enrichment vs. Differentiation

Now consider a second issue that early philosophers debated. Is the coherent reality that we experience through the senses simply "out there" to be detected; or rather, do we construct our own interpretations of that reality based on our experiences? This issue is hotly contested in two modern theories of perceptual development: enrichment theory and differentiation theory.

Both these theories argue that there is an objective reality out there to which we respond. However, **enrichment theory** (Piaget, 1954; 1960) claims that sensory stimulation is often fragmented or confusing. To interpret such ambiguous input, we must use our available cognitive schemes to add to or "enrich" it. You have probably heard radio contests where people call in to identify a song after hearing only a note or two. According to enrichment theory, contest winners can answer correctly because they draw on their memory of musical passages to add to what they have just heard and infer what the song must be. In sum, the enrichment position is that cognition "enriches" sensory experience. Our knowledge helps us construct meaning from the sensory stimulation we receive (see Figure 6.1).

Figure 6.1 *Expectations affect perception. If told to name the* animal *in this drawing, you would likely see a rat with large ears and its tail circling in front of the body. Yet, if you saw the drawing amid other drawings of faces, you would likely perceive an elderly bald man with glasses (see him?). So, as Piaget and other enrichment theorists have argued, cognition does not affect our interpretations of sensory stimulation.* Adapted from Reese, *1963.*

By contrast, Eleanor Gibson's (1969; 1987; 1992) **differentiation theory** argues that sensory stimulation provides all we need to interpret our experiences. Our task as fledgling perceivers is simply to *detect* the differentiating information, or **distinctive features,** that enable us to discriminate one form of experience from another. Consider that many 2-year-olds are apt to say "doggie" whenever they see a dog, a cat, or some other small, furry animal. They have not yet noticed the critical differences in sizes, shapes, behavior, or sounds that enable us to discriminate these creatures. Once a child masters this perceptual learning, however, his continuing quest for differentiating information may soon enable him to discriminate long-nosed collies from pug-faced boxers or spotted dalmatians, while understanding that all these animals are properly labeled dogs. Gibson's point is that the information needed to make these finer distinctions was always there in the animals themselves, and that the child's perceptual capabilities blossom as he *detects* these distinctive features.

So which theory is correct? Maybe both of them are. The research we will review in this chapter provides ample support for Gibson's view; children do get better at detecting information already contained in their sensory inputs. Yet, Piaget's view that existing knowledge provides a basis for interpreting our sensations is also well-documented as we will see in examining Piaget's theory of cognitive development in Chapter 7.

"MAKING SENSE" OF THE INFANT'S SENSORY AND PERCEPTUAL EXPERIENCES

As recently as the early 1900s, many medical texts claimed that human infants were functionally blind, deaf, and impervious to pain for several days after birth; that is, babies were believed to be unprepared to extract any "meaning" from the world around them. Today, we know otherwise. Why the change in views? It is not that babies have become any more capable or any smarter. Instead, researchers have gotten smarter, having developed some ingenious methods of persuading nonverbal infants to "tell us" what they can sense and perceive. Let's briefly discuss four of these techniques.

enrichment theory
a theory specifying that we must "add to" sensory stimulation by drawing on stored knowledge in order to perceive a meaningful world.

differentiation theory
a theory specifying that perception involves detecting distinctive features or cues that are contained in the sensory stimulation we receive.

distinctive features
characteristics of a stimulus that remain constant; dimensions on which two or more objects differ and can be discriminated (sometimes called invariances or invariant features).

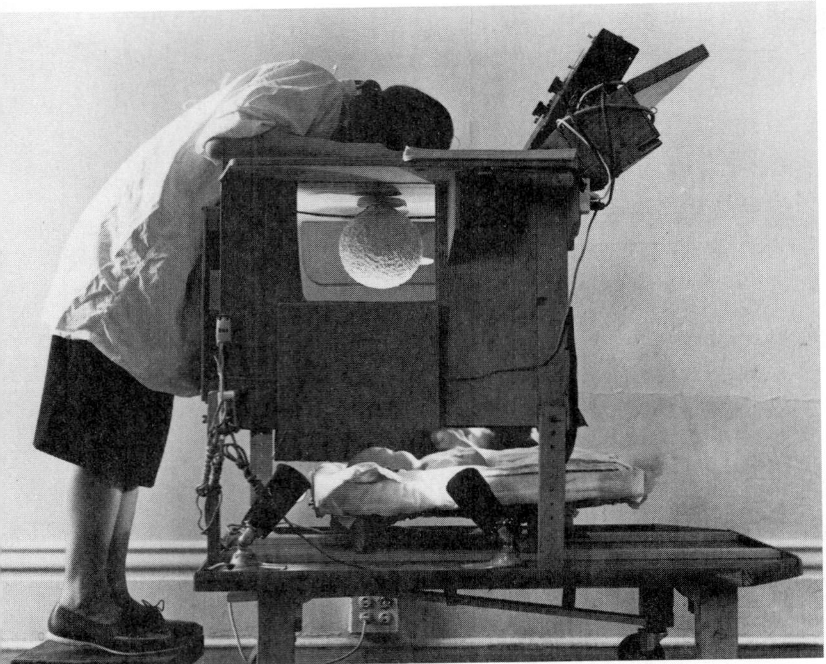

Figure 6.2 *The looking chamber that Fantz used to study infants' visual preferences.*

The Preference Method

The **preference method** is a simple procedure in which at least two stimuli are presented simultaneously to see whether infants attend more to one of them than the other(s). This approach became popular during the early 1960s after Robert Fantz used it to determine whether very young infants could discriminate visual patterns (for example, faces, concentric circles, newsprint, and unpatterned disks). Babies were placed on their backs in a *looking chamber* (see Figure 6.2) and shown two or more stimuli. An observer located above the looking chamber then recorded the amount of time the infant gazed at each of the visual patterns. If the infant looked longer at one target than the other, it was assumed that she preferred that pattern.

Fantz's early results were clear. Newborns could easily discriminate visual forms, and they preferred to look at patterned stimuli such as faces or concentric circles rather than at unpatterned disks. Apparently, the ability to detect and discriminate patterns is innate (Fantz, 1963).

The preference method has one major shortcoming. If an infant shows no preferences among the target stimuli, it is not clear whether she failed to discriminate them or simply found them equally interesting. Fortunately, each of the following methods can resolve this ambiguity.

The Habituation Method

Perhaps the most popular strategy for measuring infant sensory and perceptual capabilities is the habituation method. **Habituation** is the process whereby a repetitive stimulus becomes so familiar that responses initially associated with it (for example, head or eye movements, changes in respiration or heart rate) no longer occur. Thus, habituation is a simple form of learning. As the infant stops responding to the familiar stimulus, he is telling us that he recognizes it as "old hat"—something that he has experienced before.

To test an infant's ability to discriminate two stimuli that differ in some way, the investigator first presents one of the stimuli until the infant stops attending or otherwise responding to it (habituates). Then the second stimulus is presented. If the infant discriminates this second stimulus from the first, he will **dishabituate**—that is, attend closely to it while showing a change in respiration or heart rate. Should the infant fail to react, it is assumed that the differences between the two stimuli were too subtle for him to detect. Because babies habituate and dishabituate to so many different kinds of stimulation—sights, sounds, odors, tastes, and touches—the habituation method is very useful for assessing their sensory and perceptual capabilities.

Evoked Potentials

Yet another way of determining what infants can sense (or perceive) is to present them with a stimulus and record their brain waves. Electrodes are placed on the infant's scalp above those brain centers that process the kind of sensory information that the investigator is presenting. This means that responses to visual stimuli are recorded from the

preference method
a method used to gain information about infants' perceptual abilities by presenting two (or more) stimuli and observing which stimulus the infant prefers.

habituation
a decrease in one's response to a stimulus that has become familiar through repetition.

dishabituation
increase in responsiveness that occurs when stimulation changes.

back of the head, at a site above the occipital lobe, whereas responses to sounds are recorded from the side of the head, above the temporal lobe. If the infant detects (senses) the particular stimulus that we present, she will show a change in the patterning of her brain waves, or **evoked potential.** Stimuli that are not detected produce no changes in the brain's electrical activity. This "evoked potential" procedure can even tell us whether infants can discriminate various sights or sounds, for two stimuli that are sensed as "different" produce different patterns of electrical activity.

High-Amplitude Sucking

Finally, most infants can exert enough control over their sucking behavior to tell us what they can sense and to give us some idea of their likes and dislikes. The **high-amplitude sucking method** provides infants with a special pacifier containing electrical circuitry that enables them to exert some control over the sensory environment. After the researcher establishes an infant's baseline sucking rate, the procedure begins. Whenever the infant sucks faster or harder than she did during the baseline observations (high-amplitude sucking), she trips the electrical circuit in the pacifier, thereby activating a slide projector or tape recorder that introduces some kind of sensory stimulation. Should the infant detect this stimulation and find it interesting, she can make it last by displaying bursts of high-amplitude sucking. But once the infant's interest wanes and her sucking returns to the baseline level, the stimulation ceases. If the investigator then introduces a second stimulus that elicits a dramatic increase in high-amplitude sucking, he could conclude that the infant has discriminated the second stimulus from the first. This procedure can even be modified so the infant can indicate which of two stimuli she prefers. If we wanted to determine whether babies prefer marches to lullabies, we could adjust the circuitry in the pacifier so that high-amplitude sucking activates one kind of music and low-amplitude (or no) sucking activates the other. By then noting what the baby does, we could draw some inferences about which of these musical compositions she prefers. Clearly, this high-amplitude sucking method is a clever and versatile technique!

Let's now see what these creative methods have taught us about babies' sensory and perceptual capabilities.

INFANT SENSORY CAPABILITIES

How well do newborns "sense" their environments? Better, perhaps, than you might imagine. Let's begin our exploration of infants' sensory world by examining their visual capabilities.

Vision

Although most of us tend to think of vision as our most indispensable sense, it may be the *least* mature of the newborn's sensory capabilities. Changes in brightness elicit a subcortical *pupillary reflex,* which indicates that the neonate is sensitive to light (Pratt, 1954). Babies can also detect movement in the visual field and are likely to track a visual stimulus with their eyes as long as the target moves slowly (Banks & Salapatek, 1983). Interestingly, newborn infants are more likely to track faces (or facelike stimuli) than other patterns (Goren, Sarty, & Wu, 1975; Johnson et al., 1991) although this preference for faces disappears within a month or two. Why do babies display it? One

evoked potential
a change in patterning of the brain waves that indicates that an individual detects (senses) a stimulus.

high-amplitude sucking method
a method of assessing infants' perceptual capabilities that capitalizes on the ability of infants to make interesting events last by varying the rate at which they suck on a special pacifier.

A: Newborn's view

B: Adult's view

The newborn's limited powers of accommodation and poor visual acuity make the mother's face look fuzzy (photo A) rather than clear (photo B); even when viewed from close up.

intriguing idea is that it represents an adaptive remnant of our evolutionary history—a *reflex,* controlled by subcortical areas of the brain, that serves to orient babies to their caregivers and promote social interactions (Johnson et al., 1991).

Using the habituation method, researchers have found that neonates see the world in color, although they do have trouble discriminating blues from greens and reds from yellows. However, rapid development of the visual brain centers and sensory pathways allows their color vision to improve quickly. By 2 months of age, babies can discriminate all the basic colors (Brown, 1990). And by age 4 to 5 months, they not only recognize that an object's color doesn't change when it grows brighter or dimmer (Dannemiller, 1989), but are able to group colors of slightly different shades into the same basic categories—the reds, greens, blues, and yellows—that adults do (Bornstein, Kessen, & Weiskopf, 1976; Catherwood, Crassini, & Freiberg, 1989).

Despite these impressive capabilities, very young infants do not resolve fine detail very well. Studies of **visual acuity** suggest that a neonate's distance vision is about 20/600, which means that she sees at 20 feet what an adult with excellent vision sees at 600 feet. What's more, objects at any distance look rather blurry to a very young infant, who has trouble *accommodating*—that is, changing the shape of the lens of the eye to bring visual stimuli into focus. Given these limitations, it is perhaps not surprising that many patterns and forms are difficult for a very young infant to detect; she simply requires sharper **visual contrasts** to "see" them than adults do (Banks & Salapatek, 1983). However, vision improves very rapidly over the first few months. By age 6 months, babies' visual acuity is about 20/100 and they are accommodating well; by age 12 months, they see about as well as adults do (Aslin & Smith, 1988).

In sum, the young infant's visual system is not operating at peak efficiency, but it is certainly working. Even newborns can sense movement, colors, changes in brightness, and a variety of visual patterns as long as these patterned stimuli are not too finely detailed and have a sufficient amount of light/dark contrast.

visual acuity
a person's ability to see small objects and fine detail.

visual contrast
the amount of light/dark transition in a visual stimulus.

Hearing

Using the evoked potential procedure, researchers have found that soft sounds that adults hear must be made noticeably louder before a neonate can detect them (Aslin, Pisoni, & Jusczyk, 1983). In the first few hours of life, infants may hear about as well as an adult with a head cold. Their insensitivity to softer sounds could be due, in part, to fluids that have seeped into the inner ear during the birth process. Despite this minor limitation, habituation studies indicate that neonates are capable of discriminating sounds that differ in loudness, duration, direction, and frequency (Bower, 1982). They hear rather well indeed.

Reactions to Voices

Young infants are particularly attentive to voices, especially high-pitched feminine voices. Harriet Rheingold and Judith Adams (1980) found that caregivers often talked in a high-pitched expressive tone to their newborns and even reported that they enjoyed these "conversations." And what might adults find so interesting about a conversation with a nonverbal infant? Perhaps it is simply that babies often stop crying, open their eyes, and begin to look around or to vocalize themselves when they are spoken to (Rosenthal, 1982).

Many people would undoubtedly chuckle if a mother were to claim that her week-old baby already recognized her voice. Yet, the mother might have the last laugh, for research by Anthony DeCasper and his associates (DeCasper & Fifer, 1980; DeCasper & Spence, 1986; 1991) reveals that newborns suck faster on a nipple to hear a recording of their mother's voice than a recording of another woman. In fact, when mothers were instructed to recite a passage (for example, portions of Dr. Seuss's *Cat in the Hat*) many times during the last 6 weeks of their pregnancies, their newborns sucked faster and harder to hear *those particular stories* than to hear other samples of their mother's speech. Might these preferences reflect the experiences a baby had before birth, as he listened to his mother's muffled voice through the uterine wall? Probably so, and this special responsiveness to mother's voice may even be highly adaptive if it encourages his mother to talk to him and to provide the attention and affection that foster healthy social, emotional, and intellectual development.

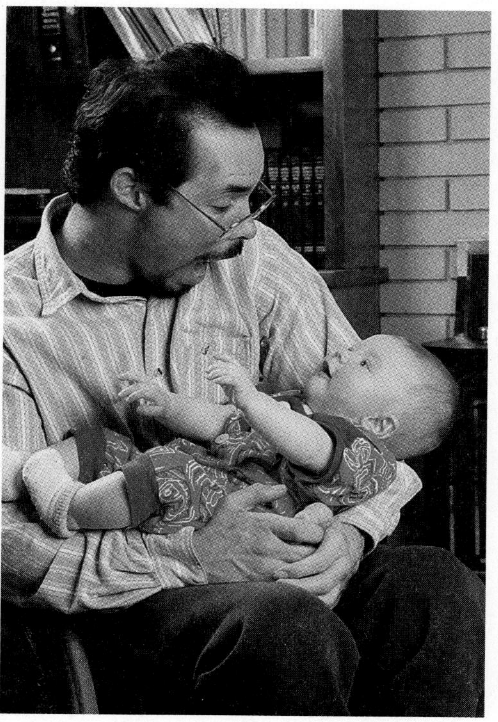

Very young infants are particularly responsive to the sound of human voices.

Reactions to Language

Not only do babies attend closely to voices, but they are also able to discriminate basic speech sounds—called **phonemes**—very early in life. Peter Eimas (1975b, 1985) pioneered research in this area by demonstrating that infants 2 to 3 months old could distinguish consonant sounds that are very similar (for example, *ba* and *pa*). In fact, infants less than 1 week old can tell the difference between the vowels *a* and *I* (Clarkson & Berg, 1983) and can even segment words into discrete syllables (Bijeljac-Babic, Bertoncini, & Mehler, 1993). Just as babies divide the spectrum of light into basic color categories, they seem to divide speech sounds into categories corresponding to the basic sound units of language (Miller & Eimas, 1996). In fact, 3- to 6-month-old infants are actually better than adults are at perceiving certain phonemes that are *not* a part of the language their companions speak (Jusczyk, 1995; Werker & Desjardins, 1995). These are impressive accomplishments indeed!

Clearly, hearing is more highly developed at birth than vision is. Although a baby's hearing improves over the first 4 to 6 months of life (Trehub et al., 1991), even newborns are remarkably well-prepared for such significant achievements as (1) using voices to identify and discriminate their companions and (2) segmenting speech into smaller units—the building blocks of language.

Consequences of Hearing Loss

How important is hearing to human development? Are children developmentally disadvantaged if they do not hear well? We gain some insight on these issues from the

phonemes
smallest meaningful sound units that make up a spoken language.

progress made by otherwise healthy youngsters whose hearing is impaired by a common childhood infection.

Otitis media, a bacterial infection of the middle ear, is the most frequently diagnosed disease among infants and preschool children. Almost all children are infected at least once, with up to one-third of them experiencing recurring infections despite receiving adequate medical care (Vernon-Feagans, Manlove, & Volling, 1996). Antibiotics can eliminate the bacteria that causes this disease but will do nothing to reduce the buildup of fluid in the middle ear, which often persists without any symptoms of pain or discomfort. Unfortunately, this fluid may produce mild to moderate hearing loss that can last for months after an infection has been detected and treated (Vernon-Feagans et al., 1996).

Otitis media strikes hardest between 6 months and 3 years of age. As a result, developmentalists have feared that youngsters with recurring infections may have difficulties understanding others' speech, which could hamper their language development as well as other cognitive and social skills that normally emerge early in childhood. And there is reason for concern. Children who have had recurring ear infections early in life do show delays in language development and poorer academic performance early in elementary school than peers whose bouts with the disease were less prolonged (Friel-Patti & Finitzo, 1990; Teele, Klein, & Chase et al., 1990). Another recent study found that 3-year-olds with chronic otitis media may be at risk of acquiring poor social skills, for they spend more time playing alone and they have fewer positive contacts with day-care classmates than other children do (Vernon-Feagans et al., 1996). Longitudinal research is needed to determine whether the problems associated with chronic otitis media persist later in childhood and adolescence, when this disease becomes less common. Nevertheless, the early returns clearly imply that young children with mild to moderate hearing loss are likely to be developmentally disadvantaged, and that otitis media, a major contributor to early hearing loss, needs to be detected early and treated aggressively.

Taste and Smell

Infants are born with some very definite taste preferences. For example, they apparently come equipped with something of a sweet tooth, for both full-term and premature babies suck faster and longer for sweet liquids than for bitter, sour, salty, or neutral (water) solutions (Crook, 1978; Smith & Blass, 1996). Different tastes also elicit different facial expressions from newborns. Sweets reduce crying and produce smiles and smacking of the lips, whereas sour substances cause infants to wrinkle their noses and purse their lips, and bitter solutions often elicit expressions of disgust—a downturning

TABLE 6.1 The Newborn's Sensory Capabilities

Sense	Newborn capabilities
Vision	Least well-developed sense; accommodation and visual acuity limited; is sensitive to brightness; can discriminate some colors; tracks moving targets.
Hearing	Turns in direction of sounds; less sensitive to soft sounds than an adult would be but can discriminate sounds that differ in such dimensions as loudness, direction, and frequency. Particularly responsive to speech; recognizes mother's voice.
Taste	Prefers sweet solutions; can discriminate sweet, salty, sour, and bitter tastes.
Smell	Detects a variety of odors; turns away from unpleasant ones. If breast-fed, can identify mother by the odor of her breast and underarm area.
Touch	Responsive to touch, temperature change, and pain.

otitis media
common bacterial infection of the middle ear that produces mild to moderate hearing loss.

of the corners of the mouth, tongue protrusions, and even spitting (Blass & Ciaramitaro, 1994; Ganchrow, Steiner, & Daher, 1983; Rosenstein & Oster, 1988). Furthermore, these facial expressions become more pronounced as solutions become sweeter, more sour, or more bitter, suggesting that newborns can discriminate different concentrations of a particular "taste."

Newborns are also capable of detecting a variety of odors, and they react vigorously by turning away and displaying expressions of disgust in response to unpleasant smells such as vinegar, ammonia, or rotten eggs (Rieser, Yonas, & Wilkner, 1976; Steiner, 1979). Even more remarkable are data indicating that a 1- to 2-week-old breast-fed infant can already recognize his mother (and discriminate her from other women) by the smell of her breasts and underarms (Cernoch & Porter, 1985; Porter et al., 1992). Like it or not, each of us has a unique "olfactory signature"—a characteristic that babies can use as an early means of identifying their closest companions.

Touch, Temperature, and Pain

Receptors in the skin are sensitive to touch, temperature, and pain. We learned in Chapter 4 that newborn infants reliably display a variety of *reflexes* if they are touched in the appropriate areas. Even while sleeping, neonates habituate to stroking at one locale but respond again if the tactile stimulation shifts to a new spot—from the ear to the chin, for example (Kisilevsky & Muir, 1984).

Sensitivity to touch clearly enhances infants' responsiveness to their environments. In Chapter 4, we learned that premature infants show better developmental progress when they are periodically stroked and massaged in their isolettes. The therapeutic effect of touch is due, in part, to the fact that gentle stroking and massaging arouses inattentive infants and calms agitated ones, often causing them to smile at and to become more involved with their companions (Field et al., 1986; Stack & Muir, 1992). Later in the first year, babies begin to use their sense of touch to explore objects—first with their lips and mouths, and later with their hands. So touch is a primary means by which infants acquire knowledge about their environment, which contributes so critically to their early cognitive development (Piaget, 1960).

WHAT DO YOU THINK? ?

Based on what you now know about newborn sensory capabilities, prepare a brief description of what a newborn might "sense" as she gazes at her attentive mother and father. Might the baby be quicker to orient to one parent than the other? If so, which parent, and why?

Newborns are also quite sensitive to warmth, cold, and changes in temperature. They refuse to suck if the milk in their bottles is too hot, and they try to maintain their body heat by becoming more active should the temperature of a room suddenly drop (Pratt, 1954).

Do babies experience much pain? Apparently so, for even 1-day-old infants cry lustily when pricked by a needle for a blood test. In fact, very young infants show greater distress upon receiving an inoculation than 6 month-olds do (Gunnar et al., 1996).

Male babies are highly stressed by circumcision, an operation that is usually done without anesthesia because giving these pain-killing drugs to infants is itself very risky (Hill, 1997). While the surgery is in progress, infants emit high-pitched wails that are similar to the cries of premature babies or those who are brain damaged (Porter, Porges, & Marshall, 1988). Moreover, plasma cortisol, a physiological indicator of stress, is significantly higher just after a circumcision than just before the surgery (Gunnar et al., 1985). Findings such as these challenge the medical wisdom of treating infants as if they are insensitive to pain. Fortunately, researchers have found that babies treated with a mild topical anesthetic before circumcision and given a sugary solution to suck afterward are less stressed by the operation and are able to sleep more peacefully (Hill, 1997).

In sum, each of the major senses is functioning at birth (see Table 6.1 on the previous page for a review) so that even neonates are well-prepared to "sense" their environments. But do they interpret this input? Can they perceive?

VISUAL PERCEPTION IN INFANCY

Although newborn infants see well enough to detect and even discriminate some patterns, we might wonder what they "see" when looking at these stimuli. If we show them a □, do they see a square; or must they learn to construct a square from an assortment of lines and angles? When do they interpret faces as meaningful social stimuli or begin to distinguish the faces of close companions from those of strangers? Can neonates perceive depth? Do they think receding objects shrink; or do they know that these objects remain the same size and only look smaller when moved away? These are precisely the kinds of questions that have motivated curious investigators to find ways of persuading nonverbal infants to "tell" us what they see.

Perception of Patterns and Forms

Recall Robert Fantz's observations of infants in his looking chamber: babies only 2 days old could easily discriminate visual patterns. In fact, of all the targets that Fantz presented, including a drawing of a face, newsprint, a bull's-eye pattern, and unpatterned red, white, and yellow disks, the most preferred stimulus was the face! Does this imply that newborns already interpret faces as a meaningful pattern? Might the nativists be correct in assuming that *form perception* is innate?

Early Pattern Perception (0 to 2 Months)

Other research implies that neonates' ability to "perceive" faces as a "meaningful" configuration is more illusory than real. When Fantz (1961) presented young infants with a face, a stimulus consisting of scrambled facial features, and a simpler stimulus that contained the same amount of light and dark shading as the facelike and scrambled face drawings, the infants were just as interested in the scrambled face as the normal one (see Figure 6.3).

Later research revealed that very young infants prefer to look at *high-contrast* patterns with many sharp boundaries between light and dark areas, and at moderately complex patterns that have curvilinear features (Banks & Ginsburg, 1985; Olson & Sherman, 1983). So faces and scrambled faces may have been equally interesting to Fantz's young subjects because these targets had the same amount of contrast, curvature, and complexity.

By analyzing the characteristics of stimuli that very young infants will or will not look at, we can estimate *what* they see. Figure 6.4, for example, indicates that babies less

Concept Check 6.1
Understanding Infants' Sensory Capabilities

Check your understanding of infants' sensory capabilities and the methods used to obtain this information by matching one or more of the following alternatives to the statements below: (a) habituation method, (b) audition (hearing), (c) vision, (d) olfaction (smell), (e) evoked potential method, (f) otitis media, (g) phoneme discrimination, (h) high-amplitude sucking, (i) circumcision. Answers appear in the Appendix at the back of the book.

_____ 1. least well-developed sense at birth
_____ 2. method especially useful for assessing taste discriminations/preferences
_____ 3. sense infants can use to discriminate their mothers from other women during the first 2 weeks
_____ 4. consequences of _________ reveal the importance of hearing to development
_____ 5. experience that points to errors in treating infants as insensitive creatures
_____ 6. sensory achievement that infants are better at than adults
_____ 7. method of assessing infant sensory capabilities from changes in psychophysiological responses

than 2 months old see only a dark blob when looking at a *highly complex* checkerboard, probably because their immature eyes don't accommodate well enough to resolve the fine detail. By contrast, the infant sees a definite pattern when gazing at the *moderately complex* checkerboard (Banks & Salapatek, 1983). Martin Banks and his associates have summarized the looking preferences of very young infants quite succinctly: *Babies prefer to look at whatever they see well* (Banks & Ginsburg, 1985), and the things they see best are moderately complex, high-contrast targets, particularly those that capture their attention by moving.

Although very young infants detect and discriminate different patterns, can they perceive forms? If shown a triangle, do they see the △ that we do; or rather, do they detect only pieces of lines and maybe an angle (such as ∠)? Although the answers to these questions are by no means established, most researchers believe 1- to 2-month-old infants detect few *if any* forms because they see so poorly and scan visual stimuli in a very limited way (see Figure 6.5 on page 200). So unless the form is very small, they are unlikely to see all of it, much less put all this information together to perceive a unified whole.

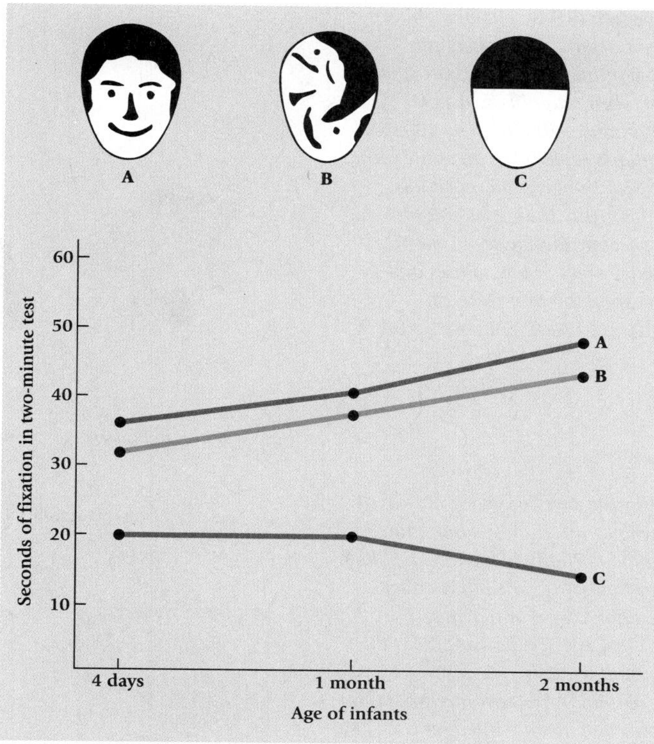

Figure 6.3 *Fantz's test of young infants' pattern preferences. Infants preferred to look at complex stimuli rather than at a simpler black-and-white oval. However, the infants did not prefer the facelike figure to the scrambled face.* Adapted from Fantz, 1961.

Later Form Perception (2 Months to 1 Year)

Between 2 and 12 months of age, the infant's visual system is rapidly maturing. She now sees better and is capable of making increasingly complex visual discriminations. She is also organizing what she sees to perceive visual forms.

The most basic task in perceiving a form is to discriminate that object from its surrounding context (that is, other objects and the general "background"). How do you suppose an infant eventually recognizes that a bottle of milk in front of a centerpiece on the dining room table is not just a part of the centerpiece? What information does she use to perceive forms and when does she begin to do so?

Philip Kellman and Elizabeth Spelke (1983; Kellman, Spelke, & Short, 1986) were among the first to explore these issues. Infants were presented with a display consisting of a rod partially hidden by a block in front of it (see Figure 6.6, displays a and b). Would they perceive the rod as a whole object, even though part of it was not available for inspection; or, rather, would they act as though they had seen two short and separate rods?

To find out, 4-month-olds were first presented with either display a (a stationary hidden rod) or display b (a moving hidden rod) and allowed to look at it until they habituated and were no longer interested. Then infants were shown displays c (a whole rod) and d (two rod segments), and their looking preferences were recorded. Infants who had habituated to the *stationary* hidden rod (display a) showed no clear preference for display c or display d in the later test. They were apparently not able to use available cues, such as the two identical rod tips oriented along the same line, to perceive a whole rod when

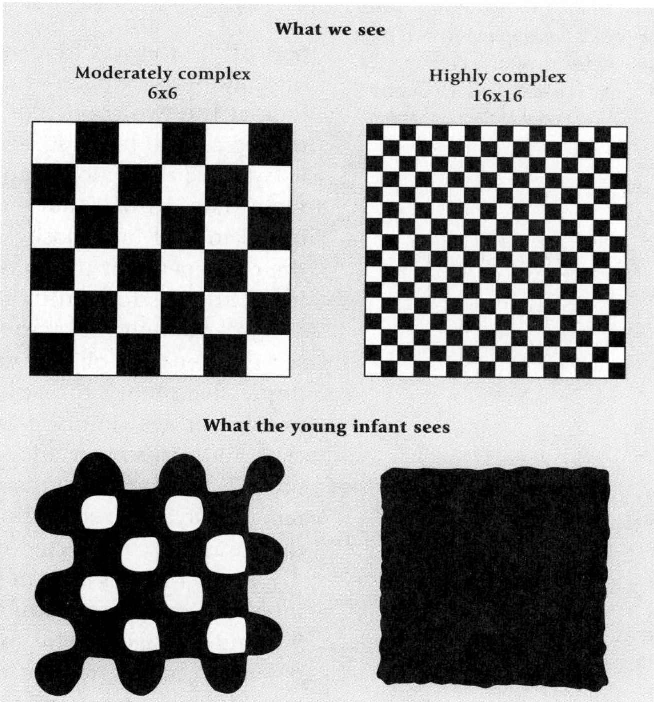

Figure 6.4 *What patterns look like to the young eye. By the time these two checkerboards are processed by eyes with poor vision, only the checkerboard on the left may have any pattern left to it. Poor vision in early infancy helps to explain a preference for moderately complex rather than highly complex stimuli.* Adapted from Banks & Salapatek, 1983.

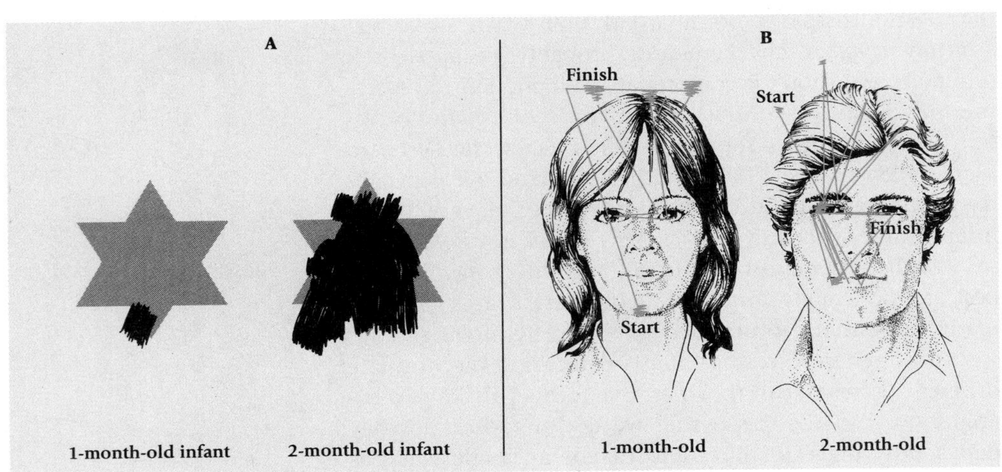

Figure 6.5 *By photographing eye movements, researchers can determine what babies are looking at when scanning a visual stimulus. Although very young infants rarely scan an entire form, 1-month-olds scan much less thoroughly than 2-month-olds do, concentrating most on specific outer edges or boundaries and least on internal features.* *ADAPTED FROM SALAPATEK, 1975.*

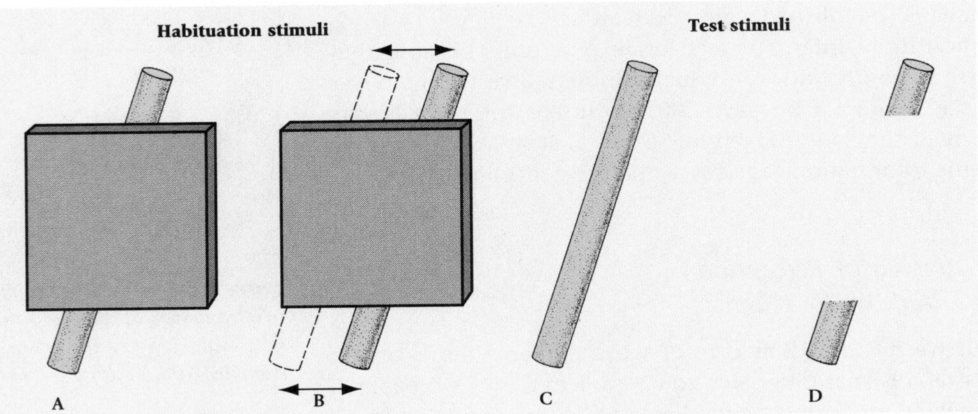

Figure 6.6 *Perceiving objects as wholes. An infant is habituated to a rod partially hidden by the block in front of it. The rod is either stationary (a) or moving (b). When tested afterward, does the infant treat the whole rod (c) as "old hat"? We certainly would, for we could readily interpret cues that tell us that there is one long rod behind the block and would therefore regard the whole rod as familiar. But if the infant shows more interest in the whole rod (c) than in the two rod segments (d), he or she has apparently not been able to use available cues to perceive a whole rod.* *ADAPTED FROM KELLMAN & SPELKE, 1983.*

part of the rod was hidden. By contrast, infants *did* apparently perceive the *moving* rod (display b) as "whole," for after habituating to this stimulus, they much preferred to look at the two short rods (display d) than at a whole rod (display c, which they now treated as "old hat"). It seems that these latter infants inferred the rod's wholeness from its synchronized movement—the fact that its parts moved in the same direction at the same time. How would 4-month-olds have responded if the two "rod tips" in display b had moved in opposite directions? They perceive them as *separate* objects based on their independent motion (Hofsten & Spelke, 1985). So infants rely heavily on kinetic (motion) cues to identify distinct forms.

Interestingly, newborns exposed to a partially screened moving rod (as in display b) see two separate objects rather than a continuous form (Slater et al., 1990b). But the impressive ability to use object movement to perceive form is already present by 2 months of age (Johnson & Aslin, 1995). By age 3 to 4 months, infants can even perceive form in some stationary scenes that capture their attention. Look carefully at Figure 6.7. Do you see a square in this display? So do 3- to 4-month-olds (Ghim, 1990)—a remarkable achievement indeed, for the boundary of this "square" is a *subjective contour* that must be constructed mentally rather than simply detected by the visual system.

Further strides in form perception occur later in the first year as infants come to detect more and more about structural configurations from the barest of cues (Craton, 1996). By 9 months of age, infants exposed to the moving point-light displays shown in Figure 6.8 pay much more attention to display a than to displays b and c, as if they were interpreting this stimulus as a representation of the human form, just as adults do (Bertenthal et al., 1987). Twelve-month-old infants are even better at constructing form from limited information. After seeing a single point of light move so as to trace a complex shape such as a ☆, 12-month-olds (but not 8- or 10-month-olds) prefer to look at actual objects with *different* shapes. This preference for novelty on the part of the 12-month-olds indicates that they have perceived the form traced earlier by the light and now find it less interesting than other novel forms (Rose, 1988b; Skouteris, McKenzie, & Day, 1992).

Face Perception

Human faces are a "form" that babies encounter often and that contain many of the features—contrast, complexity, and curvature—that capture their attention. So when do infants first respond to faces as if they were meaningful forms?

Although some researchers find that even newborns prefer to look at well-formed facial stimuli than at scrambled facial features (Valenza et al., 1996), most studies report that, for the first 8 weeks, infants lock on to high-contrast outer boundaries of facial stimuli and spend little time looking at the internal features (eyes, mouth, and lips) that might define a face as a coherent and meaningful form (Bronson, 1991; Johnson & Gilmore, 1996; and review Figure 6.5). But as 9- to 12-week-old infants begin to scan internal detail, they also come to prefer faces to scrambled faces. Indeed, 3-month-olds know what faces are supposed to look like, for they clearly prefer a normal face to an otherwise identical stimulus with its patterns of visual contrast reversed (as in a photographic negative; Dannemiller & Stephens, 1988). Three-month-old infants also recognize and prefer to look at their own mothers' faces rather than those of other women who are similar in appearance (Barrera & Maurer, 1981). And all strangers don't look alike to 3-month-olds, who gaze more at faces that adults rate as attractive rather than unattractive (Langlois et al., 1987). So between the ages of 9 and 12 weeks, infants develop a general scheme for the human face, as well as variations on that theme which enable them to recognize close companions and to discriminate strangers.

Figure 6.7 *By 3 months of age, infants are perceiving subjective contours such as the "square" shown here.* ADAPTED FROM BERTENTHAL, CAMPOS, & HAITH, *1980.*

Between 3 and 7 months of age, infants become much quicker to discriminate the faces of familiar companions from those of strangers, and they are now less likely to "forget" a face, even if they looked at it for only 2 to 3 minutes and do not see the face again for another 2 weeks (Fagan, 1979). By 8 to 10 months of age, infants begin to *interpret* emotional expressions in their mothers' faces and to respond adaptively to this information (Feinman, 1992). Although this *social referencing* ability will be discussed later in Chapter 11 as a social and emotional milestone, it illustrates that an infant's response to social interactions depends, in part, on her ability to "read" faces.

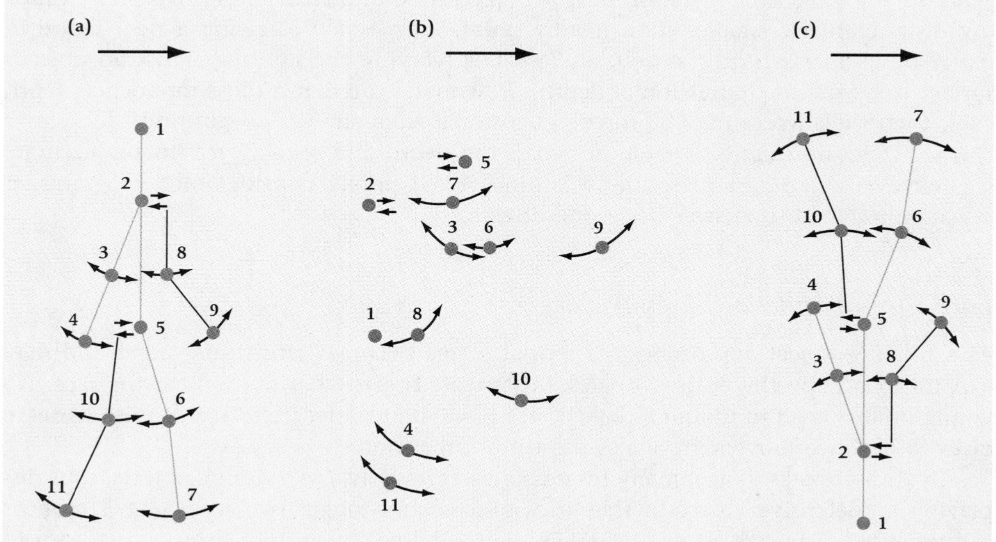

Figure 6.8 *The three point-light displays used in Bertenthal's research.* FROM BERTENTHAL, PROFFITT, & CUTTING, *1984.*

Explaining Form Perception

Perhaps you have noticed the development of face perception follows the same general course as the perception of other forms. Newborns are biologically prepared to seek visual stimulation and make visual discriminations. These early visual *experiences* are important, for they keep the visual neurons firing and contribute to the *maturation* of the visual centers of the brain (Nelson, 1995). By about 2 months of age, maturation has progressed to the point of allowing an infant to see more detail, scan more systematically, and begin to construct visual forms, including one for faces in general, as well as more specific configurations that represent the faces of familiar companions. All the while, infants are continuing their visual explorations and gaining knowledge that will permit them to make even finer distinctions among visual stimuli, and to draw some general inferences about the significance of such forms as an elongated toy that rattles when shaken or a gleeful look on a father's face.

Notice, then, that the growth of form perception results from a continuous interplay, or *interaction,* among the baby's inborn equipment (a working, but immature, visual sense), biological maturation, and visual experiences (or learning). Let's see if this same interactive model holds for spatial perception as well.

Perception of Three-Dimensional Space

Because we adults easily perceive depth and the third dimension, it is tempting to conclude that newborns can too. However, empiricists have argued that poor visual acuity and an inability to bring objects into sharp focus (that is, to accommodate) prevent the neonate from making accurate spatial inferences. In addition, infants younger than 2 to 3 months of age do not exhibit any **stereopsis**—a convergence of the visual images of the two eyes to produce a singular, nonoverlapping image that has depth (Birch, 1993). All these limitations may make it difficult for newborns to perceive depth and to locate objects in space.

However, nativists would argue that several cues to depth and distance are *monocular*—that is, detectable with only one eye. Movement of objects (such as the mother's head) toward and away from the face may be one such cue that newborns can detect. And artists make good use of other **pictorial** (or perspective) **cues** to create the illusion of three-dimensionality on a two-dimensional surface. Examples are: *linear perspective* (making linear objects converge as they recede toward the horizon), *texture gradients* (showing more detail in nearby objects than in distant ones), *sizing cues* (drawing distant objects smaller than nearby ones), *interposition* (drawing a near figure to partly obscure one further away), and *shading* (varying the lighting across an object's surface to create the impression of depth). If neonates can detect these monocular depth cues, then their world may be three-dimensional from the very beginning.

So when are infants capable of perceiving depth and making reasonably accurate inferences about size and spatial relations? We'll briefly consider four programs of research designed to answer these questions.

Early Use of Kinetic (Motion) Cues

As a moving object approaches, its retinal image becomes larger and larger and may expand to occupy the entire visual field (that is, **loom**) as it draws near the face. Do young infants react to looming objects? If so, we might infer that they can use **kinetic cues** to perceive movement across the third dimension.

By 3 to 4 weeks of age, many infants blink in response to looming objects, thus displaying a "defensive" reaction that becomes much stronger over the next 3 months (Nanez, 1987; Nanez & Yonas, 1994). Do these findings mean that babies must learn to infer movement across the third dimension, as empiricists have claimed? Maybe so, but Albert Yonas (1981) is an *interactionist* who believes that early maturation of the visual system plays a major role in this learning. Consistent with his view is the finding that preterm infants, who are neurologically immature at birth, do not begin to blink at looming objects until several weeks after full-term infants do (Petterson, Yonas, & Fisch, 1980). So it seems that a certain minimal amount of neural maturation may be necessary before infants can interpret an object's approach as a cue for depth or distance.

By 4 to 5 months of age, infants are able to use other motion cues to make spatial inferences. They know, for example, that moving objects that eclipse other stimuli are "nearer" to them than the stimuli they conceal (Craton & Yonas, 1988). So as was

stereopsis
fusion of two flat images to produce a single image that has depth.

pictorial (perspective) **cues**
depth and distance cues including linear perspective, texture gradients, sizing, interposition, and shading, that are monocular—that is, detectable with only one eye.

visual looming
the expansion of the image of an object to take up the entire visual field as it draws very close to the face.

kinetic cues
cues created by movements of objects or movements of the body; provide important information for the perception of forms and spatial relations.

6.1

FOCUS ON RESEARCH

Size Constancy in Newborns

Alan Slater and his associates (1990a) designed a clever experiment to see whether newborn babies can perceive an object's real size across changes in distance. Each of their 2-day-old subjects was given ample opportunity to gaze at either a small (5.1-cm) cube or a large (10.2-cm) cube that was presented at six different distances (although none of the babies actually saw their cube move). The purpose of these six "familiarization" trials was to expose infants to changes in the size of the retinal image of the cube in the hope that this might direct their attention to the cube's *real* (unchanging) size.

After the six familiarization trials came the test for size constancy. Each infant now saw two cubes: the small one at a distance of 30.5 cm and the large one at 61 cm. At these distances, the two cubes cast retinal images of exactly the same size (see figure). How should a baby now respond if he perceives that the real size of the "familiar" cube was constant, despite changes in the size of its retinal image? He should quickly determine that whichever cube (large or small) that he had looked at before was still the "same old cube" and should now prefer to examine the novel cube.

This is precisely what 11 of Slater's 12 newborns did, spending more than 83% of their time gazing at whichever cube (large or small) they had not previously seen. So newborn infants were able to perceive the "real" size of the cube they had examined in the familiarization trials. In other words they displayed clear evidence of size constancy in the first 2 days of life (see also Granrud, 1987).

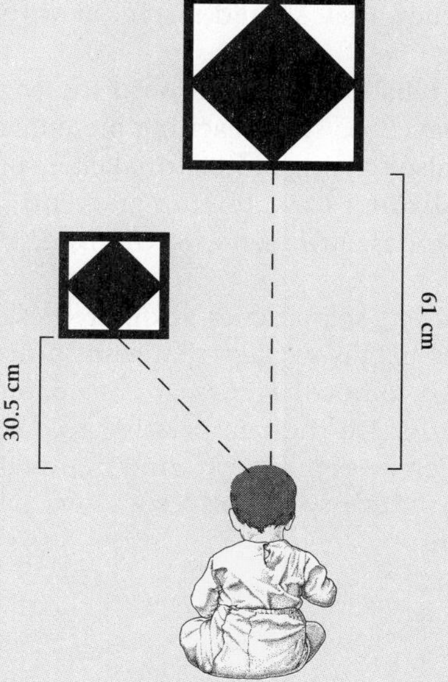

The test trial from the Slater, Mattock, & Brown (1990a) experiment. As shown at the left, babies viewed a small cube at a distance of 30.5 cm and a cube twice as large at twice that distance, or 61 cm. At these distances, the two cubes cast the same-size retinal image. The illustration at the right shows what the baby saw on this test trial.

true of early form perception, very young infants rely heavily on kinetic cues to perceive depth and distance relations.

Development of Size Constancy

If a friend who stands 5 feet 8 inches left your side and walked 20 feet away from you, the image of that person on your retina would become much smaller. Yet you realize that your friend is still the same size and simply *looks* smaller because he or she is now farther away. This realization is an example of **size constancy**—the ability to infer that the dimensions of an object remain constant over a change in distance.

Until recently, researchers claimed that size constancy could not emerge until 3 to 5 months of age, after infants had developed good binocular vision (stereopsis) that enabled them to make accurate spatial inferences. But as Box 6.1 illustrates, even newborns know something about an object's real size.

size constancy
the tendency to perceive an object as the same size from different distances despite changes in the size of its retinal image.

However, the finding that neonates display some size constancy does not mean that this ability is fully developed. Apparently, binocular vision does contribute to its development, for the 4-month-olds who show greater evidence of size constancy are those whose binocular capabilities are most mature (Aslin, 1987). Kinetic cues also contribute; inferences about real size among 4½-month-olds are more likely to be accurate if the infants have watched an object approach and recede (Day & McKenzie, 1981). Size constancy steadily improves throughout the first year; however, this ability is not fully mature until 10 to 11 years of age (Day, 1987).

Figure 6.9 *This bank of windows is actually a large photograph taken at a 45° angle, and the two edges of this stimulus are in fact equidistant from an infant seated directly in front of it. If infants are influenced by pictorial cues to depth, they should perceive the right edge of the photo to be nearer to them and indicate as much by reaching out to touch this edge rather than the more "distant" edge to their left.* *Adapted from Yonas, Cleaves, & Pettersen, 1978.*

Use of Pictorial Cues

Albert Yonas and his associates have studied infants' reactions to monocular depth cues—the tricks artists and photographers use to portray depth and distance on a two-dimensional surface. In the earliest of these studies (Yonas, Cleaves, & Pettersen, 1978), infants were exposed to a photograph of a bank of windows taken at a 45° angle. As we see in Figure 6.9, the windows on the right appear (to us at least) to be much closer than those on the left. So if infants perceive pictorial depth cues, they might be fooled into thinking that the windows on the right are closer and they should reach to the right. But if they are insensitive to pictorial cues, they should reach out with one hand about as often as they do with the other.

What Yonas found is that 7-month-olds reliably reached toward the windows that appeared nearest, whereas 5-month-olds displayed no such reaching preferences. In later research, Yonas found that 7-month-olds are also sensitive to pictorial cues such as interposition (see Figure 6.10), relative size and shading cues, texture gradients, and linear perspective, whereas 5-month-olds are not (Yonas, Arterberry, & Granrud, 1987; Arterberry, Yonas, & Bensen, 1989).

In sum, infants become sensitive to different spatial cues at different ages. From a limited capacity for size constancy at birth, babies extract spatial information from kinetic cues between 1 and 3 months of age, binocular cues at 3 to 5 months, and monocular (pictorial) cues by age 6 to 7 months. Do these impressive accomplishments imply that a 6- to 7-month-old infant perceives depth and knows enough to avoid crawling off the edge of a sofa or a staircase? Let's see what researchers have learned from their attempts to answer these questions.

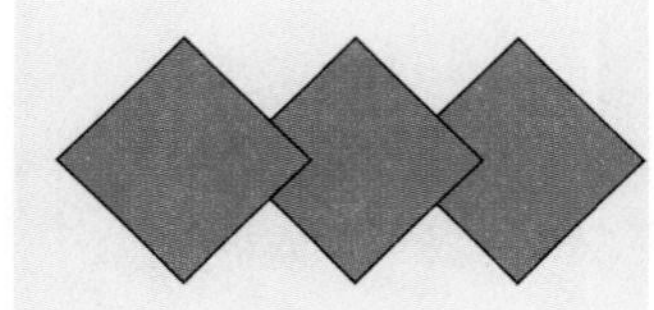

Figure 6.10 *If infants are sensitive to the pictorial cue of interposition, they should reliably reach for the "closest" area of a visual display (left side in this example). Seven-month-olds show this reaching preference, whereas 5-month-olds do not.* *From Granrud & Yonas, 1984.*

Development of Depth Perception

In the early 1960s, Eleanor Gibson and Richard Walk developed an apparatus they called the **visual cliff** to determine whether infants can perceive depth. The visual cliff (see Figure 6.11) consists of an elevated glass platform divided into two sections by a center board. On the "shallow" side, a checkerboard pattern is placed directly under the glass. On the "deep" side, the pattern is placed several feet below the glass, creating the illusion of a sharp drop-off, or a "visual cliff." The investigator tests an infant for depth perception by placing him on the center board and then asking the child's mother to try to coax the infant to cross both the "shallow" and the "deep" sides. Testing infants 6½ months of age and older, Gibson and Walk (1960) found that 90% of them would cross the shallow side but fewer than 10% would cross the deep side. Apparently, most infants of crawling age clearly perceive depth and are afraid of drop-offs.

Might children who are too young to crawl also perceive depth? To find out, Joseph Campos and his associates (1970) recorded changes in infants' heart rates when they were lowered face down over the "shallow" and "deep" sides of the apparatus. Babies as young as 2 months of age showed a *decrease* in heart rate when over the deep side but no change in heart rate on the shallow side. Why a decrease in heart rate? When we are afraid, our hearts beat faster, not slower. A decrease in heart rate is a sign of interest. So 2-month-old infants *detect a difference* between the deep and shallow sides, but they have not learned to *fear* drop-offs.

visual cliff
an elevated platform that creates an illusion of depth, used to test the depth perception of infants.

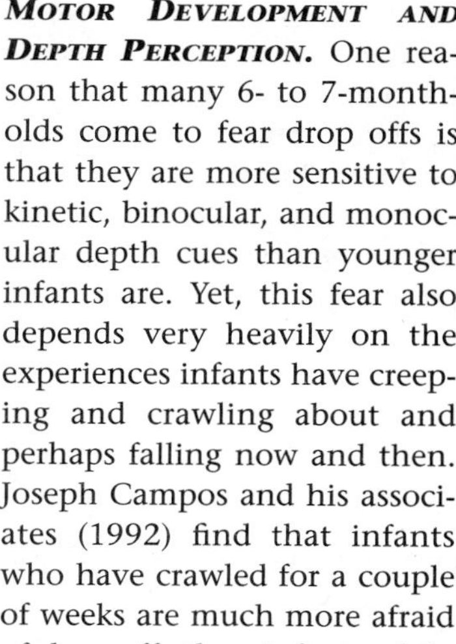

Motor Development and Depth Perception. One reason that many 6- to 7-month-olds come to fear drop offs is that they are more sensitive to kinetic, binocular, and monocular depth cues than younger infants are. Yet, this fear also depends very heavily on the experiences infants have creeping and crawling about and perhaps falling now and then. Joseph Campos and his associates (1992) find that infants who have crawled for a couple of weeks are much more afraid of drop offs than infants of the same age who are not yet crawling. In fact, precrawlers quickly develop a healthy fear of heights when given special walkers that allow them to move about on their own. So motor development provides experiences that change infants' interpretation of the meaning of depth. And as we saw in Chapter 5, infants who have began to move about on their own are better than those who haven't at solving other spatial tasks, such as finding hidden objects.

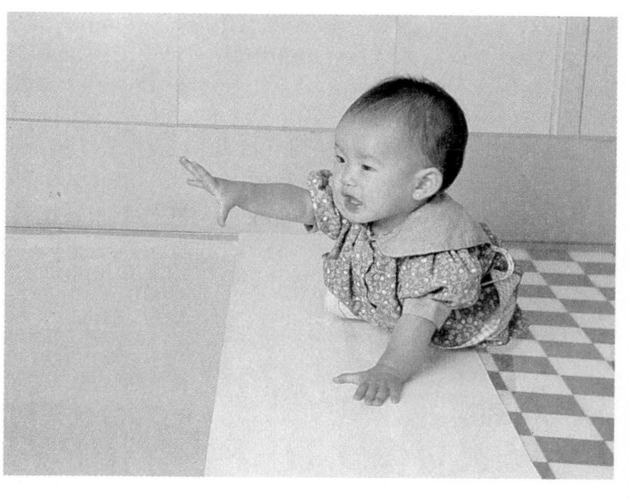

Figure 6.11 *An infant at the edge of the visual cliff.*

Why does self-produced movement make such a difference? Probably because young creepers and crawlers have discovered that the visual environment changes when they move, so that they are more inclined to use a *spatial landmark* to help them define where they (and hidden objects) are in relation to the larger spatial layout. A study by Dina Bai and Bennett Bertenthal (1992) nicely supports this interpretation. Seven- to 8-month-old creepers and precreepers saw a toy placed into one of two different-colored containers on a table. Next, either the infant or the table was rotated 180° (see Figure 6.12) and the infant was allowed to search for the toy. The results were clear. *When the table had been rotated* (and the infant did not move), both creepers and precreepers tracked the movement *of the containers* and were equally proficient at finding the hidden toy. But when the infant had been rotated (and the containers did not move), creepers were much better at finding the hidden toy than precreepers were. Why? Because creepers were more inclined to use the color of the correct cup as a spatial landmark to tell them where to search after their own position in space had changed. Self-produced movement also makes an infant more sensitive to *optical flow*—the sensation that other objects move when she does—which may promote the development of new neural pathways in the sensory and motor areas of the brain that underlie improvements in both motor skills and spatial perception (Bertenthal & Campos, 1987; Higgins et al., 1996).

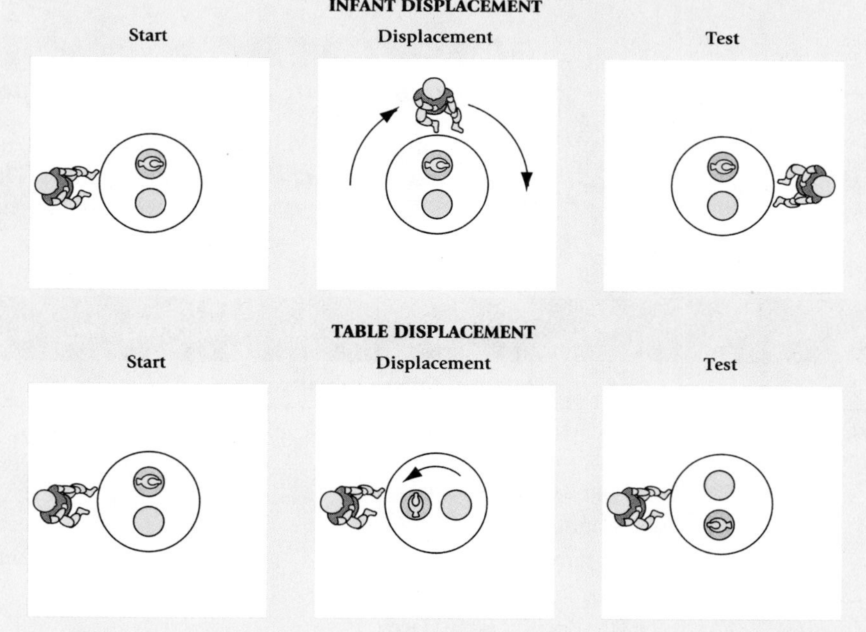

Figure 6.12 *Test trials for the Bai and Bertenthal (1992) experiment. Infants were allowed to search for a hidden toy after they had moved (top row) or the table had rotated, causing the hidden object to move (bottom row).* Adapted from Bai & Bertenthal, 1992.

Perhaps you have already inferred by now that the *interactive* model that best explains the growth of form perception applies equally well to the development of spatial abilities. Maturation of the visual sense enables infants to see better and to detect a greater variety of depth cues, while also contributing to the growth of motor skills. Yet experience is equally important: The first year is a time when curious infants are constantly making new and exciting discoveries about depth and distance relations as they become ever more skilled at reaching for and manipulating objects and at moving about to explore stairs, sloped surfaces, and other "visual cliffs" in the natural environment (Bertenthal, 1993; Bushnell & Boudreau, 1993).

Table 6.2 summarizes the remarkable changes in visual perception that occur over the first year of life. Now let's consider how infants come to integrate information from more than one sense to make perceptual inferences.

INTERMODAL PERCEPTION

Suppose you are playing a game in which you are blindfolded and are trying to identify objects by touch. A friend places a small, spherical object in your hand. As you finger it, you determine that it is about 1¼ inches in diameter, that it weighs a couple of ounces, and that it is very hard and covered with many small "dimples." You then say "aha" and conclude that the object is a ________.

A colleague who conducts this exercise in class reports that most students easily identify the object as a golf ball even if they have never touched a golf ball in their lives. This is an example of **intermodal perception**—the ability to recognize by one sensory modality (in this case, touch) an object that is familiar through another (vision). As adults, we can make many inferences of this kind. When do babies first display these abilities?

Theories of Intermodal Perception

intermodal perception
the ability to use one sensory modality to identify a stimulus or pattern of stimuli that is already familiar through another modality.

The timing of intermodal perception has been hotly debated over the years. On the one hand, *differentiation* theorists such as Thomas Bower (1982) and Eleanor Gibson (1969; 1992) believe that the senses are integrated at birth and that the defining fea-

TABLE 6.2 **Milestones in Infant Visual Perception**

Age	Pattern/form perception	Spatial perception
Birth–1 month	Seeks visual input; prefers moderately complex stimuli with high visual contrast. Scans boundaries of visual targets.	Displays some size constancy. Responds to looming objects and kinetic depth lines.
2–4 months	Visual scanning of entire stimulus. Perceives forms from their motion. Detects some subjective contours. Prefers faces to scrambled faces. Recognizes mother's face; prefers attractive to unattractive faces.	Detects depth cues on the visual cliff. Becomes sensitive to binocular depth cues.
5–8 months	Perceives form in stationary objects. Detects more subtle subjective contours.	Size constancy improves. Becomes sensitive to pictoral (monocular) depth cues. Fears drop-offs.
9–12 months	Perceives form from limited information (for example, a moving light). Interprets others' facial expressions.	All aspects of spatial perception become more refined.

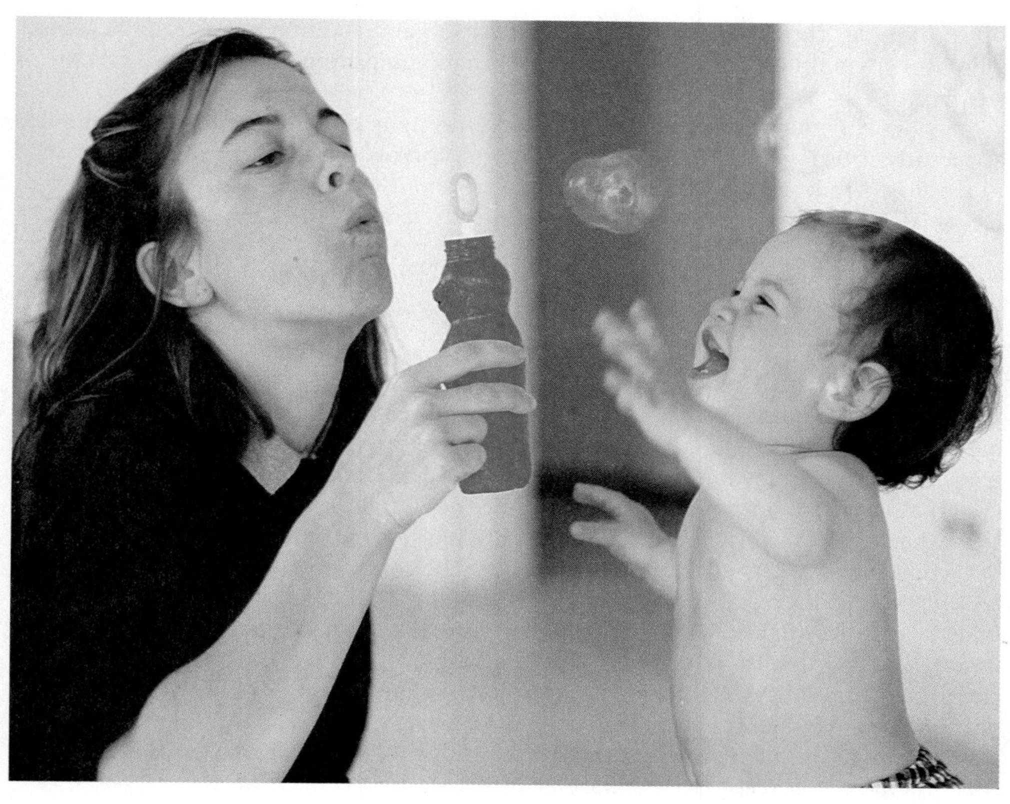

According to differentiation theory, the senses are integrated at birth, and babies expect to touch and feel objects that they can see and reach. However, vision and touch are soon differentiated, so that this year-old infant might even enjoy making an object disappear at her slightest touch.

tures of many stimuli (size, shape, texture; sight, sound, or touch sensation) cause infants to investigate further, using all their sensory modalities. Gibson (1969) adds that the "defining" features of many stimuli (shape, texture, and so on) are detectable by more than one modality. If they are correct, intermodal perception may be possible very early in life.

On the other hand, *enrichment* theorists such as Piaget (1954; 1960) believe that the senses are separate at birth and must mature independently before the infant will be able to compare and eventually integrate information from different sensory channels. So, an enrichment theorist would argue that very young infants who know an object only by sight would be unable to recognize it by touch (as in the dark).

Which theory is correct? Let's see if we can clarify the issue by examining relevant research.

Are the Senses Integrated at Birth?

Suppose that you captured a baby's attention by floating a soap bubble in front of her face. Would she reach for it? If she did, how do you think she would react when the bubble pops at her slightest touch?

Thomas Bower and his associates (Bower, Broughton, & Moore, 1970) exposed neonates to a situation similar to the soap-bubble scenario. The subjects were 8- to 31-day-old infants who could see an object well within reaching distance while they were wearing special goggles. Actually, this *virtual object* was an illusion created by a shadow caster. If the infant reached for it, his or her hand would feel nothing at all. Bower et al. found that the infants did reach for the virtual object and that they often became frustrated to tears when they failed to touch it. These results suggest that vision and touch are integrated: Infants expect to feel objects that they can see and reach, and an incongruity between vision and the tactile sense is discomforting.

Other research on auditory—visual incongruities (Aronson & Rosenbloom, 1971) reveals that 1- to 2-month-olds often become distressed when they *see* their talking mothers behind a soundproof screen but *hear* their mothers' voices through a speaker off to the side. Their discomfort implies that vision and audition are integrated; a baby who sees his mother expects to hear her voice coming from the general direction of her mouth.

So the differentiation theorists appear to be right on one point: The senses are apparently integrated early in life. Nevertheless, infants' negative emotional responses to confusing sensory stimulation say very little about their ability to use one sense to recognize objects and experiences that are already familiar through another sense.

Development of Intermodal Perception

Although intermodal perception has never been observed in newborns, it seems that babies only 1 month old have the ability to recognize by sight at least some of the objects they have previously sucked. In one study, Eleanor Gibson and Arlene Walker (1984) allowed 1-month-old infants to suck either a rigid cylinder or a spongy, pliable one. Then the two objects were displayed visually to illustrate that the spongy cylinder would bend and the rigid one would not. The results were clear: Infants who had sucked on a spongy object preferred to look at the rigid cylinder, whereas those who had sucked on a rigid cylinder now gazed more at the pliable one. Apparently, these infants could "visualize" the object they had sucked and now considered it less interesting than the other stimulus, which was new to them.

Since 30-day-old infants have had lots of experience sucking on both spongy objects (nipples) and rigid ones (their own thumbs), we cannot necessarily conclude that intermodal perception is innate. And before we get too carried away with the remarkable proficiencies of 1-month-olds, let's note that (1) oral-to-visual perception is the only cross-modal skill that has ever been observed in infants this young, and (2) this ability is weak, at best, in very young infants and improves dramatically over the first year (Rose, Gottfried, & Bridger, 1981). Even the seemingly related ability to match tactile sensations (from grasping) with visual ones does not appear until 4 to 6 months of age (Rose et al., 1981; Streri & Spelke, 1988), largely because infants younger than this cannot grasp objects well (Bushnell & Boudreau, 1993).

Intermodal perception between the vision and hearing emerges at about 4 months of age—precisely the time that infants begin to *voluntarily* turn their heads in the direction of sounds. By age 5 months, infants can even match visual and auditory cues for distance. So if they are listening to a sound track in which engine noise is becoming softer, they prefer to watch a film of a car moving away rather than one showing a vehicle approaching (Walker-Andrews & Lennon, 1985; see also Pickens, 1994). Clearly, 4- to 5-month-olds know what sights jibe with many sounds, and this auditory/visual matching continues to improve over the next several months.

Concept Check 6.2
Infant Perceptual Development

Check your understanding of selected aspects of infant perceptual development by matching one of the following alternatives to the statements below: (a) intermodal perception, (b) depth cues, (c) face perception, (d) kinetic (motion) cues, (e) depth perception, (f) pictorial cues, (g) maturation of the brain's visual centers, (h) size constancy. Answers appear in the Appendix at the back of the book.

_____ 1. type of early stimulation that sensitizes infants to forms and spatial relations

_____ 2. spatial cues that may distress a 7-month-old but interest a 2-month-old

_____ 3. spatial ability present in a rudimentary form at birth

_____ 4. spatial cues that 7-month-olds are sensitive to but 5-month-olds are not

_____ 5. early visual stimulation promotes this process, which furthers visual perception

_____ 6. locomotor skills promote this development

_____ 7. perceptual skill that predicts later intellectual performance

_____ 8. important achievement in form perception that infants display at 2 to 3 months

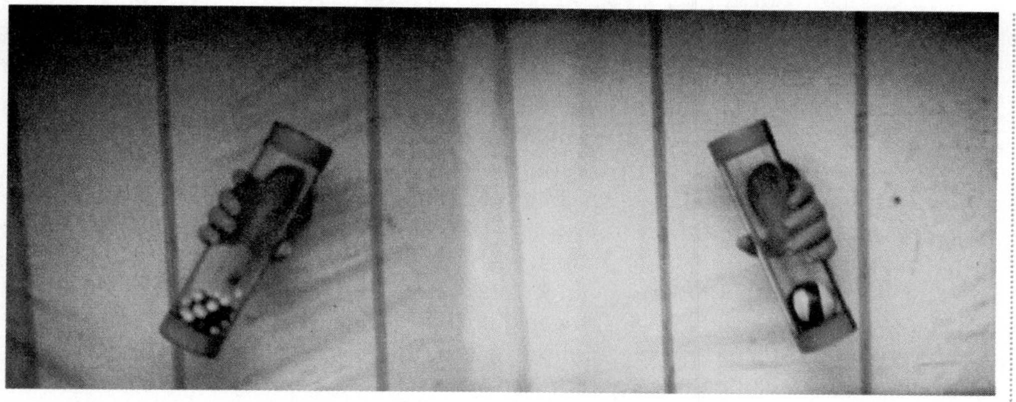

Figure 6.13 *Three-month-olds who briefly watched each cylinder rotate independently later saw both rotate* at the same time *as they listen to a tape of either one object or many objects hitting the bottom of a cylinder. As expected by differentiation theory, the infants immediately matched sights with sounds, looking to the right upon hearing the impact of one object, but to the left upon hearing impacts of many objects.* FROM BAHRICK, *1988.*

Another Look at the Enrichment/ Differentiation Controversy

So which theory—enrichment or differentiation—best explains the development of intermodal perception? The evidence we have reviewed favors differentiation theory. Not only are very young infants often upset by sensory incongruities, just as differentiation theorists had expected, but the fact that 1-month-olds show *any* intermodal matching seems more consistent with the differentiation viewpoint (simultaneous detection of defining features by different modalities) than with the enrichment perspective (independent detection of defining features followed by a gradual integration of this information across modalities).

Indeed, infants do quickly integrate *novel* sensory information to make accurate intermodal inferences. For example, 3-month-olds who have but 1 minute's experience watching the rotation of each of the two cylinders in Figure 6.13 can later match corresponding sights with sounds. That is, when they see both cylinders being rotated *at the same time,* infants who hear the tape-recorded impact of only one object look appropriately at the cylinder to the right, whereas those who hear the impact of many objects look at the cylinder to the left (Bahrick, 1988). Apparently, differentiation theorists were correct: Matching of novel information across modalities occurs almost simultaneously, as long as infants are able to detect this input in each sensory channel.

Why, then, do intermodal judgments become more accurate over time? Probably because as each sense continues to develop, it becomes a more effective means of detecting the defining features of novel stimuli. But the fact that even young infants can match sensations across modalities is very significant, for this capacity helps them to organize and interpret a bewildering array of stimuli in the natural environment and keeps their world from becoming a "blooming, buzzing confusion." Indeed, infants who were especially skilled at integrating their sensory experiences later tend to perform well at age 11 on IQ tests, thus suggesting that intermodal perceptual ability is an early indicator of future intellectual performance (Rose & Feldman, 1995).

INFANT PERCEPTION IN PERSPECTIVE— AND A LOOK AHEAD

What remarkable perceptual competencies infants display! All their senses are functioning reasonably well at birth, and babies immediately put them to work, searching for stimuli to explore and identifying similarities and differences among these sensory inputs. Within the first few months, infants are becoming accomplished perceivers:

They detect forms, react to depth and distance cues, recognize definite patterns in the language they hear, and regularly combine information from different sensory modalities to achieve a richer understanding of the natural environment.

We have concentrated heavily on the perceptual skills of infants because infancy is the period when most basic perceptual competencies emerge (Bornstein, 1992). In fact, many researchers believe that advances in perception beyond the first year stem primarily from children's increasing ability to focus their *attention* on sensory inputs and draw meaningful *inferences* from them—milestones that reflect advances in information processing and might be properly labeled *cognitive* developments. Before closing the book on perception, however, let's take note of one very influential theory of perceptual development that helps to explain why younger children may require much more information to recognize common objects than older ones do, why preschool children may have some difficulty trying to learn to read, and why people in different cultures might perceive the world in somewhat different ways.

Perceptual Learning in Childhood: Gibson's Differentiation Theory

According to Gibson (1969; 1987; 1992), **perceptual learning** occurs when we actively explore objects in our environment and detect their *distinctive (or invariant) features.* As we have noted, a distinctive feature is any cue that *differentiates* one stimulus from all others. A 3-year-old may initially confuse rabbits and cats, for both are furry animals of about the same size. However, the child will eventually discover that rabbits have long ears—a distinctive feature that differentiates them from cats, rats, squirrels, and all other small, furry animals. Gibson believes that the motivation for perceptual learning is inborn; from birth, humans are active information seekers who search for order and stability (invariants) in the natural environment.

Of course, some invariants are easier to detect than others. Even a 4-year-old whose attentional strategies are relatively immature soon notices large distinctive features such as an elephant's trunk or a rabbit's long ears. However, a 4-year-old may not easily differentiate *b* from *d* because the distinctive feature that discriminates these letters (the direction of curvature) is subtle and not very meaningful to her.

Gibson and her colleagues have conducted an experiment to study the ability of young children to distinguish different letterlike forms (Gibson, Gibson, Pick, & Osser, 1962). Children aged 4 to 8 were shown a standard letterlike stimulus and several transformations of this "standard" form (examples appear in Figure 6.14). Their task was to pick out the stimuli that were identical to the standard. The 4- and 5-year-olds had difficulties with all the transformations; they often judged these stimuli to be identical to the standard. However, 6- to 8-year-olds were generally able to detect the "distinctive features" that differentiated the transformations from the "standard" stimulus.

Perhaps you can see the relevance of Gibson's work for elementary education, particularly reading education. Clearly, the ability to discriminate and categorize letters of the alphabet is a major perceptual milestone that is necessary before children can hope to decode words and become proficient readers (Gibson & Levin, 1975). Although preschool training in letter recognition (at home, at nursery school, and on educational

perceptual learning
changes in one's ability to extract information from sensory stimulation that occur as a result of experience.

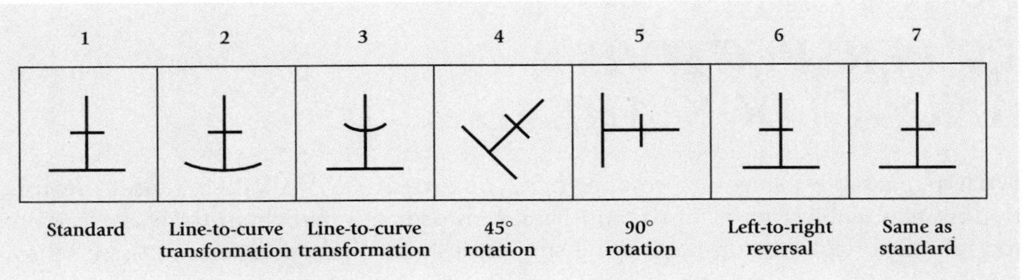

Figure 6.14 *Examples of figures used to test children's ability to detect the distinctive features of letterlike forms. Stimulus 1 is the standard. The child's task is to examine each of the comparison stimuli (stimuli 2–7) and pick out those that are the same as the standard.* Adapted from Gibson et al., *1962.*

television programs such as *Sesame Street*) helps children to recognize many letters and even a few words (such as their own names), preschoolers younger than 5 to 5½ continue to confuse letters such as *b, h,* and *d,* or *m* and *w,* that have similar perceptual characteristics (Chall, 1983). By contrast, Gibson's subjects were beginning to detect and appreciate subtle differences in *unfamiliar* letterlike forms at precisely the time (age 6) that serious reading instruction begins at school. As it turns out, learning to read is a very complex task—one that deserves a closer look. Box 6.2, on page 212, describes several of the major perceptual hurdles that children must overcome to make sense of all those funny little squiggles on the printed page.

In sum, Gibson is a *differentiation* theorist. She believes that young children are constantly extracting new and more subtle information from the environment and thereby discovering the properties, patterns, and "distinctive features" that will enable them to differentiate objects and events. As this differentiation continues, a child grows perceptually and becomes increasingly accurate at interpreting the broad array of stimuli that impinge on the sensory receptors.

However, other researchers believe that Gibson's theory is incomplete and that children do far more when making sense of their experiences than simply detecting distinctive features. Their point is that children also use their existing knowledge to *enrich* their sensory experiences and *construct* new interpretations. Indeed, unless infants used existing knowledge, to *impose meaning* on ambiguous stimuli, it is hard to see how they could ever interpret the moving light display in Figure 6.8—a stimulus with few distinctive features—as an upright human form. So as we noted at the beginning of this chapter, both the differentiation and the enrichment perspectives have some merit and have contributed substantially to our understanding of early perceptual (and cognitive) developments.

Cultural Influences on Perception

How is perception influenced by one's culture and cultural traditions? Although people in different cultures rarely differ in such basic perceptual capabilities as the ability to discriminate forms, patterns, and degrees of brightness or loudness (Berry et al., 1992), culture can have some subtle but important effects on perception.

For example, we noted earlier that there are some phonemic discriminations that an infant can make better than adults can (Werker & Desjardins, 1995). Each of us begins life biologically prepared to acquire any language that humans speak. But as we are exposed to a particular language, we become especially sensitive to the sound patterns that are important to that language (that is, to its distinctive features) and less sensitive to auditory distinctions that our language deems irrelevant. So all infants easily discriminate the consonants *r* and *l* (Eimas, 1975a). So can you if your native language is English, French, Spanish, or German. However, Chinese and Japanese make no distinction between *r* and *l,* and adult native speakers of these languages cannot make this auditory discrimination as well as infants can (Miyawaki et al., 1975).

Music is another cultural tool that influences our auditory perception. Michael Lynch and his associates (1990) had 6-month-old infants and American adults listen to melodies in either the Western major/minor scale or the Javanese pelog scale, which sounds a bit strange to Western adults. Inserted within the melodies was an occasional "mistuned" note that violated the musical scale. Remarkably, 6-month-old infants often detected these mistuned notes, regardless of whether they violated a Western or a Javanese melody. Apparently, babies are born with the potential to perceive "musicality" and to discriminate good music from bad music in a variety of musical scales. By contrast, American adults were much less sensitive to bad notes in the unfamiliar Javanese musical system than to mistuned notes in their native Western scale, suggesting that their years of experience with the Western musical system had shaped their perceptions of music.

These findings illustrate two general principles of development that are very important. First, the growth of perceptual abilities, like so many other aspects of development, is not simply a matter of adding new skills; it is also a matter of *losing* unnecessary

DEVELOPMENTAL ISSUES

How Do We Learn to Read?

One of the most challenging perceptual tasks that most children face is learning to read. How do they discover that the print on the page represents spoken words? How do they learn to translate print into spoken language?

Eleanor Gibson and Harry Levin (1975) have identified three phases in learning to read. First, children equate reading with storytelling: They may pick up a storybook and "read" very sensible sentences, most of which have no relation to the words on the page.

Next, children recognize that the squiggles on the printed page represent words. They may then try to match the spoken words of a familiar story to the symbols on the page, often incorrectly (Smith, 1977). So a 3-year-old who knows that the title of her storybook is *Santa Is Coming to Town* might try to "read" the cover by touching each letter and uttering a word or syllable, as illustrated below. This kind of activity sets the stage for learning that each letter is related to a particular sound and that combinations of letters (and sounds) make up printed words (Crain-Thoreson & Dale, 1992).

In the third and final phase of learning to read, children have become quite skilled at decoding letters; they can

Print on book cover:	S	a	n	t	a	I	s	Com...
	↓	↓	↓	↓	↓	↓	↓	↓
Child's statements (as she touches each letter)	"San	ta	is	com	ing	to	town.	What's this say?"

"sound out" unknown words by breaking them into individual sounds or syllables. Most children gain solid mastery of the rules for translating letters into sounds by third or fourth grade (Morrison, 1984).

In part, reading is an exercise in visual form perception. Readers must learn to recognize the distinctive features of letters, an ability that most youngsters begin to display by age 6 (see text). But reading is really a complex, *intermodal* task. To make sense of written words, children must not only differentiate among letters but must also learn which letters correspond to which sounds in spoken language. And detecting letter–sound correspondences seems to depend very heavily on *phonological awareness*—the realization that *spoken* words can be decomposed into basic sound units, or *phonemes.* Interestingly, the relationship between phonological processing skills and reading-related knowledge is *bidirectional.* Early phonological processing skills permit children to become more knowledgeable about reading, which makes them better phonological processors, which contributes to further advances in reading-related knowledge (Wagner, Torgesen, & Rashotte, 1994).

What does all this suggest about teaching children to read? The merits of two broad approaches to reading instruction have been debated for years. The "*phonics*" or "*code-oriented*" approach teaches children to break words down into their component sounds—that is, it systematically teaches them letter–sound correspondence rules (Vellutino, 1991). By contrast, the "*whole-language*" approach emphasizes reading for meaning and teaches children to recognize whole words by sight or to figure out what they mean using clues in the surrounding context. This approach assumes that the "parts" of printed words (the letters) are not as meaningful as the whole words and that children can learn to read as effortlessly and naturally as they learn to understand speech.

Although children can learn to read by either form of instruction, research clearly indicates that, somehow or another, they must learn exactly what the phonics or code-oriented approach attempts to teach them if they are ever to read well (Adams, 1990; Hatcher, Hulme, & Ellis, 1994; Vellutino, 1991). Today, many reading experts see advantages to combining the whole-language and phonics methods. However, they also stress that truly effective reading curricula are those that strive to maximize children's *motivation* to read by exposing them to stories and other materials that relate more closely to their interests and cultural experiences than most children's readers do (Hatcher et al., 1994; Loupe, 1997; Tharp, 1994).

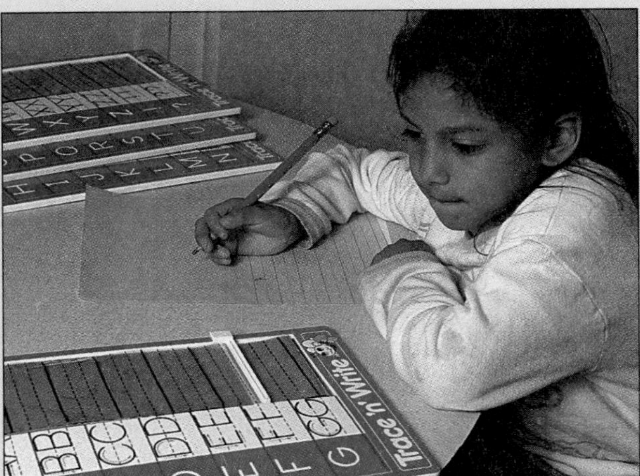

Perceiving the distinctive features of letters and the correspondence between letters and sounds are tough tasks for preschool children.

ones. Second, our culture largely determines which sensory inputs are "distinctive" and how they should be interpreted. We *learn* not to hear certain phonemes if they are not distinctive to the language we speak. We Westerners *learn* to view rats and snakes as loathful nonfood items, whereas people in many other cultures perceive them to be tasty delicacies. So the way we perceive the world depends not only on the detection of the objective aspects in our sensory inputs (*perceptual* learning) but also on *cultural* learning experiences that provide a framework for interpreting these inputs.

Let's now take a closer look at learning and see if we can determine why many developmentalists include it (along with maturation and perception) among the most fundamental developmental processes.

BASIC LEARNING PROCESSES

Learning is one of those deceptively simple terms that are actually quite complex. Most psychologists think of learning as a change in behavior (or behavior potential) that meets the following three requirements (Domjan, 1993):

1. The individual now thinks, perceives, or reacts to the environment in a *new way.*
2. This change is clearly the result of a person's *experiences*—that is, attributable to repetition, study, practice, or the observations the person has made, rather than to hereditary or maturational processes or to physiological damage resulting from injury.
3. The change is *relatively permanent.* Facts, thoughts, and behaviors that are acquired and immediately forgotten have not really been learned; and temporary changes due to fatigue, illness, or drugs do not qualify as learned responses.

Let's now consider four fundamental ways in which children learn: habituation, classical conditioning, operant conditioning, and observational learning.

Habituation: Early Evidence of Information-Processing and Memory

Earlier, we touched on one very simple and often overlooked form of learning called *habituation*—the process by which we stop attending or responding to a stimulus repeated over and over. Habituation can be thought of as learning to become disinterested in stimuli that are recognized as "old hat" and nothing to get excited about. It can occur even before a baby is born: 27- to 36-week-old fetuses initially become quite active when a vibrator is placed on the mother's abdomen, but soon stop moving (that is, habituate), as if they process these vibrations as a familiar sensation that is no longer worthy of attention (Madison et al., 1986).

How do we know that an infant is not merely fatigued when he stops responding to a familiar stimulus? We know because when a baby has habituated to one stimulus, he often *dishabituates*—that is, attends to or even reacts vigorously to a slightly different stimulus. Dishabituation, then, indicates that the baby's sensory receptors are not simply fatigued and that he can discriminate the familiar from the unfamiliar.

WHAT DO YOU THINK? ?

In a debate, your opponent claims that all humans share a uniquely human nervous system that causes them to perceive the world in pretty much the same way. Do you agree? If not, how might you respond to your opponent?

Developmental Trends

Habituation improves dramatically throughout the first year. Infants less than 4 months old may require long exposures to a stimulus before they habituate; by contrast, 5- to 12-month-olds may recognize the same stimulus as familiar after a few seconds of sustained attention and are likely to retain this knowledge for days, or even weeks (Fagan,

learning
a relatively permanent change in behavior (or behavioral potential) that results from one's experiences or practice.

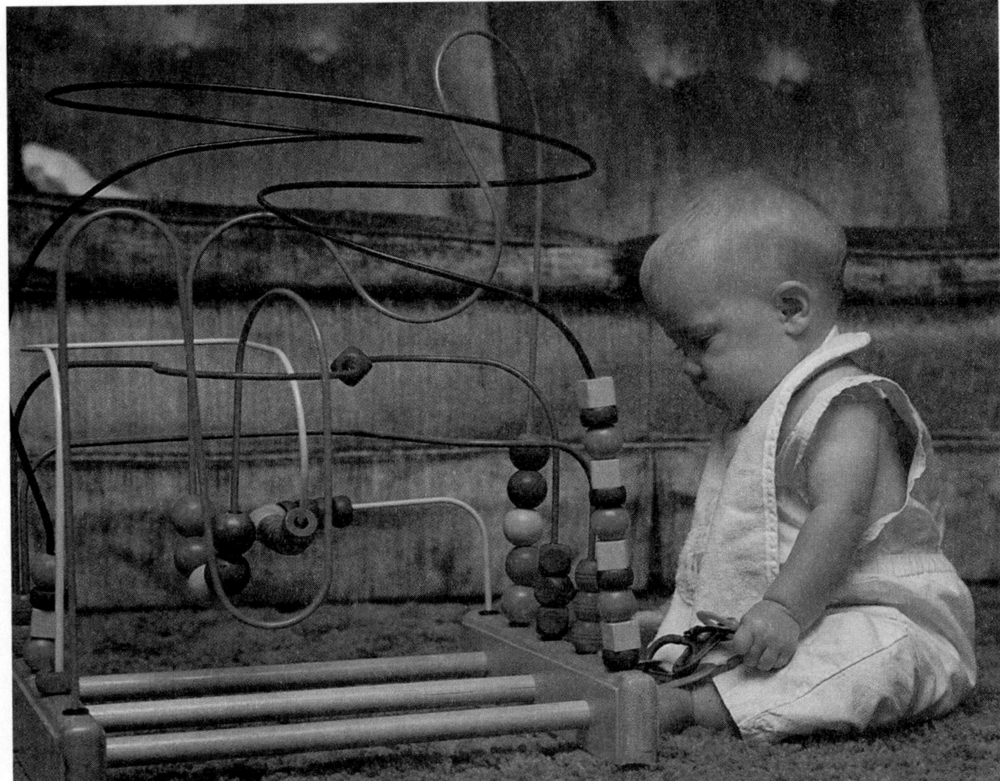

By 6 months of age, infants are quick to discriminate novel objects and events from familiar ones, and once they brand a stimulus as familiar, they may retain this knowledge for months.

1984; Richards, 1997). This trend toward rapid habituation is undoubtedly related to the maturation of the sensory areas of the cerebral cortex. As the brain and the senses continue to mature, infants process information faster and detect more about a stimulus during any given exposure (Richards, 1997; Rovee-Collier, 1987).

Individual Differences

Infants reliably differ in the rate at which they habituate. Some are highly efficient information processors: They quickly recognize repetitive sensory inputs and are very slow to forget what they have experienced. Others are less efficient: They require longer exposures to brand a stimulus as "familiar" and may soon forget what they have learned. Might these early individual differences in learning and memory have any implications for later development?

Apparently so. Infants who habituate rapidly during the first 6 to 8 months of life are quicker to understand and use language during the second year (Tamis-LeMonda & Bornstein, 1989) and reliably outscore their slower-habituating age-mates on standardized intelligence tests later in childhood (McCall & Carriger, 1993; Rose & Feldman, 1995). Why? Probably because rate of habituation measures the speed at which information is processed, as well as attention, memory, and preferences for novelty, all of which underlie the complex mental activities and problem-solving skills normally measured on IQ tests (Rose & Feldman, 1995; 1996).

classical conditioning
a type of learning in which an initially neutral stimulus is repeatedly paired with a meaningful nonneutral stimulus so that the neutral stimulus comes to elicit the response originally made only to the nonneutral stimulus.

unconditioned stimulus (UCS)
a stimulus that elicits a particular response without any prior learning.

Classical Conditioning

A second way that young children learn is through **classical conditioning.** In classical conditioning, a neutral stimulus that initially has no effect on the child eventually elicits a response of some sort by virtue of its association with a second stimulus that always elicits the response. Russian physiologist Ivan Pavlov originally discovered this form of learning while studying digestive processes in dogs. Specifically, Pavlov

Figure 6.15 *The three phases of classical conditioning. In the preconditioning phase, the unconditioned stimulus (UCS) always elicits an unconditioned response (UCR), whereas the conditioned stimulus (CS) never does. During the conditioning phase, the CS and UCS are paired repeatedly and eventually associated. At this point, the learner passes into the postconditioning phase, in which the CS alone elicits the original response (now called a conditioned response, or CR).*

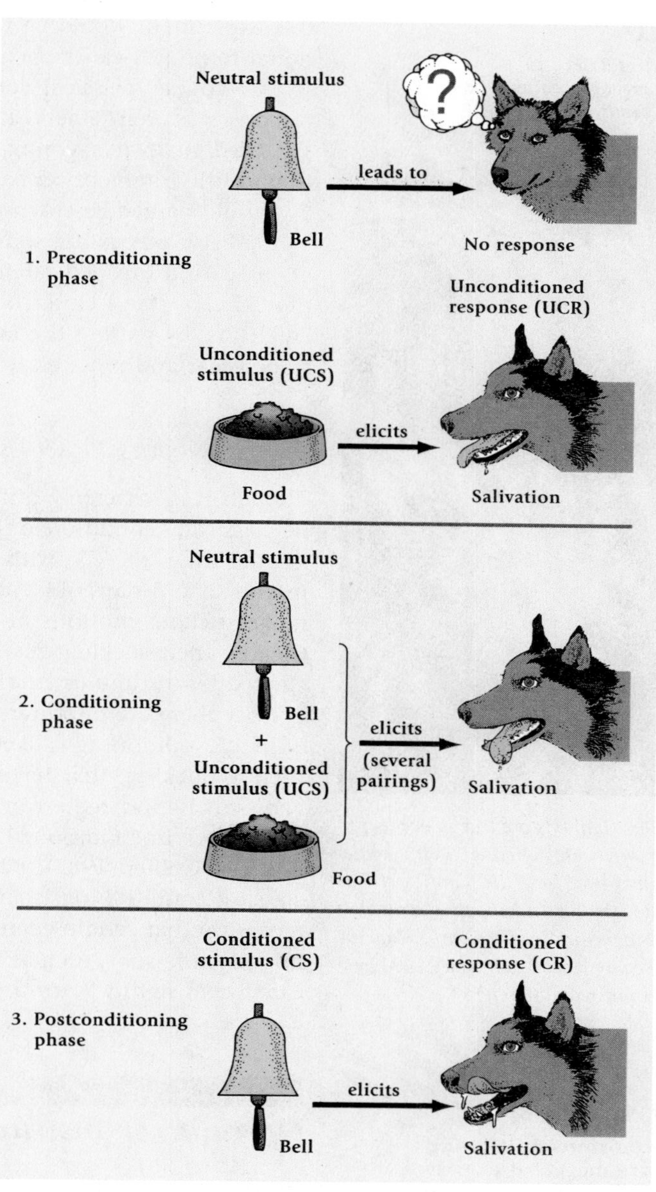

noted that his dogs would often salivate at the appearance of their caretaker who had come to feed them. He then speculated that the dogs had probably associated the caretaker (an initially neutral stimulus) with food, a nonneutral stimulus that ordinarily makes dogs salivate (an unlearned, or "reflexive," response to food). In other words, salivation at the sight of the caretaker was said to be a learned response that the dogs acquired as they made a connection between the caretaker and the presentation of food.

Pavlov then designed a simple experiment to test his hypothesis. Dogs first listened to a bell, a neutral stimulus in that bells do not ordinarily make them salivate. This neutral stimulus was sounded just before the dogs were fed. Of course, food normally elicits salivation: In the language of classical conditioning, food is an **unconditioned stimulus (UCS),** and salivation is an unlearned or **unconditioned response (UCR)** to food. After the bell and the food had been paired several times, Pavlov then sounded the bell, withheld the food, and observed that the dogs now salivated to the sound of the bell alone. Clearly, their behavior had changed as a result of their experiences. In the terminology of classical conditioning, the dogs were now emitting a **conditioned response (CR),** salivation, to an initially neutral or **conditioned stimulus (CS)**, the bell (see Figure 6.15).

Pavlov also discovered that a classically conditioned response would persist for long periods as long as the CS that elicited it was occasionally paired with the UCS to maintain their association. But if the CS (the bell) was presented alone enough times without being paired with the UCS (food), the CR (salivation) diminished in strength and eventually disappeared—a process known as **extinction.**

unconditioned response (UCR)
the unlearned response elicited by an unconditioned stimulus.

conditioned response (CR)
a learned response to a stimulus that was not originally capable of producing the response.

conditioned stimulus (CS)
an initially neutral stimulus that comes to elicit a particular response after being paired with a UCS that always elicits the response.

extinction
gradual weakening and disappearance of a learned response that occurs because the CS is no longer paired with the UCS (in classical conditioning) or the response is no longer reinforced (in operant conditioning).

Classical Conditioning of Emotions

Although the salivary responses that Pavlov conditioned may seem rather mundane, it is quite likely that every one of us has learned many, many things through classical conditioning, including some of our fears, phobias, and attitudes. Consider the plight of little Albert (Watson & Raynor, 1920), the 11-month-old we met in Chapter 2, who had learned to fear a white rat because every time he reached for it, he heard a loud, startling bang behind him (the experimenter striking a rod with a hammer). In this case, the loud banging noise was the unconditioned stimulus (UCS) because it elicited fearful behavior (the UCR) without any learning having taken place. And as the noise and the rat (an initially neutral stimulus) were repeatedly paired, Albert soon detected their association, coming to *fear* his furry companion (the CR). By today's standards, this experiment would be considered unethical; but Watson had made his point: Emotional responses can be acquired through classical conditioning.

Of course, classical conditioning may produce favorable attitudes or behavioral responses as well (Staats, 1975). Consider what Mary Cover Jones (1924) found when she tried to treat a young boy's existing phobia through **counterconditioning**—a therapeutic intervention based on classical conditioning procedures. Her patient was a 2-year-old named Peter who, like little Albert, had acquired a strong fear of furry objects. While Peter was eating some of his favorite foods (a UCS for pleasant feelings), he was exposed to a dreaded rabbit (for him, a strong CS for fear). The rabbit was gradually moved closer and closer until (after several sessions) Peter was able to hold it on his lap. Thus, by pairing the rabbit with *pleasurable stimuli,* Jones eliminated Peter's conditioned fear and replaced it with a more desirable response (playing with the rabbit).

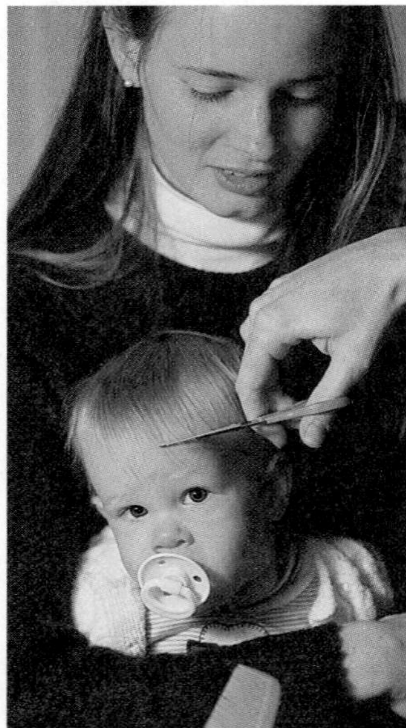

First haircuts are fearful events for many young children. With gentle treatment from the hairdresser—and perhaps a lollipop after the job is done—fear of the barbershop (or beauty parlor) will be lessened by counterconditioning.

Can Newborns Be Classically Conditioned?

Though it is extremely difficult and was once thought impossible, even newborns can be classically conditioned. Lewis Lipsitt and Herbert Kaye (1964), for example, paired a neutral tone (the CS) with the presentation of a nipple (a UCS that elicits sucking) to infants 2 to 3 days old. After several of these conditioning trials, the infants began to make sucking motions at the sound of the tone, before the nipple was presented. Clearly, their sucking qualifies as a classically conditioned response because it is now elicited by a stimulus (the tone) that does not normally elicit sucking behavior.

Yet there are important limitations on classical conditioning in the first few weeks of life. Conditioning is likely to be successful only for biologically programmed reflexes, such as sucking, that have survival value. Furthermore, neonates process information very slowly and require more time than an older participant to associate the conditioned and unconditioned stimuli in classical conditioning experiments (Little, Lipsitt, & Rovee-Collier, 1984). But despite these early limitations in information processing, classical conditioning is almost certainly one of the ways in which very young infants recognize that certain events occur together in the natural environment and learn other important lessons, such as that bottles or breasts give milk, or that other people (notably caregivers) signify warmth and comfort.

Operant (or Instrumental) Conditioning

In classical conditioning, learned responses are *elicited* by a conditioned stimulus. **Operant conditioning** is quite different: The learner first *emits* a response of some sort (that is, *operates* on the environment) and then associates this action with the pleasant or unpleasant consequences it produces. It was B. F. Skinner (1953) who made this form of conditioning famous. He argued that most human behaviors are those we emit voluntarily (that is, *operants*) and that become more or less probable, depending on their consequences. This basic principle makes a good deal of sense. We do tend to repeat behaviors that have favorable consequences and to limit those that produce unfavorable outcomes (see Figure 6.16).

Four Possible Consequences of Operant Responses

In operant conditioning, a **reinforcer** is any consequence that *strengthens* a response by making it more likely to occur in the future. If a toddler smiles at her father who then plays with her, the playful attention will probably serve as a **positive reinforcer** for smiling, as shown in Figure 6.16. *Positive* here means that something has *added to* this situation (in this case, playful stimulation); so a positive reinforcement is an event that, when introduced following a behavior, makes that behavior more probable in the future. **Negative reinforcers** also strengthen behaviors, but the behavior is strengthened because something unpleasant is *removed* from the situation (or avoided) after the

counterconditioning
a treatment based on classical conditioning in which the goal is to extinguish an undesirable response and replace it with a new and more adaptive one.

operant conditioning
a form of learning in which freely emitted acts (or operants) become either more or less probable depending on the consequences they produce.

reinforcer
any consequence of an act that increases the probability that the act will recur.

positive reinforcer
any stimulus whose presentation, as the consequence of an act, increases the probability that the act will recur.

negative reinforcer
any stimulus whose removal or termination, as the consequence of an act, increases the probability that the act will recur.

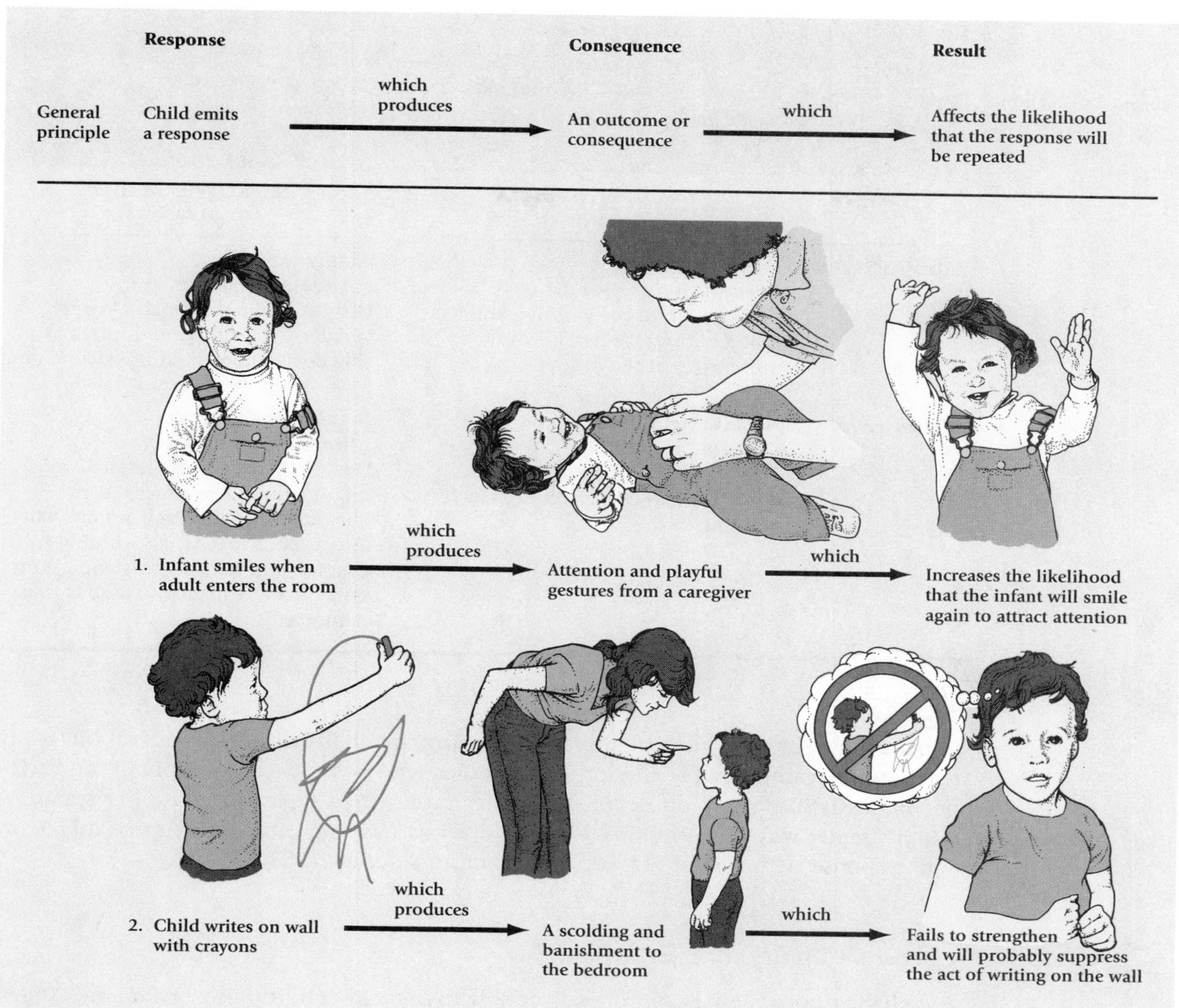
Response
Consequence
Result
General principle
Child emits a response
which produces
An outcome or consequence
which
Affects the likelihood that the response will be repeated
1. Infant smiles when adult enters the room
which produces
Attention and playful gestures from a caregiver
which
Increases the likelihood that the infant will smile again to attract attention
2. Child writes on wall with crayons
which produces
A scolding and banishment to the bedroom
which
Fails to strengthen and will probably suppress the act of writing on the wall

Figure 6.16 *Basic principles of operant conditioning.*

behavior occurs. We have all been in cars in which an obnoxious buzzer sounds until we buckle our seat belts. The idea here is that "buckling up" will become a stronger habit through *negative reinforcement;* we learn to fasten the belt because this act ends the irritating noise. Similarly, if a child finds that she can prevent an aversive scolding by picking up her crayons after using them, tidying up should become more probable through *negative reinforcement,* avoiding something unpleasant.

Is *negative reinforcement* merely a fancy name for punishment? *No, it is not!* People tend to confuse the two because they generally think of pleasant stimuli as reinforcers and unpleasant ones as punishments. This source or confusion can be overcome if we keep in mind that reinforcers and punishers are defined not by their "pleasantness" or "unpleasantness" but by their *effects:* reinforcers always *strengthen* responses whereas **punishers** inhibit or *suppress* them. There are actually two forms of punishment that parallel the two forms of reinforcement. **Positive punishment** occurs when an unpleasant consequence is *added* to the situation following a behavior (as in Figure 6.16 where a mother scolds her son for writing on the wall), whereas **negative punishment** occurs when something pleasant is *removed from* the situation following the behavior (for example, a father punishes a daughter's hitting by suspending her trip to the movies on Saturday). Both these forms of punishment are intended to suppress behaviors and decrease the likelihood that they will recur.

These four possible consequences of a behavior are summarized in Table 6.3. Which of these outcomes is most likely to encourage desirable habits? Skinner (1953) and other behavioral theorists emphasize the power of reinforcement, particularly *positive* reinforcement. They argue that punishment is less effective at producing desirable changes

punisher
any consequence of an act that suppresses the response and decreases the probability that it will recur.

positive punishment
a punishing consequence that involves the presentation of something unpleasant following a behavior.

negative punishment
a punishing consequence that involves the removal of something pleasant following a behavior.

TABLE 6.3 Four Common Consequences of an Operant Behavior

Julio comes into the TV room and sees his father joking with his sister Rita as the two watch a gymnastics meet. Soon Julio begins to whine, louder and louder, that he wants to use the TV set to play Nintendo. Here are four possible consequences of Julio's whining behavior.

	Positive stimulus (pleasant)	Negative stimulus (unpleasant)
Administered	*Positive reinforcement (strengthens the response)* Dad gives in to the whining and lets Julio use the TV, making whining more likely in the future.	*Positive punishment (weakens the response)* Dad calls Julio a "crybaby," which violates Julio's image of himself as a "big boy" and makes him less inclined to whine in the future.
Withdrawn	*Negative punishment (weakens the response)* Dad confiscates Julio's treasured Nintendo game to discourage such whining in the future.	*Negative reinforcement (strengthens the response)* Dad stops joking with Rita when Julio's whining becomes rather obvious. Since Julio gets jealous when Dad attends to Rita, his whining has enabled him to bring this unpleasant state of affairs to an end (and is thus reinforced).

in behavior because it merely suppresses ongoing or established responses without really teaching anything new. For example, a toddler who is scolded for grabbing food with her hands is likely to stop eating altogether rather than to learn to use her spoon. A much simpler way to promote the use of silverware is to positively reinforce this desirable response with lots of attention and praise (Skinner, 1953).

Operant Conditioning in Infancy

Even babies born prematurely are susceptible to operant conditioning (Thoman & Ingersoll, 1993). However, successful conditioning in very young infants is generally limited to the few biologically significant behaviors (for example, sucking, head turning) that they can control (Rovee-Collier, 1987). Newborns are also very inefficient information processors who learn very slowly. So if you hoped to teach 2-day-old infants to turn their heads to the right and offered them a nippleful of milk every time they did, you would find that they took about 200 trials, on average, to acquire this simple habit (Papousek, 1967). Older infants learn much faster. A 3-month-old requires only about 40 trials to display a conditioned head-turning response, and 5-month-olds acquire this habit in fewer than 30 trials. Apparently, older infants are quicker to associate their behavior (in this case, head turning) with its consequences (a tasty treat)—an advance in information-processing that seems to explain infants' increasing susceptibility to operant conditioning over the first few months of life.

CAN INFANTS REMEMBER WHAT THEY HAVE LEARNED? Earlier, we noted that very young infants seem to have very short memories! Minutes after they have habituated to a stimulus, they may begin to respond once again to that stimulus as if they no longer recognize it as familiar. Yet, the simple act of recognizing a stimulus as "familiar" may not be terribly meaningful to a neonate, or even a 2-month-old. Might young infants be better at remembering behaviors they have performed that have proved to be reinforcing in the past?

Yes indeed, and a program of research by Carolyn Rovee-Collier (1995, 1997; Hayne & Rovee-Collier, 1995) makes this point quite clearly. Rovee-Collier's procedure was to place an attractive mobile over the cribs of 2- to 3-month-old infants and to run a ribbon from the mobile to the infants' ankles (see Figure 6.17). Within a matter of minutes, these young participants discovered that they could make the mobile move by kicking their legs, and they took great pleasure in doing so. But would they remember how to make the mobile move a week later? To succeed at this memory task, the infant not only had to *recognize* the mobile, but also had to *recall* that it moved and that kicking was the way to get it to move.

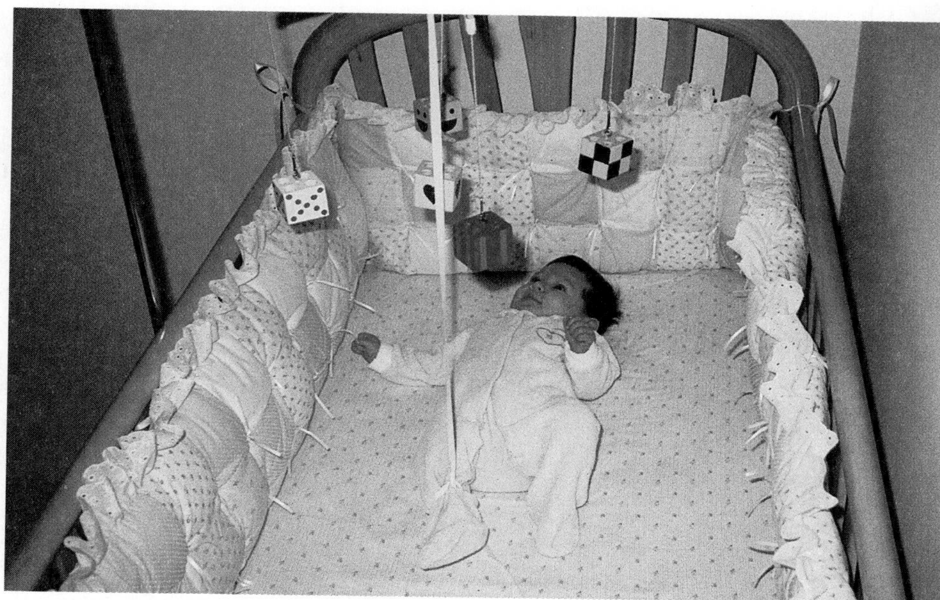

Figure 6.17 *When ribbons are attached to their ankles, 2- to 3-month-old infants soon learn to make a mobile move by kicking their legs. But do they remember how to make the mobile move when tested days or weeks after the original learning? These are the questions that Rovee-Collier has explored in her fascinating research on infant memory.*

The standard procedure for testing an infant's memory was to place the child back in the crib to see whether kicking occurred when he or she saw the mobile. Rovee-Collier and her associates found that 2-month-old infants remembered how to make the mobile move for up to 3 days after the original learning, whereas 3-month-olds recalled this kicking response for more than a week. Clearly, a very young infant's memory is much more impressive than habituation studies would have us believe.

Why do infants eventually forget how to make the mobile move? It is not that their previous learning has been lost, for even *2 to 4 weeks after the original training,* infants who were "reminded" of their previous learning by merely seeing the mobile move looked briefly at it and then kicked up a storm as soon as the ribbon was attached to their ankles (Rovee-Collier, 1987). By contrast, infants who received no reminder did not try to make the mobile move when given an opportunity. So even 2- to 3-month-old infants can *retain* meaningful information for weeks, if not longer. However, they find it hard to retrieve what they have learned from memory unless they are given explicit reminders. Interestingly, these early memories are highly *context-dependent:* If young infants are not tested under the same conditions in which the original learning occurred (that is, with the same or a highly similar mobile), they show little retention of previously learned responses (Hayne & Rovee-Collier, 1995; Howe & Courage, 1993). So a baby's earliest memories can be relatively fragile.

The Social Significance of Early Operant Learning. Since even newborns are capable of associating their behaviors with its outcomes, they should soon learn that they can elicit favorable responses from other people. For example, a baby may come to display such sociable gestures as smiling or babbling because he discovers that those responses often attract attention and affection from caregivers. At the same time, caregivers learn how to elicit favorable reactions from their baby, so that their social interactions gradually become smoother and more satisfying for both the infant and her companions. It is fortunate, then, that babies can learn, for in so doing, they are likely to become ever more responsive to other people, who, in turn, become more responsive to them. As we will see in Chapter 11, these positive reciprocal interactions provide a foundation for the strong emotional attachments that often develop between babies and their closest companions.

Punishment as a Tactic for Controlling Behavior

Should parents use punishment to suppress their children's undesirable conduct? Most parents occasionally resort to punishment as a control tactic (Hoffman, 1988), and some learning theorists have argued that there is a case to be made for its use, particularly if the prohibited act is something dangerous like playing with matches or probing electrical sockets with metallic objects. Yet other theorists believe that punishment is a two-edged sword that may prove counterproductive and even harmful in the long run.

Operant theorists are among the strongest critics of punitive controls. They believe that punishment merely suppresses an undesirable response without teaching anything new. They also stress that punishment may engender anger, hostility, or resentment, and, at best, a *temporary* suppression of the behavior it is designed to eliminate. Finally, they contend that a fear of aversive consequences can never be a totally effective deterrent, because the child may simply inhibit unacceptable conduct until it is unlikely to be detected and punished.

Despite these criticisms, research indicates that punishment, *properly applied,* can be an effective method of controlling undesirable behavior. Look first at Box 6.3, which presents some guidelines for using punishment effectively. We will then discuss why these findings make sense from a modern, information-processing perspective.

When researchers first began to study the effects of punishment, they generally favored a *conditioning viewpoint.* Presumably, punishment produces fear or anxiety, which becomes associated with the punished act. Once this conditioning occurs, the child should resist temptation to repeat the prohibited act, either to avoid the anxiety she has come to associate with it, or to avoid further punishment (Parke, 1972). Thus, conditioning theorists viewed punitive suppression as nothing more than a conditioned avoidance response.

Yet the recommendations presented in Box 6.3, particularly the finding that all forms of punishment become more effective when accompanied by a good cognitive rationale, eventually led many researchers to reject the conditioning viewpoint in favor of an *information-processing model* of punishment. Information-processing theorists agree that punishment can make children anxious or emotionally aroused. However, they argue that it is not the amount of anxiety or apprehension that the child experiences that determines whether she will inhibit a punished act. Rather, the most critical determinant of a child's future conduct is her *interpretation* of the uneasiness she is experiencing—a cognitive process that depends on the kind of rationale she has heard for modifying her conduct. To illustrate, imagine a child who is given no rationale with her punishment or, alternatively, hears a rationale that focuses her attention on her own negative consequences (for example, "I'll blister your rear if I catch you again"). If this child interprets her uneasiness as a fear of getting caught or a fear of the disciplinarian, she may well inhibit the punished act in the presence of authority figures but feel quite free to perform it when there is no one else around to detect these antics (see Figure 6.18).

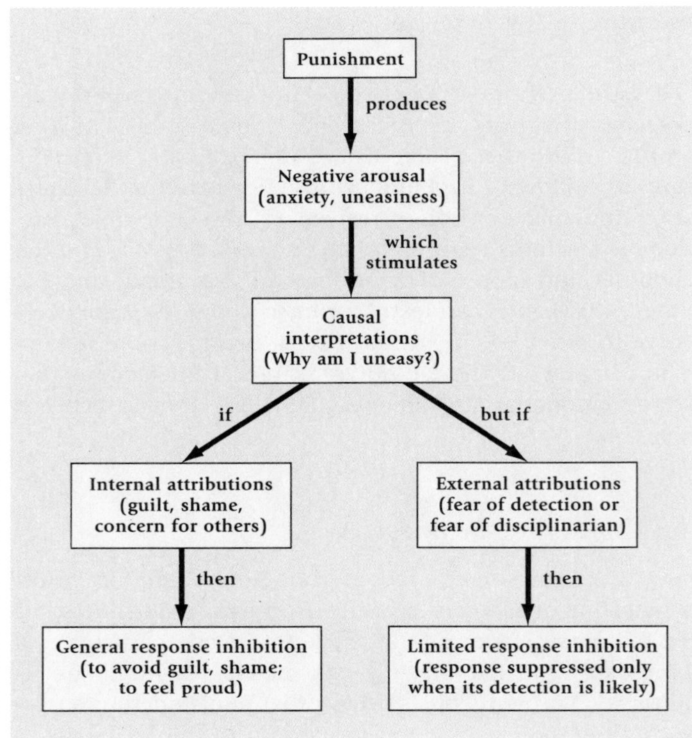

Figure 6.18 *An information-processing model of the suppressive effects of punishment.*

6.3

APPLYING DEVELOPMENTAL RESEARCH

Using Punishment Effectively

Although operant researchers emphasize the use of positive reinforcement to shape children's conduct, most parents use punishment at least occasionally to suppress undesirable behaviors. They can use it more effectively by following these guidelines, derived from the research literature (Domjan, 1993; Parke, 1977):

- *Punish as soon as possible.* It is best to punish as the child prepares to misbehave or at least during the act. Postponing punishment ("Wait til Daddy comes home") is bad practice. Young children may conclude that Daddy is punishing them for whatever they are doing at the moment—for example, putting toys back in the toy box. If delayed punishment cannot be avoided, it can be made more effective by carefully explaining to the child why she is being punished.
- *Punish firmly (but not with too much intensity).* Laboratory research with young children suggests that strong punishment, in the form of loud buzzers or noises, is more effective than mild punishment; that is, a loud "No" or "Stop that" is likely to be more effective than softer versions of the same commands. But we should not be misled into thinking that severe physical punishment is a good idea. Severe spankings, in particular, have several disadvantages. They can create high levels of anxiety that can interfere with "learning one's lesson," and they may make the child learn to fear and avoid the disciplinarian. Harsh physical punishment may also teach the child to rely on aggression as a way of dealing with problems (Weiss, Dodge, Bates, & Pettit, 1992). So firm punishment can be effective as long as it is not so intense that it has these sorts of negative side effects.
- *Punish consistently.* Acts that are punished only now and then will persist. Why? Because if the child *enjoys* the prohibited act, he is actually being reinforced when the act goes unpunished.
- *Be otherwise warm and accepting.* Children respond better to punishment when it is administered by an otherwise warm and caring person, with whom they might regain approval by behaving appropriately, than by a cold, aloof disciplinarian who has never shown them much approval.
- *Consider alternatives to physical punishment.* Although spanking a child seems to be the first punishment that many parents think of when a child misbehaves, punishment can also involve taking away desirable commodities or privileges that the child already has (for example, candy) or would ordinarily receive in the future (a movie next Saturday). Another effective alternative to physical punishment is a procedure called *time out,* in which the adult removes children from the situation in which their misbehavior is positively reinforced. A boy who thoroughly enjoys dominating his little sister might be sent to a quiet room where he is cut off from the pleasure he receives from his bullying behavior. When misbehavior is no longer reinforced, it weakens through extinction.
- *Reinforce alternative behavior.* Since punishment alone tells a child what not to do, but not *what* to do, it makes sense to strengthen acceptable alternatives to the misbehavior. The parent who does not want a toddler to play with an expensive vase might punish that behavior but also reinforce play with an unbreakable plastic pot.
- *Explain yourself.* If there is a "most important" recommendation here, this may be it. Virtually all forms of punishment become more effective if the disciplinarian explains to children why their conduct was wrong and helps them to control their behavior in the future. Older children and adolescents, in particular, want and benefit from these *cognitive rationales* that point out the harmful consequences of misbehavior (although preschool children too may benefit from rationales that are carefully tailored to their ability to understand).

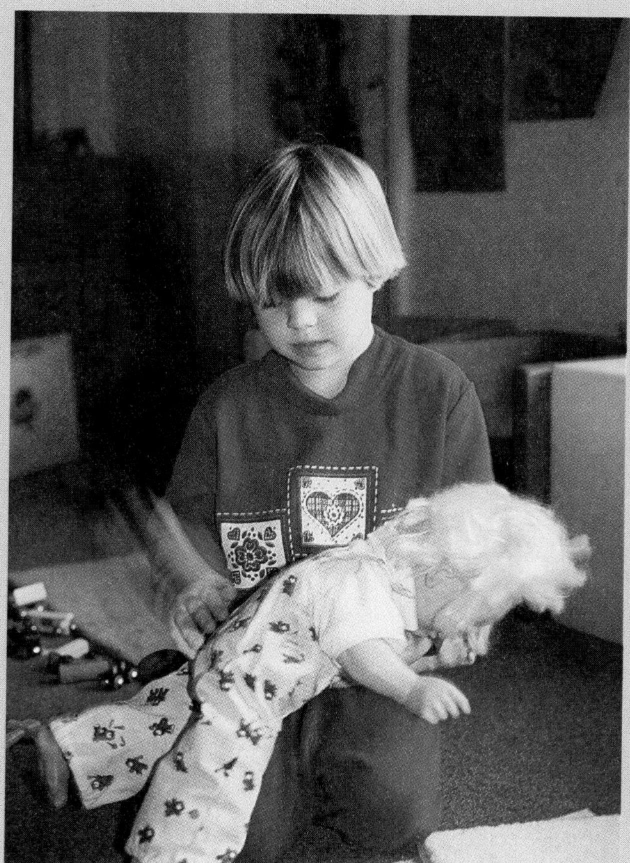

Improperly applied, physical punishment can have many undesirable side effects, including an increase in the child's aggressiveness.

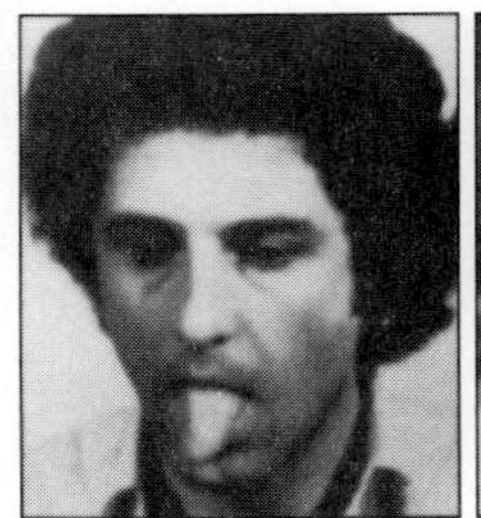
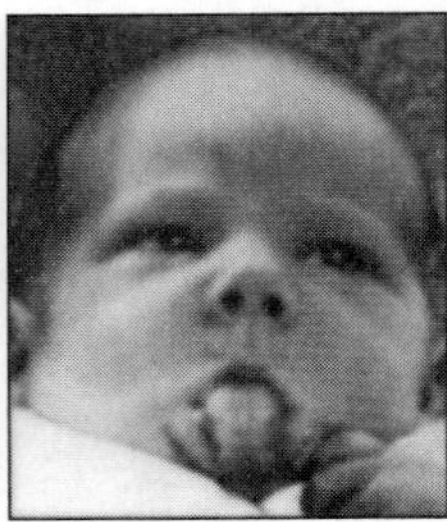
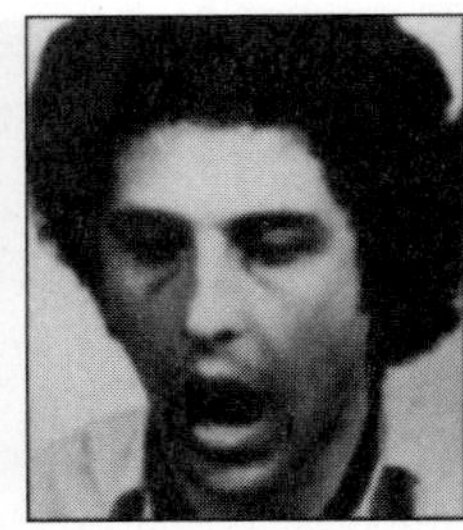
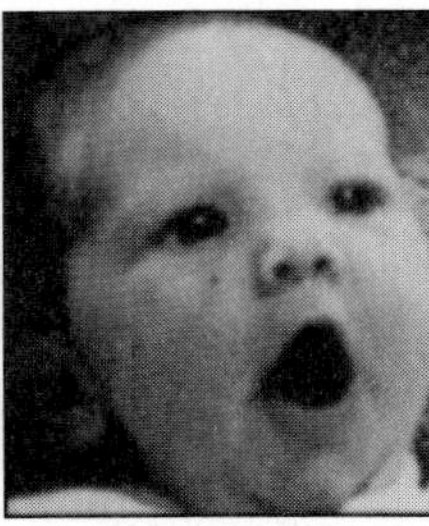

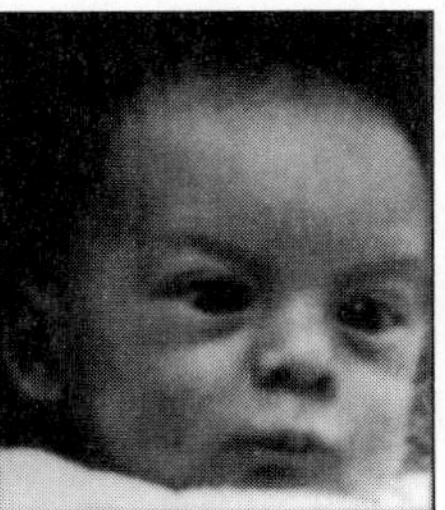

Figure 6.19 *Sample photographs from videotaped recordings of 2- and 3-week-old infants imitating tongue protrusion, mouth opening, and lip protrusion.*

By contrast, a second child who hears rationales specifying why a punished act is wrong and why he should feel bad for having performed it may be just as upset by the punishment he receives. But he has different information to process. He may now feel rather immature and even ashamed of himself for even contemplating this harmful act and, thus, be *internally* motivated to inhibit it in the future, even when there is no one else around to monitor his conduct.

In sum, punitive episodes provide children with a rich array of information to process, and it is the child's *interpretation* of this input, rather than the sheer amount of anxiety he experiences, that determines the effectiveness of punitive controls (Hoffman, 1988; Parke, 1972).

Observational Learning

The last form of basic learning we will consider is **observational learning,** which results from observing the behavior of other people. Almost anything can be learned by watching (or listening to) others. For example, a child may learn how to speak a language and tackle math problems, as well as how to swear, snack between meals, and smoke by imitating his parents. As we saw in Chapter 2, observational learning takes center stage in Albert Bandura's (1977; 1989) social learning theory. Recall that new responses acquired by observation need not be reinforced or even performed before they are learned (review Box 2.2 on page 50). Instead this *cognitive* form of learning occurs as the observer attends carefully to the model and constructs *symbolic representations* (for example, images or verbal summaries) of the model's behavior. These mental symbols are then stored in memory and retrieved later to guide the observer's performance of what he or she has observed.

Of course, successful observational learning not only requires the capacity to imitate others, but also the ability to **encode** a model's behavior and rely on mental symbols to reproduce what one has witnessed. When do these abilities first emerge?

Newborn Imitation

Researchers once believed that infants were unable to imitate the actions of another person until the latter half of the first year (Piaget, 1951). But beginning in the late 1970s, a number of studies began to report that babies less than 7 days old were apparently able to imitate a number of adult facial gestures, including sticking out their tongues, opening and closing their mouths, protruding their lower lips (as if they were sad), and even displays of happiness (Field et al., 1982; Meltzoff & Moore, 1977; see Figure 6.19).

Interestingly, these early imitative displays become much harder to elicit over the first 3 to 4 months of life (Abravanel & Sigafoos, 1984). Some have interpreted this to mean that the neonate's limited capacity for mimicry may be a largely involuntary *reflexive* scheme that disappears with age (as many other reflexes do), only to be replaced later by voluntary imitative responses (Kaitz et al., 1988; Vinter, 1986). Others have argued that the two most reliable displays—tongue protrusions and mouth openings—are not imitative responses at all, but simply reflect the baby's early attempts to explore with their mouths those sights they find particularly interesting (Jones, 1996). How-

observational learning
learning that results from observing the behavior of others.

encoding
the process by which external stimulation is converted to a mental representation.

ever, Andrew Meltzoff (1990) contends that these early expressive displays are *voluntary, imitative* responses because babies will often match an adult's facial expression after a short delay, even though the model is no longer posing that expression. Meltzoff's view is that neonatal imitation is simply another example of *intermodel* perception where babies match facial movements they can "see" in the model's face to those they can "feel" in their own faces (Meltzoff & Moore, 1992). But regardless of whether we choose to call it "imitation" or "exploration," a newborn's responsiveness to facial gestures serves a useful function in that it is likely to warm the hearts of caregivers and help ensure that they and their baby get off to a good start.

Advances in Imitation and Observational Learning

An infant's capacity to imitate *novel* responses that are not a part of her behavioral repertoire becomes much more obvious and reliable between 8 and 12 months of age (Piaget, 1951). At first, the model must be present and must continue to perform the new response before the child is able to imitate. But by age 9 months, some infants can imitate very simple acts (such as closing a wooden flap) up to 24 hours after they first observe them (Meltzoff, 1988c). This **deferred imitation**—the ability to reproduce the actions of a model at some point in the future—develops rapidly during the second year. By age 14 months, nearly half the infants in one study imitated the simple actions of a *televised* model after a 24-hour delay (Meltzoff, 1988a), and nearly all the 14-month-olds in a second experiment were able to imitate at least three (of six) novel behaviors displayed by a live model *after a delay of 1 week* (Meltzoff, 1988b). In fact, 14- to 18-month-olds who observe a *peer* operating a new toy in one context (a day-care center) are likely to imitate the model's behavior 2 days later when they finally have an opportunity to play with the toy at home (Hanna & Meltzoff, 1993).

Clearly, deferred imitation is an important developmental milestone indicating that children are not only constructing symbolic representations of their experiences, but can also retrieve this information from memory to guide their reproduction of past events. So 14- to 24-month-olds should now be prepared to learn a great deal by observing the behavior of their companions. But do they take advantage of this newly acquired ability?

Yes indeed! Leon Kuczynski and his associates (1987) asked mothers to record the immediate and the delayed reactions of their 16- and 29-month-old toddlers to the behavior of parental and peer models. The results were quite interesting. All the children imitated their models a fair percentage of the time, but there were age differences in the content of these imitations. The 16-month-olds in Kuczynski's study were more inclined to imitate emotional displays, such as laughing and cheering, as well as other high-intensity antics such as jumping, shaking the head to and fro, and pounding their fists on the table. By contrast, older toddlers more often imitated *instrumental* behaviors, such as household tasks and self-care routines, and their imitations had more of a self-instructional quality to them, as if the older children were now making an active attempt to (1) acquire skills their models had displayed or (2) understand the events they had witnessed. When imitating disciplinary encounters, for example, 16-month-olds simply repeated verbal prohibitions and physical actions such as hand slapping, usually directing these responses to themselves. However, older toddlers tended to reenact the entire scenario, including the strategies the disciplinarian had used, and they usually directed these responses to another person, an animal, or a doll. So not only do older toddlers make use of their imitative capabilities, but it appears that observational learning is already an important means by which they acquire basic personal and social competencies and gain a richer understanding of the routines and regulations that they are expected to follow (see also Rogoff et al., 1993).

Finally, grade-school children become even better at learning from social models because they are less likely than preschoolers are to rely solely on imagery to represent what they have witnessed. Instead, they *verbally describe* the model's behavior to themselves, and these verbal codes are much easier to store and retrieve than visual or auditory images are (Bandura, 1989; Coates & Hartup, 1969).

deferred imitation
the ability to reproduce a modeled activity that has been witnessed at some point in the past.

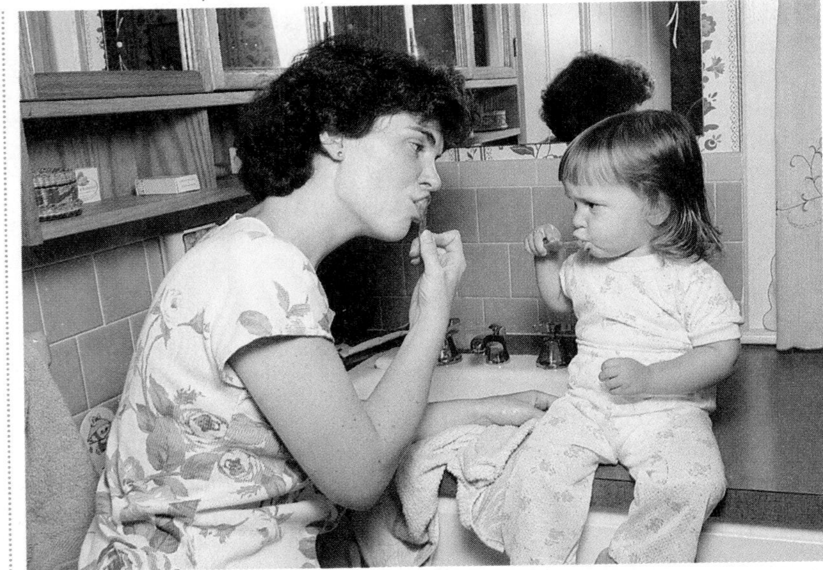

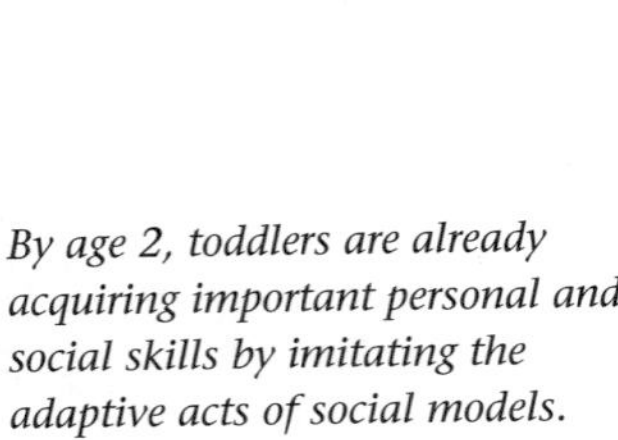

By age 2, toddlers are already acquiring important personal and social skills by imitating the adaptive acts of social models.

In sum, children can learn any number of new responses by merely attending to others' behavior and retaining mental representations of what they have witnessed. Since observational learning requires neither formal instruction nor reinforcement, it probably occurs daily, even when models are simply pursuing their own interests and are not trying to teach anything in particular. Bandura (1977; 1986; 1989) reminds us that all developing children learn from a variety of social models and that no two children are exposed to exactly the same set of modeling influences. So children should never be expected to emerge as carbon copies of their parents, siblings, or the child next door. Individual differences are an inevitable consequence of observational learning.

WHAT DO YOU THINK?

Why is it that after carefully attending to the *same sequence of actions* as they watch their dad open his combination safe, a 10-year-old may quickly succeed at cracking the safe himself, whereas a 4-year-old sibling usually will not?

REFLECTIONS ON PERCEPTION AND LEARNING

Now that we have considered the growth of basic perceptual abilities and the means by which people learn from their experiences, we might reflect for a moment on the issue: Just how important are perception and learning to the process of human development?

Perhaps we can now agree that perceptual development is the growth of *interpretive* skills—a complex process that depends on the maturation of the brain and the sensory receptors, the kinds of sensory experiences the child has available to analyze and interpret, his emerging motor skills, and even the social/cultural context in which he is raised. Although we have focused heavily on perceptual growth in this chapter, we should remember that development is a *holistic* enterprise and that a child's maturing perceptual abilities influence all aspects of development. Take intellectual development, for example. As we will see in Chapter 7, Jean Piaget argued that all the intellectual advances of the first 2 years spring from the infant's sensory and motor activities. How else, he asked, could infants ever come to understand the properties of objects without being able to see, hear, or smell them, to fondle them, or pop them into their mouths? How could infants ever use language without first perceiving meaningful regularities in the speech they hear? So Piaget (and many others) claim that perception is central to everything: There is nothing we do (consciously, at least) that is not influenced by our interpretation of the world around us.

Of course, we not only interpret (perceive) the stimuli we encounter; our behavior changes in response to these experiences. Simply stated, many of the behavioral changes that occur as we develop are the result of learning. We learn not to dwell too long on stimuli that are already familiar (habituation). We may come to like, dislike, or fear almost anything if our encounters with these objects and events have occurred under pleasant or unpleasant circumstances (classical conditioning). We form habits, some good and some bad, by associating various actions with their reinforcing and punishing consequences (operant conditioning). We acquire new attitudes, values, and patterns of conduct by observing the behaviors and listening to the pronouncements of social models (observational learning). Clearly, learning is an important developmental process. And when we recall that even newborns are capable of learning and change in response to their experiences, it is easy to see how behaviorists of the past might have championed learning as the fundamental developmental process, the mechanism by which we become like other human beings and, at the same time, develop our own idiosyncrasies.

Let's also note that human learning is most often an *active cognitive* process. Habituation and observational learning, for example, require participants to actively *attend* to the environment, to *encode* what they have witnessed, and to *retain* this information before showing any evidence of learning. And recall from Box 2.2 (p. 50) that reinforcement (or the promise of reinforcement) may make observers more inclined to *perform* responses that they have already learned by observation, but reinforcement is *not* necessary for this learning to occur in the first place. Even in operant learning, responses are not merely "stamped in" or "stamped out" by their reinforcing or punitive consequences. Instead, children treat reinforcers and punitive events as "bits of information" that they *interpret* when deciding whether or not to repeat various acts.

In sum, it is important to understand the growth of perceptual skills and the ways in which humans learn because perception and learning are *crucial cognitive foundations* that are truly at the heart of human development.

Concept Check 6.3
Basic Learning Processes

Check your understanding of some basic learning processes by completing the table below. For each vignette, decide what kind of learning is involved and identify the factor or type of consequence (if any) that is responsible for this learning. The answers appear in Appendix at the back of the book.

Vignette	*Kind of learning*	*Consequence responsible for learning*
1. The "Scumbags," a rock group, receive little response from their audience when they play new material. Consequently, they gradually begin to rely on their old "hits," which bring cheers from their fans.	____________	____________
2. Whenever Geri walks her dog, she puts on a yellow jacket. Soon she notices her dog becoming excited whenever he sees this jacket.	____________	____________
3. Having overheard a group of strangers agree that politicians are dishonest, Fred comes to look for the ulterior motive in every statement he hears a politician make.	____________	____________
4. Mosquitos consistently attack Jo in the outdoors until she applies insect repellent. Eventually, she comes to apply repellent before leaving the house.	____________	____________
5. After a week of work, Jim no longer notices the aromas that seemed so apparent when he first took his job at a bakery.	____________	____________

SUMMARY

Early Controversies about Sensory and Perceptual Development

♦ **Sensation** refers to the detection of sensory stimulation, whereas **perception** is the interpretation of what is sensed. Philosophers and developmentalists have debated whether basic perceptual skills are innate (the *nativist* position) or acquired (the *empiricist* position) and whether perception involves detection of the **distinctive features** of sensory input (**differentiation theory**) or the cognitive embellishment of sensations (**enrichment theory**). Today, most researchers favor an *interactionist* perspective, and many believe that both detection and embellishment of sensory information contribute to perceptual development.

"Making Sense" of the Infant's Sensory and Perceptual Capabilities

♦ Researchers have devised several creative methods of persuading infants to tell us what they might be sensing or perceiving. Among the more useful of these approaches are the **preference method,** the **habituation method,** the **method of evoked potentials,** and the **high-amplitude sucking method.**

Infant Sensory Capabilities

♦ Babies sense their environments reasonably well. Newborns can see patterns and colors and can detect changes in brightness. Their **visual acuity** is poor by adult standards but improves rapidly over the first 6 months. Young infants can hear very well; even newborns can discriminate sounds that differ in loudness, direction, duration and frequency. They already prefer their mother's voice to that of another women, and are quite sensitive to **phonemic** contrasts in the speech they hear. Even mild hearing losses, such as those associated with **otitis media,** may have adverse developmental effects. Babies are also born with definite taste preferences, favoring sweets over sour, bitter, or salty substances. They avoid unpleasant smells and soon come to recognize their mothers by odor alone if they are breast-fed. Newborns are also quite sensitive to touch, temperature, and pain.

Visual Perception in Infancy

♦ Visual perception develops rapidly in the first year. For the first 2 months, babies are "stimulus seekers" who prefer to look at moderately complex, high-contrast targets, particularly those that move. Between 2 and 6 months of age, infants begin to explore visual targets more systematically, become increasingly sensitive to movement, and begin to perceive visual forms and recognize familiar faces. By 9 to 12 months, infants can construct forms from the barest of cues.

♦ Although newborns display some **size constancy,** they lack **stereopsis** and are insensitive to **pictorial cues** to depth; consequently, their spatial perception is immature. By the end of the first month, they are becoming more sensitive to **kinetic cues** and are responding to **looming objects.** Their developing sensitivities to binocular cues (by 3 to 5 months) and pictorial cues (at 6 to 7 months), in conjunction with important motor developments and the experiences they provide, help to explain why older infants come to fear heights (as on the **visual cliff**) and to make more accurate judgments about size constancy and other spatial relations.

Intermodal Perception

♦ Apparently, the senses are integrated at birth, for neonates look in the direction of sound-producing sources, reach for objects they can see, and expect to see the source of sounds or to feel objects for which they are reaching. As soon as sensory information is readily detectable through two or more senses, infants display **intermodal perception**—the ability to recognize by one sensory modality an object or experience that is already familiar through another modality.

Infant Perception in Perspective—and a Look Ahead

♦ Although infancy is the period when most basic perceptual competencies emerge, much **perceptual learning** occurs later as children continue to explore objects in their environment and to detect distinctive (invariant) features. These finer perceptual discriminations underlie many new competencies, including children's readiness to read.

♦ Cultural influences affect perceptual capabilities. Some of these influences involve losing the ability to attend to and detect sensory input that has little sociocultural significance.

Basic Learning Processes

♦ **Learning** is a relatively permanent change in behavior that results from experience (repetition, practice, study, or observations) rather than from heredity, maturation, or physiological change resulting from injury.

♦ The simplest form of learning is habituation—a process in which infants come to recognize and cease responding to stimuli that are presented over and over. Although habituation may be possible even before birth, this early form of learning improves dramatically over the first few months of life.

♦ In **classical conditioning,** a neutral **conditioned stimulus (CS)** is repeatedly paired with an **unconditioned stimulus (UCS)** that always produces an **unconditioned response (UCR).** After several such pairings, the CS alone comes to elicit the response, which is now called a **conditioned response (CR).** Although newborns can be classically conditioned if the UCS and UCR have survival value, they process information very slowly and are less susceptible to this kind of learning than older infants are.

♦ In **operant conditioning,** the subject first emits a response and then associates this action with a particular outcome. **Positive** and **negative reinforcers** are outcomes that increase the probability that a response will be repeated; **positive** and **negative punishments** are outcomes that suppress an act and decrease the likelihood that it will be repeated.

♦ Punishment, properly applied, can be an effective means of suppressing undesirable conduct. Factors that influence the effectiveness of punishment include its timing, intensity, consistency, and underlying rationale, as well as the relationship between the subject and the punitive agent. When applied improperly, punishment may produce a number of undesirable side effects that limit its usefulness.

♦ **Observational learning** occurs as the observer attends to a model and constructs symbolic representations of the model's behavior. These symbolic codes are then stored in memory and may be retrieved at a later date to guide the child's attempts to imitate the behavior he or she has witnessed. Infants become better at imitating the novel responses of social models and may even display **deferred imitation** by the end of the first year. Children's capacity for observational learning continues to improve, enabling them to rapidly acquire many new habits by attending to social models.

Reflections on Perception and Learning

♦ It is important to understand the growth of perceptual skills and the ways in which humans learn because perception and learning are fundamental cognitive processes that are central to human development.

Operant conditioning is based on the basic principle that our behavior is shaped by the consequences that it produces. The principle processes outlined by B. F. Skinner were positive and negative reinforcement, and positive and negative punishment. You can complete a short interactive tutorial related to positive reinforcement by visiting: http://server.bmod.athabascau.ca/html/prtut/reinpair.htm The tutorial at this site uses illustrative examples to demonstrate the concept of positive reinforcement, and then tests your understanding using 14 novel examples.

KEY TERMS

sensation, 190
perception, 190
enrichment theory, 191
differentiation theory, 191
distinctive features, 191
preference method, 192
habituation, 192
dishabituation, 192
evoked potential, 193
high-amplitude sucking method, 193
visual acuity, 194
visual contrast, 194
phonemes, 195
otitis media, 196
stereopsis, 202
pictorial cues, 202
visual looming, 202
kinetic cues, 202
size constancy, 203
visual cliff, 204
intermodal perception, 206
perceptual learning, 210
learning, 213
classical conditioning, 214
unconditioned stimulus (UCS), 215
unconditioned response (UCR), 215
conditional response (CR), 215
conditioned stimulus (CS), 215
extinction, 215
counterconditioning, 216
operant conditioning, 216
reinforcer, 216
positive reinforcer, 216
negative reinforcer, 216
punisher, 217
positive punishment, 217
negative punishment, 217
observational learning, 222
encoding, 222
deferred imitation, 223

Cognitive Development: Piaget's Theory and Vygotsky's Sociocultural Viewpoint

If you were asked to account for the reaction of this 9-year-old, you might be tempted to conclude that he either lacks imagination or is being sarcastic. Actually, Billy's feelings about the art assignment may be rather typical (see Box 7.4 on page 253), for 9-year-olds think differently than adults do, and they often find it extremely difficult to reflect on hypothetical propositions that have no basis in reality.

TEACHER (to a class of 9-year-olds) For artwork today, I'd like each of you to draw me a picture of a person who has three eyes.

BILLY How? Nobody has three eyes!

Our next three chapters examine the growth of **cognition**—a term developmentalists use to refer to the activity of knowing and the mental processes by which human beings acquire and use knowledge to solve problems. The cognitive processes that help us to "understand" and to adapt to the environment include such activities as attending, perceiving, learning, thinking, and remembering—in short, the unobservable events and undertakings that characterize the human mind (Flavell, Miller, & Miller, 1993).

The study of **cognitive development**—the changes that occur in children's mental skills and abilities over the course of their lives—is one of the more diverse and exciting topics in all of developmental sciences. In this chapter, we begin our exploration of the developing mind, focusing first on the many important contributions of Swiss psychologist Jean Piaget, who charted what he (and others) believed to be a *universal* pattern of intellectual growth that unfolds during infancy, childhood, and adolescence. We will then compare and contrast Piaget's influential theory with Lev Vygotsky's *sociocultural* viewpoint—a theory that claims that much of cognitive growth is socially transmitted, and heavily influenced by one's culture, and may be nowhere near as universal as Piaget and his followers assumed (Wertsch & Tulviste, 1992).

Chapter 8 introduces a third influential perspective on the developing mind: information processing, a viewpoint that arose, in part, from questions left unanswered by Piaget's earlier work. Our attention will then shift to the *psychometric,* or intelligence testing, approach in Chapter 9, where we will discuss the many factors that contribute to individual differences in children's intellectual performance.

PIAGET'S THEORY OF COGNITIVE DEVELOPMENT

You were introduced to Piaget in Chapter 2. By far the most influential theorist in the history of child development, Piaget combined his earlier interests in zoology and *epistemology* (the branch of philosophy concerned with the origins of knowledge) to develop a new science that he termed **genetic epistemology,** which he defined as the experimental study of the origin of knowledge. (Piaget used the term genetic in an older sense, meaning essentially developmental.)

Piaget began his studies by carefully observing his own three children as infants: how they explored new toys, solved simple problems that he arranged for them, and generally came to understand themselves and their world. Later, Piaget studied larger samples of children through what has become known as the *clinical method,* a flexible question-and-answer technique he used to discover how children of different ages solved various problems and thought about everyday issues. From these naturalistic observations of his own children and his use of the clinical method to explore children's understanding of topics ranging from the rules of games to the laws of physics, Piaget formulated his *cognitive-developmental* theory of intellectual growth.

What Is Intelligence?

Piaget's background in zoology is quite apparent from his definition of **intelligence** as a *basic life function* that helps the organism *to adapt to its environment.* We observe such adaptation as we watch a toddler figure how to turn on the TV, a school-aged

cognition
the activity of knowing and the processes through which knowledge is acquired.

cognitive development
changes that occur in mental activities such as attending, perceiving, learning, thinking, and remembering.

genetic epistemology
the experimental study of the development of knowledge, developed by Piaget.

intelligence
in Piaget's theory, a basic life function that enables an organism to adapt to its environment.

child deciding how to divide candies among friends, or an adolescent struggle and then succeed at solving a tough geometry problem. Piaget proposed that intelligence is "a form of *equilibrium* toward which all cognitive structures tend" (1950, p. 6). His point is simply that all intellectual activity is undertaken with one goal in mind: to produce a balanced, or harmonious, relationship between one's thought processes and the environment (such a balanced state of affairs is called **cognitive equilibrium,** and the process of achieving it is called *equilibration*). Piaget stressed that children are active and curious explorers who are constantly challenged by many novel stimuli and events that are not immediately understood. He believed that these imbalances (or cognitive disequilibria) between the children's modes of thinking and environmental events prompt them to make mental adjustments that enable them to cope with puzzling new experiences and thereby restore cognitive equilibrium. So we see that Piaget's view of intelligence is an "interactionist" model that implies that mismatches between one's internal mental schemes (existing knowledge) and the external environment stimulate cognitive activity and intellectual growth.

There is a very important assumption that underlies Piaget's view of intelligence: If children are to know something, they must construct that knowledge themselves. Indeed, Piaget described the child as a **constructivist**—an organism that acts on novel objects and events and thereby gains some understanding of their essential features. Children's constructions of reality (that is, interpretations of objects and events) depend on the knowledge available to them at that point in time: The more immature the child's cognitive system, the more limited his or her interpretation of an environmental event. Consider the following example:

> A four-year-old child and his father are watching the setting sun. "Look Daddy. It's hiding behind the mountain. Why is it going away? Is it angry?" The father grasps the opportunity to explain to his son how the world works. "Well, Mark, the sun doesn't really feel things. And it doesn't really move. It's the earth that's moving. It turns on its axis so that the mountain moves in front of the sun. . . ." The father goes on to other explanations of relative motion, interplanetary bodies, and such. The boy . . . firmly and definitely responds, "But *we're* not moving. *It* is. Look, it's going down." (Cowan, 1978, p. 11)

This child is making an important assumption here that dominates his attempt at understanding—namely, that the way he sees things must correspond to the way they are. Obviously, it is the sun that is moving, ducking behind the mountain as if it were a live being who was expressing some feeling or serving a definite purpose by hiding. However, the father knows the characteristics that distinguish animate from inanimate objects (and a little about astronomy as well), so that he is able to construct a very different interpretation of the "reality" that he and his son have witnessed.

cognitive equilibrium
Piaget's term for the state of affairs in which there is a balanced, or harmonious, relationship between one's thought processes and the environment.

constructivist
one who gains knowledge by acting or otherwise operating on objects and events to discover their properties.

Cognitive Schemes: The Structure of Intelligence

Piaget uses the term *schemes* to describe the models, or mental structures, that we create to represent, organize, and interpret our experiences. A **scheme** (sometimes called a *schema* in the singular, *schemata* in the plural) is a pattern of thought or action that is similar in some respects to what the layperson calls a strategy or a concept. Piaget (1952, 1977) has described three kinds of intellectual structures: behavioral (or sensorimotor) schemes, symbolic schemes, and operational schemes.

scheme
an organized pattern of thought or action that one constructs to interpret some aspect of one's experience (also called *cognitive structure*).

Behavioral (or Sensorimotor) Schemes

A **behavioral scheme** is an organized pattern of behavior that the child uses to represent and respond to an object or experience. These are the first intellectual structures to emerge, and for much of the first 2 years of life, an infant's knowledge of objects

behavioral schemes
organized patterns of behavior that are used to represent and respond to objects and experiences.

Infants develop a broad range of behavioral schemes that they can use to explore and "understand" new objects and to solve simple problems.

and events is limited to that which she can represent through overt actions. So for a 9-month-old infant, a ball is not conceptualized as a round toy that has a formal name; instead, a ball is simply an object that she and her companions can bounce and roll.

Symbolic Schemes

During the second year, children reach a point at which they can solve problems and think about objects and events without having acted on them. In other words, they are now capable of representing experiences mentally and using these mental symbols, or **symbolic schemes,** to satisfy their objectives. Consider the following observation of the antics of Jacqueline, Piaget's 16-month-old daughter:

> Jacqueline had a visit from a little boy (18 months of age) who, in the course of the afternoon got into a terrible temper. He screamed as he tried to get out of a playpen and pushed it backward, stamping his feet. Jacqueline stood watching him in amazement, never having witnessed such a scene before. The next day, she herself screamed in her playpen and tried to move, stamping her foot . . . several times in succession (Piaget, 1951, p. 63).

symbolic schemes
internal mental symbols (such as images or verbal codes) that one uses to represent aspects of experience.

cognitive operation
an internal mental activity that one performs on objects of thought.

Clearly, Jacqueline was imitating the responses of her absent playmate, even though she had not performed those actions at the time they were modeled. It appears that she must have formed a mental representation, or image, of the boy's tantrum that preserved this scene and guided her later imitation.

Operational Schemes

According to Piaget, the thinking of children aged 7 and older is characterized by operational schemes. A **cognitive operation** is an internal mental activity that a person performs on his or her objects of thought to reach a logical conclusion. To illustrate, an 8-year-old who flattens a ball of Play-Doh into a disk is not fooled into thinking that he now has more Play-Doh as a result of spreading it out. Why? Because he can easily *reverse* this transformation in his head, thereby recognizing that the Play-Doh would become the same ball if it were rolled up once again. By contrast, 5-year-olds, who cannot "operate" on their objects of thought, are constrained to make judgments largely on the basis of overt appearances. So were they to witness the ball-to-disk transformation, they would generally assume that the disk has more dough, since it now covers more area than the ball did. And even though they can imagine (with a little prompting) that the dough can be rolled up again, they do not yet recognize the logical consequences of doing so; that is, they continue to think that there is more dough in the disk.

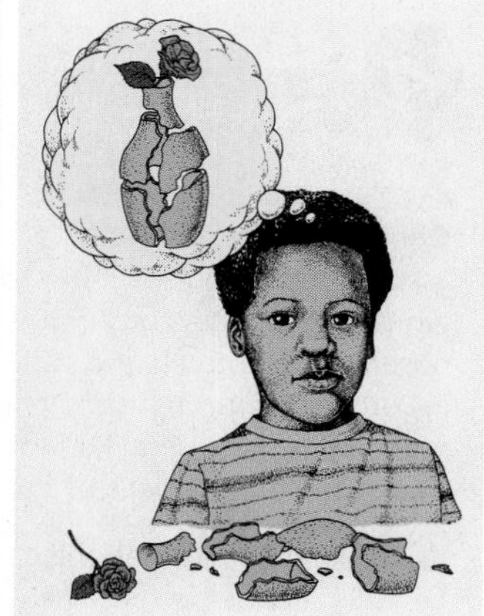

Figure 7.1 *Reversibility is an important cognitive operation that develops during middle childhood.*

According to Piaget, the most common cognitive operations are the mental activities implied by mathematical symbols such as +, −, ×, ÷, <, and >. Notice that each of these mental operations is a *reversible* activity; Mental additions, for example, can quickly be undone by mental subtractions. Piaget believed that these fluid operational abilities permit grade-school children and adolescents to construct rather elaborate intellectual schemes that enable them to think logically and systematically, first about their actual experiences and eventually about abstract or hypothetical events.

How We Gain Knowledge: Piaget's Cognitive Processes

How do children construct and modify their intellectual schemes? Piaget believed that all schemes, all forms of understanding, are created through the workings of two inborn intellectual processes that he called *organization* and *adaptation.*

Organization is the process by which children combine existing schemes into new and more complex intellectual structures. For example, a young infant who has "gazing," "reaching," and "grasping" reflexes soon organizes these initially unrelated schemes into a more complex structure—*visually directed reaching*—that enables her to reach out and discover the characteristics of many interesting objects in the environment. Although intellectual schemes may assume radically different forms at different phases of development, the process of organization is unchanging. Piaget believed that children are constantly organizing whatever schemes they have into more complex and adaptive structures.

The goal of organization is to promote **adaptation,** the process of adjusting to the demands of the environment. According to Piaget, adaptation occurs through two complementary activities: *assimilation* and *accommodation.*

Assimilation is the process by which children try to interpret new experiences in terms of their existing models of the world, the schemes that they already possess. The young child who sees a horse for the first time may try to assimilate it into one of her existing schemes for four-legged animals and thus may think of this creature as a "doggie." In other words, the child is trying to adapt to this novel stimulus by construing it as something familiar.

Yet, truly novel objects, events, and experiences may be difficult to interpret in terms of one's existing schemes. For example, our young child may soon notice that this big animal she is labeling a doggie has funny-looking feet and a most peculiar bark, and she may be inclined to seek a better understanding of the observations she has made. **Accommodation,** the complement of assimilation, is the process of modifying existing structures in order to account for new experiences. So the child who recognizes that a horse is not a dog may invent a name for this new creature or perhaps say "What dat?" and adopt the label that her companions use. In so doing, she has modified

organization
an inborn tendency to combine and integrate available schemes into coherent systems or bodies of knowledge.

adaptation
an inborn tendency to adjust to the demands of the environment.

assimilation
the process of interpreting new experiences by incorporating them into existing schemes.

accommodation
the process of modifying existing schemes in order to incorporate or adapt to new experiences.

Concept Check 7.1
Understanding Piagetian Assumptions and Concepts

Check your understanding of some of Piaget's basic assumptions about cognitive development by indicating which of the following terms best describes each of the observations listed below. Choose from the following terms: (a) organization, (b) assimilation, (c) accommodation, (d) reversibility, (e) disequilibrium. The answers appear in Appendix A at the back of the book.

_____ 1. Thinking that objects fall when dropped, Jose is flabbergasted when a helium balloon rises, thus illustrating what Piaget calls _____________.

_____ 2. Given a choice, Kai prefers a cookie that has dropped and broken over a whole one, saying that "Three little cookies are better than one big one." Kai lacks _____________.

_____ 3. Jose's construction of an explanation for the fact that helium-filled balloons rise involves the process of _____________.

_____ 4. Ten-month-old Sammie lifts a pillow to grab a toy his father has placed there. Sammie's coordination of his "lifting" and "grasping" schemes to achieve his goal is an example of _____________.

_____ 5. Freda exclaims, "Oh, look at big kitty cat," upon seeing her first tiger at the circus. Freda's response illustrates _____________.

Table 7.1 A Small Sample of Cognitive Growth from Piaget's Perspective

	Piagetian concept	Definition	Example
Start	Equilibrium	Harmony between one's schemes and one's experience.	Toddler who has never seen anything fly but birds thinks that all flying objects are "birdies."
↓	Assimilation	Tries to adapt to new experience by interpreting it in terms of existing schemes.	Seeing an airplane in the sky prompts child to call the flying object a birdie.
↓	Accommodation	Modifies existing schemes to better account for puzzling new experience.	Toddler experiences conflict or disequilibrium upon noticing that the new birdie has no feathers and doesn't flap its wings. Concludes it is not a bird and invents a new name for it (or asks, "What dat?"). Successful accommodation restores equilibrium—for the moment, at least).
Finish	Organization	Rearranges existing schemes into new and more complex structures.	Forms hierarchical scheme consisting of a superordinate class (flying objects) and two subordinate classes (birdies and airplanes).

Note: As an exercise, you may wish to apply Piaget's concepts to chart the further elaborations of the child's schemes upon encountering a butterfly and a frisbee.

(accommodated) her scheme for four-legged animals to include a new category of experience—horses.

Although Piaget distinguished assimilation from accommodation, he believed that these two processes work together to promote cognitive growth. They do not always occur equally as in the preceding example, but assimilations of experiences that do not quite "jibe" with existing schemes eventually introduce cognitive conflict and prompt accommodations to those experiences. And the end result is adaptation, a state of equilibrium between one's cognitive structures and the environment.

Table 7.1 provides one example of how cognitive growth might proceed from Piaget's point of view—a perspective that stresses that cognitive development is an *active* process in which children are regularly seeking and *assimilating* new experiences, *accommodating* their cognitive structures to these experiences, and *organizing* what they know into new and more complex schemes. So two inborn activities—adaptation and organization—make it possible for children to construct progressively greater understandings of the world in which they live.

PIAGET'S STAGES OF COGNITIVE DEVELOPMENT

Piaget has identified four major periods of cognitive development: the *sensorimotor* stage (birth to 2 years), the *preoperational* stage (2 to 7 years), the stage of *concrete operations* (7 to 11 years), and the stage of *formal operations* (11 years and beyond). These stages of intellectual growth represent qualitatively different levels of cognitive functioning and form what Piaget calls an **invariant developmental sequence;** that is, all children progress through the stages in precisely the same order, without ever skipping a stage (that is, they are universal). Piaget argued that stages can never be skipped because each successive stage builds on the accomplishments of all previous stages.

Although Piaget believed that the *sequencing* of intellectual stages is fixed, or invariant, he recognized that there are tremendous individual differences in the ages at which children enter or emerge from any particular stage. In fact, his view was that cultural factors and other environmental influences may either accelerate or retard a child's *rate* of intellectual growth, and he considered the age norms that accompany his stages (and substages) as only rough approximations at best.

invariant developmental sequence
a series of developments that occur in one particular order because each development in the sequence is a prerequisite for those appearing later.

The Sensorimotor Stage (Birth to 2 Years)

Piaget's **sensorimotor stage,** spanning the 2 years of infancy, is a period when infants coordinate their *sensory* inputs and *motor* capabilities, forming behavioral schemes that permit them to "act on" and to get to "know" their environment. How much can they really understand by relying on overt actions to generate knowledge? More than you might imagine. During the first 2 years, infants evolve from *reflexive* creatures with very limited knowledge into planful problem solvers who have already learned a great deal about themselves, their close companions, and the objects and events in their everyday world. So drastic is the infant's cognitive growth that Piaget divided the sensorimotor period into six substages (see Table 7.2, on page 239) that describe the child's gradual transition from a *reflexive* to a *reflective* organism. Our review will focus on three important aspects of sensorimotor development: *problem-solving skills* (or means/ends activities), *imitative abilities,* and the growth of the *object concept.*

Development of Problem-Solving Skills

AN INFANT ACCOMMODATING HIS MOUTH TO THE SHAPE OF AN OBJECT

Piaget characterized the first month of life as a stage of **reflex activity**—a period when an infant's actions are pretty much confined to exercising innate reflexes, assimilating new objects into these reflexive schemes (for example, sucking on blankets and toys as well as on nipples), and accommodating their reflexes to these novel objects. Granted, this is not high intellect, but these primitive adaptations represent the beginning of cognitive growth.

Primary Circular Reactions (1–4 Months). The first nonreflexive schemes emerge at 1 to 4 months of age as infants discover by chance that various responses that they can emit and control (for example, sucking their thumbs, making cooing sounds) are satisfying and, thus, worthy of repetition. These simple repetitive acts, called **primary circular reactions,** are always centered on the infant's own body. They are called primary because they are the first motor habits to appear and circular because the pleasure they bring stimulates their repetition.

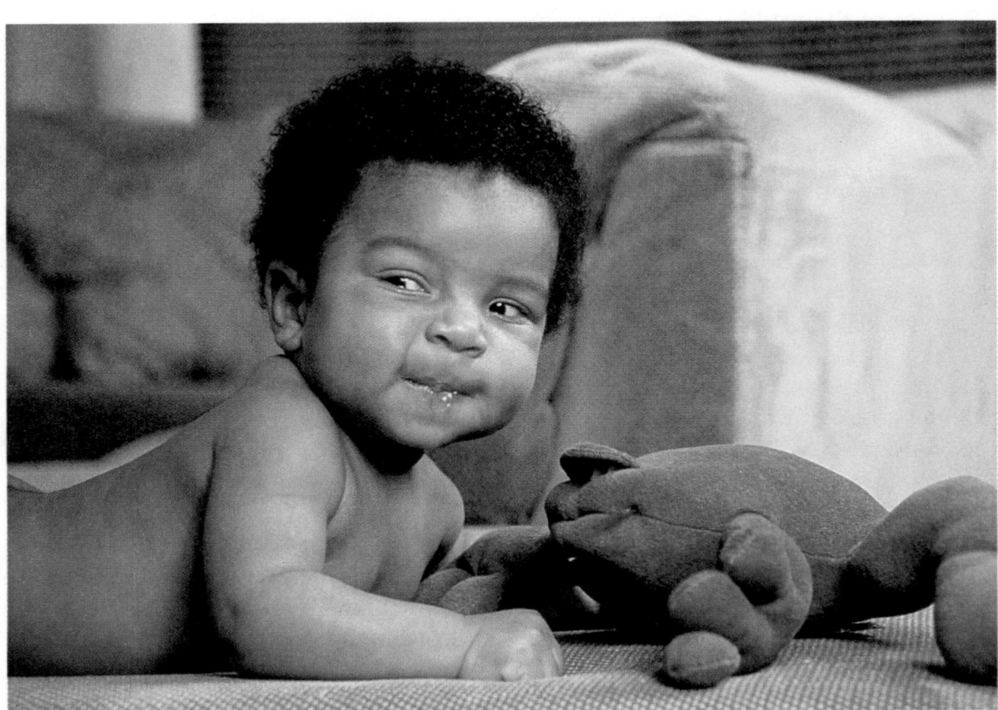

Blowing bubbles is an accommodation of the sucking reflex and one of the infant's earliest primary circular reactions.

Secondary Circular Reactions (4–8 Months). Between 4 and 8 months of age, infants discover (again by chance) that they can make interesting things happen to objects outside of their own bodies, such as making a rubber duck quack by squeezing it. These new schemes, called **secondary circular reactions,** are also repeated for the pleasure they bring. According to Piaget, 4- to 8-month olds' sudden interest in external objects indicates that they have begun to differentiate themselves from objects they can control in the surrounding environment.

Is an infant who delights in such repetitive actions as swatting a brightly colored mobile or making a toy duck quack engaging in planful or *intentional* behavior? Piaget said no: The secondary circular reaction is not a fully intentional response, because the interesting result it produces was discovered by chance and was not a purposeful goal the first time the action was performed.

Coordination of Secondary Schemes (8–12 Months). Truly planful responding first appears between 8 and 12 months of age, during the substage of the **coordination of secondary circular reactions,** as infants begin to coordinate two or more actions to achieve simple objectives. For example, if you were to place an attractive toy under a cushion, a 9-month-old might lift the cushion with one hand while using the other to grab the toy. In this case, the act of lifting the cushion is not a pleasurable response in itself, *nor is it emitted by chance.* Rather, it is part of a larger *intentional* scheme in which two initially unrelated responses—lifting and grasping—are coordinated as *a means to an end.* Piaget believed that these simple coordinations of secondary schemes represent the earliest form of true problem solving.

Tertiary Circular Reactions (12–18 Months). Between 12 and 18 months of age, toddlers begin to actively experiment with objects and try to invent totally new methods of solving problems or reproducing interesting results. For example, an infant who had originally squeezed a rubber duck to make it quack may now decide to drop it, step on it, and crush it with a pillow to see whether these actions have the same or different effects on the toy. Or she may learn from her explorations that flinging is more efficient than spitting as a means of getting food to stick to the wall. Although parents may be less than thrilled by this exciting new cognitive advance, these trial-and-error exploratory schemes, called **tertiary circular reactions,** reflect an infant's active *curiosity*—her strong motivation to learn about the way things work.

Symbolic Problem Solving (18–24 Months). The crowning achievement of the sensorimotor stage occurs as toddlers begin to internalize their behavioral schemes to construct mental symbols, or images, that they can then use to guide future conduct. Now the infant can experiment *mentally* and may show a kind of "insight" as to how to solve a problem. Piaget's son Laurent nicely illustrates this symbolic problem solving, or **inner experimentation:**

> Laurent is seated before a table and I place a bread crust in front of him, out of reach. Also, to the right . . . I place a stick, about 25 cm. long. At first, Laurent tries to grasp the bread . . . and then he gives up. . . . Laurent again looks at the bread, and without moving, looks very briefly at the stick, then suddenly grasps it and directs it toward the bread . . . [he then] draws the bread to him. (Piaget, 1952, p. 335)

Clearly, this is not trial-and-error experimentation. Instead, Laurent's problem solving occurred at an internal, symbolic level as he visualized the stick being used as an extension of his arm to obtain a distant object.

Development of Imitation

Piaget recognized the adaptive significance of imitation, and he was very interested in its development. His own observations led him to believe that infants are incapable of imitating *novel* responses displayed by a model until 8 to 12 months of age (the same

sensorimotor stage
Piaget's first intellectual stage, from birth to 2 years, when infants are relying on behavioral schemes as a means of exploring and understanding the environment.

reflex activity
first substage of Piaget's sensorimotor stage; infants' actions are confined to exercising innate reflexes, assimilating new objects into these reflexive schemes, and accommodating their reflexes to these novel objects.

primary circular reactions
second substage of Piaget's sensorimotor stage; a pleasurable response, centered on the infant's own body, that is discovered by chance and performed over and over.

secondary circular reactions
third substage of Piaget's sensorimotor stage; a pleasurable response, centered on an external object, that is discovered by chance and performed over and over.

coordination of secondary circular reactions
fourth substage of Piaget's sensorimotor stage; infants begin to coordinate two or more actions to achieve simple objectives.

tertiary circular reactions
fifth substage of Piaget's sensorimotor stage; an exploratory scheme in which the infant devises a new method of acting on objects to reproduce interesting results.

inner experimentation
the sixth substage of Piaget's sensorimotor stage, the ability to solve simple problems on a mental, or symbolic, level without having to rely on trial-and-error experimentation.

age at which they show some evidence of intentionality in their behavior). However, the imitative schemes of infants this young are rather imprecise. Were you to bend and straighten your finger, the infant might mimic you by opening and closing her entire hand (Piaget, 1951). Indeed, precise imitations of even the simplest responses may take days (or even weeks) of practice (Kaye & Marcus, 1981), and literally hundreds of demonstrations may be required before an 8- to 12-month-old will catch on and begin to enjoy sensorimotor games such as peekaboo or pat-a-cake.

Voluntary imitation becomes much more precise at age 12 to 18 months, as we see in the following example:

> At [1 year and 16 days of age, Jacqueline] discovered her forehead. When I touched the middle of mine, she first rubbed her eye, then felt above it and touched her hair, after which she brought her hand down a little and finally put her finger on her forehead. (Piaget, 1951, p. 56)

According to Piaget, **deferred imitation**—the ability to reproduce the behavior of an *absent* model—first appears at 18 to 24 months of age. When discussing symbolic schemes, we noted an example of deferred imitation—Jacqueline's reproduction of her playmate's temper tantrum 24 hours later. Piaget believed that older infants are capable of deferred imitation because they can now construct mental symbols, or images, of a model's behavior that are stored in memory and retrieved later to guide the child's recreation of the modeled sequence.

Other investigators disagree with Piaget, arguing that deferred imitation begins much earlier. Andrew Meltzoff, for example, has found that some 9-month-olds can imitate very simple acts (for example, button-pressing to activate a noise-making toy) 24 hours after observing them (Meltzoff, 1988), and later research has shown that toddlers imitate particularly memorable events up to 12 months after first witnessing them (Bauer & Werwerka, 1995; Mandler & McDonough, 1995; Meltzoff, 1995). So a capacity for deferred imitation—imitation requiring the infant to construct, store, and then retrieve mental symbols—is present much earlier than Piaget had thought (Schneider & Bjorklund, 1997).

Development of Object Permanence

One of the more notable achievements of the sensorimotor period is the development of **object permanence:** the idea that objects continue to exist when they are no longer visible or detectable through the other senses. If you removed your watch and covered it with a mug, you would still be aware that the watch continues to exist. But because very young infants rely so heavily on their senses and their motor skills to "understand" an object, they seem to operate as if objects exist only if they can be sensed or acted upon. Indeed, Piaget (1954) and others have found that 1- to 4-month-olds will not search for attractive objects that are hidden from view. If a watch that interests them is covered by a mug, they soon lose interest, almost as if they believe that the watch no longer exists or has been transformed into a mug (Bower, 1982). At age 4 to 8 months, infants will retrieve toys that are partially concealed or placed beneath a semitransparent cover; but their continuing failure to search for objects that are *completely* concealed suggested to Piaget that, from the infant's perspective, disappearing objects may no longer exist.

Clearer signs of an emerging object concept appear by 8 to 12 months of age. However, object permanence is far from complete, as we see in Piaget's demonstration with his 10-month-old daughter:

> Jacqueline is seated on a mattress without anything to . . . distract her, . . . I take her [toy] parrot from her hands and hide it twice . . . under the mattress, on her left [point A]. Both times Jacqueline looks for the object immediately and grabs it. Then I take it from her hands and move it very slowly *before her eyes* to the corresponding place on her right, under the mattress [point B]. Jacqueline watches this movement . . . but at the moment when the parrot disappears [at point B] she turns to her left and looks where it was before [at point A]. (1954, p. 51; italics added)

deferred imitation
the ability to reproduce a modeled activity that has been witnessed at some point in the past.

object permanence
the realization that objects continue to exist when they are no longer visible or detectable through the other senses.

Playing peekaboo is an exciting activity for infants who are acquiring object permanence.

Jacqueline's response is typical of 8-to-12-month-olds, who will search for a hidden object *where they found it previously* rather than where they saw it last. Piaget's account of this **A-not-B error** was straightforward: Jacqueline acted as if her *behavior* determines where the object will be found; consequently, she does not treat the object as if it exists independent of her own activity.

Between 12 and 18 months of age, the object concept improves. Toddlers now track the visible movements of objects and search for them *where they were last seen*. However, object permanence is not complete, because the child cannot make the mental inferences necessary to understand *invisible displacements*. So if you conceal a toy in your hand, place your hand behind a barrier and deposit the toy there, remove your hand, and then ask the child to find the toy, 12- to 18-month-olds will search *where the toy was last seen*—in your hand—rather than looking behind the barrier.

By 18 to 24 months of age, toddlers are capable of *mentally representing* such invisible displacements and using these mental inferences to guide their search for objects that have disappeared. At this point, they fully understand that objects have a "permanence" about them and take great pride at locating their objectives in sophisticated games of hide and seek.

Before we summarize the developments of the sensorimotor period, a caution is in order. Recent research implies that very young infants seem to know far more about objects than Piaget claimed they did and that some of this knowledge may even be inborn (Gelman & Williams, 1997; Mandler, 1997; Spelke & Newport, 1997). In Box 7.1, we consider a small portion of this intriguing research and will see why many of Piaget's ideas about object permanence have now been revised.

An Overview and Evaluation of Piaget's Sensorimotor Stage

The child's intellectual achievements during the sensorimotor period are truly remarkable. In 2 short years, infants have evolved from reflexive and largely immobile creatures into planful thinkers who can move about on their own, solve some problems in their heads, form concepts, and even communicate many of their thoughts to their

A-not-B error
tendency of 8- to 12-month-olds to search for a hidden object where they previously found it even after they have seen it moved to a new location.

7.1

DEVELOPMENTAL ISSUES

Why Infants Know More about Object Permanence Than Piaget Assumed

Do young infants really believe that vanishing objects cease to exist? Renee Baillargeon (1987) doubts it, and her research illustrates a theme that has been echoed by many contemporary researchers: Young infants know more about objects than Piaget claimed they did. In fact, they may never be totally ignorant about the permanence of objects.

The trick in demonstrating what very young infants know is to conduct tests appropriate to their developmental level. Unfortunately, 3- to 4-month-old infants have limited motor skills, so that their inability to search for things (Piaget's tests) really says very little about their knowledge of objects.

Baillargeon (1987; Baillargeon & De Vos, 1991) used the habituation/dishabituation paradigm to assess what 3½- to 4½-month-old infants may know about objects and their properties. Baillargeon (1987) first habituated each infant to a screen that moved 180°, from being flat with its leading edge facing the infant, rising continuously through an arc until it rested in the box with its leading edge being farthest away from the infant (see panel (a) of figure). Once habituated to this event, infants were shown a colorful wooden block with a clown face painted on it, placed to the rear of the flat screen. (Actually, the block was an illusion created by a mirror.) Then, as illustrated in the figure, the screen was rotated to produce either a *possible* event (the screen would stop if stopped by the block, panel (b)), or an *impossible* event (the screen rotated 180°, passing through the block, panel (c)). Baillargeon reasoned that if infants thought the block still existed, even when hidden by the screen, they would stare longer at the screen and be surprised when it appeared to pass through the solid block (an impossible event) than when it bumped the block and stopped its forward motion (possible event). That is exactly what most of the 4½-month-old and many of the 3½-month-old infants did, taking great interest in the impossible event. Clearly, these infants expected the screen to hit the block, thus illustrating their knowledge that the block continued to exist when out of their view. In a similar vein, Thomas Bower (1982) has shown that even 1- to 4-month-old infants are often surprised if a toy hidden behind a screen is no longer there when the screen is lifted a few seconds later. If the delay in lifting the screen is too long, however, infants are *not* surprised when the object is missing. These observations imply that very young infants are not ignorant about the permanence of objects; instead, they simply *forget* that the object is behind the screen if the object is hidden too long.

It was once thought that memory deficits also explained the *A-not-B error* that 8- to 12-month-olds display. But we know now that infants this old have reasonably good memories and are actually quite surprised if a hidden object turns out *not* to be where they have last seen it (at point B) (Baillargeon & Graber, 1988). So 8- to 12-month-olds who commit A-not-B errors often remember that an object has been hidden at new location B; what they may lack is the ability to

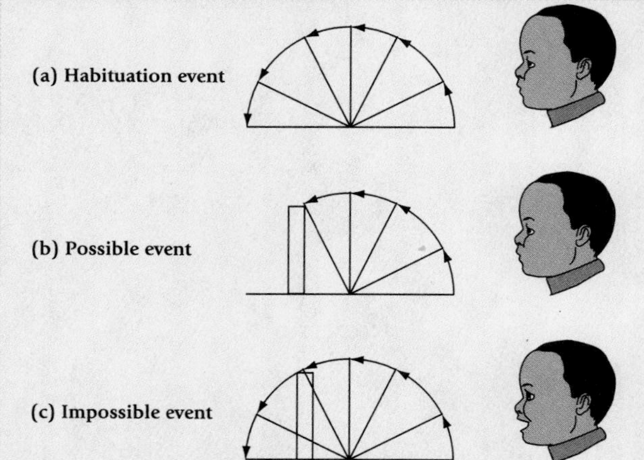

Representations of the habituation stimulus and the possible and impossible events shown to young infants in Baillargeon's (1987) experiment. Babies took great interest in the "impossible" event, thus suggesting that they knew that the box continues to exist and that the screen shouldn't have passed through it. BASED ON BAILLARGEON, *1987.*

inhibit the tendency to search where they have previously found the object. Indeed, Adele Diamond (1985) claims that some infants who search inappropriately for hidden objects at point A hardly look there at all, as if they realize that this is not the right place to search but simply cannot stop themselves. In her study, Diamond (1985) tested 25 infants in the A-not-B task, beginning at about 7 months and continuing until 12 months of age. She reported that the delay between hiding and searching that was necessary to produce the A-not-B error increased with age at a rate of about 2 seconds per month. That is, 7½-month-old infants searched for the hidden object at the erroneous A position following only a 2-second delay. By 12 months of age, infants made the error only if 10 seconds had passed between the hiding of the object and the beginning of the search.

Based on these and other data, Diamond (1991, 1995) believes that maturational changes in the frontal lobes of the cerebral cortex during the second 6 months of life permit infants to gain more control over their motor responses, thereby allowing them to inhibit an impulse to search for hidden objects at locations they know are incorrect. And she may be right. Martha Bell and Nathan Fox (1992) found that 7- to 12-month-olds who *avoid* making A-not-B errors show far more frontal lobe electrical activity while performing the task than their age-mates who search less appropriately.

Though we've considered only a portion of the evidence, it is clear that Piaget's reliance on active search procedures caused him to (1) badly underestimate what very young infants know about the "permanence" of objects and (2) misinterpret why 8- to 12-month-olds display the A-not-B error.

TABLE 7.2 **Summary of the Substages and Intellectual Accomplishments of the Sensorimotor Period**

Substage	Methods of solving problems or producing interesting outcomes	Imitation	Object concept
1. Reflex activity (0–1 month)	Exercising and accommodation of inborn reflexes.	Some reflexive imitation of motor responses.[1]	Tracks moving object but ignores its disappearance.
2. Primary circular reactions (1–4 months)	Repeating interesting acts that are centered on one's own body.	Repetition of own behavior that is mimicked by a companion.	Looks intently at the spot where an object disappeared.[2]
3. Secondary circular reactions (4–8 months)	Repeating interesting acts that are directed toward external objects.	Same as in Substage 2.	Searches for partly concealed object.
4. Coordination of secondary schemes (8–12 months)	Combining actions to solve simple problems (first evidence of intentionality).	Gradual imitation of novel responses; deferred imitation of very simple motor acts after a brief delay.	Clear signs of emerging object concept; searches for and finds concealed object that has *not* been visibly displaced.
5. Tertiary circular reactions (12–18 months)	Experimenting to find new ways to solve problems or reproduce interesting outcomes.	Systematic imitation of novel responses; deferred imitation of simple motor acts after a long delay.	Searches for and finds object that has been *visibly* displaced.
6. Invention of new means through mental combinations (18–24 months)	First evidence of insight as the child solves problems at an internal, symbolic level.	Deferred imitation of complex behavioral sequences.	Object concept is complete; searches for and finds objects that have been hidden through *invisible* displacements.

[1]Imitation of simple motor acts (such as tongue protrusions, head movements, and the opening and closing of one's lips or hands) is apparently an inborn, reflexlike ability that bears little relation to the voluntary imitation that appears later in the first year (Kaitz et al., 1988; Meltzoff & Moore, 1989; Reissland, 1988).
[2]Many researchers now believe that object permanence may be present very early and that Piaget's reliance on search procedures badly underestimated what young infants know about objects (see text).

companions. Yet, deferred imitation emerges earlier than Piaget thought, and young infants know far more about objects than he gave them credit for.

Why did Piaget often underestimate the infant's cognitive capabilities? Probably because he described what infants seem to know from their motor activities and thereby missed some of the schemes they construct through purely *perceptual learning,* by simply looking at and listening to objects and events (Gibson, 1992). Andrew Meltzoff (1990) agrees, arguing that the perceptual understandings and limited capacity for symbolism that young infants display may mean that "in a very real sense, there may be no such things as a *purely* 'sensorimotor period' in the normal human infant" (p. 20). Piaget does deserve a great deal of credit for his early work. At the level of describing infant problem-solving *behaviors* that most people (including parents) actually see, Piaget's account of infant development is generally accurate, although somewhat incomplete (Bjorklund, 1995; see Table 7.2 for a summary and some updates). Yet many researchers today believe that new theories are needed to completely capture the richness of infant intelligence (Gelman & Williams, 1997; Karmiloff-Smith, 1992; Mandler, 1997; Spelke & Newport, 1997).

The Preoperational Stage (2 to 7 Years)

As children enter Piaget's **preoperational stage,** we see a drastic increase in their use of mental symbols (words and images) to represent the objects, situations, and events they encounter. Basically, a symbol is something that stands for something else, as the word dog stands for a four-legged, medium-size, domesticated mammal. Judy DeLoache (1987; DeLoache & Marzolf, 1992) has referred to the knowledge that an entity can stand for something other than itself as **representational insight.**

preoperational stage Piaget's second stage of cognitive development, lasting from about age 2 to age 7, when children think at a symbolic level but do not yet use cognitive operations.

representational insight the knowledge that an entity can stand for (represent) something other than itself.

The most obvious evidence of symbol use for Piaget was language. Other examples of symbol use in young children are deferred imitation, drawing, mental imagery, and symbolic play (for example, pretending a shoe is a telephone or feeding imaginary cereal to a doll). Each of these forms of symbolism is available to most 2-year-olds, although how they use these symbols improves substantially over the next 10 to 12 years.

But despite this important new strength, Piaget's descriptions of preoperational intelligence focus mainly on the limitations or deficiencies in children's thinking. Indeed, he calls this period "preoperational" because he believes that preschool children have not yet acquired the cognitive operations (and operational schemes) that enable them to think logically. Let's consider what Piaget had to say about the intellectual capabilities of preschool children and then contrast his somewhat negative viewpoint with a more positive outlook that has emerged from recent research.

Piaget divided the preoperational period into two substages: the *preconceptual* period (2 to 4 years of age) and the *intuitive* period (4 to 7 years).

The Preconceptual Period

Emergence of Symbolic Thought. The **preconceptual period** is marked by the appearance of the **symbolic function:** the ability to make one thing—a word or an object—stand for, or represent, something else. This transition from the curious hands-on-everything toddler to the contemplative, symbolic preschool child is remarkable indeed. Consider, for example, that because 2- to 3-year-olds can use words and images to represent their experiences, they are now quite capable of reconstructing the past and thinking about or even comparing objects that are no longer present. And just how much does the ability to construct mental symbols transform a child's thinking? David Bjorklund (1995) answers by noting that the average, symbolic 3-year-old probably has more in common intellectually with a 21-year-old adult than with a 12-month-old infant. Although a 3-year-old's thinking changes in many ways over the next several years, it is similar to an adult's in that both preschool children and adults think by manipulating mental symbols.

preconceptual period
the early substage of preoperations, from age 2 to age 4, characterized by the appearance of primitive ideas, concepts, and methods of reasoning.

symbolic function
the ability to use symbols (for example, images and words) to represent objects and experiences.

Language is perhaps the most obvious form of symbolism that young children display. Although most infants utter their first meaningful word by the end of the first year, it is not until about 18 months of age—the point at which they show other signs of symbolism such as inner experimentation—that they combine two (or more) words to form simple sentences. Does the use of language promote cognitive development? Piaget says no, arguing instead that language merely reflects what the child *already knows* and contributes little to new knowledge. In other words, he believed that cognitive development promotes language development, not vice versa. Consistent with Piaget's view are numerous demonstrations that prelinguistic infants can form conceptual categories long before they have words to describe them (see, for example, Younger, 1990; 1993). In one such study (Roberts, 1988), 9-month-olds who had habituated to drawings of one particular kind of bird (for example, a hawk) were later shown drawings of other birds (for example, toucans, robins, and hummingbirds) as well as an out-of-category animal—a horse (see Figure 7.2). These infants explored the horse intently but paid little attention to the other birds, which they recognized as similar to the hawk. Clearly, the formation of this "bird" category could not have been based on language because 9-month-olds neither understand nor use the word bird. But having first formed a *conceptual* category for these feathery creatures, these youngsters are primed to acquire and use the word bird when they do begin to talk.

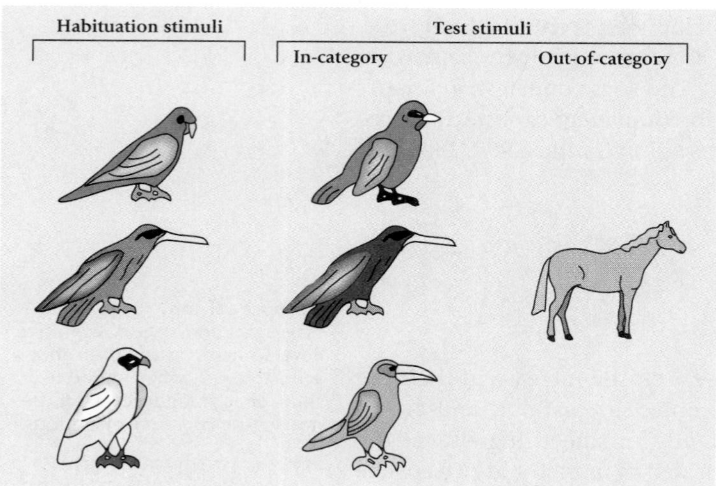

Figure 7.2 *Category stimuli used in Roberts's study.* From Roberts, 1988.

A second major hallmark of the early preconceptual period is the blossoming of *pretend play.* Toddlers often pretend to be people they are not (mommies, superheroes), and they may play these roles with props such as a shoe box or a stick that symbolize other objects such as a baby's crib or a ray gun. Although some parents are concerned when their preschool children immerse themselves in a world of make-believe and begin to invent imaginary playmates, Piaget felt that these are basically healthy activities. In Box 7.2, we focus briefly on children's play and see how these "pretend" activities may contribute in a positive way to the child's social, emotional, and intellectual development.

New Views on Symbolism. Piaget's emphasis on the symbolic nature of preoperational children's thought has captured the attention of developmentalists, who have carefully examined the development of children's symbolic abilities over the preschool years. Judy DeLoache and her colleagues, for example, have explored preschool children's abilities to use scale models and pictures as symbols (DeLoache, 1987, 1991; DeLoache, Kolstad, & Anderson, 1991; DeLoache & Marzolf, 1992; Uttal, Schreiber, & DeLoache, 1995). In DeLoache's studies, 2- to 3-year-old children are asked to find a toy hidden in a room. Prior to searching for the toys, children are shown a scale model of the room, with the experimenter hiding a miniature toy (Snoopy) behind a chair in the model. The miniature toy and the model chair correspond to a large Snoopy and real chair in the adjoining real room. Children are then asked to find the toy in the real room (Retrieval 1). After searching for the toy in the real room, they return to the model and are asked to find where the miniature toy was hidden (Retrieval 2). If children cannot find the large toy in the real room (Retrieval 1) but *can* find the miniature toy in the scale model (Retrieval 2), their failure to find the large toy cannot be due to forgetting where the miniature toy was hidden. A better interpretation would be that the children have no representational insight and cannot use the model in a symbolic fashion to guide their search.

The results of one such experiment with 2½- and 3-year old children are shown in Figure 7.3. As we see, 3-year-olds performed well in *both* retrieval tasks, indicating that they remembered where the miniature toy was hidden and used the information from the scale model to find the large toy in the real room. The 2½-year-olds showed good memory for where the miniature toy had been hidden (Retrieval 2 in the figure), but performed very poorly when trying to find the large toy in the real room (Retrieval 1 in the figure). Apparently, 2½-year-olds failed to recognize that the scale model was a symbolic representation of the large room (see also Dow & Pick, 1992).

It is not that 2½-year-olds have no representational insight. If given a *photo* that shows Snoopy's hiding place in the real room, 2½-year- olds (but not 2-year-olds) can find him there when given the opportunity. Why do they do better with a two-dimensional photo than with an actual three-dimensional scale model? DeLoache believes that scale models are harder to use as symbols because 2½-year-olds lack **dual representation**—the ability to think about an object in two different ways at the same time. Dual representation is not required with photos because the primary purpose of a photo is to represent something else. But a scale model is an interesting object in its own

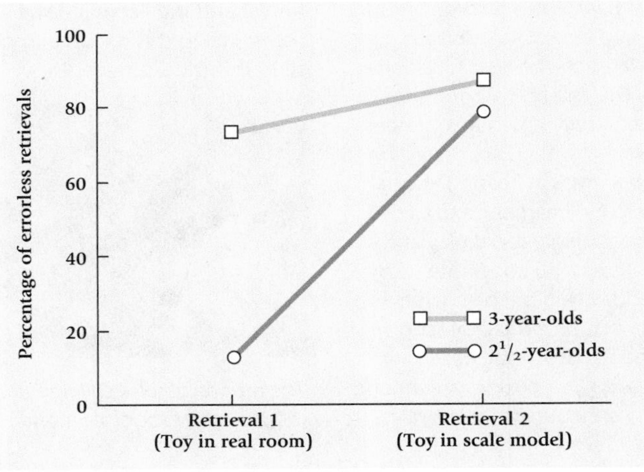

Figure 7.3 *The number of errorless retrievals (correctly locating the hidden toy) for 2½- (younger) and 3-year-olds (older) on a model task. Retrieval 1 involved locating the real toy in the real room; Retrieval 2 involved locating the miniature toy in the model.* FROM DELOACHE, 1987.

dual representation (dual encoding; dual orientation) the ability to represent an object simultaneously as an object itself and as a representation of something else.

7.2

DEVELOPMENTAL ISSUES

Play Is Serious Business

Play is an intrinsically satisfying activity that young children do for the sheer fun of it (Rubin, Fein, & Vandenberg, 1983). In contrast to earlier views that childhood play activities were a frivolous waste of time, Piaget (1951) was fascinated by the young child's play. He believed that play provides a glimpse of the child's emerging cognitive schemes in action, allowing him to practice and strengthen whatever competencies he possesses.

Sensorimotor play begins very early and develops in much the same way in all cultures (Sigman & Sena, 1993). Infants progress from playing with their own bodies (for example, sucking their thumbs), to manipulating external objects such as rattles and stuffed animals, to fully *functional play*—using objects to serve the functions they normally serve—which appears by the end of the first year. So a 12-month-old is more inclined to turn the dial on a toy phone rather than merely sucking on or banging the toy.

Perhaps the most exciting breakthrough in play activities is the emergence of *symbolic (or pretend) play* at 11 to 13 months of age. The earliest "pretend" episodes are simple ones in which infants pretend to engage in familiar activities such as eating, drinking, or sleeping. But by 18 to 24 months of age, toddlers have progressed to a point where they pretend to perform multiple acts in a meaningful sequence. They can also coordinate their actions with those of a play partner, making social games of imitating each other and sometimes even cooperating to achieve a goal (Brownell & Carriger, 1990; Howes & Matheson, 1992). Parents can foster this development by providing toddlers with a secure base of affection and by playing along with their child's little dramas (O'Reilly & Bornstein, 1993; Slade, 1987). In fact, mothers tend to respond to their toddlers with play that is at the same cognitive level or at a bit higher level than that of their children's, and mothers who are more knowledgeable about early play development introduce more complex play than less well-informed mothers (Damast, Tamis-LeMonda, & Bornstein, 1996). This is a pattern that should enhance children's play and cognitive development.

Symbolic play truly blossoms during Piaget's preoperational period. By age 2, toddlers can use one object (a block) to symbolize another (a car) and are now using language in inventive ways to create rich fantasy worlds for themselves. They clearly understand pretense. If you hand them a towel and suggest that they wipe up the imaginary tea you just spilled, they will do it (Harris, Kavanaugh, & Meredith, 1994). Think about this: Since there is no tea in sight, the child's willingness to clean it up suggests that he can construct a mental representation of someone else's pretend event and then act according to this representation. Pretend play becomes increasingly social and complex between ages 2 and 5. More importantly, children combine their capacity for increasingly social play and their capacity for understanding pretense to cooperate with each other at *planning* their pretend activities. They name and assign roles that each player will enact, propose play scripts, and may even stop playing to modify the script if necessary (Howes & Matheson, 1992). Indeed, play episodes are among the most complex social interactions that preschoolers have.

What good is play? Intellectually, play provides a context for using language to communicate and using the mind to fantasize, plan strategies, and solve problems. Children often show more advanced intellectual skills during pretend play than they do when performing other activities, suggesting that play fosters cognitive development (Lillard, 1993). Indeed, preschool children who engage in a great deal of pretend play (or who are trained to do so) perform better on tests of Piagetian cognitive development, language skills, and creativity than children who pretend less often (Fisher, 1992; Johnsen, 1991).

Preschool pretend activities may also promote social development. To be successful at social pretend play, children must adopt different roles, coordinate their activities, and resolve any disputes that may arise. Children may also learn about and prepare for adult roles by "playing house" or "school" and stepping into the shoes of their mothers, fathers, or nursery school teachers. Children who engage in more pretend play with the mothers and siblings tend to have better social perspective-taking skills than those who engage in less pretend play—a finding which implies that early experiences in social pretense clearly contribute to social understandings (Youngblade & Dunn, 1995). Perhaps due to the social skills they acquire (for example, an ability to cooperate) and the role-taking experiences they have, preschool children who participate in a lot of *social* pretend play tend to be more socially mature and more popular with peers than age-mates who often play without partners (Connolly & Doyle, 1984; Howes & Matheson, 1992).

Finally, play may foster healthy emotional development by allowing children to express feelings that bother them or to resolve emotional conflicts (Fein, 1986). If Jennie, for example, has been scolded at lunch for failing to eat her peas, she may gain control of the situation at play as she scolds her doll for picky eating or persuades the doll to "eat healthy" and consume the peas. Playful resolutions of such emotional conflicts may even be an important contributor to children's understanding of authority and the rationales that underlie all those rules they must follow (Piaget & Inhelder, 1969).

Let it never be said, then, that play is useless. Although children play because it is fun, not because it sharpens their skills, players indirectly contribute to their own social, emotional, and intellectual development, enjoying themselves all the while. In this sense, play truly is the child's work—and is serious business indeed!

The reciprocal roles children enact during pretend play promote the growth of social skills and interpersonal understanding.

right, and 2½-year-olds may not recognize that it is also a representation of the larger room. If DeLoache is right, then anything that induces young children to pay less attention to the scale model as an *object* should persuade them to use it as a symbol and thereby improve their search for the hidden toy. Indeed, DeLoache (1991) reports that 2½-year olds who are not allowed to play with the scale model but only to look through its windows do focus less on the interesting qualities of the scale model itself, treating it more like a symbol that helps them to find the hidden toy in the real room.

Although representational insight and dual-representational abilities improve drastically between 2½ and 3 years of age, they remain rather tentative and are easily disrupted. Consider, for example, that when 3-year-olds must wait 5 minutes after seeing a toy hidden in the scale model to make their initial search, they were typically unsuccessful at finding the toy in the larger room. It is not that they forget where the toy was hidden in the scale model. Instead they don't seem to remember over a 5-minute delay that the scale model is a symbolic representation of the real room (Uttal et al., 1995). So dual representation—the ability to keep in mind the relationship between a symbol and its referent—is rather fragile in 3-year olds but improves dramatically over the preschool years (Marzolf & DeLoache, 1994).

Deficits in Preconceptual Reasoning. Piaget called 2- to 4-year-olds "preconceptual" because he believed that their ideas, concepts, and cognitive processes are rather primitive by adult standards. He claimed, for example, that young children often display **animism**—a willingness to attribute life and lifelike qualities (for example, motives and intentions) to inanimate objects. The 4-year-old who believed that the setting sun was alive, angry, and hiding behind the mountain provides a clear example of the animistic logic that children are likely to display during the preconceptual period.

Several other illogical schemes, or "preconcepts," were said to stem from the child's **precausal,** or **transductive reasoning.** The transductive thinker reasons from the particular to the particular: When any two events occur together (covary), the child is likely to assume that one has caused the other. One day when Piaget's daughter had missed her usual afternoon nap, she remarked "I haven't had a nap, so it isn't afternoon." In this case, Lucienne reasoned from one particular (the nap) to another (the afternoon) and erroneously concluded that her nap determined when it was afternoon.

According to Piaget, the most striking deficiency in children's preoperational reasoning—a deficiency that contributes immensely to the other intellectual shortcomings they display—is their **egocentrism,** a tendency to view the world from one's own perspective and to have difficulty recognizing another person's point of view. Piaget demonstrated this by first familiarizing children with an asymmetrical mountain scene (see Figure 7.4) and then asking them what an observer would see as he gazed at the

animism
attributing life and lifelike qualities to inanimate objects.

precausal, or transductive, reasoning
reasoning from the particular to the particular, so that events that occur together are assumed to be causally related.

egocentrism
the tendency to view the world from one's own perspective while failing to recognize that others may have different points of view.

Figure 7.4 *Piaget's three-mountain problem. Young preoperational children are egocentric. They cannot easily assume another person's perspective and often say that another child viewing the mountain from a different vantage point sees exactly what they see from their own location.*

scene from a vantage point other than their own. Often, 3- and 4-year-olds said the other person would see exactly what they saw, thus failing to consider the other's divergent perspective. Other examples of this self-centered thinking appear in the statements young children make. Here is a sample conversation in which the egocentrism of a 4-year-old named Sandy comes through as she describes an event she has witnessed.

SANDY Uncle David, it got on your car and scratched it.

ADULT What did?

SANDY Come, I'll show you. (She takes her uncle outside and shows him a scratch on the top of his new car.)

ADULT Sandy, what made the scratch?

SANDY Not me!

ADULT (laughing) I know, Sandy, but how did the scratch get there?

SANDY It got on the car and scratched it with his claws.

ADULT What did?

SANDY (looking around) There! (She points to a cat that is walking across the street.)

ADULT Oh, a cat! Why didn't you tell me that in the first place?

SANDY I did!

In this case, Sandy assumed that her uncle shared her perspective and must already know what had caused the scratch on his car. Consequently, her speech is not adapted to the needs of her listener, reflecting instead her egocentric point of view.

Finally, Piaget claimed that the young child's egocentric focus on the way things appear to be makes it nearly impossible for her to distinguish appearances from reality. Consider Rheta DeVries's (1969) classic study of the **appearance/reality distinction.** Children 3 to 6 years of age were first introduced to a cat named Maynard. After the children had petted Maynard, DeVries hid Maynard's head and shoulders behind a screen while she strapped a realistic mask of a dog's face onto Maynard's head (see Figure 7.5). The children were then asked such questions about Maynard's identity as "What kind of animal is it now?" and "Does it bark or meow?" Even though Maynard's back half and tail remained in full view during the transformation, nearly all the 3-year-olds focused on Maynard's new appearance and concluded that he really was a dog. By contrast, most 6-year-olds could distinguish appearances from reality, correctly noting that Maynard the cat now merely looked like a dog.

appearance/reality distinction
ability to keep the true properties or characteristics of an object in mind despite the deceptive appearance that the object has assumed; notably lacking among young children during the preconceptual period.

Why do 3-year-olds fail to distinguish between the misleading visual appearance of an object and its actual identity? Their problem, according to John Flavell and his associates (1986), is that they are not yet proficient at *dual encoding*—at representing an object in more than one way at a time. Just as young children have difficulty representing a scale model as both an *object* and a *symbol* (DeLoache, 1987), they struggle to construct simultaneous mental representations of an object that looks like something other than what it really is.

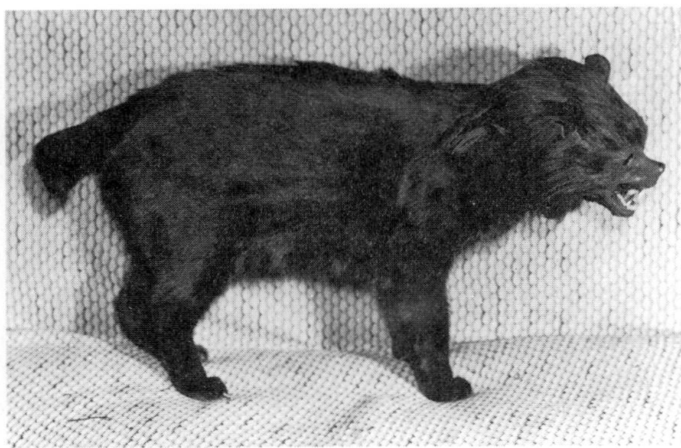

Figure 7.5 *Maynard the cat, without and with a dog mask. Three-year-olds who met Maynard before his change in appearance nonetheless believed that he had become a dog.*

To illustrate, Flavell and his colleagues (1983; 1987; 1989) found that 3-year-olds who were shown a toy sponge that looked like a rock were apt to say that, not only does it look like a rock, but it "really and truly is a rock." Their representation of the object's identity was based on its single most salient feature—its deceptive appearance. Yet, when 3-year-old children are persuaded to play a trick on someone (for example, "Let's trick Sally and make her think that this *sponge* really is a rock, and not just a sponge that looks like one."), many 3-year-olds are capable of this kind of pretense, forming dual representations of this object as a sponge (reality) that only looks like a rock (appearance) (Rice et al., 1997). Clearly, symbolic play activities, in which children pretend that objects (such as a large cardboard box) are something other than they really are (for example, a fort) are an important contributor to dual representation and to children's gradually emerging abilities to distinguish misleading appearances from reality (Golomb & Galasso, 1995). Yet, these abilities develop gradually over the preschool period. In fact, we are about to see that 6- and even 7-year-olds occasionally allow misleading visual appearances to dominate their thinking when attempting to solve logical problems that are unfamiliar to them.

The Intuitive Period

Piaget called the phase between ages 4 and 7 the **intuitive period.** Intuitive thought is little more than an extension of preconceptual thought, although children are now somewhat less egocentric and much more proficient at classifying objects on the basis of shared perceptual attributes such as size, shape, and color. The child's thinking is called "intuitive" because his understanding of objects and events is still largely based, or **"centered,"** on their single most salient perceptual feature—the way things appear to be—rather than on logical or rational thought processes.

Classification and Whole/Part Relations. The limitations of a perceptually based, intuitive logic are apparent when 4- to 7-year-olds work on **class-inclusion** problems that require them to think about whole/part relations. One such problem presents children with a set of wooden beads, most of which are brown, with a few white ones thrown in. If the preoperational child is asked whether these are all wooden beads, he answers yes. If asked whether there are more brown beads than white beads, he will again answer correctly. However, if he is then asked "Are there more brown beads or more wooden beads?," he will usually say "More brown beads." Notice that the child can conceive of a whole class (wooden beads) when responding to the first question and of two distinct classes (brown and white beads) when responding to the second. Yet the third question, which requires him to *simultaneously* relate a whole class to its component parts, is too difficult. The child's thinking about class inclusion seems to be *centered* on the one most salient perceptual feature—the color of the beads—so that he fails to consider that brown beads and white beads can be combined to form a larger class of wooden beads.

Failures to Conserve. Other examples of children's intuitive reasoning come from Piaget's famous conservation studies (Flavell, 1963). One of these experiments begins with the child adjusting the volumes of liquid in two identical containers until each is said to have "the same amount to drink." Next the child sees the experimenter pour the liquid from one of these tall, thin containers into a short, broad container. He is then asked whether the remaining tall, thin container and the shorter, broader container have the same amount of liquid (see Figure 7.6 for an illustration of the procedure). Children younger than 6 or 7 will usually say that the tall, thin receptacle contains *more* liquid than the short, broad one. The child's thinking about liquids is apparently *centered* on one perceptual feature—the relative heights of the columns (tall column = more liquid). In Piaget's terminology, preoperational children are incapable of **conservation:** they do not yet realize that certain properties of objects (such as volume, mass, or number) remain unchanged when the objects' appearances are altered in some superficial way.

intuitive period
the later substage of preoperations, from age 4 to age 7, when the child's thinking about objects and events is dominated by salient perceptual features.

centered thinking (or centration)
in Piaget's theory, the tendency of preoperational children to attend to one aspect of a situation to the exclusion of others; in contrast with *decentration.*

class inclusion
the ability to compare a class of objects with its subclasses without confusing the two.

conservation
the recognition that the properties of an object or substance do not change when its appearance is altered in some superficial way.

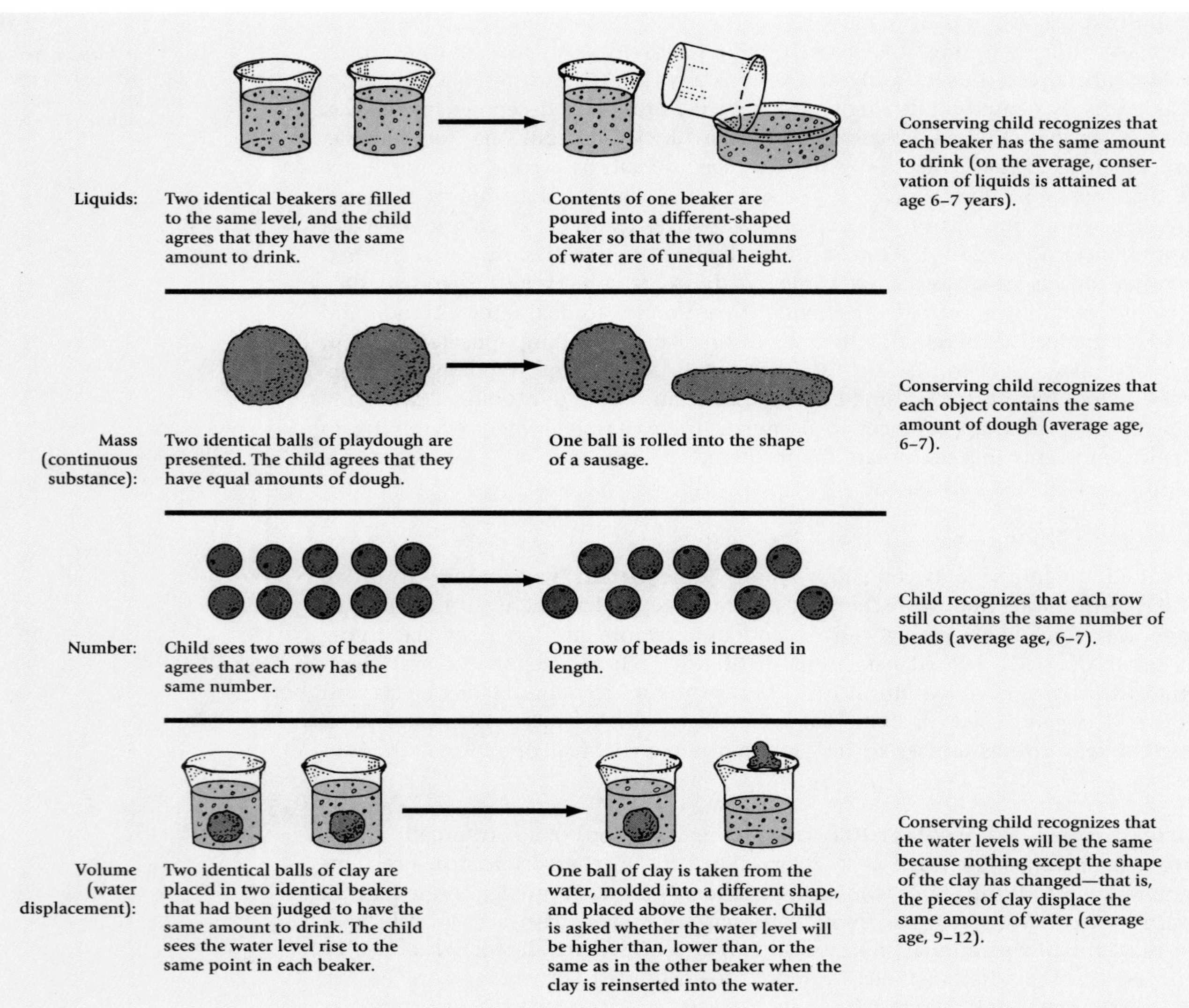

Figure 7.6 *Some common tests of the child's ability to conserve.*

Why do preschool children fail to conserve? The answer, according to Piaget, is that these *pre*operational children lack both of the cognitive operations that would help them to overcome their perceptually based intuitive reasoning. The first of these operations is **decentration**—the ability to concentrate on more than one aspect of a problem at the same time. Children at the intuitive stage are unable to attend *simultaneously* to both height and width when trying to solve the liquid conservation problem. They center their attention either on the difference in height or width and make their decisions on differences in that single dimension. Consequently, they fail to recognize that increases in the width of a column of liquid compensate for decreases in its height to preserve its absolute amount. Preschoolers also lack **reversibility**—the ability to mentally undo or negate an action. So an intuitive 5-year-old faced with the conservation-of-liquids problem is unable to mentally reverse what he has seen to conclude that the liquid in the short, broad beaker is still the same water and would attain its former height if it were poured back into its original container.

decentration
in Piaget's theory, the ability of concrete operational children to consider multiple aspects of a stimulus or situation; in contrast with *centration.*

reversibility
the ability to reverse or negate an action by mentally performing the opposite action (negation).

Does Piaget Underestimate the Preoperational Child?

Are preschool children really as intuitive, illogical, and egocentric as Piaget assumed? Can a child who has no understanding of cognitive operations be taught to conserve? Let's see what later research can tell us.

New Evidence on Egocentrism. Several experiments indicate that Piaget underestimated the ability of preschool children to recognize and appreciate another person's point of view. For example, Piaget and Inhelder's three-mountain task has been criticized as being unusually difficult, and more recent research has shown that children look much less egocentric when provided with less complicated visual displays (Gzesh & Surber, 1985; Newcombe & Huttenlocher, 1992). John Flavell and his associates (1981), for example, showed 3-year-olds a card with a dog on one side and a cat on the other. The card was then held vertically between the child (who could see the dog) and the experimenter (who could see the cat), and the child was asked which animal the experimenter could see. The 3-year-olds performed flawlessly, indicating that they could assume the experimenter's perspective and infer that he must see the cat rather than the animal they could see.

Flavell's study investigated young children's *perceptual* perspective-taking—that is, the ability to make correct inferences about what another person can see or hear. Can preoperational children engage in *conceptual* perspective-taking by making correct inferences about what another person may be thinking or feeling when these mental states differ from their own? The answer is a qualified yes, and recent experiments suggest that this ability may first emerge much earlier than Piaget believed. In one study (Hala & Chandler, 1996), 3-year-olds were asked to play a trick on a person (Lisa) by moving some biscuits from their distinctive biscuit jar to a hiding place, so that Lisa would be fooled. When later asked where Lisa will look for the biscuits and where she will think the biscuits are, children who helped plan the deception performed quite well, saying that Lisa would look in the biscuit jar. In contrast, children who merely observed the experimenter planning the deception did not perform so well. Rather, they were more likely to answer this *false-belief task* erroneously, stating that Lisa would look for the biscuits in the new hiding place. In other words, when they planned to deceive someone, 3-year-olds were later able to take the perspective of that person. When they were not actively involved in the deceit, however, they performed egocentrically, stating that the unsuspecting person would look for the biscuits where *they* knew them to be.

Clearly, preoperational children are not nearly as egocentric as Piaget thought. Nevertheless, Piaget was right in claiming that young children often rely on their own perspectives and thus fail to make accurate judgments about other people's motives, desires, and intentions; and they do often assume that if they know something, others will too (Ruffman & Olson, 1989; Ruffman et al., 1993). Today, researchers believe that children gradually become less egocentric and better able to appreciate others' points of view as they learn more and more—particularly about other people and causes of their behavior. In other words, perspective-taking abilities are not totally absent at one stage and suddenly present at another; they develop slowly and become more refined from early in life into adulthood (Bjorklund, 1995).

Another Look at Children's Causal Reasoning. Piaget was quite correct in stating that preschool children are likely to provide animistic answers to many questions and to make logical errors when thinking about cause-and-effect relationships. Yet, Susan Gelman and Gail Gottfried (1996) find that three-year-olds do *not* routinely attribute life or lifelike qualities to inanimate objects, even such inanimates as a robot that can be made to move. In addition, most 4-year-olds recognize that plants and animals grow and will heal after an injury, whereas inanimate objects (for example, a table with a broken leg) will not (Backschneider, Shatz, & Gelman, 1993). Although preschool children occasionally display animistic responses, these judgments stem not so much from a general belief that moving inanimates have lifelike qualities (Piaget's position) as from the (typically accurate) presumption that *unfamiliar* objects that appear to move *on their own* are alive (Dolgin & Behrend, 1984).

Are preoperational children truly "precausal" beings? Apparently not. Even 10-month-old infants find causal event sequences more worthy of attention than non-causal ones (Cohen & Oakes, 1993). And by age 2, children already express some awareness of causal intentions in their own language (for example, "I left it open [TV] *because* I wanna watch it") and are much more likely to recall causal event sequences than noncausal ones 2 weeks after observing them (Bauer & Mandler, 1989; Miller & Aloise, 1989). By age 3, children already know that (1) causes precede rather than follow effects and (2) an event that always precedes an effect (100% covariation) is more likely to be its cause than are other events that occasionally precede it (Sedlak & Kurtz, 1981). So even younger preschool children have some understanding of basic causal principles and do not always resort to transductive reasoning.

Can Preoperational Children Conserve? According to Piaget (1970b), children younger than 6 or 7 cannot solve conservation problems because they have not yet acquired the operation of reversibility or compensation, the two cognitive operations that would enable them to discover the constancy of attributes such as mass and volume. Piaget also argued that one cannot teach conservation to subjects younger than 6 or 7, for these *pre*operational children are much too intellectually immature to understand and use logical operations such as reversibility.

However, many researchers have demonstrated that nonconservers as young as 4 years of age, and even mentally retarded children, can be *trained* to conserve by a variety of techniques (Brainerd, 1974; Gelman, 1969; Hendler & Weisberg, 1992). One approach that has proved particularly effective is **identity training**—teaching children to recognize that the object or substance transformed in a conservation task is still the *same* object or substance, regardless of its new appearance. For example, a child being trained to recognize identities on a "conservation of liquids" task might be told "It may look like less water when we pour it from a tall, thin glass into this shorter one, but it is the *same* water, and there has to be the same amount to drink." Dorothy Field (1981) has shown that 4-year-olds who received this training not only conserved on the training task but could also use their new knowledge about identities to solve a number of conservation problems on which they had not been trained. Field also reported that nearly 75% of the 4-year-olds who had received some kind of identity training were able to solve at least three (out of five) conservation problems that were presented to them 2½ to 5 months *after* their training had ended. So contrary to Piaget's viewpoint, many preoperational children can learn to conserve, and their initial understanding of this law of nature seems to depend more on their ability to recognize identities than on their use of reversibility and decentration (see also Acredolo, 1982; Field, 1987).

Summing Up. Taken together, the evidence we have reviewed suggests that preschool children are not nearly as illogical or egocentric as Piaget assumed. Today, many researchers believe that Piaget underestimated the abilities of preschool children because his problems were too complex to allow them to demonstrate what they actually knew. If I were to ask you "What do quarks do?," you probably couldn't tell me unless you were a physics major. Surely, this is an unfair test of your "causal logic, just as Piaget's tests were when he questioned preschool children about phenomena (for example, "What causes the wind?") that were equally unfamiliar to them. Even when Piaget asked children about familiar concepts, he required them to verbally justify their answers, which these young, relatively inarticulate preschoolers were often incapable of doing (to Piaget's satisfaction, at least). Yet later research consistently indicates that Piaget's participants may have had a reasonably good understanding of many ideas that they couldn't articulate (for example, class inclusion; distinctions between animates and inanimates) and would easily have displayed such knowledge if asked different questions or given nonverbal tests of the same concepts (Bullock, 1985; Waxman & Hatch, 1992).

Clearly, Piaget was right in arguing that preschool children are more intuitive, egocentric, and illogical than older grade-school children. Yet, it is now equally clear that: (1) preschoolers are capable of reasoning logically about simple problems or concepts that are familiar to them, and (2) a number of factors other than lack of cognitive operations may account for their poor performances on Piaget's cognitive tests.

identity training
an attempt to promote conservation by teaching nonconservers to recognize that a transformed object or substance is the same object or substance, regardless of its new appearance.

The Concrete-Operational Stage (7 to 11 Years)

During Piaget's **concrete-operational** period, children rapidly acquire cognitive operations and apply these important new skills when thinking about objects, situations, and events that they have seen, heard, or otherwise experienced. Recall from our earlier discussion that a cognitive operation is an internal mental activity that enables the child to modify and reorganize her images and symbols to reach a logical conclusion (Flavell et al., 1993). With these powerful new operations in their cognitive arsenal, grade-school children progress far beyond the static and centered thinking of the preoperational stage. For every limitation of the preoperational child, we can see a corresponding strength in the concrete-operator (see Table 7.3).

Some Examples of Operational Thought

Conservation. Concrete-operational children can easily solve several of Piaget's conservation problems. Faced with the conservation-of-liquids puzzle, for example, a 7-year-old concrete-operator can *decenter* by focusing simultaneously on both the height and width of the two containers. She also displays *reversibility*—the ability to mentally undo the pouring process and imagine the liquid in its original container. Armed with these cognitive operations, then, the concrete operator now *knows* that the two different containers each have the same amount of liquid; she uses *logic,* not misleading appearances, to reach her conclusion.

Classification. Concrete-operational children find Piaget's class inclusion problems to be much simpler exercises. They are able to recognize that objects may vary on more than one dimension and thus, may be grouped or classified in many different ways. And confusing classes with subclasses is now a thing of the past. Why? Because the operations of cognitive *addition* and *subtraction* permit the concrete operator to

concrete operations
Piaget's third stage of cognitive development, lasting from about age 7 to age 11, when children acquire cognitive operations and think more logically about real objects and experiences.

Table 7.3 A Comparison of Preoperational and Concrete-operational Thought

Concept	Preoperational thought	Concrete-operational thought
Egocentrism	Children typically assume that others share their point of view.	Children may respond egocentrically at times but are now much more aware of others' divergent perspectives.
Animism	Children are likely to assume that unfamiliar objects that move on their own have lifelike qualities.	Children are more aware of the biological bases for life and do not attribute lifelike qualities to inanimates.
Causality	Limited awareness of causality. Children occasionally display transductive reasoning, assuming that one of two correlated events must have caused the other.	Children have a much better appreciation of causal principles (although this knowledge of causality continues to develop into adolescence and beyond).
Perception-bound thought/centration	Children make judgments based on perceptual appearances and focus on a single aspect of a situation when seeking answers to a problem.	Children can ignore misleading appearances and focus on more than one aspect of a situation when seeking answers to a problem (compensation).
Irreversibility/ reversibility	Children cannot mentally undo an action they have witnessed. They cannot think back to the way an object or situation was before the object or situation changed.	Children can mentally negate changes they have witnessed to make before/after comparisons and consider how changes have altered the situation.
Performance on Piagetian tests of logical reasoning	Their egocentrism and their perception-bound, centered reasoning means that children often fail conservation tasks, have difficulty grouping objects into hierarchies of classes and subclasses, and display little ability to order objects *mentally* along such quantitative dimensions as height or length.	Their declining egocentrism and acquisition of reversible cognitive operations permit concrete-operational children to conserve correctly classify objects on several dimensions, and mentally order objects on quantitative dimensions. Conclusions are now based on logic (the way things *must* necessarily be) rather than on the way they appear to be.

discover the logical relation between the two by mentally adding subclasses to form a superordinate whole and then quickly reversing this action (subtraction) to once again think of the whole class as a collection of subclasses (Flavell, 1963; Ricco, 1989).

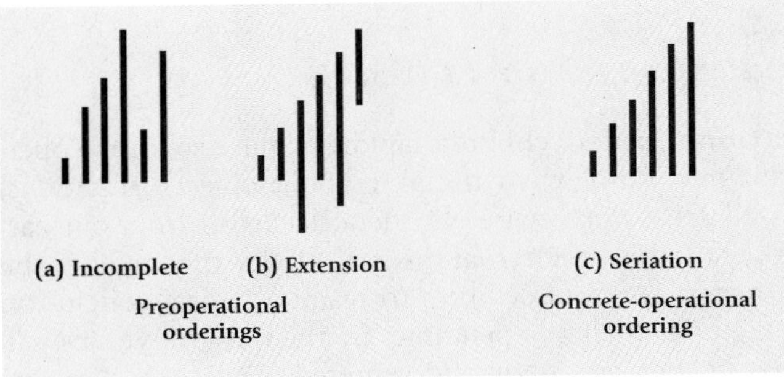

Figure 7.7 *Children's performance on a simple seriation task. If asked to arrange a series of sticks from shortest to longest, preoperational children often line up one end of the sticks and create an incomplete ordering (a) or order them so the top of each successive stick extends higher than the preceding stick (b). Concrete operators, by contrast, can use the inverse cognitive operations greater than (>) and less than (<) to quickly make successive comparisons and create a correct serial ordering.*

Relational Logic. An important hallmark of concrete-operational thinking is a better understanding of quantitative relations and relational logic. Do you remember an occasion when your gym teacher said, "Line up by height from tallest to shortest"? Carrying out such an order is really quite easy for concrete operators, who are now capable of **mental seriation**—the ability to mentally arrange items along a quantifiable dimension such as height or weight. By contrast, preoperational youngsters perform poorly on many seriation tasks (see Figure 7.7) and would struggle to comply with the gym teacher's request.

Concrete-operational thinkers have also mastered the related concept of **transitivity,** which describes the necessary relations among elements in a series. If, for example, John is taller than Mark, and Mark is taller than Sam, who is taller, John or Sam? It follows *logically* that John must be taller than Sam, and the concrete operator grasps the transitivity of these size relationships. Lacking the concept of transitivity, the preoperational child relies on perceptions to answer the question and might insist that John and Sam stand next to each other so that she can determine who is taller. Preoperational children probably have a better understanding of such transitive relations than Piaget gave them credit for (Gelman, 1978; Trabasso, 1975), but they still have difficulty grasping the logical necessity of transitivity (Chapman & Lindenberger, 1988).

? **WHAT DO YOU THINK?**

A man shaves, dons a long-haired wig, makeup, and a dress, and begins to cook and sew. What might a 3-year-old think about these events and why? How is a 7-year-old's understanding likely to differ from that of a preoperational thinker?

The Sequencing of Concrete Operations

While examining Figure 7.6, you may have noticed that some forms of conservation (for example, mass) are understood much sooner than others (volume). Piaget was aware of this and other developmental inconsistencies, and he coined the term **horizontal decalage** to describe them.

Why does the child display different levels on understanding conservation tasks that seem to require the same mental operations? According to Piaget, horizontal decalage occurs because problems that appear quite similar may actually differ in complexity. For example, conservation of volume (see Figure 7.6) is not attained until ages 9 to 12 because it is a complex task that requires the child to simultaneously consider the operations involved in the conservation of both liquids and mass *and* then to determine whether there are any meaningful relationships between these two phenomena. Although we have talked as if concrete operations were a set of skills that appeared rather abruptly over a brief period, this was not Piaget's view. Piaget always maintained that operational abilities evolve gradually and sequentially as the simpler skills that appear first are consolidated, combined, and reorganized into increasingly complex mental structures.

After reviewing some of the intellectual accomplishments of the concrete-operational period, we can see why many societies begin to formally educate their young at 6 to 7 years of age. According to Piaget, this is precisely the time when children are decentering from perceptual illusions and acquiring the cognitive operations that enable them to comprehend arithmetic, think about language and its properties, classify animals, people, objects, and events, and understand the relations between upper- and lower-case letters, letters and the printed word, and words and sentences. Although Piaget was a basic scientist, not an educator, we will see in Box 7.3 that he had some very interesting ideas about the kinds of education young children should receive.

mental seriation
a cognitive operation that allows one to mentally order a set of stimuli along a quantifiable dimension such as height or weight.

transitivity
the ability to recognize relations among elements in a serial order (for example, if A > B and B > C, then A > C).

horizontal decalage
Piaget's term for a child's uneven cognitive performance; an inability to solve certain problems even though one can solve similar problems requiring the same mental operations.

7.3

APPLYING DEVELOPMENTAL RESEARCH

Piaget on Education

Late in his career, Piaget (1971; 1976) wrote about education, offering several suggestions for change that impressed educators and had a major impact on preschool and early grade-school curricula (Gallagher & Easley, 1978; Ginsburg & Opper, 1988). Among the more widely accepted of Piaget's ideas are:

1. *Tailor education to children's readiness to learn.* Appropriate learning experiences build on existing schemes. Piaget stresses that children profit most from *moderately novel* educational experiences that pique their curiosity, challenge their current understandings, and force them to reevaluate what they already know. If the experiences are too complex, students are unable to assimilate (much less accommodate to) them, and no new learning will occur.

2. *Be sensitive to individual differences.* Because children differ in their rates of intellectual development, they are not all ready to learn precisely the same lessons. In a Piagetian-based curriculum, these individual differences are accepted by teachers, who plan activities for individual students or for small groups, rather than the whole class (Ginsburg & Opper, 1988).

3. *Promote discovery-based education.* Piaget criticized traditional educational programs for relying much too heavily on passive, verbal forms of instruction that emphasize rote learning. He believed that young children are naturally inquisitive souls who learn best when they act directly on their environments, probing objects and participating in situations that allow them to *construct* new knowledge for themselves.

Based on these principles, Piaget advised educators against lecturing or demonstrating to students sitting passively; instead, he argued that children should be encouraged to explore a variety of educational props—storybooks, arts and crafts, puzzles, and games—that enable them to learn by doing. According to Piaget: "Children should be able to do their own experimenting and their own research. Teachers, of course, can guide them by providing appropriate materials, but the essential thing is that in order for a child to understand something, he must construct it for himself; he must reinvent it" (Piaget, 1972). Piaget insisted that even formal lessons can be structured to promote active learning. For example, he believed that basic arithmetic operations are best illustrated by having children add and subtract buttons rather than showing them how to solve problems on a blackboard. He advocated teaching the concepts of space and distance by allowing children to measure their heights or the widths of their desks, as opposed to lecturing them on the relations between inches, feet, and yards. In other words, Piaget stressed that the teacher's job is not so much to transmit facts and concepts or to actively reinforce correct answers as to provide the setting, the materials, and the guidance that will enable curious children to experience the *intrinsic* satisfaction of *discovering* this knowledge for themselves. Piaget saw a "discovery-based" education as critical because he believed that "the principal goal of education is to create [adults] who are capable of doing new things, not simply of repeating what other generations have done—[people] who are creative, inventive, discoverers." (Piaget, as cited in Elkind, 1977, p. 171)

An Important Limitation of Concrete-Operational Thought

Surely, if Piaget proposed a fourth stage of cognitive development, there must be at least one important limitation to concrete-operational reasoning. And there is. Piaget called this period *concrete* operations because he believed that children can apply their operational schemes only to objects, situations, or events that are real or imaginable. The transitive inferences of concrete operators, for example, are likely to be accurate only for *real* objects that are (or have been) *physically present.* Seven- to 11-year olds cannot yet apply this relational logic to *abstract* signifiers such as the *X*s, *Y*s, and *Z*s that we use in algebra.

The Formal-Operational Stage (11–12 Years and Beyond)

formal operations
Piaget's fourth and final stage of cognitive development, from age 11 or 12 and beyond, when the individual begins to think more rationally and systematically about abstract concepts and hypothetical events.

By age 11 or 12, many children are entering the last of Piaget's intellectual stages—**formal operations.** Recall that concrete operations are mental actions performed on material aspects of experience and that concrete operators can think quite logically about tangible objects and events. By contrast, formal operations are mental actions performed on *ideas* and *propositions.* No longer is thinking tied to the factual or observable, for formal operators can reason quite logically about hypothetical processes and events that may have no basis in reality.

Hypothetico-Deductive Reasoning

The benchmark of formal operations is what Piaget referred to as **hypothetico-deductive reasoning** (Inhelder & Piaget, 1958). *Deductive reasoning,* which entails reasoning from the general to the specific, is not, in itself, a formal operational ability. Concrete-operational children can arrive at a correct conclusion if they are provided with the proper concrete "facts" as evidence. Formal-operational children, on the other hand, are not restricted to thinking about previously acquired facts, but can generate hypotheses; what is possible is more important to them than what is real. In Box 7.4, we can see the differences between concrete-operational and formal-operational thinking as children consider a hypothetical proposition presented in the form of an art assignment.

Hypothetical thinking is also critical for most forms of mathematics beyond simple arithmetic. If $2X + 5 = 15$, what does X equal? The problem does not deal with concrete entities such as apples or oranges, only with numbers and letters. It is an arbitrary, *hypothetical* problem that can be answered only if it is approached abstractly, using a symbol system that does not require concrete referents.

Thinking Like a Scientist

In addition to the development of deductive reasoning abilities, formal-operational children are hypothesized to be able to think *inductively,* going from specific observations to broad generalizations. Inductive reasoning is the type of thinking that scientists display, where hypotheses are generated and then systematically tested in experiments.

Inhelder and Piaget (1958) used a series of tasks to assess scientific reasoning, one of which was the *pendulum problem.* Given strings of different lengths, objects of different weights to attach to one end of the strings, and a hook on which to hang the other end, the child's task is to discover which factor influences how fast the string pendulum oscillates (that it, swings back and forth during a set time period). Is it the length of the string that matters? The heaviness of the weight? The force with which the weight is pushed? The height from which the weight is released? Or might two or more of these variables be important?

hypothetico-deductive reasoning
in Piaget's theory, a formal operational ability to think hypothetically.

A systematic approach to problem solving is one of the characteristics of formal-operational thinking.

The key to solving this problem is to first identify the four factors that might control the pendulum's oscillation and to then systematically test each of these hypotheses, varying one factor at a time while holding all the other factors constant. Each successive hypothesis is tested in an if–then fashion: "*If* the weight on the string matters, *then* I should see a difference in oscillation when I compare a string with a heavy weight to a same-length string with a light weight, while holding other factors constant." Formal operators, who rely on this systematic approach to hypothesis generation and testing, eventually discover that the "weight hypothesis" is wrong and that the pendulum's oscillation depends on only one factor: the length of the string.

By contrast, 9- to 10-year-old concrete operators are not able to generate and systematically test the full range of possibilities that would permit them to

7.4

FOCUS ON RESEARCH

Children's Responses to a Hypothetical Proposition

Piaget (1970a) has argued that the thinking of concrete operators is reality bound. Presumably, most 9-year-olds would have a difficult time thinking about objects that don't exist or events that could never happen. By contrast, children entering the stage of formal operations were said to be quite capable of considering hypothetical propositions and carrying them to a logical conclusion. Indeed, Piaget suspected that many formal operators would even enjoy this type of cognitive challenge.

Several years ago, a group of concrete operators (9-year-old fourth-graders) and a group of children who were at or rapidly approaching formal operations (11- to 12-year-old sixth graders) completed the following assignment:

> Suppose that you were given a third eye and that you could choose to place this eye anywhere on your body. Draw me a picture to show where you would place your extra eye, and then tell me why you would put it there.

All the 9-year-olds placed the third eye *on the forehead between their two natural eyes*. It seems as if these children called on their concrete experiences to complete their assignment: Eyes are found somewhere around the middle of the face in all people. One 9-year-old boy remarked that the third eye should go between the other two because "that's where a cyclops has his eye." The rationales for this eye placement were rather unimaginative. Consider the following examples:

> JIM (age 9½) I would like an eye beside my two other eyes so that if one eye went out, I could still see with two.
>
> VICKIE (age 9) I want an extra eye so I can see you three times.
>
> TANYA (age 9½) I want a third eye so I could see better.

In contrast, the older, formal-operational children gave a wide variety of responses that were not at all dependent on what they have seen previously. Furthermore, these children thought out the advantages of this hypothetical situation and provided rather imaginative rationales for placing the extra eye in unique locations. Here are some sample responses:

> KEN (age 11½) (draws the extra eye on top of a tuft of hair) I could revolve the eye to look in all directions.
>
> JOHN (age11½) (draws his extra eye in the palm of his left hand) I could see around corners and see what kind of cookie I'll get out of the cookie jar.
>
> TONY (age 11) (draws a close-up of a third eye in his mouth) I want a third eye in my mouth because I want to see what I am eating.

When asked their opinions of the three-eye assignment, many of the younger children considered it rather silly and uninteresting. One 9-year-old remarked, "This is stupid. Nobody has three eyes." However, the 11- to 12-year-olds enjoyed the task and continued to pester their teacher for "fun" art assignments "like the eye problem" for the remainder of the school year (Shaffer, 1973).

So the results of this demonstration are generally consistent with Piaget's theory. Older children who are at or rapidly approaching the stage of formal operations are more likely than younger, concrete operators to generate logical and creative responses to a hypothetical proposition and to enjoy this type of reasoning.

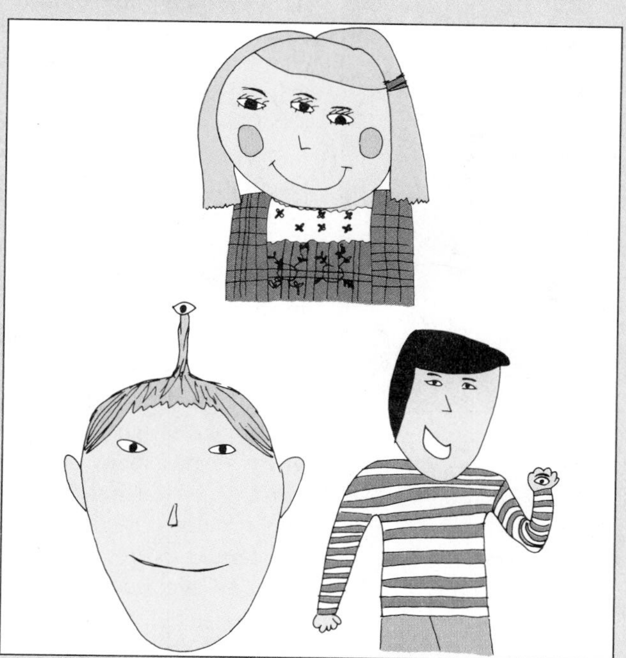

Tanya's, Ken's, and John's responses to the "third eye" assignment.

draw the appropriate conclusion. They often begin with a reasonable hypothesis ("Maybe string length matters"), but they can't isolate the effects of each variable. For example, they may test the string-length hypothesis without holding weight constant; should they find that a short string with a heavy weight oscillates faster than a longer one with a lighter weight, they are likely to erroneously conclude that both string length and weight control the pendulum's oscillation. Older concrete operators can be trained to think more like formal operators when seeking solutions to problems (Adey & Shayer, 1992; Fabricius & Steffe, 1989), but they are unable to generate these rational and methodical problem-solving strategies on their own.

In sum, formal-operational thinking is rational, systematic, and abstract. The formal operator can now think planfully about thinking and can operate on ideas and hypothetical concepts, including those that contradict reality.

Personal and Social Implications of Formal Thought

Formal-operational thinking is a powerful tool that may change adolescents in many ways—some good, and some not so good. First the good news. As we will see in Chapter 12, formal operations may pave the way for thinking about what is possible in one's life, forming a stable identity, and achieving a much richer understanding of other people's psychological perspectives and the causes of their behavior. The formal-operational thinker is also better equipped to make difficult personal decisions that involve weighing alternative courses of action and their probable consequences for herself and other people (see Chapter 14, for example, on the development of moral reasoning). So advances in cognitive growth help to lay the groundwork for changes in many other aspects of development.

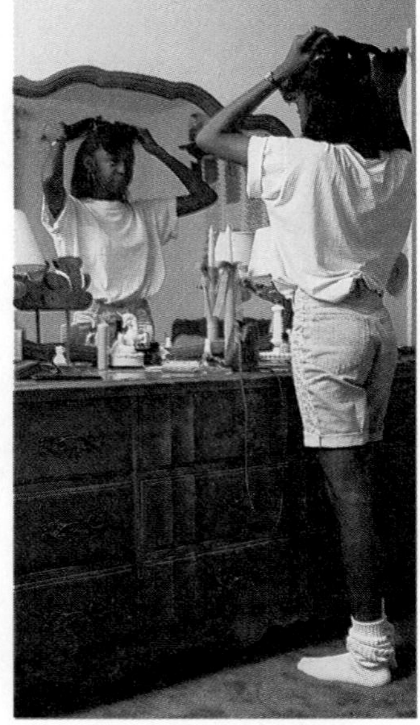

An adolescent may feel that others are as preoccupied with her appearance or her conduct as she is—a phenomenon known as the "imaginary audience."

Now the bad news: Formal operations may also be related to some of the more painful aspects of the adolescent experience. Unlike younger children who tend to accept the world as it is and to heed the dictates of authority figures, formal operators, who can imagine hypothetical alternatives to present realities, may begin to question everything from their parents' authority to impose strict curfews to the government's need for spending billions of dollars on weapons and the exploration of outer space when so many people are hungry and homeless. Indeed, the more logical inconsistencies and other flaws that adolescents detect in the real world, the more confused they become and the more inclined they are to become frustrated with or even to display rebellious anger toward the agents (for example, parents, the government) thought to be responsible for these imperfect states of affairs. Piaget (1970a) viewed this idealistic fascination with the way things "ought to be" as a perfectly normal outgrowth of the adolescent's newly acquired abstract reasoning abilities, and he thus proclaimed formal operations the primary cause of the "generation gap."

According to Piaget, adolescents can be so centered on themselves and their thinking that they actually appear more egocentric than they were during the grade-school years. Indeed, David Elkind (1967; 1981) has identified two kinds of "egocentrism" that adolescents often display. The **imaginary audience** phenomenon refers to the adolescent's feeling that she is constantly "on stage" and that everybody around her is just as concerned with and as critical of her actions or appearance as she is. Thus, a teenage girl who has spent hours making up her face to hide a few pimples may be absolutely convinced that her date is repulsed by them whenever he looks away—when, in truth, the equally self-conscious boy may be turning away because he's convinced that her concerned expressions imply that his mouthwash has failed him.

The second form of adolescent egocentrism is what Elkind calls the **personal fable**—a belief in the *uniqueness* of oneself and one's experiences. For example, a teenager who has just been "dumped" by his first love may feel that no one in human history has ever experienced anything quite like *his* crushing agony. According to Elkind, the personal fable may also explain why adolescents take risks. After all, they are *unique* and are unlikely to be harmed by reckless driving or having unsafe sex; negative consequences only happen to others, so why bother with seat belts or contraception (Arnett, 1990)?

imaginary audience
allegedly a form of adolescent egocentrism that involves confusing one's own thoughts with those of a hypothesized audience and concluding that others share one's preoccupations.

personal fable
allegedly a form of adolescent egocentrism that involves thinking that oneself and one's thoughts and feelings are special or unique.

Elkind believed that both forms of adolescent egocentrism would increase as youngsters first acquire formal operations, and would gradually decline as older adolescents enter adult roles that require them to more carefully consider others' perspectives. However, the data are not always consistent with this point of view. Apparently, teenagers perceive just as many personal dangers in risky acts such as drug use, driving while intoxicated, and having sex as middle-age adults do, thus questioning the idea that adolescents feel especially unique or invulnerable (Beyth-Marom et al., 1993). Indeed, many of the risks adolescents take reflect a desire to have exciting experiences rather than feelings of invulnerability (Arnett & Balle-Jensen, 1993). And although the imaginary audience phenomenon is stronger among 13- to 15-year-olds than among older adolescents, it is often the 13- to 15-year-olds still functioning at the *concrete-operational* level who show more of this self-consciousness (Gray & Hudson, 1984; O'Connor & Nikolic, 1990)—just the reverse of what Elkind would expect. Consequently, some developmentalists now believe that the self-preoccupation that many adolescents display may be linked less closely to formal-operational thinking than to the development of advanced social perspective-taking skills (discussed in Chapter 12) that allow teenagers to contemplate how *other people* might perceive them or react to their behavior (Lapsley et al., 1986; Vartanian & Powlishta, 1996). Viewed in this way, adolescent egocentrism is not very "egocentric" after all.

Does Everyone Reach Formal Operations?

Piaget (1970b) believed that the transition from concrete-operational to formal-operational reasoning takes place very gradually. For example, 11- to 13-year olds who are entering formal operations are able to consider simple hypothetical propositions such as the three-eye problem (see Box 7.3). However, they are not yet proficient at generating and testing hypotheses, and it may be another 3 to 4 years before they are capable of the planful, systematic reasoning that is necessary to deduce what determines how fast a pendulum will swing. Piaget never identified a stage of reasoning beyond formal operations, and he believed that most people show at least some signs of this highest level of intellect by ages 15 to 18.

Other investigators find that adolescents are much slower to acquire formal operations than Piaget had thought. In fact, Edith Neimark's (1979) review of the literature suggests that a sizable percentage of American adults do not often reason at the formal level, and apparently there are some cultures—particularly those where formal schooling is rare or nonexistent—in which no one solves Piaget's formal-operational problems (Cole, 1990; Dasen, 1977).

Why do some people fail to attain formal operations? Cross-cultural research provides one clue: They may not have had sufficient exposure to the kinds of schooling that stress logic, mathematics, and science—experiences that Piaget believed help the child to reason at the formal level (Cole, 1990; Dasen, 1977).

In the later stages of his career, Piaget (1972) suggested another possibility: Perhaps nearly all adults are capable of reasoning at the formal level, but do so only on problems that hold their interest or are of vital importance to them. Indeed, Tulkin and Konner (1973) found that preliterate Bushman hunters who fail Piaget's test problems do often reason at the formal level on at least one task: tracking prey. Clearly, this is an activity of great importance to them that requires the systematic testing of inferences and hypotheses. A similar phenomenon has been observed among high school and college students. Not only do 12th-graders reason more abstractly about relevant everyday issues with which they are already familiar (Overton et al., 1987; Ward & Overton, 1990), but as we see in Figure 7.8, physics, English, and social science majors are all more likely to perform at the formal level on problems that fall within their own academic domains (De Lisi & Staudt, 1980).

Concept Check 7.2
Understanding Deficiencies and Milestones in Children's Thinking

Check your understanding of various aspects of children's thinking. First, match each scenario below with one of the following cognitive phenomena: (a) reversibility, (b) imaginary audience, (c) seriation, (d) dual representation, (e) animism, (f) A-not-B error, (g) hypothetical reasoning. Then indicate the Piagetian stage in which each phenomenon allegedly emerges. Answers appear in the Appendix.

_____ 1. John successfully arranges his many seashells from smallest to largest.

_____ 2. "You killed him!" Ben sobs, when his mother destroys a clay pigeon while trap shooting.

_____ 3. Sarah is sure her peers will tease her because her hair is unmanageable today.

_____ 4. Knowing his sister will be surprised, Josh points a chocolate pistol at her and then takes a bite out of its muzzle.

_____ 5. Judy blissfully contemplates how nice things would be if there were no racial prejudice.

_____ 6. After seeing his brother throw his ball out the window, Sammy looks for it in his toy box.

_____ 7. Billy drops a vase and decides he'll glue it back together, hoping no one will notice.

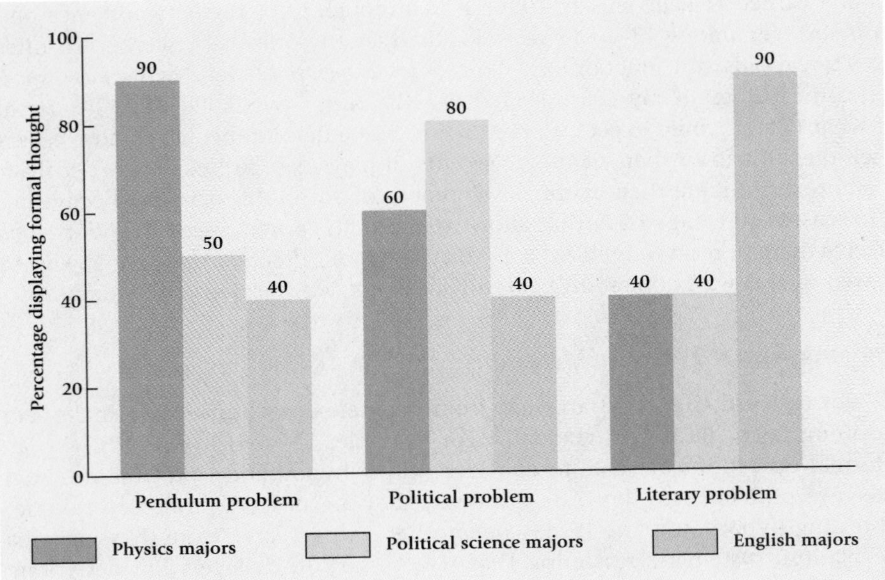

Figure 7.8 *Expertise and formal operations. College students show the greatest command of formal-operational thought in the subject area most related to their major.* *Adapted from De Lisi & Staudt, 1980.*

It seems likely, then, that each person has an optimal or "highest" level of cognitive performance that will show itself in familiar or well-trained content domains (Fischer, 1980; Fischer, Kenny, & Pipp, 1990). However, performance is likely to be inconsistent across domains unless the person has had a chance to build knowledge and to practice reasoning in all these content areas (Marini & Case, 1994). So we must be careful not to underestimate the cognitive capabilities of adolescents and adults who fail Piaget's formal-operational tests, for their less-than-optimal *performances* on these *physical science* problems may simply reflect either a lack of interest or a lack of experience with the subject matter rather than an inability to reason at the formal level.

AN EVALUATION OF PIAGET'S THEORY

Now that we have examined Piaget's theory of cognitive development, it is time to evaluate it. Let us start by giving credit where credit is due before considering the challenges to Piaget's viewpoint.

Piaget's Contributions

Piaget is a giant in the field of human development. As one anonymous scholar quoted by Harry Beilin (1992) put it, "assessing the impact of Piaget on developmental psychology is like assessing the impact of Shakespeare on English literature or Aristotle on philosophy—impossible" (p. 191). It is hard to imagine that we would know even a fraction of what we know about intellectual development had Piaget pursued his early interests in zoology and never worked with developing children.

So what exactly has Piaget contributed to the field of human development? The following list is a brief assessment of Piaget's major contributions made by several prominent researchers in honor of the 100th anniversary of Piaget's birth (Brainerd,

1996; Flavell, 1996; Elkind, 1996; Fischer & Hencke, 1996; Kessen, 1996; Gopnik, 1996; Siegler & Ellis, 1996):

1. Piaget founded the discipline we know today as cognitive development. His interest in children's thinking insured that this field would be "developmental" and not merely apply to children the ideas and methods from the study of adult thinking.
2. Piaget convinced us that children are curious, active explorers who play an important role in their own development. Although Piaget's assumptions that children actively *construct* their own knowledge may seem obvious today, this viewpoint was innovative and counter to the thinking of his time.
3. Piaget's theory was one of the first to try to explain, and not just describe, the process of development. Largely prompted by his theory, many theorists today have taken seriously the need to explain transitions in children's thinking (Case, 1992; Fischer, 1980; Fischer & Bidell, 1997; Nelson, 1996; Siegler, 1996).
4. Piaget's description of broad sequences of intellectual development provides a reasonably accurate overview of how children of different ages think. He may have been wrong about some of the specifics, but, as Robert Siegler (1991) notes, "His descriptions feel right. . . . The general trends . . . appeal to our intuitions and our memories of childhood" (p. 18).
5. Piaget's ideas have had a major influence on thinking about social and emotional development as well as many practical implications for educators.
6. Finally, Piaget asked important questions and drew literally thousands of researchers to the study of cognitive development. And as often happens when heuristic theories such as Piaget's are repeatedly scrutinized, some of his research led to new insights while pointing to problems with his original ideas.

Challenges to Piaget

Over the past 25 years, critics have pointed to several apparent shortcomings of Piaget's theory. We will briefly consider five of these criticisms.

Piaget Underestimated Developing Minds

One frequent charge is that Piaget was often incorrect about when individuals can be expected to master a concept or enter a particular stage of development. Most notably, Piaget seems to have underestimated the cognitive capabilities of infants, toddlers, and preschool children; and he also claimed that concrete-operators are incapable of reasoning abstractly, when training studies suggest otherwise. When researchers have turned to more familiar problems than Piaget used or have reduced Piaget's tasks to their bare essentials, the true competencies of young children—and of adolescents and adults, too—come through more clearly.

Piaget Failed to Distinguish Competence from Performance

Piaget was concerned with identifying the underlying *competencies,* or cognitive structures, that presumably determined how children perform on various cognitive tasks. He tended to assume that a child who failed one of his problems simply lacked the underlying concepts, or thought structures, he was testing.

We now know that this latter assumption is not valid because many factors other than a lack of critical competencies might undermine one's performance on a cognitive test. We've seen, for example, that 4- and 5-year-olds who seem to know the differences between animates and inanimates failed Piaget's tests, largely because Piaget required them to explain principles they understood (critical competency) but could not articulate. Late in his career, Piaget (1972) realized he may have erred when he observed that adolescents are more likely to display formal-operational reasoning on familiar problems that interest them and concluded that *motivation* also influences intellectual performance. But his earlier tendency to equate task performances with competencies (and to ignore motivation, task familiarity, and all other factors that influence performance) is a major reason that his age norms for various cognitive milestones were often so far off target.

Does Cognitive Development Really Occur in Stages?

Piaget maintained that his stages of intellectual development are *holistic structures,* that is, coherent modes of thinking that are applied across a broad range of tasks. To say that a child is concrete-operational, for example, implies that he relies on cognitive operations and thinks logically about the vast majority of intellectual problems that he encounters.

Recently this holistic-structures assumption has been challenged by researchers, who question whether cognitive development is at all stagelike (Bjorklund, 1995; Flavell et al., 1993). From their perspective, a "stage" of intellect implies that abrupt changes in intellectual functioning occur as the child acquires several new competencies over a relatively brief period. Yet, we've seen that cognitive growth doesn't happen that way. Major transitions in intellect occur quite gradually, and there is often very little consistency in the child's performance on tasks that presumably measure the abilities that define a given stage. For example, it may be years before a 7-year-old who can seriate or conserve number will be able to conserve volume (see Figure 7.6). Furthermore, it now appears that different concrete- and formal-operational problems are mastered in different orders by different children, a finding that suggests that there is a lot less consistency and coherence to cognitive growth than Piaget assumed (Case, 1985; Kuhn, 1992).

So is cognitive development truly stagelike? The issue is still hotly debated and far from being resolved. Some theorists insist that cognitive development is coherent and does progress through a series of stages, though not necessarily through the same stages that Piaget proposed (Case, 1992; Case & Okamoto, 1996; Flavell et al., 1993). Yet, many other theorists believe that intellectual development is a complex, multifaceted process in which children gradually acquire skills in many different content areas such as deductive reasoning, mathematics, visual–spatial reasoning, verbal skills, and moral reasoning to name a few (Bjorklund, 1995; Fischer et al. 1990). Although development within each of these domains may occur in small, orderly steps, there is no assumption of consistency across domains. Thus, a 10-year-old who enjoys solving word puzzles and playing verbal games might outperform most age-mates on tests of verbal reasoning but function at a much lower level in less familiar domains, such as hypothesis testing or mathematical reasoning.

In sum, many aspects of cognitive development are orderly and coherent (and some would say stagelike) *within particular intellectual domains*. Yet, there is very little evidence for strong consistencies in development across domains or for broad, holistic cognitive stages of the kind Piaget described.

? **WHAT DO YOU THINK?**

Joe is an excellent mechanic who systematically generates all possible causes for an automotive problem, testing them one at a time until he discovers what is wrong, and then makes the *proper* repair. Which of Piaget's stages does Joe's method of problem solving seem to illustrate? Would you change your mind if Joe failed a scientific problem said to depend on this same level of reasoning? Why or why not?

Does Piaget Explain Cognitive Development?

Even those researchers who claim that cognitive growth is stagelike are bothered by Piaget's account of how children move from one stage of intellect to the next. Recall Piaget's interactionist viewpoint: Presumably children are (1) constantly assimilating new experiences in ways that their level of maturation allows, (2) accommodating their thinking to these experiences, and (3) reorganizing their structures into increasingly complex mental schemes that enable them to reestablish cognitive equilibrium with novel aspects of the environment. As children continue to mature, assimilate more complex information, and alter and reorganize their schemes, they eventually come to view familiar objects and events in new ways and move from one stage of intellect to the next.

This rather vague explanation of cognitive growth raises more questions than it answers. What maturational changes are necessary before children can progress from sensorimotor to preoperational intellect or from concrete operations to formal operations? What kinds of experiences must a child have before he will construct mental symbols, use cognitive operations, or operate on ideas and think about hypotheticals? Piaget was simply not very clear about these or any other mechanisms that might enable a child to move to a higher stage of intellect. As a result, a growing number of researchers now look on his theory as an elaborate *description* of cognitive development that has limited explanatory power (Gelman & Baillargeon, 1983; Kuhn, 1992).

Piaget Devoted Too Little Attention to Social and Cultural Influences

Children live in very different social and cultural contexts that affect the way their world is structured. Although Piaget admitted that cultural factors may influence the rate of cognitive growth, developmentalists now know that culture influences *how* children think as well (Rogoff, 1990, 1997). Piaget also paid too little attention to the ways that children's minds develop through their *social interactions* with more competent individuals. It would be an overstatement to say that Piaget ignored social influences on cognitive development. As we will see in Chapters 12 and 14, Piaget felt that conflict among peers was a major contributor to cognitive disequilibrium and intellectual growth, particularly the growth of perspective-taking skills and moral reasoning. Nevertheless, Piaget's descriptions emphasize the *self-directed* character of cognitive growth, almost as if the child was an isolated scientist, exploring the world and making critical discoveries largely on her own. Today, we know that children develop many of their most basic (and not so basic) competencies by collaborating with parents, teachers, older siblings, and peers. Indeed, the belief that social interaction contributes importantly to cognitive growth is a cornerstone of the *sociocultural perspective* on cognitive development offered by one of Piaget's contemporaries, Lev Vygotsky.

VYGOTSKY'S SOCIOCULTURAL PERSPECTIVE

In order to view Piaget's work from a new vantage point, let's consider a perspective on cognitive development that has been arousing a great deal of interest lately—the **sociocultural theory** of Lev Vygotsky (1934/1962; 1930–1935/1978; and see Rogoff, 1990, 1997; Wertsch & Tulviste, 1992). This Russian developmentalist was an active scholar in the 1920s and 1930s when Piaget was formulating his theory. Unfortunately, Vygotsky died at the age of 38 before his work was complete. Nevertheless, he left us with much food for thought by insisting that (1) cognitive growth occurs in a sociocultural context that influences the form it takes, and (2) many of a child's most noteworthy cognitive skills evolve from *social interactions* with parents, teachers, and other more competent associates.

The sociocultural theory of Lev Vygotsky (1896–1934) views cognitive development as a socially mediated process that may vary from culture to culture.

The Role of Culture in Intellectual Development

Vygotsky (1930–1935/1978) claimed that infants are born with a few *elementary mental functions*—attention, sensation, perception and memory—that are eventually transformed by the culture into new and more sophisticated mental processes he called *higher mental functions*. Take memory, for example. Young children's early memorial capabilities

sociocultural theory
Vygotsky's perspective on cognitive development, in which children acquire their culture's values, beliefs, and problem-solving strategies through collaborative dialogues with more knowledgeable members of society.

are limited by biological constraints to the images and impressions they can produce. However, each culture provides its children **tools of intellectual adaptation** that permit them to use their basic mental functions more adaptively. Thus, children in Western societies may learn to remember more efficiently by taking notes on what to remember, whereas their age-mates in preliterate societies may have learned other memory strategies, such as representing each object they must remember by tying a knot in a string or by tying a string around their finger to remind them to perform a chore. Such socially transmitted memory strategies and other cultural tools teach children how to use their minds—in short, *how* to think. And since each culture also transmits specific beliefs and values, it teaches children *what* to think as well.

In sum, Vygotsky claimed that human cognition, even when carried out in isolation, is inherently *sociocultural* because it is affected by the beliefs, values, and tools of intellectual adaptation passed to individuals by their culture. And since these values and intellectual tools may vary dramatically from culture to culture, Vygotsky believed that neither the course nor the content of intellectual growth was as universal as Piaget assumed.

The Social Origins of Early Cognitive Competencies

Vygotsky agreed with Piaget that young children are curious explorers who are actively involved in learning and discovering new principles. However, he placed much less emphasis than Piaget did on *self*-initiated discovery, choosing instead to stress the importance of *social* contributions to cognitive growth.

According to Vygotsky, many of the truly important "discoveries" that children make occur within the context of cooperative, or collaborative, *dialogues* between a skillful tutor, who models the activity and transmits verbal instructions, and a novice pupil, who first seeks to understand the tutor's instruction and eventually internalizes this information, using it to regulate his or her own performance.

To illustrate collaborative (or guided) learning as Vygotsky viewed it, let's imagine that Annie, a 4-year-old, has just received her first jigsaw puzzle as a birthday present. She attempts to work the puzzle but gets nowhere until her father comes along, sits down beside her, and gives her some tips. He suggests that it would be a good idea to put together the corners first, points to the pink area at the edge of one corner piece and says, "Let's look for another pink piece." When Annie seems frustrated, he places two interlocking pieces near each other so that she will notice them, and when Annie succeeds, he offers words of encouragement. As Annie gradually gets the hang of it, he steps back and lets her work more and more independently.

tools of intellectual adaptation
Vygotsky's term for methods of thinking and problem-solving strategies that children internalize from their interactions with more competent members of society.

zone of proximal development
Vygotsky's term for the range of tasks that are too complex to be mastered alone but can be accomplished with guidance and encouragement from a more skillful partner.

scaffolding
process by which an expert, when instructing a novice, responds contingently to the novice's behavior in a learning situation, so that the novice gradually increases his or her understanding of a problem.

The Zone of Proximal Development

How do collaborative dialogues foster cognitive growth? First, Vygotsky would say that Annie and her father are operating in what he called the **zone of proximal development**—the difference between what a learner can accomplish independently and what he or she can accomplish with the guidance and encouragement of a more skilled partner. It is this zone in which sensitive instruction should be aimed and in which new cognitive growth can be expected to occur. Annie obviously becomes a more competent puzzle-solver with her father's help than without it. More importantly, she will internalize the problem-solving techniques that she uses in collaboration with him and will ultimately use them on her own, rising to a new level of independent mastery.

One feature of social collaboration that fosters cognitive growth is **scaffolding,** the tendency of more expert participants to carefully tailor the support they provide to the novice learner's current situation so that he can profit from that support and increase his understanding of a problem. Scaffolding occurs not just in formal educational settings, but any time a more expert person adjusts her input to guide a child

According to Vygotsky, new skills are often easier to acquire if children receive guidance and encouragement from a more competent associate.

to a level near the limits of his capabilities. The behavior of Annie's father in the preceding example reflects not only working in the zone of proximal development, but also scaffolding.

Consider another example of effective scaffolding observed in a recent research project (Bjorklund & Reubens, 1997). Five-year old Jennifer and her mother were playing a game of "Chutes and Ladders," using dice to compute their moves. On her first move, Jennifer threw the dice and just stared at them, said nothing, and then looked at her mother. Her mother asked, "How many is that?" Jennifer shrugged, and her mother said, "Count them." Jennifer shrugged again, and her mother then pointed to the dots on the first die saying, "One, two, three," then to the dots on the second die, saying "four, five. You have five. Now you count them." Jennifer complied, pointing to each dot as she counted out loud, and then moved her piece ahead five spaces on the board. This same kind of dialogue continued for six more moves. Finally, Jennifer threw the dice and counted the dots herself, without any prodding from her mother, and continued to do so, on both her and her mother's turns. The mother then adjusted her scaffolding, correcting Jennifer when she made a mistake counting; but she became less and less directive as Jennifer took more of the responsibility for the game herself.

Apprenticeship in Thinking and Guided Participation

In many cultures, children do not learn by going to school with other children, nor do their parents formally teach such lessons as weaving and hunting. Instead, they learn through **guided participation**—by actively *participating* in culturally relevant activities alongside more skilled partners who provide necessary aid and encouragement (Rogoff, 1997; Rogoff et al., 1993). Guided participation is an informal "apprenticeship in thinking" in which children's cognitions are shaped as they partake, alongside adults or other more skillful associates, in such everyday culturally relevant tasks as preparing food, tracking prey, washing clothes, harvesting crops, or simply conversing about the world around them. Barbara Rogoff believes that cognitive growth is shaped as much or more by these informal adult–child transactions as it is by more formal teaching or educational experiences.

The idea of an apprenticeship or guided participation may seem reasonable in cultures where children are integrated early into the daily activities of adult life, such as the agrarian Mayans of Guatemala and Mexico, or the !Kung of Africa whose hunting-and-gathering lifestyle has remained virtually unchanged for thousands of years. But this idea is not as easily grasped for a culture such as our own, because many aspects of cognitive development in Western culture have shifted from parents to professional educators, whose job it is to teach important cultural knowledge and skills to children. Nevertheless, learning certainly occurs at home in modern societies, particularly during the preschool years. And in many ways, these home learning experiences prepare children for the schooling that will follow. For example, formal education in the United

guided participation
adult–child interactions in which children's cognitions and modes of thinking are shaped as they participate with or observe adults engaged in culturally relevant activities.

States and Europe involves children responding to adults' questions when the adults already know the answers. It also involves learning and discussing things that have no immediate relevance—knowledge for knowledge's sake. Such **context-independent learning,** foreign to so many cultures, is fostered from infancy and early childhood in our own culture (Rogoff, 1990). Consider the following interchange between 19-month-old Brittany and her mother:

MOTHER Brittany, what's at the park?

BRITTANY Babyswing.

MOTHER That's right, the babyswing. And what else?

BRITTANY (shrugs)

MOTHER A slide?

BRITTANY (smiling, nods yes)

MOTHER And what else is at the park?

BRITTANY (shrugs)

MOTHER A see . . .

BRITTANY See-saw!

MOTHER That's right, a see-saw.

This type of conversation is typical for an American mother and her child, and it is a good example of Vygotsky's zone of proximal development. Brittany, in this case, was not only learning to recall specific objects with her mother's help, but was also learning the importance of remembering information *out of context* (mother and daughter were in their living room at the time, miles from the park). Brittany was learning that she could be called upon to state facts to her mother that her mother already knew. She was also learning that she could depend on her mother to help provide answers when she was unable to generate them herself. Yet, as Box 7.5 illustrates; the guided participation that children in traditional cultures experience is often much less verbal and less directive than that which is typical of Western societies.

It is easy to think of cognitive development as something that "just happens" exactly the same way for children worldwide. After all, evolution has provided all humans with a uniquely human nervous system, and virtually no one would deny that the center of our flexible intelligence is the brain. Yet intelligence is also rooted in the environment, particularly in the culture. Understanding how cultural beliefs and technological tools influence cognitive development through child-rearing practices helps us better comprehend the process of development and our role as guides in fostering that process.

Implications for Education

Vygotsky's theory has some rather obvious implications for education. Like Piaget, Vygotsky stressed active rather than passive learning and took great care to assess what the learner already knew, thereby estimating what he was capable of learning. The major difference in approaches concerns the role of the instructor. Whereas students in Piaget's classroom would spend more time in independent, discovery-based activities, teachers in Vygotsky's classroom would favor guided participations in which they structure the learning activity, provide helpful hints or instructions that are carefully tailored to the child's current abilities, and then monitor the learner's progress, gradually turning over more of the mental activity to their pupils. Teachers may also arrange *cooperative learning exercises* in which students are encouraged to assist each other; the idea here is that the less competent members of the team are likely to benefit from the instruction they receive from their more skillful peers, who also benefit by playing the role of teacher (Palinscar, Brown, & Campione, 1993).

context-independent learning
learning that has no immediate relevance to the present context, as is done in modern schools; acquiring knowledge for knowledge's sake.

7.5

CULTURAL INFLUENCES

Working in the Zone of Proximal Development in Different Cultures

Although the process of guided participation may be universal, how it is carried out varies from culture to culture. Rogoff and her colleagues (1993) have classified cultures into two general types: (1) cultures such as ours, where, beginning in the preschool years, children are often segregated from adults and receive much culturally important information in school; and (2) cultures where children are in close contact most of the day with adults, observing and interacting with them while they perform culturally important activities. Rogoff then observed 14 families with toddlers in each of four communities, two where culturally important information is transmitted mainly "out of context," through formal schooling (Salt Lake City, in the United States, and Kecioren, a middle-class community in Turkey), and two where culturally important information is transmitted mainly in context (the Guatemalan Mayan town of San Pedro and Dhol-Ki-Patti, a tribal village in India). Toddlers and their caregivers were observed while performing routine activities (for example, feeding, dressing), playing social games (for example, peekaboo), and playing with novel objects (for example, an embroidery hoop, a jumping jack—a marionette that kicks its legs). The following excerpts are two examples of guided participation, one from the middle-class community in Salt Lake City, and the other from the tribal Indian village of Dhol-Ki-Patti.

Salt Lake City: A 21-month-old boy and his mother, exploring a glass jar that contains a peewee doll.

Sandy's mother held the jar up and chirped excitedly, "What is it? What's inside?" and then pointed to the peewee doll inside. "Is that a little person?" When Sandy pulled down on the jar, she suggested, "Can you take the lid off?"

Sandy inspected the round knob on top and said, "Da ball."

"Da ball, yeah," his mother confirmed. "Pull the lid, she encouraged, and demonstrated pulling on the knob. "Can you pull?" Sandy put his hand on hers, and they pulled the lid off together triumphantly. "What's inside?" asked his mother, and took the peewee out. "Who is that?"

Sandy reached for the lid, and mother provided running commentary. "OK you put the lid back on." And when Sandy exclaimed "Oh!" his mother repeated "Oh!" after him. When Sandy lost interest, his mother asked with mock disappointment, "Oh, you don't want to play anymore?" and suggested, "We could make him play peekaboo."

When Sandy took the peewee out, she asked "Where did she go?" and sang, "There, she's all gone, as she covered the peewee with her hands, "Aaall gone." (Rogoff et al., 1993, p. 81)

Dhol-Ki-Patti, India: An 18-month-old girl and her mother, playing with a jumping jack.

Roopa was not holding the top and bottom strings taut enough to cause the jumping jack to jump, so her mother took Roopa's hand in her own, grasped the bottom string with both hands, and pulled on the string twice, saying, "Pull here, pull here," as she demonstrated. She then released her hold of Roopa's hand to enable Roopa to do it on her own.

But the jumping jack fell to the ground because Roopa was not holding it tight. The mother, quick to help, lifted the jumping jack as Roopa reached for it. Twice again, she pulled on the bottom string with her left hand, repeating, "Pull it here." Then she released her hold, letting Roopa take the object. She held her hands close to (but not touching) Roopa's, ready to help if necessary. (Rogoff et al., 1993, p. 114)

Although toddlers and caregivers in all communities interacted in ways permitting all participants to develop an understanding of the task at hand, there were important differences between the middle-class and more traditional communities. As illustrated in these examples, parents in Salt Lake City (and the Turkish town) placed a far greater emphasis on verbal than nonverbal instruction, with the adults providing a good deal of structure to foster children's involvement in learning, including praise and other techniques to motivate their charges. By contrast, parents in the Mayan and Indian villages used more explicit *nonverbal* communication and only occasionally instructed their children in a particular task. In these communities, children are around adults most of the day, and they can observe competent adult behavior and interact with adults while they perform the important tasks of their society. Rogoff et al. concluded that children's observation skills are more important and better developed in traditional than in middle-class communities, with children in the traditional communities being better at learning by attending to adult behavior.

Rogoff's findings make it clear that there is not one single path to becoming an effective member of society, and that different forms of guided participation are likely to be used, depending on the requirements culture places upon adults and children. One form is not necessarily better than another. It depends on how a competent adult in a society is expected to behave and on what skills a competent child is expected to acquire.

Is there any evidence that Vygotsky's collaborative-learning approach might be a particularly effective educational strategy? Consider what Lisa Freund (1990) found when she had 3- to 5-year-olds help a puppet decide which furnishings (for example, sofas, beds, bathtubs, and stoves) should be placed in each of six rooms of a dollhouse that the puppet was moving into. First, children were tested to determine what they already knew about proper furniture placement. Then each child worked at a similar task, either alone (as might be the case in Piaget's discovery-based classroom) or with his or her mother (Vygotsky's guided learning). Then to assess what they had learned, children performed a final, rather complex, furniture-sorting task. The results were clear: Children who had sorted furniture with help from their mothers showed dramatic improvements in sorting ability, whereas those who had practiced on their own showed little improvement at all, even though they had received some corrective feedback from the experimenter (see also Diaz et al., 1991; Rogoff, 1997).

Similar advances in problem-solving skills have been reported when children collaborate with peers, as opposed to working alone (Azmitia, 1992; Gauvain & Rogoff, 1989; Johnson & Johnson, 1987), and the youngsters who gain the most from these collaborations are those who were initially much less competent than their partners (Azmitia, 1988; Tudge, 1992). Johnson and Johnson (1987) conducted an analysis of 378 studies that compared achievement of people working alone versus cooperatively and found that cooperative learning resulted in superior performance in more than half of the studies; by contrast, working alone resulted in improved performance in fewer than 10% of the studies.

There appear to be at least three reasons why cooperative learning is effective. First, children are often more motivated when working problems together (Johnson & Johnson, 1989). Second, cooperative learning requires children to explain their ideas to one another and to resolve conflicts. These activities help young collaborators to examine their own ideas more closely and to become better at articulating them so that they can be understood. Finally, children are more likely to use high-quality cognitive strategies while working together—strategies that often lead to ideas and solutions that no one in the group would likely have generated alone (Johnson & Johnson, 1989).

As with other aspects of sociocultural theory, the effectiveness of collaborative learning varies by culture. American children, accustomed to competitive "do your own work" classrooms, sometimes find it difficult to adjust to the shared decision making found in cooperative learning (see Rogoff, 1997), although they get better at cooperative decision making with practice (Socha & Socha, 1994). As the structure of schools changes to support peer collaboration, with teachers' roles being that of active participants in the children's learning experiences and not simply directors of it, the benefits of cooperative learning are sure to increase (Rogoff, 1997).

So children do not always learn more when they function as solitary explorers, seeking discoveries on their own, as Piaget implied. Often, conceptual growth springs more readily from children's interactions with other people, particularly with competent people who provide just the amount of guidance and encouragement the individual needs. Those people may be parents, teachers, or peers, and the effectiveness of these collaborators will vary depending on their skills at scaffolding and working within the zone of proximal development.

The Role of Language in Cognitive Development

From Vygotsky's viewpoint, language plays two critical roles in cognitive development by (1) serving as the primary vehicle through which adults pass culturally valued modes of thinking and problem solving on to their children, and (2) eventually becoming one of the more powerful "tools" of intellectual adaptation in its own right. As it turns out, Vygotsky's perspective on language and thinking contrasts sharply with that of Piaget.

Piaget's Theory of Language and Thought

Piaget was very interested in children's language, and he observed that infants' first words were typically centered on objects and activities that they already understood through nonverbal sensorimotor processes. He then concluded that language clearly illustrates the child's *existing* schemes but plays no meaningful role in shaping thought or helping the child to construct new knowledge.

As he recorded the chatterings of preschool children, Piaget (1926) noticed that they often talked *to themselves* as they went about their daily activities, almost as if they were play-by-play announcers ("Put the big piece in the corner. Not that one, the pink one"). Indeed, two preschool children playing close to each other sometimes carried on their own separate monologues rather than truly conversing. Piaget called these self-directed utterances **egocentric speech**—talk not addressed to anyone in particular and not adapted in any meaningful way so that a companion might understand it.

What part might such speech play in a child's cognitive development? Very little, according to Piaget, who saw egocentric speech as merely reflecting the child's ongoing mental activity. However, he did observe that speech becomes progressively more social and less egocentric toward the end of the preoperational stage, which he attributed to the child's increasing ability to assume the perspective of others and thus adapt her speech so that listeners might understand. So here was another example of how cognitive development (a decline in egocentrism) was said to promote language development (a shift from egocentric to communicative speech), rather than the other way around.

Vygotsky's Theory of Language and Thought

Vygotsky agreed with Piaget that the child's earliest thinking is prelinguistic and that early language often reflects what the child already knows. However, he argued that thought and language eventually merge and that many of the nonsocial utterances that Piaget called "egocentric" actually illustrate the transition from prelinguistic to verbal reasoning.

According to Vygotsky, a preschool child's self-directed monologues occur more often in some contexts than in others. Specifically, Vygotsky observed that children are more likely to talk to themselves as they attempt to solve problems or achieve important goals, and he claimed that this nonsocial speech increased dramatically whenever these young problem solvers encountered obstacles in pursuing their objectives. He then concluded that nonsocial speech is not egocentric but communicative; it is a "speech for self," or **private speech**, that helps young children to plan strategies and regulate their behavior so that they are more likely to accomplish their goals. Viewed through this theoretical lens, language may thus play a critical role in cognitive development by making children more organized and efficient problem solvers! Vygotsky also claimed that private speech becomes more abbreviated with age, progressing from the whole phrases that 4-year-olds produce, to single words, to simple lip movements that are more common among 7- to 9-year-olds. His view was that private speech never completely disappears; it serves as a **cognitive self-guidance system** and then goes "underground," becoming silent or *inner speech*—the covert verbal thought that we use to organize and regulate our everyday activities.

egocentric speech
Piaget's term for the subset of a young child's utterances that are nonsocial—that is, neither directed to others nor expressed in ways that listeners might understand.

private speech
Vygotsky's term for the subset of a child's verbal utterances that serve a self-communicative function and guide the child's thinking.

cognitive self-guidance system
in Vygotsky's theory, the use of private speech to guide problem-solving behavior.

Which Viewpoint Should We Endorse?

Studies conducted by Vygotsky and other researchers (see Berk, 1992) side squarely with Vygotsky's theory over that of Piaget. It seems that the *social speech* that occurs during guided learning episodes (for example, the conversation between Annie and her father as they worked jointly on a puzzle) gives rise to much of the *private speech* (Annie's talking aloud as she tries to work the puzzle on her own) that preschool children display. Also consistent with Vygotsky's claims, children rely more heavily on private

WHAT DO YOU THINK? ?

Starting at a pupil's current level of mastery, many computer-assisted instructional programs present increasingly difficult problems, often diagnosing errors and intervening with hints or clues when progress has broken down. Why might both Piaget and Vygotsky see some merit in supplementing traditional classroom instruction with these computer-assisted learning activities?

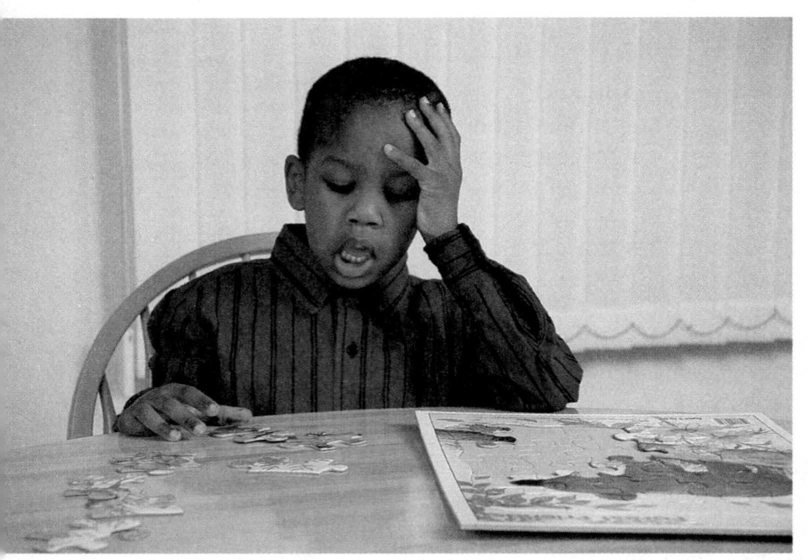

According to Vygotsky, private speech is an important tool used by preschool and young grade-school children to plan and regulate their problem-solving activities.

speech when facing difficult rather than easy tasks and deciding how to proceed after making errors (Berk, 1992), and their performance often improves after using self-instruction (Behrend, Rosengren, & Perlmutter, 1989; Berk & Spuhl, 1995). Furthermore, it is the brighter preschool children who rely most heavily on private speech, a finding that links this "self-talk" to cognitive *competence* rather than the cognitive immaturity (egocentrism) that Piaget claimed it represents (Berk, 1992; Kohlberg, Yaeger, & Hjertholm, 1968). Finally, private speech does eventually go underground, progressing from words and phrases to whispers and mutterings, to inner speech (Bivens & Berk, 1990), and this internalization process occurs earlier among the brighter members of an elementary school class (Berk & Landau, 1993; Kohlberg et al., 1968).

So private speech does appear to be an important tool of intellectual adaptation—a means by which children plan and regulate their mental activities to solve problems and make new discoveries (Vygotsky, 1934/1962).

Vygotsky in Perspective: Summary and Evaluation

Vygotsky's sociocultural theory offers a new lens through which to view cognitive development by stressing the importance of specific social processes that Piaget (and others) largely overlooked. According to Vygotsky, children's minds develop as they (1) take part in cooperative dialogues with skilled partners on tasks that are within their zone of proximal development, and (2) incorporate what skillful tutors say to them into what they say to themselves. As social speech is translated into private speech and then inner speech, the culture's preferred methods of thinking and problem solving—or tools of intellectual adaptation—work their way from the language of competent tutors into the child's own thinking.

Unlike Piaget, who stressed *universal* sequences of cognitive growth, Vygotsky's theory leads us to expect wide variations in cognitive development across cultures that reflect differences in children's cultural experiences. So children in Western cultures acquire context-independent memory and reasoning skills that prepare them for highly structured Western classrooms, whereas children of Australian and African Bushmen hunters acquire elaborate spatial reasoning skills that prepare them to successfully track the prey on which their lives absolutely depend. Neither set of cognitive capacities is necessarily any more "advanced" than the other; instead, they represent alternative forms of reasoning, or "tools of adaptation," that have evolved because they enable children to adapt successfully to cultural values and traditions (Rogoff, 1997; Vygotsky, 1978).

Concept Check 7.3
Understanding Vygotsky's Sociocultural Theory

Check your understanding of some of the basic premises of Vygotsky's theory by matching each of the following concepts with the descriptions listed below. The concepts are: (a) tools of intellectual adaptation, (b) private speech, (c) zone of proximal development, (d) elementary mental functions, (e) guided participation, (f) scaffolding. The answers appear in the Appendix.

_____ 1. important means of planning and self-regulation
_____ 2. problems that children cannot master alone but can master with skillful guidance
_____ 3. informal means by which culturally significant cognitive processes are transferred across generations
_____ 4. sensitive tailoring of guidance to a novice learner's capabilities
_____ 5. that which is transformed in the context of collaborative activities with more skillful associates
_____ 6. culturally significant cognitive processes and methods of problem solving

Table 7.4 Comparing Vygotsky's and Piaget's Theories of Cognitive Development

Vygotsky's sociocultural theory	Piaget's cognitive-developmental theory
1. Cognitive development varies across cultures.	Cognitive development is mostly universal across cultures.
2. Cognitive growth stems from social interactions (from guided learning within the zone of proximal development as children and their partners "co-construct" knowledge).	Cognitive development stems largely from independent explorations in which children construct knowledge on their own.
3. Social processes become individual-psychological processes (for example, social speech becomes private speech and, eventually, inner speech).	Individual (egocentric) processes become social processes (for example, egocentric speech is adapted in ways to allow more effective communication).
4. Adults are especially important as change agents (by transmitting their culture's tools of intellectual adaptation that children internalize).	Peers are especially important as change agents (because peer contacts promote social perspective taking, a topic we will explore in detail in Chapter 12).

As we see in Table 7.4, Vygotsky's theory challenges many of Piaget's most basic assumptions and has attracted a lot of attention lately among Western developmentalists, whose own research efforts tend to support his ideas. Yet many of Vygotsky's writings are only now being translated from Russian to other languages (Wertsch & Tulviste, 1992), and his theory has not received the intense scrutiny that Piaget's theory has. Nevertheless, at least some of his ideas have already been challenged. Barbara Rogoff (1990, 1997), for example, argues that guided participations that rely heavily on the kinds of verbal instruction that Vygotsky emphasized may be less adaptive in some cultures or less useful for some forms of learning than for others. A young child learning to stalk prey in Australia's outback or to plant, care for, and harvest rice in Southeast Asia may profit more from observation and practice than from verbal instruction and encouragement (see also Rogoff et al., 1993). Other investigators are finding that collaborative problem solving among peers does not always benefit the collaborators and may actually *undermine* task performance if the more competent collaborator is not very confident about what he knows or fails to adapt his instruction to a partner's level of understanding (Levin & Druyan, 1993; Tudge, 1992). But despite whatever criticism his theory may generate in the years ahead, Vygotsky has provided a valuable service by reminding us that cognitive growth, like all other aspects of development, is best understood when studied in the cultural and social contexts in which it occurs.

SUMMARY

♦ This and the following two chapters are devoted to an examination of **cognition,** the mental processes by which humans acquire and use knowledge, and to **cognitive development.**

Piaget's Theory of Cognitive Development

♦ Piaget's theory of **genetic epistemology** (cognitive development) defines **intelligence** as a basic life function that helps the child to adapt to the environment. Piaget described children as active explorers who **construct** three kinds of **schemes (behavioral, symbolic, and operational)** to establish **cognitive equilibrium** between their thinking and their experiences. Schemes are constructed and modified through the processes of **organization** and **adaptation.** Adaptation consists of two complementary activities: **assimilation** (attempts to fit new experiences to existing schemes) and **accommodation** (modifying existing schemes in response to new experiences). Cognitive growth results as assimilations stimulate accommodations, which induce the reorganization of schemes, permitting further assimilations, and so on.

Piaget's Stages of Cognitive Development

♦ Piaget claimed that intellectual growth proceeds through an **invariant sequence** of stages that can be summarized as follows.

♦ **Sensorimotor period** (0 to 2 years). From basic **reflex activity,** infants over the first 2 years come to know and understand objects and events by acting on them, constructing **primary, secondary,** and **tertiary circular reactions.** These behavioral schemes are eventually internalized to form mental symbols that support such achievements as **inner experimentation.** Although Piaget's general sequences of sensorimotor development have been confirmed, recent evidence indicates that Piaget's explanation of **A-not-B errors** was incorrect and that infants achieve such milestones as **deferred imitation** and **object permanence** earlier than Piaget thought.

♦ **Preoperational period** (roughly 2 to 7 years). Symbolic reasoning increases dramatically as children in the **preconceptual period** rely on **symbolic function** and display **representational insight.** Symbolism gradually becomes more sophisticated as children acquire a capacity for **dual representation.** However, Piaget described the thinking of 2- to 7-year-olds as **animistic** and **egocentric,** characterized by **centration** and **precausal (transductive) reasoning.** Although preoperational children often fail to make **appearance/reality distinctions,** recent research indicates that they are much more logical and less egocentric when thinking about familiar issues or about simplified versions of Piaget's tests. Furthermore, procedures such as **identity training** enable preoperational children to solve complex problems such as Piaget's **conservation** tasks. So preschool children possess an early capacity for logical reasoning that Piaget overlooked.

♦ **Concrete operations** (7 to 11 years). During concrete operations, children acquire such cognitive operations as **decentration** and **reversibility** that enable them to think logically and systematically about tangible objects, events, and experiences. Becoming operational in their thinking permits children to conserve, **seriate,** display **transitivity,** and understand the logical necessity of **class inclusion** and whole/part relations. However, concrete operators can only apply their logic to real or tangible aspects of experience and cannot reason abstractly.

♦ **Formal operations** (11 or 12 and beyond). Formal-operational reasoning is rational, abstract, and much like the **hypothetico-deductive** reasoning of a scientist. Attainment of formal operations may sometimes contribute to confusion, idealism, and such phenomena as the **imaginary audience** and **personal fable.** Formal operations may elude those adolescents and adults who have not been exposed to educational experiences that foster this reasoning. And even at this highest level, performance is uneven: Adults are most likely to display formal operations in areas of special interest or expertise.

An Evaluation of Piaget's Theory

♦ Piaget founded the field of cognitive development and provided the first theory that purported to explain and not simply describe cognitive growth. Many important principles about developing children were discovered by Piaget, who influenced thousands of researchers in psychology and related fields.

♦ Although Piaget seems to have adequately described general sequences of intellectual development, his tendency to infer underlying competencies from intellectual performances often led him to underestimate children's cognitive capabilities. Some investigators have challenged Piaget's assumption that development occurs in stages, whereas others have criticized his theory for failing to specify how children progress from one stage of intellect to the next, and for underestimating social and cultural influences on intellectual development.

Vygotsky's Sociocultural Perspective

♦ Vygotsky's **sociocultural theory** emphasizes social and cultural influences on intellectual growth. Each culture transmits beliefs, values, and preferred methods of thinking or problem solving—its **tools of intellectual adaptation**—to each successive generation. Thus, culture teaches children what to think and how to go about it.

♦ Children acquire cultural beliefs, values, and problem-solving strategies in the context of collaborative dialogues with more skillful partners as they gradually internalize their tutor's instructions to master tasks within their **zone of proximal development.** Learning occurs best when more skillful associates properly **scaffold** their intervention. Much of what children acquire from more skillful associates occurs through **guided participation,** a process that may be highly **context-independent** (in Western cultures) or may occur in the context of day-to-day activities (as is most common in traditional cultures).

♦ Unlike Piaget, who argued that children's self-talk, or **egocentric speech,** plays little if any role in constructing new knowledge, Vygotsky claimed that a child's **private speech** becomes a **cognitive self-guidance system** that regulates problem-solving activities and is eventually internalized to become covert, verbal thought. Recent research favors Vygotsky's position over Piaget's, suggesting that language plays a most important role in children's intellectual development.

♦ Vygotsky has provided a valuable service by reminding us that cognitive growth is best understood when studied in the social and cultural contexts in which it occurs. Although this theory has fared well to date, it has yet to receive the intense scrutiny that Piaget's theory has.

One of the cornerstone theories of cognitive development during early childhood is the theory developed by Jean Piaget. A visit to: http://snycorva.cortland.edu/~andersmd/piaget/open.html will allow you to work through an online tutorial that covers the four stages of cognitive development Piaget proposed. The same site also provides a short history of Piaget and a description of his biological theory of knowledge construction.

KEY TERMS

cognition, 229
cognitive development, 229
genetic epistemology, 229
intelligence, 229
cognitive equilibrium, 230
constructivist, 230
scheme, 230
behavioral schemes, 230
symbolic schemes, 231
cognitive operation, 231
organization, 232
adaptation, 232
assimilation, 232
accommodation, 232
invariant developmental sequence, 233
sensorimotor stage, 234
reflex activity, 234
primary circular reactions, 234
secondary circular reactions, 235
coordination of secondary circular reactions, 235
tertiary circular reactions, 235
inner experimentation, 235
deferred imitation, 236
object permanence, 236
A-not-B error, 237
preoperational stage, 239
representational insight, 239
preconceptual period, 240
symbolic function, 240
dual representation (dual encoding; dual orientation), 241
animism, 243
precausal, or transductive, reasoning, 243
egocentrism, 243
appearance/reality distinction, 244
intuitive period, 245
centered thinking (or centration), 245
class inclusion, 245
conservation, 245
decentration, 246
reversibility, 246
identity training, 248
concrete operations, 249
mental seriation, 250
transitivity, 250
horizontal decalage, 250
formal operations, 251
hypothetico-deductive reasoning, 252
imaginary audience, 254
personal fable, 254
sociocultural theory, 259
tools of intellectual adaptation, 260
zone of proximal development, 260
scaffolding, 260
guided participation, 261
context-independent learning, 262
egocentric speech, 265
private speech, 265
cognitive self-guidance system, 265

8

Cognitive Development: Information-Processing Perspectives

Piaget's and Vygotsky's theories have had a profound influence on our current understanding of cognitive development. Piaget saw children as active agents in their own development, always constructing knowledge and changing their cognitive structures to better understand the world. Vygotsky saw children as active participants in collaborative arrangements with others, acquiring the tools of thought appropriate for their culture. Yet, the shortcomings of those approaches led many cognitive scholars to believe that a fresh outlook on human cognition was necessary.

Then came the digital computer—a wondrous new invention that intrigued many scientists with its capacity for rapidly and systematically converting input (or information) into output (answers and solutions). Might the operations of a computer be similar in certain respects to the workings of the human mind? Proponents of a third influential viewpoint on cognitive development—the *information-processing perspective*—certainly thought so (Klahr & MacWhinney, 1997; Newell & Simon, 1961).

How is the human mind similar to a computer? One way is that both the mind and a computer have a *limited capacity* for processing information, associated with their hardware and software. Computer *hardware* is the machine itself—its keyboard (or input system), storage capacity, and logic units. The mind's "hardware" is the nervous system, including the brain, the sensory receptors, and their neural connections. The computer's *software* consists of the programs used to store and manipulate information—word-processing, statistics programs, and the like. The mind, too, has its software—rules, strategies, and other "mental programs" that specify how information is registered, interpreted, stored, retrieved, and analyzed.

This mind–computer analogy, then, provided the framework that information-processing theorists used to model human cognition and to provide some clues about age-related changes in children's ability to gather, store, and use information to "construct" knowledge and solve problems. Pursuing the analogy, computers have become much more sophisticated over the years. Not only have hardware improvements allowed modern computers to register and store far more information than their predecessors, but they can also perform more operations faster and more efficiently because of improvements in software. Information-processing theorists suggest that the same may be true of the developing mind. As children's brains and nervous systems mature (hardware improvements) and they adopt new strategies for attending to information, interpreting it, remembering what they have experienced, and monitoring their mental activities (software improvements), they should be able to perform increasingly complex cognitive feats with greater speed and accuracy (Bjorklund, 1995).

As we will see throughout this chapter, developmental changes in the mind's hardware and software do contribute to cognitive growth, although often in interaction with one another in ways that may not be obvious. Clearly, the information-processing perspective has proved to be a most useful and influential approach that has helped us to understand developmental changes in children's thinking.

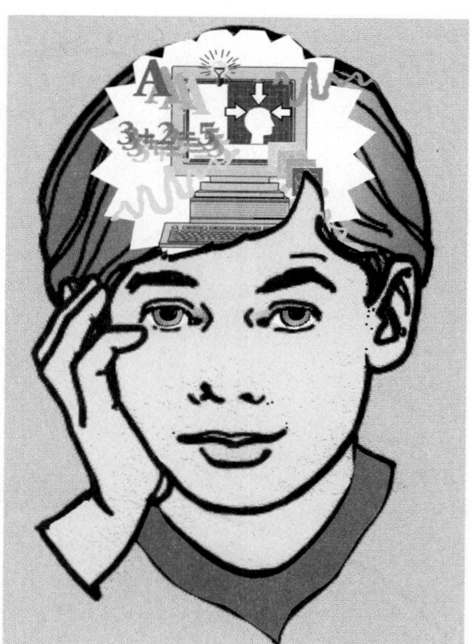

The mind-as-computer analogy provided the framework that information-processing theorists used to model human cognition.

BASIC ASSUMPTIONS OF INFORMATION-PROCESSING THEORIES

There is no single information-processing theory of cognition or cognitive development. Rather, the information-processing approach is best described as a framework for understanding cognition that is built on a set of assumptions concerning how humans acquire and use information.

The Limited-Capacity Assumption

Perhaps the most obvious assumption of information-processing approaches is that people *process* information: That is, they register, store, retrieve, and operate on input in order to "know" it or use it to solve problems. We may act on an external stimulus in order to make sense of it (such as interpreting the writing on this page), or we may act on information that already resides in our heads (for example, retrieving information to remind ourselves that Labor Day is the first Monday in September). These mental actions can be referred to as operations, control processes, strategies, or programs. Each of these terms refers to activities we undertake to make sense of information or, in other words, to think.

Most central to the information-processing approaches is the idea of *limited capacity*. Simply stated, the limited-capacity assumption implies that there are constraints on how much information we can think about at any one time, how long we can hold information in mind before it is lost, and how quickly we can process information.

The relation between capacity constraints and cognitive performance has received much attention from information-processing theorists (Hasher & Zacks, 1979; Shiffrin & Schneider, 1977). In order to execute a strategy (for example, adding the numbers 377 and 949), one must use a portion of one's limited mental resources. Some operations require more of these limited resources (require more "effort") than others, and any particular operation consumes fewer resources (that is, becomes less effortful) with practice. As processing becomes truly efficient, it is done *automatically,* without conscious awareness. So those of us who have learned to drive a standard-shift automobile no longer need to consciously represent all of the motions involved in successfully shifting gears. Rather, we execute this strategy without really thinking about the component activities.

At the outset, then, most cognitive operations consume a great deal of our limited mental resources and are very effortful. With practice, those same operations require less and less mental effort, leaving more mental resources available for the execution of other operations.

Information Flow and the Store Model

What happens as a person notices information and retains it for future use? Richard Atkinson and Richard Shiffrin (1968) assumed that information flows through a series of separate but interrelated set of processing units, or stores, and they formulated a **store model** to describe the process. A slightly modified and updated version of the important and influential model appears in Figure 8.1.

As we see in the figure, the first of these components is the **sensory store** (or **sensory register**). This is the system's log-in unit; it simply holds raw sensory input as a kind of "afterimage" (or echo) of what you have sensed. There are separate sensory registers for each sense modality, and presumably they can hold large quantities of information, but only for very brief periods of time. The contents of sensory stores are thus extremely volatile and soon disappear without further processing.

Should you attend to this information, however, it passes into the **short-term store (STS),** a processing unit that can store a limited amount of information (perhaps five to nine pieces) for several seconds. Thus, the capacity of the short-term store is sufficient to allow you to retain a telephone number for perhaps as long as it takes you to dial it. But unless this information is rehearsed or otherwise operated on, it too is soon lost. The short-term store has also been referred to as the *primary memory,* or *working memory,* because all conscious intellectual activity is thought to take place here. So short-term, or "working," memory has two functions: (1) to store information temporarily so that (2) you can do something with it.

store model
information-processing model that depicts information as flowing through three processing units (or stores): the sensory store, the short-term store (STS), and the long-term store (LTS).

sensory store (or sensory register)
first information-processing store, in which stimuli are noticed and are briefly available for further processing.

short-term store (STS)
second information-processing store, in which stimuli are retained for several seconds and operated upon (also called *working memory*).

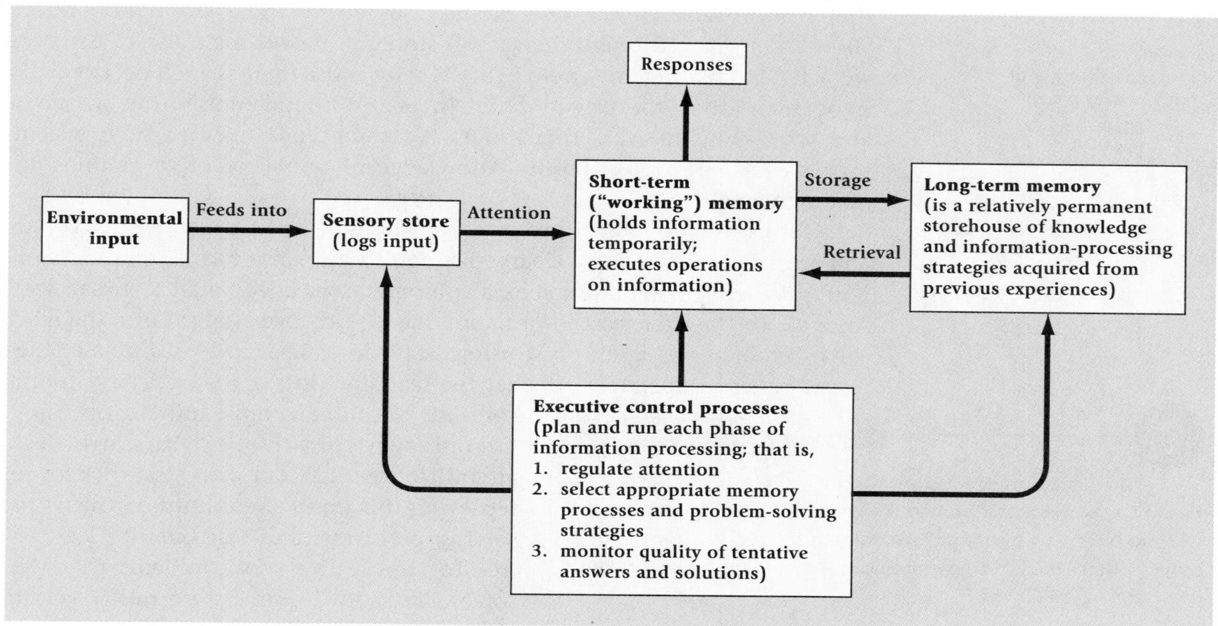

Figure 8.1 *A schematic model of the human information processing system.* ADAPTED FROM ATKINSON & SHIFFRIN, *1968.*

Finally, new information that is operated on while in the short-term store passes into the **long-term store (LTS)**—a vast and relatively permanent storehouse of information that includes your knowledge of the world, your impressions of past experiences and events, and the strategies that you use to process information and solve problems.

Let's briefly consider an example of how information might move, or flow, between the various stores of your cognitive system. Suppose that you are taking notes in your history class and you hear the instructor mention that the U.S. Constitution was ratified in 1789. Since this date is one you may need to remember, you attend to it. Consequently, the information flows from your sensory register into your short-term store, where it is *encoded* and remains long enough for you to write it in your notebook. As you later study your notes in preparation for an upcoming exam, you will probably review this information several times and eventually register it in your long-term store, where it remains until you need it while taking your test.

Now imagine that you are asked how many years have passed between the signing of the Declaration of Independence (1776, remember?) and the ratification of the Constitution. The first step, of course, is to log in, attend to, and correctly interpret the problem. You must then search long-term memory for the two dates in question and also locate your stored knowledge of the mathematical operation of subtraction. Now you must transfer all this information to short-term, or working, memory so that you can "execute" your subtraction program (1789 minus 1776) to derive the correct answer.

Metacognition: How Humans Control Cognitive Processes

Notice that to process information *successfully* and use it to solve problems, you have to know what you are doing and make the right decisions. Had you not known to log the significance of the year 1789 in your notebook, this information would have soon been lost under the barrage of names and dates that followed in your history lecture. Had you lacked any knowledge of subtraction or failed to retrieve this "program" from your long-term store, you would have been unable to determine the number of years

long-term store (LTS)
third information-processing store, in which information that has been examined and interpreted is permanently stored for future use.

that passed between the two momentous events. So, information does not simply "flow" on its own through the various stores, or processing units, of the system; instead, we actively channel the input. This is why most models include **executive control processes**—the processes involved in planning and monitoring what you attend to and what you do with this input. We sometimes refer to such executive control processes as **metacognition**—knowledge of one's cognitive abilities and processes relating to thinking.

Our executive control processes are thought to be largely under voluntary control and are, in fact, what most clearly distinguish human information processors from computers. When solving a problem, a computer does a whole lot less than we humans do. After all, the task-relevant information has already been logged into the machine, which solves problems assigned to it using strategies called up by a human "executive" (the programmer or operator). All that the machine does is the necessary computations. By contrast, we humans must initiate, organize, and monitor our own cognitive activities. We decide what to attend to; we select our own strategies for retaining and retrieving this input; we call up our own "programs" for solving problems; and last but not least, we are often free to choose the very problems that we attempt to solve. Clearly, we humans are rather versatile information processors.

WHAT DO YOU THINK?

Information-processing theorists often point to similarities in the workings of human minds and digital computers. In what important ways might the human mind *differ* from a computer? What kinds of thinking might we humans do better than computers can?

Comparisons with Piaget's Theory

Contemporary information-processing theorists differ from Piaget in many ways. Most take exception to Piaget's notion of cognitive stages. Rather than viewing younger children as qualitatively different kinds of thinkers than older children (Piaget's view), many information-processing theorists claim that cognitive development is gradual and *quantitative,* reflecting small incremental changes that occur in children's *processing capacity* (or the amount of information that can be held in STS), *processing speed,* and the kinds of strategies and the amount of general knowledge they have acquired and can apply to the problems they encounter (Bjorklund, 1995).

Another critical distinction between Piaget and virtually everyone in the information-processing camp centers on their interpretations of children's intellectual shortcomings. Consider a child who fails a conservation-of-liquids problem, claiming that the taller of two containers now has more liquid. From an information-processing perspective, there are several possible contributors to this logical error. Perhaps the child did not attend to and encode the most pertinent information. Or he might not be able to hold all the relevant information in short-term memory so that he can operate on it. He might also lack certain strategies that would enable him to transfer encoded information to long-term memory or would aid in retrieving knowledge already stored there. Of course, he may not have acquired and retained the critical rules or logical operations needed to solve the problem. And finally, he may lack the executive control processes that would enable him to coordinate all the necessary phases of problem solving to arrive at a logical conclusion. Clearly, this cognitive-processing analysis of the errors people make is much richer and more elaborate than that of Piaget, who generally assumed that the reason people fail at problems is that they lack the "cognitive structures" to solve them.

But Piaget's theory is not totally at odds with information-processing perspectives. For example, both camps see the child as playing an active role in his or her own cognitive development. Furthermore, many information-processing researchers study the growth of logical problem solving and attempt to specify the underlying schemes and strategies on which children rely to generate their solutions. And not all information-processing theorists are opposed to the stage concept (Case, 1992, 1997; Case & Okamoto, 1996; Fischer, 1980). Robbie Case and his colleagues, for example, have devel-

executive control processes
the processes involved in regulating attention and determining what to do with information just gathered or retrieved from long-term memory.

metacognition
one's knowledge about cognition and about the regulation of cognitive activities.

oped an elaborate *neo-Piagetian* model of cognitive development that emphasizes the information-processing mechanisms that children use to solve problems, focusing heavily on age-related changes in working memory and executive control processes. Yet, Case stresses that children's unique experiences and motivation play a role in their intellectual development, causing their thinking within each of his stages to be far less consistent across problems and situations than Piaget thought.

Cognitive psychologists now recognize that information processing is more complex than the Atkinson-Shiffrin store model implies (Bjorklund, 1997). For example, they now appreciate that people, like computers, engage in "parallel processing," carrying out many cognitive activities simultaneously rather than performing operations one step at a time in a sequence. Furthermore, different kinds of processing approaches are used for different problems or domains of knowledge. These latter points can be illustrated by briefly considering a recent alternative (or addendum) to traditional information-processing theories: *fuzzy-trace theory.*

Fuzzy-Trace Theory: An Alternative Viewpoint

Most traditional accounts of human information processing assume that we solve problems by encoding discrete pieces of information and then reasoning about those items. So to solve the problem "How much is 27 + 46," one must encode both numbers precisely and perform the proper mental operations to arrive at a correct answer. Not all of our thinking requires such precision. In fact, most of our thinking about everyday issues may actually be *hindered* somewhat by trying to rely on verbatim information. Instead, we also encode much of what we encounter in very general terms ("The stereo was cheaper at Circuit City than at Service Merchandise") and solve problems using this less-than-exact information ("I'll buy the stereo at Circuit City.").

Charles Brainerd's and Varerie Reyna's (1990, 1993; Reyna & Brainerd, 1995) **fuzzy-trace theory** takes this fact of mental life into account, proposing that there are important developmental differences in how children represent information to solve problems. At the core of fuzzy-trace theory is the idea that memory representations (or *memory traces*) exist on a continuum from literal verbatim representations to vague, fuzzy representations called **gists** that preserve the essential content without all of the precise details. The theory also assumes that gistlike representations, or fuzzy traces, are not merely degraded forms of our verbatim representations. Indeed, we encode both verbatim and fuzzy, gistlike representations of the information we encounter and use whichever representation is easier or more appropriate for the problem we are trying to solve.

Fuzzy and verbatim traces differ in important ways. Compared with verbatim traces, fuzzy traces are more easily accessed and generally require less effort to use. Also, verbatim traces are more susceptible to interference and forgetting than fuzzy traces are. For example, when comparing the price of two sweaters at two stores, the exact prices of the sweaters may be quickly forgotten. More resistant to forgetting, however, will be

fuzzy-trace theory
theory proposed by Brainerd & Reyna that postulates that people encode experiences on a continuum from literal, verbatim traces to fuzzy, gistlike traces.

gist
a fuzzy representation of information that preserves the central content but few precise details.

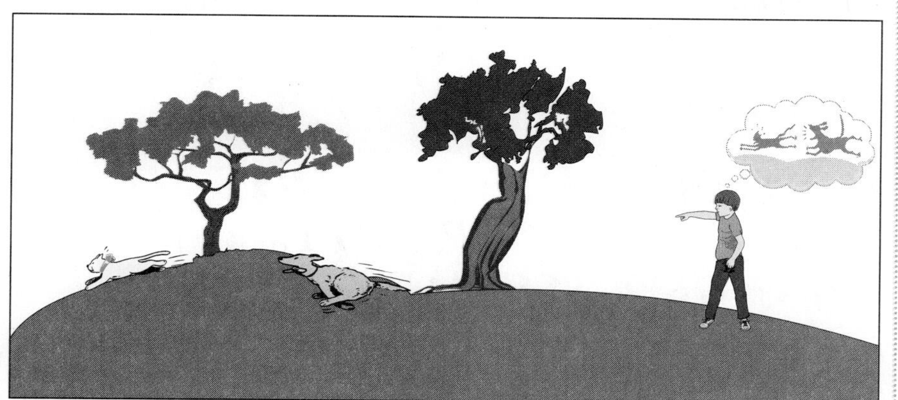

A gistlike representation, or fuzzy trace, preserves the central content of a scene or an event without all the precise details. This boy may remember that he saw a dog chasing a cat without recalling the color of the animals or the fact that the cat wore a red collar.

the information that the sweater at Sears was cheaper than the comparable sweater at JC Penney. If your problem is to decide which sweater is the better buy, you can rely on the gistlike knowledge of the relative price of the two sweaters. If, however, you are trying to decide if you have enough money to purchase either of the sweaters, you will need the verbatim information.

Although people generally find it easier and actually prefer to reason using fuzzy traces rather than verbatim representations of information, this varies with age. Prior to age 6 or 7, children seem to be biased toward encoding and remembering verbatim traces of the information they encounter, whereas older children, like adults, are more inclined to encode and remember fuzzy, gistlike traces (Brainerd & Gordon, 1994; Marx & Henderson, 1996). Brainerd and Gordon (1994), for example, gave preschool and second-grade children simple numerical problems to solve, based on the following background information:

> Farmer Brown owns many animals. He owns 3 dogs, 5 sheep, 7 chickens, 9 horses, and 11 cows.

They were then asked a series of questions, some requiring verbatim knowledge for their correct answer, such as:

> How many cows does Farmer Brown own: 11 or 9?

And others requiring only gist information, such as:

> Which of Farmer Brown's animals are the most: cows or horses?

They found that preschoolers performed better on the verbatim questions than on gist-based ones, whereas second-graders performed better on gist-based questions than on verbatim items. The second-graders performed just as well as preschoolers on the verbatim questions. The only age difference was that preschoolers were not as good as second-graders at solving gist-based problems.

Clearly, fuzzy-trace theory has been useful for describing developmental changes in the ways that children encode information and use it to solve problems. Relying on gist information is easier than trying to retrieve verbatim details and is just as effective (or more so) for solving a large number of problems that children face. Some tasks, such as mental arithmetic, do require verbatim representations. But a major reason that young children may think more slowly and less efficiently than older children do is that they often get bogged down processing unnecessary verbatim detail that consumes much of their limited cognitive resources and interferes with effective problem solving.

Other alternatives to traditional information-processing models also help to explain age differences in children's thinking. One such approach is recent research on children's **inhibition,** which is discussed in Box 8.1.

In the remaining portions of this chapter, we will trace the developmental changes that occur in children's information processing. We focus first on general changes in the hardware and software of the system and then examine the growth of such crucial information-processing skills as attention, memory, and children's arithmetic skills.

HOW DOES INFORMATION-PROCESSING CAPACITY CHANGE WITH AGE?

inhibition
the ability to prevent ourselves from executing some cognitive or behavioral response.

How much does our information-processing hardware change with age? As we saw in Chapter 5, the brain develops in regular and predictable ways over infancy and child-

8.1

DEVELOPMENTAL ISSUES

Can Age Changes in Inhibition Account for Changes in Cognitive Development?

Recently, researchers have proposed that age changes in children's abilities to *inhibit* preferred or well-established responses may play an important role in cognitive development (Bjorklund & Harnishfeger, 1990; Diamond, 1991). Where traditional information-processing theories have emphasized the *activation* of operations and knowledge, these new accounts propose that *inhibiting* an operation or preventing some piece of knowledge from getting into consciousness may be equally important for cognitive development (see also Dempster, 1993).

Deficits in inhibition are thought to influence cognition both in infancy and childhood. Recall from Chapter 7 that infants solving Piaget's A-not-B problems often reach for a hidden object at location A, even after seeing it hidden at location B. They cannot inhibit their tendency to search where they had previously found the object (at point A) despite seemingly "knowing" better.

Age-related changes in inhibitory processes have also been noted for a number of other cognitive challenges that older children face. For example, children's ability to selectively forget unimportant information is affected by their ability to keep the to-be-forgotten information out of mind. Older grade-school children are simply better able to execute these inhibitory processes than younger children are (Harnishfeger & Pope, 1996; Lehman et al., 1997; Pope & Kipp, 1998). In general, young children have a difficult time executing anything other than their preferred or predominant response. Children's ability to regulate their conduct (which involves inhibiting unacceptable responses as well as performing more desirable acts) also improves with age (Kochanska et al., 1996; Luria, 1961).

What factors contribute to the development of inhibitory control? Neurological maturation seems to. In Chapter 7, we learned that infants' ability to inhibit inappropriate responses in A-not-B search problems is related to maturation of the frontal lobes of the cerebral cortex. Furthermore, both preschool children and adults with lesions of the frontal lobes show the same difficulties at performing tasks in which verbal instructions require them to inhibit a dominant response. So if told to tap a pencil one *more* time (or one less time) than an experimenter does, both young children and brain-damaged adults have trouble in inhibiting their preferred tendency to imitate the number of taps the experimenter displays (Llamas & Diamond, 1991). Taken together, these findings imply that maturation of the frontal lobes plays a major role in permitting us to inhibit various thoughts and behaviors.

Katherine Kipp Harnishfeger and David Bjorklund (Bjorklund & Harnishfeger, 1990; Harnishfeger, 1995; Harnishfeger & Bjorklund, 1994) have proposed a model of "inefficient inhibition" to account for the influence of inhibitory mechanisms on cognitive development. The central idea in their model is that age differences in the ability to keep task-inappropriate information out of working memory influences task performance. Young children may not only have difficulty ignoring task-irrelevant input from the environment, but they also have a difficult time suppressing task-irrelevant "thoughts." This greater amount of task-irrelevant information in working memory thus results in "cognitive clutter," which effectively reduces functional working-memory space and prevents the successful execution of other cognitive strategies (see Lorsbach & Reimer, 1997).

Recognizing that inhibitory processes play an important role in cognitive development seems to be an important step forward in helping us understand children's thinking. Yet, the inhibitory perspective should be seen as supplementing information-processing views of development and not replacing them. Age changes in inhibition may *permit* certain other abilities to be expressed, but they do not *cause* them to develop in the first place. Stated another way, improvements in inhibitory control may promote cognitive growth by reducing cognitive clutter, thereby allowing more advanced information-processing abilities to emerge.

hood, and it would be surprising if these changes were not related to changes in children's information-processing abilities. So it seems plausible that older children may be more capable thinkers than younger children are because they have a better "computer"—a bigger, faster, or more efficient set of processing units. But what aspects of the system change the most and how might restrictions in information-processing capacity limit children's thinking? Interestingly, there is no consistent evidence that the capacities of the sensory register or the long-term store change appreciably after the first few months of life (Bjorklund, 1995). Our focus, then, centers on developmental changes in two interrelated aspects of information-processing capacity: the short-term store and processing speed.

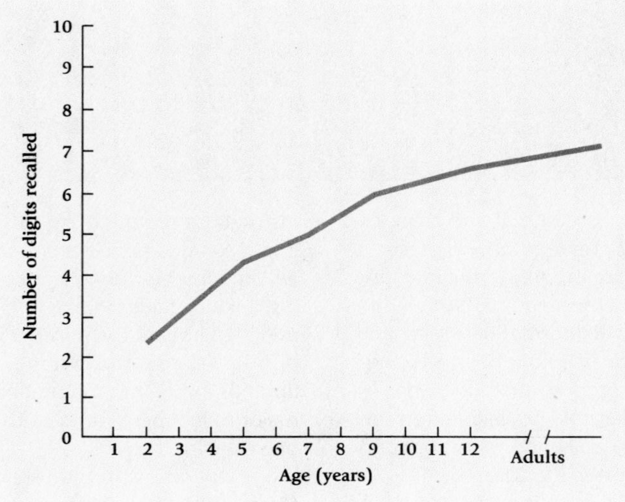

Figure 8.2 *Children's memory span for digits (digit span) shows regular increases with age.* *From Dempster, 1981.*

Development of the Short-Term Store

memory span
a measure of the amount of information that can be held in the short-term store.

working memory
the capacity to store and operate on information being held in the short-term store.

Traditionally, the capacity of the short-term store has been assessed by tests of **memory span.** Memory span refers to the number of rapidly presented and unrelated items (for example digits) that can be recalled in exact order. Age differences in memory span are highly reliable (see Figure 8.2). In fact, they are so reliable that memory span is used as one indication of general intelligence on the two most widely used intelligence tests for children.

Related to memory-span tasks are **working-memory** tasks. Since short-term memory is also the site where mental operations are performed, some researchers suggest that tasks that require children to operate on the information they are trying to remember are better indications of the capacity of the short-term store (Case, 1985). One such task provides children sets of incomplete sentences, requiring them to supply the final word (for example, "In the summer, it is very ____________ "). After listening several such sentences, children were asked to recall the final word in each sentence, in the order they were presented (Siegel & Ryan, 1989). Such a test requires not only the short-term storage of information, but also some mental work to generate the exact items to be recalled. Similar to the findings reported for digit span, reliable age differences in working memory are found, although working-memory span is usually one or two items lower than a child's short-term memory span (Case, 1985).

Do these robust age-related differences in memory span and working-memory span necessarily mean that there are age changes in the actual *physical* capacity of the short-term store? Not necessarily. In one often-cited study (Chi, 1978), a group of graduate students at the University of Pittsburgh were given two simple memory tests. The first was a digit-span task. On a second test, they were shown chess pieces on a chess board (about one chess piece per second), then given the pieces and asked to place them at their previous positions on the board. Their performance on these tasks was compared with that of a group of 10-year-olds. But, in all fairness, these were not typical 10-year-olds; they were all chess experts—winners of local tournaments or members of chess clubs. If younger children simply have smaller short-term stores than adults, the graduate students should have outperformed the 10-year-olds on both memory tests. But this is not what Chi found. As we see in Figure 8.3, the child-experts clearly outperformed the adults when memory for chess pieces was tested. However, their remarkable performance was limited to what they knew well, for they performed much worse than adults did when their memory for digits was tested (see also Schneider et al., 1993).

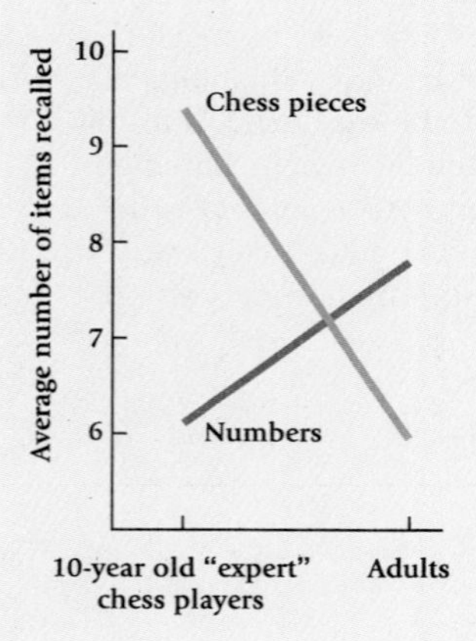

Figure 8.3 *Knowledge base affects memory. Children who are chess "experts" recall more about locations of chess pieces than "novice" adults do. However, adults recall more about numbers than children do, a finding Chi attributes to adults' greater familiarity with (or knowledge of) numbers.* *Adapted from Chi, 1978.*

These findings indicate that having a detailed knowledge base for a particular domain (in this case, chess) facilitates memory performance for information from that domain but not necessarily for information from other areas. How does being an "expert" in a subject such as chess result in improved memory span? Although a number of possibilities have been suggested, the factor that seems to play the most crucial role is *ease of item identification*—how quickly the child identifies items to be remembered. Children who are experts in a domain can process information in that domain rapidly and thus have an advantage when it comes to memory span. Their speed of item identification is an indication of their domain-specific *processing efficiency*.

Another contributor to age-related increases in memory span that has little to do with the *physical* capacity of the short-term store is increased use of memory strategies. One such strategy is *chunking,* in which to-be-remembered items are grouped in ways that make them easier to remember. To illustrate, the nine digits 236448820 are much harder to recall if we focus on each digit singly, as children often do, than if we "chunk" these digits as adolescents and adults might when recalling a Social Security number (that is, 236-44-8820).

In sum, maturational differences in the *physical capacity* of the short-term store appear to be small. However, maturation may still contribute to the development of the short-term store by influencing the speed at which people can execute a wide variety of cognitive operations (Dempster, 1985; Kail, 1993). Let's explore this idea further.

Changes in Processing Speed

It may not surprise us to learn that, overall, young children require more time to execute cognitive operations than older children do. Robert Kail (1992, 1997) finds that general developmental changes in processing speed are similar across a variety of different problems, ranging from simple tasks in which participants must determine whether the objects in two pictures have the same name (for example, are they both pictures of bananas?), to complex mental arithmetic (see also Hale, Fry, & Jessie, 1993; Miller & Vernon, 1997). Kail concedes that our past experiences (such as being a chess expert) can influence speed of processing within a particular domain, but he believes that maturationally based factors are primarily responsible for broad age-related differences in speed of information processing.

What maturational developments might underlie age-related changes in processing speed? Increased myelinization of neurons in the associative ("thinking") areas of the brain and the elimination of unnecessary (or excess) neural synapses that could interfere with efficient information processing are two possible candidates. As we noted in Chapter 5, myelin is a fatty substance that surrounds nerves and facilitates transmission of nerve impulses. Whereas myelinization of most sensory and motor areas of the brain is accomplished within the first several years of life, myelinization of the associative area is not complete until adolescence or young adulthood. Many theorists have proposed that age differences in myelinization are directly responsible for age differences in speed of information processing, and, ultimately, for age differences in the efficient use of one's limited mental capacity (Bjorklund & Harnishfeger, 1990; Case, 1985; Kail & Salthouse, 1994).

Social Influences on Processing Capacity

Yet, not all improvements in processing speed and memory span are attributable to biological maturation. One popular model of working memory proposes that the speed with which items can be *articulated* is an important contributor to developmental and individual differences in processing capacity (Baddeley, 1986; Hitch & Towse, 1995). Presumably, the faster children can articulate the names of items they are trying to process, the longer their memory spans will be. Research has shown that, with age, children are able to read or say words at a faster rate, with memory span increasing accordingly (Hitch & Halliday, 1983; Hulme et al., 1984).

There are also some interesting cross-cultural findings that support this speed-of-articulation hypotheses. For example, Chinese speakers have longer memory spans for digits than English speakers, with this difference becoming noticeable as early as age 4 and extending into adulthood (Geary et al., 1993; Stigler, Lee, & Stevenson, 1986). The reason for this cultural effect seems to be due to differences in the rate with which number words (for example, "one," "three," "seven," etc.) in the two languages can be spoken. Languages with relatively short number words that can be articulated quickly (for example, Chinese) foster longer digit spans than languages with relatively long number words that are articulated more slowly (for example, English) (Chen & Stevenson, 1988). In fact, in one study of bilingual children, participants had longer digit spans in their *second* language (English) than their first (Welsh). This surprising result was due to the fact that number words can be articulated more rapidly in English than in Welsh (Ellis & Hennelley, 1980). So the greater digit spans of Chinese children are due, not to some inherent cognitive or educational superiority of the Chinese children, but to the language they speak.

Age Differences in Processing Efficiency

The findings we've reviewed so far seem to indicate that there are few meaningful age differences in the physical capacity of the short-term store. However, there are reliable age differences in speed of processing. Also, the speed at which people process information is influenced by (1) maturationally based changes in myelinization of the associative areas of the brain and (2) by experiential factors such as what language they speak and their level of expertise in a domain. So, even though regular age differences in performance on memory-span and working-memory-span tasks are found, they do not seem to reflect changes in the physical capacity of the short-term store. Instead, children become speedier and more *efficient* information processors with age; that is, they are quicker to recognize items on memory- or working-span tasks and are more skilled at performing cognitive operations on them. If less time or effort is needed to encode and operate on the stimuli in a memory task, then more of one's *limited* working memory space can be used to store these items (Case, 1985; 1992; and see Figure 8.4).

One central assumption of this **operating efficiency hypothesis** is that many operations that take a great deal of time and effort early in life become *automatized;* that is, they are accomplished with little effort later in life. Thus, you may quickly (and almost effortlessly) arrive at an answer of 225 for the problem 9 × 25 = ______, whereas a 10-year-old might have to laboriously perform each step of the operation (that is, 9 × 5 = 45; leave the 5, carry the 4; 9 × 2 = 18 + 4 = 22 and 5 = 225) and probably could not do this problem in his head. In situations where children are experts, or in which adults experience distractions that undermine their processing efficiency, age differences in cognitive processing are greatly reduced and sometimes even reversed (Case et al., 1982; Chi, 1978). But on the whole, adults usually have longer memory spans and greater processing capacity than children do because they encode information and execute mental operations faster and more efficiently than children can.

operating efficiency hypothesis
in Case's theory, the notion that operating space in working memory increases with age because we come to process information faster or more efficiently.

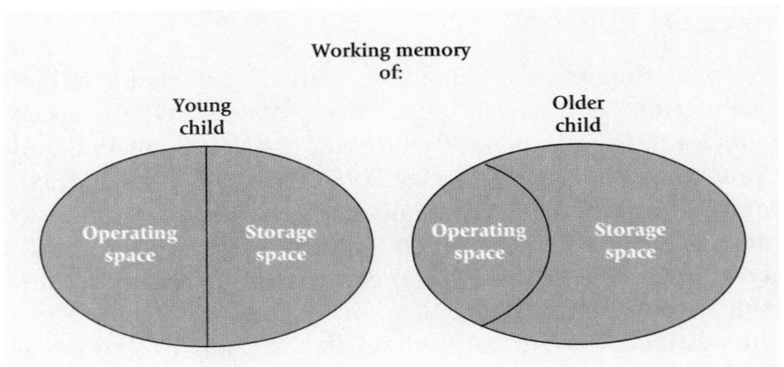

Figure 8.4 *Robbie Case's "operating efficiency" hypothesis. With age, children process information much faster and more efficiently, thus requiring less operating space and leaving more storage space.* ADAPTED FROM CASE, *1985.*

Increases in operating efficiency are due in part to *hardware* improvements. However, *software* improvements are also involved. With practice or experience, children become more familiar with items they must remember and more skilled and more strategic when performing mental operations on them (Bjorklund, 1995; Flavell et al., 1993). Let's now consider some of the developments that occur in children's cognitive strategies, or mental software.

SOFTWARE: DEVELOPMENT OF PROCESSING STRATEGIES

In addition to age differences in information-processing hardware, there are clear age differences in processing *software,* or the cognitive operations that children have available to help them solve problems or achieve other objectives. These cognitive processes vary along a number of dimensions. Some are executed automatically, so that you may not even be aware that you are "thinking." When you look at a drawing, for example, you effortlessly "see" the images without having to consciously concentrate on converting the light waves into coherent patterns. And if you tried to analyze how you performed such a complicated feat, you probably couldn't do it. Other cognitive processes are more effortful ones, of which we are quite aware. If, when looking at that same picture, for example, you were searching for a particular detail ("Find Waldo"), you would need to use more effortful and planful cognitive processes to perform the task. It is these latter type of processes, called *strategies,* that change substantially with age.

Strategies are usually defined as deliberately implemented, goal-directed operations used to aid task performance (Harnishfeger & Bjorklund, 1990; Schneider & Pressley, 1997). Much of our conscious thinking is guided by strategies, and even young children may discover or invent strategies when they encounter problems in everyday life. Yet, many strategies that children living in information-age societies find so useful are explicitly taught in school (Moely, Santulli, & Obach, 1995). These include strategies involved in mathematics, reading, memory, and scientific problem solving.

Age differences in strategy use account for a substantial portion of the age-related differences we see in children's cognitive performance. Generally speaking, younger children use fewer strategies and use them far less effectively than older children do. Yet, the development of cognitive strategies is much more complex than this statement would imply, for even young children can use some strategies effectively, and the more sophisticated strategies that older children select do not always help them as much as one might expect. Let's now examine some of the general principles governing the development of strategies before discussing the specific strategies on which developing children rely to regulate attention, improve their memories, and solve mathematical problems.

Production and Utilization Deficiencies

Developmentalists once believed that preschool children were *astrategic;* that is, they didn't use any strategies when approaching most problems, possibly because they lacked the cognitive capacity to execute strategies and to profit from their use. Later research has seriously questioned these assumptions. Consider that even 18- to 36-month olds rely on simple strategies to locate hidden objects in hide-and-seek games. If instructed to remember where a stuffed animal (Big Bird) has been hidden so that they can later wake him up from his nap, these young children strategically remind themselves where

strategies
goal-directed and deliberately implemented mental operations used to facilitate task performance.

Young children devise simple strategies for attacking the problems they face.

the animal is by repeatedly looking at or pointing to its hiding place (DeLoache, 1986; DeLoache, Cassidy, & Brown, 1985). More recently, Michael Cohen (1996) asked 3- and 4-year-olds to play "store," a game in which they had to fill customers' vegetable orders by relying on such strategies as adding, subtracting, or making no changes in the number of objects (for example, tomatoes) in an existing display. These young children used a variety of possible strategies and became more efficient (that is, made fewer moves to fill an order) with practice. Clearly, preschool children can be strategic in their thinking and problem solving, although the strategies they devise for themselves tend to be simple and to increase in efficiency with age.

Do younger children lack the cognitive capacity to execute and benefit from the more effective strategies on which older children rely? One way to find out is to try to teach them these new strategies and see if their cognitive performances improve. Dozens of training studies of this kind have been conducted, and their findings are reasonably consistent: Children who do not use a strategy on their own can be trained to do so and often benefit from its use (Bjorklund & Douglas, 1997; Harnishfeger & Bjorklund, 1990). So rather than being astrategic or lacking cognitive capacity, younger children often display **production deficiencies;** they merely fail to produce effective strategies, even though they are often quite capable of putting those strategies to good use.

Nevertheless, acquiring a new and more sophisticated strategy does not always lead to dramatic improvements in task performance or problem solving. Instead, children who spontaneously generate and use such strategies often display what Patricia Miller (1994) calls a **utilization deficiency;** they do not benefit as much from strategy use as equally strategic older children do, and they may often revert to using a less effective strategy (or no strategy). Utilization deficiencies are commonly found as children acquire new memory strategies (Coyle & Bjorklund, 1996), reading strategies (Gaultney, 1996), attentional strategies (Miller et al., 1991), and strategies for reasoning by analogy (Muir-Broaddus, 1995). Even when children are trained to use a new strategy at school or in the laboratory, they often display utilization deficiencies by failing to benefit immediately from its use (Bjorklund et al., 1997).

Why do children display utilization deficiencies if the new and more sophisticated strategies that they are acquiring are generally better ways to approach the problems they face? Information-processing theorists suggest three possible reasons. First, executing a novel strategy may require so much mental effort that children have few cognitive resources left to gather and store information relevant to the problems they face (Bjorklund & Coyle, 1995; Miller & Seier, 1994). Consequently, children who do not benefit from strategy use may fall back on less efficient procedures that work better *for them.* Teachers are well aware of this and often insist that children continue to use new strategies. Why? Because the cognitive effort involved in employing a strategy declines as children become more practiced at executing it. Consequently, their performance gradually improves as they have more cognitive capacity to devote to attending to, gathering, and storing task-relevant information.

In addition, new strategies are often intrinsically interesting to children. Much as Piaget proposed that children use a scheme just for the sheer joy of having it, children may use a strategy for the novelty of trying something different (Siegler, 1996). They may not care that much about the eventual outcome (for example, how many things they remembered or whether their arithmetic computations are correct); rather, they take pleasure in using the strategy for its own sake, even if their performance deteriorates.

Finally, younger children, in particular, may know less about how to monitor their cognitive activities and may not even be aware that they are failing to benefit from using a new strategy. However, this poor metacognition may actually be beneficial if it prompts children to practice the effortful new strategy until it can be executed much quicker and becomes a truly effective aid for problem solving (Bjorklund & Coyle, 1995).

Clearly, the fact that children display both production deficiencies and utilization deficiencies implies that the growth of strategic thinking is a slow and uneven process. In fact, Robert Siegler's recent studies of children's problem-solving strategies show just how uneven the process can be.

production deficiency
a failure to spontaneously generate and use known strategies that could improve learning and memory.

utilization deficiency
a failure to benefit from effective strategies that one has spontaneously produced; thought to occur in the early phases of strategy acquisition when executing the strategy requires much mental effort.

Multiple- and Variable-Strategy Use

Cognitive developmentalists now realize that strategy development is not stagelike, with children using one strategy at a certain age and then abandoning it for a more complicated and effective strategy at a later age. Rather, children of all ages have a variety of strategies available to them and select among those strategies when trying to solve a problem.

Consider what Robert Siegler and his colleagues (1996; Siegler & Jenkins, 1989) found when researching young children's arithmetic strategies. In learning to add, young children frequently use a *sum* strategy that involves counting both numbers out loud (for example, for 5 + 3 = ?, saying "1,2,3,4,5 [pause], 6, 7, 8."). A more sophisticated strategy is to begin with the larger number (in this case, 5) and count up from there (for example, saying "5 [pause], 6, 7, 8."). This is called the *min* strategy. A more sophisticated strategy still, known as *fact retrieval,* is "just knowing" the answer, and retrieving it directly from long-term memory without having to count at all (for example, simply saying "8" to the question "How much is 5 + 3?"). When looking at cross-sectional data across age groups, one gets the impression that children progress from using the sum strategy to using the min strategy to using fact retrieval. Yet closer examination reveals that individual children use a variety of these strategies at any given time, and the frequency that each strategy is used varies with age. Multiple- and variable strategy use has been found in other cognitive domains as well, including serial-recall (remembering a list of digits in exact order; McGilly & Siegler, 1990), free recall (Coyle & Bjorklund, 1997), tic-tac-toe (Crowley & Siegler, 1993), and scientific reasoning (Schauble, 1990).

Siegler and his colleagues (1996; Crowley, Shrager, & Siegler, 1997; Siegler & Jenkins, 1989) have formulated a **strategy choice model** to describe children's multiple strategy use and how strategies change over time. Basically, Siegler believes that children's multiple strategies compete with one another for use. Early in development or when a child is first presented with new problems, relatively simple strategies "win" most of the time. With practice and maturation, other, more effortful but more efficient strategies increase in frequency and "win" more often. So, Siegler does not see strategies developing in a steplike fashion, but rather as a series of overlapping waves, as illustrated in Figure 8.5.

strategy choice model
Siegler's model to describe how strategies change over time; the view that multiple strategies exist within a child's cognitive repertoire at any one time, with these strategies competing with one another for use.

What is the most important message from Siegler's work? Perhaps that children of all ages have multiple strategies available to them and that age changes in their selection and use of these tools is an important aspect of cognitive development that was not addressed by Piaget or earlier information-processing researchers. So the issue facing cognitive developmentalists today is not whether young children can be strategic.

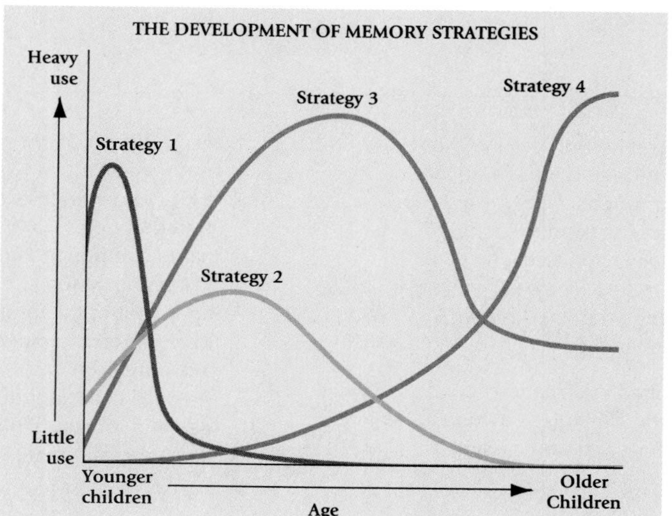

Figure 8.5 *Siegler's strategy choice model of development. Change in strategy use is seen as a series of overlapping waves, with different strategies being used more frequently at different ages.* FROM ROBERT S. SIEGLER.

Rather, developmentalists must now determine what combination of strategies children employ within different cognitive domains and explain why the simpler strategies that younger children prefer gradually give way to the more sophisticated and effective strategies used by older children, adolescents, and adults.

Now that we have described that basic premises of information-processing theory and have discussed the development of processing hardware and software in a very general way, we will trace the development of four crucial information-processing attributes—attention, strategic memory, event memory, and academic skills—and will comment on the practical as well as the theoretical importance of these developments.

THE DEVELOPMENT OF ATTENTION

Clearly, a person must first detect and *attend* to information before it can be encoded, retained, or used to solve problems. Although even young infants attend to a variety of sensory inputs, their attention is often "captured" by objects and events: A one-month-old baby does not choose to attend to a face; instead, faces attract his attention. Similarly, preschoolers who seem totally immersed in one activity can quickly lose interest and just as quickly get caught up in another activity. But as children grow older, they become better able to sustain their attention and more selective in what they attend to, and they acquire the ability to formulate and carry out systematic plans for gathering information necessary to accomplish their goals.

Changes in Attention Span

Visit a nursery school and you will see that teachers are likely to switch classroom activities every 15 to 20 minutes. Why? Because young children have very short **attention spans;** they rarely concentrate on any single activity for very long. Even when doing things they like, such as playing with toys or watching TV, 2- and 3-year-olds often look away, move about, and direct their attention elsewhere, spending far less time on the activity at hand than older children do (Ridderinkhoff & van der Molen, 1995; Ruff & Lawson, 1990). Part of the younger child's problem in trying to "concentrate" is that her attention is easily captured by distractions and she is often unable to inhibit the intrusion of task-irrelevant thoughts (Bjorklund & Harnishfeger, 1990; Dempster, 1993; Harnishfeger, 1995).

attention span
capacity for sustaining attention to a particular stimulus or activity.

Concept Check 8.1
Modeling Human Information Processing

Check your understanding of information-processing models and assumptions by matching each descriptive statement below to one of the following ideas or concepts: (a) gists, (b) long-term store, (c) short-term store/working memory, (d) sensory store, (e) operating efficiency hypothesis, (f) productive deficiency, (g) utilization deficiency, (h) executive control processes, (i) working-memory task, (j) limited capacity. Answers appear in the Appendix.

_____ 1. vast storehouse of acquired information
_____ 2. failure to benefit from the strategies one generates
_____ 3. method of assessing information-processing capacity
_____ 4. means by which we monitor information processing
_____ 5. failure to generate effective information-processing strategies
_____ 6. major assumption about the information-processing system
_____ 7. log-in unit of the information-processing system
_____ 8. fuzzy representations of information one has encountered
_____ 9. site of all conscious intellectual activity
_____ 10. idea that increases in capacity largely reflect increasing automatization of information

The capacity for sustained attention gradually improves throughout childhood and early adolescence, and these improvements may be due, in part, to maturational changes in the central nervous system. For example, the **reticular formation,** an area of the brain responsible for the regulation of attention, is not fully *myelinated* until puberty. Perhaps this neurological development helps to explain why adolescents and young adults are suddenly able to spend hours on end cramming for upcoming exams or typing furiously to make morning deadlines on term papers.

Another reason that attention capabilities increase with age is that older children use more effective strategies to regulate their attention.

Development of Planful Attentional Strategies

By age 4 or 5, children become more persistent in their attempts to solve problems and show some signs of planfulness as they gather relevant information. For example, Patricia Miller and Yvette Harris (1988) asked 3- and 4-year-olds to compare two rows of objects to determine whether the rows were identical or different. Each object in each row was covered by a door, thereby preventing the child from quickly scanning all the objects. Thus, the most efficient strategy for gathering task-relevant information was a vertical-comparison procedure in which the child examines vertically aligned pairs of objects (one in each row) as she proceeds across the rows. Three-year-olds rarely used this strategy, choosing instead to look first at all objects within a particular row before examining the second row. By contrast, the planful, vertical-comparison strategy was often used by 4-year-olds, whose "same/different" judgments were more likely to be correct on the trials they used this procedure.

With age, children become increasingly planful and systematic in their gathering of information. In a series of classic studies (Vurpillot, 1968; Vurpillot & Ball, 1979), 4- to 10-year-olds were asked to search pictures of two houses and to judge whether the contents of the windows of the houses were identical or different. As shown in Figure 8.6, 4- and 5-year-olds were not very planful; they searched only a few windows and often reached the wrong conclusion. By contrast, children older than 6½ were highly systematic. Their planned searches involved checking each window in one house with the corresponding window in the other house, pair by pair, until they arrived at a judgment (which was likely to be correct). Older children are also more likely than younger children to formulate a systematic plan for searching the environment for a lost toy, often limiting their search to areas between where the toy was last seen and where they

reticular formation
area of the brain that activates the organism and is thought to be important in regulating attention.

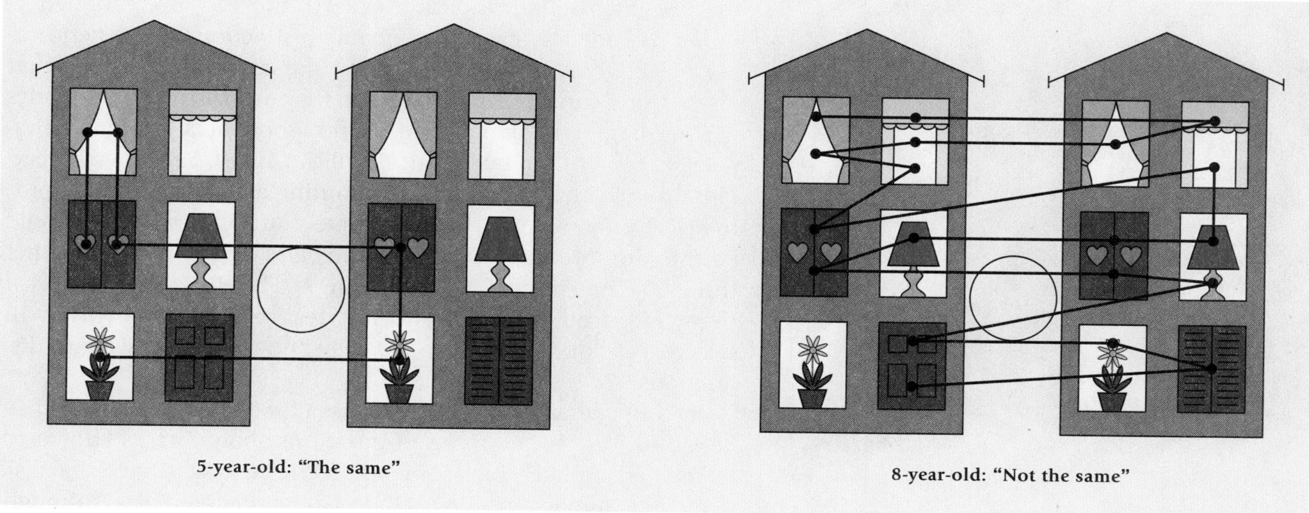

Figure 8.6 *Are the houses in each pair exactly the same or different? Preschool children often guess incorrectly because they do not systematically compare all the pairs of windows as school-aged children do.* Based on Vurpillot, 1968.

discovered it missing rather than wandering the yard aimlessly looking for it (Wellman, 1985). So the planful gathering of information that helps children to solve problems develops gradually over the course of middle childhood.

Selective Attention: Ignoring Information That Is Clearly Irrelevant

Would young children perform as well as older children if they were told in advance which information is most relevant to the tasks they face and did not have to be so planful? Probably not, for younger children display little ability to display **selective attention**—to concentrate only on task-relevant stimuli and to not be distracted by other "noise" in the environment. Consider what Patricia Miller and Michael Weiss (1981) found when they told 7-, 10-, and 13-year-olds to remember the locations of a number of *animals,* each of which was hidden behind a different cloth flap. When each flap was lifted to reveal an animal, the children could also see a household object positioned either above or below the animal. Here, then, is a learning task that requires the child to attend selectively to certain information (the animals) while ignoring other potentially distracting input (the household objects). When the children were tested to see whether they had learned where each animal was located, the 13-year-olds outperformed the 10-year-olds, who, in turn, performed slightly better than the 7-year-olds. Miller and Weiss then tested to see whether children had attended to the incidental (irrelevant) information by asking them to recall which household object had been paired with each animal. They found exactly the opposite pattern on this incidental-learning test: 13-year-olds recalled *less* about the household objects than either 7- or 10-year-olds. In fact, both of the younger groups recalled as much about the irrelevant objects as about the locations of the animals. Taken together, these findings indicate that older children are much better than younger ones at concentrating on relevant information and filtering out extraneous input that may interfere with task performance.

selective attention
capacity to focus on task-relevant aspects of experience while ignoring irrelevant or distracting information.

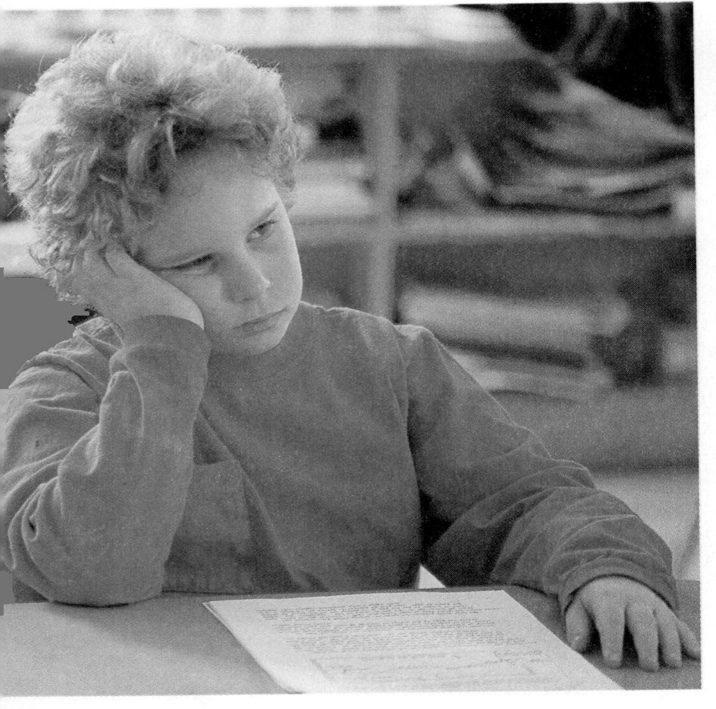

Although the ability to concentrate improves dramatically during middle childhood, grade-school students are not always successful at overcoming distractions.

What Do Children Know about Attention?

Do young children know more about attentional processes than their behavior might indicate? Indeed, they do. Even though 4-year-olds generally cannot overcome distractions when performing selective/attention tasks, they are apparently aware that distractions can be a problem, for they realize that two stories will be harder to understand if the storytellers speak simultaneously rather than taking turns (Pillow, 1988). Yet, when 4-year-olds are told that a woman is examining a set of decorative pins to select one as a gift, they are largely unaware that she would be thinking primarily about the pins and would not have other things on her mind (Flavell, Green, & Flavell, 1995). It is as if these preschoolers simply do not realize what is involved in selective attention, even though they know something about distractions.

In other research, Miller & Weiss (1982) asked 5-, 7-, and 9-year-olds to answer a series of questions about factors known to affect performance on incidental-learning task (that is, a task like the "animals and objects" test described earlier). Although knowledge about attentional processes generally increased with age, even the 5-year-olds realized that they should at least *look first* at task-relevant stimuli and then *label* these objects as an aid to remembering them. The 7- and 10-year-olds further understood that they must *attend selectively* to task-relevant stimuli and *ignore* irrelevant information in order to do well on these problems.

Why, then, do 5- to 7-year-olds not follow their own advice and perform better when actually working at incidental learning (or other selective-attention) tasks? Research by Miller and her associates (DeMarie-Dreblow & Miller, 1988; Miller & Seier, 1994; Miller, Woody-Ramsey, & Aloise, 1991) provides some clues. It seems that when children first acquire an appropriate attentional strategy, they go through a *transitional phase* in which they employ the strategy sporadically. Why? Because they often experience a *utilization deficiency;* they find that it takes so much cognitive effort to execute the strategy that they do not profit from its use and then fall back on less efficient procedures that seem to work better *for them.* But as children become more practiced at executing effective strategies, perhaps because they are prompted to do so by parents' and teachers' admonishments to "concentrate" or "pay attention," the cognitive effort to do so declines, thus leaving them more space in short-term memory to gather and hold the information they need to perform their tasks (Flavell et al., 1993; DeMarie-Dreblow & Miller, 1988).

In sum, the development of attention is apparently a lengthy process in which a child first learns to translate what she knows into appropriate actions and then gradually comes to rely on these strategies as they become more routinized and effective means of gathering information to achieve her objectives.

Despite these "normal" trends, a fair number of grade-school children find it nearly impossible to sustain their attention for long or develop planful attentional strategies. In Box 8.2, we will take a closer look at this **attention deficit-hyperactivity disorder** and its implications for children's academic, social, and emotional development.

MEMORY: RETAINING AND RETRIEVING INFORMATION

Once children have attended to information of some kind, they must find a way to retain it if they are to learn from their experiences or use this input to solve a problem. Thus, the development of *memory*—the processes by which we store and retrieve information—is central to information-processing theories of intellectual development.

In the pages that follow, we will trace the development of two general kinds of memory: *event memory* and *strategic memory.* **Event memory** refers to stored memories of such events as what you ate for breakfast this morning, Michael Stipe's opening number at last year's REM concert, or the joy your mother displayed when your baby brother was born. Memory for events, which include **autobiographical memories** of events that happened *to you,* is what most people think of as "natural" memory, and it rarely requires use of any strategies. **Strategic memory,** by contrast, refers to the processes involved when we *consciously try* to retain or retrieve such information as a telephone number, the route to a theater across town, or the text of the Gettysburg Address for a U.S. History class. Strategic memory is aided immensely by memory strategies, or **mnemonics,** many of which we may acquire because they are useful for retaining information that we are taught at school. It is hardly surprising then, that information-processing researchers have studied the development of mnemonics that might promote academic performance. These include rehearsal, organization, elaboration, and retrieval, each of which will be discussed briefly here. We will then consider some other factors that influence children's strategic memory before examining the growth of event memory, or memory for events that we have witnessed or experienced.

attention deficit-hyperactivity disorder (ADHD)
an attentional disorder involving distractibility, hyperactivity, and impulsive behavior that often leads to academic difficulties, poor self-esteem, and social/emotional problems.

event memory
long-term memory for events.

autobiographical memory
memory for important experiences or events that have happened to us.

strategic memory
processes involved as one consciously attempts to retain or retrieve information.

mnemonics (memory strategies)
effortful techniques used to improve memory, including rehearsal, organization, and elaboration.

8.2

DEVELOPMENTAL ISSUES

Attention Deficit-Hyperactivity Disorder

> They can't sit still; they don't pay attention to the teacher; they mess around and get into trouble; they try to get others into trouble; they are rude; they get mad when they don't get their way . . . (Henker & Whalen, 1989; p. 216).

These and other similar descriptions are widely endorsed by classmates of those 3 to 5% of grade-school children (mostly boys) diagnosed as having *attention deficit-hyperactivity disorder (ADHD).* ADHD youngsters display three major symptoms: (1) They are highly *impulsive,* often acting before thinking and blurting out whatever is on their minds; (2) they are *inattentive,* frequently failing to listen and displaying an inability to concentrate or to finish tasks; and (3) they are *hyperactive,* as they constantly fidget, squirm, or move about (American Psychiatric Association, 1994). As you might expect, these youngsters perform miserably on tests of sustained and selective attention (Landau, Milich, & Lorch, 1992). They also do poorly in school and often alienate both teachers and classmates by their failure to comply with requests and their disruptive and aggressive behavior (Henker & Whalen, 1989; Hinshaw & Melnick, 1995).

It was once believed that hyperactive children simply outgrew their problems after reaching puberty. Although they generally become less fidgety and overactive during the teenage years, many people diagnosed in childhood as having ADHD continue to display serious adjustment problems later in life. For example, attention-disordered adolescents are likely to struggle both socially and academically, and they frequently drop out of high school or impulsively commit reckless, delinquent acts without thinking about the consequences (Fischer et al., 1990; Greene et al., 1997). The picture is somewhat more positive by early adulthood, as about half of all ADHD individuals seem to be functioning well in their jobs. But for many with ADHD, young adulthood is characterized by above-average rates of job changes (or dismissals), marital disruptions, traffic accidents, legal infractions, and other personality problems or emotional disorders (Fischer et al., 1993; Mannuzza et al., 1993; Wender, 1995).

What causes ADHD? Unfortunately, we do not yet have a clear answer. Some people may be genetically predisposed to develop the disorder, in that one identical twin is likely to have it if the other does (Levy et al., 1997; Wender, 1995). Environment also matters. The incidence of ADHD is higher among children who were exposed *prenatally* to alcohol, drugs, and the disease rubella (Silver, 1992), and a harsh, highly controlling style of parenting may also contribute to, or at least aggravate, the problem in some cases (Jacobvitz & Sroufe, 1987; Sroufe, 1997). However, earlier theories linking the syndrome to food additives, excessive dietary intake of sugar, lead poisoning, and brain damage have received little support (Henker & Whalen, 1989).

What can be done to help children with ADHD? One treatment that seems to help 70% of them is to administer stimulant drugs such as Ritalin (Cantwell, 1996). Although it may seem odd to give overactive children drugs that increase their heart rates and respiratory levels, stimulants work because they also make ADHD children better able to focus their attention and less distractible and disruptive (Gillberg et al., 1997). Important benefits of this increased attentional focusing is that both academic performance and peer relations are likely to improve (Pelham et al., 1993; Henkler & Whalen, 1989). Gains in scholastic performance have also been achieved through cognitive-behavioral programs that teach ADHD children how to set academic goals that require sustained attention, while allowing these youngsters to reinforce their successes with tokens that can be exchanged for prizes. Indeed, ADHD children seem to benefit most from a *combination* of drug and behavior therapies (DuPaul & Barkley, 1993). And recently, researchers have found that if parents can remain warm and supportive but firm in their demands, their hyperactive sons exhibit fewer problem behaviors and are much better accepted by peers (Hinshaw & Melnick, 1995; Hinshaw et al., 1997). So, family therapies aimed at teaching often-exasperated parents to be more patient and to effectively manage the antics of a child with ADHD are likely to enhance the effectiveness of existing drug and behavioral interventions (Hinshaw et al., 1997).

A final note: Although therapeutic interventions do improve the self-esteem, social behaviors, and academic performance of ADHD children, many of these "treated" individuals are no better adjusted as adults than hyperactive peers who received no therapy (Wilens & Biederman, 1992). Undoubtedly, the long-term prognosis will improve as we learn more about this disorder. At present, we can say that the many problems associated with ADHD clearly illustrate just how important the regulation of attention is, not only to cognitive development and academic performance, but to one's social and emotional development as well.

The Development of Memory Strategies

Rehearsal

One very simple yet *effective* strategy that adults use to retain new information is **rehearsal**—repeating it over and over until we think we will remember it.

When instructed to try to remember a group of toys they have been shown, 3- to

4-year-olds look very carefully at the objects and often label them (once); but they rarely rehearse (Baker-Ward, Ornstein, & Holden, 1984; Oyen & Bebko, 1996). By contrast, John Flavell and associates (1966) gave 5- to 10-year-olds similar memory instructions and found that spontaneous use of rehearsal (as indicated by children's lip movements) increased with age. Whereas only 10% of the 5-year-olds repeated information that they were asked to recall, more than half the 7-year-olds and 85% of the 10-year-olds adopted this rehearsal strategy. In addition, the children who rehearsed remembered more than nonrehearsers.

Older children also rehearse more *efficiently* than younger children. If asked to recall a list of words presented one at a time, 5- to 8-year-olds usually rehearse each word in just that way—one at a time. By contrast, 12-year-olds are more likely to rehearse word *clusters,* repeating the earlier items over and over again as they rehearse each successive word. As a result, they remember more words than children who rehearse just one item at a time (Guttentag, Ornstein, & Siemans, 1987; Ornstein, Naus, & Liberty, 1975).

Why don't young children rehearse more efficiently? Possibly because their attempts to execute the more complex clustering strategy require so much of their limited working-memory space that they are unable to *retrieve* enough information to form useful clusters. A study by Peter Ornstein and his associates (1985) supports this interpretation. Ornstein et al. tried to teach 7-year-olds to use the "clustering" rehearsal strategy and found that the children did so *only if earlier items on the list remained visible.* So when these younger children were able to form item clusters without having to expend mental effort retrieving the items, they could execute the complex clustering strategy. By contrast, 12-year-olds relied on the clustering strategy *regardless of whether earlier items were visually displayed.* Apparently, this efficient rehearsal technique has become so automatized for most 12-year-olds that they implement it almost effortlessly, thus leaving themselves ample space in working memory for retrieving items to rehearse.

In sum, the preschooler's general failure to rehearse, coupled with the young grade-school child's less effective use of this skill, implies that the development of memory strategies is a very gradual process that may depend on both the development of working memory and the many opportunities children have to practice these techniques.

Organization

In one sense, rehearsal is a rather unimaginative memory device. If a rehearser merely repeats the names of items to be remembered, he or she may fail to notice certain meaningful relations among the stimuli that should make them easier to recall. Consider the following example:

> List 1: boat, match, hammer, coat, grass, nose, pencil, dog, cup, flower
>
> List 2: knife, shirt, car, fork, boat, pants, sock, truck, spoon, plate

Although these ten-item lists should be equally difficult to recall if one simply rehearses them, the second list is actually much easier for many people. The reason is that its items can be grouped into three semantically distinct categories (eating utensils, clothes, and vehicles) that can serve as cues for storage and retrieval. Until about age 9 to 10, children are not any better at recalling items that can be **semantically organized** (such as List 2) than those that are difficult to categorize (such as List 1) (Hasselhorn, 1992). This finding suggests that young children make few attempts to organize information for later recall.

How do children learn to organize materials in ways that could help them to remember? If we think back to Vygotsky's perspective on how many new skills are socially mediated, we might suspect that organizational strategies evolve from experiences children have had (1) categorizing highly related objects and events under a teacher's direction at school, or (2) watching as the teacher presents materials in a highly organized fashion. Interestingly, elementary school instructors in the United States spend little time teaching children explicit memory strategies, although those

rehearsal
a strategy for remembering that involves repeating the items one is trying to retain.

semantic organization
a strategy for remembering that involves grouping or classifying stimuli into meaningful (or manageable) clusters that are easier to retain.

Few experiences may contribute more to the development of effective memory skills than playing strategic games with a more competent opponent.

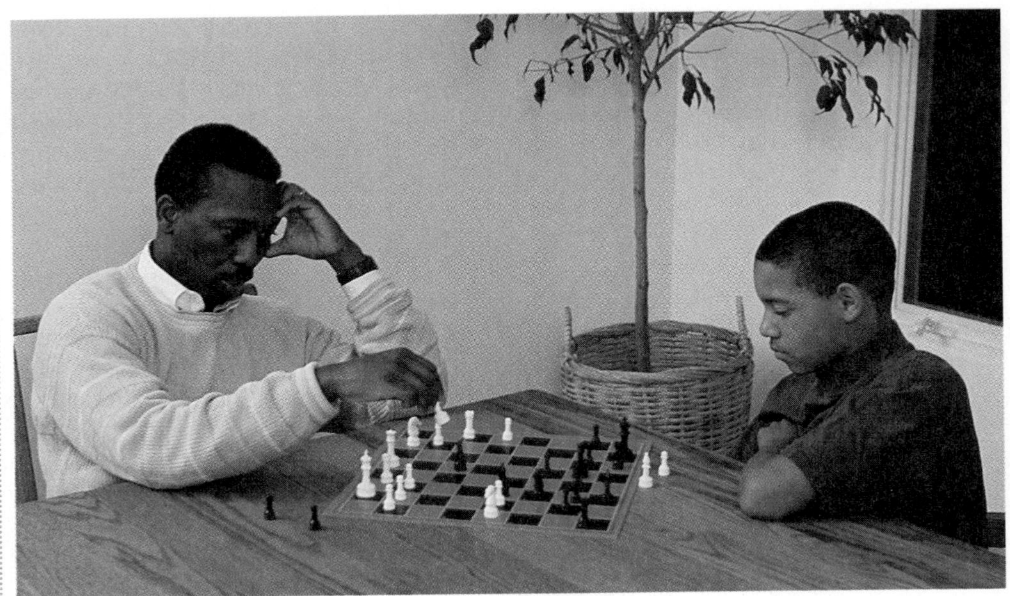

who provide more strategic suggestions do have students who tend to rely more on organizational strategies and perform better on recall tests (Moely et al., 1992).

But even in the absence of explicit instruction, children may eventually discover the benefits of organization for themselves from experiences they have categorizing highly related objects and events at school. Deborah Best (1993; Best & Ornstein, 1986) found that 9-year-olds who were instructed to sort "easily categorizable" items in any way they wished were more likely to organize their materials into semantically distinct clusters than control children, who were told to sort less categorizable items that could be organized, but with some difficulty. And there is more. Compared with the control children, those who had sorted the easily categorizable items (1) were more inclined to organize subsequent lists that were difficult to categorize, (2) performed better on recall tests of these materials, and (3) were more likely to preach the virtues of organizational strategies when asked to teach 6-year-olds how to remember.

Yet, important as schooling experience may be, memory strategies may also be fostered at home through collaborative or guided learning experiences that children have with their parents. For example, Martha Carr and her associates (1989) find that 8- to 9-year-olds who rely heavily on organizational strategies and perform well on recall tests tend to have parents who often (1) play strategy-related games with them, and (2) show them how to be planful and strategic when completing and checking their homework. So it seems that such pleasurable and strategic pursuits as chess, card games, Concentration, and the like are not only effective ways of promoting togetherness and passing leisure time, but are likely to contribute to a youngster's intellectual growth as well!

Elaboration

Another effective strategy for improving recall is to add to, or *elaborate* on, the information that we hope to remember (Kee, 1994; Pressley, 1982). **Elaboration** is particularly useful whenever our task is to associate two or more stimuli, such as a foreign word and its English equivalent. For example, one way to remember the Spanish word for duck, *pato* (pronounced "pot-o"), is to elaborate on the word *pato* by creating an image of a pot that is in some way linked to a duck (see Figure 8.7 for an example).

Figure 8.7 *An example of an elaborative image that one might create to associate* pato *(pronounced "pot-o"), the Spanish word "duck," with its English translation.*

In a review of the literature, Wolfgang Schneider and Michael Pressley (1997) found that the spontaneous use of elaborative techniques is a "latecomer to the memorizer's bag of tricks" that is rarely seen before adolescence. Furthermore, a sizable percentage of adolescents do not elaborate as a strategy for improving their recall, and these nonelaborators typically perform at lower levels on tests of associative learning than their counterparts who use elaborative techniques.

Why is elaboration so late in developing? One reason may be that younger children may have too few available mental resources to permit them to generate complex elaborative mediators (Kee, 1994; Pressley et al., 1987). However, others believe that adolescents are more proficient at elaboration because they simply know more about the world than younger children do and are better able to imagine how any two (or more) stimuli might be linked (Bjorklund, 1987). And as we will soon see, there is now some rather dramatic evidence that a person's knowledge base does indeed affect his or her performance on memory tasks.

Culture and Memory Strategies. Cultures clearly differ in the extent to which they support and encourage particular memory strategies (Kurtz, 1990; Mistry, 1997). Rehearsal, organization, and elaboration, for example, are especially helpful to children from Western industrialized societies, whose school activities involve a great deal of rote memorization and list learning. Yet, these same strategies may not be so useful to unschooled children from nonindustrialized societies, whose most important memory tasks might involve recalling the location of objects (water; game animals) in a natural setting or remembering instructions passed along in the context of proverbs or stories. In list-learning experiments, Western children rely heavily on strategies acquired at school and clearly outperform their unschooled peers from nonindustrialized societies (Cole & Scribner, 1977; Rogoff & Waddell, 1982). Yet, their superior performance does not extend to other kinds of memory tasks. Unschooled Australian aboriginal children, for example, are better than their Anglo-Australian peers at remembering the location of objects in natural settings (Kearins, 1981), and African adolescents display better recall for orally transmitted stories than American adolescents (Dube, 1982). Indeed Western children actually remember less if they try to rehearse or to organize information in these latter kinds of memory tasks (Rogoff, 1990).

These findings make perfectly good sense when viewed through the lens of Vygotsky's *sociocultural theory:* Cognitive development always occurs within a particular cultural context, which not only defines the kinds of problems that children must solve, but also dictates the strategies (or tools of intellectual adaptation) that enable them to master these challenges.

Retrieval

Once information has entered the long-term store, it is of little use unless we can get it out, or **retrieve** it. Young children are notoriously bad at retrieving information on their own. This is where the distinction between **free recall** and **cued recall** becomes important. In free recall, children are given a general prompt for information such as "Tell me what happened at school today." When these kinds of general prompts are provided, young children have a difficult time retrieving much information. However, if more focused cued-recall questions are asked, prompting younger children to retrieve more specific information, they often remember things rather well. When one 5-year-old boy who had spent the afternoon with his grandparents seeing his first play, "Little Shop of Horrors," was asked by his mother, "Well, how was your afternoon?" The child replied "OK." The mother persisted with a second general prompt: "Well, did you have a good time?" The child said, "Yeah." However, when cued by his grandmother to "Tell about Audrey II, the plant," he provided extensive details, telling how the plant ate some of the main characters, talked, sang, and how it took three people underneath it to make it move. The child had a wealth of information, but it could only be retrieved when specific cues were provided.

In a classic study of age differences in retrieval (Kobasigawa, 1974), first-, third-, and sixth-graders were given sets of pictures to remember. The pictures were grouped by categories, and a cue card picture was provided to classify the pictures in each category. Pictures of animals were grouped with a picture of a zoo, for example, and food pictures went with a picture of a grocery store. After studying the materials, children were asked to recall as many of the items as they could under one of three conditions. Children in the *free-recall* condition were simply asked to remember the items in any order they chose. Children in the *available-cue* condition were shown the cue cards that

elaboration
a strategy for remembering that involves adding something to (or creating meaningful links between) the bits of information one is trying to retain.

retrieval
class of strategies aimed at getting information out of the long-term store.

free recall
a recollection that is not prompted by specific cues or prompts.

cued recall
a recollection that is prompted by a cue associated with the setting in which the recalled event originally occurred.

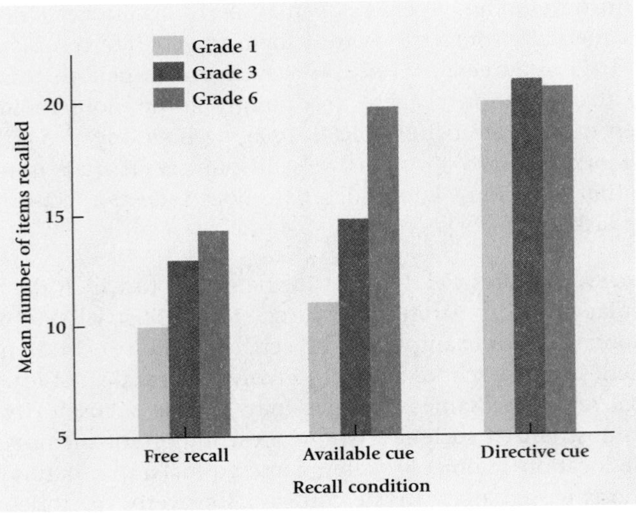

***Figure 8.8** Children's average levels of recall by grade and retrieval condition. Notice that age differences were eliminated in the directive-cue condition, where children were directed to retrieve all items from a single category before going on to the next.* FROM KOBASIGAWA, 1974.

had been paired with the items and were told that they might use these pictures to help them remember. Finally, children in the *directive-cue* condition were not only shown each cue card, one at a time, but were also told how many items had been paired with it, and were asked to recall as many of those items as they could.

Figure 8.8 shows the results. Notice that memory performance was poorest and clearly improved with age in the "free-recall" condition. Notice also that only the sixth-graders in the "available-cue" condition recalled more when the cue cards were present than in the free-recall condition. However, results were strikingly different in the "directive-cue" condition, where age differences in memory performance were all but eliminated! Apparently, first- and third-graders had gotten as much information *into* their long-term stores as older children. Their problem was getting it *out!* Even in the available-cue condition, the cue word presented to remind them of the organizational strategy that they had used to store the information was not enough to prompt first- and third-graders to use the same organizational strategy to retrieve the items they had worked so hard to store.

But why? One gets the feeling that younger children simply know less about memory aids and the circumstances under which it is appropriate to use them. They also know less in general than older children do, and their limited knowledge may hinder their attempts to categorize or elaborate on materials they are trying to remember. Let's see what researchers have learned in attempting to evaluate these hypotheses.

Metamemory and Memory Performance

Earlier in the chapter we used the term *metacognition* to refer to knowledge of the workings of one's mind, including one's mental strong and weak points. One important aspect of metacognition is **metamemory**—one's knowledge of memory and memory processes. Children display metamemory if they recognize, for example, that there are limits to what they can remember; that some things are easier to remember than others; or that certain strategies are more effective than others at helping them to remember (Schneider & Bjorklund, 1997; Schneider & Pressley, 1997).

How do we know what children know about their memories? One straightforward way of finding out is simply to ask them. Interview studies of this kind reveal that even 3- and 4-year-olds have some idea that the mind has a limited capacity and that some materials will be easier to learn and retain than others (O'Sullivan, 1997). For example, preschoolers realize that remembering many items is more difficult than remembering a few (Yussen & Bird, 1979) and that, the longer they study materials, the more likely they are to retain them (Kreutzer, Leonard, & Flavell, 1975). Yet, they usually overestimate how much they will remember and know very little about *forgetting,* even saying that it is just as easy to remember something (like a phone number) over a long period of time as over a short period (Kreutzer et al., 1975; Lyon & Flavell, 1993). It is almost as if young preschool children view information they have retained as a "mental copy"

metamemory
one's knowledge about memory and memory processes.

of reality that is filed away in one of the mind's drawers and will be available for use when they need it.

Knowledge about memory increases dramatically between ages 4 and 12 as children come to regard the mind as an active, constructive agent that stores only *interpretations* (rather than copies) of reality. Many 5-year-olds, for example, now know that items such as phone numbers are quickly forgotten unless they write them down, thus displaying an awareness that external cues can help them to remember (Kreutzer et al., 1975). Yet, knowledge about memory strategies develops very gradually. Children younger than 7 are often unaware that such strategies as rehearsal and organization may be useful to them (Justice et al., 1997); and even if they realize that related items are easier to remember than unrelated items, they often cannot say why this is so (O'Sullivan, 1996). And although 7- and 9- year-olds now realize that rehearsing and categorizing are more effective strategies than merely looking at items or labeling them once, not until age 11 do children recognize that organization is more effective than rehearsal (Justice et al., 1997).

Does a person's metamemory influence how well he or she will perform on memory tasks? The evidence is mixed. Two reviews of the literature found only low to moderate positive correlations between memory and metamemory, thus implying that *good metamemory is not always necessary for good recall* (Cavanaugh & Perlmutter, 1982; Schneider & Pressley, 1997). Nevertheless, studies that have trained children to use memory strategies are often more successful when training includes a metamemory component such as making children aware that being strategic has improved their memory performance (Ghatala et al., 1986; Leal, Crays, & Moely, 1985).

William Fabricius and Lynn Cavalier (1989) have proposed that the aspect of metamemory that is most closely related to actual memory behavior is not merely knowledge that a strategy works but, rather, knowledge of *why* that strategy works. To test this hypothesis, Fabricius and Cavalier questioned 4-, 5-, and 6-year-olds to determine whether they (1) knew that labeling objects they hoped to remember could improve recall and (2) had a mental explanation for *why* labeling is an effective technique. Then the children were observed to see if they would actually use the labeling strategy when instructed to try to remember a series of pictures that the experimenter showed them. The results clearly supported the hypotheses. Children who knew that labeling could help them recall rarely labeled the objects they were trying to remember unless they also knew *why* labeling would improve recall.

These findings dovetail nicely with studies that have attempted to help children to improve their reading comprehension by training them to use effective memory aids and other metacognitive strategies (for example, identifying the most important information in a passage; evaluating the text for clarity and monitoring how well the material has been understood). Briefly, training studies show that merely teaching strategies is not enough; to be effective, the training must also inform the child *why* each strategy is better than others she might use and *when* it is advantageous to use it. Children who receive this informed training when learning ways to extract and retain more information from their reading materials soon rely on the strategies they have learned and usually show distinct improvements in reading comprehension (a measure of retention) and other academic skills (Brown & Campione, 1990; Paris, 1988).

So a child's understanding of how or why memory strategies work seems to be the best metacognitive predictor of her use of these techniques. Indeed, the finding that measures of metamemory and memory are often more highly correlated among children 10 years of age and older (Schneider & Pressley, 1997) undoubtedly reflects the fact that older children have had more time to discover *why* various memory strategies make remembering easier.

Metamemory improves dramatically in middle childhood. This 8-year-old is now aware that writing down a phone number is an effective strategy to ensure that he retains this information.

Knowledge Base and Memory Development

As we noted earlier, children who are experts in a particular domain, such as chess, have longer memory spans when tested on information from their area of expertise (Chi, 1978). Consider an implication of this finding. Since older children generally know more about the world than younger ones do, they are relative experts on most topics. Thus, age differences in recall memory could be due as much to increases in children's **knowledge base** as to increases in their use of strategies (Bjorklund, 1987; Schneider & Bjorklund, 1997).

Consider what David and Barbara Bjorklund (1985) found when testing grade-school children's memory for one area in which they have some expertise: the identities of their classmates. Some students were given a specific strategy for performing this task (recall names row by row), whereas others were left to their own devices. Nearly all the children using the efficient row-by-row strategy listed the names they recalled in perfect row-by-row order, yet they left out (forgot) just as many classmates as did children using other schemes, even those who professed to use no strategy. In other words, use of the row-by-row strategy did not gain these children anything in the way of greater memory performance, presumably because they were all experts when it came to their current classmates, making the row-by-row strategy unnecessary.

This is not to say that strategy use is unimportant to knowledgeable individuals. In their own areas of expertise, whether the topic is math, chess, dinosaurs, or soccer, children seem to develop highly specialized strategies for processing information that make learning and remembering new information about that topic much easier (Bjorklund, 1987; Hasselhorn, 1995; Folds et al., 1990). Think about the difference between reading about a topic that you already know well and reading about an unfamiliar topic. In the first case, you can process the information quickly by linking it to existing knowledge. That is, you already have a scheme for organizing or elaborating new input. However, learning and retaining information about an unfamiliar topic is much more effortful because you have no existing conceptual pegs to hang it on.

Just how important is one's knowledge base to memory performance? In one study of third-, fifth-, and seventh-grade soccer experts and nonexperts conducted in Germany, children's ability to recall information about a soccer-related story was influenced more by their knowledge about soccer than by their general intellectual aptitude! As we see in Figure 8.9, experts recalled more than novices, even when the experts were of low general aptitude and the novices were high in general mental ability (Schneider et al., 1989). Although low-ability experts do not always outperform high-ability novices on all tasks, experts generally recall far more new information about their area of expertise than do novices of the same intellectual level (Schneider & Bjorklund, 1992; Schneider, Bjorklund, & Maier-Bruckner, 1996).

In sum, knowledge is power, and the more one knows about a topic, the more one can learn and remember. Detailed general knowledge may result in improved memory performance because the better established the information is in one's mind, the more easily it can be activated, or brought to consciousness (Bjorklund, 1987; Kee, 1994). And because older children usually know more than younger children about most subjects, they expend less mental effort to activate what they know, leaving them with more mental capacity to encode, classify, and execute other cognitive operations on the new material they encounter.

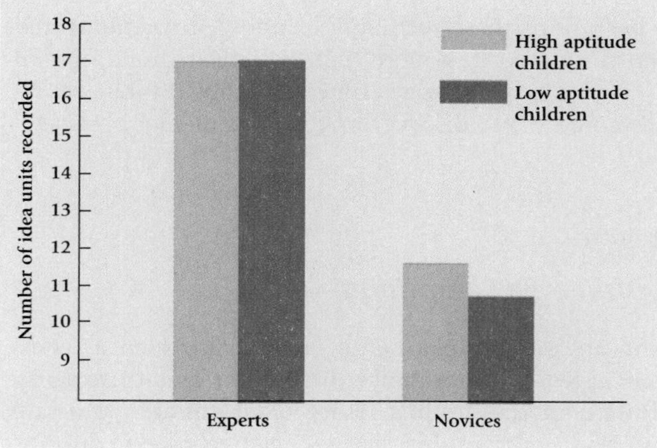

Figure 8.9 *Number of idea units remembered about a soccer story for high- and low-aptitude soccer experts and soccer novices. In this case, being an expert eliminated any effect of academic aptitude (IQ) on performance.* *Adapted from data presented in Schneider, Körkel, & Weinert, 1989.*

knowledge base
one's existing information about a topic or content area.

Table 8.1 Four Major Contributors to the Development of Learning and Memory

Contributor	Developmental trends
1. Working memory capacity	Older children have greater information-processing *capacity* than younger children do, particularly in the sense that they process information faster (and more efficiently), leaving more of their limited working memory space for storage and other cognitive processes.
2. Memory strategies	Older children use more effective *memory strategies* for encoding, storing, and retrieving information.
3. Metamemory	Older children know more about memory processes, and their greater *metamemory* allows them to select the most appropriate strategies for the task at hand and to carefully monitor their progress.
4. Knowledge base	Older children know more in general, and their greater *knowledge base* improves their ability to learn and remember.

Summing Up

How might we briefly summarize the ground we have covered? One way is to review Table 8.1, which describes four general conclusions about the development of strategic memory that have each gained widespread support.

Let's also note that these four aspects of development *interact* with each other rather than evolving independently. For example, automatization of certain information processes may leave the child with enough working memory space to use effective memory strategies that were just too mentally demanding earlier in childhood (Case, 1985; Kee, 1994; Miller et al., 1991). Or a child's expanding knowledge base may permit faster information processing and suggest ways that information can be categorized and elaborated (Bjorklund, 1995). So there is no one "best" explanation for the growth of memorial skills. All the developments that we have discussed contribute in important ways to the dramatic improvements that occur in children's strategic memory.

THE DEVELOPMENT OF EVENT AND AUTOBIOGRAPHICAL MEMORY

Although the growth of strategic memory is clearly an important aspect of cognitive development, most of what children and adolescents remember are episodes, or events, particularly those that happened to them. *Event memory* in general, and our memory for particularly important personal experiences, or *autobiographical memory,* are rarely as intentional as strategic memory is. Although we may sometimes try very hard to reconstruct a past experience, rarely do we deliberately organize or rehearse such events to ensure that we will remember them. Instead, we will see that event and autobiographical memories are closely tied to language skills and to our ability to represent our experiences in storylike narratives (Nelson, 1996).

Origins of Event Memory

Earlier in Chapter 6, we learned that the ability to *recognize* the familiar is apparently inborn, for newborns who habituate to a repetitive stimulus are telling us that they remember this object or event as something they have experienced before. When are infants capable of *pure recall*—of actively retrieving information from memory when no cues are present to remind them of their experiences? A big breakthrough occurs at age 8 to 12 months (Nelson, 1996). This is when infants begin to search for and find hidden toys in object permanence tests, thereby illustrating that they *recall* that the object exists. Other early evidence of event memory is *deferred imitation*. Many 9-month-olds are able to recall and imitate the novel actions of an adult model (for example, pushing a button to produce a beep) after a 24-hour delay (Meltzoff, 1988c). And infants less than 2 years old appear to be capable of reconstructing a noteworthy sequence of actions they had observed *8 months earlier* (Bauer, 1996).

If infants and toddlers can recall events that happened months ago, then why do we display **infantile amnesia**—an inability to remember anything that happened to us during the first few years? Though the answers remain elusive, some speculations about this fascinating memory lapse are presented in Box 8.3.

Development of Scripted Memory

What events do toddlers and preschool children remember best? The things they tend to recall very well are reccurring events that typically happen in familiar contexts. Katherine Nelson and her colleagues find that young children organize familiar routines into **scripts**—that is, schemes for certain experiences that preserve the ordering and causal relations among the events that unfold. For example, a 3-year-old describing her fast-food restaurant script might say "You drive there, go in, get in line, get hamburgers and fries, eat, and go home." Even 2-year-olds can organize information in a scriptlike fashion (Bauer, 1997; Fivush, Kuebli, & Clubb, 1992). And although scripted knowledge may become more elaborate with age, preschool children continue to learn and remember what usually happens at snack time at school, birthday parties, fast-food restaurants, at bedtime at home, and in a variety of other familiar settings (Farrar & Goodman, 1992; Fivush, 1997; Nelson, 1996).

Forming scripts thus appears to be a means by which young children organize and interpret their experiences and make predictions about what they can expect on similar occasions in the future. Yet, young children's organization of events into scripts has its costs, for it results in their tending *not* to remember much in the way of novel, atypical (or nonscript) information. In one study (Fivush & Hamond, 1990), 2½ year-olds were questioned about such recent "noteworthy" events as a trip to the beach, a camping trip, or a ride on an airplane. Rather than recalling the novel aspects of these special events, children were more likely to focus on what adults would consider to be routine information. So when describing a camping trip, one child first recalled sleeping outside, which is unusual, but then mostly remembered very mundane activities:

> INTERVIEWER You slept outside in a tent? Wow, that sounds like a lot of fun.
>
> CHILD And then we waked up and eat dinner. First we eat dinner, then go to bed, and then wake up and eat breakfast.
>
> INTERVIEWER What else did you do when you went camping? What did you do when you got up, after breakfast?
>
> CHILD Umm, in the night, and went to sleep. (p. 231)

It may seem strange that a young child would talk about such routine events as waking up, eating, and going to bed when so many new and exciting things must have happened on a camping trip. But the younger the child, the more he or she may need to embed novel events into familiar routines. According to Fivush and Hamond, everything is new to 2-year-olds, who are most concerned with making some sense of the events they experience.

As children grow older, they eventually remember more specific and atypical information over extended periods, especially if the event sequence they experienced is highly unusual and particularly noteworthy. For example, Hamond and Fivush (1991),

infantile amnesia
a lack of memory for the early years of one's life.

script
a general representation of the typical sequencing of events (that is, what occurs and when) in some familiar context.

8.3

DEVELOPMENTAL ISSUES

What Happened to Our Early Childhood Memories?

David and Barbara Bjorklund (1992) recount the following story:

> We received a letter from a woman . . . who was worried because her 10-year-old son could remember very little from his preschool days. She said that she and her husband had always tried to be good parents but thought that her son's inability to remember things from early childhood was an indication that either they hadn't done a very good job after all, or they had done a truly terrible job and her son was repressing this painful period of his life. We assured her that her son's inability to remember events much before his fourth birthday is quite normal, and is certainly not an indication that those events were unimportant . . . (p. 206).

Though infants are quite capable of remembering, most adults recall almost nothing that happened to them before the age of 3, or, if they do have memories, many turn out to be pure fiction. JoNell Usher and Ulric Neisser (1993) studied this lack of memory for the early years, or *infantile amnesia,* by questioning college students about experiences they had had early in life such as the birth of a younger sibling, a stay in the hospital, a family move, or the death of a family member. To assess recall, a series of questions was asked about each event that the participant had experienced (for example, "Who told you your mother was going to the hospital to give birth? What were you doing when she left? Where were you when you first saw the new baby?") As we see in the accompanying figure, the percentage of questions that college students could answer increased substantially the older the person was when he or she had experienced the event. Usher and Neisser concluded that the earliest age of *any* meaningful recall was about age 2 for the birth of a sibling or a hospitalization, and age 3 for the death of a family member or a family move. Even 9- and 10-year-olds who are shown photographs of their day-care classmates from 6 or 7 years earlier have difficulty discriminating these youngsters, who were once very familiar to them, from other young day-care children they have never seen before (Newcombe & Fox, 1994). So if infants can remember their experiences, why can't grade-school children and adults remember much about what their lives were like as infants and toddlers?

Sigmund Freud thought infantile amnesia simply reflected our tendency to repress the emotional conflicts of early childhood. However, contemporary researchers have rejected Freud's view in favor of more cognitive explanations. For example, infants do not use language and adults do, so it is possible that early memories are stored in some nonverbal code that we cannot retrieve once we become language users (Sheingold & Tenney, 1982). Even slightly older children, who can talk, may not represent their experiences in the same way as older children and adults. It is not until about 4 years of age that most children easily encode and remember their experiences in terms of narratives (stories about their lives)—usually with much help from adults. It is only after being guided by adults that children learn to code memories and realize that language can be used to share memories with others (Nelson, 1996). Mark Howe and Mary Courage (1993) suggest yet another interesting possibility: Maybe what is lacking in infancy is not cognitive or language ability, but a sense of self around which personal experiences can be organized. Once an infant gains a firm sense of self (to be discussed in Chapter 12) at about 18 to 24 months of age, events may become more memorable when encoded as things that happened *to me.* Though we still cannot pinpoint the exact cause (or causes) of infantile amnesia, it is quite clear that a period of life (infancy) that is so critically important to later development is a blank for most of us.

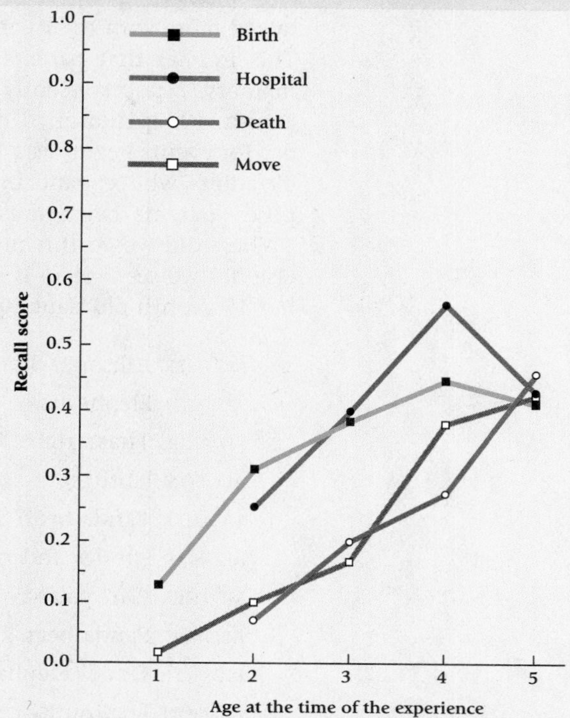

College students' recall of early life events increases as a function of their age at the time of the event. FROM USHER & NEISSER, 1993.

interviewed 3- and 4-year-olds 6 or 18 months after they had gone to Disneyworld. All children recalled a great deal of information about their trip, even after 18 months. The 4-year-olds recalled more details and required fewer prompts to describe them than 3-year-olds did. Nevertheless, recall for this single, special experience was quite good, perhaps because it deviated so far from and could not easily be assimilated into a familiar, scriptlike routine.

The Social Construction of Autobiographical Memories

One interesting aspect of Hamond and Fivish's (1991) study was that children who talked more with their parents about the Disneyworld trip recalled more about the trip. This implies that parents play an important role in the growth of autobiographical memory, a point recently made by several theorists (Fivush, 1997; Hayden, Haine, & Fivush, 1997; Hudson, 1990). Judith Hudson (1990), for example, proposes that memory for events begins as a joint activity in which children talk about past events, guided by adults who expand on their skimpy recollections. In most families, Hudson proposes, parents begin talking about the past by asking such contextual questions as "Where did we go this morning?", "What did we see?", "Who went with us?", "What else did we see?" Here is one example of a conversation in which a mother prompted her 19-month-old daughter to recall details of their morning trip to a zoo:

MOTHER Allison, what did we see at the zoo?
ALLISON Elephunts.
MOTHER That's right! We saw elephants. And what else?
ALLISON (shrugs)
MOTHER Panda bear? Did we see a panda bear?
ALLISON (smiles and nods)
MOTHER Can you say "panda bear?"
ALLISON Panda bear.
MOTHER Good! Elephants and panda bears. What else?
ALLISON Elephunts.
MOTHER That's right, elephants. And also a gorilla.
ALLISON Go-rilla!

WHAT DO YOU THINK?

To what extent do you think that each of the following experiences might prompt or inhibit the development of autobiographical memory and why: (a) watching children's shows such as *Mister Rogers' Neighborhood;* (b) watching rock videos on MTV; (c) participating in "show and tell" in nursery school?

By encouraging children to reconstruct past events in which they have participated, parents foster the development of autobiographical memory.

From these interchanges, children learn that the important facts to remember about events are the whos, whens, and wheres of their experiences. And when parents request this information in ways that reconstruct the temporal order and causal sequences among events and ask children to *evaluate* these happenings (what was *your* favorite part?), they are helping youngsters to organize their experiences into storylike *narratives* and to recall them as events that have *personal* significance—as things that happened *to me* (Fivush, Hayden, & Reese, 1996; Hayden et al., 1997). Clearly, these joint reconstructions of past experiences should remind us of Vygotsky's ideas about the social construction of knowledge and Rogoff's ideas about guided or collaborative learning. Indeed, 2- to 3½-year-olds whose parents have often collaborated with them by asking questions about past events recall more autobiographical experiences 1 to 2 years later than do age-mates whose parents have rarely questioned them about the past (Ratner, 1984; McCabe & Peterson, 1991; Reese, Hayden, & Fivush, 1993).

Interestingly, parents' co-constructions of past events become increasingly detailed as their children develop more competent language and narrative skills (Hayden et al., 1997). So over the preschool years, autobiographical memory appears and blossoms as children, guided by their parents, learn to construct increasingly detailed personal narratives in which they place their experiences in the larger context of their own lives.

Children as Eyewitnesses

The accuracy of children's autobiographical memories has received a lot of attention lately. Increasingly, children are being called on to testify in court cases involving child abuse and neglect, child custody battles, or other matters in which their recollections could play a major part in decisions that affect their welfare (Ceci & Bruck, 1995). Normally, these child-witnesses are reporting on events that were highly stressful and may even be testifying against a parent or some other relative to whom they feel some loyalty. And the stress they experience is often intensified as they are questioned in the highly unfamiliar and often emotionally charged adversarial atmosphere of a courtroom. How reliable are children's recollections under these circumstances? How susceptible are child-witnesses to suggestion?

Age Differences in Eyewitness Memory

Studies of eyewitness memory typically have children experience or watch an event and later ask these eyewitnesses for their recollections. So eyewitness memory is really no different from event memory, except that some misdeed or traumatic experience is usually imbedded in the witnessed event. When children are later asked to recall such events, typical developmental differences are found, with older children remembering far more than younger children (Ornstein, Gordon, & Larus, 1992; Poole & Lindsay, 1995). But even though preschool (and young grade-school) children recall few precise details, what they do remember is generally accurate and central to the event (Goodman, Aman, & Hirschman, 1987; Poole & White, 1995). In a video involving a boy and a girl in which the boy stole a bike, for example, young children typically recall the bike theft, but are much less likely than older children or adults to describe the participants, characteristics of the bicycle, or details of the setting (Cassel & Bjorklund, 1995). When children are prompted with more specific cues (for example, "Tell me what the girl looked like."), they recall more information. However, in addition to remembering more *correct* facts, they also tend to relate some *incorrect* "facts" as well, reducing the overall accuracy of their recall (Cassel, Roebers, & Bjorklund, 1996; Goodman et al., 1994). And unfortunately, these *false memories* often persist and may be as resistant as or more resistant to forgetting than true memories are (Brainerd & Reyna, 1996; Brainerd, Reyna, & Brandse, 1995).

How Suggestible Are Child Witnesses?

The fact that children sometimes report and retain false memories implies that their recall of witnessed or experienced events may be highly susceptible to suggestion. Research has shown that people of all ages report more inaccurate information if asked leading questions that suggest inaccurate facts or events (for example "He touched your penis, didn't he?"). And most of the available evidence implies that children younger than 8 or 9 are far more susceptible to such memory distortions than older children, adolescents, and adults are (Ackil & Zaragoza, 1995; Bruck et al., 1995a; Ceci & Bruck, 1995).

Consider what Alison Clarke-Stewart and her colleagues found in their research with preschoolers (Clarke-Stewart, Thompson, & Lepore, 1989; Goodman & Clarke-Stewart, 1991). Each child watched a man posing as a janitor who either cleaned and arranged some toys, including a doll, or played with the toys in a somewhat rough and suggestive manner. About an hour later, the janitor's "boss" interviewed the children about what they had seen. Of primary concern here is the condition in which children watched the janitor merely cleaning the toys, because the interviewer asked leading questions implying that the janitor had actually been playing with the toys improperly instead of doing his job. If a child initially did not succumb to the interviewer's suggestion, more leading questions were asked, with each question becoming increasingly stronger in suggesting misconduct. Two-thirds of these children eventually reported seeing events that the interviewer had suggested, even though they hadn't. Furthermore,

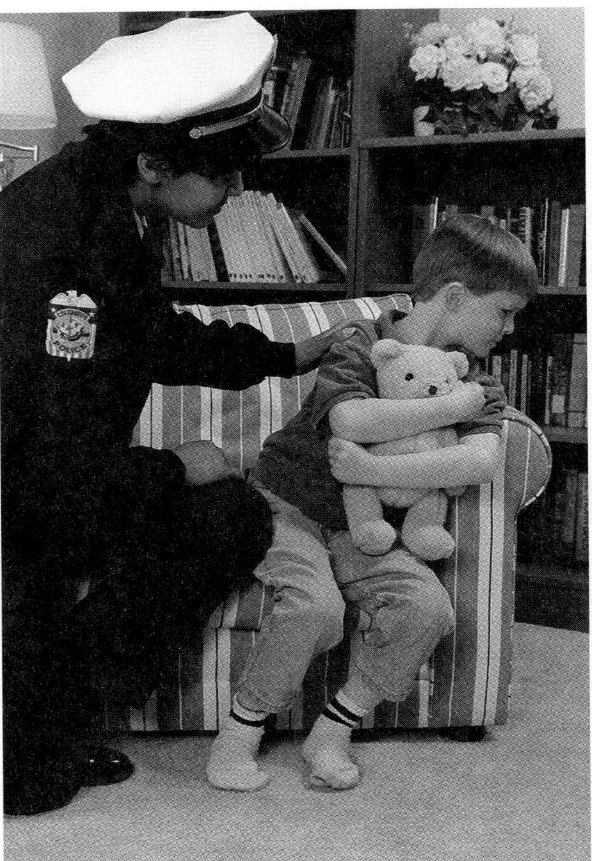

Child witnesses are susceptible to reporting false memories. To guard against this possibility, adults must be patient and supportive and must avoid asking leading questions.

when the children were questioned by their parents at the end of the session, all stuck with the false memories that they had given the interviewer.

Don't misunderstand: False memories of this kind can be induced in people of all ages (Loftus & Pickrell, 1995). Nevertheless, it is much easier to create them in preschool and young grade-school children, even when the memories address events that allegedly happened *to them* and the children initially *deny* the experiences. Stephen Ceci and his associates (1994), for example, asked preschool children and 6-year-olds if they could ever remember having experienced such events as catching a finger in a mousetrap. Although almost no one admitted to recalling these fictional events in the initial interviews, after repeated questioning, more than 50% of the younger preschool children and about 40% of the 5- and 6-year-olds said that these events had happened to them and often provided vivid accounts of their experiences! Furthermore, many children continued to believe that these events actually happened even after being told by the interviewers and their parents that the events were just made up and had never taken place.

In sum, it is often possible to convince young children to confirm an interviewer's allegations by falsely recalling information or experiences that never happened, particularly when the suggestions and accusations are strong and persistent. Why are younger children so suggestible? Such social factors as a young child's desire to please adults or to comply with their requests almost certainly contributes to their heightened suggestibility. So, too, does a young child's preference for encoding and reporting exact details (which they are more prone to forgetting) rather than gist information, which

Concept Check 8.2
Development of Attention and Memory

Check your understanding of the development of attention and memory by matching each descriptive statement below to one of the following ideas or concepts: (a) autobiographical memory, (b) knowledge base, (c) elaboration, (d) false memories, (e) storylike narratives, (f) scripts, (g) metamemory, (h) sustained attention, (i) retrieval.

_____ 1. one's increasing capacity for _____________ depends, in part, on maturation of the reticular formation

_____ 2. strategic memory strategy that rarely appears before adolescence

_____ 3. early memory device by which children organize and represent their experiences

_____ 4. excellent performance of child experts illustrates the role of _____________ in facilitating strategic memory

_____ 5. memory that infants and toddlers lack

_____ 6. memory process aided greatly by cued-recall prompts

_____ 7. representations that contribute greatly to the development of autobiographical memory

_____ 8. easily created in young children by asking leading questions

_____ 9. executive control process that can promote memory performance is easier to remember over the long run (Reyna & Brainerd, 1995). So when an interviewer suggests a fact that they haven't encoded or can't recall (for example, "The man who touched your sister had a scar on his face, didn't he?"), younger children, who are especially motivated to recall details, may answer "Yes" and remain convinced that this is what they really saw.

Implications for Legal Testimony

Although most states rarely ask children age 5 or under to testify in court, 6- to 10-year-olds are often called as witnesses. What steps might legal practitioners take to help to ensure that testimony provided by child-witnesses is accurate and not tainted by false memories?

Judging from the research on children's eyewitness memory, the most important step might be to place sensible limitations on the ways children are interviewed so as to lessen the likelihood of suggestibility. This can be accomplished by asking questions in nonleading ways, by limiting the number of times children are interviewed, and by cautioning children that it is better to say "I don't remember" or to admit to not knowing an answer than it is to guess or to go along with what an interviewer is implying (Ceci & Bruck, 1993). Remaining friendly and patient with a child, rather than stern and adversarial, also seems to lessen the probability that children will report inaccurate details or construct false memories.

Other procedures have been used to spare children the traumas of having to face an abusive parent in court or to answer pointed questions about uncomfortable issues, such as sexual abuse, that they may not understand and can easily misreport. For example, young children are sometimes asked to "act out" with dolls what they have experienced, or to answer questions about sensitive issues posed by a puppet with whom they feel more comfortable. Yet, these methods are controversial, for they may not improve the accuracy of children's testimony and can even induce some young witnesses to imply the occurrence of inappropriate physical and sexual contact that never happened (Bruck et al., 1995b). Other children are spared the discomfort of facing family members in the emotionally charged atmosphere of the courtroom by testifying on videotape, which is later entered as evidence during the trial. Although this procedure can lessen children's emotional concerns (that is anxiety, fear of punishment) and increase reporting accuracy, it is important that the interrogators be impartial and question children in nonleading ways that are unlikely to promote false memories (Bruck, Ceci, & Hembrooke, 1998).

WHAT DO YOU THINK? ?

An adult daughter accuses her father of sexual molestation once her allegedly "repressed" memories from toddlerhood have emerged after several sessions under hypnosis. Should we be skeptical of this claim? What would you want to know before treating this allegation as credible?

APPLICATIONS: INFORMATION-PROCESSING AND ACADEMIC SKILLS

Over the past 20 years, information-processing researchers have been quite concerned about the development of children's competencies and problem-solving skills in such academic domains as reading, arithmetic, and scientific reasoning. The skills and strategies that are necessary for successful performance do, of course, vary from domain to domain. Yet within each domain, the approach that researchers have taken is to identify the information-processing skills that underlie competent performance, examine how those skills change with age, and use what they have learned to devise more effective methods of instruction.

You may recall that we have already touched on certain aspects of information processing that foster the growth of scientific reasoning (see Box 2.3) and underlie children's emerging ability to learn to read (see Box 6.2). In this section, we will briefly consider some general educational implications of research we have reviewed on the development of attention and memory (see Box 8.4), and then take a closer look at the growth of children's numerical reasoning and arithmetic skills.

Development of Numerical Reasoning and Arithmetic Skills

When are human beings first capable of processing quantitative information? Remarkable as it may seem, this may be an innate ability (Geary, 1995). Very young infants can easily discriminate visual displays containing different numbers of objects and, by age 5 months, can learn that a particular numerical cue (for example, two objects rather than one or three) presented to their left means that an interesting stimulus will soon appear to their right (Canfield & Smith, 1996). By age 16 to 18 months, toddlers have even acquired a rudimentary sense of *ordinal* relationships, recognizing, for example, that three objects are *more than* two (Strauss & Curtis, 1981). These early understandings, coupled with the acquisition and use of such quantitative labels as *big, lots, small, and little,* reveal that toddlers are quite well-prepared for such feats as learning to count and to think about quantities.

Counting

Counting normally begins shortly after children begin to talk. However, early counting strategies are very imprecise, often consisting of no more than uttering a few number words (for example, "one, three, four, six") while pointing to objects that a companion has counted (Fuson, 1988). By age 3 to 4, most children can count "accurately," establishing a one-to-one correspondence between number words and the items they represent (Gallistel & Gelman, 1992). And by age 4½ to 5, most children have acquired the principle of **cardinality**—the knowledge that the last word in a counting sequence (for example, "one, two, three, four, *five*") represents the number of items in a set (Bermejo, 1996). These developments in counting are especially important, for they pave the way for the emergence of simple arithmetic strategies.

cardinality
principle specifying that the last number in a counting sequence specifies the number of items in a set.

Early Arithmetic Strategies

Although counting develops early, the growth of simple arithmetic skills is a more gradual process that unfolds over the preschool and early grade-school years. Children's earliest addition strategies are based on counting, at first out loud, and often using such props as fingers. The *sum* strategy we discussed earlier is perhaps the simplest method of adding numbers. Given the problem "What is 2 + 3?", the child begins by counting out the first number ("1, 2") and then counts out the second, starting from the cardinal value of the first (. . . 3, 4, **5**). Although this sum strategy is quite accurate, it takes a considerable amount of time to execute and is not very effective for problems where larger numbers (for example, 22 + 8) are involved.

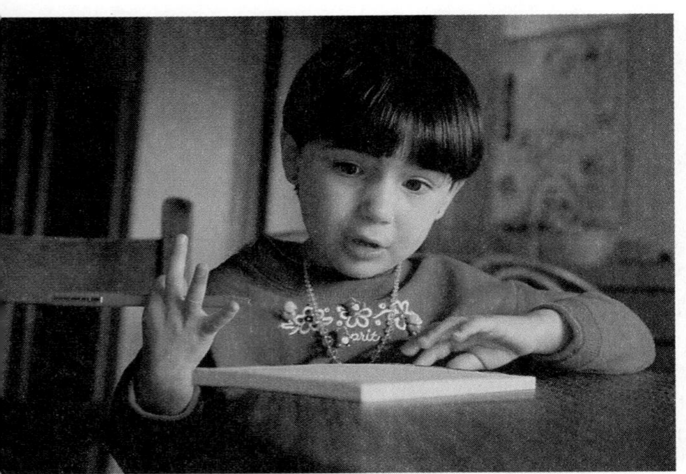

Counting on one's fingers is an early strategy that children use to solve arithmetic problems, one that is used less frequently as they develop more mathematical knowledge.

More sophisticated addition strategies take short cuts in counting. For example, a 6-year-old using the *min* strategy performs the minimum number of counts. Asked for the sum of 8 + 3, this child would start with the cardinal value of the larger number and count up from there (for example, "8 . . . 9, 10, **11.**"). Although preschoolers may use rules other than the sum and min strategies to add (and subtract) numbers, their approaches almost always involve counting out by ones the concrete objects to be added or subtracted (Carpenter & Moser, 1982).

APPLYING DEVELOPMENTAL RESEARCH

Some Educational Implications of Research on Attention and Memory

Recall that Piaget offered educators two important suggestions for helping their pupils to learn. First, teachers should view children as naturally inquisitive beings who learn best by construction knowledge from moderately novel aspects of experience—that is, from information that challenges their current understanding and forces them to reevaluate what they already know. Second, Piaget stressed that a teacher's job is not so much to transmit facts or reinforce correct answers as to provide the climate, setting, and materials that allow curious children the personal satisfaction of discovering important concepts for themselves.

Information-processing theorists can certainly agree with Piaget that children are active and curious explorers who learn best by constructing knowledge from experiences that are just beyond current levels of understanding. However, their own guidelines for effective instruction are much more explicit than Piaget's and come closer to the views of Lev Vygotsky (1978), implying that teachers should take a more *active, directive* role than Piaget had envisioned. The following five implications for instruction flow directly from the research we have reviewed on the development of attentional and strategic memory processes.

1. *Analyze the requirements of problems that you present to your pupils.* Know what information must be encoded and what mental operations must be performed to arrive at a correct answer or to otherwise grasp the lesson to be learned. Without such knowledge, it may be difficult to tell why students are making errors or help them overcome their mistakes.

2. *Reduce short-term memory demands to a bare minimum.* Problems that require young grade-school children to encode more than three or four bits of information are likely to overload their short-term storage capacity and prevent them from thinking logically about this input. The simplest possible version of a new problem or concept is what teachers should strive to present. If a problem involves several steps, students might be encouraged to break it down into parts (or subroutines) and perhaps to record the solutions to these parts in their notes in order to reduce demands on their short-term storage. Once children grasp a concept and their information-processing becomes more "automatized," they will have the short-term storage capacity to succeed at more complex versions of these same problems (Case, 1985; 1992).

3. *Encourage children to have fun using their memories.* Strategic games such as 20 Questions or Concentration not only are enjoyable to grade-school children but help them to appreciate the advantages of being able to retain information and to retrieve it for a meaningful purpose.

4. *Provide opportunities to learn effective memory strategies.* A teacher can do this by grouping materials into distinct categories as she talks about them or by giving children easily categorizable sets of items to sort and classify (Best, 1993). Question-and-answer games of the form "Tell me why leopards, lions, and house cats are alike" or "How do dragonflies and hummingbirds differ from helicopters and missiles?" are challenging to young children and make them aware of conceptual similarities and differences on which organizational strategies depend.

5. *Structure lessons so that children are likely to acquire metacognitive knowledge and to understand why they should plan, monitor, and control their cognitive activities.* Simply teaching appropriate information-processing strategies does not guarantee that your pupils will use them. If these skills are to transfer to settings other than the training task, it is important that children understand *why* these strategies will help them to achieve their objectives and *when* it is appropriate to use them. As an instructor, you can help by making your own metacognitive knowledge more explicit (I'll have to read this page more than once to understand it"), offering suggestions to the child ("You might find it easier to remember the months of the year if you group them according to seasons. Summer includes . . ."), or asking questions that remind children of strategies already taught ("Why is it important to summarize what you've read?", "Why do you need to double-check your answer?"). All these approaches have proved quite successful at furthering children's metacognitive skills and persuading them to apply this knowledge to the intellectual challenges they face (Brown et al., 1983; Brown & Campione, 1990; Paris, 1988).

Development of Mental Arithmetic. At some point during the early grade-school years, children's solutions to simple arithmetic problems become more covert. They no longer rely on counting objects on their fingers because they can perform arithmetic operations in their heads. The earliest mental arithmetic strategies may still be such counting strategies as covert sum or min solutions. However, the many experiences they have adding and subtracting numbers, coupled with knowledge about number systems that is often taught at school, soon permit grade-school children to employ other, more efficient arithmetic strategies. For example, knowledge of the base-10 number system underlies *decomposition* strategies, in which children transform an original problem into two simpler problems. Given 13 + 3 = ?, for example, a child might think "13 is 10 + 3; 3 + 3 = 6; 10 + 6 = 16; so the answer is 16." Initially, use of a decomposition strategy may be slower than a min strategy, particularly for simple problems where not many "counts" are involved. But as children become practiced at decomposing numbers into base-10 components, they solve problems faster by decomposition, particularly if they are working with larger numbers (for example, 26 + 17) for which counting strategies are laborious (Siegler, 1996). Finally, children come to solve many simple arithmetic problems by *fact retrieval;* they simply know the correct answer (that is, 8 + 6 is 14) and retrieve it from long-term memory.

Once children begin to perform arithmetic computations "in their heads," knowing precisely what they are doing becomes more difficult. However, it is possible to infer their arithmetic strategies from the time it takes for them to arrive at a correct answer. If children are using a min strategy, for example, their reaction times for addition problems should increase as the size of the smaller of the two numbers (that is, the number of counts it requires) increases. If children are using fact retrieval, by contrast, they should answer very quickly.

Using this reaction time paradigm, researchers have found that children's mental arithmetic strategies become more complex with age (Ashcraft, 1990; Ashcraft & Fierman, 1982). Third-graders have progressed from the counting-based procedures used by first-graders, to a transitional phase in which they rely on both counting-based and more complex strategies, whereas most fourth- through sixth-graders, like adults, rapidly solve many simple arithmetic problems by fact retrieval. However, Robert Siegler and his associates find that the growth of arithmetic strategies is not a simple stagelike process. Based on his analyses of kindergarten, first-grade, and second-grade children's reaction times, errors, and verbal reports, Siegler (1987) identified five general strategies children use to solve addition problems: the sum, min, decomposition, and fact-retrieval approaches we have discussed, and a strategy of simply guessing at the answer. Interestingly, most children used more than one strategy to solve mental addition problems; in fact 62% reported using three or more strategies. The min strategy was used most frequently, but even so, it accounted for less than 40% of the solutions by children of any age. Consistent with past research, the older second-graders more often used the sophisticated decomposition and fact retrieval strategies. But the most striking finding was the sheer variety of strategies on which all children relied. Similar variability in strategy use has been reported for adults performing mental arithmetic problems (Siegler, 1996; Siegler & Jenkins, 1989).

Siegler's findings should remind us of the *strategy choice model* of problem solving that we touched on earlier. The model claims that children of any age have a variety of tools, or strategies, that compete for use on problems for which they are relevant. Sometimes one strategy will "win" the mental competition (the min strategy, for example) and sometimes another strategy will win (fact retrieval, for example). With age, experience, and improved information-processing abilities, more sophisticated strategies are apt to "win," so that min, on average, replaces sum as a preferred strategy, and later on, decomposition or fact retrieval replaces min. But for new problems or problems with which children are less familiar, the older "fall-back" strategies often come up as the winners. So from Siegler's perspective, strategy development is not the simple matter of abandoning older, less sophisticated strategies for newer, more powerful ones. Rather, multiple strategies reside side by side in one's mind and old strategies never die; they simply lie in wait for a chance to be used when a newer, more preferred strategy doesn't quite fit or fails to produce the correct answer. So faced with 38 − 12 = ?, even we adults who know many arithmetic facts may quickly revert to a decomposition strategy (that is 30 − 10 = 20; 8 − 2 = 6; answer is 26) if we cannot immediately retrieve the answer from memory.

Complex Computations. Obviously, not all mathematical proficiencies rest on our abilities to retrieve numerical facts or perform computations in our heads. Children in schooled societies are explicitly taught a number of computational procedures, such as the carrying and borrowing rules that enable them to solve multidigit addition and subtraction problems, multiply large numbers, and perform long division. Many pupils have trouble learning and applying these rules, and often educators can quickly correct these deficiencies if, as suggested by the first point of Box 8.4, they have carefully analyzed the requirements of the problems they present and have inferred what a child is doing wrong from the kinds of errors he makes. If Johnny, for example, is presented with 350 − 131 and answers 221 rather than 219, he is using a faulty strategy that says "when subtracting from 0, enter the bottom digit." He will require different instruction than Susie, who works the same problem and comes up with an answer of 119. Can you diagnose the faulty strategy Susie is using? (If not, the answer appears at the bottom of the page.)

Cultural Influences on Mathematics Performance

One of the major claims that Vygotsky made in his *sociocultural* theory was that cognitive development always occurs in a cultural context that influences the way one thinks and solves problems. Can this important principle possibly hold for a rule-bound domain such as arithmetic? Let's see if it does.

Arithmetic Competencies of Unschooled Children

Although children in most cultures learn to count and acquire some very simple arithmetic strategies during the preschool years, the computational procedures on which higher mathematics are based are typically taught at school. Does this imply that children who receive minimal or no schooling are hopelessly incompetent in math?

One might answer "yes" if math competencies are assessed by the paper-and-pencil tests so often used to assess arithmetic and other quantitative skills in Western societies. However, these tests often badly underestimate the skills that unschooled children display.

Kpelle children from Liberia typically struggle to master arithmetic in Westernized schools, performing very poorly on paper-and-pencil arithmetic exercises. However, J. Gay and Michael Cole (1967) found that the Kpelle did have a consistent way of measuring one commodity, rice—their only cash crop that was of vital importance to their livelihood. Gay and Cole then assessed Kpelle farmers' ability to estimate quantities of rice in bowls of varying size and contrasted their performance with those of Americans. The Kpelle were consistently more accurate in this task than were the Americans, reflecting a mathematical competence not apparent by previous tests. Stated another way, the Kpelle had devised some rather sophisticated mathematical strategies for solving problems of practical importance to them.

In later research, T. N. Carraher and associates (1985) examined the mathematical competencies of unschooled 9- and 15-year-old street vendors in Brazil. They found that problems embedded in real-life contexts (for example, "If a large coconut costs 76 cruzeiros, and a small one costs 50, how much do the two cost together?") were solved correctly *98% of the time.* By contrast, the same problems presented in a standard, out-of-context way (that is, "How much is 76 + 50?") were answered correctly only 37% of the time. Street vendors can quickly and accurately add and subtract currency values *in their heads,* just as they must when conducting street transactions, where mistakes can have economic consequences. By contrast, the same numerical problems presented in out-of-context paper-and-pencil format have little practical application, and unschooled participants are apparently less motivated to expend the effort

---

Susie uses an inappropriate borrowing rule. She thinks that whenever she needs to borrow she must borrow from every column—that is,

24
3̸5̸0
−131
119

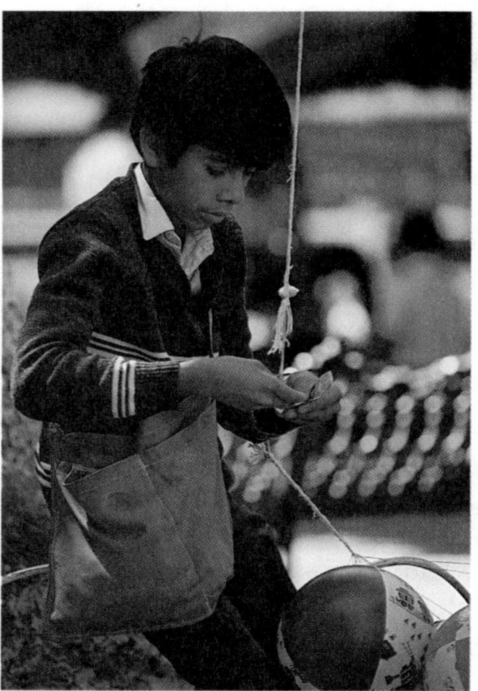

Although unschooled street vendors may often fail at paper-and-pencil math problems, they display sophisticated arithmetic skills by quickly and accurately making change during sales transactions.

necessary to serve them. Other unschooled participants, such as bricklayers and lottery bookies, also develop flexible arithmetic competencies that they use with great skill in their own work (Schliemann, 1992).

These findings are clearly consistent with Vygotsky's most basic sociocultural premise: Children acquire the skills they need within their own cultural context. Parents of unschooled Brazilian children, for example, construct arithmetic tasks for them (such as buying things at local stores with currency) that are appropriate for their current developmental level and contribute to a brand of arithmetic reasoning that is functional in their daily lives (Guberman, 1996).

Cultural Variations in Arithmetic among Schooled Children

Much has been written lately, both in the popular and the scholarly presses, about the fact that East Asian youngsters from China, Taiwan, and Japan typically outperform American children in certain academic subjects, most notably mathematics. Figure 8.10 shows the math test performance of first- and fifth-grade children from the United States (Minneapolis), Japan (Sendai), and Taiwan (Taipei). Clearly, U.S. children performed much worse that age-mates from the two Asian cultures, even in the first grade, and this cultural difference in math performance becomes more apparent with age.

In attempting to explain these findings, researchers quickly ruled out the possibility that East Asian students are inherently smarter than Americans, for first-graders in all three cultures do equally well on standardized intelligence tests (Stevenson et al., 1985). Yet, East Asian first-graders already rely on a more sophisticated mix of basic arithmetic strategies than American first-graders do, including the relatively sophisticated (for first-graders) decomposition and fact retrieval strategies (Geary, Fan, & Bow-

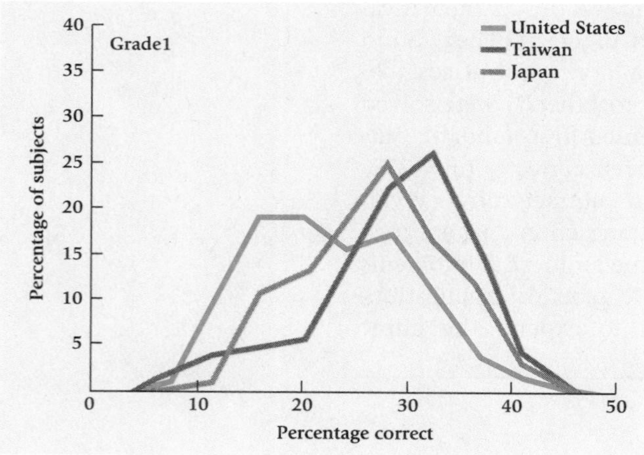

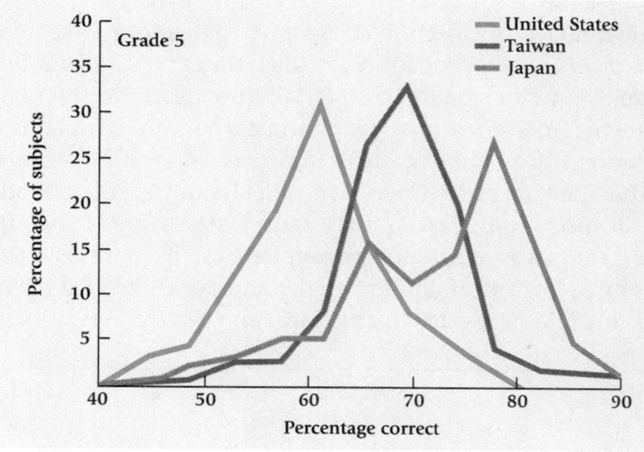

Figure 8.10 *Frequency distributions of mathematics scores for first- and fifth-grade children in the United States, Japan, and Taiwan.* FROM STEVENSON & LEE, 1990.

Thomas, 1992). And later research reveals that the math-strategy advantage that East Asian children display is already apparent during the *preschool* period (Geary et al., 1993).

Now a critic might argue "So what?" We are talking here about the most basic of arithmetic strategies which American children clearly master by the end of elementary school. Yet, David Geary and his colleagues have shown that the sophistication of early arithmetic strategies and speed of fact retrieval predicts later performance in more complex forms of mathematics (Geary & Burlingham-Dubre, 1989; Geary & Widaman, 1992). So if early mastery of basic skills promotes more complex mathematical competencies, it may not be surprising that East Asian students display a consistent mathematical advantage over their American peers at all levels of schooling.

Now the obvious question becomes "Why are young East Asians so advantaged in acquiring basic mathematical skills?" Let's briefly consider some linguistic and instructional supports for acquiring mathematical concepts that are available to East Asian children but not to their American counterparts.

Linguistic Supports. Earlier in the chapter, we learned that Chinese children have larger digit spans than American children do, largely because Chinese number words can be articulated more quickly than English number words—a fact that is generally true of East Asian languages. This implies that young East Asian children may be mathematically advantaged in at least two ways: Not only can they hold more of those quickly articulated number words in short-term memory, which should facilitate use of counting strategies, but the brevity of those number words increases the speed with which they can retrieve math facts from long-term memory (Geary et al., 1993).

The structure of East Asian languages differs from English in another important way that promotes mathematical understandings. Although children in all cultures learn the same base-10 number system, the system is more obvious or transparent in Asian languages (Fuson & Kwon, 1992; Geary, Bow-Thomas, Liu, & Siegler, 1996). For example, in Chinese, the number words for 11, 12, and 13 are translated as "ten-one," "ten-two," and "ten-three," which helps children to understand that the 1 in 13 has a place value of 10 (rather than 1). By contrast, English words for two-digit numbers (that is, *eleven* through *nineteen*) are irregular and do not convey the idea of tens and ones. In one recent study, Korean second- and third-graders had an excellent understanding of the meaning of digits in multidigit numbers, knowing that the 1 in 186 stood for "hundreds" and the eight stands for "eight-tens." Consequently, they performed very well on three-digit addition and subtraction problems (What is 142 + 318?), even though they had not yet received any formal instruction on adding or subtracting numbers this large (Fuson & Kwon, 1992). By contrast, the irregular form of many English multidigit numbers makes the meaning of larger numbers less intuitive and may even contribute to the problems English-speaking children experience with the borrowing and carrying rules they must acquire to perform multidigit addition and subtraction.

Instructional Supports. Finally, several East Asian instructional practices support the rapid learning of math facts and computational procedures involved in multidigit addition and subtraction. East Asian students practice computational procedures more than American students do (Stevenson & Lee, 1990), and practice of this sort fosters the retrieval of math facts from memory (Geary et al., 1992). And the type of instruction provided seems to matter. For example, Asian teachers instructing students how to carry a sum from one column of a multidigit number to the next higher will say to "bring up" the sum instead of "carrying" it. The term "bring *up*" (rather than "carry") may help children learning multidigit addition to remember that each digit to the left in a multidigit number is a base-10 increment of the cardinal value of that digit (that is, the *5* in 350 represents "50" rather than "5" and the *3* represents "300"). Furthermore, Asian math texts also help children to avoid confusing place values by having different color codes for the "hundreds," "tens," and "ones" column of multidigit numbers (Fuson, 1992).

How much do these linguistic and instructional supports contribute to the superior math performance of East Asian students? They almost certainly matter, but are hardly

Linguistic supports, instructional supports, and a lot of practice help to explain the high proficiency that East Asian students display in mathematics.

the sole contributors. Consider that Asian students have always had the linguistic advantages over their American counterparts; and yet, American children who received their elementary school educations during the 1930s were quicker to acquire basic mathematical competencies than today's American students are, showing a proficiency for mathematics that rivals today's East Asian students (Geary, Salthouse, Chen, & Fan, 1996). So cross-national differences in mathematical competencies between East Asian and American students seem to be a relatively recent phenomenon that undoubtedly reflects broader cultural differences in educational philosophies and supports for education, as well as the differences in linguistic and instructional supports for mathematics learning that we have discussed here. Indeed, we will see just how true this speculation is in Chapter 16, where we will examine the many roles that schooling plays in the social, emotional, and intellectual lives of developing children and adolescents.

EVALUATING THE INFORMATION-PROCESSING PERSPECTIVE

Today, the information-processing perspective has become the dominant approach to the study of children's intellectual development, and justifiably so. Simply stated, information-processing researchers have provided a reasonably detailed description of how such cognitive processes as attention, memory, and metacognition—processes that Piaget did not emphasize—change with age and influence children's thinking. Furthermore, the detailed examination of certain domain—specific academic skills that information-processing theorists have undertaken have led to important instructional changes that enhance scholastic performances.

Despite these obvious strengths, the information-processing approach has several drawbacks that render it woefully incomplete as an explanation of cognitive development. Some of the stronger challenges have come from the developing field of cognitive neuroscience, which is concerned with identifying evolutionary and neurological contributors to cognition and intellectual growth. Research on the neural correlates of inhibition that we reviewed in Box 8.1 is one small step in this direction. But because information-processing theorists have chosen not to emphasize and explore the biological underpinnings of the mind's activities, critics have argued that new theories that "take the brain as seriously as the mind" are sorely needed (Bjorklund, 1997; Tooby & Cosmides, 1992).

Still other critics point out that information-processing theorists have paid little attention to important social and cultural influences on cognition that Vygotsky and others (for example, Rogoff, 1997) have emphasized. And those who favor the elegant coherence of Piaget's stage model question what they see as the "fragmented" approach of information-processing theorists, who focus on specific cognitive processes and view development as the gradual acquisition of skills in many different domains. These critics contend that information-processing researchers have succeeded in breaking cognition into pieces, but haven't been able to put it back together into a broad, comprehensive theory of intellectual development. Although this criticism has some merit, information-processing theorists would reply by noting that it was the many, many problems with Piaget's broad-brush account of cognitive development that helped to stimulate their work in the first place.

Even some of the central assumptions on which information-processing theory rests have been assailed in some quarters. For example, critics have argued that the classic mind–computer analogy badly underestimates the richness of human cognitive activity. After all, people can dream, speculate, create, and reflect on their own (and other people's) cognitive activities and mental states, whereas computers most certainly cannot (Kuhn, 1992). Furthermore, the classic assumption that all cognitive activities take place in a single, limited-capacity working memory store has now been challenged. Charles Brainerd and Johannas Kingma (1985), for example, propose that working memory should be viewed as a series of independent stores, each with its own resources and each performing such specific operations as information encoding, information retrieval, and execution of strategies. Of course, we have already discussed another alternative to traditional information-processing models—*fuzzy-trace theory*—which claims that we process information at more than one level rather than merely making verbatim mental copies of what we experience.

In sum, the information-processing approach is itself a developing theory that has greatly advanced our understanding of children's intellectual growth while experiencing some very real "growing pains" of its own. We like to think of this model as a necessary complement to, rather than a replacement for, Piaget's earlier framework. And our guess is that this new look at cognitive development will continue to evolve, aided by advances in cognitive neuroscience and other complementary perspectives (see Fischer & Bidell, 1997), eventually filling in many of the gaps that remain in its own framework and that of Piaget, and thereby contributing to a comprehensive theory of intellectual growth that retains the best features of both approaches.

SUMMARY

Basic Assumptions of Information-Processing Theories

♦ Information-processing theorists approach the topic of intellectual growth by charting the development of cognitive skills such as attention, memory, metacognition, and academic skills. Many analogies are drawn between human minds and computers. The mind, like a computer, is thought to be a *limited-capacity* system composed of mental "hardware" and "software." The **store model** depicts the human-information-processing system as consisting of a **sensory store** to detect, or "log in" input, a **short-term store (STS),** where information is stored temporarily until we can operate on it, and a "permanent," or **long-term store (LTS).** Also included in most information-processing models is a concept of **executive control processes,** or **metacognition,** which include processes by which we plan, monitor, and control all phases of information-processing.

♦ Recent alternatives to the store model of information processing include neo-Piagetian theories that reinterpret many of Piaget's ideas in information-processing terms, **fuzzy-trace theory,** which claims that we process information at both a **gist** and a verbatim level and accounts for some age differences in memory and problem solving, and theories that emphasize the role of **inhibition** in children's intellectual development.

How Does Information-Processing Capacity Change with Age?

♦ Age differences in information-processing "hardware" have been examined by assessing **memory span** and

working-memory span to evaluate capacity of the STS and speed of processing. Although substantial age differences have been found in speed of processing, many developmental differences in memory and working-memory span can be attributed to differences in efficiency of processing, as reflected by Case's **operating efficiency hypothesis.**

♦ Research on developmental changes in information-processing "software" have focused mainly on **strategies**—goal-directed operations used to aid task performance. Frequent findings include production **deficiencies,** in which children fail to produce a strategy spontaneously but can do so when instructed, and **utilization deficiencies,** in which children experience little or no benefit when they use a new strategy. Children of all ages have been found to use multiple- and variable-strategies in solving problems, a phenomenon that is explained by Robert Siegler's **strategy choice model.**

The Development of Attention

♦ With age, the **attention spans** of children and adolescents increase dramatically, owing, in part, to increasing myelinization of the central nervous system.

♦ Attention also becomes more planful and more **selective** with age, as children and adolescents steadily improve in their ability to seek and to concentrate on task-relevant stimuli and to not be distracted by other "noise" in the environment. **Attention deficit-hyperactivity disorder (ADHD)** describes children who find it nearly impossible to sustain their attention for long or to develop planful attentional strategies.

Memory: Retaining and Retrieving Information

♦ The effective use of **strategic memory** strategies, or **mnemonics,** increases with age. Frequently used memory strategies include **rehearsal, semantic organization, elaboration,** and **retrieval.** Memory strategies are usually assessed on either **free-recall** or **cued-recall** tasks, the latter of which provide specific cues, or prompts, to aid retrieval. The particular memory strategies that one acquires are heavily influenced by culture and the kinds of information that children are expected to remember.

♦ **Metamemory** (or knowledge of the workings of memory) increases with age and contributes to developmental and individual differences in strategic memory.

♦ Another reason for the dramatic improvements in strategic memory between infancy and adolescence is that older persons know more than younger ones do, and this larger **knowledge base** improves one's ability to access information and to devise memory strategies for use in learning and remembering.

The Development of Event and Autobiographical Memory

♦ **Event memory** in general, and our memory for personal experiences, or **autiobiographical memory,** are rarely as intentional as strategic memory is. Although infants can recall events that happened earlier in time, most of us display **infantile amnesia**—an inability to recall much about the first few years of life.

♦ Early autobiographical memory is based on **scripts,** or schematic organizations of recurring real-world events organized in terms of their causal and temporal sequences. Even very young children organize their experiences in terms of scripts, which become more detailed with age.

♦ Autobiographical memory expands dramatically during the preschool years. Parents play an important role in the growth of autobiographical memories by discussing past events, providing clues about what information is important to remember, and helping children to recall their experiences in rich personal narratives.

♦ One aspect of autobiographical memory that has received much attention is age differences in eyewitness memory and suggestibility. As in general episodic memory, the accuracy of children's eyewitness memory increases with age. Young children are generally more susceptible to suggestion than older children and are more likely to form false memories. Steps to increase the accuracy of children's eyewitness testimony in legal proceedings include limiting the number of times child witnesses are interrogated, asking questions in nonleading ways, and cautioning the child against guessing or providing answers merely to satisfy the interrogator.

Applications: Information-Processing and Academic Skills

♦ Information-processing researchers have studied the development of such academic competencies as reading, arithmetic, and scientific reasoning and have made positive instructional contributions in these (and other) areas.

♦ Even infants are capable of processing and using quantitative information, and toddlers have already acquired a rudimentary understanding of ordinal relationships. Counting begins once children begin to talk, and preschoolers gradually construct such basic mathematical understandings as the principle of **cardinality.** Early arithmetic strategies usually involve counting out loud, but eventually, children perform simple arithmetic operations in their heads, using increasingly sophisticated arithmetic strategies. Yet, children of any age actually use a variety of strategies to solve math problems, as described by Siegler's *strategy choice model.*

♦ There are sizable cultural variations in mathematics performance and the use of arithmetic strategies. Unschooled children develop arithmetic strategies that they apply quite skillfully to the practical problems they encounter. Among those who are taught arithmetic strategies at school, East Asian children consistently outperform their American agemates, owing, in part, to the structure of their languages and to instructional practices that aid them in retrieving math facts and acquiring computational skills and other mathematical knowledge.

Evaluating the Information-Processing Perspective

♦ Despite its many strengths, the information-processing perspective has been criticized for largely ignoring neurological, evolutionary, and sociocultural influences on cognitive growth, for failing to provide a broad, integrative theory of children's intelligence, and for underestimating the richness and diversity of human cognitive activities.

To understand the basics of information-processing theory, it is necessary to understand how your own attentional system and memory systems work. A visit to: **http://www.psych.purdue.edu/~coglab/start.html** will allow you to actively experience some classic experiments in memory and attention.

KEY TERMS

store model, 272

sensory store (or sensory register), 272

short-term store (STS), 272

long-term store (LTS), 273

executive control processes, 274

metacognition, 274

fuzzy-trace theory, 275

gist, 275

inhibition, 276

memory span, 278

working memory, 278

operating efficiency hypothesis, 280

strategies, 281

production deficiency, 282

utilization deficiency, 282

strategy choice model, 283

attention span, 284

reticular formation, 285

selective attention, 286

attention deficit-hyperactivity disorder (ADHD), 287

event memory, 287

autobiographical memory, 287

strategic memory, 287

mnemonics (memory strategies), 287

rehearsal, 288

semantic organization, 289

elaboration, 290

retrieval, 291

free recall, 291

cued recall, 291

metamemory, 292

knowledge base, 294

infantile amnesia, 296

script, 296

cardinality, 302

Intelligence: Measuring Mental Performance

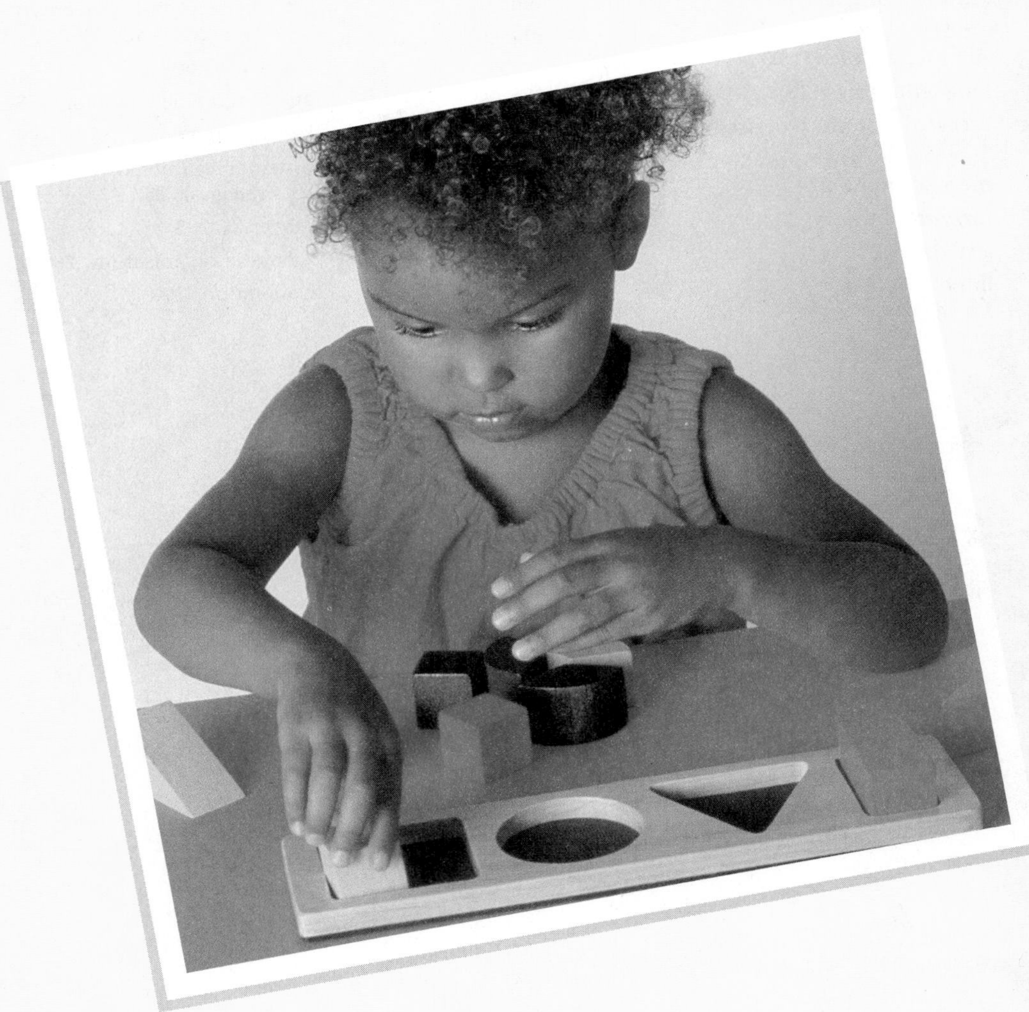

"When he was 3 years old, the 19th-century philosopher John Stuart Mill began to study Greek under his father's direction. At age 6½ he wrote a history of Rome. He tackled Latin at age 8 [when] he also began his study of geometry and algebra. Mill's IQ score has been estimated at 190, on a scale on which 100 is average" (Cox, 1926).

At age 27, Susan lives in an institution for the mentally retarded. She has been labeled profoundly retarded, has an IQ of 37, and usually responds to people with smiles. She cannot read and write or even feed or dress herself. Yet, remarkably, she can flawlessly recite just about any poem after having heard it only once.

As these examples indicate, the range of human cognitive potentials is immense. So far, our explorations of cognitive development have focused mainly on what human minds have in common. Piaget, after all, was interested in identifying *universal* stages in the way thinking is organized or structured. Similarly, information-processing theorists have been primarily concerned with understanding the basic cognitive processes on which all people rely to learn, remember, and solve problems.

In this chapter, we continue our exploration of how the human mind changes over the course of childhood and adolescence, but with a greater emphasis on *individual differences* in cognitive performance. We will begin by introducing yet another perspective on intellectual development—the *psychometric* approach—which has led to the creation and widespread use of intelligence tests. Unlike the Piagetian and information-processing approaches, which focus on cognitive *processes,* psychometricians are more *product oriented.* They seek to determine how many and what kinds of questions children can answer *correctly* at different ages and whether or not this index of intellectual performance can predict such developmental outcomes as scholastic achievement, occupational attainments, and even health and life satisfaction.

There may be some surprises ahead as we consider what a person's score on an intelligence test implies about his or her ability to learn, to perform in academic settings, or to succeed at a job. Perhaps the biggest surprise for many people is learning that intelligence test scores, which can vary dramatically over the course of one's life, are assessments of intellectual *performance* rather than innate potential or intellectual *capacity*. True, heredity does affect intellectual performance. But so too do a variety of environmental factors that we will examine, including one's cultural and socioeconomic background, the character of one's home environment, the schooling one receives, and even social and emotional factors surrounding the testing situation itself. We will then evaluate the merits of preschool educational programs, such as *Project Head Start,* designed to promote the scholastic performances of children who perform poorly on intelligence tests. Finally, we will conclude by exploring the growth of highly valued *creative* talents that are not adequately represented on our current intelligence tests.

WHAT IS INTELLIGENCE?

Go out and ask five people to summarize in a single sentence what intelligence means to them, and then, to list up to five attributes that characterize highly intelligent people. Chances are their summary sentences will state that intelligence is how "smart" someone is compared with other people, or perhaps that it represents one's capacity for learning or problem solving. However, you can almost bet that your five interviewees will show some meaningful differences in the attributes they view as characterizing highly intelligent individuals. Simply stated, intelligence does not mean the same thing to all people (Neisser et al., 1996).

And so it goes with behavioral scientists. Although few topics have generated as much research as intelligence and intelligence testing, even today there is no

WHAT DO YOU THINK? ?

Before reading further, list five attributes that you think characterize people you would consider "highly intelligent" and say why these attributes define intelligence for you. As you read the section entitled "What Is Intelligence?", think about whose views of intelligence are most compatible with your own.

clear consensus about what intelligence is. Clearest agreement comes in "one-sentence" characterizations. Piaget (1970), for example, defined intelligence as "adaptive thinking or action." And in a recent survey, 24 experts provided somewhat different one-sentence definitions of what intelligence meant to them, but virtually all these definitions centered in some way on the ability to think abstractly or to solve problems effectively (Sternberg, 1997).

So why is there still no singular definition of intelligence? Simply because different theorists have very different ideas about which attributes (and how many of them) are core aspects of this construct they call intelligence. Let's now consider some of the more influential viewpoints on the nature of intelligence, beginning with the psychometric perspective.

Psychometric Views of Intelligence

The research tradition that spawned the development of standardized intelligence tests is the **psychometric approach** (Thorndike, 1997). According to psychometric theorists, intelligence is a trait or a set of traits that characterizes some people to a greater extent than others. Their goal, then, was to identify precisely what those traits might be and to measure them so that intellectual differences among individuals could be described. But from the start, psychometricians could not agree on the structure of intelligence. Was it a single ability that influenced how people performed on all cognitive tests; or, alternatively, was intelligence best described as many distinct abilities?

Alfred Binet's Singular Component Approach

Alfred Binet (1857–1911), the father of intelligence testing.

Alfred Binet and a colleague, Theodore Simon, produced the forerunner of modern intelligence tests. In 1904, Binet and Simon were commissioned by the French government to construct a test that would identify "dull" children who might profit from remedial instruction. They then devised a large battery of tasks measuring skills presumed to be necessary for classroom learning: attention, perception, memory, numerical reasoning, verbal comprehension, and so on. Items that successfully discriminated normal children from those described by teachers as dull or slow were kept in the final test.

In 1908, the Binet-Simon test was revised, and all test items were age-graded. For example, problems that were passed by most 6-year-olds but few 5-year-olds were assumed to reflect the mental performance of a typical 6-year-old; those passed by most 12-year-olds but few 11-year-olds were said to measure the intellectual skills of an average 12-year-old, and so on. This age-grading of test items for ages 3 to 13 allowed a more precise assessment of a child's level of intellectual functioning. A child who passed all items at the 5-year-old level but none at the 6-year-old level was said to have a **mental age (MA)** of 5 years. A child who passed all items at the 10-year-old level and half of those at the 11-year-old level would have an MA of 10½ years.

In sum, Binet had created a test that enabled him to identify slow learners and to estimate their levels of intellectual development. This information proved particularly useful to school administrators, who began to use children's mental ages as a guideline for planning curricula for both normal and retarded students.

psychometric approach
a theoretical perspective that portrays intelligence as a trait (or set of traits) on which individuals differ; psychometric theorists are responsible for the development of standardized intelligence tests.

mental age (MA)
a measure of intellectual development that reflects the level of age-graded problems a child is able to solve.

Factor Analysis and the Multicomponent View of Intelligence

Other psychometric theorists were quick to challenge the notion that a single score, such as mental age, adequately represents human intellectual performance. Their point was that intelligence tests (even Binet's earliest versions) require people to perform a variety of tasks such as defining words or concepts, extracting meaning from written passages, answering general information questions, reproducing geometric designs with blocks, and solving arithmetic puzzles (see Figure 9.1 for some sample items). Couldn't

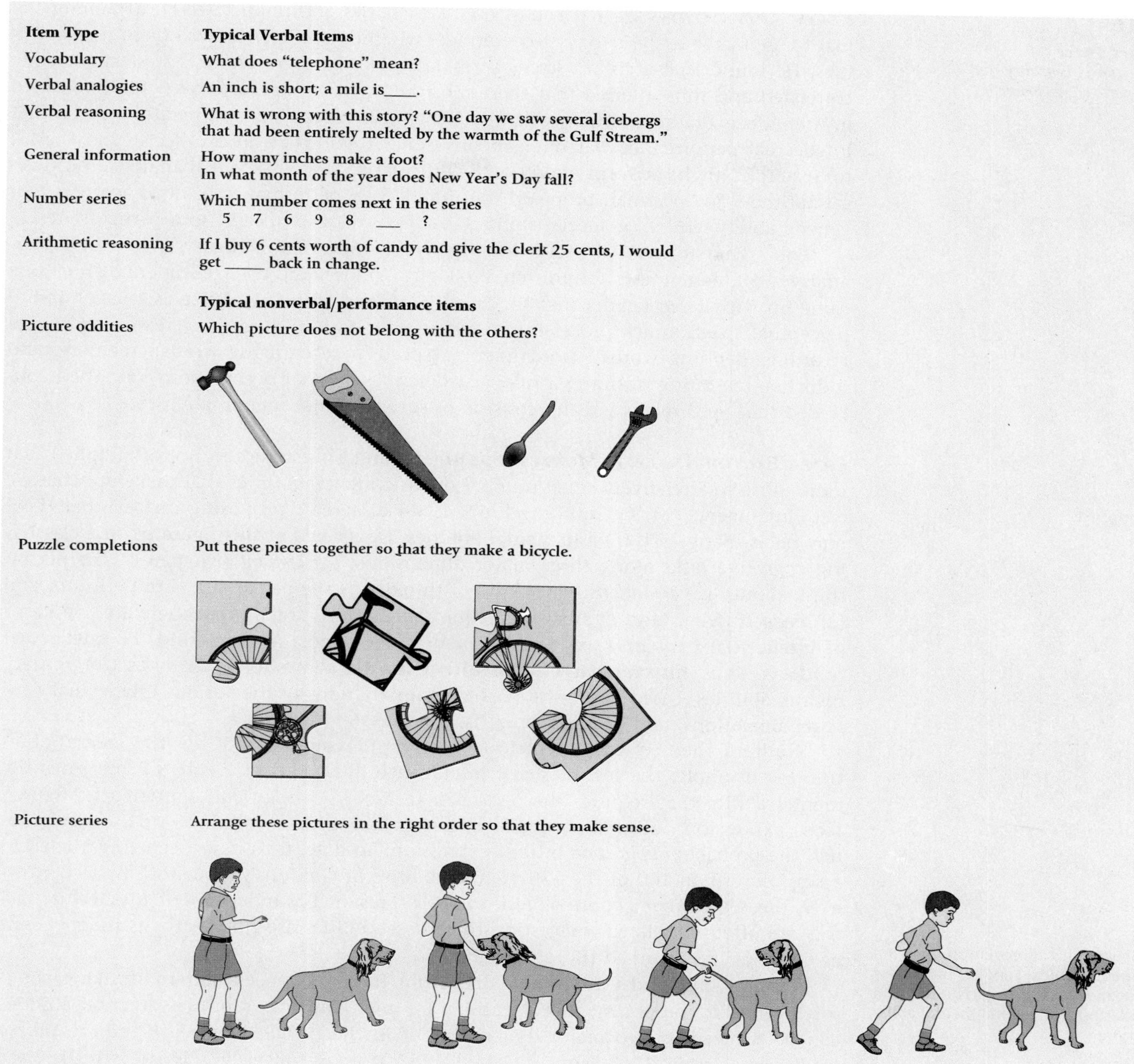

Item Type
Typical Verbal Items
Vocabulary
What does "telephone" mean?
Verbal analogies
An inch is short; a mile is____.
Verbal reasoning
What is wrong with this story? "One day we saw several icebergs that had been entirely melted by the warmth of the Gulf Stream."
General information
How many inches make a foot?
In what month of the year does New Year's Day fall?
Number series
Which number comes next in the series
5 7 6 9 8 ___ ?
Arithmetic reasoning
If I buy 6 cents worth of candy and give the clerk 25 cents, I would get_____ back in change.
Typical nonverbal/performance items
Picture oddities
Which picture does not belong with the others?
Puzzle completions
Put these pieces together so that they make a bicycle.
Picture series
Arrange these pictures in the right order so that they make sense.

Figure 9.1 *Items similar but not identical to those appearing on intelligence tests for children.*

these different subtests be measuring a number of distinct mental abilities rather than a single, overarching ability?

One way of determining whether intelligence is a single attribute or many different attributes is to ask participants to perform a large number of mental tasks and then analyze their performances using a statistical procedure called **factor analysis.** This technique identifies clusters of tasks, or test items, called *factors*, that are highly correlated with one another and unrelated to other items on the test. Each factor (if more than one are found) presumably represents a distinct mental ability. Suppose, for example, we found that examinees performed very similarly on four items that require verbal skills and on three items that require mathematical skills, but that their verbal-skill score was not correlated with their score on the math items. Under these circumstances, we might conclude that verbal ability and mathematical ability are distinct intellectual factors. But if subjects' verbal and math scores were highly correlated with each other and with scores for all other kinds of mental problems on the test, we might conclude that intelligence is a singular attribute rather than a number of distinct mental abilities.

factor analysis
a statistical procedure for identifying clusters of tests or test items (called factors) that are highly correlated with one another and unrelated to other test items.

Early Applications of Factor Analysis. Charles Spearman (1927) was among the first to use factor analysis to try to determine whether intelligence was one or many abilities. He found that a child's scores across a variety of cognitive tests were moderately correlated and thus inferred that there must be a *general mental factor,* which he called **g,** that affects one's performance on most cognitive tasks. However, he also noticed that intellectual performance was often inconsistent. A student who excelled at most tasks, for example, might perform poorly on a particular test, such as verbal analogies or musical aptitude. So Spearman proposed that intellectual performance has two aspects: *g,* or general ability, and **s,** or special abilities, each of which is specific to a particular test.

Louis Thurstone (1938) soon took issue with Spearman's theory. When he factor-analyzed 50 mental tests administered to eighth-graders and college students, Thurstone came up with *seven* factors that he called **primary mental abilities:** spatial ability perceptual speed (quick processing of visual information), numerical reasoning, verbal meaning (defining words), word fluency (speed at recognizing words), memory, and inductive reasoning (forming a rule that describes a set of observations). He then concluded that Spearman's *g* really consists of seven distinct mental abilities.

Later Factor-Analytic Models. Spearman's and Thurstone's early work implied that there must be a relatively small number of basic mental abilities that make up what we call "intelligence." J. P. Guilford (1967; 1988) disagreed, proposing instead that there may be as many as 180 basic mental abilities. He arrived at this figure by first classifying cognitive tasks along three major dimensions: (1) *content* (what must the person think about), (2) *operations* (what kind of thinking is the person asked to perform), and (3) *products* (what kind of answer is required). Guilford argued that there are five kinds of intellectual contents, six kinds of mental operations, and six kinds of intellectual products. Thus, his **structure-of-intellect model** allows for as many as 180 primary mental abilities, based on all the possible combinations of the various intellectual contents, operations, and products (that is, $5 \times 6 \times 6 = 180$).

Guilford then set out to construct tests to measure each of his 180 mental abilities. For example, the test of social intelligence illustrated in Figure 9.2 measures the mental ability that requires the test taker to act on a *behavioral* content (the figure's facial expression), using a particular operation, *cognition,* to produce a particular product, the probable *implication* of that expression. To date, tests have been constructed to assess more than 100 of the 180 mental abilities in Guilford's model of intellect. However, the scores that people obtain on these presumably independent intellectual factors are often correlated, suggesting that these abilities are not nearly as independent as Guilford has assumed (Brody, 1992).

Finally, Raymond Cattell and John Horn have influenced current thinking about intelligence by proposing that Spearman's *g* and Thurstone's primary mental abilities can be reduced to two major dimensions of intellect: *fluid intelligence* and *crystallized intelligence* (Cattell, 1963; Horn & Cattell, 1982; Horn & Noll, 1997). **Fluid intelligence**

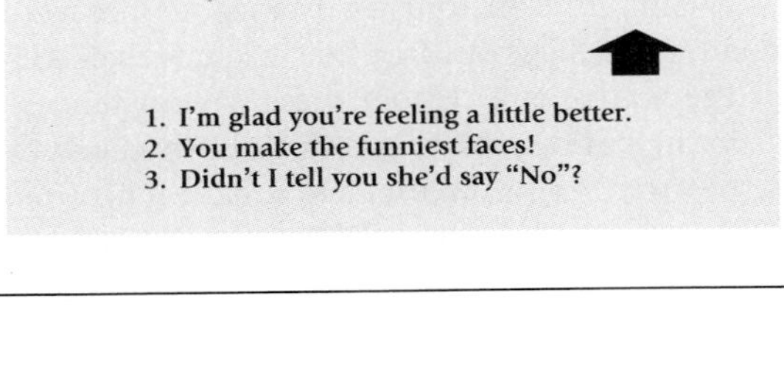

1. I'm glad you're feeling a little better.
2. You make the funniest faces!
3. Didn't I tell you she'd say "No"?

Figure 9.2 *An item from one of Guilford's tests of social intelligence. The task is to read the characters' expressions and to decide what the person marked by the arrow is most probably saying to the other person. You may wish to try this item yourself (the correct answer appears below).* Adapted from Guilford, 1967.

g
Spearman's abbreviation for *neogenesis,* which, roughly translated, means one's ability to understand relations (or general mental ability).

s
Spearman's term for mental abilities that are specific to particular tests.

primary mental abilities
seven mental abilities, identified by factor analysis, that Thurstone believed to represent the structure of intelligence.

structure-of-intellect model
Guilford's factor-analytic model of intelligence, which proposes that there are 180 distinct mental abilities.

fluid intelligence
the ability to perceive relationships and solve relational problems of the type that are not taught and are relatively free of cultural influences.

Answer to Figure 9.2: 3.

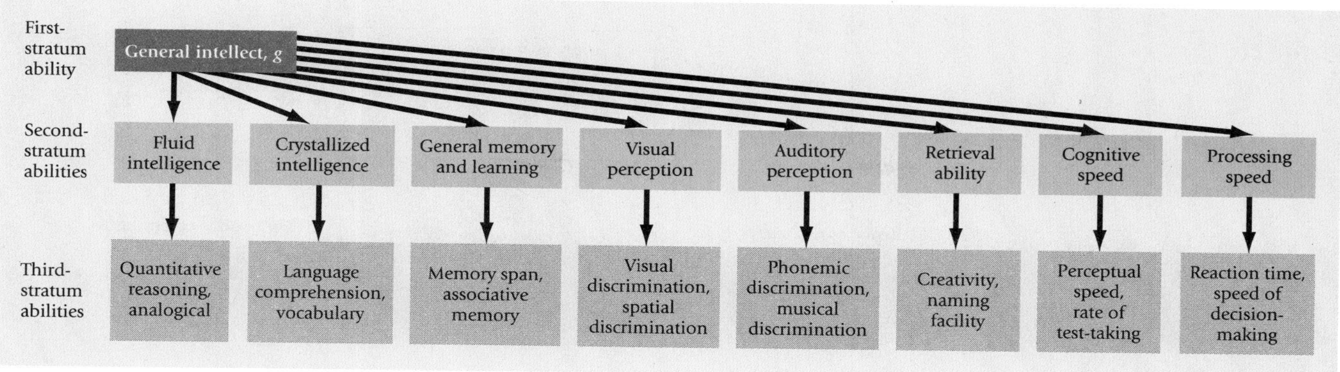

Figure 9.3 *John Carroll's three-stratum hierarchical model of intelligence. Second-stratum abilities are arranged from left to right in terms of their decreasing correlation with* g. *So fluid intelligence and the reasoning it supports (for example, quantitative reasoning) are more closely associated with general mental ability* g *than are auditory perception, cognitive speed, and the third-stratum skills that these abilities support.* FROM CARROLL, *1993.*

refers to one's ability to solve novel and abstract problems of the sort that are not taught and are relatively free of cultural influences. Examples of the kinds of problems that tap fluid intelligence are the verbal analogies and number series tests from Figure 9.1, as well as tests of one's ability to recognize relationships among otherwise meaningless geometric figures (see Figure 9.9, on page 337, for an example). By contrast, **crystallized intelligence** is the ability to solve problems that depend on knowledge acquired as a result of schooling and other life experiences. Tests of general information ("At what temperature does water boil?"), word comprehension ("What is the meaning of *duplicate*?"), and numerical abilities are all measures of crystallized intelligence.

A Recent Hierarchical Model. So what have we learned from factor-analytic studies of intelligence? Perhaps that Spearman, Thurstone, and Cattell and Horn were all partially correct. Indeed, many psychometricians today favor **hierarchical models of intellect** in which intelligence is viewed as consisting of (1) a general ability factor at the top of the hierarchy, which influences one's performance on many cognitive tests, and (2) a number of specialized ability factors (something similar to Thurstone's primary mental abilities) that influence how well one performs in particular intellectual domains (for example, on tests of numerical reasoning or tests of spatial skills). The most elaborate of these hierarchical models, based on analyses of hundreds of studies of mental abilities conducted over the past 50 years, is John Carroll's **three-stratum theory of intelligence.** As shown in Figure 9.3, Carroll (1993) represents intelligence as a pyramid, with *g* at the top and eight broad intellectual abilities at the second level. This model implies that each of us may have particular intellectual strengths or weaknesses depending on the patterns of second-stratum intellectual abilities we display. It also explains how a person of below-average general ability (*g*) might actually excel in a narrow third-stratum domain (for example, reciting poems heard only once) if she displays an unusually high second-stratum ability (general memory) that fosters good performance in that domain.

So hierarchical models depict intelligence as *both* an overarching general mental ability *and* a number of more specific abilities that each pertain to a particular intellectual domain. Are we now closer to a consensus on the definition of intelligence? No indeed, for a growing number of researchers believe that no psychometric theory of intelligence fully captures what it means to be intelligent (Neisser et al., 1996). Let's now examine two alternative viewpoints that should help us to appreciate some of the limitations of today's intelligence tests.

crystallized intelligence
the ability to understand relations or solve problems that depend on knowledge acquired from schooling and other cultural influences.

hierarchical model of intelligence
model of the structure of intelligence in which a broad, general ability factor is at the top of the hierarchy, with a number of specialized ability factors nested underneath.

three-stratum theory of intelligence
Carroll's hierarchical model of intelligence with *g* at the top of the hierarchy, eight broad abilities at the second level, or stratum, and narrower domains of each second-stratum ability at the third stratum.

A Modern Information-Processing Viewpoint

One recurring criticism of psychometric definitions of intelligence is that they are very narrow, focusing primarily on intellectual content, or what a person knows, rather than on the processes by which this knowledge is acquired, retained, and used to solve problems. Furthermore, traditional intelligence tests measure one's proficiency at mathematical, verbal, and spatial reasoning while ignoring other attributes that people

Figure 9.4 Sternberg's triarchic theory of intelligence.

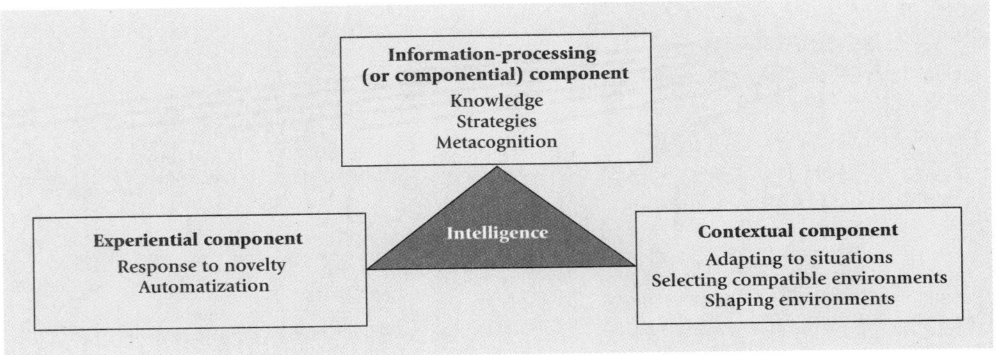

commonly think of as indications of intelligence, such as common sense, social and interpersonal skills, and the talents that underlie creative accomplishments in music, drama, and athletics (Gardner, 1983).

Recently, Robert Sternberg (1985; 1991) proposed a **triarchic theory of intelligence** that emphasizes three aspects, or components, of intelligent behavior: *context, experience,* and *information-processing* skills (see Figure 9.4). As we will see in reviewing this model, Sternberg's view of intelligence is much, much broader than that of psychometric theorists.

Context

The contextual component of Sternberg's model is a relatively simple idea: Whether an act qualifies as intelligent behavior depends to a large extent on the context in which it occurs. According to Sternberg, intelligent people are those who can successfully adapt to their environments or who are successful at shaping their environments to suit them better. In everyday language, we might describe this kind of intelligence as practical intelligence or "street smarts." Unfortunately, this ability to adapt to or cope with real-life problems or challenges is not assessed by traditional intelligence tests (Sternberg, 1997).

Notice that from a contextual perspective, what is meant by intelligent behavior may vary from one culture or subculture to another, from one historical epoch to another, and from one period of the life span to another. Sternberg describes an occasion when he attended a conference in Venezuela and showed up on time, at 8:00 A.M., only to find that he and four other North Americans were the only ones there. In North American society, it is considered smart to be punctual for important engagements. However, strict punctuality is not so adaptive in Latin cultures, where people are rather lax (by our standards, at least) about being on time. And consider the effects of history on assessments of intelligence. Thirty years ago, it was considered quite intelligent to be able to perform arithmetic operations quickly and accurately. However, an individual who spends countless hours perfecting those same skills today might be considered somewhat less than intelligent given that computers and calculators can perform these computations much faster.

The sophisticated ability that this child displays is considered intelligent in his culture, but is not measured by traditional IQ tests.

The Experiential Component

According to Sternberg, one's experience with a task helps to determine whether one's performance qualifies as intelligent behavior. He believes that relatively novel tasks require active and conscious information-processing and are the best measures of one's reasoning abilities, as long as these tasks are not so foreign that the person is unable to apply what he may know (as would be the case if geometry problems were presented to 5-year-olds). So responses to novel challenges are an indication of the person's ability to generate good ideas or fresh insights.

In daily life, however, people also perform more or less intelligently on familiar tasks (such as driving, balancing a checkbook, or quickly extracting the most important content from a newspaper). This second kind of experiential intelligence reflects *automatization*, or increasing efficiency of information processing with practice. According to Sternberg, it is a sign of intelligence when we develop automatized routines or "programs of the mind" for performing everyday tasks accurately and efficiently, so that we don't have to waste much time thinking about them.

The experiential component of Sternberg's theory has a most important implication for intelligence testers: In order to properly assess a person's intellectual prowess from the answers she gives, you have to know how familiar the task is to the test taker and, thus, which aspect of intelligence—response to novelty or automatization—her answer reflects. A child who struggles with and finally solves a problem after 2 to 3 minutes might be considered highly intelligent if the problem is novel, but rather dull if this task is like others he has performed many times before. Similarly, if the items on an intelligence test are familiar to members of one cultural group but unfamiliar to members of another, the second group will perform much worse than the first, thereby reflecting a **cultural bias** in the test itself. So if one is seeking to compare the intellectual performances of people from diverse cultural backgrounds, the test items must be equally familiar (or unfamiliar) to all test takers.

The Componential (or Information-Processing) Component

Sternberg's major criticism of psychometric theorists is that they estimate a person's intelligence from the quality, or correctness, of her answers while completely ignoring how she produces intelligent responses. Sternberg is an information-processing theorist who believes that we must focus on the componential aspects of intelligent behavior—that is, the cognitive processes by which we size up the requirements of problems, formulate strategies to solve them, and then monitor our cognitive activities until we've accomplished our goals. He argues that some people process information faster and more efficiently than others and that our cognitive tests could be improved considerably were they to measure these differences and treat them as important aspects of intelligence.

In sum, Sternberg's triarchic theory provides us with a very rich view of the nature of intelligence. It suggests that if you want to know how intelligent Charles, Chico, and Chenghuan are, you had better consider (1) the context in which they are performing (that is, the culture and historical period in which they live; their ages); (2) their *experience* with the tasks and whether their behavior qualifies as responses to novel or automatized processes, and (3) the *information-processing skills* that reflect how each person is approaching these tasks. Unfortunately, the most widely used intelligence tests are not based on such a broad and sophisticated view of intellectual processes.

triarchic theory
a recent information-processing theory of intelligence that emphasizes three aspects of intelligent behavior not normally tapped by IQ tests: the *context* of the action; the person's *experience* with the task (or situation); and the *information-processing strategies* the person applies to the task (or situation).

Gardner's Theory of Multiple Intelligences

Howard Gardner (1983, 1998) is another theorist who criticizes the psychometricians for trying to describe a person's intelligence with a single score. In his book *Frames of Mind*, Gardner (1983) outlines his **theory of multiple intelligences,** proposing that humans display at least seven distinctive kinds of intelligence, which are described in Table 9.1.

Gardner (1998) does not claim that these seven abilities represent the universe of intelligences. But he makes the case that each ability is distinct, is linked to a specific area of the brain, and follows a different developmental course. As support for these ideas, Gardner points out that injury to a particular area of the brain usually influences only one ability (linguistic or spatial, for example), leaving others unaffected.

cultural bias
the situation that arises when one cultural or subcultural group is more familiar with test items than another group and therefore has an unfair advantage.

theory of multiple intelligences
Gardner's theory that humans display at least seven distinct kinds of intelligence, each linked to a particular area of the brain, several of which are not measured by IQ tests.

TABLE 9.1	Gardner's Multiple Intelligences	
Type of intelligence	**Intellectual processes**	**Vocational end-states**
Linguistic	Sensitivity to the meaning and sounds of words, to the structure of language, and to the many ways language can be used.	Poet, novelist, journalist
Spatial	Ability to perceive visual-spatial relationships accurately, to transform these perceptions, and to re-create aspects of one's visual experience in the absence of the pertinent stimuli.	Engineer, sculptor, cartographer
Logical-mathematical	Ability to operate on and to perceive relationships in abstract symbol systems and to think logically and systematically in evaluating one's ideas.	Mathematician, scientist
Musical	Sensitivity to pitch, melody; ability to combine tones and musical phrases into larger rhythms; understanding of the emotional aspects of music.	Musician, composer
Body-kinesthetic	Ability to use the body skillfully to express oneself or achieve goals; ability to handle objects skillfully.	Dancer, athlete
Interpersonal	Ability to detect and respond appropriately to the mood, temperaments, motives, and intentions of others.	Therapist, minister, public relations specialist
Intrapersonal	Sensitivity to one's own inner states; recognition of personal strengths and weaknesses and ability to use information about the self to behave adaptively.	Contributes to success in almost any walk of life

SOURCE: Adapted from Gardner, 1983.

As further evidence for the independence of these abilities, Gardner notes that some individuals are truly exceptional in one ability but poor in others. This is dramatically clear in cases of the *savant syndrome*—mentally retarded people with an extraordinary talent. Leslie Lemke is once such individual. He is blind, has cerebral palsy, and is mentally retarded, and he could not talk until he was an adult. Yet he can hear a musical piece once and play it flawlessly on the piano or imitate songs in German or Italian perfectly even though his native language is still primitive. And despite their abysmal performance on intelligence tests, other mentally retarded individuals with savant skills can draw well enough to gain admittance to art school or calculate almost instantaneously what day of the week January 16, 1909 was (O'Connor & Hermelin, 1991). Finally, Gardner notes that different intelligences mature at different times. Many of the great composers and athletes, for example, begin to display their immense talents in childhood, whereas logical-mathematical intelligence often shows up much later in life.

Gardner's ideas have had an impact, particularly on investigators who study the development of creativity and special talents—a topic we will explore later in this chapter. Nevertheless, the major criticism of Gardner's theory is that his multiple intelligences are nowhere near as independent as he claims them to be. For example, individuals who are exceptionally talented in one area (for example, music) are often talented in several other areas as well (Feldman & Goldsmith, 1991). Furthermore, current intelligence tests do tap Gardner's linguistic, spatial, and logical-mathematical intelligences, which are moderately correlated rather than highly distinct. Perhaps it is too early, then, to reject the concept of *g*, or general mental ability. Yet Gardner is almost certainly correct in arguing that we surely misrepresent and underestimate the talents of many individuals by trying to characterize their intelligence with a single test score.

HOW IS INTELLIGENCE MEASURED?

When psychometricians began to construct intelligence tests at the beginning of this century, their concern was not with defining the nature of intelligence but with the more practical goals of determining which schoolchildren were likely to be slow learners. Recall that Binet and Simon produced a test that accomplished this goal and characterized each child's intellectual development with a single score, or *mental age*. Among the more popular of our contemporary intelligence tests for children is a direct descendant of Binet and Simon's early test.

The Stanford-Binet Intelligence Scale

In 1916, Lewis Terman of Stanford University translated and published a revised version of the Binet scale for use with American children. This test came to be known as the **Stanford-Binet Intelligence Scale.**

Like Binet's scale, the original version of the Stanford-Binet consisted of age-graded tasks designed to measure the average intellectual performance of children aged 3 through 13. Terman first gave his test to a sample of about 1,000 middle-class American schoolchildren in order to establish performance norms against which an individual child could be compared. But unlike Binet, who classified children according to mental age, Terman used a ratio measure of intelligence, developed by Stern (1912), that came to be known as an **intelligence quotient,** or **IQ.** The child's IQ, which was said to be as a measure of his brightness or rate of intellectual development, was calculated by dividing his mental age by his chronological age and then multiplying by 100:

Stanford-Binet Intelligence Scale
modern descendent of the first successful intelligence test which measures general intelligence and four factors: verbal reasoning, quantitative reasoning, spatial reasoning, and short-term memory.

$$IQ = MA/CA \times 100$$

intelligence quotient (IQ)
a numerical measure of a person's performance on an intelligence test relative to the performance of other examinees.

Notice that an IQ of 100 indicates average intelligence; it means that a child's *mental age is exactly equal to her chronological age*. An IQ greater than 100 indicates that the child's performance is comparable to that of people older than she is, whereas an IQ less than 100 means that her intellectual performance matches that of children somewhat younger than herself.

Concept Check 9.1
Recognizing Different Perspectives on Intelligence

Check your understanding of various theories on the nature of intelligence by matching the names of their originators with brief descriptions of the theories' main themes that appear below. Choose from among the following theorists: (a) Raymond Cattell/John Horn, (b) Howard Gardner, (c) J. P. Guilford, (d) Charles Spearman, (e) Robert Sternberg, (f) Louis Thurstone. The answers appear in the Appendix at the back of the book.

_____ 1. This theorist proposes that there may be as many as 180 distinct mental abilities.

_____ 2. This theorist claims that intelligence consists of a general mental factor, or *g*, and a number of special abilities, *s*, each of which is specific to a particular kind of reasoning.

_____ 3. This theorist thinks that there are seven distinctive kinds of intelligence, several of which (for example, musical intelligence) are not measured on intelligence tests.

_____ 4. This psychometrician also claims that there are seven forms of intelligence that he identified through factor analysis and called *primary mental abilities*.

_____ 5. This theory claims that *g*, or general mental ability, and the so-called primary mental abilities can be divided into two kinds of intelligence: *fluid* and *crystallized*.

_____ 6. This person's theory emphasizes three aspects of intelligence: the *contextual, experiential,* and *componential* (or information-processing) components.

A revised version of the Stanford-Binet is still in use (Thorndike, Hagen, & Sattler, 1986). Its **test norms** are now based on representative samples of people (6-year-olds through adults) from many socioeconomic and racial backgrounds rather than merely reflecting the performance of white middle-class schoolchildren. The revised test continues to measure abilities thought to be important to academic success, namely, verbal reasoning, quantitive reasoning, visual–spatial reasoning, and short-term memory. However, the concept of mental age is no longer used to calculate IQ on the Stanford-Binet or any other modern intelligence test. Instead, individuals receive IQ scores that reflect how well or poorly they do *compared with others of the same age.* An IQ of 100 is still average, and the higher (or lower) the IQ score an individual attains, the better (or worse) her performance is compared with age-mates.

The Wechsler Scales

David Wechsler has constructed two intelligence tests for children, both of which are widely used. The **Wechsler Intelligence Test for Children III (WISC-III)** is appropriate for schoolchildren aged 6 to 16, whereas the *Wechsler Preschool and Primary Scale of Intelligence Revised (WPPSI-R),* is designed for children between ages 3 and 8 (Wechsler, 1989, 1991).

One reason Wechsler constructed his own intelligence tests is that he believed that earlier versions of the Stanford-Binet were overloaded with items that require verbal skills. Specifically, he felt that this heavy bias toward verbal intelligence discriminated against children who have certain language handicaps—for example, those for whom English is a second language or those who have reading difficulties or are hard of hearing. To overcome this problem, Wechsler's scales contain verbal subtests similar to those on the Stanford-Binet as well as *nonverbal,* or "performance" subtests. Items on the performance subtests are designed to measure such predominantly nonverbal skills as the ability to assemble puzzles, to solve mazes, to reproduce geometric designs with colored blocks, and to rearrange sets of pictures so that they tell a meaningful story. Test takers receive three scores: a *verbal IQ,* a *Performance IQ,* and a *full-scale IQ* based on a combination of the verbal and performance measures.

The Wechsler scales soon became quite popular. Not only did the new performance subscales allow children from all backgrounds to display their intellectual strengths, but the tests were also sensitive to inconsistencies in mental skills that may be early signs of neurological problems or learning disorders. For example, children who display reading disorders often do much worse on the verbal component of the WISC.

Distribution of IQ Scores

If a young girl scores 130 on the Stanford-Binet or the WISC, we know that her IQ is above average. But how bright is she? To tell, we would have to know something about the way IQs are distributed in the population at large.

One interesting feature of all modern IQ tests is that people's scores are **normally distributed** around an IQ of 100 (see Figure 9.5). This patterning of scores is hardly an accident. By definition, the average score made by examinees from each age group is set at 100, and this is the most common score that people make (Neisser et al., 1996). Note that approximately half the population scores below 100 and half above. Moreover, roughly equal numbers of examinees obtain IQs of 85 and 115 (15 points from the average) or 70 and 130 (30 points from average). To determine the meaning of an IQ of 130, we can look at Table 9.2, which shows what percentage of the population the person outperforms by scoring at that level. Here we see that an IQ of 130 equals or exceeds the IQs of 97% of the population; it is a very high IQ indeed. Similarly, fewer than 3% of all test takers obtain IQs below 70, a cutoff that is commonly used today to define mental retardation.

test norms
standards of normal performance on psychometric instruments that are based on the average scores and the range of scores obtained by a large, representative sample of test takers.

Wechsler Intelligence Scale for Children (WISC-III)
widely used individual intelligence test that includes a measure of general intelligence and both verbal and performance intelligence.

normal distribution
a symmetrical, bell-shaped curve that describes the variability of certain characteristics within a population; most people fall at or near the average score, with relatively few at the extremes of the distribution.

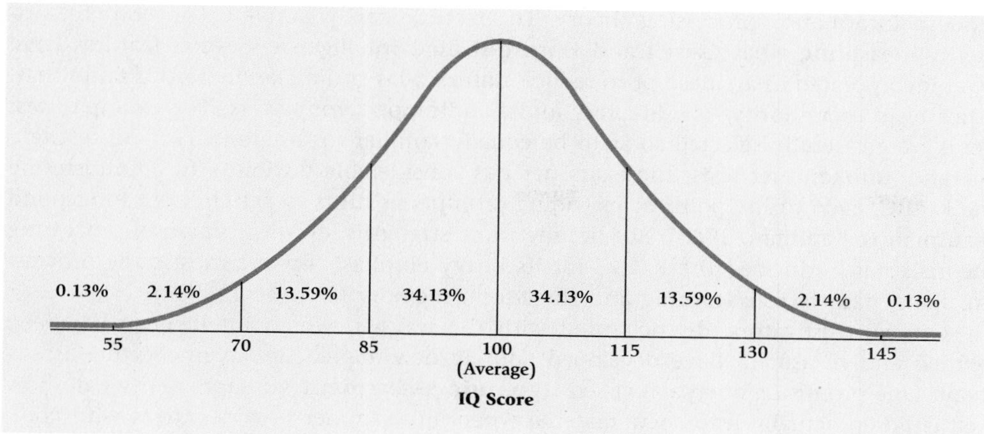

Figure 9.5 *The approximate distribution of IQ scores people make on contemporary intelligence tests. These tests are constructed so that the average score made by examinees in each age group is equivalent to an IQ of 100. Note that more than two-thirds of all examinees score within 15 points of this average (that is, IQs of 85–115) and that 95% of the population score within 30 points of average (IQs of 70–130).* ADAPTED FROM SATTLER, *1992.*

Group Tests of Mental Performance

Because the Stanford-Binet and the Wechsler scales must be administered individually by a professional examiner and can take more than an hour to assess each person's IQ, psychometricians soon saw the need for more cost-effective, paper-and-pencil measures—tests that could be group-administered to quickly assess the intellectual performance of large numbers of army recruits, job applicants, or students in a city's public schools.

Indeed, you have almost certainly taken a *group test* of intelligence (or scholastic aptitude) at some point in your life. Among the more widely used of these tests are the Large-Thorndike Test, which is designed for grade school and high school students, the Scholastic Assessment Test (SAT) and the American College Test (ACT) taken by many college applicants, and the Graduate Record Examination (GRE) often required of applicants to graduate school. These instruments are sometimes called "achievement" tests because they call for specific information that the examinee has learned at school (that is, what Cattell and Horn call crystallized intelligence) and are designed to predict future academic achievement.

Newer Approaches to Intelligence Testing

Although traditional IQ tests are still heavily used, new tests are constantly being developed. For example, there are intelligence scales based on Piagetian concepts and developmental milestones (see Humphreys, Rich, & Davey, 1985). The **Kaufman Assessment Battery for Children (K-ABC)** is another recent test, based on

Kaufman Assessment Battery for Children (K-ABC) an individual intelligence test for children; grounded heavily in information-processing theory.

TABLE 9.2 **The Meaning of Different IQ Scores**

An IQ of	Equals or exceeds (% of the population)	An IQ of	Equals or exceeds (% of the population)
160	99.99	100	50
140	99.3	95	38
135	98	90	27
130	97	85	18
125	94	80	11
120	89	75	6
115	82	70	3
110	73	65	2
105	62	62	1

modern information-processing theory. The test is heavily nonverbal in content, primarily measuring what Cattell and Horn call fluid intelligence. Several features have been incorporated in an attempt to reduce cultural bias and make the K-ABC fairer than other tests to minority, low-income, and handicapped youngsters. For example, test items were carefully selected so as to be equally familiar (or unfamiliar) to all test takers, and, unlike other tests, the examiner has considerable flexibility in administering the K-ABC, even to the point of providing prompts or hints to get children to respond (Kaufman & Kaufman, 1983). But despite these strengths, even information-processing theorists have criticized the K-ABC for its heavy emphasis on the most basic processing skills, namely rote learning and short-term memory (Sternberg, 1984).

Other investigators, disenchanted with the ways in which intelligence has been defined and measured, have developed entirely new approaches to intellectual assessment. One promising approach called **dynamic assessment** attempts to evaluate how well children actually learn new material when an examiner provides them with competent instruction (Campione et al., 1984; Lidz, 1997). Reuven Feuerstein and his colleagues (1997), for example, have argued that, even though intelligence is often defined as a *potential* to learn from experience, IQ tests typically assess what has been learned, not what *can be* learned. Thus, the traditional psychometric approach may be biased against children from culturally diverse or economically disadvantaged backgrounds who lack opportunities to learn what the tests measure. Feuerstein's *Learning Potential Assessment Device* asks children to learn new things with the guidance of an adult who provides increasingly helpful hints—precisely the kind of collaborative learning that Vygotsky emphasized in his sociocultural theory. This test interprets intelligence as the ability to learn quickly with minimal guidance. Robert Sternberg (1985, 1991) used a similar approach in a test he constructed based on his triarchic theory of intelligence. To better understand the information processes involved in verbal comprehension, for example, Sternberg does not ask people to define words they learned in the past, as IQ testers so often do. Instead, he places an unfamiliar word in a set of sentences and asks people to learn, from its *context*, what the new word means, just as they must do in real life.

In sum, modern perspectives on intelligence are now beginning to be reflected in the content of intelligence tests (Sternberg, 1997). However, these new tests and testing procedures have a very short history, and it remains to be seen whether they will eventually replace more traditional assessments of mental performance, such as the WISC and the Stanford-Binet.

Assessing Infant Intelligence

None of the standard intelligence tests can be used with children much younger than 2½ because the test items require verbal skills and attention spans that infants do not have. However, attempts have been made to measure infant "intelligence" by assessing the rate at which babies achieve important developmental milestones. Perhaps the best known and most widely used of the infant tests is the *Bayley Scales of Infant Development* (Bayley, 1969; 1993). This instrument, designed for infants aged 2 to 30 months, has three parts:

1. The *motor* scale (which assesses such motor capabilities as grasping a cube, throwing a ball, or drinking from a cup).
2. The *mental* scale (which includes adaptive behaviors such as categorizing objects, searching for a hidden toy, and following directions).
3. The *Infant Behavioral Record* (a rating of the child's behavior on dimensions such as goal directedness, fearfulness, and social responsivity).

On the basis of the first two scores, the infant is given a **developmental quotient, or DQ**, rather than an IQ. The DQ summarizes how well or poorly the infant performs in comparison with a large group of infants the same age.

dynamic assessment
an approach to assessing intelligence that evaluates how well individuals learn new material when an examiner provides them with competent instruction.

developmental quotient (DQ)
a numerical measure of an infant's performance on a developmental schedule relative to the performance of other infants of the same age.

Do DQs Predict Later IQs?

Infant scales are very useful for charting babies' developmental progress and for diagnosing neurological disorders and other signs of mental retardation, even when these conditions are fairly mild and difficult to detect in a standard neurological exam (Columbo, 1993; Honzik, 1983). Yet, these instruments generally fail to predict a child's later IQ or scholastic achievements (Honzik, 1983; McCall, 1983; Rose et al., 1989). In fact, a DQ measured early in infancy may not even predict the child's DQ later in infancy!

Why do infant tests do such a poor job at predicting children's later IQs? Perhaps the main reason is that infant tests and IQ tests tap very different kinds of abilities. Infant scales are designed to measure sensory, motor, language, and social skills, whereas standardized IQ tests such as the WISC and the Stanford-Binet emphasize more abstract abilities such as verbal reasoning, concept formation, and problem solving. So to expect an infant test to predict the later results of an IQ test is like expecting a yardstick to tell us how much someone weighs. There may be some correspondence between the two measures (a yardstick indicates height, which is correlated with weight; DQ indicates developmental progress, which is related to IQ), but the relationship is not very great.

New Evidence for Continuity in Intellectual Performance

Is it foolish, then, to think that we might ever accurately forecast a child's later IQ from his or her behavior during infancy? Maybe not. As we learned in Chapter 6, information-processing theorists have discovered that certain measures of infant attention and memory are much better at predicting IQ during the preschool and grade-school years than are the Bayley scales or other measures of infant development. Three attributes appear especially promising: how quickly infants look when presented with a visual target *(visual reaction time)*, the rate at which they *habituate* to repetitive stimuli, and the extent to which they prefer novel stimuli to familiar ones *(preference for novelty)*. Measures of these information-processing skills obtained during the first 4 to 8 months of life have an average correlation of .45 with IQ in childhood, with visual reaction time corresponding more closely to later measures of performance IQ, and the other measures predicting better for verbal IQ (Dougherty & Haith, 1997; McCall & Carriger, 1993). Infant information-processing skills also predict the childhood IQs of babies born prematurely (Rose & Feldman, 1995).

So there is some continuity between infant intelligence and childhood intelligence after all. Perhaps we can now characterize the "smart" infant as one who prefers and seeks out novel experiences and who soaks up new information quickly—in short, a speedy and efficient information processor.

Stability of IQ in Childhood and Adolescence

It was once assumed that a person's IQ reflected his or her genetically determined intellectual *capacity* and remained quite stable over time. In other words, a child with an IQ of 120 at age 5 was expected to obtain a similar IQ at age 10, 15, or 20.

How much support is there for this idea? As we have seen, infant DQs do not predict later IQ test scores very well at all. But starting at about age 4, there is a meaningful relationship between early and later IQs (Sameroff et al., 1993), and the relationship grows even stronger during middle childhood. Table 9.3 summarizes the results of a longitudinal study of more than 250 children conducted at the University of California (Honzik, MacFarlane, & Allen, 1948). In examining these data, we see that the shorter the interval between two testings, the higher the correlations between children's IQ scores. But even after a number of years have passed, IQ seems to be a reasonably stable attribute. After all, the scores that children obtain at age 8 are still clearly related to those they obtain 10 years later at age 18.

TABLE 9.3 **Correlations of IQs Measured during the Preschool Years and Middle Childhood, with IQs Measured at Ages 10 and 18**

Age of child	Correlation with IQ at age 10	Correlation with IQ at age 18
4	.66	.42
6	.76	.61
8	.88	.70
10	–	.76
12	.87	.76

SOURCE: Adapted from Honzik, MacFarlane, & Allen, 1948.

There is something that these correlations are not telling us, however. Each of them is based on a large group of children, and they do not necessarily mean that the IQs of *individual children* remain stable over time. Robert McCall and his associates looked at the IQ scores of 140 children who had taken intelligence tests at regular intervals between age 2½ and 17 (McCall, Applebaum, & Hogarty, 1973). Their findings were remarkable. More than half of these individuals displayed meaningful fluctuations in IQ over time, and the average range of variation in the IQ scores of these fluctuators was more than 20 points (see also Gottfried et al., 1994).

So it seems that IQ is more stable for some children than for others. Clearly, these findings challenge the notion that IQ is a reflection of one's absolute potential for learning or intellectual capacity; if it were, the intellectual profiles of virtually all children would be highly stable, showing only minor variations due to errors of measurement.

What, then, does an IQ represent, if not one's intellectual competence or ability? Today, many experts believe that an IQ score is merely an estimate of the examinee's intellectual *performance* at one particular point in time—an estimate that may or may not be a good indication of the examinee's intellectual capacity.

Interestingly, children whose IQs change the most usually do not fluctuate randomly; their scores tend to either increase or decrease over time. Who are the gainers and who are the losers? Gainers typically come from homes in which parents are interested in their intellectual accomplishments, urge them to achieve, and are neither too strict nor too lax in their child-rearing practices (Honzik et al., 1948; McCall et al., 1973). On the other hand, meaningful declines in IQ often occur among children who live in poverty, especially when the child's parents are not only poor but are low in intellectual functioning themselves (Jensen, 1977; Ramey & Ramey, 1992).

cumulative-deficit hypothesis the notion that impoverished environments inhibit intellectual growth and that these inhibiting effects accumulate over time.

Although both genes and environments contribute to a person's intellectual performance, environmental factors clearly seem to be most responsible for the *declining* IQs that poverty-stricken children often display. Otto Klineberg (1963) proposed a **cumulative-deficit hypothesis** to explain this: Presumably, impoverished environments dampen intellectual growth, and these inhibiting effects accumulate over time. Consequently, the longer children remain in a barren intellectual environment, the worse they perform on IQ tests.

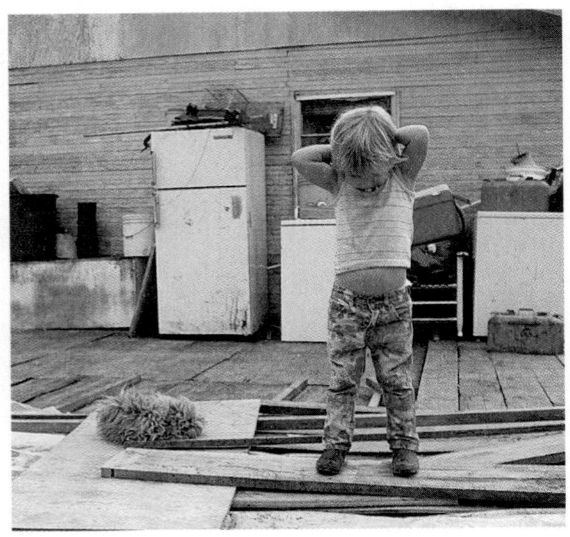

Impoverished environments dampen intellectual growth leading to a progressive decline in children's IQ scores.

Arthur Jensen (1977) tested the cumulative-deficit hypothesis by comparing the intellectual performance of economically disadvantaged African-American siblings living in California and Georgia. If a cumulative-deficit mechanism is operating, older siblings should obtain lower IQs than their younger brothers and sisters. This is precisely what Jensen found for children in the Georgia sample, whose environmental disadvantages were markedly greater than those of the California group. In addition, children who have always lived in poverty score lower on IQ tests than those whose poverty status is not so consistent (Duncan & Brooks-Gunn, 1997)—another finding that suggests that poverty has cumulative effects on children's intellectual performance.

WHAT DO INTELLIGENCE TESTS PREDICT?

We have seen that IQ tests measure intellectual performance rather than capacity and that a person's IQ may vary considerably over time. Given these qualifications, it seems reasonable to ask whether IQ scores can tell anything very meaningful about the people who were tested. For example, does IQ predict future academic accomplishments? Is it in any way related to a person's health, occupational status, or general life satisfaction? Let's first consider the relationship between IQ and academic achievement.

IQ as a Predictor of Scholastic Achievement

Since the original purpose of IQ testing was to estimate how well children would perform at school, it should come as no surprise that modern intelligence tests do predict academic achievement. The average correlation between children's IQ scores and their current and future grades at school is about .50 (Neisser et al., 1996). In addition, scholastic aptitude tests such as the ACT or SAT are also reliable predictors of the grades that high school students will make in college.

Not only do children with high IQs tend to do better in school, but they stay there longer (Brody, 1997). Students who perform well on IQ tests are less likely to drop out of high school and more likely than other high school graduates to attempt and to complete college.

Some have argued that IQ tests predict scholastic performance because both measures depend on the abstract reasoning abilities that make up Spearman's *g*, or general mental ability (Jensen, 1980). However, critics of this viewpoint argue that both IQ tests and measures of scholastic achievement reflect knowledge and reasoning skills that are culturally valued. One line of evidence consistent with this viewpoint is that schooling, which largely reflects cultural values, actually *improves* IQ test performance (Ceci & Williams, 1997). How? By transmitting factual knowledge pertinent to test questions, promoting memory strategies and categorization skills that are measured on IQ tests, and encouraging attitudes and behaviors, such as trying hard and working under pressure, that foster successful test-taking skills (Ceci, 1991; Neisser et al., 1996). Viewed from this perspective, then, IQ tests could almost be considered tests of academic achievement.

Finally, let's keep in mind that the moderate correlations between IQ and scholastic performance are based on *group* trends and that the IQ score of any individual student may not accurately reflect her current or future academic accomplishments. Clearly, academic performance also depends very heavily on such factors as a student's work habits, interests, and motivation to succeed (Neisser et al., 1996). So even though IQ (and aptitude) tests predict academic achievement better than *any other type of test*, judgments about a student's prospects for future success *should never be based on a test score alone*. Indeed, studies have consistently shown that the best single predictor of a student's future grades is not an IQ or aptitude score but, rather, the grades the student has previously earned (Minton & Schneider, 1980).

IQ as a Predictor of Vocational Outcomes

Do people with higher IQs land better jobs? Are they more successful in their chosen occupations than co-workers who test lower in intelligence?

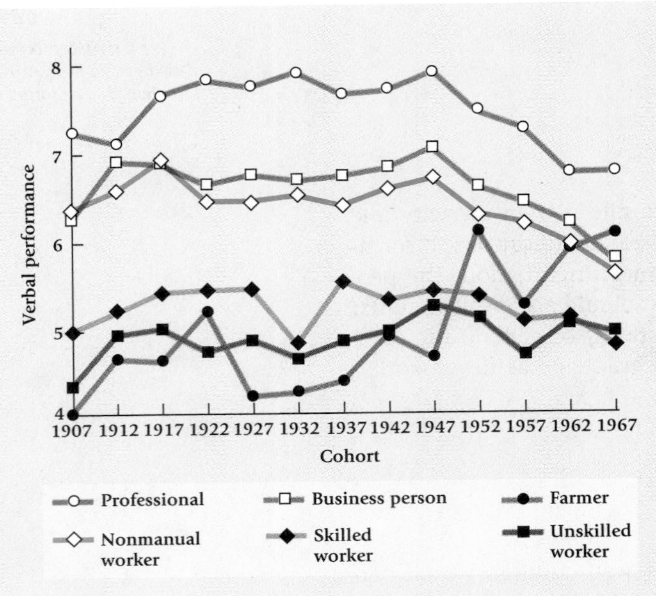

Figure 9.6 *Mean verbal ability scores differ across occupational groups, but the size of the gap seems to be narrower for people born in the 1960s than for people born early in the century.* FROM WEAKLIEM, MCQUILLAN, & SCHAUER, 1995.

WHAT DO YOU THINK?

The correlation between IQ (or SAT) scores and future college grades is approximately +.50, which means that these tests account for about 25% of the variability in students' grade point averages (that is, variance accounted for = r^2, or .50 × .50 = .25). Does this imply to you that college admissions offices may be placing too much emphasis on standardized test scores? Why or why not?

There is a clear relationship between IQ and occupational status. Figure 9.6 shows that (1) professional and other white-collar business persons consistently score higher in IQ than blue collar, or manual, workers, and (2) the IQ gap across occupations is smaller for recent cohorts than for earlier ones, perhaps due to improvements over time in educational opportunities for the less wealthy (Weakliem, McQuillan, & Schauer, 1995). Generally, the average IQ for an occupation increases as the prestige of the occupation increases (Gottfredson, 1986). And one contributor to this relationship is the link between IQ and education: It undoubtedly takes more intellectual ability to complete law school and become a lawyer than it does to become a farmhand (Brody, 1997). Yet IQs vary considerably in every occupational group, and many people in low-status jobs have high IQs.

Does IQ predict job *performance*? Are bright lawyers, electricians, or farmhands more successful or productive than their less intelligent colleagues? The answer here is also yes. The correlations between mental test scores and such indications of job performance as ratings from supervisors average about +.50—about as high as IQ correlates with academic achievement (Hunter & Hunter, 1984; Neisser et al., 1996). However, an astute manager or personnel officer would never rely exclusively on an IQ score to decide who to hire or promote. One reason for looking beyond IQ is that people differ in **tacit (or practical) intelligence**—the ability to size up everyday problems and take steps to solve them—which is not closely related to IQ, but which predicts job performance rather well (Sternberg et al., 1995). In addition, other variables such as prior job performance, interpersonal skills, and motivation to succeed may be as important or even more important than IQ as predictors of future job performance (Neisser et al., 1996).

IQ as a Predictor of Health, Adjustment, and Life Satisfaction

Are bright people any healthier, happier, or better adjusted than those of average or below-average intelligence? Let's see what researchers have learned by considering the life outcomes of people at opposite ends of the IQ continuum: the *intellectually gifted* and the *mentally retarded.*

In 1922, Lewis Terman began a most interesting longitudinal study of more than 1,500 California schoolchildren who had IQs of 140 or higher—a study that continues today. The purpose of the project was to collect as much information as possible about the abilities and personal characteristics of these "gifted" children and to follow up on them every few years for the rest of their lives to see what they were accomplishing.

It soon became clear that these children were exceptional in many respects other than intelligence. For example, they had learned to walk and talk much sooner than most toddlers, and their general health, as determined from physicians' reports, was much better than average. The gifted children were rated by teachers as better adjusted emotionally and more morally mature than their less intelligent peers. And although they were no more popular, on average, than their classmates, the gifted children were quicker to take charge and assume positions of leadership. Taken together, these find-

tacit (or practical) intelligence
ability to size up everyday problems and solve them; only modestly related to IQ.

ings demolish the stereotype of child prodigies as frail, sickly youngsters who are socially inadequate and emotionally immature.

Another convincing demonstration of the personal and social maturity of gifted individuals comes from a study of high-IQ children who skipped high school entirely and entered the University of Washington as part of a special program to accelerate their education (Robinson & Janos, 1986). Contrary to the common wisdom that gifted children suffer if they skip grades and must fit in with much older students, these youngsters showed no signs at all of maladjustment. Yet, a decision to accelerate the education of gifted children should always be made on an individual basis, for some accelerated children do become anxious and depressed at being so far behind their older classmates both socially and emotionally (Winner, 1997).

What becomes of gifted children as adults? Most of Terman's gifted sample remained remarkable in many respects. Fewer than 5% were rated as seriously maladjusted, and the incidence of problems such as ill health, alcoholism, and delinquent behavior was but a fraction of that normally observed in the general population (Terman, 1954). The occupational attainments of the gifted men were impressive. The vast majority were working in professional or semiprofessional jobs by age 40. As a group they had taken out more than 200 patents and written some 2,000 scientific reports, 100 books, 375 plays or short stories, and more than 300 essays, sketches, magazine articles, and critiques. Due to the influence of gender-role expectations during the period covered by Terman's study, most of the gifted women sacrificed career aspirations to raise families (Schuster, 1990; Tomlinson-Keasey & Little, 1990). However, more recent cohorts of gifted women are pursuing careers more vigorously and seem to have a greater sense of well-being than Terman's gifted women did (Schuster, 1990; Subotnik, Karp, & Morgan, 1989).

In short, most of Terman's participants were well-adjusted people living happy, healthy, and highly productive lives. Nevertheless, approximately 15% of the sample were not particularly happy or successful as middle-aged adults (Shurkin, 1992; Terman, 1954). In their analysis of factors that predicted the paths these adults' lives took over a 40-year period, Carolyn Tomlinson-Keasey and Todd Little (1990) found that the most well-adjusted and successful participants had highly educated parents who offered them lots of love and intellectual stimulation; by contrast, the least successful of the group were likely to have experienced disruption of family ties due to their parents' divorce and less social support and encouragement (see also Friedman et al., 1995). So a high IQ, by itself, does not guarantee health, happiness, or success. Even among a select sample of children with superior IQs, the quality of the home environment contributes substantially to future outcomes and accomplishments.

What about the other end of the IQ continuum? Do mentally retarded individuals have much hope of succeeding in life or achieving happiness? Although our stereotypes about **mental retardation** might persuade us to say "no," the research presented in Box 9.1 suggests a very different conclusion.

Some gifted children as young as 11 or 12 thrive as college students, particularly if they have the support and encouragement of their parents.

mental retardation
significant subaverage intellectual functioning associated with impairments in adaptive behavior in everyday life.

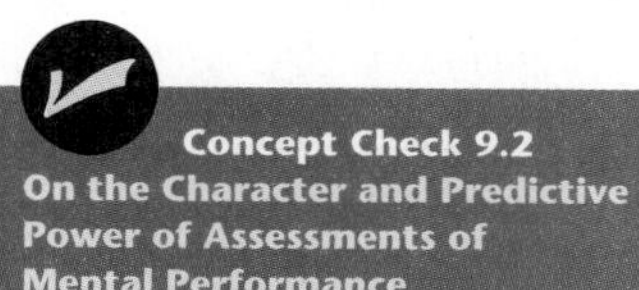

Concept Check 9.2
On the Character and Predictive Power of Assessments of Mental Performance

Check your understanding of the character and usefulness of various assessments of mental performance by matching each of the following alternatives to a statement that appears below: (a) Wechsler Intelligence Scale for Children (WISC-III), (b) Stanford-Binet Intelligence Scale, (c) cumulative deficit, (d) dynamic assessment, (e) grades previously earned, (f) tacit (or practical) intelligence, (g) developmental quotient (DQ), (h) habituation rate. Answers appear in the Appendix at the back of the book.

_____ 1. assessment of how well children learn from competent instruction
_____ 2. measure of infant functioning that does *not* forecast childhood IQ
_____ 3. IQ test designed to overcome the heavily verbal bias of earlier tests
_____ 4. concept explaining how IQs might decline over time
_____ 5. measure of infant functioning that forecasts childhood IQs moderately well
_____ 6. although not closely related to IQ, this attribute predicts future job performance rather well
_____ 7. first American IQ test
_____ 8. predicts future academic success as well or better than IQ scores

DEVELOPMENTAL ISSUES

9.1

Mental Retardation: A Closer Look

As many as 3% of school-age children are classified as mentally retarded—that is, as significantly below average in intellectual functioning, with limitations in such adaptive behaviors as self-care and social skills (American Association of Mental Retardation, 1992; Roeleveld, Zielhuis, & Gabreels, 1997). Individuals with mental retardation differ greatly in their levels of functioning. Severely retarded individuals with IQs lower than 55 are often affected by *organic retardation*—deficits caused by such identifiable causes are Down syndrome, diseases, or injuries. These individuals may require basic care throughout life, often in institutions. More common, however, are mildly retarded individuals (IQs 55 to 70) who usually display *cultural-familial retardation*—deficits reflecting a combination of low genetic potential and an unstimulating rearing environment (Simonoff et al., 1996). Mildly retarded individuals can learn both academic and practical lessons at school, and they can often work and live independently or with occasional help as adults.

What kinds of life outcomes do mildly retarded individuals display? We gain some clues from a follow-up study of men and women (average IQ = 67) who had been placed in special education classes for the mentally retarded during the 1920s and 1930s (Ross et al., 1985). Nearly 40 years later, their life outcomes were compared with those of siblings and nonrelated peers, and with the highly favorable attainments of Terman's gifted sample.

Generally, the mentally retarded adults had less favorable life outcomes in middle age than the nonretarded groups (see also Schalock et al., 1992). As we see in the table, about 80% of the retarded men were employed, but they usually held semiskilled or unskilled jobs that required little education or intellectual ability. (Retarded women usually married and became homemakers.) Compared with nonretarded peers, retarded men and women fared worse on other counts as well. For example, they had lower incomes, less adequate housing, poorer social skills, and a greater dependency on others.

Yet the authors of this study still found grounds for optimism. After all, the vast majority of these mildly retarded individuals had worked and married, and they were generally satisfied with their accomplishments. In fact, only one in five reported having *any* need for public assistance in the 10 years before they were interviewed. Clearly, they were faring much better than common stereotypes about the mentally retarded would lead us to believe.

So this study, like others before it, reveals that many individuals labeled mildly retarded by schools, and who do indeed have some difficulty mastering academic lessons, often "vanish" into the adult population after they leave school. Apparently, they adapt to the demands of adult life, displaying a fair amount of the practical intelligence or "street smarts" that Sternberg (1997) talks about—and that is not measured by standardized IQ tests. As the authors put it, "It does not take as many IQ points as most people believe to be productive . . . and self-fulfilled" (Ross et al., 1985, p. 149).

Midlife Occupations of Mentally Retarded, Nonretarded, and Gifted Males

Occupational classification	Mentally retarded subjects (n = 54), %	Nonretarded siblings (n = 31), %	Nonretarded peers (n = 33), %	Terman's gifted sample (n = 757), %
Professional, managerial	1.9	29.1	36.4	86.3
Retail business, skilled trade, agricultural	29.6	32.3	39.4	12.5
Semiskilled, minor or business, clerical	50.0	25.8	15.2	1.2
Slightly skilled, unskilled	18.5	13.0	9.4	0.0

Source: Adapted from Ross et al., 1985.

FACTORS THAT INFLUENCE IQ SCORES

Why do people differ so dramatically in the scores that they make on IQ tests? In addressing this issue, we will briefly review the evidence for hereditary and environmental influences and then take a closer look at several important social and cultural correlates of intellectual performance.

The Evidence for Heredity

In Chapter 3, we reviewed two major lines of evidence indicating that heredity affects intellectual performance and that about half the variation in IQ scores within a particular population of test takers is due to genetic differences among these individuals.

Twin Studies

The intellectual resemblance between pairs of individuals living in the same home increases as a function of their kinship (that is, genetic similarity). For example, the IQ correlation for identical twins, who inherit identical genes, is substantially higher than the IQ correlations for fraternal twins and normal siblings, who have half their genes in common.

Adoption Studies

Adopted children's IQs are more highly correlated with the IQs of their biological parents than with those of their adoptive parents. This finding can be interpreted as evidence for a genetic influence on IQ, for adoptees share genes with their biological parents but not with their adoptive caregivers.

We also learned in Chapter 3 that a person's genotype may influence the type of environment that he or she is likely to experience. Indeed, Scarr and McCartney (1983) have proposed that people seek out environments that are compatible with their genetic predispositions, so that identical twins (who share identical genes) select and experience more similar environments than fraternal twins or ordinary siblings do. This is a major reason that identical twins resemble each other intellectually throughout life, whereas the intellectual resemblances between fraternal twins or ordinary siblings become progressively smaller over time (McCartney et al., 1990).

Do these observations imply that a person's genotype *determines* his environment and exerts the primary influence on his intellectual development? *No, they do not!* A child who has a genetic predisposition to seek out intellectual challenges could hardly be expected to develop a high IQ if she is raised in a barren environment that offers few such challenges for her to meet. Alternatively, a child who does not gravitate toward intellectual activities might nevertheless obtain an average or above-average IQ if raised in a stimulating environment that continually provides him with cognitive challenges that he must master. Let's now take a closer look at how environment might influence intellectual performance.

The Evidence for Environment

The evidence for environmental effects on intelligence comes from a variety of sources. For example, we learned in Chapter 3 that there is a small to moderate intellectual resemblance between pairs of *genetically unrelated* children who live in the same household—a resemblance that can only be attributable to their common rearing environment since they share no genes. And earlier in this chapter, we noted that children from impoverished backgrounds show a progressive decline (or cumulative deficit) in IQ as they grow older, thus implying that economic disadvantage inhibits intellectual growth.

Might we then promote intellectual development and improve children's IQs by enriching the environments in which they live? Indeed we can, and at least two lines of evidence tell us so.

Natural Experiments of Social Change

During the 1930s and 1940s, several studies assessed the impact of social and economic change on the intellectual performance of children from poverty-stricken communities where education had been substandard. For example, when children from an isolated mountain community in Eastern Tennessee were first tested in the early 1930s, they obtained an average IQ of 82 (Wheeler, 1932). Ten years later, the children in this same community were retested. During the decade between testings, this community had changed in many ways: Roads had been built, the school system had been modernized, and economic conditions had improved to the point that most people could now afford radios. In other words, this formerly isolated and impoverished community was coming into the social and economic mainstream of American life. As a result, the average IQ of children there rose by 11 points (to 93) in the ten years between testings (Wheeler, 1942). Other studies conducted in Hawaii and the American Midwest found similar increases in children's intellectual performance in communities where dramatic social and educational improvements had taken place (Finch, 1946; Smith, 1942).

Adoption Studies

Other investigators have charted the intellectual growth of adopted children who left disadvantaged family backgrounds and were placed with highly educated adoptive parents (Scarr & Weinberg, 1983; Skodak & Skeels, 1949). By the time these adoptees were 4 to 7 years old, they were scoring well above average on standardized IQ tests (about 110 in Scarr and Weinberg's study and 112 in Skodak and Skeels's). Interestingly, the IQ scores of these adoptees were still correlated with the IQs of their *biological* mothers, thus reflecting the influence of heredity on intellectual performance. And yet, the *absolute* IQs these adoptees attained were considerably *higher* (by 10 to 20 points) than one would expect on the basis of the IQs and educational levels of their biological parents, and their levels of academic achievement remained slightly above the national norm well into adolescence (Weinberg, Scarr, & Waldman, 1992; Waldman, Weinberg, & Scarr, 1994). So the *phenotype* that one displays on a genetically influenced attribute like intelligence is clearly influenced by one's environment. Since the adopting parents in these studies were themselves highly educated and above average in intelligence, it seems reasonable to assume that they were providing enriched, intellectually stimulating home environments that fostered the cognitive development of their adoptees.

So environment is truly a powerful force that may either promote or inhibit intellectual growth. Yet our use of the term *environment* here is very global, and the evidence that we have reviewed does not really tell us which of the many life experiences that children have are most likely to affect their intellectual development. In the next section, we will look more closely at environmental influences and see that a child's performance on IQ tests depends to some extent on parental attitudes and child-rearing practices, the structure and socioeconomic status of the family, and even the sociocultural group to which the family belongs.

SOCIAL AND CULTURAL CORRELATES OF INTELLECTUAL PERFORMANCE

Home Environment and IQ

Earlier, we implied that the quality or character of the home environment may play an important role in determining children's intellectual performance and eventual life outcomes. Recently, Arnold Sameroff and his colleagues (1993) listed ten environmental factors that place children at risk of displaying low IQ scores, nine of which were characteristics of children's homes and families (or family members). These researchers measured each of the IQ risk factors shown in Table 9.4 at age 4, and again when the children in their sample were 13 years old. Every one of these risk factors was related

Table 9.4 Ten Environmental Risk Factors Associated with Low IQ and Mean IQs at Age 4 of Children Who Did or Did Not Experience Each Risk Factor

	Mean IQ at age 4	
Risk factor	**Child experienced risk factor**	**Child did not experience risk factor**
Child is member of minority group	90	110
Head of household is unemployed or low-skilled worker	90	108
Mother did not complete high school	92	109
Family has four or more children	94	105
Father is absent from family	95	106
Family experienced many stressful life events	97	105
Parents have rigid child-rearing values	92	107
Mother is highly anxious/distressed	97	107
Mother has poor mental health/diagnosed disorder	99	107
Mother shows little positive affect toward child	88	107

Source: Data and descriptions compiled from Sameroff et al., 1993

to IQ at age 4, and most also predicted IQ at age 13. In addition, the greater the number of these risk factors affecting a child, the lower his or her IQ; which particular risk factors a child experienced were less important than how many he or she experienced. It is clearly not conducive to intellectual development to grow up in an economically disadvantaged home with highly stressed or poorly educated parents who are unable to provide much intellectual stimulation.

Assessing the Character of the Home Environment

Exactly how do parents influence a child's intellectual development? In an attempt to find out, Bettye Caldwell and Robert Bradley have developed a widely used instrument, called the **HOME inventory** (*H*ome *O*bservation for *M*easurement of the *E*nvironment), that allows an interviewer/observer to visit an infant, preschooler, or school-age child at home and determine how intellectually stimulating (or impoverished) that home environment is (Caldwell & Bradley, 1984). The infant version of the HOME inventory, for example, consists of 45 statements, each of which is scored yes (the statement is true of this family) or no (the statement is not true of this family). To gather the information necessary to complete the inventory, the researcher (1) asks the child's parent (usually the mother) to describe her daily routine and child-rearing practices, (2) carefully observes the parent as she interacts with her child, and (3) notes the kinds of play materials that the parent makes available to the child. The 45 bits of information collected are then grouped into the six subscales in Table 9.5. The home then receives a score on each subscale. The higher the scores across all six subscales, the more intellectually stimulating the home environment.

Does the HOME Predict IQ?

Research conducted in the United States consistently indicates that the scores that homes obtain on the HOME Inventory do predict the intellectual performances of toddlers, preschoolers, and grade-school children, regardless of their social class or ethnic backgrounds (Bradley et al., 1988; 1989, Luster & Dubow, 1992). Furthermore, gains in IQ from age 1 to age 3 are likely to occur among children from stimulating homes, whereas children from families with low HOME scores often experience 10- to 20-point declines in IQ over the same period (Bradley et al., 1989).

HOME inventory
a measure of the amount and type of intellectual stimulation provided by a child's home environment.

TABLE 9.5 Subscales and Sample Items for the HOME Inventory (Infant Version)

Subscale 1: Emotional and verbal responsivity of parent (11 items)

Sample items:	Parent responds verbally to child's vocalizations or verbalizations
	Parent's speech is distinct, clear, and audible
	Parent caresses or kisses child at least once

Subscale 2: Avoidance of restriction and punishment (8 items)

Sample items:	Parent neither slaps nor spanks child during visit
	Parent does not scold or criticize child during visit
	Parent does not interfere with or restrict child more than three times during visit

Subscale 3: Organization of physical and temporal environment (6 items)

Sample items:	Child gets out of house at least four times a week
	Child's play environment is safe

Subscale 4: Provision of appropriate play materials (9 items)

Sample items:	Child has a push or pull toy
	Parent provides learning facilitators appropriate to age: mobile, table and chairs, highchair, playpen, and so on
	Parent provides toys for child to play with during visit

Subscale 5: Parental involvement with child (6 items)

Sample items:	Parent talks to child while doing household work
	Parent structures child's play periods

Subscale 6: Opportunities for variety in daily stimulation (5 items)

Sample items:	Father provides some care daily
	Child has three or more books of his or her own

SOURCE: Adapted from Caldwell & Bradley, 1984.

WHICH ASPECTS OF THE HOME ENVIRONMENT MATTER MOST? Although all of the HOME subscales are moderately correlated with children's IQ scores, some are better predictors of intellectual performance than others. During infancy, HOME subscales measuring *parental involvement* with the child, provision of *age-appropriate play materials,* and opportunities for *variety in daily stimulation* are the best predictors of children's later IQs and scholastic achievement (Bradley et al., 1988; Gottfried et al., 1994). And preschool measures of *parental warmth, stimulation of language,* and *academic behaviors* are also closely associated with children's future intellectual performances (Bradley & Caldwell, 1982; Bradley et al., 1988).

What these findings imply, then, is that an intellectually stimulating home is one in which parents are warm, verbally engaging, and eager to be involved with their child (Fagot & Gauvain, 1997; Hart & Risley, 1995; MacPhee, Ramey, & Yeates, 1984). These parents describe new objects, concepts, and experiences clearly and accurately, and they provide the child with a variety of challenges that are appropriate for her age or developmental level. They encourage the child to ask questions, solve problems, and think about what she is learning. As the child matures and enters school, they stress the importance of academic achievement and expect her to get good grades (Luster & Dubow, 1992). When you stop and think about it, it is not at all surprising that children from these "enriched" home settings often have high IQs; after all, their parents are obviously concerned about their cognitive development and have spent several years encouraging them to acquire new information and to practice many of the cognitive skills that are measured on intelligence tests.

Orderly home environments in which family members are warm, responsive, and eager to be involved with one another are precisely the kind of setting that promotes children's intellectual development.

A HIDDEN GENETIC EFFECT? It turns out that brighter parents are likely to provide more intellectually stimulating home environments (Coon et al., 1990; Longstreth et al., 1981). Is it possible, then, that any correlation between the quality of the home environment and children's IQ scores simply reflects the fact that bright parents transmit genes for high intelligence to their children?

There is some support for this idea in that correlations between HOME scores and IQ scores are higher for biological children, who share genes with their parents, than for adopted children, who are genetically unrelated to other members of their family (Braungart, Fulker, & Plomin, 1992). So does the quality of the home environment have any effect on children's intellectual development that does not reflect the influence of genes?

The answer is yes, and there are two lines of evidence that tell us so. First, adopted children's IQ scores rise considerably when they are moved from less stimulating to more stimulating homes (Turkheimer, 1991). Clearly, this change in IQs has to be an *environmental* effect because adoptees share no genes with their adoptive parents. Equally revealing are the results of a longitudinal study of 112 mothers and their 2- to 4-year-old children conducted by Keith Yeates and his associates (1983). These investigators measured the mothers' IQs, the IQ of each child at ages 2, 3, and 4, and the quality of the families' home environments (as assessed by the HOME). The best predictor of a child's IQ at age 2 was the mother's IQ, just as a genetic hypothesis would suggest. But the picture had changed by the time children were 4 years old; now the quality of the home environment was a strong predictor of children's IQs, even after the influence of mothers' IQ was taken into account (see also Luster & Dubow, 1992; Sameroff et al., 1993).

So it appears that the quality of the home environment is truly an important contributor to a child's intellectual development that becomes more apparent later in the preschool period, when IQ becomes a more stable attribute (Sameroff et al., 1993; Yeates et al., 1983). However, let's also note that the relationship between HOME scores and children's IQs does decline somewhat during the elementary-school years (Luster & Dubow, 1992), probably because older children are away from home more often and are exposed to other people, such as teachers, who also influence their intellectual development.

Birth Order, Family Size, and IQ

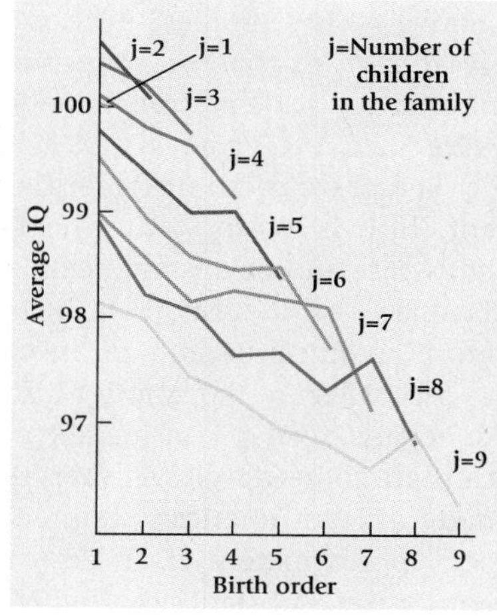

Figure 9.7 *Average scores on a nonverbal measure of intelligence as a function of the examinee's birth order and the size of his family. Note that subjects from smaller families score higher on this test than do subjects from large families. We also see that, within a given family size, children born early tend to obtain higher IQs than those born late.* *Adapted from Zajonc & Markus, 1975.*

Two other "family" characteristics that influence children's performance on IQ tests are *family size* and the child's position within the family, or *birth order*. These effects are clearly illustrated in a large-scale study based on military records of almost all males born in the Netherlands between 1944 and 1947 (Belmont & Marolla, 1973). As shown in Figure 9.7, the brighter children tended to come from smaller families. The figure also reveals a birth-order effect: On average, first-borns outperformed second-borns, who outperformed third-borns, and so on down the line. These findings are not unique to Dutch males; they have now been replicated in samples of males and females from several countries (Markus & Zajonc, 1977).

Robert Zajonc (Zajonc & Markus, 1975; Zajonc & Mullally, 1997) has offered an interesting explanation for these birth-order and family-size effects. According to his **confluence hypothesis,** a child's intellectual development depends on the unique intellectual climate that he or she experiences at home. First-borns have an advantage because they are initially exposed only to adults, whose intellectual levels are very high. By contrast, a second child experiences a less stimulating intellectual environment because she must deal with a cognitively immature older sibling as well. The third child is further disadvantaged by the presence of two relatively immature older siblings. So

confluence hypothesis
Zajonc's notion that a child's intellectual development depends on the average intellectual level of all family members.

later-borns and children from large families are said to score lower on IQ tests because they spend more time in a world of child-sized minds, less time with adults, and have fewer opportunities to maximize their intellectual potential.

Zajonc's interesting theory has some merit in that first-borns do tend to receive more intellectual stimulation at home than later-borns (Bradley & Caldwell, 1984; Rothbart, 1971). However, other confluence predictions do not always ring true. For example, children who live with only one parent rather than two do not always show the poorer intellectual performances that confluence theory predicts (Duncan et al., 1994; Entwisle & Alexander, 1990). Let's also note that the birth-order and family-size effects that confluence theory seeks to explain are rather modest (accounting for 3 to 4 IQ points, at best), and are detectable only when large numbers of families are compared. So the trends that emerge for the population as a whole may not apply to children within any particular family (Zajonc & Mullally, 1997).

Social Class, Racial, and Ethnic Differences in IQ

One of the most reliable findings in the intelligence literature is a social class effect: Children from lower- and working-class homes average some 10 to 15 points below their middle-class age-mates on standardized IQ tests (Helms, 1997). Infants are apparently the only exception to this rule, as there are no reliable social class differences on infant information-processing measures of habituation and preference for novelty that predict later IQ scores (McCall & Carriger, 1993) or in the developmental quotients (DQs) that infants obtain on infant "intelligence" tests (Golden et al., 1971).

There are also racial and ethnic differences in intellectual performance. In the United States, children of African-American and Native-American ancestry score, on average, about 12 to 15 points below their European-American classmates on standardized IQ tests. The average IQ scores of Hispanic-American children lie in between those of African-American and European-American classmates, whereas Asian-American children score at about the same level on IQ tests that European-American children do (Flynn, 1991; Neisser et al., 1996). Different subcultural groups may also display distinctive ability profiles. African-American children, for example, often perform better on verbal tests than on other subtests, whereas Hispanic and Native-American children may do particularly well on nonverbal items assessing spatial abilities (Neisser et al., 1996; Suzuki & Valencia, 1997; Taylor & Richards, 1991).

Before we try to interpret these social class, racial, and ethnic differences, an important truth is worth stating here—one that is often overlooked when people discover that white and Asian-American children outperform their African-American or Hispanic classmates on IQ tests. This fact is that we cannot predict anything about the IQ or the future accomplishments of an *individual* on the basis of his ethnicity or skin color. As we see in Figure 9.8, the IQ distributions for samples of African Americans and white Americans overlap considerably. So even though the average IQ scores of African Americans are somewhat lower than those of whites, the overlapping distributions mean that many African-American children obtain higher IQ scores than many white children. In fact, approximately 15 to 25% of the African-American population scores higher—in many cases, substantially higher—than most of the white population.

Why Do Groups Differ in Intellectual Performance?

Over the years, developmentalists have proposed three general hypotheses to account for racial, ethnic, and social class differences in IQ: (1) a *cultural test bias* hypothesis, that standardized IQ tests and the ways they are administered are geared toward white,

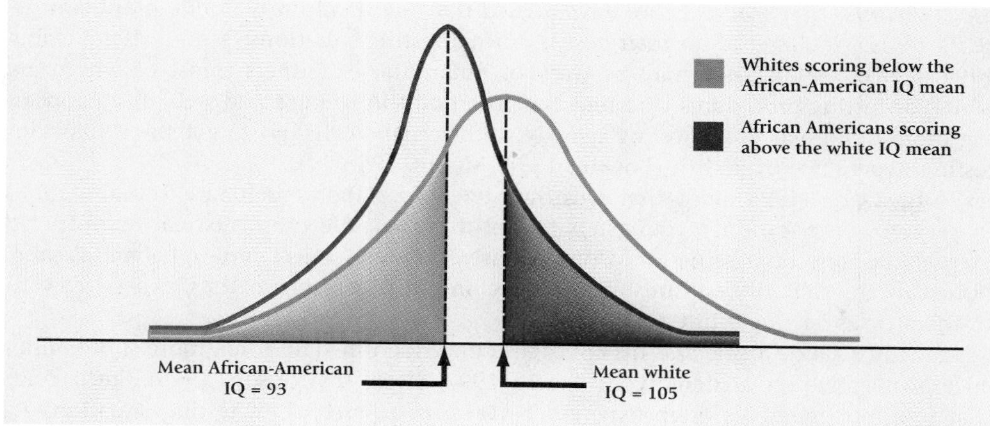

Figure 9.8 *Approximate distributions of IQ scores for African-American and white children reared by their biological parents.* BASED ON BRODY, 1992; NEISSER ET AL., 1996.

middle-class cultural experiences and seriously underestimate the intellectual capabilities of economically disadvantaged children, especially those from minority subcultures; (2) a *genetic* hypothesis that group differences in IQ are hereditary; and (3) an *environmental* hypothesis, that the groups scoring lower in IQ come from intellectually impoverished backgrounds—that is, neighborhoods and home environments that are not very conducive to intellectual growth.

The Cultural Test Bias Hypothesis

Those who favor the **cultural test bias hypothesis** believe that group differences in IQ are an artifact of our tests and testing procedures (Helms, 1992). To illustrate, they point out that IQ tests currently in use were designed to measure cognitive skills (for example, assembling puzzles), general information (for example, "What is a 747?") that white, middle-class children are more likely to have acquired. They note that subtests measuring vocabulary and word usage may be harder for African Americans and Latinos, who often speak a different English dialect from that of the white middle class. Even the way language is used varies across ethnic groups. For example, white parents ask a lot of "knowledge-training" questions ("What does a doggie say?"; "Where do Eskimos live?") that require brief answers and are similar to the kinds of questions asked on IQ tests. By contrast, African-American parents are more inclined to ask *real questions* (for example, "Why didn't you come right home after school?") that they may not know the answer to—questions that often require elaborate, story-type responses that are quite unlike those called for at school or when taking an IQ test (Heath, 1989). So if IQ tests assess proficiency in the white culture, as many critics contend, minority children are bound to appear deficient (Helms, 1992).

cultural test bias hypothesis
the notion that IQ tests and testing procedures have a built-in, middle-class bias that explains the substandard performance of children from lower-class and minority subcultures.

culture-fair tests
intelligence tests constructed to minimize any irrelevant cultural biases in test content that could influence test performance.

DOES TEST BIAS EXPLAIN GROUP DIFFERENCES IN IQ? Several attempts have been made to construct **culture-fair IQ tests** that do not place poor people or those from minority subcultures at an immediate disadvantage. For example, the *Raven Progressive Matrices Test* requires the examinee to scan a series of abstract designs, each of which has a missing section. The examinee's task is to complete each design by selecting the appropriate section from a number of alternatives (see Figure 9.9). These problems are assumed to be equally familiar (or unfamiliar) to people from all ethnic groups and social classes, there is no time limit on the test, and the instructions are very simple. Nevertheless, middle-class whites continue to outperform their lower-income and/or African-American age-mates on these culture-fair measures of intelligence (Jensen, 1980). Translating existing tests into the English dialect spoken by urban African-American children also does not appear to increase the scores that these children make (Quay, 1971). And finally, IQ tests and various tests of intellectual aptitude (such as the SAT) predict future academic successes just as well as or even better for African Americans and other minorities as for whites (Neisser et al., 1996). Taken together, these findings imply that group differences in IQ scores are not solely attributable to biases in the *content* of our tests or the dialect in which they are administered. But another possibility remains.

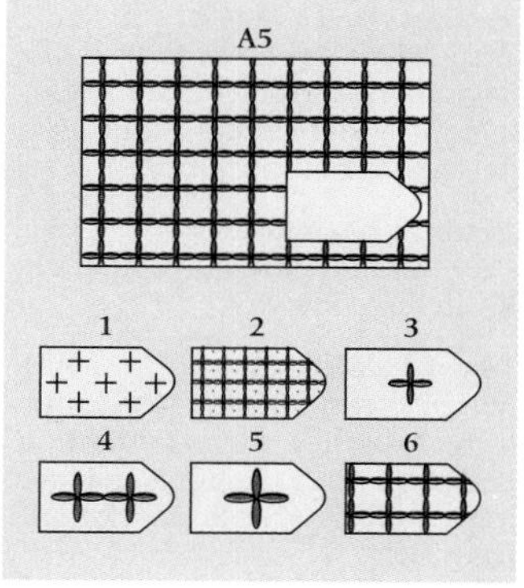

Figure 9.9 *An item similar to those appearing in the Raven Progressive Matrices Test.*

Motivational Factors. Critics have argued that many minority children and adolescents are not inclined to do their best in formal testing situations (Moore, 1986; Ogbu, 1994; Steele, 1997). They may be wary of unfamiliar examiners (most of whom are white) or testing procedures, and may see little point in trying to do well, often appearing more interested in answering quickly (rather than correctly) to get the unpleasant testing experience over with (Boykin, 1994; Moore, 1986).

John Ogbu (1994) adds that negative stereotypes about their intellectual abilities may cause some minority youngsters to feel that their life prospects will be restricted by prejudice and discrimination. Consequently, they may reject certain behaviors sanctioned by the majority culture, such as excelling in school or on tests, as less relevant to them or as "acting white."

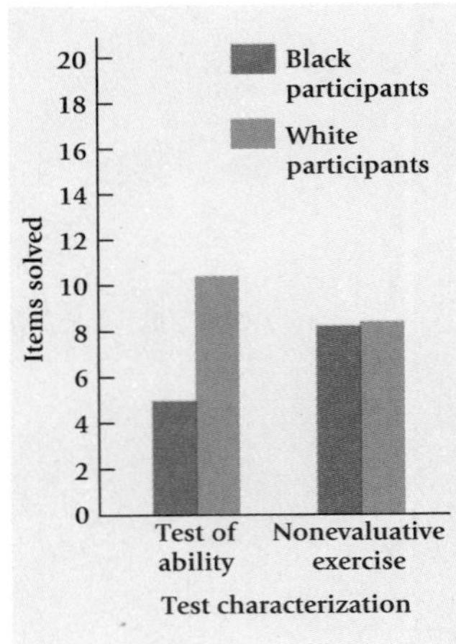

Figure 9.10 *Average performance on a difficult verbal test as a function of race and test characterization. African-American students perform poorly on tests of mental abilities when they think they are taking a test that may result in their being stereotyped as unintelligent.*
Adapted from Steele & Aronson, 1995.

Finally, Claude Steele and his colleagues have identified another, more subtle influence of negative social stereotypes (Steele, 1997; Steele & Aronson, 1995). Steele finds that minority members often experience **stereotype threat** in testing situations—a fear that they will be judged to have traits associated with negative racial or ethnic stereotypes—which then makes them anxious and unable to do their best. In one study, female students took a difficult verbal skills test after learning that these problems were either (1) designed to assess their abilities or (2) simply of interest to the researchers. As Figure 9.10 indicates, African-American adolescents performed *poorly* when they thought their abilities would be assessed, but performed *as well as white students* when the test was portrayed as a nonevaluative exercise. So the fear of displaying lesser ability, or *stereotype threat,* can make minority students anxious and undermine their performance when taking "ability" tests (Steele & Aronson, 1995).

Changes in testing procedures to make minority examinees more comfortable and less threatened can make a big difference. When minority children are allowed to become comfortable with a friendly examiner who is patient and supportive, they score 7 to 10 points higher on IQ tests than they normally would when tested in the traditional way by a strange examiner (Kaufman, Kamphaus, & Kaufman, 1985; Zigler et al., 1982). Even minority youngsters from *middle-class* homes may benefit from those procedural changes, for they are often much less comfortable in testing situations than middle-class whites are (Moore, 1986; Steele, 1997).

The Genetic Hypothesis

Controversy surrounding the causes of racial and ethnic differences in IQ scores was fueled by publication of Richard Herrnstein and Charles Murray's book, *The Bell Curve,* in 1994. These authors argued that racial differences in average IQ scores cannot be explained entirely by test biases or by socioeconomic differences between racial groups. Instead, these IQ differences were said to be heavily influenced by genetic differences between the races.

Arthur Jensen (1980; 1985) agrees with this **genetic hypothesis.** He claims that there are two broad classes of intellectual abilities which are equally heritable among different racial and ethnic groups. **Level I abilities** include attentional processes, short-term memory, and associative skills that are important for simple kinds of rote learning. **Level II abilities** allow one to reason abstractly and to manipulate words and symbols to form concepts and solve problems. According to Jensen, Level II abilities are highly correlated with school achievement, whereas Level I abilities are not. Of course, it is predominantly Level II abilities that are measured on IQ tests.

Jensen (1985) finds that Level I tasks are performed equally well by children from all races, ethnic groups, and social classes. However, middle-class and white children outperform lower-income and African-American children on the more advanced Level II tasks. Since Level I and Level II tasks are equally heritable *within* each social class and ethnic group, Jensen proposes that the IQ differences *between* groups must be hereditary.

stereotype threat
a fear that one will be judged to have traits associated with negative social stereotypes about his or her racial or ethnic group.

genetic hypothesis
a notion that group differences in IQ are hereditary.

Level I abilities
Jensen's term for lower-level intellectual abilities (such as attention and short-term memory) that are important for simple association learning.

Level II abilities
Jensen's term for higher-level cognitive skills that are involved in abstract reasoning and problem solving.

Criticisms of the Genetic Hypothesis. Although Jensen's arguments may sound convincing, there are reasons to suspect that genetic influences do not explain group differences in IQ. For example, Jensen's critics have noted that within-group heritability estimates imply absolutely nothing about between-group differences in an attribute (Lewontin, 1976). As we see in Box 9.2, it is possible for individual differences *within*

9.2

DEVELOPMENTAL ISSUES

Why Heritability Estimates Do Not Explain Group Differences In IQ

Let's suppose that a group of white children obtains an average IQ of 105 and their African-American classmates average 93 on the same test. Further, we will assume that the heritability estimates for the African-American and white populations are comparable. Jensen might use these data to argue that the 12-point difference in IQ between the white and African-American children is attributable to the genetic differences between African Americans and whites. On the surface, this reasoning seems to make sense, because IQ is equally heritable within each group.

However, the argument is flawed. Let's recall that heritability is the amount of variation in a trait that is attributable to genetic factors. If two groups have comparable heritability estimates for a trait, this simply means that, *within* each group, the amount of variability on that trait that is attributable to genetic factors is approximately the same. It says nothing about any differences *between* the groups on that trait.

An example should clarify the point. Suppose a farmer randomly draws corn seed from a bag containing several genetic varieties. He then plants half the seed in a barren field and half in soil that is quite fertile. When the plants are fully grown, the farmer discovers that those *within* each field have grown to different heights. Since all plants within each field were grown in the same soil, their different heights reflect the genetic variability among the seeds that were planted. Therefore, the heritability estimates for plants within each plot should be very high. But notice that the plants growth in the fertile soil are taller, on the average, than those grown in the barren soil. The most logical explanation for this *between-field variation* is an environmental one: Plants grown in fertile soil simply grew taller than those grown in barren soil, and this is true even though the heritability estimates for the heights of the plants *within* each field are comparable (Lewontin, 1976).

The same argument can be applied to explaining group differences in intellectual performance. Even though the heritability estimates for IQ are comparable *within* our samples of African-American and white schoolchildren, the 12-point differences in average IQ *between* the groups may reflect differences in the home environments of African Americans and whites rather than a genetic difference between the races.

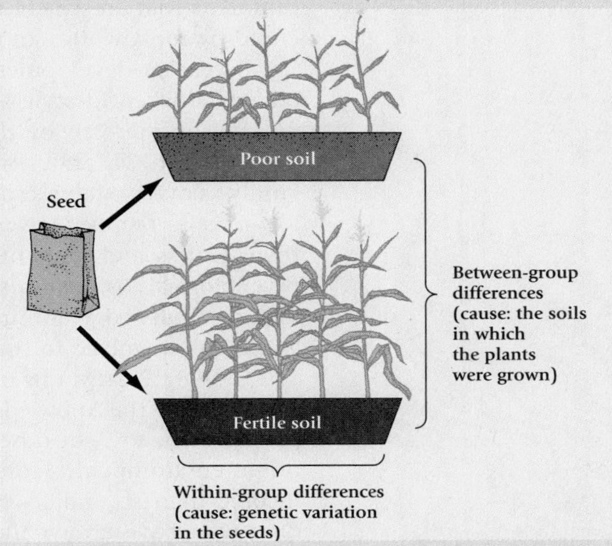

Why within-group differences do not necessarily imply anything about between-group differences. Here we see that the difference in the heights of the plants within each field reflects the genetic variation in the seeds that were planted there, whereas the difference in the average heights of the plants across the fields is attributable to an environmental factor: the soils in which they were grown. ADAPTED FROM GLEITMAN, 1991.

a group to be entirely genetic in character whereas differences *between* two groups are largely the result of environment.

Data available on mixed-race children also fails to support the genetic hypothesis. Eyferth (as cited in Loehlin et al., 1975) obtained the IQ scores of German children fathered by African-American soldiers, and compared these mixed-race children to a group of German children fathered by white-American servicemen. Clearly, the mixed-race group should have scored lower than their white age-mates if their African-American fathers had had fewer IQ-enhancing genes to pass along to them. However, Eyferth found that these two groups of children did not differ in IQ. Similarly, extremely bright African-American children have no higher percentage of white ancestors than is typical of the African-American population as a whole (Scarr et al., 1977).

Despite this negative evidence, the genetic hypothesis lives on. T. Edward Reed (1997), for example, points to methodological problems with existing studies of mixed-race children that, in his opinion, call their findings into question. Other investigators claim that race differences in head and brain size (with whites having larger heads and brains than African Americans) provide strong evidence that race differences in IQ are largely hereditary (Lynn, 1997; Rushton, 1997). Are these *physical* differences between blacks and whites truly evidence that *genes* are responsible for black/white differences in IQ? Ulric Neisser (1997) certainly doesn't think so. He points out that both head and brain size are heavily influenced by such factors as adequacy of prenatal care and nutrition—*environmental* variables that differ across racial and ethnic groups and can strongly affect children's intellectual performances. So even though IQ is a genetically influenced attribute within all racial and ethnic groups, conclusions drawn in *The Bell Curve* are badly overstated. Simply stated, there is no evidence to conclusively demonstrate that *group differences* in IQ are genetically determined (Neisser et al., 1996).

The Environmental Hypothesis

A third explanation for group differences in IQ is the **environmental hypothesis** that poor people and members of various minority groups tend to grow up in environments that are much less conducive to intellectual development than those experienced by most whites and other members of the middle class.

Recently, developmentalists have carefully considered how a low-income or poverty-stricken lifestyle is likely to influence a family's children, and several of these findings bear directly on the issue of children's intellectual development (Duncan et al., 1994; Garrett, Ng'andu, & Ferron, 1994; McLoyd, 1998). Consider, for example, that a family's poverty status and lack of adequate income may mean that many children from low-income families are undernourished, which may inhibit brain growth and make them listless and inattentive (Pollitt, 1994). Furthermore, economic hardship creates psychological distress—a strong dissatisfaction with life's conditions that makes lower-income adults edgy and irritable and reduces their capacity to be sensitive, supportive, and highly involved in their children's learning activities (Conger et al., 1992; McLoyd, 1990; 1998). Finally, low-income parents are often poorly educated themselves and may have neither the knowledge nor the money to provide their children with age-appropriate books, toys, or other experiences that contribute to an intellectually stimulating home environment. Scores on the HOME inventory are consistently lower in low-income than in middle-class homes (Bradley et al., 1989; Gottfried, 1984). And children who have always lived in poverty and whose parents have the fewest financial resources are the ones who experience the least stimulating home environments (Garrett et al., 1994). So there are ample reasons for suspecting that social class differences in intellectual performance are largely *environmental* in origin.

Carefully conducted transracial adoption studies lead to a similar conclusion. Sandra Scarr and Richard Weinberg (1983; Waldman et al., 1994; Weinberg et al., 1992) have studied more than 100 African-American (or interracial) children who were adopted by white, middle-class families. The adoptive parents were well above average in IQ and highly educated, and many had biological children of their own. Although Scarr and Weinberg found that the childhood IQs of the adoptees were about 6 points lower than IQs of white offspring of these same families, this small racial difference seems rather insignificant when we look at the *absolute* performance of the transracial adoptees. As a group, the African-American adoptees obtained an average IQ of 106—6 points above the average for the population as a whole and 15 to 20 points above comparable children who are raised in low-income African-American communities. Ten years later, the average IQs of the transracial adoptees had declined somewhat (average = 97), although direct comparisons may be misleading since the IQ test used in the follow-up was different from that administered in childhood. Nevertheless, these transracial adolescent adoptees remained well above the average IQ obtained by low-income African-American youth, and they scored slightly higher than the national norm in academic achievement. Scarr and Weinberg (1983) concluded that:

> The high IQ scores for the black and interracial [adoptees] . . . mean that (a) genetic differences do not account for a major portion of the IQ performance difference between racial groups, and (b) African-American and interracial children *reared in the [middle class] culture of the tests and the schools* perform as well as other . . . children in similar families [p. 261, italics added].

environmental hypothesis
the notion that groups differ in IQ because the environments in which they are raised are not equally conducive to intellectual growth.

Let's note, however, that Scarr and her associates are not suggesting that white parents are better parents or that disadvantaged children would be better off if they were routinely placed in middle-class homes. In fact, they caution that debates about who might make better parents only distract us from the more important message of the transracial adoption study, namely, that much of the intellectual and academic discrepancies that have been attributed to race or ethnicity may largely reflect ethnic differences in socioeconomic status. Indeed Charlotte Patterson and her associates (1990) found that variation in family income is a better predictor of the academic competencies of African-American and white schoolchildren than race is. The research described in Box 9.3, on page 342, proceeds one step further by suggesting that almost all of the differences in IQ test performance between African-American and white preschool children reflect differences in the social and economic environments in which these children are raised.

IMPROVING COGNITIVE PERFORMANCE THROUGH COMPENSATORY EDUCATION

Perhaps the most enduring legacy of President Lyndon B. Johnson's War on Poverty in the United States is a variety of preschool education programs that are designed to enrich the learning experiences of economically disadvantaged children. Project Head Start is perhaps the best known of these **compensatory interventions.** Specifically, the goal of **Head Start** (and similar programs) was to provide disadvantaged children with the kinds of educational experiences that middle-class youngsters were presumably getting in their homes and nursery school classrooms. It was hoped that these early interventions would compensate for the disadvantages that these children may have already experienced and place them on a roughly equal footing with their middle-class peers by the time they entered first grade.

The earliest reports suggested that Head Start and comparable programs were a smashing success. Program participants were posting an average gain of about 10 points on IQ tests, whereas the IQs of nonparticipants from similar social backgrounds remained unchanged. However, this initial optimism soon began to wane. When program participants were reexamined after completing a year or two of grade school, the gains they had made on IQ tests had largely disappeared (Gray & Klaus, 1970). In other words, few if any lasting intellectual benefits seemed to be associated with these interventions, thus prompting Arthur Jensen (1969, p. 2) to conclude that "compensatory education has been tried and it apparently has failed."

However, many developmentalists were reluctant to accept this conclusion. They felt that it was shortsighted to place so much emphasis on IQ scores as an index of program effectiveness. After all, the ultimate goal of compensatory education is not so much to boost IQ as to improve children's academic performance. Others have argued that the impact of these early interventions might be cumulative, so that it may be several years before the full benefits of compensatory education are apparent.

compensatory interventions
special educational programs designed to further the cognitive growth and scholastic achievements of disadvantaged children.

Head Start
a large-scale preschool educational program designed to provide children from low-income families with a variety of social and intellectual experiences that might better prepare them for school.

Long-Term Follow-ups

As it turns out, Jensen's critics may have been right on both counts. In 1982 Irving Lazar and Richard Darlington reported on the long-term effects of 11 high-quality, university-based early intervention programs initiated during the 1960s. The program participants were disadvantaged preschool children from several areas of the United States. At regular intervals throughout the grade-school years, the investigators examined the

CULTURAL INFLUENCES

Do Socioeconomic Differences between the Races Explain Race Differences in IQ?

In 1994, nearly 22% of American children—some 16 million in all—were living in families in which total income was not sufficient to meet the families' most basic needs (U.S. Bureau of the Census, 1996). Furthermore, children from minority groups are much more likely to be living under these marginal conditions than white youngsters are, especially African-American children, for whom living in poverty early in life is more the rule than the exception (Duncan et al., 1994).

To what extent do socioeconomic differences between African Americans and whites account for race differences in IQ? One way to approach this question is to (1) select a large number of African-American and white families, (2) carefully measure several indicators and correlates of each family's socioeconomic status, and (3) determine whether any race differences in these socioeconomic variables are associated with (and thus might conceivably explain) race differences in children's intellectual performance.

Jeanne Brooks-Gunn and her associates (1996) conducted such a study as part of a larger longitudinal investigation of low-birth-weight children. All of the children in this sample, who were now healthy 5-year-olds, had recently taken a standardized IQ test. In addition, such social class indicators and correlates as family income, average neighborhood income, mother's educational level, mother's verbal ability, number of parents living at home, and quality of the home environment (as assessed by the HOME inventory) were available for the family of each child. Like other investigators, Brooks-Gunn et al. found that African-American children obtained lower IQs, on average, than white children did. Furthermore, the African-American families scored lower on each of the above indicators and correlates of socioeconomic status. So how close was the association between race differences in IQ and race differences in socioeconomic status?

To find out, Brooks-Gunn and her associates (1996) submitted their data to a sophisticated correlational analysis that allowed them to estimate how much of the race difference in intellectual performance is accounted for by each indicator/correlate of socioeconomic status. This is accomplished statistically by holding each socioeconomic variable constant for all children and then estimating what the IQ difference between African Americans and whites would be had they been raised under the same conditions—that is, with the same financial circumstances, home environments, and so on.

The results of this analysis appear in the table. Since African-American children and white children differed in ways other than socioeconomic status that are known to influence intellectual performance (for example, in birth weight), it was necessary to first estimate the contribution of these background variables to race differences in intellectual performance. As we see in the table, race differences in IQ are hardly affected, dropping from 18.1 points actually observed to an estimated 17.8 points after controlling for background differences between the races. However, after adjusting for the lower average incomes of African-American families, estimated race differences in IQ drop 52%, to 8.5 points. Further adjustments to compensate for the lower levels of maternal education, maternal verbal ability, and the greater number of single-parent households among the African-American sample reduced the IQ differences only minimally, from 8.5 to 7.8 points. But when the data were further analyzed to compensate for the less stimulating home environments in which African-American children lived, there remained an IQ difference of only 3.4 points that was not accounted for by race differences in socioeconomic status and home environments!

Of course, these findings are correlational data that we must interpret cautiously. Nevertheless, they strongly suggest that much of the IQ difference between African Americans and whites is really a social class effect and that African-American children would perform comparably with whites if raised under similar socioeconomic circumstances. Indeed, we have reviewed other evidence that supports this conclusion, namely Scarr and Weinberg's transracial adoption study. When raised in similar middle-class environments, African-American and white children differ only minimally in intellectual performance and score at or above the national average on tests of academic achievement.

Estimated Differences in Intellectual Performance of African-American and White Preschool Children after Adjusting for Race Differences in Background Variables, Socioeconomic Status, and Other Family Characteristics

Analysis performed	Race difference in IQ (points)
Unadjusted (actual IQ scores)	18.1
After adjusting for race differences in:	
Background variables	17.8
Family/neighborhood income	8.5
Mother's education, mother's verbal ability, number parents living at home	7.8
Home environment (HOME scores)	3.4

participants' scholastic records and administered IQ and achievement tests. The participants and their mothers were also interviewed to determine the children's feelings of self-worth, attitudes about school and scholastic achievement, and vocational aspirations, as well as mothers' aspirations for their children and their feelings about their children's progress at school. Other longitudinal follow-ups of these or similar high-quality interventions have been conducted since 1982 (Barnett, 1993; Berrueta-Clement et al., 1984; Darlington, 1991). Together, these longitudinal studies suggest that program participants score higher in IQ than nonparticipants for 2 to 3 years after the interventions are over, but that their IQ scores eventually decline. Did the program fail then?

No, indeed! Children who participated in the interventions were much more likely to meet their school's basic requirements than nonparticipants were. They were less likely to be assigned to special education classes or to be retained in a grade, and they were more likely than nonparticipants to complete high school. Program participants had more positive attitudes about school and (later) about job-related successes than nonparticipants did, and their mothers were more satisfied with their academic performances and held higher occupational aspirations for them as well. There was even some evidence that teenagers who had participated in these high-quality interventions earlier in life were less likely to become pregnant or to be involved in delinquent activities and were more likely to be employed than nonparticipants were.

Can we expect to do better than this in the future? Many believe that we can if compensatory education begins earlier in life and lasts longer, and ways are found to help parents become more involved in their children's learning activities (Murray, 1997; Ramey & Ramey, 1998).

The Importance of Parental Involvement

Comparisons of the impact of early intervention programs suggest that the most effective ones almost always involve parents in one way or another. For example, Joan Sprigle and Lyn Schaefer (1985) evaluated the long-term benefits of two preschool interventions—*Head Start* and *Learning to Learn*, a program that educated parents about its goals, provided them with informational updates about their children's progress, and repeatedly emphasized that a partnership between home and school was necessary to ensure the program's success. When the disadvantaged students who participated in these interventions were later observed in the fourth, fifth, and sixth grades, the outcomes consistently favored the Learning to Learn (LTL) program, in which parents had been heavily involved. Although LTL students did not necessarily outperform those from Head Start on IQ tests, they were making better grades in basic academic subjects (such as reading) and were less likely to have failed a grade in school or to have been placed in costly special education classes for the learning disabled.

Other investigators favor **two-generation interventions** that not only provide children with high-quality preschool education, but also provide disadvantaged parents with social support and the educational and vocational training they need to lift themselves out of poverty (Ramey & Ramey, 1998). The research described in Box 9.4 suggests that this kind of family intervention is likely to improve parents' psychological well-being, which may translate into more effective patterns of parenting and, ultimately, into long-term gains in children's intellectual performances.

The Importance of Intervening Early

Critics of *Head Start* have argued that it begins too late (often after age 3) and is simply too brief to have any lasting impact. Might interventions that begin *in infancy* and

two-generation intervention
interventions with goals to both stimulate children's intellectual development through preschool day-care/education and to assist parents to move out of poverty.

APPLYING DEVELOPMENTAL RESEARCH

An Effective Compensatory Intervention for Families

Earlier in Chapter 5, we learned that disadvantaged children of teenage mothers are at risk of displaying poor cognitive development and of becoming academic underachievers throughout childhood and adolescence. Recently, Victoria Seitz and Nancy Apfel (1994b; Seitz et al., 1985) described a two-generation family intervention that looks very promising as a means of preventing these outcomes.

Seitz and Apfel's family intervention was a 30-month program targeting poverty-stricken mothers who had recently delivered healthy first-born children. It provided pediatric care, developmental evaluations, and monthly home visits by a psychologist, nurse, or social worker, who gave mothers social support, information about child-rearing and other family matters, and assistance in obtaining education or vocational training needed to land a job (or a better paying job). The children received stimulating, high-quality day-care from a provider who met frequently with mothers to discuss their children's developmental progress and to help them deal constructively with any child-rearing problems they had encountered. Other mothers and their first-borns from the same socioeconomic backgrounds received no intervention and served as a control group.

Ten years later, Seitz and her associates (1985) followed up on the first-born children of these families to assess their academic progress. They found that children who had received the intervention were doing well. They were much more likely than control children to be attending school regularly and making normal progress, and were much less likely to have been retained in a grade or required costly remedial services such as special education. Clearly, this intervention appeared to benefit the children who had participated.

Two-generation family interventions that target disadvantaged children and their parents lead to changes in parenting that benefit all children in the family.

But there was more—what might be called a *diffusion* effect. Specifically, the *younger* siblings of the "intervention" and the "control" participants displayed precisely the same differences in scholastic outcomes that the older children did, even though these younger brothers and sisters of children who participated in the intervention had not been born *until after the intervention was over* (Seitz & Apfel, 1994b). Apparently, this family intervention had made disadvantaged mothers who participated more involved in their children's lives and more confident and effective in their parenting—a change that not only benefited their first-born child who received stimulating day-care, but *all of their subsequent children* as well. It was an effective intervention indeed!

last for several years produce more enduring gains in the IQs and academic performances of disadvantaged children?

The Carolina Abecedarian Project (Campbell & Ramey, 1994; 1995) is a particularly ambitious early intervention that was designed to answer these questions. Program participants were selected from families considered to be at risk for producing mildly retarded children. These families were all on welfare, and most were headed by a single parent, the mother, who had scored well below average on a standardized IQ test (obtaining IQs of 70 to 85). The project began when the participating children were only 6 to 12 weeks old, and it continued for the next 5 years. Half of the high-risk children took part in a special day-care program designed to promote their intellectual development. The program was truly a full-time endeavor, running from 7:15 A.M. to 5:15 P.M., five days a week for 50 weeks each year, until the child entered school. The remaining control children received exactly the same dietary supplements, social services, and pediatric care given to their agemates in the experimental group, but they did not attend day-care. At regular intervals over the next 15 years, the progress of these two groups of high-risk children was assessed by administering IQ tests. Periodic tests of academic achievement were also given at school.

Figure 9.11 summarizes the IQ data through age 12. Notice that the high-risk day-care children began to outperform their counterparts in the control group by 18 months of age and that they *maintained* this IQ advantage over the long run (now through age 15). Here, then, is evidence that high-quality preschool education that begins very early

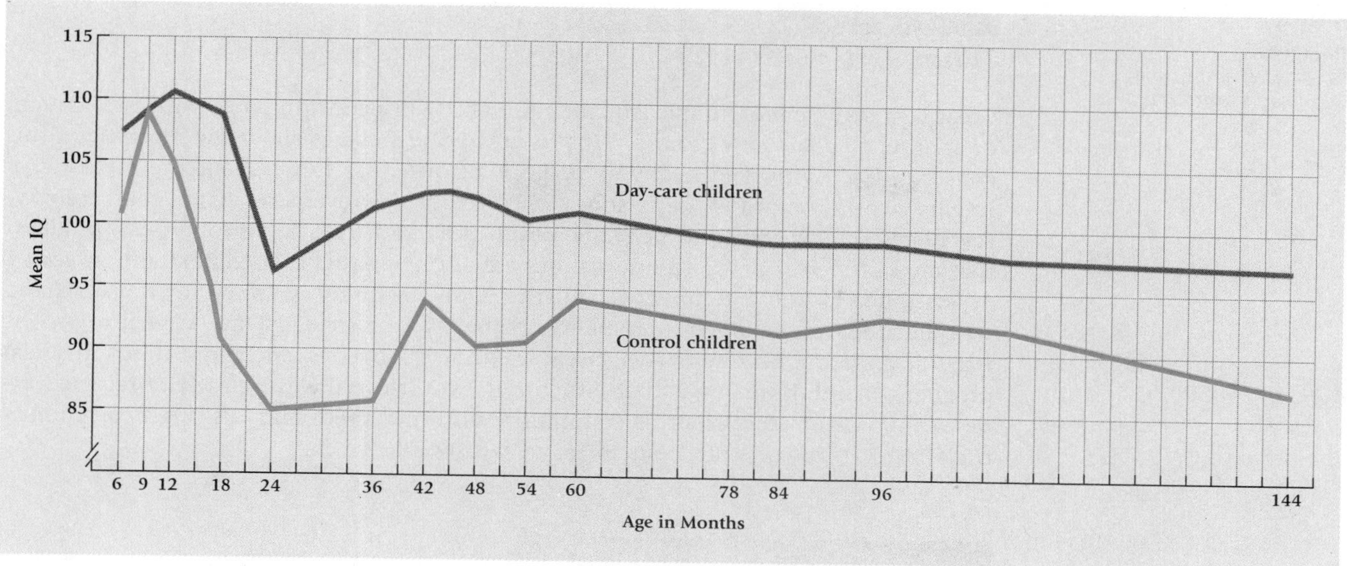

Figure 9.11 *IQ scores of day-care and control children from the Abecedarian Project between 6 months and 12 years of age.* ADAPTED FROM CAMPBELL & RAMEY, 1994.

can have *lasting* intellectual benefits. It can have lasting educational benefits, too, for the day-care children outperformed the control group in all areas of academic achievement from the third year of school onward (Campbell & Ramey, 1994; 1995; see also Reynolds & Temple, 1998).

Programs such as the family intervention described in Box 9.4 and the Abecedarian project are expensive to administer, and there are critics who claim that they would be not worth the high costs of providing them to all disadvantaged families. However, such an attitude may be "penny wise and pound foolish," for Victoria Seitz and her associates (1985) found that extensive two-generation interventions emphasizing quality day-care often pay for themselves by (1) allowing more parents freedom from full-time child care to work, thereby reducing their need for public assistance, and (2) providing the foundation for cognitive growth that enables most disadvantaged children to avoid special education in school—a service that costs in excess of $1,500 per pupil per year. And when we consider the long-term economic benefits that could accrue later in life, when gainfully employed adult graduates of highly successful interventions pay more taxes than disadvantaged nonparticipants, need less welfare, and are less often maintained at public expense in penal institutions, the net return on each dollar invested in compensatory education could be impressive indeed.

WHAT DO YOU THINK?

How do you feel about providing two-generation interventions on a large scale to economically disadvantaged populations? Do the demonstrated benefits justify the expenditures (which may be high)? Why or why not?

CREATIVITY AND SPECIAL TALENTS

What do we mean when we say that a child or an adolescent is "gifted"? This term was once limited to people such as those in Terman's longitudinal study with IQs of 140 or higher. Yet, despite their lofty IQs and generally favorable life outcomes, not one of Terman's gifted children ever became truly eminent. Recent definitions of **giftedness** have been broadened to include not only a high IQ but also special talents in particular areas such as music, art, literature, or science. Over the years, we have learned that certain abilities not measured by traditional IQ tests help some people to become innovators in their chosen fields. In other words, gifted individuals are not only bright but are also "creative."

giftedness
the possession of unusually high intellectual potential or other special talents.

What Is Creativity?

Creativity may be more important than a high IQ in permitting a Mozart, an Einstein, or a Piaget to break new ground. What is creativity? Debates about the meaning of this construct have provoked nearly as much controversy as those about the meaning of intelligence (Mumford & Gustafson, 1988). Yet, almost everyone agrees that **creativity** represents an ability to generate novel ideas and innovative solutions—products that are not merely new and unusual but are also appropriate in context and *valued* by others (Lubart, 1994; Sternberg & Lubart, 1996). Creativity is important *to individuals,* who must solve challenging problems on the job and in daily life, as well *to society,* when it underlies new inventions, new scientific discoveries, and innovations in social programs or the humanities that enrich our lives. Nevertheless, creativity received little attention from the scientific community until the 1960s and 70s, when psychometricians began to construct tests to try to measure it.

The Psychometric Perspective

In his structure-of-intellect model, J. P. Guilford (1967; 1988) proposed that creativity represents divergent rather than convergent thinking. **Convergent thinking** requires individuals to generate the one best answer to a problem and is precisely what IQ tests measure. By contrast, **divergent thinking** requires one to generate a variety of solutions to problems for which there is no one right answer. Figure 9.12 presents a *figural* measure of divergent thinking, whereas a *verbal* measure might ask respondents to list all words that can be made from the letters in the word *baseball,* and a *"real-world" problem* measure might ask them to devise as many practical uses as possible for common objects such as a clothespin or a cork (Runco, 1992; Torrance, 1988).

Interestingly, divergent thinking is only modestly correlated with IQ (Wallach, 1985; Sternberg & Lubart, 1996) and seems to be more heavily influenced by children's home environments than by their genes (Plomin, 1990). Specifically, children who score high in divergent thinking have parents who encourage their intellectual curiosity and who grant them a great deal of freedom to select their own interests and to explore them in depth (Getzels & Jackson, 1962; Harrington, Block, & Block, 1987; Runco, 1992). So divergent thinking is a cognitive skill that is distinct from general intelligence and can be nurtured. However, many researchers became disenchanted with the psychometric approach to creativity once it became rather obvious that the scores people make on tests of divergent thinking during childhood and adolescence are, at best, only modestly related to their creative accomplishments later in life (Feldhusen & Goh, 1995; Runco, 1992). Clearly, divergent thinking may foster creative solutions; but, by itself, it is a woefully incomplete account of what it means to be creative (Amabile, 1983; Lubart, 1994).

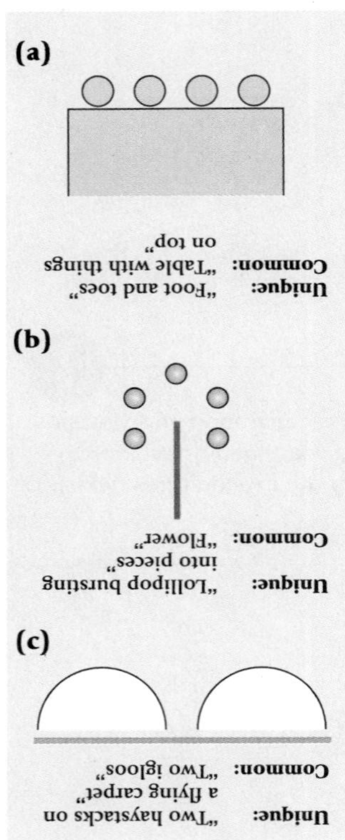

Figure 9.12 *Are you creative? Indicate what you see in each of the three drawings. Below each drawing you will find examples of unique and common responses, drawn from a study of creativity in children.* ADAPTED FROM WALLACH & KOGAN, *1965.*

The Multicomponent (or Confluence) Perspective

Think for a moment about the characteristics of people whom you consider creative. Chances are that you view them as reasonably intelligent; but it is also likely that they display such characteristics as being highly inquisitive and flexible individuals who love their work, make connections between ideas that others don't, and may be a bit unorthodox and nonconforming. This creativity syndrome may be no accident, for researchers today generally believe that creativity results from a *convergence* of many personal and situational factors (Amabile, 1983; Gardner, 1993; Gruber, 1982; Sternberg & Lubart, 1996; Weisberg, 1993).

If creativity truly reflects *all* of the attributes above, then it is perhaps understandable why many people with high IQs are not particularly creative or why so few are truly eminent (Richert, 1997). Yet, Robert Sternberg and Todd Lubart (1996) have argued that most people have the potential to be creative and will be, at least to some degree, if they can marshal the *resources* that foster creativity and can invest themselves in the right kinds of goals. Let's briefly consider this new but influential **investment theory of creativity** and its implications for promoting the creative potential of children and adolescents.

Parents of creative children encourage their intellectual curiosity and allow them to explore their interests in depth.

Sternberg and Lubart's Investment Theory

According to Sternberg and Lubart (1996), creative people are willing to "buy low and sell high" in the realm of ideas. "Buying low" means that they invest themselves in ideas or projects that are novel (or out of favor) and may initially encounter resistance. But by persisting in the face of such skepticism, a creative individual generates a product that is highly valued, and can now "sell high" and move on to the next novel or unpopular idea that has growth potential.

What factors determine whether an individual will invest in an original project and bring it to a creative end? Sternberg and Lubart believe that creativity depends on a convergence, or confluence, of six distinct but interrelated sets of resources. Let's briefly consider these components of creativity and how we might seek to promote them.

Intellectual Resources. Sternberg and Lubart (1996) believe that three intellectual abilities are particularly important to creativity. One is the ability to *find new problems* to solve or to see old problems in new ways. Another is the ability to *evaluate* one's ideas to determine which are worth pursuing and which are not. Finally, one must be able to *sell others* on the value of new ideas in order to gain the support that may be necessary to fully develop them. All three abilities are important. If one cannot evaluate new ideas one has generated or sell others on their value, they are unlikely to ever blossom into creative accomplishments.

Knowledge. A child, an adolescent, (or an adult) must be familiar with the current state of the art in her chosen area if she is to ever advance or transform it as the ground-breaking artist, musician, or science-fair winner does. As Howard Gruber (1982) puts it "Insight comes to the prepared mind . . ." (p. 22).

Cognitive Style. A *legislative cognitive style*—that is, a preference for thinking in novel and divergent ways of *one's own choosing*—is important to creativity. It also helps to think in broad, *global* terms—to be able to distinguish the forest from the trees—which will help in deciding which of one's ideas are truly novel and worth pursuing.

Personality. Previous research indicates that the personality variables most closely associated with high creativity are a willingness to take sensible risks, to persevere in the face of uncertainty or ambiguity, and to have the self-confidence to defy the crowd and pursue ideas that will eventually win recognition.

Motivation. People rarely do creative work in an area unless they have a passion for what they are trying to accomplish and focus on *the work itself* rather than its potential rewards (Amabile, 1983). The ground-breaking Olympic gymnast Olga Korbut put it well: "If gymnastics did not exist, I would have invented it" (Feldman, 1982, p. 35). This does not mean that the prospect of winning Olympic medals had nothing to do with Ms. Korbut's success, for prizes and other incentives indicate what goals are socially valued and encourage people to work on innovative projects. But creativity can truly suffer if children focus too much on the rewards and lose their intrinsic interest in the work they are pursuing (Lubart & Sternberg, 1995).

creativity
the ability to generate novel ideas or works that are useful and valued by others.

convergent thinking
thinking that requires one to come up with a single correct answer to a problem; what IQ tests measure.

divergent thinking
thinking that requires a variety of ideas or solutions to a problem when there is no one correct answer.

investment theory of creativity
recent theory specifying that the ability to invest in innovative projects and to generate creative solutions depends on a convergence of creative resources, namely, background knowledge, intellectual abilities, personality characteristics, motivation, and environmental support/encouragement.

A Supportive Environment. Several studies of children with special talents in such domains as chess, music, or mathematics reveal that these child prodigies are blessed with an environment that nurtured their talents and motivations and rewarded their accomplishments (Feldman & Goldsmith, 1991; Hennessay & Amabile, 1989; Monass & Engelhard, 1990). Parents of creative youngsters generally encourage intellectual activities and accept their children's idiosyncrasies (Albert, 1994; Runco, 1992). They are also quick to recognize unusual talents and help to foster their growth by soliciting the assistance of expert coaches or tutors. Furthermore, some societies value creativity more than others do and devote many financial and human resources to nurturing creative potential (Simonton, 1988; 1994). Indeed, Olga Korbut's brilliant talent might not have bloomed had gymnastics not been so highly valued in Russian society when she was growing up.

A Test of Investment Theory

If investment theory is sound, then people who have more creative resources at their disposal should generate more creative solutions to problems. Lubart and Sternberg (1995) tested this hypothesis in a study of adolescents and adults. A battery of questionnaires, cognitive tests, and personality measures was first administered to measure five of the six sets of creative resources (environment was not assessed). Participants then worked at innovative problems in writing (for example, create a story about the octopus's sneakers), *art* (draw a picture to illustrate "hope"), *advertising* (create an ad for brussels sprouts) and *science* (How might we detect extraterrestrials among us?). Their solutions were then rated for creativity by a panel of judges, who showed high levels of agreement in their ratings.

The results supported investment theory in that all five sets of creativity resources were moderately to highly correlated with the creativity ratings participants received, and participants whose solutions were rated most creative were those who had higher scores across all five kinds of creative resources. Apparently, creativity does reflect the convergence of many factors rather than the possession of a dominant cognitive attribute such as divergent thinking.

Promoting Creativity in the Classroom

How might educators foster creativity in the classroom? Most current programs for gifted students concentrate on enriching and accelerating traditional learning and may do little, beyond providing background knowledge, to promote creativity (Sternberg, 1995; Winner, 1997). Gardner's theory of multiple intelligences has been used as a framework for promoting the growth of intelligences that are not heavily stressed in school. These programs enrich the experiences of all pupils to foster such abilities as *spatial intelligence* (through sculpting or painting), *kinesthetic-body intelligence* (through dance or athletics), and *linguistic intelligence* (through storytelling). Whether these efforts truly foster creativity is not yet clear, although they have been successful at identifying special talents of children who are not at all exceptional in traditional academic subjects (Ramos-Ford & Gardner, 1997).

Programs to encourage the development of "intelligence" not usually stressed at school often identify hidden talents and may foster creativity.

The investment theory of creativity suggests several possible means of fostering creative potential. Were teachers to allow students more freedom to design their own art projects or science experiments and to explore any unusual interests in depth, they would more closely approximate the kind of home environment that nurtures curiosity, risk taking, perseverance, intrinsic interest, and a concern with task performance (rather than with such performance outcomes as earning a passing grade). Less emphasis on memorizing facts and obtaining correct answers (convergent thinking) and more emphasis on discussing complex problems that have many possible answers may also help students to develop divergent thinking skills, tolerance for ambiguity, and a global analytic style that fosters creative solutions. Unfortunately, attempts to further the creative potential of children are in their infancy, and it is not yet clear just what procedures work best. However, the research we have reviewed implies that parents and educators might try to be a bit more enthusiastic when youngsters display an unusual passion for an offbeat or otherwise nontraditional interest. By providing such support (and exposure to experts if any are available), we may be helping to nurture the creative potential of future innovators.

SUMMARY

What Is Intelligence?

◆ The **psychometric** (or testing) **approach** defines intelligence as a trait (or set of traits) that allows some people to think and solve problems more effectively than others. Alfred Binet developed the first successful intelligence test, which conceived of intelligence as a general mental ability. Yet, researchers relying on **factor analysis** argue that intelligence is not a singular trait. Spearman viewed intelligence as a *general mental ability* (or **g**) and *special abilities* (or **s**), each of which was specific to a particular test. Thurstone claimed that intelligence consists of seven **primary mental abilities.** Guilford's **structure-of-intellect model** proposed that intelligence consists of 180 mental abilities, whereas Cattel and Horn make a distinction between **fluid intelligence** and **crystallized intelligence. Hierarchical models,** such as Carroll's **three-stratum theory of intelligence,** are the most elaborate psychometric classifications of mental abilities to date.

◆ New viewpoints on intelligence are becoming increasingly influential. Robert Sternberg's **triarchic theory** criticizes psychometric theories of intelligence for their failure to consider the *contexts* in which intelligent acts are displayed, the test taker's *experience* with test items, and the *information-processing strategies* on which people rely when thinking or solving problems.

◆ Gardner's **theory of multiple intelligences,** which is currently influencing research on creativity and special talents, contends that human beings display at least seven distinctive kinds of intelligence, several of which are not assessed by traditional intelligence tests.

How Is Intelligence Measured?

◆ Today, there are literally hundreds of intelligence tests, and the **Stanford-Binet Intelligence Scale** and the **Wechsler Intelligence Test for Children (WISC-III)** are widely used. Both scales compare children's performance against **test norms** for age-mates and assign them **intelligence quotients (IQs),** which are normally distributed around the average score of 100.

◆ New approaches to intelligence testing include the **Kaufman Assessment Battery for Children (K-ABC),** which is grounded in information-processing theory, and **dynamic assessment,** which is compatible with Vygotsky's theory and Sternberg's triarchic theory.

◆ Infant intelligence tests, which tap perceptual and motor skills and assign **developmental quotient (DQ)** scores, are poor predictors of childhood IQs. Newer measures of infant information-processing capabilities are much better predictors of later intellectual performance.

◆ IQ is a relatively stable attribute for some individuals. However, many others will show wide variations in their IQ scores over the course of childhood. The fact that IQ can wander upward or downward over time suggests that IQ tests measure intellectual *performance* rather than an inborn capacity for thinking and problem solving. Children whose home environments are stable and stimulating often display IQ stability or increases over time, whereas children from impoverished backgrounds often display a **cumulative deficit** in IQ.

What Do Intelligence Tests Predict?

◆ When we consider trends for the population as a whole, IQ scores predict important outcomes such as future academic accomplishments, occupational status, and even health and happiness. But at the individual level, an IQ score is not always a reliable indicator of one's future health, happiness, or success. Besides IQ, one's family background, work habits, education, **tacit (or practical) intelligence,** and motivation to succeed are important contributors to the successes one attains.

Factors That Influence IQ Scores

◆ Both heredity and environment contribute heavily to intellectual performance. The evidence from twin studies and studies of adopted children indicates that about half the variation among individuals in IQ is attributable to hereditary factors. But regardless of one's genetic predispositions, barren intellectual environments clearly inhibit cognitive growth, whereas enriched, intellectually stimulating environments can clearly promote it.

Social and Cultural Correlates of Intellectual Performance

◆ Research with the **HOME Inventory** reveals that parents who create a stimulating home environment by becoming involved in their children's learning activities, explaining new concepts, and providing age-appropriate challenges and consistent encouragement are likely to have children who score relatively high in academic achievement and IQ.

◆ First-borns and children from smaller families tend to develop slightly higher IQs than later-borns and children from larger families. Zajonc's **confluence hypothesis,** which seeks to explain these findings, has received mixed support.

♦ On average, African-American, Native American, Hispanic-American, and other children from lower-income backgrounds score lower on IQ tests than middle-class whites and Asian-Americans do. These differences are still apparent on **culture-fair IQ tests,** and although some minority students may be less motivated in testing situations, or may display the effects of **stereotype threat, cultural test bias** does not explain all the group differences in IQ. Nor is there any conclusive evidence for the **genetic hypothesis** (or the **Level I–Level II** distinction) which posits that group differences in IQ are hereditary. The best explanation for group differences in IQ is the **environmental hypothesis:** many poor people and minority group members score lower on IQ tests because they grow up in impoverished environments that are much less conducive to intellectual development than those of their middle-class age-mates.

Improving Cognitive Performance Through Compensatory Education

♦ **Head Start** and other **compensatory interventions** for disadvantaged preschoolers rarely produce lasting gains in IQ. However, the best of these interventions do improve children's chances of succeeding in the classroom, and they help to prevent the progressive decline in intellectual performance and academic achievement so often observed among students from disadvantaged backgrounds.

♦ Compensatory education is most effective when it starts early, lasts through the preschool period, and involves children's parents. Recent **two-generation interventions** and those beginning early in infancy look especially promising.

Creativity and Special Talents

♦ Definitions of **giftedness** have been expanded to include not only a high IQ but special talents, including **creativity.**

♦ Psychometricians distinguish IQ (which rests on **convergent thinking**) from creativity, or **divergent thinking.** Although divergent thinking is only modestly correlated with IQ, it also fails to predict future creativity very well.

♦ Recent multicomponent (or confluence) perspectives, such as the **investment theory of creativity,** specify that a variety of cognitive, personal, motivational, and environmental resources combine to foster creative problem solving. This theory looks very promising, both in terms of its existing empirical support and its suggestions for fostering creativity.

Tests designed to measure an individual's intelligence can come in many forms. A visit to: http://www.iglobal.net/psman/intelligence.html will let you test your own intelligence using a variety of assessment tools. By looking through all the tests at this site you will discover the diversity of testing methods that can be used to get at the puzzle of intelligence.

KEY TERMS

psychometric approach, 314
mental age (MA), 314
factor analysis, 315
g, 316
s, 316
primary mental abilities, 316
structure-of-intellect model, 316
fluid intelligence, 316
crystallized intelligence, 317
hierarchical model of intelligence, 317
three-stratum theory of intelligence, 317
triarchic theory, 318
cultural bias, 319
theory of multiple intelligences, 319
Stanford-Binet Intelligence Scale, 321
intelligence quotient(IQ), 321
test norms, 322
Wechsler Intelligence Scale for Children (WISC-III), 322
normal distribution, 322
Kaufman Assessment Battery for Children (K-ABC), 323
dynamic assessment, 324
development quotient (DQ), 324
cumulative-deficit hypothesis, 326
tacit (or practical) intelligence, 328
mental retardation, 329
HOME inventory, 333
confluence hypothesis, 335
cultural test bias hypothesis, 337
culture-fair tests, 337
stereotype threat, 338
genetic hypothesis, 338
Level I abilities, 338
Level II abilities, 338
environmental hypothesis, 340
compensatory interventions, 341
Head Start, 341
two-generation intervention, 343
giftedness, 345
creativity, 346
convergent thinking, 346
divergent thinking, 346
investment theory of creativity, 347

Development of Language and Communication Skills

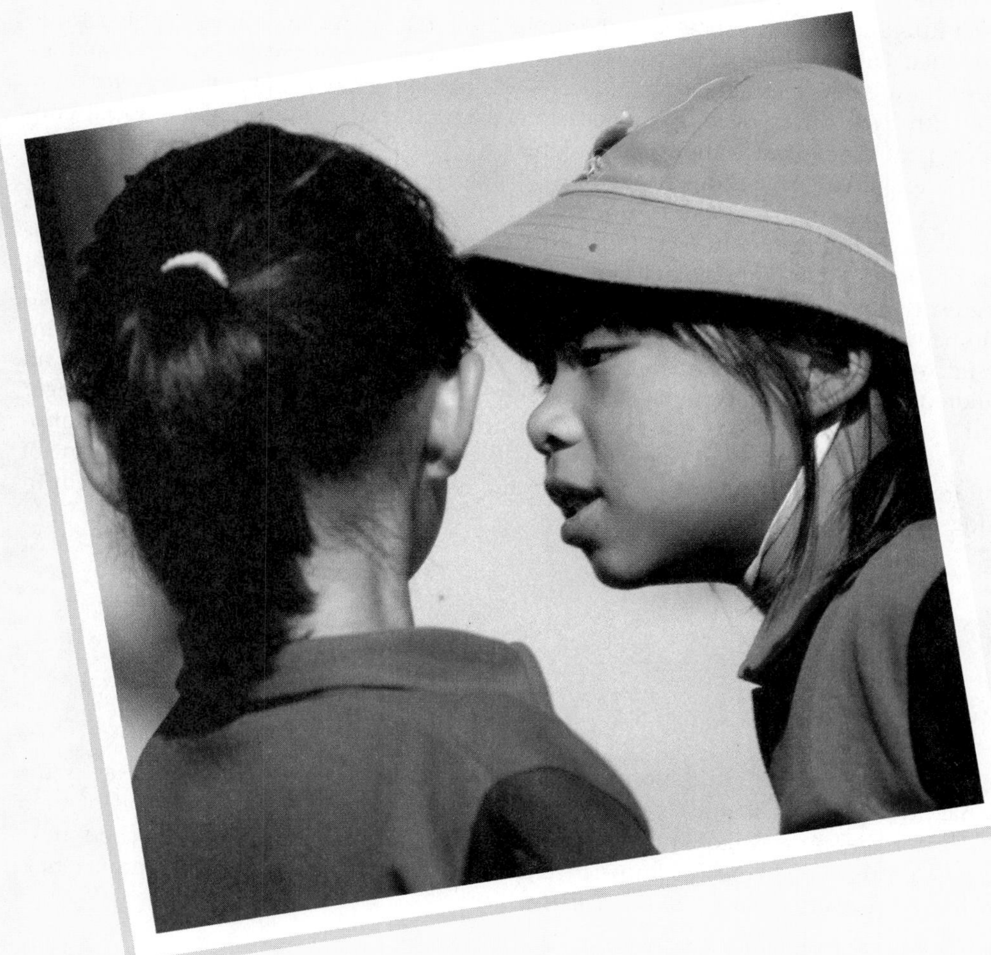

"Rrrrrruh! Rrrrrruh!" exclaims 11-month-old Jacob as he sits in his walker looking out the window. "What are you saying, little man?" asks his aunt Pam. "He's saying Daddy's car is in the driveway; he's home from work!" Jacob's mother replies.

"Oops! It broked. Fix it daggy." (18-month-old Amy responding to the arm that has come loose from her doll).

"I can see clearly now . . . I see all icicles *in my way" (2½-year-old Todd singing his rendition of a popular song; the correct lyric is "obstacles").*

One truly astounding achievement that sets humans apart from the rest of the animal kingdom is our creation and use of **language.** Although animals can **communicate** with one another, their limited number of calls and gestures are merely isolated signals that convey very specific messages (for example, a greeting, a threat, a summons to congregate) in much the same way that single words or stereotyped phrases do in a human language (Tomasello & Camaioni, 1997). By contrast, human languages are amazingly *flexible* and *productive*. From a small number of individually meaningless sounds, children come to generate thousands of meaningful auditory patterns (syllables, words, and even idiosyncratic vocables such as Jacob's "Rrrrrruh!") that are eventually combined according to a set of grammatical rules (with a few missteps, such as Amy's use of the word *broked*) to produce an infinite number of messages. Language is also an *inventive* tool with which we express our thoughts and interpretations (or in Todd's case, misinterpretations) of what we have seen, heard, or otherwise experienced. In singing the lyrics above, Todd was trying to faithfully reproduce what he had heard. However, most of what children say in any given situation is not merely a repetition of what they have said or heard before; speakers create many novel utterances on the spot, and the topics they talk about may have nothing to do with their current state or the stream of ongoing events. Yet creative as they may be in generating new messages, even 3- and 4-year-olds are generally able to converse quite well with each other, as long as their statements adhere to the rules and social conventions of the language they are speaking.

Although language is one of the most abstract bodies of knowledge we ever acquire, children in all cultures come to understand and use this intricate form of communication very early in life. In fact, some infants are talking before they can walk. How is this possible? Are infants biologically programmed to acquire language? What kinds of linguistic input must they receive in order to become language users? Is there any relation between a child's cooing, gesturing, or babbling and the later production of meaningful words? How do infants and toddlers come to attach meaning to words? Do all children pass through the same steps or stages as they acquire their native language? And what practical lessons must children learn to become truly effective communicators? These are but a few of the issues we will consider as we trace the development of children's linguistic skills and try to determine how youngsters become so proficient in using language at such an early age.

FOUR COMPONENTS OF LANGUAGE

Perhaps the most basic question that **psycholinguists** have tried to answer is the "what" question: what must children learn in order to master the intricacies of their native tongue? After many years and literally thousands of studies, researchers have concluded that four kinds of knowledge underlie the growth of linguistic proficiency: *phonology, semantics, syntax,* and *pragmatics.*

Phonology

Phonology refers to the basic units of sound, or **phonemes,** that are used in a language and the rules for combining these sounds. Each language uses only a subset of sounds that humans are capable of generating, and no two languages have precisely the same phonologies, which explains why foreign languages may sound rather strange to us. Clearly, children must learn how to discriminate, produce, and combine the speechlike sounds of their native tongue in order to make sense of the speech they hear and to be understood when they try to speak.

language
a small number of individually meaningless symbols (sounds, letters, gestures) that can be combined according to agreed-on rules to produce an infinite number of messages.

communication
the process by which one organism transmits information to and influences another.

psycholinguists
those who study the structure and development of children's language.

phonology
the sound system of a language and the rules for combining these sounds to produce meaningful units of speech.

phonemes
the basic units of sound that are used in a spoken language.

Animals communicate through a series of calls and gestures that convey a limited number of very specific messages.

Semantics

Semantics refers to the *meanings* expressed in words and sentences. The most basic meaningful units of language are called **morphemes;** they include words and grammatical markers (such as *-ed* for past tense, or *-s* to signify a plural noun) with meanings that are arbitrarily assigned. For example, the relation of the word *dog* to the furry, four-legged creature we know as a dog is completely arbitrary. We could just as easily have labeled the animal a *chien,* as the French have. Clearly, children must recognize that words convey meanings—that they symbolize particular objects, actions, and relations and can be combined to form larger and more complex meanings—before they can comprehend the speech of others or be understood when they speak.

Syntax

Language also involves **syntax,** or the rules that specify how words are to be combined to form meaningful phrases and sentences. Consider these three sentences:

1. Garfield Odie bit.
2. Garfield bit Odie.
3. Odie bit Garfield.

Even very young speakers of English recognize that the first sentence violates the rules of English sentence structure, although this word order would be perfectly acceptable in languages with a different syntax, such as French. The second and third sentences are grammatical English sentences that contain the same words but convey very different meanings. They also illustrate how word meanings (semantics) interact with sentence structure (word order) to give the entire sentence a meaning. Clearly, children must acquire a basic understanding of the syntactical features of their native tongue before they can become very proficient at speaking or understanding that language.

Pragmatics

Language learners must also master the **pragmatics** of language—knowledge of how language might be used to *communicate effectively.* Imagine a 6-year-old who is trying to explain a new game to her 2-year-old brother. Clearly, she cannot speak to the

semantics
the expressed meaning of words and sentences.

morphemes
the smallest meaningful units of language; these include words and grammatical markers such as prefixes, suffixes, and verb-tense modifiers (for example, *-ed, -ing*).

syntax
the structure of a language; the rules specifying how words and grammatical markers are to be combined to produce meaningful sentences.

pragmatics
principles that underlie the effective and appropriate use of language in social contexts.

A pragmatic error: Messages can have unintended consequences when we fail to adapt them to the social or situational context.
REPRINTED WITH SPECIAL PERMISSION OF KING FEATURES SYNDICATE.

toddler as if he were an adult or an age-mate; she has to adjust her speech to his linguistic capabilities if she hopes to be understood.

Pragmatics also involves **sociolinguistic knowledge**—culturally specified rules that dictate how language should be used in particular social contexts. A 3-year-old may not yet realize that the best way of obtaining a cookie from Grandma is to say "Grandma, may I please have a cookie?" rather than demanding "Gimme a cookie, Grandma!" In order to communicate most effectively, children must become "social editors" and take into account where they are, with whom they are speaking, and what the listener already knows, needs, and wants to hear.

Finally, the task of becoming an effective communicator requires not only a knowledge of the four aspects of language, but an ability to properly interpret and use *nonverbal signals* (facial expressions, intonational cues, gestures, and so on) that often help to clarify the meaning of verbal messages and are important means of communicating in their own right. This brings us to a second basic question: *How* do young, cognitively immature toddlers and preschool children acquire all this knowledge so quickly?

THEORIES OF LANGUAGE DEVELOPMENT

As psycholinguists began to chart the course of language development, they were amazed that children could learn such a complex symbol system at such a breathtaking pace. After all, many infants are using arbitrary and *abstract signifiers* (words) to refer to objects and activities before they can walk. And by age 5, children already seem to know and use most of the syntactical structures of their native tongue, even though they have yet to receive their first formal lesson in grammar. How do they do it?

In addressing the "how" question, we will once again encounter a nativist/empiricist (nature/nurture) controversy. Learning theorists represent the empiricist point of view. From their perspective, language is obviously *learned:* after all, Japanese children acquire Japanese, French children acquire French, and profoundly deaf children of hearing parents may acquire few formal communication skills unless they receive instruction in sign language. However, other theorists point out that children the world over seem to display similar linguistic achievements at about the same age: They all babble by 4 to 6 months of age, utter their first meaningful word by age 12 to 13 months, begin to combine words by the end of the second year, and know the meanings of many thousands of words and are constructing a staggering array of grammatical sentences by the tender age of 4 or 5. These **linguistic universals** suggested to *nativists* that language acquisition is a *biologically programmed* activity that may even involve highly specialized linguistic processing capabilities that operate most efficiently early in childhood.

Of course, there is an intermediate point of view favored by an increasing number

sociolinguistic knowledge
culturally specific rules specifying how language should be structured and used in particular social contexts.

linguistic universal
an aspect of language development that all children share.

of *interactionists* who believe that language acquisition reflects a complex interplay among a child's biological predispositions, her cognitive development, and the characteristics of her unique linguistic environment.

The Learning (or Empiricist) Perspective

Ask most adults how children learn language and they are likely to say that children imitate what they hear, are reinforced when they use proper grammar, and are corrected when they say things wrong. Indeed, learning theorists have emphasized these same processes—imitation and reinforcement—in their own theories of language learning.

In 1957, B. F. Skinner published a book entitled *Verbal Behavior* in which he argued that children learn to speak appropriately because they are reinforced for grammatical speech. He believed that adults begin to shape a child's speech by selectively reinforcing those aspects of babbling that most resemble words, thereby increasing the probability that these sounds will be repeated. Once they have "shaped" sounds into words, adults then withhold further reinforcement (attention or approval) until the child begins combining words, first into primitive sentences and then into longer grammatical utterances. Other social-learning theorists (for example, Bandura, 1971; Whitehurst & Vasta, 1975) add that children acquire much of their linguistic knowledge by carefully listening to and *imitating* the language of older companions. So according to the learning perspective, caregivers "teach" language by modeling and reinforcing grammatical speech.

Evaluation of the Learning Perspective

Imitation and reinforcement clearly play some part in early language development. Certainly, it is no accident that children end up speaking the same language their parents speak, down to the regional accent. In addition, young children are quicker to acquire and use the proper names for novel toys when reinforced for doing so by receiving the toys to play with (Whitehurst & Valdez-Menchaca, 1988). Finally, children whose parents frequently encourage them to converse by asking questions and making requests are more advanced in their early language development (and later reading proficiencies) than age-mates whose parents are less conversational (Hart & Risley, 1995; Valdez-Menchaca & Whitehurst, 1992; Walker et al., 1994).

Despite these observations, learning theorists have had little success accounting for the development of syntax. If parents really "shaped" grammar, as Skinner claimed, then they ought to reliably praise or otherwise reinforce the child's grammatical utterances. Yet, careful analyses of conversations between mothers and young children reveal that a mother's approval or disapproval depends far more on the *truth value* (semantics) of what a child says, *not* on the statement's grammatical correctness (Baron, 1992; Brown, Cazden, & Bellugi, 1969). So if a child gazing at a cow says "Him cow" (truthful but grammatically incorrect), his mother is likely to approve ("That's right!"); yet, if the child had said "There's a dog!" (grammatically correct, but untruthful), mom would probably correct him ("No, silly—that's a *cow!*"). Clearly, these findings cast doubt on the notion that parents shape syntax by directly reinforcing grammatical speech.

Nor is there much evidence that children acquire grammatical rules by imitating adult speech. Many of a child's earliest sentences are highly creative statements such as "Allgone cookie" or "It broked" that do not appear in adult speech and could not have been learned by imitation. And when young children do try to imitate an adult utterance such as "Look, the kitty is climbing the tree," they condense it to conform to their existing level of grammatical competence, saying something like "Kitty climb tree" (Baron, 1992; Bloom et al., 1974).

How, then, might young children acquire grammatical knowledge if they do not

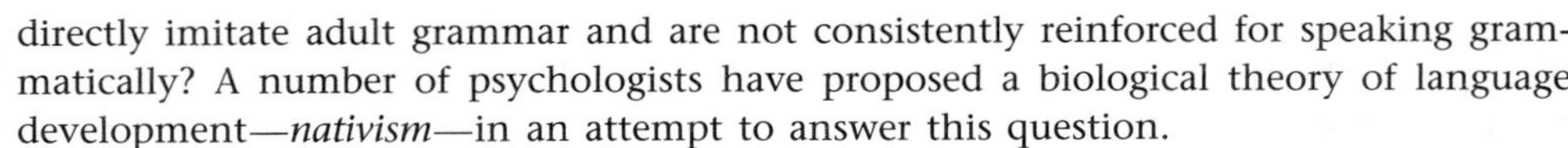

directly imitate adult grammar and are not consistently reinforced for speaking grammatically? A number of psychologists have proposed a biological theory of language development—*nativism*—in an attempt to answer this question.

The Nativist Perspective

Noam Chomsky's nativist theory dominated thinking about language development in the 1960s and 1970s.

According to the nativists, human beings are biologically programmed to acquire language. Linguist Noam Chomsky (1959; 1968) has argued that the structure of even the simplest of languages is incredibly elaborate—far too complex, he believed, to be either taught by parents (as Skinner proposed) or discovered via simple trial-and-error processes by cognitively immature toddlers and preschool children. Instead, Chomsky proposed that we humans (and only humans) come equipped with a **language acquisition device (LAD)**—an inborn linguistic processor that is activated by verbal input. According to Chomsky, the LAD contains a *universal grammar,* or knowledge of rules that are common to all languages. So regardless of the language (or languages) a child has been listening to, the LAD should permit any child who has acquired a sufficient vocabulary to combine words into novel, rule-bound utterances and to understand much of what he hears.

Other nativists make similar claims. Dan Slobin (1985), for example, does not assume that children have any innate knowledge of language (as Chomsky did), but he thinks that they have an inborn **language-making capacity (LMC)**—a set of cognitive and perceptual abilities that are highly specialized for language learning. Presumably, these innate mechanisms (a LAD or LMC) enable young children to process linguistic input and to infer the phonological regularities, semantic relations, and rules of syntax that characterize whatever language they are listening to. These inferences about the meaning and structure of linguistic information represent a "theory" of language that children construct for themselves and use to guide their own attempts to communicate (see Figure 10.1). Of course, young children are likely to make some erroneous inferences because their linguistic database is very limited; but as they continue to process more and more input, their underlying theories of language become increasingly elaborate until they eventually approximate those used by adults. For the nativists, then, language acquisition is quite natural and almost automatic, as long as children have linguistic data to process.

Support for the Nativist Perspective

Are children biologically programmed to acquire language? Several observations seem to suggest that they are. For example, we've noted that children the world over reach certain linguistic milestones at about the same age, despite cultural differences in the structure of their languages. Nativists interpret these *linguistic universals* as clear evidence that language must be guided by some species-specific biological blueprint. Even retarded children who perform very poorly on a broad range of cognitive tasks nevertheless acquire a near-normal knowledge of syntax and become quite adequate conversationalists (Flavell et al., 1993; Pinker, 1991).

Also consistent with the nativist viewpoint is the observation that language is species-specific. Although animals can communicate with each other, no species has ever devised anything in the wild that closely resembles an abstract, rule-bound linguistic system. Is this because they lack a LAD (or LMC)? Are animals truly incapable of acquiring a language? Box 10.1 on page 358 explores this intriguing issue.

Brain Specialization and Language. As we learned in Chapter 5, the brain is a lateralized organ with major language centers in the left cerebral hemisphere. Damage to one of these language areas typically results in *aphasia*—a loss of one or more language functions; the symptoms that an aphasic displays depend on the site and the extent of the injury. Injuries to **Broca's area,** near the frontal lobe of the left hemisphere, typ-

language acquisition device (LAD)
Chomsky's term for the innate knowledge of grammar that humans were said to possess, which might enable young children to infer the rules governing others' speech and to use these rules to produce language.

language-making capacity (LMC)
a hypothesized set of specialized linguistic processing skills that enable children to analyze speech and to detect phonological, semantic, and syntactical relationships.

Broca's area
structure located in the frontal lobe of the left hemisphere of the cerebral cortex that controls language production.

Wernicke's area
structure located in the temporal lobe of the left hemisphere of the cerebral cortex that is responsible for interpreting speech.

sensitive-period hypothesis (of language acquisition)
the notion that human beings are most proficient at language learning before they reach puberty.

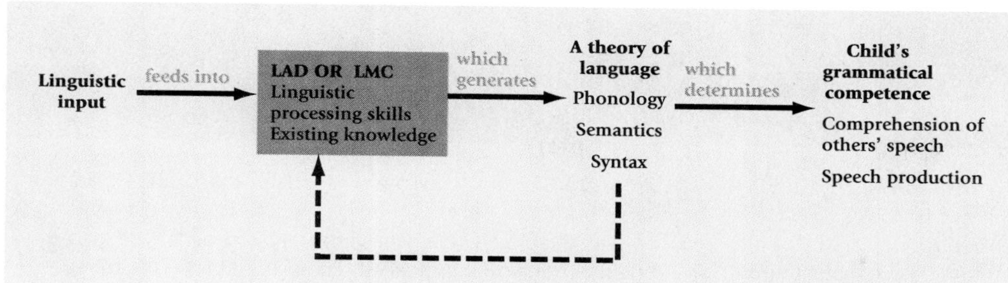

Figure 10.1 *A model of language acquisition proposed by nativists.*

ically affect speech production rather than comprehension (Slobin, 1979). By contrast, patients who suffer an injury to **Wernicke's area,** on the temporal lobe of the left hemisphere, may speak fairly well but have difficulty understanding speech.

Apparently, the left hemisphere is sensitive to some aspects of language from birth. In the first day of life, speech sounds already elicit more electrical activity from the left side of an infant's brain, while music and other nonspeech sounds produce greater activity from the right cerebral hemisphere (Molfese, 1977). Furthermore, we learned in Chapter 6 that infants are quite capable of discriminating important phonetic contrasts in the first few days and weeks of life (Miller & Eimas, 1996). These findings seem to imply that the neonate is "prewired" for speech perception and is prepared to analyze speechlike sounds.

The Sensitive-Period Hypothesis. Many years ago, nativist Erik Lenneberg (1967) proposed that languages should be most easily acquired between birth and puberty, the period when the lateralized human brain is becoming increasingly specialized for linguistic functions. This **sensitive-period hypothesis** for language development was prompted by observations that child aphasics often recover their lost language functions without special therapy, whereas adult aphasics usually require extensive therapeutic interventions to recover even a portion of their lost language skills. Lenneberg's explanation for this intriguing age difference was straightforward. Presumably, the right hemisphere of a child's relatively unspecialized brain can assume any linguistic functions lost when the left hemisphere is damaged. By contrast, the brain of a person who is past puberty is already fully specialized for language and other neurological duties. So aphasia may persist in adolescents and adults because the right hemisphere is no longer available to assume linguistic skills lost from a traumatic injury to the left side of the brain.

If language really is most easily acquired before puberty, then children who were largely deprived of a normal linguistic environment should find it difficult to acquire language later in life. Two excellent case studies reflect nicely on this idea. One is the case of Genie, a child who was locked away in a back room as an infant and was not discovered by the authorities until she was nearly 14 years old. While confined, Genie heard very little language; no one was permitted to talk to her, and she was beaten by an abusive father if she made any noise (Curtiss, 1977). Then there is Chelsea, a deaf woman who—because of her deafness and her family's isolation—was 32 years old before she was ever exposed to a formal language system. Extensive efforts were undertaken to teach these women language, and each made remarkable progress, learning the meaning of many words and even producing lengthy sentences that were rich in their semantic content. Yet neither woman has mastered the rules of syntax that virtually all children acquire without formal instruction (Curtiss, 1977; 1988), thus suggesting that learning a first language is easier early in life.

What about learning a second language? Is acquiring a foreign language a tougher task for a postpubertal adolescent whose sensitive period for language learning is over? Research by Jacqueline Johnson and Elissa Newport suggests that this may be the case. In one study (Johnson & Newport, 1989), native speakers of Korean or Chinese who had emigrated to the United States at different ages were tested as adults for mastery of English grammar. As we see in Figure 10.2, immigrants who began to learn English between 3 and 7 years of age were as proficient in English as native speakers are. By

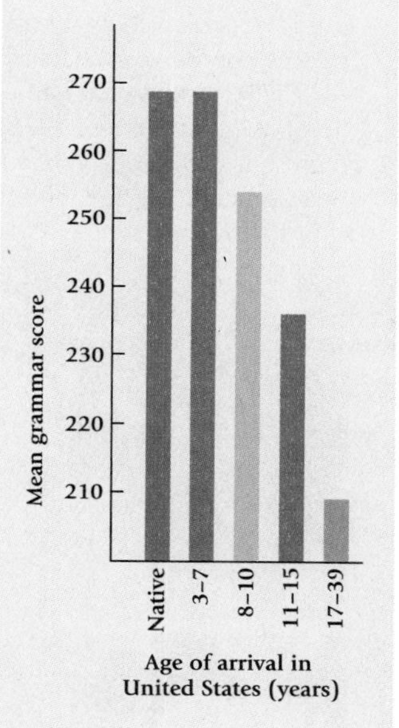

Figure 10.2 *As shown here, there is a clear relationship between the age at which immigrants arrived in the United States and their eventual adult performance in English grammar. Those who arrived early in childhood end up performing like native speakers of English, whereas those who arrived as teenagers or adults perform much more poorly.* ADAPTED FROM JOHNSON & NEWPORT, *1989.*

FOCUS ON RESEARCH

10.1

Language Learning in Chimpanzees

Perhaps it is only natural for humans to wonder whether chimpanzees and other primates who look so much like us could ever express themselves through some form of language. Earlier in this century, attempts were made to raise chimpanzees like children and to teach them to speak English (see Savage-Rumbaugh et al., 1993 for a review). Unfortunately, these projects were destined to fail, for the vocal apparatus of a chimpanzee is structurally incapable of producing the many phonemes of human speech.

In recent years, however, a number of researchers have shown that chimpanzees (and at least one gorilla) can learn to use linguistic signs and symbols to communicate a variety of messages. For example, several chimps have each acquired more than 100 signs from American Sign Language for the deaf (ASL) and can combine these signs to describe objects and events (for example, referring to a duck as a "water bird"), to make requests (such as "Give milk"), and to both ask and answer questions (for example, correctly answering "bed" in response to the question "What is that?" and answering "red" in response to the follow-up question "What color is it?") (Gardner & Gardner, 1974; Slobin, 1979). Other chimps introduced to linguistic hieroglyphics printed on computer keys have demonstrated similar communicative skills and have even used the code to type messages that permit trained chimpanzee companions to comply with their simple requests (such as "Give [chimp's own name] spoon") (Savage-Rumbaugh, Rumbaugh, & Boysen, 1978). Clearly, these accomplishments represent a form of *communication* that relies on abstract symbols and is far more elaborate than the calls and gestures that chimpanzees use in the wild (see Goodall, 1986). But is it language?

Remarkable as these achievements may be, nativists conclude that none of the so-called "linguistic" apes has acquired a language. One of the more vocal skeptics, Herbert Terrace (1979), actually began as an advocate of chimp language. But after attempting to teach sign language to a chimp pupil named Nim Chimpsky (an obvious play on the name of nativist Noam Chomsky), Terrace discovered that the internal structure of Nim's sign sentences was essentially arbitrary. To illustrate, Nim often produced blatantly ungrammatical constructions such as "Give banana, banana, banana" or "Play me Nim play" that were (1) highly similar to the "sentences" produced by all other "linguistic" apes and (2) very different from the speech of a 2-year-old child (Terrace at al., 1980). Lieberman (1984) reached a similar conclusion, noting that, after years of hard work, an ape may grasp many semantic relations but will display little if any knowledge of syntax—a critical feature of a true language.

These conclusions may have to be revised, however, in light of Sue Savage-Rumbaugh's recent findings when testing language *comprehension* in highly sociable pygmy chimps (Savage-Rumbaugh et al., 1993). In one study, Savage-Rumbaugh and her associates compared the linguistic abilities of a 2-year-old child, Alia, with those of Kanzi, an 8-year-old pygmy chimp who had been spoken to like a child since infancy. Two-year-olds respond appropriately to commands a majority of time. Could Kanzi comprehend the *verbal* instructions he received? Yes, indeed! In fact, he performed slightly better than 2-year-old Alia did, and his correct responses to hundreds of *novel* commands (for example, "Get the tomato that's in the microwave," "Put the egg in the juice") implies that he correctly interpreted both the semantics *and* the syntax of these statements. Nevertheless, it took years in a language-rich environment for Kanzi to attain an understanding of grammar comparable to that of a typical 2- to 3-year-old. Apparently, apes lack something that humans have that allows even severely retarded children who receive no formal training to easily surpass the linguistic accomplishments of the brightest chimpanzees.

Is that "something" we humans have a specialized linguistic processor—a LAD or LMC? Nativists say yes and offer several additional observations (described in the text) that they believe to be consistent with their biological perspective on language development.

This figure illustrates the array in front of Kanzi (top left) as he hears the sentence "Put the egg in the juice" (bottom left). It is possible for Kanzi either to put the juice in the egg, to put the egg in the juice, or to do something else entirely. Kanzi responds to this sentence by picking up the bowl containing the egg (top right) and tilting it until the egg falls into the juice (bottom right).

10.2

DEVELOPMENTAL ISSUES

On the "Invention" of Language by Children

Suppose that ten children were raised in isolation by an adult caregiver who attended to their basic needs but never talked or even gestured to them in any way. Would these youngsters devise some method of communicating among themselves? No one can say for sure, for children such as these have never been studied. However, the results of two recent programs of research suggest that our hypothetical children not only would learn to communicate but might even invent their own language.

Home Sign among the Deaf

Susan Goldin-Meadow and Carolyn Mylander (1984) have observed the progress of ten deaf children aged 1½ to 3 years, all of whom had hearing parents who knew little if anything about sign language. Clearly, these children were exposed to very atypical linguistic environments in that they couldn't hear oral speech and their parents were unable to instruct them in the use of signs. Would these youngsters invent a system of communicating in the absence of a language model? Could they create their own unique sign language?

Maybe so, for each of these children not only came to use signs and gestures to represent *actions* (for example, a fist at the mouth accompanied by chewing to represent eating), *objects* (for example, digging motions to refer to a snow shovel), and *attributes* (for example, a thumb and forefinger joined to signify "roundness"), but they soon began to combine their individualized signs into "sentences" that their companions could easily understand. However, critics have argued that these competencies may not reflect the child's inventiveness at all, for they may have resulted from subtle gestural exchanges with parents (Bohannon & Warren-Leubecker, 1989). So let's consider a second set of observations.

Transforming Pidgins to True Languages

When adults from different cultures migrate to the same area, they often begin to communicate in *pidgin*—a hybrid of their various languages that enables them to convey basic meanings and thus understand each other. In the 1870s, for example, large numbers of immigrants from China, Korea, Japan, the Philippines, Portugal, and Puerto Rico migrated to Hawaii to work in the sugar fields. What evolved from this influx was Hawaiian Pidgin English, a communication system with a small vocabulary and a few basic rules for combining words that enabled residents from different linguistic communities to communicate well enough to get by. Yet in the course of a generation, this pidgin was transformed into a *creole*—that is, a true language that evolves from a pidgin. Indeed, Hawaiian Creole English was a rich language with a vocabulary that sprang from the pidgin and its foreign language predecessors and had formal syntactical rules. How did this transformation from marginal pidgin to true language occur so rapidly?

Linguist Derek Bickerton (1983; 1984) claims that children of pidgin-speaking parents do not continue to speak pidgin. Instead, they spontaneously invent syntactical rules that creolize the pidgin to make it a true language that future generations in these multilingual communities will use. How did he decide that children were responsible? One clue was that whenever pidgins arise, they are quickly transformed into creoles, usually within a single generation. But the more important clue was that creole syntax closely resembles the (often inappropriate) sentences that young children construct when acquiring virtually any language. For example, questions of the form "Where he is going?" and double negatives such as "I haven't got none" are perfectly acceptable in creole languages. Finally, the structure of different creoles is similar the world over—so similar that it cannot be attributed to chance. Bickerton believes that only a nativist model can account for these observations. In his own words: "The most cogent explanation of this similarity . . . is that it derives from . . . a species-specific program for language, genetically coded and expressed . . . in the structures . . . and operation of the human brain" (1984, p. 173).

So it seems that children who lack a formal linguistic model—be they deaf or subjected to marginally linguistic pidgins—will create languagelike codes to communicate with their companions. Apparently, they have some linguistic predispositions that serve them well.

contrast, immigrants who arrived after puberty (particularly after age 15) performed rather poorly. Similarly, deaf adults show much better mastery of sign language if they were exposed to it as young children than if their training began later in life (Newport, 1991).

Finally, nativists interpret the research presented in Box 10.2 as a rather dramatic illustration that language acquisition is a fundamental human characteristic—even if children must "invent" the language they acquire.

Problems with the Nativist Approach

Though most everyone today agrees that language learning is influenced by biological factors, many developmentalists have serious reservations about the nativist approach.

Some have challenged the findings that nativists cite as support for their theory. We now know, for example, that the human brain retains some of its plasticity well into adulthood (Nelson & Bloom, 1997), and later research has challenged Lenneberg's sensitive-period notion that young children are more likely than adolescents or adults to recover from traumatic aphasia (Bishop, 1988; Piacentini & Hynd, 1988). Furthermore, the fact that human infants can make important phonemic distinctions in the first days and weeks of life no longer seems to be such compelling support for the existence of a uniquely human LAD. Why? Simply because the young of other species (for example, rhesus monkeys and chinchillas) show similar powers of auditory discrimination (Passingham, 1982). Even the seemingly amazing linguistic inventions that young children display (see Box 10.2) have been challenged. For example, no one has yet carefully observed the language development of children whose parents speak pidgins; thus, it is not completely clear that children transform pidgins to creole languages by themselves, without adult assistance (Bohannon et al., 1990; Tomasello, 1995).

Others have argued that nativists don't really *explain* language development by attributing it to a built-in language acquisition device. An explanation would require knowing *how* such an inborn processor sifts through linguistic input and infers the rules of language; yet nativists are not at all clear about how a LAD (or LMC) might operate (Moerk, 1989). In some ways, attributing language development to the mysterious workings of a LAD or LMC is like saying that physical growth is biologically programmed—*and then stopping there, failing to identify the underlying variables (nutrition, hormones, and so forth) that explain why growth follows the course that it takes.* Clearly, the nativist approach is woefully incomplete; it is really more a description of language learning than a true explanation.

Finally, there are those who claim that nativists, who focus almost exclusively on biological mechanisms and on the deficiencies of learning theories, have simply overlooked the many ways in which a child's language environment promotes linguistic competencies. Let's now turn to a third theoretical viewpoint which claims that language development reflects an interaction of nature and nurture.

The Interactionist Perspective

Proponents of the **interactionist theory** believe that *both* learning theorists and nativists are partially correct: Language development results from a complex interplay among biological maturation, cognitive development, and an ever-changing linguistic environment that is heavily influenced by the child's desire to communicate with her companions (Bohannon & Bonvillian, 1997; Tomasello, 1995).

Biological and Cognitive Contributors

Clearly, the remarkable similarities that young children display when learning very different languages imply that biology contributes to language acquisition. But must we attribute language development to the mysterious workings of a LAD or LMC to explain these linguistic universals?

Apparently not. According to the interactionist viewpoint, young children the world over talk alike and display other linguistic universals because they are all members of the same species *who share many common experiences.* What is inborn is not any specialized linguistic knowledge or processing skills but, rather, a sophisticated brain that *matures* very slowly and predisposes children to develop similar ideas at about the same age—ideas that they are then motivated to express in their own speech (Bates, 1993; Tomasello, 1995). Indeed, there is ample support for links between general cognitive development and language development. For example, words are symbols, and infants speak their first meaningful words at about 12 months of age, shortly after they first display some capacity for symbolism in their *deferred imitation* of adult models (Meltzoff, 1988c). Furthermore, we will see that infants' first words center heavily on

interactionist theory
the notion that biological factors and environmental influences interact to determine the course of language development.

objects they have manipulated or on actions they have performed—in short, on aspects of experience they can understand through their sensorimotor schemes (Pan & Gleason, 1997). Finally, words like *gone* and *oh oh* emerge during the second year, about the same time infants are mastering *object permanence* and are beginning to appraise the success or failure of their problem-solving activities (Gopnik & Meltzoff, 1987). So infants and toddlers often seem to talk about whatever cognitive understandings they are acquiring at the moment.

Like the nativists, then, interactionists believe that children are biologically prepared to acquire a language. However, the preparation consists *not* of a LAD or LMC but, rather, of a powerful human brain that slowly matures, allowing children to gain more and more knowledge, which gives them more to talk about. However, this does not mean that cognitive development explains language development, for even after acquiring new understandings, children must learn how to express this knowledge in their own speech. How do they make these discoveries? Here is where the linguistic environment comes into play.

Environmental Supports for Language Development

Interactionists stress that language is primarily a means of *communicating* that develops in the context of social interactions as children and their companions strive to get their messages across one way or another (Bohannon & Bonvillian, 1997; Tomasello, 1995). Over the years, psychologists have discovered that parents and older children have distinctive ways of talking to and interacting with infants and toddlers—that is, strategies for communicating with them that seem to foster language learning. Let's see what they have learned.

Lessons from Joint Activities. Long before infants use words, their caregivers show them how to take turns in conversations, even if the only thing these young infants can contribute when their turn comes is to laugh or babble (Bruner, 1983). As adults converse with young children, they create a supportive learning environment (zone of proximal development) that helps the children grasp the regularities of language (Bruner, 1983; Harris, 1992). For example, parents may go through their children's favorite picture books at bedtime, asking "What's this?" or "What does the kitty say?" This gives their children repeated opportunities to learn that conversing involves taking turns, that things have names, and that there are proper ways to pose questions and give answers.

Lessons from Child-Directed Speech. Cross-cultural research points to a nearly universal tendency of parents and older siblings to address infants and toddlers with very short, simple sentences that psycholinguists call *child-directed speech,* or **motherese** (Gelman & Shatz, 1977; Pine, 1994). Typically, these utterances are spoken slowly in a high-pitched voice, are often repeated, and emphasize key words (usually words for objects and activities). For example, a mother trying to get her young son to throw a ball might say "*Throw* the *ball,* Billy! Not the rattle. See the *ball?* Yeah, that's the *ball; throw* it!" From the earliest days of life, infants pay more attention to the high-pitched sounds and varied intonational patterns of motherese than to the "flatter" speech that adults use when communicating with each other (Cooper & Aslin, 1990; Pegg, Werker, & McLeod, 1992), and they process more information about objects introduced by infant-directed speech as well (Kaplan et al., 1996). Indeed, infants even seem to grasp certain messages carried in their parents' tone of voice (for example, "Pay attention!" or "That's good!") long before they can understand a word about what is being said (Fernald, 1989; 1993).

Interestingly, parents gradually increase both the length and the complexity of their simplified child-directed speech as their children's language becomes more elaborate (Shatz, 1983). And at any given point in time, a parent's sentences are slightly longer and slightly more complex than the child's (Bohannon & Bonvillian, 1997; Sokolov, 1993). Here then, is a situation that might seem ideal for language learning. The child is constantly exposed to new semantic relations and grammatical rules that appear in

motherese
the short, simple, high-pitched (and often repetitive) sentences that adults use when talking with young children (also called *child-directed speech*).

Reprinted with special permission of King Features Syndicate.

simple utterances that he will probably understand, particularly if older companions frequently repeat or paraphrase the ideas they are trying to communicate (Harris, 1992). Clearly, this is a form of modeling by the parent. However, children do not acquire new grammatical principles by mimicking them directly, nor do adults consciously attempt to teach these principles by illustration. Parents speak in motherese for one main reason—to *communicate effectively* with their children (Fernald & Morikawa, 1993; Penner, 1987).

Lessons from Negative Evidence. Although parents do not reliably attempt to reinforce correct grammar, they do provide the child with *negative evidence;* that is, they respond to ungrammatical speech in ways that subtly communicate that an error has been made and provide information that might be used to correct these errors (Bohannon & Bonvillian, 1997; Saxton, 1997). For example, if a child, says "Doggie go," an adult may respond with an **expansion**—a grammatically correct and enriched version of the child's ungrammatical statement ("Yes, the doggie is going away"). A slightly different form of expansion occurs when adults **recast** the child's sentences into new grammatical forms. For example, a child who says "Doggie eat" might have his sentence recast as "What is the doggie eating?" or "Yes, the doggie is hungry." These recasts are moderately novel utterances that probably command the child's attention and thereby increase the likelihood that he will notice the new grammatical forms that appear in the adult's speech. Finally, parents are likely to respond to grammatically *appropriate* sentences by simply maintaining and extending the conversation *(topic extension).* By carrying on without revising the child's utterance, adults provide a strong clue that the utterance was grammatical (Bohannon & Stanowicz, 1988; Penner, 1987).

Do children profit from negative evidence? Apparently so, for adults who frequently expand, recast, or otherwise extend their children's speech have youngsters who are quicker to acquire grammatical rules and who score relatively high on tests of expressive language ability, compared with children whose parents rely less on these conversational techniques (Bohannan et al., 1996; Valdez-Menchaca & Whitehurst, 1992).

The Importance of Conversation. Would young children learn language just as well by merely listening to others converse? Apparently not. Nativists, who claimed that all children need to acquire language is regular exposure to speech samples, have clearly underestimated the role of *social* interactions in language learning. Mere exposure to speech is simply not enough; children must be actively involved in using language (Locke, 1997)! Catherine Snow and her associates, for example, found that a group of Dutch-speaking children, despite the fact that they watched a great deal of German television, did not acquire any German words or grammar (Snow et al., 1976). Furthermore, hearing children of profoundly deaf parents often show an approximately normal pattern of language development as long as they spend 5 to 10 hours a week in the company of a hearing/speaking adult who *converses* with them (Schiff-Myers, 1988). True, there are cultures (for example, the Katuli of New Guinea, the natives of American Samoa, and the Trackton people of the Piedmont Carolinas) in which chil-

expansions
responding to a child's ungrammatical utterance with a grammatically improved form of that statement.

recasts
responding to a child's ungrammatical utterance with a nonrepetitive statement that is grammatically correct.

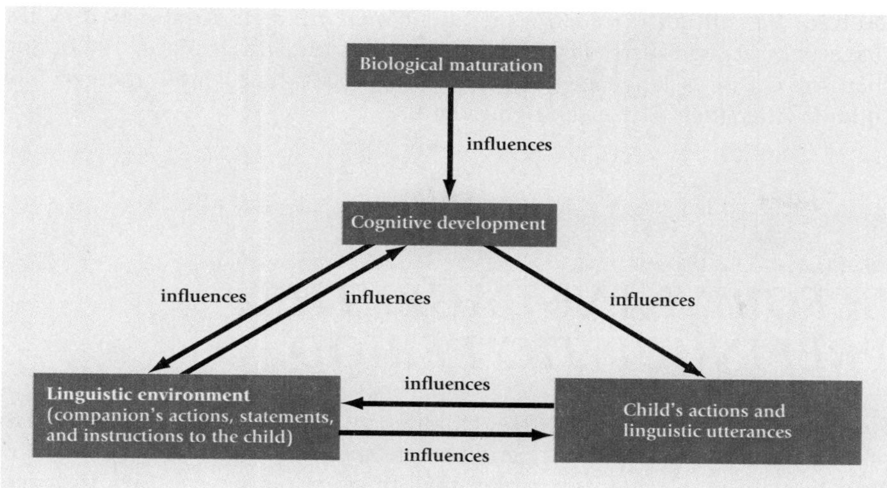

Figure 10.3 *An overview of the interactionist perspective on language development.*

dren acquire language without noticeable delays, even though adults rarely restructure their primitive sentences or address them in motherese (Gordon, 1990; Ochs, 1982; Schieffelin, 1986). Yet, even these youngsters regularly participate in *social* interactions in which language is used, and that is what seems to be most essential in mastering a language (Lieven, 1994).

Summing Up. From an interactionist perspective, then, language development is the product of a complex transaction between nature and nurture. Children are born with a powerful human brain that *matures* slowly and predisposes them to acquire new understandings that they are *motivated to share with others* (Bates, 1993; Tomasello, 1995). Yet interactionists emphasize—as Vygotsky (1978) did in his model of collaborative learning—how conversations with older companions foster cognitive and language development. As their nervous systems continue to mature and children grow intellectually, they express their new understandings in increasingly complex utterances that prompt close companions to increase the complexity of their replies (Bohannon & Bonvillian, 1977; Sokolov, 1993). As illustrated in Figure 10.3, the pattern of influence is clearly reciprocal: The child's early attempts to communicate influence the speech of older companions, which, in turn, provides information that the child can process to infer linguistic principles and speak more clearly, and influence the speech of companions once again. Stated another way, the interactionists propose that the language of young children is heavily influenced by a rich, responsive, and ever more complex linguistic environment that they have had a hand in creating (Bloom et al., 1996).

One final note: Although the interactionist perspective is the approach that many developmentalists favor, the question of how children acquire language is by no means

Concept Check 10.1
Theories of Language Development

Check your understanding of theories of language development by matching each descriptive statement below with one of the following concepts or hypotheses: (a) appropriate grammar, (b) recasts, (c) language acquisition device, (d) sensitive-period hypothesis, (e) creolizing of pidgins by children, (f) universals in cognitive development, (g) conversations with language users, (h) appropriate semantics. Answers appear in the Appendix at the back of the book.

_____ 1. explains why adolescents might have a harder time acquiring foreign languages than children do

_____ 2. means by which companions introduce new linguistic forms to children

_____ 3. offered as support for the *nativist* perspective on language acquisition

_____ 4. aspect of early speech that parents are most likely to reinforce

_____ 5. essential input for mastering a language

_____ 6. mechanism that *interactionists* cite to explain linguistic universals

_____ 7. proposed inborn linguistic processor with a "universal" grammar common to all languages

_____ 8. aspect of early speech that *learning theorists* claim that parents reinforce resolved. We still know much more about *what* children acquire as they learn a language than about exactly *how* they acquire this knowledge (Rice, 1989). So let's now chart the course of language development, a process that is well underway long before children utter their first meaningful word.

BEFORE LANGUAGE: THE PRELINGUISTIC PERIOD

For the first 10 to 13 months of life, children are said to be in the **prelinguistic phase** of language development—the period before speaking their first meaningful words. But even though young infants are preverbal, they are quite responsive to language from the day they are born.

Early Reactions to Speech

In Chapter 6, we learned that newborns may be programmed to "tune in" to human speech. When spoken to, neonates often open their eyes, gaze at the speaker, and sometimes even vocalize themselves (Rheingold & Adams, 1980; Rosenthal, 1982). By 3 days of age, an infant already recognizes his or her mother's voice and clearly prefers it to the voice of a female stranger (DeCasper & Fifer, 1980), and newborns suck faster to hear recorded speech than to hear instrumental music or other rhythmic sounds (Butterfield & Siperstein, 1972). So babies can discriminate speech from other sound patterns, and they pay particularly close attention to speech from the very beginning.

Do different samples of speech all sound alike to the very young infant? Apparently not. Within the first few days after birth, babies begin to discriminate different stress patterns, or rhythms, in two-syllable and three-syllable words (Sansavini, Bertoncini, & Giovanelli, 1997), and they already prefer the sound pattern of the language their mother speaks to that of a foreign tongue (Moon, Cooper, & Fifer, 1993). As we noted in Chapter 6, 1-month-old infants are as capable as adults of discriminating consonant sounds such as *ba* and *da* and *ta,* and by 2 months of age even recognize that a particular vowel (an *a,* for example) is still the same sound when spoken at different pitches or intensities by different speakers (Jusczyk, 1995; Marean, Werner, & Kuhl, 1992). In fact, very young infants are actually able to discriminate a wider variety of phonemes than adults can, for as we learned in Chapter 6, we lose the ability to make phonemic distinctions that are not important in our native language (Werker & Desjardins, 1995).

It seems, then, that the abilities to discriminate speech from nonspeech and to differentiate a variety of speechlike sounds are either (1) innate or (2) acquired in the first few days and weeks of life. In either case, young infants are remarkably well prepared for the task of decoding the speech they hear.

The Importance of Intonational Cues

Earlier, we noted that adults typically speak to infants in a highly intonated motherese that attracts their attention. Furthermore, adults reliably vary their tone of voice when trying to communicate different "messages" to their preverbal infants (Fernald, 1989; Katz, Cohn, & Moore, 1996). Rising intonations (for example, "Look at mom^{my}") are used to recapture the attention of a baby who looks away, whereas falling intonations such as "HEY $_{there}$!" are often used to comfort or to *elicit positive affect* (smiles, bright eyes) from a somber baby. These intonational prompts are often successful at affect-

prelinguistic phase
the period before children utter their first meaningful words.

ing a baby's mood or behavior (Fernald, 1989; 1993), and 2- to 6-month-old infants frequently produce a vocalization in return that matches the intonation of what they have just heard (Masataka, 1992). So it is tempting to conclude that preverbal infants not only discriminate different intonational patterns but soon recognize that certain tones of voice have a particular meaning. In fact, some researchers believe that a 2- to 6-month-old's successful interpretation of intonational cues may provide some of the earliest evidence that speech is a *meaningful* enterprise—and is something she might try to perfect (Fernald, 1989; 1993).

During the second half of the first year, infants become increasingly attuned to the "rhythm" of a language, which helps them to segment what they hear, first into phrases, and eventually into words. Phrase boundaries in infant-directed speech are characterized by long pauses that are preceded by very long vowel sounds—acoustic cues that provide ample information about where one phrase ends and another begins (Fisher & Tokura, 1996). By 7 months of age, infants can detect phrase units and clearly prefer to listen to speech that contains natural breaks and pauses to that in which pauses are inserted at unnatural places, such as the middle of a phrase (Hirsh-Pasek et al., 1987). By age 9 months, infants are becoming sensitive to smaller speech units. They now prefer to listen to speech samples that match the syllabic stress patterns and phonemic combinations of the language their caregivers speak (Jusczyk, Cutler, & Redanz, 1993), and they can even integrate this information into two-syllable wordlike segments (Morgan & Saffran, 1995). At the same time, they are rapidly losing the ability to discriminate phonemes that are *not* a part of their native language (Werker & Desjardins, 1995). So by the last quarter of the first year, infants' increasing familiarity with the phonological aspects of their native tongue provides important clues about which patterns in an ongoing stream of speech represent individual words.

Producing Sounds: The Infant's Prelinguistic Vocalizations

The first vocal milestone other than crying occurs by 2 months of age as babies make vowellike noises called **cooing.** These "oooohs" and "aaaaahs" are likely to be heard after a feeding when the baby is awake, alert, dry, and otherwise contented. By 4 to 6 months of age, infants have added consonant sounds to their vocal repertoires and are now **babbling**—that is, repeating vowel/consonant combinations such as "mamama" or "papapa" that may sound like words but convey no meaning. Interestingly, deaf infants whose parents are deaf and communicate in sign language will, themselves, babble manually, experimenting with gestures in much the same way that hearing infants experiment with sounds (Petitto & Marentette, 1991).

For the first 6 months, infants the world over (even deaf ones) sound pretty much alike, which suggests that early babbling is heavily influenced by maturation of the brain and the muscles controlling verbal articulation (Hoff-Ginsberg, 1997). Yet, the effects of experience soon come into play. Deaf infants, who hear no speech, now begin to fall far behind hearing infants in their ability to produce well-formed, languagelike phonemes (Eilers & Oller, 1994; Oller & Eilers, 1988). By contrast, hearing infants attend very carefully to others' speech. By the end of the first year, they match the intonation of their babbles to the tonal qualities of the language they hear, and they actually begin to sound as if they are speaking that language (Blake & Boysson-Bardies, 1992). Apparently, babies are "learning the tune before the words" (Bates, O'Connell, & Shore, 1987, p. 154).

As babbling progresses, 10- to 12-month-olds often reserve certain sounds for particular situations. For example, one infant began to use the *m* sound (*"mmmm"*) when making requests and various vowel sounds ("aaaach") when manipulating objects (Blake & Boysson-Bardies, 1992). According to Charles Ferguson (1977), infants who produce these **vocables** are now aware that certain speech sounds have consistent meanings and are about ready to talk.

coos
vowellike sounds that young infants repeat over and over during periods of contentment.

babbles
vowel-consonant combinations that infants begin to produce at about 4 to 6 months of age.

vocables
unique patterns of sound that a prelinguistic infant uses to represent objects, actions, or events.

What Do Prelinguistic Infants Know about Language and Communication?

Do young infants know more about language than they can possibly tell? It now appears that they do and that one of the first things they learn about speech is a practical lesson. During the first 6 months, babies often coo or babble *while* their caregivers are speaking (Rosenthal, 1982). It is almost as if very young infants view "talking" as a game of noisemaking in which the object is to "harmonize" with their speaking companions. But by 7 to 8 months of age, infants are typically silent while a companion speaks and wait to respond with a vocalization when their partner stops talking. Apparently, they have learned their first rule in the *pragmatics* of language: Don't talk while someone else is speaking, for you'll soon have an opportunity to have your say.

Vocal turn-taking may come about because parents typically say something to the baby, wait for the infant to smile, cough, burp, coo, or babble, and address the infant again, thereby inviting another response (Snow & Ferguson, 1977). Of course, infants may also learn about the importance of turn-taking from other contexts in which they assume reversible roles with their companions (Bruner, 1983). Examples of these reciprocal exchanges might include bouts of nose touching, pat-a-cake, and sharing toys. By 9 months of age, infants clearly understand the alternation rules of many games, and if such activities are interrupted by the adult's failure to take her turn, the infant is likely to vocalize, to urge the adult to resume by offering her a toy, or to wait for a second or two and take the adult's turn before looking once again at the adult (Ross & Lollis, 1987). So it seems that the ways caregivers structure interactions with an infant may indeed help the child to recognize that many forms of social discourse, including "talking," are patterned activities that follow a definite set of rules.

Gestures and Nonverbal Responses

By 8 to 10 months of age, preverbal infants begin to use gestures and other nonverbal responses (for example, facial expressions) to communicate with their companions (Acredolo & Goodwyn, 1990). Two kinds of preverbal gestures are common: *declarative gestures,* in which the infant directs others' attention to an object by pointing at or touching it, and *imperative gestures,* in which the infant tries to convince others to grant his requests through such actions as pointing at candy he wants or tugging at a caregiver's pantleg when he hopes to be picked up. Eventually, some of these gestures become entirely representational and function like words. For example, a 1- to 2-year-old might raise her arms to signify that she wishes to be picked up, hold her arms out to signify an airplane, or even pant heavily to represent the family dog (Acredolo & Goodwyn, 1990; Bates et al., 1989). Once children begin to speak, they often supplement their one- and two-word utterances with a gesture or an intonational cue to ensure that their messages are understood (Ingram, 1989). However, the use of gestures eventually declines as parents encourage their children to talk, and children learn that their words are more likely to be understood.

? WHAT DO YOU THINK?

Suppose three male and three female infants are raised on an island and only have contact with one nonlinguistic adult who gives them love and cares for their basic needs? Would these children come to communicate with each other? Do you think they would devise a language? Why or why not?

Do Preverbal Infants Understand the Meaning of Words?

Although most babies do not utter their first meaningful words until the end of the first year, parents are often convinced that their preverbal infants can understand at least some of what is said to them. Yet, well-controlled tests of word comprehension suggest that preverbal infants understand the meaning of few, if any, words. In one study, 11- and 13-month-olds were told by their mothers to look at an object that was familiar to them. Mothers were *out of sight* and could not use gestures or other nonverbal cues to direct the infants' attention. Clearly, the 13-month-olds did understand

Pointing is an early but very effective means of communication. By the end of the first year, children are calling attention to interesting objects and activities by pointing at them with the index finger.

the meaning of the word that named this object, for they gazed intently at its referent when told to, and they looked very little at other distractor stimuli. By contrast, most 11-month-olds did *not* understand the meaning of this word, for they were as likely to gaze at distractor stimuli as at the word's referent (Thomas et al., 1981). By age 12 to 13 months, however, infants are beginning to realize that individual words do have meaning. In fact, Sharon Oviatt (1980) found that 12- to 17-month-olds understand the meaning of many nouns and verbs long before they use them in their own speech. So infants seem to know much more about language than they can possibly say. Apparently, **receptive language** (comprehension) is ahead of **productive language** (expression) from the 12th or 13th month of life and possibly even sooner.

ONE WORD AT A TIME: THE HOLOPHRASTIC PERIOD

In the first stage of meaningful speech, the **holophrastic period,** infants utter single words that often seem to represent an entire sentence's worth of meaning (that is, **holophrases**). At first, the child's productive vocabulary is constrained, in part, by the sounds she can pronounce, so that her very first words may be intelligible only to close companions—for example, "ba" (for "ball") or "awa" (for "I want," as the child points to a cookie) (Hura & Echols, 1996). Sounds that begin with consonants and end with vowels are easiest for infants, whose longer words are often repetitions of the syllables they can pronounce (for example, "mama," "bye-bye").

However, phonological development occurs very rapidly. By the middle of the second year, infants' cute and creative pronunciations are already guided by rules, or strategies, that enable them to produce simplified but more intelligible versions of adult words (Ingram, 1986; Vihman et al., 1994). For example, they often delete the unstressed syllable of a multisyllable word (saying "ghetti" for "spaghetti"), or replace an ending consonant syllable with a vowel (saying "appo" for "apple"). The fact that these early pronunciation errors are somewhat similar across languages and are resistant to adults' attempts to correct them implies that they stem, in part, from biological constraints, namely, an immature vocal tract. Yet, there are tremendous individual differences: All toddlers do not sound alike, even if they have been exposed to the same

receptive language
that which the individual comprehends when listening to others' speech.

productive language
that which the individual is capable of expressing (producing) in his or her own speech.

holophrastic period
the period when the child's speech consists of one-word utterances, some of which are thought to be holophrases.

holophrase
a single-word utterance that represents an entire sentence's worth of meaning.

language (Vihman et al., 1994). Why? Probably because articulating phonemes and combining them into words is a vocal-*motor* skill, which like all of the dynamic motor systems we discussed in Chapter 5, reflects the unique paths that individual children follow as they combine the sounds that *they* have been attending closely to and producing themselves into new and more complex patterns in an attempt to achieve a most important goal: communicating effectively with their companions (Thelen, 1995; Vihman et al., 1994). As the vocal tract matures during the preschool period, and children have more and more opportunities to decipher and to produce the phonemic combinations in the speech of older models, their pronunciation errors become much less frequent. Indeed, most 4- to 5-year-olds already pronounce most words in pretty much the same way that adults do (Ingram, 1986).

Early Semantics: Building a Vocabulary

As infants begin to speak, the growth of their vocabularies literally proceeds one word at a time (Bloom, 1973). In fact, 3 to 4 months may pass before most children have a vocabulary of 10 words. Yet, the pace of word learning quickens dramatically between 18 and 24 months of age, when infants may add anywhere from 10 to 20 new words a week (Reznick & Goldfield, 1992). This vocabulary spurt is sometimes called the **naming explosion,** for as most parents will attest, toddlers seem to arrive at the wonderful realization that everything has a name and they want to learn all the names they can (Reznick & Goldfield, 1992). A typical 2-year-old may now produce nearly 200 words (Nelson, 1973) and may comprehend a far greater number (Benedict, 1979).

A large percentage of children's first words are the names of objects that move or can be acted on.

What do infants talk about? Katherine Nelson (1973) studied 18 infants as they learned their first 50 words and found that nearly two-thirds of these early words referred to *objects,* including familiar people (see Table 10.1). Furthermore, these objects were nearly all either manipulable by the child (for example, balls or shoes) or capable of moving themselves (for example, animals, vehicles); rarely do infants mention objects such as plates or chairs that simply sit there without doing anything. Toddlers' first words also include many references to familiar *actions* as well (Nelson, Hampson, & Shaw, 1993; see Table 10.1). So it seems that infants talk mostly about those aspects of experience that they already understand through their sensorimotor activities.

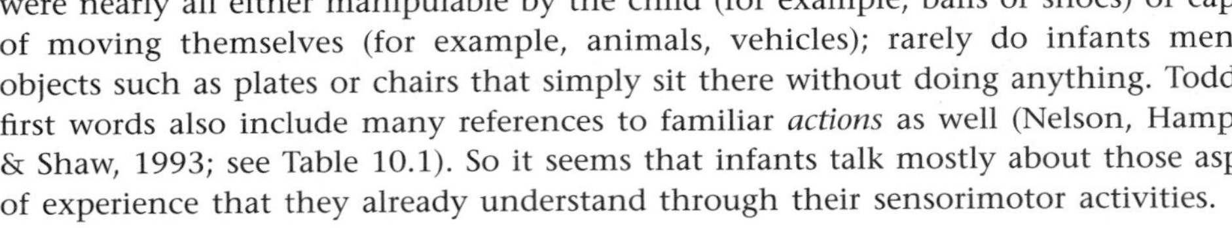

Individual and Cultural Variations in Early Language

Nelson's (1973) early study revealed an interesting individual difference in the kinds of words infants produced. Most infants displayed what she called a **referential style;** their early vocabularies consisted mainly of words that referred to people or objects. By

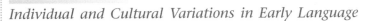

Table 10.1 Types of Words Used by Children with Productive Vocabularies of 50 Words

Word category	Description and examples	Percentage of utterances
Object words	Words used to refer to classes of objects *(car, doggie, milk)* Words used to refer to unique objects *(Mommy, Rover)*	65
Action words	Words used to describe or accompany actions or to demand attention *(bye-bye, up, go)*	13
Modifiers	Words that refer to properties or quantities of things *(big, hot, mine, allgone)*	9
Personal/social words	Words used to express feelings or to comment about social relationships *(please, thank you, no, ouch)*	8
Function words	Words that have a grammatical function *(what, where, is, to, for)*	4

Source: Adapted from Nelson, 1973.

contrast, a smaller number of infants displayed an **expressive style.** Their vocabularies were more diverse and contained a larger number of personal/social words such as *please, thank you, don't,* and *stop it.* Apparently, language serves somewhat different functions for these two groups of children. Referential children seem to think words are for naming objects, whereas expressive children use words to call attention to their own and others' feelings and to regulate their social interactions (Nelson, 1981).

Interestingly, a child's birth order seems to influence the linguistic environment in ways that could affect her language style. Most first-borns in Western cultures adopt a referential style, perhaps reflecting parents' willingness to label and to ask questions about interesting objects that have captured their attention (Nelson, 1973). By contrast, later-borns hear a great deal of speech directed to an older sibling that first-borns haven't heard (Pine, 1995). So later-borns may spend somewhat less time talking with parents about objects and more time listening to speech designed to control their own or their siblings' conduct. As a result, they are more likely than first-borns to conclude that the function of language is to regulate social interactions, prompting them to adopt an expressive language style (Nelson, 1973).

Culture also influences language styles. When talking about a stuffed animal, American mothers treat the interaction as an opportunity to teach the infant about objects ("It's a doggie! Look at its big ears."), thereby encouraging a referential style. Japanese mothers, by contrast, are more inclined to emphasize social routines and consideration for others ("Give the doggie love!") that seem to promote an expressive style (Fernald & Morikawa, 1993). Indeed, in Asian cultures such as Japan, China, and Korea that stress interpersonal harmony, children are much quicker to acquire verbs and personal/social words than American children are (Gopnik & Choi, 1995; Tardif, 1996).

By emphasizing social routines and concern for others, Japanese mothers encourage their children to adopt an "expresseive" language style.

Attaching Meaning to Words

How do toddlers figure out what words mean? In many cases, they seem to employ a **fast-mapping** process, quickly acquiring (and retaining) a word after hearing it applied to its referent only a time or two (Taylor & Gelman, 1988; 1989; Woodward, Markman, & Fitzsimmons, 1994). Early fast mapping apparently reflects a toddler's desire to share meaning with the speaker, for it occurs among 18- to 20-month-olds only if both toddler and speaker are *jointly attending* to the object that is labeled (Baldwin et al., 1996).

Common Errors in Word Use

Despite their remarkable fast-mapping capabilities, toddlers often attach meanings to words that differ from those of adults (Pan & Gleason, 1997). One kind of error that they frequently make is to use a word to refer to a wider variety of objects or events than an adult would. This phenomenon, called **overextension,** is illustrated by a child's use of the term *doggie* to refer to all furry, four-legged animals. **Underextension,** the opposite of overextension, is the tendency to use a general word to refer to a smaller range of objects than an adult would—for example, applying the term *cookie* only to chocolate chip cookies. Why young children overextend or underextend particular words is not always clear, but it is likely that fast mapping contributes to these errors. Suppose, for example, that a mother points to a collie and says "doggie," and then turns toward a fox terrier and says "Look, another doggie." Her toddler may note that about the only things these two beasts seem to have in common are four legs and a hairy exterior, thus leading him to fast map the word *doggie* onto these perceptual attributes. And having done so, he may then be inclined to *overextend* the word *doggie* to all other animals (cats, horses) that share similar perceptual (semantic) features (Clark, 1973). Fast mapping could lead to underextensions as well. If the only dog a toddler has ever seen is the family pet, which he has heard his mother refer to as "doggie" a couple of times, he may initially assume that *doggie* is the proper name of this particular companion and use the term only when referring to his pet.

naming explosion
term used to describe the dramatic increase in the pace at which infants acquire new words in the latter half of the second year; so named because many of the new words acquired are the names of objects.

referential style
early linguistic style in which toddlers use language mainly to label objects.

expressive style
early linguistic style in which toddlers use language mainly to call attention to their own and others' feelings and to regulate social interactions.

fast mapping
process of linking a word with its referent after hearing the word a time or two.

overextension
the young child's tendency to use relatively specific words to refer to a broader set of objects, actions, or events than adults do (for example, using the word *car* to refer to all motor vehicles).

underextension
the young child's tendency to use general words to refer to a smaller set of objects, actions, or events than adults do (for example, using *candy* to refer only to mints).

Of course, deciphering the meaning of many new words is more difficult than these examples imply because it is often unclear exactly what new words refer to. For example, if mother sees a cat walking alongside a car and exclaims "Oh, there is a kitty!", the child must first decide whether mom is referring to the car or to the animal. If he rules out the car, it is still not obvious whether the word *kitty* refers to four-legged animals, to this particular animal, to the cat's pointed ears, leisurely gait, or even the meowing sound it made. How does the child decide among these many possibilities, all of which may seem plausible to him?

Strategies for Inferring Word Meanings

Determining how young children figure out what new words mean when their referents are *not* immediately obvious (as in the *kitty* example) has proved to be a challenging task that is far from complete. Nameera Akhtar and associates (1996) believe that 2-year-olds are already especially sensitive to *social* and *contextual* cues that help them to determine what novel aspects of a companion's speech might mean. To illustrate this point, Akhtar and associates had 2-year-olds and two adults play with three *unnamed* objects that were unfamiliar to the children. Then one adult left the room, and a fourth unnamed object was added to the mix. Later, when the absent adult returned, she exclaimed "Look, I see a gasser! A gasser!" without pointing or displaying any other clue to indicate which of the four objects she was referring to. Even though *gasser* could have referred to any of the four unnamed objects, a substantial percentage of these 2-year-olds correctly inferred the speaker's referential intent, picking the novel object (which was novel *only for the speaker* and not for them) when asked to show a *gasser.* They realized that the second adult had not previously seen this fourth object and then assumed that she must be talking about whichever object was new to her.

In addition to using social or contextual cues to infer word meanings, 2-year-olds have a number of other cognitive strategies, or **processing constraints,** that help them narrow down what a new word might possibly mean (de Villiers & de Villiers, 1992; Golinkoff et al., 1996; Hall & Waxman, 1993; Littschwager & Markman, 1994). Several of the more basic constraints that seem to guide children's inferences about word meanings are described in Table 10.2.

processing constraints cognitive biases or tendencies that lead infants and toddlers to favor certain interpretations of the meaning of new words over other interpretations.

Of course, these constraints may often work together to help children infer word meanings. For example, when 2-year-olds hear the words *horn* and *clip* applied to two

Table 10.2 Some Processing Strategies, or Constraints, That Guide Young Children's Inferences about the Meaning of New Words

Constraint	Description	Example
Object scope constraint	The assumption that words refer to whole objects rather than to parts of the objects or to object attributes.	The child concludes that the word *kitty* refers to the animal he sees rather than to than to the animal's ears, tail, meowing vocalizations, or color.
Taxonomic constraint	The assumption that words label categories of *similar* objects that share common perceptual features.	The child concludes that the word *kitty* refers to the animal he has seen *and* to other small, furry, four-legged animals.
Lexical contrast constraint	The assumption that each word has a unique meaning.	The child who already knows the meaning of *doggie* assumes that a label such as *dalmatian,* applied to a dog, refers to that particular kind of dog (subordinate class).
Mutual exclusivity	The assumption that each object has one label and that different words refer to separate, nonoverlapping categories.	The child who already knows the word for *doggie* assumes that the word *kitty* refers to the fleeing animal if he hears someone say "Look at the doggie chasing the kitty."

very different objects, they assign each word correctly to a whole object, rather than to its parts or attributes (**object scope constraint**), and they display **mutual exclusivity** by almost never calling the horn a *clip* (or vice versa) when tested later (Waxman & Senghas, 1992).

However, the mutual exclusivity constraint is not very helpful when adults use more than one word to refer to the same object (for example, "Oh, there is a *doggie—a cocker spaniel*"). Under these circumstances, 2-year-olds who already know the word *doggie* often apply the **lexical contrast constraint,** concluding that *cocker spaniel* must refer to a particular kind of dog that has the distinctive features (long floppy ears, heavy coat) that this one displays (Taylor & Gelman, 1988, 1989; Waxman & Hatch, 1992). Indeed, this tendency to contrast novel with familiar words may explain how children form hierarchical linguistic categories, eventually recognizing, for example, that a dog is also an animal and a mammal (superordinate designations) as well as a cocker spaniel who has a proper name such as Pokey (subordinate designations) (Mervis, Golinkoff, & Bertrand, 1994). And by age 3 to 5, many children have learned that some objects really can have more than one name. So when they hear two speakers apply different labels (for example, *shades* and *sunglasses*) to the same pair of dark glasses, they may override both the mutual exclusivity and lexical contrast constraints and accept both labels as synonyms, finally coming to prefer whichever word they reencounter first (Savage & Au, 1996).

object scope constraint
the notion that young children assume that a new word applied to an object refers to the whole object rather than to parts of the object or to object attributes (for example, its color).

mutual exclusivity constraint
notion that young children assume that each object has only one label and that different words refer to separate and nonoverlapping categories.

lexical contrast constraint
notion that young children make inferences about word meanings by contrasting new words with words they already know.

syntactical bootstrapping
notion that young children make inferences about the meaning of words by analyzing the way words are used in sentences and inferring whether they refer to objects (nouns), actions (verbs), or attributes (adjectives).

Syntactical Clues to Word Meaning. Finally, young language learners may often infer word meanings by paying close attention to the way that the word is used in a sentence. For example, a 2-year-old who hears a new word, *zav,* used as a noun to refer to a toy ("This is a *zav*") is likely to conclude that this new word refers to the toy itself. However, a child who hears *zav* used as an adjective ("This is a *zav* one") is more likely to conclude that *zav* refers to some characteristic of the toy, such as its shape or color (Taylor & Gelmen, 1988).

Notice, then, children infer word meanings from sentence structure, or *syntactical* clues. Indeed, this **syntactical bootstrapping** may be particularly important in helping them to decipher the meaning of new verbs (Gleitman, 1990). Consider the following two sentences:

1. The duck is gorping the bunny. (Gorping refers to a causative action.)
2. The duck and the bunny are gorping. (Gorping is a synchronized action.)

When 2-year-olds hear one or the other of these sentences, they prefer to look at a video that matches what they have heard—for example, looking at a duck *causing* a rabbit to bend back after hearing Sentence 1 (Naigles, 1990). Clearly the verb's syntax—the form that it takes in a sentence—provides important clues as to what it means (Naigles & Hoff-Ginsberg, 1995).

Syntactical bootstrapping. Young children can use the form of a verb to infer that the sentence "The duck is gorping the bunny," refers to the causative action in the first drawing, whereas the sentence "The duck and the bunny are gorping," refers to the synchronized action in the second drawing.

Summing Up. Toddlers are remarkably well prepared for the task of figuring out what new words mean. Their strong desire to share meaning with companions makes them especially sensitive to novel aspects of the speech they hear and highly motivated to use contextual cues and other available information to decode new words. By age 2, toddlers already produce nearly 200 words—a sufficient baseline for lexical contrast. And apparently they already understand enough about sentence structure (syntax) to determine whether many new words are nouns, verbs, or adjectives—a second important clue to word meaning. While it is true that toddlers make many semantic errors, they often seem to know much more about the meaning of words than their errors might indicate. For example, 2-year-olds who say "doggie" when they see a horse can usually discriminate dogs from other animals if they are given a set of animal pictures and asked to find a horse (Naigles & Gelman, 1995). Why, then, might they choose to call a horse a doggie when they can easily tell the animals apart?

One possibility is that toddlers who know relatively few words may use overextension as yet another strategy for learning the names of new objects and activities. A child who sees a horse may call it a *doggie,* not because he believes it is a dog, but because he has no better word in his vocabulary to describe this animal and he has learned from experience that an incorrect label is likely to elicit reactions such as "No, Johnny, that's a *horse.* Can you say *horsie?* C'mon, say *horsie*" (Baron, 1992; Ingram, 1989).

When a Word Is More Than a Word

Many psycholinguists characterize an infant's one-word utterances as *holophrases* because they often seem less like labels and more like attempts to convey an entire sentence's worth of meaning. These single-word "sentences" can serve different communication functions, depending on how they are said and the context in which they are said (Greenfield & Smith, 1976). For example, 17-month-old Shelley used the word *ghetti* (spaghetti) three times over a 5-minute period. First, she pointed to the pan on the stove and seemed to be *asking* "Is that spaghetti?" Later, the function of her holophrase was to *name* the spaghetti when shown the contents of the pan, as in "It is spaghetti!" Finally, she left little question that she was *requesting* spaghetti when she tugged at her companion's sleeve as he was eating and used a whining tone.

Of course, there are limits to the amount of meaning that can be packed into a single word, but infants in the holophrastic phase of language development do seem to display such basic language functions as naming, questioning, requesting, and demanding—functions that they will later serve by producing different kinds of sentences. They are also learning an important *pragmatic* lesson: that their one-word messages are often ambiguous and may require an accompanying gesture or intonational cue if they are to be understood (Ingram, 1989).

FROM HOLOPHRASES TO SIMPLE SENTENCES: THE TELEGRAPHIC PERIOD

At about 18 to 24 months of age, children begin to combine words into simple "sentences" such as "Daddy eat," "Kitty go," and "Mommie drink milk" that are remarkably similar across languages as diverse as English, German, Finnish, and Samoan (see Table 10.3). These early sentences have been called **telegraphic speech** because, like telegrams, they contain only critical content words, such as nouns, verbs, and adjectives, and leave out such frills as articles, prepositions, and auxiliary verbs.

Why do young children stress nouns and verbs and omit many other parts of speech in their earliest sentences? Certainly not because the omitted words serve no function. Children clearly encode these words in others' speech, for they respond more appropriately to fully grammatical sentences (for example, "Get the ball") than to telegraphic (or otherwise ungrammatical) versions of the same idea (such as "Get ball" or "Point to gub ball") (Gerken & McIntosh, 1993; Petretic & Tweney, 1977). Current thinking is that telegraphic children omit words because of their own processing and production constraints. A child who can only generate very short utterances will choose to deemphasize smaller less important words in favor of those heavily stressed nouns and verbs that are necessary for effective communication (Gerken et al., 1990; Valian, Hoeffner, & Aubry, 1996).

Interestingly, telegraphic speech is not nearly as universal as earlier researchers had thought. Russian and Turkish children, for example, produce short but reasonably grammatical sentences from the very beginning. Why? Because their languages place more stress on small grammatical markers and have less rigid rules about word order than other languages do (de Villiers & de Villiers, 1992; Slobin, 1985). So it seems whatever is most noticeable about the structure of a language is what children acquire first. And if content words and word-order rules are most heavily stressed (as in English), then young children will include this information and omit the lightly stressed articles, prepositions, and grammatical markers to produce what appear to be "telegraphic" utterances.

telegraphic speech
early sentences that consist of content words and omit the less meaningful parts of speech, such as articles, prepositions, pronouns, and auxiliary verbs.

TABLE 10.3 Similarities in Children's Spontaneous Two-Word Sentences in Four Languages

	Language			
Function of sentence	**English**	**Finnish**	**German**	**Samoan**
To locate or name	There book	Tuossa Rina (there Rina)	Buch da (book there)	Keith lea (Keith there)
To demand	More milk Give candy	Annu Rina (give Rina)	Mehr milch (more milk)	Mai pepe (give doll)
To negate	No wet Not hungry	Ei susi (not wolf)	Nicht blasen (not blow)	Le'ai (not eat)
To indicate possession	My shoe Mama dress	Täti auto (aunt's car)	Mein ball (my ball) Mamas hut (Mama's hat)	Lole a'u (candy my)
To modify or qualify	Pretty dress Big boat	Rikki auto (broken car)	Armer wauwau (poor dog)	Fa'ali'i pepe (headstrong baby)
To question	Where ball	Missa pallo (where ball)	Wo ball (where ball)	Fea Punafu (where Punafu)

Source: Adapted from Slobin, 1979.

A Semantic Analysis of Telegraphic Speech

Psycholinguists have approached early child language as if it were a foreign language and have tried to describe the rules that young children use to form their sentences. Early attempts to specify the structural characteristics, or syntax, of telegraphic speech made it quite clear that many of children's earliest two-word sentences followed at least some grammatical rules. English-speaking children, for example, usually say "Mommy drink" rather than "Drink mommy" or "My ball" rather than "Ball my," thus suggesting that they already realize that some word orders are better than others for conveying meaning (de Villiers & de Villiers, 1992).

However, it soon became obvious that analyses of telegraphic speech based on syntax alone grossly underestimated the young child's linguistic capabilities. Why? Because young children often use the *same* two-word utterance to convey *different* meanings (or semantic relations) in different contexts. For example, one of Lois Bloom's (1970) young subjects said "Mommy sock" on two occasions during the same day—once when she picked up her mother's sock and once while her mother was putting a sock on the child's foot. In the first instance, "Mommy sock" seems to imply a possessive relationship—"Mommy's sock." But in the second instance, the child was apparently expressing a different idea, namely "Mommy is putting on my sock." So to properly interpret telegraphic statements, one must determine the child's *meaning* or *semantic intent* by considering not only the words that she generates but also the contexts in which these utterances take place.

Roger Brown (1973) has analyzed the "telegraphese" of several young children from around the world and written a "*semantic grammar*" to describe the basic categories of meaning that they often express in their two-word sentences. The most common of these semantic relations appear in Table 10.4.

The Pragmatics of Early Speech

Because early sentences are incomplete and their meanings often ambiguous, children continue to supplement their words with gestures and intonational cues to ensure that their messages are understood (O'Neill, 1996). Although adults who are proficient with the spoken language may consider nonverbal gestures a rather limited and inefficient form of communication, such an attitude is extremely shortsighted. Indeed, many deaf

Table 10.4 Common Meanings (Semantic Relations) Expressed in Children's Earliest Sentences

Semantic relation	Examples
Agent + action	Mommy come; Daddy sit
Action + object	Drive car; eat grape
Agent + object	Mommy sock; baby book
Action + location	Go park; sit chair
Entity + location	Cup table; toy floor
Possessor + possession	My teddy; Mommy dress
Entity + attribute	Box shiny; crayon big
Demonstrative + entity	Dat money; dis telephone
Notice + noticed object	Hi belt; Hi Mommy
Recurrence	More milk
Nonexistence	Allgone cookie; No wet

Source: Based on Brown, 1973.

10.3

DEVELOPMENTAL ISSUES

Learning a Gestural Language

Children who are born deaf or who lose their hearing very early in childhood have a difficult time learning an oral language. Contrary to popular opinion, the deaf do not learn much from lip reading. In fact, many deaf children (especially those of hearing parents) may be delayed in their language development unless they are exposed early to a gestural system known as American Sign Language (ASL) (Mayberry, 1994).

Although ASL is produced by the hands rather than orally, it is a remarkably flexible medium (Bellugi, 1988). Some signs represent entire words; others stand for grammatical morphemes such as the progressive ending *-ing,* the past tense *-ed,* and auxiliaries. Each sign is constructed from a limited set of gestural components in much the same way that the spoken word is constructed from a finite number of distinctive sounds (phonemes). In ASL, the components that make up a sign are (1) the position of the signing hand(s), (2) the configuration of the hand(s) and fingers, and (3) the motions of the hand(s) and fingers. Syntactical rules specify how signs are to be combined to form declarative sentences, to ask questions, and to negate a proposition. And, like an oral language, ASL permits the user to sign plays on words (puns), metaphorical statements, and poetry. So people who are proficient in this gestural system can transmit and understand an infinite variety of highly creative messages. They are true language users!

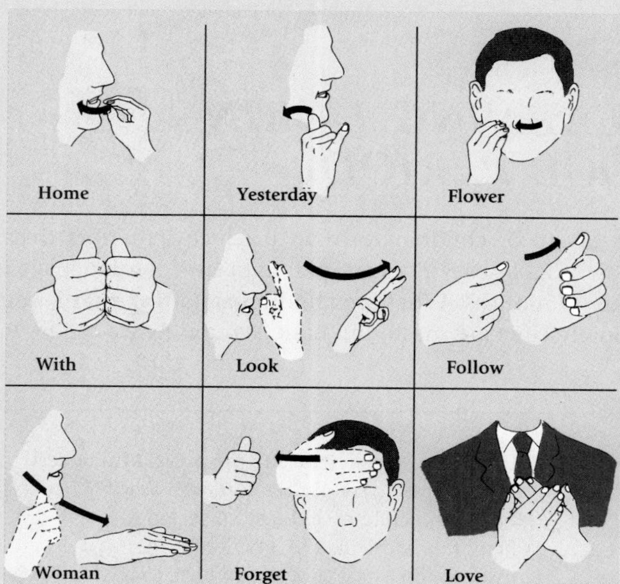

Some signs in American Sign Language. FROM REIKEHOF, 1963.

Deaf children who are exposed early to ASL acquire it in much the same way that hearing children acquire an oral language (Bellugi, 1988; Locke, 1997). Indeed, signs are readily visible to the infant and grow from sensorimotor schemes, perhaps explaining why many children produce their first truly referential sign or gesture at about the same time or slightly before hearing children utter their first meaningful words (Folven & Bonvillian, 1991; Goodwyn & Acredolo, 1993). Deaf mothers support sign learning by signing to their infants in "motherese"—that is, signing slowly with exaggerated movements that are repeated often to ensure comprehension (Masataka, 1996). And the deaf child usually begins by "babbling" in sign, forming rough approximations of signs that parents use, before proceeding to one-word, or "holophrastic," phrases, in which a single sign is used to convey a number of different messages. Furthermore, the linguistic advances of both deaf and hearing children are closely linked to advances in cognitive development; for example, putting signs or words together in sentences happens at about the same age that children put sequences of actions together in their play (Spencer, 1996). And when deaf children begin to combine signs, their two-sign sentences are "telegraphic" statements that express the same set of semantic relations that appears in the early speech of hearing children.

Finally, it seems that language areas of the brain develop much the same in deaf children exposed early to sign language as in hearing children exposed to speech. Helen Neville and her colleagues (1997) examined the brain activity of deaf ASL users and hearing individuals as they processed sentences in their respective languages. For the most part, reliance on areas of the left hemisphere of the cerebral cortex to process sentences was just as strong among participants who acquired ASL early in life as among hearing individuals who acquired English early in life. However, early learners of ASL also used their right hemisphere in responding to sentences, perhaps because spatial skills controlled by the right hemisphere come into play in interpreting the gestures of someone who is signing.

What do these striking parallels tell us about theories of language acquisition? They surely imply that language learning depends, in part, on biological processes (Meier, 1991). What isn't clear, however, is whether the linguistic milestones and abilities that deaf children share with hearing children reflect (1) the operation of a specialized linguistic capacity that enables children to acquire any and all languages (nativist position), or (2) the gradual maturation of the human brain and achievement of *general* cognitive milestones that children are then motivated to express in their own language (interactionist position).

children learn and use a rather sophisticated language that is based entirely on nonverbal signs and gestures (see Box 10.3).

Toddlers are also becoming quite sensitive to many of the social and situational determinants of effective communication. For example, 2-year-olds are rather proficient at vocal turn taking; they know that speakers "look up" at the listener when they are about to yield the floor, and they now use this same nonverbal cue to signal the end of their own utterances (Rutter & Durkin, 1987). By age 2 to 2½, children know that they must either stand close to a listener or compensate for distance by raising their voices if they are to communicate with that person (Johnson et al., 1981; Wellman & Lempers, 1977). And remarkably, 2- to 2½-year-olds are already considering what a partner knows (or doesn't know) when choosing a conversational topic or making a request. They much prefer to talk about events that their partners haven't shared with them or don't already know about (Shatz, 1994), and their requests for assistance in obtaining a toy that is out of reach are much more elaborate and more likely to include a gesture when they know that their partners are unaware of the toy's whereabouts (O'Neill, 1996). In fact, 2½-year-olds can even monitor others' *verbal* responses to their messages and clarify requests that an adult has misunderstood. So a child who requested a toy duck and hears an adult say "You asked for the sock" will often repair his failed message with a statement such as "I don't want that! Want duck!" (Shwe & Markman, 1997).

Finally, young children also learn certain sociolinguistic prescriptions, such as the need to be polite when making requests, and they begin to understand what is polite and what isn't in other people's speech (Baroni & Axia, 1989; Garton & Pratt, 1990). Although we have seen that parents do not intentionally teach grammar to their children, they *do* instruct them in etiquette (Flavell et al., 1993). Such common parental prompts as "What do you say?" or "Say the magic word and the cookie is yours" play an important part in this learning.

In sum, most 2- to 2½-year-olds have learned many pragmatic lessons about language and communication and are usually able to get their meaning across to conversational partners. But even though toddlers can converse with adults and older children, their communication skills pale in comparison with those of a 5-year-old, a 4-year-old, or even many 3-year-olds. Our next task is to determine what it is that preschool children acquire that enables them to become rather sophisticated users of language by the time they enter kindergarten.

LANGUAGE LEARNING DURING THE PRESCHOOL PERIOD

In the short period from age 2½ to 5, children learn to produce sentences that are remarkably complex and adultlike. Table 10.5 gives an inkling of how fast language progresses in the brief span of 7 to 10 months. What are children acquiring that accounts for this language explosion? Surely they are mastering basic syntax: As we see in Table

Concept Check 10.2
Language Learning among Infants and Toddlers

Check your understanding of *selected aspects* of early language learning by matching each descriptive statement below with one of the following terms or concepts: (a) vocal turn-taking, (b) syntactical bootstrapping, (c) expressive style, (d) telegraphic speech, (e) holophrastic speech, (f) intonational cues, (g) overextension, (h) referential style, (i) object scope constraint. Answers appear in the Appendix at the back of the book.

_____ 1. early linguistic style more common among laterborns and children in Asian societies

_____ 2. very early clue that caregivers' speech conveys distinct meanings

_____ 3. term to describe children's one-word utterances

_____ 4. early linguistic style more common among firstborns and children in Western societies

_____ 5. first pragmatic rule that children learn

_____ 6. assumption that a new word refers to a whole object rather than to its parts

_____ 7. term characterizing a child's earliest sentences

_____ 8. inferring word meaning from the way the word is used in a sentence

_____ 9. semantic "error" that may promote vocabulary development by virtue of its impact on older companions

Table 10.5 Samples of One Boy's Speech at Three Ages

Age		
28 months (telegraphic speech)	**35 months**	**38 months**
Somebody pencil	No—I don't know	I like a racing car
Floor	What dat feeled like?	I broke my racing car
Where birdie go?	Lemme do again	It's broked
Read dat	Don't—don't hold with me	You got some beads
Hit hammer, Mommy	I'm going to drop it—inne dump truck	Who put dust on my hair?
Yep, it fit	Why—cracker can't talk?	Mommy don't let me buy some
Have screw	Those are mines	Why it's not working?

Source: Adapted from McNeill, 1970.

10.5, a child of 35 to 38 months is now inserting articles, auxiliary verbs, and grammatical markers (for example, *-ed, -ing*) that were previously omitted, as well as negating propositions and occasionally asking a well-formed question (Hoff-Ginsberg, 1997). And although it is not as obvious from the table, we will see that preschool children are also beginning to understand much more about the pragmatics of language and communication.

Grammatical Development

Development of Grammatical Morphemes

Grammatical morphemes are modifiers that give more precise meaning to the sentences we construct. These meaning modifiers usually appear sometime during the third year as children begin to pluralize nouns by adding *-s,* to signify location with the prepositional morphemes *in* and *on,* to indicate verb tense with the present progressive *-ing* or the past tense *-ed,* and to describe possessive relations with the inflection *'s.*

Roger Brown (1973) kept records on three children as they acquired 14 grammatical morphemes that frequently appear in English sentences. He found these three children varied considerably with respect to (1) the age at which they began to use grammatical markers and (2) the amount of time it took them to master all 14 rules. However, all three children in this longitudinal study learned the 14 grammatical morphemes in the exact order in which they appear in Table 10.6 on page 378, a finding confirmed in a cross-sectional study of 21 additional children (de Villiers & de Villiers, 1973).

Why do children who have very different vocabularies learn these 14 grammatical markers in one particular order? Brown (1973) soon rejected a frequency-of-mention hypothesis when he found that the grammatical morphemes learned first appear no more often in parents' speech than morphemes acquired later. What he did discover is that the morphemes acquired early are less semantically and syntactically complex than those acquired later. For example, the present progressive *-ing,* which describes an ongoing action, appears before the past regular *-ed,* which describes both action and a sense of "earlier in time." Moreover, *-ed,* which conveys two semantic features, is acquired earlier than the uncontractible forms of the verb *to be* (*is, are, was, were*), all of which are more syntactically complex and specify *three* semantic relations: number (singular or plural), tense (present or past), and action (ongoing process).

Once young children have acquired a new grammatical morpheme, they apply this rule to new as well as to familiar contexts. For example, if the child realizes that the way to pluralize a noun is to add the grammatical inflection *-s,* he or she has no problem

grammatical morphemes prefixes, suffixes, prepositions, and auxiliary verbs that modify the meaning of words and sentences.

Table 10.6 Order of Acquisition of English Grammatical Morphemes

Morpheme	Example
1. Present progressive: *-ing*	He is sitt*ing* down.
2. Preposition: *in*	The mouse is *in* the box.
3. Preposition: *on*	The book is *on* the table.
4. Plural: *-s*	The dog*s* ran away
5. Past irregular: for example, *went*	The boy *went* home.
6. Possessive: *-'s*	The girl*'s* dog is big.
7. Uncontractible copula *be:* for example, *are, was*	*Are* they boys or girls? *Was* that a dog?
8. Articles: *the, a*	He has *a* book.
9. Past regular: *-ed*	He jump*ed* the stream.
10. Third person regular: *-s*	She run*s* fast.
11. Third person irregular: for example, *has, does*	*Does* the dog bark?
12. Uncontractible auxiliary *be:* for example, *is, were*	*Is* he running? *Were* they at home?
13. Contractible copula *be:* for example, *-'s, -'re*	That*'s* a spaniel.
14. Contractible auxiliary *be:* for example, *-'s, -'re*	They*'re* running very slowly.

Source: Adapted from Clark & Clark, 1977.

This is a wug.
Now there is another one.
There are two of them.
There are two ______

Figure 10.4 *A linguistic puzzle used to determine young children's understanding of the rule for forming plurals in English.* From Berko, 1958.

solving the puzzle in Figure 10.4: These two funny-looking creatures are obviously wugs (Berko, 1958).

Overregularization. Interestingly, children occasionally overextend new grammatical morphemes to cases in which the adult form is irregular—a phenomenon known as **overregularization.** Statements such as "I brushed my *tooths,*" "She *goed,*" or "It *runned* away" are common examples of the kind of overregularization errors that 2½- to 3-year-olds make. Oddly enough, children have often used the *correct* forms of many irregular nouns and verbs (for example, "It *ran* away"; "My *feet* are cold") *before* they learn any grammatical morphemes (Brown, 1973; Mervis & Johnson, 1991). Even after acquiring a new rule, a child's overregularizations are relatively rare, occurring on only about 2.5 to 5% of those occasions in which irregular verbs are used (Marcus et al., 1992). So overregularization is not a serious grammatical defect that must be unlearned. Instead, most of their errors seem to occur because children occasionally fail to retrieve the irregular form of a noun or a verb from memory and must then apply their new morpheme (overregularize) to communicate the idea they are trying to express (Marcus et al., 1992).

Mastering Transformational Rules

In addition to grammatical morphemes, each language has rules for creating variations of the basic declarative sentence. Applying these rules of **transformational grammar,** the declarative statement "I was eating pizza" can easily be modified to produce a *question* ("What was I eating?") or to generate *negative* sentences ("I was *not* eating pizza"), *imperatives* ("Eat the pizza!"), *relative clauses* ("I, who hate cheese, was eating pizza"), and *compound sentences* ("I was eating pizza, and John was eating spaghetti").

Between the ages of 2 and 2½, most children begin to produce some variations of declarative sentences, many of which depend on their mastery of the auxiliary verb *to be* (de Villiers & de Villiers, 1992). However, children acquire transformational rules in a step-by-step fashion, so that their earliest transformations are very different from those of an adult. We can easily illustrate this point by considering the phases that children go through as they learn to ask questions, negate propositions, and generate complex sentences.

overregularization
the overgeneralization of grammatical rules to irregular cases where the rules do not apply (for example, saying *mouses* rather than *mice*).

transformational grammar
rules of syntax that allow one to transform declarative statements into questions, negatives, imperatives, and other kinds of sentences.

Asking Questions. There are two kinds of questions that are common to virtually all languages. *Yes/no questions,* the simpler form which is mastered first, ask whether particular declarative statements are true or false (for example, "Is that a doggie?"). By contrast, *wh- questions* call for responses other than a simple yes or no. These queries are called *wh-* questions because, in English, they almost always begin with a *wh-* word such as *who, what, where, when,* or *why.*

The child's earliest questions often consist of nothing more than a declarative sentence uttered with a rising intonation that transforms it into a yes/no question (for example, "See doggie?"). However, *wh-* words are occasionally placed at the beginning of telegraphic sentences to generate simple *wh-* questions such as "Where doggie?" or "What daddy eat?" During the second phase of question asking, children begin to use the proper auxiliary, or helping, verbs, but their questions are of the form "What daddy is eating?" or "Where doggie is going?". Finally, children learn the transformational rule that calls for moving the auxiliary verb ahead of the subject, and they begin to produce adultlike questions such as "What is daddy eating?"

Interestingly, children begin to ask *what, where,* and *who* questions long before they request information about *why, when,* and *how* (Bloom, Merkin, & Wootten, 1982; Tyack & Ingram, 1977). One explanation for this finding ties it to general cognitive development: *What, where,* and *who* questions have concrete referents (objects, locations, and persons) that a cognitively immature toddler can easily understand, whereas *when, why,* and *how* questions require an appreciation of *abstract* concepts, such as time and causality, that develops a little later, between ages 3 and 5 (French, 1989).

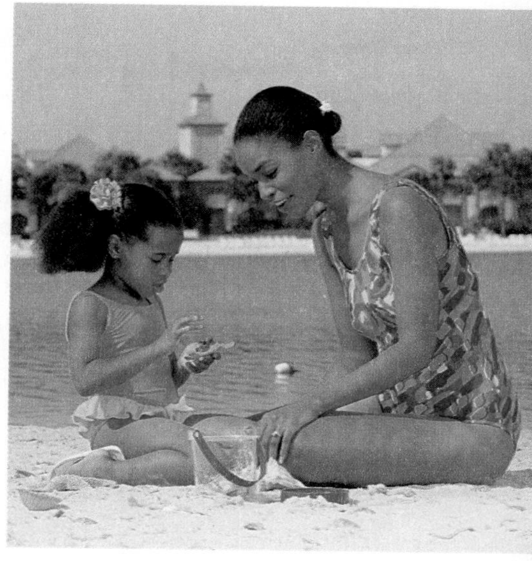

Curious 3- to 5-year-olds display their knowledge of transformational grammar by asking many "who," "what," and "why" questions of their companions.

Producing Negative Sentences. Like questions, children's negative sentences develop in a steplike fashion. Children the world over initially express negations by simply placing a negative word in front of the word or statement they wish to negate, producing such utterances as "No mitten" or "No I go." Notice, however, that these first negatives are ambiguous: "No mitten" can convey *nonexistence* ("There's no mitten"), *rejection* ("I won't wear a mitten"), or *denial* ("That's not a mitten") (Bloom, 1970). This ambiguity is clarified once the child begins to insert the negative word inside the sentence, in front of the word that it modifies (for example, "I not wear mitten" or "That not mitten"). Finally, children learn to combine negative markers with the proper auxiliary verbs to negate sentences in much the same way adults do. Indeed, Peter and Jill de Villiers (1979) describe a delightful experiment in which young children were persuaded to argue with a talking puppet. Whenever the puppet made a declarative statement, such as "He likes bananas," the child's task was to negate the proposition (argue) in any way he or she could. Most 3- to 4-year-olds thoroughly enjoyed this escalating verbal warfare between themselves and the puppet. But more important, these young children were quite capable of using a wide variety of negative auxiliaries, including *wouldn't, wasn't, hasn't,* and *mustn't,* to properly negate almost any sentence the puppet produced.

Producing Complex Sentences. By age 3, most children have begun to produce complex sentences. Relative clauses that modify nouns (for example, "That's the box *that they put it in*"), and conjunctions to join simple sentences ("He was stuck *and* I got him out") are usually the first to appear, followed by embedded sentences (for example, "The man *who fixed the fence* went home") and more intricate forms of questions as well (for example, "John will come, won't he?"; "Where did you say you put my doll?") (de Villiers & de Villiers, 1992). By the end of the preschool period, at age 5 to 6, children are using most of the grammatical rules of their language and speaking much like adults do, even though they have never had a formal lesson in grammar.

Semantic Development

Another reason that preschoolers' language becomes more complex is that 2- to 5-year-olds are beginning to understand and express relational contrasts such as big/little, tall/short, in/on, before/after, here/there, and I/you (de Villiers & de Villiers, 1979;

1992). *Big* and *little* are usually the first spatial adjectives to appear, and these terms are soon used to specify a variety of relations. By age 2 to 2½, for example, children can use *big* and *little* to draw proper *normative* conclusions (a 10-cm egg, viewed by itself, is "big" relative to other eggs the child remembers seeing) and *perceptual* inferences (a 10 cm egg placed next to an even larger egg is "little") (Ebeling & Gelman, 1988; 1994). By age 3, children are even capable of using these terms to make appropriate *functional* judgments such as deciding that an oversized article of doll clothing, which is little relative to what the child wears, is nonetheless too "big" to fit the doll in question (Gelman & Ebeling, 1989).

Several researchers have devised linguistic games such as the argumentative-puppet technique to test children's knowledge and use of relational opposites such as big/little, tall/short, long/short, wide/narrow, and deep/shallow. They have found that children acquire these spatial contrasts in the following order:

	tall/short		wide narrow	
big/little →		→ high/low →		→ deep/shallow
	long/short		thick/thin	

There appear to be two reasons that spatial adjectives are learned in this particular order. First, children hear some adjectives more than others: *big* and *little* are by far the most frequent spatial terms in English, and adjectives such as *tall* and *short* are used more often than *thick, narrow,* or *shallow.* In addition, *big* and *little* may be acquired first because they are so broadly applicable, referring to variations in size along *any* spatial dimension; by contrast, *wide* and *narrow* are more limited in meaning, pertaining only to variations on the horizontal dimension (Flavell et al., 1993).

Although preschoolers are becoming increasingly aware of a variety of meaningful relations and are rapidly learning how to express them in their own speech, their incomplete knowledge of syntax leads them to make some interesting semantic errors. Consider the following sentences:

1. The girl hit the boy.
2. The boy was hit by the girl.

Children younger than 5 or 6 frequently misinterpret *passive* constructions, such as sentence number 2 above. They can easily understand the *active* version of the same idea—that is, sentence 1. But if asked to point to a picture that shows "The boy was hit by the girl," preschoolers usually select a drawing that shows a boy hitting a girl. What they have done is to assume that the first noun is the agent of the verb and that the second is the object; consequently, they interpret the passive construction as if it were an active sentence. Passive sentences based on mental-state verbs such as *like* and *know* (for example, "Goofy was liked by Donald") are particularly difficult and are not understood until later in grade school (Sudhalter & Braine, 1985). Yet, preschoolers can often interpret *irreversible* passives that make little sense if processed as an active sentence. For example, even a 3-year-old might correctly interpret "The candy was eaten by the girl" because it is nonsense to assume that the candy was doing the eating (de Villiers & de Villiers, 1979).

Development of Pragmatics and Communication Skills

During the preschool period, children acquire a number of conversational skills that help them to communicate more effectively and accomplish their objectives. For example, 3-year-olds are already beginning to understand *illocutionary intent*—that the real underlying meaning of an utterance may not always correspond to the literal meaning of the words speakers use. Notice how the 3-year-old in the following example uses this knowledge to her advantage as she turns a declarative statement into a successful command (Reeder, 1981, p. 135):

SHEILA Every night I get an ice cream.

BABYSITTER That's nice, Sheila.

SHEILA Even when there's a babysitter, I get an ice cream.

BABYSITTER (to himself) [B]acked into a corner by a 3-year-old's grasp of language as a social tool!

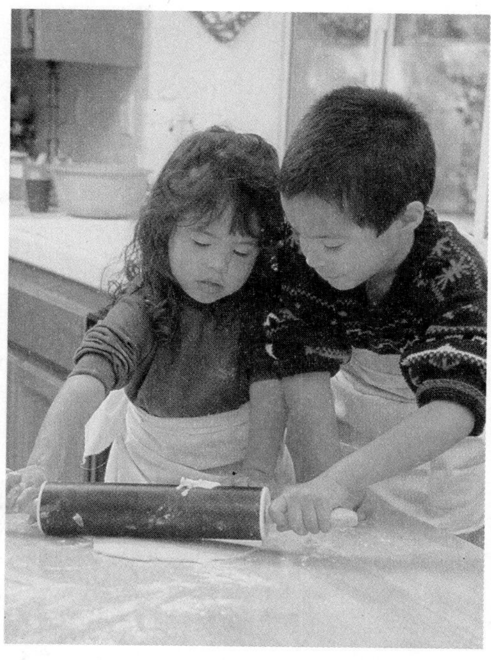

Communication skills develop rapidly during the preschool years. Four-year-olds are already quite proficient at adjusting their messages to a listener's level of understanding.

Three- to five-year-olds are also learning that they must tailor their messages to their audience if they hope to communicate effectively. Marilyn Shatz and Rochel Gelman (1973) recorded the speech of several 4-year-olds as they introduced a new toy to either a 2-year-old or an adult. An analysis of the tapes revealed that 4-year-old children are already beginning to adjust their speech to their listener's level of understanding. When talking to a 2-year-old, the older children used short sentences and were careful to choose phrases such as "Watch," "Look, Perry," and "Look here" that would attract and maintain the toddler's attention. By contrast, 4-year-olds explaining how the toy worked to an adult used complex sentences and were generally more polite.

Referential Communication

An effective communicator is one who not only produces clear, unambiguous messages, but is able to detect any ambiguities in others' speech and ask for clarification. These aspects of language are called **referential communication skills.**

It was once generally assumed that preschool children lacked the abilities to detect uninformative messages and resolve most problems in communication. Indeed, if asked to evaluate the quality of an ambiguous message such as "Look at *that* horse" when a number of horses are in view, preschool children are more likely than their grade-school counterparts to say that this is an *informative* message. Apparently, they often fail to detect linguistic ambiguities because they are focusing on what they *think* the speaker means rather than on the (ambiguous) *literal* meaning of the message (Beal & Belgrad, 1990; Flavell et al., 1993). Why do preschoolers guess at the meaning of uninformative messages? Possibly because they are often quite successful at inferring the true meaning of ambiguous utterances from other contextual cues, such as their knowledge of a particular speaker's attitudes, preferences, and past behaviors (cf. Ackerman, Szymanski, & Silver, 1990). Four-year-olds are also less likely than 7-year-olds to detect and rephrase their own uninformative messages. In fact, they often assume that their own statements are perfectly informative and that failures to communicate should be blamed on their listeners (Flavell et al., 1993).

However, most 3- to 5-year-olds display better referential communication skills in the natural environment than on laboratory tasks, particularly when there are contextual cues to help them clarify an otherwise ambiguous message (Ackerman, 1993; Beal & Belgrad, 1990). Furthermore, even 3-year-olds know that they cannot carry out an unintelligible request made by a yawning adult, and they quickly realize that other impossible requests (such as "Bring me the refrigerator") are problematic as well (Revelle, Wellman, & Karabenick, 1985). These young children also know how they might resolve such breakdowns in communication, for they often say "What?" or "Huh?" to a yawning adult or ask "How? It's too heavy!" when told to retrieve a refrigerator.

In sum, 3- to 5-year-olds are not very good at detecting ambiguities in the *literal* meaning of oral messages. Nevertheless, they are better communicators than many laboratory studies of comprehension monitoring might suggest because they are often successful at inferring what an ambiguous message must mean from nonlinguistic contextual information.

referential communication skills
abilities to generate clear verbal messages, to recognize when others' messages are unclear, and to clarify any unclear messages one transmits or receives.

LANGUAGE LEARNING DURING MIDDLE CHILDHOOD AND ADOLESCENCE

Although 5-year-olds have learned a great deal about language in a remarkably brief period, many important strides in linguistic competence are made from ages 6 to 14—the grade-school and junior high school years. Not only do schoolchildren use bigger words and produce longer and more complex utterances, they also begin to think about and manipulate language in ways that were previously impossible.

Later Syntactic Development

During middle childhood, children correct many of their previous syntactical errors and begin to use a number of complex grammatical forms that did not appear in their earlier speech. For example, 5- to 8-year-olds are beginning to iron out the kinks in their use of personal pronouns, so that sentences such as "Him and her went" become much less frequent (Dale, 1976). By age 7 to 9, children understand and may occasionally even produce such complex *passive* sentences as "Goofy was liked by Donald" (Sudhalter & Braine, 1985) and *conditional sentences* such as "If Goofy had come, Donald would have been delighted" (Boloh & Champaud, 1993).

So middle childhood is a period of syntactical refinement. Children are learning subtle exceptions to grammatical rules and coming to grips with the more complex syntactical structures of their native tongue. However, this process of syntactic elaboration occurs very gradually, often continuing well into adolescence or young adulthood (Clark & Clark, 1977; Eisele & Lust, 1996).

Semantics and Metalinguistic Awareness

Children's knowledge of semantics and semantic relations continues to grow throughout the grade-school years. Vocabulary development is particularly impressive. Six-year-olds already understand approximately 10,000 words and continue to expand their *receptive vocabularies* at the rate of about 20 words a day, until they comprehend some 40,000 words by age 10 (Anglin, 1993). Of course grade-school children do not use all these new words in their own speech and may not even have heard many of them before. What they have gained is **morphological knowledge**—knowledge of the meaning of morphemes that make up words—which enables them to analyze the structure of such unfamiliar words as "sourer," "custom-made," or "hopelessness" and quickly figure out what they mean (Anglin, 1993). Finally, adolescents' capacity for formal-operational reasoning permits them to further expand their vocabularies, adding a host of abstract words (for example, "ironic," "eradicate") that they rarely heard (or didn't understand) during the grade-school years (McGhee-Bidlack, 1991).

Grade-school children are also becoming more proficient at *semantic integrations*—that is, at drawing linguistic inferences that enable them to understand more than is actually said. For example, if 6- to 8-year-olds hear "John did not see the rock; the rock was in the path; John fell," they are able to infer that John must have tripped over the rock. Interestingly, however, 6- to 8-year-olds often assume that the story explicitly described John tripping and are not consciously aware that they have drawn an inference (Beal, 1990). By age 9 to 11, children are better able to make these kinds of linguistic inferences and recognize them as *inferences* (Beal, 1990; Casteel, 1993), even

morphological knowledge
one's knowledge of the meaning of morphemes that make up words.

when the two or more pieces of information that are necessary to draw the "appropriate" conclusion are separated by a number of intervening sentences (Johnson & Smith, 1981; van den Broek, 1989). And once children begin to integrate different kinds of linguistic information, they are able to detect *hidden* meanings that are not immediately obvious from the content of an utterance. For example, if a noisy 6-year-old hears her teacher quip "My, but you're quiet today," the child will probably note the contradiction between the literal meaning of the sentence and its satirical intonation or its context and thereby detect the *sarcasm* in her teacher's remark (Dews et al., 1996).

One reason that school-age children are able to go beyond the information given when making linguistic inferences is that they are rapidly developing **metalinguistic awareness**—an ability to think about language and to comment on its properties. This reflective ability is present to some degree among preschoolers, particularly 4- to 5-year-olds, who are beginning to display much more *phonological awareness* (for example, if you take the *s* sound of scream, what's left?) and *grammatical awareness* (for example, is "I be sick" the right or wrong way to say it?) than younger children do (de Villiers & de Villiers, 1979). Yet, the metalinguistic competencies that 5-year-olds display are limited compared with those of a 9-year-old, a 7-year-old, or even a 6-year-old (Bialystok, 1986; Ferreira & Morrison, 1994).

An emerging awareness that language is an arbitrary and rule-bound system may have important educational implications, for children who score relatively high in metalinguistic awareness (particularly phonological awareness) at ages 5 and 6 are likely to be the most proficient readers during the first and second grades (Warren-Leubecker & Carter, 1988; Wolf & Dickinson, 1985). So metalinguistic skills are related to reading abilities, but how? Some think that reading instruction and other early literary experiences promote metalinguistic awareness, whereas others argue that the development of a certain amount of metalinguistic knowledge makes reading easier. Amye Warren-Leubecker and Beth Carter (1988) think that both views may be correct. They found that (1) informal literary experiences (for example, having stories read to them) do predict preschool children's levels of phonological awareness, but (2) phonological awareness was a better predictor of future reading achievement than were informal literary experiences or traditional tests of reading readiness, implying that some degree of phonological awareness may be necessary before a child learns to read (see also Wagner et al., 1997). Indeed, 7- to 10-year-olds who are poor readers tend to display poor phonological awareness and phonological processing skills (McBride-Chang, 1996). And one particularly effective way of improving their reading is a program that combines phonological awareness training with reading instruction, thus highlighting the connections between the phonemic aspects of oral language and the decoding of written words (Hatcher et al., 1994; Seppa, 1997).

By reading to young children, a parent promotes phonological awareness—an important contributor to the development of reading skills.

metalinguistic awareness
a knowledge of language and its properties; an understanding that language can be used for purposes other than communication.

Further Development of Communication Skills

Earlier, we examined a study (Shatz & Gelman, 1973) in which preschool children adjusted the style and content of their speech to a listener's level of understanding. Recall that the 4-year-olds in this study were face to face with their 2-year-old or their adult companion and thus could see whether or not the listener was responding appropriately to their messages or following their instructions. Could children this young have communicated effectively with their partners if they had been asked to deliver their messages over a telephone?

Probably not. In one early study of children's referential communication skills, 4- to 10-year-olds were asked to describe blocks with unfamiliar graphic designs on them to a peer who was on the other side of an opaque screen so that the peer could identify them (Krauss & Glucksberg, 1977). As shown in Table 10.7, preschool children described these designs in highly idiosyncratic ways that neither communicated much to their listeners nor enabled them to identify which blocks the speaker was talking about. By contrast, 8- to 10-year-olds provided much more informative messages. They realized that their listener could not see what they were referring to, thus requiring them to somehow *differentiate* these objects and make each distinctive if their messages were to be understood.

WHAT DO YOU THINK?

How would you seek to improve 5-year-olds' referential communication skills? Might having them play games in which they must seek limiting information (for example, 20 Questions) be of any help?

Four- and five-year-olds perform much better on referential communication tasks that require them to describe the whereabouts of *real* (rather than abstract) objects that are hidden or missing (Plumert, Ewert, & Spear, 1995). But even so, their messages are more ambiguous than those of grade-school children (Craton et al., 1990).

Dramatic improvements in referential communication skills during the early grade-school years are due, in part, to the growth of cognitive skills and sociolinguistic understanding. Six- to seven-year-olds have learned from earlier miscommunications about the importance of generating more informative messages. This is also the age at which they are becoming notably less egocentric and acquiring some role-taking skills, two *cognitive developments* that help them to adapt their speech to the needs of their listeners in such highly demanding situations as talking on the phone (or participating in a referential communication experiment), where it may be difficult to tell whether one's message has been interpreted correctly (Hoff-Ginsberg, 1997). Furthermore, *sociolinguistic understanding* is required to make the right kinds of speech adjustments, for messages that are clear for one listener may not be for others. For example, a listener who is unfamiliar with the stimuli in a referential communication task may require more differentiating information and more message redundancy than a second person who is already familiar with these objects. Six- to ten-year-olds do provide longer mes-

Table 10.7 **Typical Idiosyncratic Descriptions Offered by Preschool Children When Talking about Unfamiliar Graphic Designs in the Krauss and Glucksberg Communication Game**

Form	Child 1	Child 2	Child 3	Child 4	Child 5
	Man's legs	Airplane	Drapeholder	Zebra	Flying saucer
	Mother's hat	Ring	Keyhold	Lion	Snake
	Daddy's shirt	Milk jug	Shoe hold	Coffeepot	Dog

Source: Adapted from Krauss & Glucksberg, 1977.

sages to unfamiliar than to familiar listeners. Yet, only the 9- and 10-year-olds among them adjusted the *content* of their communications to the listeners' needs by providing richer *differentiating* information to an unfamiliar listener (Sonnenschein, 1986, 1988).

What Role Do Siblings Play in the Growth of Communication Skills?

Most studies of social influences on language development have focused on mother–child pairs (usually mothers and their *first-born* children). Yet, children with siblings spend a fair amount of time conversing with them or listening as a sibling converses with a parent (Barton & Tomasello, 1991). Might conversations involving siblings contribute in any meaningful way to the growth of communication skills?

Indeed, it appears that interactions among linguistically immature siblings may actually *promote* effective communication. Consider, for example, that because older children are less likely than parents to adjust their speech to a younger sibling's ability to understand (Tomasello, Conti-Ramsden, & Ewert, 1990), the comprehension errors that a younger sibling displays may make older brothers and sisters more aware of listeners' needs and more inclined to monitor and repair their own ambiguous messages. And because older siblings are also less likely than parents are to correctly *interpret* a younger sibling's uninformative messages and grant her wishes, the younger sibling may learn from her failures to communicate and be prompted to speak in ways that are more widely understood (Perez-Granados & Callanan, 1997). So if children truly learn from breakdowns in communication, then opportunities to converse with relatively immature linguistic partners (siblings and peers) would seem to provide fertile ground for the growth of communication skills.

In sum, the rapid pace at which cognitively immature children master the fundamentals of language and communication is truly awe-inspiring. Table 10.8, on page 386, briefly summarizes the ground we have covered in tracing the evolution of young human beings from preverbal creatures, who are prepared for language learning and motivated to share meaning with their companions, to highly articulate adolescents, who can generate and comprehend an infinite number of messages.

BILINGUALISM: CHALLENGES AND CONSEQUENCES OF LEARNING TWO LANGUAGES

Most American children speak only English. However, many children around the world grow up bilingual, acquiring two (or more) languages by the time they reach puberty.

Concept Check 10.3
Language Development from Toddlerhood to Adolescence

Check your understanding of *selected aspects* of language development from the preschool period through early adolescence by matching each statement below with one of the following terms/concepts: (a) referential communication skills, (b) overregularization, (c) metalinguistic awareness, (d) transformational grammar, (e) phonological awareness, (f) morphological knowledge, (g) grammatical morphemes. Answers appear in the Appendix at the back of the book.

_____ 1. rules enabling children to produce variations of declarative sentences
_____ 2. enables children to reflect on language and its properties
_____ 3. enables children to expand their receptive vocabularies at a dramatic rate
_____ 4. helps speakers tailor messages to listeners' needs and characteristics
_____ 5. modifiers that give more precise meaning to sentences
_____ 6. grammatical "error" that reflects new linguistic understandings
_____ 7. especially good predictor of preschool children's future reading achievement

Table 10.8 Important Milestones in Language Development

Age (years)	Phonology	Semantics	Grammar/syntax	Pragmatics	Metalinguistic awareness
0–1	Receptivity to speech and discrimination of speech sounds Babbling begins to resemble the sounds of native language	Some interpretation of intonational cues in others' speech Preverbal gestures appear Vocables appear Little if any understanding of individual words	Preference for phrase structure and stress patterns of native language	Joint attention with caregiver to objects and events Turn-taking in games and vocalizations Appearance of preverbal gestures	None
1–2	Appearance of strategies to simplify word pronunciations	First words appear Rapid expansion of vocabulary after age 18 months Overextensions and underextensions of word meanings	Holophrases give way to 2-word telegraphic speech Sentences express distinct semantic relations Acquisition of some grammatical morphemes	Use of gestures and intonational cues to clarify messages Richer understanding of vocal turn-taking rules First signs of etiquette in children's speech	None
3–5	Pronunciations improve	Vocabulary expands Understanding of spatial relations and use of spatial words in speech	Grammatical morphemes added in regular sequence Awareness of most rules of transformational grammar	Beginning understanding of illocutionary intent Some adjustment of speech to different audiences Some attempts at clarifying obviously ambiguous messages	Some phonemic and grammatical awareness
6–adolescence	Pronunciations become adultlike	Acquisition of morphological knowledge Dramatic expansion of vocabulary, including abstract words during adolescence Appearance and refinement of semantic integrations	Correction of earlier grammatical errors Acquisition of complex syntactical rules	Referential communication improves, especially the ability to detect and repair uninformative messages one sends and receives	Metalinguistic awareness blossoms and becomes more extensive with age

In fact, some 6½ *million* American schoolchildren speak a language other than English at home (U.S. Bureau of the Census, 1997), and many of them display at least some limitations in their use of the English language.

Does learning two languages rather than one hinder a child's language proficiency or slow her intellectual development? Before 1960, many researchers claimed that it did, pointing to several demonstrations that bilingual children score significantly lower than their monolingual peers on tests of linguistic knowledge and general intelligence (Hakuta, 1988). Yet, these early studies were seriously flawed. The bilinguals were often first- or second-generation immigrants from lower socioeconomic backgrounds who were not very proficient in English. Furthermore, the tests they took were administered in English (rather than in their language of greatest proficiency), and their performances were compared with samples largely comprised of middle-class, English-speaking monolinguals (Diaz, 1983). No wonder the bilinguals performed so poorly! Unfortunately, these findings were often taken at face value by educators and lawmakers, who have used them as justification for prohibiting the teaching of foreign languages until after age 10, so as not to " . . . distract from [students'] ability to assimilate their normal studies in the English language and . . . cause serious emotional disturbances . . ." (Kendler, as cited in Hakuta, 1988, p. 303).

Spurred on in part by the nativist contention that young children should easily acquire any language that they hear regularly, psycholinguists in the 1960s began to look more carefully at the process of becoming bilingual. Their findings were clear. Children exposed early (before age 3) to two languages had little difficulty becoming proficient in both. Bilingual toddlers occasionally mixed phonologies and applied the grammar and vocabulary of one language to the second tongue they were acquiring. But by age 3, they were well aware that the two languages were independent systems and that each was associated with particular contexts in which it was to be spoken (Lanza, 1992; Reich, 1986). By age 4, they displayed normal language proficiency in the language of their community and solid to excellent linguistic skills in the second language, depending on how much they had been exposed to it. Even when preschool children acquired a second language *sequentially* (that is, after age 3, when they were already conversant in their native tongue), it often took no more than a year to achieve near-native abilities in that language (Reich, 1986).

What about the cognitive consequences of bilingualism? Recent well-controlled studies that have matched bilinguals and monolinguals on important variables such as socioeconomic status consistently find that there are cognitive *advantages* to bilingualism. Not only do bilingual children score as high or higher than monolingual peers on tests of language proficiency, concept formation, and nonverbal intelligence (see, for example, Diaz, 1985), but they also outperform monolinguals on measures of metalinguistic awareness (Bialystok, 1988)—particularly those that call for them to recognize the correspondence between letters, words, and their phonological components (Bialystok, 1997), or to detect grammatical errors in speech and written prose (Campbell & Sais, 1995; Galambos & Goldin-Meadow, 1990). The metalinguistic advantages that bilinguals display may arise from the many experiences they have had translating messages back and forth across two linguistic systems, an activity that young bilinguals often treat as a game and perform for the fun of it (Reich, 1986).

Despite these positive findings and increased federal support for bilingual education in the United States, public opinion in this country does not support this policy. In fact, 18 states have even passed laws making English the official language, providing a strong incentive for instructing nonnative English speakers only in English. This may be unfortunate for at least two reasons. First, a total immersion in English-speaking classrooms causes students whose English is poor to lose some proficiency in their native language, thus placing them at risk of becoming *semilingual*—that is, less than fully competent, or literate, in either language. Second, and even more important, there appear to be clear benefits to **two-way bilingual education**—programs in which

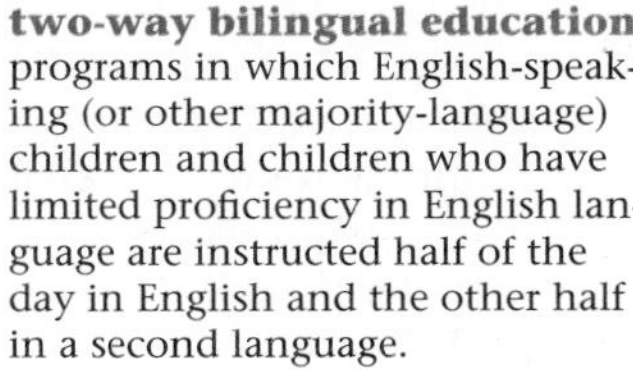
two-way bilingual education programs in which English-speaking (or other majority-language) children and children who have limited proficiency in English language are instructed half of the day in English and the other half in a second language.

Contrary to popular belief, learning two (or more) languages rather than one neither hinders a child's language proficiencies nor retards her intellectual growth. Indeed, recent research suggests that there are cognitive advantages to bilingualism.

native English speakers and limited-English-proficient (LEP) minority students are taught half of the day in English and half in a second language. Not only has two-way bilingualism been found to foster the academic achievement of LEP students, but the English-speaking students (1) perform just as well academically (or slightly better) than other comparable native English speakers who receive English-only instruction and (2) often achieve near-native proficiency in the second language as well (Sleek, 1994). Furthermore, both English-speaking and minority-language students in two-way bilingual programs are more optimistic about their academic and personal competencies than their counterparts who receive English-only instruction (Sleek, 1994).

It is rather ironic that an American educational system that so often tries to convert its LEP bilinguals into English-speaking monolinguals also deplores American citizens' lack of competence in foreign languages. How might we resolve this paradox? Although highly controversial (see Delcampo & Delcampo, 1998), one solution might be to provide all children with two-way bilingual education. Such an approach may not only promote broader linguistic proficiency and better academic performance, but may also foster a greater appreciation of ethnic diversity and address our increasing societal need for a bilingually competent workforce (Hakuta & Garcia, 1989; Sleek, 1994).

? **WHAT DO YOU THINK?**

What would your reaction be if the federal government mandated two-way bilingual education for all elementary school children by the year 2004? How could this order be implemented, given that most elementary-school teachers are monolingual and some classrooms have LEP students from a variety of linguistic backgrounds (for example, Spanish, Hmong, Vietnamese, etc.)?

SUMMARY

Four Components of Language

◆ The four aspects of **language** that children must acquire to **communicate** effectively in their native tongue are **phonology,** a knowledge of the language's sound system; **semantics,** an understanding of the meaning of **morphemes,** words, and sentences; **syntax,** the rules that specify how words are combined to produce sentences; and **pragmatics,** the principles governing how language is to be used in different social situations.

Theories of Language Development

◆ There are three major theoretical perspectives on language acquisition. Learning theorists propose that children acquire language as they imitate others' speech and are reinforced for grammatically correct utterances. However, research provides very little support for the notions that parents shape grammatical speech or that children acquire language by mimicking the sentences they hear. Adults speak in **motherese** to young children, as well as reshaping their primitive sentences with **expansions** and **recasts;** but as long as children have partners with whom to converse, they will acquire language, even without these environmental supports.

◆ Nativists believe that human beings are innately endowed with linguistic processing capabilities (that is, a **language acquisition device** or **language-making capacity**) that function most efficiently prior to puberty. Presumably, children require nothing other than being exposed to speech in order to learn any and all languages. The identification of **linguistic universals** is consistent with the nativist viewpoint, as are the observations that language functions are served by **Broca's** and **Wernicke's areas** of the brain, and that deaf children of hearing parents and other children exposed to ungrammatical pidgins may create languages of their own. Furthermore, both first- and second-language learning seem to proceed more smoothly during the **"sensitive period"** prior to puberty. Yet many of these findings have been challenged; and unfortunately, nativists are not very clear about how children sift through verbal input and make the crucial discoveries that further their linguistic competencies.

◆ Proponents of the **interactionist perspective** acknowledge that children are biologically prepared to acquire language. However, they suggest that what may be innate is not any specialized linguistic processor but, rather, a nervous system that gradually matures and predisposes children to develop similar ideas at about the same age, which they are motivated to share with their companions. Thus, biological maturation is said to affect cognitive development, which, in turn, influences language development. However, interactionists stress that the environment plays a crucial role in language learning, for companions continually introduce new linguistic rules and concepts in engaging conversations that children can easily comprehend.

Before Language: The Prelinguistic Period

◆ Infants are well-prepared for language learning. During the **prelinguistic phase** they easily discriminate speechlike sounds and are sensitive to a wider variety of phonemes than adults are. They are sensitive to intonational cues from the beginning and, by 7 to 10 months of age, are already segmenting others' speech with phrases and wordlike units.

♦ Infants begin **cooing** by age 2 months and start to **babble** by age 4 to 6 months. Later in the first year, infants match the intonation of their babbles to the tonal qualities of the language they hear and may produce their own **vocables** to signify meaning.

♦ Although infants less than 1 year old understand the meaning of few, if any, individual words, they have already learned that people take turns while vocalizing and that gestures can be used to communicate and share meaning with companions. Once infants begin to understand individual words, their **receptive language** is ahead of their **productive language.**

One Word at a Time: The Holophrastic Period

♦ During the one-word, or **holophrastic, period,** infants speak in **holophrases** and spend several months expanding their vocabularies one word at a time. They talk mostly about moving or manipulable objects that interest them and show a vocabulary spurt, or **naming explosion,** between 18 and 24 months of age. Most children in Western cultures develop a **referential style** of language; however, a smaller number of Western infants and a larger number from cultures emphasizing social harmony adopt an **expressive style** of language.

♦ Toddlers are quite adept at using social and contextual cues to **fast map** words onto objects, actions, and attributes. Other strategies, or **processing constraints,** that help them to figure out what new words mean include the **object scope constraint, mutual exclusivity, lexical context,** and **syntactic bootstrapping.** Nevertheless, toddlers frequently make such semantic errors as **overextensions** and **underextensions.**

♦ Many psycholinguists call a toddler's one-word utterances *holophrases* because they often seem less like labels and more like attempts to communicate an entire sentence's worth of meaning.

From Holophrases to Simple Sentences: The Telegraphic Period

♦ At 18 to 24 months of age, toddlers begin to produce two- and three-word sentences known as **telegraphic speech** because they omit grammatical markers and smaller, less important words. Although telegraphic sentences are not grammatical by adult standards, they are far more than random word combinations. Not only do children follow certain rules of word order when combining words, but they also express the same categories of meaning (semantic relations) in their earliest sentences.

♦ Telegraphic toddlers are also becoming highly sensitive to pragmatic constraints, including the realization that speakers must be more directive and elaborate when a listener doesn't share their knowledge. Young children are also learning certain sociolinguistic prescriptions such as the need to be polite when making requests.

Language Learning during the Preschool Period

♦ During the preschool period (ages 2½ to 5), the child's language becomes much more similar to an adult's. As children produce longer utterances, they begin to add **grammatical morphemes** such as the *-s* for plurality, the *-ed* for past tense, the *-ing* for present progressive, articles, prepositions, and auxiliary verbs. Although individual children acquire grammatical markers at different rates and occasionally **overregularize** them, there is a striking uniformity in the order in which these morphemes appear. The preschool period is also the time when a child learns rules of **transformational grammar** that will enable him or her to change declarative statements into questions, negations, imperatives, relative clauses, and compound sentences. By the time they enter school, children have mastered most of the syntactical rules of their native language and can produce a wide variety of sophisticated, adultlike messages.

♦ Another reason that language becomes increasingly complex during the preschool years is that youngsters are beginning to appreciate and use semantic and relational contrasts such as big/little, wide/narrow, more/less, and before/after.

♦ Preschool children are beginning to understand such pragmatic lessons as the need to tailor their messages to a listener's ability to comprehend if they hope to be understood. Children's **referential communication skills** are not well developed, although they have begun to detect at least some of the uninformative messages they receive and to ask for clarification.

Language Learning during Middle Childhood and Adolescence

♦ Middle childhood and early adolescence is a period of linguistic refinement. Children learn subtle exceptions to grammatical rules and begin to understand even the most complex syntactical structures of their native language. Vocabulary grows rapidly, as children acquire **morphological knowledge,** as well as **metalinguistic awareness**—an ability to think about language and to comment on its properties, which is a good predictor of reading achievement. School-age children also display much better referential communication skills as they attend more carefully to literal meanings of ambiguous utterances and are more likely to clarify the uninformative messages they send and receive. Cognitive development, the growth of sociolinguistic knowledge, and opportunities to communicate with linguistically immature siblings and peers all contribute to the development of communication skills.

Bilingualism: Challenges and Consequences of Learning Two Languages

♦ Bilingualism is becoming increasingly common in the United States, and children exposed early and regularly to two languages can easily acquire them both. There are cognitive advantages to bilingualism, and recent **two-way bilingual education** programs appear to promote the language skills and the self-perceived academic and social competencies of both majority-language and minority-language students.

Babies go from prelinguistic coos and babbles to speaking single words by their first birthday and telegraphic sentences before their second birthday. By visiting: **http://www.kidsears.com/milestones/milestone_intro.htm** you can trace the major milestones in infant language development. For each of the age ranges listed at this site you can access an online video of children as they master the fundamentals of speech.

KEY TERMS

language, 352
communication, 352
psycholinguists, 352
phonology, 352
phonemes, 352
semantics, 353
morphemes, 353
syntax, 353
pragmatics, 353
sociolinguistic knowledge, 354
linguistic universal, 354
language acquisition device (LAD), 356
language-making capacity (LMC), 356
Broca's area, 356
Wernicke's area, 357
sensitive-period hypothesis, 357
interactionist theory, 360
motherese, 361
expansions, 362
recasts, 362
prelinguistic phase, 364
coos, 365
babbles, 365
vocables, 365
receptive language, 367
productive language, 367
holophrastic period, 367
holophrase, 367
naming explosion, 368
referential style, 368
expressive style, 369
fast mapping, 369
overextension, 369
underextension, 369
processing constraints, 370
object scope constraint, 371
mutual exclusivity constraint, 371
lexical contrast constraint, 371
syntactical bootstrapping, 371
telegraphic speech, 373
grammatical morphemes, 377
overregularization, 378
transformational grammar, 378
referential communication skills, 381
morphological knowledge, 382
metalinguistic awareness, 383
two-way bilingual education, 388

Emotional Development and the Establishment of Intimate Relationships

Two 18-month-olds, Terry and Toni, are playing in Terry's living room when a delivery truck enters the driveway and backfires loudly. Terry, obviously startled and fearful, whimpers, stands, and moves nearer his mother on the sofa. Toni is more curious. She looks wide-eyed at her mother, who smiles and exclaims "That truck went boom!" Toni then runs to the window and gazes out at the two delivery men, who are now unloading the washer and dryer that Terry's mother has ordered.

Clearly, these toddlers had very different emotional reactions to the startling event they had experienced. Terry, noticeably upset, sought comfort from his mother, whereas Toni, more intrigued than scared, first looked to her mother for clarification before exploring the situation for herself. Why might these two children have reacted so differently to the same novel experience?

In this chapter, we will address this issue by turning to the literature on children's emotions and the development of emotional ties to parents and other close companions. We begin by charting age-related changes in children's displays and interpretations of emotions, and by considering some of the roles that emotions play in early social and personality development. We will then look at individual differences in emotional reactivity, or *temperament,* and see that the early temperamental attributes that so often explain why young children react differently to everyday events are now considered by many developmentalists to be important building blocks of adult personalities. We will then turn to emotional *attachments* and explore the processes by which infants and their closest companions establish these intimate affectional ties. Finally, we will review a rapidly expanding base of evidence suggesting that the kind of emotional attachments that infants are able to establish can have important implications for their later social, emotional, and intellectual development.

AN OVERVIEW OF EMOTIONAL DEVELOPMENT

Do babies have feelings? Do they experience and display specific emotions such as happiness, sadness, fear, and anger the way older children and adults do? Most parents think so. In one study, more than half the mothers of 1-month-old infants said that their babies displayed at least five distinct emotional expressions: interest, surprise, joy, anger, and fear (Johnson et al., 1982). Although one might argue that this is simply a case of proud mothers reading much too much into the behavior of their babies, there is now reliable evidence that even very young infants are emotional creatures.

Displaying Emotions: The Development (and Control) of Emotional Expressions

Carroll Izard and his colleagues at the University of Delaware have studied infants' emotional expressions by videotaping babies' responses to such events as grasping an ice cube, having a toy taken away, or seeing their mothers return after a separation (Izard, 1982; 1993). Izard's procedure is to ask raters, who are unaware of the events that an infant has experienced, to tell him what emotion the infant is experiencing from the facial expression the infant displays. These studies reveal that different adult raters observing the same expressions reliably see the same emotion in a baby's face (see Figure 11.1). Other investigators find that adults can usually tell what *positive* emotion a baby is experiencing (for example, interest versus joy) from facial expressions, but that negative emotions (fear versus anger, for example) are much more difficult to discriminate on the basis of facial cues alone (Izard et al., 1995; Matias & Cohn, 1993). Nev-

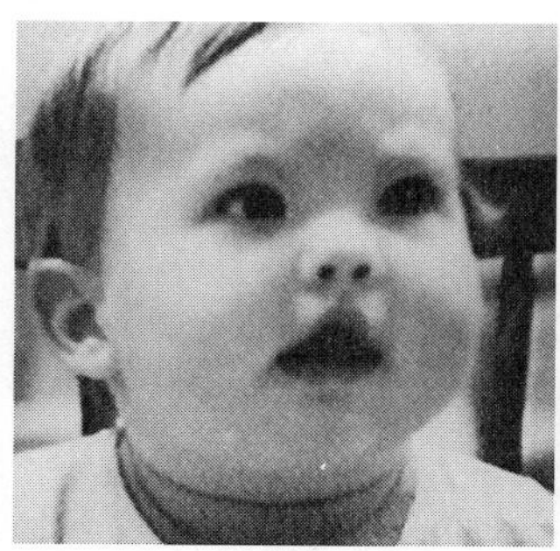

Interest: brows raised; mouth may be rounded; lips may be pursed.

Fear: mouth retraced; brows level and drawn up and in; eyelids lifted.

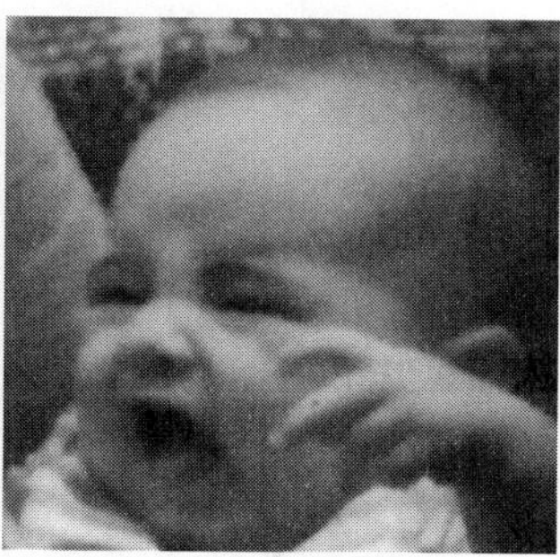

Disgust: tongue protruding; upper lip raised; nose wrinkled.

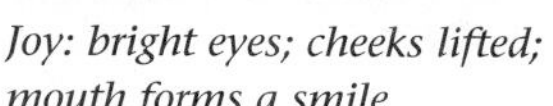

Joy: bright eyes; cheeks lifted; mouth forms a smile.

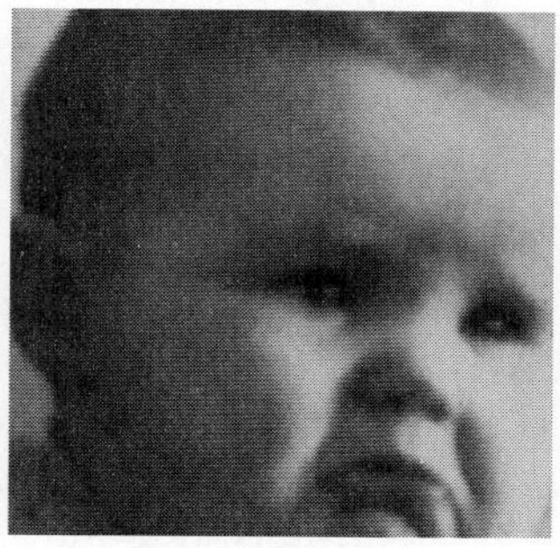

Sadness: corners of mouth turned down; inner portion of brows raised.

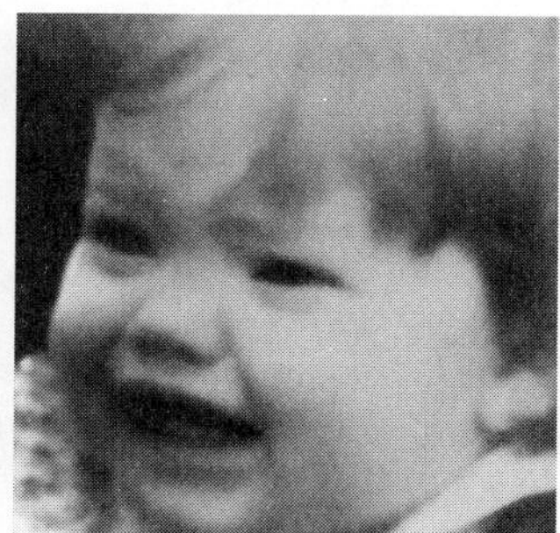

Anger: mouth squared at corners; brows drawn together and pointing down; eyes fixed straight ahead.

Figure 11.1 *Young infants display a variety of emotional expressions.*

ertheless, most researchers agree that babies communicate a variety of feelings through their facial expressions, and that each expression becomes a more recognizable sign of a particular emotion with age (Camras et al., 1992; Izard et al., 1995).

Sequencing of Discrete Emotions

Various emotions appear at different times over the first two years. At birth, babies show interest, distress, disgust, and contentment (as indicated by a rudimentary smile). Other **primary (or basic) emotions** that emerge between 2½ and 7 months of age are anger, sadness, joy, surprise, and fear (Izard et al., 1995). These so-called primary emotions seem to be biologically programmed, for they emerge in all normal infants at roughly the same ages and are displayed and interpreted similarly in all cultures (Camras et al., 1992; Izard, 1982; 1993; Malatesta et al., 1989). Yet some learning (or cognitive development) may be necessary before babies express any emotion not present at birth. Indeed, one of the strongest elicitors of surprise and joy among 2- to 8-month olds is their discovery that they can exert some control over objects and events. And disconfirmation of these *learned* expectancies (as when someone or something prevents them from exerting control) is likely to *anger* many 2- to 4-month-olds and may *sadden* 4- to 6-month-olds as well (Lewis, Alessandri, & Sullivan, 1990; Sullivan, Lewis, & Alesandri, 1992).

Later in the second year, infants begin to display such **secondary (or complex emotions** as embarrassment, shame, guilt, envy, and pride. These feelings are sometimes called *self-conscious emotions* because each involves some damage to or enhancement of our sense of self. Michael Lewis and his associates (1989) believe that embarrassment, the simplest self-conscious emotion, does not emerge until the child can recognize herself in a mirror or a photograph (a self-referential milestone that we will discuss in detail in Chapter 12), whereas *self-evaluative* emotions such as shame, guilt, and pride may require both self-recognition *and* an understanding of rules or standards for evaluating one's conduct.

primary (or basic) emotions
the set of emotions present at birth or emerging early in the first year that some theorists believe to be biologically programmed.

secondary (or complex) emotions
self-conscious or self-evaluative emotions that emerge in the second year and depend, in part, on cognitive development.

Most of the available evidence is consistent with Lewis's theory. For example, the only toddlers who become noticeably embarrassed by lavish praise or by requests to "show off" for strangers are those who display self-recognition (Lewis et al., 1989). By about age 3, when children are better able to evaluate their performances as good or bad, they begin to show clear signs of *pride* (smiling, applauding, or shouting "I did it") when they succeed at a difficult task, as well as *shame* (a downward gaze with a slumped posture, often accompanied by statements such as "I'm no good at this") should they fail at an easy task (Lewis, Alessandri, & Sullivan, 1992; Stipek, Recchia, & McClintic, 1992).

Of course, parents can clearly influence a child's experience and expression of self-evaluative emotions. In one recent study (Alessandri & Lewis, 1996), mothers' reactions were observed as their 4- to 5-year-olds succeeded or failed at a variety of puzzles. As expected, children generally showed some signs of pride over their successes and shame over their failures. Yet, the amounts of pride and shame they displayed largely depended on their mothers' reactions to these outcomes. Mothers who accentuated the negative by being especially critical of failures tended to have children who displayed high levels of shame after a failure and little pride after successes. By contrast, mothers who were more inclined to react positively to successes had children who displayed more pride in their accomplishments and less shame on those occasions when they failed to achieve their objectives.

Interestingly, toddlers and young preschool children are likely to display self-evaluative emotions only when an adult is present to observe their conduct (Harter & Whitesell, 1989; Stipek et al., 1992). So it seems that young children's self-evaluative emotions may stem largely from the reactions they anticipate receiving from adult evaluators. In fact, it may be well into the elementary school period before children fully internalize many rules or evaluative standards and come to feel especially prideful, shameful, or guilty about their conduct in the absence of external surveillance (Bussey, 1992; Harter & Whitesell, 1989).

Socialization of Emotions and Emotional Self-regulation

Each society has a set of **emotional display rules** that specify the circumstances under which various emotions should or should not be expressed (Gross & Ballif, 1991; Harris, 1989). Children in the United States, for example, learn that they are supposed to express happiness or gratitude when they receive a gift from grandma and, by all means, to suppress any disappointment they may feel should the gift turn out to be underwear. In some ways, these emotional codes of conduct are similar to the pragmatic rules of language: Children must acquire and use them in order to get along with other people and to maintain their approval. When does this learning begin?

Earlier than you might imagine! Consider that when mothers play with 7-month-old infants, they restrict themselves mainly to displays of joy, interest, and surprise, thus serving as models of positive emotions for their babies (Malatesta & Haviland, 1982). Mothers also respond selectively to their infants' emotions; over the first several months, they become increasingly attentive to babies' expressions of interest or surprise and less responsive to the infants' negative emotions (Malatesta et al., 1986). Through basic learning processes, then, babies are trained to display more pleasant faces and fewer unpleasant ones, and they do just that over time.

However, the emotions that are considered socially acceptable may be quite different in one culture than in another. American parents love to stimulate their babies until they reach peaks of delight. By contrast, Gusii mothers in Kenya hardly ever take part in face-to-face play with their babies, seeking instead to keep young infants as calm and contented as possible (LeVine et al., 1994). So American babies learn that intense emotion is okay as long as it is positive, whereas Gusii babies learn to restrain both positive and negative emotions.

emotional display rules
culturally defined rules specifying which emotions should or should not be expressed under which circumstances.

emotional self-regulation
strategies for managing emotions or adjusting emotional arousal to a comfortable level of intensity.

Regulating Emotions. To comply with these emotional lessons, however, babies must devise strategies for **regulating** and controlling their emotions. This is a difficult task for very young infants, who manage to reduce at least some of their negative arousal by turning their bodies away from unpleasant stimuli or by sucking vigorously on objects (Mangelsdorf, Shapiro, & Marzolf, 1995). Nevertheless, young infants must often depend on caregivers to soothe them when they are experiencing strong emotional distress (Cole, Michel, & Teti, 1994). By the end of the first year, infants develop other strategies for reducing negative arousal such as rocking themselves, chewing on objects, and moving away from people or events that upset them (Kopp, 1989; Mangelsdorf et al., 1995). And by age 18 to 24 months, toddlers are more likely to try to control the actions of people or objects (for example, mechanical toys) that upset them (Mangelsdorf et al., 1995), and they begin to cope with frustrations of having to wait for snacks or gifts by talking to companions, playing with toys, or otherwise distracting themselves from the source of their disappointments (Grolnick, Bridges, & Connell, 1996). In fact, toddlers this young have even been observed to knit their brows or to compress their lips as they actively attempt to suppress their anger or sadness (Malatesta et al., 1989).

As young preschool children become more talkative and begin to discuss their feelings, parents and other close companions often help them to deal constructively with negative emotions by distracting them from the most distressing aspects of unpleasant situations (for example, telling a child who is about to receive an inoculation to look at a brightly colored poster on the wall) or by otherwise helping them to understand frightening, frustrating, or disappointing experiences (Thompson, 1994; 1997). These supportive interventions are a form of guided instruction of the kind that Vygotsky wrote about—experiences that should help preschoolers to devise effective strategies for regulating their own emotions. Indeed, 2- to 6-year-olds do become better and better at coping with unpleasant emotional arousal by directing their attention away from frightening events ("I scared of the shark. Close my eyes."), by thinking pleasant thoughts to overcome unpleasant ones ("Mommy left me but when she comes back, we are going to the movies.") and by reinterpreting the cause of their distress in a more satisfying way ("He [story character] didn't *really* die . . . it's just pretend.") (Thompson, 1994). Unfortunately, youngsters who experience a good deal of negative emotionality and do not learn how to regulate it are likely to alienate both adults and peers when they act out their anger or frustrations (Eisenberg et al., 1995; 1997).

Interestingly, adaptive regulation of emotions may sometimes involve *maintaining* or *intensifying* one's feelings rather than suppressing them. For example, children may learn that *conveying* their anger helps them to stand up to a bully (Thompson, 1994). And as we will see in Chapter 14, parents often call attention to (and thereby seek to maintain) the uneasiness that young children experience after causing another person distress or breaking a rule. Why? Because they hope to persuade youngsters to *reinterpret* these feelings in ways that cause them to (1) *sympathize* with victims of distress and act on this concern, or (2) feel *guilty* about their transgressions and become less inclined to repeat them (Dunn, Brown, & Maguire, 1995; Kochanska, 1991). Another form of emotional arousal that parents may seek to maintain or enhance in children is *pride* in their accomplishments, an important contributor to a healthy sense of achievement motivation and to the development of a positive academic self-concept (see Chapter 12 for further discussion of this point). So effective regulation of emotions involves an ability to suppress, maintain, or even intensify our emotional arousal in order to remain productively engaged with the challenges we face or the people we encounter (Thompson, 1994).

Acquiring Emotional Display Rules. An ability to regulate emotions is only the first skill that children must acquire in order to comply with a culture's emotional display rules. Indeed, these prescriptions often dictate that we not only suppress whatever "unacceptable" emotions that we are actually experiencing, but also *replace* them (outwardly, at least) with whatever feeling that the display rule calls for in that situation (for example, acting happy rather than sad upon receiving a disappointing gift).

By about age 3, children are beginning to show some limited ability to hide their true feelings. Michael Lewis and his associates (Lewis, Stanger, & Sullivan, 1989), for example, found that 3-year-olds who had lied about peeking at a forbidden toy showed subtle signs of anguish (detectable on film played in slow motion); however, they were

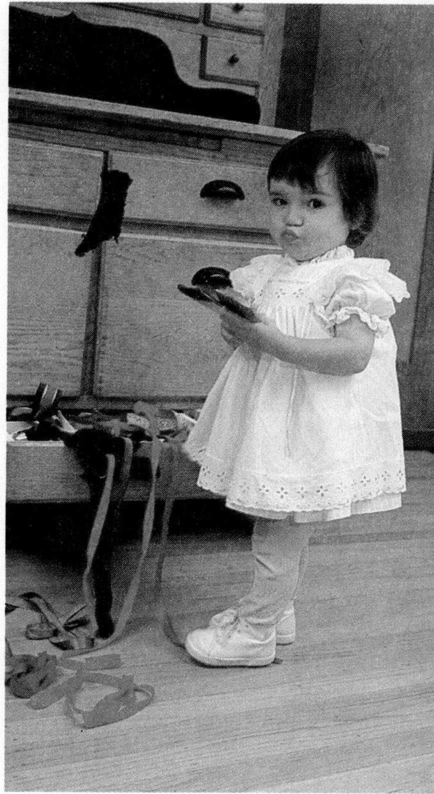

Toddlers and preschool children are not very skilled at masking their true feelings.

able to mask their feelings well enough to make it impossible for uninformed adult judges to discriminate them from other children who truthfully reported that they hadn't peeked. With each passing year, preschool children become a little better at posing outward expressions that differ from their inner feelings (Peskin, 1992; Ruffman et al., 1993). Still, preschoolers are not especially skilled at disguising their true emotions; they typically wear their feelings on their face and express them freely.

Throughout the grade-school years, children become increasingly aware of socially sanctioned display rules, learning more about which emotions to express (and which to suppress) in particular social situations (Zeman & Shipman, 1997). Perhaps because parents place stronger pressures on girls to "act nice" in social situations, girls are both more motivated and more skilled at complying with display rules than boys are (Davis, 1995). Furthermore, mothers who emphasize positive emotions in their parent–child interactions tend to have children who are better able to mask disappointment and other negative feelings (Garner & Power, 1996). Yet even simple display rules take some time to fully master. As we see in Figure 11.2, many 7- to 9-year-olds (especially boys) are still unable to act thrilled and to totally mask their disappointment upon receiving an undesirable gift. And even many 12- to 13-year-olds fail to suppress all their anger when a respected adult exercises authority and thwarts their plans (Underwood, Coie, & Herbsman, 1992).

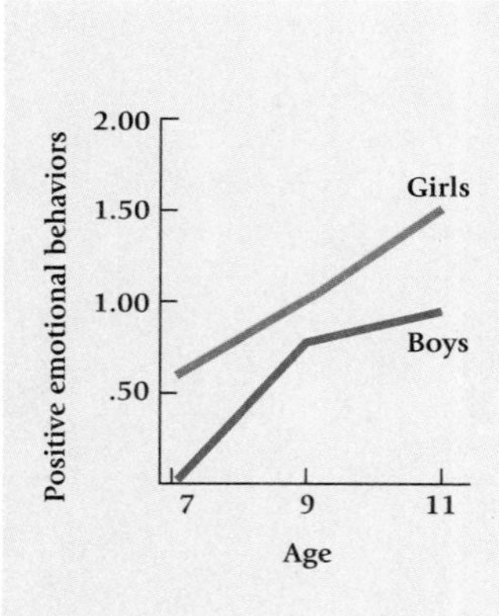

Figure 11.2 *With age, children are better able to display positive emotional reactions after receiving a disappointing gift.* ADAPTED FROM SAARNI, *1984.*

Compliance with culturally specified rules for displaying emotions occurs earlier and is especially strong in communal societies like Japan that stress social harmony and place the needs of the social order over those of the individual (Matsumoto, 1990). Clearly, this socialization of emotions works for the good of society. Even in an individualistic culture like the United States, children's increasing compliance with emotional display rules is largely motivated by a desire to maintain social harmony and to avoid the disapproval of both adults and peers (Saarni, 1990; Zeman & Garber, 1996).

Recognizing and Interpreting Emotions

Currently, there is some debate about when babies begin to recognize and interpret the emotional expressions that others display. As we learned in Chapter 6, 3-month-olds can discriminate different emotions posed by adults in photos; however, these demonstrations may simply reflect their powers of visual discrimination and do not necessarily imply that infants this young *interpret* various expressions as happy, angry, or sad (Ludemann, 1991; Nelson, 1987).

Social Referencing

Infants' ability to interpret emotional expressions becomes rather obvious between 8 and 10 months of age, the point at which they begin to monitor parents' emotional reactions to uncertain situations and to use this information to regulate their own behavior (Feinman, 1992). This **social referencing** becomes more common with age (Walden & Baxter, 1989) and soon extends to people other than parents. By the end of the first year, for example, infants typically approach and play with unfamiliar toys if a nearby stranger is smiling, but are apt to avoid these objects if the stranger displays a fearful expression (Klinnert et al., 1986). An adult's *vocal* expressions of emotion seem to convey as much or more information for a 12-month-old infant as an adult's facial expressions do (Mumme, Fernald, & Herrera, 1996), and some investigators have wondered whether these emotional signals might not best be interpreted as commands (for example, "don't touch") rather than as active information-seeking on the infant's part (Baldwin & Moses, 1996). But during the second year, toddlers often look to their companions *after* they have appraised a new object or situation, thereby suggesting that they are now using other's emotional reactions as information to assess the accuracy of their *own* judgments (Hornik & Gunnar, 1988).

social referencing
the use of others' emotional expressions to infer the meaning of otherwise ambiguous situations.

Conversations that focus on the emotional experiences that family members have had promote emotional understanding, empathy, and social competencies in young children.

Conversations about Emotions

Once toddlers begin to talk about emotions at 18 to 24 months of age, family conversations that center on emotional experiences can help them achieve a much richer understanding of their own and others' feelings. In fact, Judy Dunn and her associates (1991; Herrera & Dunn, 1997) found that the more often 3-year-olds had discussed emotional experiences with other family members, the better they were at interpreting others' emotions and at settling disputes with friends 3 years later in grade school (see also Denham, Zoller, & Couchoud, 1994; Oppenheim et al., 1997). Of course, the ability to identify how others are feeling and to understand why they feel that way is a central aspect of social cognition that may have important social consequences. We will see in Chapter 14, for example, that understanding the *causes* of others' emotions is an important contributor to **empathy,** which often motivates children to comfort or otherwise assist distressed companions. In fact, these "prosocial" inclinations may largely explain why children who score high on tests of emotional understanding tend to be rated high in social competence by teachers and enjoy especially good relations with their peers (Cassidy et al., 1992; Garner, Jones, & Miner, 1994; Oppenheim et al., 1997).

Later Milestones in Emotional Understanding. The ability to recognize and interpret others' emotional displays steadily improves throughout childhood. By age 4 to 5, children can offer explanations for why playmates are happy, angry, or sad, although they tend to focus more on *external* events as causes of emotions than on internal needs, desires, moods, or motives (Fabes et al., 1991). As grade-school children gradually begin to rely more on both internal and external information to interpret emotions, they achieve several important breakthroughs in emotional understanding. For example, they eventually recognize at about age 8 that many situations (for example, the approach of a big dog) elicit different emotional reactions (for example, fear versus joy) from different individuals (Gnepp & Klayman, 1992). Furthermore, 6- to 9-year-olds also begin to understand that a person can experience more than one emotion (for example, excitement and wariness) at the same time (Arsenio & Kramer, 1992; Brown & Dunn, 1996), and they display some ability to integrate contrasting facial, behavioral, and situational cues to infer what those emotions might be (Hoffner & Badzinski, 1989; see also Friend & Davis, 1993).

Notice that these latter advances in emotional understanding emerge at about the same age that children can integrate more than one piece of information (for example, height and width of a column of liquid) in Piagetian conservation tasks, and they may depend, in part, on the same underlying cognitive developments. However, social experiences are also important. Jane Brown and Judy Dunn (1996), for example, found that 6-year-olds who show an early understanding of conflicting emotions had often

empathy
the ability to understand and to experience the emotions that others display.

discussed the *causes* of emotions with their parents earlier in childhood. Apparently, these discussions prepared them to analyze mixed feelings that may have arisen from squabbles with siblings and peers.

Emotions and Early Social Development

What role do emotions play in early social development? Clearly, a baby's displays of emotion serve a *communicative* function that is likely to affect the behavior of caregivers. For example, cries of distress summon close companions. Early suggestions of a smile or expressions of interest may convince caregivers that their baby is willing and even eager to strike up a social relationship with them. Later expressions of fear or sadness may indicate that the infant is insecure or feeling blue and needs some attention or comforting. Anger may imply that the infant wishes her companions to cease whatever they are doing that is upsetting her, whereas joy serves as a prompt for caregivers to prolong an ongoing interaction or perhaps signals the baby's willingness to accept new challenges. So infant emotions are adaptive in that they promote social contact and help caregivers to adjust their behavior to the infant's needs and goals. Stated another way, the emotional expressions of infancy help infants and their close companions get to know each other (Tronick, 1989).

At the same time, the infant's emerging ability to recognize and interpret others' emotions is an important achievement that enables him to infer how he should be feeling or behaving in a variety of situations. The beauty of this "social referencing" is that children can quickly acquire *knowledge* in this way. For example, a sibling's joyful reaction to the family dog should indicate to an infant that this "ball of fur" is a friend rather than an unspeakable monster. A mother's worried expression and accompanying vocal concern might immediately suggest that the knife in one's hand is an implement to be avoided. And given the frequency with which expressive caregivers direct an infant's attention to important aspects of the environment or display their feelings about an infant's appraisal of objects and events, it is likely that the information contained in their emotional displays contribute in a major way to the child's understanding of the world in which he lives (Rosen, Adamson, & Bakeman, 1992).

TEMPERAMENT AND DEVELOPMENT

As parents well know, every baby has a distinct personality. In trying to describe infant personality, researchers have focused on aspects of **temperament**—an individual's tendency to respond in predictable ways to environmental events that many believe to be the emotional and behavioral building blocks of the adult personality (Caspi & Silva, 1995; Goldsmith et al., 1987). Although different researchers do not always define or

Concept Check 11.1
Understanding Early Emotional Development

Check your understanding of selected aspects of early emotional development by matching each descriptive statement below with one of the following concepts: (a) emotional self-regulation, (b) self-recognition, (c) social referencing, (d) disconfirmed expectancies, (e) ability to interpret emotions (emotional understanding), (f) infant emotional expressions. The answers appear in the Appendix at the back of the book.

_____ 1. thought to be necessary for the development of all complex emotions

_____ 2. communicative signals that affect the behavior of caregivers

_____ 3. correlate of children's social competence/peer relations in grade school

_____ 4. using others' emotional expressions to regulate one's conduct

_____ 5. may underlie early expressions of anger, surprise, and sadness

_____ 6. necessary to comply with emotional display rules

Table 11.1 An Overview of Emotional Development

Age	Emotional expressions/regulations	Emotional understandings
Birth–6 months	All primary emotions appear. Displays of positive emotion are encouraged and become more commonplace. Attempts to regulate negative emotions by sucking or turning away are observed.	Discriminates such facial expressions as happiness, anger, and sadness.
7–12 months	Primary emotions such as anger, fear, and sadness become more apparent. Emotional self-regulation improves as infants rock themselves, chew on objects, or move away from distressing stimuli.	Recognition of others' primary emotions improves. Social referencing appears.
1–3 years	Secondary (self-conscious) emotions appear. Emotional regulation improves as toddlers distract themselves from or attempt to control stimuli that upset them.	Toddlers begin to talk about and play-act emotions. Empathic responding appears.
3–6 years	Appearance and refinement of cognitive strategies for regulating emotions. Some masking of emotions and compliance with simple display rules.	Understanding of the external causes and consequences of emotions improves. Empathic responding becomes more common.
6–12 years	Compliance with display rules improves. Self-conscious emotions become more closely tied to internalized standards of "right" or "competent" behavior. Self-regulation strategies (including those allowing one to intensify emotions when appropriate) become more varied and more complex.	Children integrate internal and external cues to understand others' emotions. Empathetic responding becomes stronger. Awareness that people may differ in their emotional reactions to the same event. Understanding that others may experience mixed emotions.

measure temperament in precisely the same ways, most would agree that the following five attributes are important components of temperament (Buss & Plomin, 1984; Goldsmith et al., 1987; Rothbart, 1981):

1. *Activity level*—typical pace or vigor of one's activities,
2. *Irritability/negative emotionality*—how easily or intensely upset one becomes over negative events,
3. *Soothability*—ease with which one calms after becoming upset,
4. *Fearfulness*—wariness of intense or highly unusual stimulation, and
5. *Sociability*—receptiveness to social stimulation.

Hereditary and Environmental Influences on Temperament

To many, the very term *temperament* implies a biological foundation for individual differences in behavior, a foundation that is genetically influenced and stable over time (Buss & Plomin, 1984; DiLalla, Kagan, & Reznick, 1994). Behavioral geneticists have looked for hereditary influences by comparing the temperamental similarities of pairs of identical and fraternal twins. By the middle of the first year, identical twins are already more similar than fraternal twins are on most temperamental attributes, including activity level, demands for attention, irritability, and sociability (Braungart et al., 1992; Emde et al., 1992; and see Figure 11.3). Although the heritability coefficients for most temperamental attributes are moderate at best throughout infancy and the preschool period (Goldsmith, Buss, & Lemery, 1997), it seems that many important components of temperament are genetically influenced.

temperament
a person's characteristic modes of responding emotionally and behaviorally to environmental events, including such attributes as activity level, irritability, fearfulness, and sociability.

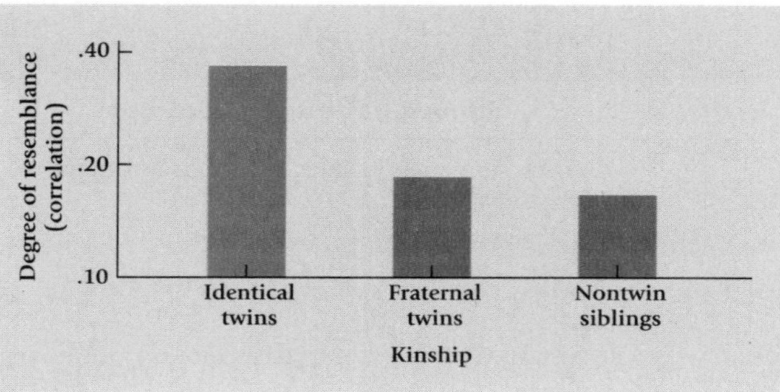

Figure 11.3 *Average correlations in infant temperament among identical twins, fraternal twins, and nontwin siblings born at different times.* Based on Braungart et al., *1992;* Emde et al., *1992.*

Environmental Influences

Of course, the fact that most temperamental attributes are only moderately heritable tells us that environment is also implicated in shaping children's temperaments. Which aspects of environment are most important? The home environment that siblings share clearly influences one temperamental attribute—the tendency to smile and display positive affect (Goldsmith et al., 1997). Yet, shared environment plays little part in shaping other temperamental attributes, for genetically unrelated adoptees and nontwin siblings who live together often barely resemble each other in activity level, fearfulness, and the like (Plomin et al., 1997; Schmitz et al., 1996). Thus, behavioral geneticists now believe that the strongest environmental contributors to temperament are *nonshared environmental influences*—those aspects of environment that siblings do not share and that conspire to make them temperamentally *dissimilar.* This can easily happen if parents notice early behavioral differences among their children and adjust their parenting to them. For example, if a mother observes that her infant son Jimmy is much less outgoing with strangers than her 3-year-old Jennifer was at Jimmy's age, she may allow Jimmy more freedom to avoid social contacts and to pursue solitary activities, thereby encouraging him to become more reclusive and socially inhibited than his sister is (Park et al., 1997).

Stability of Temperament

How stable is early temperament over time? Is the "fearful" 8-month-old who is highly upset by a strange face likely to remain wary of strangers at 24 months and to shun new playmates as a 4-year-old? Longitudinal research indicates that several components of temperament—namely, activity level, irritability, sociability, and shyness—are moderately stable through infancy, childhood, and sometimes even into the early adult years (Caspi & Silva, 1995; Pedlow et al., 1993; Ruff et al., 1990). In fact, one longitudinal study in New Zealand found that several components of temperament measured at age 3 were not only moderately stable between ages 3 and 18, but also predicted individual differences in participants' antisocial tendencies and the quality of their personal and family relationships at ages 18 to 21 (Caspi & Silva, 1995; Henry et al., 1996; Newman et al., 1997). Findings such as these illustrate why many developmentalists consider temperament to be the cornerstone of the adult personality. However, not all individuals are so temperamentally stable.

Consider what Jerome Kagan and his associates found while conducting longitudinal studies of a temperamental attribute they call **behavioral inhibition,** the tendency to withdraw from unfamiliar people or situations (Kagan; 1992; Kagan & Snidman, 1991; Snidman et al., 1995). At age 4 months, inhibited infants are already fussing and showing heightened motor activity to such novel objects as a brightly colored mobile, and they often displayed intense physiological arousal (for example, high heart rates) to situations that barely phased uninhibited infants. When tested at age 21 months, toddlers classified as inhibited were rather shy and sometimes even fearful when they encountered unfamiliar people, toys, or settings, whereas most uninhibited children responded quite adaptively to these events. And when retested at ages 4, 5½, and 7½, inhibited youngsters were still less sociable with strange adults and peers and more cautious than uninhibited children were about engaging in activities that involved an element of risk (for example, walking a balance beam).

behavioral inhibition
a temperamental attribute reflecting one's tendency to withdraw from unfamiliar people or situations.

So behavioral inhibition is a moderately stable attribute that may have deep biological roots. Indeed, researchers have been finding that infants easily upset by novelty show greater electrical activity in the right cerebral hemisphere of the brain (the center for negative emotions) than in the left hemisphere, whereas infants who are less reactive show either the opposite pattern or no hemispheric differences in electrical activity (Calkins, Fox, & Marshall, 1996; Fox, Bell, & Jones, 1992). In addition, family studies clearly indicate that behavioral inhibition is a genetically influenced attribute (DiLalla et al., 1994; Robinson et al., 1992). Nevertheless, both Kagan and his associates and a research team in Sweden (Kerr et al., 1994) found that only those children at the *extremes* of the continuum—the most highly inhibited and most highly uninhibited youngsters—displayed such long-term stability, with most other children showing considerable fluctuation in their levels of inhibition over time. What those latter observations imply is that genetically influenced aspects of temperament are often modified by environmental influences. Interestingly, a similar conclusion emerges from Alexander Thomas and Stella Chess's classic longitudinal research on the stability of temperamental profiles from infancy to adulthood.

Early Temperamental Profiles and Later Development

easy temperament
temperamental profile in which the child quickly establishes regular routines, is generally good natured, and adapts easily to novelty.

difficult temperament
temperamental profile in which the child is irregular in daily routines and adapts slowly to new experiences, often responding negatively and intensely.

slow-to-warm-up temperament
temperamental profile in which the child is inactive and moody and displays mild passive resistance to new routines and experiences.

In their earliest reports, Thomas and Chess (1977; Thomas, Chess, & Birch, 1970) noted that certain aspects of infant temperament tend to cluster in predictable ways, forming broader temperamental profiles. In fact, the majority of the 141 infants in their *New York Longitudinal Study* could be placed into one of three temperamental profiles:

1. **Easy temperament** (40% of the sample). Easygoing children are even-tempered, are typically in a positive mood, and are quite open and adaptable to new experiences. Their habits are regular and predictable.
2. **Difficult temperament** (10% of the sample). Difficult children are active, irritable, and irregular in their habits. They often react very vigorously to changes in routine and are very slow to adapt to new persons or situations.
3. **Slow-to-warm-up temperament** (15% of the sample). These children are quite inactive, somewhat moody, and can be slow to adapt to new persons and situations. But, unlike the difficult child, they typically respond to novelty in mildly, rather than intensely, negative ways. For example, they may resist cuddling by looking away rather than by kicking or screaming.

The remaining children fit none of these profiles, showing their own unique patterns of temperamental attributes.

Temperamental Profiles and Children's Adjustment

Apparently, these broader temperamental patterns may persist over time and influence a child's adjustment to a variety of settings later in life. For example, temperamentally difficult children are more likely than other children to have problems adjusting to school activities, and they are often irritable and aggressive in their interactions with siblings and peers (Lytton, 1990; Thomas, Chess, & Korn, 1982). By contrast, about half of all children who are slow to warm up show a different kind of adjustment problem, as their hesitancy to embrace new activities and challenges may cause them to be ignored or neglected by peers (Chess & Thomas, 1984).

Difficult children are likely to retain their difficult temperaments if parents are impatient and forceful with them.

Child-rearing and Temperament

Do those observations imply that early temperamental profiles are difficult to alter and largely determine our personalities and social adjustment? No, they do not! Thomas and Chess (1986; Chess & Thomas, 1984) found that early temperamental characteristics *sometimes do* and *sometimes do not* carry over into later life. In other words, temperament can change, and one factor that often determines whether it does change is the **"goodness of fit"** between the child's temperamental style and patterns of child-rearing used by parents. Let's first consider a good fit between temperament and child-rearing. Difficult infants who fuss a lot and have trouble adapting to new routines often become less cranky and more adaptable over the long run if parents remain calm, exercise restraint, and allow these children to respond to novelty at a more leisurely pace. Indeed, many difficult infants who experience such patient and sensitive caregiving are no longer classifiable as temperamentally difficult later in childhood or adolescence (Chess & Thomas, 1984). Yet it is not always easy for parents to be patient and sensitive with a highly active, moody child who resists their bids for attention; in fact, many parents become irritable, impatient, demanding, and punitive with difficult children (van den Boom, 1995). Unfortunately, these attitudes and behaviors constitute a poor fit with a difficult child, who is apt to become all the more fussy and resistant in response to the parent's forceful and punitive tactics. And true to form, Chess and Thomas (1984) found that difficult infants were especially likely to remain difficult and to display behavior problems later in life if their parents had been impatient, demanding, and forceful with them.

Finally, there is a great deal of variation across cultures in what qualifies as a desirable temperament and in the developmental outcomes that are associated with particular temperamental attributes. Box 11.1 briefly examines some cross-cultural differences in the developmental implications of childhood and adolescent shyness.

? **WHAT DO YOU THINK?**

Do you think that Terry and Toni, the 18-month-olds in the vignette that opened this chapter, display different temperamental qualities? If so, characterize the qualities they display, and see if you think they fit any of Thomas and Chess's temperamental profiles.

"goodness-of-fit" model
Thomas and Chess's notion that development is likely to be optimized when parents' child-rearing practices are sensitively adapted to the child's temperamental characteristics.

attachment
a close emotional relationship between two persons, characterized by mutual affection and a desire to maintain proximity.

WHAT ARE EMOTIONAL ATTACHMENTS?

Although babies can communicate many of their feelings right from the start, their social lives change rather dramatically as they become emotionally attached to their caregivers. What is an emotional **attachment**? John Bowlby (1969) uses the term to describe the strong affectional ties that we feel for the special people in our lives. According to Bowlby (1969), people who are securely attached take pleasure in their interactions and feel comforted by their partner's presence in times of stress or uncertainty. So 10-month-old Michael may reflect the attachment relationship he shares with his mother by reserving his biggest grins for her and by crying out to her or crawling in her direction whenever he is upset, discomforted, or afraid.

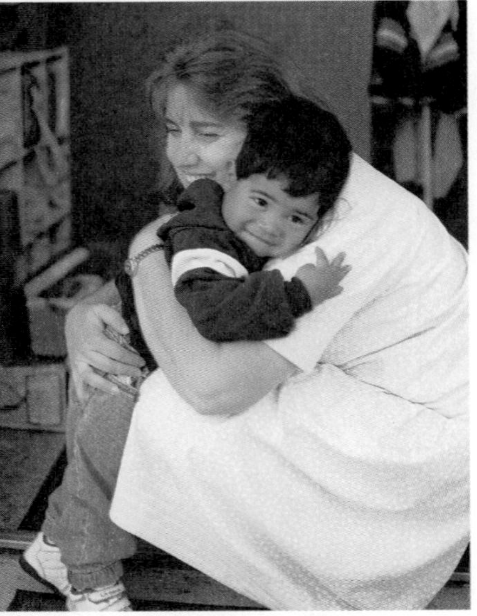

Young children and caregivers who are securely attached interact often and try to maintain proximity.

Reciprocal Relationships

Bowlby (1969) also stressed that parent–infant attachments are *reciprocal* relationships: Infants become attached to parents, and parents become attached to infants.

Parents clearly have an edge on infants when it comes to forming these intimate affectional ties. Even before their baby is born, they often display their readiness to become attached by talking blissfully about the baby, formulating grand plans for him or her, and expressing delight in such milestones as feeling the fetus kick or hearing his heart beat with the aid of a stethoscope (Grossman, Eichler, Winickoff, & Associates, 1980). And as we learned in Chapter 4, close contact with a newborn in the first few hours after birth can intensify positive feelings parents already have for their baby (Klaus & Kennell, 1982), particularly if they are younger, economically disadvantaged, and know very little about babies or infant care (Eyer, 1992). Yet, it is important to emphasize that genuine emotional *attachments* build slowly from parent–infant inter-

11.1

CULTURAL INFLUENCES

Is Shyness a Social Disadvantage? It Depends on One's Culture

In the United States, children who are shy and reserved are at a social disadvantage. They run the risk of being neglected or even rejected by peers, which can lead to low self-esteem, depression, and a number of other adjustment problems that we will discuss in detail in Chapter 16. Furthermore, even if shy adolescents or young adults are otherwise well-adjusted, they often fail to act boldly or assertively enough to take advantage of many opportunities, and they typically lag far behind bolder peers in getting married, having children, and firmly establishing themselves in a career (Caspi et al., 1988).

By contrast, many Asian cultures *value* what Americans would call a shy and somewhat inhibited demeanor. In China, for example, children who are shy and reserved are perceived as socially mature by their teachers (Chen, Rubin, & Li, 1995), and they are much more likely than active, assertive children to be popular with their peers—precisely the opposite pattern to what we see in the U.S. and Canada (Chen, Rubin, & Sun, 1992). And the boisterous classroom behaviors that many Western children display on occasion (and that American teachers view as normal) are likely to be branded *conduct disorders* by teachers in Thailand, who expect their pupils to be reserved, respectful, and obedient (Weisz et al., 1995).

There are even differences among Western cultures in outcomes associated with shyness. Swedes, for example, view shyness somewhat more positively than Americans do and prefer shy, reserved behaviors to bold, assertive, or attention-seeking antics. Consequently, shyness is not really a disadvantage for Swedish men. Like shy American men, shy Swedish men married and had children later than their less shy counterparts; however shyness did not constrain their careers in the same way it does for American men (Kerr, Lambert, & Bem, 1996). What about Swedish women? Shyness posed no problems for them in establishing intimate relationships, for shy Swedish girls married and had children at roughly the same age as their less shy peers. But unlike shy American women, who were generally well educated and who married successful men, shy Swedish women completed *fewer* years of education than their bolder counterparts and married men who made less money, thus suggesting that shyness may place them at some risk of economic disadvantage. Why did shy Swedish girls receive less education than less shy peers? Margaret Kerr and her associates (1996) speculate that Swedish teachers are more likely to encourage shy students to continue their education if the students are males. So lacking the initiative to approach teachers and seek their guidance, shy Swedish girls end up having fewer educational opportunities than nonshy girls or shy boys do.

We see, then, that outcomes associated with shyness vary dramatically across cultures (and even within a culture, depending on one's gender). Clearly, some temperamental qualities provide better fits with a culture's specific values and traditions than others do. And because cultural traditions vary so widely, we can safely conclude that there is no one temperamental profile that is most adaptive in all cultures.

actions that occur over the first several months and can become highly intimate, even when there is no early contact between parents and their newborn (Brockington, 1996).

Establishment of Interactional Synchrony

One important contributor to the growth of attachments is the **synchronized routines** that caregivers and infants often establish over the first few months of a baby's life (Stern, 1977; Tronick, 1989). These coordinated interactions, which have been likened to dances, are most likely to develop if the caregiver attends carefully to her baby's state, provides playful stimulation when the baby is alert and attentive, and avoids pushing things when an overexcited or tired infant is fussy and sending the message "Cool it! I just need a break from all this excitement." Edward Tronick (1989, p. 112) described one very synchronous interaction that unfolded as a mother played peekaboo with her infant:

> . . . The infant abruptly turns away from his mother as the game reaches its "peek" of intensity and begins to suck on his thumb and stare into space with a dull facial expression. The mother stops playing and sits back watching. . . . After a few seconds the infant turns back to her with an inviting expression. The mother moves closer, smiles, and says in a high-pitched, exaggerated voice,

synchronized routines generally harmonious interactions between two persons in which participants adjust their behavior in response to the partner's actions.

"Oh, now you're back!" He smiles in response and vocalizes. As they finish crowing together, the infant reinserts his thumb and looks away. The mother again waits. [Soon] the infant turns . . . to her and they greet each other with big smiles.

Notice that much information is exchanged in this simple but synchronous exchange. By turning away and sucking, the excited infant is saying "Hey, I need to slow down and regulate my emotional state." His mother tells him she understands by patiently awaiting his return. As he returns, mom tells him she's glad he's back, and he acknowledges that signal with a smile and an excitable blurt. And when the baby becomes overstimulated a minute or two later, his mother waits for him to calm once again, and he communicates his thanks by smiling wide for her when he turns back the second time. Clearly, this is a dyad that not only interacts smoothly but quickly repairs any interactive errors.

Daniel Stern (1977) believes that synchronized interactions between infants and their caregivers may occur several times a day and are particularly important contributors to emotional attachments. As an infant continues to interact with a particular caregiver, he learns what this person is like and how he can regulate her attention. Of course, the caregiver should become better at interpreting the baby's signals and learn how to adjust her behavior to successfully capture and maintain his attention. As the caregiver and the infant practice their routines and become better "dance partners," their relationship should become more satisfying for both parties and eventually blossom into a strong reciprocal attachment (Isabella, 1993; Isabella & Belsky, 1991).

HOW DO INFANTS BECOME ATTACHED?

Although many parents do find themselves emotionally drawn to their infant very soon after their baby is born, an infant requires some time before she is developmentally ready to form a genuine attachment to another human being. Many theories have been proposed to explain how and why infants become emotionally involved with the people around them. But before we consider these theories, we should briefly discuss the phases that babies go through in becoming attached to a close companion.

The Growth of Primary Attachments

Many years ago, Rudolph Schaffer and Peggy Emerson (1964) studied the development of emotional attachments by following a group of Scottish infants from early infancy to 18 months of age. Once a month, mothers were interviewed to determine (1) how the infant responded when separated from close companions in seven situations (for example, being left in a crib; being left in the presence of strangers) and (2) the persons to whom the infant's separation responses were directed. A child was judged to be attached to someone if separation from that person reliably elicited a protest.

Schaffer and Emerson found that infants pass through the following phases as they develop close ties with their caregivers:

The Asocial Phase (0 to 6 Weeks)

asocial phase (of attachment)
approximately the first 6 weeks of life, in which infants respond in an equally favorable way to interesting social and nonsocial stimuli.

The very young infant is somewhat "asocial" in that many kinds of social or nonsocial stimuli produce a favorable reaction, and few produce any kind of protest. By the end of this period, infants are beginning to show a preference for such social stimuli in a smiling face.

The Phase of Indiscriminate Attachments (6 Weeks to 6 to 7 Months)

Now infants clearly enjoy human company but tend to be somewhat indiscriminate. They smile more at people than at such other lifelike objects as talking puppets (Ellsworth, Muir, & Hains, 1993) and are likely to fuss whenever *any* adult puts them down. Although 3- to 6-month-olds reserve their biggest grins for familiar companions (Watson et al., 1979) and are more quickly soothed by a regular caregiver, they seem to enjoy the attention they receive from just about anyone (including strangers).

The Specific Attachments Phase (about 7 to 9 Months)

Between 7 and 9 months of age, infants begin to protest only when separated from one particular individual, usually the mother. Now able to crawl, infants often try to follow along behind their mother, to stay close and greet mothers warmly when they return. They also become somewhat wary of strangers. According to Schaffer and Emerson (1964), these babies have established their first genuine attachments.

The formation of a strong attachment to a caregiver has another important consequence: It promotes the development of exploratory behavior. Mary Ainsworth (1979) emphasizes that an attachment figure serves as a **secure base** for exploration, a point of safety from which an infant can feel free to venture away. Thus Juan, a securely attached infant visiting a neighbor's home with his mother, may be quite comfortable exploring the far corners of the living room so long as he can check back occasionally to see that Mom is still seated on the sofa. But should she disappear into the bathroom, Juan may become wary and reluctant to explore. Paradoxical as it may seem, then, infants apparently need to rely on another person in order to feel confident about acting independently.

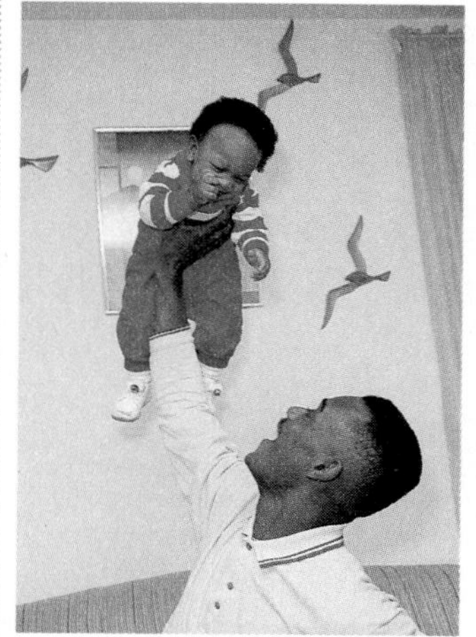

For many infants, fathers assume the role of special playmate.

The Phase of Multiple Attachments

Within weeks after forming their initial attachments, about half the infants in Schaffer and Emerson's study were becoming attached to other people such as fathers, siblings, grandparents, or perhaps even a regular babysitter. By 18 months of age, very few infants were attached to only one person, and some were attached to five or more.

Theories of Attachment

If you have ever had a kitten or a puppy, you may have noticed that pets often seem especially responsive and affectionate to the person who feeds them. Might the same be true of human infants? Developmentalists have long debated this very point, as we will see in examining four influential theories of attachment: psychoanalytic theory, learning theory, cognitive-developmental theory, and ethological theory.

Psychoanalytic Theory: I Love You because You Feed Me

According to Freud, young infants are "oral" creatures who derive satisfaction from sucking and mouthing objects and should be attracted to any person who provides oral pleasure. Since it is usually mothers who "pleasure" oral infants by feeding them, it seemed logical to Freud that the mother would become the baby's primary object of security and affection, particularly if she was relaxed and generous in her feeding practices.

Erik Erikson also believed that a mother's feeding practices influence the strength or security of her infant's attachments. However, he claimed that a mother's *overall responsiveness* to her child's needs is more important than feeding itself. According to Erikson, a caregiver who consistently responds to all an infant's needs fosters a sense

phase of indiscriminate attachments
period between 6 weeks and 6 to 7 months of age in which infants prefer social to nonsocial stimulation and are likely to protest whenever any adult puts them down or leaves them alone.

phase of specific attachment
period between 7 and 9 months of age when infants are attached to one close companion (usually the mother).

secure base
an infant's use of a caregiver as a base from which to explore the environment and to which to return for emotional support.

phase of multiple attachments
period when infants form attachments to companions other than their primary attachment object.

of *trust* in other people, whereas unresponsive or inconsistent caregiving breeds mistrust. He adds that children who have learned *not* to trust caregivers during infancy may come to avoid close mutual-trust relationships throughout life.

Before we examine the research on feeding practices and attachments, we need to consider another viewpoint that assumes that feeding is important: learning theory.

Learning Theory: Rewardingness Leads to Love

For quite different reasons, some learning theorists have also assumed that infants become attached to persons who feed them and gratify their needs. Feeding was thought to be particularly important for two reasons (Sears, 1963). First, it should elicit positive responses from a contented infant (smiles, coos) that are likely to increase a caregiver's affection for the baby. Second, feeding is often an occasion when mothers can provide an infant with *many comforts*—food, warmth, tender touches, soft, reassuring vocalizations, changes in scenery, and even a dry diaper (if necessary)—*all in one sitting.* Over time, then, an infant should come to associate his mother with pleasant or pleasurable sensations, so that the mother herself becomes a valuable commodity. Once the mother (or any other caregiver) has attained this status as a **secondary reinforcer,** the infant is attached; he or she will now do whatever is necessary (smile, cry, coo, babble, or follow) in order to attract the caregiver's attention or to remain near this valuable and rewarding individual.

Just how important *is* feeding? In 1959, Harry Harlow and Robert Zimmerman reported the results of a study designed to compare the importance of feeding and tactile stimulation for the development of attachments in infant monkeys. The monkeys were separated from their mothers in the first day of life and reared for the next 165 days by two surrogate mothers. As you can see in the photograph, each surrogate mother had a face and well-proportioned body constructed of wire. However, the body of one surrogate (the "cloth mother") was wrapped in foam rubber and covered with terry cloth. Half the infants were always fed by this warm, comfortable cloth mother, the remaining half by the rather uncomfortable "wire mother."

secondary reinforcer
an initially neutral stimulus that acquires reinforcement value by virtue of its repeated association with other reinforcing stimuli.

The research question was simple: Would these infants become attached to the "mother" who fed them, or would they instead prefer the soft, cuddly "cloth mother"? It was no contest! Even if their food had come from the "wire mother," infants spent time with "her" *only while feeding* and ran directly to the "*cloth* mother" whenever they were upset or afraid. So all infants became attached to the "cloth mother," thereby implying that *contact comfort* is a more powerful contributor to attachment in monkeys than feeding or the reduction of hunger.

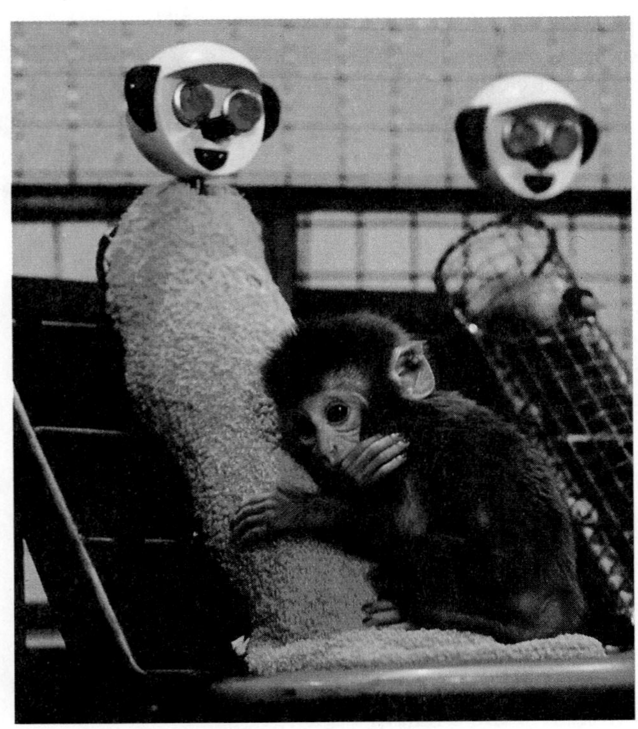

The "wire" and "cloth" surrogate mothers used in Harlow's research. Infants became attached to the cloth mother even if it was the wire mother who fed them.

Apparently, feeding is not any more important to human infants than to baby monkeys. When Schaffer and Emerson (1964) asked mothers about the feeding schedules (regular interval versus demand feeding) they had used and the age at which they had weaned their infants, they found that the generosity of a mother's feeding practices simply did not predict the quality of her infant's attachment to her. In fact, for 39% of these infants, the person who usually fed, bathed, and changed them (typically the mother) was not even the child's primary attachment object!

Current Viewpoints. Although it is now quite clear that feeding is *not* the primary contributor to attachments in either monkeys or humans, modern learning theorists continue to argue that *reinforcement* is the mechanism responsible for social attachments (Gewirtz & Petrovich, 1982). Their revised viewpoint, which is similar to that of Erik Erikson, is that infants are attracted to any individual who is quick to respond to all their needs and who provides them with a variety of pleasant or rewarding experiences. Indeed, Schaffer and Emerson (1964) found that the two aspects of a mother's behavior that predicted the character of her infant's attachment to her were her *responsiveness* to the infant's behavior and the *total amount of stimulation* that she provided. Mothers who responded reliably and appropriately to their infants' bids for attention and who often played with their babies had infants who were closely attached to them.

Cognitive-Developmental Theory: To Love You, I Must Know You Will Always Be There

Cognitive-developmental theory has little to say about which adults are most likely to appeal to infants, but it does remind us of the holistic character of development by suggesting that the ability to form attachments depends, in part, on the infant's level of intellectual development. Before an attachment can occur, the infant must be able to discriminate familiar companions from strangers. He must also recognize that familiar companions have a "permanence" about them (object permanence), for it would be difficult indeed to form a stable relationship with a person who ceases to exist whenever she passes from view (Schaffer, 1971). So perhaps it is no accident that attachments first emerge at age 7 to 9 months—precisely the time when infants are entering Piaget's *fourth sensorimotor substage,* the point at which they first begin to search for and find objects that they've seen someone hide from them.

Barry Lester and his associates (1974) evaluated this hypothesis by giving 9-month-old infants a test of object permanence before exposing them to brief separations from their mothers, their fathers, and a stranger. They found that 9-month-olds who scored high (substage 4 or above) in object permanence only protested when separated from their mothers, whereas age-mates who scored lower (Stage 3 or below) showed little evidence of *any* separation protest. So it seemed that only the cognitively advanced 9-month-olds had formed a primary attachment (to their mothers), which implies that the timing of this important emotional milestone depends, in part, on the infant's level of object permanence.

Ethological Theory: Perhaps I Was Born to Love

Ethologists have proposed a most interesting and influential explanation for emotional attachments that has strong evolutionary overtones. A major assumption of the ethological approach is that all species, including human beings, are born with a number of innate behavioral tendencies that have in some way contributed to the survival of the species over the course of evolution. Indeed, John Bowlby (1969; 1980), who was originally a psychoanalyst, came to believe that many of these built-in behaviors are specifically designed to promote attachments between infants and their caregivers. Even the attachment relationship itself is said to have adaptive significance, serving to protect the young from predators and other natural calamities and to ensure that their needs are met. Of course, ethologists would argue that the long-range purpose of the primary attachment is to permit members of each successive generation to live long enough to reproduce, thereby enabling the species to survive.

Origins of the Ethological Viewpoint. Interestingly, the ethological theory of attachment was prompted by research with animals. In 1937, Konrad Lorenz reported that very young goslings followed almost any moving object—their mothers, a duck, or even a human being, a behavior he labeled **imprinting.** Lorenz also noted that imprinting (1) is automatic—young fowl do not have to be taught to follow, (2) occurs only within a narrowly delimited *critical period* after the bird has hatched, and (3) is irreversible—once the bird begins to follow a particular object, it will remain attached to it.

imprinting
an innate or instinctual form of learning in which the young of certain species follow and become attached to moving objects (usually their mothers).

Lorenz then concluded that imprinting was an adaptive response. Young birds generally survive if they follow their mothers so that they are led to food and afforded protection. Those that wander away may starve or be eaten by predators and thus fail to

Figure 11.4 *Infants of many species display the "kewpie-doll" effect that makes them appear lovable and elicits caregivers' attention.* ADAPTED FROM LORENZ, 1943.

pass their genes to future generations. So over the course of many, many generations, then, the imprinting response eventually became an inborn, **preadapted characteristic** that attaches a young fowl to its mother, thereby increasing its chances of survival.

ATTACHMENT IN HUMANS. Although human infants do not imprint on their mothers in the same way that young fowl do, they seem to have inherited a number of attributes that help them to maintain contact with others and to elicit caregiving. Lorenz (1943), for example, suggested that a baby's **"kewpie doll"** appearance (that is, large forehead, chubby cheeks, and soft, rounded features; see Figure 11.4) makes the infant appear cute or lovable to caregivers. Thomas Alley (1981) agrees. Alley found that adults judged line drawings of infant faces (and profiles) to be "adorable"—much cuter than those of 2-, 3-, and 4-year-old children. So babyish facial features may well help to elicit the kinds of positive attention from others that promote social attachments, and the more attractive the baby, the more favorably mothers and other companions respond to him or her (Barden et al., 1989; Langlois et al., 1995). Nevertheless, babies need not be adorable to foster close attachments, for a clear majority of unattractive infants end up securely attached to their caregivers (Speltz et al., 1997).

preadapted characteristic
an innate attribute that is a product of evolution and serves some function that increases the chances of survival for the individual and the species.

kewpie doll effect
the notion that infantlike facial features are perceived as cute and lovable and elicit favorable responses from others.

Not only do most infants have "cute" faces, but many of their inborn, reflexive responses may have an endearing quality about them (Bowlby, 1969). For example, the rooting, sucking, and grasping reflexes may lead parents to believe that their infant enjoys being close to them. Smiling, which is initially a reflexive response to almost any pleasing stimulus, is a particularly potent signal to caregivers, as are cooing, excitable blurting, and spontaneous babbling (Keller & Scholmerich, 1987). In fact, an adult's typical response to a baby's smiles and positive vocalizations is to smile at (or vocalize to) the infant (Gewirtz & Petrovich, 1982; Keller & Scholmerich, 1987), and parents often interpret their baby's grins, laughs, and babbles as an indication that the child is contented and that they are effective caregivers. So a smiling or babbling infant can reinforce caregiving activities and thereby increase the likelihood that parents or other nearby companions will want to attend to this happy little person in the future.

Few signals attract as much attention as a baby's social smile.

Finally, Bowlby insists that under normal circumstances, adults are just as biologically predisposed to respond favorably to a baby's signals as the baby is to emit them. It is difficult, he claims, for parents to ignore an urgent cry or to fail to warm up to a baby's big grin. In sum, human infants and their caregivers are said to have evolved in ways that predispose them to respond favorably to each other and to form close attachments, thus enabling infants (and ultimately, the species) to survive.

Does this mean that attachments are automatic? No, indeed! Bowlby claims that secure attachments develop gradually as parents become more proficient at reading and reacting appropriately to the baby's signals and the baby *learns* what his parents are like and how he might regulate their behavior. Yet, the process can easily go awry, as illustrated by the finding that an infant's preprogrammed signals eventually wane if they fail to produce favorable reactions from an unresponsive companion, such as a depressed mother or an unhappily married father (Ainsworth et al., 1978). So while Bowlby believes that human beings are biologically *prepared* to form close attachments, he also stresses that secure emotional bonds will not develop unless each participant has *learned* how to respond appropriately to the behavior of the other.

Comparing the Four Theoretical Approaches

Although the four theories we have reviewed differ in many respects, each has something to offer. Clearly, feeding practices are not as important to human attachments as psychoanalysts originally thought; but it was Freud who stressed that we need to know more about mother–infant interactions if we hope to understand how babies form attachments. Erik Erikson and the learning theorists pursued Freud's early leads and concluded that caregivers do play an important role in the infant's emotional development. Presumably, infants are likely to view a responsive companion who provides many comforts as a trustworthy and rewarding individual who is worthy of affection. Ethologists can agree with this point of view, but they add that infants are *active participants* in the attachment process who emit preprogrammed responses that enable them to promote the very interactions from which attachments are likely to develop. Finally, cognitive theorists have contributed by showing that the timing of emotional attachments is related to the infant's level of cognitive development. So it makes little sense to tag one of these theories as "correct" and to ignore the others, for each theory has helped us to understand how infants become attached to their most intimate companions.

Two Attachment-Related Fears of Infancy

At about the same time that infants are establishing close affectional ties to a caregiver, they often begin to display negative emotional reactions that may puzzle or perhaps even annoy their companions. In this section, we will briefly look at two of the common fears of infancy: *stranger anxiety* and *separation anxiety.*

Stranger Anxiety

Nine-month-old Billy is sitting on the floor in the den when his mother leads a strange person into the room. The stranger suddenly walks closer, bends over, and says "Hi, Billy! How are you?" If Billy is like many 9-month-olds, he may stare at the stranger for a moment and then turn away, whimper, and crawl toward his mother.

This wary reaction to a stranger, or **stranger anxiety,** stands in marked contrast to the smiling, babbling, and other positive greetings that infants often display when approached by a familiar companion. Most infants react positively to strangers until they form their first attachment, and then become apprehensive shortly thereafter (Schaffer & Emerson, 1964). Wary reactions to strangers, which are often mixed with signs of interest, peak at 8 to 10 months of age, and gradually decline in intensity over the second year (Sroufe, 1977). However, even an 8- to 10-month-old is not afraid of every strange face she sees and may occasionally react rather positively to strangers. In Box 11.2, we consider the circumstances under which stranger anxiety is most likely to occur and see how medical personnel and other child-care professionals might use this knowledge to head off outbreaks of fear and trembling in their offices.

stranger anxiety
a wary or fretful reaction that infants and toddlers often display when approached by an unfamiliar person.

APPLYING DEVELOPMENTAL RESEARCH

11.2

Combating Stranger Anxiety: Some Helpful Hints for Doctors and Child-Care Professionals

It is not at all unusual for toddlers visiting the doctor's office to break into tears and to cling tenaciously to their parents. Some youngsters who remember previous visits may be suffering from "shot anxiety" rather than stranger anxiety, but many are simply reacting fearfully to the approach of an intrusive physician who may poke, prod, and handle them in ways that are atypical and upsetting. Fortunately, there are steps that caregivers and medical personnel (or any other stranger) can take to make such encounters less terrifying for an infant or toddler. What can we suggest?

1. *Keep familiar companions available.* Infants react much more negatively to strangers when they are separated from their mothers or other close companions. Indeed, most 6- to 12-month-olds are not particularly wary of an approaching stranger if they are sitting on their mother's lap; however, they frequently whimper and cry at the stranger's approach if seated only a few feet from their mothers (Morgan & Ricciuti, 1969; and see Bohlin & Hagekull, 1993). Clearly, doctors and nurses can expect a more constructive response from their youngest patients if they can avoid separating them from their caregivers.

2. *Arrange for companions to respond positively to the stranger.* Stranger anxiety is less likely to occur if the caregiver issues a warm greeting to the stranger or uses a positive tone of voice when talking to the infant about the stranger (Feinman, 1992). These actions permit the child to engage in *social referencing* and to conclude that maybe the stranger really isn't all that scary if mom and dad seem to like him. It might not hurt, then, for medical personnel to strike up a pleasant conversation with the caregiver before directing their attention to the child.

3. *Make the setting more "familiar."* Stranger anxiety occurs less frequently in familiar settings than in unfamiliar ones. For example, few 10-month-olds are especially wary of strangers at home, but most react negatively to strange companions when tested in an unfamiliar laboratory (Sroufe, Waters, & Matas, 1974). Although it may be unrealistic to advise modern physicians to make home visits, they could make at least one of their examination rooms more homelike for young children, perhaps by placing an attractive mobile in one corner and posters of cartoon characters on the wall, or by having a stuffed toy or two available for the child to play with. The infant's familiarity with a strange setting also makes a difference: Whereas the vast majority (90%) of 10-month-olds become upset if a stranger approaches them within a minute after being placed in an unfamiliar room, only about half will react negatively to the stranger when they have had 10 minutes to grow accustomed to this setting (Sroufe et al., 1974). Perhaps trips to the doctor would become more tolerable for an infant or a toddler if medical personnel gave the child a few minutes to familiarize himself with the examination room before making their entrance.

4. *Be a sensitive, unobtrusive stranger.* Not surprisingly, an infant's response to a stranger depends on the stranger's behavior (Sroufe, 1977). The meeting is likely to go best if the stranger initially keeps his or her distance and then approaches slowly while smiling, talking, and offering a familiar toy or suggesting a familiar activity (Bretherton, Stolberg, & Kreye, 1981; Sroufe, 1977). It also helps if the stranger, like any sensitive caregiver, takes his or her cues from the infant (Mangelsdorf, 1992). Babies prefer strangers they can control! Intrusive strangers who approach quickly and force themselves on the child (for example, by trying to pick infants up before they have time to adjust) probably get the response they deserve.

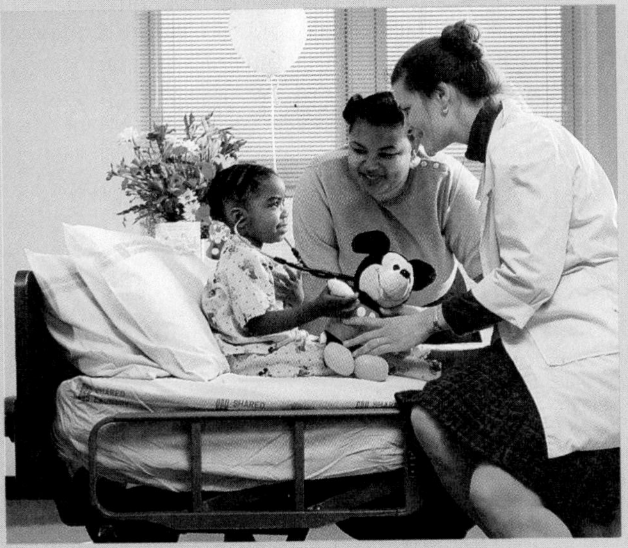

Most toddlers respond favorably to a friendly stranger—even a doctor—who offers a toy.

5. *Try looking a little less strange to the child.* Stranger anxiety depends, in part, on the stranger's physical appearance. Jerome Kagan (1972) has argued that infants form mental representations, or *schemas,* for the faces that they encounter in daily life and are most likely to be afraid of people whose appearance is not easily assimilated into these existing schemas. So a doctor in a sterile white lab coat with a strange stethoscope around her neck (or a nurse with a pointed hat that may give her a "witchlike" look) can make infants and toddlers rather wary indeed! Pediatric professionals may not be able to alter various physical features (for example, a huge nose or a facial scar) that might make children wary; but they can and often do shed their strange instruments and white uniforms in favor of more "normal" attire that will help their youngest patients to recognize them as members of the human race. Babysitters with spiked hair or nose rings might also heed this advice if they hope to establish rapport with their young companions.

Separation Anxiety

Many infants who have formed primary attachments also begin to display obvious signs of discomfort when separated from their mothers or other attachment objects. Ten-month-old Tony, for example, is likely to cry as he sees his mother put on a coat and pick up her purse as she prepares to go shopping, whereas 15-month-old Doris might even follow her mother to the door while whining and pleading not to be left at home. These reactions reflect the children's **separation anxiety.** Separation anxiety normally appears at 6 to 8 months of age (at about the time infants are forming emotional attachments, peaks at 14 to 18 months, and gradually becomes less frequent and less intense throughout infancy and the preschool period (Kagan, Kearsley, & Zelazo, 1978; Weinraub & Lewis, 1977). However, grade-school children and even adolescents may still show signs of anxiety and depression when separated for long periods from their loved ones (Thurber, 1995).

Why Do Infants Fear Strangers and Separations?

Why do infants who are just beginning to experience the pleasures of love suddenly become wary of strangers and anxious when separated from their objects of affection? Let's consider two views that have received some support.

The Ethological Viewpoint. Ethologist John Bowlby (1973) claims that many situations that infants face qualify as *natural clues to danger;* they have been so frequently associated with danger throughout human evolutionary history that a fear or avoidance response has become "biologically programmed." Among the situations that infants may be programmed to fear, once they can readily discriminate familiar objects and events from unfamiliar ones, are strange faces (which, in earlier eras, may have been a predatory animal), strange settings, and the "strange circumstance" of being separated from familiar companions.

Consistent with this ethological viewpoint, infants show stronger reactions to strangers and separations in an unfamiliar laboratory than at home; presumably the "strangeness" of the laboratory magnifies the apprehension they ordinarily experience upon encountering a stranger or having to endure a separation. This ethological viewpoint also explains an interesting cross-cultural variation in separation anxiety: Infants from many nonindustrial societies, who sleep with their mothers and are nearly always in close contact with them, begin to protest separations about 2 to 3 months earlier than Western infants do. Why? Because those infants are so rarely apart from their caregivers that almost any separation is a very "strange" and fear-provoking event for them (Ainsworth, 1967).

Ethological theory also explains why stranger and separation anxieties decline during the second year. Once infants begin to walk and can use their attachment objects as *secure bases* for exploration, they actively initiate separations, becoming much more tolerant of them and much less wary of other novel stimuli (including friendly strangers) that had previously been a source of concern (Ainsworth, 1989; Posada et al., 1995).

The Cognitive-Developmental Viewpoint. Cognitive theorists view both stranger anxiety and separation anxiety as natural outgrowths of the infant's perceptual and cognitive development. Jerome Kagan (1972; 1976) suggests that 6- to 10-month-olds have finally developed stable schemes for (1) the faces of familiar companions and (2) these companions' probable whereabouts at home (if they are not present). Suddenly, a strange face that is discrepant with the infants' schemes for caregivers now upsets children because they can't *explain* who this is or what has become of familiar caregivers. Kagan also proposes that 7- to 10-month-olds will *not* protest most separations at home because they have a pretty good idea where a caregiver has gone should he leave them in the living room and proceed to a familiar area, such as the kitchen. But should a caregiver violate this "familiar faces in familiar places" scheme by lifting his briefcase and walking out the front door, an infant cannot easily account for his whereabouts and will probably cry.

separation anxiety
a wary or fretful reaction that infants and toddlers often display when separated from the person(s) to whom they are attached.

Indeed, infants observed at home are more likely to protest when caregivers depart through an unfamiliar doorway (such as the entry to the cellar) than through a familiar one (Littenberg, Tulkin, & Kagan, 1971). And 9-month-old infants who have played quietly during a separation soon become extremely upset after looking for their mother and discovering that she is not where they thought she was (Corter et al., 1980). Clearly, these observations support Kagan's theory: Infants are most likely to protest separations from a caregiver when they are uncertain about her whereabouts.

In sum, stranger anxiety and separation anxiety are relatively complex emotional responses that stem, in part, from an infant's *general apprehension of the unfamiliar* (the ethological viewpoint), and her inability to *explain* who a stranger may be or what has become of familiar companions (cognitive-developmental viewpoint). Yet, it is important to note that infants vary dramatically in their responses to separations and strangers: Some are almost indifferent to these events, whereas others act as if they are terrified. Why the variations? Developmentalists now believe that they often reflect individual differences in the quality, or security, of infants' attachment relationships.

INDIVIDUAL DIFFERENCES IN ATTACHMENT QUALITY

The attachment relationships that virtually all home-reared infants establish with their caregivers clearly differ in quality. Some infants are quite secure and relaxed around caregivers, whereas others seem highly anxious or uncertain about what to expect next. Why are some infants secure and others insecure in their attachment relationships? And does the security of a child's early attachments have any impact on later development? To answer these questions, researchers first had to find ways of measuring attachment quality.

strange situation
a series of eight separation and reunion episodes to which infants are exposed in order to determine the quality of their attachments.

secure attachment
an infant–caregiver bond in which the child welcomes contact with a close companion and uses this person as a secure base from which to explore the environment.

Assessing Attachment Security

The most widely used technique for measuring the quality of attachments that 1- to 2-year-olds have established with their mothers or other caregivers is Mary Ainsworth's **strange situation** procedure (Ainsworth et al., 1978). The strange situation consists of a series of eight episodes (summarized in Table 11.2) that attempt to simulate (1) naturalistic caregiver–infant interactions in the presence of toys (to see if the infant uses the caregiver as a *secure base* from which to explore); (2) brief separations from the caregiver and encounters with strangers (which often stress the infant); and (3) reunion

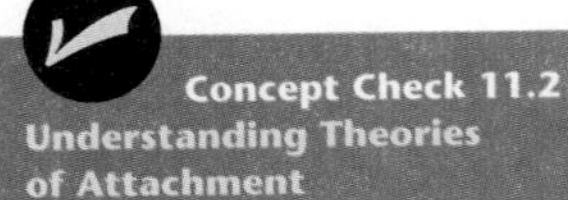

Concept Check 11.2
Understanding Theories of Attachment

Check your understanding of various theories of attachment by matching each descriptive statement below to one of the following theories or theorists: (a) Sigmund Freud, (b) Erik Erikson, (c) learning perspective, (d) John Bowlby, (e) Mary Ainsworth, (f) cognitive-developmental perspective. The answers appear in the Appendix at the back of the book.

_____ 1. believes that stranger/separation anxieties gradually decline as infants use their attachment objects as secure bases for exploration

_____ 2. proposes that infants are attached once the caregiver attains the status of a secondary reinforcer

_____ 3. claims that infants protest separations when they cannot account for the caregiver's whereabouts

_____ 4. proposes that caregivers' feeding practices determine the strength or character of infant attachments

_____ 5. thinks that strange faces and separations from attachment objects are natural clues to danger that infants are programmed to fear

_____ 6. emphasizes caregiver responsiveness and the infant's feelings of trust as the primary determinants of attachment security

Table 11.2 The Eight Episodes of the Strange Situation

Episode	Events	Potential attachment behaviors noted
1.	Experimenter introduces parent and baby to playroom and leaves.	
2.	Parent sits while baby plays.	Parent as a secure base
3.	Stranger enters, sits, and talks to parent.	Stranger anxiety
4.	Parent leaves, stranger offers comfort if the baby is upset.	Separation anxiety
5.	Parent returns, greets baby, and offers comfort if baby is upset. Stranger leaves.	Reunion behaviors
6.	Parent leaves room.	Separation anxiety
7.	Stranger enters and offers comfort.	Ability to be soothed by stranger
8.	Parent returns, greets baby, offers comfort if necessary, and tries to interest baby in toys.	Reunion behaviors

Note: All episodes except the first last 3 minutes, although separation episodes may be abbreviated and reunion episodes extended for babies who become extremely upset.
Source: Based on Ainsworth et al., 1978.

episodes (to determine whether a stressed infant derives any comfort and reassurance from the caregiver and can once again become involved with toys). By recording and analyzing an infant's responses to these episodes—that is, exploratory activities, reactions to strangers and to separations, and, in particular, behaviors when reunited with the close companion—it is usually possible to characterize his or her attachment to the caregiver in one of four ways.

Secure Attachment

About 65% of 1-year-old North American infants fall into this category. The **securely attached** infant actively explores while alone with the mother and may be visibly upset by separations. The infant *often greets the mother warmly when she returns and, if highly distressed, often seeks physical contact with her,* which helps to alleviate that distress. The child is outgoing with strangers while the mother is present.

Resistant Attachment

About 10% of 1-year-olds show this type of "insecure" attachment. These infants try to stay close to their mother but explore very little while she is present. They become very distressed as the mother departs. But when she returns, the infants are ambivalent: They *remain near her,* although they seem angry at her for having left them and are likely to *resist physical contact initiated by the mother.* Resistant infants are quite wary of strangers, even when their mothers are present.

Avoidant Attachment

These infants (about 20% of 1-year-olds) also display an "insecure" attachment. They often show little distress when separated from the mother and generally *turn away from and may continue to ignore their mothers, even when mothers try to gain their attention.* Avoidant infants are often rather sociable with strangers but may sometimes avoid or ignore them in much the same way that they avoid or ignore their mothers.

Disorganized/Disoriented Attachment

This recently discovered attachment pattern characterizes the 5 to 10% of American infants who are most stressed by the strange situation and who may be the most insecure (Hertsgaard et al., 1995). It appears to be a curious combination of the resistant

resistant attachment
an insecure infant–caregiver bond, characterized by strong separation protest and a tendency of the child to remain near but resist contact initiated by the caregiver, particularly after a separation.

avoidant attachment
an insecure infant–caregiver bond, characterized by little separation protest and a tendency of the child to avoid or ignore the caregiver.

and the avoidant patterns that reflects confusion about whether to approach or avoid the caregiver (Main & Solomon, 1990). When reunited with their mothers, these infants may act dazed and freeze; or they may move closer but then abruptly move away as the mother draws near; or they may show both patterns in different reunion episodes.

Unfortunately, the strange situation is not as useful for characterizing the attachments of children much older than 2, who are becoming quite accustomed to (and less stressed by) brief separations and encounters with strangers. Recently, an alternative assessment of attachment quality—the **Attachment Q-set (AQS)**—has become quite popular. Appropriate for use with 1- to 5-year-olds, the Attachment Q-set requires an observer—usually a parent or trained observer—to sort a set of 90 descriptors of attachment-related behaviors (for example, "Child looks to mother for reassurance when wary"; "Child greets mother with big smiles. . . .") into categories ranging from "most like" to "least like" the child's behavior at home. The resulting profile represents how secure the child is with his or her caregiver (Waters et al., 1995). Trained observers' Q-set assessments for infants and toddlers are usually concordant with strange situation attachment classifications (Pederson & Moran, 1996; Vaughn & Waters, 1990). And the ability to classify the attachment security of older preschool children *in their natural environments* makes the AQS a rather versatile alternative to the Strange Situation.

disorganized/disoriented attachment
an insecure infant–caregiver bond, characterized by the infant's dazed appearance on reunion or a tendency to first seek and then abruptly avoid the caregiver.

Attachment Q-set
alternative method of assessing attachment security that is based on observations of the child's attachment-related behaviors at home; can be used with infants, toddlers, and preschool children.

Cultural Variations in Attachment Classifications

Although child-rearing traditions vary dramatically across cultures, secure attachments are more common than insecure attachments around the world.

The percentages of infants and toddlers who fall into the various attachment categories differ somewhat from culture to culture and seem to reflect cultural variations in child-rearing. For example, parents in northern Germany deliberately encourage their infants to be independent and tend to discourage clingy close contact, perhaps explaining why more German than American babies show reunion behaviors characteristic of the avoidant attachment pattern (Grossmann et al., 1985). Furthermore, intense separation and stranger anxieties, which characterize resistant attachments, are much more common in cultures such as Japan, where caregivers rarely leave their infants with substitute caregivers, and Israel, where communally reared kibbutz children sleep in infant houses without their parents being accessible to them at night (Sagi et al., 1994). But despite these cultural variations, parents around the world prefer that their young children feel secure in their relationships with them (Posada et al., 1995), and more infants around the world fall into the secure attachment category than into any of the insecure categories (van IJzendoorn & Kroonenberg, 1988).

FACTORS THAT INFLUENCE ATTACHMENT SECURITY

Among the many factors that seem to influence the kinds of attachments that infants establish are the quality of caregiving they receive, the character or emotional climate of their homes, and their own health conditions and temperaments.

Quality of Caregiving

Mary Ainsworth (1979) believes that the quality of an infant's attachment to his mother (or any other close companion) depends largely on the kind of attention he has received. According to this **caregiving hypothesis,** mothers of *securely attached* infants are thought to be sensitive, responsive caregivers from the very beginning. And apparently they are. One recent review of 66 studies found that mothers who display the characteristics described in Table 11.3 tend to have infants who form secure attachments with them (De Wolff & van IJzendoorn, 1997). So if a caregiver has a positive attitude toward her baby, is usually sensitive to his needs, has established interactional synchrony with him, and provides ample stimulation and emotional support, the infant often derives comfort and pleasure from their interactions and is likely to become securely attached.

Babies who show a *resistant* rather than secure pattern of attachment sometimes have irritable and unresponsive temperaments (Cassidy & Berlin, 1994; Waters et al., 1980); but more often they have parents who are *inconsistent* in their caregiving—reacting enthusiastically or indifferently depending on their moods and being unresponsive a good deal of the time (Ainsworth, 1979; Isabella, 1993; Isabella & Belsky, 1991). The infant copes with this inconsistent caregiving by trying desperately—through clinging, crying, and other attachment behaviors—to obtain emotional support and comfort and then becomes sad and resentful when these efforts often fail.

There are at least two patterns of caregiving that place infants at risk of developing *avoidant* attachments. Ainsworth and others (for example, Isabella, 1993) find that some mothers of avoidant infants are often impatient with their babies and unresponsive to their signals, are likely to express negative feelings about their infants, and seem to derive little pleasure from close contact with them. Ainsworth (1979) believes that these mothers are rigid, self-centered people who are likely to *reject* their babies. In other cases, however, avoidant babies have overzealous parents who chatter endlessly and provide high levels of stimulation even when their babies do not want it (Belsky et al., 1984; Isabella & Belsky, 1991). Infants may be responding quite adaptively by learning to avoid adults who seem to dislike their company or who bombard them with stimulation they cannot handle. Whereas resistant infants make vigorous attempts to gain emotional support, avoidant infants seem to have learned to do without it (Isabella, 1993).

Finally, Mary Main believes that infants who develop *disorganized/disoriented* attachments are often drawn to but also *fearful* of caregivers because of past episodes in which they were neglected or physically abused (Main & Soloman, 1990). Indeed, the infant's approach/avoidance (or totally dazed demeanor) at reunion is quite understandable if she has experienced cycles of acceptance and abuse (or neglect) and doesn't know whether to approach the caregiver for comfort or to retreat from her to safety.

TABLE 11.3 Aspects of Caregiving that Promote Secure Mother–Infant Attachments

Characteristic	Description
Sensitivity	Responding promptly and appropriately to the infant's signals
Positive attitude	Expressing positive affect and affection for the infant
Synchrony	Structuring smooth, reciprocal interactions with the infant
Mutuality	Structuring interactions in which mother and infant attend to the same thing
Support	Attending closely to and providing emotional support for the infant's activities
Stimulation	Frequently directing actions toward the infant

NOTE: These six aspects of caregiving are moderately correlated with each other.
SOURCE: Based on data from De Wolff and van IJzendoorn, 1997.

caregiving hypothesis
Ainsworth's notion that the type of attachment that an infant develops with a particular caregiver depends primarily on the kind of caregiving he has received from that person.

Available research supports Main's theorizing: Although disorganized/disoriented attachments are occasionally observed in research samples, they seem to be the *rule* rather than the exception among groups of abused infants (Carlson et al., 1989). And this same curious mixture of approach and avoidance, coupled with sadness upon reunion, also characterizes many infants of severely depressed mothers, who may be inclined to mistreat or neglect their babies (Lyons-Ruth et al., 1990; Murray et al., 1996; Teti et al., 1995).

Who Is at Risk of Becoming an Insensitive Caregiver?

Several personal characteristics place parents at risk of displaying the insensitive patterns of parenting that contribute to insecure attachments. For example, insecure attachments of one kind or the other are the *rule* rather than the exception when a child's primary caregiver has been diagnosed as clinically depressed (Radke-Yarrow et al., 1985; Teti et al., 1995). Depressed parents often ignore babies' social signals and generally fail to establish satisfying and synchronous relationships with them. And infants often become angry at these caregivers' lack of responsiveness and may soon begin to match their depressive symptoms, even when interacting with other *nondepressed* adults (Campbell, Cohn, & Meyers, 1995; Field et al., 1988; Pickens & Field, 1993).

Another group of parents who are often insensitive caregivers are those who themselves felt unloved, neglected, or abused as children. These formerly mistreated caregivers often start out with the best intentions, vowing never to do to their children what was done to them, but they often expect their infants to be perfect and to love them right away. So when their babies are irritable, fussy, or inattentive (as all infants are at times), these emotionally insecure adults are likely to feel as if they are being rejected once again (Steele & Pollack, 1974). They may then back off or withdraw their own affection (Biringen, 1990; Crowell & Feldman, 1991), sometimes to the point of neglecting or even abusing their babies.

Finally, caregivers whose pregnancies were unplanned and their babies unwanted can be particularly insensitive caregivers whose children fare rather poorly in all aspects of development. In one longitudinal study in Czechoslovakia (Matejcek, Dytrych, & Schuller, 1979), mothers who had been denied permission to abort an unwanted pregnancy were judged to be less closely attached to their children than a group of same-aged mothers of similar marital and socioeconomic status who had not requested an abortion. Although both the wanted and the unwanted children were physically healthy at birth, over the next 9 years, the unwanted children were more frequently hospitalized, made lower grades in school, had less stable family lives and poorer relations with peers, and were generally more irritable than the children whose parents had wanted them. Follow-up observations in young adulthood tell much the same story: Compared with their wanted peers, the formerly unwanted children were now much less satisfied with their marriages, jobs, friendships, and general mental health, having more often sought treatment for a variety of psychological disorders (David, 1992; 1994). Clearly, parents are unlikely to be very sensitive or to foster the development of children they do not care to raise.

Ecological Constraints on Caregiving Sensitivity

Of course, parent–child interactions always take place in a broader ecological context that may influence how caregivers respond to their children. Insensitive parenting, for example, is much more likely among caregivers who are experiencing health-related, legal, or financial problems, and it is hardly surprising that the incidence of insecure attachments is highest among poverty-stricken families that receive inadequate health care (Murray et al., 1996; NICHD Early Child Care Research Network, 1997).

The quality of a caregiver's relationship with his or her spouse can also have a dramatic effect on parent–infant interactions. Consider that parents who were unhappily married *prior* to the birth of their child (1) are less sensitive caregivers after the baby is born, (2) express less favorable attitudes about their infants and the parenting role, and (3) establish less secure ties with their infants and toddlers, compared with other parents from similar socioeconomic backgrounds whose marriages are close and confiding (Cox et al., 1989; Howes & Markman, 1989). Happily married couples, on the other hand, usually support each other's parenting efforts, and this positive social support for parenting is especially important if the baby has already shown a tendency to be irritable and unresponsive. In fact, Jay Belsky (1981) found that newborns who are at risk for later emotional difficulties (as indicated by their poor performance on the Brazelton Neonatal Behavioral Assessment Scale) are likely to have nonsynchronous interactions with their parents *only when the parents are unhappily married*. So it seems that a stormy marriage is a major environmental hazard that can hinder or even prevent the establishment of secure emotional ties between parents and their infants.

Insensitive parenting is more likely to occur in families experiencing health-related, financial, or marital distress.

What Can Be Done to Assist Insensitive Caregivers?

Fortunately, there are ways of assisting at-risk parents to become more sensitive and responsive caregivers. In one intervention, depressed poverty-stricken mothers were visited regularly by a professional, who first established a friendly, supportive relationship, and then taught them how to elicit more favorable responses from their babies and encouraged their participation in weekly parenting groups. Toddlers whose mothers received this support later scored higher on intelligence tests and were much more likely to be securely attached than those of other depressed mothers who hadn't participated in an intervention (Lyons-Ruth et al., 1990).

In another intervention in Holland, economically disadvantaged mothers whose babies were extremely irritable received a 3-month intervention designed to improve their sensitivity and responsiveness to their infants' social signals. Not only did those mothers become more sensitive caregivers, but their infants were more likely than those of comparable mothers who received no intervention to be securely attached at age 12 months and to remain more secure with their mothers at age 3½ (van den Boom, 1995).

So the intervention studies clearly indicate that caregiving sensitivity can be fostered and that it promotes secure attachments. Unfortunately, most of the research conducted to date has focused exclusively on caregiving provided by mothers and has largely ignored fathers. In Box 11.3, we take a closer look at fathers as caregivers and at the contributions that fathers can make to their infants' social and emotional development.

Infant Characteristics

Thus far, we have talked as if parents are responsible for the kind of attachments that infants establish. But since it takes two people to form an attachment *relationship,* we might suspect that babies can also influence the quality of parent–infant emotional ties. For example, the sluggish and often irritable demeanor that characterizes many low-birth-weight babies (and those born seriously ill or addicted to drugs) is a behavioral profile that can alienate caregivers and contribute to insensitive parenting and insecure

DEVELOPMENTAL ISSUES

11.3 Fathers as Attachment Objects

In 1975, Michael Lamb described fathers as the "forgotten contributors to child development." And he was right. Until the mid-1970s, fathers were treated as biological necessities who played only a minor role in the social and emotional development of their infants and toddlers. One reason for overlooking or discounting the father's early contributions may have been that most fathers spend less time interacting with babies than mothers do (Belsky, Gilstrap, & Rovine, 1984; Parke, 1995). However, fathers appear to be just as engrossed with their newborn infants as mothers are (Nichols, 1993), and they become increasingly involved with their babies over the first year of life (Belsky et al., 1984), spending an average of nearly an hour a day interacting with their 9-month-olds (Ninio & Rinott, 1988). Fathers are most highly involved with their infants and hold more favorable attitudes about them when they are happily married (Belsky, 1996; Cox et al., 1989; 1992) and when their wives encourage them to become an important part of their babies' lives (Palkovitz, 1984).

Many infants form secure attachments to their fathers during the latter half of the first year (Lamb, 1981), particularly if the father has a positive attitude about parenting, is extroverted and agreeable, spends a lot of time with them, and is a sensitive caregiver (Cox et al., 1992; van IJzendoorn & De Wolff, 1997). And how do fathers compare with mothers as companions? Research conducted in Australia, Israel, India, Italy, Japan, and the United States reveals that mothers and fathers in all these societies tend to play somewhat different roles in a baby's life. Mothers are more likely than fathers to hold their infants, to soothe and talk to them, to play traditional games, such as peekaboo, and to care for their physical needs; fathers are more likely than mothers to provide playful physical stimulation and to initiate unusual or unpredictable games that infants often enjoy. Although most infants prefer their mothers' company when upset or afraid, fathers are often preferred as playmates (Lamb & Oppenheim, 1989; Roopnarine et al., 1990).

However, the playmate role is but one of many that modern fathers fulfill, particularly if their wives are working and they must necessarily assume at least some of the caregiving responsibility (Cox et al., 1992). And what kinds of caregivers do dads make? Many of them are (or soon become) rather skillful at virtually all phases of routine care (including diapering, bathing, and soothing a distressed infant). Moreover, once fathers become objects of affection, they begin to serve as a secure base from which their babies will venture to explore the environment (Hwang, 1986; Lamb, 1981). So fathers are rather versatile companions who can assume any and all functions normally served by the other parent (of course, the same is true of mothers).

Although many infants form the same kind of attachment with their fathers that they have established with their mothers (Fox, Kimmerly, & Schafer, 1991; Rosen & Rothbaum, 1993), it is not at all unusual for a child to be securely attached to one parent and insecure with the other (Cox et al., 1992; van IJzendoorn & De Wolff, 1997). For example, when Mary Main and Donna Weston (1981) used the Situation to measure the quality of 44 infants' attachments to their mothers and their fathers, they found that 12 infants were securely attached to both parents, 11 were secure with

attachments (Field, 1987; Lester et al., 1991). Indeed, low-birth-weight babies are more likely than full-term healthy ones to establish insecure primary attachments (Mangelsdorf et al., 1996), although most of these at-risk infants who receive sensitive parenting end up quite secure with their caregivers (Goldberg et al., 1986; Pederson & Moran, 1995).

Do the large temperamental variations that infants display influence attachment classifications? Jerome Kagan (1984; 1989) certainly thinks so. He argues that the Strange Situation really measures individual differences in infants' temperaments rather than the quality of their attachments. This idea grew from his observation that the percentages of 1-year-olds who have established *secure, resistant,* and *avoidant* attachments corresponds closely to the percentages of babies who fall into Thomas and Chess's *easy, difficult,* and *slow-to-warm-up* temperamental profiles (see Table 11.4). And the linkages even make some sense. Kagan suggests that a temperamentally difficult infant who actively resists changes in routine and is upset by novelty may become so distressed by the Strange Situation that he is unable to respond constructively to his mother's comforting and is thus classified as *resistant.* By contrast, a friendly, easygoing child is apt to be classified as *securely attached,* whereas one who is shy or slow to warm up may appear distant or detached in the Strange Situation and will probably be classified as *avoidant.* So Kagan's **temperament hypothesis** implies that infants, not caregivers, are the primary architects of their attachment classifications. Presumably, the attachment behaviors that a child displays reflect his or her own temperament.

temperament hypothesis Kagan's view that the Strange Situation measures individual differences in infants' temperaments rather than the quality of their attachments.

the mother but insecure with the father, 10 were insecure with the mother but secure with the father, and 11 were insecurely attached to both parents.

What does the father add to a child's social and emotional development? One way to find out is to compare the social behavior of infants who are securely attached to their fathers with those whose relationships with their fathers are insecure. Main and Weston did just that by exposing their four groups of infants to a friendly stranger in a clown outfit who spent several minutes trying to play with the child and then turned around and cried when a person at the door told the clown he would have to leave. As the clown went through his routine, the infants were each observed and rated for (1) the extent to which they were willing to establish a positive relationship with the clown (low ratings indicated that the infant was wary or distressed) and (2) signs of emotional conflict (that is, indications of psychological disturbance such as curling up in the fetal position on the floor or vocalizing in a "social" manner to a wall). The table shows the results of this stranger test. Note that infants who were securely attached to both parents were the most socially responsive group. Equally important is the finding that infants who were securely attached to *at least one parent* were more friendly toward the clown and less emotionally conflicted than infants who had insecure relationships with both parents. So this study illustrates the important role that fathers can play in their infants' social and emotional development. Not only are infants more socially responsive when they are securely attached to *both* the mother and the father, but it also appears that secure attachment with the father may buffer the potentially negative effects of an insecure mother–infant attachment (see also Biller, 1993).

Average Levels of Social Responsiveness and Emotional Conflict Shown by Infants Who Were Either Securely or Insecurely Attached to Their Mothers and Fathers

	Patterns of attachment			
Measure	*Securely attached to both parents*	*Secure with mother, insecure with father*	*Insecure with mother, secure with father*	*Insecurely attached to both parents*
Social responsiveness	6.04	4.87	3.30	2.45
Emotional conflict	1.17	1.00	1.80	2.50

Note: Social responsiveness ratings could vary from 1 (wary, distressed) to 9 (happy, responsive). Conflict ratings could vary from 1 (no conflict) to 5 (very conflicted).
Source: Adapted from Main & Weston, 1981.

Does Temperament Explain Attachment Security?

Although such components of temperament as irritability and negative emotionality predict certain attachment behaviors (for example, intensity of separation protests) and can certainly contribute to the quality of an infant's attachments (Goldsmith & Alansky, 1987; Seifer et al., 1996; Vaughn et al., 1992), most experts view Kagan's temperament hypothesis as far too extreme. Consider, for example, that many infants are securely attached to one close companion and insecurely attached to another—a pattern that we would not expect to see if attachment classifications were merely reflections of the child's relatively stable temperamental characteristics (Goossens & van

TABLE 11.4 Percentage of 1-Year-Olds Who Can Be Classified as Temperamentally "Easy," "Difficult," and "Slow to Warm Up" Who Have Established Secure, Resistant, and Avoidant Attachments with Their Mothers

Temperamental profile	Percentage of "classifiable" infants	Attachment classification	Percentage of 1-year-olds
Easy	60	Secure	65
Difficult	15	Resistant	10
Slow to warm up	23	Avoidant	20

SOURCE: Ainsworth, Blehar, Waters, & Wall, 1978; Thomas & Chess, 1977.

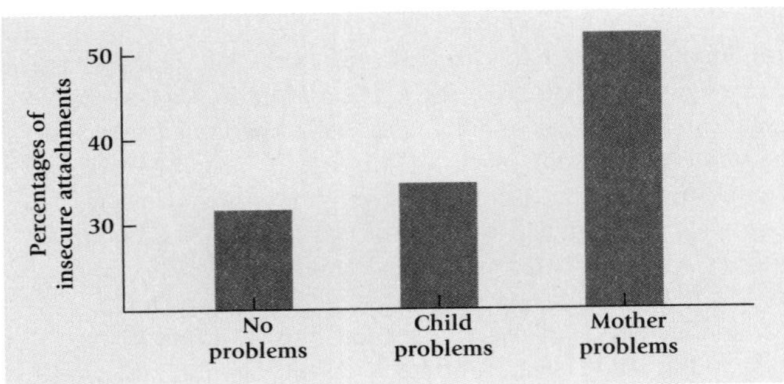

Figure 11.5 *Comparing the impact of maternal and child problem behaviors on the incidence of insecure attachments. Maternal problems were associated with a sharp increase in insecure attachments, whereas child problems were not.* BASED ON VAN IJZENDOORN ET AL., *1992.*

IJzendoorn, 1990; Sroufe, 1985). In addition, we have already seen that when mothers of temperamentally difficult Dutch infants are trained to be more sensitive, the vast majority of their babies establish secure rather than insecure attachments, which indicates that sensitive caregiving is causally related to attachment quality (van den Boom, 1995). Finally, one review of 34 studies revealed that maternal characteristics that often predict insensitive parenting, such as illness, depression, and child maltreatment, were associated with a sharp increase in insecure attachments (see Figure 11.5). However, child problems such as prematurity, illness, and other psychological disorders had virtually no impact on attachment quality (van IJzendoorn et al., 1992).

So it seems that caregivers, not infants, are the *primary* architects of the quality of infant attachments. This is not to say that infant temperament is unimportant, for it is harder for a caregiver to be consistently sensitive and responsive to a temperamentally difficult infant than to an easygoing one (van den Boom, 1995). However, it should be emphasized that a clear majority of temperamentally difficult babies establish *secure* attachments with caregivers who display lots of patience and adapt their caregiving to their baby's temperamental characteristics (Mangelsdorf et al., 1990; van den Boom, 1995; van IJzendoorn et al., 1992). By contrast, even many babies who are good-natured may end up establishing insecure relationships with mothers who are experiencing serious psychological difficulties that prevent them from being sensitive, responsive companions (van IJzendoorn et al., 1992).

Perhaps these findings are best summarized in terms of Thomas and Chess's (1977) *goodness-of-fit model* that we introduced earlier in the chapter. Secure attachments evolve from relationships in which there is a good fit between the caregiving that a baby receives and his or her own temperament, whereas insecure attachments are more likely to develop when highly stressed or otherwise inflexible caregivers fail to accommodate to their infants' temperamental qualities (van den Boom, 1995). Indeed, one reason why caregiver sensitivity predicts attachment security is that the very notion of *sensitive* care implies an ability to tailor one's routines to whatever temperamental qualities a baby might display (Sroufe, 1985; van den Boom, 1997).

ATTACHMENT AND LATER DEVELOPMENT

Both psychoanalytic theorists (Erikson, 1963; Freud, 1905/1930) and ethologists (Bowlby, 1969) believe that the feelings of warmth, trust, and security that infants gain from secure attachments set the stage for healthy psychological development later in life. Of course, one implication of this viewpoint is that insecure attachments may forecast less-than-optimal developmental outcomes in the years ahead.

Long-Term Correlates of Secure and Insecure Attachments

Although the existing data are somewhat limited in that they focus almost exclusively on infants' attachments to their mothers, it seems that infants who have established secure primary attachments are likely to display more favorable developmental outcomes. For example, babies who were securely attached at age 12 to 18 months are better problem solvers as 2-year-olds (Frankel & Bates, 1990), more complex and creative in their symbolic play (Pipp, Easterbrooks, & Harmon, 1992), and more attractive to toddlers as playmates (Fagot, 1997; Jacobson & Wille, 1986) than children who were insecurely attached. In fact, infants whose primary attachments are disorganized/disoriented are at risk of becoming hostile and aggressive preschool and grade-school children whom peers are likely to reject (Lyons-Ruth, Alpern, & Repacholi, 1993; Lyons-Ruth, Easterbrooks, & Cibelli, 1997).

Many other studies of securely and insecurely attached children paint a similar picture. Everett Waters and his associates (1979), for example, first measured the quality of children's attachments at 15 months of age and then observed these children in a nursery school setting at age 3½. Children who had been securely attached to their mothers at age 15 months were now social leaders in the nursery school: They often initiated play activities, were generally sensitive to the needs and feelings of other children, and were very popular with their peers. Observers described these children as curious, self-directed, and eager to learn. By contrast, children who had been insecurely attached at age 15 months were socially and emotionally withdrawn, were hesitant to engage other children in play activities, and were described by observers as less curious, less interested in learning, and much less forceful in pursuing their goals. A follow-up in a camp setting when these children were 11 to 12 years old revealed that those who had been securely attached still displayed better social skills, enjoyed better peer relations, and were more likely to have close friends than age-mates whose primary attachments had been insecure (Elicker, Englund, & Sroufe, 1992; Shulman, Elicker, & Sroufe, 1994). So it seems that children can be influenced by the quality of their early attachments for many years to come. And one reason is that attachments are often stable over time; most children (84% in one American sample and 82% in a German sample) experienced the same kind of attachment relationships with their parents during the grade-school years that they did in infancy (Main & Cassidy, 1988; Wartner et al., 1994). In fact, young adults who characterize their early parental attachments as secure, resistant, or avoidant tend to establish the same kind of attachment relationships with their current romantic partners (Feeney & Noller, 1990; Hazan & Shaver, 1987).

Why Might Attachment Quality Forecast Later Outcomes?

Why is the quality of one's early attachments so often stable over time? And how might attachments shape one's behavior and influence the character of one's future interpersonal relationships?

Attachments as Working Models of Self and Others

Ethologists John Bowlby (1980; 1988) and Inge Bretherton (1985; 1990) have proposed an interesting explanation for both the stability and the enduring effects of early attachment classifications. They believe that as infants continue to interact with primary caregivers, they develop **internal working models**—that is, cognitive representations of *themselves* and *other people*—that are used to interpret events and to form expectations about the character of human relationships. Sensitive, responsive caregiving should lead the child to conclude that people are dependable (positive working model of others), whereas insensitive, neglectful, or abusive caregiving may lead to insecurity and a lack of trust (negative working model of others). Although this sounds very similar to Erik Erikson's earlier ideas about the importance of trust, ethologists proceed one step further, arguing that infants also develop a working model of the *self* based largely on their ability to elicit attention and comfort *when they need it.* So an infant whose caregivers respond quickly and appropriately to her bids for attention is apt to believe that "I'm lovable" (positive working model of self), whereas one whose signals are ignored or misinterpreted

internal working models
cognitive representations of self, others, and relationships that infants construct from their interactions with caregivers.

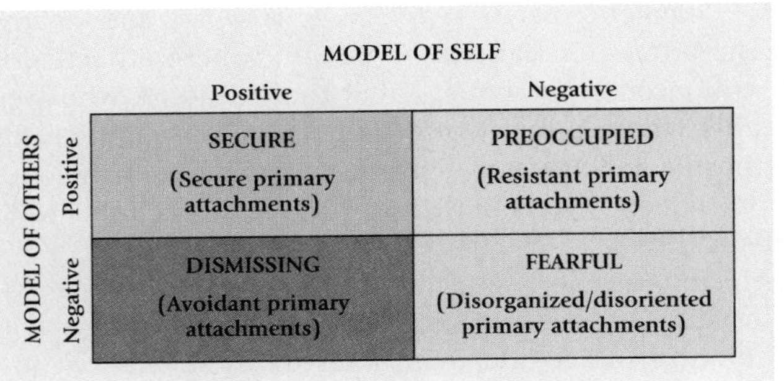

Figure 11.6 *Four perspectives on close emotional relationships that evolve from the positive or negative "working models" of self and others that people construct from their experiences with intimate companions.* ADAPTED FROM BARTHOLOMEW & HOROWITZ, 1991.

may conclude that "I'm unworthy or loathsome" (negative working model of self). Presumably, these two models combine to influence the quality of the child's primary attachments and the expectations she has about future relationships. What kinds of expectations might she form?

A recent version of this working-models theory appears in Figure 11.6. As shown, infants who construct positive working models of themselves and their caregivers are the ones who should (1) form secure primary attachments, (2) have the *self*-confidence to approach and to master new challenges, and (3) be inclined to establish secure, mutual-trust relationships with friends and spouses later in life. By contrast, a positive model of self coupled with a negative model of others (as might result when infants can successfully attract the attention of an insensitive, overintrusive caregiver) is thought to predispose the infant to form *avoidant* attachments and to dismiss the importance of close emotional bonds. A negative model of self and a positive model of others (as might result when infants sometimes can but often cannot attract the attention they need) should be associated with *resistant* attachments and a preoccupation with establishing secure emotional ties. Finally, a negative working model of both the self and others is thought to underlie *disorganized/disoriented* attachments and an emerging fear of being hurt (either physically or emotionally) in intimate relationships (Bartholomew & Horowitz, 1991).

Although the working-models hypothesis is relatively new and researchers may find it rather difficult to measure the cognitive representations of nonverbal infants (and toddlers), early returns with preschool and grade-school children have been highly informative. Consider that 3½- to 6-year-olds with secure and resistant attachment histories—the very children who presumably have formed a *positive* working model of others—already perceive peers in more positive ways than do age-mates with avoidant attachments. Furthermore, children with more positive cognitive representations of peers have established more reciprocated friendships than those whose peer representations are less positive (Cassidy et al., 1996). Other research with grade-school students indicates that children with negative *self*-representations make lower grades later in adolescence than do those with positive working models of self (Jacobsen & Hofmann, 1997). They also have negative representations of peers and are often rather unpopular with them (Rudolph, Hammen, & Burge, 1995). So the available evidence is quite consistent with the notion that working models established at home may persist for long periods, influencing our reactions to cognitive challenges and the character of our future interpersonal relationships.

Parents' Working Models and Attachment

Interestingly, parents also have positive or negative working models of themselves and others based on their own life experiences. Several methods now exist to measure adults' working models, based either on a detailed analysis of their memories of childhood attachment experiences or on their current view of themselves, other people, and the character of interpersonal relationships (Bartholomew & Horowitz, 1991; Main & Goldwyn, 1994). Using these instruments, adults can be reliably cast into the classifications described earlier in Figure 11.6. Do their own working models influence the kinds of attachments that their babies form?

Indeed they do. Peter Fonagy and his associates (1991), for example, found that English mothers' working models of attachment relationships measured *before their babies were born* accurately predicted about 75% of the time whether their infants would establish secure or insecure attachments with them. Similar results have now been reported in studies conducted in Canada, Germany, the Netherlands, and the United States (Benoit & Parker, 1994; Das Eiden, Teti, & Corns, 1995; Steele, Steele, & Fonagy,

1996; van IJzendoorn, 1995), with an exact matching of working models occurring in 60 to 70% of the mother–infant dyads. And at least one study found that mothers' working models of attachment relationships were actually better predictors of infants' attachment classifications than was the sensitivity of caregiving that mothers displayed (Ward & Carlson, 1995).

So it seems that cognitive representations of intimate relationships are often transmitted from generation to generation. Indeed, Bowlby (1988) proposed that once formed early in life, working models may stabilize, becoming an aspect of personality that continues to influence the character of one's close emotional ties throughout life.

Is Attachment History Destiny?

Although it appears that early working models can be long-lasting, and that there are some clear advantages to having formed secure emotional attachments early in life, the future is not always so bleak for infants who are insecurely attached. As we learned in Box 11.3, a secure relationship with another person such as the father (or perhaps a grandparent or a day-care provider) can help to offset whatever undesirable consequences might otherwise result from an insecure attachment with the mother (Clarke-Stewart, 1989).

Let's also note that secure attachments sometimes become insecure should a mother return to work, place her infant in day-care, or experience such life stresses as marital problems, a major illness, or financial woes that drastically alter the ways that she and her infant respond to each other (Thompson, Lamb, & Estes, 1982). One reason why Bowlby (and later Bretherton) used the term *working* models was to underscore that a child's cognitive representations of self, others, and close emotional relationships are dynamic and can change (for better or for worse) if later experiences with caregivers, close friends, romantic partners, or spouses imply that a revision is necessary.

In sum, secure attachment histories are no guarantee of positive adjustment later in life; nor are insecure early attachments a certain indicator of poor life outcomes (Fagot & Kavanagh, 1990). Yet, we should not underestimate the adaptive significance of secure early attachments, for children who have functioned adequately as infants but very poorly during the preschool period are more likely to recover and to display good social skills and self-confidence during the grade-school years if their early attachment histories were secure rather than insecure (Sroufe, Egeland, & Kreutzer, 1990).

THE UNATTACHED INFANT

Some infants have very limited contacts with adults during the first year or two of life and do not appear to become attached to anyone. Occasionally, these socially deprived youngsters are reared at home by very abusive or neglectful caregivers, but most of them are found in understaffed institutions where they may see a caregiver only when it is time to be fed, changed, or bathed. Will these infants suffer as a result of their early experiences?

Effects of Social Deprivation in Infancy and Childhood

In the 1940s, physicians and psychologists began to discover and study infants who were living under conditions of extreme social deprivation. For example, it was not uncommon for the impoverished institutions in which these infants lived to have but one caregiver for every 10 to 20 infants. Adult caregivers rarely interacted with the

Children raised in barren, understaffed institutions show many signs of developmental retardation.

infants except to bathe and change them or to prop a bottle against their pillows at feeding time. Infants were often housed in separate cribs with sheets hung over the railings so that, in effect, they were isolated from the world around them. By today's standards, these babies were victims of extreme neglect (DeAngelis, 1997).

Infants raised under these conditions appear quite normal for the first 3 to 6 months of life: They cry for attention, smile and babble at caregivers, and make the proper postural adjustments when they are about to be picked up. But in the second half of the first year, their behavior changes. Now they seldom cry, coo, or babble; they become rigid and fail to accommodate to the handling of caregivers, and they often appear rather depressed and uninterested in social contact (Goldfarb, 1943; Provence & Lipton, 1962; Ribble, 1943; Spitz, 1945). Here is a description of one such infant:

> **? WHAT DO YOU THINK?**
>
> Imagine that you are a researcher who studies the developmental significance of infant emotions (both emotional expression and emotional understanding). Knowing what you do, how would you explain the sober, depressed behavior of infants in understaffed institutions?

> Outstanding were his soberness, his forlorn appearance, and lack of animation. . . . He did not turn to adults to relieve his distress. . . . He made no demands. . . . As one made active and persistent efforts at a social exchange he became somewhat more responsive, animated and . . . active, but lapsed into his depressed . . . appearance when the adult became less active. . . . If you crank his motor you can get him to go a little; but he can't start on his own. (Provence & Lipton, 1962, pp. 134–135).

What are these institutionalized infants like as schoolchildren and adolescents? The answer depends, in part, on how long they remain in the institution. William Goldfarb (1943; 1947) compared children who left an understaffed orphanage during the first year with similar children who spent their first 3 years at the orphanage before departing for foster homes. After interviewing, observing, and testing these children at ages 3½, 6½, 8½, and 12, Goldfarb found that youngsters who had spent 3 years in the institution lagged behind the early adoptees in virtually all aspects of development. They scored poorly on IQ tests, were socially immature, remarkably dependent on adults, had poor language skills, and were prone to behavior problems such as aggression and hyperactivity. By early adolescence, they were often loners who had a difficult time relating to peers or family members.

More recent observations of late-adopted institution children from England and Romania, and of neglected or mistreated infants placed into foster care late in the first year, find many of the same developmental impairments that characterized the institution children from earlier eras (DeAngelis, 1997; Fischer et al., 1997; Hodges & Tizard, 1989). Particularly disturbing is the finding that many children raised under these adverse conditions display **reactive attachment disorder,** an inability to become *securely* attached to adoptive or foster parents, even when these new caregivers have secure working models of attachment relationships (DeAngelis, 1997). Indeed, the insecure attachments that these children form may help to explain why they are often restless, troubled, and have few close friends later in childhood and adolescence.

Why Is Early Deprivation Harmful?

No one questions that early social deprivation can have lasting effects, but there is some disagreement about why this is so. Proponents of the **maternal deprivation hypothesis** (Bowlby, 1969; Spitz, 1965) think that neglected children and those in understaffed institutions develop abnormally because they lack the warm, loving attention of a single mother-figure to whom they can become attached. But despite its popularity, there are many observations that the maternal deprivation hypothesis cannot easily explain. Studies of adequately staffed institutions in Russia and Israel, for example, reveal that infants who are cared for by dozens of responsive caregivers appear quite normal and are as well adjusted later in childhood as those who are reared at home (Bronfenbrenner, 1970; Kessen, 1975; Oppenheim, Sagi, & Lamb, 1988). Similarly, Efe (Pygmy) infants in Zaire seem to thrive from birth on being cared for and even nursed by a variety of caregivers (Tronick, Morelli, & Ivey, 1992). So it seems that the impairments characterizing children in understaffed institutions probably reflect something other than their lack of an exclusive attachment to a singular mother figure.

Might socially deprived infants develop abnormally simply because they have little contact with anyone who responds to their social signals? Proponents of the **social stimulation hypothesis** think so, arguing that the normal development of Chinese, Russian, Israeli, and Efe infants raised by a multitude of caregivers implies that infants need *sustained* interactions with *responsive* companions—either one or several—in order to develop normally. Such stimulation may be particularly important because it often depends, in part, on the infant's own behavior: People often attend to the infant *when* he or she cries, smiles, babbles, or gazes at them. This kind of association between one's own behavior and the behavior of caregivers may lead an infant to believe that she has some *control* over the social environment—an important contributor to a positive working model of self. And as she exerts this "control" and receives others' attention and affection, she develops a positive working model of others and becomes more outgoing.

Now consider the plight of socially deprived infants who may emit many signals and rarely receive a response from their overburdened or inattentive caregivers. What are these children likely to learn from their early experiences? Probably that *their* attempts to attract the attention of others are useless (negative working model of self), for nothing they do seems to matter to anyone (negative working model of others). Consequently, they may develop a sense of **"learned helplessness"** and simply stop trying to elicit responses from other people (Finkelstein & Ramey, 1977). Here, then, is a very plausible reason why socially deprived infants are often rather passive, withdrawn, and apathetic.

reactive attachment disorder
inability to form *secure* attachment bonds with other people; characterizes many victims of early social deprivation and/or abuse.

maternal deprivation hypothesis
the notion that socially deprived infants develop abnormally because they have failed to establish attachments to a primary caregiver.

social stimulation hypothesis
the notion that socially deprived infants develop abnormally because they have had little contact with companions who respond contingently to their social overtures.

learned helplessness
the failure to learn how to respond appropriately in a situation because of previous exposures to uncontrollable events in the same or similar situations.

Can Children Recover from Early Deprivation Effects?

Fortunately, socially deprived children can overcome many of their initial handicaps if placed in homes where they receive lots of attention from affectionate and responsive caregivers (Clarke & Clarke, 1976; Rutter, 1981). Recovery seems to go especially well if children are deprived for less than 2 years, have not been physically abused, and are placed with *highly educated, relatively affluent* parents who, as we learned in Chapter 9, have the personal, social, and financial resources to foster adaptive development (DeAngelis, 1997; Hodges & Tzard, 1989). Audrey Clark and Jeannette Hanisee (1982), for example, studied a group of Asian orphans who had lived in institutions, foster homes, or hospitals before coming to the United States. Many were war orphans who had early histories of malnutrition or serious illness. But despite the severe environmental insults they had endured, these children made remarkable progress. After only 2 to 3 years in their highly stimulating, middle-class adoptive homes, the Asian adoptees scored significantly *above* average on both a standardized intelligence test and an assessment of social maturity.

In sum, infants who have experienced social and emotional deprivation over the first 2 years often show a strong capacity for recovery when they are placed in a stimulating home environment and receive individualized attention from responsive caregivers. However, the lingering deficiencies and reactive attachment disorders that many abuse victims and late adoptees display suggest that infancy and toddlerhood may be a *sensitive period* for the establishment of *secure* affectional ties and other capacities that these ties may foster. Can they make complete recoveries? Many researchers think so, although they remind us that especially severe or prolonged adversity may take longer to overcome and may require stronger interventions than merely placing these children in good homes. Fortunately, recently developed *attachment therapies,* specifically aimed at building emotional bridges to adoptive parents and at fostering more positive working models of others, look quite promising. One recent study found that 85% of children who had undergone attachment therapy eventually established secure bonds to their caregivers (although the success rate with *teenage* victims of reactive attachment disorder was very poor) (DeAngelis, 1997). So there is hope that new and improved interventions that begin as soon as children show signs of reactive attachment disorders will eventually enable victims of prolonged social adversity to place their lingering deficiencies behind them.

MATERNAL EMPLOYMENT, DAY-CARE, AND EARLY EMOTIONAL DEVELOPMENT

In recent years, an important question has arisen about the ways in which infants in our society spend their time. Should they be cared for at home by a parent, or can they pursue their developmental agendas just as well in a day-care setting? Now that more than 60% of all mothers work outside the home at least part time, more and more

Concept Check 11.3
Understanding Individual Differences in Attachment

Check your understanding of individual differences in attachment by matching each descriptive statement below with one of the following models/hypotheses: (a) Ainsworth's caregiving hypothesis, (b) Kagan's temperament hypothesis, (c) Thomas & Chess's goodness-of-fit model, (d) the Bowlby/Bretherton internal working models hypothesis, (e) maternal deprivation hypothesis, (f) social stimulation hypothesis. The answers appear in the Appendix at the back of the book.

_____ 1. best summarizes how characteristics of infants and caregivers combine to influence attachment quality

_____ 2. has difficulty explaining why an infant might be securely attached to one parent and insecure with the other

_____ 3. easily explains why institutionalized infants show no developmental impairments when exposed to many responsive caregivers

_____ 4. claims that babies may be responding adaptively by forming avoidant attachments with unresponsive caregivers who seem to dislike their company

_____ 5. explains how early attachments can affect the character of one's interpersonal relationships later in life

_____ 6. now-discredited explanation for the developmental delays shown by children in understaffed institutions young children are receiving alternative forms of care. According to recent U.S. Department of Labor statistics, 40% of infants and toddlers and preschool children are cared for full-time by their parents, whereas 21% receive day-care from other relatives, 4% are cared for at home by a sitter, 14% receive care in day-care homes (typically run by a woman who cares for a few children in her own home during the day for payment), and 31% are enrolled in large day-care centers (Scarr, 1998).[1]

Do infants who attend day-care homes or centers suffer in any way compared with those who stay at home with a parent? Research to date suggests that they usually do not (Clarke-Stewart, 1993; NICHD Early Child Research Network, 1997). In fact, we learned in Chapter 9 that high-quality day-care promotes both the social responsiveness and the intellectual development of children from disadvantaged backgrounds, who are otherwise at risk of experiencing developmental delays (Burchinal et al., 1996; Campbell & Ramey, 1995). Furthermore, a large, well-controlled longitudinal study of 1,153 children in alternative care revealed that neither the age at which children enter day-care nor the amount of day-care they receive was related to the security of their attachments to their mothers or their emotional well-being (NICHD Early Child Care Research Network, 1997).

However, this broad generalization does not tell the full story. Let's briefly consider two factors that are likely to influence how an infant or toddler adjusts to maternal employment and day-care.

Quality of Alternative Care

Table 11.5 lists what experts believe to be the most important characteristics of high-quality day-care for infants and toddlers (Howes, Phillips, & Whitebrook, 1992; Zigler & Gilman, 1993). Unfortunately, the quality of alternative care in the United States is very uneven compared with that widely available in many Western European countries. Large numbers of American infants and toddlers are cared for by sitters who have little knowledge of or training in child development, or in unlicensed day-care homes that often fail to meet minimum health and safety standards (Zigler & Gilman, 1993).

TABLE 11.5 Characteristics of High-Quality Infant and Toddler Day-Care

Physical setting	The indoor environment is clean, well-lighted and ventilated; outdoor play areas are fenced, spacious, and free of hazards and include age-appropriate implements (slides, swings, sandbox, etc.).
Child:caregiver ratio	No more than 3 infants or 4–6 toddlers per adult caregiver.
Caregiver characteristics/ qualifications	Caregivers should have some training in child development and first aid, and should be warm, emotionally expressive, and responsive to children's bids for attention. Ideally, staffing is consistent so that infants and toddlers can form relationships (even attachment relationships) with their caregivers.
Toys/activities	Toys and activities are age appropriate; infants and toddlers are *always* supervised, even during free play indoors.
Family links	Parents are always welcome, and caregivers confer freely with them about their child's progress.
Licensing	Day-care setting is licensed by the state and (ideally) accredited by the National Family Day Care Program or the National Academy of Early Childhood Programs.

[1]These figures total more than 100% because about 9% of children have more than one regular care assignment (for example, part-time, center-based care and part-time care by a parent).

How important is high-quality care? Apparently, there is far less risk that children will display insecure attachments (or any other adverse outcome) when children receive excellent day-care—*even when that care begins very early.* Jerome Kagan and his associates (1978), for example, found that the vast majority of infants who entered a high-quality, university-sponsored day-care program at age 3½ to 5½ months not only developed secure attachments to their mothers but were just as socially, emotionally, and intellectually mature over the first 2 years of life as children from similar backgrounds who had been cared for at home. Studies conducted in Sweden (where day-care is government subsidized, closely monitored, and typically of high quality) report similar positive outcomes (Broberg et al., 1997), and it seems that the earlier that Swedish infants enter high-quality day-care, the better their cognitive, social, and emotional development 6 to 8 years later in elementary and junior high school (Andersson, 1989; 1992) Finally, Carollee Howes' (1990) longitudinal study of middle-class families in California indicates that early entry into day-care is associated with poor social, emotional, and intellectual outcomes later in childhood *only* when the day-care that children received was of low quality (see also Vandell, Henderson, & Wilson, 1988).

Unfortunately, children who receive the poorest and most unstable day-care are often those whose parents are living complex, stressful lives of their own that may constrain their sensitivity as parents and their involvement in children's learning activities (Fuller, Holloway, & Liang, 1996; Howes, 1990). So a child's poor progress in day-care may often stem as much from a disordered home life, in which parents are not all that enthused about parenting, as from the less-than-optimal alternative care that he or she receives (NICHD Early Child Care Research Network, 1997). Let's explore this idea further.

Parenting and Parents' Attitudes about Work

According to Lois Hoffman (1989), a mother's attitudes about working and child care may be as important to her child's social and emotional well-being as her actual employment status. Mothers tend to be much happier and more sensitive as caregivers when their employment status matches their attitudes about working (Crockenberg & Litman, 1991; Hock & DeMeis, 1990; Stuckey, McGhee, & Bell, 1982). So, if a woman

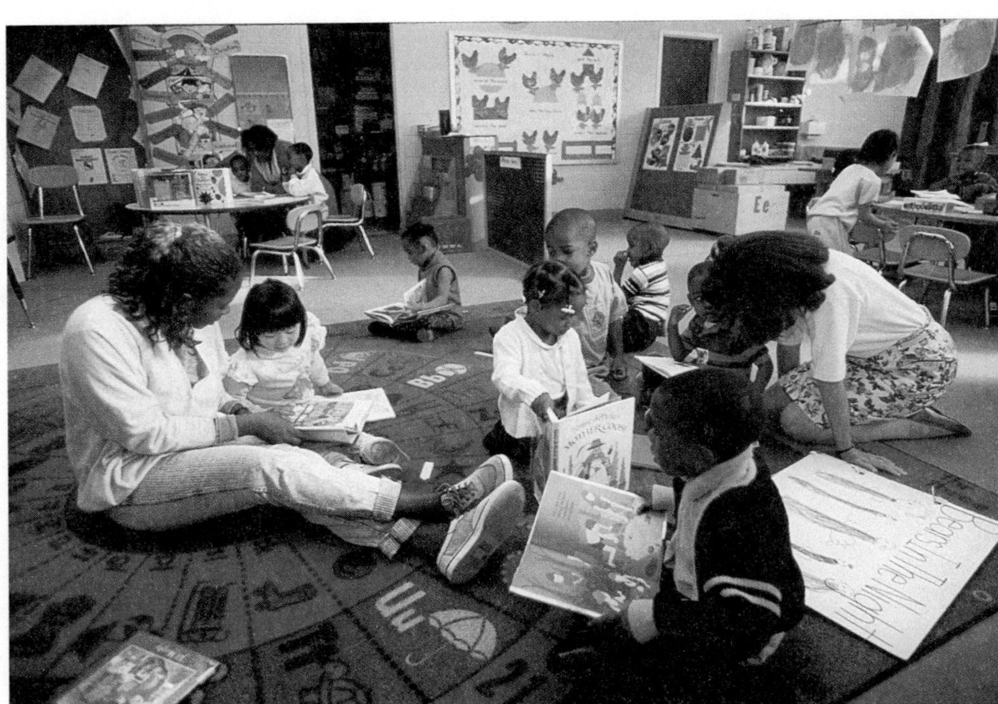

High-quality day-care can have beneficial effects on children's social, emotional, and intellectual development.

wants to work, it may make little sense to pressure her into staying home to care for her child when she might be depressed, hostile, or otherwise unresponsive in that role.

Even when children receive less-than-optimal alternative care, their outcomes depend greatly on the parenting they receive (NICHD Early Child Care Research Network, 1997). Outcomes are likely to be better if a working mother has positive attitudes *both* about working and about being a mother (Belsky & Rovine, 1988; Crockenberg & Litman, 1991). And it also helps immensely if her spouse approves of her working and supports her in her parenting role (Spitze, 1988). Ultimately, parents' attitudes about parenting and the quality of care they provide at home have far more to do with an infant's development than the kind of alternative care he receives (Broberg et al., 1997; NICHD Early Child Care Research Network, 1997; Scarr, 1998).

Do such findings then imply that quality of alternative care doesn't matter? *No, they do not.* As we have seen, high-quality alternative care has social and intellectual benefits and it clearly buffers young children against risks of forming insecure attachments when they receive far less than optimal care at home (Broberg et al., 1997; NICHD Early Child Care Research Network, 1997). Yet, the weight of the evidence suggests that neither maternal employment nor a child's experiences in alternative care are likely to impair early emotional development *as long as the child receives sensitive, responsive care from his or her parents* (NICHD Early Child Care Research Network, 1997).

What, then, might be done to help working parents to establish and maintain more secure ties with their infants and toddlers and to otherwise optimize their development? A national policy governing parental leave for child care is certainly one step in the right direction. The United States Congress passed the Family Leave and Medical Act of 1993 guaranteeing workers in firms with 50 or more employees the right to take 12 weeks of *unpaid* leave to spend time with their newborns, without jeopardizing their jobs. Yet this guarantee (1) does not apply to the *majority* of American workers (who are employed by firms with fewer than 50 employees) and (2) seems almost miserly compared with the often-generous parental-leave policies that many other industrialized societies have enacted (see Table 11.6).

An early report on the impact of maternal leave reveals that longer leaves are more beneficial than shorter ones. Specifically, American mothers who took 4-month leaves after the birth of their babies displayed less negative affect when interacting with their babies than did mothers whose leaves lasted only 2 months (Clark et al., 1997). The benefits of longer leaves were most noticeable among mothers who reported depressive symptoms or who had babies with difficult temperaments: These mothers were much more *positively* involved with their infants and more sensitive in their face-to-face interactions if their leave had lasted a full 4 months. Longer leaves may allow depressed

Table 11.6 **Sample Parental-Leave Policies in Modern Industrialized Nations**

Country	Policy
Denmark	Mothers receive 14 weeks' paid maternity leave after childbirth; at their option, either the mother or father may take an additional 10 weeks without pay.
Finland	Leave for a mother or a father consists of 70 working days at full pay and an additional 188 working days at 70% pay. Unpaid leave may be extended for 3 years without jeopardizing the parent's employment.
France	Working mothers receive 16 weeks of leave at 85% pay.
Israel	Working mothers receive 12 weeks' paid leave and up to 40 weeks' unpaid leave.
Japan	Working mothers receive 14 weeks paid leave.
Poland	Working mothers can take up to 6 months' leave with full pay and up to 2½ additional years with partial pay.
Sweden	Working mothers receive 6 months' leave at 90% pay and an additional 6 months' unpaid leave. Mothers and fathers may share leave benefits if they wish.
United States	Either parent may take 12 weeks of unpaid leave in firms of 50 or more employees.

mothers to become more confident as caregivers, while allowing more time for those with difficult infants to establish a "good fit" between their parenting and their babies' temperamental attributes. Unfortunately, many mothers cannot afford to take 4-month, *unpaid* leaves, thus prompting Clark et al. to recommend that the Family Leave and Medical Act of 1993 be revised to provide 4 to 6 months of leave with partial pay to employees in all firms, regardless of their size.

WHAT DO YOU THINK?

Assume that you live in a country in which parents can share leave benefits at half-pay for 9 months after a baby is born. Should you and your spouse share these benefits, or should the mother take them all? How would you justify your point of view?

A workable national policy governing day-care may be equally (or more) important. At present, middle-class families are the ones caught most directly in a day-care squeeze. Upper-income families have the resources to purchase excellent day-care; and the compensatory education (or other subsidized alternative care) that many lower-income children receive is typically of higher quality than that middle-class parents can afford to purchase (Scarr, 1998). Meanwhile, parents from all social backgrounds must often struggle to find and keep competent sitters or other high-quality day-care placements, which are in short supply, due, in part, to the continuing reluctance of the U.S. government to subsidize day-care for all citizens and carefully monitor its quality, as many European countries have done (Scarr, 1998). Increasingly, employers are realizing that it is in their best interest to help workers obtain quality day-care, and a few have even established day-care centers at the work site (Hymes, 1990). But, until more options are available, working parents will continue to face the challenges of finding good alternative care at a cost they can afford.

SUMMARY

An Overview of Emotional Development

♦ Human infants are clearly emotional beings. At birth, babies reliably display interest, distress, disgust, and contentment (as indicated by their facial expressions), with the remaining **primary emotions** (that is, anger, sadness, surprise, and fear) normally appearing by the middle of the first year. Such **secondary emotions** as embarrassment, pride, guilt, and shame emerge in the second (or third) year, after children reach such cognitive milestones as self-recognition and have acquired standards for evaluating their conduct.

♦ The socialization of emotions and **emotional self-regulation** begin very early, as parents model positive emotions for their infants, attend carefully to and try to prolong their infants' pleasant feelings, and become less responsive to infants' negative emotional displays. By the end of the first year, infants develop simple strategies for regulating aversive arousal; soon thereafter, they make active attempts to suppress their sadness or anger. However, the ability to regulate and control emotions develops very slowly, and it may be well into the grade-school years before children become proficient at complying with culturally defined **emotional display rules.**

♦ The infant's ability to recognize and interpret others' emotions improves dramatically over the first year. By 8 to 10 months of age, infants are capable of **social referencing,** and their ability to identify and interpret others' emotions continues to improve throughout childhood, aided, in part, by cognitive development and by family conversations centering on the causes of one's own and others' emotions.

♦ Emotions play at least two important roles in an infant's life. The child's emotional displays promote social contact with caregivers and help them to adjust their behaviors to her needs and goals. The infant's ability to recognize and interpret others' emotions serves an important *knowledge* function by helping the child to infer how she should feel, think, or behave in uncertain situations.

Temperament and Development

♦ Many components of **temperament**—a person's tendency to respond in predictable ways to environmental events—are genetically influenced. Environment also contributes heavily to temperament, with nonshared environmental influences having the larger impact.

♦ Such components of temperament as activity level, irritability, sociability, and **behavioral inhibition** are moderately stable over time and forecast later variations in adult personality. Stability is greatest for individuals at the extremes of a temperamental dimension.

♦ Temperamental attributes often cluster in predictable patterns such as the **easy, difficult,** and **slow-to-warm-up** profiles. Although children with difficult and slow-to-warm-up temperaments are at greater risk of experiencing adjustment problems, whether they actually develop these problems depends on the **goodness of fit** between parenting and their own temperamental attributes.

What Are Emotional Attachments?

◆ Infants form affectional ties to their close companions during the first year of life. These **attachments** are reciprocal relationships, for an infant's attachment objects (parents and other intimate companions) will normally become attached to him or her. Parents' initial *bonding* with their infant builds in strength as they gear their behavior to the infant's social signals and establish **synchronized routines.** These exquisite interactions are pleasing for both parents and infants and are thought to contribute to strong reciprocal attachments.

How Do Infants Become Attached?

◆ Infants pass through an **asocial phase** and a **phase of indiscriminate attachment** before forming their first true attachments at 7 to 9 months of age during the **phase of specific attachments.** Attached infants become more curious, using their attachment object as a **secure base** for exploration. They eventually enter the **phase of multiple attachments,** forming affectional ties to more than one person.

◆ Early *psychoanalytic* and *learning* theories were largely discredited by the finding that feeding plays much less of a role in human attachments than these models expected. The *cognitive-developmental* notion that attachments depend, in part, on cognitive development has received some support. *Ethological* theory, which specifies that humans have **preadapted characteristics** that predispose them to form attachments, has become especially influential in recent years. Yet, all those theories have contributed to our understanding of infant attachments.

◆ At about the time infants are becoming attached to a close companion, they often begin to display **stranger anxiety** and **separation anxiety.** These two fears, which stem from infants' wariness of strange situations and their inability to explain who strangers are and the whereabouts of absent companions, usually decline dramatically in the second year as toddlers mature intellectually and venture away from their secure bases to explore.

Individual Differences in Attachment Quality

◆ Ainsworth's **strange situation** is most commonly used to assess the quality of attachments that 1- to 2-year-olds have formed, although the **Attachment Q-set** is a versatile alternative that is becoming quite popular. Four attachment classifications have been identified: **secure, resistant, avoidant,** and **disorganized/disoriented.**

◆ Although the distributions of various attachment classifications varies across cultures and often reflects cultural differences in child-rearing, more infants around the world establish secure attachments than any other pattern.

Factors that Influence Attachment Security

◆ Sensitive responsive caregiving is associated with the development of secure attachments, whereas inconsistent, neglectful, overintrusive, and abusive caregiving predict insecure attachments. Thus, there is ample support for the **caregiving hypothesis.**

◆ Infant characteristics and temperamental attributes may also influence attachment quality by affecting the character of caregiver–infant interactions. However, the **temperament hypothesis**—that attachments are merely reflections of infant temperament—is clearly an overstatement.

Attachment and Later Development

◆ Secure attachment during infancy predicts intellectual curiosity and social competence later in childhood. One reason for this is that infants form **internal working models** of themselves and others that are often stable over time and influence their reactions to people and challenges for years to come. Parents' working models correspond closely with those of their children and are sometimes better predictors of attachment than parenting sensitivity is. However, children's working models can change, so that a secure attachment history is no guarantee of positive adjustment later in life; nor are insecure attachments a certain indication of poor life outcomes.

The Unattached Infant

◆ Infants who are socially deprived or abused are likely to be withdrawn, and apathetic and may later display intellectual deficits, behavior problems, and **reactive attachment disorders.** Their problems appear to stem more from their lack of responsive social stimulation **(social stimulation hypothesis)** than from failure to receive care from a singular mother figure **(maternal deprivation hypothesis),** and they often display a strong capacity for recovery, overcoming many of their initial handicaps. However, special interventions are needed for those whose early adversities were prolonged or severe.

Maternal Employment, Day-Care, and Early Emotional Development

◆ It was once feared that regular separations from working parents and placement into day-care might prevent infants from establishing secure attachments. However, there is little evidence that either a mother's employment outside the home or alternative caregiving have such effects, provided that the day-care is of good quality and that parents are sensitive and responsive caregivers when they are at home.

Emotional attachments are strong affectionate ties to another person. Children's first attachment relationships are formed during infancy as they become emotionally attached to their caregivers. By visiting: http://www.psy.sunysb.edu/ewaters/mainmenu.htm you can find out how attachment is measured. From here you can also link to other sites all over the world that are devoted to the study of attachment relationships.

KEY TERMS

primary (or basic) emotions, 393
secondary (or complex) emotions, 393
emotional display rules, 394
emotional self-regulation, 394
social referencing, 396
empathy, 397
temperament, 398
behavioral inhibition, 400
easy temperament, 401
difficult temperament, 401
slow-to-warm-up temperament, 401
"goodness-of-fit" model, 402
attachment, 402
synchronized routines, 403
asocial phase (of attachment), 404
phase of indiscriminate attachments, 405
phase of specific attachment, 405
secure base, 405
phase of multiple attachments, 405
secondary reinforcer, 406
imprinting, 407
preadapted characteristic, 408
"kewpie doll," 408
stranger anxiety, 409
separation anxiety, 411
strange situation, 412
secure attachment, 412
resistant attachment, 413
avoidant attachment, 413
disorganized/disoriented attachment, 413
Attachment Q-set, 414
caregiving hypothesis, 415
temperament hypothesis, 418
internal working models, 421
reactive attachment disorder, 425
maternal deprivation hypothesis, 425
social stimulation hypothesis, 425
learned helplessness, 425

12

Development of the Self and Social Cognition

Who am I?

I'm a person who says what I think . . . not [one] who's going to say one thing and do the other. I'm really lucky. I've never [drunk or] done drugs, but I'm always high. I love life. I've got a lot of different business interests . . . a construction company, oil wells, land . . . I'm trying everything. I travel a lot . . . it's difficult to be traveling and in school at the same time. [People] perceive me as being unusual . . . very mysterious, and I hope they see me as being a competitor, because I do all my talking on the field.

HERSCHEL WALKER, former college student and Olympic bobsledder, and now running back of the Dallas Cowboys (as quoted by Blount, 1986)

How would you answer the "Who am I?" question to the left? If you are like most adults, you would probably respond by mentioning some of your noteworthy personal characteristics (honesty, friendliness), some roles you play in life (student, volunteer), your religious or moral views, and perhaps your political leanings. In doing so, you would be describing that elusive concept that psychologists call the **self.**

Although no one else knows you as well as you do, it is a safe bet that much of what you know about yourself stems from your contacts and experiences with other people. When a college sophomore says that he is a friendly, outgoing person who is active in his fraternity, the Young Republicans, and the Campus Crusade for Christ, he is telling us that his past experiences with others and the groups to which he belongs are important determinants of his personal identity. Many years ago, sociologists Charles Cooley (1902) and George Herbert Mead (1934) proposed that the self-concept evolves from social interactions and undergoes many changes over the course of a lifetime. Cooley used the term **looking-glass self** to emphasize that a person's understanding of self is a reflection of how other people react to him: The self-concept is the image cast by a social mirror.

Cooley and Mead believed that the self and social development are completely intertwined, that they emerge together and that neither can progress far without the other. Presumably, newborns experience people and events as simple "streams of impressions" and have absolutely no concept of "self" until they realize that they exist independent of the objects and individuals that they encounter regularly. Once infants make this important distinction between self and nonself, they establish interactive routines with close companions (that is, develop socially) and learn that their behavior elicits predictable reactions from others. In other words, they are acquiring information about the "social self" based on the ways that people respond to them. Mead (1934) concluded that

> the self has a character that is different from that of the physiological organism proper. The self is something which . . . is not initially there at birth but arises in the process of social development. That is, it develops in a given individual as a result of his relations to that process as a whole and to other individuals within the process.

Do babies really have no sense of self at birth? We explore this issue in the first section of the chapter, as we trace the growth of the self-concept from infancy through adolescence. We will then consider how children and adolescents evaluate the self and construct a sense of self esteem. Our focus next shifts to two very important contributors to self-esteem, as we examine the growth of self-control and explore how children develop an interest (or disinterest) in achievement and form positive or negative academic self-concepts. We will then discuss a major developmental hurdle faced by adolescents: the need to establish a firm, future-oriented self-portrait, or *identity,* with which to approach the responsibilities of young adulthood. Finally, we will consider what developing children know about other people and interpersonal relationships and will see that this aspect of **social cognition,** which parallels the development of the self-concept, nicely illustrates Cooley's and Mead's point that personal (self) and social aspects of development are complexly intertwined.

Of course, we all develop conceptions of ourselves (and others) as males or females and as moral (or immoral) beings. Research on these topics is now so extensive that they merit chapters of their own (see Chapters 13 and 14). For now, let's return to the starting point and see how children come to know this entity we call the *self.*

self
the combination of physical and psychological attributes that is unique to each individual.

looking-glass self
the idea that a child's self-concept is largely determined by the ways that other people respond to him or her.

social cognition
thinking people display about the thoughts, feelings, motives, and behaviors of themselves and other people.

DEVELOPMENT OF THE SELF-CONCEPT

When do infants first distinguish themselves from other people, objects, and environmental events? At what point do they sense their uniqueness and form self-images?

What kinds of information do young children use to define the self? And how do their self-images and feelings of self-worth change over time? These are some of the issues that we will explore as we trace the development of the **self-concept** from infancy through adolescence.

The Emerging Self: Differentiation and Self-recognition

Like Mead, many developmentalists believe that infants are born without a sense of self. Psychoanalyst Margaret Mahler (Mahler, Pine, & Bergman, 1975) likens the newborn to a "chick in an egg" who has no reason to differentiate the self from the surrounding environment. After all, every need that the child has is soon satisfied by his or her ever-present companions, who are simply "there" and have no identities of their own. And yet, other developmentalists (see Brown, 1998) claim that even newborns may have the capacity to distinguish themselves from their surroundings. So when do infants first gain a sense of themselves as beings separate from the world around them?

This is not an easy question to answer, but it is helpful to recall Piaget's (and others') descriptions of cognitive development early in infancy. During the first 2 months, babies exercise their reflexive schemes and repeat pleasurable acts centered in their own bodies (for example, sucking their thumbs and waving their arms). In other words, they are becoming acquainted with their own physical capabilities, and, by 3 to 4 months of age, an infant who sees legs kicking on a TV monitor can already use proprioceptive and spatial cues about the directionality of those kicks to decide whether the legs on the TV are his own (Rochat & Morgan, 1995). We also learned in Chapters 6 and 11 that infants only 2 to 3 months old delight at producing interesting sights and sounds by kicking their legs or pulling their arms which are attached by strings to mobiles or to audiovisual machinery (Lewis, Alessandri, & Sullivan, 1990; Rovee-Collier, 1995). Even an 8-week-old infant can recall how to produce these interesting events for 2 or 3 days; and if the strings are disconnected so she can no longer exert any control, she may pull or kick all the harder and become rather distressed (Lewis et al., 1990; Sullivan et al., 1992). Thus it seems that 2-month-old infants may have some limited sense of *personal agency,* or understanding that *they* are responsible for at least some of the events that so fascinate them.

It is certainly possible, then, that infants learn the limits of their own bodies during the first month or two and differentiate this "physical self" from the external objects that they can control shortly thereafter (Samuels, 1986). So if a 2- to 6-month-old could talk, he might answer the "Who am I?" question by saying "I am a looker, a chewer, a reacher, and a grabber who acts on objects and makes things happen."

WHAT DO YOU THINK? ?

Newborn babies distinguish their own cries from those of other babies (review Box 2.4) and visually orient themselves to moving objects (Brown, 1998). Do you think that these achievements imply that newborns differentiate the self from the environment? Why or why not?

Self-recognition

Once infants know that they *are* (that they exist independent of other entities), they are in a position to find out *who* or *what* they are (Harter, 1983). When, for example, do infants recognize their own physical features and become able to tell themselves apart from other infants?

Michael Lewis and Jeanne Brooks-Gunn (1979) have studied the development of **self-recognition** by asking mothers to surreptitiously apply a spot of rouge to their infants' noses (under the pretext of wiping the infants' faces) and then place the infants before a mirror. If infants have a scheme for their own faces and recognize their mirror images as themselves, they should soon notice the new red spot and reach for or wipe their *own* noses. When infants 9 to 24 months old were given this rouge test, the younger ones showed no self-recognition. They seemed to treat the image in the mirror as if it were "some other kid." Signs of self-recognition were observed among a few

self-concept
one's perceptions of one's unique attributes or traits.

self-recognition
the ability to recognize oneself in a mirror or a photograph.

of the 15- to 17-month-olds, but only among the 18- to 24-month-olds did a majority of infants touch their own noses, apparently realizing that they had a strange mark on their faces. They knew exactly who that kid in the mirror was (see also Asendorph, Warkentin, & Baudonniere, 1996)!

Interestingly, infants from nomadic tribes, who have no experience with mirrors, begin to display self-recognition on the rouge test at the same age as city-reared infants (Priel & deSchonen, 1986). And many 18- to 24-month-olds can even recognize themselves in current photographs and often use a personal pronoun ("me") or their own name to label their photographic image (Lewis & Brooks-Gunn, 1979). Yet, children this young are not fully aware that the self is an entity that is stable over time. Not until age 3½ will they retrieve a brightly colored sticker placed surreptitiously on their heads if their first glimpse of it comes after a 2- to 3-minute delay on videotape or in a photograph (Povinelli, Landau, & Perilloux, 1996). Apparently, 2- to 3-year-olds who display some self-recognition do not retrieve the sticker because they don't yet seem to realize that earlier events in which they have participated have happened to *them!*

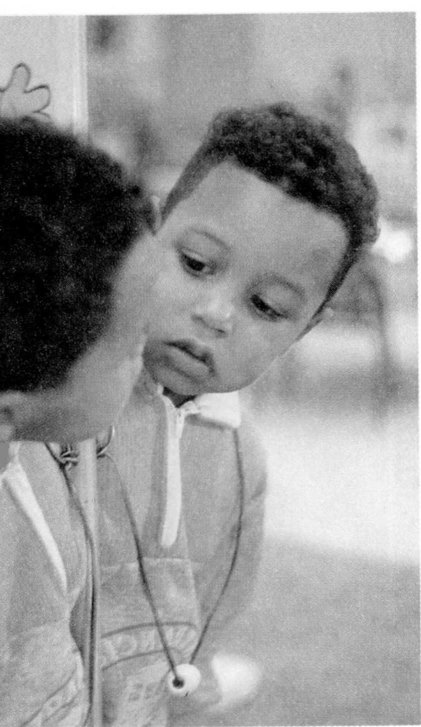

Recognizing one's mirror image as "me" is a crucial milestone in the development of self.

Contributors to Self-recognition

Why do 18- to 24-month-olds suddenly recognize themselves in a mirror? Recall that this is precisely the age when toddlers are said to internalize their sensorimotor schemes to form mental images, at least one of which may be an image of their own facial features. Even children with Down syndrome can recognize themselves in a mirror if they have attained a mental age of 18 to 20 months (Hill & Tomlin, 1981). And once 3- to 4-year-olds finally begin to encode earlier events as autobiographical memories and to overcome the infantile amnesia we discussed earlier in Chapter 8, they realize that the self is a stable entity and that earlier events that they remember did indeed happen to *them* (Nelson, 1993; Povinelli et al., 1996).

Although a certain level of cognitive development may be necessary for self-recognition, social experiences are probably of equal importance. Gordon Gallup (1979) found that adolescent chimpanzees easily recognized themselves in a mirror (as shown by the rouge test) unless they had been reared in complete social isolation. In contrast to normal chimps, social isolates react to their mirror images as if they were looking at another animal! So the term *looking-glass self* may apply to chimpanzees as well as to humans: Reflections in a "social mirror" enable normal chimps to develop some self-awareness, whereas a chimpanzee that is denied these experiences fails, to acquire a clear self-image.

One social experience that contributes to self-awareness in humans is a secure attachment to a primary caregiver. Sandra Pipp and her associates (1992) administered a complex test of self-knowledge to 2- and 3-year-olds—a test that assessed the child's awareness of his name and gender as well as tasks to assess self-recognition. As we see in Figure 12.1, securely attached 2-year-olds outperformed their insecurely attached agemates on the test, and differences in self-knowledge between secure and insecure 3-year-olds were even greater.

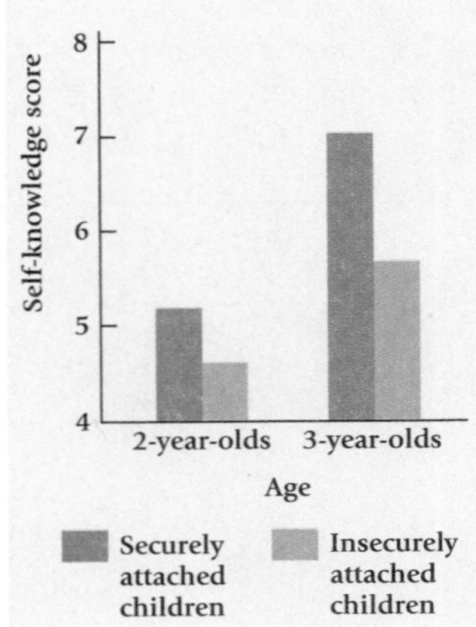

Figure 12.1 *Average scores on a test of self-knowledge as a function of age and attachment quality.* ADAPTED FROM PIPP, EASTERBROOKS, & HARMON, 1992.

Social and Emotional Consequences of Self-recognition

The growth of self-recognition and an emerging awareness of oneself as a participant in *social* interactions pave the way for many new social and emotional competencies (Pipp-Siegel & Foltz, 1997). For example, we saw in Chapter 11 that the ability to experience *self-conscious* emotions such as embarrassment depends on self-recognition. Furthermore, toddlers who have reached this self-referential milestone soon become more outgoing and socially skilled. They now take great pleasure in imitating a playmate's activities (Asendorph & Baudonniere, 1993; Asendorph et al., 1996) and occasionally even *cooperate* (as illustrated by one child's operating a handle so that another can retrieve toys from a container) to achieve shared goals (Brownell & Carriger, 1990).

Once toddlers display self-recognition, they also become more sensitive to the ways in which people differ and begin to categorize themselves on these dimensions—a classification called the **categorical self** (Stipek, Gralinski, & Kopp, 1990). Age, sex, and evaluative dimensions are the first social categories that toddlers incorporate into their self-concepts, as illustrated by such statements as "I *big boy,* not a *baby*" or "Jennie *good girl.*"

Interestingly, young children are even becoming aware of racial and ethnic categories, although it may take a while before they can classify themselves correctly. Native-American 3- to 5-year-olds, for example, can easily discriminate Indians from whites in photographs but are less often accurate in specifying which category they most resemble (Spencer & Markstrom-Adams, 1990). A similar "misidentification" phenomenon has been observed among African-American preschoolers, who show a clear pro-white bias and associate fewer positive attributes with the color black or with African-American people (Cross, 1985; Spencer, 1988). However, these "misidentifications" and pro-white biases do not necessarily mean that minority youngsters are unaware of their own ethnicity. Instead, they may simply reflect the same early awareness of negative stereotypes about minorities that white children display (Bigler & Liben, 1993) and a desire to align themselves with what they believe to be the most socially desirable group (Spencer & Markstrom-Adams, 1990).

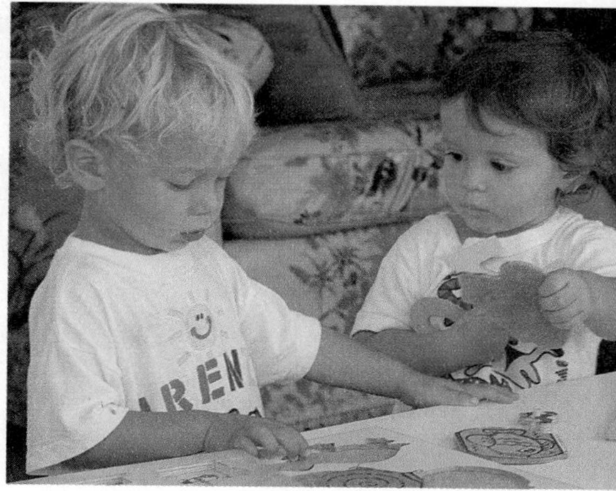

Toddlers who display self-recognition become much more socially skilled and can now cooperate to achieve shared goals.

Who Am I? Responses of Preschool Children

Until very recently, developmentalists believed that the self-concepts of preschool children were concrete, physicalistic, and nearly devoid of any *psychological* self-awareness. Why? Because when 3- to 5-year-olds are asked to describe themselves, they talk mostly about their physical attributes ("I have blue eyes"), their possessions ("I have a new bike"), or about *actions* of which they feel especially proud, such as hitting a baseball or walking to nursery school on their own. By contrast, psychological descriptors such as "I'm happy," "I'm good at sports," or "I like people" are rarely used by children this young (Damon & Hart, 1988; Keller, Ford, & Meachum, 1978).

categorical self
a person's classification of the self along socially significant dimensions such as age and sex.

However, not everyone agrees that preschoolers' self-concepts are limited to observable characteristics. Rebecca Eder (1989; 1990) finds that when 3½- to 5-year-olds are asked to respond to contrasting forced-choice statements that require fewer verbal skills than open-ended "Who am I?" questions, they can quickly characterize themselves on *psychological* dimensions such as sociability (by choosing, for example, between such statements as "I like to play by myself" versus "I like to play with my friends"). Furthermore, they characterize themselves differently on different dimensions, and these self-characterizations are stable over time (Eder, 1990). Although preschool children may not be consciously aware of what it means to be "sociable" or "athletic" or to be an "achiever," Eder's research implies that they have rudimentary psychological conceptions of self long before they can express this knowledge in traitlike terminology (see also Flavell et al., 1993).

Preschool children are already aware of their behavioral patterns and preferences and are using this information to form an early portrait of the self.

Children's Theory of Mind and Emergence of the Private Self

When adults think about the self, they know that it consists of a **public self** (or **me**) that others can see and a **private self** (or **I**) that has an inner, reflective (thinking) character not available to others. Are young children aware of both the public and private aspects of self? Such a distinction implies that they have a *theory of mind,* an understanding of how the human mind works and a knowledge that humans are cognitive beings whose mental states are not always shared with or accessible to others.

Early Understandings of Mental States

By 18 months of age, toddlers demonstrate some awareness of their own and others' mental states. They imitate the purposeful actions of human models but not those of a mechanical toy, thereby illustrating an early awareness that *human* behaviors reflect definite goals and intentions (Meltzoff, 1995). They can also reason accurately about other peoples' *desires.* So having seen an experimenter express disgust at the thought of eating crackers, they know that she would prefer raw vegetables to the crackers that they prefer when offered a choice between these snacks (Repacholi & Gopnik, 1997).

By age 2 to 3, children often talk about such mental states as needs, feelings, and desires, and they are aware that (1) they may know something that others don't (O'Neill, 1996) and (2) people cannot actually observe their thoughts (Flavell et al., 1993). But despite these early glimmerings of an emerging private self, 2- to 3-year-olds have a very primitive understanding of the connections between various mental states and behaviors. They think, for example, that a person's actions reflect his *desires* and do not yet understand that a person's beliefs might also affect his behavior (Wellman & Woolley, 1990). But between the ages of 3 and 4, children develop a **belief-desire theory** of mind in which they recognize, as we adults do, that beliefs and desires are different mental states and that either or both can influence one's conduct (Wellman, 1990). So, a 4-year-old who has broken a vase while roughhousing may try to overcome his mother's *desire* to punish him by trying to make her *believe* that his breaking the vase was unintentional ("I didn't mean to, Mama. It was an accident!").

Origins of a Belief-Desire Theory

Very young children may view desire as the most important determinant of behavior because their own actions are so often triggered by desires and they may assume that other people's conduct reflects similar motives. In addition, 3-year-olds have a very curious view of beliefs: They assume that beliefs are accurate reflections of reality that everyone shares. They don't seem to appreciate, as older children do, that beliefs are merely *interpretations* of reality that may differ from person to person and may be *inaccurate.* Consider children's reactions to the following story.

> A boy puts some chocolate in a blue cupboard and goes out to play. In his absence, his mother moves the chocolate to the green cupboard. When the boy returns, he wants his chocolate. Where does he look for it?

Three-year-olds say "in the green cupboard." They know where the chocolate is, and because beliefs represent reality, they assume that the boy will be driven by his *desire* for chocolate to look in the right place. By contrast, 4- to 5-year-olds display a *belief-desire theory of mind:* They now understand that beliefs are merely mental representations of reality that may be inaccurate and that someone else may not share; thus, they know that the boy will look for his chocolate in the blue cupboard where he *believes* it is (beliefs determine behavior, even if they are false) rather than in the green cupboard where they know it is (Wellman & Woolley, 1990).

Once children understand that people act on the basis of false beliefs, they may use this knowledge to their own advantage by lying or attempting other deceptive ploys.

public self (or **me**)
those aspects of self that others can see or infer.

private self (or **I**)
those inner, or subjective, aspects of self that are known only to the individual and are not available for public scrutiny.

belief-desire theory
theory of mind that develops between ages 3 and 4; the child now realizes that both beliefs and desires may determine behavior and that people act on their beliefs, even if they are inaccurate.

In Chapter 7, for example, we noted that 4-year-olds (but not 3-year-olds) who are playing hide-the-object games will spontaneously generate false clues, trying to mislead their opponent about the object's true location (Sodian et al., 1991). Notice that 4-year-olds make a clear distinction between public and private self, for they recognize that their deceptive *public* behavior will lead their opponent to adopt a belief that differs from their own *private* knowledge.

It's not that younger children haven't the capacity to recognize a false belief or its implications. With a little prompting, they can tell from thought-bubble depictions when a story character holds a belief that misrepresents reality (Wellman, Hollander, & Schult, 1996). And if they have collaborated with an adult in formulating a deceptive strategy in a hide-the-object game, their performance improves dramatically on other false-belief tasks (Hala & Chandler, 1996). Nevertheless, between 3 and 4 is when children normally achieve a much richer understanding of mental life and clearly discriminate the private self-as-knower from the public self that they present to others. How important are those developments? John Flavell and his colleagues (1993) answer by saying that if children had no theory of mind and no awareness that public appearances do not necessarily reflect private realities, they would be largely incapable of drawing meaningful *psychological* inferences about their own or others' behavior; in other words, the rich social-cognitive abilities that humans display would be impossible.

How Does a Theory of Mind Originate?

How do children manage to construct a theory of mind so early in life? One perspective is that human infants may be just as biologically prepared and as motivated to acquire information about mental states as they are to share meaning through language. Andrew Meltzoff (1995), for example, suggests that early *imitative* acts may reflect an infant's or toddler's attempts to share meaning by representing and understanding others' motives and intentions.

But even if humans are biologically predisposed to develop a theory of mind, there are many social experiences that foster its development. Pretend play, for example, is an activity that prompts children to think about mental states. As toddlers and preschool children conspire to make one object represent another or to enact pretend roles such as cops and robbers, they become increasingly aware of the creative potential of the human mind—an awareness that beliefs are merely mental constructions that can influence behavior (Taylor & Carlson, 1997; Youngblade & Dunn, 1995). Young children also have ample opportunity to learn how the mind works from family interactions centering on the discussion of motives and intentions, resolution of conflicts among siblings, and reasoning about moral issues (Dunn, 1994). Indeed, researchers have been finding that preschoolers with siblings, especially those with two or more, do better on false-belief tasks than only children do (Jenkins & Astington, 1996; Lewis et al., 1996; Perner, Ruffman, & Leekam, 1994). Having siblings may provide more opportunities for pretend play, as well as more interactions involving deception or trickery—experiences that may illustrate the links between beliefs and behaviors. However, preschoolers who perform especially well on false-belief tasks also interact with a

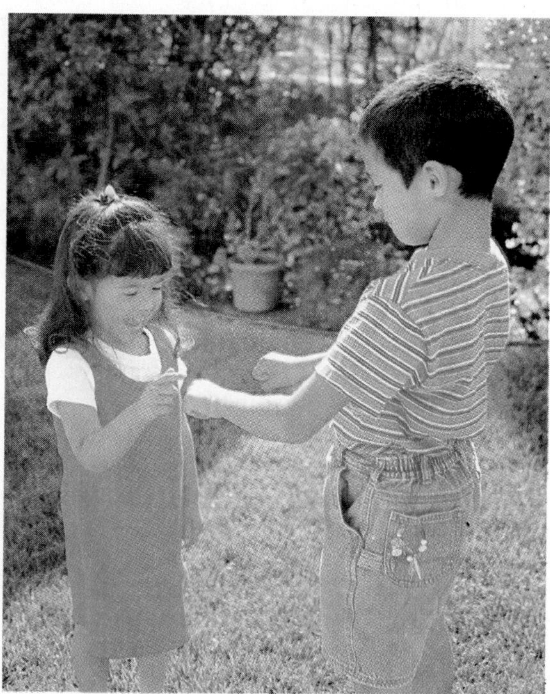

Sibling interactions involving deception or trickery contribute to the development of a theory of mind.

larger number of adults, which implies that children are apprentices to a variety of tutors as they acquire a theory of mind (Lewis et al., 1996).

Cultural Influences. Do children in all cultures construct such a rich understanding of how the mind works during the preschool period? Apparently not. Even 8-year-olds among the Junin Quechua people of Peru have difficulties understanding that beliefs can be false (Vinden, 1996). Why? Probably because Junin Quechua speakers do not often talk about their own or others' mental states. Most of these people are subsistence farmers who work from dawn to dusk just to survive, and they do not need to reflect very often on what they or others may feel or believe in order to live productive lives. In fact, their language has few mental-state words, and references to mental states are largely absent from their folktales. So the appearance of a belief-desire theory of mind by age 4 is not universal and is likely to be delayed in cultures that lack the social supports for its emergence.

Conceptions of Self in Middle Childhood and Adolescence

Once children develop a theory of mind and clearly differentiate their public and private selves, their self-descriptions gradually evolve from listings of their physical, behavioral, and other "external" attributes to sketches of their enduring *inner* qualities—that is, their traits, values, beliefs, and ideologies (Damon & Hart, 1988; Livesley & Bromley, 1973). This developmental shift toward a more abstract or "psychological" portrayal of self can be seen in the following three responses to the "Who am I?" question (Montemayor & Eisen, 1977, pp. 317–318):

> *9-year-old:* My name is Bruce C. I have brown eyes. I have brown hair. I love! sports. I have seven people in my family. I have great! eye site. I have lots! of friends. I live at. . . . I have an uncle who is almost 7 feet tall. My teacher is Mrs. V. I play hockey! I'm almost the smartest boy in the class. I love! food. . . . I love! school.
>
> *11½-year-old:* My name is A. I'm a human being . . . a girl . . . a truthful person. I'm not pretty. I do so-so in my studies. I'm a very good cellist. I'm a little tall for my age. I like several boys. . . . I'm old fashioned. I am a very good swimmer. . . . I try to be helpful. . . . Mostly I'm good, but I lose my temper. I'm not well liked by some girls and boys. I don't know if boys like me. . . .
>
> *17-year-old:* I am a human being . . . a girl . . . an individual . . . I am a Pisces. I am a moody person . . . an indecisive person . . . an ambitious person. I am a big curious person. . . . I am lonely. I am an American (God help me). I am a Democrat. I am a liberal person. I am a radical. I am conservative. I am a pseudoliberal. I am an Atheist. I am not a classifiable person (i.e., I don't want to be) (pp. 317–318).

In addition to using more psychological terms to describe the self than grade-school children do, adolescents are also becoming much more aware that they are not the same person in all situations—a fact that may puzzle or even annoy them. Susan Harter and Ann Monsour (1992) asked 13-, 15-, and 17-year-olds to describe themselves when they are with (1) parents, (2) friends, (3) romantic partners, and (4) teachers and classmates. Then each participant was asked to sort through the four self-descriptions, picking out any inconsistencies and indicating how confusing or upsetting they were. As we see in Figure 12.2, 13-year-olds reported few inconsistencies and were not bothered much by those they did detect. By contrast, 15-year-olds listed many oppositional attributes and were often confused about them. One 15-year-old talked about her tendency to be happy with friends but depressed at home. " 'I

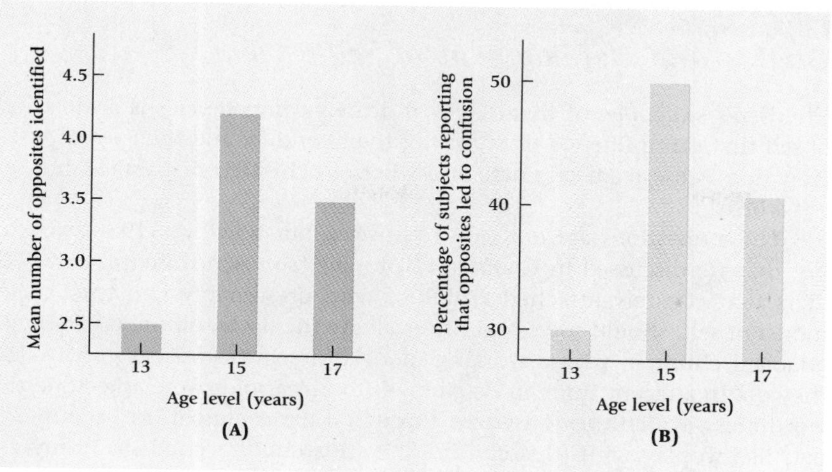

Figure 12.2 *Average number of oppositional attributes reported by 13-, 15-, and 17-year-olds (panel A) and the percentages of 13-, 15-, and 17-year-olds who said they were confused or "mixed up" by these inconsistencies in their self-portraits (panel B).* ADAPTED FROM HARTER & MONSOUR, 1992.

really think of myself as happy—and want to be that way because I think that's my true self, but I get depressed with my family and it bugs me. . .'" (Harter & Monsour, 1992, p. 253). These 15-year-olds seemed to feel that there were several different selves inside them and were concerned about finding the "real me." Interestingly, adolescents who are most upset over inconsistencies in their self-portrayals are those who put on false fronts, acting out of character in an attempt to improve their images or win the approval of parents or peers. Unfortunately, those who most often display these **false-self behaviors** are the ones who feel least confident that they know who they truly are (Harter et al., 1996).

Inconsistent self-portrayals are somewhat less bothersome to older adolescents, who have often integrated them into a higher-order, more coherent view of themselves. A 17-year-old boy, for example, might conclude that it is perfectly understandable to be relaxed and confident in most situations but nervous on dates if one has not yet had much dating experience, or that *moodiness* can explain his being *cheerful* with friends on some occasions but *irritable* on others. Harter and Monsour believe that cognitive development—specifically the formal-operational ability to compare abstract traits like *cheerful* and *irritable* and to ultimately integrate them into more general concepts like *moodiness*—is behind this change in self-perceptions.

In sum, one's self-concept becomes more psychological, more abstract, and more of a coherent, integrated self-portrait from childhood throughout adolescence. Truly, the adolescent becomes a sophisticated self-theorist who can reflect on and understand the workings of his or her personality.

SELF-ESTEEM: THE EVALUATIVE COMPONENT OF SELF

As children develop, they not only understand more and more about themselves and construct more intricate self-portraits, but they also begin to *evaluate* the qualities that they perceive themselves as having. This evaluative aspect of self is called **self-esteem.** Children with high self-esteem are fundamentally satisfied with the type of person they are; they recognize their strong points, can acknowledge their weaknesses (often hoping to overcome them), and generally feel quite positive about the characteristics and competencies they display. By contrast, children with low self-esteem view the self in a less favorable light, often choosing to dwell on perceived inadequacies rather than on any strengths they may happen to display (Brown, 1998; Zupan, Hammen, & Jaenicke, 1987).

false-self behavior
acting in ways that do not reflect one's true self or the "true me."

self-esteem
one's evaluation of one's worth as a person based on an assessment of the qualities that make up the self-concept.

Origins and Development of Self-esteem

Children's *evaluation* of themselves and their competencies is a most important aspect of self that can influence all aspects of their conduct and their psychological well being. How does self-esteem originate and when do children first establish a realistic sense of self-worth?

These questions are not easy to answer, but Bowlby's (1988) working-models theory that we discussed in Chapter 11 provides some meaningful clues. The theory predicts that securely attached children, who presumably construct a *positive* working model of self, should soon begin to evaluate themselves more favorably than insecurely attached children, whose working models of self are not so positive. And apparently they do. In a recent study in Belgium, 4- to 5-year-olds were asked questions about their worthiness, which they answered through a hand puppet (for example, "Do you [puppet] like to play with [this child]?"; "Is [this child] a good [bad] boy/girl?"). Children with secure ties to their mothers not only described themselves more favorably (through the puppet) than did children who were insecurely attached, but they were also rated as more competent and socially skilled by their preschool teachers (Verschueren, Marcoen, & Schoefs, 1996). So it seems that by age 4 or 5 (and possibly sooner), children have already established an early and meaningful sense of self-esteem that is influenced by their attachment history and is a reasonably accurate reflection of how teachers evaluate their competencies.

Determinants of Global Self-esteem

When we adults think about self-esteem, a global appraisal of self comes to mind based on the strengths and weaknesses we display in several different domains. The same is true for children, who first evaluate their competencies in many different areas and only later integrate these impressions into an overall self-evaluation.

Susan Harter (1982, 1990) has asked children of different ages to evaluate their competencies in such domains as *social acceptance, task/scholastic competence, physical/athletic competence,* and *behavioral conduct* by indicating the extent to which statements such as "Some kids are good at figuring out answers at school!" (scholastic competence) and "Some kids are always chosen for games" (athletic competence) are true of themselves. Before age 7, children clearly distinguish how well they think others like them (social acceptance) from how good they think they are at accomplishing tasks (general competence). And by about age 8, children are not only evaluating their competencies in three domains—*physical competence, academic competence,* and *social acceptance,* but their appraisals now more accurately reflect other people's evaluations of them (Harter, 1982). For example, ratings of social self-esteem are now confirmed by peers who were asked to rate their classmates' social competencies; and children with high athletic self-esteem are more frequently chosen for team sports and are rated higher in physical competence by gym teachers than are classmates who feel physically inadequate. Taken together, these findings suggest that both self-knowledge and self-esteem may depend to a large extent on the way that others perceive and react to our behavior. This is precisely the point that Charles Cooley (1902) was making when he coined the term *looking-glass self* to explain how we construct a self-image.

In adolescence, the quality of one's friendships becomes one of the strongest determinants of self-esteem.

During adolescence, new dimensions such as *job competence, romantic appeal,* and *close friendships* become important contributors to global self-esteem (Masden et al., 1995), although they affect the self-appraisals of boys and girls in somewhat different ways (Thorne & Michaelieu, 1996). Girls who enjoy high self-esteem have had *supportive* relationships with friends, whereas boys are more likely to derive high self-esteem from their ability to successfully *influence* their friends. Low self-esteem in girls is most strongly associated with a failure to win friends' approval, whereas a major contributor to low self-esteem in adolescent boys is a lack of romantic competence, as reflected by their failure to win or maintain the affection of girls.

Changes in Self-esteem

How stable are one's feelings of self-worth? Is a child who enjoys high self-esteem as an 8-year-old likely to feel especially good about himself as an adolescent? Or is it more reasonable to assume that the stresses and strains of adolescence cause most teenagers to doubt themselves and their competencies, thereby undermining their self-esteem?

Erik Erikson (1963) favored the latter point of view, arguing that young adolescents who experience the many physical, cognitive, and social changes associated with puberty often become confused and show at least some decline in self-esteem as they leave childhood behind and begin to search for stable adult identity. Indeed, some young adolescents experience a decline of self-esteem as they leave elementary school as the oldest and most revered students and enter junior high, where they are the youngest and least competent (Seidman et al., 1994; Simmons et al., 1987). This dip in self-esteem is likely to be greatest when multiple stressors pile up—for example, when adolescents are not only making the transition to junior high school but coping with pubertal changes, beginning to date, and perhaps dealing with family transitions, such as a divorce, all at the same time (Simmons et al., 1987). Furthermore, adolescents experience more daily hassles and other negative events, both at home and at school, than younger children do, and these stresses largely account for the increased sulkiness and other negative emotions that seventh to ninth graders display (Larson & Ham, 1993; Seidman et al., 1994). So early adolescence can be a somewhat painful experience that can even drive some teenagers to consider taking their own lives (see Box 12.1).

But before we conclude that adolescence is hazardous to our sense of self-worth, let's note that *most* 11- to 14-year-olds show no appreciable decline in self-esteem (Nottelmann, 1987). In fact, teenagers generally display gradual though modest *increases* in self-esteem over the course of adolescence (Marsh, 1989; Mullis, Mullis, & Normandin, 1992; Savin-Williams & Demo, 1984). Perhaps owing to the greater autonomy they are granted, boys are more likely than girls to show such increases in self-esteem (Thorne & Michaelieu, 1996), but most youths emerge from their teenage years with their self-worth intact, particularly if they enjoyed good self-esteem upon entering adolescence (Block & Robins, 1993; Brown, 1998).

Social Contributors to Self-esteem

Parenting Styles

Parents can play a crucial role in shaping a child's self-esteem. As we noted in Chapter 11, the sensitivity of parenting early in childhood clearly influences whether infants and toddlers construct positive or negative working models of self. Furthermore, grade-school children and adolescents with high self-esteem tend to have parents who are warm and supportive, set clear standards for them to live up to, and allow them a voice in making decisions that affect them personally (Coopersmith, 1967; Isberg et al., 1989; Lamborn et al., 1991). The link between high self-esteem and this nurturing, democratic parental style is much the same in Taiwan and Australia as it is in the United States and Canada (Scott, Scott, & McCabe, 1991). Although these child-rearing studies are correlational and we cannot be sure that warm, supportive parenting *causes* high self-esteem, it is easy to imagine such a causal process at work. Certainly, sending a message that "You're a good kid whom I trust to follow rules and make good decisions" is apt to promote higher self-esteem than more aloof or more controlling styles in which parents may be saying, in effect, "Your inadequacies turn me off."

12.1

DEVELOPMENTAL ISSUES

Adolescent Suicide: The Tragic Destruction of Self

Surprising as it may seem to anyone who has never contemplated taking his own life, suicidal thoughts are shockingly common among adolescents and young adults (Committee on Adolescent Suicide, 1996). In one survey of adolescents, 56% reported at least one instance of suicidal thinking, and 5% had actually attempted suicide (Windle & Windle, 1997). Suicide rates among 15- to 13-year-olds have increased dramatically over the past 30 years, so much so that suicide is now the third leading cause of death for this age group, ranking behind only accidents and homicides (U.S. Bureau of the Census, 1996). Among some Native American groups, suicidal thoughts and behaviors are even more widespread (Garland & Zigler, 1993); in one sample of Zuni adolescents, for example, fully 30% had attempted suicide, most of them more than once (Howard-Pitney et al., 1992). Overall, females *attempt* suicide more often than males do; but males are more often successful in their attempts—by a ratio of about 3 to 1, a difference that holds up across most cultures studied (Girard, 1993). Males succeed more often simply because they shun slower-acting pills in favor of more abruptly lethal techniques such as nooses and guns.

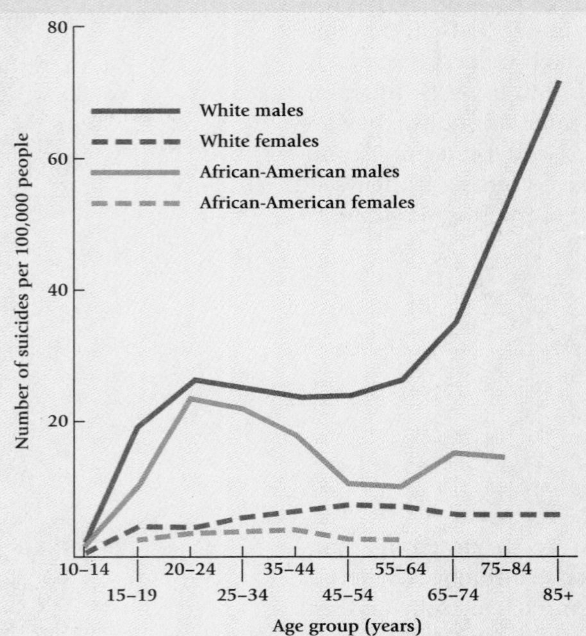

Number of suicides per 100,000 people by age and sex among whites and African-Americans in the United States. Data about the oldest African-Americans are not shown because too few cases were studied. DATA FROM U.S. BUREAU OF THE CENSUS, 1996.

Although teenagers *attempt* suicide more often than adults do, we see in the figure that adults are more likely to actually commit suicide. The suicide rate for women peaks in middle age, whereas it climbs for white males throughout adulthood. Because adolescents are far less successful than adults at killing themselves when they try, some researchers believe that their suicide attempts are often a desperate "cry for help." Unlike suicidal adults, who are often determined to end it all, many suicidal adolescents hope to *improve* their lives; they may see their suicide attempts as a way of forcing others to take their problems seriously, but by miscalculation or sudden impulse, they often die before they can be helped (Berman & Jobes, 1991; Rubenstein et al., 1989).

Unfortunately, there is no sure way to identify young people who will try to kill themselves. Suicidal adolescents come from all racial and ethnic groups, all social classes, and even popular adolescents of superior intelligence may take their own lives. Yet, there are some telltale warning signs. Suicidal adolescents are often severely depressed, abusing drugs, or displaying other forms of antisocial conduct (Committee on Adolescence, 1996; Vannatta, 1996). They often have experienced deteriorating relationships with parents, peers, or romantic partners, suffered academic failures, and lost all interest in hobbies or other enjoyable activities as they sink into a state of hopelessness and despair and feel incapable of coping with their problems (Berman & Jobes, 1991; Wagner, 1997).

Friends and associates can play an important role in preventing adolescent suicide by recognizing the warning signs and encouraging their deeply depressed or suddenly hostile young companions to talk about their problems—a step that adults often fail to take, thinking that the teenager's unruly or depressed demeanor reflects the typical "storm and stress" of adolescence. Should a troubled youngster divulge suicidal thoughts, companions might try to convince him or her that there are ways other than suicide to cope with distress. But perhaps the most important thing friends and associates can do is to tell what they have learned to other people who are in a better position to help, such as the adolescent's parents, a teacher, or a school counselor. Clearly, it is better to break a confidence than to let the person die.

As for parents, perhaps the best advice is to take *all* suicidal thinking seriously. And professional assistance is definitely called for after an unsuccessful suicide attempt, for adolescents who try once are at risk of succeeding in the future if they receive little help and continue to feel incapable of coping with their problems (Berman & Jobes, 1991).

Peer Influences

As early as age 5 or 6, children begin to recognize differences among themselves and their classmates as they use **social comparison** information to tell them whether they perform better or worse in various domains than their peers (Pomerantz et al., 1995). For example, they glance at each others' papers and say "How many did you miss?" or will make such statements as "I'm faster than you" after winning a footrace (Frey & Ruble, 1985). This kind of comparison increases and becomes more subtle with age (Pomerantz et al., 1995) and plays an important role in shaping children's self-esteem, particularly in Western cultures where competition and individual accomplishments are stressed. Interestingly, this preoccupation with evaluating oneself in comparison with peers is not nearly as strong among communally reared kibbutz children in Israel, perhaps because cooperation and teamwork are so strongly emphasized there (Butler & Ruzany, 1993).

Peer influences on self-esteem become even more apparent during adolescence. Recall that some of the strongest contributions to adolescent self-appraisals are the quality of one's relationships with particularly close friends. In fact, when young adults reflect back on life experiences that were noteworthy to them and that may have influenced their self-esteem, they mention experiences with friends and romantic partners far more frequently than experiences with parents and family members (Thorne & Michaelieu, 1996).

Now that we have considered how developing children and adolescents gain information about the self and evaluate this information to gain a sense of self-esteem, we turn to another critical aspect of self: the development of *self-control.*

WHAT DO YOU THINK?

Today, some people offering child-rearing advice argue that children simply need to feel good about themselves to succeed in life. They contend that adults should always strive to boost self-esteem by complimenting children, regardless of the level of their accomplishments or the appropriateness of their conduct. Do you agree with this philosophy? Why or why not?

DEVELOPMENT OF SELF-CONTROL

Developmentalists use the term **self-control** to refer to our ability to regulate our conduct and to *inhibit* actions (for example, rule violations) that we might otherwise be inclined to perform. Self-control is unquestionably an important attribute. If we never learned to control our immediate impulses, we would constantly be at odds with other people for violating their rights, breaking rules, and failing to display the patience and self-sacrifice that permit us to achieve important *long-range* objectives (for example, earning a diploma). Although many theorists have commented on the development of self-control (for example, Bandura, 1986; Freud, 1935/1960; Kopp, 1987; Mischel, 1986), all of them make two assumptions: (1) young children's behavior is almost completely controlled by external agents (for example, parents); (2) over time, control is gradually *internalized* as children adopt standards, or norms, that stress the value of self-control and acquire self-regulatory skills that permit them to adhere to these prescriptions.

Emergence of Self-control in Early Childhood

When do children first display any evidence of self-regulation and self-control? Most theorists assume that these milestones occur at some point during the second year, after infants realize that they are separate, autonomous beings and that their actions have consequences that *they* have produced. By age 18 to 24 months, toddlers are showing clear evidence of **compliance.** They are now aware of a caregiver's expectations and can obey many of her requests and commands (Crockenberg & Litman, 1990; Kaler & Kopp, 1990). They are also beginning to show clear signs of distress when they break things or otherwise do something that is prohibited, such as snitching a forbidden cookie (Cole, Barrett, & Zahn-Waxler, 1992; Kochanska, Casey, & Fukumoto, 1995). Yet, their behavior is still largely *externally* controlled by the approval they anticipate for compliance and the disapproval they associate with noncompliance.

social comparison
the process of defining and evaluating the self by comparing oneself with other people.

self-control
ability to regulate one's conduct and to inhibit actions that are unacceptable or that conflict with a goal.

compliance
the act of obeying the requests or commands of others.

However, anyone who has ever spent much time with 2- to 3-year-olds knows that they can become extremely uncooperative and noncompliant upon entering a phase that parents sometimes call the "terrible twos" (Bullock & Lutkenhaus, 1990; Erikson, 1963). According to Erikson, these toddlers are struggling with the psychosocial conflict of *autonomy versus shame and doubt.* They are resolved to display their independence and self-determination by doing things their own way, even if that means occasionally being noncompliant and risking others' disapproval.

An autonomy-seeking toddler who refuses to comply may do so through **self-assertion** (simply refusing a command or request) or **defiance** (saying "NO!" and becoming angry or intensifying one's ongoing behavior). Susan Crockenberg and Cindy Litman (1990) find that the strategies that caregivers use to resolve autonomy conflicts with their self-assertive toddlers play a major role in determining whether children become negative and defiant toward authority figures or adopt a more cooperative and compliant posture that is likely to promote self-control. Specifically, mothers who reacted to their 2-year-olds' self-assertive refusals by intervening physically or threatening and criticizing were likely to elicit *defiance,* whereas those who took an initial "NO" as an opportunity to remain firm in their demands while offering a rationale for complying were likely to elicit *compliance.* Grazyna Kochanska (1997; Kochanska & Aksan, 1995) adds that a warm mother–child relationship in which a mother is responsive to her toddler's needs and requests and sets reasonable expectations for mature conduct promotes **committed compliance**—an eagerness and readiness on the child's part to cooperate with the mother by internalizing her rules and obeying her commands. But if parents have often been insensitive to toddlers' needs and have shared few mutually enjoyable activities with them, their children are much more likely to display **situational compliance**—generally nonoppositional behavior that stems more from the parent's power to control the child's conduct than from the child's eagerness to cooperate and to embrace the parent's agenda. Clearly, 2- to 3-year-olds are quite capable of cooperation and are more likely to willingly comply with a sensitive, caring parent who has demonstrated a willingness to cooperate with them. Sensitive, responsive parenting is particularly important for fostering the committed compliance and later self-control of temperamentally impulsive children, who are prone to tantrums when they don't get their own way (Kochanska, 1995).

self-assertion
noncompliant acts that are undertaken by children in the interest of doing things for themselves or otherwise establishing autonomy.

defiance
active resistance to others' requests or demands; noncompliant acts that are accompanied by anger and an intensification of ongoing behavior.

committed compliance
compliance based on an eagerness or readiness to cooperate with a responsive parent who has been willing to cooperate with the child.

situational compliance
compliance based primarily on the parent's power to control the child's conduct.

As children acquire language, they begin to incorporate adult standards into their own speech, using those vocalizations to describe the implications of their actions and, eventually, to regulate and control their conduct. Even 2- to 2½-year-olds occasionally say things like "No" or "Don't" when they are about to commit a prohibited act, such as jumping on the sofa (Kochanska, 1993). The self-instructional role that language may play in early self-control is also apparent in other contexts. In one study, Brian Vaughn and his associates (1984) presented 18- to 30-month-old toddlers with three challenges: (1) to refrain from touching a nearby toy telephone, (2) to not eat raisins hidden under a cup until told that they could, and (3) to not open a gift until the experimenter had finished her work. The child was then observed to see how long he or she could wait before succumbing to these powerful temptations. As shown in Figure 12.3, the ability to wait increased dramatically between 18 and 30 months of age. Furthermore, there were clear individual differences in the patience displayed by the 30-month-olds; those who were further along in their language development showed the most self-control. So it seems that the private speech that Vygotsky wrote about not only helps young children to master cognitive challenges, but may also be involved in helping toddlers to control their impulses.

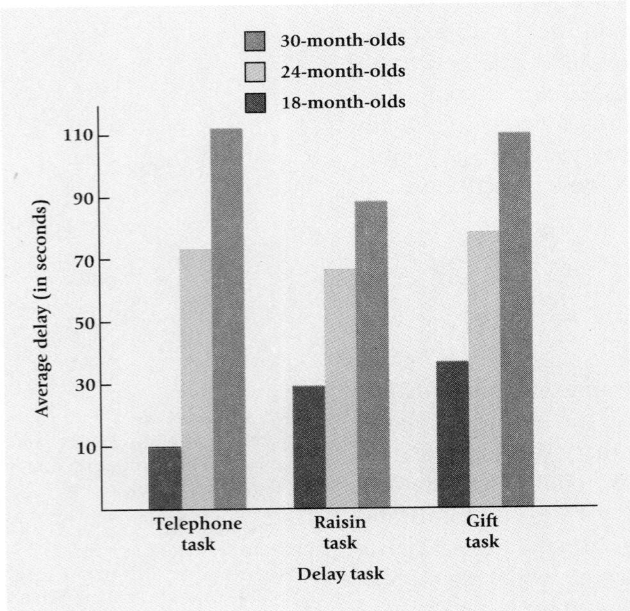

30-month-olds
24-month-olds
18-month-olds
Average delay (in seconds)
110
90
70
50
30
10
Telephone task
Raisin task
Gift task
Delay task

Figure 12.3 *Average delay of gratification (in seconds) of 18-, 24-, and 30-month-olds exposed to three strong temptations.* ADAPTED FROM VAUGHN, KOPP, & KRAKOW, 1984.

Delay of Gratification in Childhood and Adolescence

One of the more fruitful approaches for studying the development of self-control has been the **delay of gratification** paradigm. In a typical delay-of-gratification study, participants are offered a choice between a small incentive available immediately and a larger (or more desirable) incentive for which they must wait. What these studies find is that (1) preschool children find it exceedingly difficult to be patient when the smaller incentives they must resist are in plain sight, although (2) they do become better and better at delaying gratification over the grade-school years, eventually showing a strong preference to wait for larger delayed incentives by age 10 to 12 (Mischel, 1986). Why does this aspect of self-control improve so dramatically with age? Let's consider two possibilities.

Knowledge of Delay Strategies

In an early delay-of-gratification study, Walter Mischel and Ebbe Ebbesen (1970) found that 3- to 5-year-olds simply cannot keep their minds off tempting objects for long. The children in this study were told that if they waited 15 minutes, they would receive a very attractive snack; but, if they couldn't wait that long, they could signal the experimenter by ringing a bell and would receive a less desirable snack. When both kinds of snacks were visible during the delay period, preschoolers waited an average of only a minute or two before losing their patience, signaling the experimenter, and receiving the less desirable treat. Only a handful of children were able to wait the entire 15-minute delay period to earn the more valuable incentive. How did they do it? By covering their eyes, singing songs, inventing games, or otherwise *distracting* themselves from the temptations they faced.

However, it should be emphasized that the vast majority of preschoolers do *not* know that distraction can help them to resist immediate temptations. They can be *taught* by adults to use distractive strategies (Mischel & Patterson, 1976)—even very complex ones that require them to mentally transform tempting objects (for example, marshmallows) into less tempting stimuli (for example, white, puffy clouds)—to help them maintain their resolve (Mischel & Baker, 1975). But they do not generate these distractive strategies on their own. In fact, if it is suggested to them that they might become more patient by choosing a self-instructional strategy, preschoolers are much more inclined to focus attention on the *desirable qualities* of the incentives they are trying to resist (Toner, 1981)—a very ineffective means of coping with the frustrations of a delay.

By age 6 to 8, most children realize that creating physical distractions (for example, by covering their eyes or the tempting objects) can help them to be more patient. And by age 11 to 12, they know that *abstract ideation* (that is, cognitive distractions such as the marshmallows-are-clouds transformation or even such untrue self-instructions as "I hate marshmallows") can reduce their frustrations and make waiting easier (Mischel & Mischel, 1983). Abstract ideation probably takes so long to develop because it rests on hypothetical transformations of present realities—a formal-operational ability. Younger children can use abstract ideation if adults supply these distractors for them, but they will not generate them on their own. So one reason why self-control improves over the grade-school years is that children mature intellectually and are able to devise more effective strategies for regulating their thinking and conduct.

Self-control as a Valued Attribute

Another reason why older children and adolescents are better able to delay gratification, to comply with rules, or to otherwise control their impulses is that they are internalizing norms that stress the value of self-regulation and self-control. Evidence of this

delay of gratification
a form of self-control that involves the capacity to inhibit impulses to seek small rewards available immediately in the interest of obtaining larger, delayed incentives.

can be seen in the self-descriptions of preadolescents and adolescents. When asked what they like about themselves, adolescents often mention conduct that reflects their self-discipline (for example, being persistent at pursuing their goals or being slow to lose their tempers), and teenagers are often quite concerned about breakdowns in self-control (for example, blowing up at someone over nothing or failing to complete their homework) (Rosenberg, 1979). So by early adolescence, a capacity for self-control is viewed as a highly desirable and almost obligatory attribute that many teenagers hope to incorporate into their own self-concepts.

Instructing children that they can be patient is an important step parents can take to foster self-control and delay of gratification.

Could we foster children's self-control by working on their self-concepts—that is, by trying to convince them that they can be patient, persistent, honest, and even-tempered whenever they have shown some signs of displaying these attributes? Might children who are labeled as "honest" or "patient" incorporate these attributions into their self-concepts and try to live up to this new self-image? Indeed, they may. Nace Toner and his associates (1980) attempted to influence children's self-concepts by labeling them as "patient" individuals. Before beginning a typical delay-of-gratification experiment, the experimenter casually mentioned to half of the 5½- to 9-year-old participants "I hear that you are patient because you can wait for nice things when you can't get them right away." The remaining children heard a task-irrelevant attribution: "I hear that you have some very nice friends." The results were clear: Even when no one was present to monitor their conduct, children who had been labeled as "patient" were able to delay gratification far longer than those who had been labeled as having nice friends. So in addition to suggesting effective self-instructional strategies for regulating conduct, it appears that adults can promote self-control by bolstering children's images of themselves as patient, honest, or otherwise self-disciplined individuals (see also Casey & Burton, 1982).

Early Self-control as a Predictor of Later Life Outcomes

Developmentalists who study self-control cannot help but notice that some children are much more self-disciplined than others. Individual differences in compliance with rules and requests are already quite apparent by age 2; and relatively noncompliant toddlers whose mothers are either emotionally unresponsive or are critical and forceful with them (and who remain that way over time) are likely to become *defiant* and often continue to display undercontrolled antisocial and disruptive behaviors from the preschool period throughout early adolescence (Beckwith, Rodning, & Cohen, 1992; Henry et al., 1996; Shaw, Keenan, & Vondra, 1994). So there is reason to believe that a lack of self-discipline early in life can be a very maladaptive attribute.

Do children who display early evidence of self-control experience more *favorable* life outcomes? Indeed, they may. Walter Mischel and his associates have conducted 10-year follow-up studies of individuals who participated as preschoolers in Mischel's early delay-of-gratification experiments. In the follow-ups, parents completed questionnaires in which they described the competencies and shortcomings of their now-adolescent sons and daughters. These descriptions were highly informative. Apparently, self-control is a reasonably stable attribute, for adolescents who had been unable to delay gratification for long during the preschool years were the ones whom parents were now most likely to characterize as impatient and impulsive (Shoda, Mischel, & Peake, 1990). Adolescents who had been better at delaying gratification 10 years earlier were generally described in more favorable terms (that is, more academically competent, socially skilled, confident and self-reliant, and better able to cope with stress) than their counterparts who had shown less self-control as preschoolers (Mischel, Shoda, & Peake, 1988; Shoda et al., 1990). And, consistent with the parents' reports of their teenagers' academic competencies, adolescents who had displayed the most self-control as preschoolers were the ones who made the highest scores on the Scholastic Assessment Test (SAT) (Shoda et al., 1990).

Perhaps we can now appreciate why developmentalists consider the establishment of self-regulatory skills and the emergence of self-control to be such important developmental hurdles. Not only is self-control a moderately stable characteristic, but it is reliably associated with the very attributes (cognitive competencies, social skills, self-confidence, self-reliance) that forecast high self-esteem in adolescence (Harter, 1990) and occupational success and good interpersonal relations in adulthood (Hunter & Hunter, 1984; Newman et al., 1997). So one's capacity for self-control is a crucial component of this entity we call the "self"—one that enables children (among other things) to persist when faced with academic challenges and to develop positive academic self-concepts. Let's now take a closer look at the growth of children's propensities to achieve.

DEVELOPMENT OF ACHIEVEMENT MOTIVATION AND ACADEMIC SELF-CONCEPT

In Chapter 9, we learned that even though IQ predicts academic achievement, the relationship is far from perfect. Why? Because children also differ in **achievement motivation**—their willingness to strive to succeed at challenging tasks and to meet high standards of accomplishment. Although the meaning of achievement varies somewhat from society to society, one survey conducted in 30 cultures revealed that people around the world value personal attributes such as self-reliance, responsibility, and a willingness to work hard to attain important objectives (Fyans et al., 1983).

Many years ago, psychoanalyst Robert White (1959) proposed that from infancy onward, human beings are intrinsically motivated to "master" their environments—to have an effect on or to cope successfully with a world of people and objects. We see this **mastery motive** in action as we watch infants struggle to turn knobs, open cabinets, and operate toys, and then notice their pleasure when they succeed (Mayes & Zigler, 1992). Even infants and toddlers who are mentally retarded actively seek out challenges just for the joy of mastering them (Hausen-Corn, 1996).

But even though all babies may be curious, mastery-oriented beings, it is obvious that some children try harder than others to master their school assignments, music lessons, or the positions they play on the neighborhood softball team. How do we explain these individual differences? Let's begin by tracing the development of achievement motivation early in life and examining some of the factors that promote (or inhibit) its growth.

achievement motivation
a willingness to strive to succeed at challenging tasks and to meet high standards of accomplishment.

mastery motivation
an inborn motive to explore, understand, and control one's environment.

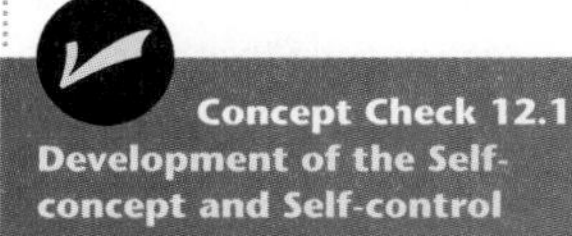
Concept Check 12.1
Development of the Self-concept and Self-control

Check your understanding of important processes and milestones in the development of the self by matching each descriptive statement below with one of the following concepts: (a) delay of gratification, (b) categorical self, (c) self-esteem, (d) looking-glass self, (e) self-assertion, (f) parental warmth/responsiveness, (g) belief-desire theory of mind, (h) private self, (i) social comparison, (j) self-recognition, (k) friendship quality. Answers appear in the Appendix.

_____ 1. evaluative component of the self that becomes more realistic by age 8
_____ 2. inner, reflective component of self
_____ 3. healthy form of noncompliance among autonomy-seeking toddlers
_____ 4. self-portrait based on other's reactions to one's behaviors and attributes
_____ 5. early predictor of favorable life outcomes
_____ 6. early contributor to socially skilled play activities
_____ 7. early self-description along such socially significant dimensions as age and sex
_____ 8. appears to underlie successful use of deceptive ploys
_____ 9. strong contributor to self-esteem beginning in adolescence
_____ 10. important contributor to self-esteem in cultures that stress individual accomplishments
_____ 11. promotes high self-esteem in childhood

Early Origins of Achievement Motivation

How does a baby's mastery motivation evolve into a grade-school child's achievement motivation? Deborah Stipek and her associates (Stipek, Recchia, & McClintic, 1992) have conducted a series of studies with 1- to 5-year-olds to find out when children develop the capacity to evaluate their accomplishments against performance standards—a capacity central to achievement motivation. In Stipek's research, children were observed as they undertook activities that had clear-cut achievement goals (for example, hammering pegs into pegboards, working puzzles, knocking down plastic pins with a bowling ball). Tasks were structured so that children either could or could not master them in order to observe reactions to success or failure. Based on this research, Stipek and her colleagues suggest that children progress through three phases in learning to evaluate their performances in achievement situations, phases we will call *joy in mastery, approval seeking,* and *use of standards.*

Phase 1: Joy in Mastery

Before the age of 2, infants are visibly pleased to master challenges, displaying the mastery motivation that White (1959) wrote about. However, they do not call other people's attention to their triumphs or otherwise seek recognition, and, rather than being bothered by failures, they simply shift goals and attempt to master other toys. They are not yet evaluating their outcomes in relation to performance standards that define success and failure.

Phase 2: Approval-Seeking

As they near age 2, toddlers begin to anticipate how others will evaluate their performances. They seek recognition when they master challenges and expect disapproval when they fail. For example, children as young as 2 who succeeded on a task often smiled, held their heads and chins up high, and made such statements as "I did it" as they called the experimenter's attention to their feats. Meanwhile, 2-year-olds who failed to master a challenge often turned away from the experimenter as though they hoped to avoid criticism. It seems, then, that 2-year-olds already appraise their outcomes as mastery successes or nonsuccesses and have already learned that they can expect approval after successes and disapproval after failures (see also Bullock & Lutkenhaus, 1988).

Three-year-olds are highly motivated to master challenges and can take pride in their accomplishments.

Phase 3: Use of Standards

An important breakthrough occurs around age 3 as children begin to react more independently to their successes and failures. They seem to have adopted objective standards for appraising their performance and are not as dependent on others to tell them when they have done well or poorly. These Phase 3 children seemed capable of experiencing real *pride* (rather than mere pleasure) in their achievements and real *shame* (rather than mere disappointment) after failure.

In sum, infants are guided by a mastery motive and take pleasure in their everyday accomplishments; 2-year-olds begin to anticipate others' approval or

Figure 12.4 *Scenes like this one were used by David McClelland and his associates to measure achievement motivation.*

disapproval of their performances; and children 3 and older evaluate their accomplishments against performance standards and are capable of experiencing pride or shame depending on how successfully they match those standards.

Achievement Motivation during Middle Childhood and Adolescence

In their pioneering studies of achievement motivation, David McClelland and his associates (1953) gave children and adolescents a series of four somewhat ambiguous pictures and asked them to write stories about them as part of a test of creative imagination. Assuming that people project their own motives into their stories, one can measure their achievement motivation by counting the number of achievement-related themes they mention. What kind of story would you tell about the scene portrayed in Figure 12.4? A person high in achievement motivation might respond by saying that the individual in the photo has been working for months on a new scientific breakthrough that will revolutionize the field of medicine, whereas a person who scores low might say that this worker is glad the day is over so that she can go home and relax. Early research revealed that children and adolescents who scored high in achievement motivation on this and other measures tended to receive better grades in school than those who scored low (McClelland et al., 1953). These findings prompted investigators to look more closely at parent–child interactions to determine how the home setting influences achievement motivation.

Home Influences on Mastery Motivation and Achievement

Over the years, researchers have identified three especially potent home influences on children's mastery/achievement motivation and actual achievement behavior: the quality of the child's attachments, the character of the home environment, and the child-rearing practices that parents use, which can either foster or inhibit a child's will to achieve.

Quality of Attachment. In Chapter 11, we learned that children who were securely attached to primary caregivers at age 12 to 18 months were more likely than those who were insecurely attached to solve problems successfully as 2-year-olds and to display a

TABLE 12.1 Relation between Quality of Home Environment at 12 Months of Age and Children's Grade-School Academic Achievement 5 to 9 Years Later

	Academic achievement	
Quality of home environment at age 12 months	**Average or high (top 70%)**	**Low (bottom 30%)**
Stimulating	20 children	10 children
Unstimulating	6 children	14 children

SOURCE: Adapted from van Doorninck, Caldwell, Wright, & Frankenberg, 1981.

strong sense of curiosity, self-reliance, and an eagerness to solve problems some 4 to 5 years later as they enter elementary school. It is not that securely attached preschoolers are any more intellectually competent; instead, they seem to be more *eager* than insecurely attached children to *apply* their competencies to the new problems they encounter (Belsky, Garduque, & Hrncir, 1984). So children apparently need the secure base provided by a loving, responsive parent to feel comfortable about taking risks and *seeking* challenges.

THE HOME ENVIRONMENT. The young child's tendency to explore, acquire new skills, and solve problems also depends on the kind of challenges the home environment provides. In one study (van Doorninck et al., 1981), researchers visited the homes of fifty 12-month-old infants from lower-income families and used the *Home Inventory* (described in Chapter 9) to classify the child's early environment as intellectually stimulating or unstimulating. Five to nine years later, the research team followed up on these children by looking at their standardized achievement test scores and the grades they had earned at school. As we see in Table 12.1, the quality of the home environment at 12 months of age predicted children's academic achievement several years later. Two out of three children from stimulating homes were now performing quite well at school, whereas 70% of those from unstimulating homes were doing very poorly (see also Bradley, Caldwell, & Rock, 1988). Although the seeds of mastery motivation may well be innate, it seems that the joy of discovery and problem solving is unlikely to blossom in a barren home environment where the child has few problems to solve and limited opportunities for learning.

CHILD-REARING AND ACHIEVEMENT. In their book *The Achievement Motive,* McClelland and his associates (1953) proposed that parents who stress *independence training*—doing things on one's own—and who warmly reinforce such self-reliant behavior contribute in a positive way to achievement motivation. And research bears this out (Grolnick & Ryan, 1989; Winterbottom, 1958). Furthermore, direct *achievement training*—setting *high standards* and encouraging children to do things *well*—also fosters achievement motivation (Rosen & D'Andrade, 1959). Finally, patterns of praise (or punishment) that accompany the child's accomplishments are also important: Children who seek challenges and display high levels of achievement motivation have parents who *praise their successes and are not overly critical of an occasional failure;* by contrast, children who shy away from challenges and are low in achievement motivation have parents who are slow to acknowledge their successes (or who do so in a matter-of-fact way) and are inclined to *punish* their failures (Burhans & Dweck, 1995; Teeven & McGhee, 1972).

We see, then, that parents of youngsters high in achievement motivation possess three characteristics: (1) they are warm, accepting, and quick to praise the child's accomplishments; (2) they provide guidance and control by setting standards for the child to live up to and then monitoring her progress to ensure that she does; and (3) they permit the child some independence or autonomy, allowing her a say in deciding how best to master challenges and meet their expectations. Diana Baumrind calls this warm, firm, but democratic parenting an **authoritative parenting** style—a style that she and others have found to foster positive attitudes about achievement and considerable

authoritative parenting
flexible, democratic style of parenting in which warm, accepting parents provide guidance and control while allowing the child some say in deciding how best to meet challenges and obligations.

Parents who encourage achievement and who respond warmly to success are likely to raise mastery-oriented children who enjoy challenges.

academic success among grade-school children and adolescents, both in Western societies (Glasgow et al., 1997; Lamborn et al., 1991; Steinberg, Elmen, & Mounts, 1989) and in Asia (Lin & Fu, 1990). If children are encouraged and supported in a positive manner as they tackle their schoolwork, they are likely to enjoy new challenges and feel confident of mastering them (Connell, Spencer, & Aber, 1994). By contrast, parents can undermine a child's school performance and motivation to succeed if they (1) are uninvolved and offer little in the way of guidance or (2) are highly controlling and do such things as nag continually about homework, offer tangible bribes for good grades, or harp incessantly about bad ones (Ginsburg & Bronstein, 1993).

Peer Group Influences

Peers are also an important source of influence on grade-school children and adolescents who may sometimes support and at other times undermine parents' efforts to encourage academic achievement. Peer pressures that interfere with academic achievement may be especially acute for many lower-income African-American and Latino students and may help explain why they often lag behind Anglo-American and Asian-American students in school achievement (Slaughter-Defoe et al., 1990; Tharp, 1989). Lawrence Steinberg and his colleagues (Steinberg, Dornbusch, & Brown, 1992) found that the African-American and Latino peer cultures in many low-income areas actively discourage academic achievement, whereas Anglo- and Asian-American peer groups tend to value and encourage it. High-achieving African-American students in some inner-city schools actually run the risk of being rejected by their African-American peers if their academic accomplishments cause them to be perceived as "acting white" (Ford & Harris, 1996; Fordham & Ogbu, 1986).

By contrast, children whose parents value education highly and work hard to promote their achievement tend to associate with peers who share those values. In his recent study of Latino, East Asian, Filipino, and European immigrant families, Andrew Fuligni (1997) found that immigrant adolescents tend to make higher grades at school than native-born U.S. adolescents do, despite the fact that their parents are not highly educated and often speak little English at home. Why? Because the parents of these high achievers strongly endorsed the value of academics, a value that was clearly reinforced by their friends, who often studied together with them, shared class notes, and encouraged them to do well in school. This kind of peer support for parental values also fosters the academic achievement of talented African-American students (Ford & Harris, 1996) and preadolescents in Shanghai, China (Chen, Rubin, & Li, 1997), and is probably a strong contributor to the academic successes of students from any background. Clearly, it is easier to remain focused on academic goals if one is not receiving mixed messages about their value from parents and peers.

Beyond Achievement Motivation: Development of Achievement-Related Attributions

Many contemporary researchers acknowledge that the concept of achievement motivation has some value, but they believe it is naive to presume that this one global motive predicts behavior in all achievement situations. Why? Because they have also discovered that children's achievement behavior and academic self-concepts depend very heavily on their **achievement attributions,** or how they *interpret* their successes and failures.

Types of Achievement Attributions

Bernard Weiner (1974; 1986) finds that adolescents and young adults tend to attribute their successes and failures to any of four possible causes: *ability* (or the lack thereof), *effort, task difficulty,* or *luck* (either good or bad). As shown in Table 12.2, two of these causes, ability and task difficulty, are *stable* causes, which foster strong *achievement expectancies,* whereas effort and luck are *unstable,* or highly variable from situation to situation, and promote weaker expectancies. To illustrate, if you do poorly on a test and attribute your failure to a *stable* cause like low ability, you should feel less confident of future success (strong negative expectancy) than if you attributed that failure to low effort, which you might overcome by studying harder next time. Notice also that two of the causes in the table, ability and effort, are *internal* causes (characteristics of the individual), whereas the other two are *external* causes (characteristics of the situation). Weiner proposes that the internality–externality of our achievement attributions affects how much we *value* our achievement outcomes. So if we attribute an A on a test to an *internal* cause such as our high ability or hard work, we are more likely to value our success than if we attributed it to such external factors as blind luck or a ridiculously easy exam.

Perhaps you can see that it is adaptive to attribute our successes to high ability, for this internal and stable attribution causes us to *value* what we have accomplished and leads us to *expect* that we can repeat our success. By contrast, it is more adaptive to attribute *failures* to low effort (rather than low ability) because effort is unstable and we are more likely to believe that we can do better in the future if we just try harder.

Age Differences in Achievement-Related Attributes

If it seems to you as if Weiner's theory sounds a little too cognitive and abstract to explain the achievement attributions that young children display, you would be right. Before age 7 or so, children tend to be unrealistic optimists who think they have the ability to succeed on almost any task, even those that they have repeatedly failed to master in the past (Stipek & Mac Iver, 1989). Preschool and primary-grade teachers may

TABLE 12.2 Weiner's Classification of the Causes of Achievement Outcomes (and Examples of How You Might Explain a Terrible Test Grade)

	Locus of causality	
	Internal cause	**External cause**
Stable cause	*Ability* "I'm hopeless in math."	*Task difficulty* "That test was incredibly hard and much too long."
Unstable cause	*Effort* "I should have studied more instead of going out to the concert."	*Luck* "What luck! Every question seemed to be about information taught on the days of class I missed."

achievement attributions
causal explanations that one provides for his/her successes and failures.

contribute to this rosy optimism by setting mastery goals and by praising children more for their efforts than for the quality of their work, thus leading them to believe that they can accomplish much and "be smart" by working hard (Rosenholtz & Simpson, 1984; Stipek & Mac Iver, 1989). Indeed, young children do seem to have an **incremental view of ability:** They believe that ability is changeable, not stable, and that they can get smarter or become more capable through increased effort and lots of practice (Droege & Stipek, 1993; Dweck & Leggett, 1988).

When do children begin to distinguish ability from effort? When do they move toward an **entity view of ability**—a perspective that ability is a fixed or stable trait that is not influenced much by effort or practice? It turns out that many 8- to 12-year-olds begin to distinguish effort from ability (Nicholls & Miller, 1984) due, in part, to the changing character of their experiences at school. Teachers gradually place more and more emphasis on *ability* appraisals; they assign grades that reflect the quality of work that students perform rather than the amount of effort expended, and these performance evaluations are supplemented by such competitive activities as science fairs and spelling bees, which also place a premium on the *quality* rather than the quantity of students' work. Furthermore, older grade-school children are often placed into "ability groups" based on the teacher's appraisal of their competencies (Rosenholtz & Simpson, 1984; Stipek & Mac Iver, 1989). So all these practices, coupled with children's increased use of social comparison to appraise their outcomes (Pomerantz et al., 1995), help to explain why older grade-school students begin to distinguish effort from ability and make the kind of causal attributions for their successes and failures that Weiner's theory anticipates.

Interestingly, the late elementary school period (4th to 6th grades) is also the time when many students begin to value academic achievement less and to develop rather negative academic self-concepts, a trend that becomes even stronger during the junior high school years (Eccles et al., 1993; Seidman et al., 1994). And as we are about to see, children's tendency to distinguish ability and effort and to adopt an *entity view* of ability is a major contributor to these trends.

Dweck's Learned-Helplessness Theory

Carol Dweck and her colleagues (Dweck & Elliott, 1983; Dweck & Leggett, 1988) find that middle-school children clearly differ in the attributions they offer for their achievement outcomes, particularly for their failures. Some children are **mastery oriented:** They attribute their successes to their high ability but tend to externalize the blame for their failures ("That test was ambiguous and unfair") or to attribute them to *unstable* causes that they can easily overcome ("I'll do better if I try harder"). These students are called "mastery oriented" because they persist in the face of failure, believing that their increased effort will allow them to succeed. Although they see their ability as a reasonably stable attribute that doesn't fluctuate radically from day to day (which allows them to feel confident about repeating their successes), they still think that they can improve their competencies (an *incremental* viewpoint) by trying harder after a failure. So mastery-oriented youngsters are highly motivated to "master" new challenges, regardless of whether they have previously succeeded or failed at similar tasks (see Figure 12.5 on page 456).

By contrast, other children often attribute their successes to the *unstable* factors of hard work or luck; they do not experience the pride and self-esteem that come from viewing themselves as highly competent. Yet they often attribute their failures to a stable and internal factor—namely, their *lack of ability*—which causes them to form low expectations of future successes and give up. It appeared to Dweck as if these youngsters were displaying a **learned helplessness orientation:** If failures are attributed to a *stable* cause—lack of ability—that the child thinks he can do little about (an *entity view* of ability), he becomes frustrated and sees little reason to try to improve. So he stops trying and acts helpless (see also Pomerantz & Ruble, 1997). Unfortunately, even talented students may adopt this unhealthy attributional style which, once established, tends to persist over time and eventually undermines their academic performances (Fincham, Hokada, & Sanders, 1989; Phillips, 1984).

incremental view of ability
belief that one's ability can be improved through increased effort and practice.

entity view of ability
belief that one's ability is a highly stable trait that is not influenced much by effort or practice.

mastery orientation
a tendency to persist at challenging tasks because of a belief that one has high ability and/or that earlier failures can be overcome by trying harder.

learned helplessness orientation
a tendency to give up or to stop trying after failing because these failures have been attributed to a lack of ability that one can do little about.

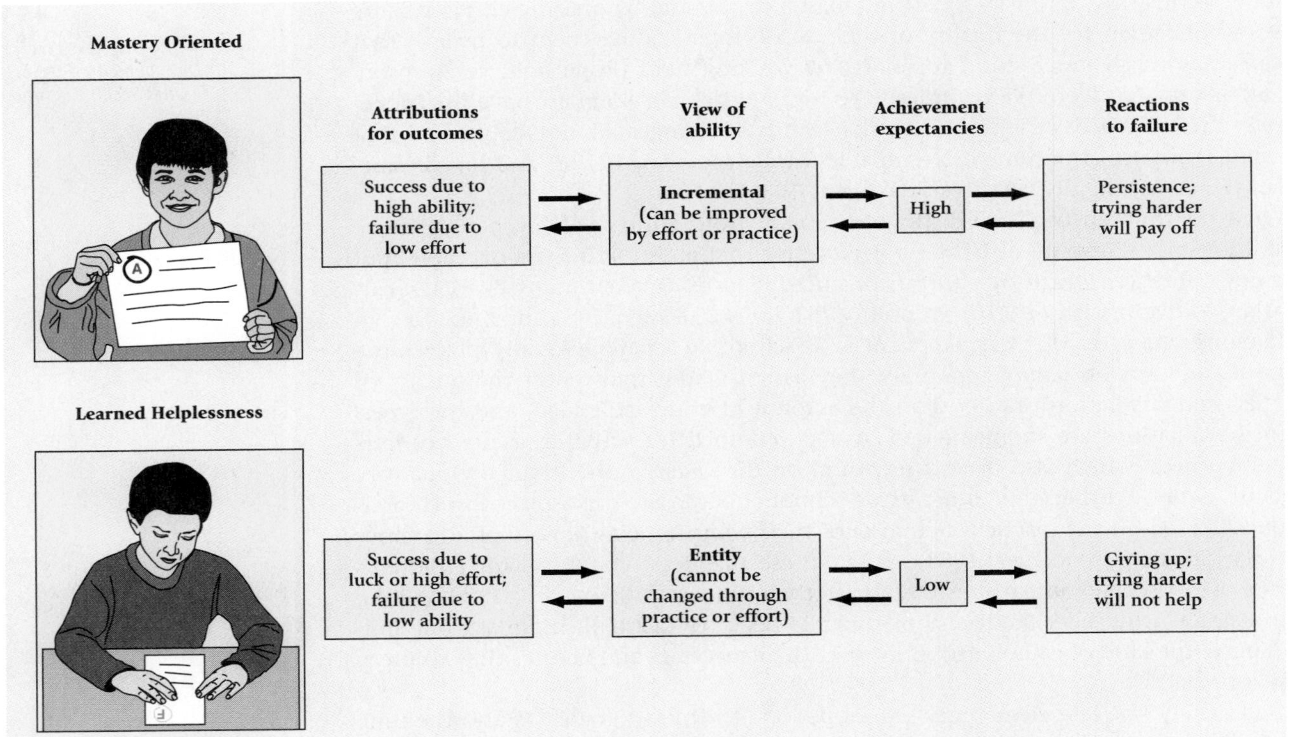

Figure 12.5 *Characteristics of the mastery-oriented and learned-helplessness achievement orientations.*

How Does Learned Helplessness Develop? According to Dweck (1978), parents and teachers may unwittingly foster the development of a helpless achievement orientation if they praise the child for *working hard* when she succeeds but criticize her *lack of ability* when she fails. Apparently, even 4- to 6-year-olds can begin to develop a helpless orientation if their failures are often punished or otherwise criticized in ways that cause them to doubt their abilities (Burhans & Dweck, 1995; Heyman, Dweck, & Cain, 1992). By contrast, if parents and teachers praise the child's *abilities* when she succeeds but emphasize her *lack of effort* when she fails, the child may conclude that she is certainly smart enough and would do even better if she tried harder—precisely the viewpoint adopted by mastery-oriented youngsters. In one clever experiment, Dweck and her associates (1978) demonstrated that fifth-graders who received the *helplessness-producing* pattern of evaluation while working at unfamiliar problems began to attribute their failures to a lack of ability, whereas classmates who received the *mastery-oriented* evaluative pattern attributed their failures to a lack of effort, saying, in effect, "I need to try harder." These strikingly different attributional styles were created in less than 1 hour in this experiment, thus implying that similar patterns of evaluative feedback from parents or teachers, given consistently over a period of months or years, might well contribute to the development of the contrasting helpless and mastery orientations so often observed among grade-school (and older) students.

On Helping the Helpless to Achieve. Obviously, giving up as soon as one begins to founder is not the kind of achievement orientation that adults hope to encourage. What can be done to help these "helpless" children to persist at tasks where they have failed? According to Dweck, one effective therapy might be a form of **attribution retraining** in which children with a learned-helplessness orientation are persuaded to attribute their failures to unstable causes—namely, insufficient effort—that they can do something about, rather than continuing to view them as stemming from their lack of ability, which is not so easy to change.

attribution retraining therapeutic intervention in which helpless children are persuaded to attribute failures to their lack of effort rather than a lack of ability.

Dweck (1975) tested her hypothesis by exposing children who had become "helpless" after failing a series of tough math problems to either of two "therapies." Over a period of 25 therapy sessions, half the children received a *success-only* therapy in which they worked problems they could solve and received tokens for their successes. The other half received *attribution retraining:* They experienced nearly as many successes over the 25 sessions as did the children in the other group but were also told after each of several prearranged failures that they had not worked fast enough and *should have tried harder.* Thus, an explicit attempt was made to convince these youngsters that failures can reflect a lack of effort rather than a lack of ability. Did this therapy work? Yes, indeed! At the end of the experiment, "helpless" children in the attribution-retraining condition now performed much better on the tough math problems they had initially failed to solve; and when they did fail one, they usually attributed their outcome to a lack of effort and tried harder. By contrast, children in the success-only condition showed no such improvements, giving up once again after failing the original problems. So merely showing children who act helpless that they are capable of succeeding is not enough! To alleviate learned helplessness, one must teach children to respond more constructively to their *failures* by viewing these experiences as something they can overcome if they try harder.

Can we do better than this? Certainly we can by taking steps to *prevent* learned helplessness from developing. Parents and teachers can play a major part in these preventive efforts by simply praising the child's *abilities* when she succeeds and taking care not to undermine her self-worth by suggesting that failures reflect a lack of ability. Indeed, one of the reasons that *authoritative parenting* is so consistently linked to high achievement is that these warm, supportive companions (1) convince their child that he has the *ability* to meet high standards, while (2) praising successes and not becoming overly concerned about occasional failures, thereby fostering the development of a *mastery-oriented* attributional style.

Finally, some restructuring of classroom goals may go a long way toward preventing learned helplessness. Whether pursuing academic or social objectives, children with a learned-helplessness orientation tend to adopt **performance goals:** They are motivated to *display their competencies* and give up when they experience difficulty because their goal has been undermined (Elliott & Dweck, 1988; Erdley et al., 1997). By contrast, mastery-oriented children adopt **learning goals,** in which they seek to *increase their abilities.* Their failures simply tell them that they need to change their approach and keep working to master new skills. Today, many researchers believe that restructuring curricula to emphasize *individual mastery* and improving one's competencies not only convince children to adopt learning goals, but are particularly helpful to slower learners who fare poorly by comparison with their peers should they try to demonstrate their competencies through such competitive performance appraisals as grades (Butler, 1990; Stipek & Mac Iver, 1989). Such a focus on mastering new skills *for their own sake* should persuade students to view initial failures as evidence that they need to change strategies and keep on working rather than treating them as proof that they have little ability and simply cannot master their assignments.

WHO AM I TO BE? FORGING AN IDENTITY

According to Erik Erikson (1963), the major developmental hurdle that adolescents face is establishing an **identity**—a firm and coherent sense of who they are, where they are heading, and where they fit into society. Forging an identity involves grappling with many important choices: What kind of career do I want? What religious, moral, and political values should I adopt? Who am I as a man or a woman, and as a sexual being? Just where do I fit into society? All this is, of course, a lot for teenagers to have on their minds, and Erikson used the term **identity crisis** to capture the sense of confusion, and even anxiety, that adolescents may feel as they think about who they are today and try to decide "What kind of self can (or should) I become?"

Can you recall a time during the teenage years when you were confused about who

performance goal
state of affairs in which one's primary objective in an achievement context is to display one's competencies (or to avoid looking incompetent).

learning goal
state of affairs in which one's primary objective in an achievement context is to increase one's skills or abilities.

identity
a mature self-definition; a sense of who one is, where one is going in life, and how one fits into society.

identity crisis
Erikson's term for the uncertainty and discomfort that adolescents experience when they become confused about their present and future roles in life.

you were, what you should be, and what you were likely to become? Is it possible that you have not yet resolved these identity issues and are still seeking answers? If so, does that make you abnormal or maladjusted?

James Marcia (1980) has developed a structured interview that allows researchers to classify adolescents into one of four *identity statuses—identity diffusion, foreclosure, moratorium,* and *identity achievement*—based on whether or not they have explored various alternatives and made firm commitments to an occupation, a religious ideology, a sexual orientation, and a set of political values. These identity statuses are as follows:

1. **Identity diffusion.** Persons classified as diffuse have not yet thought about or resolved identity issues and have failed to chart future life directions. *Example:* "I haven't really thought much about religion, and I guess I don't know exactly what I believe."
2. **Foreclosure.** Persons classified as foreclosed are committed to an identity but have made this commitment without experiencing the crisis of deciding what really suits them best. *Example:* "My parents are Baptists and so I'm a Baptist; it's just the way I grew up."
3. **Moratorium.** Persons in this status are experiencing what Erikson called an identity crisis and are actively asking questions about life commitments and seeking answers. *Example:* "I'm evaluating my beliefs and hope that I will be able to decide what's right for me. I like many of the answers provided by my Catholic upbringing, but I'm skeptical about some teachings as well. I have been looking into Unitarianism to see if it might help me answer my questions."
4. **Identity achievement.** Identity-achieved individuals have solved identity issues by making *personal* commitments to particular goals, beliefs, and values. *Example:* "After a lot of soul-searching about my religion and other religions too, I finally know what I believe and what I don't."

identity diffusion
identity status characterizing individuals who are not questioning who they are and have not yet committed themselves to an identity.

foreclosure
identity status characterizing individuals who have prematurely committed themselves to occupations or ideologies without really thinking about these commitments.

moratorium
identity status characterizing individuals who are currently experiencing an identity crisis and are actively exploring occupational and ideological positions in which to invest themselves.

identity achievement
identity status characterizing individuals who have carefully considered identity issues and have made firm commitments to an occupation and ideologies.

Developmental Trends in Identity Formation

Although Erikson assumed that the identity crisis occurs in early adolescence and is often resolved by age 15 to 18, his age norms were overly optimistic. When Philip Meilman (1979) measured the identity statuses of males between the ages of 12 and 24, he observed a clear developmental progression. But as shown in Figure 12.6, the vast majority of 12- to 18-year-olds were identity diffuse or foreclosed, and not until age 21 or older had the majority of participants reached the moratorium status or achieved stable identities.

Is the identity formation process different for girls and women than it is for boys and men? In most respects, no (Archer, 1992; Kroger, 1996). Girls make progress toward achieving a clear sense of identity at about the same ages that boys do (Streitmatter, 1993). However, one intriguing sex difference has been observed: Although today's college women are just as concerned about establishing a career identity as men are, they attach greater importance to the aspects of identity that center on interpersonal relationships, gender roles, and sexuality (Archer, 1992; Kroger, 1996; Patterson, Sochting, & Marcia, 1992). They are also more concerned than men with the issue of how to balance career and family goals (Archer, 1992; Matula et al., 1992).

Judging from this research, identity formation takes quite a bit of time. Not until late adolescence—during the college years—do many young men and women move from the diffusion or foreclosure status into the moratorium status and then achieve a sense of identity (Waterman, 1982). But this is by no means the end of the identity formation process. Many adults are *still* struggling with identity issues or have reopened the question of who they are after thinking they had all the answers earlier in life

? **WHAT DO YOU THINK?**

In the United States, 17- to 20-year-olds are often encouraged to enlist in the armed services to see the world and prepare themselves for adult life. What identity status do you think the services are encouraging youth to assume? To whom do you think this pitch is most likely to appeal and why?

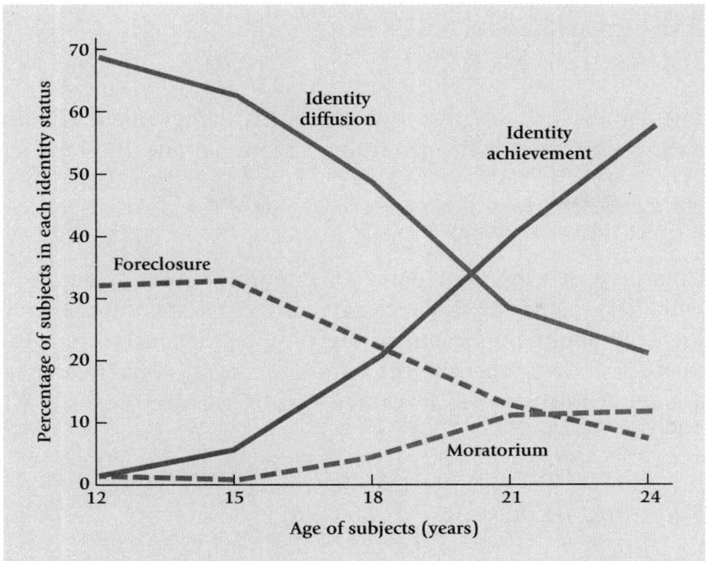

Figure 12.6 *Percentages of participants in each of Marcia's four identity statuses as a function of age. Note that resolution of the identity crisis occurs much later than Erikson assumed: Only 4% of the 15-year-olds and 20% of the 18-year-olds had achieved a stable identity.* FROM MEILMAN, 1979.

(Waterman & Archer, 1990). A divorce, for example, may cause a homemaker to rethink what it means to be a woman and raise questions about other aspects of her identity as well.

The process of achieving identity is also quite uneven (Archer, 1982; Kroger, 1996). For example, Sally Archer (1982) assessed the identity statuses of sixth to twelfth graders in four domains: occupational choice, gender-role attitudes, religious beliefs, and political ideologies. Only 5% of her adolescents were in the same identity status in all four areas, with 95% being in two or even three statuses across the four domains. So adolescents can achieve a strong sense of identity in one area and still be searching in others.

How Painful Is Identity Formation?

Perhaps it is unfortunate that Erikson used the term *crisis* to describe the adolescent's active search for an identity (or identities), because adolescents in the moratorium status do not appear all that "stressed out." In fact, James Marcia and his associates (1993) find that these active identity seekers feel much better about themselves and their futures than do age-mates in the diffusion and foreclosure statuses. Yet, Erikson was right in characterizing identity achievement as a very healthy and adaptive development, for identity achievers do enjoy higher self-esteem and are less self-conscious or preoccupied with personal concerns than their counterparts in the other three identity statuses (Adams, Abraham, & Markstrom, 1987; O'Connor, 1995).

What may be most painful or crisislike about identity seeking is a long-term failure to establish one. Erikson believed that individuals without a clear identity eventually become depressed and lacking in self-confidence as they drift aimlessly, trapped in the diffusion status. Or alternatively, they might heartily embrace what Erikson called a *negative identity,* becoming a "black sheep," a "delinquent," or a "loser." Why? Because for these foundering souls, it is better to become everything that one is not supposed to be than to have no identity at all (Erikson, 1963). Indeed, many adolescents who are stuck in the diffusion status are highly apathetic and express a sense of hopelessness about the future (Waterman & Archer, 1990). Others who enter high school with very low self-esteem often drift into delinquency and view their deviant self-image as having provided them with a boost in self-worth (Bynner, O'Malley, & Bachman, 1981; Wells, 1989). So it seems that a small minority of adolescents and young adults experience what might be termed an identity *crisis* after all.

Influences on Identity Formation

The adolescent's progress toward identity achievement is influenced by at least four factors: cognitive growth, parenting, schooling, and the broader social-cultural context.

Cognitive Influences

Cognitive development plays an important role in identity achievement. Adolescents who have achieved solid mastery of formal-operational thought and who can reason logically about hypotheticals are now better able to imagine and contemplate future identities. Consequently, they are more likely to raise and resolve identity issues than are age-mates who are less intellectually mature (Boyes & Chandler, 1992; Waterman, 1992).

Parenting Influences

The relationships that adolescents have with their parents can also affect their progress at forging an identity (Markstrom-Adams, 1992; Waterman, 1982). Adolescents in the diffusion status are more likely than those in other statuses to feel neglected or rejected by their parents and to be distant from them (Archer, 1994). Perhaps it is difficult to establish one's own identity without first having the opportunity to identify with respected parental figures and take on some of their desirable qualities. At the other extreme, adolescents in the identity foreclosure status are often extremely close to and sometimes fear rejection from relatively controlling parents (Kroger, 1995). Foreclosed adolescents may never question parental authority or feel any need to forge a separate identity.

By contrast, adolescents in the moratorium and identity achievement statuses appear to have a solid base of affection at home combined with considerable freedom to be individuals in their own right (Grotevant & Cooper, 1986). In family discussions, for example, these adolescents experience a sense of closeness and mutual respect while feeling free to disagree with their parents. So the same loving and democratic style of parenting that fosters academic achievement and helps children gain a strong sense of self-esteem is also associated with healthy and adaptive identity outcomes in adolescence.

Scholastic Influences

Does attending college help one to forge an identity? The answer is yes—and no. Attending college does seem to push people toward setting career goals and making stable occupational commitments (Waterman, 1982), but college students are often far behind their working peers in terms of establishing firm political and religious identities (Munro & Adams, 1977). In fact, some collegians regress from identity achievement to the moratorium or even the diffusion status in certain areas, most notably religion. But let's not be too critical of the college environment, for, like college students, many adults later reopen the question of who they are if exposed to people or situations that challenge old viewpoints and offer new alternatives (Waterman & Archer, 1990).

Social-Cultural Influences

Finally, identity formation is strongly influenced by the broader social and historical context in which it occurs—a point that Erikson himself emphasized. In fact, the very idea that adolescents should choose a personal identity after carefully exploring many options may well be peculiar to industrialized societies of the 20th century (Cote & Levine, 1988). As in past centuries, adolescents in many nonindustrialized societies today simply adopt the adult roles they are expected to adopt, without any soul-searching or experimentation: Sons of farmers become farmers; the children of fishermen become (or perhaps marry) fishermen, and so on. For many of the world's adolescents, then, what Marcia calls identity foreclosure is probably the most adaptive route to adulthood.

On the other hand, the process of forging an identity may be especially difficult for members of minority racial and ethnic groups in modern industrialized societies. As Box 12.2, on page 462, indicates, they face the additional task of establishing a positive ethnic identity.

THE OTHER SIDE OF SOCIAL COGNITION: KNOWING ABOUT OTHERS

Being appropriately social requires us to interact with other people, and these interactions are more likely to be harmonious if we know what our social partners are thinking or feeling and can predict how they are likely to behave. The development of children's knowledge about other people—their descriptions of others' characteristics and the inferences they make about others' thoughts and behaviors—constitutes perhaps the largest area of social-cognitive research. And there are so many questions to be answered. For example, what kinds of information do children use to form impressions of others? How do these impressions change over time? And what skills do children acquire that might explain such changes in person perception? These are the issues that we will now explore.

Age Trends in Person Perception

Children younger than 7 or 8 are likely to characterize people they know in the same concrete, observable terms that they use to describe the self (Livesley & Bromley, 1973; Ruble & Dweck, 1995; and see Box 12.3 on page 463). Five-year-old Jenny, for example, said: "My daddy is big. He has hairy legs and eats mustard. Yuck! My daddy likes dogs—do you?" Not much of a personality profile there! When young children do use a psychological term to describe others, it is typically a very general attribute such as "He's *nice*" or "She's *mean*" that they may use more as a label for the other person's recent behavior than as a description of the person's enduring qualities (Rholes & Ruble, 1984; Ruble & Dweck, 1995).

Concept Check 12.2
Establishing an Achievement Orientation and a Personal Identity

Check your understanding of identity formation and the development of achievement orientations by matching each descriptive statement below to one of the following concepts: (a) strong parental criticism of failures, (b) negative peer influences, (c) stability of achievement attributions, (d) children with a mastery orientation, (e) children with a learned helplessness orientation, (f) identity foreclosure, (g) identity diffusion, (h) identity achievement. Answers appear in the Appendix.

_____ 1. thought to be an adaptive route to identity formation in nonindustrialized societies
_____ 2. strong contributor to academic underachievement among disadvantaged minorities
_____ 3. attribute successes to high ability and failures to lack of effort
_____ 4. adolescents displaying this status often feel distant from their parents
_____ 5. attribute successes to high effort (or luck) and failures to lack of ability
_____ 6. solid mastery of formal operations promotes this status
_____ 7. correlate of low achievement motivation
_____ 8. predictor of future achievement expectancies

12.2

CULTURAL INFLUENCES

Identity Formation among Minority Adolescents

In addition to the identity issues that confront all adolescents, members of ethnic minority groups must also establish an *ethnic identity*—a personal identification with an ethnic group and its values and traditions (Phinney, 1996). This is not always an easy task. As we saw earlier, some minority children may even identify at first with the culture's ethnic majority, apparently wanting to affiliate with the group that has the most status in society (Spencer & Markstrom-Adams, 1990). One Hispanic adolescent who had done this said, "I remember I would not say I was Hispanic. My friends . . . were White and Oriental and I tried so hard to fit in with them" (Phinney & Rosenthal, 1992, p. 158). It is not that young children have no knowledge of their subcultural traditions. Mexican-American preschoolers, for example, may learn such culturally relevant behaviors as giving a Chicano handshake; yet, not until about age 8 are they likely to fully understand which ethnic labels apply to them, what they mean, or that their ethnicity is a lifelong attribute (Bernal & Knight, 1997).

Forming a positive ethnic identity during adolescence seems to involve the same steps, or statuses, as forming a vocational or religious identity (Phinney, 1993). Young adolescents often say that they identify with their racial or ethnic group because their parents and other members of the group influenced them to do so (foreclosure status) or because that is what they are and they have not given the issue much thought (diffusion status) (Markstrom-Adams & Adams, 1995). But between ages 16 and 19, many minority youths move into the moratorium or achievement phases of ethnic identity. One Mexican-American girl described her moratorium period this way: "I want to know what we do and how our culture is different from others. Going to festivals and cultural events helps me to learn more about my own culture and about myself" (Phinney, 1993, p. 70). Once ethnic identity is achieved, minority youth tend to enjoy higher self-esteem and better relations with parents and peers than their counterparts who merely label themselves as a minority and are still ethnically diffuse or foreclosed (Phinney, 1996).

Interestingly, minority adolescents sometimes lag behind their majority-group peers at resolving other, more traditional identity issues. Why is this? Spencer and Markstrom-Adams (1990) suggest several possibilities. For one thing, minority adolescents may come to realize that prejudice and discrimination in society may limit their educational and vocational prospects, thus causing them to be less than optimistic about the future and hindering their establishment of an occupational identity (Ogbu, 1988). In addition, minority youths frequently encounter conflicts between the values of their subculture and those of the majority culture, and members of their subcultural communities (especially peers) often discourage identity explorations that clash with the social traditions of their own group. Virtually all North American minorities have a term for community members who are "too white" in orientation, be it the "apple" (red on the outside, white on the inside) for Native Americans, the Hispanic "coconut," the Asian "banana," or the African-American "Oreo." Clearly, minority adolescents must resolve these value conflicts and decide for themselves what *they* are inside.

Interestingly, biracial adolescents and minority adoptees in white adoptive homes sometimes face even greater conflicts. These youngsters may feel pressured to choose between minority and white peer groups, thereby encountering social barriers to achieving an identity as *both* African-American (for example) and white (DeBerry, Scarr, & Weinberg, 1996; Kerwin et al., 1993). About half the transracial adoptees in Scarr's classic Minnesota Transracial Adoption Study showed some signs of social maladjustment at age 17. Although African-American in appearance, many of these adoptees regarded whites as their primary reference group. Thus, their maladjustment could reflect the fact that they were (1) not prepared to function effectively within the African-American community and (2) likely to face some prejudice and discrimination as a black trying to fit into a white ecological niche (DeBerry et al., 1996). Yet a stronger identification with either a white or an African-American reference group predicted better adjustment outcomes than did maintaining a more racially diffuse orientation. So here is another sign that establishing some kind of ethnic identity, or point of reference, is an adaptive developmental outcome for members of a minority group.

How can we help minority youths to forge positive ethnic identities? Their parents can play a major role by (1) teaching them about their group's cultural traditions and fostering ethnic pride, (2) preparing them to deal constructively with the prejudices and value conflicts they may encounter, and (3) simply being warm and supportive confidants (Bernal & Knight, 1997; Rosenthal & Feldman, 1992). Schools and communities can also help by promoting a greater understanding and appreciation of ethnic diversity and racism, starting early in the preschool years (Burnette, 1997) and continuing their efforts to ensure that educational and economic opportunities are extended to all (Spencer & Markstrom-Adams, 1990).

Forging a positive ethnic identity is an adaptive development for minority youths.

12.3 DEVELOPMENTAL ISSUES

Racial Categorization and Racism in Young Children

Because toddlers and preschool children tend to define others in terms of their observable characteristics and to place people into categories, it may come as no surprise to learn that even 3- and 4-year-olds have formed racial categories and can apply labels such as *black* and *white* to different people or to photos of blacks and whites. Furthermore, studies conducted in Australia, Canada, and the U.S. reveal that, by age 5, most white children have some knowledge of racial stereotypes (Bigler & Liben, 1993) and display at least some prejudicial attitudes toward blacks and Native Americans (Black-Gutman & Hickson, 1996; Doyle & Aboud, 1995).

Interestingly, parents often believe that their own children are largely oblivious to race, and that racist attitudes and behaviors in other children arise when their bigoted parents pass their own intolerant views to them (Burnette, 1997). However, research suggests otherwise, for the racial attitudes of young children often bear little relationship to those of their parents or their friends (Aboud, 1988; Burnette, 1997). So the origins of racial prejudice may be more *cognitive* than social, reflecting the tendency of egocentric youngsters to rigidly categorize people by skin color (and other physical correlates of ethnicity) and to favor the group to which they belong.

As children enter concrete operations and become more flexible in their thinking, prejudicial attitudes often decline in strength. This increased tolerance of 8- to 9-year-olds reflects their more realistic evaluation of racial groups in which out-groups are viewed more favorably and their own group somewhat less favorably than was true during the preschool years (Doyle & Aboud, 1995). Nevertheless, social forces can obviously play a role in maintaining or even intensifying racial prejudice. Daisa Black-Gutman and Fay Hickson (1996) found that Euro-Australian children's prejudice toward black Aborigines declined between ages 5 and 9, and then intensified at age 10 to 12, returning to the high levels displayed by 5- to 6-year-olds! Since the 10- to 12-year-olds were no longer constrained by the egocentrism and rigid categorization schemes of a 5- or 6-year-old, their increased prejudice apparently reflected the influence of adult attitudes, namely, the deep-seated animosity that many Euro-Australians feel toward black Aborigines.

Developmentalists now believe that the best way to combat racism is for parents and teachers to talk openly about race and ethnic diversity, beginning in the preschool period when prejudicial attitudes often take root (Burnette, 1997). One especially promising program in the public schools of western Massachusetts takes a three-pronged approach:

1. *Teacher training.* Teachers receive a 4-month course that defines racism, explores how educators and children display it, and provides guidance for handling it at school.

2. *Youth groups.* Children of different races and ethnicities first meet for 7 weeks with ethnic peers to discuss the values and traditions of their own subcultures. Then participants meet for 7 more weeks in mixed-ethnicity groups to discuss their different perspectives and to devise strategies for getting along.

3. *Parent groups.* Once a month, parents of program participants attend classes to learn more about racism and how to comfortably discuss racial issues with their children.

This program is based on the proposition that the key to combating racism is to be honest about it with children rather than shunning the topic or trying to cover it up. As developmentalist Vonnie McLoyd (cited in Burnette, 1997, p. 33) has noted, "Racism is so deeply rooted that [overcoming it] is going to take hard work by open, honest, fair-minded people who are not easily discouraged."

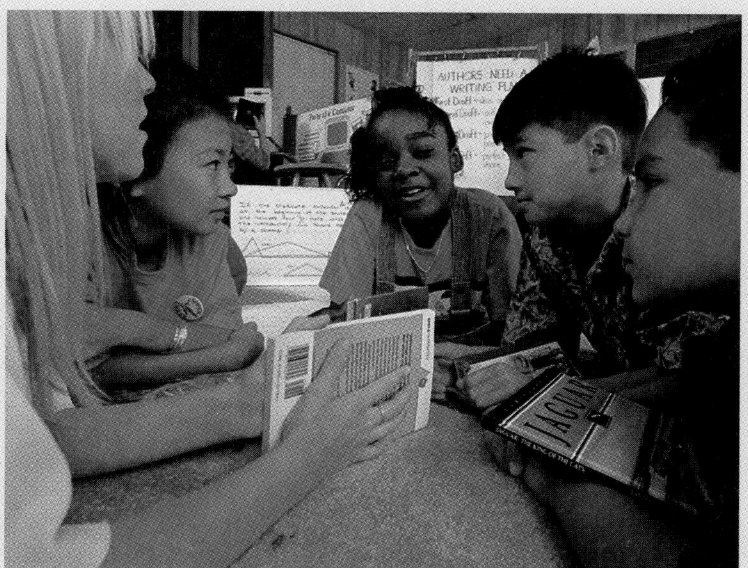

Mixed-ethnicity discussion groups can foster an appreciation of diverse subcultural traditions and combat the formation of prejudicial attitudes.

It's not that preschoolers have *no* appreciation for the inner qualities that people display. As we noted earlier in the chapter, even 18-month-olds initiate the purposeful acts of humans but not mechanical toys, thus reflecting an awareness that human behaviors are guided by intentions (Meltzoff, 1995). By age 3 to 5, children are aware of how their closest peer companions typically behave in a variety of different situations (Eder, 1989). And kindergartners already know that their classmates differ in academic competencies and social skills; furthermore, they reliably choose the smart ones as teammates for academic competitions and the socially skilled classmates as partners for play activities (Droege & Stipek, 1993). Nevertheless, it appears that traitlike descriptions are often less meaningful for younger than for older children. Five- to 7-year-olds are not especially interested in playing with a child merely because he is "nice"; but describe the same child as owning an attractive toy and his popularity skyrockets. By contrast, 9-year-olds are much more inclined to want to play with a child described as "nice" than with one whose most noteworthy quality is owning an attractive toy (Boggiano, Klinger, & Main, 1986).

Between ages 7 and 16, children come to rely less and less on concrete attributes and more on psychological descriptors to characterize their friends and acquaintances. These changes are nicely illustrated in a program of research by Carl Barenboim (1981) who asked 6- to 11-year-olds to describe three persons they know well. Rather than simply listing the behaviors that close companions display, 6- to 8-year-olds often *compared* others on noteworthy behavioral dimensions, making such statements as "Billy *runs faster* than Jason" or "She *draws the best* pictures in our whole class." As shown in Figure 12.7, use of these **behavioral comparisons** increased between ages 6 and 8 and declined rapidly after age 9. One outgrowth of the behavioral comparison process is that children become increasingly aware of regularities in a companion's behavior and eventually begin to attribute them to stable **psychological constructs,** or traits, that the person is now presumed to have. So a 10-year-old who formerly described one of her acquaintances as drawing better than anyone in her class may now convey the same impression by saying that the acquaintance is "very artistic." Notice in reexamining the figure that children's use of these psychological constructs increased rapidly between ages 8 and 11, the same period when behavioral comparisons became less common. Eventually, children begin to compare and contrast others or important psychological *dimensions,* making statements such as "Bill is more shy than Ted" or "Susie is the most artistic person in our class." Although few 11-year-olds generate these **psychological comparisons** when describing others (see Figure 12.7), the majority of 12- to 16-year-olds in Barenboim's second study actively compared their associates on noteworthy psychological dimensions.

behavioral comparisons phase
the tendency to form impressions of others by comparing and contrasting their overt behaviors.

psychological constructs phase
tendency to base one's impressions of others on the stable traits that these individuals are presumed to have.

psychological comparisons phase
tendency to form impressions of others by comparing and contrasting these individuals on abstract psychological dimensions.

By age 14 to 16, adolescents are not only aware of the *dispositional* similarities and dissimilarities that characterize their acquaintances, but they are also beginning to recognize that any number of *situational* factors (for example, illness, family strife) can cause a person to act "out of character" (Damon & Hart, 1988). So by midadolescence, young people are becoming sophisticated "personality theorists" who are able to look both inside and outside a companion to explain her conduct and form coherent impressions of her character.

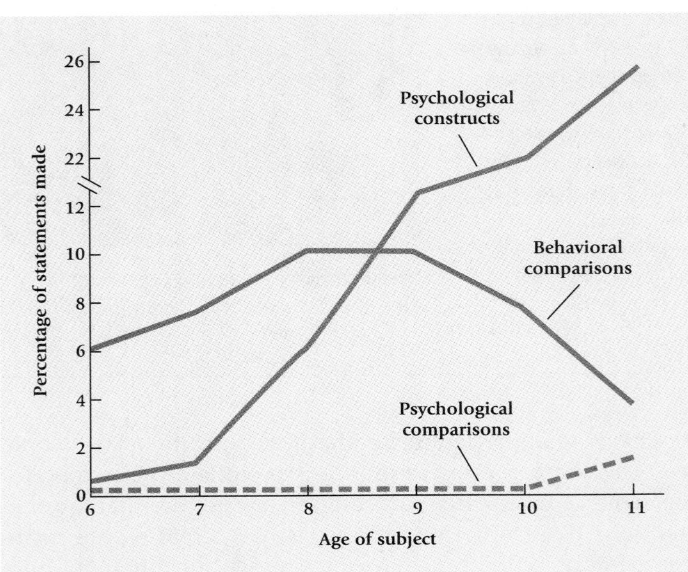

Figure 12.7 *Percentages of descriptive statements classified as behavioral comparisons, psychological (traitlike) constructs, and psychological comparisons for children between the ages of 6 and 11. From Barenboim, 1981.*

Why do children progress from behavioral comparisons, to psychological constructs, to psychological comparisons? Why do their own self-concepts and their impressions of others become increasingly abstract and coherent over time? In addressing these issues, we will first examine two cognitive points of view before considering how social forces might contribute, both directly and indirectly, to the growth of social cognition.

Theories of Social-Cognitive Development

Cognitive Theories of Social Cognition

The two cognitive theories that are most often used to explain developmental trends in social cognition are Piaget's cognitive-developmental approach and Robert Selman's role-taking analysis.

Cognitive-Developmental Theory. According to cognitive-developmental theorists, the ways that children think about the self and other people largely depend on their own levels of cognitive development. Recall that the thinking of 3- to 6-year-old "preoperational" children tends to center on the most salient perceptual aspects of stimuli and events. So it would hardly surprise a Piagetian to find that 3- to 6-year-olds describe their associates in very concrete, observable terms, mentioning their appearances and possessions, their likes and dislikes, and the actions that they can perform.

The thinking of 7- to 10-year-olds changes in many ways as these youngsters enter Piaget's concrete-operational stage. Not only is egocentrism becoming less pronounced, but children are now *decentering* from perceptual illusions and beginning to recognize that certain properties of an object remain unchanged despite changes in the object's appearance *(conservation).* Clearly, these emerging abilities to look beyond immediate appearances and to infer underlying invariances might help to explain why 7- to 10-year-olds, who are actively comparing themselves with their peers, become more attuned to regularities in their own and others' conduct and use psychological constructs, or traits, to describe these patterns.

By age 12 to 14, children are entering formal operations and are now able to think more logically and systematically about abstractions. Although the concept of a psychological trait is itself an abstraction, it is one based on regularities in concrete, observable behaviors, perhaps explaining why *concrete* operators can think in these terms. However, a trait *dimension* is even more of a mental inference or abstraction that has few if any concrete referents. Thus, the ability to think in dimensional terms and to reliably order people along these continua (as is necessary in making psychological comparisons) implies that a person is able to operate on abstract concepts—a formal-operational ability (O'Mahoney, 1989).

Although children begin to make behavioral comparisons at ages 6 to 8 and psychological comparisons at age 12—precisely the times that Piaget's theory implies that they should—Robert Selman (1980) believes that there is one particular aspect of cognitive development that underlies a mature understanding of the self and other people: the growth of **role-taking** skills.

Selman's Role-Taking Theory. According to Selman (1980; Yeates & Selman, 1989), children gain much richer understandings of themselves and other people as they acquire the ability to discriminate their own perspectives from those of their companions and to see the relationships between these potentially discrepant points of view. Simply stated, Selman believes that in order to "know" a person, one must be able to assume his perspective and understand his thoughts, feelings, motives, and intentions—in short, the *internal* factors that account for his behavior. If a child has not yet acquired these important role-taking skills, she may have little choice but to describe her acquaintances in terms of their external attributes—that is, their appearance, their activities, and the things they possess.

role taking
the ability to assume another person's perspective and understand his or her thoughts, feelings, and behaviors.

Selman has studied the development of role-taking skills by asking children to comment on a number of interpersonal dilemmas. Here is one example (from Selman, 1976, p. 302):

> Holly is an 8-year-old girl who likes to climb trees. She is the best tree climber in the neighborhood. One day while climbing down from a tall tree, she falls . . . but does not hurt herself. Her father sees her fall. He is upset and asks her to promise not to climb trees any more. Holly promises.
>
> Later that day, Holly and her friends meet Shawn. Shawn's kitten is caught in a tree and can't get down. Something has to be done right away or the kitten may fall. Holly is the only one who climbs trees well enough to reach the kitten and get it down but she remembers her promise to her father.

To assess how well a child understands the perspectives of Holly, her father, and Shawn, Selman asks: Does Holly know how Shawn feels about the kitten? How will Holly's father feel if he finds out she climbed the tree? What does Holly think her father will do if he finds out she climbed the tree? What would you do? Children's responses to these probes led Selman to conclude that role-taking skills develop in a stagelike manner, as shown in Table 12.3.

TABLE 12.3 Selman's Stages of Social Perspective Taking

Stage of role taking	Typical responses to the "Holly" dilemma
0. Egocentric or undifferentiated perspective (roughly 3 to 6 years) Children are unaware of any perspective other than their own. They assume that whatever they feel is right for Holly to do will be agreed on by others.	Children often assume that Holly will save the kitten. When asked how Holly's father will react to her transgression, these children think he will be "happy because he likes kittens." In other words, these children like kittens themselves, and they assume that Holly and her father also like kittens.
1. Social-informational role taking (roughly 6 to 8 years) Children now recognize that people can have perspectives that differ from their own but believe that this happens *only* because these individuals have received different information.	When asked whether Holly's father will be angry because she climbed the tree, the child may say "If he didn't know why she climbed the tree, he would be angry. But if he knew why she did it, he would realize that she had a good reason."
2. Self-reflective role taking (roughly 8 to 10 years) Children now know that their own and others' points of view may conflict even if they have received the same information. They are now able to consider the other person's viewpoint. They also recognize that the other person can put himself in their shoes, so that they are now able to anticipate the person's reactions to their behavior. However, the child cannot consider his own perspective and that of another person at the same time.	If asked whether Holly will climb the tree, the child might say "Yes. She knows that her father will understand why she did it." In so doing, the child is focusing on the father's consideration of Holly's perspective. But if asked whether the father would want Holly to climb the tree, the child usually says no, thereby indicating that he is now assuming the father's perspective and considering the father's concern for Holly's safety.
3. Mutual role taking (roughly 10 to 12 years) The child can now simultaneously consider her own and another person's points of view and recognize that the other person can do the same. The child can also assume the perspective of a disinterested third party and anticipate how each participant (self and other) will react to the viewpoint of his or her partner.	At this stage, a child might describe the outcome of the "Holly" dilemma by taking the perspective of a disinterested third party and indicating that she knows that both Holly and her father are thinking about what each other is thinking. For example, one child remarked: "Holly wanted to get the kitten because she likes kittens, but she knew that she wasn't supposed to climb trees. Holly's father knew that Holly had been told not to climb trees, but he couldn't have known about [the kitten]."
4. Societal role taking (roughly 12 to 15 and older) The adolescent now attempts to understand another person's perspective by comparing it with that of the social system in which he operates (that is, the view of the "generalized other"). In other words, the adolescent expects others to consider and typically assume perspectives on events that most people in their social group would take.	When asked if Holly should be punished for climbing the tree, the stage 4 adolescent is likely to say "No" and claim that the value of humane treatment of animals justifies Holly's act and that most fathers would recognize this point.

Source: Adapted from Selman, 1976.

Notice in examining the table that children progress from largely egocentric beings, who may be unaware of any perspective other than their own (stage 0), to sophisticated social-cognitive theorists, who can keep several perspectives in mind and compare each with the viewpoint that "most people" would adopt (Stage 4). Apparently, these role-taking skills represent a true developmental sequence, for 40 of 41 boys who were repeatedly tested over a 5-year period showed a steady forward progression from stage to stage, with no skipping of stages (Gurucharri & Selman, 1982). Perhaps the reason that they develop in one particular order is that they are closely related to Piaget's invariant sequence of cognitive stages (Keating & Clark, 1980): Preoperational children are at Selman's first or second level of role taking (stage 0 or 1), whereas most concrete operators are at the third or fourth level (stage 2 or 3), and formal operators are about equally distributed between the fourth and fifth levels of role taking (stages 3 and 4).

Role-Taking and Thinking about Relationships. As children acquire role-taking skills, their understanding of the meaning and character of human relationships begins to change. Consider what children of different ages say about the meaning of *friendship.*

Preschoolers at Selman's egocentric (level 0) stage think that virtually any pleasant interactions between themselves and available playmates qualify those playmates as "friends." So 5-year-old Chang might describe Terry as a close friend simply because "He lives next door and plays games with me" (Damon, 1977).

Common activity continues to be the principal basis for friendship among 6- to 8-year-olds (Hartup, 1992). But because these youngsters have reached Selman's stage 1 and recognize that others may not always share their perspectives, they begin to view a friend as someone who *chooses* to "do nice things for me." Friendships are often one-way at this stage, for the child feels no strong pressure to reciprocate these considerations. And should a friend fail to serve the child's interests (for example, by spurning an invitation to camp out in the back yard), she may quickly become a nonfriend.

Later, at Selman's stage 2, 8- to 10-year-olds show increasing concern for the needs of a friend and begin to see friendships as reciprocal relationships, based on *mutual trust,* in which two people exchange respect, kindness, and affection (Selman, 1980). No longer are common activities sufficient to brand someone a friend; as children appreciate how their own interests and perspectives and those of their peers can be similar or different, they insist that their friends be *psychologically* similar to themselves.

By early adolescence, many children have reached Selman's stage 3 or 4. Although they still view friends as psychologically similar people who like, trust, and assist each other, they have expanded their notions of the obligations of friendship to emphasize the exchange of intimate thoughts and feelings (Berndt & Perry, 1990). They increasingly expect their friends to stick up for them and be *loyal,* standing ready to provide close emotional support whenever they may need it (Berndt & Perry, 1990; Buhrmester, 1990).

So, with the growth of role-taking skills, children's conceptions of friendship gradually change from the one-sided, self-centered view of friends as "people who benefit me" to a harmonious, reciprocal perspective in which each party truly understands the other, enjoys providing him or her with emotional support and other niceties, and expects these same considerations in return. Perhaps because they rest on a firmer basis of intimacy and interpersonal understanding, the close friendships of older children and adolescents are viewed as more important and are more stable, or long-lasting, than those of younger children (Berndt, 1989; Berndt & Hoyle, 1985; Furman & Buhrmester, 1992).

Table 12.4 briefly summarizes the changes in thinking about the self and others that we have discussed—changes that are clearly influenced by cognitive development. Yet, as we will see in concluding the chapter, the growth of *social* cognition is also heavily influenced by *social* interactions and experiences that children and adolescents have had.

Social Influences on Social-Cognitive Development

Many developmentalists have wondered whether the growth of children's self-awareness and their understanding of other people are as closely tied to cognitive development as cognitive theorists have assumed. Consider, for example, that even though

Table 12.4 Milestones in the Development of Self and Social Cognition

Age (years)	Self-concept/Self-esteem	Self-control	Social cognition
0–1	Differentiation of self from the external environment Sense of personal agency emerges		Discriminates familiar from unfamiliar people Prefers familiar companions (attachment objects)
1–2	Self-recognition emerges Categorical self develops	Compliance emerges	Recognition that others act on intentions Categorization of others on socially significant dimensions
3–5	Self-concept emphasizes actions Evaluation of accomplishments emerge Undifferentiated self-esteem emerges Appearance of belief-desire theory of mind and private self Achievement attributions reflect incremental view of ability	Compliance improves Can use adult-generated strategies to self-regulate and delay gratification	Impressions are based on other's actions and concrete attributes Knowledge of racial stereotypes and prejudicial attitudes emerge Friendships are based on shared activities
6–10	Self-concepts come to emphasize personality traits Self-esteem is based on one's academic, physical, and social competencies Achievement attributions progress toward an entity view of ability	Appearance of self-generated strategies for self-control Begins to value self-regulation/self-control	Impressions come to be based on the traits others display (psychological constructs) Prejudicial attitudes often decline in strength Friendships are based largely on psychological similarities and mutual trust
11 and beyond	Friendships, romantic appeal, and job competence become important to one's self-esteem Self-concepts now reflect one's values and ideologies, and become more integrated and abstract Identity is achieved	Generates abstract strategies to regulate conduct and defer gratification Internalizes norms that stress the value of self-control	Impressions are now based on others' dispositional similarities and dissimilarities (psychological comparisons) Prejudicial attitudes may decline or intensify, depending on social influences Friendships are based on loyalty and sharing of intimacies

children's role-taking abilities are related to their performances on Piagetian measures and IQ tests (Pellegrini, 1985), it is quite possible for a child to grow less egocentric and to mature intellectually without becoming an especially skillful role taker (Shantz, 1983). So, there must be other, *noncognitive* factors that contribute to the growth of role-taking skills and that may even exert their own unique effects on children's social-cognitive development. Might social experiences play such a role? No less an authority than Jean Piaget thought so.

Social Experience as a Contributor to Role-Taking. Many years ago, Piaget (1965) argued that playful interactions among grade-school children promote the development of role-taking skills and mature social judgments. Piaget's view was that, by assuming different roles while playing together, young children become more aware of discrepancies between their own perspectives and those of their playmates. When conflicts arise in play, children must learn to coordinate their points of view with those of their companions (that is, compromise) in order for play to continue. So Piaget assumed that *equal-status contacts among peers* are an especially important contributor to social perspective taking and the growth of interpersonal understanding.

Not only has research consistently supported Piaget's viewpoint, but it appears that some forms of peer contact may be better than others at fostering the growth of interpersonal understanding. Specifically, Janice Nelson and Francis Aboud (1985) propose that disagreements among *friends* are particularly important because children tend to be more open and honest with their friends than with mere acquaintances and are more motivated to resolve disputes with friends. As a result, disagreeing friends should be more likely than disagreeing acquaintances to provide each other with the information needed to understand and appreciate their conflicting points of view. Indeed, when 8- to 10-year-olds discuss an interpersonal issue on which they disagree, pairs of friends are much more critical of their partners than pairs of acquaintances are; but friends are also more likely to fully explain the rationales for their own points of view. Furthermore, disagreeing friends display increases in social understanding after these discussions are over, whereas disagreeing acquaintances do not (Nelson & Aboud, 1985). So it seems that equal-status contacts among friends may be especially important for the growth of role-taking skills and interpersonal understanding.

Disagreements among peers are important contributors to role-taking skills and the growth of interpersonal understanding.

Social Experience as a Direct Contributor to Person Perception. Social contacts with peers not only contribute *indirectly* to person perception by fostering the development of role-taking skills, but they are also a form of *direct experience* by which children can learn what others are like. In other words, the more experience a child has with peers, the more *motivated* she should be to try to understand them and the more *practiced* she should become at appraising the causes of their behavior (Higgins & Parsons, 1983).

Popularity is a convenient measure of social experience; that is, popular children interact more often with a wider variety of peers than do their less popular age-mates (LeMare & Rubin, 1987). So, if the amount of direct experience that a child has with peers exerts its own unique influence on his or her social-cognitive judgments, then popular children should outperform less popular age-mates on tests of social understanding, *even when their role-taking skills are comparable.* This is precisely what Jackie Gnepp (1989) found when she tested the ability of popular and less popular 8-year-olds to make appropriate traitlike inferences about an unfamiliar child from a small sample of the child's previous behaviors. So it seems that both social experience (as indexed by popularity) and cognitive competence (role-taking skills) contribute in their own ways to the development of children's understanding of other people. Apparently, Cooley (1902) and Mead (1934) were quite correct in suggesting that social cognition and social experience are completely intertwined—that they develop together, are reciprocally related, and that neither can progress very far without the other.

Concept Check 12.3
Understanding Social Cognition

Check your understanding of the growth of social-cognitive abilities by matching each descriptive statement below with one of the following terms: (a) loyalty/sharing of intimacies, (b) common activities, (c) psychological similarities, (d) role-taking skills, (e) behavioral comparisons, (f) psychological constructs, (g) psychological comparisons, (h) social experiences with peers. Answers appear in the Appendix.

_____ 1. principal basis for friendships among 9- to 12-year-olds

_____ 2. impressions derived by noting and comparing the *actions* of one's associates

_____ 3. principal basis for friendships among adolescents

_____ 4. impressions based on the *traits* that others are presumed to have

_____ 5. major contributor to children's thinking about the meaning of friendships

_____ 6. principal basis for friendship among 3- to 7-year-olds

_____ 7. contribute in two ways to the growth of social cognition

_____ 8. impressions stemming from dispositional similarities/dissimilarities that others display

SUMMARY

♦ The **self** is thought to arise from social interactions and to largely reflect other people's reactions to us (that is, a **looking-glass self**). The development of **social cognition** deals with how children's understanding of the self and other people changes with age.

Development of the Self-concept

♦ Most developmentalists believe that infants are born without a **self-concept** and gradually come to distinguish themselves from the external environment over the first 2 to 6 months of life. By 18 to 24 months of age, toddlers display **self-recognition** and have begun to form a **categorical self** as they classify themselves along socially significant dimensions such as age and sex.

♦ Although preschool children know how they typically behave in many situations and can classify themselves along psychological dimensions if asked to do so in ways that do not tax their verbal skills, the self-descriptions of 3- to 5-year-olds are typically very concrete, focusing mostly on their physical features, possessions, and the activities they can perform.

♦ Between ages 3 and 4, children's theory of mind becomes a **belief-desire theory** that more closely resembles adults' conception of how the mind works. Once children achieve this milestone, which is fostered by interactions with siblings and adults, they more clearly distinguish their **private self** from their **public self** and are better prepared to make meaningful psychological inferences about their own and others' behavior.

♦ By about age 8, children begin to describe themselves in terms of their inner and enduring psychological attributes. Adolescents have an even more integrated and abstract self-concept that includes not only their dispositional qualities (that is, traits, beliefs, attitudes, and values) but a knowledge of how these characteristics might interact with each other and with situational influences to affect their behavior. However, frequent displays of **false self behaviors** can leave adolescents confused about who they really are.

Self-esteem: The Evaluative Component of Self

♦ **Self-esteem,** the judgments we make about our self-worth, begin to take shape early in life as infants form positive or negative working models of self from their interactions with caregivers. By age 8, children evaluate themselves in three domains: physical competence, academic competence, and social acceptance; in adolescence, new dimensions such as job competence, romantic appeal, and quality of close friendships also become important contributors to global self-esteem. Except for a temporary decline associated with transition to junior high school, self-esteem is reasonably stable over time and often increases throughout adolescence, particularly for boys.

♦ Warm, responsive, democratic parenting fosters self-esteem, whereas aloof or controlling parenting styles seem to undermine it. Peers influence each other's self-esteem through **social comparison** during the grade-school years. For adolescents, some of the strongest determinants of self-worth are the quality of one's relationship with peers, particularly with close friends and prospective romantic partners.

Development of Self-control

♦ The emergence of **self-control** is a major development. Although 2-year-olds voluntarily comply with others' directives, their conduct is still largely externally controlled by the consequences they anticipate for **compliance** (or noncompliance). All toddlers can be **self-assertive** at times, but whether or not they display **defiance** largely depends on the parent–child relationship and on how parents respond to their bids for autonomy. Warm, responsive parenting is associated with **committed compliance** and internalization of parental rules, whereas control based on the parent's superior power leads to **situational compliance** and a hesitancy to fully embrace the parent's agenda. By the middle of the third year, children display an increasing capacity to regulate and control their own thinking and behavior, aided, in part, by private speech as a regulatory mechanism.

♦ **Delay of gratification** is an important aspect of self-control that improves dramatically with age as children become more knowledgeable about effective delay strategies and internalize norms that stress the value of self-regulation and self-control. Preschoolers who have already developed a relatively strong capacity for delaying gratification tend to become self-disciplined adolescents whom parents describe as displaying attributes that contribute to high self-esteem and to favorable outcomes later in life.

Development of Achievement Motivation and Academic Self-concept

♦ Children clearly differ in **achievement motivation**—their willingness to strive for success and to master new challenges **(mastery motivation).** Infants who are securely attached to responsive caregivers who provide them with a stimulating home environment are likely to become curious nursery-school children who will later do well at school. Parents may also foster the development of achievement motivation by encouraging their children to do things on their own and to do them well and by reinforcing a child's successes without becoming overly distressed about an occasional failure. Parents who combine all of these practices into one parenting style **(authoritative parenting)** tend to raise children who seek challenges and who achieve considerable academic success. However, peers may either foster or undermine parents' efforts to encourage academic achievement.

♦ Academic self-concepts also depend very heavily on children's **achievement attributions. Mastery-oriented** children and adolescents attribute their successes to stable, internal causes (such as high ability) and their failures to unstable causes (lack of effort), and they adopt an **incremental view of ability;** consequently, they feel quite competent and will work hard to overcome failures. By contrast, **helpless children** often stop trying after a failure because they display an **entity view of ability** and attribute their failures to a lack of ability that they feel they can do little about. Children who are often criticized for their lack of ability and who feel pressured to adopt **performance goals** rather than **learning goals** are at risk of becoming helpless. Helpless children can become more mastery-oriented if they are taught (through **attribution retraining**) that their failures can and often should be attributed to unstable causes, such as a lack of effort, that they can overcome by trying harder.

Who Am I to Be? Forging an Identity

◆ One of the more challenging tasks of adolescence is that of resolving one's **identity crisis** and forming a stable **identity** (or identities) with which to embrace the responsibilities of young adulthood. From the **diffusion** and **foreclosure** statuses, many college-age youths progress to the **moratorium** status (where they are experimenting to find an identity) and ultimately to **identity achievement.** Identity formation is an uneven process that often continues well into adulthood.

◆ The process of seeking an identity is a lot less crisislike than Erik Erikson assumed. Identity achievement and moratorium are psychologically healthy statuses. If there is a crisis, it is a long-term failure to form an identity, for adolescents stuck in the diffusion status often assume a *negative identity* and display poor psychological adjustment.

◆ Healthy identity outcomes are fostered by cognitive development, by warm, supportive parents who encourage individual self-expression, and by a culture that permits and expects adolescents to find their own niches. For minority youth, achieving a positive *ethnic identity* fosters healthy identity outcomes.

The Other Side of Social Cognition: Knowing about Others

◆ Children younger than 7 or 8 are likely to describe friends and acquaintances in the same concrete observable terms that they use to describe the self. As they compare themselves and others on noteworthy behavioral dimensions, they become more attuned to regularities in their own and others' conduct (**behavioral comparisons** phase) and begin to rely on stable psychological constructs, or traits, to describe these patterns (**psychological constructs** phase). Young adolescents' impressions of others become even more abstract as they begin to make **psychological comparisons** among their friends and acquaintances. And by age 14 to 16, adolescents are becoming sophisticated "personality theorists" who know that any number of situational influences can cause a person to act "out of character."

◆ The growth of children's social-cognitive abilities is related to cognitive development in general and to the emergence of **role-taking** skills in particular: To truly "know" a person, one must be able to assume her perspective and understand her thoughts, feelings, motives, and intentions. However, *social interactions*—particularly equal-status contacts with friends and peers—are crucial to social-cognitive development. They contribute indirectly by fostering the growth of role-taking skills and in a more direct way by providing the experiences children need to learn what others are like.

Self-esteem is the evaluative component of an individual's self-image. Children who have high self-esteem are fundamentally satisfied with the type of person they are. If you visit: http://childparenting.miningco.com/msub6a.htm you will find some practical suggestions for building a sense of positive self-esteem in children. There are also a number of activities designed to help foster self-esteem.

KEY TERMS

self, 434
looking-glass self, 434
social cognition, 434
self-concept, 435
self-recognition, 435
categorical self, 437
public self (or me), 438
private self (or I), 438
belief-desire theory, 438
false-self behavior, 441
self-esteem, 441
social comparison, 445
self-control, 445
compliance, 445
self-assertion, 446
defiance, 446
committed compliance, 446
situational compliance, 446
delay of gratification, 447
achievement motivation, 449
mastery motivation, 449
authoritative parenting, 452
achievement attributions, 454
incremental view of ability, 455
entity view of ability, 455
mastery orientation, 455
learned helplessness orientation, 455
attribution retraining, 456
performance goal, 457
learning goal, 457
identity, 457
identity crisis, 457
identity diffusion, 458
foreclosure, 458
moratorium, 458
identity achievement, 458
behavioral comparisons phase, 464
psychological constructs phase, 464
psychological comparisons phase, 464
role taking, 465

13

Sex Differences and Gender-Role Development

How important is a child's gender to his or her development? Many people would say "Very important!" Often the first bit of information that parents receive about their child is his or her sex, and the question "Is it a boy or a girl?" is the very first one that most friends and relatives ask when proud new parents telephone to announce the birth of their baby (Intons-Peterson & Reddel, 1984). Indeed, the ramifications of this gender labeling are normally swift and rather direct. In the hospital nursery or delivery room, parents often call an infant son things like "big guy" or "tiger," and they are likely to comment on the vigor of his cries, kicks, or grasps. By contrast, infant daughters are more likely to be labeled "sugar" or "sweetie" and described as soft, cuddly, and adorable (Maccoby, 1980; MacFarlane, 1977). A newborn infant is usually blessed with a name that reflects his or her sex, and in many Western societies boys are immediately adorned in blue and girls in pink. Mavis Hetherington and Ross Parke (1975, pp. 354–355) describe the predicament of a developmental psychologist who "did not want her observers to know whether they were watching boys or girls.

> Even in the first few days of life some infant girls were brought to the laboratory with pink bows tied to wisps of their hair or taped to their little bald heads. . . . When another attempt at concealment of sex was made by asking mothers to dress their infants in overalls, girls appeared in pink and boys in blue overalls, and "Would you believe overalls with ruffles?"

Sex-role socialization begins very early as parents provide their infants with "gender-appropriate" clothing, toys, and hairstyles.

This gender indoctrination continues during the first year as parents provide their children with "gender-appropriate" clothing, toys, and hairstyles (Pomerleau et al., 1990). They also play differently with and expect different reactions from their young sons and daughters (Caldera, Huston, & O'Brien, 1989). So it is clear that a child's companions view gender as an important attribute that often determines how they respond to him or her.

Why do people react differently to males and females, especially *infant* males and females? One explanation centers on the biological differences between the sexes. Recall that fathers determine the sex of their offspring. A zygote that receives an X chromosome from each parent is a genetic (XX) female that develops into a baby girl, whereas a zygote that receives a Y chromosome from the father is a genetic (XY) male that normally assumes the appearance of a baby boy. Could it be that this basic genetic difference between the sexes is ultimately responsible for *sex differences in behavior* that might explain why parents often do not treat their sons and daughters alike? We will explore this interesting idea in some detail in a later section of the chapter.

However, there is more to sex differences than biological heritage. Virtually all societies expect males and females to behave differently and to assume different roles. In order to conform to these expectations, the child must understand that he is a boy or that she is a girl and must incorporate this information into his or her self-concept. In this chapter, we will concentrate on the interesting and controversial topic of **gender typing**—the process by which children acquire not only a gender identity but also the motives, values, and behaviors considered appropriate in their culture for members of their biological sex.

We begin the chapter by summarizing what people generally believe to be true about sex differences in cognition, personality, and social behavior. As it turns out, some of these beliefs have an element of truth to them, although many others are best described as fictions or fables that have no basis in fact. We will then look at developmental trends in gender typing and see that youngsters are often well aware of gender-role stereotypes and display gender-typed patterns of behavior long before they are old enough to go to kindergarten. And how do children learn so much about the sexes and gender roles at such an early age? We will address this issue by reviewing several influential theories that specify how biological forces, social experiences, and cognitive development might combine or interact to influence the gender-typing process. And after examining a new perspective that asserts that traditional gender-roles have outlived their usefulness in today's modern society, the chapter concludes by briefly considering how the constraining and potentially harmful effects of gender stereotypes might be reduced.

gender typing
the process by which a child becomes aware of his or her gender and acquires motives, values, and behaviors considered appropriate for members of that sex.

CATEGORIZING MALES AND FEMALES: GENDER-ROLE STANDARDS

Most of us have learned a great deal about males and females by the time we enter college. In fact, if you and your classmates were asked to jot down ten psychological dimensions on which men and women are thought to differ, it is likely that every member of the class could easily generate such a list. Here's a head start: Which gender is most likely to display emotions? to be tidy? to be competitive? to use harsh language?

A **gender-role standard** is a value, a motive, or a class of behavior that is considered more appropriate for members of one sex than the other. Taken together, a society's gender-role standards describe how males and females are expected to behave and reflect the stereotypes by which we categorize and respond to members of each sex.

The female's role as childbearer is largely responsible for the gender-role standards and stereotypes that have prevailed in many societies, including our own. Girls have typically been encouraged to assume an **expressive role** that involves being kind, nurturant, cooperative, and sensitive to the needs of others (Parsons, 1955). These psychological traits, it was assumed, would prepare girls to play the wife and mother roles—to keep the family functioning, and raise children successfully. By contrast, boys have been encouraged to adopt an **instrumental role,** for as a traditional husband and father, a male would face the tasks of providing for the family and protecting it from harm. Thus, young boys are expected to become dominant, assertive, independent, and competitive. Similar norms and role prescriptions are found in many, though certainly not all, societies (Williams & Best, 1990). In one rather ambitious project, Herbert Barry, Margaret Bacon, and Irving Child (1957) analyzed the gender-typing practices of 110 nonindustrialized societies, looking for sex differences in the socialization of five attributes: nurturance, obedience, responsibility, achievement, and self-reliance. As shown in Table 13.1, achievement and self-reliance were more strongly encouraged in young boys, whereas young girls were encouraged to become nurturant, responsible, and obedient.

Children in modern industrialized societies also face strong gender-typing pressures, though not always to the same extent and in the same ways that children in nonindustrialized societies do. (For example, parents in many Western societies place roughly equal emphasis on achievement for sons and for daughters; Lytton & Romney, 1991). Furthermore, the findings in Table 13.1 do not imply that self-reliance in girls is frowned on or that disobedience by young boys is acceptable. In fact, all

gender-role standard
a behavior, value, or motive that members of a society consider more typical or appropriate for members of one sex.

expressive role
a social prescription, usually directed toward females, that one should be cooperative, kind, nurturant, and sensitive to the needs of others.

instrumental role
a social prescription, usually directed toward males, that one should be dominant, independent, assertive, competitive, and goal-oriented.

TABLE 13.1 **Sex Differences in the Socialization of Five Attributes in 110 Societies**

	Percentage of societies in which socialization pressures were greater for:	
Attribute	**Boys**	**Girls**
Nurturance	0	82
Obedience	3	35
Responsibility	11	61
Achievement	87	3
Self-reliance	85	0

Note: The percentages for each attribute do not add to 100 because some of the societies did not place differential pressures on boys and girls with respect to that attribute. For example, 18% of the societies for which pertinent data were available did not differentiate between the sexes in the socialization of nurturance.
Source: Adapted from Barry, Bacon, & Child, 1957.

five attributes that Barry et al. studied were encouraged in *both* boys and girls, but with different emphases on different attributes depending on the sex of the child (Zern, 1984). So it appears that the first goal of socialization is to encourage children to acquire those traits that will enable them to become well-behaved, contributing members of society. A second goal (but one that adults view as important nevertheless) is to "gender type" the child by stressing the importance of relationship-oriented (or expressive) attributes for girls and individualistic (or instrumental) attributes for boys.

Because cultural norms specify that girls should assume an expressive role and boys an instrumental role, we may be inclined to assume that girls and women actually display expressive traits and that boys and men possess instrumental traits (Broverman et al., 1972; Williams & Best, 1990). If you assume that these stereotypes have disappeared as attention to women's rights has increased and as more women have entered the labor force, think again. Although some change has occurred, adolescents and young adults still endorse many traditional stereotypes about men and women (Bergen & Williams, 1991; Twenge, 1997; and test yourself in Box 13.1). Might these beliefs about sex differences have any basis in fact? Let's see if they do.

13.1

DEVELOPMENTAL ISSUES

What Traits Characterize Males and Females?

Several recent surveys have asked college students to respond to lists of various mannerisms and personal characteristics by saying which of these traits characterize the "typical" man or "typical" woman (or by judging which are clearly "masculine" or clearly "feminine" attributes). Although you may not agree with peer consensus, see if you can anticipate how they have responded by indicating whether each trait in the list below is more characteristic of men or more characteristic of women. (The results of the survey are given at the bottom of the page.)

	More characteristic of:	
Trait	Men	Women
1. Active	____	____
2. Aware of others' feelings	____	____
3. Adventurous	____	____
4. Considerate	____	____
5. Aggressive	____	____
6. Creative	____	____
7. Ambitious	____	____
8. Cries easily	____	____
9. Competitive	____	____
10. Other-oriented	____	____
11. Dominant	____	____
12. Emotional	____	____
13. Independent	____	____

Trait	Men	Women
14. Artistic	____	____
15. Displays leadership	____	____
16. Excitable	____	____
17. Mathematical	____	____
18. Empathic	____	____
19. Makes decisions easily	____	____
20. Feelings hurt easily	____	____
21. Mechanical	____	____
22. Gentle	____	____
23. Outspoken	____	____
24. Kind	____	____
25. Persistent	____	____
26. Neat	____	____
27. Self-confident	____	____
28. Seeks approval	____	____
29. Skilled in business	____	____
30. Tactful	____	____
31. Takes a stand	____	____
32. Understanding	____	____

SOURCE FOR THESE TRAITS: RUBLE, 1983.

Answers for Box 13.1: College students generally indicate that the even-numbered traits characterize women, whereas the odd-numbered ones are more characteristic of men.

SOME FACTS AND FICTIONS ABOUT SEX DIFFERENCES

The old French maxim "Vive la difference" reflects a fact we all know to be true: Males and females are anatomically different. Adult males are typically taller, heavier, and more muscular than adult females, while females may be hardier in the sense that they live longer. But although these physical variations are fairly obvious, the evidence for sex differences in psychological functioning is not as clear as most of us might think.

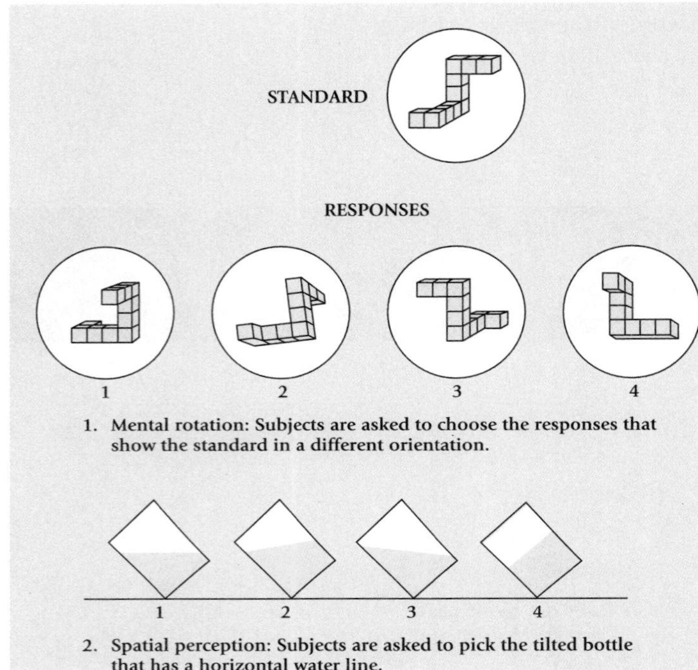
STANDARD
RESPONSES
1
2
3
4
1. Mental rotation: Subjects are asked to choose the responses that show the standard in a different orientation.
1
2
3
4
2. Spatial perception: Subjects are asked to pick the tilted bottle that has a horizontal water line.

Figure 13.1 *Two spatial tasks for which sex differences in performance have been found.* FROM LINN & PETERSEN, 1985.

Actual Psychological Differences between the Sexes

In a classic review of more than 1,500 studies comparing males and females, Eleanor Maccoby and Carol Jacklin (1974) concluded that few traditional gender stereotypes have any basis in fact. In fact, their review pointed to only four *small* but reliable differences between the sexes that were consistently supported by research. Here are their conclusions, with some updates and amendments.

Verbal Ability

Girls have greater verbal abilities than boys. Girls acquire language and develop verbal skills at an earlier age than boys and display a small but consistent verbal advantage on tests of reading comprehension and speech fluency throughout childhood and adolescence (Halpern, 1997; Hedges & Nowell, 1995).

Visual/Spatial Abilities

Boys outperform girls on tests of **visual/spatial abilities**—that is, the ability to draw inferences about or otherwise mentally manipulate pictorial information (see Figure 13.1 for two kinds of visual/spatial tasks on which sex differences have been found). The male advantage in spatial abilities is not large, although it is detectable by middle childhood and persists across the life span (Kerns & Berenbaum, 1991; Voyer, Voyer, & Bryden, 1995).

Mathematical Ability

Beginning in adolescence, boys show a small but consistent advantage over girls on tests of *arithmetic reasoning* (Halpern, 1997; Hyde, Fennema, & Lamon, 1990; and see Figure 13.2 on page 477). Girls actually exceed boys in computational skills; but boys have acquired more mathematical problem-solving strategies that enable them to outperform girls on complex word problems, geometry, and the mathematics portion of the Scholastic Assessment Test (SAT) (Byrnes & Takahira, 1993; Casey, 1996). The male advantage in mathematical problem solving is most apparent among high math achievers; more males than females are exceptionally talented in math (Stumpf & Stanley, 1996). And it seems that sex differences in visual/spatial abilities and the problem-solving strategies they sup-

visual/spatial abilities
the ability to mentally manipulate or otherwise draw inferences about pictorial information.

port contribute to sex differences in arithmetic reasoning (Casey, Nuttal, & Pezaris, 1997). However, we will soon see that social forces—namely the messages boys and girls receive about these respective abilities—can also influence their mathematical, verbal, and visual/spatial reasoning skills.

Aggression

Finally, boys are more physically and verbally *aggressive* than girls, starting as early as age 2, and are about ten times more likely than girls are to be involved in antisocial behavior and violent crime during adolescence (U.S. Department of Justice, 1995). However, girls are more likely than boys to display covert forms of hostility toward others by snubbing or ignoring them or by trying to undermine their relationships or social status (Crick et al., 1997; Crick & Grotpeter, 1995).

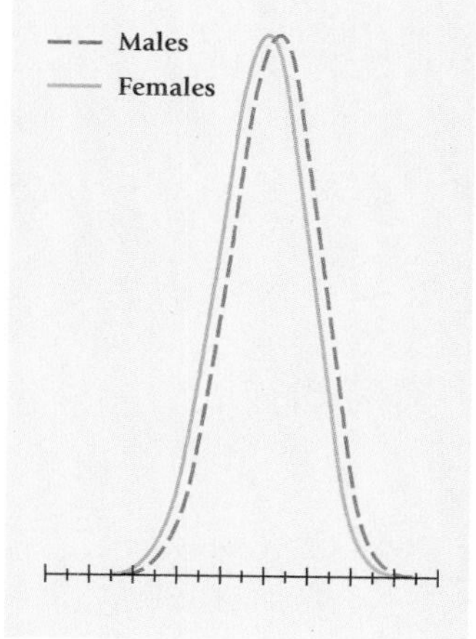

Figure 13.2 *These two distributions of scores—one for males, one for females—give some idea of the size of the gap between the sexes in abilities for which sex differences are consistently found. Despite a small difference in average performance, the scores of males and females overlap considerably.* ADAPTED FROM HYDE, FENNEMA, & LAMON, 1990.

Other Sex Differences

Critics were quick to challenge Maccoby and Jacklin's review, claiming that the procedures they used to gather and tabulate their results led them to underestimate the number of sex differences that actually exist (Block, 1976; Huston, 1983). More recent research, which often combines the results of several studies and provides a better estimate of the reliability of sex-related differences, points to several additional sex differences in personality and social behavior. For example:

Activity Level

Even before they are born, boys are more physically active than girls (DiPietro et al., 1996) and they remain more active throughout childhood, especially when interacting with peers (Eaton & Enns, 1986; Eaton & Yu, 1989). In fact, the heightened activity that boys display may help to explain why they are more likely than girls to initiate and to be receptive to bouts of nonaggressive, *rough-and-tumble* play (Humphreys & Smith, 1987).

Fear, Timidity, and Risk Taking

As early as the first year of life, girls appear to be more fearful or timid in uncertain situations than boys are. They are also more cautious and less assertive in these situations than boys are, taking far fewer risks than boys do (Christophersen, 1989; Feingold, 1994).

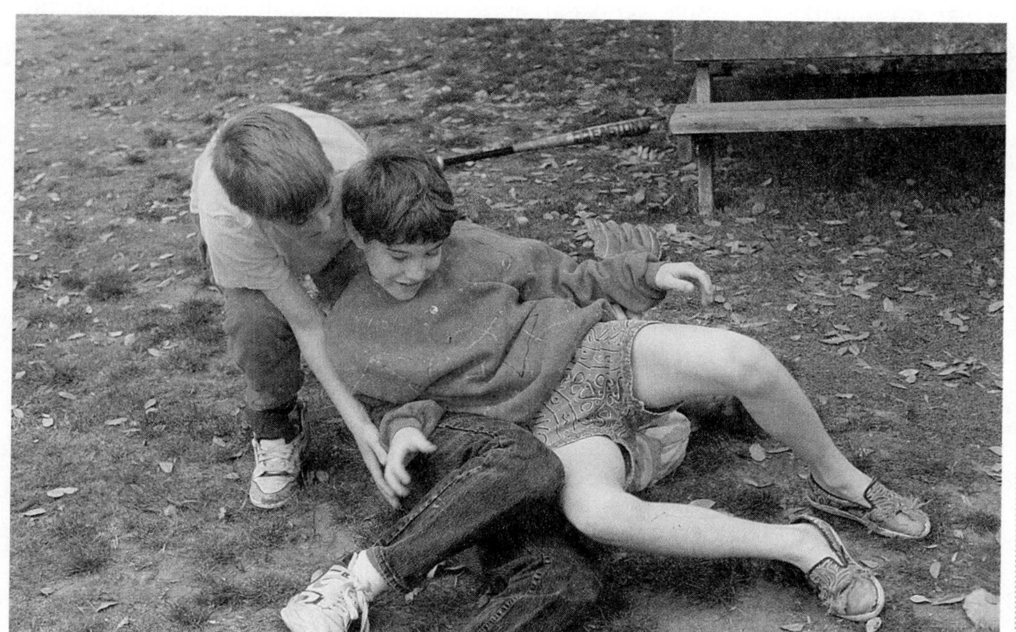

Rough-and-tumble play is more common among boys than among girls.

Developmental Vulnerability

From conception, boys are more physically vulnerable than girls to prenatal and perinatal hazards and to the effects of disease (Raz et al., 1994; 1995). Boys are also more likely than girls to display a variety of developmental problems, including reading disabilities, speech defects, hyperactivity, emotional disorders, and mental retardation (Halpern, 1997; Henker & Whalen, 1989).

Emotional Expressivity/Sensitivity

In some ways, females appear to be more emotionally expressive than males. Two-year-old girls are already using more emotion-related words than 2-year-old boys do (Cervantes & Callanan, 1998), and parents of preschoolers talk more with daughters than with sons about emotions and memorable emotional events (Kuebli, Butler, & Fivush, 1995; Reese & Fivush, 1993). Indeed, this social support for reflecting on their feelings may help to explain why girls and women characterize their emotions as deeper, or more intense, and feel freer to express them than boys and men do (Diener, Sandvik, & Larson, 1985; Fuchs & Thelen, 1988; Saarni, 1993).

The evidence for sex differences in empathic sensitivities is mixed. Girls and women consistently *rate themselves* (and are described by others) as more nurturant and empathic than boys and men (Cohen & Strayer, 1996; Feingold, 1994). Yet, boys often appear no less empathic or compassionate than girls when studied in naturalistic settings (Fabes, Eisenberg, & Miller, 1990; Zahn-Waxler et al., 1992). For example, boys display at least as much affection toward and concern for the welfare of their pets and older relatives as girls do (Melson, Peet, & Sparks, 1991).

Compliance

From early in the preschool period, girls are more compliant than boys with the requests and demands of parents, teachers, and other authority figures (Feingold, 1994; Maccoby, 1990). And when trying to persuade others to comply with them, girls are more likely to rely on tact and polite suggestions, whereas many boys are inclined to adopt more forceful or demanding strategies (Cowan & Avants, 1988; Maccoby, 1990).

In reviewing the evidence for "real" sex differences, we must keep in mind that the data reflect *group averages* that may or may not characterize the behavior of any particular individual. For example, gender accounts for about 5% of the variation that children display in aggressive behavior (Hyde, 1984), so that the remaining 95% is due to differences between people other than their sex. Furthermore, the sex differences in verbal, spatial, and mathematical abilities that Maccoby and Jacklin identified are also small, are most apparent at the extreme (that is, very high or very low) ends of the ability distributions (Halpern, 1997), and may not be evident elsewhere (Daubman, Heatherington, & Ahn, 1992). For example, women do better on tests of mathematical ability, sometimes even outperforming men, in societies like Israel, where women have excellent opportunities in technical training and technical occupations (Baker & Jones, 1992). Findings such as these imply that most sex differences are not biologically inevitable and that cultural and other social influences play an important role in the development of males and females (Halpern, 1997).

What, then, should we conclude about psychological differences between the sexes? Although contemporary scholars may quibble at times about which sex differences are real or meaningful (Eagly, 1995; Hyde & Plant, 1995), most developmentalists can agree on this: *Males and females are far more psychologically similar than they are different,* and even the most well-documented differences seem to be modest. So it is impossible to accurately predict the aggressiveness, mathematical skills, activity level, or emotional expressivity of any individual simply by knowing his or her gender. Only when group averages are computed do sex differences emerge.

Cultural Myths

Another conclusion that most developmentalists now endorse is Maccoby and Jacklin's (1974) proposition that many (perhaps most) gender-role stereotypes are "cultural myths" that have no basis in fact. The most widely accepted of these myths are listed in Table 13.2.

Why do these inaccuracies persist? Maccoby and Jacklin (1974) propose that:

> a . . . likely explanation for the perpetuation of "myths" is the fact that stereotypes are such powerful things. An ancient truth is worth restating here: if a generalization about a group of people is believed, whenever a member of the group behaves in the expected way the observer notes it and his belief is confirmed and strengthened; when a member of the group behaves in a way that is not consistent with the observer's expectations, the instance is likely to pass unnoticed, and the observer's generalized belief is protected from disconfirmation. . . . [This] well-documented [selective attention] . . . process . . . results in the perpetuation of myths that would otherwise die out under the impact of negative evidence (p. 355).

In other words, gender-role stereotypes are well-ingrained cognitive schemes that we use to interpret and often distort the behavior of males and females (Martin & Halverson, 1981; see also Box 13.2). People even use these schemas to classify the behavior of infants. In one study (Condry & Condry, 1976), college students watched a videotape of a 9-month-old child who was introduced as either a girl ("Dana") or a boy ("David"). As the students observed the child at play, they were asked to interpret his/her reactions to toys such as a teddy bear or a jack-in-the-box. The resulting impressions of the infant's behavior clearly depended on his or her presumed sex. For example, a strong reaction to the jack-in-the-box was labeled "anger" when the child was presumed to be a boy and "fear" when the child had been introduced as a girl (see also Burnham & Harris, 1992).

TABLE 13.2 Some Unfounded Beliefs about Sex Differences

Beliefs	Facts
1. Girls are more "social" than boys.	The two sexes are equally interested in social stimuli, equally responsive to social reinforcement, and equally proficient at learning from social models. At certain ages, boys actually spend more time than girls with playmates.
2. Girls are more "suggestible" than boys.	Most studies of children's conformity find no sex differences. However, sometimes boys are more likely than girls to accept peer-group values that conflict with their own.
3. Girls have lower self-esteem than boys.	The sexes are highly similar in their overall self-satisfaction and self-confidence throughout childhood and adolescence. More boys than girls show gains in self-esteem over the course of adolescence, possibly reflecting the greater freedom and encouragement that males receive to pursue instrumental roles (Block & Robins, 1993).
4. Girls are better at simple repetitive tasks, whereas boys excel at tasks that require higher-level cognitive processing.	The evidence does not support these assertions. Neither sex is superior at rote learning, probability learning or concept formation.
5. Boys are more "analytic" than girls.	With the exception of the *small* sex differences in cognitive abilities that we have already discussed, boys and girls do *not* differ on tests of analytical or logical reasoning.
6. Girls lack achievement motivation.	No such differences exist! Perhaps the myth of lesser achievement motivation for females has persisted because males and females have generally directed their achievement strivings toward different goals.

SOURCE: Adapted from Maccoby & Jacklin, 1974.

FOCUS ON RESEARCH

13.2

Do Gender Stereotypes Color Children's Interpretations of Counterstereotypic Information?

Maccoby and Jacklin (1974) proposed that, once people learn gender stereotypes, they are more likely to attend to and remember events that are consistent with these beliefs than events that would disconfirm them. Carol Martin and Charles Halverson (1981) agree, arguing that gender stereotypes are well-ingrained schemes or naive theories that people use to organize and represent experience. Once established, these gender schemes should have at least two important effects on a child's (or an adult's) cognitive processes: (1) an *organizational* effect on memory, such that information consistent with the scheme will be easier to remember than counterstereotypic events, and (2) a *distortion* effect, such that counterstereotypic information will tend to be remembered as much more consistent with one's gender scheme than the information really is. For example, it should be easier for people to remember that they saw a girl at the stove cooking (gender-consistent information) than a boy partaking in the same activity (gender-inconsistent information). And if people were to witness the latter event, they might distort what they had seen to make it more consistent with their stereotypes—perhaps by remembering the actor as a girl rather than a boy or by reconstructing the boy's activities as *fixing* the stove rather than cooking.

Martin and Halverson (1983) tested their hypotheses in an interesting study with 5- and 6-year-olds. During a first session, each child was shown 16 pictures, half of which depicted a child performing *gender-consistent* activities (for example, a boy playing with a truck) and half showing children displaying *gender-inconsistent* behaviors (for example, a girl chopping wood). One week later, children's memory for what they had seen was assessed.

The results of this experiment were indeed interesting. Children easily recalled the sex of the actor for scenes in which actors had performed gender-consistent activities. But when the actor's behavior was gender *inconsistent,* these youngsters often distorted the scene by saying that the actor's sex was consistent with the activity they recalled (for example, they were likely to say that it had been a boy rather than a girl who had chopped wood). As predicted, children's *confidence* about the sex of the actors was greater for gender-consistent scenes than for gender-inconsistent ones, suggesting that counterstereotypic information is harder to remember. But it was interesting to note that, when children actually distorted a gender-inconsistent scene, they were just as confident about the sex of the actor (which they recalled *incorrectly*) as they were for the gender-consistent scenes in which they correctly recalled the actor's sex. So it seems that children are likely to distort counterstereotypic information to be more consistent with their stereotypes and that these memory distortions are as "real" to them as stereotypical information that has not been distorted.

Why, then, do inaccurate gender stereotypes persist? Because we find disconfirming evidence harder to recall and, in fact, often distort that information in ways that will confirm our initial (and inaccurate) beliefs.

As it turns out, the persistence of unfounded or inaccurate sex-role stereotypes has important consequences for both boys and girls. Some of the more negative implications of these cultural myths are discussed in the following section.

Do Cultural Myths Contribute to Sex Differences in Ability (and Vocational Opportunity)?

In 1968 Phillip Goldberg asked college women to judge the merits of several scientific articles that were attributed to a male author ("John McKay") or to a female author ("Joan McKay"). Although these manuscripts were identical in every other respect, participants judged the articles written by a male to be of higher quality than those by a female.

These young women were reflecting a belief, common to people in many societies, that girls and women lack the potential to excel in either math and science courses or in occupations that require this training. Kindergarten and first-grade girls already believe that they are not as good as boys are in arithmetic; and throughout the grade-school years, children increasingly come to regard

? WHAT DO YOU THINK?

Imagine you meet a 1-year-old named Taylor who is dressed in gender-neutral clothing and is sporting a pudding-bowl hairstyle, so that you cannot tell whether Taylor is a boy or a girl. How long would it be before you became curious about Taylor's sex? How would you determine whether a 1-year-old like Taylor is a boy or a girl?

reading, art, and music as girls' domains and mathematics, athletics, and mechanical subjects as more appropriate for boys (Eccles et al., 1990; 1993; Entwisle & Baker, 1983). Furthermore, an examination of the percentages of male and female practitioners in various occupations reveals that women are over-represented in fields that call for verbal ability (for example, library science; elementary education) and are seriously underrepresented in most other professions, particularly the sciences and other technical fields (for example, engineering) that require a math/science background (U.S. Bureau of the Census, 1997). How do we explain these dramatic sex differences? Are the small sex-related differences in verbal, mathematical, and visual/spatial performances responsible? Or rather, do gender-role stereotypes create a **self-fulfilling prophecy** that *promotes* sex differences in cognitive performance and steers boys and girls along different career paths? Today, many developmentalists favor the latter viewpoint. Let's take a closer look.

Home Influences

Parents may often contribute to sex differences in ability and self-perceptions by treating their sons and daughters differently. Jacquelynne Eccles and her colleagues (1990) have conducted a number of studies aimed at understanding why girls tend to shy away from math and science courses and are underrepresented in occupations that involve math and science. They find that parental expectations about sex differences in mathematical ability become self-fulfilling prophecies. The plot goes something like this.

1. Parents, influenced by gender stereotypes, expect their sons to outperform their daughters in math. Even before their children receive any formal math instruction, mothers in the United States, Japan, and Taiwan express a belief that boys have more mathematical ability than girls (Lummis & Stevenson, 1990).
2. Parents attribute their sons' successes in math to ability but credit their daughters' successes to hard work (Parsons, Adler, & Kaczala, 1982). These attributions further reinforce the belief that girls lack mathematical talent and turn in respectable performances only through plodding effort.
3. Children begin to internalize their parents' views, so that girls come to believe that they are "no good" in math (Jacobs & Eccles, 1992).
4. Thinking they lack ability, girls become less interested in math, less likely to take math courses, and less likely than boys to pursue career possibilities that involve math after high school (Benbow & Arjimand, 1990; U.S. Bureau of the Census, 1997).

In short, parents who expect their daughters to have trouble with numbers may get what they expect. In their research, Eccles and her colleagues have ruled out the possibility that parents (and girls themselves) expect less of girls because girls actually do worse in math than boys do. The negative effects of low parental expectancies on girls' self-perceptions are evident even when boys and girls perform *equally well* on tests of math aptitude and attain similar grades in math (Eccles et al., 1990). Parental beliefs that girls excel in English and that boys excel in sports contribute to sex differences in interests and competencies in these areas as well (Eccles et al., 1990).

Scholastic Influences

Teachers also have stereotyped beliefs about the relative abilities of boys and girls in particular subjects. Sixth-grade math instructors, for example, believe that boys have more ability in math but that girls try harder at it (Jussim & Eccles, 1992). And even though these teachers often reward girls' greater efforts by assigning them equal or higher grades than they give to boys (Jussim & Eccles, 1992), their message that girls must try harder to succeed in math may nonetheless convince many girls that their talents might be best directed toward other nonquantitative achievement domains for which they are better suited . . . like music or English

self-fulfilling prophecy
phenomenon whereby people cause others to act in accordance with the expectations they have about those others.

In sum, unfounded beliefs about sex differences in cognitive abilities may indeed contribute to the small sex-related ability differences we have discussed and, ultimately, to the large underrepresentation of women in the sciences and other occupations requiring quantitative skills. Even as we approach the 21st century, most high school students continue to prepare for occupations dominated by members of their own sex (Associated Press, 1994; Hannah & Kahn, 1989), and there is a clear need for programs to educate parents, teachers, and counselors about the subtle ways that gender stereotypes can undermine the educational and occupational aspirations of talented female students (Benbow & Arjimand, 1990). Fortunately, there are some hopeful signs that times are changing. Although we still see few females among the engineering graduates of most colleges, women now make up nearly 50% of first-year law classes and about 40% of the enrollment in the School of Business at my home institution (University of Georgia Fact Book, 1997). So there is reason to suspect that many of the constraining stereotypes about women's competencies will eventually crumble as women, in ever-increasing numbers, enter politics, professional occupations, and the sciences, skilled trades, and virtually all other walks of life. To oppose such a trend is to waste a most valuable resource: the abilities and efforts of more than half the world's population.

Now let's examine the gender-typing process to see why it is that boys and girls may come to view themselves so differently and often choose to assume different roles.

DEVELOPMENTAL TRENDS IN GENDER TYPING

Gender-typing research has traditionally focused on three separate but interrelated topics: (1) the development of **gender identity,** or the knowledge that one is either a boy or a girl and that gender is an unchanging attribute, (2) the development of *gender-role stereotypes,* or ideas about what males and females are supposed to be like; and (3) the development of *gender-typed* patterns of *behavior*—that is, the child's tendency to favor same-sex activities over those normally associated with the other sex.

Development of the Gender Concept

The first step in the development of a gender identity is to discriminate males from females and to place oneself into one of these categories. By 6 months of age, infants use differences in vocal pitch to discriminate female speech from that of males (Miller, 1983); and by the end of the first year, they can reliably discriminate photographs of men and women (women are the long-haired ones) and are beginning to match male and female voices with faces in tests of intermodal perception (Leinbach & Fagot, 1993; Poulin-Dubois et al., 1994).

Between ages 2 and 3, children begin to tell us what they know about gender as they acquire and correctly use such labels as "mommy" and "daddy" and (slightly later) "boy" and "girl" (Leinbach & Fagot, 1986). By age 2½ to 3, almost all children can accurately label themselves as either boys or girls (Thompson, 1975), although it takes longer for them to grasp the fact that gender is a permanent attribute. Many 3- to 5-year-olds, for example, think that boys could become mommies or girls daddies if they really wanted to, or that a person who changes clothing and hairstyles can become a member of the other sex (Fagot, 1985b; Marcus & Overton, 1978; Slaby & Frey, 1975). Children normally begin to understand that sex is an unchanging attribute between the ages of 5 and 7, so that most youngsters have a firm, future-oriented identity as a boy or a girl by the time they enter grade school.

gender identity
one's awareness of one's gender and its implications.

By age 2½ to 3, children know that boys and girls prefer different kinds of activities, and they have already begun to play in gender-stereotyped ways.

Development of Gender-Role Stereotypes

Remarkable as it may seem, toddlers begin to acquire gender-role stereotypes at about the same time that they become aware of their basic identities as boys or girls. Deanna Kuhn and her associates (1978) showed a male doll ("Michael") and a female doll ("Lisa") to 2½- to 3½-year-olds and then asked each child which of the two dolls would engage in sex-stereotyped activities such as cooking; sewing; playing with dolls, trucks, or trains; talking a lot; giving kisses; fighting; or climbing trees. Almost all the 2½-year-olds had some knowledge of gender-role stereotypes. For example, boys and girls agreed that girls talk a lot, never hit, often need help, like to play with dolls, and like to help their mothers with chores such as cooking and cleaning. By contrast, these young children felt that boys like to play with cars, help their fathers, and build things, and are apt to make statements such as "I can hit you." The 2- to 3-year-olds who know most about gender stereotypes are those who can correctly label photographs of other children as boys and girls (Fagot, Leinbach, & O'Boyle, 1992). So an understanding of gender labels seems to accelerate the process of gender stereotyping.

Over the preschool and early grade-school years, children learn more and more about the toys, activities, and achievement domains considered appropriate for boys and for girls (Serbin, Powlishta, & Gulko, 1993; Welch-Ross & Schmidt, 1996). Eventually, grade-school children draw sharp distinctions between the sexes on *psychological* dimensions, learning first the positive traits that characterize their own gender and the negative traits associated with the other sex (Serbin et al., 1993). By age 10 to 11, children's stereotyping of personality traits begins to rival that of adults. In one well-known cross-cultural study, Deborah Best and her colleagues (1977) found that fourth- and fifth-graders in England, Ireland, and the United States generally agreed that women are weak, emotional, soft-hearted, sophisticated, and affectionate, whereas men are ambitious, assertive, aggressive, dominating, and cruel.

How seriously do children take the gender-role prescriptions they are rapidly learning? Do they believe that they must conform to these stereotypes? Many 3- to 7-year-olds do; they often reason like little chauvinists, treating sex-role standards as blanket rules that are not to be violated (Biernat, 1991; Martin, 1989). Consider the reaction of one 6-year-old to a boy named George who likes to play with dolls:

> *(Why do you think people tell George not to play with dolls?)* Well, he should only play with things that boys play with. The things that he is playing with now is girls' stuff. . . . *(Can George play with Barbie dolls if he wants to?)* No sir! . . . *(What should George do?)* He should stop playing with girls' dolls and start playing with G.I. Joe. *(Why can a boy play with G.I. Joe and not a Barbie doll?)* Because if a boy is playing with a Barbie doll, then he's just going to get people teasing him . . . and if he tries to play more, to get girls to like him, then the girls won't like him either (Damon, 1977, p. 255; italics added).

Why are young children so rigid and intolerant of sex-role transgressions? Possibly because gender-related issues are very important to them between ages 3 and 7: After all, this is the time when they are firmly classifying themselves as boys or girls and beginning to suspect that they will *always be* boys and girls. Thus, they may exaggerate gender-role stereotypes to "get them cognitively clear" so that they can live up to their self-images (Maccoby, 1980).

By age 8 to 9, however, children are becoming more flexible and less chauvinistic in their thinking about gender (Damon, 1977; Levy, Taylor, & Gelman, 1995; Serbin et al., 1993). Notice how 9-year-old James makes a clear distinction between moral rules that people are obligated to obey and gender-role standards that are customary but *nonobligatory.*

> *(What do you think his parents should do?)* They should . . . get him trucks and stuff, and see if he will play with those. *(What if . . . he kept on playing with dolls? Do you think they would punish him?)* No. *(How come?)* It's not really doing anything bad. *(Why isn't it bad?)* Because . . . if he was breaking a window, and he kept on doing that, they could punish him because you're not supposed to break windows. But if you want to you can play with dolls. *(What's the difference? . . .)* Well, breaking windows you're not supposed to do. And if you play with dolls, you can, but boys usually don't (Damon, 1977, p. 263; italics added).

However, just because grade-school children say that boys and girls can legitimately pursue cross-sex interests and activities does not necessarily imply that they *approve* of those who do. When asked about whether they could be friends with a boy who wears lipstick or a girl who plays football and to evaluate such gender-role transgressions, grade-school children (and adults) were reasonably tolerant of violations by girls. However, participants (especially boys) came down hard on boys who behaved like girls, viewing these transgressions as almost as bad as violating a moral rule. Here, then, is an indication of the greater pressure placed on boys to conform to gender roles (Levy et al., 1995).

Thinking about the traits that males and females might display and the hobbies and occupations they might pursue becomes increasingly flexible during early adolescence, as children make the transition from elementary school to junior high. But soon thereafter, gender-role prescriptions once again become less flexible, with both boys and girls showing a strong intolerance of cross-sex mannerisms displayed by either males or females (Alfieri, Ruble, & Higgins, 1996; Sigelman, Carr, & Begley, 1986; Signorella et al., 1993; and see Figure 13.3). How might we explain this second round of gender chauvinism?

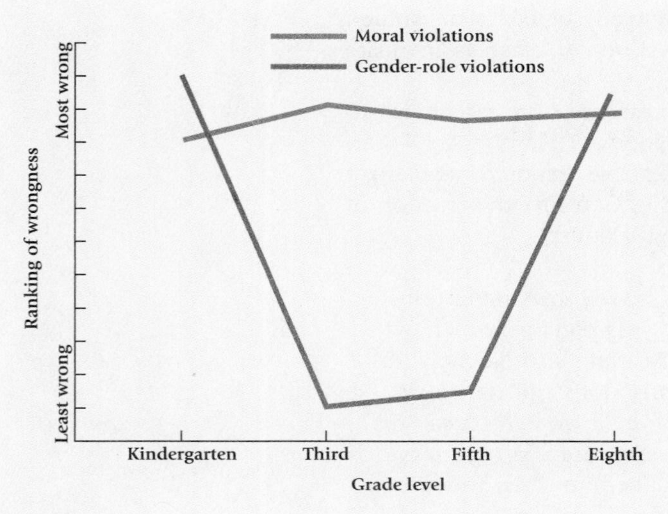

Figure 13.3 *Children's rankings of the wrongness of gender-role transgressions (such as a boy's wearing nail polish) and violations of moral rules (such as pushing another child from a swing). Notice that children of all ages deplore immoral acts but that only kindergartners and adolescents view gender-role violations as wrong. Elementary school children come to think about gender-role standards in a more flexible way than they did earlier in life, but adolescents become concerned about the psychological implications of deviating from one's "proper" gender identity.* ADAPTED FROM STODDART & TURIEL, 1985.

Apparently, an adolescent's increasing intolerance of cross-sex mannerisms and behaviors is tied to a larger process of **gender intensification**—a magnification of sex differences that is associated with increased pressure to conform to gender roles as one reaches puberty (Boldizar, 1991; Galambos, Almeida, & Petersen, 1990; Hill & Lynch, 1983). Boys begin to see themselves as more masculine; girls emphasize their feminine side. Why might gender intensification occur? Parental influence is one contributor: As children enter adolescence, mothers become more involved in joint activities with daughters and fathers more involved with sons (Crouter, Manke, & McHale, 1995). However, peer influences may be even more important. For example, adolescents increasingly find that they must conform to traditional gender norms in order to succeed in the dating scene. A girl who was a tomboy and thought nothing of it may find during adolescence that she must dress and behave in more "feminine" ways to attract boys, and a boy may find that he is more popular if he projects a more "masculine" image (Burn, O'Neil, & Nederend, 1996; Katz, 1979). Social pressures on adolescents to conform to traditional roles may even help explain why sex differences in cognitive abilities sometimes become more noticeable as children enter adolescence (Hill & Lynch, 1983; Roberts et al., 1990). Later in high school, teenagers become more comfortable with their identities as young men or women and more flexible once again in their thinking about gender (Urberg, 1979). Yet, even adults may remain highly intolerant of males who blatantly disregard gender-role prescriptions (Levy et al., 1995).

Development of Gender-Typed Behavior

The most common method of assessing the "gender-appropriateness" of children's behavior is to observe whom and what they like to play with. Sex differences in toy preferences develop very early, even before the child has established a clear gender identity or can correctly label various toys as "boy things" or "girl things" (Blakemore, LaRue, & Olejnik, 1979; Fagot, Leinbach, & Hagan, 1986; Weinraub et al., 1984). Boys aged 14 to 22 months usually prefer trucks and cars to other objects, whereas girls of this age would rather play with dolls and soft toys (Smith & Daglish, 1977). In fact, 18- to 24-month-old toddlers often refuse to play with cross-sex toys, even when there are no other objects available for them to play with (Caldera et al., 1989).

Gender Segregation

Children's preferences for same-sex playmates also develop very early. In nursery school, 2-year-old girls already prefer to play with other girls (La Freniere, Strayer, & Gauthier, 1984), and by age 3, boys reliably select boys rather than girls as companions. This **gender segregation,** which has been observed in a variety of cultures (Leaper, 1994; Whiting & Edwards, 1988), becomes progressively stronger with each passing year (Serbin et al., 1993). Four- and 5-year-olds have already begun to actively *reject* playmates of the other sex (Ramsey, 1995), and by age 6½, children spend more than 10 times as much time with same-sex as with opposite-sex companions (Maccoby, 1988). Alan Sroufe and his colleagues (1993) find that those 10- to 11-year-olds who insist most strongly on maintaining clear gender boundaries and who avoid consorting with the "enemy" tend to be viewed as socially competent and popular, whereas children who violate gender segregation rules tend to be much less popular and less well-adjusted. In fact, children who display a *preference* for cross-sex friendships are likely to be *rejected* by their peers (Kovacs, Parker, & Hoffman, 1996). However, gender boundaries and biases against other-sex companions decline in adolescence when the social and physiological events of puberty trigger an interest in members of the opposite sex (Serbin et al., 1993).

Why does gender segregation occur? Eleanor Maccoby (1990) believes that it largely reflects differences between boys' and girls' play styles—an incompatibility that may stem from boys' heightened levels of androgen, which fosters active, rambunctious

gender intensification
a magnification of sex differences early in adolescence; associated with increased pressure to conform to traditional gender roles.

gender segregation
children's tendency to associate with same-sex playmates and to think of the other sex as an out-group.

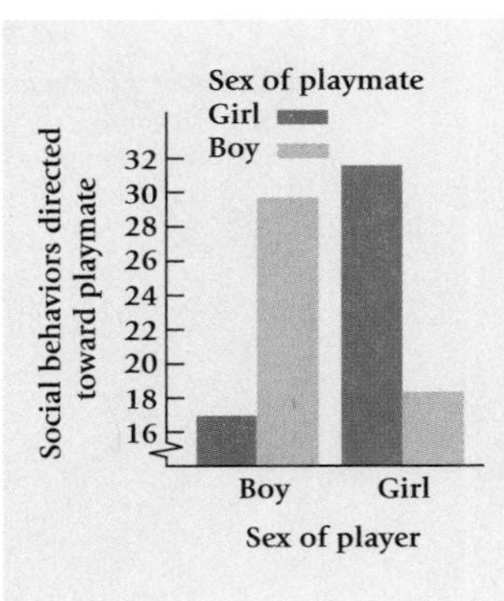

Figure 13.4 *Two- to 3-year-old toddlers already prefer playmates of their own sex. Boys are much more social with boys than with girls, whereas girls are more outgoing with girls than with boys.* ADAPTED FROM JACKLIN & MACCOBY, 1978.

behavior. In one study (Jacklin & Maccoby, 1978), an adult observer recorded how often pairs of same-sex and mixed-sex toddlers played together or played alone when placed in a playroom with several interesting toys. As we see in Figure 13.4, boys directed far more social responses to boys than to girls, whereas girls were more sociable with girls than with boys. Interactions between playmates in the same-sex pairings were lively and positive in character. By contrast, girls tended to withdraw from boys in the mixed-sex pairs. Boys were simply too boisterous and domineering to suit the taste of many girls, who preferred less roughhousing and would rather rely on polite negotiations rather than demands or shows of force when settling disputes with their playmates (see also Alexander & Hines, 1994; Moller & Serbin, 1996).

Cognitive and social-cognitive development also contribute to the increasing gender segregation children display. Once preschoolers label themselves as boys or girls and begin to acquire gender stereotypes, they come to favor the group to which they belong and eventually view the other sex as a homogeneous out-group with many negative characteristics (Martin, 1994; Powlishta, 1995). In fact, children who hold the more stereotyped views of the sexes are most likely to maintain gender segregation in their own play activities and to make few if any opposite-sex friends (Kovacs et al., 1996; Martin, 1994).

Sex Differences in Gender-Typed Behavior

Many cultures, including our own, assign greater status to the male gender role (Turner & Gervai, 1995), and boys face stronger pressures than girls to adhere to gender-appropriate codes of conduct (Bussey & Bandura, 1992; Lobel & Menashri, 1993). Consider that fathers of baby girls are generally willing to offer a truck to their 12-month-old daughters, whereas fathers of baby boys are likely to withhold dolls from their sons (Snow, Jacklin, & Maccoby, 1983). And boys are quicker than girls to adopt gender-typed toy preferences. Judith Blakemore and her associates (1979), for example, found that 2-year-old boys clearly favor gender-appropriate toys whereas some 2-year-old girls may not. And by age 3 to 5, boys (1) are much more likely than girls to say that they *dislike* opposite-sex toys (Bussey & Bandura, 1992; Eisenberg, Murray, & Hite, 1982) and (2) *may* even prefer a girl playmate who likes "boy" toys to a boy playmate who prefers girls' activities (Alexander & Hines, 1994).

Between the ages of 4 and 10, both boys and girls are becoming more aware of what is expected of them and conforming to these cultural prescriptions (Huston, 1983). Yet, girls are more likely than boys to retain an interest in cross-sex toys, games, and activities. Consider what John Richardson and Carl Simpson (1982) found when recording the toy preferences of 750 5- to 9-year-olds as expressed in their letters to Santa Claus. Although most requests were clearly gender-typed, we see in Table 13.3 that more

TABLE 13.3 Percentages of Boys and Girls Who Requested Popular "Masculine" and "Feminine" Items from Santa Claus

	Percentage of boys requesting	Percentage of girls requesting
Masculine items		
Vehicles	43.5	8.2
Sports equipment	25.1	15.1
Spatial/temporal toys (construction sets, clocks, and so on)	24.5	15.6
Feminine items		
Dolls (adult female)	.6	27.4
Dolls (babies)	.6	23.4
Domestic accessories	1.7	21.7

SOURCE: Adapted from Richardson & Simpson, 1982.

girls than boys asked for "opposite-sex" items (see also Etaugh & Liss, 1992). With respect to their actual gender-role preferences, young girls often wish they were boys, and nearly half of today's college women claim that they were tomboys when they were young (Burn et al., 1996). Yet it is unusual for a boy to wish he were a girl (Martin, 1990).

There are probably several reasons that girls are drawn to male activities and the masculine role during middle childhood. For one thing, they are becoming increasingly aware that masculine behavior is more highly valued, and perhaps it is only natural that girls would want to be what is "best" (or at least something other than a second-class citizen) (Frey & Ruble, 1992). Furthermore, girls are given much more leeway than boys are to partake in cross-sex activities; it is okay to be a "tomboy" but a sign of ridicule and rejection should a boy be labeled a "sissy" (Martin, 1990). Finally, fast-moving masculine games and "action" toys may simply be more interesting than the familiar household playthings and pastimes (dolls, dollhouses, dish sets, cleaning and caretaking utensils) often imposed on girls to encourage their adoption of a nurturant, expressive orientation. Consider the reaction of Gina, a 5-year-old who literally squealed with delight when she received an "action garage" (complete with lube racks, gas pumps, cars, tools, and spare parts) from Santa one Christmas. At the unveiling of this treasure, Gina and her three female cousins (aged 3, 5, and 7) immediately ignored their dolls, dollhouses, and unopened gifts to cluster around and play with this unusual and intriguing toy.

In spite of their earlier interest in masculine activities, most girls come to prefer (or at least to comply with) many of the prescriptions for the feminine role by early adolescence. Why? Probably for biological, cognitive, and social reasons. Once they reach puberty and their bodies assume a more womanly appearance *(biological growth),* girls often feel the need to become more "feminine" if they hope to be attractive to members of the other sex (Burn et al., 1996; Katz, 1979). Furthermore, these young adolescents are also attaining formal operations and advanced role-taking skills *(cognitive growth),* which may help to explain why they become (1) self-conscious about their changing body images (Von Wright, 1989), (2) so concerned about other people's evaluation of them (Elkind, 1981; remember the *imaginary audience* phenomenon) and; (3) more inclined to conform to the *social* prescriptions of the female role.

In sum, gender-role development proceeds at a remarkable pace (see Table 13.4 on page 488). By the time they enter school, children have long been aware of their basic gender identities, have acquired many stereotypes about how the sexes differ, and have come to prefer gender-appropriate activities and same-sex playmates. During middle childhood, their knowledge continues to expand as they learn more about gender-stereotyped *psychological* traits, and they become more flexible in their thinking about gender roles. Yet their *behavior,* especially if they are boys, becomes even more gender-typed, and they segregate themselves even more from the other sex. Now the most intriguing question: How does all this happen so fast?

Concept Check 13.1
Understanding Sex Differences and Gender-Role Development

Check your understanding of sex differences and selected aspects of gender-role development by matching each descriptive statement below with one of the following terms: (a) achievement motivation, (b) gender identity, (c) gender intensification, (d) gender segregation, (e) reading comprehension, (f) self-fulfilling prophecy, (g) gender-role stereotypes, (h) visual/spatial ability, (i) gender-role standard. The answers appear in the Appendix.

_____ 1. attribute for which girls show a small but consistent advantage
_____ 2. knowledge about one's gender and its permanence
_____ 3. value, motive, or behavior considered more appropriate for members of one sex than the other
_____ 4. process by which others' expectancies may promote sex differences in behavior
_____ 5. attribute for which boys show a small but consistent advantage
_____ 6. affiliative preference that becomes stronger with age across childhood
_____ 7. attribute on which boys and girls *do not* differ
_____ 8. process that seems responsible for young teens' renewed intolerance of cross-sex mannerisms
_____ 9. can cause us to distort or misinterpret gender-atypical behaviors that we observe

TABLE 13.4 An Overview of Gender Typing

Age (years)	Gender identity	Gender stereotyping	Gender-typed behavior
0–2½	Ability to discriminate males from females emerges and improves. Child accurately labels the self as a boy or a girl.	Some gender stereotypes emerge.	Gender-typed toy/activity preferences emerge. Preferences for same-sex playmates emerge (gender segregation).
3–6	Conservation of gender (recognition that one's gender is unchanging) emerges.	Gender stereotyping of interests, activities, and occupations become quite rigid.	Gender-typed play/toy preferences become stronger, particularly for boys. Gender segregation intensifies.
7–11		Gender stereotyping of personality traits and achievement domains emerge. Gender stereotyping becomes less rigid.	Gender segregation continues to strengthen. Gender-typed toy/activity preferences continue to strengthen for boys; girls develop (or retain) interests in some masculine activities.
12 and beyond	Gender identity becomes more salient, reflecting gender intensification pressures.	Intolerance of cross-sex mannerisms increases early in adolescence. Gender stereotyping becomes more flexible in most respects later in adolescence.	Conformity to gender-typed behaviors increases early in adolescence, reflecting gender intensification. Gender segregation becomes less pronounced.

THEORIES OF GENDER TYPING AND GENDER-ROLE DEVELOPMENT

Several theories have been proposed to account for sex differences and the development of gender roles. Some theories emphasize the role of biological differences between the sexes, whereas others emphasize *social* influences on children. Some emphasize how society influences children, others the choices children make as they try to understand gender and all its implications. Let's briefly examine a biologically oriented theory and then consider the more "social" approaches offered by psychoanalytic theory, social learning theory, cognitive-developmental theory, and gender schema theory.

Money and Ehrhardt's Biosocial Theory

"Once there was a baby named Chris . . . [who] went to live on a beautiful island . . . [where] there were only boys and men; Chris was the only girl. Chris lived a very happy life on this island, but she never saw another girl or woman" (Taylor, 1996, p. 1559). What would Chris be like?

When Marianne Taylor (1996) asked 4- to 10-year-olds to indicate Chris's toy preferences, occupational aspirations, and personality traits, 4- to 8-year olds assigned stereotypically feminine attributes to her, despite the fact that she was raised in a masculinizing environment and never saw a girl or woman. In other words, preschool and young grade-school children display an *essentialist bias,* assuming that Chris's biological status as a girl determines what she will become. Only the 9- to 10-year-olds in this study showed any awareness that Chris's masculinizing environment might influence her activities, aspirations, and personality characteristics.

Many scholars once displayed a similar essentialist bias by assuming that virtually all sex differences were largely attributable to biological variations between males and females. What biological differences might be so important? For one, males have a Y chromosome and hence, some genes that all females lack. For another, the sexes clearly differ in hormonal balance, with males having higher concentrations of androgens (including testosterone) and lower levels of estrogen than females do. But do these biological *correlates* of gender and gender differences actually cause sex differences in behavior? Do they predispose boys and girls to prefer and to adopt different gender roles?

Today, even biologically oriented theorists take a more moderate stance, arguing that biological and social influences *interact* to determine a person's behaviors and role preferences. Nowhere is this interactive emphasis more apparent than in the *biosocial theory* proposed by John Money and Anke Ehrhardt (1972). Although biosocial theory concentrates on biological forces that may channel and constrain the development of boys and girls, it also acknowledges that early biological developments affect other people's *reactions* to the child and suggests that these social forces play a major part in steering the child toward a particular gender role. Let's take a closer look at this influential theory.

An Overview of Gender Differentiation and Sex-Role Development

Money and Ehrhardt (1972) propose that there are a number of critical episodes or events that affect a person's eventual preference for the masculine or the feminine gender role. The first critical event occurs at conception as the child inherits either an X or a Y chromosome from the father. Over the next 6 weeks, the developing embryo has only an undifferentiated gonad, and the sex chromosomes determine whether this structure becomes the male testes or the female ovaries. If a Y chromosome is present, the embryo develops testes; otherwise, ovaries form.

These newly formed gonads then determine the outcome of episode 2. The testes of a male embryo secrete two hormones: *testosterone,* which stimulates the development of a male internal reproductive system, and *mullerian inhibiting substance (MIS),* which inhibits the development of female organs. In the absence of these hormones, the embryo develops the internal reproductive system of a female.

At a third critical point, 3 to 4 months after conception, secretion of testosterone by the testes normally leads to the growth of a penis and scrotum. If testosterone is absent (as in normal females) or if the male fetus has inherited a rare recessive disorder, called **testicular feminization syndrome (TFS),** that makes his body insensitive to male sex hormones, female external genitalia (labia and clitoris) form. Testosterone also alters the development of the brain and nervous system. For example, it signals the male brain to stop secreting hormones in a cyclical pattern so that males do not experience menstrual cycles at puberty.

Once a child is born, *social* factors immediately come into play. Parents and other people label and begin to react to the child based on the appearance of his or her genitals. If one's genitals are abnormal so that he or she is mislabeled as a member of the other sex, this incorrect label can affect his or her future development. For example, if a biological male were consistently labeled and treated as a girl (as a boy with TFS syndrome and female external genitalia might be), he would, by about age 2½ to 3, acquire the gender identity (though not the biological characteristics) of a girl. Finally, biological factors enter the scene again at puberty when large quantities of hormones are released, stimulating the growth of the reproductive system, the appearance of secondary sex characteristics, and the development of sexual urges. These events, in combination with one's earlier self-concept as a male or a female, provide the basis for an adult gender identity and gender role preference (see Figure 13.5).

testicular feminization syndrome (TFS)
a genetic anomaly in which a male fetus is insensitive to the effects of male sex hormones and develops femalelike external genitalia.

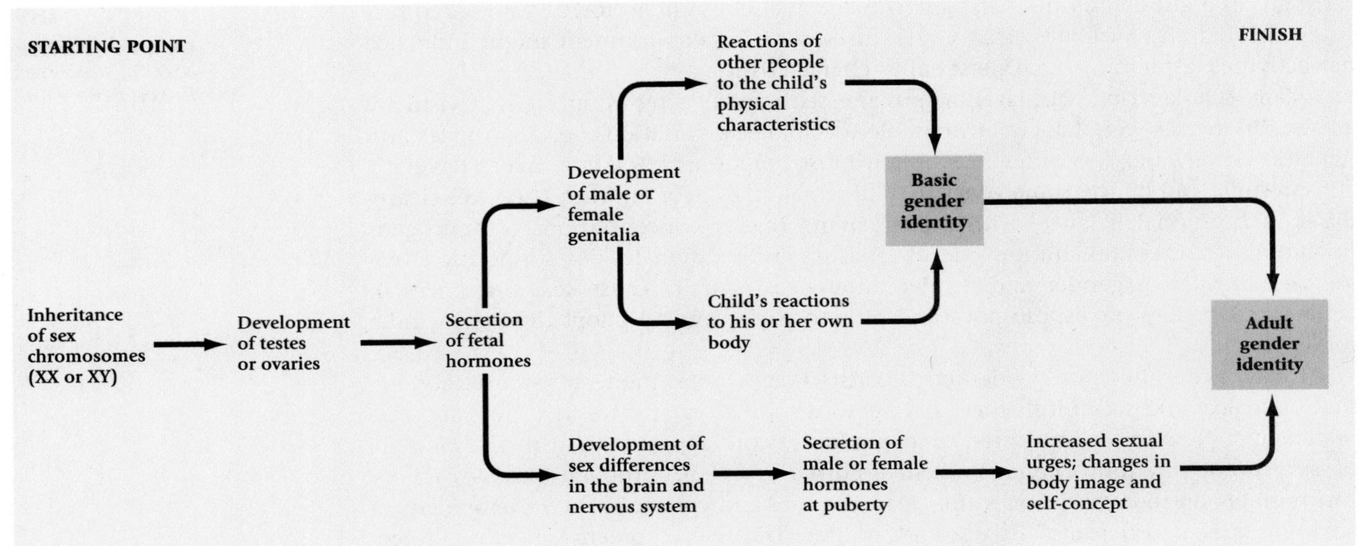

Figure 13.5 *Critical events in Money and Ehrhardt's biosocial theory of sex typing.* From Money & Ehrhardt, 1972.

Evidence for Biological Influences on Gender-Role Development

How much influence *do* biological factors have on the behavior of males and females? To answer this question, we must consider what investigators have learned about genetic and hormonal influences.

Genetic Influences. Genetic factors may contribute to some sex differences in personality, cognitive abilities, and social behavior. Corrine Hutt (1972), for example, suspects that several of the developmental disorders more commonly seen among boys may be X-linked recessive traits. (Recall from Chapter 3 that boys are more likely to display such traits because they have but one X chromosome and need only inherit one recessive gene to be affected). Furthermore, **timing of puberty,** a biological variable regulated in part by our genotypes, has a slight effect on visual/spatial performances. Both boys and girls who mature *late* tend to outperform early maturers of their own sex on some visual/spatial tasks, allegedly because slow maturation promotes increasing specialization of the brain's right hemisphere, which serves spatial functions (see Newcombe & Dubas, 1987). However, later research indicates that the spatial performances of both boys and girls are more heavily influenced by their *previous involvement* in spatial activities and their *self-concepts* than by the timing of puberty (Newcombe & Dubas, 1992; Signorella, Jamison, & Krupa, 1989). Specifically, it appears that having a strong masculine self-concept and ample experience with spatial toys and activities fosters the growth of spatial skills in both boys and girls, whereas having restricted spatial experiences and a feminine self-concept seems to inhibit spatial abilities.

How closely are our masculine and feminine self-concepts related to the genes that we have inherited? Results from several behavioral genetics studies of adolescent twins suggest that genotype accounts for about 50% of the variability in people's masculine self-concepts but only 0 to 20% of the variability in their feminine self-concepts (Loehlin, 1992; Mitchell, Baker, & Jacklin, 1989). So even though genes determine our biological sex and may have some influence on the outcome of gender typing, it appears that at least half the variability in people's masculine and feminine self-concepts is attributable to environmental influences.

timing-of-puberty effect
the finding that people who reach puberty late perform better on visual/spatial tasks than those who mature early.

Hormonal Influences. Biological influences on development are also evident in studies of children who have been exposed to the "wrong" hormones during the prenatal period (Ehrhardt & Baker, 1974; Money & Ehrhardt, 1972; Gandelman, 1992). Before

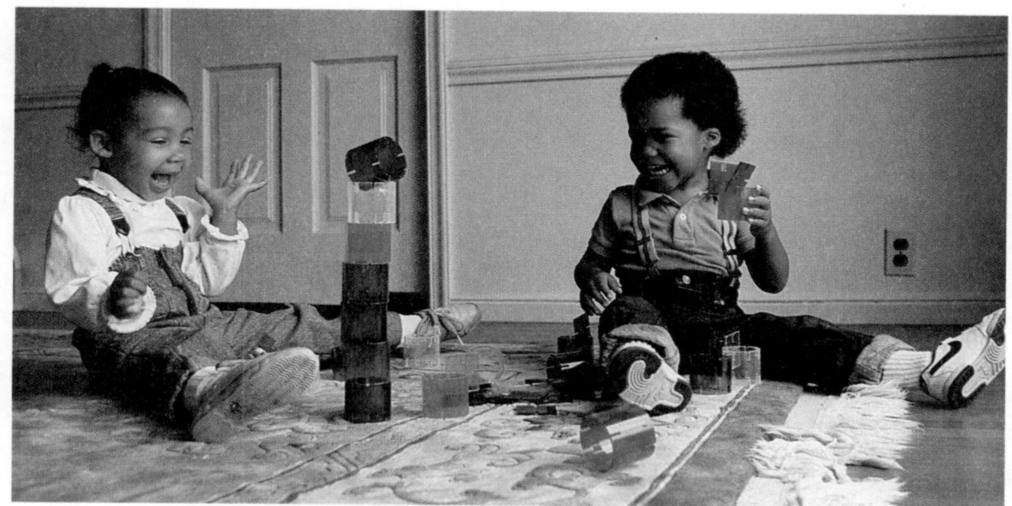

Girls who often play with visual/spatial toys tend to perform better on tests of spatial ability.

the consequences were known, some mothers who had had problems carrying pregnancies to term were given drugs containing progestins, which are converted to the male hormone testosterone by the body. Other children with a condition known as **congenital adrenal hyperplasia (CAH)** have a genetic defect that causes their adrenal glands to produce unusually high levels of androgen from the prenatal period onward. These conditions usually have no effect on males; but female fetuses are often masculinized so that, despite their XX genetic endowment and female internal organs, they are born with external genitalia that resemble those of a boy (for example, a large clitoris that looks like a penis and fused labia that resemble a scrotum).

Money and Ehrhardt (1972; Ehrhardt & Baker, 1974) have followed several of these **androgenized females** whose external organs were surgically altered and who were then raised as girls. Compared with their sisters and other girls, many more androgenized girls were tomboys who often played with boys and who preferred boys' toys and activities to traditionally feminine pursuits (see also Berenbaum & Snyder, 1995; Hines & Kaufman, 1994). As adolescents, they began dating somewhat later than other girls and felt that marriage should be delayed until they had established their careers. A high proportion (37%) described themselves as homosexual or bisexual (Money, 1985; see also Dittman, Kappes, & Kappes, 1992). Androgenized females also perform better than most girls and women on tests of spatial ability, further suggesting that early exposure to male hormones may have "masculinizing" effects on a female fetus's brain (Kimura, 1992; Resnick et al., 1986). Yet it is still not entirely clear that the masculine interests and abilities these girls display are a direct result of their prenatal exposure to androgen. Many of those girls received cortisone therapy to control their androgen levels and prevent further masculinization of their bodies, and one side effect of cortisone is to dramatically increase a person's activity level. So, a plausible alternative interpretation is that the high-intensity "masculine" behaviors and the interest patterns that androgenized girls display are really due more to the medical treatments that they received than to their prenatal exposure to male sex hormones (Huston, 1983).

It has also been suggested that males are more aggressive than females because of their higher levels of testosterone—the male sex hormone that is thought to promote heightened activity, a readiness to anger, and hence, a predisposition to behave aggressively (Archer, 1991; 1996). The evidence seems quite convincing when experiments are conducted with animals. Female rhesus monkeys exposed prenatally to the male hormone testosterone later display patterns of social behavior more characteristic of males: They often threaten other monkeys, initiate rough-and-tumble play, and try to "mount" a partner as males do at the beginning of a sexual encounter (Wallen, 1996; Young, Goy, & Phoenix, 1964). By contrast, genetically male rat pups that are castrated and cannot produce testosterone tend to be passive and to display feminine sexual behavior (Beach, 1965).

congenital adrenal hyperplasia (CAH)
a genetic anomaly that causes one's adrenal glands to produce unusually high levels of androgen from the prenatal period onward; often has masculinizing effects on female fetuses.

androgenized females
females who develop malelike external genitalia because of exposure to male sex hormones during the prenatal period.

What about humans? Dan Olweus and his associates (1980) found that 16-year-old boys who label themselves physically and verbally aggressive have higher testosterone levels than boys who view themselves as nonaggressive, and men with extremely high testosterone levels tend to display higher rates of delinquency, abusiveness, and violence (Dabbs & Morris, 1990). Yet we must be extremely cautious in interpreting these correlational findings, because a person's hormonal level may depend on his or her experiences. To illustrate, Irwin Bernstein and his associates (Rose, Bernstein, & Gordon, 1975) found that the testosterone levels of male rhesus monkeys rose after they had won a fight but fell after they had been defeated. So it appears that higher concentrations of male sex hormones might be either a cause or an effect of aggressive behavior, and it is difficult to establish conclusively that these hormones either *cause* one to act aggressively or explain sex differences in aggression (Archer, 1991).

Evidence for Social-Labeling Influences

Although biological forces may steer boys and girls toward different activities and interests, Money and Ehrhardt (1972) insist that social-labeling influences are also important—so important, in fact, that they can modify or even *reverse* biological predispositions. Indeed, some of the evidence for this provocative claim comes from Money's own work with androgenized girls.

Recall that these androgenized girls were born with the internal reproductive organs of a normal female even though their external genitalia resembled a penis and scrotum. These children are sometimes labeled boys at birth and raised as such until their abnormalities are detected. Money (1965) reports that the discovery and correction of this condition (by surgery and gender reassignment) presents few if any adjustment problems, provided that the sex change occurs *before age 18 months.* But after age 3, gender reassignment is exceedingly difficult because these genetic females have experienced prolonged masculine gender typing and have already labeled themselves as boys. These data led Money to conclude that there is a "critical period" between 18 months and 3 years of age for the establishment of gender identity. As illustrated in Box 13.3, it may be more accurate to call the first 3 years a *sensitive* period, for other investigators have claimed that it is possible to assume a new identity later in adolescence. Nevertheless, Money's findings indicate that early social labeling and gender role socialization can play a very prominent role in determining a child's gender identity and role preferences.

Gender-role behaviors are often specific to one's culture. Like many Peruvian boys, this youngster routinely washes clothes and attends to other household tasks.

Cultural Influences. The fact that most societies promote instrumental traits in males and expressive traits in females has led some theorists to conclude that traditional gender roles are part of the natural order of things—a product of our bioevolutionary history (Archer, 1996; Buss, 1995). Yet, there are sizable differences across cultures in what people expect of boys and girls (Whiting & Edwards, 1988). Consider Margaret Mead's (1935) classic study of three tribal societies in New Guinea. *Both* males and females among the Arapesh were taught to be cooperative, nonaggressive, and sensitive to the needs of others. This behavioral profile would be considered "expressive" or "feminine" in Western cultures. By contrast, *both* men and women of the Mundugumor tribe were expected to be assertive, aggressive, and emotionally unresponsive in their interpersonal relationships—a masculine pattern of behavior by Western standards. Finally, the Tchambuli displayed a pattern of gender-role development opposite to that of Western societies: Males were passive, emotionally dependent, and socially sensitive, whereas females were dominant, independent, and assertive. So members of these three tribes developed in accordance with the gender roles that were

13.3 CURRENT CONTROVERSIES

Is Biology Destiny?

When biological sex and social labeling conflict, which wins out? Consider the case of a male identical twin whose penis was damaged beyond repair during circumcision (Money & Tucker, 1975). After seeking medical advice and considering the alternatives, the parents agreed to a surgical procedure that made their 21-month-old son a girl anatomically. After the operation, the family began to actively gender type this boy-turned-girl by changing her hairstyle, dressing her in frilly blouses, dresses, and the like, purchasing feminine toys for her to play with, and teaching such feminine behaviors as sitting to urinate. By age 5, the "girl" twin was quite different from her *genetically identical* brother: She knew she was a girl and was far neater and daintier than her brother. Here, then, was a case in which assigned sex and gender-role socialization seemed to overcome biological predispositions. Or did they?

Milton Diamond and Keith Sigmundson (1997) followed up on this "John" turned "Joan" and found that the story had a twist ending. Over time, Joan became quite uncomfortable with doll play and other traditionally feminine pursuits; she preferred to dress up in men's clothing, play with her twin brother's toys, and take things apart to see how they worked. Somewhere around the age of 10, she had the distinct feeling that she was not a girl: "I began to see how different I felt and was . . . I thought I was a freak or something . . . but I didn't want to admit it. I figured I didn't want to wind up opening a can of worms" (pp. 299–300). Being rejected by other children because of her masculine looks and feminine dress also took their toll, as did continued pressure from psychiatrists to behave in a more feminine manner. Finally, at age 14 after years of inner turmoil and suicidal thinking, Joan had had it and simply refused to take female hormones and pretend to be a girl any longer. She then received male hormone shots, a mastectomy, and surgery to construct a penis and emerged as a quite handsome and popular young man who dated girls, married at age 25, and appears to be comfortable with his hard-won identity as a man. Perhaps, then, we should back off from the conclusion that early gender-role socialization is all that matters. Biology matters, too.

A second source of evidence that biology matters is a study of 18 biological males in the Dominican Republic who had a genetic condition (TFS syndrome) that made them insensitive prenatally to the effects of male hormones (Imperato-McGinley, Peterson, Gautier, & Sturla, 1979). They had begun life with ambiguous genitals, and were labeled and raised as girls. However, under the influence of male hormones produced at puberty, they sprouted beards and became masculine in appearance. How, in light of Money and Ehrhardt's critical-period hypothesis, could a person adjust to becoming a man after leading an entire childhood as a girl?

Amazingly, 16 of these 18 individuals seemed able to accept their late conversion from female to male and to adopt masculine lifestyles, including the establishment of heterosexual relationships. One retained a female identity and gender role, and the remaining individual switched to a male gender identity but still dressed as a female. Clearly, this study also casts doubt on the notion that socialization during the first three years is absolutely critical to later gender-role development. Instead, it suggests that hormonal influences may be more important than social influences.

However, Imperato-McGinley's conclusions have been challenged (Ehrhardt, 1985). Little information was reported about how these individuals were raised, and it is quite possible that Dominican parents, knowing this genetic disorder was common in their society, treated these "girls" differently from other "girls" when they were young. Furthermore, the girls-turned-boys had genitals that were not completely normal in appearance, and the practice of river bathing in Dominican culture almost certainly means that these youngsters compared themselves to normal girls (and boys) and may have recognized early on that they were different. So these children may not have received an exclusively feminine upbringing and may never have fully committed themselves to being girls. Nor should we automatically assume that their later incorporation of the masculine role was due to hormones. One study of TFS males raised as females among the Sambia of New Guinea found that *social pressures*—namely, the argument that they could not bear children—appeared to be most responsible for the gender switches that occurred after puberty (Herdt & Davidson, 1988).

Studies like these of individuals with genital abnormalities teach us that we are predisposed by our biology to develop as males or females; the first 3 years of life are a *sensitive period* perhaps, but not a critical period, for gender-role development; and *neither* biology nor social labeling can fully account for gender-role development.

socially prescribed by their culture, none of which matched the female/expressive—male/instrumental pattern seen in Western societies. Clearly, social forces contribute heavily to gender typing.

In sum, Money and Ehrhardt's biosocial theory stresses the importance of early biological developments that influence how parents and other social agents label a child at birth and that possibly also affect behavior more directly. However, the theory also holds that whether children are socialized as boys or girls strongly influences their gender-role development—in short, that biological and social forces *interact*. But how, exactly, do they interact?

A Psychobiosocial Viewpoint. Diane Halpern (1997) has recently proposed a *psychobiosocial model* to explain how nature and nurture might jointly influence the development of gender-typed attributes. According to the model, prenatal exposure to male or female hormones influences the organization of male and female brains in ways that might make boys, for example, somewhat more receptive to spatial activities and girls somewhat more susceptible to quiet verbal exchanges. These heightened sensitivities, in concert with others' beliefs about the kinds of experiences most appropriate for boys and for girls, means that boys are likely to receive a richer array of spatial experiences than girls do, whereas girls are exposed more often to verbal play activities. These differential experiences then influence the neural pathways laid down in a young child's immature and highly plastic brain, so that boys become even more receptive to spatial activities and to acquiring spatial competencies, while girls become ever more receptive to verbal activities and to acquiring verbal skills. From a psychobiosocial perspective then, nature and nurture feed on each other and are a false dichotomy. In Halpern's words, " . . . biology and environment are as inseparable as conjoined twins who share a common heart" (p. 1097).

WHAT DO YOU THINK?

Do you think that an interactive model such as Halpern's *psychobiosocial approach* can explain the late conversion from female-to-male gender identities seen among the TFS males we discussed in Box 13.3? Why or why not?

What both biosocial theory and the psychobiosocial model do *not* do is to specify the precise social processes that contribute most heavily to children's emerging gender identities and gender-typed patterns of behavior. Let's turn now to the social theories of gender typing, the first of which was Sigmund Freud's psychoanalytic approach.

Freud's Psychoanalytic Theory

phallic stage
Freud's third stage of psychosexual development (from 3 to 6 years of age) in which children gratify the sex instinct by fondling their genitals and developing an incestuous desire for the parent of the other sex.

identification
Freud's term for the child's tendency to emulate another person, usually the same-sex parent.

castration anxiety
in Freud's theory, a young boy's fear that his father will castrate him as punishment for his rivalrous conduct.

Recall from Chapter 2 that Freud thought that sexuality (the sex instinct) was inborn. However, he believed that one's gender identity and preference for a gender role emerge during the **phallic stage** as children begin to emulate and to **identify** with their same-sex parent. Specifically, Freud claimed that a 3- to 6-year-old boy internalizes masculine attributes and behaviors when he is forced to identify with his father as a means of renouncing his incestuous desire for his mother, reducing his **castration anxiety,** and thus resolving his **Oedipus complex.** However, Freud believed that gender typing is more difficult for a young girl who lacks a penis, already feels castrated, and experiences no overriding fear that would compel her to identify with her mother and resolve her **Electra complex.** Why, then, would a girl ever develop a preference for the feminine role? Freud offered several suggestions, one of which was that the object of a girl's affection, her father, was likely to encourage her feminine behavior—an act that increases the attractiveness of the mother, who serves as the girl's model of femininity. So by trying to please her father (or to prepare for relationships with other males after she recognizes the implausibility of possessing her father), a girl is motivated to incorporate her mother's feminine attributes and eventually becomes gender typed (Freud, 1924/1961a).

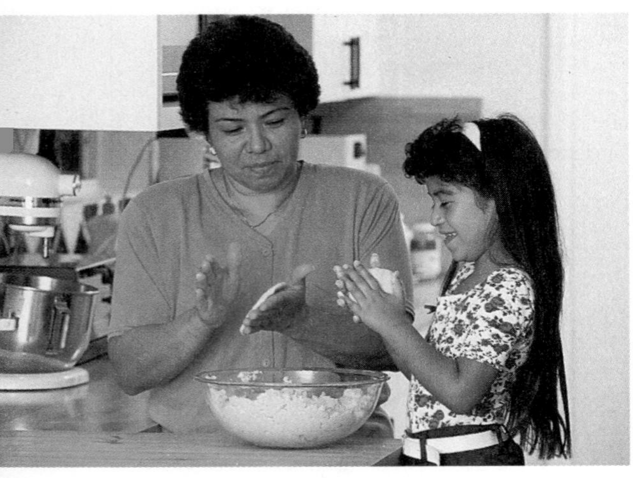

According to Freud, children become appropriately "masculine" or "feminine" by identifying with the same-sex parent.

Although children are rapidly learning gender stereotypes and developing gender-typed playmate and activity preferences at roughly the ages Freud says they should, his psychoanalytic theory of gender-typing has not fared well at all. Many 4- to 6-year-olds are so ignorant about differences between male and female genitalia that it is hard to see how most boys could fear castration or how most girls could feel castrated as Freud says they do (Bem, 1989; Katcher, 1955). Furthermore, Freud assumed that a boy's identification with his father is based on fear; but most researchers find that boys identify more strongly with fathers who are warm and nurturant rather than overly punitive and threatening (Hetherington & Frankie, 1967; Mussen & Rutherford, 1963). Finally, studies of parent–child resemblances reveal that school-age children and adolescents are not all that similar psychologically to either parent (Maccoby & Jacklin, 1974). Clearly, these findings are damaging to the Freudian notion that children acquire important personality traits by identifying with the same-sex parent.

Let's now consider the social learning interpretation of gender typing to see whether this approach looks any more promising.

Social Learning Theory

According to social learning theorists such as Albert Bandura (1989) and Walter Mischel (1970), children acquire their gender identities and gender-role preferences in two ways. First, through **direct tuition** (or *differential reinforcement*), children are encouraged and rewarded for gender-appropriate behaviors and are punished or otherwise discouraged for behaviors considered more appropriate for members of the other sex. Second, through *observational learning,* children adopt the attitudes and behaviors of a variety of same-sex models.

Direct Tuition of Gender Roles

Are parents actively involved in teaching boys how to be boys and girls how to be girls? Yes, indeed (Leaper, Anderson, & Sanders, 1998; Lytton & Rommney, 1991), and their shaping of gender-typed behaviors begins rather early. Beverly Fagot and Mary Leinbach (1989), for example, found that parents are already encouraging gender-appropriate activities and discouraging cross-gender play during the second year of life, *before* children have acquired their basic gender identities or display clear preferences for male or female activities. By age 20 to 24 months, daughters are consistently reinforced for dancing, dressing up (as women), following parents around, asking for help, and playing with dolls; and they are generally discouraged from manipulating objects, running, jumping, and climbing. By contrast, sons are often reprimanded for such "feminine" behaviors as doll play or seeking help and are actively encouraged to play with masculine items such as blocks, trucks, and push-and-pull toys that require large muscle activity (Fagot, 1978).

Are children influenced by the "gender curriculum" their parents provide? They certainly are! In fact, parents who show the clearest patterns of differential reinforcement have children who are relatively quick to (1) label themselves as boys or girls, (2) develop strong gender-typed toy and activity preferences, and (3) acquire an understanding of gender stereotypes (Fagot & Leinbach, 1989; Fagot, Leinbach, & O'Boyle, 1992). And fathers are even more likely than mothers to encourage "gender-typed" behaviors and to discourage behavior considered more appropriate for the other sex (Leve & Fagot, 1997; Lytton & Romney, 1991). So it seems that a child's earliest preferences for gender-typed toys and activities may well result from their parents' (particularly fathers') successful attempts to reinforce these interests.

Throughout the preschool period, parents become less and less inclined to carefully monitor and differentially reinforce their children's gender-typed activities (Fagot & Hagan, 1991; Lytton & Romney, 1991). Why? Because many other factors conspire to maintain these interests, not the least of which is the behavior of same-sex peers (Beal, 1994). Even before they have established their basic gender identities, 2-year-old boys often belittle or disrupt each other for playing with "girl toys" or with girls, and 2-year-old girls are quite critical of other girls who choose to play with boys (Fagot, 1985a). So peers differentially reinforce gender-typed attitudes and behaviors even as parents become somewhat less likely to do so.

Oedipus complex
Freud's term for the conflict that 3- to 6-year-old boys were said to experience when they develop an incestuous desire for their mothers and a jealous and hostile rivalry with their fathers.

Electra complex
female version of the Oedipus complex, in which a 3- to 6-year-old girl was thought to envy her father for possessing a penis and to choose him as a sex object in the hope that he would share with her this valuable organ that she lacked.

direct tuition
teaching young children how to behave by reinforcing "appropriate" behaviors and by punishing or otherwise discouraging inappropriate conduct.

Observational Learning

According to Bandura (1989), children acquire many of their gender-typed attributes and interests by observing and imitating a variety of same-sex models. The assumption is that boys will see which toys, activities, and behaviors are "for boys" and girls will learn which activities and behaviors are "for girls" by selectively attending to and imitating a variety of *same-sex* models, including peers, teachers, older siblings, and media personalities, as well as their mothers or their fathers.

Yet, there is some question just how important *same-sex* modeling influences are during the preschool period, for researchers often find that 3- to 6-year-olds learn from models of both sexes. For example, children of employed mothers (who play the *masculine* instrumental role) or of fathers who routinely perform such *feminine* household tasks as cooking, cleaning, and child care are less aware of gender stereotypes than children of more traditional parents are (Serbin et al., 1993; Turner & Gervai, 1995). Furthermore, John Masters and his associates (1979) found that preschool children are much more concerned about the sex-appropriateness of the *behavior* they are observing than the sex of the model who displays it. Four- to 5-year-old boys, for example, will play with objects labeled "boys' toys" even after they have seen a girl playing with them. However, these youngsters are reluctant to play with "girls' toys" that boy models have played with earlier, and they think that other boys would also shun objects labeled as girls' toys (Martin, Eisenbud, & Rose, 1995). So children's toy choices are affected more by the labels attached to the toys than by the sex of the child who served as a model. But once they recognize that gender is an unchanging aspect of their personalities (at age 5 to 7), children do begin to attend more selectively to same-sex models and are now likely to avoid toys and activities that other-sex models seem to enjoy (Frey & Ruble, 1992; Ruble et al., 1981).

Media Influences. Not only do children learn by observing other children and adult models with whom they interact, but they also learn about gender roles from reading stories and watching television. Although sexism in children's books has declined over the past 50 years, male characters are still more likely than female characters to engage in active, instrumental pursuits such as riding bikes or making things, whereas female characters are often depicted as passive and dependent individuals who spend much of their time playing quietly indoors and "creating problems that require masculine solutions" (Kortenhaus & Demarest, 1993; Turner-Bowker, 1996). It is similar in the world of television: Males are usually featured as the central characters who work at professions, make important decisions, respond to emergencies, and assume positions of leadership, whereas females are often portrayed as relatively passive and emotional creatures who manage a home or work at "feminine" occupations such as waitressing or nursing (Liebert & Sprafkin, 1988).

Apparently, children are influenced by these highly sexist media portrayals, for those who watch a lot of television are more likely to prefer gender-typed activities and to hold highly stereotyped views of men and women than their classmates who watch little television (McGhee & Frueh, 1980; Signorielli & Lears, 1992). But as more women play detectives and more men raise families on television, children's perceptions of male and female roles are likely to change. In fact, children who regularly watch *The Cosby Show* and other relatively nonsexist programs do hold less stereotyped views of the sexes (Rosenwasser, Lingenfelter, & Harrington, 1989).

In sum, there is a lot of evidence that differential reinforcement and observational learning contribute to gender-role development. However, social learning theorists have often portrayed children as *passive pawns* in the process: Parents, peers, and TV characters show them what to do and reinforce them for doing it. Might this perspective miss something—namely, the child's *own* contribution to gender-role socialization? Consider, for example, that children do not always receive gender-stereotyped presents because their sexist parents force these objects upon them. Many parents who would rather buy gender-neutral or educational toys end up "giving in" to sons who beg for machine guns or daughters who want tea sets (Robinson & Morris, 1986).

Kohlberg's Cognitive-Developmental Theory

Lawrence Kohlberg (1966) has proposed a cognitive theory of gender typing that is quite different from the other theories we have considered and helps to explain why boys and girls adopt traditional gender roles even when their parents may not want them to. Kohlberg's major themes are:

1. Gender-role development depends on cognitive development; children must acquire certain understandings about gender before they will be influenced by their social experiences.
2. Children *actively socialize themselves;* they are not merely passive pawns of social influence.

According to both psychoanalytic theory and social learning theory, children first learn to do "boy" or "girl" things because their parents encourage these activities; then, they come to identify with or habitually imitate same-sex models, thereby acquiring a stable gender identity. By contrast, Kohlberg suggests that children *first* establish a stable gender identity and then *actively* seek out same-sex models and other information to learn how to act like a boy or a girl. To Kohlberg, it's not "I'm treated like a boy; therefore, I must be one" (social learning position). It's more like "Hey, I'm a boy; therefore, I'd better do everything I can to find out how to behave like one" (cognitive–self-socialization position).

Kohlberg believes that children pass through the following three stages as they acquire a mature understanding of what it means to be a male or a female:

1. **Basic gender identity.** By age 3, children have labeled themselves as boys or girls.
2. **Gender stability.** Somewhat later, gender is perceived as *stable over time.* Boys invariably become men and girls grow up to be women.
3. **Gender consistency.** The gender concept is complete when the child realizes that one's sex is also *stable across situations.* Five- to 7-year-olds who have reached this stage are no longer fooled by appearances. They know, for example, that one's gender cannot be altered by cross-dressing or taking up cross-sex activities.

When do children become motivated to socialize themselves—that is, to seek out same-sex models and learn how to act like males and females? According to Kohlberg, self-socialization begins only after children reach *gender consistency.* So for Kohlberg, a mature understanding of gender (1) instigates true sex typing and (2) is the *cause* rather than the consequence of attending to same-sex models.

Studies conducted in more than 20 different cultures reveal that preschool children do proceed through Kohlberg's three stages of gender identity in the sequence he describes and that attainment of gender consistency (or conservation of gender) is clearly associated with other relevant aspects of cognitive development, such as the conservation of liquids and mass (Marcus & Overton, 1978; Munroe, Shimmin, & Munroe, 1984). Furthermore, boys who have achieved gender consistency begin to pay more attention to male than to female characters on television (Luecke-Aleksa et al., 1995) and favor novel toys that male models prefer to those that female models like—even when the toys they pass on are the *more attractive objects* (Frey & Ruble, 1992). So children with a mature gender identity (especially boys) often play it safe and select the toy or activity that other members of their gender view as more appropriate for them.

basic gender identity
the stage of gender identity in which the child first labels the self as a boy or a girl.

gender stability
the stage of gender identity in which the child recognizes that gender is stable over time.

gender consistency
the stage of gender identity in which the child recognizes that a person's gender is invariant despite changes in the person's activities or appearance (also known as *gender constancy*).

Criticisms of Kohlberg's Theory

The major problem with Kohlberg's theory is that gender typing is well underway before the child acquires a mature gender identity. We have seen, for example, that 2-year-old boys prefer masculine toys before they have achieved a basic gender identity, and that 3-year-olds of each sex have learned many gender-role stereotypes and already prefer same-sex activities and playmates long before they begin to attend more selectively to same-sex models. Furthermore, we've noted that gender reassignment is exceedingly difficult after children reach age 3 (Kohlberg's basic identity stage) and have initially categorized themselves as boys or girls. In fact, one's level of gender identity may rest as much on social experience as on cognitive development, for even 3- and 4-year olds who have often seen members of the other sex naked may display gender consistency on gender identity tests (Bem, 1989). Finally, measures of gender identity simply do not predict how much children know about gender stereotypes or how gender typed their behaviors are (Bussey & Bandura, 1992; Lobel & Menashri, 1993; Martin & Little, 1990). So Kohlberg badly overstates the case in arguing that a mature understanding of gender is necessary for gender typing to begin. As we will see in the next section, only a rudimentary understanding of gender permits children to acquire gender stereotypes and develop strong gender-typed toy and activity preferences.

Gender Schema Theory

Carol Martin and Charles Halverson (1981; 1987) have proposed a somewhat different cognitive theory of gender typing (actually, an information-processing theory) that appears quite promising. Like Kohlberg, Martin, and Halverson believe that children are intrinsically motivated to acquire interests, values, and behaviors that are consistent with their "boy" or "girl" self-images. But unlike Kohlberg, they argue that this self-socialization begins as soon as the child acquires a *basic gender identity* at age 2½ or 3 and is well underway by age 6 to 7 when the child achieves gender consistency.

According to Martin and Halverson's gender schema theory, establishment of a basic gender identity motivates a child to learn about the sexes and to incorporate this information into **gender schemas**—that is, organized sets of beliefs and expectations about males and females that influence the kinds of information he attends to, elaborates, and remembers. First, children acquire a simple **in-group/out-group schema** that allows them to classify some objects, behaviors, and roles as "for boys" and others as "for girls" (for example, trucks are for boys; girls can cry but boys should not, and so on). This is the kind of information that researchers normally tap when studying children's knowledge of gender stereotypes. And this initial categorization of objects and activities clearly affects children's thinking. In one research program, 4- and 5-year-olds were shown unfamiliar gender-neutral toys (for example, spinning bells; a magnet stand), told that these objects were either "for boys" or "for girls," and asked whether they and other boys or girls would like them. Children clearly relied on the labels to guide their thinking. Boys, for example, liked "boy" objects better than girls did, and children assumed that other boys would also like these objects better than other girls would. Just the opposite pattern of reasoning was observed when these same objects were labeled as "for girls." Even highly attractive toys soon lost their luster if they were labeled as for the other gender (Martin et al., 1995).

In addition, children are said to construct an **own-sex schema,** which consists of detailed plans of action that they will need to perform various gender-consistent behaviors and enact a gender role. So a girl who has a basic gender identity might first learn that sewing is "for girls" and building model airplanes is "for boys." Then, because she is a girl and wants to act consistently with her own self-concept, she will gather a great deal of information about sewing to add to her own-sex schema, while largely ignoring information about building model airplanes (see also Figure 13.6). To test this notion, 4- to 9-year-olds were given boxes of gender-neutral objects (for example, burglar alarms, pizza cutters) and told that these objects were either "boy" items or "girl" items (Bradbard et al., 1986). As predicted, boys subsequently explored "boy" items more than girls did, whereas girls explored more than boys when the objects were described as things girls enjoy. One week later, boys recalled much more in-depth information about "boy" items than girls did, whereas girls recalled more than boys about these very same objects if they had been labeled "girl" items. If children's information-gathering efforts are consistently guided by their own-sex schemas in this way, we can easily see how boys and girls might acquire very different stores of knowledge and develop different interests and competencies as they mature.

Once formed, gender schemas serve as scripts for processing social information. Recall from Chapter 8 that preschool children often have a difficult time recalling infor-

gender schemas
organized sets of beliefs and expectations about males and females that guide information processing.

in-group/out-group schema
one's general knowledge of the mannerisms, roles, activities, and behaviors that characterize males and females.

own-sex schema
detailed knowledge or plans of action that enable a person to perform gender-consistent activities and to enact his or her gender role.

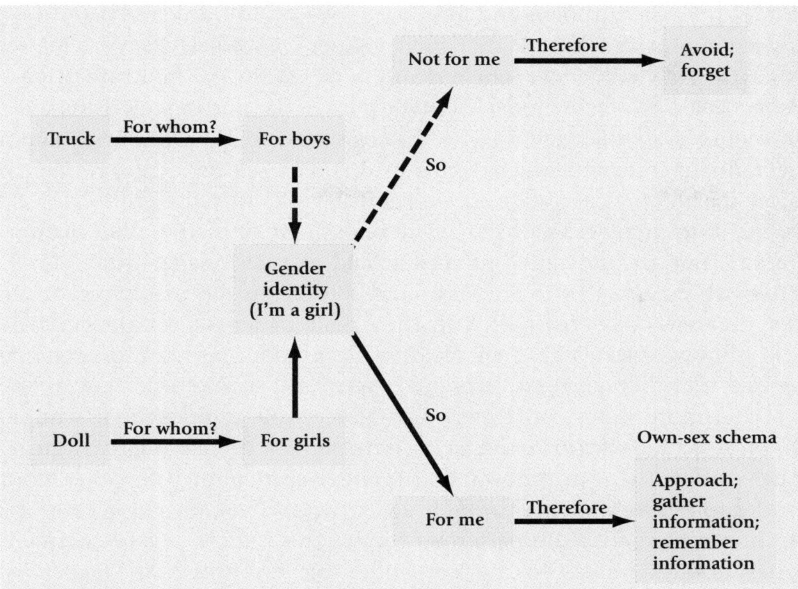

Figure 13.6 *Gender-schema theory in action. A young girl classifies new information according to an in-group/out-group schema as either "for boys" or "for girls." Information about boys' toys and activities is ignored, but information about toys and activities for girls is relevant to the self and so is added to an ever-larger own-sex schema.* ADAPTED FROM MARTIN & HALVERSON, 1987.

mation that deviates from their scripted knowledge of everyday events. And so it goes with gender-related knowledge: Children are likely to encode and remember information consistent with their gender schemas and to forget schema-inconsistent information or to otherwise distort it so that it becomes more consistent with their stereotypes (Liben & Signorella, 1993; Martin & Halverson, 1983), especially if they have reached age 6 to 7, when their own stereotyped knowledge and preferences have crystallized and are especially strong (Welch-Ross & Schmidt, 1996). Support for this idea was presented in Box 13.2; recall that children who heard stories in which actors performed gender-atypical behaviors (for example, a girl chopping wood) tended to recall the action but to alter the scene to conform to their gender stereotypes (saying that a boy had been chopping). Surely, these strong tendencies to forget or to distort counter-stereotypic information help to explain why unfounded beliefs about males and females are so slow to die.

In sum, Martin and Halverson's gender schema theory is an interesting new look at the gender-typing process. Not only does this model describe how gender-role stereotypes might originate and persist over time, but it also indicates how these emerging gender schemas might contribute to the development of strong gender-role preferences and gender-typed behaviors long before a child may realize that gender is an unchanging attribute.

An Integrative Theory

Biological, social learning, cognitive-developmental, and gender schema perspectives have each contributed in important ways to our understanding of sex differences and gender-role development (Huston, 1983; Serbin et al., 1993). In fact, the processes that different theories emphasize seem to be especially important at different periods. Biological theories account for the major biological developments that occur before birth that induce people to label the child as a boy or a girl and to treat him or her accordingly. The differential reinforcement process that social learning theorists emphasize seems to account rather well for early gender typing: Young children display gender-consistent behaviors largely because other people encourage these activities and often discourage behaviors considered more appropriate for members of the other sex. As a result of this early socialization and the growth of categorization skills, 2½- to 3-year-olds acquire a basic gender identity and begin to form *gender schemas* that tell them (1) what boys and girls are like and (2) how they, as boys and girls, are supposed to think and act. And when they finally understand, at age 6 or 7, that their gender will never change, children begin to focus less exclusively on gender schemas and to pay more and more attention to same-sex models to decide which attitudes, activities, interests, and mannerisms are most appropriate for members of their own sex (Kohlberg's viewpoint). Of course, summarizing developments in an integrative model such as this one (see Table 13.5 for an overview) does not mean that biological forces play no further role after the child is born or that differential reinforcement ceases to affect development once the child acquires a basic gender identity. But an integrative theorist would emphasize that from, age 3 on, children are active *self-socializers* who try very hard to acquire the masculine or feminine attributes that they view as consistent with their male or female self-images. This is why parents who hope to discourage their children from adopting traditional gender roles are often amazed that their sons and daughters seem to become little "sexists" all on their own.

One more point: All theories of gender-role development would agree that what children actually learn about being a male or a female depends greatly on what their society offers them in the way of a "gender curriculum." In other words, we must view gender-role development through an *ecological* lens and appreciate that there is nothing inevitable about the patterns of male and female development that we see in our society today. (Indeed, recall the gender-role reversals that Mead observed among the Tchambuli tribe of New Guinea.) In another era, in another culture, the gender-typing process can produce very different kinds of boys and girls.

Should we in Western cultures be trying to raise different kinds of boys and girls? As we will see in our next section, some theorists would answer this question with a resounding "Yes!"

PSYCHOLOGICAL ANDROGYNY: A PRESCRIPTION FOR THE FUTURE?

Throughout this chapter, we have used the term *gender-appropriate* to describe the mannerisms and behaviors that societies consider more suitable for members of one sex than the other. Today, many developmentalists believe that these rigidly defined gender-role standards are actually harmful because they constrain the behavior of both males and females. Sandra Bem (1978), for example, has stated that her major purpose in studying gender roles is "to help free the human personality from the restrictive prison of sex-role stereotyping and to develop a conception of mental health that is free from culturally imposed definitions of masculinity and femininity."

For many years, psychologists assumed that masculinity and femininity were at

Concept Check 13.2
Understanding Theories of Gender-Role Development

Check your understanding of theories of gender-role development by matching each descriptive statement below with one of the following concepts or viewpoints: (a) Money and Ehrhardt's biosocial theory, (b) Halpern's psychobiosocial model, (c) Freud's psychoanalytic theory, (d) social-learning theory, (e) Kohlberg's cognitive-developmental theory, (f) Martin and Halverson's gender schema theory, (g) basic gender identity, (h) gender consistency.

_____ 1. starting point for self-socialization, according to Kohlberg's theory

_____ 2. claims there is a critical period for gender typing between 18 months and 3 years

_____ 3. claims that children adopt gender roles by identifying with the same-sex parent

_____ 4. starting point for self-socialization, according to gender schema theory

_____ 5. claims that gender-typed experiences influence development of the brain's neural pathways

_____ 6. claims that early gender typing largely reflects the gender curriculum that parents provide

_____ 7. explains why unfounded beliefs about males and females are likely to persist

_____ 8. cannot easily explain why gender reassignment usually fails with 3- to 5-year-olds

TABLE 13.5	An Overview of the Gender-Typing Process from the Perspective of an Integrative Theorist	
Developmental period	**Events and outcomes**	**Pertinent theory(ies)**
Prenatal period	The fetus develops male or female genitalia which others will react to once the child is born.	Biosocial/psychobiosocial
Birth to 3 years	Parents and other companions label the child as a boy or a girl, frequently remind the child of his or her gender, and begin to encourage gender-consistent behavior while discouraging cross-sex activities. As a result of these social experiences and the development of very basic classification skills, the young child acquires some gender-typed behavioral preferences and the knowledge that he or she is a boy or a girl (basic gender identity).	Social-learning (differential reinforcement)
3 to 6 years	Once children acquire a basic gender identity, they begin to seek information about sex differences, form gender schemas, and become intrinsically motivated to perform those acts that are viewed as "appropriate" for their own sex. When acquiring gender schemas, children attend to *both* male and female models. Once their gender schemas are well established, these youngsters are likely to imitate behaviors considered appropriate for their sex, regardless of the gender of the model who displays them.	Gender schema
7 to puberty	Children finally acquire a sense of gender consistency—a firm, future-oriented image of themselves as boys who must necessarily become men or girls who will obviously become women. At this point, they begin to rely less exclusively on gender schemas and to look to the behavior of same sex models to acquire those mannerisms and attributes that are consistent with their firm categorization of self as a male or female.	Cognitive-developmental (Kohlberg)
Puberty and beyond	The biological upheavals of adolescence, in conjunction with new social expectations (gender intensification), cause teenagers to reexamine their self-concepts, forming an adult gender identity.	Biosocial/psychobiosocial Social learning Gender schema Cognitive-developmental

opposite ends of a single dimension. If one possessed highly masculine traits, one must be very unfeminine; being highly feminine implied being unmasculine. Bem (1974) challenged this assumption by arguing that individuals of either sex can be characterized by psychological **androgyny**—that is, by a balancing or blending of *both* desirable masculine-stereotyped traits (for example, being assertive, analytical, forceful, and independent) and desirable feminine-stereotyped traits (for example, being affectionate, compassionate, gentle, and understanding). In Bem's model, then, masculinity and femininity are *two separate dimensions* of personality. A male or female who has many desirable masculine-stereotyped traits and few feminine ones is defined as a *masculine gender-typed* person. One who has many feminine- and few masculine-stereotyped traits is said to be *feminine gender typed.* The androgynous person possesses both masculine and feminine traits, whereas the *undifferentiated* individual lacks both of these kinds of attributes (see Figure 13.7).

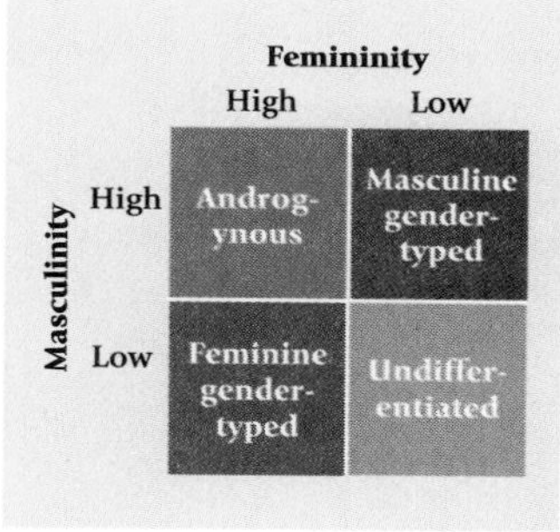

Figure 13.7 *Categories of sex-role orientation based on viewing masculinity and femininity as separate dimensions of personality.*

Do Androgynous People Really Exist?

Bem (1974) and other investigators (Spence & Helmreich, 1978) have developed self-perception inventories that contain both a masculinity (or instrumentality) scale and a femininity (or expressivity) scale. In one large sample of college students (Spence & Helmreich, 1978), roughly 33% of the test takers proved to be "masculine" men or "feminine" women, about 30% were androgynous, and the remaining individuals were either undifferentiated or "sex-reversed" (masculine gender-typed females or feminine gender-typed males). Janet Boldizar (1991) has developed a similar gender-role inventory for grade-school children (see Table 13.6 for sample items) and finds that approximately 25 to 30% of third through seventh graders can be classified as androgynous. So androgynous individuals do exist, and in sizable numbers.

androgyny
a gender-role orientation in which the individual has incorporated a large number of both masculine and feminine attributes into his or her personality.

TABLE 13.6 Sample Items from a Gender-Role Inventory for Grade-school Children

Personality trait	Item
Masculine	
Dominant	I can control a lot of the kids in my class.
Authoritative	I am a leader among my friends.
Self-sufficient	I can take care of myself.
Ambitious	I am willing to work hard to get what I want.
Masculine	I like to do what boys and men do.
Feminine	
Compassionate	I care about what happens to others.
Cheerful	I am a cheerful person.
Loyal	I am faithful to my friends.
Nurturant	I like babies and small children a lot.
Feminine	I like to do what girls and women do.

Format: The child is asked to respond to each item on a four-point scale, with options ranging from 1 = "not at all true of me" to 4 = "very true of me."

SOURCE: Adapted from Boldizar, 1991.

Are There Advantages to Being Androgynous?

When we consider the idea that a person can be both assertive and sensitive, both independent and understanding, we can't help but think that being androgynous is psychologically healthy. Is it? Bem (1975, 1978) demonstrated that androgynous men and women behave more flexibly than more traditionally gender-typed individuals. For example, androgynous people, like masculine gender-typed people, can display the "masculine" instrumental trait of *independence* by resisting social pressure to judge very unamusing cartoons as funny just because their companions do. Yet they are as likely as feminine gender-typed individuals to display the "feminine" expressive quality of *nurturance* by interacting positively with a baby. Androgynous people seem to be more highly adaptable, able to adjust their behavior to the demands of the situation at hand (Shaffer, Pegalis, & Cornell, 1992). Furthermore, androgynous children and adolescents appear to enjoy higher self-esteem and are perceived as more likable and better adjusted than their traditionally gender-typed peers (Allgood-Merten & Stockard, 1991; Boldizar, 1991; O'Heron & Orlofsky, 1990). It has also become clear that androgynous men can still feel quite masculine and androgynous women appropriately feminine even though they sometimes express traits traditionally associated with the other sex (Spence, 1993).

But before we conclude that androgyny is a thoroughly desirable attribute, let's note that it is the possession of "masculine" traits rather than androgyny per se that is most strongly associated with good adjustment and high self-esteem (Spence & Hall, 1996; Whitley, 1983). This finding should not surprise us, for people in many societies value masculine characteristics more highly than feminine attributes (Turner & Gervai, 1995). But even so, there are signs that the times may be changing. In her study of grade-school children, Boldizar (1991) found that (1) androgyny was by far the best single predictor of children's impressions of their global self-worth, and (2) femininity predicted some aspects of self-esteem (physical attractiveness; behavioral conduct) just as well as or better than masculinity did.

? WHAT DO YOU THINK?

In some Islamic societies (for example, Iran), gender roles are much more sharply delineated than is true of Western societies such as our own. Do you think that there are any advantages to being psychologically androgynous in such a society?

So it may be premature to conclude that one is better off in *all* respects to be androgynous rather than masculine or feminine in orientation. But given the behavioral flexibility that androgynous people display and the strong contribution that androgyny makes to children's perceived self-worth, we can safely assume that it is probably adaptive and certainly not harmful for girls and women to become a little more "masculine," and for boys and men to become a little more like women.

Applications: On Changing Gender-Role Attitudes and Behavior

Today, many people believe that the world would be a better place if sexism were eliminated and boys and girls were no longer steered toward adopting confining "masculine" or "feminine" roles. In a nonsexist culture, women would no longer suffer from a lack of assertiveness and confidence in the world of work, and men would be freer to display their sensitive, nurturant sides that many now suppress in the interest of appearing "masculine." How might we reduce sexism and encourage children to be more flexible about the interests and attributes they might display?

Bem (1983; 1989) believes that parents must take an active role by (1) teaching their young children about genital anatomy as part of a larger lesson that one's biological sex is unimportant outside the domain of reproduction, and (2) delaying children's exposure to gender stereotypes by encouraging cross-sex as well as same-sex play and by dividing household chores more equitably (with fathers sometimes cooking and cleaning and mothers gardening or making repairs). If preschoolers come to think of sex as a purely biological attribute and often see themselves and their parents pursuing cross-sex interests and activities, they should be less inclined to construct the rigid gender stereotypes that might otherwise evolve in a highly sexist early environment. Research suggesting that androgynous parents tend to raise androgynous children is consistent with Bem's prescriptions for change (Orlofsky, 1979; see also Weisner & Wilson-Mitchell, 1990). So, too, are findings that children whose mothers work or whose fathers routinely perform "feminine" household and child-care tasks are less aware of gender stereotypes and are more likely to be androgynous themselves, compared with youngsters whose mothers are not employed and whose fathers display more traditional patterns of gender-typed behavior (Hoffman, 1989; Turner & Gervai, 1995).

How might we reach children from more traditional backgrounds, who have already received thousands of gender-stereotyped messages from family members, television, and their peers? Apparently, interventions that simply show children the benefits of cross-gender cooperation or that praise them for playing with other-sex toys and play partners have no lasting effect; children soon retreat to same-sex play and continue to prefer same-sex peers after the interventions are over (Maccoby, 1988). One particularly ambitious program (Guttentag & Bray, 1976) exposed kindergarten, fifth-grade, and ninth-grade students to age-appropriate readings and activities designed to teach them about the capabilities of women and about the problems created by stereotyping and sexism. This program worked quite well with the younger children, particularly the girls, who often became outraged about what they had learned about sexism. However, it actually had a boomerang effect among ninth-grade boys, who seemed to resist the new ideas they were being taught and actually expressed more stereotyped views after the training than before. And although ninth-grade girls took many of the lessons to heart, they still tended to cling to the idea that women should run the family and that men should be the primary breadwinners.

By encouraging and engaging in counterstereotypic activities, parents may deter their children from developing rigid gender stereotypes.

13.4

APPLYING DEVELOPMENTAL RESEARCH

Combatting Gender Stereotypes with Cognitive Interventions

During the preschool period when children are constructing gender schemas, their thinking tends to be intuitive and one-dimensional. As we have seen, children who encounter a violation of their gender schemas, hearing of a boy who likes to cook, for example, are unlikely to process and retain this information. After all, their one-dimensional, intuitive thinking makes it extremely hard to separate the gender-typed activity (cooking) from the gender category (for girls). So the information doesn't compute and is likely to be distorted or forgotten.

Rebecca Bigler and Lynn Liben (1990; 1992) have devised and compared two cognitive interventions aimed at reducing children's gender schematic thinking about the occupations that men and women might pursue. The 5- to 11-year-olds who participated in this research were assigned to one of three conditions:

1. *Rule training.* Through a series of problem-solving discussions, children were taught that (1) the most important considerations in deciding who would perform well at such traditionally masculine and feminine occupations as construction worker and beautician are the person's interests and willingness to learn, and (2) the person's gender was irrelevant.

2. *Classification training.* Children were given multiple classification tasks that required them to sort objects into two categories at once (for example, men and women engaged in masculine and feminine activities). This training was designed to illustrate that objects can be classified in many ways—knowledge that would hopefully help children to see that occupations can be classified independently of the kinds of people who normally enact these roles.

3. *Control group.* Children were simply given lessons on the contributions of various occupations to the community.

Compared with children in the control group, those who either received rule training or who improved in classification skills showed clear declines in occupational stereotyping. Furthermore, later tests of information processing provided further evidence for the weakening of children's stereotypes. Specifically, children who received rule training or who had gained in classification skills after the classification training were much more likely than "control" children to remember counterstereotypic information in stories (for example, recalling that the garbage man in a story was actually a woman). It seems, then, that gender stereotypes can be modified by directly attacking their accuracy (rule training) or by promoting the cognitive skills (classification training) that help children to see the fallacies in their own rigid gender schemas.

Unfortunately, teachers may unwittingly foster gender schematic thinking should they group children on the basis of gender and emphasize gender differences during the first few years of school. In a recent experiment, Bigler (1995) randomly assigned some 6- to 11-year-old summer school students to "gender classrooms" in which teachers created separate boy and girl bulletin boards, seated boys with boys and girls with girls, and often made statements that distinguished boys from girls (for example, "All the boys should be sitting down"; "All the girls put their bubble-makers in the air."). Other children were assigned to classrooms in which teachers were instructed to refer to their pupils only by name and to treat the entire class as a unit. After only 4 weeks, children in the "gender classrooms" endorsed more gender stereotypes than those in control classrooms, particularly if they were one-dimensional thinkers who had trouble understanding that a person can belong to more than one social category at the same time. So it seems that teachers can help to combat gender stereotyping by avoiding grouping pupils on the basis of gender during the early grades, when young one-dimensional thinkers are prone to construct rigid gender schemas.

Interventions that show men and women participating side by side at traditionally "masculine" or traditionally "feminine" occupations can be highly effective at combating rigid gender stereotypes.

Calvin and Hobbes **by Bill Watterson**

CALVIN AND HOBBES © WATTERSON. DIST. BY UNIVERSAL PRESS SYNDICATE. REPRINTED WITH PERMISSION. ALL RIGHTS RESERVED.

This study and others (see Katz & Walsh, 1991, for a review) suggest that efforts to change gender-role attitudes are more effective with younger children than with older ones and possibly with girls than with boys. It makes some sense that it is easier to alter children's thinking early on, before their stereotypes have become fully crystallized; and many researchers now favor *cognitive interventions* that either attack the stereotypes directly or remove constraints on children's thinking that permit them to construct these rigid gender schemas. As we see in Box 13.4, these cognitive interventions can be quite effective indeed.

Finally, there is some evidence that programs designed to modify children's gender-stereotyped attitudes and behaviors may be more effective when the adult in charge is a man (Katz & Walsh, 1991). Why? Possibly because men normally make stronger distinctions between "gender-appropriate" and "gender-inappropriate" behaviors than women do; thus, men may be particularly noteworthy as *agents of change.* In other words, children may feel that cross-gender activities and aspirations are quite legitimate indeed if it is a man who encourages (or fails to discourage) these pursuits.

So new gender-role attitudes can be taught, although it remains to be seen whether such change persists and generalizes to new situations should these attitudes not be reinforced at home or in the culture at large. Sweden is one culture that has made a strong commitment to gender equality: Men and women have the same opportunities to pursue traditionally masculine (or traditionally feminine) careers, and fathers and mothers are viewed as equally responsible for housework and child care. Swedish adolescents still value masculine attributes more highly than feminine characteristics. However, they are much less adamant about it than American adolescents are and are much more inclined to view gender roles as acquired domains of expertise rather than biologically programmed duties (Intons-Peterson, 1988).

Although our society has not made the commitment to gender equality that Sweden has, it is slowly becoming more egalitarian, and some people believe that these changes are having an impact on children (Etaugh, Levine, & Mennella, 1984). Judith Lorber (1986) sees much hope in her 13-year-old's response to her inquiry about whether a pregnant acquaintance of theirs had delivered a boy or girl: "Why do you want to know?" this child of a new era asked (p. 567).

Concept Check 13.3
On Altering Sexist Attitudes

You are an educator who hopes to modify children's rigid gender stereotypes. Design a program based on the research literature that should help you to achieve this objective. One such program is described in the Appendix.

SUMMARY

◆ **Gender typing** is the process by which children acquire a gender identity as well as the motives, values, and behaviors considered appropriate in their society for members of their biological sex.

Categorizing Males and Females: Gender-Role Standards

◆ A **gender-role standard** is a motive, value, or behavior considered more appropriate for members of one sex than the other. Many societies are characterized by a gender-based division of labor in which females are encouraged to adopt an **expressive role** and males an **instrumental role.**

Some Facts and Fictions about Sex Differences

◆ Girls outperform boys in many assessments of verbal ability and are more emotionally expressive, compliant, and timid than boys are. Boys are more active and more physically and verbally aggressive than girls and tend to outperform girls on tests of arithmetic reasoning and **visual/spatial skills.** In all, however, these sex differences are small, and males and females are far more psychologically similar than they are different.

◆ Of the many traditional gender-role stereotypes that have no basis in fact are the notions that females are more sociable, suggestible, and illogical and less analytical and achievement oriented than males. The persistence of these "cultural myths" can create **self-fulfilling prophecies** that promote sex differences in cognitive performance and steer males and females along different career paths.

Developmental Trends in Gender Typing

◆ By age 2½ to 3, children firmly label themselves as boys or girls, taking their first step in the development of **gender identity.** Between ages 5 and 7, they come to realize that gender is an unchanging aspect of self.

◆ Children begin to learn gender-role stereotypes at about the same age that they display a basic gender identity. By age 10 to 11, children's stereotyping of male and female personality traits rivals that of an adult. At first, stereotypes are viewed as obligatory prescriptions, but children become more flexible in their thinking about gender during middle childhood before becoming somewhat more rigid once again during the adolescent period of **gender intensification.**

◆ Even before reaching basic gender identity, many toddlers display gender-typed toy and activity preferences. By age 3, they display **gender segregation** by preferring to spend time with same-sex associates and developing clear prejudices against members of the other sex. Boys face stronger gender-typing pressures than girls do and are quicker to develop gender-typed toy and activity preferences.

Theories of Gender Typing and Gender-Role Development

◆ Money and Ehrhardt's biosocial theory emphasizes biological developments that occur before birth and influence the way a child is socialized. The behavior of **androgenized females** implies that prenatal androgen levels may contribute to sex differences in play styles, and males' heightened levels of testosterone may contribute to sex differences in aggression. Yet, the development of children raised as members of the other sex (for example, those with **testicular feminization syndrome)** illustrates that social labeling and gender-role socialization play a crucial role in determining one's gender identity and role preferences.

◆ Freud believed that children become gender typed as they **identify** with the same-sex parent during the **phallic stage** of development in order to resolve their **Oedipus** or **Electra complexes.** However, several lines of research have failed to confirm Freud's theory.

◆ Consistent with social learning theory, children acquire many of their earliest gender typed toy and activity preferences through **direct tuition** (or differential reinforcement). *Observational learning* also contributes to gender typing as preschool children attend to models of *both sexes* and become increasingly aware of gender stereotypes.

◆ Kohlberg's cognitive-developmental theory claims that children are self-socializers who must pass through **basic gender identity** and **gender stability** before reaching **gender consistency,** the point at which they begin to selectively attend to same-sex models and become gender typed. However, research consistently reveals that gender typing begins much earlier than Kohlberg thought and that measures of gender consistency do not predict the strength of gender typing.

◆ According to Martin and Halverson's *gender schema* theory, children who have established a basic gender identity construct **in-group/out-group** and **own-sex gender schemas,** which serve as scripts for processing gender-related information and socializing themselves into gender roles. Schema-consistent information is gathered and retained, whereas schema-inconsistent information is ignored or distorted, thus perpetuating gender stereotypes that have no basis in fact.

◆ The best account of gender typing is an eclectic, integrative theory that recognizes that processes emphasized in biosocial, social learning, cognitive-developmental, and gender schema theories all contribute to gender-role development.

Psychological Androgyny: A Prescription for the Future?

◆ The psychological attributes "masculinity" and "femininity" are generally considered to be at opposite ends of a single dimension. However, one new look at gender roles proposes that masculinity and femininity are two separate dimensions and that the **androgynous** person is someone who possesses a fair number of masculine *and* feminine characteristics. Recent research shows that androgynous people do exist, are relatively popular and well adjusted, and may be adaptable to a wider variety of environmental demands than people who are traditionally gender typed.

◆ Parents and teachers (particularly males) may prevent rigid sex typing by emphasizing that one's sex is largely irrelevant outside the domain of reproduction, by encouraging and modeling other-sex as well as same-sex activities, and by highlighting and discussing the many exceptions to any unfounded gender stereotypes that children may have acquired.

The U.S. Census Bureau and the Bureau of Labor Statistics have both reported that women tend to be underrepresented in professions that require a math or science background. By visiting: http://math.rice.edu/~lanius/club/girls.html you can find suggestions for helping girls develop an interest in science or computing. This site is part of a teacher training program designed to include girls in computing, without excluding boys.

KEY TERMS

gender typing, 473
gender-role standard, 474
expressive role, 474
instrumental role, 474
visual/spatial abilities, 475
self-fulfilling prophecy, 481
gender identity, 482
gender intensification, 485
gender segregation, 485
testicular feminization syndrome (TFS), 489
timing-of-puberty effect, 490
congenital adrenal hyperplasia (CAH), 491
androgenized females, 491
phallic stage, 495
identification, 495
castration anxiety, 495
Oedipus complex, 495
Electra complex, 495
direct tuition, 495
basic gender identity, 497
gender stability, 497
gender consistency, 497
gender schemas, 498
in-group/out-group schema, 498
own-sex schema, 498
androgyny, 501

Aggression, Altruism, and Moral Development

What would *you* say is the most important aspect of a child's social development? Surely this is a question that might generate any number of answers. But when one sample of new parents encountered this item in a child-rearing survey conducted by one of my laboratory classes, 74% of them indicated that they hoped, above all, that their children would acquire a strong sense of *morality*—right and wrong—to guide their transactions with other people.

When then asked what sort of moral principles they hoped to instill, these new parents provided many answers. However, most of their responses fit into one of the following three categories:

1. *Avoid hurting others.* Parents generally hoped their children could learn to become appropriately autonomous and to serve their needs without harming others. In fact, unprovoked and intentional acts of harmdoing—or *aggression*—was one class of behavior that most parents said they would try to suppress.
2. *Prosocial concern.* Another value that many parents hoped to instill was a sense of *altruism*—that is, a selfless concern for the welfare of other people and a willingness to act on that concern. In fact, it is not at all unusual for parents to encourage such altruistic acts as sharing, comforting, or helping others while their children are still in diapers.
3. *A personal commitment to abide by rules.* Finally, almost all of our survey respondents mentioned the importance of persuading children to comply with socially condoned rules of conduct and monitoring their behavior to ensure that these rules are followed. They felt that the ultimate goal of this *moral socialization* is to help the child acquire a set of *personal* values, or ethical principles, that will enable her to distinguish right from wrong and to do the "right" things, even when there may be no one else present to monitor and evaluate her conduct.

This chapter explores these three interrelated aspects of social development that people often consider when making judgments about one's moral character. We begin with the topic of aggression by asking how it develops and changes over time and then considering some of the ways that adults might effectively control such conduct. Our focus will then shift from harmdoing to a seemingly incompatible form of social activity—altruism and prosocial behavior—as we consider how young and reputedly selfish children might learn to make personal sacrifices to benefit others. Finally, we turn to the broader issue of moral development as we trace the child's evolution from a seemingly self-indulgent creature who appears to respect no rules to a moral philosopher of sorts who has internalized certain ethical principles to evaluate his own and others' conduct.

THE DEVELOPMENT OF AGGRESSION

What qualifies as **aggression**? According to the most widely accepted definition, an aggressive act is any form of behavior designed to harm or injure a living being who is motivated to avoid such treatment (Baron & Byrne, 1994). Notice that it is the actor's *intent* that defines an act as "aggressive," not the act's consequences. So this *intentional definition* would classify as aggressive all acts in which harm was intended but not done (for example, a violent kick that misses its target; an undetected snub) while excluding accidental harmdoing or rough-and-tumble play in which participants are enjoying themselves with no harmful intent.

Aggressive acts are often divided into two categories: **hostile aggression** and **instrumental aggression.** If an actor's major goal is to harm a victim, his or her behavior qualifies as hostile aggression. By contrast, instrumental aggression describes those situations in which one person harms another as a means to some other end.

aggression
behavior performed with the intention of harming a living being who is motivated to avoid this treatment.

hostile aggression
aggressive acts for which the perpetrator's major goal is to harm or injure a victim.

instrumental aggression
aggressive acts for which the perpetrator's major goal is to gain access to objects, space, or privileges.

Clearly, the same overt act could be classified as either hostile or instrumental aggression depending on the circumstances. If a young boy clobbered his sister and then teased her for crying, we might consider this hostile aggression. But these same actions could be labeled instrumentally aggressive (or a mixture of hostile and instrumental aggression) had the boy also grabbed a toy that his sister was using.

Origins of Aggression in Infancy

Although young infants get angry and may occasionally strike people, it is difficult to think of these actions as having an aggressive intent. Piaget (1952) describes an incident in which he frustrated 7-month-old Laurent by placing his hand in front of an interesting object that Laurent was trying to reach. The boy then smacked Piaget's hand, as if it merely represented an obstruction that must be removed.

However, the picture soon changes. Marlene Caplan and her associates (1991) found that 1-year-old infants can be quite forceful with each other when one infant controls a toy that the other wants. Even when duplicate toys were available, 12-month-olds occasionally ignored these unused objects and tried to overpower a peer in order to control *that child's* toy. And the intimidators in these tussles appeared to be treating the other child as an *adversary* rather than an inanimate obstacle, implying that the seeds of instrumental aggression may already have been sown by the end of the first year.

Although 2-year-olds have just as many (or more) conflicts over toys as 1-year-olds do, they are more likely than 1-year-olds to resolve these disputes by negotiating and sharing than by fighting, particularly when toys are in short supply (Caplan et al., 1991). So early conflicts need not be training grounds for aggression and can even be adaptive, serving as a context in which infants, toddlers, and preschool children can learn to negotiate and achieve their aims without resorting to shows of force—especially when adults intervene and encourage harmonious means of conflict resolution (Perlman & Ross, 1997). Indeed, Japanese mothers are especially intolerant of harmdoing and encourage their children to suppress anger in the interest of promoting social harmony. As a result, Japanese *preschoolers* are already less angered by interpersonal conflicts and less likely to respond aggressively to them than American children are (Zahn-Waxler et al., 1996).

Developmental Trends in Aggression

The squabbles of young children usually center around toys, candy, or other treasured resources and qualify as examples of instrumental aggression.

The character of children's aggression changes dramatically with age. In her classic study of the development of aggression among preschoolers, Florence Goodenough (1931) asked mothers of 2- to 5-year-olds to keep diaries in which they recorded the details of their children's angry outbursts. In examining these data, Goodenough found that unfocused temper tantrums become less and less common between ages 2 and 3 as children began to *physically retaliate* (by hitting or kicking) when playmates frustrated or attacked them. However, physical aggression gradually declined between ages 3 and 5, only to be replaced by teasing, tattling, name-calling, and other forms of verbal aggression. What were these preschoolers squabbling about? Goodenough found that they fought most often over toys and other possessions, so that their aggression was usually *instrumental* in character. And though the majority of tussles among older (4- to 7-year-old) children are still centered around the control of objects, Willard Hartup (1974) found that an increasing percentage of their aggressive outbursts are *hostile* exchanges designed primarily to harm an adversary.

One reason that hostile aggression increases with age is that older children are acquiring the role-taking skills to better infer others' *harmful intent*—to which they sometimes react by retaliating against the harmdoer (Coie et al., 1991; Hartup, 1974).

As children mature, an increasing percentage of their aggressive acts qualify as examples of hostile aggression.

In fact, grade-school children (particularly boys) are reluctant to condemn this **retaliatory aggression,** often viewing "fighting back" as a normal (though not necessarily moral) response to provocation (Astor, 1994; Coie et al., 1991).

Sex Differences

Although the trends we've described hold for both boys and girls, data from more than 100 countries around the world reveal that boys and men are more physically and more verbally aggressive, on average, than girls and women are (Harris, 1992; Maccoby & Jacklin, 1974). As we noted in Chapter 13, boys' higher levels of male sex hormones—namely, testosterone—may contribute to sex differences in aggression. Yet, proponents of a social learning viewpoint are quick to point out that very young boys are *not* more aggressive than girls. Marlene Caplan and her associates (1991), for example, found that forceful, aggressive resolutions of disputes over toys were actually more numerous among 1-year-olds when the play groups were dominated *by girls!* Even at age 2, groups dominated by boys were more likely than those dominated by girls to negotiate and share when toys were scarce. It is not until age 2½ to 3 that sex differences in aggression are reliable, and this is clearly enough time for gender-typing to have steered boys and girls in different directions (Fagot, Leinbach, & O'Boyle, 1992).

What social influences might conspire to make boys more aggressive than girls? For one, parents play rougher with boys than with girls and react more negatively to the aggressive behaviors of daughters than to those of sons (Mills & Rubin, 1990; Parke & Slaby, 1983). Furthermore, the ray-guns, tanks, missile launchers, and other symbolic implements of destruction that boys often receive as gifts encourage the enactment of aggressive themes—and actually promote aggressive behavior (Feshbach, 1956; Watson & Peng, 1992). During the preschool years, children came to view aggression as a male attribute in their gender schemas; and by middle childhood, boys expect aggressive acts to provide them with more tangible benefits and to elicit less disapproval from either parents or peers than girls do (Hertzberger & Hall, 1993; Perry, Perry, & Weiss, 1989). So even though biological factors may contribute, it is clear that sex differences in aggression depend to no small extent on gender typing and gender differences in social learning.

One final point: Some investigators today believe that boys may appear much more aggressive than girls because researchers have focused on overt aggressive behaviors and have failed to consider *covertly* hostile acts that may be more common among girls than boys. The research in Box 14.1 clearly supports this point of view.

retaliatory aggression
aggressive acts elicited by real or imagined provocations.

FOCUS ON RESEARCH

14.1

How Girls Are More Aggressive Than Boys

Recently, Nicki Crick and Jennifer Grotpeter (1995) proposed that both boys and girls can be quite hostile and aggressive, but they display their aggression in very different ways. Boys, who often pursue competitive, instrumental goals, are likely to strike, insult, or display other *overt* forms of aggression toward others who displease them or who interfere with their objectives. Girls, by contrast, are more likely to focus on *expressive* or *relational* goals—on establishing close, intimate connections with others rather than attempting to compete with or dominate their associates. So Crick and Grotpeter proposed that girls' aggressive behavior would be more consistent with the *social* goals they pursue, consisting largely of covert forms of **relational aggression**—actions such as withdrawing acceptance of an adversary, excluding her from one's social network, or taking some sort of action (for example, spreading rumors) that might damage her friendships or general status in the peer group.

To test this hypothesis, 3rd- through 6th-graders were asked to nominate classmates who often displayed (1) overtly aggressive acts (for example, hitting or insulting others) and (2) *relationally manipulative* acts (for example, withdrawing acceptance; snubbing or excluding others). As we see in the figure, far more boys than girls were viewed as high in overt aggression—a finding that replicates past research. However, far more girls than boys were perceived to be high in relational aggression. Clearly, such subtle or indirect expressions of hostility may be difficult at times for victims to detect, and may thus allow the perpetrator to behave aggressively while avoiding open conflict. Even 3- to 5-year-old girls are learning this lesson, for they are already more inclined than preschool boys are to try to exclude rather than hit a peer who provokes them (Crick, Casas, & Mosher, 1997; Crick et al., 1998).

Do other children perceive these attempts to undermine a person's status or the quality of his or her personal relationships as clear examples of aggression? Crick and her associates (1996) addressed this issue by asking 9- to 12-year-olds to indicate the ways in which peers of each sex try to get back at or "to be mean to" someone who makes them mad. Overwhelmingly, children said that boys will hit or insult their adversaries, whereas they felt that the most likely response for girls was to try to undermine an adversary's social standing. So children clearly do view these relationally manipulative acts as harmful and "aggressive"—a viewpoint that grows even stronger among adolescents (Galen & Underwood, 1997). Furthermore, girls who frequently display relational aggression are often lonely and are rejected by their peers in much the same way that boys high in overt aggression are at risk of poor peer relations (McNeilly-Choque et al., 1996; Tomada & Schneider, 1997).

In sum, boys and girls often tend to express their hostilities in very different ways. Since most prior research on children's aggression has focused on physical and verbal assaults and has largely ignored relationally manipulative acts, it clearly underestimates girls' aggressive inclinations.

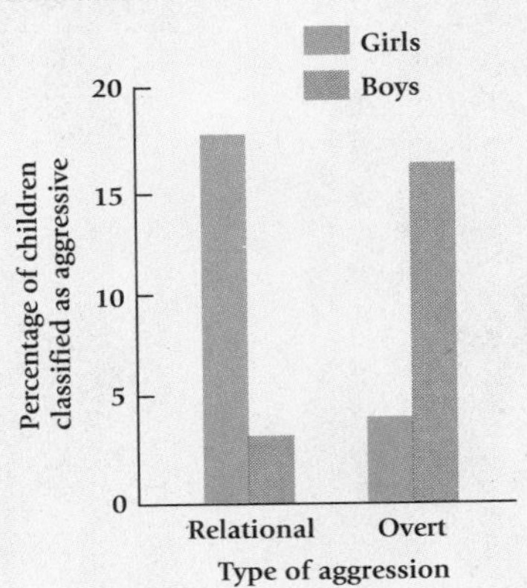

Percentage of girls and boys nominated by classmates as high in relationally manipulative behaviors and overt aggression (physical or verbal assaults) by a sample of 3rd- through 6th-graders.
ADAPTED FROM CRICK & GROTPETER, 1995.

From Aggression to Antisocial Conduct

The incidence of hostile and other overt, easily detectable forms of aggression peaks early in adolescence (at ages 13–15) and gradually declines (Cairns et al., 1989; Loeber & Stouthamer-Loeber, 1998). However, this does not necessarily mean that adolescents are becoming any better behaved. Apparently relational aggression in girls becomes more widespread, more subtle, and more malicious during the adolescent period (Bjorkqvist, Lagerspetz, & Kaukiainen, 1992; Galen & Underwood, 1997), and teenage boys become more inclined to express their anger and frustrations indirectly, through such acts as theft, truancy, substance abuse, and sexual misconduct (U.S. Department of Justice, 1995). So it seems that adolescents who are becoming less overtly aggressive may simply turn to other forms of antisocial conduct to express their aggressive impulses.

relational aggression
acts such as snubbing, exclusion, withdrawing acceptance, or spreading rumors that are aimed at damaging an adversary's self-esteem, friendships, or social status.

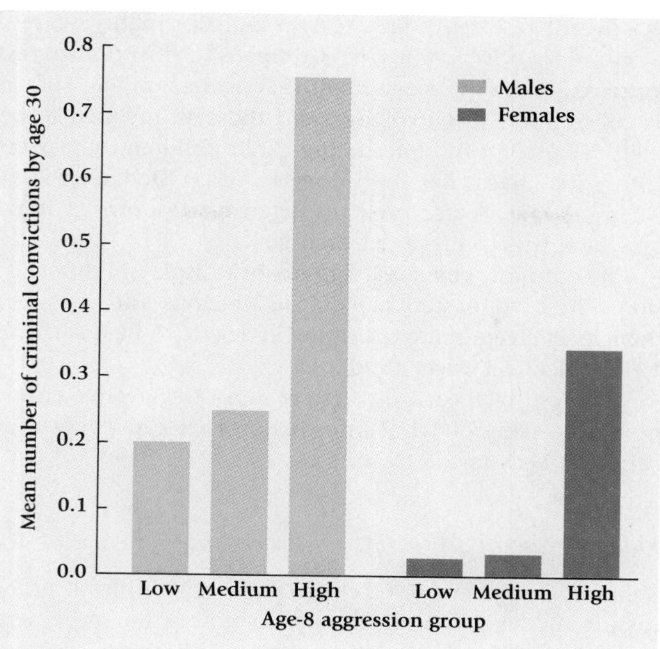

Figure 14.1 *Aggression in childhood predicts criminal behavior in adulthood for both males and females.* *From Huesmann, Eron, Lefkowitz, & Walder, 1984.*

Is Aggressiveness a Stable Attribute?

Apparently, aggression is a reasonably stable attribute. Not only are aggressive toddlers likely to become aggressive 5-year-olds (Cummings, Iannotti, & Zahn-Waxler, 1989), but longitudinal research conducted in Iceland, New Zealand, and the United States reveals that the amount of moody, ill-tempered, and aggressive behavior that children display between ages 3 and 10 is a fairly good predictor of their aggressive or other antisocial inclinations later in life (Hart et al., 1997; Henry et al., 1996; Newman et al., 1997). Rowell Huesman and his associates (1984), for example, tracked one group of 600 participants for 22 years. As we see in Figure 14.1, highly aggressive 8-year-olds often became relatively hostile 30-year-olds who were likely to batter their spouses or children and to be convicted of criminal offenses.

Clearly, these findings reflect group trends and do not necessarily imply that all highly aggressive children remain highly aggressive over time. Yet, we should not be surprised to find that aggression is a reasonably stable attribute for many children. Twin studies imply that some individuals are genetically predisposed to be temperamentally irritable and to partake in aggressive behaviors and other antisocial acts (Plomin, 1990; Rushton et al., 1986). And regardless of their genetic predispositions, other children may remain highly aggressive because they are raised in social environments that *nurture* and *maintain* aggressive habits (Bandura, 1991; Dodge, 1993). Before examining these "training grounds" for aggression, let's briefly consider the characteristics that aggressive children display.

Individual Differences in Aggressive Behavior

Although children vary dramatically in their levels of aggression, only a small percentage can be described as chronically aggressive. In fact, some researchers who have charted aggressive incidents among grade-school and high-school students find that a small minority of youngsters are involved in a large majority of the conflicts. Who is involved? In many groups, the participants are a handful of highly aggressive instigators and the 10 to 15% of their classmates who are regularly abused by these bullies (Olweus, 1984; Perry, Kusel, & Perry, 1988).

Recent research points to two kinds of highly aggressive children: *proactive aggressors* and *reactive aggressors*. Compared with nonaggressive youngsters, **proactive aggressors** are quite confident that aggression will "pay off" in tangible benefits (such as control of a disputed toy), and they are inclined to believe that they can enhance their self-esteem by dominating other children, who generally submit to them before any serious harm has been done (Crick & Dodge, 1996; Quiggle et al., 1992; Slaby & Guerra, 1988). So for proactive aggressors, shows of force are an *instrumental* strategy by which they achieve personal goals.

By contrast, **reactive aggressors** display high levels of hostile, retaliatory aggression. These youngsters are quite suspicious and wary of other people, often viewing them as belligerent adversaries who *deserve* to be dealt with in a forceful manner (Astor, 1994; Crick & Dodge, 1996).

Interestingly, each of these groups of aggressive children displays distinct biases in their processing of social information that contribute to their high levels of aggressive behavior. Let's take a closer look.

Dodge's Social Information-Processing Theory of Aggression

Kenneth Dodge (1986; Crick & Dodge, 1994) has formulated a social information-processing model that seeks to explain how children come to favor aggressive or nonaggressive solutions to social problems. To illustrate, let's suppose that a child is harmed under somewhat ambiguous circumstances, as a peer nudges his table and says "Oops!", scattering the child's nearly completed jigsaw puzzle. As shown in Figure 14.2, the child who is harmed first encodes and interprets the available social cues (What is the harmdoer's reaction? Did he/she mean to do it?). After interpreting the meaning of these cues, the child then formulates a goal (to resolve the situation), thinks about and evaluates possible strategies for achieving this goal, selects a response and then enacts it.

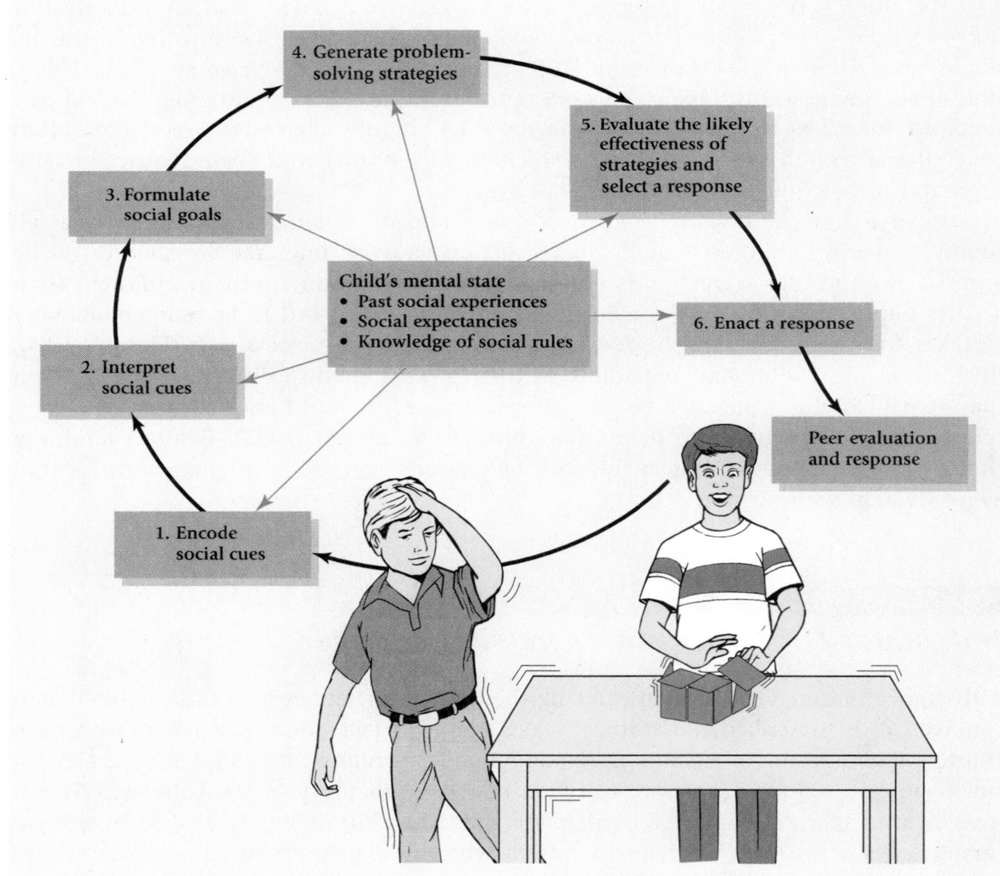

Figure 14.2 *Dodge's social information-processing model of the steps children take when deciding how to respond to harmdoing or other social problems. The boy whose creation is destroyed by the other boy's nudging the table must first encode and interpret the social cues (i.e., did he mean it or was it accidental?) and then proceed through the remaining steps to formulate a response to this harmdoing.* ADAPTED FROM CRICK AND DODGE, 1994.

proactive aggressors
highly aggressive children who find aggressive acts easy to perform and who rely heavily on aggression as a means of solving social problems or achieving other personal objectives.

reactive aggressors
children who display high levels of hostile, retaliatory aggression because they overattribute hostile intents to others and can't control their anger long enough to seek nonaggressive solutions to social problems.

Notice that the model proposes that a child's *mental state*—that is, his or her past social experiences, social expectancies, and knowledge of social rules—can influence any of the model's six phases of information processing.

According to Dodge, the mental states of *reactive aggressors,* who have a history of bickering with peers, are likely to include an expectancy that "others are hostile to me." So when harmed under ambiguous circumstances (such as having their puzzle scattered by a careless peer), they are much more inclined than nonaggressive children to (1) search for and find cues compatible with this expectancy, (2) attribute hostile intent to the harmdoer, and (3) become very angry and quickly retaliate in a hostile manner without carefully considering other nonaggressive solutions. Not only does research consistently indicate that reactive aggressors overattribute hostile intent to peers (Crick & Dodge, 1996; Dodge, 1980), but by virtue of their own hostile retaliations, these children have many negative experiences with teachers and peers (Dodge et al., 1990; Trachtenberg & Viken, 1994), who come to dislike them, thereby reinforcing their expectancy that "others are hostile to me" (see Figure 14.3). Interestingly, girls can be as reactively aggressive as boys, displaying the same kind of **hostile attributional bias** and a strong readiness to react aggressively to ambiguous harmdoing (Crick & Dodge, 1996; Guerra & Slaby, 1990).

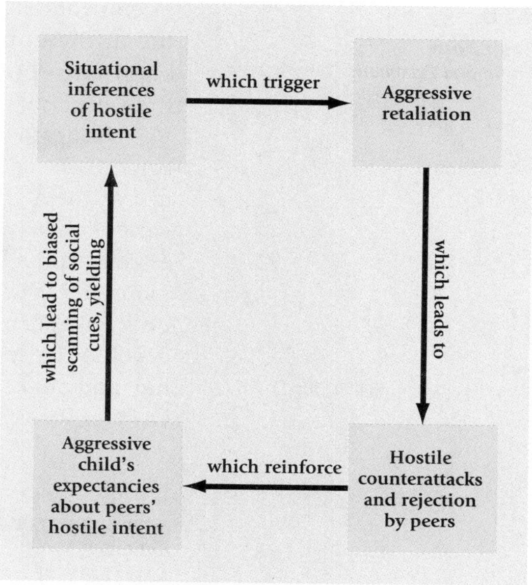

Figure 14.3 *A social-cognitive model of the reactive aggressor's biased attributions about ambiguous harmdoing and their behavioral outcomes.*

Proactive aggressors display a different pattern of social information processing. Rather than quickly attributing hostile intent when harmed under ambiguous circumstances, these children are more inclined to carefully formulate an *instrumental* goal (for example, I'll teach careless peers to be more careful around me) and to *consciously decide* that an aggressive response is likely to be most effective at achieving this aim. Their mental states favor aggressive solutions to conflict because they expect positive outcomes to result from their use of force, and they feel quite capable of dominating their adversaries (Crick & Dodge, 1996).

Perpetrators and Victims of Peer Aggression

Each of us has probably known at least one victimized peer—a youngster who repeatedly serves as a target for other children's hostile acts. Who are these children and who singles them out for abuse?

Research with Swedish male adolescents (Olweus, 1984; 1993) and American grade-school children of both sexes (Kochenderfer & Ladd, 1996; Perry et al., 1988) provides some clues. Based on teacher ratings, about 10% of Olweus's adolescent sample could be described as habitual bullies who regularly subjected another 10% of the sample (their whipping boys) to physical and verbal harassment. Victimization rates are even higher among younger children; about one child in five reports moderate to high levels of victimization in kindergarten (Kochenderfer & Ladd, 1996), and grade-school girls bully other girls and are victimized (usually in verbally aggressive ways) about as often as grade-school boys are (Pepler & Craig, 1995; Perry et al., 1988). Habitual bullies have often observed adult conflict and aggression at home but have rarely themselves been the target of aggression (Schwartz et al., 1997). Their home experiences suggest that aggression pays off, and they come to view victims as "easy marks" who will surrender tangible resources or otherwise submit to their dominance without putting up much of a fight. So bullies appear to harass their victims for personal or instrumental reasons (Olweus, 1993) and are usually classifiable as *proactive* aggressors.

Although chronic victims are generally disliked by their peers (Boivin & Hymel, 1997), they are not at all alike. Most are *passive victims* who are socially withdrawn, physically weak, reluctant to fight back, and appear to do little (other than being "easy marks") to invite the hostilities they receive (Olweus, 1993). But a smaller number in both Olweus's Swedish sample and Perry's American sample could be described as *provocative victims*—that is, oppositional, restless, and hot-tempered individuals who

hostile attributional bias
tendency to view harm done under ambiguous circumstances as having stemmed from a hostile intent on the part of the harmdoer; characterizes reactive aggressors.

often irritated peers, were inclined to fight back (unsuccessfully), and displayed the hostile attributional bias that characterizes reactive aggressors. Provocative victims have often been physically abused or otherwise victimized at home and have learned from their experiences to view other people as hostile adversaries (Schwartz et al., 1997).

Unfortunately, many children and adolescents who become chronic victims continue to be victimized, especially if they have no friends who are capable of sticking up for them (Hodges, Malone, & Perry, 1997). And victimized children are at risk for a variety of adjustment problems, including loneliness, anxiety, depression, low self-esteem, and a growing dislike for and avoidance of school (Ladd, Kochenderfer, & Coleman, 1997; Olweus, 1993). Clearly there is a pressing need for interventions that not only take strong steps to discourage bullying, but that also help chronic victims to develop the social skills and supportive friendships that will improve their social standing and make them less inviting targets for their tormentors (Hodges et al., 1997; Olweus, 1993).

Cultural and Subcultural Influences on Aggression

Cross-cultural studies consistently indicate that some societies and subcultures are more violent and aggressive than others. Peoples such as the Arapesh of New Guinea, the Lepchas of Sikkim, and the Pygmies of central Africa all use weapons to hunt but rarely show any kind of interpersonal aggression. When these peace-loving societies are invaded by outsiders, their members retreat to inaccessible regions rather than stand and fight (Gorer, 1968).

In marked contrast to these groups are the Gebusi of New Guinea, who teach their children to be combative and emotionally unresponsive to the needs of others and who show a murder rate that is more than 50 times higher than that of any industrialized nation (Scott, 1992). The United States is also an "aggressive" society. On a percentage basis, the incidence of rape, homicide, and assault is higher in the United States than in any other industrialized nation, and the U.S. ranks a close second to Spain (and far above third-place Canada) in the incidence of armed robbery (Wolff, Rutten, & Bayer, 1992).

Studies conducted in the United States and in England also point to social-class differences in aggression: Children and adolescents from the lower socioeconomic strata, particularly males from larger urban areas, exhibit more aggressive behavior and higher levels of delinquency than their age-mates from the middle class (see Atwater, 1992; Feshbach, 1970, for reviews). African-American males, in particular, are overrepresented among school-aged children labeled as aggressive and among juveniles arrested for delinquency—so much so that researchers who study childhood aggression often include large numbers of black males in their samples (Graham et al., 1992). Yet, this finding may simply reflect the fact that more African Americans live in poverty, for other researchers are finding that economically disadvantaged white children and adolescents are every bit as aggressive and are just as inclined to commit violent crimes as disadvantaged African Americans are (Farrington, 1987; Dodge, Pettit, & Bates, 1994).

Several factors contribute to social class differences in aggression and antisocial conduct. For example, parents from lower-income families are more likely than middle-class parents to rely on physical punishment to discipline aggression and noncompliance, thereby *modeling aggression* even as they try to suppress it (Dodge et al., 1994; Patterson, DeBaryshe, & Ramsey, 1989; Sears et al., 1957). A child who learns that he will be hit, kicked, or shoved when he displeases his parents will probably direct the same kinds of responses toward playmates who displease him (Hart, Ladd, & Burleson, 1990). Low-SES parents are also more inclined to endorse aggressive

WHAT DO YOU THINK?

Why do you think that the incidence of violent crimes such as murder and rape are nearly twice as high in the relatively affluent United States as in the countries ranked second for each of these offenses (that is, Canada for murder and Sweden for rape; Wolff et al., 1992)? How might you evaluate your hypotheses?

solutions to conflict and to encourage their children to respond forcefully when provoked by peers (Dodge et al., 1994; Jagers, Bingham, & Hans, 1996)—practices that may foster the development of the *hostile attributional bias* that highly aggressive youngsters so often display. Finally, low-SES parents often live complex, stressful lives that may make it difficult for them to manage or monitor their children's whereabouts, activities, and choice of friends. Unfortunately, this lack of parental monitoring is consistently associated with such aggressive or delinquent activities as fighting, disobeying teachers, destroying property, using drugs, and generally breaking rules outside the home (Barber, Olsen, & Shagle, 1994; Patterson, 1993), especially when members of a child's or adolescent's peer group are inclined to endorse antisocial conduct (Mason et al., 1996).

Antisocial or delinquent conduct is rather common among teenagers whose parents fail to monitor their activities, whereabouts, and choice of friends.

In sum, a person's aggressive or antisocial inclinations depend, in part, on the extent to which the culture or subculture condones or fails to discourage such behavior. Yet not all people in pacifistic societies are kind, cooperative, and helpful, and the vast majority of people raised in relatively aggressive societies or subcultures are not especially prone to violence. Why are there such dramatic individual differences in aggression within a given culture or subculture? Gerald Patterson and his associates answer by claiming that highly aggressive children often live in homes that can be described as "breeding grounds" for hostile, antisocial conduct.

Coercive Home Environments: Breeding Grounds for Aggression and Delinquency

Patterson (1982; Patterson, Reid, & Dishion, 1992) has observed patterns of interaction among children and their parents in families that have at least one highly aggressive child. The aggressive children in Patterson's sample seemed "out of control"; they fought a lot at home and at school and were generally unruly and defiant. These families were then compared with other families of the same size and socioeconomic status that had no problem children.

Families as Social Systems

Patterson soon discovered that he could not explain "out of control" behavior by merely focusing on the child-rearing practices that parents used. Instead, it seemed that highly aggressive children lived in rather atypical family environments that were characterized by a social climate that *they had helped to create.* Unlike most homes, where people frequently display approval and affection, the highly aggressive problem child usually lived in a setting in which family members were constantly bickering with one another. They were reluctant to initiate conversations, and, when they did talk, they tended to needle, threaten, or otherwise irritate other family members rather than conversing amiably. Patterson called these settings **coercive home environments** because a high percentage of interactions centered on one family member's attempts

coercive home environment
a home in which family members often annoy one another and use aggressive or otherwise antisocial tactics as a method of coping with these aversive experiences.

to force another to stop irritating him or her. He also noted that **negative reinforcement** was important in maintaining these coercive interactions: When one family member makes life unpleasant for another, the second learns to whine, yell, tease, or hit because these actions often force the antagonist to stop (and thus are reinforced). Consider the following sequence of events, which may be fairly typical in a coercive home environment:

1. A girl teases her older brother, who makes her stop teasing by yelling at her (yelling is negatively reinforced).
2. A few minutes later, the girl calls her brother a nasty name. The boy then chases and hits her.
3. The girl stops calling him names (which negatively reinforces hitting). She then whimpers and hits him back, and he withdraws (negatively reinforcing her hits). The boy then approaches and hits his sister again, and the conflict escalates.
4. At this point, the mother intervenes. However, her children are too emotionally disrupted to listen to reason, so she finds herself applying punitive and coercive tactics to make them stop fighting.
5. The fighting stops (thus reinforcing the mother for using coercive methods). However, the children soon begin to whine, cry, or yell at the mother. These countercoercive techniques are then reinforced if the mother backs off and accepts peace at any price. Unfortunately, backing off is only a temporary solution. The next time the children antagonize each other and become involved in an unbearable conflict, the mother is likely to use even more coercion to get them to stop. The children once again apply their own methods of countercoercion to induce her to "lay off," and the family atmosphere becomes increasingly unpleasant for everyone.

Mothers of problem children rarely use social approval as a means of behavior control, choosing instead to largely ignore prosocial conduct, interpret many innocuous acts as antisocial, and rely almost exclusively on coercive tactics to deal with perceived misconduct (Patterson et al., 1992; Strassberg, 1995). Perhaps the overwhelmingly negative treatment that these problem children receive at home (including parents' tendency to label ambiguous events as antisocial) helps to explain why they generally mistrust other people and display the *hostile attributional bias* so commonly observed among highly aggressive children (Dishion, 1990; Weiss et al., 1992)). And ironically, children from highly coercive home environments eventually become resistant to punishment. They have learned to fight coercion with countercoercion and often do so by defying the parent and *repeating the very act that she is trying to suppress.* Why? Because this is one of the few ways that the child can successfully command the attention of an adult who rarely offers praise or shows any signs of affection. No wonder Patterson calls these children "out of control"! By contrast, children from noncoercive families receive much more positive attention from siblings and parents, so that they don't have to irritate other family members to be noticed (Patterson, 1982).

So we see that the flow of influence in the family setting is *multidirectional:* Coercive *interactions* between parents and their children and the children themselves affect the behavior of *all* parties and contribute to the development of a hostile family environment—a true breeding ground for aggression. Unfortunately, these problem families may never break out of this destructive pattern of attacking and counterattacking one another unless they receive help. In Box 14.2, we consider one particularly effective approach to this problem—a method that necessarily focuses on the family as a social system rather than simply on the aggressive child who has been referred for treatment.

Coercive Home Environments as Contributors to Chronic Delinquency

How serious are the risks faced by "out of control" children who grow up in a coercive home environment? Patterson and his associates (1989) have addressed this issue by reviewing the literature on problem children and have drawn some strong conclusions.

negative reinforcer
any stimulus whose removal or termination as the consequence of an act increases the probability that the act will recur.

14.2 APPLYING DEVELOPMENTAL RESEARCH

Helping Children (and Parents) Who Are "Out of Control"

How does one treat a problem child who is hostile, defiant, and "out of control"? Rather than focusing on the problem child, Gerald Patterson's (1981, 1982) approach is to work with the entire family. Patterson begins by carefully observing the family's interactions and determining just how family members are reinforcing one another's coercive activities. The next step is to describe the nature of the problem to parents and to teach them a new approach to managing their children's behavior. Some of the principles, skills, and procedures that Patterson stresses are the following:

1. Don't give in to the child's coercive behavior.

2. Don't escalate your own coercion when the child becomes coercive.

3. Control the child's coercion with the *time-out* procedure in which the child is sent to her room (or some other location) until she calms down and stops using coercive tactics.

4. Identify those of the child's behaviors that are most irritating, and then establish a point system in which the child can earn credits (rewards, privileges) for acceptable conduct or lose them for unacceptable behavior. Parents with older problem children are taught how to formulate "behavioral contracts" that specify how the child is expected to behave at home and at school, as well as how deviations from this behavioral code will be punished. Whenever possible, children should have a say in negotiating these contracts.

5. Be on the lookout for occasions when you can respond to the child's prosocial conduct with warmth and affection. Although this is often difficult for parents who are accustomed to snapping at their children and accentuating the negative. Patterson believes that parental affection and approval reinforce good conduct and eventually elicit displays of affection from the child—a clear sign that the family is on the road to recovery.

A clear majority of problem families respond quite favorably to these methods. Not only do problem children become less coercive, defiant, and aggressive, but the mother's depression fades as she gradually begins to feel better about herself, her child, and her ability to resolve family crises (Patterson, 1981). Some problem families show an immediate improvement. Others respond more gradually to the treatment and may require periodic "booster shots"—that is, follow-up treatments in which the clinician visits the family, determines why progress has slowed (or broken down), and then retrains the parents or suggests new procedures to correct the problems that are not being resolved. Clearly, this therapy works, because it recognizes that "out of control" behavior stems from a *family system* in which both parents and children influence each other and contribute to the development of a hostile family environment. Therapies that focus exclusively on the problem child are not enough!

As shown in Figure 14.4, coercive parenting early in childhood contributes to the development of children's hostile attributional biases, defiant, aggressive behaviors, and general lack of self-restraint which, by middle childhood, can cause these youngsters to be rejected by grade-school peers, criticized by teachers, and to founder academically. These poor outcomes may then cause parents to feel less invested in their children and less inclined to closely monitor their activities (Patterson et al., 1989; Vuchinich et al., 1992).

Furthermore, the rejection that problem children experience from peers, coupled with their likely placement in classes with other academically deficient children, often means that they have ample exposure to other relatively defiant, aggressive, and socially unskilled youngsters like themselves. By age 11 to 14, these youngsters associate mainly with other hostile, antisocial classmates, banding together to form deviant peer cliques that tend to devalue academics, encourage aggression, and promote such dysfunctional activities as sexual misconduct, substance abuse, dropping out of school, and a variety of other antisocial or delinquent behaviors (Cairns et al., 1988; Dishion et al., 1991, 1995; Patterson et al., 1989; 1992). So, to return to the question raised earlier, Patterson claims that living in a coercive home environment poses serious risks indeed and is often a crucial first step along the road to chronic aggression and delinquency.

Although boys are more likely than girls to take the developmental path described in Figure 14.4 (McFadyen-Ketchum et al., 1996), the delinquency "gender gap" is narrowing. Male delinquents still dominate violent crime statistics; but females are about as likely as males to be involved in larcenies, sexual misconduct, and substance abuse,

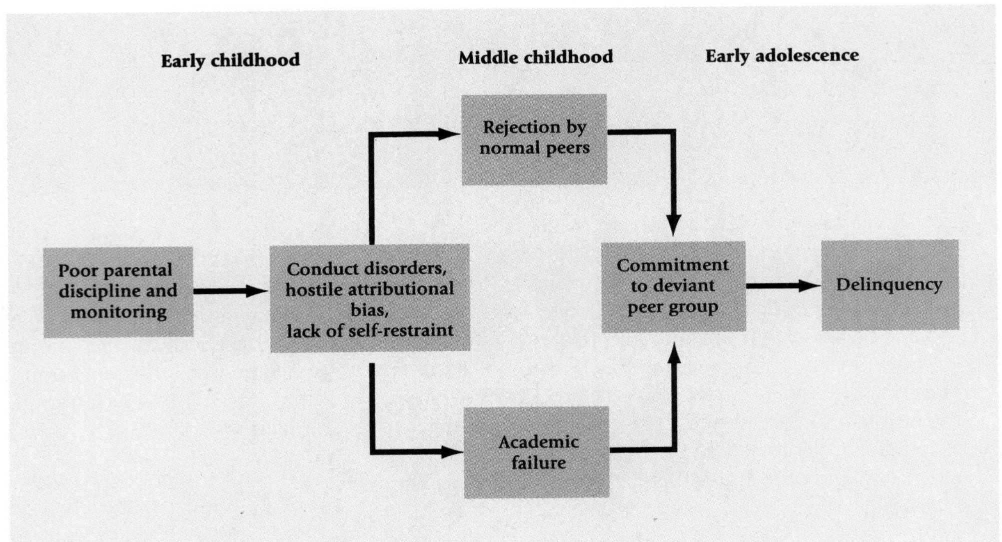

Figure 14.4 *A model of the development of chronic antisocial behavior.* ADAPTED FROM PATTERSON, DEBARYSHE, & RAMSEY, 1989.

and they are more likely than males to be arrested for such status offenses as running away from home and engaging in prostitution (*Uniform Crime Reports,* 1997). It may take a more disordered home environment to push girls along the path to delinquency, but girls can become just as chronically antisocial as boys (Loeber & Stouthamer-Loeber, 1998).

Family interventions of the kind described in Box 14.2 can be quite effective at modifying the antisocial tendencies of preadolescent (and younger) children. However, once antisocial patterns continue into adolescence, so many factors conspire to maintain them that interventions are usually unsuccessful (Kazdin, 1995). Note the implication here: To cope with the problem of chronic delinquency, we must think in terms of *preventive* interventions—ideally, programs that (1) teach parents more effective child-management techniques, (2) foster children's social skills to prevent them from being rejected by their peers, and (3) provide any academic remediation that may be necessary to keep children on track at school and to lessen the likelihood that they will fall in with deviant peer groups and/or become high school dropouts. Of course, any intervention that makes aggressive, antisocial conduct a less viable or attractive option is a step in the right direction. Let's now consider some of the procedures that developmentalists have used in attempting to control children's hostilities.

Methods of Controlling Aggression and Antisocial Conduct

What approaches other than family therapy might assist parents and teachers in suppressing the aggressive antics of young children so that antisocial solutions to conflict do not become habitual? Let's look at three general strategies that have achieved some success.

Creating Nonaggressive Environments

One simple but effective approach for reducing children's aggression is to create play areas that minimize the likelihood of conflict. For example, parents and teachers might remove (or refuse to buy) "aggressive" toys such as guns, tanks, and rubber knives that are known to provoke hostilities (Watson & Peng, 1992). Providing ample space for vigorous play also helps to eliminate the accidental bumps, shoves, and trips that often escalate into full-blown hostilities (Hartup, 1974). Finally, shortages of play materials sometimes contribute to conflicts and aggression; yet, children are likely to play quite harmoniously if adults provide enough balls, slides, swings, and other toys to keep them from having to compete for scarce resources (Smith & Connolly, 1980).

How might one reach children who have already become highly aggressive? Developmentalists now recognize that different forms of aggression require different kinds of interventions (Coie & Koeppl, 1990; Crick & Dodge, 1996). Recall that proactive aggressors rely on forceful strategies because they are easy to enact and often enable these youngsters to achieve personal goals. An effective intervention for these children might teach them that aggression doesn't pay and that alternative prosocial responses, such as cooperation or sharing, are better ways to achieve their objectives. By contrast, hotheaded reactive aggressors may profit more from programs that teach them to control their anger and suppress their tendency to overattribute hostile intentions to companions who displease them. Let's take a closer look at these two kinds of intervention.

Eliminating the Payoffs for Aggression

Parents and teachers can reduce the incidence of proactive aggression by identifying and eliminating its reinforcing consequences and encouraging alternative means of achieving one's objectives. For example, if 4-year-old Lennie were to hit his 3-year-old sister Gail in order to take possession of a toy, Lennie's mother could teach him that this instrumental aggression doesn't pay by simply returning the toy to Gail and denying him his objective. However, this strategy wouldn't work if Lennie is an insecure child who feels neglected and has attacked his sister *in order to attract his mother's attention;* under these circumstances, the mother would be reinforcing Lennie's aggression if she attended to it at all! So what is she to do?

One proven method that she might use is the **incompatible-response technique**—a strategy of *ignoring* all but the most serious of Lennie's aggressive antics (thereby denying him an "attentional" reward) while reinforcing such acts as cooperation and sharing that are incompatible with aggression. Teachers who have tried this strategy find that it quickly produces an increase in children's prosocial conduct and a corresponding decrease in their hostilities (Brown & Elliot, 1965; see also Slaby & Crowley, 1977). And how might adults handle *serious* acts of harmdoing without "reinforcing" them with their attention? One effective approach is the **time-out technique** that Patterson favors, in which the adult removes the offender from the situation in which his aggression is reinforced (for example, by sending him to his room until he is ready to behave appropriately). Although this approach may generate some resentment, the adult in charge is not physically abusing the child or serving as an aggressive model and is not likely to unwittingly reinforce the child who misbehaves as a means of attracting attention. The time-out procedure is most effective at controlling children's hostilities when adults also reinforce cooperative or helpful acts that are incompatible with aggression (Parke & Slaby, 1983).

Responses that are incompatible with aggression may also be instilled by modeling or coaching strategies. When children see a model choose a nonaggressive solution to a conflict or are explicitly coached in the use of nonaggressive methods of problem solving, they become more likely to enact similar solutions to their own problems (Shure, 1989; Zahavi & Asher, 1978).

Social-Cognitive Interventions

Highly aggressive youngsters, particularly those high in reactive aggression, can profit from social-cognitive interventions that help them to (1) regulate their anger and (2) become more skilled at empathizing with and taking others' perspectives so that they will not be so likely to overattribute hostile intentions to their peers (Crick & Dodge, 1996; Rabiner, Lenhart, & Lochman, 1990). In one study (Guerra & Slaby, 1990), a group of violent adolescent offenders were coached in such skills as (1) looking for nonhostile cues that might be associated with harmdoing, (2) controlling their impulses (or anger), and (3) generating nonaggressive solutions to conflict. Not only did these violent offenders show dramatic improvements in their social problem-solving skills, but

incompatible-response technique
a nonpunitive method of behavior modification in which adults ignore undesirable conduct, while reinforcing acts that are incompatible with these responses.

time-out technique
a form of discipline in which children who misbehave are removed from the setting until they are prepared to act more appropriately.

they also became less inclined to endorse beliefs supporting aggression and less aggressive in their interactions with authority figures and other inmates. Michael Chandler (1973) found a similar reduction in the hostile social cognitions and aggressive behaviors of a group of 11- to 13-year-old delinquents who had participated in a 10-week program designed specifically to make them more aware of other people's intentions and feelings.

Some researchers now believe that the best interventions are likely to be comprehensive ones that minimize the rewards for aggression, replace aggressive with prosocial responses, and include all of the elements of successful social-cognitive training programs (Gibbs, Potter, & Goldstein, 1995). Yet, it is important to note that any reduction in hostilities that result from successful interventions of any kind could be short-lived if lessons that participants have learned are quickly undermined in a coercive home environment (Pettit, Dodge, & Brown, 1988) or in the company of chronically aggressive friends who value and endorse aggression (Dishion et al., 1995).

Finally, highly aggressive children are often found to be deficient in **empathy** (Cohen & Strayer, 1996)—a social cognitive attribute that parents can easily foster by modeling empathic concern and by using disciplinary techniques that (1) point out the harmful consequences of their child's aggressive acts while (2) encouraging him to put himself in the victim's place and imagine how the victim feels. In the next section of the chapter, we will see that parents who rely mainly on these rational, nonpunitive disciplinary techniques tend to raise sympathetic children who seem genuinely concerned about the welfare of others.

ALTRUISM: DEVELOPMENT OF THE PROSOCIAL SELF

empathy
the ability to experience the same emotions that someone else is experiencing.

altruism
a selfless concern for the welfare of others that is expressed through prosocial acts such as sharing, cooperating, and helping.

As we noted in opening this chapter, most parents hope that their children acquire a sense of **altruism**—that is, a selfless concern for the welfare of other people and a willingness to act on that concern. In fact, many parents encourage altruistic acts such as sharing, cooperating, or helping while their children are still in diapers! Experts in child development once would have claimed that these well-intentioned adults were wasting their time, for infants and toddlers were thought to be incapable of considering the needs of anyone other than themselves. But the experts were wrong!

Concept Check 14.1
Understanding Aggression and Antisocial Conduct

Check your understanding of the development of aggression and antisocial conduct by matching each descriptive statement below with one of the following concepts or processes: (a) deviant peer cliques, (b) hostile aggression, (c) instrumental aggression, (d) relational aggression, (e) coercive home environment, (f) peer rejection, (g) negative reinforcement, (h) proactive aggressors, (i) reactive aggressors. Answers appear in the Appendix.

_____ 1. type of aggression for which girls exceed boys
_____ 2. these individuals think that aggression pays off and are high in instrumental aggression
_____ 3. process by which unpleasant interactions are maintained in coercive home environments
_____ 4. thought to be a strong, *direct* contributor to chronically antisocial conduct
_____ 5. this kind of aggression is first to appear, often by age 12 months
_____ 6. aggression of these individuals often stems from a hostile attributional bias
_____ 7. type of aggression that becomes more common with the growth of role-taking skills
_____ 8. thought to be a strong, *direct* contributor to one's affiliation with deviant peer cliques
_____ 9. often the *first step* along the road to chronic delinquency

Origins of Altruism

Long before children receive any formal moral or religious training, they may act in ways that resemble the prosocial behavior of older people. Twelve- to 18-month-olds, for example, occasionally offer toys to companions (Hay et al., 1991) and even attempt to help their parents with such chores as dusting or setting the table (Rheingold, 1982). And the prosocial conduct of very young children even has a certain "rationality" about it. For example, 2-year-olds are more likely to offer toys to a peer when playthings are scarce rather than plentiful (Hay et al., 1991). Furthermore, a type of *reciprocity* appears by the end of the third year. In one study (Levitt et al., 1985), 29- to 36-month-old toddlers who had previously received a toy from a peer when they had had none of their own typically returned the favor when they later found themselves with several toys to play with and the peer without any. Yet, if that peer had earlier refused to share, the toddlers almost invariably hoarded the toys when it was their turn to control them.

Are toddlers capable of expressing sympathy and behaving compassionately toward their companions? Yes, indeed, and these displays of prosocial concern are not all that uncommon (Radke-Yarrow et al., 1983; Zahn-Waxler et al., 1992). Consider the reaction of 21-month-old John to his distressed playmate, Jerry:

> Today Jerry was kind of cranky; he just started . . . bawling and he wouldn't stop. John kept coming over and handing Jerry toys, trying to cheer him up. . . . He'd say things like "Here Jerry," and I said to John "Jerry's sad; he doesn't feel good; he had a shot today." John would look at me with his eyebrows wrinkled together like he really understood that Jerry was crying because he was unhappy. . . . He went over and rubbed Jerry's arm and said "Nice Jerry," and continued to give him toys (Zahn-Waxler, Radke-Yarrow, & King, 1979, pp. 321–322).

Clearly, John was concerned about his little playmate and did what he could to make him feel better.

Although some toddlers often try to comfort distressed companions, others rarely do. These individual differences are due, in part, to cognitive development, for 23- to 25-month-olds who have achieved self-recognition (as assessed by the rouge test and other similar measures) are more likely than those who haven't to display sympathy for and to try to comfort a victim of distress (Zahn-Waxler et al., 1992). By contrast, younger toddlers often became *personally distressed* (rather than concerned) by others' distress and were less inclined to show compassion, sometimes even behaving aggressively.

Individual differences in early compassion also depend on parents' reactions to occasions in which their toddler has harmed another child. Carolyn Zahn-Waxler and her associates (1979) found that mothers of less compassionate toddlers typically used coercive tactics such as verbal rebukes or physical punishment to discipline harmdoing. By contrast, mothers of highly compassionate toddlers frequently disciplined harmdoing with *affective explanations* that may foster sympathy (and perhaps some remorse) by helping children to see the relation between their own acts and the distress they have caused (for example, "You made Doug cry; it's not nice to bite!").

Developmental Trends in Altruism

Although many 2- to 3-year-olds show sympathy and compassion toward distressed companions, they are not particularly eager to make truly self-sacrificial responses, such as sharing a treasured toy with a peer. Sharing and other benevolent acts are more likely to occur if adults instruct a toddler to consider others' needs (Levitt et al., 1985), or if a peer actively elicits sharing through a request or a threat of some kind, such as

Preschool children must often be coaxed to share.

"I won't be your friend if you won't gimme some" (Birch & Billman, 1986). But, on the whole, acts of *spontaneous* self-sacrifice in the interest of others are relatively infrequent among toddlers and young preschool children. Is this because toddlers are largely oblivious to others' needs and to the good they might do by sharing or helping their companions? Probably not, for at least one observational study in a nursery-school setting found that 2½- to 3½-year-olds often took pleasure in performing acts of kindness for others during *pretend play;* by contrast, 4- to 6-year-olds performed more *real* helping acts and rarely "play-acted" the role of an altruist (Bar-Tal, Raviv, & Goldberg, 1982).

Many studies conducted in cultures from around the world find that sharing, helping, and most other forms of prosocial conduct become more and more common from the early elementary school years onward (see, for example, Underwood & Moore, 1982; Whiting & Edwards, 1988). Indeed, much of the research that we will examine seeks to explain why older children and adolescents tend to become more prosocially inclined.

Before turning to this research, let's address one other issue that developmentalists have pondered: Are there sex differences in altruism? Although people commonly assume that girls are (or will become) more helpful, generous, or compassionate than boys (see Shigetomi, Hartmann, & Gelfand, 1981), there is little evidence for this notion in either laboratory experiments or survey studies (Grusec, Goodnow, & Cohen, 1996; Radke-Yarrow et al., 1983). Girls sometimes emit stronger *facial* expressions of sympathy than boys do (Eisenberg et al., 1988; Fabes, Eisenberg, & Miller, 1990; Zahn-Waxler et al., 1992). However, the vast majority of studies find that girls and women do not reliably differ from boys and men in either the amount of sympathy that they *say* they experience or in their willingness to comfort, help, or share resources with people in need. Nor is there much evidence for the idea that girls are more likely than boys to reliably *seek* assistance. From 1st through 5th grade, children of both sexes become less and less dependent on others to accomplish tasks for them, and they are equally likely to favor indirect help (such as hints) that will enable them to master tasks on their own (Shell & Eisenberg, 1996). So the notions that girls are any more altruistic than boys or any less capable of accomplishing tasks without direct assistance are probably best described as cultural myths that have little basis in fact.

Social-Cognitive and Affective Contributors to Altruism

Children with well-developed role-taking skills are often found to be more helpful or compassionate than poor role takers, largely because they are better able to infer a companion's needs for assistance or comforting (Shaffer, 1994b). In fact, evidence for a causal link between *affective* and *social* perspective taking (recognizing what another person is feeling, thinking, or intending) and altruism is quite clear in studies showing that children and adolescents who receive training to further these role-taking skills subsequently become more charitable, cooperative, and concerned about the needs of others when compared with age-mates who receive no training (Chalmers & Townsend, 1990; Iannotti, 1978). However, role taking is only one of several personal attributes that play a part in the development of altruistic behavior. Two especially important contributors are children's level of **prosocial moral reasoning** and their empathic reactions to the distress of other people.

Prosocial Moral Reasoning

prosocial moral reasoning the thinking that people demonstrate when deciding whether to help, share with, or comfort others when these actions could prove costly to themselves.

Over the past 20 years, researchers have charted the development of children's reasoning about prosocial issues and its relationship to altruistic behavior. Nancy Eisenberg and her colleagues, for example, presented children with stories in which the central character has to decide whether or not to help or comfort someone when the prosocial act would be personally costly. The following story illustrates the kinds of dilemmas that children were asked to resolve (Eisenberg-Berg & Hand, 1979):

> One day a girl named Mary was going to a friend's birthday party. On her way she saw a girl who had fallen down and hurt her leg. The girl asked Mary to go to her house and get her parents so that [they] could come and take her to a doctor. But if Mary did . . . , she would be late to the party and miss the ice-cream, cake, and all the games. What should Mary do?

As illustrated in Table 14.1, reasoning about these prosocial dilemmas may progress through as many as five levels between early childhood and adolescence. Notice that preschoolers' responses are frequently *self-serving:* These youngsters often say that Mary should go to the party so as not to miss out on the goodies. But as children mature, they tend to become increasingly responsive to the needs and wishes of others—so much so that some high school students feel that they could no longer respect themselves were they to ignore the appeal of a person in need in order to pursue their own interests (Eisenberg, 1983; Eisenberg, Miller et al., 1991).

WHAT DO YOU THINK?

Despite ample evidence to the contrary, many people simply refuse to believe that girls and women are not any more prosocially inclined than boys and men. Why might the weight of the research evidence be so hard for so many people to accept?

Does a child's or adolescent's level of prosocial moral reasoning predict his or her altruistic behavior? Apparently so. Preschoolers who have progressed beyond the hedonistic level of prosocial moral reasoning are more likely to help and to *spontaneously* share valuable commodities with their peers than are those who still reason in a self-serving way (Eisenberg-Berg & Hand, 1979; Miller et al., 1996). Studies of older participants tell a similar story. Mature moral reasoners among a high school sample often said they would help someone they *disliked* if that person really needed their help, whereas immature moral reasoners were apt to ignore the needs of a person they dislike (Eisenberg, 1983; Eisenberg, Miller et al., 1991). Another study conducted recently in Brazil found that adolescents rated high by their peers in prosocial behavior were more likely than those who were less prosocially inclined to reason at Eisenberg's highest level of prosocial moral reasoning (Carlo et al., 1996).

Why are mature moral reasoners so sensitive to the needs of others—even *disliked* others? Eisenberg's view is that the child's growing ability to *empathize* with others contributes heavily to mature prosocial reasoning and to the development of a selfless concern for promoting the welfare of *whomever* might require assistance (Eisenberg et al., 1987; Eisenberg, Miller et al., 1991). Let's now consider what researchers have learned about the relationship between empathy and altruism.

TABLE 14.1 Eisenberg's Levels of Prosocial Moral Reasoning

Level	Approximate age	Brief description and typical response
Hedonistic	Preschool, early elementary school	Concern is for one's own needs. Giving help is most likely if it will benefit the self. *Example:* "I wouldn't help 'cause I'd miss the party."
Needs oriented	Elementary school and a few preschoolers	Others' needs are recognized as a legitimate basis for helping, but there is little evidence of sympathy or guilt for failing to help. *Example:* "I'd help because she needs help."
Stereotyped, approval oriented	Elementary school and some high school students	Concern for approval and stereotyped images of good and bad heavily influence one's thinking. *Example:* "My mother would hug me for helping."
Empathic orientation	Older elementary school and high school students	Judgments now include evidence of sympathetic feelings; vague references are sometimes made to duties and values. *Example:* "I'd feel good about helping because she was in pain."
Internalized values orientation	A small minority of high school students; no elementary school students	Justifications for helping (or not helping) are based on internalized values, norms, convictions, and responsibilities; violating these principles could undermine self-respect. *Example:* "I refused to make a donation because the [charity] wastes too much money fundraising and gives little to its intended recipients."

SOURCE: Adapted from Eisenberg, Lennon, & Roth, 1983.

Empathy: An Important Affective Contributor to Altruism

Empathy refers to a person's ability to experience the emotions of other people. According to Martin Hoffman (1981; 1993), empathy is a universal human response that has a neurological basis and can be either fostered or suppressed by environmental influences. Hoffman believes that empathic arousal eventually becomes an important mediator of altruism. Why else, Hoffman asks, would we set aside our own selfish motives to help other people or to avoid harming them unless we had the capacity to share their emotions and experience their distress?

Although infants and toddlers seem to recognize and often react to the distress of their companions (Zahn-Waxler et al., 1979, 1992; see also Box 2.4), their responses are not always helpful ones. In fact, some young children experience *personal* distress upon witnessing the distress or misfortunes of others (this may be the predominant response early in life) and may turn away from a person in need in order to relieve their *own* discomfort. Yet other children (even some young ones) are more inclined to interpret their empathic arousal as concern for distressed others, and it is this **sympathetic empathic arousal,** rather than **self-oriented distress,** that should eventually promote altruism (Batson, 1991; Miller et al., 1996; Hoffman, 1993).

Socialization of Empathy. As we noted earlier when discussing the origins of compassion in toddlers, parents can help to promote sympathetic empathic arousal by (1) modeling empathic concern and (2) relying on affectively oriented forms of discipline that help young children to understand the harmful effects of any distress they may have caused others (Barnett, 1987; Eisenberg, Fabes et al., 1991; Zahn-Waxler et al., 1979; 1992). Interestingly, mothers who use more *positive* facial expressions while modeling sympathy and who explicitly verbalize their own sympathetic feelings have children who act more sympathetically—probably because the mother's positivity and her affective explanations help to counteract the negative reactions that young children may have to others' misfortunes, thus making them less inclined to interpret their own arousal as *personal* distress (Fabes et al., 1994).

Age Trends in the Empathy-Altruism Relationship. So what is the relationship between empathy and altruism? The answer depends, in part, on how empathy is measured and how old the research participants are. In studies that assess empathy by having children report their own feelings about the misfortunes of story characters, researchers have found little association between empathy and altruism. However, teacher ratings of children's empathic sensitivities and children's own *facial* expressions of emotion in response to others' misfortunes are better predictors of prosocial behavior (Chapman et al., 1987; Eisenberg et al., 1990). Overall, it seems that the evidence for a link between empathy and altruism is modest at best for preschool and young grade-school children but stronger for preadolescents, adolescents, and adults (Underwood & Moore, 1982).

One possible explanation for these age trends is that it simply takes some time for children to become better at suppressing personal distress to others' misfortunes so that they can respond more sympathetically. And it is likely that social-cognitive development plays an important part in this process, for younger children may lack the role-taking skills and insight about their own emotional experiences to fully understand and appreciate (1) *why* others are distressed and, thus, (2) *why* they are feeling aroused (Roberts & Strayer, 1996). For example, when kindergartners see a series of slides showing a boy becoming depressed after his dog runs away, they usually attribute his sadness to an external cause (the dog's disappearance) rather than to a more personal or internal one, such as the boy's longing for his pet (Hughes, Tingle, & Sawin, 1981). And, although kindergartners report that they feel sad after seeing the slides, they usually provide egocentric explanations for their empathic arousal that seem to reflect *personal distress* (for example, "I might lose my dog"). However, 7- to 9-year-olds begin to associate their own empathic emotions with those of the story character as they put themselves in his place and infer the psychological basis for his sadness (for example, "I'm sad because he's sad . . . because, if he really liked the dog, then . . . "). So empathy may become a stronger contributor to altruism once children become better at infer-

sympathetic empathic arousal
feelings of sympathy or compassion that may be elicited when one experiences the emotions of (that is, empathizes with) a distressed other; thought to become an important mediator of altruism.

self-oriented distress
feeling of *personal* discomfort or distress that may be elicited when we experience the emotions of (that is, empathize with) a distressed other; thought to inhibit altruism.

ring others' points of view (role taking) and understanding the causes of their own empathic emotions—causes that can help them to feel *sympathy* for distressed or needy companions (Roberts & Strayer, 1996).

As children mature and develop better role-taking skills, they are more likely to sympathize with distressed companions and to provide them with comfort or assistance.

The Felt-Responsibility Hypothesis. Now an important question: *How* exactly does empathy promote altruism? One possibility is that a child's *sympathetic* empathic arousal causes him to reflect on altruistic lessons that he has learned, such as the Golden Rule, the *norm of social responsibility* (that is, help others who need help), or even the knowledge that other people approve of helping behavior. As a result of this reflection, the child is likely to assume some personal *responsibility* for aiding a victim in distress (see Figure 14.5) and would now feel guilty for callously ignoring that obligation (Chapman et al., 1987; Williams & Bybee, 1994). Notice that this **"felt responsibility" hypothesis** is reflected in Eisenberg's higher levels of prosocial moral reasoning (see Table 14.1) and may help to explain why the link between empathy and altruism becomes stronger with age. Since older children are likely to have learned (and internalized) more altruistic principles than younger children, they should have much more to reflect on as they experience empathic arousal. Consequently, they are more likely than younger children to feel responsible for helping a distressed person and to follow through by rendering the necessary assistance.

Cultural and Social Influences on Altruism

Cultural Influences

Cultures clearly differ in their endorsement or encouragement of altruism. In one interesting cross-cultural study, Beatrice and John Whiting (1975) observed the altruistic behavior of 3- to 10-year-olds in six cultures—Kenya, Mexico, the Philippines, Okinawa,

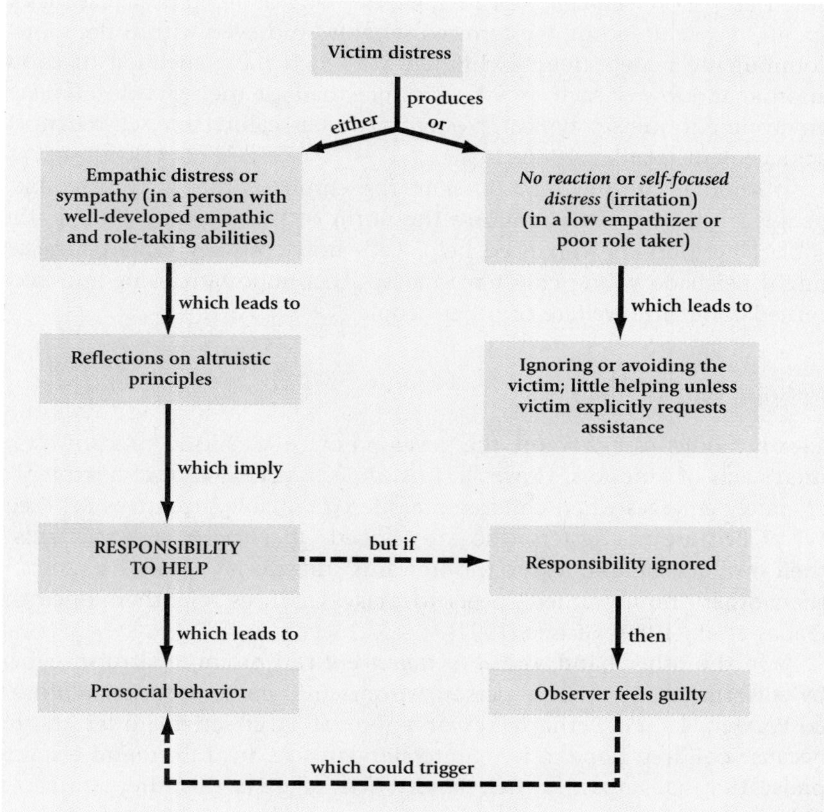

Figure 14.5 *How empathy promotes altruism: A "felt responsibility" interpretation.*

"felt responsibility" hypothesis
the theory that empathy may promote altruism by causing one to reflect on altruistic norms and, thus, to feel some obligation to help distressed others.

Table 14.2 Prosocial Behavior in Six Cultures: Percentages of Children in Each Culture Who Scored above the Median Altruism Score for the Cross-Cultural Sample as a Whole

Type of society	Percentage scoring high in altruism	Type of society	Percentage scoring high in altruism
Nonindustrialized		*Industrialized*	
Kenya	100	Okinawa	29
Mexico	73	India	25
Philippines	63	United States	8

Source: Based on Whiting & Whiting, 1975.

India, and the United States. As we see in Table 14.2, the cultures in which children were most altruistic were the less industrialized societies in which people live in large families and children *routinely contribute to the family welfare* by processing food, preparing meals, fetching wood and water, or caring for younger brothers and sisters. Although children in Western industrialized societies are involved in relatively few family-maintenance activities, those who are assigned housework or other tasks that *benefit family members* are more prosocially inclined than age-mates whose responsibilities consist mainly of *self*-care routines, such as cleaning their own rooms (Grusec et al., 1996).

Another factor contributing to the low altruism scores of children from Western industrialized nations is the tremendous emphasis that these societies place on competition and on individual rather than group goals. By contrast, Native American and Mexican children (and those raised in such communal settings as the Israeli kibbutz) are taught to suppress individualism, to cooperate with others for the greater good of the group, and to avoid interpersonal conflicts. The impact of these cultural teachings can be seen in a number of contexts. For example, Anne Marie Tietjen (1986) found that children from a communal society in New Guinea typically become less other-oriented and more self-centered in their thinking about prosocial issues once they have spent 3 years attending Westernized schools. And even within the same society (Israel), communally reared kibbutz children are much more inclined to cooperate with one another and to *seek* each other's assistance than are their city-dwelling age-mates, whose environment stresses typical Western attitudes calling for self-reliance and individual achievement (Nadler, 1986; 1991).

Although cultures may differ in the emphasis that they place on altruism, most people in most societies endorse the norm of social responsibility—the rule that one should help others who need help. Let's now consider some of the ways that adults might persuade young children to adopt this important value and become more concerned about the welfare of other people.

Reinforcing Altruism

Clearly, adults can promote the development of altruistic concern by reinforcing children's acts of kindness. However, it is important to note that a strong concern for others rarely emerges when children are offered tangible incentives for their prosocial acts. Why? Because youngsters who are "bribed" to perform prosocial acts often attribute their own acts of kindness to the "rewards" they receive, and they are actually less likely than other "nonrewarded" peers to make sacrifices for others once the rewards stop (Fabes et al., 1989; Grusec, 1991).

On the other hand, *verbal reinforcement* can promote altruism when administered by a warm and charitable person whom children respect and admire (Yarrow, Scott, & Waxler, 1973). Perhaps verbal approval is effective under these circumstances because children hope to live up to standards set by a liked and respected person, and praise that accompanies their kindly acts suggests that they are accomplishing that objective.

Practicing and Preaching Altruism

Social-learning theorists have assumed that adults who encourage altruism and who practice what they preach affect children in two ways. By practicing altruism, the adult model may induce the child to perform similar acts of kindness. In addition, regular exposure to the model's **altruistic exhortations** provides the child with opportunities to internalize principles such as the norm of social responsibility that contribute to the development of an altruistic orientation.

Laboratory experiments consistently indicate that young children who observe charitable or helpful models become more charitable or helpful themselves, especially if the model has established a warm relationship with them, provides a compelling justification (rationale) for his acts of kindness, and regularly *practices what he preaches* (Rushton, 1980; Yarrow et al., 1973). Furthermore, it appears that exposure to these altruistic models can have *long-term* effects on children's behavior—effects that generalize to new situations. For example, Elizabeth Midlarsky and James Bryan (1972) found that a model who donated valuable tokens to a charity increased children's willingness to donate candy to the same charity, even though the candy donations were solicited ten days later in a different setting by a person whom the children had never seen. Other investigators have noted that children who observe charitable models are more generous than those who observe selfish models, even when they are tested *2 to 4 months later* (Rice & Grusec, 1975; Rushton, 1980). So it seems that encounters with altruistic models may indeed foster the development of prosocial habits and altruistic values.

Children learn many prosocial lessons by observing the behavior of prosocial models.

Now let's turn to the child-rearing literature to see if the variables that promote altruism in the laboratory have similar effects on children in the natural environment.

Who Raises Altruistic Children?

Studies of unusually charitable adults indicate that these "altruists" have enjoyed a warm and affectionate relationship with parents who themselves were highly concerned about the welfare of others. For example, Christians who risked their lives to save Jews from the Nazis during World War II reported that they had had close ties to moralistic parents who always acted in accordance with their ethical principles (London, 1970). And interviews of white "freedom riders" from the U.S. civil rights movement of the 1960s reveal that "fully committed" activists (volunteers who gave up their homes and/or careers to work full-time for the cause) differed from "partially committed" (part-time) activists in two major ways: They had enjoyed warmer relations with their parents, and they had had parents who advocated altruism and backed up these exhortations by performing many kind and compassionate deeds. By contrast, parents of partially committed activists had often preached but rarely practiced altruism (Rosenhan, 1970; see also Clary & Snyder, 1991). Clearly, these findings are consistent with the laboratory evidence we have reviewed, which indicates that warm and compassionate models who practice what they preach are especially effective at eliciting prosocial responses from young children.

Parental reactions to a child's harmdoing also play an important role in the development of altruism. Recall that mothers of less compassionate infants and toddlers react to harmdoing in punitive or forceful ways, whereas mothers of compassionate toddlers rely more heavily on nonpunitive, affective explanations in which they persuade the child to accept personal responsibility for her harmdoing and urge her to direct some sort of comforting or helpful response toward the victim (Zahn-Waxler et al., 1979; 1992). Research with older children paints a similar picture: Parents who continue to rely on rational, nonpunitive disciplinary techniques in which they regularly display sympathy and concern for others tend to raise children who are sympathetic and self-sacrificing, whereas frequent use of forceful and punitive discipline appears to inhibit altruism and lead to the development of self-centered values (Brody & Shaffer, 1982; Eisenberg et al., 1992; Krevans & Gibbs, 1996).

altruistic exhortations
verbal encouragements to help, comfort, share, or cooperate with others.

There are probably several reasons why rational affectively oriented discipline that is heavy on reasoning might inspire children to become more altruistic. First, it encourages children to assume another person's perspective (role taking) and to experience that person's distress (empathy training). It also teaches children to perform helpful or comforting acts that make both themselves and the other person feel better. And last but not least, these reparative responses might convince children that they can be caring or helpful people, thereby fostering a *positive self-image* that they may try to live up to by performing other acts of kindness in the future.

Now let's look at the broader issue of moral development, which encompasses both the encouragement of altruistic values and the inhibition of hostile, antisocial impulses.

WHAT IS MORALITY?

During the course of development, most of us arrive at a point at which we wish to behave responsibly and to think of ourselves (and be thought of by others) as *moral* individuals (Blasi, 1990; Hoffman, 1988). What is **morality**? College students generally agree that morality implies a capacity to (1) *distinguish right from wrong,* (2) *act on this distinction,* and (3) *experience pride in virtuous conduct and guilt or shame over acts that violate one's standards* (Quinn, Houts, & Graesser, 1994; Shaffer, 1994a).

Implicit in this definition is the idea that *morally mature* individuals do not submit to society's dictates because they expect tangible rewards for complying or fear punishments for transgressing. Rather, they eventually *internalize* the moral principles that they have learned and conform to these ideals, even when authority figures are not present to enforce them. As we will see, virtually all contemporary theorists consider **internalization**—the shift from externally controlled actions to conduct that is governed by internal standards and principles—to be a most crucial milestone along the road to moral maturity.

morality
a set of principles or ideals that help the individual to distinguish right from wrong, to act on this distinction, and to feel pride in virtuous conduct and guilt (or shame) for conduct that violates his or her standards.

internalization
the process of adopting the attributes or standards of other people; taking these standards as one's own.

How Developmentalists Look at Morality

Developmental theorizing and research have centered on the same three moral components that college students mention in their consensual definition of morality:

1. An *affective,* or emotional, component that consists of the feelings (guilt, concern for others' feelings, and so on) that surround right or wrong actions and that motivate moral thoughts and actions.
2. A *cognitive* component that centers on the way we conceptualize right and wrong and make decisions about how to behave.
3. A *behavioral component* that reflects how we actually behave when we experience the temptation to lie, cheat, or violate other moral rules.

Concept Check 14.2
Understanding Cognitive and Social Contributors to Altruism

Check your understanding of cognitive and affective contributors to prosocial conduct by matching each of the descriptive statements below with one of the following concepts or processes: (a) altruistic lessons (or norms), (b) felt responsibility, (c) role-taking skills, (d) competitive orientation, (e) self-oriented distress, (f) sympathetic empathic arousal, (g) altruistic exhortations. Answers appear in the Appendix.

_____ 1. others' attempts to foster this attribute may undermine prosocial conduct

_____ 2. empathic arousal that is thought to *inhibit* altruism

_____ 3. what altruistic individuals may focus on when experiencing others' distress

_____ 4. may be the most *direct* contributor to an empathizer's prosocial conduct

_____ 5. permits children to interpret empathic arousal as sympathy rather than personal distress

_____ 6. effectively promotes altruistic behavior among children of *charitable* parents

_____ 7. empathic arousal that is thought to *promote* altruism

As it turns out, each of the three major theories of moral development has focused on a different component of morality. Psychoanalytic theorists emphasize the affective component, or powerful **moral affects.** They believe that children are motivated to act in accordance with their ethical principles in order to experience positive affects such as pride and to avoid such negative moral emotions as guilt and shame. Cognitive-developmental theorists have concentrated on the cognitive aspects of morality, or **moral reasoning,** and have found that the ways children think about right and wrong may change rather dramatically as they mature. Finally, the research of social-learning and social information-processing theorists has helped us to understand how children learn to resist temptation and to practice **moral behavior,** inhibiting actions such as lying, stealing, and cheating that violate moral norms.

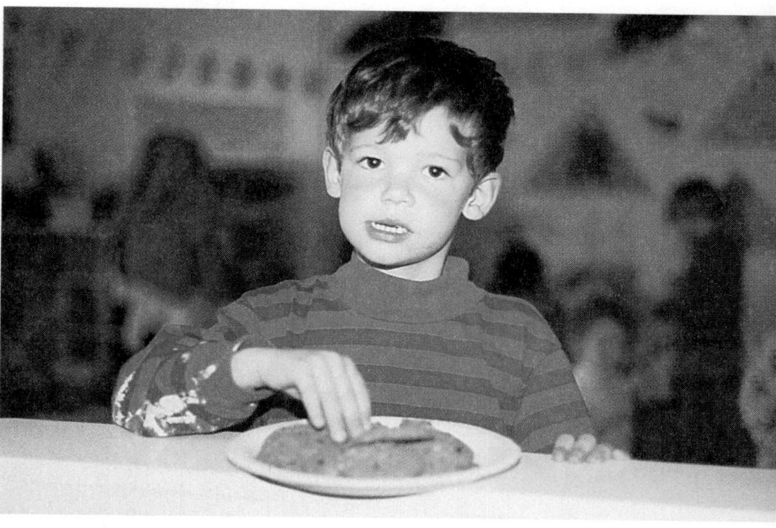

Resisting temptation is a difficult feat for young children to accomplish, particularly when there is no one around to help the child exercise willpower.

In examining each of these theories and the research it has generated, we will look at the relationships among moral affect, moral reasoning, and moral behavior. This information should help us to decide whether a person really has a unified moral character that is stable over time and across situations. Then, we will consider how various child-rearing practices may affect a child's moral development and then will attempt to integrate much of the information we have reviewed.

PSYCHOANALYTIC EXPLANATIONS OF MORAL DEVELOPMENT

In Chapter 2, we learned that psychoanalysts view the mature personality as having three components: an irrational *id* that seeks the immediate gratification of instinctual needs, a rational *ego* that formulates *realistic* plans for meeting these needs, and a moralistic *superego* (or conscience) that monitors the acceptability of the ego's thoughts and deeds. Freud claimed that infants and toddlers lack a superego and act on their selfish impulses unless parents control their behavior. But once the superego emerges, it was said to function as an *internal* censor that has the power to make a child feel proud of his virtuous conduct and guilty or shameful about committing moral transgressions. So children who are morally mature should generally resist temptation to violate moral norms in order to maintain self-esteem and avoid experiencing negative moral affects.

Freud's Theory of Oedipal Morality

According to Freud (1935/1960), the superego develops during the phallic stage (age 3 to 6), when children were said to experience an emotional conflict with the same-sex parent that stemmed from their incestuous desire for the other-sex parent. To resolve this *Oedipus complex,* a boy was said to *identify* with and pattern himself after his father, particularly if his father was a threatening figure who aroused fear. Not only does he learn his masculine role in this manner, but he also internalizes his father's moral standards. Similarly, a girl resolves her *Electra complex* by identifying with her mother and internalizing her mother's moral standards. However, Freud claimed that because girls do not experience the intense fear of castration that boys experience, they develop weaker superegos than boys do.

moral affect
the emotional component of morality, including feelings such as guilt, shame, and pride in ethical conduct.

moral reasoning
the cognitive component of morality; the thinking that people demonstrate when deciding whether various acts are right or wrong.

moral behavior
the behavioral component of morality; actions that are consistent with one's moral standards in situations in which one is tempted to violate them.

Evaluating Freud's Theory and Newer Psychoanalytic Ideas about Morality

We might credit Freud for pointing out that moral emotions such as pride, shame, and guilt are potentially important determinants of ethical conduct and that the internalization of moral principles is a crucial step along the way to moral maturity. Yet, the specifics of his theory are largely unsupported. For example, threatening and punitive parents do not raise children who are morally mature. Quite the contrary: Parents who rely on harsh forms of discipline tend to have children who often misbehave and rarely express feelings of guilt, remorse, shame, or self-criticism (Brody & Shaffer, 1982; Kochanska, 1997b). Furthermore, there is simply no evidence boys develop stronger superegos than girls. Finally, Freud's proposed age trends for moral development are actually rather pessimistic. Two-year-olds, for example, are already beginning to show clear signs of distress when they violate rules (Kochanska et al., 1995), and they sometimes try to correct any mishaps they think they have caused, *even when no one else is present to tell them to* (Cole, Barrett, & Zahn-Waxler, 1992). In addition, 3-year-olds are already displaying complex emotions that look very much like *pride* when they live up to a standard and *shame* when they fail to do so (Lewis et al., 1992; Stipek et al., 1992). These observations imply that the process of moral internalization may have already begun long before young children would have even experienced an Oedipus or Electra complex, much less have resolved it. So even though Freud's broader themes about the significance of moral emotions have some merit, perhaps it is time to lay his theory of **oedipal morality** to rest.

This is exactly what modern psychoanalytic theorists have done. They argue that children may begin to form a conscience *as toddlers* if they are *securely attached* to warm and responsive parents who have often cooperated with their wishes during joint play and have shared many positive emotional experiences with them. Within the context of a warm, mutually responsive emotional relationship (rather than a fear-provoking one), toddlers are likely to display the kind of *committed compliance* we discussed in Chapter 12—an orientation in which they are (1) highly motivated to embrace the parent's agenda and to comply with her rules and requests, (2) sensitive to a parent's emotional signals indicating whether they have done right or wrong, and (3) beginning to internalize those parental reactions to their triumphs and transgressions, coming to experience the pride, shame, and (later) guilt that will help them to evaluate and regulate their own conduct (Emde et al., 1991; Kochanska, 1997b). Although data to evaluate those newer psychoanalytic ideas are not extensive, Grazyna Kochanska (1997b) reports that preschoolers who had earlier enjoyed warm, mutually responsive emotional relationships with their mothers as 2- to 3½-year-olds show more signs of having a strong internalized conscience (for example, a reluctance to break rules) at ages 3½ to 5 than do age-mates whose earlier mother–toddler relationships had been less warm and mutually responsive.

Unfortunately, modern psychoanalytic theorists have had less to say about moral development beyond the preschool period or about children's *moral reasoning*—the very issue that cognitive-developmentalists emphasize.

COGNITIVE DEVELOPMENTAL THEORY: THE CHILD AS A MORAL PHILOSOPHER

oedipal morality
Freud's theory that moral development occurs during the phallic period (ages 3 to 6) when children internalize the moral standards of the same-sex parent as they resolve their Oedipus or Electra conflicts.

Cognitive developmentalists study morality by charting the development of *moral reasoning* that children display when deciding whether various acts are right or wrong. According to cognitive theorists, both cognitive growth and social experiences help children to develop progressively richer understandings of the meaning of rules, laws, and interpersonal obligations. As children acquire these new understandings, they are said to progress through an *invariant sequence* of moral stages, each of which evolves from and replaces its predecessor and represents a more advanced or "mature" perspective on moral issues. In this part of the chapter, we will first examine Jean Piaget's early theory of moral development before turning to Lawrence Kolberg's revision and extension of Piaget's approach.

Piaget's Theory of Moral Development

Piaget's (1932/1965) early work on children's moral judgments focused on two aspects of moral reasoning. He studied the development of *respect for rules* by playing marbles with Swiss children between ages 5 and 13. As they played, Piaget asked questions such as "Where do these rules come from? Must everyone obey a rule? Can these rules be changed?" To study children's conceptions of *justice,* Piaget gave them moral-decision stories to ponder. Here is one example:

> *Story A.* A little boy who is called John is in his room. He is called to dinner. He goes into the dining room. But behind the door there was a chair, and on the chair there was a tray with 15 cups on it. John couldn't have known that there was all this behind the door. He goes in, the door knocks against the tray, bang go the 15 cups, and they all get broken.
> *Story B.* Once there was a little boy whose name was Henry. One day when his mother was out he tried to reach some jam out of the cupboard. He climbed onto a chair and stretched out his arm. But the jam was too high up, and he couldn't reach it . . . While he was trying to get it, he knocked over a cup. The cup fell down and broke [Piaget, 1932/1965, p. 122].

Having heard the stories, participants were asked such questions as "Which child is naughtier? Why?" and "How should the naughtier child be punished?" Using these research techniques, Piaget formulated a theory of moral development that includes a premoral period and two moral stages.

The Premoral Period

According to Piaget, preschool children show little concern for or awareness of rules. In a game of marbles, these **premoral** children do not play systematically with the intent of winning. Instead, they seem to make up their own rules, and they think the point of the game is to take turns and have fun.

The Stage of Moral Realism, or Heteronomous Morality

Between ages of 5 and 10, children develop a strong respect for rules as they enter Piaget's stage of **heteronomous morality** ("heteronomous" means "under the rule of another"). Children now believe that rules are laid down by powerful authority figures such as God, the police, or their parents, and they think that these regulations are sacred and unalterable. Try breaking the speed limit with a 6-year-old at your side and you may see what Piaget was talking about. Even if you are rushing to the hospital in a medical emergency, the young child may note that you are breaking a "rule of the road" and consider your behavior unacceptable conduct that deserves to be punished. Heteronomous children think of rules as *moral absolutes.* They believe that there is a "right" side and a "wrong" side to any moral issue, and right always means following the rules.

Heteronomous children are also likely to judge the naughtiness of an act by its objective consequences rather than the actor's intent. For example, many 5- to 9-year-olds judged John, who broke 15 cups while performing a well-intentioned act, to be naughtier than Henry, who broke one cup while stealing jam.

premoral period
in Piaget's theory, the first 5 years of life, when children have little respect for or awareness of socially defined rules.

heteronomous morality
Piaget's first stage of moral development, in which children view the rules of authority figures as sacred and unalterable.

"HEY, CAREFUL, JOEY! GOD SEES EVERYTHING WE DO, THEN HE GOES AN' TELLS SANTA CLAUS!"

Heteronomous children also favor *expiatory punishment*—punishment for its own sake, with no concern for its relation to the nature of the forbidden act. So a 6-year-old might favor spanking a boy who had broken a window rather than making the boy pay for the window from his allowance. Furthermore, the heteronomous child believes in **immanent justice**—the idea that violations of social rules will invariably be punished in one way or another (see, for example, Dennis's warning to Joey in the cartoon). So if a 6-year-old boy were to fall and skin his knee while stealing cookies, he might conclude that this injury was the punishment he deserved for his transgression. Life for the heteronomous child is fair and just.

The Stage of Moral Relativism, or Autonomous Morality

By age 10 or 11, most children have reached Piaget's second moral stage—moral relativism, or **autonomous morality.** Older, autonomous children now realize that social rules are arbitrary agreements that can be challenged and even changed with the consent of the people they govern. They also feel that rules can be violated in the service of human needs. Thus, a driver who speeds during a medical emergency is no longer considered immoral, even though she is breaking the law. Judgments of right and wrong now depend more on the actor's intent to deceive or to violate social rules rather than the objective consequences of the act itself. So 10-year-olds reliably say that Henry, who broke one cup while stealing some jam (bad intent), is naughtier than John, who broke 15 cups while coming to dinner (good or neutral intent).

When deciding how to punish transgressions, the morally autonomous child usually favors *reciprocal punishments*—that is, treatments that tailor punitive consequences to the "crime" so that the rule breaker will understand the implications of a transgression and perhaps be less likely to repeat it. So an autonomous child may decide that the boy who deliberately breaks a window should pay for it out of his allowance (and learn that windows cost money) rather than simply submitting to a spanking. Finally, autonomous youngsters no longer believe in immanent justice, because they have learned from experience that violations of social rules often go undetected and unpunished.

immanent justice
the notion that unacceptable conduct will invariably be punished and that justice is ever present in the world.

autonomous morality
Piaget's second stage of moral development, in which children realize that rules are arbitrary agreements that can be challenged and changed with the consent of the people they govern.

Moving from Heteronomous to Autonomous Morality

According to Piaget, both cognitive maturation and social experience play a role in the transition from heteronomous to autonomous morality. The cognitive advances that are necessary for this shift are a general decline in egocentrism and the development of role-taking skills that enable the child to view moral issues from several perspectives. The kind of social experience that Piaget considers important is *equal-status* contact with peers. As we noted in Chapter 12, peers must learn to take each other's perspectives and resolve their disagreements in mutually beneficial ways, often without any adult intervention, if they are to play cooperatively or accomplish other group goals. So equal-status contacts with peers may lead to a more flexible, autonomous morality because they (1) lessen the child's respect for adult authority, (2) increase his or her self-respect and respect for peers, and (3) illustrate that rules are arbitrary agreements that can be changed with the consent of the people they govern.

And what role do parents play? Interestingly, Piaget claimed that unless parents relinquish some of their power, they may *slow* the progress of moral development by reinforcing the child's respect for rules and authority figures. If, for example, a parent enforces a demand with a threat or a statement such as "Do it because I told you to!", it is easy to see how the young child might conclude that rules are absolutes that derive their "teeth" from the parent's power to enforce them.

An Evaluation of Piaget's Theory

Many researchers in many cultures have replicated Piaget's findings when they rely on his research methods. For example, younger children around the world are more likely than older ones to display such aspects of heteronomous morality as a belief in immanent justice or a tendency to emphasize consequences more than intentions when judging how wrong an act is (Jose, 1990; Lapsley, 1996). In addition, the maturity of children's moral judgments is related to such indications of cognitive development as IQ and role-taking skills (Ambron & Irwin, 1975; Lapsley, 1996). There is even some support for Piaget's "peer participation" hypothesis: Popular children who often take part in peer-group activities and who assume positions of leadership tend to make mature moral judgments (Bear & Rys, 1994; Keasey, 1971).

Nevertheless, there is ample reason to believe that Piaget's theory clearly underestimates the moral capacities of preschool and grade-school children.

Figure 14.6 *Example of drawings used by Nelson to convey an actor's intentions to preschool children.* ADAPTED FROM NELSON, 1980.

Do Younger Children Ignore an Actor's Intentions?

Consider Piaget's claim that children younger than 9 or 10 judge acts as right or wrong based on the consequences that the acts produce rather than the intentions that guided them. Unfortunately, Piaget's moral-decision stories were flawed in that they (1) confounded intentions and consequences by asking whether a person who caused little harm with a bad intent was naughtier than one who caused a larger amount of harm while serving good intentions, and (2) made information about the consequences of an act *much clearer* than information about the actor's intentions.

Sharon Nelson (1980) overcame these flaws in an interesting experiment with 3-year-olds. Each child listened to stories in which a character threw a ball to a playmate. The actor's motive was described as *good* (his friend had nothing to play with) or *bad* (the actor was mad at his friend), and the consequences of his act were either *positive* (the friend caught the ball and was happy to play with it) or *negative* (the ball hit the friend in the head and made him cry). To ensure that her 3-year-olds understood the actor's intentions, Nelson showed them drawings such as Figure 14.6, which depicts a negative intent.

Not surprisingly, the 3-year-olds in this study judged acts that had positive consequences more favorably than those that caused harm. However, as Figure 14.7 shows,

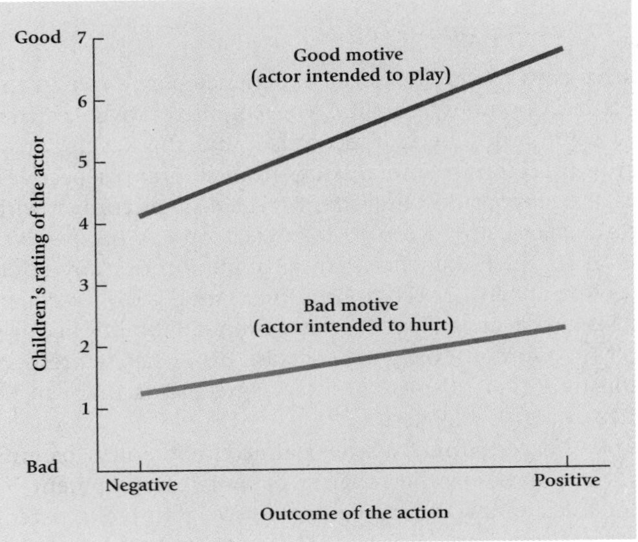

Figure 14.7 *Average ratings of an actor's behavior for actors who produced positive or negative outcomes while serving either good or bad intentions.* ADAPTED FROM NELSON, 1980.

they also judged the well-intentioned child who had wanted to play much more favorably than the child who intended to hurt his friend, *regardless of the consequences of his actions*. So even *preschool* children consider an actor's intentions when making moral judgments. In fact, young children often attempt to escape punishment through such intentional pleas as, "I didn't *mean* to, mommy!" But Piaget was right in one respect: Younger children do assign more weight to consequences and less weight to intentions than older children do, even though both younger and older children consider both sources of information when evaluating others' conduct (Lapsley, 1996; Zelazo, Helwig, & Lau, 1996).

Do Younger Children Respect All Rules (and Adult Authority)?

According to Piaget, young children think of rules as sacred and obligatory prescriptions that are laid down by respected authority figures and are not to be questioned or changed. However, Elliot Turiel (1983) notes that children actually encounter two kinds of rules. **Moral rules** focus on the welfare and basic rights of individuals and include prescriptions against hitting, stealing, lying, cheating, or otherwise harming others or violating their rights. By contrast, **social-conventional rules** are determined by social consensus and regulate conduct in particular social situations. These standards are more like rules of social etiquette and include the rules of games as well as school rules that forbid snacking in class or using the restroom without permission. Do children treat these two kinds of rules as equivalent?

Apparently not. Judith Smetana (1981; 1985; Smetana, Schlagman, & Adams, 1993) finds that even 2½- to 3-year-olds consider moral transgressions such as hitting, stealing, and refusing to share to be much more serious and more deserving of punishment than social conventional violations such as snacking in class or not saying "please" when requesting a toy. When asked whether a violation would be okay if there were no rule against it, children said that moral transgressions are always wrong but social-conventional violations are okay in the absence of any explicit rule. Clearly, parents view themselves as responsible for enforcing both moral and social-conventional rules. However, they attend more closely to moral violations and place much more emphasis on the harm such violations do to others (Nucci & Smetana, 1996; Nucci & Weber, 1995), perhaps explaining why children understand the need for and importance of *moral* prescriptions by age 2½ to 3—much sooner than Piaget had assumed they would.

Furthermore, Piaget's theory predicts that 6- to 10-year-old heteronomous children should be even more inclined than younger children are to respect pronouncements laid down by adults. Yet children of this age are quite capable of questioning adult authority. They believe that parents are justified in enforcing rules against stealing and other *moral* transgressions, but they feel that a parent is clearly abusing authority should he arbitrarily impose rules that restrict their choice of friends or leisure activities—areas that they perceive as under their own *personal* jurisdiction (Tisak & Tisak, 1990). In addition, they increasingly recognize that adult authority may be limited to certain con-

moral rules
standards of acceptable and unacceptable conduct that focus on the rights and privileges of individuals.

social-conventional rules
standards of conduct determined by social consensus that indicate what is appropriate within a particular social context.

texts, acknowledging, for example, that teachers have a right to regulate smoking at school but not in the neighborhood (Smetana & Bitz, 1996). Perhaps the best illustration that older heteronomous children are not totally cowed by adult authority is this: Ten-year-olds who are relatively religious believe that not even the endorsement of the ultimate authority figure—God—would make a *moral* transgression (such as stealing) morally right (Nucci & Turiel, 1993). So 6- to 10-year-olds do have ideas about what constitutes *legitimate* authority, and those ideas are not based solely on an unwavering respect for the sanctity or wisdom of adults, as Piaget had assumed.

Do Parents Impede Children's Moral Development?

Finally, Piaget was partially right and partially wrong in his views of parents as agents of moral socialization. He was right in assuming that parents can impede moral growth by adopting a heavy-handed, authoritarian approach in which they *challenge* the child's moral reasoning and present their own ideas in a lecturelike format as lessons to be learned (Walker & Taylor, 1991). But he was very wrong in assuming that parents typically operate in this way when discussing moral issues with their children. Consider that 6- to 7-year-olds, who should be at Piaget's heteronomous stage, often make *autonomous* moral judgments—*as long as their parents do* (Leon, 1984). How is this possible? Research by Lawrence Walker and John Taylor (1991) suggests an answer: By carefully tailoring their own reasoning to the child's ability to understand, and by presenting new moral perspectives in a supportive (rather than challenging) way, parents may often *promote* their children's moral development.

Developmentalists are indebted to Piaget for suggesting that children's moral reasoning develops in stages that are closely tied to cognitive growth. Even today, his theory continues to stimulate research and new insights—including the findings above, which reveal that children younger than 10 are considerably more sophisticated in their moral reasoning than Piaget made them out to be. But is moral reasoning fully developed by age 10 to 11, as Piaget had assumed? Lawrence Kohlberg certainly didn't think so.

Kohlberg's Theory of Moral Development

Kohlberg (1963, 1984; Colby & Kohlberg, 1987) has refined and extended Piaget's theory of moral development by asking 10-, 13-, and 16-year-old boys to resolve a series of moral dilemmas. Each dilemma challenged the respondent by requiring him to choose between (1) obeying a rule, law, or authority figure and (2) taking some action that conflicted with these rules and commands while serving a human need. The following story is the best known of Kohlberg's moral dilemmas:

> In Europe, a woman was near death from a special kind of cancer. There was one drug that doctors thought might save her. It was a form of radium that a druggist in the same town had recently discovered. The drug was expensive to make, but the druggist was charging $2000, or 10 times the cost of the drug, for a small (possibly life-saving) dose. Heinz, the sick woman's husband, borrowed all the money he could, about $1000, or half of what he needed. He told the druggist that his wife was dying and asked him to sell the drug cheaper or to let him pay later. The druggist replied "No, I discovered the drug, and I'm going to make money from it." Heinz then became desperate and broke into the store to steal the drug for his wife. Should Heinz have done that?

Kohlberg was actually less interested in the respondent's decision (that is, what Heinz should have done) than in the underlying rationale, or "thought structures," that the individual used to justify his decision. So, if a participant says "Heinz should steal the drug to save his wife's life," it is necessary to determine why her life is so important. Is it because she cooks and irons for Heinz? Because it's a husband's duty to save his wife? Or because the preservation of life is among the highest of human values? To determine the "structure" of a person's moral reasoning, Kohlberg asked probing questions: Does Heinz have an obligation to steal the drug? If Heinz doesn't love his wife, should he steal it for her? Should Heinz steal the drug for a stranger? Is it important for people to do everything they can to save another life? Is it against the law to steal? Does that make it morally wrong? The purpose of these probes was to clarify how individual participants reasoned about obedience and authority on the one hand and about human needs, rights, and privileges on the other.

Through his use of these elaborate *clinical interviews,* Kohlberg's first discovery was that moral development is far from complete when the child reaches age 10 to 11, or Piaget's autonomous stage. Indeed, moral reasoning seems to evolve and become progressively more complex throughout adolescence and into young adulthood. Careful analyses of his participants' responses to several dilemmas led Kohlberg to conclude that moral growth progresses through an *invariant sequence* of three moral levels, each of which is composed of two distinct moral stages. According to Kohlberg, the order of these moral levels and stages is invariant because they depend on the development of certain cognitive abilities that evolve in an invariant sequence. Like Piaget, Kohlberg assumes that each succeeding stage evolves from and replaces its predecessor; once the individual has attained a higher stage of moral reasoning, he or she should never regress to earlier stages.

Before examining Kohlberg's moral stages, it is important to emphasize that each stage represents a particular perspective, or *method of thinking* about moral dilemmas, rather than a particular type of moral decision. As we will see, decisions are not very informative in themselves, because people at each moral stage might well endorse either of the alternative courses of action when resolving one of these ethical dilemmas. (However, participants at Kohlberg's highest moral level generally favor serving human needs over complying with rules or laws that would compromise others' welfare.)

The basic themes and defining characteristics of Kohlberg's three moral levels and six stages are as follows:

Level 1: Preconventional Morality

In **preconventional morality,** rules are truly external to the self rather than internalized. The child conforms to rules imposed by authority figures to avoid punishment or obtain personal rewards. Morality is self-serving: What is right is what one can get away with or what is personally satisfying.

Stage 1: Punishment-and-Obedience Orientation. The goodness or badness of an act depends on its consequences. The child obeys authorities to avoid punishment, but may not consider an act wrong if it is not detected and punished. The greater the harm done or the more severe the punishment is, the more "bad" the act is. The following two responses reflect a punishment-and-obedience orientation to the Heinz dilemma:

> *Protheft:* It isn't really bad to take the drug—he did ask to pay for it first. He wouldn't do any other damage or take anything else, and the drug he'd take is only worth $200, not $2,000.
>
> *Antitheft:* Heinz doesn't have permission to take the drug. He can't just go and break through a window. He'd be a bad criminal doing all that damage . . . and stealing anything so expensive would be a big crime.

preconventional morality
Kohlberg's term for the first two stages of moral reasoning, in which moral judgments are based on the tangible punitive consequences (Stage 1) or rewarding consequences (Stage 2) of an act for the actor rather than on the relationship of that act to society's rules and customs.

Stage 2: Naive Hedonism. A person at this second stage conforms to rules in order to gain rewards or satisfy personal objectives. There is some concern for the perspective of others, but other-oriented behaviors are ultimately motivated by the hope of benefiting in return. "You scratch my back and I'll scratch yours" is the guiding philosophy. Here are two samples of this hedonistic, self-serving morality (see also Calvin's moral philosophy in the cartoon).

Calvin and Hobbes

by Bill Watterson

Protheft: Heinz isn't really doing any harm to the druggist, and he can always pay him back. If he doesn't want to lose his wife, he should take the drug.
Antitheft: Hey, the druggist isn't wrong, he just wants to make a profit like everybody else. That's what you're in business for, to make money.

Level 2: Conventional Morality

The individual with **conventional morality** strives to obey rules and social norms in order to win others' approval or to maintain social order. Social praise and the avoidance of blame have now replaced tangible rewards and punishments as motivators of ethical conduct. The perspectives of other people are clearly recognized and given careful consideration.

Stage 3: "Good Boy" or "Good Girl" Orientation. Moral behavior is that which pleases, helps, or is approved of by others. Actions are evaluated on the basis of the actor's intent. "He means well" is a common expression of moral approval at this stage. As we see in the following responses, the primary objective of a Stage 3 respondent is to be thought of as a "good" person.

Protheft: Stealing is bad, but Heinz is only doing something that is natural for a good husband to do. You can't blame him for doing something out of love for his wife. You'd blame him if he didn't save her.
Antitheft: If Heinz's wife dies, he can't be blamed. You can't say he is heartless for failing to commit a crime. The druggist is the selfish and heartless one. Heinz tried to do everything he really could.

Stage 4: Social-Order-Maintaining Morality. At this stage, the individual considers the perspectives of the generalized other—that is, the will of society as reflected in law. Now what is right is what conforms to the rules of *legal* authority. The reason for conforming is not a fear of punishment, but a belief that rules and laws maintain a social order that is worth preserving. As we see in the following responses, laws always transcend special interests:

Protheft: The druggist is leading the wrong kind of life if he just lets somebody die; so it's Heinz's duty to save [his wife]. But Heinz just can't go around breaking laws—he must pay the druggist back and take his punishment for stealing.
Antitheft: It's natural for Heinz to want to save his wife, but it's still always wrong to steal. You have to follow the rules regardless of your feelings or the special circumstances.

conventional morality
Kohlberg's term for the third and fourth stages of moral reasoning, in which moral judgments are based on a desire to gain approval (Stage 3) or to uphold laws that maintain social order (Stage 4).

Level 3: Postconventional (or Principled) Morality

A person at the level of **postconventional morality** defines right and wrong in terms of broad principles of justice that could conflict with written laws or with the dictates of authority figures. Morally right and legally proper are not always one and the same.

STAGE 5: THE SOCIAL-CONTRACT ORIENTATION. At Stage 5, the individual views laws as instruments for expressing the will of the majority and furthering human values. Laws that accomplish these ends and are impartially applied are viewed as social contracts that one has an obligation to follow; but imposed laws that compromise human rights or dignity are considered unjust and worthy of challenge. Notice how distinctions between what is legal and what is moral begin to appear in the following Stage 5 responses to Heinz's dilemma:

> *Protheft:* Before you say stealing is morally wrong, you've got to consider this whole situation. Of course, the laws are quite clear about breaking into a store. And . . . Heinz would know that there were no legal grounds for his actions. Yet it would be reasonable for anybody, in that kind of situation, to steal the drug.
>
> *Antitheft:* I can see the good that would come from illegally taking the drug. But the ends don't justify the means. The law represents a consensus of how people have agreed to live together, and Heinz has an obligation to respect these agreements. You can't say Heinz would be completely wrong to steal the drug, but even these circumstances don't make it right.

STAGE 6: MORALITY OF INDIVIDUAL PRINCIPLES OF CONSCIENCE. At this "highest" moral stage, the individual defines right and wrong on the basis of the self-chosen ethical principles of his or her own conscience. These principles are not concrete rules such as the Ten Commandments. They are abstract moral guidelines or principles of universal justice (and respect for the rights of *all* human beings) that *transcend* any law or social contract that may conflict with them. Here are two Stage 6 responses to the Heinz dilemma:

> *Protheft:* When one must choose between disobeying a law and saving a human life, the higher principle of preserving life makes it morally right to steal the drug.
>
> *Antitheft:* With many cases of cancer and the scarcity of the drug, there may not be enough to go around to everybody who needs it. The correct course of action can only be the one that is "right" by all people concerned. Heinz ought to act not on emotion or the law, but according to what he thinks an ideally just person would do in this case.

Stage 6 is Kohlberg's vision of ideal moral reasoning. But because it is so very rare and virtually no one functions consistently at this level, Kohlberg came to view it as a hypothetical construct—that is, the stage to which people would progress were they to develop beyond Stage 5. In fact, the later versions of Kohlberg's manual for scoring moral judgments no longer attempt to measure Stage 6 reasoning (Colby & Kohlberg, 1987).

Support for Kohlberg's Theory

Although Kohlberg believes that his stages form an invariant and universal sequence of moral growth that is closely tied to cognitive development, he also claims that cognitive growth, by itself, is not sufficient to guarantee moral development. In order to ever move beyond the preconventional level of moral reasoning, children must be

postconventional morality
Kohlberg's term for the fifth and sixth stages of moral reasoning, in which moral judgments are based on social contracts and democratic law (Stage 5) or on universal principles of ethics and justice (Stage 6).

exposed to persons or situations that introduce *cognitive disequilibria*—that is, conflicts between existing moral concepts and new ideas that force them to reevaluate their viewpoints. So, like Piaget, Kohlberg believes that both cognitive development and *relevant social experiences* underlie the growth of moral reasoning.

How much support is there for these ideas? Let's review the evidence, starting with data bearing on Kohlberg's invariant-sequence hypothesis.

Are Kohlberg's Stages an Invariant Sequence?

If Kohlberg's stages represent a true developmental sequence, we should find a strong positive correlation between age and maturity of moral reasoning. This is precisely what researchers have found in studies conducted in the U.S., Mexico, the Bahamas, Taiwan, Turkey, Honduras, India, Nigeria, and Kenya (Colby & Kohlberg, 1987). So it seems that Kohlberg's levels and stages of moral reasoning are "universal" structures that are age-related, just as we would expect them to be if they formed a developmental sequence. But do these studies establish that Kohlberg's stages form a fixed, or *invariant,* sequence?

No, they do not! The problem is that participants at each age level were *different* people, and we cannot be certain that a 25-year-old at Stage 5 has progressed through the various moral levels and stages in the order specified by Kohlberg's theory.

The Longitudinal Evidence. Clearly, the most compelling evidence for Kohlberg's invariant-sequence hypothesis would be a demonstration that individual children progress through the moral stages in precisely the order that Kohlberg says they should. Ann Colby and her associates (1983) have conducted a 20-year longitudinal study of Kohlberg's original research participants, who were reinterviewed five times at 3- to 4-year intervals. As shown in Figure 14.8, moral reasoning developed very gradually, with use of preconventional reasoning (Stages 1 and 2) declining sharply in adolescence—the same period in which conventional reasoning (Stages 3 and 4) is on the rise. Conventional reasoning remained the dominant form of moral expression in adulthood, with very few participants ever moving beyond it to postconventional morality (Stage 5). But even so, Colby et al. found that participants proceeded through the stages they did attain in precisely the order Kohlberg predicted and that no one ever skipped a stage. Similar results have been reported in a 9-year longitudinal study of adolescents in Israel and a 12-year longitudinal project conducted in Turkey (Colby & Kohlberg, 1987). So Kohlberg's moral stages do seem to represent an invariant sequence (see also Rest, Thoma, & Edwards, 1997). Let's note, however, that people progress in an orderly fashion to *their* highest stage of reasoning and that Stage 3 or 4 is the end of this developmental journey for most individuals worldwide (Snarey, 1985).

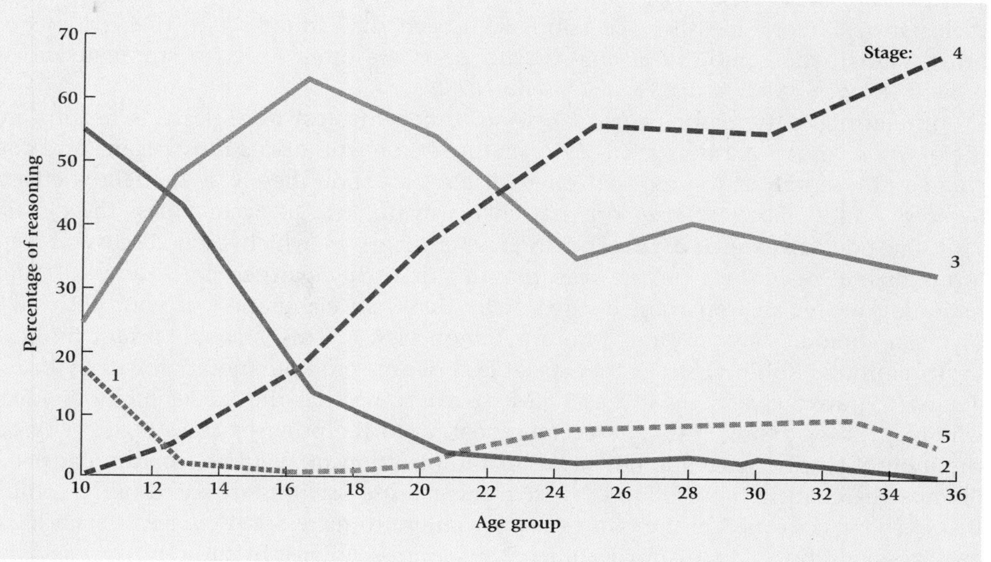

Figure 14.8 *Use of Kohlberg's moral stages at ages 10 through 36 by male participants studied longitudinally over a 20-year period.* ADAPTED FROM COLBY, KOHLBERG, GIBBS, & LIEBERMAN, 1983.

Cognitive Prerequisites for Moral Growth

According to Kohlberg (1963), the young, preconventional child reasons about moral issues from an egocentric point of view. At Stage 1, the child thinks that certain acts are bad because they are punished. At Stage 2, the child shows a limited awareness of the needs, thoughts, and intentions of others but still judges *self-serving* acts as more appropriate. However, conventional reasoning clearly requires some *role-taking* abilities. A person at Stage 3, for example, must necessarily recognize others' points of view before she will evaluate intentions that would win their approval as "good" or morally acceptable. Furthermore, Kohlberg proposed that postconventional moral reasoning requires *formal operations*. A Stage 5 individual who bases moral judgments on abstract principles must be able to reason abstractly rather than simply adhering to the rule of law or concrete moral norms.

These hypotheses have received ample support. Lawrence Walker (1980), for example, found that all 10- to 13-year-olds who had reached Kohlberg's Stage 3 ("good boy-good girl" morality) were quite proficient at mutual role taking, although not all proficient role takers had reached Stage 3 in their moral reasoning. Similarly, Carolyn Tomlinson-Keasey and Charles Keasey (1974) and Deanne Kuhn and her associates (1977) found that (1) all participants who showed any evidence of postconventional (Stage 5) moral reasoning had reached formal operations but that (2) most formal operators had not reached Kohlberg's postconventional level of moral reasoning. What these findings imply is that role-taking skills are *necessary but not sufficient* for the development of conventional morality and that formal operations are *necessary but not sufficient* for the emergence of postconventional morality. This pattern is precisely what Kohlberg had expected, as he viewed cognitive growth as only one prerequisite for moral development. The other prerequisite is *relevant social experience*—that is, exposure to persons or situations that force a person to reevaluate and alter his current moral perspectives.

Evidence for Kohlberg's Social-Experience Hypothesis

Does research support the proposition that social experience contributes to moral development? Yes, indeed, and we've already discussed an important example—the fact that parents can promote the growth of a child's moral reasoning if they are sensitive to the child's viewpoint when discussing moral issues and present their own perspectives in a supportive (and nonthreatening) way.

Peer Interactions. Like Piaget, Kohlberg felt that interactions with peers probably contribute more to moral growth than one-sided discussions with adult authority figures. And they were right to call attention to the role that peers play as agents of moral socialization. Children do seem to think more actively and deeply about their own and their partners' moral ideas in discussions with peers than in talks with their parents or other adults; what's more, discussions with peers are more likely to stimulate moral growth (Kruger, 1992; Kruger & Tomasello, 1986).

Interestingly, the participants who seem to benefit most from peer discussions are those whose moral reasoning was least mature before the discussions began. And the changes in moral reasoning that they display are not merely a modeling effect. Berkowitz and Gibbs (1983) report that change is unlikely to occur unless the discussions include **transactive interactions**—exchanges in which each discussant performs mental operations on the reasoning of his or her partner (for example, "Your reasoning misses an important distinction"; "Here's an elaboration of your position"; "We can combine our positions into a common view"). This is an important finding, for it reinforces Kohlberg's idea that social experiences promote moral growth by introducing cognitive challenges to one's current reasoning that the *less mature* individual will adapt to by assimilating and accommodating to the other person's logic. Why do the more mature discussants not move in the direction of their less mature partners? Because the challenges introduced by their less mature partners are based on reasoning that they have already rejected. In fact, their failure to regress in the face of such logic provides additional support for Kohlberg's invariant-sequence hypothesis.

transactive interactions
verbal exchanges in which individuals perform mental operations on the reasoning of their discussion partners.

Discussing weighty ethical issues with peers often promotes the growth of moral reasoning.

Advanced Education. Another kind of social experience that promotes moral growth is receiving an advanced education. Consistently, adults who go on to college and receive many years of education reason more complexly about moral issues than those who are less educated (Pratt et al., 1991; Speicher, 1994), and differences in the moral reasoning between college students and their nonstudent peers become greater with each successive year of school that the college students complete (Rest & Thoma, 1985). Advanced education may foster moral growth in two ways: by (1) contributing to cognitive growth and (2) exposing students to diverse moral perspectives that produce cognitive conflict and soul searching (Kohlberg, 1984; Mason & Gibbs, 1993).

Cultural Influences. Finally, simply living in a complex, diverse, and democratic society can stimulate moral development. Just as we learn the give-and-take of mutual perspective taking by discussing issues with our friends, we learn in a diverse democracy that the opinions of many groups must be weighed and that laws reflect a consensus of the citizens rather than the arbitrary rulings of a dictator. Cross-cultural studies suggest that postconventional moral reasoning emerges primarily in Western democracies and that people in rural villages in many nonindustrialized countries show no signs of it (Harkness, Edwards, & Super, 1981; Snarey & Keljo, 1991; Tietjen & Walker, 1985). People in these homogeneous communities may have less experience with the kinds of political conflicts and compromises that take place in a more diverse society and so may never have any need to question conventional moral standards. By adopting a contextual perspective on development, we can appreciate that the conventional (mostly Stage 3) reasoning typically displayed by adults in these societies—with its emphasis on cooperation and loyalty to the immediate social group—is adaptive and mature within their own social systems (Harkness et al., 1981).

In sum, Kohlberg has described an invariant sequence of moral stages and identified some of the cognitive factors and major environmental influences that determine how far an individual progresses in this sequence. Yet, critics have offered many reasons for suspecting that Kohlberg's theory is far from a complete account of moral development.

Criticisms of Kohlberg's Approach

Many of the criticisms of Kohlberg's theory have centered on the possibilities that it is biased against certain groups of people, that it underestimates the moral sophistication of young children, and that it says much about moral reasoning but little about moral affect and moral behavior.

Is Kohlberg's Theory Biased?

CULTURAL BIAS. Although research indicates that children and adolescents in many cultures proceed through the first three or four of Kohlberg's stages in order, we have seen that postconventional morality as Kohlberg defines it simply does not exist in some societies. Critics have charged that Kohlberg's highest stages reflect a Western ideal of justice and that his stage theory is therefore biased against people who live in non-Western societies or who do not value individualism and individual rights highly enough to want to challenge society's rules (Gibbs & Schnell, 1985; Shweder, Mahapatra, & Miller, 1990). People in communal societies that emphasize social harmony and place the good of the group ahead of the good of the individual may be viewed as conventional moral thinkers in Kohlberg's system but may actually have very sophisticated concepts of justice (Snarey & Keljo, 1991; Vasudev & Hummel, 1987). Although there are some aspects of moral development that do seem to be common to all cultures, the research presented in Box 14.3 indicates that other aspects of moral growth can vary considerably from society to society.

GENDER BIAS. Critics have also charged that Kohlberg's theory, which was developed from data provided by *male* participants, does not adequately represent female moral reasoning. Carol Gilligan (1982, 1993), for example, has been disturbed by the fact that, in some early studies, women seemed to be the moral inferiors of men, typically reasoning at Kohlberg's Stage 3 while men usually reasoned at Stage 4. Her response was to argue that differential gender typing causes boys and girls to adopt different moral orientations. The strong independence and assertiveness training that boys receive encourages them to view moral dilemmas as inevitable conflicts of interest between *individuals* that laws and other social conventions are designed to resolve. Gilligan calls this orientation the **morality of justice,** a perspective that approximates Stage 4 in Kohlberg's scheme. By contrast, girls are taught to be nurturant, empathic, and concerned about others—in short, to define their sense of "goodness" in terms of their interpersonal *relationships.* So for females, morality implies a sense of caring or compassionate concern for human welfare—a **morality of care** that may seem to represent Stage 3 in Kohlberg's scheme. However, Gilligan insists that the morality of care that females adopt can become quite abstract or "principled," even though Kohlberg's scheme might place it at Stage 3 because of its focus on interpersonal obligations.

At this point, there is little support for Gilligan's claim that Kohlberg's theory is biased against women. Most studies indicate that women reason just as complexly about moral issues as men do when their answers are scored by Kohlberg's criteria (Jadack et al., 1995; Walker, 1995). Nor is there much evidence for sex differences in moral orientations: When reasoning about real-life dilemmas they have faced, *both* males and females raise issues of compassion and interpersonal responsibility about as often as or more often than they talk about issues of law, justice, and individual rights (Walker, 1995; Wark & Krebs, 1996). Although there are some indications that females tend to raise care issues more than males do (Wark & Krebs, 1996) and to place somewhat more emphasis on the interpersonal aspects of everyday problem solving (Strough, Berg, & Sansone, 1996; Williams & Bybee, 1994), it has become quite clear that the justice and care orientations are *not* sex-specific moralities, as Gilligan had claimed.

Nevertheless, Gilligan's theory and the research designed to test it have broadened our view of morality by illustrating that both men and women often think about moral issues—especially real-life as opposed to hypothetical moral issues—in terms of their responsibilities for the welfare of other people. Kohlberg emphasized only one way, a very legalistic way, of thinking about right and wrong. There seems to be merit in tracing the development of *both* a morality of justice and a morality of care in *both* males and females (Brabeck, 1983; Gilligan, 1993).

morality of justice
Gilligan's term for what she presumes to be the dominant moral orientation of males, focusing more on socially defined justice as administered through law than on compassionate concerns for human welfare.

morality of care
Gilligan's term for what she presumes to be the dominant moral orientation of females—an orientation focusing more on compassionate concerns for human welfare than on socially defined justice as administered through law.

14.3

CULTURAL INFLUENCES

Cultural Differences in Moral Reasoning

Is each of the following acts wrong? If so, how serious a violation is it?

1. A young married woman is beaten black and blue by her husband after going to a movie without his permission despite having been warned not to do so again.

2. A brother and sister decide to get married and have children.

3. The day after his father died, the oldest son in a family has a haircut and eats chicken.

These are three of 39 acts presented by Richard Shweder, Manamahan Mahapatra, and Joan Miller (1990) to children ages 5 to 13 and adults in India and the United States. You may be surprised to learn that Hindu children and adults rated the son's having a haircut and eating chicken after his father's death as among the very more morally offensive of the 39 acts they rated, and the husband's beating of his disobedient wife as not wrong at all. American children and adults, of course, viewed wife beating as far more serious than breaking seemingly arbitrary rules about appropriate mourning behavior. Although Indians and Americans could agree that a few acts like brother–sister incest were serious moral violations, they did not agree on much else.

Furthermore, Indian children and adults viewed the Hindu ban against behavior disrespectful of one's dead father as a *universal moral rule;* they thought it would be best if *everyone in the world* followed it (see also Wainryb, 1993) and strongly disagreed that it would be acceptable to change the rule if most people in their society wanted to change it. Hindus also believed that it is a serious moral offense for a widow to eat fish or wear brightly colored clothes or for a woman to cook food for her family during her menstrual period. To orthodox Hindus, rules against such behavior are required by natural law; they are not just arbitrary social conventions created by members of society. Hindus also regard it as morally necessary for a man to beat his disobedient wife in order to uphold his obligations as head of the family.

What effects do cultural beliefs of this sort have on moral development? The developmental trend in moral thinking that Shweder detected in India was very different from the developmental trend he observed in the United States, as the figure shows. With age, Indian children saw more and more issues as matters of universal moral principle, whereas American children saw fewer and fewer issues in the same light (and more and more as matters of arbitrary social convention that can legitimately differ from society to society). Even the youngest children in both societies expressed moral outlooks very similar to those expressed by adults in their own society and very different from those expressed by either children or adults in the other society.

Based on these cross-cultural findings, Shweder calls into question Kohlberg's claims that all children everywhere construct similar moral codes at similar ages and that certain universal moral principles exist. Shweder also questions Turiel's claim that children everywhere distinguish from an early age between moral rules and social-conventional rules, for Shweder found that the concept of social-conventional rules was simply not very meaningful to Indians of any age. There are also important subcultural influences on moral reasoning. For example, individuals who occupy a subordinate position within their societies (for example, Arab women and Brazilian children from the lower socioeconomic strata) are more inclined than age-mates of higher status to view themselves as having relatively few personal choices about how to behave and as under greater moral obligation to submit to authority (Nucci, Camino, & Sapiro, 1996; Wainryb & Turiel, 1994).

Clearly, these findings challenge the cognitive-developmental position that *all* important aspects of moral growth are universal. Instead, they tend to support a contextual perspective on moral development by suggesting that children's moral judgments are shaped by the culture and subculture in which they live. Perhaps children all over the world think in more and more complex ways about issues of morality and justice as they get older, as Kohlberg claimed, but at the same time adopt different notions about what is right and what is wrong (or a personal choice versus a moral obligation) as Shweder and others claim.

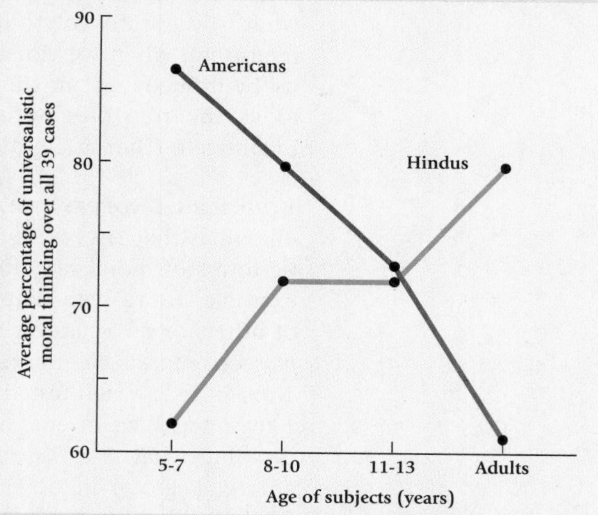

Universalistic moral thinking—the tendency to view rules of behavior as universally valid and unalterable—increases with age among Hindu children in India but decreases with age in the United States. The course of moral development is likely to be different in different societies. ADAPTED FROM SHWEDER, MAHAPATRA, & MILLER, 1987.

Is Kohlberg's Theory Incomplete?

Another common criticism of Kohlberg's theory is that it focuses too heavily on moral reasoning and neglects moral affect and behavior. Yet, Kohlberg did assume that mature moral reasoners should be more inclined to behave morally and that the links between moral reasoning and moral behavior would become stronger as individuals progress toward higher levels of moral understanding (Blasi, 1990).

Does Moral Reasoning Predict Moral Conduct? Most of the available data are consistent with Kohlberg's viewpoint. With few exceptions (for example, Kochanska, Padavich, & Koenig, 1996), most researchers have found that the moral judgments of young children do *not* predict their behavior in situations where they are induced to cheat or violate other moral norms (Nelson, Grinder, & Biaggio, 1969; Santrock, 1975; Toner & Potts, 1981). However, studies of older grade-school children, adolescents, and young adults often find that individuals at higher stages of moral reasoning are more likely than those at lower stages to behave altruistically and conscientiously and are less likely to cheat or take part in delinquent or criminal activity (Colby & Kohlberg, 1987; Rest et al., 1997). Kohlberg (1975), for example, found that only 15% of college students who reasoned at the postconventional level actually cheated on a test when given an opportunity, compared with 55% of the conventional students and 70% of those at the preconventional level. Yet the relationship between stage of moral reasoning and moral behavior is only moderate at best (Bruggerman & Hart, 1996). Why? Largely because people at any stage occasionally revert to lower stages of moral reasoning (that is, regress), especially when resolving dilemmas in which strong punishment for wrongdoing is a distinct possibility (Sobesky, 1983; Wark & Krebs, 1996). So it seems that personal qualities other than moral reasoning, and many situational factors as well, may also influence a person's moral conduct in daily life (Thoma, Rest, & Davison, 1991). One such influence is moral affect.

Kohlberg Ignores Moral Emotions. Norma Haan and her associates (1985) point out that moral dilemmas in everyday life arouse powerful emotions (moral affects). We care about moral issues and how our decisions affect other people; we agonize about what to do and want to feel that we are moral beings; and we do often feel guilty or remorseful when we violate moral norms. These emotions play a central role in morality by influencing our thoughts and motivating our actions, and any theory that overlooks the role of emotions, as Kohlberg's tends to, would seem to be woefully incomplete (Hart & Chmiel, 1992; LeCapitaine, 1987).

Kohlberg Underestimates Young Children. Finally, Kohlberg's focus on legalistic dilemmas that laws were designed to address caused him to overlook other nonlegalistic forms of moral reasoning that influence the behavior of grade-school children. For example, we've seen that young elementary-school children often consider the needs of others or do whatever they think people will approve of when resolving Eisenberg's *prosocial* moral dilemmas, even though these youngsters are hopelessly mired in Stage 1 (or Stage 2) when tested on Kohlberg's dilemmas. Furthermore, 8- to 10-year-old Stage 1 reasoners have often developed some sophisticated notions about *distributive justice*—deciding what is a "fair and just" allocation of limited resources (toys, candies, etc.) among a group of deserving recipients (see Damon, 1988; Sigelman & Waitzman, 1991)—reasoning not adequately represented in Kohlberg's theory. Interestingly, fear of punishment, deference to authority, and other legalistic themes that Kohlberg believes to characterize the moral judgments of 8- to 10-year-olds do not even appear in children's distributive-justice reasoning. So by focusing so heavily on legalistic concepts, Kohlberg has clearly underestimated the moral sophistication of grade-school children.

In sum, Kohlberg's theory of moral development has become prominent for good reason. It describes a universal sequence of changes in moral reasoning extend-

? **WHAT DO YOU THINK?**

Do you think it is acceptable for public schools in a multicultural society, such as the United States, to provide a "moral education" to pupils whose own moral beliefs may depend very heavily on their diverse religious, subcultural, and familial backgrounds? Why or why not?

Although children this young usually display preconventional moral reasoning on Kohlberg's legalistic dilemmas, they actually have some reasonably sophisticated standards of distributive justice.

ing from childhood through adulthood. Furthermore, the evidence supports Kohlberg's view that both cognitive growth and social experiences contribute to moral development. However, there is also some merit to his critics' concerns. Kohlberg's theory does not fully capture the morality of people who live in non-Western societies or who choose to emphasize a morality of care rather than a morality of justice, and it clearly underestimates the moral reasoning of young children. And because Kohlberg concentrates so heavily on moral reasoning, we must rely on other perspectives to help us to understand how moral affect and moral behavior develop, and how thought, emotions, and behavior interact to make us the moral beings that most of us ultimately become.

MORALITY AS A PRODUCT OF SOCIAL LEARNING (AND SOCIAL INFORMATION PROCESSING)

Social learning theorists such as Albert Bandura (1986; 1991) and Walter Mischel (1974) have been primarily interested in the *behavioral* component of morality—what we actually do when faced with temptation. They claim that moral behaviors are learned in the same way that other social behaviors are—through the operation of reinforcement and punishment and through observational learning. They also consider moral behavior to be strongly influenced by the specific situations in which people find themselves. It is not at all surprising, they say, to see a person behave morally in one situation but transgress in another situation, or proclaim that nothing is more important than honesty but then lie or cheat.

How Consistent Are Moral Conduct and Moral Character?

Perhaps the most extensive study of children's moral conduct is one of the oldest—the Character Education Inquiry reported by Hugh Hartshorne and Mark May (1928–1930). The purpose of this 5-year project was to investigate the "moral character" of 10,000 children aged 8 to 16 by tempting them to lie, cheat, or steal in a variety of situations.

Sometimes it is difficult to tell whether children are working together, helping each other, or using each other's work. Although there is some consistency to moral behavior, a child's conduct in any particular situation is likely to be influenced by factors such as the importance of the goal that might be achieved by breaking a moral rule and the probability of being caught should he or she commit a transgression.

The most noteworthy finding of this massive investigation was that children tended *not* to be consistent in their moral behavior; a child's willingness to cheat in one situation did not predict his willingness to lie, cheat, or steal in other situations. Of particular interest was the finding that children who cheated in a particular setting were just as likely as those who did not to state that cheating is wrong! Hartshorne and May concluded that "honesty" is largely specific to the situation rather than a stable character trait.

This **doctrine of specificity** has been questioned by other researchers. Roger Burton (1963; 1976) reanalyzed Hartshorne and May's data using newer and more sophisticated statistical techniques. His analyses provide some support for behavioral consistency. For example, a child's willingness to cheat or not cheat in one context (for example, on tests in class) is reasonably consistent, although the same child might behave very differently in highly unrelated contexts (for example, at competitive games on the playground). Other investigators have since discovered that moral behaviors of *a particular kind* (for example, sharing, refusing to break rules) are reasonably consistent over time and across situations (Rushton, 1980; Kochanska et al., 1996). Finally, the correlations among measures of moral affect, moral reasoning, and moral behavior become progressively stronger with age (Blasi, 1980; 1990).

So the doctrine of specificity is clearly an overstatement. However, the finding that all three moral components become more consistent and more highly interrelated with age does not mean that morality ever becomes a wholly stable and unitary attribute: Willingness to lie, cheat, or violate other moral norms may always depend to some extent on contextual factors, such as the importance of the goal that might be achieved by transgressing or the amount of encouragement provided by peers for deviant conduct (Burton, 1976). In other words, the moral character of even the most mature of adults is unlikely to be perfectly consistent across all situations.

Learning to Resist Temptation

From society's standpoint, one of the more important indexes of morality is the extent to which an individual is able to resist pressures to violate moral norms, *even when the possibility of detection and punishment is remote* (Hoffman, 1970). A person who resists temptation in the absence of external surveillance not only has learned a moral rule but is *internally* motivated to abide by that rule. How do children acquire moral standards, and what motivates them to obey these learned codes of conduct? Social-learning theorists have attempted to answer these questions by studying the effects of reinforcement, punishment, and social modeling on children's moral behavior.

Reinforcement as a Determinant of Moral Conduct

We have seen on several occasions that the frequency of many behaviors can be increased if these acts are reinforced. Moral behaviors are certainly no exception. When warm, accepting parents set clear and reasonable standards for their children and often *praise* them for behaving well, even toddlers are likely to meet their expectations and to display strong evidence of an internalized conscience by age 4 to 5 (Kochanska, 1997b; Kuczynski & Kochanska, 1995). Children are generally motivated to comply with the wishes of a warm, socially reinforcing adult, and the praise that accompanies their desirable conduct tells them that they are accomplishing that objective.

The Role of Punishment in Establishing Moral Prohibitions

doctrine of specificity
a viewpoint shared by many social-learning theorists which holds that moral affect, reasoning, and behavior may depend as much or more on the situation that one faces than on an internalized set of moral principles.

Although reinforcing acceptable behaviors is an effective way to promote desirable conduct, adults often fail to recognize that a child has *resisted* a temptation and is deserving of praise. By contrast, adults are quick to correct a child's misdeeds by *punishing* these moral transgressions. Is punishment an effective way to foster the development of **inhibitory controls**? As we will see, the answer depends critically on the child's *interpretation* of these aversive experiences.

Early Research. Ross Parke (1977) used the *forbidden-toy paradigm* to study the effects of punishment on children's resistance to temptation. During the first phase of a typical experiment, participants are punished (by hearing a noxious buzzer) whenever they touch an attractive toy; however, nothing happens when they play with unattractive toys. Once the child has learned the prohibition, the experimenter leaves and the child is surreptitiously observed to determine whether he or she plays with the forbidden toys.

Recall from our discussion in Chapter 6 (see Box 6.3) that *firm* (rather than mild) punishments, administered *immediately* (rather than later) and *consistently* by a *warm* (rather than an aloof) disciplinarian proved most effective at inhibiting a child's undesirable conduct. Yet, Parke's most important discovery was that all forms of punishment became more effective if accompanied by a cognitive rationale that provides the transgressor with reasons for inhibiting a forbidden act.

Explaining the Effects of Cognitive Rationales. Why do rationales increase the effectiveness of punishment, even mild or delayed punishments that produce little moral restraint by themselves? Probably because rationales provide children with information specifying why the punished act is wrong and why *they* should feel guilty or shameful for repeating it. So when these youngsters think about committing the forbidden act in the future, they should experience a general uneasiness (stemming from previous disciplinary encounters), should be inclined to make an *internal attribution* for this arousal (for example, "I'd feel guilty if I did something wrong"; "I wouldn't be good like I usually am") and should now be more likely to inhibit the forbidden act and to feel rather good about their "mature and responsible" conduct. By contrast, children who receive no rationales or who have been exposed to reasoning that focuses their attention on the negative consequences that they can expect for future transgressions (for example, "You'll be spanked again if you do it") experience just as much uneasiness when they think about committing the forbidden act. However, these youngsters tend to make *external attributions* for their emotional arousal (for example, "I'm worried about getting caught and punished") that might make them comply with moral norms in the presence of authority figures but probably won't inhibit deviant conduct if there is no one around to detect their transgressions.

We see, then, that fear of detection and punishment is not enough to persuade children to resist temptations in the absence of external surveillance. In order to establish truly internalized *self*-controls, adults must structure disciplinary encounters to include an appropriate rationale that informs the child why the prohibited act is wrong and why *she* should feel guilty or otherwise less than virtuous about repeating it (Hoffman, 1988). Clearly, true *self*-restraint is largely under *cognitive* control; it depends more on what's in children's heads rather than on the amount of fear or uneasiness in their guts.

Moral Self-Concept Training. If making internal attributions about one's conduct truly promotes moral self-restraint, we should be able to convince children that they can resist temptations to violate moral norms *because* they are "good," "honest," or otherwise "responsible" persons (an internal attribution). This kind of moral self-concept training really does work. William Casey and Roger Burton (1982) found that 7- to 10-year-olds became much more honest while playing games if honesty was stressed and the players learned to remind themselves to follow the rules. Yet when honesty was *not* stressed, players often cheated. Furthermore, David Perry and his associates (1980) found that 9- to 10-year-olds who had been told that they were especially good at carrying out instructions and following rules (moral self-concept training) behaved very differently after succumbing to a nearly irresistible temptation (leaving a boring task to watch an exciting TV show) than did peers who had not been told they were especially good. Specifically, children who had heard positive attributions about themselves were

inhibitory control
an ability to display acceptable conduct by resisting the temptation to commit a forbidden act.

more inclined than control participants to *punish their own transgressions* by giving back many of the valuable prize tokens they had been paid for working at the boring task. So it seems that labeling children as "good" or "honest" may not only increase the likelihood that they will resist temptations, but also contributes to children's feelings of guilt or remorse should they behave inappropriately and violate their positive self-images.

In sum, moral self-concept training, particularly when combined with praise for desirable conduct, can be a most effective alternative to punishment as a means of establishing inhibitory controls—one that should help convince the child that "I'm resisting temptation because *I* want to" and lead to the development of truly *internalized* controls rather than a response inhibition based on a fear of detection and punishment. Furthermore, this positive, nonpunitive approach should produce none of the undesirable side effects (for example, resentment) that often accompany punishment.

Effects of Social Models on Children's Moral Behavior

Might children be influenced by rule-following models who exhibit moral behaviors in a "passive" way by failing to commit forbidden acts? Indeed, they may, as long as they are aware that the "passive" model is resisting the temptation to violate a rule. Joan Grusec and her associates (1979) found that a rule-following model can be particularly effective at inspiring children to behave in kind if he clearly verbalizes that he is following a rule *and* states a rationale for not committing the deviant act. Furthermore, rule-following models whose rationales match the child's customary level of moral reasoning are more influential than models whose rationales are well beyond that level (Toner & Potts, 1981).

Finally, consider what Nace Toner and his associates (1978) found: 6- to 8-year-olds who were persuaded to serve as *models* of moral restraint for other children became more likely than age-mates who had not served as models to obey other rules during later tests of resistance to temptation. It was almost as if serving as a model produced a change in children's self-concepts, so that they now defined themselves as "people who follow rules." The implications for child-rearing are clear: Parents can succeed in establishing inhibitory controls in their older children by appealing to their maturity and persuading them to serve as models of self-restraint for their younger brothers and sisters.

WHO RAISES CHILDREN WHO ARE MORALLY MATURE?

love withdrawal
a form of discipline in which an adult withholds attention, affection, or approval in order to modify or control a child's behavior.

power assertion
a form of discipline in which an adult relies on his or her superior power (for example, by administering spankings or withholding privileges) to modify or control a child's behavior.

induction
a nonpunitive form of discipline in which an adult explains why a child's behavior is wrong and should be changed by emphasizing its effects on others.

Many years ago, Martin Hoffman (1970) reviewed the child-rearing literature to see whether the disciplinary techniques that *parents* actually use have any effect on the moral development of their children. Three major approaches were compared.

1. **Love withdrawal:** withholding attention, affection, or approval after a child misbehaves or, in other words, creating anxiety over a loss of love.
2. **Power assertion:** use of superior power to control the child's behavior (including techniques such as forceful commands, physical restraint, spankings, and withdrawal of privileges that may generate fear, anger, or resentment).
3. **Induction:** explaining why a behavior is wrong and should be changed by emphasizing how it affects other people, often suggesting how the child might repair any harm done.

Suppose that little Suzie has just terrorized the family dog by chasing him with a lit sparkler during a Fourth of July celebration. Using *love withdrawal,* a parent might say "How could you? Get away! I can't bear to look at you." Using *power assertion,* a parent might spank Suzie or say "That's it! No movie for you this Saturday." Using *induction,* the parent might say "Suzie, look how scared Pokey is. You could have set him on fire, and you know how sad we'd all be if he was burned." Induction, then, is a matter of providing rationales that focus special attention on the consequences of one's wrongdoing for other people (or dogs, as the case may be).

Although only a limited number of child-rearing studies had been conducted by 1970, their results suggested that (1) neither love withdrawal nor power assertion were particularly effective at promoting moral maturity, but that (2) induction seemed to foster the development of all three aspects of morality—moral emotions, moral reasoning, and moral behavior (Hoffman, 1970). Table 14.3 summarizes the relationships among the three patterns of parental discipline and various measures of children's moral maturity that emerged from a later review of the literature which included many more studies (Brody & Shaffer, 1982). Clearly, these data confirm Hoffman's conclusions: Parents who rely on inductive discipline tend to have children who are morally mature, whereas frequent use of power assertion is more often associated with moral *immaturity* than with moral maturity. The few cases in which induction was *not* associated with moral maturity all involved children under age 4. However, recent research indicates that induction can be highly effective with 2- to 5-year-olds, reliably promoting sympathy and compassion for others as well as a willingness to comply with parental requests. By contrast, use of such high-intensity power-assertive tactics as becoming angry and physically restraining or spanking the child is already associated with and seems to promote noncompliance, defiance, and a lack of concern for others (Crockenberg & Litman, 1990; Kochanska; 1997b; Kochanska et al., 1996; Zahn-Waxler et al., 1979).

Why is inductive discipline effective? Hoffman cites several reasons. First, it provides children with *cognitive standards* (or rationales) to evaluate their conduct. Second, this form of discipline helps children to sympathize with others (Krevans & Gibbs, 1996) and allows parents to talk about such *moral affects* as pride, guilt, and shame that are not easily discussed with a child who is made emotionally insecure by love withdrawal or angry by power-assertive techniques. Finally, parents who use inductive discipline are likely to explain to the child (1) what he or she *should have done* when tempted to violate a prohibition and (2) what he or she *can now do* to make up for a transgression. So induction may be an effective method of moral socialization because it calls attention to the cognitive, affective, and behavioral aspects of morality and may help the child to integrate them.

Finally, it is important to note that few if any parents are totally inductive, love oriented, or power assertive in their approach to discipline; most make at least some use of all three disciplinary techniques. Although parents classified as "inductive" rely heavily on inductive methods, they occasionally take punitive measures whenever punishment is necessary to command the child's attention or to discipline repeated transgressions. So the style of parenting that Hoffman calls induction may be very similar to the "rationale + mild punishment" treatment that Parke (1977) found most effective in laboratory studies of resistance to temptation.

TABLE 14.3 **Relationships between Parents' Use of Three Disciplinary Strategies and Children's Moral Development**

	Type of discipline		
Direction of relationship between parents' use of a disciplinary strategy and children's moral maturity	**Power assertion**	**Love withdrawal**	**Induction**
+ (positive correlation)	7	8	38
− (negative correlation)	32	11	6

NOTE: Table entries represent the number of occasions on which a particular disciplinary technique was found to be associated (either positively or negatively) with a measure of children's moral affect, reasoning, or behavior.
SOURCE: Adapted from Brody & Shaffer, 1982.

DENNIS THE MENACE® USED BY PERMISSION OF HANK KETCHAM AND © BY NORTH AMERICAN SYNDICATE.

"IF YOU'RE TRYIN' TO GET SOMETHING INTO MY HEAD, YOU'RE WORKIN' ON THE WRONG END!"

CRITICISMS OF HOFFMAN'S IDEAS ABOUT DISCIPLINE. Several investigators have wondered whether Hoffman's conclusions about the effectiveness of inductive discipline might not be overstated. For example, inductive discipline used by white, middle-class mothers is consistently associated with measures of children's moral maturity; however, the same findings don't always hold for fathers or for parents from other socioeconomic backgrounds (Brody & Shaffer, 1982; Grusec & Goodnow, 1994). Furthermore, one recent study found that the positive association between parents' use of power-assertive discipline and children's aggressive, antisocial conduct held for European-American but not for African-American children (Deater-Deckard & Dodge, 1997). Clearly, more research is needed to establish how culturally specific Hoffman's ideas may be.

Other critics have raised the *direction-of-effects* issue: Does induction promote moral maturity, or, rather, do morally mature children elicit more inductive forms of discipline from their parents? Since child-rearing studies are based on correlational data, either of these possibilities can explain Hoffman's findings. Hoffman (1975) responds by claiming that parents exert far more control over their children's behavior than children exert over parents. In other words, he believes that parental use of inductive discipline promotes moral maturity rather than the other way around. And there is some *experimental* support for Hoffman's claim in that induction is much more effective than other forms of discipline at persuading children to keep their promises and to comply with rules imposed by *unfamiliar* adults (Kuczynski, 1983).

Nevertheless, children clearly have a hand in determining how they are disciplined by their parents. For example, the research presented in Box 14.4 reveals that a child's *temperament* can influence how he or she reacts to different kinds of discipline which, in turn, may affect how he or she is treated. Other research indicates that children who react unfavorably to discipline by acting out and repeating their transgressions often drive adults to use more and more power-assertive (and less and less effective) means of discipline over time (Anderson, Lytton, & Romney, 1986; Lytton, 1990).

14.4

FOCUS ON RESEARCH

Temperament, Discipline, and Moral Internalization

Recently, Grazyna Kochanska (1993; 1997a) proposed that the kind of parenting most likely to foster moral internalization depends on a child's temperament. Some children are temperamentally *fearful*—that is, prone to become highly anxious and to burst into tears when they receive a sharp reprimand from their parents. According to Kochanska, fearful children respond much more favorably to gentle, psychological forms of discipline that de-emphasize power assertion—something akin to Hoffman's induction. Other children are highly impulsive and temperamentally *fearless.* Kochanska believes that these emotionally nonreactive youngsters may not be sufficiently aroused by mild psychological forms of discipline to internalize parental rules or even to stop performing the behavior for which they are being reprimanded! Although their parents may be inclined to become forceful with them when gentle forms of discipline do not work, Kochanska claims that resorting to power assertion proves no more effective with a fearless child than with a fearful one. Instead, she proposes that the route to moral internalization for a fearless child is warm, sensitive parenting of the kind that promotes secure attachments and a mutually cooperative parent–child relationship. Her view is that a secure and mutually positive orientation fosters *committed compliance* from the child, who wants to cooperate with and please his parents.

To test her theory, Kochanska (1995; 1997a) classified a sample of 2- to 3-year-olds as temperamentally fearful or fearless. She then observed each of them interacting with their mothers to assess the mothers' warmth and responsiveness to social signals and the kinds of discipline that the mother used. Data on the security of the child's attachment to his or her mother were also available. The strength of children's moral internalization was assessed at three times: ages 2 to 3, 4, and 5. Measures of moral internalization included complying with requests and following rules (that is, refusing to touch prohibited toys) at age 2 to 3, as well as refusing to cheat at games and maturity of moral reasoning at ages 4 and 5.

The results of this longitudinal study provided clear support for Kochanska's theory. For the *fearful* children, use of gentle, inductive discipline that was low in power assertion predicted higher levels of moral internalization at all three ages. Yet this same discipline bore no relationship to the levels of moral internalization that *fearless* participants displayed. Instead, a secure attachment to a mother who was highly responsive to their social signals is what predicted strength of conscience among fearless children.

Here, then, is another example of how "goodness of fit" between parenting practices and children's temperaments foster adaptive outcomes. Judging from the child-rearing literature, most children probably are sufficiently aroused by gentle, inductive disciplinary techniques to learn moral lessons, although this approach may be essential to foster moral internalization among especially fearful youngsters. However, continued reliance on this same discipline constitutes a poor fit for highly fearless children, who are more likely to internalize moral lessons in the context of a secure relationship with a parent whose discipline is firm and reminds the child of the desirability of maintaining the warm, mutually cooperative relationship they have enjoyed. Finally, Kochanska and her associates (1996) find that mothers' frequent use of power assertion consistently *inhibits* children's moral internalization and represents a poor fit with all temperaments.

So moral socialization at home is a two-way street: Although inductive discipline does indeed promote moral maturity, children who respond more favorably to these rational, nonpunitive techniques are the ones who are most likely to be treated this way by their parents.

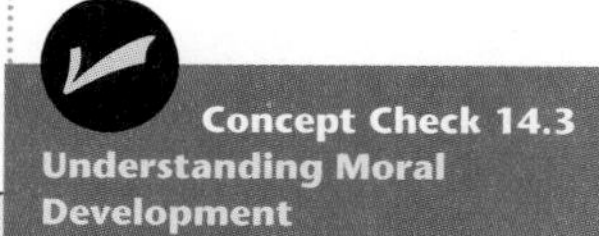

Concept Check 14.3
Understanding Moral Development

Check your understanding of theories and selected aspects of moral development by matching each descriptive statement below with one of the following concepts or processes: (a) role-taking skills, (b) formal operations, (c) disequilibrating social experiences, (d) induction, (e) moral rules, (f) morality of care, (g) peer interactions, (h) power assertion, (i) secure attachment to parent, (j) warm, responsive parenting. Answers appear in the Appendix.

_____ 1. preschoolers' strong respect for _________ contradicts Piaget's theory

_____ 2. Freud's oedipal morality is discredited by this strong contributor to moral maturity

_____ 3. both Piaget and Kohlberg emphasize this *social* contributor to moral development

_____ 4. according to Gilligan, Kohlberg overlooks the growth of this moral aspect

_____ 5. discipline consistently associated with moral *immaturity*

_____ 6. most children, particularly fearful ones, respond well to this discipline

_____ 7. may be particularly important for successful moral socialization of fearless children

_____ 8. cognitive prerequisite for Kohlberg's postconventional morality

_____ 9. cognitive prerequisite for Kohlberg's conventional morality

_____ 10. prerequisite for all moral growth beyond Kohlberg's preconventional level

A Child's-Eye View of Discipline. What do children think about various disciplinary strategies? Do they feel (as many developmentalists do) that physical punishment and love withdrawal are ineffective methods of promoting moral restraint? Would they favor inductive techniques or perhaps prefer that their parents adopt more permissive attitudes about transgressions?

Michael Siegal and Jan Cowen (1984) addressed these issues by asking children and adolescents between the ages of 4 and 18 to listen to stories describing different kinds of misdeeds and to evaluate strategies that parents had used to discipline these antics. Five kinds of transgressions were described: (1) simple disobedience (the child refusing to clean his room), (2) causing physical harm to others (the child punching a playmate), (3) causing physical harm to oneself (ignoring an order not to touch a hot stove), (4) causing psychological harm to others (making fun of a physically disabled person), and (5) causing physical damage (breaking a lamp while roughhousing). The four disciplinary techniques on which parents were said to have relied were *induction,* (reasoning with the culprit by pointing out the harmful consequences of his or her actions), *physical punishment* (striking the child), *love withdrawal* (telling the child to stay away), and *permissive nonintervention* (ignoring the incident and assuming that the child would learn important lessons on his or her own). Each participant heard 20 stories that resulted from pairing each of the four disciplinary strategies with each of the five transgressions. After listening to or reading each story, the participant indicated whether the parent's approach to the problem was "very wrong," "wrong," "half right–half wrong," "right," or "very right."

Although the perceived appropriateness of each disciplinary technique varied somewhat across transgressions, the most interesting findings overall were that (1) induction was the most preferred disciplinary strategy for participants of all ages (even preschoolers), and (2) physical punishment was the next most favorably evaluated technique. So all participants seemed to favor a rational disciplinarian who relies heavily on reasoning that is occasionally backed by power assertion. By contrast, love withdrawal and permissiveness were favorably evaluated by no age group. In fact, the 4- to 9-year-olds in the sample favored *any* form of discipline, even love withdrawal, over a permissive attitude on the parent's part (which they viewed as "wrong" or "very wrong"). Apparently, young children see the need for adults to step in and restrain their inappropriate conduct, for they were disturbed by stories in which youngsters were generally free to do their own thing, largely unencumbered by adult constraints.

In sum, the disciplinary style that children favor (induction backed by occasional use of power assertion) is the one most closely associated with measures of moral maturity in child-rearing studies and with resistance to temptation in the laboratory. Perhaps another reason that inductive discipline may promote moral maturity is simply that children view this approach as the "right" way to deal with transgressions, and they may be highly motivated to accept influence from a disciplinarian whose "world view" matches their own. By contrast, children who favor induction but are usually disciplined in other ways may see little justification for internalizing the values and exhortations of a disciplinarian whose very methods of inducing compliance seem unwise, unjust, and hardly worthy of their respect.

SUMMARY

♦ Three interrelated aspects of social development are often considered when making judgments about a child's moral character: the emergence and control of aggression, the development of altruism, and the establishment of an internalized sense of morality.

The Development of Aggression

♦ Intentional acts of harmdoing, or **aggression,** are often divided into two categories: **hostile aggression** and **instrumental aggression.** Instrumental aggression appears by the end of the first year as infants begin to quarrel with siblings and peers over toys and other possessions.

♦ During early childhood, aggression becomes less physical and increasingly verbal, and somewhat less instrumental and increasingly hostile or **retaliatory** in nature. Boys are more overtly aggressive than girls are, but girls exceed boys in **relational aggression.** Although overt aggression declines with age, more covert forms of antisocial conduct show a corresponding rise. Aggressiveness is a moderately stable attribute for both males and females.

♦ Two types of highly aggressive children have been identified. **Proactive aggressors** rely on aggression to satisfy personal objectives and are quite confident that aggression will "pay off" for them. By contrast, **reactive aggressors** display a **hostile attributional bias** that causes them to overattribute hostile intents to others and to retaliate in a hostile manner to imagined provocations. Proactive aggressors may become bullies, whereas reactive aggressors may often be victimized. However, most victims of abuse are passive youngsters whom bullies find easy to dominate.

♦ A person's aggressive inclinations depend, in part, on the cultural, subcultural, and family settings in which he or she is raised. Due in part to social class differences in parenting, children and adolescents from disadvantaged backgrounds are more aggressive and display higher rates of delinquency than their middle-class peers.

♦ Children from any social background can become highly aggressive and find themselves on a path leading to chronic delinquency if they live in a **coercive home environment** where family members are quick to **negatively reinforce** bickering and fighting. In order to help these highly combative children, it is often necessary to treat the entire family.

♦ The incidence of children's aggression can be reduced by taking care to create "nonaggressive" play environments. *Proactive aggressors* can benefit when adults rely on such control procedures as **time-out** and the **incompatabile-response technique,** which teaches them that aggression doesn't pay and that nonaggressive means of problem solving are better ways to achieve their objectives. And all aggressive youngsters, particularly hot-headed *reactive aggressors,* can benefit from social-cognitive interventions that help them to regulate their anger and to become more skilled at **empathizing** with others and taking others' perspectives, thus becoming less inclined to attribute hostile intents to other people.

Altruism: Development of the Prosocial Self

♦ Early indications of **altruism,** such as sharing toys and comforting distressed companions, appear in infancy and toddlerhood, particularly among youngsters whose parents emphasize a concern for others as part of their disciplinary strategies.

♦ Sharing, helping, and other forms of prosocial conduct become more and more common from the preschool period onward. Contrary to widely held stereotypes, girls are neither more altruistic than boys nor any less capable than boys are of accomplishing tasks without seeking assistance.

♦ The growth of altruistic concern is linked to the development of role-taking skills, **prosocial moral reasoning,** and **sympathetic empathic arousal.** Although young children often interpret empathic arousal as personal, or **self-oriented distress,** they eventually acquire the role-taking skills to interpret their reactions as sympathy for others, which promotes altruism by making them feel responsible for others' welfare (the **"felt responsibility" hypothesis**).

♦ Like aggression, a person's altruistic tendencies are influenced by his or her cultural and family environments. Parents can promote altruistic behavior through their **altruistic exhortations,** by praising their child's kindly deeds, and by practicing themselves the prosocial lessons that they have preached. Furthermore, parents who discipline harmdoing with nonpunitive, affective explanations that point out the negative effects of children's misconduct on victims are likely to raise children who become sympathetic, self-sacrificing, and concerned about the welfare of others.

What Is Morality?

♦ **Morality** has been defined in many ways, although almost everyone agrees that it implies a set of **internalized** principles or ideals that help the individual to distinguish right from wrong and to act on this distinction. Morality has three basic components: **moral affect, moral reasoning,** and **moral behavior.**

Psychoanalytic Explanations of Moral Development

♦ According to Freud's theory of **oedipal morality,** children internalize the moral standards of the same-sex parent during the phallic stage as they resolve their Oedipus or Electra complexes and form a conscience or superego.

♦ Research has consistently discredited Freud's theory. However, newer psychoanalytic ideas that the conscience forms earlier in toddlerhood in the context of a warm supportive (rather than fear-provoking) parent–child relationship has received some support.

Cognitive Development Theory: The Child as a Moral Philosopher

♦ Cognitive-developmental theorists have emphasized the cognitive component of morality by studying the development of moral reasoning. Jean Piaget formulated a two-stage model of moral development based on changes that occur in children's conceptions of rules and their sense of social justice. From a **premoral period** in which children allegedly respect no rules, they progress to **heteronomous morality,** in which they view rules as moral absolutes and believe in **immanent justice** and finally to **autonomous morality,** in which they regard rules as flexible and justice as relative rather than absolute.

♦ Piaget clearly identified some important trends in the development of moral reasoning. However, shortcomings of his research methods and his failure to capture children's distinctions between **moral rules** and **social conventional rules** caused him to underestimate the moral sophistication of preschool and young grade-school children.

♦ Lawrence Kohlberg's revision and extension of Piaget's theory views moral reasoning as progressing through an invariant sequence of three levels, **(preconventional, conventional,** and **postconventional moralities),** each composed of two distinct stages. According to Kohlberg, the order of progression through the levels and stages is invariant because each of these modes of thinking depends, in part, on the development of cognitive abilities that evolve in a fixed sequence. Yet, Kohlberg also claimed that no moral growth occurs in the absence of social experiences that would cause a person to reevaluate her existing moral concepts.

◆ Research indicates that Kohlberg's stages do form an invariant sequence. Furthermore, both cognitive development and such relevant social experiences as exposure to divergent moral perspectives in the context of discussions with parents, peers, and other participants in higher education or democratic activities do contribute to the growth of moral reasoning. However, Kohlberg's theory may not adequately describe the morality of people who live in many non-Westernized societies or who emphasize a **morality of care** rather than a **morality of justice;** and, like Piaget, Kohlberg clearly underestimates the moral reasoning of young children. Critics also claim that the theory says too little about moral affect and moral behavior.

Morality as a Product of Social Learning (and Social Information Processing)

◆ Although their **doctrine of specificity** is clearly an overstatement, social learning theorists have helped to explain how children learn to resist temptation and inhibit acts that violate moral norms. Among the factors that promote the development of **inhibitory controls** are praise given for virtuous conduct, punishments that include appropriate rationales, and exposing children to (or having them serve as) models of moral restraint. Other nonpunitive techniques such as moral self-concept training are also quite effective at promoting moral behavior.

Who Raises Children Who Are Morally Mature?

◆ Child-rearing studies consistently imply that use of **inductive discipline** promotes moral maturity, whereas **love withdrawal** has little effect, and **power assertion** is associated with moral *immaturity.* The effectiveness of induction may vary, however, depending on the child's temperament. But children generally prefer inductive discipline to other approaches, and most seem highly motivated to accept influence from an inductive adult whose methods they can respect.

Lawrence Kohlberg's theory of moral development suggests there are three main levels of moral development, with two stages at each of these levels. You can review your understanding of Kohlberg's theory by visiting: http://snycorva.cortland.edu/~andersmd/kohl/content.html The online tutorial at this site reviews the basics of Kohlberg's theory and also shows how Kohlberg's ideas can be applied in classroom settings, or in the analysis of U.S. congressional debates.

KEY TERMS

aggression, 509
hostile aggression, 509
instrumental aggression, 509
retaliatory aggression, 511
relational aggression, 512
proactive aggressors, 514
reactive aggressors, 514
hostile attributional bias, 515
coercive home environment, 517
negative reinforcer, 518
incompatible-response technique, 521
time-out technique, 521
empathy, 522
altruism, 522
prosocial moral reasoning, 524
sympathetic empathic arousal, 526
self-oriented distress, 526
"felt responsibility" hypothesis, 527
altruistic exhortations, 529
morality, 530
internalization, 530
moral affect, 531
moral reasoning, 531
moral behavior, 531
oedipal morality, 532
premoral period, 533
heteronomous morality, 533
immanent justice, 534
autonomous morality, 534
moral rules, 536
social-conventional rules, 536
preconventional morality, 538
conventional morality, 539
postconventional morality, 540
transactive interactions, 542
morality of justice, 544
morality of care, 544
doctrine of specificity, 548
inhibitory control, 549
love withdrawal, 550
power assertion, 550
induction, 550

15

The Family

When Burnam and Addie Ledford hosted the Ledford family reunion, he was 102, she 93. They had married in 1903 and were nearing their 75th wedding anniversary. They had 13 children, 9 of them still surviving; the oldest was age 69. They also had 32 grandchildren and 39 great-grandchildren—so many that Burnam marveled, "It's like planting seeds. . . . They just keep coming up." Burnam and Addie clearly valued their bonds to past, present, and future generations of Ledfords.

(EGERTON, 1983)

The Ledfords' emphasis on family ties is not at all unusual. More than 99% of children in the United States are raised in a family of one kind or another (U.S. Bureau of the Census, 1997), and the vast majority of children in all societies grow up in a home setting with at least one biological parent or other relative. So virtually all of us are bound to families. We are born into them, work our way toward adulthood in them, start our own as adults, and remain connected to them in old age. We are part of our families, and they are part of us.

Our focus in this chapter is on the family as a *social system,* an institution that both influences and is influenced by its young. What functions do families serve? How does the birth of a child affect other family members? Do the existing (or changing) relationships among other members of the family have any effect on the care and training that a child or adolescent receives? Are some patterns of parenting better than others? Do parents decide how they will raise their children, or might children influence their parents? Does the family's cultural heritage and socioeconomic status affect parenting and parent–child interactions? How important are siblings as socialization agents? How are children affected by the increasing diversity of family life that we see today: by growing up with gay or lesbian parents or by having to adjust to maternal employment, divorce, or a return to a two-parent family when a single parent remarries? And why do some parents abuse their offspring? These are some of the major issues that we will consider as we look at the important roles that families play in the cognitive, social, and emotional development of children and adolescents.

FUNCTIONS OF THE FAMILY

Families serve society in many ways. They produce and consume goods and services, thereby playing a role in the economy. Traditionally, the family has served as an outlet for the sexual urges of its adult members and as the means of replenishing the population. Families provide social and emotional supports that help family members cope with crises. They also care for their elderly, although this function in Western societies is often shared with such institutions as Social Security, Medicare (or other kinds of socialized medicine), and nursing homes. But perhaps the most widely recognized and universal functions of the family are the caregiving and training that parents and other family members provide for their young.

Socialization is the process by which children acquire the beliefs, values, and behaviors deemed significant and appropriate by the older members of their society. The socialization of each generation serves society in at least three ways. First, it is a means of regulating children's behavior and controlling their undesirable or antisocial impulses. Second, socialization promotes the personal growth of the individual. As children interact with and become like other members of their culture, they acquire the knowledge, skills, motives, and aspirations that should enable them to adapt to their environment and function effectively within their communities. Finally, socialization perpetuates the social order: Appropriately socialized children become competent, adaptive, prosocial adults who will impart what they have learned to their own children.

Of course, families are only one of many institutions involved in the socialization process. Religious institutions, for example, provide important emotional supports and moral socialization that often increase family cohesion and promote healthy developmental outcomes (Brody, Stoneman, & Flor, 1996). And as we will see in Chapter 16, such institutions as schools, the mass media, and children's groups (for example, Boy and Girl Scouts) frequently supplement the training and emotional support functions served by families. Nevertheless, many children have limited exposure to people outside the family for their first several years, until they are placed in day-care or nursery school or begin their formal schooling. So the family has a clear head start on other institutions when it comes to socializing a child. And since the events of the early years are so very important to the child's social, emotional, and intellectual development, it is appropriate to think of the family as society's primary instrument of socialization.

socialization
the process by which children acquire the beliefs, values, and behaviors considered desirable or appropriate by the society to which they belong.

For many families, religious activities provide an important source of social/emotional support that increases family cohesion and helps to promote healthy developmental outcomes.

THE FAMILY AS A SOCIAL SYSTEM

When developmentalists began to study socialization in the 1940s and 50s, they focused almost entirely on the mother–child relationship, operating under the assumption that mothers (and, to a lesser extent, fathers) were the agents who molded children's conduct and character (Ambert, 1992). However, modern family researchers have rejected this simple unidirectional model in favor of a more comprehensive "systems" approach (Minuchin, 1988) that is similar to Urie Bronfenbrenner's (1993; 1995) ecological systems theory that we discussed in Chapter 2. The systems approach recognizes that parents influence their children. But it also stresses that (1) children influence the behavior and child-rearing practices of their parents, and (2) families are complex **social systems**—that is, networks of *reciprocal* relationships and alliances that are constantly evolving and are greatly affected by community and cultural influences. Now consider some implications of this systems perspective.

Direct and Indirect Influences

What does it mean to say that a family is a social system? To Jay Belsky (1981), it means that the family, much like the human body, is a *holistic structure* consisting of interrelated parts, each of which affects and is affected by every other part, and each of which contributes to the functioning of the whole.

To illustrate, consider the simplest of **traditional nuclear families,** consisting of a mother, a father, and a first-born child. According to Belsky (1981), even this man–woman–infant "system" is quite complex. An infant interacting with his or her mother is already involved in a process of *reciprocal influence,* as is evident when we notice that the infant's smile is likely to be greeted by the mother's smile or that a mother's concerned expression often makes her infant wary. These influences, in which each family member affects and is affected by another's behavior, are called **direct effects.** And what happens when Dad arrives? As shown in Figure 15.1, the mother–infant dyad is suddenly transformed into a "*family system* [comprising] a husband–wife as well as mother–infant and father–infant relationships" (Belsky, 1981, p. 17).

One implication of viewing the family as a system is that interactions between any two family members are likely to be influenced by the attitudes and behaviors of a third family member—a phenomenon known as an **indirect,** or **third-party, effect.** To illustrate, fathers clearly influence the mother–infant relationship: Happily married

family social system
the complex network of relationships, interactions, and patterns of influence that characterizes a family with three or more members.

traditional nuclear family
a family unit consisting of a wife/mother, a husband/father, and their dependent child(ren).

direct effect
instances in which any pair of family members affects and is affected by each other's behavior.

indirect, or third-party, effect
instances in which the relationship between two individuals in a family is modified by the behavior or attitudes of a third family member.

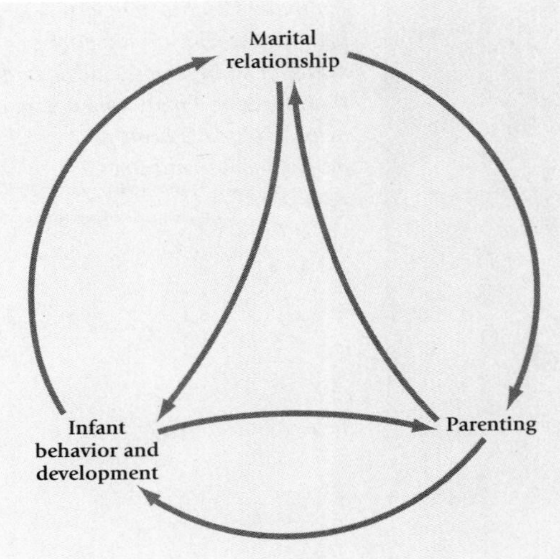

Figure 15.1 *A model of the family as a social system. As implied in the diagram, a family is bigger than the sum of its parts. Parents affect infants, who affect each parent and the marital relationship. Of course, the marital relationship may affect the parenting that the infant receives, the infant's behavior, and so on. Clearly, families are complex social systems. As an exercise, you may wish to rediagram the patterns of influence within a family after adding a sibling or two.* FROM BELSKY, 1981.

mothers who have close, supportive relationships with their husbands tend to interact much more patiently and sensitively with their infants than mothers who experience marital tension and feel that they are raising their children on their own (Cox et al., 1989; 1992). Meanwhile, mothers indirectly influence the father–infant relationship: Fathers tend to be more involved with their infants when their wives believe that a father should play an important role in a child's life (Palkovitz, 1984) and when the two parents talk frequently about the baby (Belsky, Gilstrap, & Rovine, 1984; Levy-Shiff, 1994). Overall, children fare best when couples **coparent**—that is, mutually support each other's parenting efforts and function as a cooperative (rather than an antagonistic) team. Unfortunately, effective coparenting is difficult for couples experiencing marital discord and other life stresses (Belsky, Crnic, & Gable, 1995; McHale, 1995), and disputes between parents over child-rearing issues can be particularly harmful, often forecasting increases in childhood and adolescent adjustment problems over and above those attributable to other aspects of marital conflict (Jouriles et al., 1991; Vaughn et al., 1988). Clearly, both mothers and fathers can influence their children *indirectly* through their interactions with their spouses.

Of course, children also exert direct and indirect effects on their parents. A highly impulsive toddler who shows little inclination to comply with requests may drive a mother to punitive coercive methods of discipline (direct child-to-mother effect; Kochanska, 1993), which, in turn, may make the child more defiant than ever (a direct mother-to-child effect; Crockenberg & Litman, 1990). Alarmed by this state of affairs, the exasperated mother may then criticize her husband for his nonintervention, thereby precipitating an unpleasant discussion about parental obligations and responsibilities (an indirect effect of the child's impulsivity on the husband–wife relationship).

In short, every person and every relationship within the family affects every other person and relationship through pathways of reciprocal influence, as illustrated in Figure 15.1. Now we begin to see why it was rather naive to think we might understand how families influence children by concentrating exclusively on the mother–child relationship.

Now think about how complex the family system becomes with the birth of a second child and the addition of sibling–sibling and sibling–parent relationships. Or consider the complexity of an **extended family** household, a nearly universal practice in some cultures in which parents and their children live with other kin such as grandparents, aunts, uncles, nieces, and nephews. It turns out that living in extended families is a fairly common arrangement for African Americans—and an adaptive one in that large members of economically disadvantaged black mothers must work, are often supporting their offspring without the father, and can surely use the assistance they receive from grandparents, siblings, uncles, aunts, and cousins who live with them and serve as alternative caregivers for young children (Pearson et al., 1990; Wilson, 1989).

Until recently, family researchers had largely ignored extended families or had viewed them as *unhealthy* contexts for development, due largely to the fact that so many of these families were raising children without a father living at home (Wilson, 1989). This view is rapidly changing because of research showing how social support from members of extended families (for example, grandmothers, aunts and uncles, and even fathers residing elsewhere) can help economically disadvantaged mothers to cope with the many stresses they face and to become more sensitive, responsive parents (Burton, 1990; Taylor & Roberts, 1995). Regardless of whether their kin live in their homes, disadvantaged African-American schoolchildren and adolescents whose families receive ample kinship support usually experience competent parenting at home which, in turn, is associated with such positive outcomes as a strong sense of self-reliance, good psychological adjustment, solid academic performances, and fewer behavioral problems (Taylor, 1996; Taylor & Roberts, 1995; Zimmerman, Salem. & Maton, 1995). And in cultures such as the Sudan, where social life is governed by ideals stressing communal

coparenting
circumstance in which parents mutually support each other and function as a cooperative parenting team.

extended family
a group of blood relatives from more than one nuclear family (for example, grandparents, aunts, uncles, nieces, and nephews) who live together, forming a household.

interdependence and intergenerational harmony, children routinely display better patterns of psychological adjustment if raised in extended-family households than in Westernized, two-parent nuclear families (Al-Awad & Sonuga-Barke, 1992). So it seems that the healthiest family contexts for development depend heavily on both the needs of individual families and the values that families within particular cultural (and subcultural contexts) are trying to promote.

Older members of extended families serve many useful functions. In addition to providing information and emotional support to young parents, grandmothers, and even great-grandmothers may figure prominently in the care and guidance of the family's children.

Families Are Developing Systems

Families are not only complex social systems, they are also dynamic systems as well. Consider that every family member is a *developing* individual and that relationships between husband and wife, parent and child, and sibling and sibling also change in ways that can influence the development of each family member (Klein & White, 1996). Many such changes are planned, as when parents allow toddlers to do more things on their own as a means of encouraging autonomy and developing individual initiative. Yet, a host of unplanned or unforeseen changes (such as the death of a sibling or a strained husband–wife relationship) can greatly affect family interactions and growth of its children. So a family is not only a system in which developmental change takes place; its dynamics also change with development of its members.

Families Are Embedded Systems

The social systems perspective also emphasizes that all families are embedded within larger cultural and subcultural contexts and that the ecological niche that a family occupies (for example, the family's religion, its socioeconomic status, and the values that prevail within a subculture, a community, or even a neighborhood) can affect family interactions and the development of a family's children (Bronfenbrenner, 1993; 1995). As we will see later in the chapter, economic hardship exerts a strong influence on parenting: Parents often become depressed over their financial situation which, in turn, can cause them to become less nurturant toward and involved with their children (Conger et al., 1992, 1995; McLoyd, 1990). And yet, economically distressed parents who have close ties to a community—a church group, a volunteer organization, or a circle of close friends and other confidants—experience far less stress and less disruption of their parenting routines (Burchinal, Follmer, & Bryant, 1996; Hashima & Amato, 1994). Clearly, the broader social contexts that families experience can greatly affect the ways that family functions are carried out.

In sum, even the simplest of families is a true social system that is much bigger than the sum of its parts. Not only does each family member influence the behavior of every other, but the relationship between any two family members can affect the interactions and relationships of all other family members. And when we consider that family members develop, relationships change, and all family dynamics are influenced by the broader social contexts in which families are embedded, it becomes quite clear that socialization within the family is best described not as a two-way street between parents and children, but as the busy intersection of many, many avenues of influence.

A Changing Family System in a Changing World

Not only is the family a complex, developing system, but it exists and develops in a world that is constantly changing. During the last half of the 20th century, several dramatic social changes have affected the makeup of the typical family and the character of family life. Drawing on U.S. census data and other surveys, we highlight the following changes:

More Single Adults

More adults are living as singles today than in the past. Marriage isn't "out," however, as about 90% of young adults eventually marry (Chadwick & Heaton, 1992).

Active Postponement of Marriage

Many young singles postpone marriage to pursue educational and career goals. Although the average age of first marriage actually decreased during the first half of this century, it has risen again to about 24 for women and 26 for men (U.S. Bureau of the Census, 1997).

Decreased Childbearing

Today's adults not only wait longer after they marry to have children, but they also have fewer of them—about 1.8 on average (U.S. Bureau of the Census, 1997). The Baby Boom period after World War II was an unusual departure from an otherwise consistent trend toward smaller family sizes. Today, about 12% of married women remain childless, many by choice (U.S. Bureau of the Census, 1997).

More Women Are Employed

In 1950, 12% of married women with children under age 6 worked outside the home; now the figure is 63%, a truly dramatic social change (U.S. Bureau of the Census, 1997). Although women still carry the lion's share of child-rearing and housework responsibilities, fewer and fewer children have a mother whose full-time job is to be a mother.

More Divorces

The divorce rate has been increasing over the past several decades, to the point where an additional one *million* children each year are affected by their parents' divorce (Teegartin, 1994). By one estimate, up to 60% of newly married couples can expect to divorce (Bumpass, 1990).

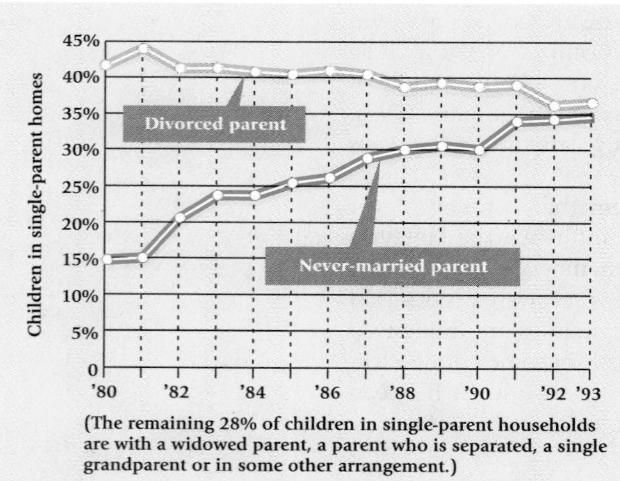

Figure 15.2 *The single-parent, postdivorce family is a common phenomenon of the past two decades; now, however, the number of children living with single parents who never married is almost equal to the number living with single parents who are divorced. In 1970, just 7% of American children in single-parent homes had a never-married parent.* SOURCE: *U.S. CENSUS DATA CITED IN TEEGARTIN, 1994.*

More Single-Parent Families

Nearly 60% of all children born in the 1980s and 90s will spend some time in a **single-parent family** (Teegartin, 1994). In 1960, only 9% of children lived with one parent, usually a widowed one; now 24% live with a single parent, usually a never-married or divorced one (see Figure 15.2). Father-headed single-parent homes are more common than they used to be, now accounting for about 17% of all single-parent families (U.S. Bureau of the Census, 1997).

More Children Living in Poverty

Unfortunately, the increase in the number of single-parent families has contributed to an increase in the proportion of children living below the poverty line; 54% of children living in female-headed homes live in poverty, compared with 10% of children in two-parent homes (Eggebeen & Lichter, 1991). Spending at least some time living in poverty is the rule rather than the exception for African-American children (Brooks-Gunn, Klebanov, & Duncan, 1996), 65% of whom have spent some time in single-parent homes (Teegartin, 1994).

Because divorce and remarriage are so common, many children now live in blended (stepparent) families with stepsiblings.

More Remarriages

Because more married couples are divorcing, more adults (about 72% of divorced mothers and 80% of divorced fathers) are remarrying, forming **blended,** (or **reconstituted**), **families** that involve at least one child, his or her biological parent, and a stepparent. Often multiple children from two families are blended into a new family system (Glick, 1989). About 25% of American children will spend some time in a stepparent family (Hetherington & Jodl, 1994).

What these changes tell us is that modern families are much more diverse than ever. Our stereotyped image of the model family—the *Leave It to Beaver* nuclear aggregation with a breadwinning father, a housewife mother, and at least two children—is just that: a stereotype. By one estimate, this "typical" family represented about 50% of American households in 1960, but only 12% in 1995 (Hernandez, 1997). Although the family is by no means dying, we must broaden our image of it to include the many dual-career, single-parent, and blended families that exist today, which are influencing the development of the *majority* of our children. Bear that in mind as we begin our discussion of family life, seeking to determine how families influence the development of their children.

single-parent family
a family system consisting of one parent (either the mother or the father) and the parent's dependent child(ren).

blended, or reconstituted, families
new families resulting from cohabitation or remarriage that include a parent, one or more children, and step-relations.

Concept Check 15.1
Families as Social Systems

Check your understanding of families and family processes by matching each descriptive statement below with one of the following principles or concepts: (a) traditional nuclear family, (b) extended family, (c) single-parent family, (d) blended family, (e) direct effect, (f) indirect, or third-party, effect, (g) families are "embedded" entities, (h) families are "developing" entities. Answers appear in the Appendix.

_____ 1. child abuse is more common in cultures that sanction the use of physical punishment
_____ 2. a sensitive, responsive father gains his infant's trust and affection
_____ 3. arrangement in which a child lives with a biological parent and a nonbiological parent
_____ 4. still the dominant family model but becoming less common
_____ 5. as soon as he is able, Billy's parents allow him to dress himself
_____ 6. living arrangement experienced at one time or another by nearly 60% of American children
_____ 7. type of family in which children show better psychological adjustment in societies that stress communal interdependence
_____ 8. a husband's aloofness toward his son causes his wife to criticize him, thus precipitating marital discord

PARENTAL SOCIALIZATION DURING CHILDHOOD AND ADOLESCENCE

In previous chapters, we considered the results of a large body of research aimed at understanding how parents might affect the social, emotional, and intellectual development of their infants and toddlers. Recall that this work was remarkably consistent in its implications: Warm and sensitive parents who often talk to their infants and try to stimulate their curiosity contribute in a positive way to the establishment of secure emotional attachments, as well as to the child's curiosity and willingness to explore, sociability, and intellectual development. It also helps if *both* parents are sensitive, responsive caregivers who can agree on how their infant should be raised and support each other in their roles as parents. Indeed, Jay Belsky (1981) has argued that caregiver warmth and sensitivity "is the most influential dimension of [parenting] in infancy. It not only fosters healthy psychological functioning during this developmental epoch, but also . . . lays the foundation on which future experiences will build" (p. 8).

During the second year, parents continue to be caregivers and playmates, but they also become much more concerned with teaching children how to behave (or how not to behave) in a variety of situations (Fagot & Kavanaugh, 1993). According to Erik Erikson (1963), this is the period when socialization begins in earnest. Parents must now manage the child's budding autonomy in the hope of instilling a sense of social propriety and self-control, while taking care not to undermine his or her curiosity, initiative, and feelings of personal competence.

Two Major Dimensions of Parenting

Erikson and others (for example, Maccoby & Martin, 1983) claim that two aspects of parenting are especially important throughout childhood and adolescence: *Parental acceptance/responsiveness* and *parental demandingness/control* (sometimes called permissiveness-restrictiveness).

Acceptance/responsiveness refers to the amount of support and affection that a parent displays. Parents classified as accepting and responsive often smile at, praise, and encourage their children, expressing a great deal of warmth, even though they can become quite critical when a child misbehaves. By contrast, less accepting and relatively unresponsive parents are often quick to criticize, belittle, punish, or ignore a child; they rarely communicate to children that they are valued or loved. Throughout the text, we have discussed a wealth of evidence suggesting that parental affection/responsiveness is a powerful contributor to such healthy developmental outcomes as secure attachments and the problem-solving and social skills that such attachments foster (see Chapter 11), competent intellectual and academic performances during the grade-school years (Pettit, Bates, & Dodge, 1997; and see Chapters 9 and 12), high self-esteem, good role-taking skills, and positive identity outcomes (see Chapter 12), more flexible (and androgynous) gender identities (see Chapter 13), and a strong conscience coupled with a healthy sense of prosocial concern (see Chapter 14).

Now compare this behavioral profile with that of the "unwanted" Czechoslovakian children we met in Chapter 11, whose mothers had tried repeatedly to gain permission to abort them (David, 1994). Compared with "wanted" children from similar family backgrounds, the unwanted children had less stable family ties; were described as anxious, emotionally frustrated, and irritable; had more physical health problems; made poorer grades in school (even though they were comparable in IQ to the "wanted" children); were less popular with peers; and were more likely to require psychiatric attention for serious behavior disorders throughout childhood, adolescence, and young adulthood. Other investigators are also finding that a primary contributor to poor peer

acceptance/responsiveness
a dimension of parenting that describes the amount of responsiveness and affection that a parent displays toward a child.

relations, clinical depression, and other psychosocial problems later in life is a family setting in which one or both parents have treated the child as if he or she was unworthy of their attention and affection (Ge et al., 1996; MacKinnon-Lewis et al., 1997; MacDonald, 1992). Children simply do not thrive when they are often ignored or rejected; nor are they apt to become happy, well-adjusted adults (MacDonald, 1992).

Demandingness/control refers to the amount of regulation or supervision that parents undertake with their children. Controlling/demanding parents place limits on their children's freedom of expression by imposing many demands and actively surveying their children's behavior to ensure that these rules and regulations are followed. Uncontrolling/undemanding parents are much less restrictive; they make fewer demands and allow children considerable freedom to pursue their interests and to make decisions about their own activities.

Is it better for parents to be highly controlling, or to impose few restrictions and grant their children considerable autonomy? To answer these questions, we need to be more specific about the degrees of control that parents display and to look carefully at patterns of parental acceptance.

Warmth and affection are crucial components of effective parenting.

Four Patterns of Parenting

It turns out that the two major parenting dimensions are reasonably independent, so that we find parents who display each of the four possible combinations of acceptance/responsiveness and control/demandingness shown in Figure 15.3. How are these four parenting styles related to a child's or an adolescent's social, emotional, and intellectual development?

demandingness/control
a dimension of parenting that describes how restrictive and demanding parents are.

authoritarian parenting
a restrictive pattern of parenting in which adults set many rules for their children, expect strict obedience, and rely on power rather than reason to elicit compliance.

authoritative parenting
a flexible style of parenting in which adults allow their children autonomy, but are careful to explain the restrictions they impose and to ensure that their children follow these guidelines.

Baumrind's Early Research

Perhaps the best-known research on parenting styles is Diana Baumrind's (1967; 1971) early studies of preschool children and their parents. Each child in Baumrind's sample was observed on several occasions in nursery school and at home. These data were used to rate the child on such behavioral dimensions as sociability, self-reliance, achievement, moodiness, and self-control. Parents were also interviewed and observed while interacting with their children at home. When Baumrind analyzed the parental data, she found that individual parents generally used one of three parenting styles shown in Figure 15.3 (none of her parents could be classified as "uninvolved"). These three patterns of parenting were described as follows.

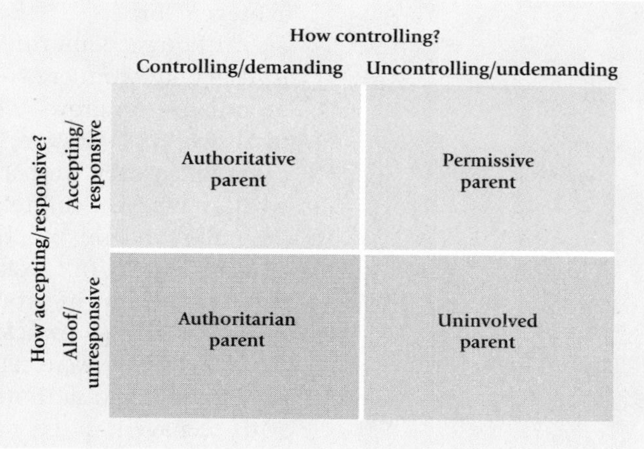

Figure 15.3 *Two major dimensions of parenting. When we cross the two dimensions, we come up with four parenting styles: accepting/controlling (or "authoritative"); accepting/uncontrolling (or "permissive"); aloof/controlling (or "authoritarian"); and aloof/uncontrolling (or "uninvolved"). Which parenting style do you think would be associated with the most favorable outcomes? The least favorable outcomes?* DATA FROM MACCOBY & MARTIN, 1983.

AUTHORITARIAN PARENTING. A very restrictive pattern of parenting in which adults impose many rules, expect strict obedience, rarely if ever explain to the child why it is necessary to comply with all these regulations, and often rely on punitive, forceful tactics (that is, power assertion or love withdrawal) to gain compliance. Authoritarian parents are not sensitive to a child's conflicting viewpoints, expecting instead for the child to accept their word as law and to respect their authority.

AUTHORITATIVE PARENTING. A controlling but flexible style in which involved parents make many reasonable demands of their children. They are careful to provide rationales for complying with the limits they set, and ensure that their children follow those guidelines. However, they are much more accepting of and responsive to their children's points of view than authoritarian parents are and often seek their

Table 15.1 Relationships between Child-rearing Patterns and Developmental Outcomes in Middle Childhood and Adolescence

Child-rearing pattern	Outcomes: Childhood	Outcomes: Adolescence
Authoritative	High cognitive and social competencies	High self-esteem, excellent social skills, strong moral/prosocial concern, high academic achievement
Authoritarian	Average cognitive and social competencies	Average academic performance and social skills; more conforming than adolescents of permissive parents
Permissive	Low cognitive and social competencies	Poor self-control and academic performance; more drug use than adolescents of authoritative or authoritarian parents

Sources: Baumrind, 1977; 1991; Steinberg et al., 1994.

children's participation in family decision making. So authoritative parents exercise control in a *rational, democratic* (rather than a domineering) way that recognizes and respects their children's perspectives.

Permissive Parenting. An accepting but lax pattern of parenting in which adults make relatively few demands, permit their children to freely express their feelings and impulses, do not closely monitor their children's activities, and rarely exert firm control over their behavior.

When Baumrind (1967) linked these three parenting styles to the characteristics of the preschool children who were exposed to each style, she found that children of authoritative parents were developing rather well. They were cheerful, socially responsible, self-reliant, achievement oriented, and cooperative with adults and peers. By contrast, children of authoritarian parents tended to be moody and seemingly unhappy much of the time, easily annoyed and unfriendly, relatively aimless, and generally not very pleasant to be around. Finally, children of permissive parents were often impulsive and aggressive, especially if they were boys. They tended to be bossy and self-centered, lacking in self-control, and quite low in independence and achievement.

Although Baumrind's findings clearly favor authoritative parenting, one might legitimately wonder whether children of authoritarian or permissive parents might eventually "outgrow" whatever shortcomings they displayed as preschoolers. Seeking to answer this question, Baumrind (1977) observed her participants (and their parents) again when they were 8 to 9 years old. As we see in Table 15.1, children of authoritative parents were still relatively high in both *cognitive competencies* (that is, they showed originality in thinking, had high achievement motivation, liked intellectual challenges) and *social skills* (for example, they are sociable and outgoing, participate actively and show leadership in group activities), whereas children of authoritarian parents were generally average to below average in cognitive and social skills, and children of permissive parents were relatively unskilled in both areas. Indeed, the strengths of children exposed to authoritative parenting were still evident in adolescence: Compared with teenagers raised by either permissive or authoritarian parents, those raised by authoritative parents were relatively confident, achievement-oriented, and socially skilled, and they tended to stay clear of drug abuse and other problem behaviors (Baumrind, 1991). The link between authoritative parenting and positive developmental outcomes seems to hold for all racial and ethnic groups studied to date in the United States (Glasgow et al., 1997; Luster & McAdoo, 1996; Lamborn et al., 1991; Steinberg et al., 1994) and in a variety of different cultures as well (Pinto, Folkers, & Sines, 1991; Scott, Scott, & McCabe, 1991).

permissive parenting
a pattern of parenting in which otherwise accepting adults make few demands of their children and rarely attempt to control their behavior.

Uninvolved Parenting

In recent years, it has become quite clear that the least successful parenting style is what might be termed **uninvolved parenting**—an extremely lax and undemanding approach displayed by parents who have either *rejected* their children or are so overwhelmed with their own stresses and problems that they haven't much time or energy to devote to child-rearing (Maccoby & Martin, 1983). By age 3, children of uninvolved parents are already relatively high in aggression and such externalizing behaviors as temper tantrums (Miller et al., 1993). Furthermore, they tend to perform very poorly in the classroom later in childhood (Eckenrode, Laird, & Doris, 1993), and often become hostile, selfish, and rebellious adolescents who lack meaningful long-range goals and are prone to commit such antisocial and delinquent acts as alcohol and drug abuse, sexual misconduct, truancy, and a wide variety of criminal offenses (Lamborn et al., 1991; Kurdek & Fine, 1994; Patterson et al., 1992; Weiss & Schwarz, 1996). In effect, these youngsters have neglectful, "detached" parents whose actions (or lack thereof) seem to be saying "I don't care about you or about what you do"—a message that undoubtedly breeds resentment and the motivation to strike back at these aloof, uncaring adversaries or other authority figures.

Explaining the Effectiveness of Authoritative Parenting

Why is authoritative parenting so consistently associated with positive social, emotional, and intellectual outcomes? Probably for several reasons. First, authoritative parents are warm and accepting: They communicate a sense of *caring concern* that may motivate their children to comply with the directives they receive in a way that children of more aloof and demanding (authoritarian) parents are not. Then there is the issue of how control is exercised. Unlike the authoritarian parent who sets *inflexible* standards and *dominates* the child, allowing little if any freedom of expression, the authoritative parent exercises control in a *rational* way, carefully explaining his or her point of view, while also considering the child's viewpoint. Demands that come from a warm, accepting parent and that appear to be fair and reasonable rather than arbitrary and dictatorial are likely to elicit committed compliance rather than complaining or defiance (Kochanska, 1997b). Finally, authoritative parents are careful to tailor their demands to the child's ability to regulate his or her own conduct. In other words, they set standards that children can *realistically* achieve and allow the child some freedom, or *autonomy,* in deciding how best to comply with these expectations. This kind of treatment carries a most important message—something like "You are a capable human being whom I trust to be self-reliant and accomplish important objectives." Of course, we've seen in earlier chapters that feedback of this sort fosters the growth of self-reliance, achievement motivation, and high self-esteem in childhood, and provides the kind of support that adolescents need to feel comfortable about exploring various roles and ideologies to forge a personal identity.

In sum, it appears that authoritative parenting—warmth combined with *moderate* and *rational* parental control—is the parenting style most consistently associated with positive developmental outcomes. Children apparently need love *and* limits, a set of rules that help them to structure and to evaluate their conduct. Without such guidance, they may not learn self-control and may become quite selfish, unruly, and lacking in clear achievement goals, particularly if their parents are also aloof or uncaring (Steinberg et al., 1994). But, if they receive too much guidance and are hemmed in by inflexible restrictions, they may have few opportunities to become self-reliant and may lack confidence in their own decision-making abilities (Grolnick & Ryan, 1989; Steinberg et al., 1994).

The Direction of Effects Issue. Does authoritative parenting really foster positive traits in children? Or is it that easygoing, manageable children cause parents to be authoritative? Baumrind (1983; 1993) insists that authoritative parenting causes children to be well behaved rather than the other way around. She notes that children of authoritative

uninvolved parenting
a pattern of parenting that is both aloof (or even hostile) and overpermissive, almost as if parents neither cared about their children nor about what they may become.

parents often resist parental demands at first, but they eventually come around *because* parents are firm in their demands and sufficiently patient to allow their children time to comply without caving in to the children's unreasonable demands or turning to power-assertive tactics. Indeed, longitudinal studies of early parental control strategies used by mothers with their 1½- to 3-year-olds clearly supports Baumrind's parental-influence hypothesis. Specifically, authoritative mothers who demanded that their children perform competent actions (or do's) and who dealt firmly but patiently with noncompliance had toddlers who became more compliant over time and displayed few problem behaviors. By contrast, authoritarian mothers whose demands emphasized don'ts (don't touch; don't yell) and who used arbitrary, power-assertive control strategies had children who were less competent and cooperative, and who displayed an increase in problem behaviors over time (Crockenberg & Litman, 1990; Kuczynski & Kochanska, 1995).

Yet, it is also true that extremely stubborn and impulsive children who show little self-control tend to elicit more coercive forms of parenting (Kuczynski & Kochanska, 1995) and may eventually wear their parents out, causing them to become more lax, less affectionate, and possibly even hostile and uninvolved (Lytton, 1990; Stice & Barrera, 1995). So as we concluded when considering the impact of discipline on moral development in Chapter 14, socialization within the family is a matter of *reciprocal* influence. Parents certainly influence their children, but children have some influence on the kind of parenting they receive.

? WHAT DO YOU THINK?

In view of the data suggesting that parenting styles clearly differ in effectiveness, some developmentalists believe that a course in parenting should become a required part of the high school curriculum. Do you agree with this proposal? Why or why not?

Social Class and Ethnic Variations in Child-rearing

Associations between authoritative parenting and healthy psychological development have been found in many cultures and subcultures. Yet, people from different social strata and ethnic backgrounds face different kinds of problems, pursue different goals, and adopt different values about what it takes to adapt to their environments, and these ecological considerations often affect their approaches to child-rearing.

Social Class Differences in Child-rearing

How, then, do parenting styles differ by social class? Compared with middle- and upper-class parents, economically disadvantaged and working-class parents tend to:

1. stress obedience and respect for authority more and place somewhat less emphasis on fostering independence, curiosity, and creativity.
2. be more restrictive and authoritarian, more frequently using power-assertive discipline.
3. talk to and reason with their children less frequently.
4. show less warmth and affection (Maccoby, 1980; McLoyd, 1990).

According to Eleanor Maccoby (1980), these class-linked differences in parenting have been observed in many cultures and across racial and ethnic groups in the United States. However, we should keep in mind that what we are talking about here are *group trends* rather than absolute contrasts. Some middle-class parents are highly restrictive, power-assertive, and aloof in their approach to child-rearing, whereas many lower- and working-class parents function more like their counterparts in the middle class (Kelley, Power, & Wimbush, 1992; Laosa, 1981). But on average, it appears that lower-SES and working-class parents are somewhat more critical, punitive, and intolerant of disobedience than are parents from the middle and upper socioeconomic strata.

Explaining Social Class Differences in Child-rearing

Undoubtedly, many factors contribute to social-class differences in child-rearing, and economic considerations seem to head the list. Consider that a low income may mean that living quarters are crowded, that family members must occasionally make do without adequate food, clothing, or medical care, and that parents are constantly tense or anxious about living under these marginal conditions. Eleanor Maccoby (1980) suggests that low-income living is probably much more *stressful* for parents and that stress affects the ways in which parental functions are carried out. Vonnie McLoyd (1989; 1990) agrees. Her reviews of the literature suggest that economic hardship creates its own psychological distress—a most pervasive discomfort that makes lower-income adults more edgy and irritable and more vulnerable to all negative life events (including the daily hassles associated with child-rearing), thereby diminishing their capacity to be warm, supportive parents who are highly involved in their children's lives.

Recently, Rand Conger and his associates (1992, 1994, 1995; see also Bolger et al., 1995) offered support for this economic-distress hypothesis by finding clear links between family economic hardships, nonnurturant/uninvolved parenting, and poor adolescent outcomes. The causal sequence, shown in Figure 15.4, goes like this: Parents who experience economic pressure or feel that they cannot cope with their financial problems tend to become depressed, which increases marital conflict. Marital conflict, in turn, disrupts each parent's ability to be a supportive, involved parent, which contributes to such adolescent problems as low self-esteem, poor school performance, poor peer relations, and such adjustment problems as depression, hostility, and antisocial conduct. Many of the conflicts that economically distressed parents have with their adolescents center on money matters—a highly sensitive topic that can make a financially strapped parent feel downright hostile toward his or her children (Conger et al., 1994). And the adolescent adjustment problems and antisocial conduct that nonnurturant/insensitive parenting helps to create may further exasperate parents, causing them to back away and become even less nurturant and less involved in the lives of their children (Vuchinich, Bank, & Patterson, 1992). So it seems that Maccoby and McLoyd were right in assuming that economic hardships are a very important contributor to the relatively aloof and coercive style of parenting often observed in low-income, economically distressed families.

Another explanation for the link between social class and parenting styles focuses on the skills needed by workers in white-collar and blue-collar jobs (Arnett, 1995; Kohn, 1979). A large percentage of lower-SES and working-class breadwinners are blue-collar workers who must please a supervisor and defer to his or her authority. So many lower-income parents may emphasize obedience and respect for authority because these are precisely the attributes that they view as critical for success in the blue-collar economy. By contrast, middle- and upper-class parents may reason and negotiate more with their

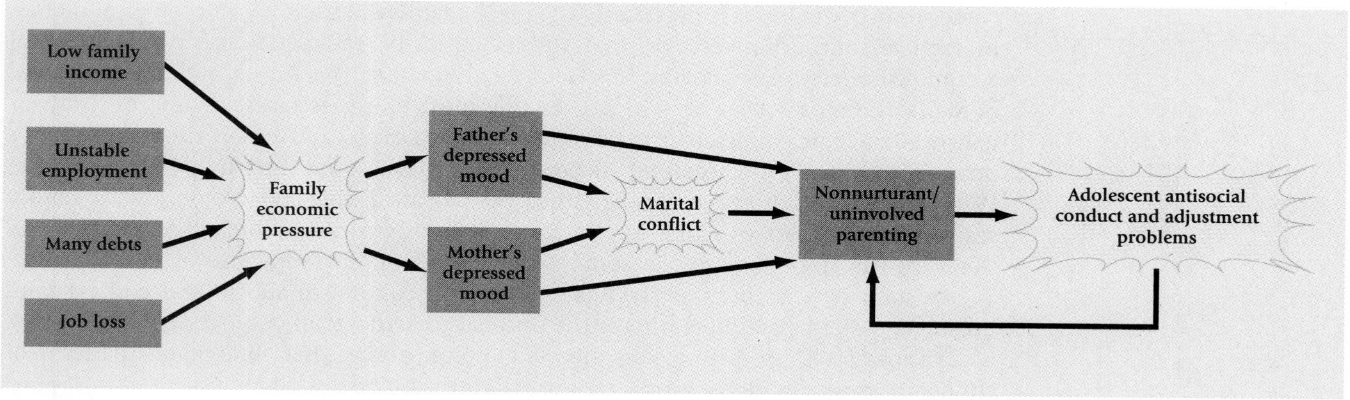

Figure 15.4 *A model of the relationship among family economic stress, patterns of parenting, and adolescent adjustment.* ADAPTED FROM CONGER ET AL., 1992.

children while emphasizing individual initiative, curiosity, and creativity because these are the skills, attributes, and abilities that matter in their own occupations as business executives, white-collar workers, or professionals (Greenberger, O'Neil, & Nagel, 1994).

Ethnic Variations in Child-rearing

Parents of different ethnicities may also hold distinct child-rearing beliefs and values that are products of their cultural backgrounds or the ecological niches they occupy in society (MacPhee, Fritz, & Miller-Heyl, 1996). For example, Native American and Hispanic parents, whose cultural backgrounds stress communal rather than individual goals, are more inclined than European-American parents to (1) maintain close ties to a variety of kin and (2) insist that their children display calm, proper, and polite behaviors and a strong respect for others, as opposed to independence, competitiveness, and the pursuit of individual goals (Harwood et al., 1996; MacPhee et al., 1996). These parents foster such attributes by displaying ample warmth and affection while teaching their children to respect parental authority, particularly the father's legitimate right to set limits and promote their welfare (Harrison et al., 1994).

Asian and Asian-American parents also tend to stress self-discipline and interpersonal harmony and, if anything, are even more authoritarian than parents of other ethnicities (Greenberger & Chen, 1996; Uba, 1994). Yet, authoritarian parenting may mean something quite different for these children than for European Americans. Ruth Chao (1994) notes, for example, that Chinese children perform very well in school despite the fact that their parents are highly authoritarian rather than authoritative. In Chinese culture, parents believe that strictness is the best way to express love for children and to train them properly; and children accept longstanding cultural values specifying that they obey elders and honor their families. Thus, an authoritarian style that may be too controlling to work well for European Americans appears highly effective indeed in China (and among Asian immigrant families in the United States; see Fuligni, 1997).

Although it is difficult to summarize the diversity of child-rearing practices that characterize African-American families, research suggests that urban black mothers (particularly if they are younger, single, and less educated) are inclined to demand strict obedience from their children and to use coercive forms of discipline to ensure that they get it (Kelley et al., 1992; Ogbu, 1994). Yet, a somewhat coercive and controlling pattern of parenting may be adaptive for single mothers who lack social support if it protects children who reside in dangerous neighborhoods from becoming victims of crime (Ogbu, 1994) or associating with antisocial peers (Mason et al., 1996). In fact, use of coercive discipline within the normal range does not foster heightened aggression and antisocial conduct in African-American youth in the same way it does for European Americans, possibly because it may be viewed by African-American children as a sign of caring and concern rather than a symptom of parental hostility (Deater-Deckard & Dodge, 1997).

Considering the findings we have reviewed, one must be careful *not* to assume that a middle-class pattern of authoritative parenting that seems to promote favorable outcomes in many cultures is necessarily the most adaptive pattern for all ecological niches. In fact, an authoritative style that fosters curiosity, independence, and individual accomplishments may actually represent "incompetent" parenting among the Temne of Sierra Leone, a society in which everyone must pull together and suppress individualism if the community is to successfully plant, harvest, and ration the meager crops on which its livelihood absolutely depends (Berry, 1967). And since many children from Western societies choose a career within the so-called blue-collar economy, it hardly seems reasonable to conclude that a lower-SES pattern of child-rearing that prepares them for this undertaking is in some way deficient or "incompetent."

In sum, development always takes place in a cultural or subcultural context, and no single pattern of child-rearing is the optimal pattern for all cultures and subcultures. Louis Laosa (1981, p. 159) makes this same point, noting that "indigenous patterns of child care throughout the world represent largely successful adaptations to conditions of life that have long differed from one people to another. [Adults] are 'good [parents]' by the only relevant standards, those of their own culture."

The Quest for Autonomy: Renegotiating the Parent–Child Relationship during Adolescence

One of the most important developmental tasks that adolescents face is to achieve a mature and healthy sense of **autonomy.** This complex attribute has two major components: (1) *emotional autonomy,* or an ability to serve as one's own source of emotional strength rather than childishly depending on parents to provide comfort, reassurance, and emotional security, and (2) *behavioral autonomy,* or an ability to make one's own decisions, to govern one's own affairs, and to take care of oneself (Steinberg, 1996). If adolescents are to "make it" as adults, they can't be rushing home for loving hugs after every little setback. Nor can they continue to rely on parents to get them to work on time or to remind them of their duties and obligations.

So what happens within the family system as children mature and begin to act more autonomously? Sparks fly! In cultures as diverse as Hong Kong and the United States, conflicts between parents and children about self-governance issues become much more frequent, at least temporarily, as children reach puberty (Holmbeck & Hill, 1991; Steinberg, 1996; Yau & Smetana, 1996). These squabbles are usually neither prolonged nor severe, often centering around such issues as the adolescent's physical appearance, her choice of friends, or her neglect of schoolwork and household chores. And much of the friction stems from the different perspectives that parents and adolescents adopt. Parents view conflicts through a moral or *social-conventional* lens, feeling that they have a responsibility to monitor and regulate their child's conduct, whereas the adolescent, locked in his quest for autonomy, often views his nagging parents as infringing on *personal* rights and choices (Smetana, 1995; Yau & Smetana, 1996). As teenagers continue to assert themselves and parents slowly loosen the reins, the parent–child relationship gradually evolves from an enterprise in which the parent is dominant to one in which parents and adolescents are on a more equal footing (Feldman & Gehring, 1988; Furman & Buhrmester, 1992). Yet, Chinese and Asian-American parents tend to exert their authority far longer than European-American parents do (Greenberger & Chen, 1996; Yau & Smetana, 1996), a practice that often bothers and may depress Asian-American adolescents (Greenberger & Chen, 1996).

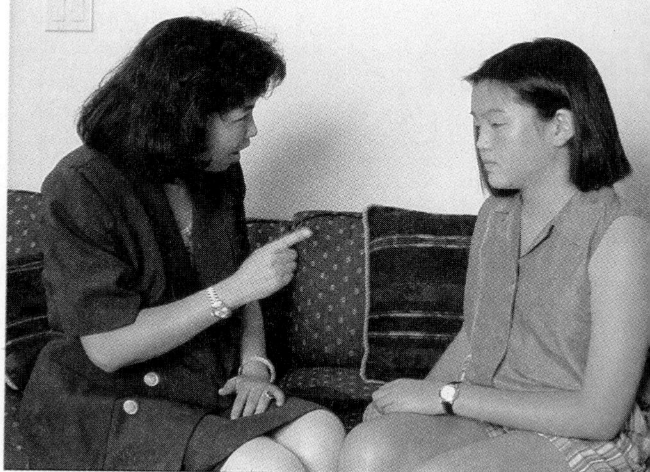

As adolescents begin their quest for autonomy, conflicts with parents become more commonplace.

Researchers once believed that the most adaptive route to establishing autonomy was for adolescents to separate from parents by cutting the emotional cords. Indeed, teenagers who perceive their relationships with parents to be very conflictual and nonsupportive appear to be better adjusted when they distance themselves from their families and become emotionally autonomous (Fuhrman & Holmbeck, 1995). Yet adolescents who are warmly received at home would be ill-advised to cut the emotional cords, for those who gradually achieve more behavioral autonomy while maintaining *close attachments* to family members display the best overall pattern of psychosocial adjustment (Lamborn & Steinberg, 1993; Steinberg, 1996).

Encouraging Autonomy

How might parents successfully promote adolescent autonomy and healthy psychological outcomes? It seems that parents of well-adjusted adolescents gradually relinquish control as their teenagers display a readiness to accept more responsibility, but they also continue to monitor their adolescents' conduct and demand more in the way of self-governance as well (Lamborn et al., 1991; Youniss & Smollar, 1985). Furthermore, parents of well-adjusted adolescents keep their rules and regulations to a reasonable minimum, strive to explain them, and continue to be warm and supportive, even in the face of the inevitable conflicts that arise (Steinberg, 1996). Does this parenting style sound familiar? It should, for this winning combination of parental

autonomy
the capacity to make decisions independently, to serve as one's own source of emotional strength, and to otherwise manage life tasks without depending on others for assistance; an important developmental task of adolescence.

acceptance and a pattern of flexible control that is neither too lax nor overly restrictive is an *authoritative* approach—the same style that fosters high self-esteem and solid academic performances in childhood and healthy identity outcomes later in adolescence. (Indeed, becoming appropriately autonomous seems to be a necessary prerequisite for achieving a stable personal identity.) It is mainly when parents react negatively to a teenager's push for autonomy and become overly strict or overly permissive that adolescents are likely to experience personal distress or to rebel and to get into trouble (Barber, Olsen, & Shagle, 1994; Fuhrman & Holmbeck, 1995; Lamborn et al., 1991). Of course, we must remind ourselves that socialization within the family is a matter of reciprocal influence, and that it may be much easier for a parent to respond authoritatively to a responsible, level-headed adolescent than to one who is rude, hostile, and unruly.

In sum, conflicts and power struggles are an almost inevitable consequence of an adolescent's quest for autonomy. Yet, most teenagers and their parents are able to resolve these differences while maintaining positive feelings for one another as they renegotiate their relationship so that it becomes more equal (Furman & Buhrmester, 1992). As a result, young autonomy seekers become more self-reliant while also developing a more "friendlike" attachment to their parents.

Might an adolescent's experiences in the world of work help to foster a healthy sense of autonomy? Box 15.1 explores this issue.

THE INFLUENCE OF SIBLINGS AND SIBLING RELATIONSHIPS

Although families are getting smaller, the majority of American children still grow up with at least one sibling, and there is certainly no shortage of speculation about the roles that brothers and sisters play in a child's life. Many parents, distressed by the fighting and bickering that their children display, often fear that such rivalrous conduct will undermine the growth of children's prosocial concerns and their ability to get along with others. At the same time, the popular wisdom is that only children are likely to be lonely, overindulged "brats" who would profit both socially and emotionally from having siblings to teach them that they are not nearly as "special" as they think they are (Falbo, 1992).

Although rivalries among siblings are certainly commonplace, we will see that siblings can play some very positive roles in a child's life, often serving as caregivers, teachers, playmates, and confidants. And yet, we will also see that only children may not be nearly as disadvantaged by their lack of sibling relationships as people have commonly assumed.

Changes in the Family System When a New Baby Arrives

Judy Dunn and Carol Kendrick (1982; see also Dunn, 1993) have studied how children adapt to a new baby, and the account they provide is not an entirely cheerful one. After the baby arrives, mothers typically devote less warm and playful attention to their older children, who may respond to this perceived "neglect" by becoming difficult and disruptive and less securely attached, particularly if they are 2 years of age or older and can more readily appreciate that their "exclusive" relationship with caregivers has been undermined by the baby's birth (Teti et al., 1996). Clearly, older children often resent losing their mothers' attention and may harbor animosities toward a new baby for stealing it; and their own difficult behavior may make matters worse by alienating their parents.

DEVELOPMENTAL ISSUES

Does Part-Time Employment Foster a Healthy Sense of Autonomy (and Positive Developmental Outcomes)?

More than 60% of high school students in the United States work part time, and it is reasonable to assume that their work experiences could have any number of effects on their development. On the positive side, Michael Shanahan and his associates (1996) find that the money that teenagers make often fosters a sense of self-efficacy and economic autonomy. Other investigators have reported that working youth feel that they have become more punctual, dependable, responsible, and self-reliant as a result of having held a job (see Mortimer et al. (1996) for a review). However, some potential disadvantages of adolescent employment have been reported as well.

Lawrence Steinberg and his associates have compared working and nonworking youth on such outcome measures as their autonomy from parents, academic performances, psychological adjustment, and involvement in delinquent activities (Greenberger & Steinberg, 1986; Steinberg & Dornbusch, 1991; Steinberg, Fegley, & Dornbusch, 1993). Overall, this research reports far more bad news than good about teenagers who work, particularly about those who work more than 20 hours per week during the school year. Specifically, adolescents who worked such long hours had much more autonomy over day-to-day decisions than age-mates who worked 10 hours a week or less. Yet, this greater autonomy seemed to be directed toward "cutting the cords" to parents, for teenagers who were heavily invested in work were much less involved in family activities and were monitored less closely by older family members. And the psychological and behavioral correlates of all this freedom were downright gloomy. Compared with peers who worked 10 hours a week or less, teenagers who worked 20 or more hours a week were lower in self-esteem, made lower grades at school, and reported higher levels of anxiety, depression, and somatic complaints (for example headaches, stomach aches), and more frequent involvement in alcohol and drug use and other delinquent activities. So would adolescents be better off by avoiding employment, if possible, and by concentrating on their schooling?

Not necessarily. Critics have argued that working may look like such a negative influence because the adolescents who worked long hours in the earlier reports often came from nonsupportive home environments or were already experiencing academic (or other) difficulties that may have *caused* them to separate from parents and to seek greater involvement in the world of work. In other words, their preexisting problems, rather than their heavy work involvement, could have been the primary contributor to their poor psychosocial outcomes. In agreement with earlier reports, Michael Shanahan and his associates (1996) found that younger (7th to 10th grade) working youth spent less time with their families and were monitored less closely than were nonworking peers. Yet, within this rural sample, adolescent employment was associated with more sharing of advice with older family members and with *improved* emotional relationships with them. In another 4-year longitudinal study of 1,000 high school students that controlled for such other variables as family background and prior academic performance that might influence developmental outcomes, Jeylen Mortimer and associates (1996) found that working 20 hours or more per week did *not* undermine teenagers' academic achievement, self-esteem, or other aspects of their psychological adjustment. In fact, the figure shows that high school seniors who worked a moderate number (1 to 20) of hours per week actually made better grades than those who didn't work. The sole cause for concern was that high school seniors who worked more than 20 hours a week used alcohol more frequently than those who were not employed.

Clearly, the question of whether adolescents are affected positively or negatively by their working experiences is a complex one, although it now seems clear that even a heavy work involvement need not be harmful. Some developmentalists believe that adolescents are much more likely to benefit from challenging jobs that provide opportunities for self-direction and decision making than from menial, repetitive fast food or manual labor positions that require few academic skills and do little to foster a sense of self-efficacy or self-esteem. Indeed, Michael Shanahan and his associates (1991; Call, Mortimer, & Shanahan, 1995) found that adolescent boys displayed clear increases in mastery motivation and became less depressed when the work they performed offered opportunities for advancement and provided skills that would be useful in the future. By contrast, boys showed declines in mastery motivation and became more depressed while working menial jobs with demands that conflicted with their involvement in school. So whether working fosters a healthy sense of autonomy and has positive or negative effects on adolescent adjustment may depend far more on the *quality* of adolescents' work experiences than the quantity of work they perform.

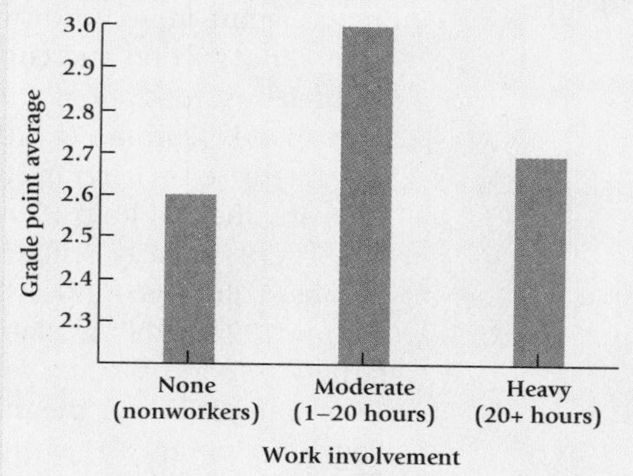

Grade-point averages of high school seniors as a function of work involvement. Notice that students who worked a moderate amount made the best grades and that even the students who were heavily invested in work performed just as well as their nonworking peers. ADAPTED FROM MORTIMER ET AL., 1996.

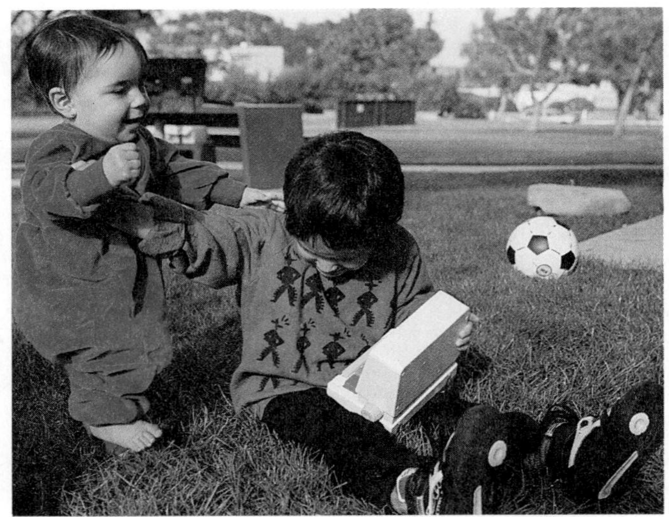

Coercive and rivalrous conduct between siblings is a normal aspect of family life.

Thus, **sibling rivalry**—a spirit of competition, jealousy, or resentment between siblings—often begins as soon as a younger brother or sister arrives. How can it be minimized? The adjustment process is easier if the first-born had secure relationships with both parents before the baby arrived and continues to enjoy close ties afterward (Dunn & Kendrick, 1982; Volling & Belsky, 1992). Parents are advised to continue to provide love and attention to their older children and to maintain their normal routines as much as possible. It also helps to encourage older children to become aware of the baby's needs and assist in the care of their new brother or sister (Dunn & Kendrick, 1982; Howe & Ross, 1990). Yet Dunn & Kendrick (1982) find that parents may have to walk a thin line between two traps: becoming so attentive to the new baby that they deprive the older child of attention, and becoming so indulgent of the first-born that he or she becomes a "spoiled brat" who resents any competition from the younger sibling.

Sibling Relationships over the Course of Childhood

Fortunately, most older siblings adjust fairly quickly to having a new brother or sister, becoming much less anxious and less inclined to display the problem behaviors that they showed early on. But even in the best of sibling relationships, conflict is normal. Indeed, Judy Dunn (1993) reports that the number of skirmishes between very young siblings can range as high as 56 per hour! Rivalrous conduct continues throughout the preschool and grade-school years, with older siblings often becoming the more domineering and aggressive parties and younger siblings the more compliant ones (Abramovitch et al., 1986; Berndt & Bulleit, 1985). Yet, older sibs also initiate more helpful, playful, and other prosocial behaviors, a finding that may reflect the pressure that parents place on them to demonstrate their maturity by caring for a younger brother or sister.

In some ways, sibling relationships are truly paradoxical because they are often both *close* and *conflictual* (Furman & Buhrmester, 1985). Grade-school siblings who are similar in age report more warmth and closeness than do other sibling pairs—but, at the same time, more friction and conflict! Yet grade-school children consistently say that their sibling relationships are as important or more important to them than their relationships with friends (Furman & Buhrmester, 1985), and highly aggressive children or those who are otherwise socially unskilled are much better adjusted if they have maintained close ties with their siblings (Dunn et al., 1994; East & Rook, 1992; Stormshak et al., 1996).

Parents clearly influence just how smooth or stormy the sibling relationship becomes. Brothers and sisters are more likely to get along if their parents get along (Dunn, 1993). Sibling relationships are also friendlier and less conflictual if mothers and fathers respond warmly and sensitively to *all* their children and do not consistently favor one child over the other (Brody, Stoneman, & McCoy, 1994; McHale et al., 1995). Younger siblings are particularly sensitive to unequal treatment, often reacting negatively and displaying adjustment problems if they perceive that the older sib is favored by parents (McHale et al., 1995; Tarullo et al., 1995). It is not that older siblings are unaffected by differential treatment; but because they are older, they are usually better able to understand that siblings may have different needs and that unequal treatment may be justified, even if that means that parents may sometimes favor a younger sib in certain respects (Kowal & Kramer, 1997).

sibling rivalry
the spirit of competition, jealousy, and resentment that may arise between two or more siblings.

As is true of parent–child relationships, sibling relationships become much more egalitarian during the adolescent years. Siblings now quarrel less frequently and their relationships otherwise become less intense, probably because teenagers spend less time with brothers and sisters who are, after all, part of the family from whom they want to develop some autonomy (Furman & Buhrmester, 1992; Larson et al., 1996). But even though they immerse themselves in close friendships and romantic relationships, adolescents continue to perceive their siblings as important and intimate associates—people to whom they can turn for support and companionship, despite the fact that relations with them have often been rather stormy (Buhrmester & Furman, 1990; Furman & Buhrmester, 1992).

Perhaps these seemingly paradoxical data make perfectly good sense if we carefully examine the findings on the nature of sibling–sibling interactions. Yes, rivalries and conflicts among siblings are a very normal part of family life. Yet, the observational record consistently shows that brothers and sisters often do nice things for one another and that these acts of kindness and affection are typically much more common than hateful or rivalrous conduct (Abramovitch et al., 1986; Baskett & Johnson, 1982).

Contributions of Siblings to Development

What positive roles might siblings play in one another's development? One of their most important functions is to provide *emotional support.* Brothers and sisters confide in one another and protect and comfort one another in rough times. Older children are especially inclined to comfort a distressed infant or toddler sibling if they are securely attached themselves to their mothers (Teti & Ablard, 1989) and have developed the role-taking skills to understand why their younger brother or sister is distressed (Garner, Jones, & Palmer, 1994; Stewart & Marvin, 1984). And as we have noted, a secure tie to a sibling can help to prevent the anxiety and adjustment problems that grade-school children often display if they are ignored or rejected by their peers (East & Rook, 1992; Stormshak et al., 1996).

Second, older siblings often provide *caretaking* services for younger ones. In one cross-cultural study, older siblings were the *principal* caregivers for infants and toddlers in 57% of the 186 cultures surveyed (Weisner & Gallimore, 1977). In our society as well, older sibs, especially girls, are frequently asked to babysit or otherwise tend to their young brothers and sisters (McHale & Gamble, 1989).

Third, older siblings often *teach* new skills to younger brothers and sisters. Even infants are quite attentive to older sibs, often choosing to imitate their behaviors or taking over toys that they have abandoned (Abramovitch, Corter, & Pepler, 1980). Younger children tend to admire their older siblings, who continue to serve as important models and tutors throughout childhood (Buhrmester & Furman, 1990). Given a problem to master, children are likely to learn more when they have an older sibling available to guide them than when they have access to an equally competent older peer (Azmitia & Hesser, 1993). Why? Because (1) older siblings feel a greater responsibility to teach if the pupil is a younger *sibling,* (2) they provide more detailed instructions and encouragement than older peers do, and (3) younger children are more inclined to seek the older sibling's guidance. This kind of informal instruction clearly pays off: When older siblings play school with younger brothers and sisters, teaching them such lessons as the ABCs, younger siblings have an easier time learning to read (Norman-Jackson, 1982). What's more, older siblings who often tutor younger ones may profit

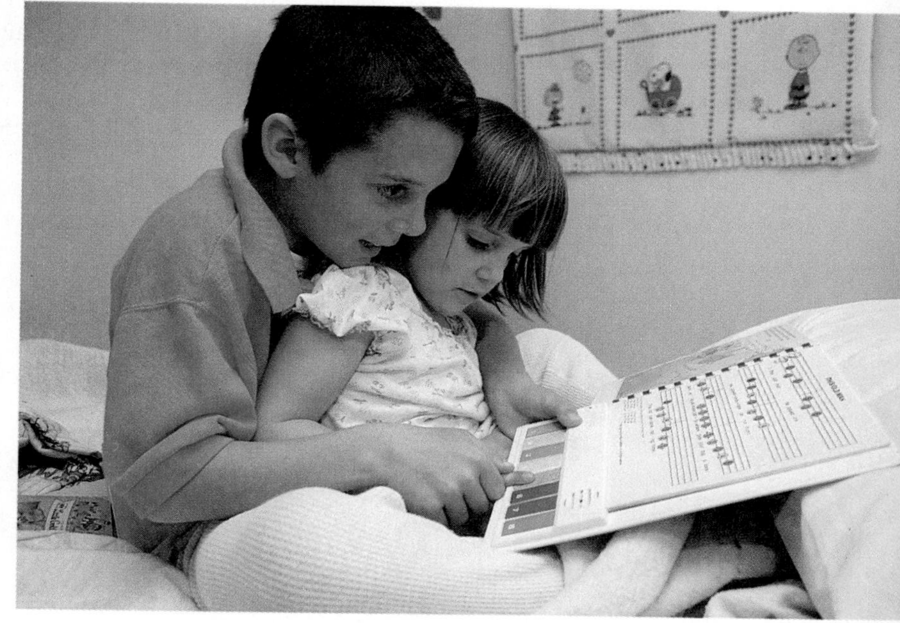

Older siblings often serve as teachers for their younger brothers and sisters.

as well, for they score higher on tests of academic aptitude and achievement than peers who have not had these tutoring experiences (Paulhus & Shaffer, 1981; Smith, 1990).

Finally, the sheer frequency and intensity of sibling interactions imply that these contacts may foster the growth of many other competencies. In Chapters 10 and 12, for example, we learned that playful interactions among siblings contribute to the growth of effective communication skills and to children's emerging theory of mind. Furthermore, siblings are not at all shy about communicating their wants, needs, and emotional reactions to conflict, thus providing each other with information that fosters the growth of perspective-taking skills, emotional understanding, a capacity for negotiation and compromise, and more mature forms of moral reasoning (Brown & Dunn, 1996; Dunn et al., 1995). Clearly, there are many ways in which children may benefit from their experiences with siblings.

Characteristics of Only Children

Are only children who grow up without siblings the spoiled, selfish, overindulged brats that people often presume them to be? Hardly! Two major reviews of hundreds of pertinent studies found that only children are (1) relatively high, on average, in self-esteem and achievement motivation, (2) more obedient and slightly more intellectually competent than children with siblings, and (3) likely to establish good relations with peers (Falbo, 1992; Falbo & Polit, 1986). Since only children enjoy an exclusive relationship with their parents, they may receive more quality time from adults and more direct achievement training than children with siblings do, perhaps explaining their tendency to be relatively friendly, well-behaved, and instrumentally competent (Baskett, 1985). Furthermore, these singletons have no younger sibs that they can dominate and may soon learn that they must negotiate and be accommodating if they hope to play successfully with *peer* playmates, most of whom are probably at least as powerful as they are.

Might these findings simply reflect the fact that parents who choose to have only one child differ systematically from those who have more children? Probably not. In 1979, the People's Republic of China implemented a one-child family policy in an attempt to control its burgeoning population. So regardless of the number of children that parents may have wanted, most Chinese couples, in urban areas at least, have been limited to one child. Contrary to the fears of many critics, there is no evidence that China's one-child policy has produced a generation of spoiled, self-centered brats who behave like "little emperors." Only children in China closely resemble only children in Western countries, scoring slightly higher than children with siblings on measures of intelligence and academic achievement and showing few meaningful differences in personality (Falbo & Poston, 1993; Jaio, Ji, & Jing, 1996). In fact, only children in China actually report *less* anxiety and depression than children with siblings do, a finding that may reflect China's social condemnation of multichild families and only children's tendency to taunt children with siblings with such remarks as "You shouldn't be here" or "Your parents should have only one child" (Yang et al., 1995).

So evidence from very different cultural settings suggests that only children are hardly disadvantaged by having no brothers and sisters. Apparently, many singletons are able to gain through their friendships and peer alliances whatever they may miss by not having siblings at home.

DIVERSITY IN FAMILY LIFE

As we noted earlier in the chapter, modern families are more diverse today than ever before: The *majority* of our children are growing up in dual-career, single-parent, or blended families that may be very different than the two-parent, single-breadwinner aggregation with two or more children that people often think of as the typical family unit. So let's examine some of these variations in family life.

Adoptive Families

If one member of the pair is infertile, couples who hope to become parents often seek to adopt a child. Yet, those who are successful in adopting may face many challenges. For example, adults who remain distressed about their own infertility may have some difficulties relating to adoptive children (Burns, 1990; Humphrey & Humphrey, 1988). However, the clear majority of adoptive parents develop strong emotional ties to their adoptees (Levy-Shiff et al., 1991), and it now appears as if an adult's desire to be a parent is much more important to a child's outcome than the adult's genetic ties (or lack thereof) to his or her children (Golombok et al., 1995). Nevertheless, since adoptive parents and their children share no genes, the rearing environments that adoptive parents provide may not be as closely compatible with an adoptee's own genetic predispositions as they are for a biological child. These environmental incompatibilities, coupled with the fact that many adoptees have been previously neglected, abused, or have other special needs (Kirchner, 1998), help to explain why adoptees display more learning difficulties and emotional problems than their nonadopted peers later in childhood and adolescence (Verhulst & Versluis-Den Bieman, 1995).

Don't misunderstand. Adopted children typically fare much better in adoptive homes than in foster care, where their foster parents may not be very invested in them or their long-range prospects (Bohman & Sigvardsson, 1990). Even transracially adopted children from lower socioeconomic backgrounds usually fare quite well intellectually and academically and often display healthy patterns of psychosocial adjustment when raised in supportive, relatively affluent middle-class adoptive homes (Brodzinsky et al., 1987; DeBerry et al., 1996). So adoption is a quite satisfactory arrangement for most adoptive parents and their adoptees.

Adoption practices in the United States are changing from a confidential system, in which the identities of the birth mother and adoptive parents are withheld from each other, to a more open system that allows for varying amounts of direct or indirect contact between birth mothers and members of adoptive families. Since adoptees are often curious about their biological origins and may be upset about the prospect of never knowing their birth parents, more open arrangements may prove beneficial to them. Preliminary research with 5- to 13-year-old adoptees reveals that children (particularly older ones) are both more curious and more satisfied with information about their roots when

Concept Check 15.2
Understanding Parental and Sibling Influences

Check your understanding of selected influences that parents and siblings may have on developing children by matching each descriptive statement below with one of the following groups or concepts: (a) authoritarian parenting, (b) authoritative parenting, (c) economic distress, (d) emotional support, (e) increased academic aptitude, (f) mastery motivation, (g) only children, (h) uninvolved parenting, (i) unwanted children. Answers appear in the Appendix.

_____ 1. can undermine an adult's ability to be a supportive, involved parent

_____ 2. benefit that older siblings may receive by instructing younger siblings

_____ 3. their outcomes dramatically illustrate that acceptance/responsiveness is a crucial aspect of effective parenting

_____ 4. children exposed to this inflexible, controlling parenting style show average to below-average cognitive and social competencies

_____ 5. contrary to popular belief, they are not developmentally disadvantaged

_____ 6. very ineffective parenting style that is consistently associated with poor developmental outcomes

_____ 7. benefit that younger siblings often receive from older siblings

_____ 8. often increases among adolescents working a moderate number of hours in *challenging* jobs

_____ 9. parenting style that illustrates that *rational* exercise of control contributes to positive developmental outcomes they can share information or even have contact with their birth mothers (Wrobel et al., 1996); yet, there was no evidence in this study that providing information about birth mothers had such harmful effects as confusing children about the meaning of adoption or undermining their self-esteem, as some critics of open adoption policies had feared.

Gay and Lesbian Families

In the United States, several million gay men or lesbians are parents, most through previous heterosexual marriages, although some have adopted children or conceived through donor insemination (Flaks et al., 1995; Patterson, 1995b). Historically, many courts have been so opposed to the prospect of lesbians and gay men raising children that they have denied the petitions of homosexual parents in child custody hearings solely on the basis of these parents' sexual orientations. Among the concerns people have are that gay and lesbian parents may be less mentally healthy or that they will molest their children who, in turn, are at risk of being stigmatized by peers because of their parents' sexual orientation. But perhaps the greatest concern is the fear that children raised by gay or lesbian parents are likely to become gay or lesbian themselves (Bailey et al., 1995).

Interestingly, there is virtually no basis for any of these speculations. As shown in Figure 15.5, more than 90% of adult children of lesbian mothers or gay fathers develop a heterosexual orientation, a figure that is not significantly different from the percentages of heterosexuals raised by heterosexual parents. Furthermore, children of gay and lesbian parents are just as cognitively, emotionally, and morally mature, on average, and are otherwise as well adjusted as children of heterosexual parents (Flaks et al., 1995; Patterson, 1994). Finally, gay fathers and lesbian mothers are every bit as knowledgeable about effective child-rearing techniques as heterosexual parents are (Bigner & Jacobsen, 1989; Flaks et al., 1995), and partners of homosexual parents are usually attached to the children and assume some caregiving responsibilities. In fact, lesbian mothers are happiest and their children somewhat better adjusted when child care responsibilities are more evenly distributed between the biological parent and her partner (Patterson, 1995a).

In sum, there is no credible scientific evidence that would justify denying a person's rights of parenthood on the basis of his or her sexual orientation. Aside from the possibility of being stigmatized by their parent's lifestyle, children raised in gay and lesbian families are virtually indistinguishable from those of heterosexual couples.

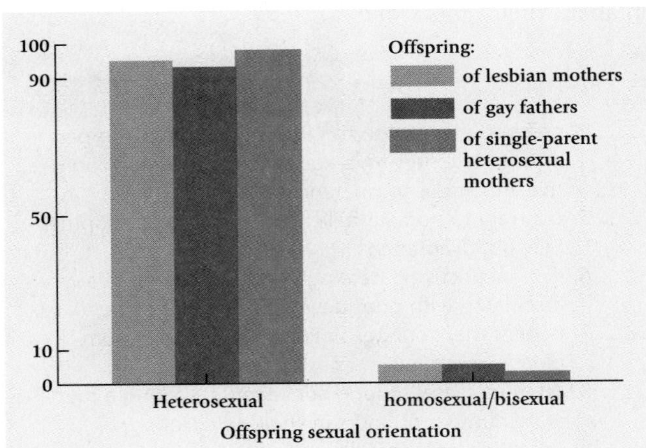

Figure 15.5 *Sexual orientation of adult children raised by lesbian mothers, gay fathers, and single-parent heterosexual mothers. (Notice that children with homosexual parents are just as likely to display a heterosexual orientation as children raised by heterosexuals.)*
Adapted from Bailey et al., 1995; Golombok & Tasker, 1996.

The Impacts of Family Conflict and Divorce

Earlier, we noted that about half of today's marriages will end in divorce and that as many as 60% of all children born in the 1980s and 90s will spend some time (about 5 years, on average) in a single-parent home, usually one headed by the mother (Teegartin, 1994). What effects might a divorce have on developing children? As we address this issue, let's first note that divorce is *not* a singular life event; instead, it represents a series of stressful experiences for the entire family that begins with marital conflict before the actual separation and includes a multitude of life changes afterward. As Mavis Hetherington and Kathleen Camara (1984) see it, families must often cope with "the diminution of family resources, changes in residence, assumption of new roles and responsibilities, establishment of new patterns of [family] interaction, reorganization of routines . . . , and [possibly] the introduction of new relationships [that is, steppar-ent/child and stepsibling relationships] into the existing family" (p. 398).

Youngsters who live in conflict-ridden nuclear families often suffer physically and emotionally. In the long run, children of divorce are usually better adjusted than those whose unhappily married parents stay together "for the sake of the children."

Before the Divorce: Exposure to Marital Conflict

The period prior to divorce is often accompanied by a dramatic rise in family conflict that may include many heated verbal arguments and even physical violence between parents. How are children influenced by their exposure to marital conflict? A growing body of evidence indicates that they often become extremely distressed and that continuing conflict at home increases the likelihood that children will have hostile, aggressive interactions with siblings and peers (Cummings & Davies, 1994). Furthermore, regular exposure to marital discord is a contributor to a number of other child and adolescent adjustment problems, including anxiety, depression, and externalizing conduct disorders (Davies & Cummings, 1998; Harold et al., 1997; McCloskey, Figueredo, & Koss, 1995). Marital discord can have both *direct effects* on children and adolescents by putting them on edge emotionally and undermining the maturity of their behavior, as well as *indirect effects* by undermining parental acceptance/sensitivity and the quality of the parent/child relationship (Erel & Burman, 1995; Harold et al., 1997). So conflict-ridden homes are not healthy contexts for child or adolescent development, and many researchers now believe that children in strife-ridden homes often fare better in the long run if their parents separate or divorce (Barber & Eccles, 1992; Hetherington, 1989). Nevertheless, divorce is often a highly unsettling life transition that may have its own effects on the well-being of all family members.

Immediate Effects of Divorce: Crisis and Reorganization

Most families going through a divorce experience a *crisis period* of a year or more in which the lives of all family members are seriously disrupted (Booth & Amato, 1991; Hetherington, 1989; Hetherington, Cox, & Cox, 1982; Kitson & Morgan, 1990). Typically, both parents experience emotional as well as practical difficulties. The mother, who obtains custody of any children in about 83% of divorcing families, may feel angry, depressed, lonely, or otherwise distressed, although often relieved as well. The father is also likely to be distressed, particularly if he did not seek the divorce and feels shut off from his children. Having just become single adults, both parents often feel isolated from former married friends and other bases of social support on which they relied as marrieds. Divorced women with children usually face the added problem of getting by with less money—about half the family income they had before, on average (Smock, 1993). And life may seem especially difficult if they must move to a lower-income neighborhood, and try to work and raise young children singlehandedly (Emery & Forehand; 1994; Kitson & Morgan, 1990).

As you might suspect, psychologically distressed adults do not make the best parents. Hetherington and her associates (1982) find that custodial mothers, overwhelmed by responsibilities and by their own emotional reactions to divorce, often become edgy, impatient, and insensitive to their children's needs, and they typically adopt more restrictive and coercive methods of child-rearing. Noncustodial fathers, on the other hand, often undermine the mother's parenting efforts by becoming more permissive and indulging. And the children of divorce, who are often anxious, angry, or depressed over the family breakup, may react to these changes in parenting by becoming whiney and argumentative, disobedient, and downright disrespectful. Parent–child relationships during this crisis phase are best described as a vicious cycle in which the child's emotional distress and problem behaviors and the adults' ineffective parenting styles feed on each other and make everyone's life unpleasant (Baldwin & Skinner, 1989). However, children's initial reactions to divorce vary somewhat as a function of their ages, temperaments, and sex.

Children's Age. Younger, cognitively immature preschool and early grade-school children often display the most visible signs of distress as a divorce unfolds. They may not understand why their parents have divorced and are even inclined to feel guilty if they think they are somehow responsible for the break-up of their families (Hetherington, 1989). Older children and adolescents are better able to understand the personality conflicts and lack of caring that may lead distressed parents to divorce and to resolve any loyalty conflicts that may arise; however, they often remain highly distressed over their parents' divorce and may react by withdrawing from family members and becoming more involved in such undesirable peer-sponsored activities as truancy, sexual misconduct, substance abuse, and other forms of delinquent behavior (Amato, 1993; Doherty & Needle, 1991). So even though they are better able to comprehend the reasons for the parents' divorce and to feel less responsible for having caused it, older children and adolescents seem to suffer no less than younger children do (Amato, 1993; Hetherington & Clingempeel, 1992).

Children's Temperament and Sex. The stresses associated with parental conflict and divorce hit particularly hard at temperamentally difficult children, who display more immediate and long-range adjustment problems to these events than easygoing children do (Henry et al., 1996; Hetherington & Clingempeel, 1992). Often, the highly volatile behavior of a temperamentally difficult child elicits more coercive forms of parenting from his impatient and highly distressed caregiver which, in turn, represents an extremely "poor fit" with a difficult child's reactive demeanor and contributes substantially to his adjustment difficulties.

Although the finding is by no means universal (see Allison & Furstenberg, 1989), many investigators report that the impact of marital strife and divorce is more powerful and enduring for boys than for girls. Even before a divorce, boys already display more overt behavioral problems than girls do (Block, Block, & Gjerde, 1986; 1988). And at least two longitudinal studies found that girls had largely recovered from their social and emotional disturbances 2 years after a divorce, whereas boys, who improved dramatically over this same period, were nevertheless continuing to show signs of emotional stress and problems in their relationships with parents, siblings, teachers, and peers (Hetherington et al., 1982; Wallerstein & Kelly, 1980).

Why might marital turmoil and divorce strike harder at boys? One explanation is that boys may feel closer to fathers than girls do, so that they experience more frustration and a deeper sense of loss when the father is no longer readily available to them (Hetherington, Bridges, & Insabella, 1998; Lamb, 1981). And because boys are normally more active and less compliant than girls are (see Chapter 13), they may respond more negatively and vigorously to new restrictions imposed by the custodial parent—reactions that often elicit the kinds of coercive discipline that are likely to perpetuate their whiney, surly, and defiant behavior (Hetherington et al., 1982). However, some developmentalists believe that boys appear to be poorly adjusted because investigators have focused more on overt behavior problems that are easy to detect than on other, more subtle adjustment measures, such as covert psychological distress (Zaslow, 1989). Indeed, at least three recent studies suggest that even prior to a divorce (and for up to 10 years afterward), girls experience more *covert* distress than boys do (Allison & Furstenberg, 1989; Chase-Lansdale, Cherlin, & Kiernan, 1995; Doherty & Needle, 1991). What's more, a disproportionate number of girls from divorced families show precocious sexual activity at adolescence and a persistent lack of self-confidence in their relationships with boys and men (Cherlin, Kiernan, & Chase-Lansdale, 1995; Fernandez, 1997). So divorce seems to affect boys and girls in different ways.

Yet another reason why boys may look bad is that most researchers have limited their studies to the most common custodial arrangement: mother-headed households. Interestingly, boys whose fathers assume custody fare much better than boys who live with their mothers; in fact, children and adolescents of *both* sexes seem to be better adjusted and are less likely to drop out of high school when they live with their same-sex parent (Camara & Resnick, 1988; Zaslow, 1989; Zimiles & Lee, 1991).

So a divorce can strike very hard at children of either sex. Clearly, we would be overstating the case (not to mention being insensitive to girls) were we to conclude that this disruptive life experience is anything but a struggle for the majority of boys *and* girls.

Long-term Reactions to Divorce

Although many of the emotional and behavioral disturbances that accompany a divorce diminish considerably over the next 2 years, there may be aftereffects. Compared with children in harmonious, two-parent families, some children of divorce show signs of academic difficulties and psychological distress throughout adolescence and into young adulthood (Fernandez, 1997; Chase-Lansdale et al., 1995; Jonsson & Gahler, 1997). But most children from divorced families improve dramatically over time and display healthy patterns of psychological adjustment (Chase-Lansdale et al., 1995).

Nevertheless, even the well-adjusted children of divorce may show some long-term effects (Hetherington et al., 1998). In one longitudinal study, children from divorced families were still rather negative in their assessments of the impact of divorce on their lives when interviewed more than 20 years after the break-up of their families (Wallerstein & Lewis, as cited by Fernandez, 1997). Another interesting long-term reaction is that adolescents from divorced families are more likely than those from nondivorced families to fear that their own marriages will be unhappy (Franklin, Janoff-Bulman, & Roberts, 1990; Wallerstein & Blakeslee, 1989). There may well be some basis for this concern, for adults whose parents divorced are more likely than adults from intact families to experience an unhappy marriage and a divorce themselves (Amato, 1996).

In sum, divorce tends to be a most unsettling and troubling life event that few children feel very positive about, even after 20 to 25 years have elapsed. But despite the gloomy portrait of divorce that we have painted here, there are some more encouraging messages. First, researchers consistently find that children in stable, single-parent (or stepparent) homes are usually better adjusted than those who remain in conflict-ridden two-parent families (Hetherington, 1989; Long & Forehand, 1987). Indeed, many of the behavior problems that children display after a divorce are actually evident well *before* the divorce and may be more closely related to long-standing family conflict than to the divorce itself (Amato & Booth, 1996; Davies & Cummings, 1998). Take away the marital discord and the breakdown in parenting often associated with divorce and the experience, while always stressful, need not always be damaging (Amato, 1993). So today's conventional wisdom holds that unhappily married couples who have unreconcilable differences might well *divorce* for the good of the children; that is, children are likely to *benefit* if the ending of a stormy marriage ultimately reduces the stress they experience and enables either or both parents to be more sensitive and responsive to their needs (Barber & Eccles, 1992; Hetherington, 1989).

A second encouraging message is that not all divorcing families experience all the difficulties we have described. In fact, some adults and children manage this transition quite well and may even grow psychologically as a result of it (Bursik, 1991; Hetherington, 1989). Who are these survivors? Box 15.2 provides some clues by exploring the factors that seem to promote a positive adjustment to divorce.

Remarriage and Blended Families

Within 3 to 5 years after a divorce, about 75% of single-parent families experience yet another major change when the custodial parent remarries or *cohabits* (lives with) a partner outside of marriage, and the children acquire a stepparent, and perhaps new siblings as well (Hetherington, 1989; U.S. Bureau of the Census, 1997). Remarriage often improves the financial and other life circumstances of custodial parents, and most newly remarried adults report that they are satisfied with their second marriages. Yet, these blended families introduce new challenges for children, who must now adjust not only to the parenting of an unfamiliar adult, but to the behavior of stepsiblings

APPLYING DEVELOPMENTAL RESEARCH

15.2

Smoothing the Rocky Road to Recovery from a Divorce

Some individuals adjust rather well to a divorce, whereas others may suffer negative and long-lasting effects. Who is likely to fare well and what factors make the process of adjustment easier for members of divorcing families?

Adequate financial support

Divorcing families fare much better if they have adequate finances (Hetherington, 1989; Simons et al., 1993). Unfortunately, many mother-headed families experience a precipitous drop in income, which may necessitate a move to a lower-income neighborhood and a mother's return to work at precisely the time that her children need stability and increased attention. Furthermore, a lack of money for trips, treats, and other amenities to which children may be accustomed can be a significant contributor to family quarrels and bickering. Unfortunately, only about half of noncustodial fathers pay any child support (Sorensen, 1997) and recent efforts to require noncustodial parents to pay their fair share are a step in the right direction.

Adequate parenting by the custodial parent

The custodial parent obviously plays a crucial role in the family's adjustment to divorce. If he or she can continue to respond in a warm, consistent, and authoritative manner, children are much less likely to experience serious problems (Hetherington & Clingempeel, 1992; Kline et al., 1989). Of course, it is difficult to be an effective parent when one is highly stressed or depressed. Yet, both the custodial parent and the children can benefit immensely from receiving outside social support, not the least important of which is that provided by the noncustodial parent.

Social/emotional support from the noncustodial parent

If divorced parents continue to squabble and are hostile to each other, both are likely to be upset, the custodial parent's parenting is likely to suffer, and the children will likely feel "caught in the middle," torn in their loyalties, and will probably have difficulties adjusting (Amato, 1993; Buchanan, Maccoby, & Dornbusch, 1991). Recently, the state of Arizona passed a law requiring couples hoping to divorce to complete a 4½-hour seminar to understand the impact of the divorce on their children before their divorce action may proceed (Associated Press, 1996). The purpose of the seminar is to make parents aware that (1) their children are likely to be more traumatized by the parents' postdivorce wranglings than by the separation itself, and (2) *regular contact* with a noncustodial parent who *supports* the custodial guardian in his or her parenting role is a strong contributor to children's positive adjustment to life in a single-parent home. Ideally, then, children should be permitted to maintain close, affectionate ties with *both* parents and shielded from any continuing conflict between them (Amato, 1993).

Is *joint physical custody* the answer? Obviously, living part of the time in each parent's home does prevent loss of contact with noncustodial fathers, which happens all too often and can be very upsetting to children (Kline et al., 1989). Yet, this "contact advantage" may be offset by new kinds of instability (that is, by changes in residence, and sometimes, in schools and peer groups) that can leave some children distressed and confused (Kline et al., 1989). It may not really matter whether parents obtain joint custody if they both maintain high-quality relationships with their children (Emery & Tuer, 1993; Kline et al., 1989). But when parents' relationship is hostile and conflictual, living in dual residencies may heighten children's perception of being "caught in the middle," which is associated with high levels of stress and poor adjustment outcomes (Buchanan et al., 1991).

Additional social support

Divorcing adults are less depressed if they participate in support groups such as *Parents without Partners* (a national organization with local chapters that attempt to help single parents cope with their problems) or if they have relatives or close confidants to whom they can turn (Emery, 1988; Hetherington et al., 1998). Children also benefit from the support they receive from close friends (Lustig, Wolchik, & Braver, 1992), as well as from participating in peer-support programs at school, in which they and other children of divorce are encouraged to share their feelings, correct their misconceptions, and learn positive coping skills (Grych & Fincham, 1992; Pedro-Carroll & Cowen, 1985). In sum, friends, peers, school personnel, and other sources of social support outside the nuclear family can do much to help families adjust to divorce.

Minimizing additional stress

Generally, families respond more positively to divorce if additional disruptions are kept to a minimum—for example, if parents do not have to go through messy divorce trials and custody hearings, seek new jobs or residences, cope with the loss of their children, and soon. One way to accomplish some of these aims is through *divorce mediation*—meetings prior to the divorce in which a trained professional tries to help divorcing parents reach amiable agreements on disputed issues such as child custody and property settlements. Divorce mediation does increase the likelihood of out-of-court settlements and often promotes better feelings between divorcing adults (Emery & Wyer, 1987); thus it may well have a beneficial effect on children's adjustment to the family break-up (although this latter effect remains to be confirmed by research).

Here, then, we have some effective first steps in the path toward a positive divorce experience, as well as a better understanding of why divorce is more disruptive for some families than for others. This research also serves as yet another excellent example of the family as a social system embedded in larger social systems. Mother, father, and children all influence one another's adjustment to divorce, and the family's experience also depends on the supports available within the neighborhood, the schools, the community, and family members' own social networks.

(if any) and to the possibility of receiving less attention from both their custodial and noncustodial parents (Hetherington, 1989). Furthermore, second marriages are somewhat more likely to end in divorce than first marriages are (Booth & Edwards, 1992). Imagine, then, the stresses experienced by families that find themselves in a recurring cycle of marriage, marital conflict, divorce, single parenthood, and remarriage. Indeed, recent studies reveal that the more marital transitions that grade-school children have experienced, the poorer their academic performances and the less well-adjusted they are (Capaldi & Patterson, 1991; Kurdek, Fine, & Sinclair, 1995; and see Figure 15.6).

So how do children fare in relatively *stable* blended families? The answer depends in part on their ages and gender and on whether their mother or father has formed the new family.

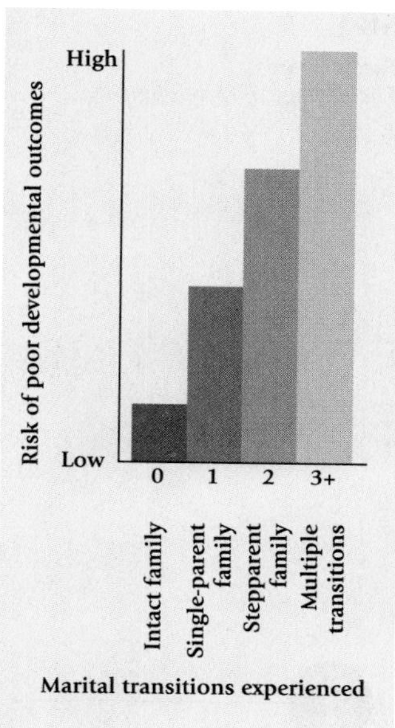

Figure 15.6 *Boys' risk for poor adjustment outcomes (that is, antisocial behavior, low self-esteem, peer rejection, drug use, depression, poor academic performance, and deviant peer associations) as a function of number of marital transitions experienced.* From Capaldi & Patterson, *1991.*

Mother–Stepfather Families

After an initial period of disruption and confusion that occurs as new family roles iron themselves out, boys seem to benefit more than girls by gaining a *stepfather.* Stepfathers who are warm and accepting offer relief from the coercive cycles that boys may have experienced with a custodial mother, so that these stepsons often enjoy a boost in self-esteem and eventually overcome many of the adjustment problems they displayed before their mothers remarried (Hetherington, 1989; Vucinich et al., 1991). Why do girls not fare as well? Certainly *not* because stepfathers are treating stepdaughters any worse than stepsons; in fact, just the opposite is true during the early stages of remarried life, and no matter how hard stepfathers try, their stepdaughters often remain rather cool and aloof. Girls often view stepfathers as threats to their relationships with their mothers and may even resent their mothers for remarrying and becoming less attentive to their needs (Hetherington, 1989; Vucinich et al., 1991).

Father–Stepmother Families

Less is known about children's reactions to *stepmothers* because stepmother families are still relatively uncommon (recall that fathers currently receive custody of their children in only about 17% of all custody hearings). What research there is indicates that introduction of a stepmother into the family system is somewhat more disruptive initially than the introduction of a stepfather, in part because (1) fathers granted custody typically have very close relations with their children that stepmothers may disrupt (Mekos, Hetherington, & Reiss, 1996), and (2) stepmothers play more active roles as behavior monitors and disciplinarians than stepfathers do (Furstenberg, 1988; Santrock & Sitterle, 1987). Furthermore, the transition from a father-custody single-parent home to a two-parent *stepmother* family is once again more disruptive and difficult for girls than for boys, particularly if the biological mother maintains frequent contact with her children (Brand, Clingempeel, & Bowen-Woodward, 1988; Clingempeel & Segal, 1986). Girls are often so closely allied with their mothers that they are bothered by either a stepfather competing for their mother's attention or a stepmother attempting to play a substitute-mother role. But the emotional disruption and resentment that daughters may initially experience in stepmother families is often short-lived, for most girls eventually warm up to their stepmothers and may benefit from the support of a second mother figure (Brand et al., 1988).

Age and Family Constellation

Interestingly, preadolescent and young adolescent children of both sexes find it more difficult to adjust to life in a blended family than younger children do. In fact, Mavis Hetherington and Glenn Clingempeel (1992) found that even after spending more than 2 years in a blended family, many adolescents were less well adjusted than age-mates from nondivorced families and had shown little improvement over the 26-month course of the study. Problems are more common when each adult brings a child into the family, in part because parents tend to be warmer and more involved with their biological offspring than with their stepchild, and adolescents pick up on this differential treatment and react negatively to it (Mekos et al., 1996). Of course, many adolescents in blended families adjust quite well, and authoritative parenting within these homes is associated with more favorable adjustment outcomes (Hetherington & Clingempeel, 1992; Maccoby, 1992). Nevertheless, a fair number (perhaps one-third) of adolescents disengage from their blended families, and the incidence of deviant or delinquent behavior is higher among adolescents from stepparent homes than among age-mates from nondivorced families (Capaldi & Patterson, 1991; Hetherington & Jodl, 1994; Steinberg, 1987).

How might we explain this finding? One possibility that has received some support (see Fine & Kurdek, 1994; Mekos et al., 1996), is that many stepparents are hesitant to impose restrictions on adolescents or to carefully monitor their activities, preferring to leave these tasks to the biological parent. And because grandparents often become less involved in their grandchildren's lives once a custodial parent remarries (Clingempeel et al., 1992), the biological parent may now have little social support for the rules she imposes and may find it extremely difficult to adequately monitor the activities of adolescents on her own (Dornbusch et al., 1985; Steinberg, 1987). But before we get too carried away about the antisocial tendencies of adolescents in blended families, an important truth should be stated here: most adolescents who experience this marital transition turn out to be perfectly normal teenagers who may experience some initial problems adjusting, but are unlikely to display any prolonged psychopathological tendencies (Maccoby, 1992). In fact, disengagement from a blended family may even be beneficial if a teenager's time away from home is spent at a job or at extracurricular activities that foster constructive, supportive relationships with adult mentors or peers.

WHAT DO YOU THINK?

Prior to the 1970s, grandparents did not have the right to petition for visitation privileges with their grandchildren after the children's parents had divorced. Now grandparents in the United States can seek such visitation privileges in court. How do you feel about this policy? What limitations might be placed on grandparent visitation to protect the best interests of the custodial parent? The child?

Maternal Employment

In Chapter 11, we learned that a clear majority of American mothers now work outside the home and that this arrangement need not undermine the emotional security of their children. Infants and toddlers are likely to become or to remain securely attached to their working parents if they have good day-care, if their mothers (and fathers) have favorable attitudes about both working and parenting, and if they receive sensitive responsive care at home.

Looking beyond primary attachments, research with older children suggests that maternal employment, in itself, is unlikely to impede a child's social or intellectual development. In fact, the opposite may be true, for children of working mothers (particularly daughters) tend to be more independent, to enjoy higher self-esteem, and to

Concept Check 15.3
Understanding Family Diversity and Family Transitions

Check your understanding of variations and changes in families and their developmental implications by matching each descriptive statement below with one of the following responses: (a) boys, (b) girls, (c) coercive parenting, (d) delinquent conduct, (e) gay/lesbian parenting, (f) adoption, (g) noncustodial parental support, (h) unhappy marital relations. Answers appear in the Appendix.

_____ 1. more common among adolescents in blended families than among those from traditional nuclear families

_____ 2. seem to adjust better to living with a custodial mother

_____ 3. factor that helps children adjust to a divorce

_____ 4. postdivorce change in family dynamics that may contribute to children's adjustment difficulties

_____ 5. seem to adjust better life in a blended family

_____ 6. long-term risk of being a child of divorce

_____ 7. highly satisfactory family transition for most who experience it

_____ 8. fears about the possible consequences of _____ have proved to be unfounded hold higher educational and occupational aspirations and less stereotyped views of men and women than those whose mothers are not employed (Richards & Duckett, 1994; Hoffman, 1989). Indeed, one recent study of a national sample of *low-income* families linked maternal employment to children's cognitive *competence:* Second-graders whose mothers had worked a great deal outperformed those whose mothers had worked less (if at all) in mathematics, reading, and language achievement (Vandell & Ramanan, 1992; see also Williams & Radin, 1993).

Parenting of Employed Mothers

One reason that children of employed mothers often experience favorable (rather than unfavorable) developmental outcomes and look so socially mature is that employed mothers are more inclined than nonemployed mothers to grant their children independence and autonomy when their youngsters are ready for it (Hoffman, 1989). And when mothers have stimulating jobs, receive adequate social support from their husbands or partners and other close associates, and are highly committed to being a parent, they have generally favorable impressions of their children, rely less on power-assertion to control their behavior, and are inclined to take an authoritative approach to child-rearing—precisely the parenting style so often associated with favorable cognitive, social, and emotional outcomes (Crockenberg & Litman, 1991; Greenberger & Goldberg, 1989; Greenberger, O'Neil, & Nagel, 1994). Of course, employed mothers may be less effective parents if they are dissatisfied with their jobs, are not highly committed to parenting, or receive little support in their parenting role (Greenberger & Goldberg, 1989; Greenberger & O'Neil, 1993).

Against this backdrop of generally favorable outcomes associated with maternal employment is a recurring finding that has caused some concern: *middle-class* boys (but not girls) of employed mothers tend to score lower in intelligence and academic achievement than boys whose mothers are not employed (Bronfenbrenner, 1986; Gold & Andres, 1978), particularly when their mothers work long hours (Goldberg, Greenberger, & Nagel, 1996; Gottfried, Gottfried, & Bathurst, 1988). Yet even these results must be qualified, for Ann Crouter and her associates (1990) found that maternal employment is associated with lower academic achievement only when a boy's working parents failed to carefully monitor his behavior. Indeed, boys in dual-career families are just as competent academically as boys (and girls) with nonemployed mothers when parents monitor their activities and ensure that they devote sufficient attention to their schoolwork (Crouter et al., 1990; see also Moorehouse, 1991).

So it seems that maternal employment may often foster the development of daughters without impeding that of sons, as long as working mothers are motivated to work, are highly committed to parenting, and have the supports they need to be effective parents.

The Importance of Good Day-care

As we noted in Chapter 11, one of the strongest supports that working parents could hope for is *high-quality* day-care for their children. Recall that children who enter high-quality day-care centers early in life tend to display positive social, emotional, and intellectual outcomes from infancy through early adolescence (Andersson, 1989; 1992; Broberg et al., 1997). Much of the research which points to the long-term benefits of excellent day-care comes from Western European countries, where day-care for infants, toddlers, and preschool children is often government subsidized, staffed with trained, well-paid child care professionals, and widely available to all citizens at a modest fee (usually less than 10% of an average woman's

Children fare rather well, both socially and academically, if their working parents are authoritative and carefully monitor their activities.

wages; Scarr et al., 1993). By comparison, day-care in the United States is often woefully inadequate. Typically run as a for-profit enterprise, U.S. day-care centers and day-care homes are generally staffed by poorly compensated caregivers who have little training or experience in early childhood education and who rarely stay in the profession long enough to gain much expertise (Scarr, 1998; Zigler & Gilman, 1993). Furthermore, American day-care is expensive; providing one child with what is often far less than optimal care can run $3,200–$4,500 per year, or about 30–40% of the annual income of a minimum-wage worker (U.S. Bureau of the Census, 1997). In 1990, the U.S. Congress passed a bill granting some tax relief to parents to help offset the cost of day-care. But the absence of a national day-care policy that would ensure the availability of *high-quality* care at a *reasonable cost* to *all* who may need it means that many American workers will have to struggle to find and finance the kind of alternative care that would help them to optimize the development of their children.

Self-care

The importance of adequate alternative care raises another employment-related issue: the after-school care of children whose mothers work. In the United States, some 2 to 4 *million* grade-school students between the ages of 6 and 13 qualify as **self-care** (or **latchkey**) **children** who care for themselves after school with little or no adult supervision (Zigler & Finn-Stevenson, 1993). Are these children at risk of being victimized, led astray by peers, or experiencing other less than desirable outcomes?

Research designed to answer these questions is often contradictory. Some studies find that self-care children display higher levels of anxiety, poorer academic performances, and more delinquent or antisocial conduct than supervised youngsters do (Marshall et al., 1997; Pettit et al., 1997), whereas other studies find no such effects (Galambos & Maggs, 1991; Vandell & Corasantini, 1988). Why the inconsistencies? Let's begin by noting that the risks of self-care do seem to be greater for lower-income children in urban neighborhoods that may present many opportunities for unsupervised children to associate with deviant peer groups and to take part in antisocial conduct (Posner & Vandell, 1994; Vandell & Ramanan, 1991). And regardless of the neighborhood, the way self-care children spend their time may be crucial. Grade-school children and adolescents who have received authoritative parenting, who are required to come home after school to complete homework or other chores, and who are monitored at a distance by telephone calls are generally responsible and well-adjusted. By contrast, unmonitored age-mates who are allowed to "hang out" after school are more inclined to be influenced by peers and to engage in delinquent or antisocial conduct (Galambos & Maggs, 1991; Steinberg, 1986).

So it appears that there are steps that working parents can take to minimize some of the potential risks of leaving schoolchildren to care for themselves—namely, by requiring them to go home after school, by supervising them *in absentia* to ensure that they do, and by parenting them in an authoritative manner. Nevertheless, leaving children younger than 8 or 9 to fend for themselves may be asking for trouble (Pettit et al., 1997). Not only is the practice illegal in many states, but 5- to 7-year-olds often lack the cognitive skills to avoid high-risk hazards such as swimming pools or heavy traffic or to cope with such emergencies as personal injuries or fires (Peterson, Ewigman, & Kivlahan, 1993). Younger children in self-care also appear to be more vulnerable to sexual abuse and to harm at the hands of burglars as well (Zigler & Finn-Stevenson, 1993). Fortunately, organized after-school care for school-aged children is becoming more common in American communities, now serving an estimated 2½ million children nationwide (Rosenthal & Vandell, 1996). These programs differ in quality, ranging from "social addresses" where children hang out largely unsupervised, to well-run programs with trained staff, reasonable child-to-staff ratios, and curricula that include a variety of age appropriate activities including sports, games, dance, art projects, music, computer activities, and academic assistance. Not only do children prefer the higher-quality after-school care programs (Rosenthal & Vandell, 1996), but they fare better in these programs as well. Jill Posner and Deborah Vandell (1994), for example, found that 9-year-olds from high-risk neighborhoods who attended *closely supervised* after-school care programs providing ample recreational opportunities and/or academic assistance were more aca-

self-care, or latchkey, children
children who care for themselves after school or in the evenings while their parents are working.

demically competent, were rated as better adjusted by teachers, and were much *less* likely to be involved in antisocial activities than age-mates who were not supervised after school by an adult. However, the same benefits of after-school care are not found if the programs children attend are primarily custodial and provide little stimulation or adult guidance (Vandell & Corasantini, 1990). So the *quality* of day-care that children receive is important at all ages. Given the success of the publicly funded programs that Posner and Vandell (1994) evaluated, we might encourage politicians and community leaders to look carefully at them as a potentially affordable means of (1) optimizing developmental outcomes and (2) preventing more children of working mothers from having to face the risks of being alone in the afternoon and early evening.

Children of working mothers may benefit, both socially and academically, from organized after-school care that is closely supervised by adults.

WHEN PARENTING BREAKS DOWN: THE PROBLEM OF CHILD ABUSE

Family relationships can be our greatest source of nurturance and support, but they can also be a powerful source of anguish. Nowhere is this more obvious than in cases of **child abuse.** Every day, thousands of infants, children, and adolescents are burned, beaten, starved, suffocated, sexually molested, or otherwise mistreated by their caregivers. Other children are not targets of these "physical" forms of abuse, but are victims of such *psychological abuse* as rejection, ridicule, or even being terrorized by their parents (Wiehe, 1996). Still others are *neglected* and deprived of the basic care and stimulation that they need to develop normally. Although instances of severe battering are the most visible forms of child abuse and are certainly horrible, many investigators now believe that strong and recurrent psychological abuse and neglect may prove to be even more harmful to children in the long run (Emery, 1989; Grusec & Walters, 1991).

Child abuse is a very serious problem. In 1994, over 3.1 *million* reports of child maltreatment of all sorts were filed in the United States (American Humane Association, as cited in Wiehe, 1996). In another recent national sample of families in the United States, almost 11% of the children had reportedly been kicked, bitten, punched, hit with an object, or threatened with a knife or a gun by their parents in the past year (Wolfner & Gelles, 1993). What's more, surveys of sexual abuse find that more than 400,000 American children a year are coerced into oral, anal, or genital intercourse (Finkelhor & Dziuba-Leatherman, 1994), usually by a father, a stepfather, an older sibling, or another male relative or family friend (Trickett & Putnam, 1993; Wiehe, 1996). It is not a pretty picture, is it? And since many cases of child abuse are never reported or detected, these figures may represent only the tip of the iceberg.

There are many, many factors that contribute to a social problem as widespread as child abuse. Fortunately, researchers are beginning to gain a better understanding of why abuse occurs through a social systems perspective that recognizes why (1) some adults may be more inclined than others to abuse children, (2) some children may be more likely than others to be abused, and (3) abuse may be more likely to occur in some contexts, communities, and cultures than in others.

Who Are the Abusers?

Researchers have found that there is no single abusive personality syndrome that accurately characterizes adults who commit child abuse (Wiehe, 1996). Child abusers come from all races, ethnic groups, and social classes, and many of them even appear on the surface to be rather normal, loving parents who would never harm their children.

Yet there are at least some differences between parents who abuse their children and those who do not. Although most maltreated children do not abuse their own

child abuse
any extreme maltreatment of children, involving physical batterings, sexual molestations, psychological insults such as persistent ridicule, rejection, and terrorization, and physical or emotional neglect.

children when they become parents, roughly 30% do (Kaufman & Zigler, 1989). In other words, abusive parenting is often passed from generation to generation (Simons et al., 1991; van IJzendoorn, 1992). In addition, abusive mothers are often battered women, victims of abuse in their own romantic relationships (Coohey & Braun, 1997; McCloskey et al., 1995). They may have learned through their experiences as a child and a romantic partner that violence is a common reaction to frustrations. Abusive mothers are also often young, poverty-stricken, poorly educated, and raising children without partners to share their burdens (Wiehe, 1996; Wolfner & Gelles, 1993). And many abusive parents are *emotionally insecure* individuals who are likely to interpret children's irritability or quests for autonomy as signs of *disrespect* or *rejection.* Finally, abusive parents generally favor authoritarian control over authoritative techniques (which they view as largely ineffective). Although abusive parents do not report using physical punishment any more *often* than nonabusive parents do, they do admit to relying heavily on the most severely punitive tactics such as yanking children's hair, hitting them in the face, or striking them with objects (Trickett & Susman, 1988).

In sum, abusive parents are often highly stressed younger women with little social support who have a history of abuse, believe that coercive discipline is more effective than reasoning, and find parenting more unpleasant and ego-threatening than nonabusive parents do. Still, there are many *nonabusive* parents who display all these characteristics, and it has been difficult to predict, in advance, exactly who will become a child abuser (Trickett et al., 1991).

Who Is Abused?

Abusive parents often single out only one child in the family as a target, implying that some children may bring out the worst in their parents (Gil, 1970). No one is suggesting that children are to *blame* for this abuse, but some children do appear to be more at risk than others. For example, infants who are emotionally unresponsive, hyperactive, irritable, impulsive, or sickly are far more likely to be abused than quiet, healthy, and responsive babies who are easy to care for (Ammerman & Patz, 1996; Belsky, 1993). Yet it is important to emphasize that many such "difficult" children are never abused, while many cheerful and seemingly easygoing children are mistreated. Just as caregiver characteristics cannot fully predict or explain why abuse occurs, neither can characteristics of children, although it is likely that the combination of a high-risk parent and a high-risk child spells trouble (Bugental, Blue, & Cruzcosa, 1989).

But even the match between high-risk children and caregivers does not invariably result in child abuse. The broader social contexts in which families are embedded matter, too.

Social-Contextual Triggers: The Ecology of Child Abuse

Child abuse is much more likely to occur in families under stress. Such significant life changes as a divorce, the death of a family member, the loss of a job, or moving to a new home can disrupt social and emotional relationships within a family and contribute to neglectful or abusive parenting (Bronfenbrenner, 1986; McLoyd et al., 1994; Wolfner & Gelles, 1993). Children are also much more likely to be abused or neglected if their parents are unhappily married (Belsky, 1993; Egeland et al., 1988).

High-Risk Neighborhoods

high-risk neighborhood
a residential area in which the incidence of child abuse is much higher than in other neighborhoods with the same demographic characteristics.

Families are embedded in broader social contexts (that is, a neighborhood, a community, and a culture) that can affect a child's chances of being abused. Some residential areas can be labeled **high-risk neighborhoods** because they have much higher rates of child abuse than other neighborhoods with similar demographic characteristics (Coulton et al., 1995). What are these high-risk areas like? According to James Garbarino (Garbarino & Kostelny, 1992; Garbarino & Sherman, 1980), they tend to be impoverished and deteriorating neighborhoods that offer struggling parents little in the way of *community services,* such as organized support groups, recreation centers, preschool programs, churches, and parks, or *informal support systems,* such as contact with friends and relatives. Consequently, socially isolated parents who live in these neighborhoods have nowhere to turn for advice and assistance during particularly stressful periods, and they often end up taking out their frustrations on their children.

The incidence of child abuse is relatively high in deteriorating neighborhoods that offer few services and little if any social support to financially troubled families.

Cultural Influences

Finally, the broader cultural contexts in which families live can affect the likelihood that children will be abused. Some developmentalists believe that child abuse is rampant in the United States because this society (1) has a permissive attitude toward violence and (2) generally sanctions the use of physical punishment as a means of controlling children's behavior (Whipple & Richey, 1997). There may well be some truth to these assertions, for cross-cultural studies reveal that children are less often abused in societies that discourage the use of physical punishment and advocate nonviolent ways of resolving interpersonal conflicts (Belsky, 1993; Gilbert, 1997). In fact, several Scandinavian countries, where children are rarely abused, have *outlawed* the use of corporal punishment (spanking), even by parents (Finkelhor & Dziuba-Leatherman, 1994).

Clearly, child abuse is a very complex phenomenon with many causes and contributing factors (see Table 15.2 for a brief review). It is not always easy to recognize probable abusers, but we know that abuse is most likely to occur when a psychologically vulnerable parent faces overwhelming stress with insufficient social support (Wolfner & Gelles, 1993).

Consequences of Abuse and Neglect

Children who are neglected or abused tend to display a number of serious problems, including intellectual deficits, academic difficulties, depression, social anxiety, low self-esteem, and disturbed relationships with teachers and peers (Bagley, 1995; Trickett & McBride-Chang, 1995; and see Box 15.3 for some noteworthy consequences of childhood sexual abuse). The behavioral correlates of physical abuse differ somewhat from those of neglect. Neglected children are more likely than those who are physically and sexually abused to founder academically and have to repeat a grade (Eckenrode et al., 1993). Victims of neglect may receive very little stimulation from nurturing adults that

TABLE 15.2 Factors Contributing to Child Abuse and Neglect

Contributing factor	Examples
Parental characteristics	Younger age (under 25); low educational level; depression or other psychological disturbance; history of rejection or abuse; belief in effectiveness of coercive discipline; general insecurity or low ego strength
Child characteristics	Irritable or impulsive temperament; hyperactivity; prematurity; inattentiveness; sickliness or other chronic developmental problems
Family characteristics	Financial strain or poverty; job loss; frequent moves; marital instability; lack of spousal support; many children to care for; divorce
Neighborhood	High-risk areas characterized by few community services and little opportunity for informal social support from friends and relatives
Culture	Approval of coercive methods of resolving conflicts and use of corporal punishment to discipline children

15.3

DEVELOPMENTAL ISSUES

Childhood Sexual Abuse

In the 1970s, developmentalists began to discover that the sexual abuse of children was far more common than they had thought. We noted earlier that approximately 400,000 children a year are sexually abused in the United States. And if we count all those individuals who report that they were *ever* molested as children, as David Finkelhor and his associates (1990) did in a national survey, 27% of women and 16% of men had experienced some form of sexual abuse, ranging from being fondled in ways they considered inappropriate to actually being raped. About 25% of the victims were first victimized before age 8, usually by a father, stepfather, grandfather, uncle, teacher, or other male authority figure whom the victim knew well and trusted (Burkhardt & Rotatori, 1995; Wiehe, 1996). Women also commit sexual abuse, although female-initiated sex offenses are often underreported because boys are less likely than girls to disclose their abuse (Rudin, Zalewski, & Bodmer-Turner, 1995).

Sexual abuse is more common in poverty-stricken families, particularly those in which parents are unhappily married and one or both of them abuse alcohol or drugs and were molested themselves as children (Emery & Laumann-Billings, 1998). Yet sexual abuse can and does occur (and is probably underreported) in middle-class families that display none of these risk factors. In many cases, the perpetrator entices and entraps the victim by implying that the child is special and that their sexual activity will be a mutual secret. This pretext is then reinforced by the offender giving the victim gifts, special favors, or privileges (Wiehe, 1996). And often the victim has little choice but to comply because he or she either did not understand what was happening or was operating under threats of reprisal for noncompliance.

Effects of abuse

After reviewing 45 studies, Kathleen Kendall-Tackett and her associates (1993) concluded that there is no one distinctive "syndrome" of psychological disorders that characterizes all who experience sexual abuse. Instead, these victims display any number of problems commonly seen in emotionally disturbed individuals, including anxiety, depression, low self-esteem, acting out, aggression, withdrawal, and academic difficulties. Roughly 20 to 30% of sexual abuse victims experience each of these problems, and boys seem to display the same types and degrees of disturbance as girls do.

Many of these after-effects boil down to feelings of shame, a lack of self-worth, and a strong reluctance to trust other people (Cole & Putnam, 1992; Wiehe, 1996). And there are two problems that seem to be uniquely associated with sexual abuse. First, about a third of the victims engage in "sexualized behaviors"—acting out sexually by placing objects in their vaginas, masturbating in public, behaving seductively, or, if they are older, becoming sexually promiscuous (Kendall-Tackett et al., 1993). Perhaps it is not surprising, then, that adults who were sexually abused as children are more likely than nonabused individuals to be sexually victimized as adults and to report dissatisfaction with their sexual relationships and marriages (Bagley, 1995). Second, about a third of abuse victims show the symptoms of *posttraumatic stress disorder,* a clinical syndrome that includes nightmares, flashbacks to the traumatizing events, and feelings of helplessness and anxiety in the face of danger (Kendall-Tackett et al., 1993; McNew & Abell, 1995). Victims who are extremely traumatized are also at risk of displaying such self-destructive acts as drug and alcohol abuse, reckless behavior, and suicide attempts (Wiehe, 1996). And yet, about half of all sexually abused children and adolescents display no long-term psychological symptoms as young adults (Bagley, 1995; Kilpatrick, 1992).

Preventing and treating child abuse

Overcoming the harmful effects of sexual abuse can be very difficult, particularly if it occurred frequently over a long period, if the perpetrator was a close relative such as the father of an older sibling, and if the child's mother looked the other way, refused to believe the child's story, or was hostile toward the victim for making such accusations (Kendall-Tackett et al., 1993; Trickett et al., 1993). Yet many symptoms fade within a year or two, and recovery may proceed particularly well if the nonabusing parent believes the child's story, puts a stop to the abuse, and provides a stable and loving home environment thereafter (Kendall-Tackett, 1993). Psychotherapy aimed at treating the anxiety, depression, and self-blame that many victims experience and teaching them to avoid being victimized again can also contribute to the healing process (O'Donohue & Elliott, 1992).

Perhaps the best way to combat child sexual abuse is to identify it early and prevent it from continuing. Sex education programs at school are one promising strategy: When children learn how to recognize inappropriate "touches" and other sexual advances, they are more inclined to report them to teachers (Bagley, 1995). It is also important that teachers be trained to recognize the signs of sexual abuse and how to report any child disclosures or their own suspicions to the appropriate child protection or law enforcement agencies (Burkhardt & Rotatori, 1995). Early identification of a problem is crucial to limit the victims' suffering and ensure that they get the help that they need.

would foster their intellectual or academic competencies. By contrast, hostility, aggression, and disordered social relationships are more common among physically abused youngsters, who often create disciplinary problems at school (Eckenrode et al., 1993) and are likely to be rejected by peers (Haskett & Kistner, 1991; Salzinger et al., 1993).

One particularly disturbing correlate of physical abuse is a lack of normal empathy in response to the distress of peers. When Mary Main and Carol George (1985) observed the responses of abused and nonabused toddlers to the fussing and crying of peers, they found that nonabused children typically attended carefully to the distressed child, showed concern, or even attempted to provide comfort. But as shown in Figure 15.7, not one abused child showed appropriate concern; instead, abused toddlers were likely to become angry and attack the crying child (see also Klimes-Dougan & Kistner, 1990). So it seems that physically abused children are likely to become abusive companions who have apparently learned from their own experiences at home that distress signals are particularly irritating to others and often elicit angry responses rather than displays of sympathy. Other forms of domestic violence (for example, spouse battering) are also common in families that abuse children (McCloskey et al., 1995), so that victims of abuse may have few occasions to learn to respond compassionately to others' distress but many opportunities to learn aggressive solutions to conflict. No wonder these children are often rejected by their peers.

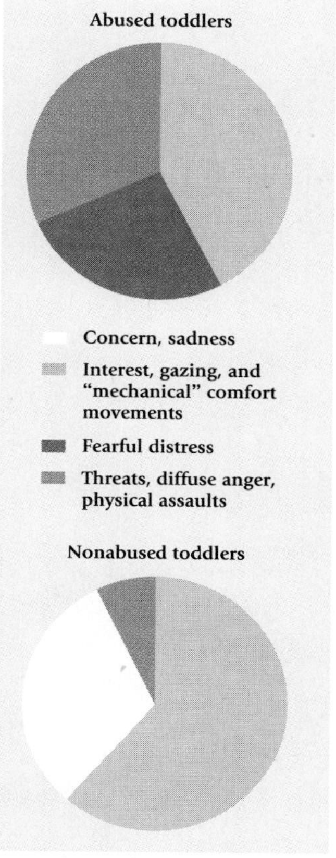

Figure 15.7 *Responses to the distress of peers observed in abused and nonabused toddlers in the day-care setting. (The circles show the mean proportion of responses falling into each category for the nine abused and nine nonabused toddlers.)* ADAPTED FROM MAIN & GEORGE, *1985.*

Unfortunately, the harmful social and emotional consequences of abuse and neglect can be long lasting, and some adolescents try to escape their pain, anxieties, self-doubts, and disordered social lives by attempting to take their own lives (Bagley, 1995; Sternberg et al., 1993). Furthermore, many adults who were abused as children are prone to violence, both inside and outside the family, and they show higher-than-average rates of criminal activity, substance abuse, depression, and other psychological disturbances (Bagley, 1995; Malinosky-Rummell & Hansen, 1993).

The good news is that many abused or neglected youngsters are remarkably resilient, especially if they are able to establish a warm, secure, and supportive relationship with a nonabusive parent, a grandparent, or some other member of the extended family (Egeland et al., 1988). And even though abused children are at risk of becoming abusive parents, it is worth emphasizing once again that the majority of abuse victims do *not* abuse their own children (Kaufman & Zigler, 1989). Abused parents who succeed at breaking the cycle of abuse are more likely than those who do not to have (1) received emotional support from a nonabusive parent (or parent substitute), a therapist, and their spouses and (2) have avoided severe stress as adults (Egeland et al., 1988; Vondra & Belsky, 1993).

Despite our better understanding of the causes of child abuse and observations that its often severe consequences can be lessened or even overcome, we are still a long way from solving the problem. Rather than conclude on that depressing note, let's consider some of the methods that have been used to assist abused children and their abusers.

How Might We Solve the Problem?

It can be discouraging to realize that so many factors contribute to the maltreatment of children. Where do we begin to intervene? How many problems must be corrected to prevent or stop the violence and discourage the neglect? Despite the complexity of the problem, progress has been made.

Preventing Abuse and Neglect

Let's first consider the task of preventing child maltreatment before it starts. This requires identifying high-risk families, a task that is greatly aided by the kinds of studies we have reviewed. For example, once neonatal assessment indicates that an infant may be at risk of abuse or neglect because he or she is particularly irritable or unresponsive, it makes sense to help the child's parents learn to handle the frustrations of dealing with those traits and to appreciate and evoke the baby's positive qualities.

Indeed, we have already seen that Brazelton testing and training programs (see Box 4.3) are effective methods of preventing the "miscommunications" between infants and caregivers that can contribute to child abuse.

Other efforts to prevent abuse directly target high-risk parents. Steven Schinke and his associates (1986), for example, worked with one high-risk group of mothers—single teenagers who were under a great deal of stress. The goal was to teach a wide range of stress-management skills: relaxation techniques, problem-solving strategies, communication skills that would enable mothers to request help and to calmly refuse a child's unreasonable demands, and even techniques for building stronger social support networks. Three months later, mothers who received the training outperformed mothers in a control group on several measures. They had improved their problem-solving skills, established stronger support networks, now enjoyed higher self-esteem, and were more confident about their parenting skills. It seems likely that high-risk parents who learn effective techniques for coping with stress will be better able to deal with the sometimes overwhelming challenges they face without resorting to violence. These parents can also benefit from programs to teach them effective child management skills (Emery & Laumann-Billings, 1998).

The demonstrated success of these and other similar interventions has led child-welfare agencies in several states to develop family support and education programs designed to prevent child abuse (Zigler & Finn-Stevenson, 1993). For example, the *Ounce of Prevention program,* a collaborative effort of the Illinois Department of Children and Family Services and the Pittway Corporation, attempts to head off child abuse by offering parent-education classes that teach effective child-management techniques and by providing such support services (through churches, medical clinics, and schools) as child-care programs, medical assistance, and job training. Other similar family support systems, which are regularly evaluated to ensure that they are meeting families' needs, are now available in Arkansas, Iowa, Massachusetts, Oregon, and Vermont (Wiehé, 1996; Zigler & Finn-Stevenson, 1993).

At the community level, steps might be taken to assess the probable impact on children of actions undertaken by the government or industry. For example, a local planning board's decision to rezone a stable residential area or to locate a highway there can create a high-risk neighborhood by causing property values to decline, destroying play areas, and ultimately isolating families from friends, community services (which may no longer exist), or other bases of social support. James Garbarino (1992) is one of many theorists who believe that significant numbers of American children are likely to be mistreated because of political or economic decisions that undermine the health and stability of low-risk, family-oriented neighborhoods.

Controlling Abuse

How do we deal with parents who are already abusive? It seems clear that a few visits from a social worker are unlikely to solve the problem. Kempe and Kempe (1978) report that a fair percentage of abusive parents stop physically maltreating their children if they are persuaded to use certain services, such as 24-hour "hot lines" or crisis nurseries, that enable them to discuss their hostile feelings with a volunteer or to get away from their children for a few hours when they are about to lose control. However, these are only stopgap measures that will probably not work for long unless the abuser also takes advantage of other services, such as **Parents Anonymous** or family therapy, that are designed to help the caregiver to understand his or her problem while providing the friendship and emotional support that an abusive parent so often lacks.[1] Ultimately, however, a comprehensive approach is likely to be most effective. Abusive parents need emotional support *and* opportunities to learn more effective parenting and coping skills, whereas the victims of abuse and neglect need stimulating day-care programs *and* spe-

Parents Anonymous
an organization of reformed child abusers that functions as a support group and helps parents to understand and overcome their abusive tendencies (modeled after Alcoholics Anonymous).

[1] Fortunately these services are often free. Chapters of Parents Anonymous are now located in many cities and towns in the United States (for the location of a nearby chapter, one can consult a telephone directory or write to Parents Anonymous, 675 W. Foothill Blvd., Suite 220, Claremont, CA 91711). In addition, many cities and counties provide free family therapy to abusive parents.

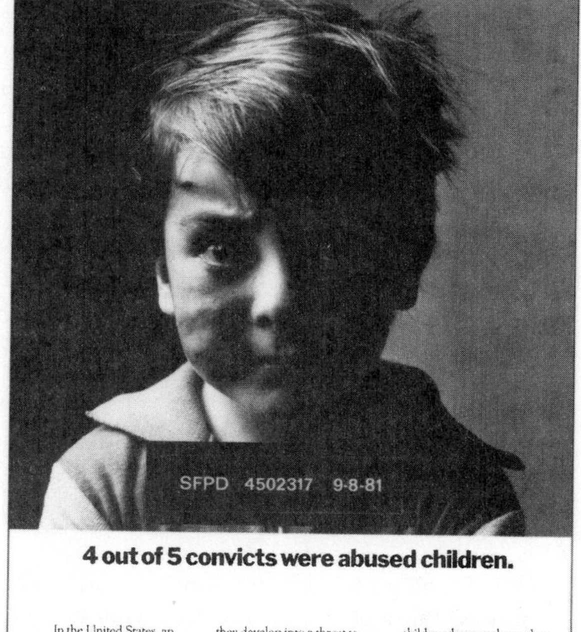

SFPD 4502317 9-8-81
4 out of 5 convicts were abused children.
In the United States, an average of 80% of our prisoners were abused children. That is why we are working so hard to help these children today, before they develop into a threat to others tomorrow.
With your support, we can have a full staff of trained people available 24 hours a day. Abused children desperately need us. Please let us be there to help. Write for our free brochure, or send in your tax-deductible donation today.
San Francisco Child Abuse Council, Inc.
4093 24th Street, San Francisco, CA 94114

A number of programs and services have arisen as attempts to prevent or control the problem of child abuse.

cialized training to help then overcome the cognitive, social, and emotional problems associated with abuse (Culp et al., 1991; Oates & Bross, 1995; Wiehe, 1996). In short, the ultimate goal in attempting to prevent or control child abuse must be to convert a pathological family system into a healthy one.

In recent years, another control tactic has become more common in cases of severe or repeated abuse: arresting and prosecuting parents for acts of violence that would qualify as criminal assault if they occurred between strangers. Yet, child abuse is often difficult to prove (beyond the reasonable doubt required for criminal conviction), and American courts are quite hesitant to take children away from parents, even when there is reason to suspect repeated abuse (Gelles, 1996). One reason for this reluctant attitude is that, historically, children have been treated as their parents' possessions (Hart & Brassard, 1987). Another is that abused children and their parents are often attached to each other, so that neither the abusive adult nor the mistreated child wishes to be separated. However, it is essential that we carefully weigh the child's rights against the rights and wishes of parents, for some abusive adults (between 1,000 and 2,000 per year in the United States) will go so far as to kill their children, regardless of the counseling they receive (Emery & Laumann-Billings, 1998; Wiehe, 1996).

Although some people may disagree, developmentalists the world over have argued that no caregiver has the right to abuse a child (Hart, 1991). And in cases of severe abuse or neglect, developmentalists generally agree that our first priority must be to provide for the health and safety of mistreated children, even if that means terminating the abusers' legal rights of parenthood and placing their children in foster care or adoptive homes. The challenge that we now face is to become much more successful at preventing and controlling child abuse so that the difficult decision of whether to separate children from their parents needs to be made far less frequently than it is at present.

WHAT DO YOU THINK? ?

In the United States, the Clinton administration endorsed a new approach to combating child abuse that makes it easier to sever parental rights and free abused children to be adopted. What, in your opinion, are reasonable grounds for severing legal rights of parenthood in cases of neglect or abuse? How do your criteria compare with those currently used in your state or province?

REFLECTIONS ON THE FAMILY

James Garbarino (1992) characterizes the family as "the basic unit of human experience" (p. 7). To fully appreciate the awesome significance of the family for children and adolescents, think for a moment about how very badly things can go when the family does not fulfill its important functions. Start with a neglected infant who may not only fail to thrive physically (see Chapter 5), but also does not experience anything faintly resembling warm, sensitive, and responsive care. How is this child to form the secure attachments that serve as foundations for later social and intellectual competencies? Or think about the child whose parents are downright hostile and who either provide no guidance at all or who control the child with strict rules and punish his every misstep. How is this child to learn how to care about other people, to become appropriately autonomous, and to fit into society?

Regina Campos and her associates (1994) have studied homeless street youths in Brazil whose families have failed them by neglecting, abusing, or otherwise dismissing them as unimportant. Compared with age-mates who worked on the streets but lived at home, homeless youths fare very poorly. They struggle daily to survive, often begging if necessary to get by. What's more, they live in constant fear of being victimized and are themselves heavily involved in such antisocial behaviors as prostitution, drug abuse, thievery, and a host of other criminal activities. In short, these youngsters who have no family life pursue a highly atypical and deviant lifestyle that may place them on the fast track to psychopathology, as we see in one 16-year-old's account of his daily routine:

> When you go to sleep it's about 5 in the morning; we wake up around 2 or 3 in the afternoon . . . get up, wash your face, if you have money you have breakfast [then] go out to steal, then you start to sell the stuff and the money all goes on drugs, because in the street it's all drugs! . . . Then, you get high, you're all set, then you come down and sleep (Campos et al., 1994, p. 322).

What happens to these homeless street youths when they grow up? Clearly, there is reason to suspect that their outcomes will be grim, in view of the fact that 80% of the prison population of one major Brazilian city consists of former street youth (Campos et al., 1994).

You get the picture. It is often easier to illustrate the grave importance of families by accentuating the negative. Fortunately, most of us have fared much better than this, even though we do not always acknowledge just how significant our families may have been in underwriting our developmental successes. So think about what you have learned in this chapter the next time you gather with the closest members of your own family. Chances are you will understand why children and adults who are asked to reflect on what or whom is most important in their lives almost invariably speak of their families (Furman & Buhrmester, 1992; Whitbourne, 1986). Although we change and our families change as we get older, it seems that most of us never cease to affect, or to be affected by, those folks we call "family."

SUMMARY

◆ The family is the primary agent of **socialization,** the context in which children begin to acquire the beliefs, attitudes, values, and behaviors considered appropriate in their society.

The Family as a Social System

◆ Both a **traditional nuclear family** and an **extended family,** are best viewed as **social systems** in which each family member has **direct effects** and **indirect,** or **third-party, effects** on all other family members. Children fare better when adult members of the family can effectively **coparent,** mutually supporting each other's parenting efforts.

◆ Families are also developing social systems embedded in community and cultural contexts that affect family functioning.

◆ Social changes affecting family life today include greater numbers of single adults, later marriages, a decline in childbearing, more female participation in the work force, and more divorces, **single-parent families,** and **blended** or **reconstituted families,** as well as greater numbers of families living in poverty.

Parental Socialization during Childhood and Adolescence

◆ Parents differ along two broad child-rearing dimensions: **acceptance/responsiveness** and **demandingness/control** that, when considered together, yield four patterns of parenting. Generally speaking, accepting and demanding (or **authoritative**) parents who appeal to reason in order to enforce their demands tend to raise highly competent, well-adjusted children. Children of less accepting but more demanding (or **authoritarian**) parents and accepting but undemanding (or **permissive**) parents display somewhat less favorable developmental outcomes, and children of unaccepting, unresponsive, and undemanding (or **uninvolved**) parents are often deficient in virtually all aspects of psychological functioning.

◆ Parents from different cultures, subcultures, and social classes have different values, concerns, and outlooks on life that influence their child-rearing practices. Yet, parents from all social backgrounds emphasize the characteristics that contribute to *success as they know it* in their own ecological niches, and it is inappropriate to conclude that one particular style of parenting is somehow better or more competent than all others.

◆ Parent–child relationships are renegotiated when adolescents begin to seek **autonomy.** Although family conflict escalates during this period, adolescents are likely to become appropriately autonomous if their parents willingly grant them more freedom, explain the rules and restrictions that they impose, and continue to be loving and supportive guides.

The Influence of Siblings and Sibling Relationships

◆ **Sibling rivalry** is a normal aspect of family life that may begin as soon as a younger sibling arrives; yet there is a positive side to having siblings. Siblings are typically viewed as intimate associates who can be counted on for support. Older sibs frequently serve as caregivers, sources of security, models, and teachers for their younger siblings, and they often profit themselves from the instruction and guidance that they provide. Yet, sibling relationships are not essential for normal development, for only children are just as socially, emotionally, and intellectually competent (or slightly more so), on average, than are children with siblings.

Diversity in Family Life

◆ Infertile couples and single adults who desire to be parents often adopt a child to start a family. Although adoptees display more emotional and learning problems than biological children do, adoption is a highly satisfactory arrangement for the vast majority of adoptive parents and their children. Adopted children are often more satisfied with their family lives in open adoption systems that permit them to learn about their biological roots.

◆ Gay and lesbian parents are just as effective as heterosexual parents are. Their children tend to be well adjusted and are overwhelmingly heterosexual in orientation.

◆ Divorce represents a major transition in family life that is stressful and unsettling for children and their parents. Children's initial reactions often include anger, fear, depression, and guilt, which may last more than a year. The emotional upheaval that follows a divorce often influences the parent–child relationship. Children often become cranky, disobedient, or otherwise difficult, while the custodial parent may suddenly become more punitive and controlling. The stresses resulting from a divorce and this new coercive lifestyle often affect the child's peer relations and schoolwork. Visible signs of distress may be most apparent in younger children and those with difficult temperaments, and girls adjust better than boys to life in a single-parent, mother-headed home. Although some after-effects of divorce can be seen even 10 to 20 years later, children of divorce are usually better adjusted than those who remain in conflict-ridden two-parent families. Among the factors that help children to make positive adjustments to divorce are adequate financial and emotional support from the noncustodial parent, additional social support (from friends, relatives, and the community) for custodial parents and their children, and a minimum of additional stressors surrounding the divorce itself.

◆ As long as working mothers are satisfied with their jobs, committed to parenting, and receive adequate support from their spouses or partners and other close associates, their employment is associated with such favorable child outcomes as self-reliance, sociability, competent intellectual and academic performances, and less stereotyped views of men and women. One of the strongest supports that working parents could hope for is stimulating day-care for their children, a support system that is woefully inadequate in the United States, compared with that provided by many other Western industrialized nations. Large numbers of American grade-school children whose mothers work must care for themselves after school. When monitored from a distance by authoritative parents, these **self-care** (or **latchkey**) **children** fare well. After-school day-care programs are becoming more common in the United States, and well-managed ones that offer children meaningful activities can help to optimize developmental outcomes and lessen the chances that children of working mothers will engage in antisocial conduct.

When Parenting Breaks Down: The Problem of Child Abuse

◆ **Child abuse** is related to conditions within the family, the community, and the larger culture. Abusers come from all social strata and walks of life, although many of them are young, highly stressed caregivers who favor coercive forms of discipline and were themselves abused as children. Children who are highly impulsive, irritable, emotionally unresponsive, or ill are more vulnerable to abuse than are healthy, even-tempered children who are easy to care for. The incidence of child abuse is highest when stressed caregivers live in **high-risk neighborhoods** where they are isolated from sources of social support and the broader culture approves of force as a means of resolving conflicts. The long-term consequences of abuse are often severe and long lasting. Programs designed to assist abused children and their abusive parents have achieved some noteworthy success. However, we are still a long way from solving the problem.

The family influences development in a variety of ways. The influence of siblings, the need to discipline, and the impact of blended families are just a few of the challenges that face many modern parents. By visiting: http://family.disney.com/Categories/Parenting you can search for online resources that deal with these topics along with a variety of other topics related to family interactions. The site allows you to search for general information, or to narrow your search to information that relates to children at a specific stage of development.

KEY TERMS

socialization, 558
family social system, 559
traditional nuclear family, 559
direct effect, 559
indirect, or third-party, effect, 559
coparenting, 560
extended family, 560
single-parent family, 563
blended, or reconstituted, families, 563
acceptance/responsiveness, 564
demandingness/control, 565
authoritarian parenting, 565
authoritative parenting, 565
permissive parenting, 566
uninvolved parenting, 567
autonomy, 571
sibling rivalry, 574
self-care, or latchkey, children, 586
child abuse, 587
high-risk neighborhood, 588
Parents Anonymous, 592

Extrafamilial Influences: Television, Computers, Schools, and Peers

In Chapter 15, we considered the family as an agent of socialization, looking at the ways that parents and siblings affect developing children. Although families have an enormous impact on their young, it is only a matter of time before other societal institutions begin to exert their influence. For example, infants, toddlers, and preschool children are often exposed to alternative caregivers and a host of new playmates when their working parents place them in some kind of day-care or nursery school. Yet, even those toddlers who remain at home soon begin to learn about a world beyond the family once they develop an interest in television. And by age 6 to 7, virtually all children in Western societies go to elementary school, a setting that requires them to interact with other little people who are similar to themselves and to adjust to rules and practices that may be very dissimilar to those they follow at home.

So as they mature, children become increasingly familiar with the outside world and spend much less time under the watchful eyes of their parents. How do these experiences affect their lives? This is the issue to which we will now turn as we consider the impact of four **extrafamilial influences** on development: television, computers, schools, and the society of one's peers

EARLY WINDOWS: IMPACTS OF TELEVISION AND COMPUTER TECHNOLOGIES ON CHILDREN AND ADOLESCENTS

extrafamilial influences social agencies other than the family that influence a child's or an adolescent's cognitive, social, and emotional development.

It seems almost incomprehensible that the average American of only 50 years ago had never seen a television. Now more than 98% of American homes have one or more TV sets, and children between the ages of 3 and 11 watch an average of 3 to 4 hours of TV a day (Comstock, 1993; Huston et al., 1992). As we see in Figure 16.1, TV viewing begins in infancy, increases until about age 12, and then declines somewhat during adolescence—a trend that holds in Australia, Canada, and several European countries, as well as in the United States. By age 18, a child born today will have spent more time watching television than in any other single activity except sleeping (Liebert & Sprafkin, 1988). Boys watch more TV than girls do, and ethnic minority children living in poverty are especially likely to be heavy viewers (Signorielli, 1991). Is all this time in front of the tube damaging to children's cognitive, social, and emotional development, as many critics have feared?

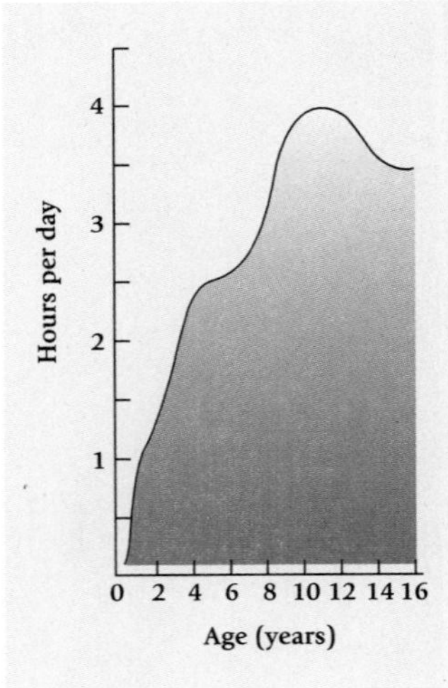

Figure 16.1 *Average number of hours per day that American children and adolescents spend watching television.* FROM LIEBERT & SPRAFKIN, 1988.

One way to assess the global impact of television is to see whether children who have access to the medium differ systematically from those who live in remote areas not served by television. One such study of Canadian children gave some cause for concern. Prior to the introduction of television to the isolated town, "Notel," children living there tested higher in creativity and reading proficiency than did age-mates in comparable Canadian towns served by television. Yet, 2 to 4 years after television was introduced, the children of Notel showed declines in their reading skills and creativity (to levels shown by peers in other towns), less community involvement, and dramatic increases in aggression and gender stereotyping (Corteen & Williams, 1986; Harrison & Williams, 1986).

Although sobering, these findings may be somewhat misleading. Other investigators report that the biggest impact of the coming of television is that children substitute TV viewing for such other leisure activities as listening to the radio, reading comics, or going to movies (Huston et al., 1992; Liebert & Sprafkin, 1988). And as long as TV viewing is not excessive, children exposed to the medium show no significant cognitive or academic deficiencies and spend no less time playing with peers (Liebert & Sprafkin, 1988). In fact, one review of the literature found that children may actually learn a great deal of useful information from television, particularly educational programming (Anderson & Collins, 1988).

So in moderate doses, television neither deadens young minds nor impairs children's social development. Yet, we will see that this medium does have the potential to do good or harm, depending on *what* children are watching and their ability to understand and interpret what they have seen.

Development of Television Literacy

Television literacy refers to one's ability to understand how information is conveyed on the small screen. It involves the ability to process program *content* to construct a story line from characters' activities and the sequencing of scenes. It also involves an ability to interpret the *form* of the message—production features such as zooms, fade-outs, split-screens, and sound effects—that are often essential to understanding a program's content (Fitch, Huston, & Wright, 1993).

Prior to age 8 or 9, children process program content in a piecemeal fashion. They are likely to be captivated by zooms, fast-paced action, loud music, and children's (or cartoon characters') voices, and often direct their attention elsewhere during slower scenes that contain quiet dialogue (Anderson et al., 1981). Consequently, preschool children are usually unable to construct a causal chain of events leading from the beginning to the end of a story. Even 6-year-olds have trouble recalling a coherent story line due, in part, to their tendency to remember the *actions* that characters perform rather than the motives or goals that characters pursue and the events that shaped these goals (van den Broek, Lorch, & Thurlow, 1996). Furthermore, children younger than 7 do not fully grasp the fictional nature of television programming, often believing that characters retain their roles (and scripted characteristics) in real life (Wright et al., 1994). And even though 8-year-olds may know that TV programming is fiction, they may still view it as an *accurate* portrayal of everyday events (Wright et al., 1995).

Comprehension of TV programming increases sharply from middle childhood throughout adolescence. Experience watching TV helps children to properly interpret the zooms, fade-outs, musical scores, and other production features that assist viewers in inferring characters' motives and connecting nonadjacent scenes. Furthermore, older children and adolescents are increasingly able to draw inferences about scenes that are widely separated in time, in much the same way that they integrate semantic information that is separated by intervening paragraphs in a written story (van den Broek, 1997; and see Chapter 10). So if a character were to act nice and gain someone's trust in order to dupe him later, a 10-year-old would eventually recognize the character's deceptive intent and evaluate him negatively. By contrast, a 6-year-old, who focuses more on concrete behaviors than on subtle intentions, will often brand this con artist as a "nice guy" and is likely to evaluate his later self-serving acts much more positively (van den Broek et al., 1996).

Does their strong focus on actions and general lack of television literacy increase the likelihood that younger children will imitate the particularly vivid behaviors that TV characters display? Yes, indeed; and whether these imitations are beneficial or harmful depends critically on *what* children happen to be viewing (Liebert & Sprafkin, 1988).

Some Potentially Undesirable Effects of Television

Effects of Televised Violence

As early as 1954, complaints raised by parents, teachers, and experts in child development prompted Senator Estes Kefauver, then chairman of the Senate Subcommittee on Juvenile Delinquency, to question the violence in television programming. Indeed, the National Television Violence Study, a 2-year survey of the frequency, nature, and context

television literacy
one's ability to understand and interpret how information is conveyed in television programming.

of TV violence, reveals that American television programming is incredibly violent (Mediascope, 1996; Seppa, 1997). Fifty-eight percent of programs broadcast between 6 A.M. and 11 P.M. contained *repeated* acts of overt aggression, and 73% contained violence in which the perpetrator neither displayed any remorse nor received any penalty or criticism. In fact, the most violent TV programs are those intended for children, especially cartoons, and nearly 40% of the violence on TV is initiated by heroes or other characters portrayed as attractive role models for children (Seppa, 1997). Furthermore, nearly two-thirds of the violent incidents in children's programming are couched in humor.

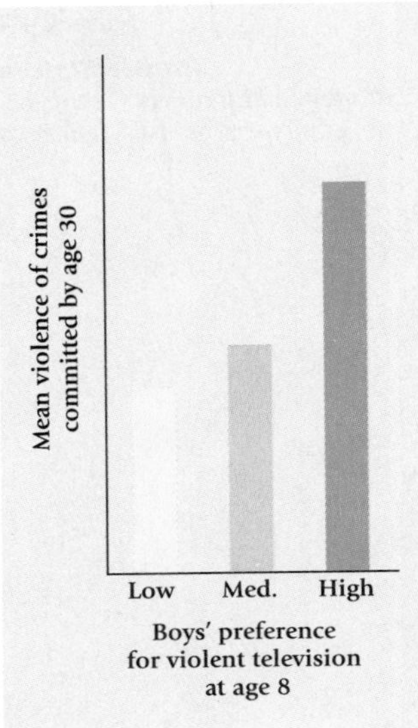

Figure 16.2 *Relationship between boys' preference for violent TV programming at age 8 and mean violence of crimes committed by age 30.* ADAPTED FROM HUESMANN, *1986.*

DOES TV VIOLENCE INSTIGATE AGGRESSION? It has been argued that the often-comical violence portrayed in children's programming is unlikely to affect the behavior of young viewers. Yet, hundreds of experimental studies and correlational surveys suggest otherwise (Huston et al., 1992; Liebert & Sprafkin, 1988; Slaby et al., 1995). Simply stated, children and adolescents who watch a lot of televised violence tend to be more hostile and aggressive than their classmates who watch little violence. This positive relationship between exposure to TV violence and aggressive behavior in naturalistic settings has been documented over and over with preschool, grade school, high school, and adult participants in the United States and with grade school boys and girls in Australia, Canada, Finland, Great Britain, and Poland (Liebert & Sprafkin, 1988; Parke & Slaby, 1983). Furthermore, longitudinal studies suggest that the link between TV violence and aggression is *reciprocal:* Watching TV violence increases children's aggressive tendencies, which stimulates interest in violent programming, which promotes further aggression (Eron, 1982; Huesmann et al., 1984b). Although longitudinal surveys are correlational research and do *not* demonstrate causality, their results are at least consistent with the argument that early exposure to a heavy diet of televised violence can lead to the development of hostile, antisocial habits that persist over time. Indeed, when Rowell Huesmann (1986) followed up on boys from an earlier study when they were 30 years old, he found that their earlier preferences for violent television at age 8 predicted not only their aggressiveness as adults, but their involvement in serious criminal activities as well (see Figure 16.2).

OTHER EFFECTS OF TELEVISED VIOLENCE. Even if children do not act out the aggression that they observe on television, they may be influenced by it nonetheless. For example, a steady diet of televised violence can instill **mean-world beliefs**—a tendency to view the world as a violent place inhabited by people who typically rely on aggressive solutions to their interpersonal problems (Comstock, 1993; Slaby et al., 1995). In fact, 7- to 9-year-olds who show the strongest preferences for violent television are the ones most likely to believe that violent shows are an accurate portrayal of everyday life.

In a similar vein, prolonged exposure to televised violence can *desensitize* children—that is, make them less emotionally upset by violent acts and more willing to tolerate them in real life. Margaret Thomas and her colleagues (1977; Drabman & Thomas, 1974) tested this **desensitization hypothesis** with 8- to 10-year-olds. Each participant watched either a violent detective show or a nonviolent but exciting sporting event while hooked up to a physiograph that recorded his or her emotional reactions. Then the participant was told to watch over two kindergartners, visible in the next room on a TV monitor, and to come to get the experimenter should *anything* go wrong. A prepared film then showed the two kindergartners getting into an intense battle that escalated until the screen went blank. Participants who had earlier watched the violent program were now less physiologically aroused by the fight they observed and were more inclined to tolerate it (by being much slower to intervene) than their counterparts who had watched an equally arousing but nonviolent sporting event. Apparently, TV violence can desensitize viewers to real-world instances of aggression.

mean-world belief
a belief, fostered by televised violence, that the world is a more dangerous and frightening place than is actually the case.

desensitization hypothesis
the notion that people who watch a lot of media violence will become less aroused by aggression and more tolerant of violent and aggressive acts.

Television as a Source of Social Stereotypes

Another unfortunate effect that television may have on children is to reinforce a variety of potentially harmful social stereotypes (Huston et al., 1992). In Chapter 13, for example, we noted that sex-role stereotyping is common on television and that children who watch a lot of commercial TV are likely to hold more traditional views of men and women than their classmates who watch little television. Yet, television might also be employed to counter gender stereotypes. Early attempts to accomplish this aim by showing males performing competently at traditionally feminine activities and females excelling at traditionally masculine pursuits are enjoying some limited success (Johnston & Ettema, 1982; Rosenwasser et al., 1989). However, these programs would undoubtedly be more effective if they were combined with the kinds of cognitive training procedures, described in Chapter 13, that undermine the inflexible and erroneous *beliefs* on which gender stereotypes rest (Bigler & Liben, 1990; 1992).

Stereotyped views of minorities are also common on television. Largely due to the influence of the civil rights movement, African Americans now appear on television in a much wider range of occupations, and their numbers equal or exceed their proportions in the population. However, Latinos and other ethnic minorities remain underrepresented. And when nonblack minorities do appear, they are usually portrayed in an unfavorable light, often cast as villains or victims (Associated Press, 1994b; Liebert & Sprafkin, 1988).

Although the evidence is limited, it seems that children's ethnic and racial attitudes are influenced by televised portrayals of minority groups. Earlier depictions of African Americans as comical, inept, or lazy led to negative racial attitudes (Graves, 1975; Liebert & Sprafkin, 1988), whereas positive portrayals of minorities in cartoons and on such educational programs as *Sesame Street* appear to reduce children's racial and ethnic stereotypes and increase their likelihood of having ethnically diverse friends (Graves, 1993; Gorn, Goldberg, & Kanungo, 1976). Apparently, television has the power to bring people of different racial and ethnic backgrounds closer together or to drive them further apart, depending on the ways in which these social groups are depicted on the small screen.

Heavy exposure to media violence may blunt children's emotional reactions to real-life aggression and convince them that the world is a violent place populated mainly by hostile and aggressive people.

Children's Reactions to Commercial Messages

In the United States, the average child is exposed to nearly 20,000 television commercials each year, many of which extol the virtues of toys, fast foods, and sugary treats that parents may not wish to purchase. Nevertheless, young children continue to ask for products that they have seen on television, and conflicts often ensue when parents refuse to honor their requests (Atkin, 1978; Kunkel & Roberts, 1991). Young children may be so persistent because they rarely understand the manipulative (selling) intent of ads, often regarding them like public service announcements that are intended to be helpful and informative (Liebert & Sprafkin, 1988). By age 9 to 11, most children realize that ads are designed to persuade and sell, and by 13 to 14, they have acquired a healthy skepticism about advertising and product claims (Linn, de Benedictis, & Delucchi, 1982; Robertson & Rossiter, 1974). Nevertheless, even adolescents are often persuaded by the ads they see, particularly if the product endorser is a celebrity or the appeals are deceptive and misleading (Huston et al., 1992).

Is it any wonder, then, that many parents are concerned about the impact of commercials on their children? Not only do children's ads often push products that are unsafe or of poor nutritional value, but the many ads for over-the-counter drugs and glamorous depictions of alcohol use could cause children to underestimate the consequences of such risky behaviors as drinking, self-medication, and drug use (Tinsley, 1992). *Action for Children's Television,* an organization of parents that monitors and works to improve children's television, considers the potentially harmful influence of TV commercials to be an even greater problem than televised violence! And policymakers are beginning to respond to the outcries, as evidenced by a recent law limiting the number of commercials on children's programs and requiring broadcasters to offer more educational programming or risk losing their licenses (Zigler & Finn-Stevenson, 1993).

Reducing the Harmful Effects of Television Exposure

How might concerned parents limit the potentially harmful effects of commercial television? Table 16.1 lists several effective strategies recommended by experts, including monitoring children's home viewing habits to limit their exposure to highly violent or otherwise offensive fare, while trying to interest them in programs with prosocial or

Table 16.1 Effective Strategies for Regulating Children's Exposure to Television

Strategy	Implementation
Limit TV viewing	Set clear rules that limit when children may watch TV. Don't use the medium as an electronic babysitter or increase its attractiveness by withholding TV privileges as a punishment.
Encourage appropriate viewing	Encourage children to watch child-appropriate informational or prosocial programs. Use lock-out features available on cable or satellite systems to restrict child access to channels with excessive violent or sexual content.
Explain televised information to children	Watch TV with children and point out subtleties that they may miss, such as an aggressor's antisocial motives and the unpleasant consequences that perpetrators may suffer as a result of their violent acts. Critical discussions centering on the violence and negative social stereotypes portrayed on television help children to evaluate what they see and to view it as less "real."
Model good viewing habits	Parental viewing practices influence children's viewing practices so avoid watching too much television, particularly programs that are inappropriate for children.
Parent authoritatively	Warmth coupled with reasonable and rational limit setting make children more responsive to parental control, including restrictions on TV viewing.

Sources: Slaby et al., 1995; Seppa, 1997.

educational themes. Information about programs that experts consider inappropriate for children can be obtained from *The National Foundation to Improve Television,* 60 State Street, Boston, MA 02109 (phone: [781] 523-6353).

WHAT DO YOU THINK?

The Mighty Morphin Power Rangers, one of the most popular and yet most violent television programs for children, has been shown to dramatically increase the incidence of aggressive behavior among 5- to 8-year-olds (see Boyatzis et al., 1995). How would you attempt to combat its influence on your own children if you felt incapable of preventing them from watching it away from home?

Television as an Educational Tool

Thus far, we've cast a wary eye at television, talking mostly about its capacity to do harm. Yet, this "early window" could become a most effective way of teaching a number of valuable lessons if only its content were altered to convey such information. Let's examine some of the evidence to support this claim.

Educational Television and Children's Prosocial Behavior

Many TV programs—especially offerings such as *Sesame Street* and *Mister Roger's Neighborhood* that are broadcast on public television—are designed, in part, to illustrate the benefits of such prosocial activities as cooperation, sharing, and comforting distressed companions. One major review of the literature found that young children who often watch prosocial programming become more prosocially inclined (Hearold, 1986). However, it is important to emphasize that these programs may have few if any *lasting* benefits unless an adult monitors the broadcasts and encourages children to rehearse and enact the prosocial lessons that they have learned (Friedrich & Stein, 1975; Friedrich-Cofer et al., 1979). Furthermore, young children are more likely to process and enact any prosocial lessons that are broadcast when the programming is free of violent acts that otherwise compete for their attention. But despite these important qualifications, it seems that the positive effects of prosocial programming greatly outweigh the negatives (Hearold, 1986), especially if adults encourage children to pay close attention to episodes that emphasize constructive methods of resolving interpersonal conflicts.

In 1968, the U.S. government and a number of private foundations provided funds to create *Children's Television Workshop (CTW),* an organization committed to producing TV programs that would hold children's interest and foster their intellectual development. CTW's first production, *Sesame Street,* became the world's most popular children's series—seen an average of three times a week by about half of America's preschool children and broadcast to nearly 50 other countries around the world (Liebert & Sprafkin, 1988). Targeted at 3- to 5-year-olds, *Sesame Street* attempts to foster important cognitive skills such as counting, recognizing and discriminating numbers and letters, ordering and classifying objects, and solving simple problems. It was hoped that children from disadvantaged backgrounds would be much better prepared for school after viewing this programming on a regular basis.

Evaluating Sesame Street. During the first season that *Sesame Street* was broadcast, its impact was assessed by the Educational Testing Service. About 950 3- to 5-year-olds from five areas of the United States took a pretest that measured their cognitive skills and determined what they knew about letters, numbers, and geometric forms. At the end of the season, they took this test again to see what they had learned.

When the data were analyzed, it was clear that *Sesame Street* was achieving its objectives. As shown in Figure 16.3, children who watched *Sesame Street* the most (groups Q3 and Q4, who watched four or more times a week) showed the biggest improvements in their total test scores (panel a), their scores on the alphabet test (panel b), and their ability to write their names (panel c). The 3-year-olds posted bigger gains than the 5-year-olds, probably because the younger children knew less to begin with (Ball & Bogatz, 1970). The results of a second similar study which included only urban disadvantaged preschoolers paralleled those of the original study (Bogatz & Ball, 1972), and others have found that regular exposure to *Sesame Street* is associated with impressive gains in preschoolers' vocabularies and prereading skills as well (Rice et al., 1990). Finally, disadvantaged children who had been heavy viewers of *Sesame Street* were later rated by their first-grade teachers as better prepared for school and more interested in school activities than classmates who had rarely watched the program (Bogatz & Ball, 1972).

Other Educational Programs. The success of *Sesame Street* has prompted CTW and other noncommercial producers to create programs that teach children subjects such as reading skills *(The Electric Company),* math *(Square One),* logical reasoning *(Think About),* science *(3-2-1 Contact),* and social studies *(Big Blue Marble).* Designed for first- through fourth-graders, *The Electric Company* does produce gains in reading skills, but only when children watch at school where teachers can help them to apply what they have learned

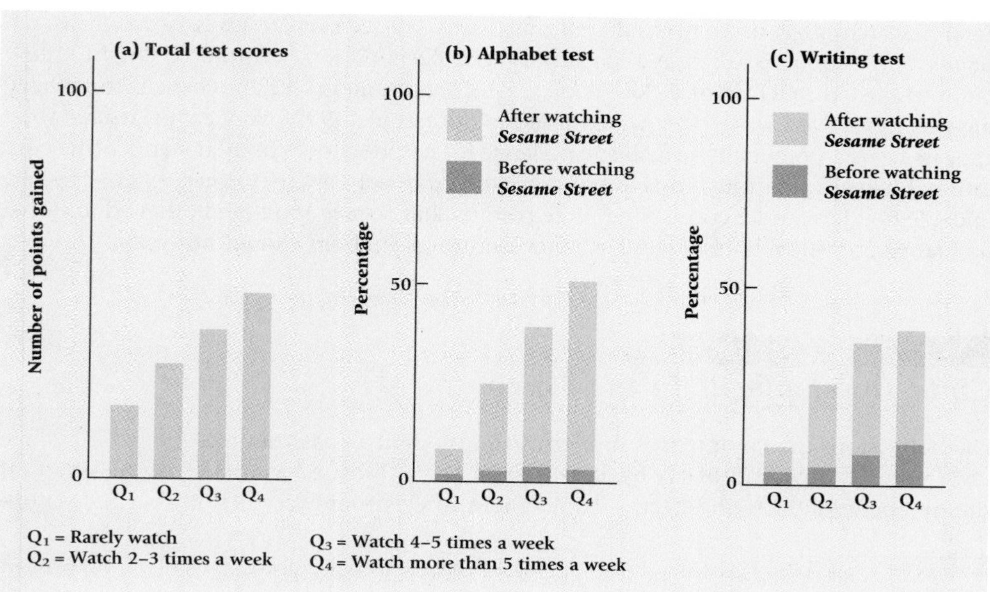

Figure 16.3 *Relationship between amount of viewing of* Sesame Street *and children's abilities: (a) improvement in total test scores for children grouped into different quartiles according to amount of viewing; (b) percentage of children who recited the alphabet correctly, grouped according to quartiles of amount of viewing; (c) percentage of children who wrote their first names correctly, grouped according to quartiles of amount of viewing.* From Liebert & Sprafkin, 1988.

Children learn many valuable lessons from educational TV programs such as Sesame Street.

(Ball & Bogatz, 1973).[1] Unfortunately, recent educational programs produced by commercial networks and aimed at older children have largely failed to attract a wide viewership, although such offerings as ABC's *Science Court* and the syndicated show *Popular Mechanics For Kids* rate as qualified successes (Farhl, 1998).

Criticisms of Educational Programming. One recurring criticism of educational television is that it is essentially a one-way medium in which the pupil is a passive recipient of information rather than an active constructor of knowledge. Critics fear that heavy TV viewing (be it educational TV or otherwise) blunts children's curiosity, and they believe that a child's viewing time would be more profitably spent in active, imaginative activities under the guidance of an adult (Singer & Singer, 1990). Indeed, we've seen that programs such as *The Electric Company* (as well as those stressing prosocial behavior) are unlikely to achieve their objectives unless children watch *with an adult* who encourages them to apply what they have learned. Perhaps John Wright and Aletha Huston (1983) were correct in arguing that television's potential as a teaching device will be greatly enhanced once it becomes *computer-integrated* and interactive, thereby allowing the viewer to be more actively involved in the learning process.

Although *Sesame Street* was primarily targeted at disadvantaged preschoolers in an attempt to narrow the intellectual gap between these youngsters and their advantaged peers, early research suggested that children from advantaged backgrounds were the ones who were more likely to watch the program. Thus, it was feared that *Sesame Street* might actually end up *widening* the intellectual and academic gaps between advantaged and disadvantaged youth (Cook et al., 1975). Yet, this particular concern now appears unfounded. Later research suggests that children from disadvantaged backgrounds not only watch *Sesame Street* about as often as their advantaged peers (Pinon, Huston, & Wright, 1989) but learn just as much from it (Rice et al., 1990). What's more, children benefit from viewing this series even when they watch it alone (Rice et al., 1990). So viewing *Sesame Street* appears to be a potentially valuable experience for *all* preschool children—and a true educational bargain that only costs about a penny a day per viewer (Palmer, 1984). The formidable task lies ahead: convincing more parents that *Sesame Street* (and other educational programs) are valuable resources that they and their children should not miss.

Child Development in the Computer Age

Like television, the computer is modern technology that has the potential to influence children's learning and lifestyles. But in what ways? Most educators today believe that the microcomputer is an effective supplement to classroom instruction that helps chil-

[1]In 1985, *The Electric Company* went off the air. However, episodes are still available to schools on videocassette for classroom use.

dren to learn more and to have more fun doing so. By 1996, over 98% of American public schools were using computers as instructional tools, and more than 35 million machines were available for use in American homes (U.S. Bureau of the Census, 1997). So computers are now widely accessible; but do they really help children to learn, think, or create? Is there a danger that young "hackers" will become so enamored of computer technology and so reclusive or socially unskilled that they risk being ostracized by their peers?

Computers in the Classroom

The results of literally hundreds of studies reveal that classroom use of computers produces many, many benefits. For example, elementary school students do learn more and report that they enjoy school more when they receive at least some **computer-assisted instruction (CAI)** (Clements & Nastasi, 1992; Collis, 1996; Lepper & Gurtner, 1989). Many CAI programs are simply drills that start at a student's current level of mastery and present increasingly difficult problems, often intervening with hints or clues when progress breaks down. Other, more elaborate forms of CAI are guided tutorials that rely less on drill and more on the discovery of important concepts and principles in the context of highly motivating, thought-provoking games. Regular use of drill programs during the early grades does seem to improve children's basic reading and math skills, particularly for disadvantaged students and other low achievers (Clements & Nastasi, 1995; Fletcher-Flinn & Gravatt, 1995; Lepper & Gurtner, 1989). However, the benefits of CAI are greatest when children receive at least some exposure to highly involving guided tutorials as well as simple drills.

Word Processing. Aside from their drill function, computers are also *tools* that can further children's basic writing and communication skills (Clements, 1995). Once children can read and write, using word-processing programs eliminates much of the drudgery of handwriting and increases the likelihood that they will revise, edit, and polish their writing (Clements & Nastasi, 1992). Furthermore, computer-prompted metacognitive strategies also help students to think about what they wish to say and to organize their thoughts into more coherent essays (Lepper & Gurtner, 1989).

Computer Programming and Cognitive Growth. Finally, it seems that teaching students to *program* (and thus *control*) a computer can have such important benefits as fostering mastery motivation and self-efficacy, as well as promoting novel modes of thinking that are unlikely to emerge from computer-assisted academic drills. In his own research, Douglas Clements (1991; 1995) trained first- and third-graders in Logo, a computer language that allows children to translate their drawings into input statements so that they can reproduce their creations on the computer monitor. Although Clements's "Logo" children performed no better on achievement tests than age-mates who participated in the more usual kinds of computer-assisted academic exercises, Logo users scored higher on tests of Piagetian concrete-operational abilities, mathematical problem-solving strategies, and creativity (Clements, 1995; Nastasi & Clements, 1994). And because children must learn to detect errors and debug their Logo programs to get them to work, programming fosters thinking about one's own thinking and is associated with gains in metacognitive knowledge (Clements, 1990). Clearly, these findings are important, for they suggest that computers are useful not only for teaching children academic lessons but for helping them to *think* in new ways as well.

Social Impacts. Are young computer users at risk of becoming reclusive, socially unskilled misfits, as some people have feared? Hardly! Children often use home computers as a toy to *attract* playmates (Crook, 1992; Kee, 1986). And research conducted in classrooms reveals that students who are learning to program or solve problems with a computer are (1) likely to *seek* collaborative solutions to the challenges they face and (2) more inclined to persist after experiencing problems when they are collaborating with a peer (Nastasi & Clements, 1993; 1994; Weinstein, 1991). Conflicts may arise between collaborators over how to approach a problem; yet the strong interest that collaborators frequently display when facing a programming challenge often supersedes

computer-assisted instruction (CAI)
use of computers to teach new concepts and practice academic skills.

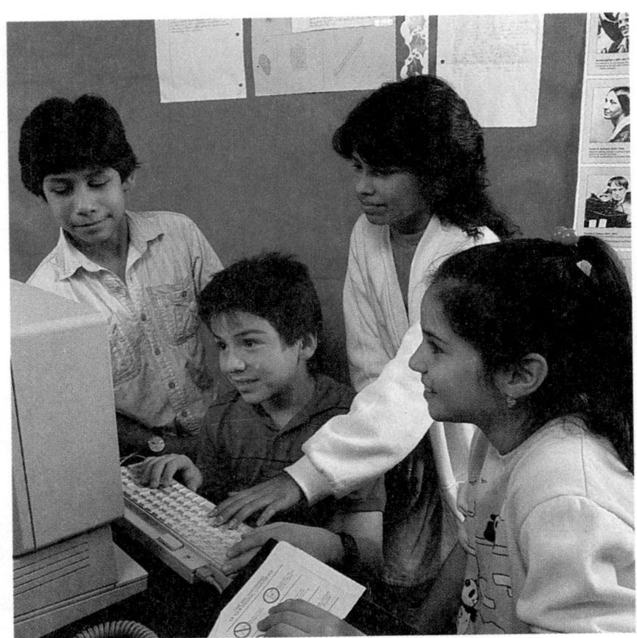

Learning by computer is an effective complement to classroom instruction and an experience that can teach young children to collaborate.

their differences and encourages amiable methods of conflict resolution (Nastasi & Clements, 1993). So computers seem to promote (rather than impede) peer interactions—contacts that are often lively and challenging and that appear to foster the growth of socially skilled behaviors.

Concerns about Computers

What are the danger signs of exposing children to computer technology? Three concerns are raised most often.

Concerns about Video Games. The results of one recent survey revealed that more than 80% of U.S. adolescents spend 2 or more hours a week playing computer video games (Williams, 1998). It is not that this activity necessarily diverts children from schoolwork and peer activities, as many parents have assumed; time spent playing at the computer is usually a substitute for other leisure activities, most notably TV viewing. Nevertheless, critics have feared (and early evidence suggests) that heavy exposure to such popular and incredibly violent video games such as *Alien Intruder* and *Mortal Kombat* can instigate aggression and cultivate aggressive habits in the same ways that televised violence does (Fling et al., 1992; Williams, 1998).

Concerns about Social Inequalities. Other critics are convinced that the computer revolution may leave some groups of children behind, lacking in skills that are required in our increasingly computer-dependent society. For example, children from economically disadvantaged families may be exposed to computers at school but are unlikely to have them at home (Rocheleau, 1995). Also, boys are far more likely than girls to take an interest in computers and to sign up for computer camps. Why? Probably because computers are often viewed as involving mathematics, a traditionally masculine subject, and many available computer games are designed to appeal to boys (Lepper, 1985; Ogletree & Williams, 1990). Yet, this gender gap is narrowing, largely due to the increasing use of computers to foster *cooperative* classroom learning activities that girls typically enjoy (Collis, 1996; Rocheleau, 1995).

Concerns about Internet Exposure. The proliferation of home computers and online services means that literally millions of children and adolescents around the world may now have unsupervised access to the Internet and the *World Wide Web*. Clearly, exposure to information available on the Web can be a boon to students researching topics pertinent to their school assignments. Nevertheless, many parents and teachers are alarmed about potentially unsavory Web influences. For example, children and adolescents chatting with acquaintances on line have been drawn into cybersexual relationships and, occasionally, to meetings with and exploitation by their adult chat-mates (Williams, 1998). Furthermore, the Web is (or has been) a primary recruiting tool for such dangerous cults as the *Manson family* and *Heaven's Gate,* as well as hate organizations such as the *Ku Klux Klan* (Downing, 1998). So there are reasons to suspect that unrestricted Web access could prove harmful to some children and adolescents, and additional research aimed at estimating those risks is sorely needed.

Like television sets, then, computers may prove to be either a positive or a negative force on development, depending on how they are used. Outcomes may be less than positive if a young person's primary uses of the machine are to fritter away study time chatting about undesirable topics on line, or to hole up by himself, zapping mutant aliens from space. But the news may be rather positive indeed for youngsters who use computers to learn, create, and collaborate amicably with siblings and peers.

SCHOOL AS A SOCIALIZATION AGENT

Of all the formal institutions that children encounter away from home, few have as much opportunity to influence their development as the schools they attend. Obviously, students acquire a great deal of knowledge and many academic skills at school. But schooling also promotes cognitive and *metacognitive* growth by teaching children a variety of rules, strategies, and problem-solving skills (including an ability to concentrate and an appreciation for abstraction) that they can apply to many different kinds of information (Ceci, 1991). Consider what Frederick Morrison and his associates (1995; 1997) found when comparing the cognitive performance of children who had just made the age cutoff for entering first grade with that of youngsters who had just missed the cutoff and had spent the year in kindergarten. When tested at the end of the school year, the youngest first-graders clearly outperformed the nearly *identically aged* kindergartners in reading, memory, language, and arithmetic skills. In another study of fourth-, fifth-, and sixth-graders in Israel (Cahan & Cohen, 1989), children at any given grade performed at higher levels on a variety of intellectual tests than their chronological *age-mates* in the next lower grade—another indication that intellectual performance is influenced, in part, by the *amount* of schooling one has had.

In addition to the cognitive and academic challenges they provide, schools expose children to an **informal curriculum** that teaches them how to fit into their culture. Students are expected to obey rules, cooperate with their classmates, respect authority, and become good citizens. And much of the influence that peers may have on developing children occurs in the context of school-related activities and may depend very critically on the type of school that a child attends and the quality of a child's school experiences. So it is quite proper to think of the school as an agent of socialization that is likely to affect children's social and emotional development as well as imparting knowledge and helping to prepare students for a job and economic self-sufficiency.

The vast majority of children in our society now begin their schooling well before age 6—attending kindergarten as 5-year-olds and, in many cases, going to nursery school or day care before that (Clarke-Stewart, 1993). Is this a healthy trend? As we will see in Box 16.1, there are advantages as well as some possible disadvantages associated with early entry into a school-like environment.

informal curriculum
noncurricular objectives of schooling such as teaching children to cooperate, respect authority, obey rules, and become good citizens.

Concept Check 16.1
Understanding Some Impacts of Television and Computer Technology

Check your understanding of *selected impacts* of television and computer technology by matching each descriptive statement below with one of the following alternatives: (a) ethnic/gender stereotypes, (b) mean-world beliefs, (c) television literacy, (d) aggressive children, (e) disadvantaged children, (f) adult monitoring/encouragement, (g) poor peer relations, (h) ads for children, (i) metacognitive development. Answers appear in the Appendix.

_____ 1. they display the strongest preference for and effects of exposure to violent programming
_____ 2. often displayed and reinforced in commercial television programs
_____ 3. thought by some critics to be more harmful than televised violence
_____ 4. hypothesized consequence of computer use that proved to be unfounded
_____ 5. their cognitive gains illustrated important benefits of *Sesame Street*
_____ 6. demonstrated effect of computer programming experience
_____ 7. promotes children's enactment of lessons from prosocial television programming
_____ 8. possible consequence of heavy exposure to televised violence
_____ 9. attribute that young children lack that causes them to misinterpret TV programming

CURRENT CONTROVERSIES

16.1

Should Preschoolers Attend School?

In recent years, children in the United States have begun their schooling at increasingly younger ages. Not only is kindergarten for 5-year-olds compulsory in most states, but there is talk of requiring school for 4-year-olds (Zigler, 1987). And already many preschoolers spend 4- to 8-hour days in day-care settings or nursery schools that have a strong academic emphasis and attempt to ready them for the classroom.

Is attending preschool beneficial? Developmentalists such as Edward Zigler (1987) and David Elkind (1981), author of *The Hurried Child,* express some concerns that the current push for earlier and earlier education may be going too far. They feel that many young children today are not given enough time simply to be children—to play and socialize as they choose. Elkind even worries that children may lose their self-initiative and enjoyment of learning if their lives are orchestrated by parents who incessantly push them to achieve.

Three recent studies seem to confirm Elkind's concerns (Hart, Burts, et al., 1998; Hyson, Hirsch-Pasek, & Rescorla, 1989; Stipek et al., 1995). Three- to-6-year-olds in academically oriented preschools or kindergartens displayed an initial advantage in such basic academic competencies as a knowledge of letters and reading skills but had lost it by the end of kindergarten. What's more, students in these highly structured, academically oriented programs proved to be *less creative, more stressed, and more anxious about tests, less prideful* about their successes, *less confident* about succeeding in the future, and generally *less enthused* about school than children who attended preschool or kindergarten programs that emphasized child-centered social agendas and flexible, hands-on, discovery-based learning. So there may well be dangers in overemphasizing academics during the preschool period, after all.

On the other hand, preschool programs that offer a healthy mix of play and basic skill-building activities can be very beneficial to young children, especially to disadvantaged children. Children who attend high-quality preschools often develop social skills at an earlier age than those who remain at home (Clarke-Stewart, 1993). And, although most children who attend preschool classes are no more or less intellectually advanced than those who remain at home, *disadvantaged* preschoolers who attend programs designed to prepare them for school display more cognitive growth and achieve more success in school than other disadvantaged youngsters (Burchinal et al., 1997). So as long as preschool programs allow plenty of time for play and for skill building in the context of group social interactions, they can help children from all social backgrounds acquire social and communication skills, as well as an appreciation of rules and routines, that will smooth the transition from individual learning at home to group learning in an elementary school classroom (Zigler & Finn-Stevenson, 1993).

Determinants of Effective (and Ineffective) Schooling

One of the first questions that parents often ask when searching for a residence in a new town is "Where should we live so that our children will get the best education?" This concern reflects the common belief that some schools are "better" or "more effective" than others. But are they?

Michael Rutter (1983) certainly thinks so. According to Rutter, **effective schools** are those that promote academic achievement, social skills, polite and attentive behavior, positive attitudes toward learning, low absenteeism, continuation of education beyond the age at which attendance is mandatory, and acquisition of skills that enable students to find and hold a job. Rutter argues that some schools are more successful than others at accomplishing these objectives, regardless of the students' racial, ethnic, or socioeconomic backgrounds. Let's examine the evidence for this claim.

In one study, Rutter and his associates (1979) conducted extensive interviews and observations in 12 high schools serving lower- to lower-middle-income populations in London, England. As adolescents entered these schools, they were given a battery of achievement tests to measure their prior academic accomplishments. At the end of high school, the pupils took another major exam to assess their academic progress. Other information, such as attendance records and teacher ratings of classroom behavior, was also available. When the data were analyzed, Rutter found that the 12 schools clearly differed in "effectiveness": students from the "better" schools exhibited fewer problem behaviors, attended school more regularly, and made more academic progress than students from the less effective schools. We get some idea of the importance of these

effective schools
schools that are generally successful at achieving curricular and noncurricular objectives, regardless of the racial, ethnic, or socioeconomic background of the student population.

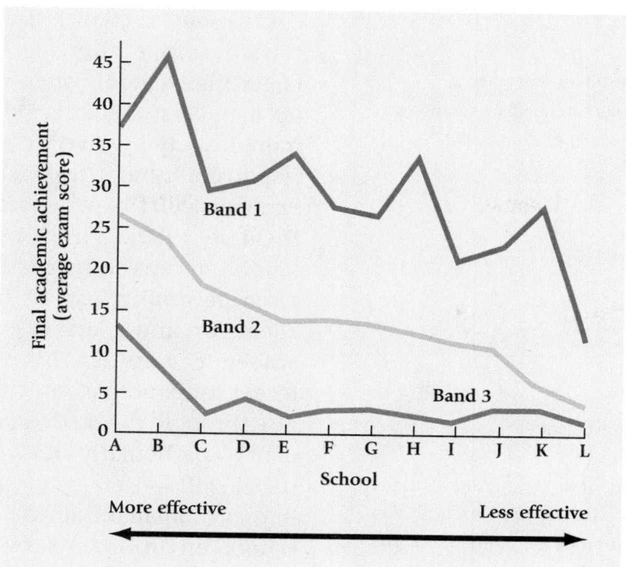

Figure 16.4 *Average level of academic achievement in secondary school as a function of initial achievement at the time of entry (Bands 1–3) and the school that pupils were attending (Schools A–L). Note that pupils in all three bands performed at higher levels on this final academic assessment if they attended the more effective schools. Furthermore, students in Band 2 performed like Band 1 students in the more effective schools but like Band 3 students in the least effective schools.* FROM RUTTER ET AL., *1979.*

"schooling effects" from Figure 16.4. The "bands" on the graph refer to the pupils' academic accomplishments *at the time they entered* high school (Band 3, low achievers; Band 1, high achievers). In all three bands, students attending the "more effective" schools outperformed those in the "less effective" schools on the final assessment of academic achievement. Even more revealing is the finding that the initially poor students (Band 3) who attended the "better" schools ended up scoring just as high on this final index of academic progress as the initially good (Band 1) students who attended the least effective schools. Similar findings were obtained in other large studies of elementary and high schools in the United States. Even after controlling for important variables such as the racial composition and socioeconomic backgrounds of the student bodies and the type of communities served, some elementary schools were found to be much more "effective" than others (Brookover et al., 1979; Hill, Foster, & Gendler, 1990).

So the school that children attend can make a difference. And you may be surprised by some of the factors that do and do not have a bearing on how "effective" a school is.

Some Misconceptions about Effective Schooling

MONETARY SUPPORT. Surprising as it may seem, a school's level of *financial* support has little to do with the quality of education that students receive. Seriously inadequate funding *can* undermine the quality of education; but as long as a school has qualified teachers and a reasonable level of support, the precise amount of money spent per pupil, the number of books in the school library, and teachers' salaries and academic credentials play only a minor role in determining student outcomes (Rutter, 1983).

SCHOOL AND CLASS SIZE. Another factor that has relatively little to do with a school's effectiveness is average class size. In typical elementary- and secondary-school classes ranging from 20 to 40 students, class size has little or no effect on academic achievement (Cooper, 1989; Odden, 1990). However, classes smaller than 15 to 20 pupils are beneficial in the primary grades (kindergarten through grade 3) (Finn & Achilles, 1990), and primary students in larger classes—especially disadvantaged or low-ability students—do much better in reading and math when they are tutored part of the day in smaller study groups (Odden, 1990; Slavin, 1989). So if a school district has money available to hire additional instructors, the wisest allocation might be to devote these "personnel resources" to the primary grades—precisely the settings in which smaller classes promote academic achievement.

There is some evidence that the size of one's school affects older students' participation in structured extracurricular activities, where such aspects of the "informal

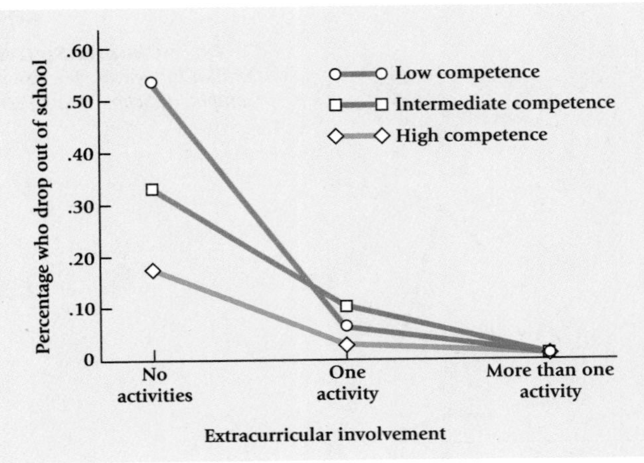

Figure 16.5 *Rates of high school dropout as a function of student social/academic competencies and participation in extracurricular activities. Clearly, students of low or intermediate competence are more likely to stay in school if they participate in extracurricular activities and maintain a positive and voluntary connection to peers and the school environment.* MAHONEY & CAIRNS, 1997.

curriculum" as cooperation, fair play, and healthy attitudes toward competition are likely to be stressed. Although larger high schools offer a greater number of extracurricular activities, students in smaller schools tend to be (1) more heavily involved, (2) more likely to hold positions of responsibility and leadership, and (3) more satisfied with extracurricular experiences (Barker & Gump, 1964; Jacobs & Chase, 1989). Why? One reason is that students in larger schools receive much less encouragement to participate, often becoming lost in the crowd and feeling a sense of alienation and a lack of connectedness with peers and the academic culture. This is indeed unfortunate, for one recent longitudinal study that tracked adolescents from the 7th through the 12th grade found that high school students—particularly less competent students with poor social skills—were much less likely to drop out of school if they had maintained a voluntary connection to their school environments by participating in one or more extracurricular activities (Mahoney & Cairns, 1997; see Figure 16.5). The implications of these findings are clear: To better accomplish their mission of educating students and properly preparing them for adult life, middle and secondary schools—large and small—should encourage *all* students to participate in extracurricular activities and avoid denying them those opportunities because of marginal academic performances (Mahoney & Cairns, 1997).

ABILITY TRACKING. The merits of **ability tracking**—a procedure in which students are grouped by IQ or academic achievement and then taught in classes made up of students of comparable "ability"—have been debated for years. Some educators believe that students learn more when surrounded by peers of equal ability. Others argue that ability tracking undermines the self-esteem of lower-ability students and contributes to their poor academic achievement and high dropout rate.

In his early review of the literature, Rutter (1983) found that neither ability tracking nor mixed-ability teaching has decisive advantages: Both procedures are common in highly effective and less effective schools. Yet, recent research suggests some qualifications. Apparently, ability tracking does widen the gap between high and low achievers (Dornbusch, Glasgow, & Lin, 1996; Slavin, 1987), whereas mixed-ability instruction in elementary and middle schools seems to promote the academic achievement of less capable students without undermining the performance of their more capable peers (Kulik & Kulik, 1992). Ability tracking *can* be beneficial to high-ability students, *if* they are exposed to a curriculum tailored to their learning needs (Fuligni, Eccles, & Barber, 1995; Kulik & Kulik, 1992). However, lower-ability students are unlikely to benefit and may well suffer if they are stigmatized as "dummies" and are not challenged academically, or if they are denied access to the more effective instructors who might help them to master such challenges (Fuligni et al., 1995; Kulik & Kulik, 1992).

ability tracking
the educational practice of grouping students according to ability and then educating them in classes with students of comparable educational or intellectual standing.

traditional classroom
a classroom arrangement in which all pupils sit facing an instructor, who normally teaches one subject at a time by lecturing or giving demonstrations.

open classroom
a less structured classroom arrangement in which there is a separate area for each educational activity and children distribute themselves around the room, working individually or in small groups.

CLASSROOM ORGANIZATION. Chances are that you were educated in a **traditional classroom** with seats arranged in neat rows facing the teacher, who lectured or gave demonstrations at a desk or a chalkboard. In a traditional classroom, the curriculum is highly structured: Normally, everybody studies the same subject at a given moment, and students are expected to interact with the teacher rather than with each other.

In an **open classroom,** children are viewed as active, autonomous agents who learn better by becoming more actively involved in their education. Rarely do children in open classrooms do the same thing at once. A more typical scenario is for students to distribute themselves around the room, working individually or in small groups at reading stories, playing word games, solving math puzzles, creating art, or working on a science project. And rather than being centers of attention or central authority figures, teachers in open classrooms help children to decide what to learn about and then circulate around the room, guiding and instructing students in response to their individual needs (Minuchin & Shapiro, 1983).

There are some clear social and emotional advantages associated with open classrooms: Students express more positive attitudes about school, are more self-directed in pursuing learning objectives, and display a greater ability to cooperate with classmates while creating fewer disciplinary problems than students in traditional classrooms (Minuchin & Shapiro, 1983). However, many investigators find no difference in the academic performance of students in open and traditional classrooms (Minuchin & Shapiro, 1983), and others have concluded that students actually learn more in a *traditional* classroom whenever the subject matter involves learning abstract concepts that may be difficult for students to grasp on their own (Good, 1979; Slavin, as cited in Associated Press, 1994a). Clearly, each of these classroom arrangements has its advantages and disadvantages, and both are common in effective (and in less effective) schools (Associated Press 1994a; Rutter, 1983).

Factors that Contribute to Effective Schooling

Composition of the Student Body. To some extent, the "effectiveness" of a school is a function of what it has to work with. On average, academic achievement is lowest in schools with a preponderance of economically disadvantaged students (Brookover et al., 1979; Rutter, 1983), and it appears that *any* child is likely to make more academic progress if taught in a school with a higher concentration of intellectually capable peers. However, this *does not* mean that a school is only as good as the students it serves, for many schools that draw heavily from disadvantaged minority populations are highly effective at motivating students and preparing them for jobs or higher education (Reynolds, 1992).

The Scholastic Atmosphere of Successful Schools. So what is it about the learning environment of some schools that allows them to accomplish so much? Reviews of the literature (Linney & Seidman, 1989; Reynolds, 1992; Rutter, 1983) point to the following values and practices that characterize effective schools:

1. *Academic emphasis.* Effective schools have a clear focus on academic goals. Children are regularly assigned homework, which is checked, corrected, and discussed with them.
2. *Classroom management.* In effective schools, teachers waste little time getting activities started or dealing with distracting disciplinary problems. Lessons begin and end on time. Pupils are told exactly what is expected of them and receive clear and unambiguous feedback about their academic performance. The classroom atmosphere is comfortable; all students are actively encouraged to work to the best of their abilities, and ample praise acknowledges good work.
3. *Discipline.* In effective schools, the staff is firm in enforcing rules and does so on the spot rather than sending offenders off to the principal's office. Rarely do instructors resort to physical sanctions (slapping or spanking), which contribute to truancy, defiance, and a tense classroom atmosphere.
4. *Teamwork.* Effective schools have faculties that work as a team, jointly planning curricular objectives and monitoring student progress, under the guidance of a principal who provides active, energetic leadership.

In sum, the effective school environment is a *comfortable* but *businesslike* setting in which academic successes are expected and students are *motivated* to learn.

The "Goodness of Fit" between Students and Schools. There is another important point to make about effective schooling: Characteristics of the student and of the school environment often *interact* to affect student outcomes—a phenomenon that Lee Cronbach and Richard Snow (1977) call **aptitude–treatment interaction (ATI).** Over the years, much educational research has been based on the assumption that a particular teaching method, philosophy of education, or organizational system will prove

aptitude–treatment interaction (ATI)
phenomenon whereby characteristics of the student and of the school environment interact to affect student outcomes, such that any given educational practice may be effective with some students, but not with others.

superior for all students, regardless of their abilities, personalities, and cultural backgrounds. This assumption is often wrong. Instead, many approaches to education are highly effective with *some* kinds of students but quite ineffective with others. The secret to being effective is to find an appropriate fit between learners and educational practices.

For example, teachers tend to get the most out of *high-ability, middle-class* students by moving at a quick pace and insisting on high standards of performance—that is, by challenging these students. By contrast, *low-ability* and *disadvantaged* students often respond more favorably to a teacher who motivates them by being warm and encouraging rather than intrusive and demanding (Good & Brophy, 1994).

Sensitivity to students' *cultural* traditions is also crucial for designing an effective instructional program. European-American students come from cultures that stress individual learning, perhaps making them especially well-suited for the individual mastery expectations that are emphasized in traditional classrooms. By contrast, ethnic Hawaiians and other students from cultures that stress cooperation and collaborative approaches to learning often founder in traditional classrooms. They pay little attention to the teacher or their lessons and spend a lot of time seeking the attention of classmates—behaviors that are perceived by teachers as reflecting their lack of interest in school (Tharp, 1989). Yet, when instruction is made more culturally compatible for these youngsters by having teachers circulate among small groups, instructing and encouraging group members to pull together and assist each other to achieve learning objectives, Hawaiian children become much more enthusiastic about school and achieve much more as well (see Figure 16.6).

WHAT DO YOU THINK?

Some school districts now require students to dress in school uniforms (DelCampo & DelCampo, 1998). Proponents believe that this policy improves the educational atmosphere by (among other things) decreasing the incidence of fighting and other misconduct. Critics, however, claim that requiring uniforms imposes economic hardships and restricts students' First Amendment rights to self-expression. What do you think about requiring students to wear uniforms and why?

Unfortunately, young adolescents from any social background may begin to lose interest in academics should they experience a mismatch between their school environments and their changing developmental needs—a point well illustrated by the findings presented in Box 16.2.

In sum, the "goodness of fit" between students and their classroom environments is a crucial aspect of effective schooling. Education that is carefully tailored to students' cultural backgrounds, personal characteristics, and developmental needs is much more likely to succeed.

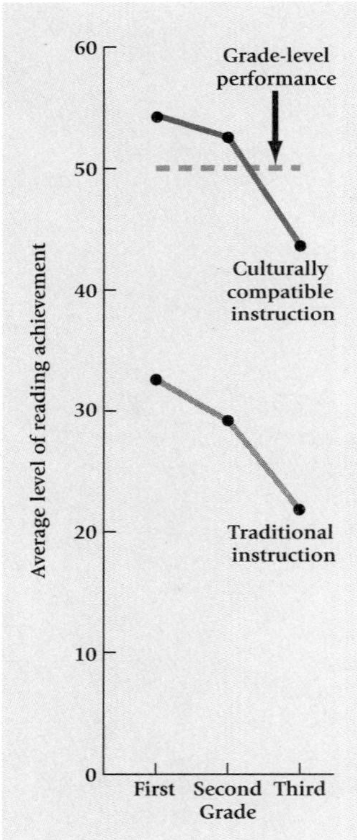

Figure 16.6 *Reading achievement of ethnic Hawaiian first- through third-grade students who received traditional or culturally compatible classroom instruction. The students who received culturally compatible instruction read at grade level, whereas those receiving traditional instruction read far below grade level.* ADAPTED FROM THARP & GALLIMORE, 1988.

Do Our Schools Meet the Needs of All of Our Children?

Public education in the United States arose not so much from a desire to educate a work force (most 19th-century workers were farmers or unskilled laborers who required little education) as from the need to "Americanize" a nation of immigrants—to bring them into the mainstream of American society (Rudolph, 1965). So our public schools have traditionally been majority-culture, middle-class institutions staffed by white instructors who promote middle-class values.

However, more and more of the students educated in our public schools come from nonwhite social backgrounds; in fact, a *majority* of students in California's public schools now belong to various "minority" groups (Garcia, 1993). How well are minority students served by our schools? And how well do schools meet the needs of students with developmental disabilities and other special needs?

Educational Experiences of Ethnic Minorities

African-American, Latino, and Native American children tend to earn poorer grades in school and lower scores on standardized achievement tests than their European-American classmates, whereas Asian Americans (particularly recent immigrants) tend to outperform European-American students at school (Chen & Stevenson, 1995; Fuligni, 1997;

16.2

DEVELOPMENTAL ISSUES

On the Difficult Transition to Secondary Schools

For some time now, educators have been concerned about a number of undesirable changes that often occur when students make the transition from elementary school to junior high school: loss of self-esteem and interest in school, declining grades, and increased troublemaking, to name a few (Eccles et al., 1993; 1996; Seidman et al., 1994). Why is this a treacherous move?

One reason that the transition is difficult is because young adolescents, particularly girls, are often experiencing major physical and psychological changes at the same time that they are required to change schools. Roberta Simmons and Dale Blyth (1987), for example, found that girls who were reaching puberty as they were making the transition from 6th grade in an elementary school to 7th grade in a junior high school were more likely to experience drops in self-esteem and other negative changes than girls who remained in a kindergarten–8th grade (K-8) school during this vulnerable period. Adolescents at greatest risk of academic and emotional difficulties are those who must also cope with other life transitions, such as family turmoil or a change in residence, at about the time that they change schools (Flanagan & Eccles, 1993). Could it be, then, that more adolescents would remain interested in academics and show better adjustment outcomes if they weren't forced to change schools at the precise time that they are experiencing many other changes often associated with puberty? This has been part of the rationale for the development of *middle schools,* serving grades 6 through 8, which are now more common than junior high schools in the United States (Braddock & McPartland, 1993).

Yet Jacquelynne Eccles and her colleagues (Eccles, Lord, & Midgley, 1991; Eccles et al., 1993) report that students do not necessarily find the transition to middle school any easier than the transition to junior high school. This has led them to suspect that it is not as important *when* adolescents make a school change as *what* their new school is like. Specifically, they have proposed a "goodness of fit" hypothesis stating that the transition to a new school is likely to be especially difficult when that school, whether a junior high or middle school, is ill-matched to the developmental needs of early adolescents.

Eccles and her associates have found that the transition to junior high school often involves going from a small school with close student–teacher relationships, a good deal of choice regarding learning activities, and reasonable discipline to a larger, more bureaucratized environment where student–teacher relationships are impersonal, good grades are harder to come by, opportunities for choice are limited, assignments are not very intellectually stimulating, and discipline is rigid—all this at a time when adolescents are seeking *more,* rather than less, autonomy and are more intellectually capable.

Eccles and others have demonstrated that the "fit" between developmental needs and school environment is indeed an important influence on adolescent adjustment to school. In one study (Mac Iver & Reuman, 1988), the transition to junior high brought about a decline in intrinsic interest in learning mainly among students who wanted more involvement in classroom decisions but ended up with fewer such opportunities than they had had in elementary school.

Moving from small, close-knit elementary schools to highly bureaucratic and impersonal secondary schools is stressful for adolescents, many of whom lose interest in academics and become more susceptible to peer-group influences.

Furthermore, the lack of close, supportive relations with teachers makes many autonomy-seeking adolescents in impersonal secondary schools much more susceptible to peer values and influences, which they often perceived as antisocial (Seidman et al., 1994). Finally, a third study illustrates just how important a *good* fit between students and school environments can be. Students experienced negative changes in their attitudes toward mathematics if their transition to junior high resulted in less personal and supportive relations with math teachers; but for those few students whose transition to junior high involved gaining more supportive teachers than they had in elementary school, interest in academics actually *increased* (Midgley, Feldlaufer, & Eccles, 1989).

The message? Declines in academic motivation and performance are not inevitable as students move from elementary to secondary schools. These declines occur primarily when the fit between student and school environment goes from good to poor. How might we improve the fit? Parents can help by recognizing how difficult school transitions can be and communicating this understanding to their teens. Indeed, one study found that adolescents whose parents were in tune with their developmental needs and who fostered autonomy in decision making generally adjusted well to the transition to junior high and posted *gains* in self-esteem (Lord, Eccles, & McCarthy, 1994). Teachers can also help by seeking parents' opinions about scholastic matters and keeping them involved during this transitional period—a time when collaborative relations between parents and teachers normally decline and adolescents often feel that they are facing the stresses of this new, impersonal academic atmosphere with little social support (Eccles & Harold, 1993). Finally, The Carnegie Council on Adolescent Development (1989) advises secondary schools to reorganize into smaller communities for learning in order to provide young adolescents with more social support and to make them feel less anonymous. The key elements of this "communities" approach involve forming (1) "schools within schools," in which subsets of students and teachers grouped together as "teams" become more familiar with (and, hopefully, supportive of) each other, and (2) small group advisories, or homerooms, to ensure that every student has access to at least one adult who knows him or her well.

Children are more likely to do well in school if their parents value education and are interested and involved in school activities.

Slaughter-Defoe et al., 1990). These racial and ethnic differences in academic achievement are still found even after group differences in socioeconomic status are controlled, and they are not merely the product of group differences in intellectual ability (Alexander & Entwisle, 1988; Pungello et al., 1996; Sue & Okazaki, 1990). Why, then, do such differences exist?

Parental Attitudes and Involvement. One widely held notion is that parents of underachieving ethnic minority students do not value education or encourage school achievement as much as other parents do. This is a serious misconception. African-American and Latino-American parents seem to value education at least as much as European-American parents do (Galper, Wigfield, & Seefeldt, 1997; Steinberg et al., 1992), and they are actually *more* likely to appreciate the value of homework, competency testing, and a longer school day (Stevenson, Chen, & Uttal, 1990). However, minority parents are often less knowledgeable about the school system and less involved in many school activities, and this lack of participation may partially counteract their message to children that school is important. Yet, when minority parents *are* highly involved in school activities, their children feel more confident about mastering academic challenges and tend to do well in school (Connell, Spencer, & Aber, 1994; Luster & McAdoo, 1996; Slaughter-Defoe et al., 1990). So active parental involvement can make a big difference.

Patterns of Parenting and Peer Influences. Although minority parents often play an important role in fostering their children's school achievement, we cannot fully appreciate their contribution without also understanding how peers influence academic achievement. Lawrence Steinberg and his colleagues (1992) have conducted a large-scale study of school achievement among African-, Latino-, Asian-, and European-American high school students. They found that academic success and good personal adjustment are usually associated with *authoritative parenting*. However, this positive parental influence on academic achievement may be undermined by African-American peers, who often devalue academic achievement and pressure many African-American students to choose between academic success and peer acceptance (see also Ogbu, 1994).

Latino parents tend to be strict and somewhat authoritarian rather than flexible and authoritative. As a result, Latino students may have relatively few opportunities at home to act autonomously and acquire decision-making skills that would serve them well in school (Steinberg et al., 1992). Furthermore, Latino students from low-income areas also tend to associate with peers who do not strongly value academics and who may undercut their parents' efforts to promote academic achievement. By contrast, European-American students are more likely than either African-American or Latino students to have *both* authoritative parents and peer support for education working in their favor.

Interestingly, high-achieving Asian-American students often experience restrictive, authoritarian parenting at home. However, this highly controlling pattern, coupled with a *very strong* emphasis on education and the *very high* achievement standards that many Asian-American parents set for their children, actually *fosters* academic success. Why? Because Asian-American children are also taught from a very early age to be respectful of and obey their elders, who have a duty to train them to be socially responsible and competent human beings (Chao, 1994). Given this kind of socialization in Asian-American homes, it is hardly surprising that the Asian-American peer group strongly endorses education and encourages academic success (Fuligni, 1997). The result? Asian-American students typically spend more hours studying, often with their supportive friends, than other students do, which undoubtedly accounts for much of their academic success (Fuligni, 1997; Steinberg et al., 1992).

Teacher Expectancies. Finally, we must consider another hypothesis about ethnic differences in school achievement: the possibility that underachievement by some minority students is rooted in subtle stereotyping and discrimination on the part of teachers. According to social stereotypes, Asian Americans are expected to be bright and hard-working, whereas African Americans and Latino students from low-income neighborhoods are expected to perform poorly in school. And teachers are hardly immune to these stereotypes. Minority students often feel that white teachers do not understand them and that they could do better in school were they given more respect and understanding (Ford & Harris, 1996). Consistent with this viewpoint, teachers in one study were asked to select from a checklist those attributes that best described their lower-income minority pupils. Teachers consistently selected adjectives such as *lazy, fun-loving,* and *rebellious,* thus implying that they did not expect much of these students (Gottlieb, 1966).

In a classic study, Robert Rosenthal and Lenore Jacobson (1968) demonstrated that a teacher's expectancies about a student can influence a child's achievement through what they called the **Pygmalion effect:** A student actually performs better when expected to do well than when expected to do poorly, so that teacher expectancies may become *self-fulfilling prophecies.* To demonstrate this, Rosenthal and Jacobsen gave each elementary school teacher in their study a list of five students who were supposed to be "rapid bloomers." In fact, the so-called rapid bloomers had been randomly selected from class rosters. The only way that they differed from other students is that their teachers expected more of them. Yet planting these high expectancies in the minds of first- and second-grade teachers was sufficient to cause the so-called rapid bloomers to show greater gains in IQ and reading achievement than their unlabeled classmates.

Although some investigators have failed to replicate Rosenthal and Jacobson's results (Cooper, 1979), many others have reported similar findings, showing that (1) students expected by teachers to do well are likely to live up to these positive expectancies, whereas (2) those expected to perform poorly often do earn lower grades and score lower on standardized tests than classmates of comparable ability for whom the teacher has no negative expectancies (see Harris & Rosenthal, 1986; Weinstein et al., 1987). Clearly, the positive or negative expectancies that most teachers form often reflect *real* differences between students: Those expected to perform well (or poorly) in the future have typically performed well (or poorly) in the past (Jussim & Eccles, 1992). Still, even if two students have equal aptitude and motivation, the one whose teacher expects great things is likely to outperform the one whose teacher expects less (Jussim & Eccles, 1992).

Pygmalion effect
the tendency of teacher expectancies to become self-fulfilling prophecies, causing students to perform better or worse depending on their teacher's estimation of their potential.

How exactly does the Pygmalion effect work? It seems that teachers expose high-expectancy students to more challenging materials, demand better performances from them, and are more likely to praise them for answering questions correctly (perhaps leading them to infer that they have *high ability*). And when high-expectancy students do not answer correctly, they often hear the question rephrased so that they can get it right, thus implying that failures can be overcome by *persisting* and *trying harder* (Dweck & Elliott, 1983). Meanwhile, a Mexican-American or African-American student from a poverty-stricken neighborhood might be tagged by a teacher as a low-ability student—one who may rarely be challenged or often be criticized if he does not know the answer to questions. Unfortunately, these practices could convince the child that he has little ability, thereby undermining his will to achieve and causing him to confirm the teacher's low expectations (see Sorensen & Hallinan, 1986).

In sum, parents' values and styles of parenting, peers' level of support for academic achievement, and teacher expectancies probably all contribute to racial and ethnic differences in school achievement. Some theorists believe that children from lower-income minority subcultures are at an immediate disadvantage when they enter a middle-class scholastic setting and that schools must change dramatically if they are to motivate and better educate these children. Among the positive changes that we see today are stronger bilingual education programs designed to meet the needs of children from the over 100 distinct language groups in the United States (Garcia, 1993), and multicultural education programs designed to bring the perspectives of many cultural and subcultural groups into the classroom so that all students feel more welcome there (Banks, 1993).

Educating Students with Special Needs

One major challenge that educators face is successfully educating students with special needs: learning disabilities, mental retardation, physical and sensory handicaps, and other developmental disorders. These youngsters used to be placed in separate schools or classrooms—or in some cases, were rejected as unteachable by public schools—until the U.S. Congress passed the *Education for all Handicapped Children Act* in 1975. Revised in 1990, this law requires school districts to provide an education to all youngsters with special needs comparable with that received by other children. The intent of the law was to better prepare children with special needs to participate in society by ensuring that their educational experiences were as similar as possible to pupils in typical public school classrooms. How might the law be served? Many school districts opted for **mainstreaming,** the practice of integrating special-needs children into regular classrooms for all or large parts of the day, as opposed to segregating them in special schools or classrooms.

Has mainstreaming accomplished its objectives? Not very well, unfortunately. Compared with other special-needs children who attend segregated special education classes, mainstreamed youngsters sometimes fare better academically and socially but often do not (Buysse & Bailey, 1993; Siegel, 1996). Furthermore, their self-esteem often declines because classmates tend to ridicule them and are reluctant to choose them as friends or playmates (Guralnick & Groom, 1988; Taylor, Asher, & Williams, 1987).

Do these findings imply that mainstreaming has failed? No, they do not! Robert Slavin and his colleagues (1991; 1996; Stevens & Slavin, 1995a; 1995b) have had much success with **cooperative learning methods** in which a mainstreamed child and several classmates are assigned to work teams and are reinforced for performing well *as a team*. For example, each member of a math team is given problems to solve that are appropriate to his or her ability level. Yet members of a work team also monitor one another's progress and offer each other aid when needed. To encourage this cooperation, the teams that complete the most math units are rewarded, for example, with special certificates that designate them as "superteams." Similarly, the "jigsaw method" of instruction developed by Elliot Aronson and his colleagues (1978) to facilitate racial integration involves giving each member of a small learning team one portion of the material to be learned and requiring him or her to teach it to teammates. Here, then, is a formula for ensuring that children of different social backgrounds and ability levels will interact in a context where the efforts of even the least capable team members are important to the *group's* success.

Clearly, these cooperative learning methods work. Mainstreamed second- to sixth- graders in classrooms stressing cooperative learning come to like school better

mainstreaming
the educational practice of integrating developmentally disabled students with special needs into regular classrooms rather than placing them in segregated special educational classes.

cooperative learning methods
an educational practice whereby children of different races or ability levels are assigned to teams; each team member works on problems geared to his or her ability level, and all members are reinforced for "pulling together" and performing well as a team.

By stressing teamwork to achieve shared goals, cooperative learning activities make mainstreaming a more fruitful experience for children of all ability levels.

and to outperform mainstreamed peers in traditional classrooms in vocabulary, reading and language skills, and tests of metacognitive knowledge, posting even bigger advantages in the second year of cooperative learning than in the first (Stevens & Slavin, 1995a). What's more, both special-needs children and gifted children thrive in the cooperative learning classrooms, often displaying clear gains in self-esteem and becoming more fully accepted by peers (Stevens & Slavin, 1995b). So mainstreaming *can* succeed if educators deliberately design learning experiences that encourage students from different backgrounds or ability levels to pool their efforts in order to achieve common goals.

How Well-Educated Are Our Children? A Cross-Cultural Comparison

How successful are our schools at imparting academic skills to their pupils? Large surveys of the reading, writing, and mathematical achievement of 9- to 17-year-old American students reveal that most of them do learn to read during the elementary school years and have acquired such mathematical proficiencies as basic computational skills and graph-reading abilities by the time they finish high school (Dossey et al., 1988; National Education Goals Panel, 1992). Yet, only about one American student in four could be described as truly proficient in reading and mathematics achievement (National Assessment of Educational Progress, as cited in Greene, 1997). Furthermore, American youth do not write very well; in fact, more than one-third of all 17-year-olds could not produce a well-formed and coherent paragraph. Are these findings cause for alarm?

Many educators think so (Short & Talley, 1997; Tirozzi & Uro, 1997), especially in view of the results of several cross-national surveys of children's academic achievement—studies indicating that the average scores obtained by American schoolchildren in mathematics, science, and verbal skills are consistently lower, and sometimes much lower, than those made by students in many other industrialized nations (National Education Goals Panel, 1992; Stevenson, Chen, & Lee, 1993).

Cross-cultural research conducted by Harold Stevenson and his colleagues (Chen & Stevenson, 1995; Stevenson, Lee, & Stigler, 1986; Stevenson et al., 1993) leaves no doubt that schoolchildren in Taiwan, the People's Republic of China, and Japan outperform students in the United States in math, reading, and other school subjects. The gap in math performance is especially striking; in recent testings of fifth graders, for example, only 4% of Chinese children and 10% of Japanese students had scores on a math achievement test as low as those of the average American child (Stevenson et al., 1993). Achievement differences of this sort are evident from the time children enter school and grow larger each year as children progress from first to fifth to eleventh grade (Geary et al., 1996; Stevenson et al., 1993). Why do these differences exist, and what can they tell us about improving American education?

Children in traditional Asian classrooms are required to stay in their seats working on assignments or paying close attention to their teacher.

The problem is not that American students are any less intelligent, for they enter school performing just as well on IQ tests as their Asian counterparts (Stevenson et al., 1985), and they score at least as well as Japanese and Chinese students on general information tests covering material *not* typically covered in school (Stevenson et al., 1993). In Chapter 8, we touched on some linguistic and instructional supports that help East Asian children to acquire mathematical knowledge. Yet, most of the achievement gap between American and Asian students seems to reflect cultural differences in educational attitudes and practices. For example:

Classroom Instruction

Asian students spend more time being educated than American students do. Elementary school teachers in Asian countries devote more class time to core academic subjects: for example, two to three times as many hours a week on math instruction. The Asian classroom is a comfortable but businesslike setting where little time is wasted; Asian students spend about 95% of their time on "on-task" activities such as listening to the teacher and completing assignments, whereas American students spend only about 80% of their time "on task" (Stigler, Lee, & Stevenson, 1987). Asian students also attend school for more hours per day and more days per year (often attending half the day on Saturdays) than American students do (Fuligni & Stevenson, 1995; Stevenson et al., 1986).

Parental Involvement

Asian parents are strongly committed to the educational process. They hold higher achievement expectancies for their children than American parents do, and even though their children excel by American standards, Asian parents are much less likely than American parents to be satisfied with their children's current academic performance (Chen & Stevenson, 1995; Stevenson et al., 1993). Asian parents think that homework is more important than American parents do, and they also receive frequent communications from their children's teachers in notebooks that children carry to and from school each day. These communications enable Asian parents to keep close tabs on how their children are progressing and to follow teachers' suggestions about how they can encourage and assist their children at home (Stevenson & Lee, 1990). By contrast, communications between U.S. parents and teachers are often limited to brief annual parent–teacher conferences.

Student Involvement

Not only do Asian students spend more days in class and more class time on academic assignments than American children do, but they are assigned and complete more homework as well (Stevenson et al., 1993). During the high school years, Asian students continue to devote more time to scholastic activities and spend much less time working, dating, or socializing with friends than American students do (Fuligni & Stevenson, 1995).

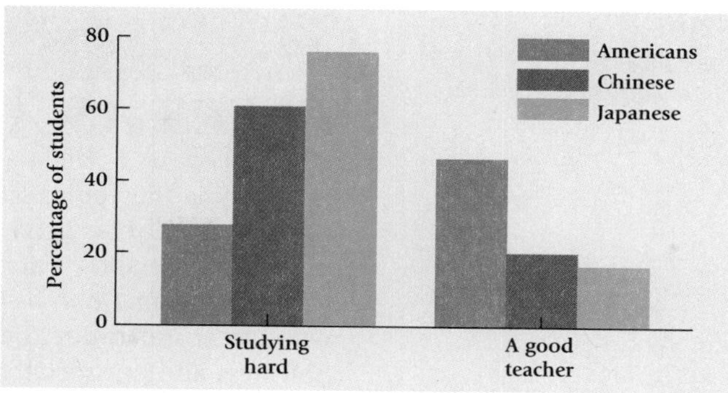

Figure 16.7 *Percentages of Chinese, Japanese, and American high school students who picked "studying hard" or having "a good teacher" as the most important factor influencing their performance in mathematics.* ADAPTED FROM CHEN & STEVENSON, *1995*.

A Strong Emphasis on Effort

A major reason that Asian students apply themselves so diligently to academic activities is that their parents, teachers, and they themselves share the strong belief that *all* youngsters have the potential to master their studies if they work hard enough. By contrast, their American counterparts are more inclined to believe that academic success reflects other factors such as the quality of the child's teachers (see Figure 16.7) or one's native intelligence (Chen & Stevenson, 1995; Stevenson et al., 1993). Asian students face especially strong pressures to excel in the classroom because their prospects for obtaining a college education largely depend on the results of a competitive exam taken in high school. Yet, their strong belief that effort will ultimately pay off in better learning (and higher test scores) helps to explain why Asian youngsters are no more anxious about school or otherwise psychologically maladjusted than American students are (Chen & Stevenson, 1995; Crystal et al., 1994).

So the formula for more effective education may not be so mysterious after all, judging from the success of the Chinese and Japanese educational systems. The secret is to get teachers, students, and parents working together to make education a top priority for youth, to set high achievement goals, and to invest the day-by-day effort required to attain those objectives. In response to evidence that American schools are being outclassed by those in other countries, the U.S. Congress passed *Goals 2000: Educate America Act of 1994* which aimed at making U.S. students first in the world in science and mathematics achievement by the year 2000 (Short & Talley, 1997). Although this goal is unlikely to be met that soon (Greene, 1997), many states and local school districts have taken up the challenge. How? By strengthening curricula, tightening standards for teacher certification, raising standards for graduation and promotion from grade to grade, implementing alternative academic calendars to shorten summer vacations and increase student retention in previously learned material, and, most importantly, seeking ways to involve parents as partners with teachers, at both the elementary and secondary school levels, to create more supportive learning environments and foster higher standards of academic achievement (Tirozzi & Uro, 1997; U.S. Department of Education, 1996). These educational reformers are well aware that improving the scholastic and vocational preparation of America's youth is crucial if Americans are to maintain a leadership role in an ever-changing and ever more competitive world (Goals 2000: Educate America Act, 1994).

Concept Check 16.2
Schools as Socialization Agents

Check your understanding of selected impacts of schools and educational practices on children by matching each descriptive statement below with one of the following terms, principles, or concepts: (a) ability tracking, (b) aptitude-treatment interaction, (c) cooperative learning methods, (d) group differences in IQ, (e) informal curriculum, (f) mainstreaming, (g) monetary support, (h) parental involvement, (i) peer influences, (j) extracurricular activities. Answers appear in the Appendix.

_____ 1. may undermine the self-esteem of special-needs students
_____ 2. contributes to ethnic differences in achievement
_____ 3. likely to undermine the academic achievement of low-ability students
_____ 4. aimed at teaching students how to fit into the culture
_____ 5. not a strong contributor to school effectiveness
_____ 6. strong contributor to academic success of minority youth and students in Asian cultures
_____ 7. protects against adolescents' dropping out of school
_____ 8. factor that best describes the effectiveness (or ineffectiveness) of particular educational practices
_____ 9. does *not* account for cross-cultural differences in academic achievement
_____ 10. successful method of promoting the objectives of mainstreaming

PEERS AS AGENTS OF SOCIALIZATION

By the time they enter school, most children spend the majority of their leisure time in the company of peers. What roles might peers play in a child's or an adolescent's development? If we allow ourselves to be influenced by such popular novels and films as *Lord of the Flies* and *Dead Poets Society,* we might conclude that peers are subversive agents who often undermine the best-laid plans of adults and lead the child into a life of rebelliousness and antisocial conduct. However, developmentalists now know that this perspective on peer influences is highly distorted and unnecessarily negative (Hartup, 1983). Yes, peers are occasionally "bad influences"; but they clearly have the potential to affect their playmates in a number of positive ways. Consider the viewpoint of a lonely farmer from the midwestern United States whose own life experiences convinced him that normal peer interactions foster healthy and adaptive developmental outcomes:[2]

> Dear Dr. Moore:
> . . . I am an only child, now 57 years old, and I want to tell you some things about my life. . . . I grew up in the country where there were no nearby children to play with . . . [and] from the first year of school, I was teased and made fun of. . . . I dreaded to get on the school bus and go to school because the other children on the bus called me "Mommy's baby." In about the second grade I heard the boys use a vulgar word. I asked what it meant and they made fun of me. So I learned a lesson—don't ask questions. I never went out with a girl while I was in school—in fact I hardly talked to them . . . [and] I didn't learn anything about girls. When we got into high school and boys and girls started dating, I could only listen to their stories about their experiences. . . . I could tell you a lot more, but the important thing is I have never married or had any children. I have not been very successful in an occupation or vocation. I believe my troubles are not all due to being an only child . . . but I do believe you are right in recommending playmates for preschool children, and I will add playmates for . . . school agers and *not* have them strictly supervised by adults. . . . Parents of only children should make special efforts to provide playmates for them.
>
> Sincerely yours,

If we assume that peers are important agents of socialization, there are a number of questions that remain to be answered. Who qualifies as a peer? How do peers influence one another? What is it about peer influence that is unique? What are the consequences (if any) of poor peer relations? Is it important to have special peer alliances, or friendships? Do peers eventually become a more potent source of influence than parents or other adults? These are some of the issues that we will explore in the pages that follow.

Who or What Is a Peer and What Functions Do Peers Serve?

Webster's New Collegiate Dictionary defines a **peer** as "one that is of equal standing with another." Developmentalists also think of peers as *"social equals"* or as individuals *who, for the moment at least, are operating at similar levels of behavioral complexity* (Lewis & Rosenblum, 1975). According to this activity-based definition, children who differ somewhat in age could still be considered "peers" as long as they can adjust their behaviors to suit one another's capabilities as they pursue common interests or goals.

peers
two or more persons who are operating at similar levels of behavioral complexity.

[2]This letter appears with the permission of its author and its recipient, Dr. Shirley G. Moore.

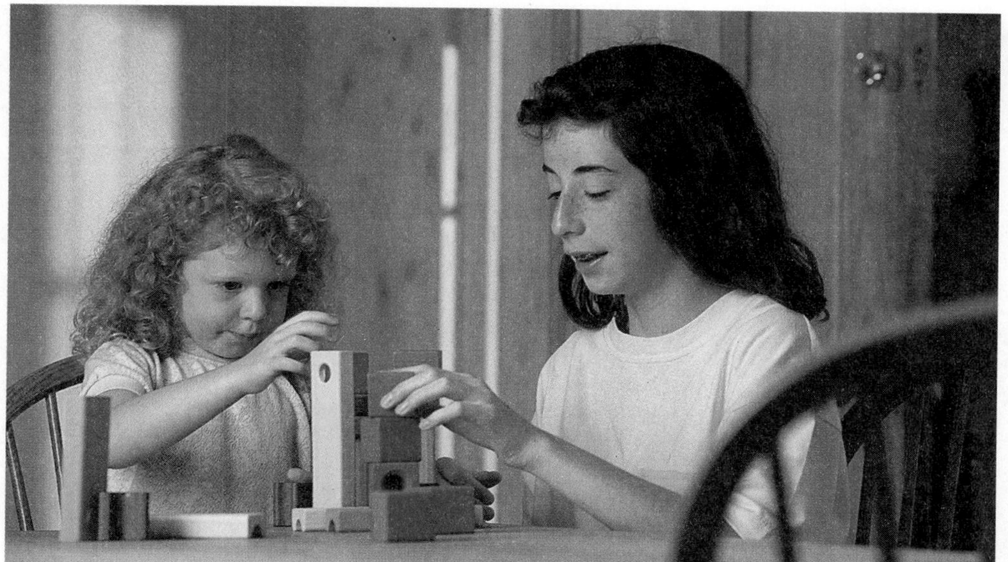

Both older and younger children benefit from mixed-age interactions.

Same-Age (or Equal-Status) Contacts

We gain some idea of why peer contacts among age-mates may be important by contrasting them to exchanges that occur at home. A child's interactions with parents and older siblings are rarely equal-status contacts; typically, children are placed in a subordinate position by an older member of the family who instructs them, issues orders, or otherwise oversees their activities. By contrast, age-mates are much less critical and directive, and children are freer to try out new roles, ideas, and behaviors when interacting with someone of similar status. And in so doing, they are likely to learn important lessons about themselves and others, such as "She quits when I don't take turns," "He hits me when I push him," or "Nobody likes a cheater." Many theorists believe that peer contacts are important precisely because they are *equal-status* contacts—that is, they teach children to understand and appreciate the perspectives of people *just like themselves* and thereby contribute to the development of social competencies that are difficult to acquire in the nonegalitarian atmosphere of the home.

Mixed-Age Interactions

According to Hartup (1983), interaction among children of *different* ages is also a critically important context for development. Although cross-age interactions tend to be somewhat *asymmetrical,* with one child (typically the elder) possessing more power than the other, these asymmetries may help children to acquire certain social competencies. One cross-cultural survey revealed that the presence of younger peers fostered the development of compassion, caregiving, and prosocial inclinations, assertiveness, and leadership skills in older children (Whiting & Edwards, 1988). At the same time, younger children benefitted from mixed-age interactions by acquiring a variety of new skills from older playmates and learning how to seek assistance from and defer gracefully to these more powerful associates. Older children usually took charge of mixed-age interactions and adjusted their behavior to the competencies of their younger companions (see also Brody, Graziano, & Musser, 1983; Graziano et al., 1976). Even 2-year-olds show such powers of leadership and accommodation, for they are more inclined to take the initiative and to display simpler and more repetitive play routines when paired with an 18-month-old toddler than with an age-mate (Brownell, 1990).

Perhaps you have noticed that mixed-age peer interactions seem to benefit older and younger children in many of the same ways that sibling interactions benefit older and younger siblings (see Chapter 15). But there is a crucial difference between sibling and peer contacts, for one's standing as either a younger or an older sibling is *fixed* by order of birth, whereas one's position among peers is more *flexible,* depending on the associates one chooses. Thus, mixed-age *peer* interactions may provide children with experiences that they might otherwise miss in their mixed-age sibling interactions and, in fact, may be the primary context in which (1) an habitually domineering elder sibling learns to be more accommodating (when interacting with older peers), (2) an oppressed younger sib learns to lead and to show compassion (when dealing with even younger children), and (3) an only child (who has no sibs) acquires both sets of social competencies. Viewed in this way, mixed-age peer associations may be important experiences indeed.

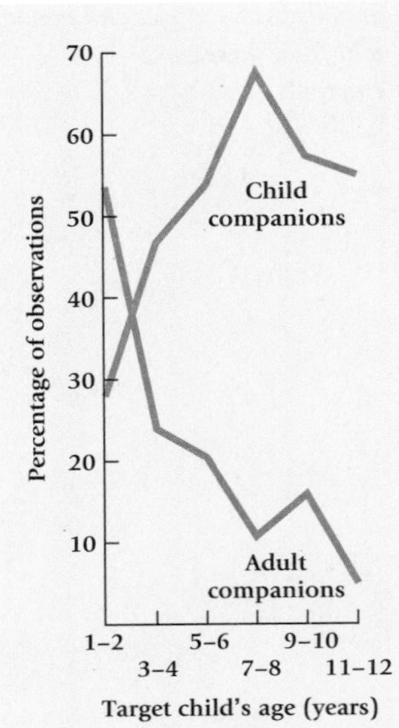

Figure 16.8 *Developmental changes in children's companionship with adults and other children.* ADAPTED FROM ELLIS, ROGOFF, & CROMER, 1981.

Frequency of Peer Contacts

Between the ages of 2 and 12, children spend more and more time with peers and less and less time with adults. This trend is illustrated in Figure 16.8, which summarizes what Sherri Ellis and her colleagues (1981) found while observing 436 children playing in their homes and around the neighborhood. Interestingly, this same study revealed that youngsters of all ages spent *less* time with age-mates (defined as children whose ages were within a year of their own) than with children who were more than a year older or younger than they were. Apparently, we must take seriously the idea that peers are "social equals" rather than age-mates.

Another finding of this study is a familiar one: Even 1- to 2-year-olds played more often with same-sex companions than with other-sex companions, and this *gender segregation* increased with age. Once in their sex-segregated worlds, boys and girls experience different kinds of social relationships. Boys tend to form "packs," whereas girls form "pairs"; that is, a boy often plays competitive games or team sports in groups, whereas a girl more often establishes a longer and more cooperative relationship with one playmate (Archer, 1992; Benenson, Apostoleris, & Parnass, 1997).

Overall, then, children spend an increasing amount of time with peers, and those peers are typically *same*-sex children who are only *roughly similar* in age but who enjoy the same kinds of gender-typed activities.

How Important Are Peer Influences?

To this point, we have speculated that peer interactions may foster many social and personal competencies that are not easily acquired within nonegalitarian parent–child or sibling–sibling relationships. Is there truly any basis for such a claim? And if so, just how important are these peer influences? Developmentalists became very interested in these questions once they learned of Harry Harlow's research with rhesus monkeys.

HARLOW'S WORK WITH MONKEYS. If youngsters have little or no contact with peers, will they turn out to be abnormal or maladjusted? To find out, Harlow and his associates (Alexander & Harlow, 1965; Suomi & Harlow, 1978) raised groups of rhesus monkeys with their mothers and denied them the opportunity to play with peers. These "**mother-only" monkeys** failed to develop normal patterns of social behavior. When finally exposed to age-mates, the peer-deprived youngsters preferred to avoid them. On those occasions when they did approach a peer, these social misfits tended to be highly (and inappropriately) aggressive, and their antisocial tendencies often persisted into adulthood.

Monkeys raised only with peers form strong mutual attachments and often attack other monkeys from outside their peer group.

Is peer contact the key to normal social development? Not entirely. In later experiments, Harlow and his colleagues separated rhesus monkey infants from their mothers and raised them so that they had continuous exposure to peers. These "**peer-only" monkeys** were observed to cling tenaciously to one another and to form strong mutual attachments. Yet their social development was somewhat atypical in that they became highly agitated over minor stresses or frustrations (see also Higley et al., 1992), and as adults they were unusually aggressive toward monkeys from outside their peer groups.

A Human Parallel. In 1951, Anna Freud and Sophie Dann reported a startling human parallel to Harlow's peer-only monkeys. During the summer of 1945, six 3-year-olds were found living by themselves in a Nazi concentration camp. By the time these children were 12 months old, their parents had been put to death. Although they received minimal caregiving from a series of inmates who were periodically executed, these children had, in effect, reared themselves.

When rescued at the war's end, the six orphans were flown to a treatment center in England, where attempts were made to "rehabilitate" them. How did these "peer-only" children respond to this treatment? They began by breaking nearly all their toys, damaging their furniture, and displaying cold indifference or open hostility toward the staff at the center. Like Harlow's peer-only monkeys, these children were strongly attached to each other and often became upset when separated from other members of the group, even for brief periods. They also showed a remarkable prosocial concern for one another:

> There was no occasion to urge the children to "take turns"; they did it spontaneously. They were extremely considerate of each other's feelings. . . . At mealtimes handing food to the neighbor was of greater importance than eating oneself (Freud & Dann, 1951, pp. 132–133).

Although these youngsters displayed many signs of anxiety and were highly suspicious of outsiders, they eventually established positive relationships with their adult caregivers and acquired a new language during their first year at the center. The story even has a happy ending, for 35 years later, these orphans were leading productive lives as middle-aged adults (Hartup, 1983).

Taken together, Harlow's monkey research and Freud and Dann's observations of their war orphans suggest that parents and peers each contribute something essential but different and perhaps unique to a child's (or a monkey's) social development. Regular contacts with sensitive, responsive parents not only permit infants to acquire some basic social interactive skills, but also provide a sense of *security* that enables them to venture forth to explore the environment and to discover that other people can be interesting companions (Hartup, 1989; Higley et al., 1992). By contrast, later contacts with peers may allow children to elaborate their basic social skills, acquiring increasingly competent and adaptive patterns of social behavior with associates who are more or less similar to themselves. Indeed, Harlow's "peer-only" monkeys lacked the security of a mother–infant relationship, perhaps explaining why they clutched at one another, were reluctant to explore, and were terrified by (and aggressive toward) outsiders. But *within their own peer groups,* they developed competent interactive routines and displayed normal patterns of social behavior (Suomi & Harlow, 1978).

Just how important is it for humans to establish and maintain *harmonious* relations with their peers? Apparently, it is very important. One review of more than 30 studies revealed that youngsters who had been rejected by their peers during grade school are much more likely than those who had enjoyed good peer relations to drop out of school, become involved in delinquent or criminal activities, and display serious psychological difficulties later in adolescence and young adulthood (Parker & Asher, 1987; Parker et al., 1995; see also Crick, 1996, 1997; Morison & Masten, 1991). So merely having contact with peer associates is not enough to ensure positive developmental outcomes; getting along with peers is important, too.

In sum, peers do seem to be meaningful agents of socialization, and the task of becoming *appropriately* sociable with peers is a most important developmental hurdle. In our next section, we will focus on the growth of peer sociability and on some of the factors that influence how appropriately (or inappropriately) sociable a child turns out to be.

"mother-only" monkeys
monkeys who are raised with their mothers and denied any contact with peers.

"peer-only" monkeys
monkeys who are separated from their mothers (and other adults) soon after birth and raised with peers.

The Development of Peer Sociability

Sociability is a term that describes a person's willingness to engage others in social interaction and to seek their attention or approval. In Chapter 11, we learned that even young infants are sociable creatures: Months before forming their first attachments,

sociability
willingness to interact with others and to seek their attention or approval.

they are already smiling, cooing, or otherwise trying to attract the attention of caregivers and are likely to protest whenever *any* adult puts them down or walks off and leaves them alone. But would they be so positively disposed to a peer?

Peer Sociability in Infancy and Toddlerhood

Although babies show an interest in other babies from the first months of life, they do not really *interact* until about the middle of the first year. By then, infants often smile or babble at their tiny companions, vocalize, offer toys, and gesture to one another (Vandell & Mueller, 1995; Vandell, Wilson, & Buchanan, 1980). However, many of these friendly gestures go unnoticed and unreciprocated.

Between 12 and 18 months of age, toddlers begin to react more appropriately to each other's behavior. Yet, there is some question about whether these action/reaction episodes qualify as true social discourse, for 12- to 18-month-olds often seem to treat peers as particularly responsive "toys" that they can control by making them look, gesture, smile, and laugh (Brownell, 1986).

By 18 months of age, however, almost all toddlers begin to display *coordinated interactions* with age-mates that are clearly social in character. They now take great delight in *imitating* each other and often gaze and smile at their partners as they turn their imitative sequences into social games (Eckerman & Stein, 1990; Howes & Matheson, 1992). By age 20 to 24 months, toddlers' play has a strong verbal component: Playmates often describe their ongoing play activities to each other ("I fall down!" "Me too, I fall down") or attempt to influence the role that their partner should assume ("You go in playhouse") (Eckerman & Didow, 1996). This coordinated social speech makes it easier for 2- to 2½-year-olds to assume *complementary roles,* such as chaser or chasee in a game of tag, or to cooperate to achieve a shared goal, as illustrated by one child's operating a handle, thereby enabling the second to retrieve attractive toys from a container (Brownell & Carriger, 1990).

Both social and cognitive developments contribute to the growth of peer sociability over the first 2 years. In Chapter 11, we learned that toddlers who are securely attached to their caregivers are generally more outgoing and even more "popular" as playmates than those who are insecurely attached, implying that the sensitive, responsive caregiving that securely attached infants receive contributes in a positive way to development of social skills. And 18- to 24-month-olds begin to display truly coordinated, reciprocal interactions at precisely the time that they first recognize themselves in a mirror and can discriminate photographs of themselves from those of peers (see

With age, toddlers' interactions with one another become increasingly skilled and reciprocal.

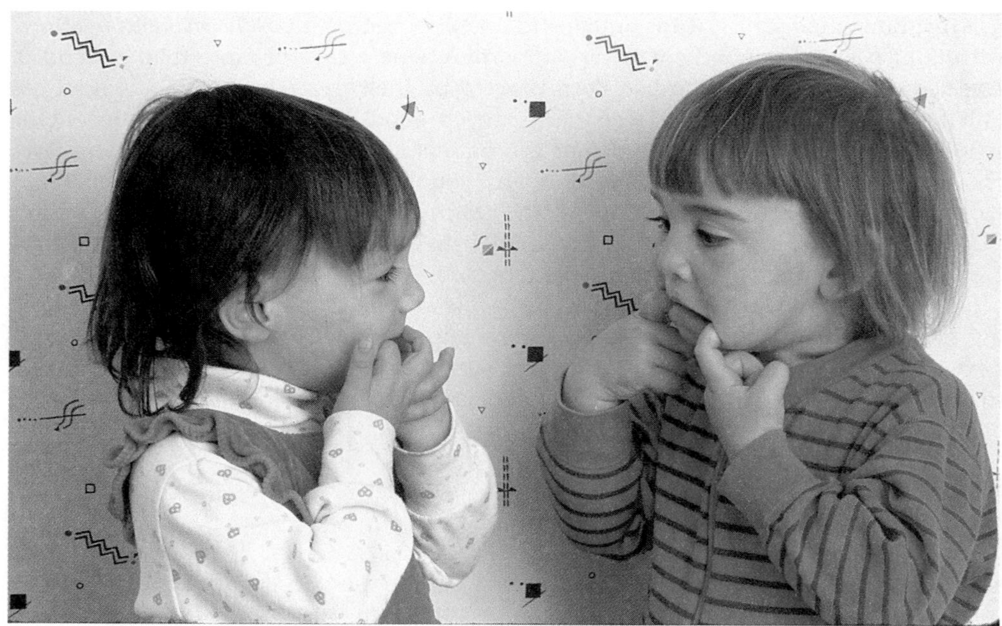

Chapter 12). This may be no accident. Celia Brownell and Michael Carriger (1990) propose that toddlers must first realize that both they and their companions are autonomous causal agents who can make things happen before they are likely to play complementary games or try to coordinate their actions to accomplish a goal. Indeed, they found that toddlers who cooperated successfully to achieve a goal scored higher on a test of self–other differentiation than their less cooperative age-mates, thus implying that early interactive skills may depend heavily on social-cognitive development.

Sociability during the Preschool Period

Between the ages of 2 and 5, children not only become more outgoing but also direct their social gestures to a wider audience. Observational studies suggest that 2- to 3-year-olds are more likely than older children to remain near an adult and to seek physical affection, whereas the sociable behaviors of 4- to 5-year-olds normally consist of playful bids for attention or approval that are directed at *peers* rather than adults (Harper & Huie, 1985; Hartup, 1983).

As children become more peer oriented during the preschool years, the character of their interactions changes as well. In a classic study, Mildred Parten (1932) observed 2½- to 4-year-olds during free-play periods at nursery school, looking for developmental changes in the *social complexity* of peer interactions. She found that preschoolers' play activities could be divided into four categories, arranged from least to most socially complex:

1. **Nonsocial activity.** Children watch others play or engage in their own solitary play and largely ignore what others are doing.
2. **Parallel play.** Children play side by side but interact very little and do not try to influence the behavior of other players.
3. **Associative play.** Children now share toys and swap materials, but pursue their own agendas and do not cooperate to achieve shared goals.
4. **Cooperative play.** Children now act out make-believe themes, assume reciprocal roles, and collaborate to achieve shared goals.

nonsocial activity
onlooker behavior and solitary play.

parallel play
largely noninteractive play in which players are in close proximity but do not often attempt to influence each other.

associative play
form of social discourse in which children pursue their own interests but swap toys or comment on each other's activities.

cooperative play
true social play in which children cooperate or assume reciprocal roles while pursuing shared goals.

As we see in Figure 16.9, solitary and parallel play decline with age, whereas associative and cooperative play become more common. However, all four kinds of play were observed among children of *all* ages, and even a nonsocial activity like solitary play need not be considered "immature" if the child is doing something constructive such as drawing pictures or completing a puzzle (Hartup, 1983).

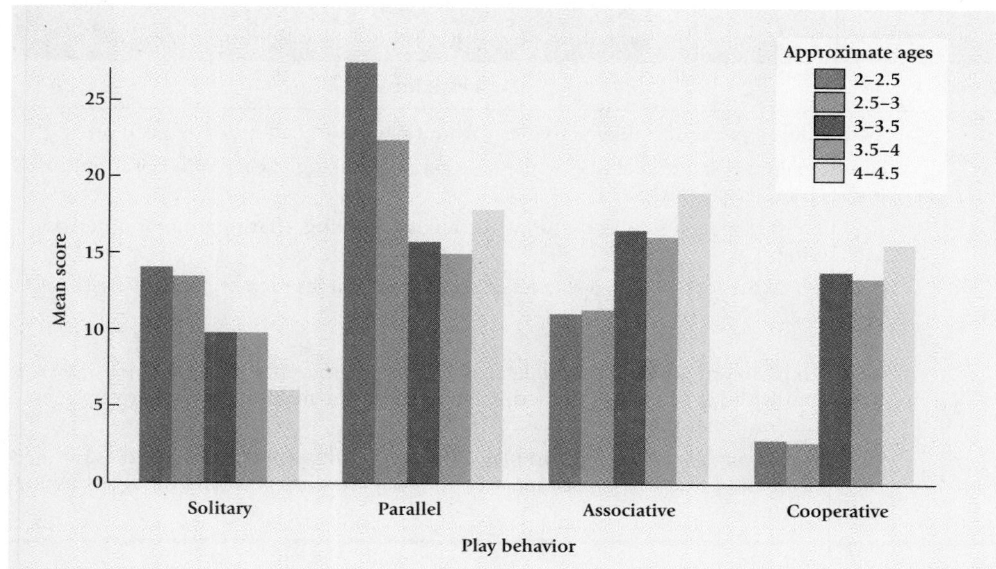

Figure 16.9 *Frequency of activities engaged in by preschool children of different ages. With age, solitary and parallel play occur less frequently, whereas associative and cooperative play occur more frequently.* ADAPTED FROM PARTEN, *1932.*

Could it be, then, that the "maturity" of preschool play depends as much (or more) on its *cognitive complexity* as on its social or nonsocial character? Indeed, it could, and the cognitive and social characteristics of preschool play are clearly interrelated. In a longitudinal study in which the play activities of a group of 1- to 2-year-olds were observed at 6-month intervals for 3 years, Carolee Howes and Catherine Matheson (1992) found that play became more and more cognitively complex with age, as described by the six-category sequence in Table 16.2. What's more, there was a clear relationship between the complexity of a child's play and the child's social competence with peers: Children whose play was more complex at any given age were rated as more outgoing and prosocially inclined and as less aggressive and withdrawn at the next observation period 6 months later. So it seems that the *cognitive complexity* of a child's play (particularly pretend play) is a reliable predictor of his or her future social competencies with peers (see also Doyle et al., 1992; Rubin, Fein, & Vandenberg, 1983).

Peer Sociability in Middle Childhood and Adolescence

Peer interactions become increasingly sophisticated throughout the grade-school years. Not only do cooperative forms of complex pretend play become more commonplace, but, by age 6 to 10, children are becoming enthusiastic participants in games (such as tee-ball and *Monopoly*) that are governed by formal sets of rules (Hartup, 1983; Piaget, 1965).

Another very noticeable way that peer interactions change during middle childhood is that contacts among 6- to 10-year-olds more often occur in true **peer groups.** When psychologists talk about peer groups, they are referring not merely to a collection of playmates but, rather, to a true confederation that (1) interacts on a regular basis, (2) defines a sense of belonging, (3) formulates its own *norms* that specify how members are supposed to dress, think, and behave, and (4) develops a structure or hierarchical organization (for example, leader and other roles) that enables group members to work together toward the accomplishment of shared goals. Furthermore, elementary school children clearly *identify* with their groups: being a Brownie, a "Blue Knight," or "one of Smitty's gang" is often a source of great personal pride. So between ages 6 and 10, children expose themselves to a most potent social context—the *peer group*—in which they are likely to discover the value of teamwork, develop a sense of commitment and loyalty to shared goals, and learn a number of other important lessons about how social organizations pursue their objectives (Hartup, 1983; Sherif et al., 1961).

peer group
a confederation of peers that interacts regularly, defines membership in the group, and formulates norms that specify how members are supposed to look, think, and act.

clique
a small group of friends that interacts frequently.

By early adolescence, youngsters spend more time with peers, particularly with small groups of close friends known as **cliques,** than with parents, siblings, or any other agent of socialization (Berndt, 1989; Larson & Richards, 1991). Early peer cliques

TABLE 16.2 **Changes in Play Activities from Infancy through the Preschool Period**

Play type	Age of appearance	Description
Parallel play	6–12 months	Two children perform similar activities without paying any attention to each other.
Parallel aware play	By age 1	Children engage in parallel play while occasionally looking at each other or monitoring each other's activities.
Simple pretend play	1–1½ years	Children engage in similar activities while talking, smiling, sharing toys, or otherwise interacting.
Complementary and reciprocal play	1½–2 years	Children display action-based role reversals in social games such as run-and-chase or peekaboo.
Cooperative social pretend play	2½–3 years	Children play complementary *nonliteral,* or "pretend," roles (for example, mommy and baby), but without any planning or discussion about the meaning of these roles or about the form that the play will take.
Complex social pretend play	3½–4 years	Children actively *plan* their pretend play. They name and explicitly assign roles for each player and propose a play script, and may stop playing to modify the script if play breaks down.

SOURCE: Adapted from Howes & Matheson, 1992.

Young adolescents spend more time socializing with their peers than with their parents or siblings. Much time is spent with small numbers of same-sex associates who genuinely like each other and prefer similar activities. These same-sex cliques often evolve into mixed-sex (heterosexual) cliques by mid-adolescence.

usually consist of four to eight *same-sex* members who share similar values and activity preferences; but by midadolescence, boy cliques and girl cliques begin to interact more frequently, eventually forming *heterosexual cliques* (Dunphy, 1963; Richards et al., 1998). Once formed, cliques often develop distinct and colorful dress codes, dialects, and behaviors that set the cliques apart and help members establish a firm sense of belongingness, or a group identity (Cairns et al., 1995).

Often, several cliques with similar norms and values coalesce into larger, more loosely organized aggregations known as **crowds.** Crowds do not replace cliques; membership in a crowd is based on reputation, and individual members within a particular clique may even belong to different crowds (Urberg et al., 1995). Crowds come into play mainly as a mechanism for defining an adolescent's niche within the larger social structure of a high school and, occasionally, for organizing such social activities as parties, trips to the football game, and so on. The names may vary, but most schools have crowds of "brains," "populars," "jocks," "druggies," and "burnouts," each consisting of a loose aggregation of cliques that are similar to one another in some fundamental way (Brown et al., 1993; Brown & Lohr, 1987).

Not only do cliques and crowds permit adolescents to express their values and try out new roles as they begin their quest to forge an identity apart from their families, but they also pave the way for the establishment of dating relationships (Brown, 1990; Dunphy, 1963). Gender segregation usually breaks down early in adolescence as members of boys' and girls' cliques begin to interact. Same-sex cliques provide what amounts to a secure base for exploring ways to behave with members of the other sex; talking to girls when your buddies are there is far less threatening than doing so on your own. And as heterosexual cliques and crowds take shape, adolescents are likely to have many opportunities to get to know members of the other sex in casual social situations, without having to be intimate. Eventually, strong cross-sex friendships develop and couples form, often double-dating or spending time with a small number of other couples. At this point, cliques and crowds gradually begin to disintegrate, having served their purposes of helping adolescents to establish a social identity and bringing the boys and girls together (Brown, 1990; Dunphy, 1963).

Parental Effects on Peer Sociability

Some children are drawn to peers and seem to thrive on social interaction, whereas others appear rather unsociable or even withdrawn. Although we learned in Chapter 11 that sociability is influenced to some extent by one's genotype, it is also clear that the path to positive or negative peer relations often begins at home and that parents may either foster or inhibit peer sociability.

Promoting Peer Contacts. There are many ways in which parents may influence the sheer amount of contact their children have with peers. Their choice of a residence is one such influence: A decision to live in a neighborhood with widely spaced homes and few available playgrounds or playmates could seriously restrict access to peers.

crowd
a large, loosely organized peer group made up of several cliques that share similar norms, interests, and values.

When young children cannot easily get together on their own, their contact with peers depends heavily on whether their parents serve as "booking agents" for peer interaction—whether parents arrange visits with playmates, enroll their children in day-care or nursery school, or encourage their participation in other organized activities for children (Hart et al., 1997; Parke & Kellum, 1994). As we noted earlier in Box 16.2, children who receive good day-care or attend nursery schools that emphasize a social curriculum tend to develop social skills at an earlier age than those who remain at home. Why? Although the guidance offered by nursery school teachers and day-care providers undoubtedly plays a part in improving children's social skills (Howes, Hamilton, & Matheson, 1994), children may also become more outgoing with day-care or nursery-school classmates because they have gotten to know them better. Indeed, preschoolers' play is much more cooperative, complex, and socially skilled among familiar companions than among strangers (Brody et al., 1983; Doyle, Connolly, & Rivest, 1980; Harper & Huie, 1985).

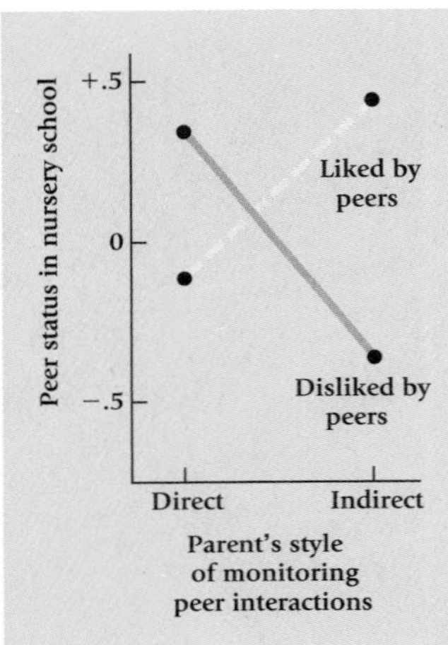

Figure 16.10 *Nursery school children enjoy a more favorable status with peers when parents have indirectly monitored their interactions with playmates.*
Based on Ladd & Golter, 1988.

Monitoring and Controlling Play Activities. Of course, parents who arrange home visits with peer playmates are also in a position to influence their child by monitoring his or her peer interactions to ensure that play proceeds smoothly and amiably, without major conflicts. This brings us to an interesting issue.

Should parents closely monitor or intrude upon playful interactions between young children? Gary Ladd and Beckie Golter (1988) attempted to answer this question by asking parents of preschool children how they had supervised any recent interactions that their child had had with peers at home. Some parents reported that they had closely watched over the children or had even participated in their play activities (direct monitoring), whereas others said they had checked occasionally on the children without often intruding or becoming involved as a playmate (indirect monitoring). Which form of monitoring is associated with successful and harmonious peer interactions? Ladd and Golter's findings clearly favor indirect parental monitoring. As we see in Figure 16.10, preschoolers whose parents had indirectly monitored their peer interactions were much better liked (and less often disliked) by their nursery school classmates than those whose parents closely monitored and often intruded on their play activities.

Interestingly, mothers who believe that their children are not very socially skilled are most likely to intrude in their children's play activities—a finding which implies that conflictual peer interactions may promote direct monitoring rather than the other way around (Mize, Pettit, & Brown, 1995). Nevertheless, the quality of monitoring and intervention that parents provide clearly matters. If a parent's coaching is supportive and optimistic and focuses heavily on prosocial strategies, the child often displays more harmonious interactions with peers (Mize & Pettit, 1997; Russell & Finnie, 1990). By contrast, parents who become agitated and issue commands rather than constructive solutions usually elicit negative responses from their children, who continue to display poor social skills and nonharmonious peer interactions (Carson & Parke, 1996; Russell & Finnie, 1990). A negative and controlling parent who is always barking orders may inhibit sociability by simply taking all the fun out of play activities. Or, alternatively, these parents may be teaching their children to be bossy and dictatorial themselves, a style that is likely to elicit negative reactions from playmates and convince the child that contacts with peers are not all that pleasant (Kochanska, 1992; Russell & Finney, 1990).

In sum, parents of appropriately sociable preschool children tend to be warm, accepting companions who (1) indirectly monitor their children's interactions with peers to ensure that they comply with rules of social etiquette while (2) allowing children considerable freedom to structure their own play activities and to resolve minor disputes on their own (Ladd & Hart, 1992). Clearly, this pattern of warmth, sensitivity, and moderate control sounds very much like the *authoritative* pattern of child-rearing that we have commented favorably upon throughout the text—a pattern that is consistently associated with children's socially skilled behaviors and acceptance by peers (Baumrind, 1971; Hinshaw et al., 1997; Mize & Pettit, 1997). By contrast, highly authoritarian (or uninvolved) parents who rely heavily on power assertion as a control tactic tend to raise youngsters who are often aggressive or otherwise socially unskilled when interacting with other children and are likely to be *rejected* by peers (Dekovic & Janssens, 1992; Hart et al., 1998; MacKinnon-Lewis et al., 1994). So there is ample evidence that the path to positive (or negative) peer interactions often begins at home. As Putallaz and Heflin have noted:

> Parental involvement, warmth, and moderate control appear to be important [to] children's social competence. Within the social context of the family, children appear to learn certain interactional skills and behaviors that then transfer to their interactions with peers (1990, p. 204).

Peer Acceptance and Popularity

Perhaps no other aspect of children's social lives has received more attention than **peer acceptance:** the extent to which a child is viewed by peers as a worthy or likable companion. Typically, researchers assess peer acceptance through self-report instruments called **sociometric techniques.** In a sociometric survey, children might be asked to nominate several classmates whom they like and several whom they dislike; or they may be asked to rate each of their classmates with respect to their desirability as social companions (Terry & Coie, 1991). Even 3- to 5-year-olds can respond appropriately to sociometric surveys (Denham et al., 1990); and the choices (or ratings) that children provide correspond reasonably well to teacher ratings of peer popularity, thus suggesting that sociometric surveys provide *valid* assessments of children's social standing in their peer groups (Hymel, 1983).

When sociometric data are analyzed, it is usually possible to classify each child into one of the following categories: **popular children,** who are liked by many peers and disliked by few; **rejected children,** who are disliked by many peers and liked by a few; **neglected children,** who receive very few nominations as a liked or a disliked companion and who seem almost invisible to their peers; and **controversial children,** who are liked by many peers but disliked by many others. Together, these four types of children make up about two-thirds of the pupils in a typical elementary school classroom; the remaining one-third are **average-status children,** who are liked (or disliked) by a moderate number of peers (Coie, Dodge, & Coppotelli, 1982).

Notice that both neglected children and rejected children are low in acceptance and are not well received by their peers. Yet it is not nearly so bad to be ignored by other children as to be rejected by them. Neglectees do not feel as lonely as rejectees do (Cassidy & Asher, 1992; Crick & Ladd, 1993), and they are much more likely than rejected children to eventually attain a more favorable sociometric status should they enter a new class at school or a new play group (Coie & Dodge, 1983). Furthermore, rejected children are the ones who face the greater risk of displaying deviant, antisocial behavior and other serious adjustment problems later in life (Asher & Coie, 1990; Morison & Masten, 1991; Parker & Asher, 1987).

peer acceptance
a measure of a person's likability (or dislikability) in the eyes of peers.

sociometric techniques
procedures that ask children to identify those peers whom they like or dislike or to rate peers for their desirability as companions; used to measure children's peer acceptance (or nonacceptance).

popular children
children who are liked by any members of their peer group and disliked by very few.

rejected children
children who are disliked by many peers and liked by few.

neglected children
children who receive few nominations as either a liked or a disliked individual from members of their peer group.

controversial children
children who receive many nominations by peers as a liked individual and many as a disliked individual.

average-status children
children who receive a moderate number of nominations as a liked and/or a disliked individual from members of their peer group.

Calvin and Hobbes by Bill Watterson

Why Are Children Accepted, Neglected, or Rejected by Peers?

At several points throughout the text, we have discussed factors that seem to contribute to children's popularity with peers. By way of brief review:

Parenting Styles. Warm, sensitive, and authoritative parents who rely on reasoning rather than power to guide and control children's conduct tend to raise youngsters who are *liked* by adults and peers. By contrast, highly authoritarian and/or uninvolved parents who rely heavily on power assertion as a control tactic often have youngsters who are surly, uncooperative, and aggressive, and are actively *disliked* by peers.

The fact that parents influence their children's social skills implies that the long-term adjustment problems that many rejected children display may stem as much from a rejectee's disordered home life as from poor peer relations. Nevertheless, we will see that rejected youngsters' patterns of social interaction often alienate peers and elicit negative reactions that can perpetuate and even intensify the problems that these children display.

Cognitive Skills. Popular children tend to have well-developed role-taking skills (LeMare & Rubin, 1987). Popular, average-status, and neglected youngsters also tend to perform better academically and to score higher on IQ tests than rejected children and adolescents do (Bukowski et al., 1993; Chen, Rubin, & Li, 1997; Wentzel & Asher, 1995).

At least two additional characteristics seem to reliably predict children's standing among their peers: their physical attractiveness (particularly facial attractiveness) and their patterns of interpersonal behavior.

Facial Attractiveness. Despite the maxim that "beauty is only skin deep," many of us seem to think otherwise. Even 6-month-old infants can easily discriminate attractive from unattractive faces (Langlois et al., 1991), and 12-month-old infants already prefer to interact with attractive rather than unattractive strangers (Langlois, Roggman, & Rieser-Danner, 1990). By the preschool period, attractive youngsters are often described in more favorable ways (that is, friendlier, smarter) than their less attractive classmates by both teachers and peers (Adams & Crane, 1980; Langlois, 1986), and attractive children are generally more popular than unattractive children from elementary school onward (Langlois, 1986). This link between facial attractiveness and peer acceptance even begins to make some sense when we consider how attractive and unattractive children interact with their playmates. Although attractive and unattractive 3-year-olds do not yet differ a great deal in the character of their social behaviors, by age 5, unattractive youngsters are more likely than attractive ones to be active and boisterous during play sessions and to respond aggressively toward peers (Langlois & Downs, 1979). So unattractive children seem to develop patterns of social interaction that could alienate other children.

Why might this happen? Some theorists have argued that parents, teachers, and other children may contribute to a self-fulfilling prophecy by subtly (or not so subtly) communicating their expectancies to attractive youngsters, letting them know that they are smart and are supposed to do well in school, behave pleasantly, and be likable. Information of this sort undoubtedly has an effect on children: Attractive youngsters may become progressively more confident, friendly, and outgoing, whereas unattractive children may resent the less favorable feedback that they receive and become more defiant and aggressive. This is precisely how a "beautiful is good" stereotype could become a reality (Langlois & Downs, 1979).

Behavioral Contributors. Although one's physical characteristics and cognitive/scholastic/athletic prowess are all meaningfully related to peer acceptance, even the brightest and most attractive children may be unpopular if peers consider their behavior inappropriate or antisocial (Dodge, 1983). What behavioral characteristics are most important in influencing a child's standing with peers?

Several studies of preschool, elementary, and middle school (young adolescent) children report pretty much the same findings. *Popular* children are observed to be relatively calm, outgoing, friendly, and supportive companions who can successfully initiate and maintain interactions and resolve disputes amicably (Coie, Dodge, & Kupersmidt, 1990; Denham et al., 1990; Ladd, Price, & Hart, 1988). Stated another way, these "sociometric stars" are warm, cooperative, and compassionate individuals who display many prosocial behaviors and are seldom disruptive or aggressive (Newcomb, Bukowski, & Pattee, 1993; Parkhurst & Asher, 1992).

Neglected children, by contrast, often appear shy or withdrawn. They are not very talkative; they make fewer attempts than children of average status to enter play groups; and they seldom call attention to themselves (Coie et al., 1990; Harrist et al., 1997). Nevertheless, these "neglectees" are no less socially skilled than children of average status; nor are they any more lonely or more distressed about the character of their social relationships (Cassidy & Asher, 1992; Wentzel & Asher, 1995). Their withdrawn behavior appears to stem more from their own social anxieties and their beliefs that they are not socially skilled than from any active ostracism or exclusion by their peer groups (Cassidy & Asher, 1992; Younger & Daniels, 1992).

There are at least two kinds, or categories, of *rejected* children, each with a distinct behavioral profile. **Rejected-aggressive children** often alienate peers by using forceful means to dominate them or their resources. These disruptive braggarts tend to be uncooperative and critical of peer group activities and display very low levels of prosocial behavior (Newcomb et al., 1993; Parkhurst & Asher, 1992). Rejected-aggressive children are prone to interpret others' behavior as hostile, even when it isn't; yet, they clearly overestimate their social standing, often saying that they are liked just as well as, or better than, most children (Zakriski & Coie, 1996). These are the youngsters who display the greatest risk of becoming chronically hostile and displaying externalizing conduct disorders and even criminal acts of violence later in adolescence and adulthood (Crick & Ladd, 1993; Parker & Asher, 1987).

Rejected-withdrawn children, on the other hand, are typically socially awkward companions who display many unusual and immature behaviors and are insensitive to peer group expectations. Unlike rejected-aggressive children, they are well aware that other children do not like them and eventually begin to withdraw as peers actively exclude them from their activities (Harrist et al., 1997; Hymel, Bowker, & Woody, 1993; Zakriski & Coie, 1996). These withdrawn rejectees feel especially lonely and are at risk of experiencing low self-esteem, depression, and other emotional disorders (Hymel et al., 1993; Rabiner, Keane, & MacKinnon-Lewis, 1993). And because of their unusual behaviors, hypersensitivity to criticism, and lack of close friends to stick up for them, they are particularly inviting targets for abuse at the hands of bullies (Hodges et al., 1997; Parkhurst & Asher, 1992).

Do popular children become popular because they are friendly, cooperative, and nonaggressive? Or is it that children become friendlier, more cooperative, and less aggressive after achieving their popularity? One way to test these competing hypotheses is to place children in play groups with *unfamiliar* peers and then see whether the behaviors they display predict their eventual status in the peer group. Several studies of this type have been conducted (Coie & Kupersmidt, 1983; Dodge, 1983; Dodge et al., 1990; Ladd et al., 1988), and the results are reasonably consistent: The patterns of behavior that children display predict the statuses they achieve with their peers. Children who are ultimately accepted by unfamiliar peers are effective at initiating social interactions and at responding positively to others' bids for attention. When they want to join a group activity, for example, these socially skilled, *soon-to-be-accepted* children first watch and attempt to understand what is going on, and then comment constructively about the proceedings as they blend smoothly into the group. By contrast, children who are ultimately *rejected* are pushy and self-serving; they often criticize or disrupt group activities and may even threaten reprisals if they are not allowed to join in. Other children who end up being *neglected* by their peers tend to hover around the edges of a group, initiating few interactions and shying away from other children's bids for attention.

In sum, peer popularity is affected by many factors. It may help to have an attractive face and academic skills, but it is even more important to display good social-cognitive

rejected-aggressive children
a subgroup of rejected children who display high levels of hostility and aggression in their interactions with peers.

rejected-withdrawn children
a subgroup of rejected children who are often passive, socially unskilled, and insensitive to peer-group expectations.

skills and to behave in socially competent ways. Definitions of desirable social behavior, of course, may vary from culture to culture and change over time. In Box 11.1, for example, we learned that shyness, which may undermine one's popularity in Western societies, actually promotes peer acceptance in China, where being quiet and reserved are more socially desirable traits. The ingredients of popularity also change with age: Although establishing close relationships with members of the other sex enhances popularity during adolescence, frequent consorting with "the enemy" violates norms of gender segregation during childhood and *detracts* from one's popularity (Kovacs et al., 1996; Sroufe et al., 1993). In short, contextual factors influence who is popular and who is not.

Unfortunately, children who are rejected by peers are likely to retain their rejected status throughout their school years and are at risk of experiencing some (or all) of the adjustment problems associated with peer rejection (Cillessen et al., 1992; Coie et al., 1990). In Box 16.3, we will examine some of the programs that have helped rejected children to improve their social skills and their prospects for experiencing healthier psychological outcomes.

Children and Their Friends

As young children become more outgoing and are exposed to a wider variety of peers, they typically form close ties to one or more playmates—bonds that we call **friendships.** Recall from Chapter 12 that children have some pretty firm ideas about what qualifies someone as a friend. Before age 8, the principal basis for friendship is *common activity:* Children view a friend as someone who likes them and who enjoys similar kinds of play activities. By contrast, 8- to 10-year-olds, equipped with more sophisticated social perspective-taking skills, begin to see friends as individuals who are *psychologically similar* and who can be trusted to be loyal, kind, cooperative, and sensitive to each other's feelings and needs (Berndt, 1989; Pataki, Shapiro, & Clark, 1994). And although adolescents continue to think that loyalty and shared psychological attributes are characteristics that friends display, their conceptions of friendship now focus more on *reciprocal emotional commitments.* That is, friends are viewed as *intimate* associates who truly understand each other's strengths and accept each other's weaknesses and are willing to share their innermost thoughts and feelings (Hartup, 1992).

Social Interactions among Friends and Acquaintances

As early as age 1 to 2, children may become attached to a preferred play partner and respond very differently to these "friends" than to other playmates (Hartup, 1992). For example, friends display more advanced forms of pretend play than acquaintances do, as well as more affection and more approval (Howes, Droege, & Matheson, 1994; Whaley & Rubenstein, 1994). Friends often do nice things for each other, and many altruistic behaviors may first appear within these early alliances of the preschool era. Frederick Kanfer and his associates (1981), for example, found that 3- to 6-year-olds were generally willing to give up their own valuable play time to perform a dull task if their efforts would benefit a friend; yet, this same kind of self-sacrifice was almost never made for a mere acquaintance (see also Zarbatany et al., 1996). Young children also express more sympathy in response to the distress of a friend than to that of an acquaintance, and they are more inclined to try to relieve the friend's distress as well (Costin & Jones, 1992; Farver & Branstetter, 1994).

It is often said that there is a "chemistry" to close friendships and that best friends seem to be "in tune with each other." Research clearly supports this notion. Casual conversations among pairs of sixth-graders are much more cheerful, playful, and relaxed when the members of these pairings are good friends rather than mere acquaintances (Field et al., 1992). In fact, a measure of participants' saliva cortisol levels (a physiological correlate of stress) taken after the conversations suggested that casual interactions between acquaintances are more stressful than those between friends. Even when

friendship
a close and often enduring relationship between two individuals which may be characterized by loyalty and mutual affection.

16.3

APPLYING DEVELOPMENTAL RESEARCH

On Improving the Social Skills of Unpopular Children

The finding that peer rejection is a strong predictor of current and future psychological difficulties has prompted many investigators to devise interventions aimed at improving the social skills of unpopular children. Here are some of the more effective techniques.

Reinforcement and Modeling Therapies

Many early approaches to social-skills training were based on learning theory and involved (1) reinforcing children (with tokens or praise) for displaying such socially appropriate behaviors as cooperation and sharing, or (2) exposing children to social models who displayed a variety of socially skilled acts. Both approaches have been successful at increasing the frequency of children's socially skilled behaviors. And when teachers and peers *participate* in the intervention, they are much more likely to notice changes in the rejected child's behavior and are more inclined to change their opinion of him or her (Bierman & Furman, 1984; White & Kistner, 1992). Similarly, some modeling therapies are more effective than others. Modeling programs work best when the model is similar to the target child and when his socially skillful actions are accompanied by some form of commentary that directs the child's attention to the purposes and benefits of behaving appropriately toward peers (Asher, Renshaw, & Hymel, 1982).

Cognitive Approaches to Social-Skills Training

The fact that modeling strategies work better when accompanied by verbal rationales and explanations implies that interventions that prompt the child to think about or to imagine the consequences of various social overtures are likely to be effective. Why? Because the child's active cognitive involvement in the social-skills training may increase her understanding and appreciation of the principles that are taught, thereby persuading her to internalize and then rely on these lessons when interacting with peers.

Coaching is a cognitive social-learning technique in which the therapist displays one or more social skills, carefully explains the rationales for using them, allows children to practice such behavior, and then suggests how the children might improve on their performances. Sherri Oden and Steven Asher (1977) coached third- and fourth-grade social isolates on four important skills: how to participate in play activities, how to take turns and share, how to communicate effectively, and how to give attention and help to peers. Not only did the children who were coached become more outgoing and positive, but follow-up measures a year later revealed that these former isolates had achieved even further gains in social status (see also Bierman, 1986; Mize & Ladd, 1990; Schneider, 1992).

Other cognitive interventions, firmly grounded in cognitive-developmental theory, include attempts to improve children's *role-taking* skills and *social problem-solving abilities* (Chandler, 1973; Rabiner, Lenhart, & Lochman, 1990). These techniques can be especially effective with rejected-aggressive children who often display a *hostile attributional bias* (a tendency to overattribute hostile intentions to their companions) that has been acquired at home from coercive parents who mistrust other people and endorse aggression (Keane, Brown, & Crenshaw, 1990; Pettit, Dodge, & Brown, 1988). In order to help these aggressive rejectees, the training must not only emphasize that aggression is inappropriate but also demonstrate ways to generate nonaggressive solutions to conflict. One approach that looks promising is the **social problem-solving training** that Myrna Shure and George Spivack (1978; Shure, 1989) devised to help preschoolers generate and then evaluate amicable solutions to interpersonal problems. Over a 10-week period, children role-played conflict scenarios with puppets and were encouraged to discuss the impact of their solutions on the feelings of all parties involved in a conflict. Shure and Spivack found that fewer aggressive solutions were offered the longer the children had participated in the program. Furthermore, the children's classroom adjustment (as rated by teachers) improved as they became better able to think through the social consequences of their own actions.

Academic-Skills Training

Children who are failing miserably at school are often rejected by their classmates (Dishion et al., 1995). Might we elevate their social status by improving their academic skills and bringing them back into the mainstream of school activities? One research team tried this approach, providing extensive academic-skills training to low-achieving, socially rejected fourth-graders (Coie & Krehbiel, 1984). This training not only improved the children's reading and math achievement, but their social standing improved as well. One year after the intervention ended, these former rejectees now enjoyed average status in their peer group.

So there are a variety of techniques on which adults might rely to improve the social skills of unpopular children and help them to establish a more favorable standing among their peers. Yet a caution is in order, for the long-term success of any intervention could easily be compromised if the new social skills and problem-solving strategies that children have acquired are likely to be undermined by coercive, mistrusting parents who endorse aggressive solutions to conflict or by highly aggressive friends. For these reasons, Gregory Pettit and his associates (1988) favor *preventive* therapies—family-based interventions in which parents who accept and even encourage aggression are identified early and retrained themselves, thus possibly preventing their children from ever being rejected by peers. Academic-skills training is also a preventive strategy; children who gain in scholastic competence not only become better liked, but are also less likely to select highly aggressive children as friends or to become members of deviant peer cliques (Dishion et al., 1995). Today, we are seeing a much stronger emphasis on preventive interventions that are undertaken as soon as a child's problems with peers become apparent. And such an emphasis is clearly warranted, for (as we learned in Chapter 14) social-skills training programs rarely succeed once a child's deviant, antisocial conduct has continued beyond the first few grades at school (Kadzin, 1995).

collaborating on school assignments, friends tend to be more "in synch," agreeing more readily with each other and spending more time "on task" than collaborating acquaintances do (Hartup, 1996). So perhaps it is fair to say that interactions between friends are often characterized by a sense of mutuality and positive affect and do have a favorable chemistry about them.

How long do children's friendships last? It may surprise you to learn that even preschool friendships can be highly stable. Carollee Howes (1988), for example, found that children who attend the same day-care center for several years often keep the same close friends for more than a year. Although they may wax and wane in strength, close friendships often remain stable from year to year during middle childhood (Berndt & Hoyle, 1985; Cairns et al., 1995). However, friendship networks (the list of *all* individuals that a child might nominate as "friends") tend to shrink in size as children approach adolescence (Berndt, Hawkins, & Hoyle, 1986; Berndt & Hoyle, 1985). This loss of friends may simply reflect the young adolescent's growing awareness that the obligations of friendship, which now include the exchange of intimate information and the provision of emotional support, are easier to live up to if one selects a smaller circle of very close friends.

Are There Distinct Advantages to Having Friends?

Do friends play a unique role in shaping a child's development? Do children who have established adequate peer relations but no close friends turn out any differently from those who have one or more of these special companions? Although the well-controlled longitudinal studies needed to answer these questions have not yet been conducted (Hartup, 1996), we can draw some tentative conclusions about the roles that friends play as socializing agents.

Friends as Providers of Security and Social Support. One strong clue that friends play an important role in children's lives is the finding that having at least one supportive friend can go a long way toward reducing the loneliness and the victimization of unpopular children who are excluded from the larger peer group (Hodges et al., 1997; Parker & Asher, 1993; Parker & Seal, 1996). A close relationship with one or more friends may provide an emotional safety net, a kind of security that not only helps children to deal more constructively with new challenges but may also make almost any other form of life stress (for example, coping with a divorce or with a rejecting parent) a little easier to bear (Bagwell, Newcomb, & Bukowski, 1998). Indeed, Gary Ladd and his associates (1987; 1990; 1997) found that children who enter kindergarten along with their friends seem to like school better and have fewer adjustment problems than those who enter school without many friends. Furthermore, we saw in Chapter 15 that children who respond most constructively to their parents' divorce are often those who have the support of friends, particularly those whose parents are also divorced. Close supportive friendships play an especially important role in promoting the social competencies and self-esteem of children from nonnurturant, noncohesive families; and should youngsters from such nonsupportive family environments lose a particularly close friend, they often experience sizable declines in their feelings of self-worth (Gauze et al., 1996).

So friends are potentially important sources of security and **social support,** and they become increasingly important in fulfilling this role as children grow older. Fourth-graders, for example, say that their parents are their primary sources of social support; however, friends are perceived to be (1) as supportive as parents by seventh-graders and (2) the most frequent providers of social support by tenth-grade adolescents (Furman & Buhrmester, 1992).

coaching
method of social-skills training in which an adult displays and explains various socially skilled behaviors, allows the child to practice them, and provides feedback aimed at improving the child's performances.

social problem-solving training
method of social-skills training in which an adult helps children (through role playing or role-taking training) to make less hostile attributions about harmdoing and to generate nonaggressive solutions to conflict.

social support
tangible and intangible resources provided by other people in times of uncertainty or stress.

Friends as Contributors to Social Problem-Solving Skills. Since friendships are usually described as pleasant and rewarding relationships that are worth preserving, children should be highly motivated to resolve any conflicts with these "special" companions (Hartup, 1992). And apparently they are: Even during the preschool period, disagreeing friends are more likely than disagreeing acquaintances to step away before

Sometimes nothing is as reassuring as the affection and encouragement of a friend.

the squabbles become intense, to make concessions by accepting equal outcomes, and to continue playing together after the conflict is over (Hartup et al., 1988). By middle childhood, friends are much more inclined than acquaintances are to follow the rules (and not cheat) while playing competitive games and to respect the opinions, needs, and wishes of their partner while negotiating to settle a dispute (Fonzi et al., 1997; Nelson & Aboud, 1985). These experiences at amicably resolving conflicts with a friend are undoubtedly important contributors to the growth of mature social problem-solving skills—one of the strongest predictors of a healthy sociometric status with peers.

Friendships as Preparation for Adult Love Relationships. We've seen that *close* friendships are characterized by increasing intimacy and mutuality from middle childhood through adolescence. Could these relatively intense and intimate ties to what are overwhelmingly *same-sex* companions be necessary for the development of the deep interpersonal sensitivity and commitment so often observed in stable adult love relationships? Harry Stack Sullivan (1953) thought so. Sullivan reported that many of his lonely, mentally depressed patients had failed to form close friendships when they were young (see also Bagwell et al., 1998), and he concluded that the close bonds that develop between same-sex friends (or "chums") during preadolescence provide the foundation of caring and compassion that a person needs to establish and maintain intimate love relationships later in life. Consistent with Sullivan's ideas, preadolescents who have established *intimate* same-sex friendships are more likely than their friendless agemates to have broken through the gender segregation barrier and begun to forge closer ties with members of the opposite sex (George & Hartmann, 1996).

Quality of Friendships and Adjustment

One more point, and an important one. Friendships clearly differ in quality, and the very children who tend to have poor social skills—those who are insecurely attached to their parents, who have highly controlling or uninvolved parents, or who are rejected by peers—also tend to have friendships that are conflictual, nonsupportive, and lacking in trust (Dishion et al., 1995; Kerns et al., 1996; Parker & Asher, 1993; Youngblade & Belsky, 1992). Does the *quality* of a child's friendships influence his or her adjustment and developmental outcomes?

Apparently so. Studies of both kindergartners (Ladd, Kochenderfer, & Coleman, 1996) and seventh- and eighth-grade preadolescents (Berndt & Keefe, 1995) reveal that children who entered a school year with close, supportive friendships typically showed an increase in their liking for or involvement with school, whereas students whose friendships were more rivalrous and conflictual displayed poorer attitudes toward school, often becoming less engaged in scholastic activities and increasingly disruptive. In addition, Cyma Gauze and associates (1996) found that only when friendships are close and supportive do they foster the social competencies and self-esteem of children from nonnurturant and disordered families. Clearly, these findings have an important practical implication: In view of the crucial roles that intimate, supportive friendships can play in a child's life, perhaps our interventions for at-risk, unpopular children should be broadened to include lessons in how to make and keep close friends as well as more general kinds of social skills training (Murphy & Schneider, 1994).

How Do Peers Exert Their Influence?

To this point, we have seen that it is important for children to establish good peer relations and close supportive friendships because they acquire many competent and adaptive patterns of social behavior through their interactions with peers. How do peers exert their influence? In many of the same ways that parents do: by reinforcing, modeling, discussing, and even pressuring one another to comply with the values and behaviors that they condone.

Peer Reinforcement and Modeling Influences

It is easy to see that parents, teachers, and other powerful authority figures are in a position to reward or punish the behavior of children. But can a peer, who shares a similar status with the child, truly become an effective reinforcing agent?

Yes, indeed. Recall from Chapter 13 that 22- to 24-month-old toddlers have already begun to encourage gender-appropriate play and to criticize or disrupt a playmate's cross-sex activities. And playmates are influenced by these reactions: Children who receive peer approval for sex-appropriate play tend to keep playing, whereas those who are criticized for cross-sex play usually stop such activity in less than a minute (Lamb, Easterbrooks, & Holden, 1980).

Many of the reinforcers that peers provide one another are quite subtle or unintentional. For example, a child who "caves in" to a bully not only reinforces the bully's aggressive tactics without meaning to, but sets herself up to be victimized again. Yet, when a potential victim "punishes" a tormentor by fighting back, she may persuade him to seek other victims and possibly even learn that fighting "pays off," thus becoming more aggressive herself (Patterson, Littman, & Bricker, 1967).

So peers *are* important sources of social reinforcement. Although we have sampled but two studies from a voluminous literature, the evidence clearly indicates that children's social behaviors are often strengthened, maintained, or virtually eliminated by the favorable or unfavorable reactions that they elicit from peers.

Modeling Influences. Peers also influence one another by serving as social models for a multitude of behaviors—some good, and some not so good. Among the attributes and activities that are easily acquired by observing peer models are socially skilled behaviors (Cooke & Apolloni, 1976), achievement behaviors (Sagotsky & Lepper, 1982), moral judgments (Kruger, 1992), an ability to delay gratification (Stumphauzer, 1972), and sex-typed attitudes and behaviors (Frey & Ruble, 1992), to name a few. You may recall that several of these findings were discussed at length in earlier chapters.

Finally, peers clearly influence each other by serving as objects for *social comparison.* You may recall from our discussion in Chapter 12 that grade-school children often reach conclusions about their competencies and sense of self-worth by comparing their behaviors and accomplishments with those displayed by peers.

Peer Conformity

A major reason that peers become increasingly important as agents of socialization is that, from middle childhood onward, an increasing percentage of peer interactions occur in true *peer groups* that influence their members by setting norms specifying how group members are supposed to look, dress, think, and act. And children do become increasingly responsive to normative peer pressures as they grow older, although they are hardly the blind conformists that many people assume.

In his classic study of **peer conformity,** Thomas Berndt (1979) asked third- through 12th-graders to indicate the likelihood that they would bend to peer pressure when peers were advocating various prosocial or antisocial acts. He found that conformity to peer pressure for prosocial behaviors did not change much with age. Instead, the most striking developmental change was a sharp increase in conformity with peers urging *antisocial* behavior. This receptivity to peer-sponsored misconduct peaked in the ninth grade (or about age 15; see Figure 16.11) and then declined throughout the high school years (see also Brown, Clasen, & Eicher, 1986; Steinberg & Silverberg, 1986). So parents may have some grounds for worrying that their 13- to 15-year-olds could wind up in trouble by going along with the crowd. Peer pressure of all kinds is especially strong at this age (Gavin & Furman, 1989), and there is nothing worse than being viewed as a "dweeb" who does not fit in (Kinney, 1993).

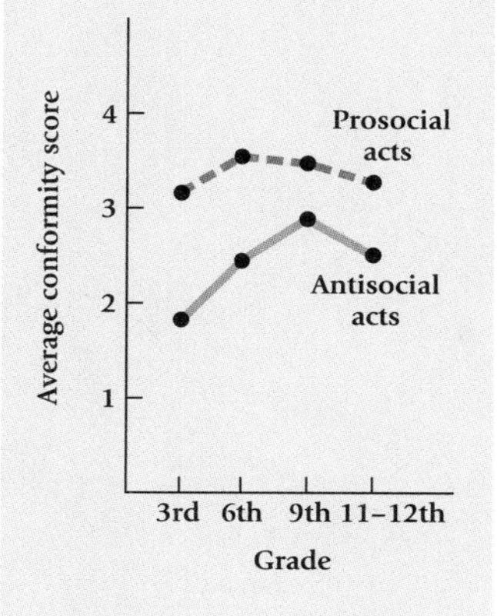

Figure 16.11 *Average scores by grade for conformity to peer pressure for prosocial and antisocial behaviors.* ADAPTED FROM BERNDT, *1979.*

Why does conformity to peer-sponsored misconduct *decrease* by the end of high school? Perhaps this trend reflects the progress that older adolescents have made in their quest for autonomy: They are now better able to make their own decisions and are less dependent on the opinions of *either* parents or peers. According to Lawrence Steinberg and Susan Silverberg (1986), strong conformity to peer pressure early in adolescence may even be a necessary step in the development of autonomy: Young adolescents who are struggling to become less dependent on their parents may need the security that peer acceptance provides before they develop confidence to take their own stands and stick by them. And they are unlikely to gain such acceptance if they conform too closely to adult rules and values without taking a chance and going along with peers every now and then (Allen, Weissberg, & Hawkins, 1989). Although the parent whose teenager is nabbed with his friends for cherry-bombing mailboxes or deflating tires may not be totally comforted by this thought, it does seem that a period of heavy peer influence may pave the way for later independence.

WHAT DO YOU THINK? ?

Do you think that Steinberg and Silverberg (1986) are correct in arguing that strong peer conformity early in adolescence fosters autonomy later on? Why or why not, and how might you test your hypothesis?

Peer versus Adult Influences: The Question of Cross-Pressures

In years gone by, adolescence was often characterized as a stormy period when all youths experience **cross-pressures**—strong conflicts that stem from differences in the values or practices advocated by parents and those favored by peers. How accurate is this "life portrait" of the teenage years? It may have some merit for some adolescents, especially those "rejected" youth who form deviant peer cliques and endorse antisocial behaviors that are likely to alienate their parents, teachers, and most other peers (Dishion et al., 1991; 1995; Patterson et al., 1989; Vitaro et al., 1997). But there are several reasons to believe that the "cross-pressures problem" is not a problem for most adolescents.

One reason that parent–peer conflicts are kept to a minimum is that parents and peers tend to exert their influence in different domains. Hans Sebald (1986), for example, has asked adolescents whether they would seek the advice of their parents or the advice of their peers on a number of different issues. *Peers* were likely to be more influ-

peer conformity
the tendency to go along with the wishes of peers or to yield to peer-group pressures.

cross-pressures
conflicts stemming from differences in the values and practices advocated by parents and those favored by peers.

ential than parents on such issues as what styles to wear and which clubs, social events, hobbies, and other recreational activities to choose. By contrast, adolescents claimed that they would depend more on their *parents* when the issue involved scholastic or occupational goals or other future-oriented decisions. Teenagers are unlikely to be torn between parent and peer pressures as long as parents and peers have different areas of influence.

A second and more important reason why parent–peer warfare is typically kept to a minimum is that parents have a good deal of influence on the company that their adolescents keep. Authoritative parents who are warm, neither too controlling nor too lax, and who are consistent in their discipline generally find that their adolescents are closely attached to them and have internalized their values. These adolescents have little need to rebel or to desperately seek acceptance from peers when they are so warmly received at home (Brown et al., 1993; Fuligni & Eccles, 1993). In fact, they tend to associate with friends who share their values, which largely protects them from unhealthy peer influences (Fletcher et al., 1995).

Interestingly, problems for youths who *do* "fall in with the wrong crowd" and display antisocial behavior usually begin at home. One way that parents can go wrong is by being too strict, failing to adjust to an adolescent's needs for greater autonomy. This may cause adolescents to become alienated from parents and overly susceptible to negative peer influences, to the point that they would let schoolwork slide or break parental rules to please their friends (Fuligni & Eccles, 1993). Parents can also go wrong by failing to provide enough discipline and by not monitoring their children's activities closely enough (Barber et al., 1994; Brown et al., 1993; Dishion et al., 1991; 1995). So parents have a good deal of power to influence, through their parenting, whether their adolescents end up in "good" or "bad" crowds and are exposed to healthy or unhealthy peer pressures.

Of course, there are some issues for which parental opinions are likely to conflict with those of many peers (for example, opinions about acceptable conduct on dates or about the harm involved in experimenting with tobacco, alcohol, or marijuana). But even so, peer group values are rarely as deviant as adults commonly assume, and the adolescent's behavior is usually a product of *both* parental and peer influences. Denise Kandel (1973), for example, studied a group of adolescents whose best friends either did or did not smoke marijuana and whose parents either did or did not use psychoactive drugs. Among those teenagers whose parents used drugs but whose friends did not, only 17% were marijuana users. When parents did not use drugs but best friends did, 56% of the adolescents used marijuana. From these findings, we might conclude that the peer group is more influential than parents over marijuana use (see also Bentler, 1992). However, the highest rate of marijuana smoking (67%) occurred among teenagers whose parents and peers *both* used psychoactive drugs, and a similar pattern emerges when we look at parental and peer influences on use of alcohol, tobacco, and other illicit drugs (Chassin et al., 1996; Newcomb & Bentler, 1989).

Concept Check 16.3
Understanding Peer Sociability and Peer Influences

Check your understanding of *selected aspects* of peer sociability and peer influences by matching each descriptive statement below with one of the following concepts or processes: (a) neglected children, (b) rejected-aggressive children, (c) rejected-withdrawn children, (d) crowd, (e) same-sex clique; (f) deviant peer clique, (g) authoritarian/uninvolved parenting, (h) patterns of social behavior, (i) close friends, (j) play complexity. Answers appear in the Appendix.

_____ 1. social contributor to nonharmonious peer interactions
_____ 2. personal characteristic that predicts the future social competencies of toddlers and preschool children
_____ 3. important mechanism for promoting cross-sex friendships
_____ 4. at greatest risk of becoming chronically hostile and antisocial
_____ 5. passive youngsters who often improve their sociometric statuses
_____ 6. perhaps the strongest contributor to sociometric status
_____ 7. cross-pressures are often a problem for members of these aggregations
_____ 8. strongest providers of social support by mid-adolescence
_____ 9. at greatest risk of experiencing depression and low self-esteem
_____ 10. form that the peer group takes in early adolescence

Although teenagers are often characterized as wild or rebellious, many of their norms and values are a reflection of adult society.

In sum, adolescent socialization is not a continual war of parents *versus* peers; instead, these two important sources of influence interact to influence one's development (Mounts & Steinberg, 1995). Most adolescents have cordial relationships with their parents, accept many of their parents' values, and are reluctant to stray too far from these guidelines and undermine their parents' approval. And most parents know how important it is for their children and adolescents to establish close relationships with their social equals. They seem to appreciate what the lonely farmer whose letter opened this section learned the hard way: Many of the social competencies that serve people well are the fruits of their alliances with close friends and peers.

SUMMARY

Early Windows: Impacts of Television and Computer Technologies on Children and Adolescents

◆ Although children spend more time watching television than in any other waking activity, TV viewing, in moderate doses, is unlikely to impair their cognitive growth, academic achievement, or peer relations. Cognitive development and experience watching television leads to increases in **television literacy** during middle childhood and adolescence.

◆ Televised violence can instigate aggressive behavior, cultivate aggressive habits and **mean-world beliefs,** and **desensitize** children to aggression. TV also presents stereotypes that influence viewers' beliefs about ethnicity, race, and gender, and children are easily manipulated by TV commercials that push products that parents may be reluctant to purchase.

◆ On the positive side, children are likely to learn prosocial lessons and to put them into practice after watching acts of kindness on television. Parents can help by watching shows such as *Mister Rogers' Neighborhood* with their children and then encouraging them to verbalize or role-play the prosocial lessons that they have observed. Educational programs such as *Sesame Street* have been quite successful at fostering basic cognitive skills, particularly when children watch with an adult who discusses the material with them and helps them to apply what they have learned.

◆ Children seem to benefit, both intellectually and socially, from their use of computers. **Computer-assisted instruction (CAI)** often improves children's basic academic skills; word processing programs foster the growth of writing skills; and computer programming facilitates cognitive and metacognitive development. Furthermore, computers promote rather than inhibit social interactions with peers. Nevertheless, critics fear that (1) disadvantaged children and girls may reap fewer of these benefits, (2) violent computer games may instigate aggression, and (3) harm may result from youngsters' unrestricted access to the Internet and the World Wide Web.

School as a Socialization Agent

◆ Schools influence many aspects of development. Formal scholastic curricula are intended to impart academic knowledge, and schooling promotes cognitive and metacognitive development by teaching rules and problem-solving strategies that can be applied to many different kinds of information. Schools also pursue an **informal curriculum** that teaches children skills that help them to become good citizens.

◆ Some schools are more "effective" than others at producing positive outcomes such as low absenteeism, an enthusiastic attitude about learning, academic achievement, occupational skills, and socially desirable patterns of behavior. What makes a school effective is not its physical characteristics, **open** or **traditional classroom** structure, whether students experience **ability tracking,** or the amount of money spent per pupil. Instead, **effective schools** are those in which (1) students are motivated to learn, (2) teachers create a classroom environment that is comfortable, engaging, and task-focused, and (3) there are positive **aptitude-treatment interactions**—that is, a "good fit" between students' personal or cultural characteristics and the kinds of instruction they receive.

◆ Racial and ethnic differences in academic achievement can often be traced to parental and peer influences and to teacher expectancies (the **Pygmalion effect**). At best, **mainstreaming** has produced modest improvements in the academic performance of students with developmental disabilities, while failing to enhance their peer acceptance or self-esteem. Among the steps that might be taken to better meet the educational needs of all of our students are creating stronger bilingual and multicultural educational programs and making greater use of **cooperative learning methods** in the classroom.

◆ Cross-national surveys of academic achievement clearly brand American students as "underachievers," especially in math and science. The achievement gap that exists between American schoolchildren and those in other industrialized societies centers around cultural differences in educational attitudes, educational practices, and the involvement of both parents and students in the learning process.

Peers as Agents of Socialization

◆ **Peer** contacts represent a second world for children—a world of equal-status interactions that is very different from the nonegalitarian environment of the home. Contacts with peers increase dramatically with age, and during the preschool or early elementary school years, children are spending at least as much of their leisure time with peers as with adults. The "peer group" consists mainly of *same sex* associates of somewhat *different ages.*

Research with **mother-only** and **peer-only monkeys** and young children indicates that peer contacts are important for the development of competent and adaptive patterns of social behavior. Children who fail to establish and maintain adequate relations with their peers will run the risk of experiencing any number of serious adjustment problems later in life.

◆ **Sociability** between peers emerges by the middle of the first year. By age 18–24 months, toddlers' sociable interactions are becoming much more complex and coordinated as they reliably imitate each other, assume complementary roles in simple social games, and occasionally coordinate their actions to achieve shared goals. During the preschool years, **nonsocial activities** and **parallel play** become less common, whereas **associative play** and **cooperative play** become more common. During middle childhood, more peer interactions occur in true **peer groups**—confederations that associate regularly, define a sense of group membership, and formulate norms that specify how group members are supposed to behave. By early adolescence, youngsters are spending even more time with peers—particularly with their closest friends in small **cliques,** and in larger confederations of like-minded cliques, known as **crowds.** Cliques and crowds help adolescents to forge an identity apart from their families and pave the way for the establishment of dating relationships.

◆ Parents influence their children's sociability with peers by virtue of the neighborhood in which they choose to live, their willingness to serve as "booking agents" for peer contacts, and their monitoring of peer interactions. Warm, sensitive, authoritative parents tend to raise appropriately sociable children who establish good relations with peers, whereas highly authoritarian or uninvolved parents—particularly those who rely on power assertion as a control tactic—tend to raise disruptive, aggressive youngsters whom peers often dislike.

◆ Children clearly differ in **peer acceptance**—the extent to which other youngsters view them as likable (or dislikable) companions. Using **sociometric techniques,** developmentalists find that there are five categories of peer acceptance: (1) **popular children** (liked by many and disliked by few), (2) **rejected children** (disliked by many and liked by few), (3) **controversial children** (liked by many and disliked by many), (4) **neglected children** (seldom nominated by others as likable or dislikable), and (5) **average-status children** (those who are liked or disliked by a moderate number of peers). Neither neglected children nor rejected children are well received by peers; however, it is the rejected child who is typically the lonelier of the two and at greater risk of displaying serious adjustment problems later in life.

◆ Although physical attractiveness, cognitive prowess, and the parenting one has received may contribute to a child's popularity with peers, one's patterns of social behavior are the strongest predictor of peer acceptance. Popular children are generally warm, cooperative, and compassionate companions who display many prosocial behaviors and are rarely disruptive or aggressive. Neglected children often have adequate social skills, but they experience social anxieties that cause them to appear shy and to hover at the edge of peer-group activities. Rejected children display many unpleasant and annoying behaviors and few prosocial ones. **Rejected-aggressive** children are hostile, impulsive, highly uncooperative, and aggressive, whereas **rejected-withdrawn children** are socially awkward and immature companions who are hypersensitive to criticism and have actively isolated themselves from peers. Programs to improve social skills of rejectees work better (1) with younger children than with adolescents, and (2) when the target children's classmates also participate in the intervention.

◆ Children typically form close ties, or **friendships,** with one or more members of their play groups. Younger children view a friend as a harmonious playmate, whereas older children and adolescents come to think of friends as close companions who share similar interests and values and are willing to provide them with intimate social and emotional support. Interactions among friends are warmer, more cooperative, more compassionate, and more synchronous than those among acquaintances. Close friendships seem to promote positive developmental outcomes by (1) providing security and **social support,** (2) promoting the growth of social-problem-solving skills and an ability to compromise, and (3) fostering caring and compassionate feelings which are the foundation of intimate love relationships later in life. However, friendships differ in quality, and only close, supportive friendships seem to foster adaptive developmental outcomes.

◆ Peers influence a child in many of the same ways that parents do—by modeling, reinforcing, discussing, and pressuring associates to conform to the behaviors and values they condone. **Peer conformity** pressures peak at midadolescence, when teenagers are most susceptible to peer-sponsored misconduct. Yet, severe **cross-pressures** are not a problem for most adolescents, who have established warm relations with their parents, and have generally internalized many of their parents' values. What's more, peer-group values are often very similar to those of parents, and peers are more likely to discourage than to condone antisocial conduct. So adolescent socialization is not a continual battle between parents and peers; instead, these two important influences interact to affect one's development.

One major influence on early development is mass media in general, and television in particular. By visiting The Media Literacy Online project at: **http://interact.uoregon.edu/MediaLit/FA/MLmediaviolence.html** you can access more than 20 on-line articles dealing with the impact of television on children and adolescents. There are also numerous links to other sites that host Web resources on this topic.

KEY TERMS

extrafamilial influences, 598
television literacy, 599
mean-world belief, 600
desensitization hypothesis, 600
computer-assisted instruction (CAI), 605
informal curriculum, 607
effective schools, 608
ability tracking, 610
traditional classroom, 610
open classroom, 610
aptitude–treatment interaction (ATI), 611
Pygmalion effect, 615
mainstreaming, 616
cooperative learning methods, 616
peers, 620
"mother-only" monkeys, 623
"peer-only" monkeys, 623
sociability, 623
nonsocial activity, 625
parallel play, 625
associative play, 625
cooperative play, 625
peer group, 626
clique, 626
crowd, 627
peer acceptance, 629
sociometric techniques, 629
popular children, 629
rejected children, 629
neglected children, 629
controversial children, 629
average-status children, 629
rejected-aggressive children, 631
rejected-withdrawn children, 631
friendship, 632
coaching, 633
social problem-solving training, 633
social support, 634
peer conformity, 637
cross-pressures, 637

Appendix: Answers to Concept Checks

CHAPTER 1

Concept Check 1.1

1. *d. structured observation.* Obvious transgressions are events that children may not admit to in an interview, may not be detected by a case study, or may not occur while they are being monitored by an adult observer.

2. *a. structured interview.* If young children listening to the same vignettes regularly guess that the characters who display the most negative traits are the minority rather than majority group members, we might infer that they have already acquired some negative stereotypes about members of minority groups.

3. *e. psychophysiological methods.* By recording changes in such physiological responses as heart rate or event-related potentials, even a nonverbal 6-month-old can "tell us" if she can discriminate stimuli that differ only in their color.

4. *c. naturalistic observation.* To answer this question, you would probably want to observe boys and girls in the natural environment where conflicts are likely to occur.

5. *b. ethnography.* Close and enduring contact with members of Sambia culture provides a richer understanding of the impact of cultural traditions than do limited observations or questionnaire methods.

Note: Of course, most of the above research questions *can* be addressed by a variety of research methods.

Concept Check 1.2

1. *b.* The other conclusions make inappropriate causal inferences from correlational data.

2. *d.* Chang has failed to control for any potentially confounding variables. For example, the boys may have earned higher grades than the girls because they were smarter to begin with (intelligence is a confounding variable). Moreover, having boys in the treatment group and girls in the control group confounds treatment with gender. Had Chang wanted to see if increases in self-esteem *cause* increases in academic performance, he should have *randomly assigned* boys and girls to the treatment and control groups, thereby helping to ensure that all potentially confounding variables were roughly equivalent across these two conditions. If children in the treatment group subsequently earned higher grades than their counterparts in the control group, a causal inference would then be warranted.

Concept Check 1.3

1. *a. cross-sectional design.* Although either the longitudinal or the sequential design could provide similar information, neither of these alternatives is very quick.

2. *c. sequential design.* The researcher's question concerns the long-term effects of interventions given to children of different ages, thus calling for a sequential design.

3. *d. cross-cultural design.* The only way to determine whether there are any true "universals" in development is to conduct cross-cultural research to see whether children show the same developmental patterns despite differences in their rearing environments.

4. *b. longitudinal design.* Because our researcher is interested in the stability of children's intellectual performance relative to their peers between ages 2 and 6, he could answer his question by following a group of 2-year-olds over a four-year period in a simple longitudinal comparison. The cross-sectional design is inappropriate here because each child is observed only once, thus providing no information about the *development* of individuals.

CHAPTER 2

Concept Check 2.1

This person is a *discontinuity theorist* (as evidenced by the claim that all children progress through the same phases (stages) of intellectual development). The spokesman's claims that intelligence is passed from parents to child and that children will develop their own intellectual potential imply the opinions that intelligence is heavily influenced by *nature* (rather than nurture) and that children are *actively* (rather than passively) involved in their intellectual development.

Concept Check 2.2

1. *b. Eric Erikson* (1950, p. 32) explaining that humans are biological beings whose development is heavily influenced by the cultural contexts in which they live.

2. *d. Albert Bandura* (1977, p. 10) criticizing the radical behaviorist views of B. F. Skinner and emphasizing cognitive contributors to social learning.

3. *c. B. F. Skinner* (1971, p. 17) explaining why he thinks that free will is an illusion and that behavior is controlled by its external (reinforcing or punitive) consequences.

4. *a. Sigmund Freud* (1905, p. 78) arguing that it is possible to probe into the unconscious depths of the mind and reveal the conflicts that motivate many behaviors.

Concept Check 2.3

1. *c. Ethology*

2. *a. Piaget's cognitive-developmental theory*

3. *d. Ecological systems theory*

4. *b. Information-processing theory*

5. *all of the above* theories view developing persons as "active" rather than "passive" agents.

CHAPTER 3

Concept Check 3.1

1. *a. 100%.* Monozygotic twins have 100% of their genes in common and are always the same sex.

2. *c. 50%.* Your mother cannot curl her tongue and can pass only recessive (non-tongue-curling) genes to her children. And because your sister cannot curl her tongue, she received a recessive gene from each parent. So your father is a *heterozygous* for tongue curling. Half his sperm will carry the dominant tongue-curling gene, thus implying that your odds of being able to curl your tongue are 50%.

3. *a. 100%.* Since both parents cannot curl their tongues, they can pass only recessive genes to their children.

Concept Check 3.2

1. *e.* Down syndrome
2. *f.* Tay-Sachs disease
3. *g.* ultrasound
4. *a.* mutation
5. *b.* supermale syndrome
6. *d.* phenylketonuria (PKU)
7. *c.* chorionic villus sampling (CVS)

Concept Check 3.3

1. *c. low.* $H = (r_{mz} - r_{dz}) \times 2 = (.61 - .50) \times 2 = \mathbf{.22}$

2. *a.* This is a trait for which both SE and NSE contribute more than heredity does. The contribution of NSE (i.e., $1 - r_{mz}$ twins, or **.39**) is about twice as large as the hereditary contribution. And a rough estimate of the contribution of SE (that is, $1 - (NSE + H) = 1 - (.39 + .22)$, or **.39** is comparable in magnitude to that of NSE.

CHAPTER 4

Concept Check 4.1

Event	*Period*	*Timing*	*Name for organism*
Implantation	germinal	10–14 days	zygote
Age of viability	fetal	7th month	fetus
First heartbeats	embryonic	4th week	embryo
Kicks first felt by mother	fetal	4th month	fetus
Organs form	embryonic	2 weeks–2 months	embryo
Sexual differentiation (external genitalia)	fetal	3rd month	fetus

Concept Check 4.2

1. *g. syphilis*
2. *c. diethylstilbestrol (DES)*
3. *a. alcohol*
4. *b. toxoplasmosis*
5. *e. folic acid*
6. *d. rubella*
7. *a. severe malnutrition*

Concept Check 4.3

1. *d. NBAS training*
2. *a. cranial bleeding*
3. *c. respiratory distress syndrome*
4. *e. RH incompatibility*
5. *f. natural (or prepared) childbirth*
6. *b. emotional bonding/engrossment*

CHAPTER 5

Concept Check 5.1

1. *c.* Establishment of *lateral preferences* is one consequence of cerebral lateralization.

2. *d.* Many subcortical *reflexes disappear* as the higher cortical centers mature.

3. *f.* The formation of glia and proliferation of synapses early in life are important contributors to the *brain growth spurt.*

4. *a.* With the loss of unused neural pathways, the brain becomes *less plastic.*

5. *b.* Increasing myelinization of the nervous system over the course of childhood is thought to underlie the *increases in attention span* that children display.

6. *e. Neurons will degenerate* if not properly stimulated.

Concept Check 5.2

1. *f. sex-role socialization*
2. *d. peak of pubertal changes*
3. *a. early maturation*
4. *a. early maturation*
5. *g. menarche/ejaculation*
6. *e. locomotor skills*
7. *b. late maturation*
8. *b & c. on-time maturation; late maturation*

Concept Check 5.3

1. *b. malnutrition*
2. *a. increase in GH production* (testosterone plays a secondary role for boys).
3. *d. stress-induced inhibition of GH*
4. *f. sedentary lifestyle*
5. *c. increase in testosterone/estrogen production*
6. *a & e. malnutrition; insensitive/abusive caregiving*

CHAPTER 6

Concept Check 6.1

1. *c. vision*
2. *h. high-amplitude sucking*
3. *b & d. audition (hearing); olfaction (smell)*
4. *f. otitis media*
5. *i. circumcision*
6. *g. phoneme discrimination*
7. *a & e. habituation method; evoked potential method*

Concept Check 6.2

1. *d. kinetic (motion) cues*
2. *b. depth cues*
3. *h. size constancy*
4. *f. pictorial cues*
5. *g. maturation of the brain's visual centers*
6. *e. depth perception*
7. *a. intermodal perception*
8. *c. face perception*

Concept Check 6.3

Vignette	*Kind of Learning*	*Consequence responsible for learning*
1. Scumbags learn to stick with old hits.	Operant learning	Positive reinforcement for playing old hits.
2. Dog becomes excited at the sight of a yellow jacket.	Classical conditioning	By pairing the yellow jacket with a UCS (walking) that elicits excitement, the yellow jacket becomes a CS for excitement.
3. Fred distrusts politicians after hearing a group of strangers who are unanimous in questioning their integrity.	Observational learning	None, learning occurs at a symbolic level, without reinforcement or punishment.
4. Jo comes to apply insect repellent before venturing outdoors.	Operant conditioning	Negative reinforcement (applying repellent ends the aversive insect attacks).
5. Jim no longer notices an initially powerful odor.	Habituation	Becoming bored or disinterested in a now-familiar stimulus.

CHAPTER 7

Concept Check 7.1

1. *e. disequilibrium*
2. *d. reversibility*
3. *c. accommodation*
4. *a. organization*
5. *b. assimilation*

Concept Check 7.2

1. *c. seriation (concrete operations)*
2. *e. animism (preoperational stage)*
3. *b. imaginary audience (formal operations)*
4. *d. dual representation (preoperational stage)*
5. *g. hypothetical reasoning (formal operations)*
6. *f. A-not-B error (sensorimotor stage)*
7. *a. reversibility (concrete operations)*

Concept Check 7.3

1. *b. private speech*
2. *c. zone of proximal development*
3. *e. guided participation*
4. *f. scaffolding*
5. *d. elementary mental functions*
6. *a. tools of intellectual adaptation*

CHAPTER 8

Concept Check 8.1

1. *b. long-term store*
2. *g. utilization deficiency*
3. *i. working-memory task*
4. *h. executive control processes*
5. *f. production deficiency*
6. *j. limited capacity*
7. *d. sensory store*
8. *a. gists*
9. *c. short-term store/working-memory*
10. *e. operating efficiency hypothesis*

Concept Check 8.2

1. *h. sustained attention*
2. *c. elaboration*
3. *f. scripts*
4. *b. knowledge base*
5. *a. autobiographical memory*
6. *i. retrieval*
7. *e. story-like narratives*
8. *d. false memories*
9. *g. metamemory*

Concept Check 8.3

1. *b. strategy choice model*
2. *f. knowledge of why and when a strategy works*
3. *h. higher intellectual abilities*
4. *c. quickly articulated number words*
5. *a. cardinality principle*
6. *e. insufficient attention to biological underpinnings of cognitive growth*
7. *g. mind-computer analogy*
8. *d. provides in-depth understanding of domain-specific cognitive skills*

CHAPTER 9

Concept Check 9.1

1. *c. J. P. Guilford* (structure of intellect model)
2. *d. Charles Spearman* (early factor-analytic model of intelligence)
3. *b. Howard Gardner* (theory of multiple intelligences)
4. *f. Louis Thurstone* (early factor-analytic model of intelligence)
5. *a. Raymond Cattell/John Horn* (a modern psychometric view of intelligence)
6. *e. Robert Sternberg* (triarchic theory of intelligence)

Concept Check 9.2

1. *d. dynamic assessment*
2. *g. developmental quotient (DQ)*
3. *a. Webster Intelligence Scale for Children (WISC—III)*
4. *c. cumulative deficit*
5. *h. habituation rate*
6. *f. tacit (or practical) intelligence*
7. *b. Stanford-Binet Intelligence Scale*
8. *e. grades previously earned*

Concept Check 9.3

1. *d. confluence hypothesis*
2. *b. socioeconomic risk factors*
3. *a. quality of home environment*
4. *f. stereotype threat* (*b* is another alternative that applies here)
5. *e. genetic hypothesis for group differences in IQ*
6. *c. unequal rearing environments*

CHAPTER 10

Concept Check 10.1

1. *d. sensitive-period hypothesis*
2. *b. recasts*
3. *e. creolizing of pidgins by children*
4. *h. appropriate semantics*
5. *g. conversations with language users*
6. *f. universals in cognitive development*
7. *c. language acquisition device*
8. *a. appropriate grammar*

Concept Check 10.2

1. *c. expressive style*
2. *f. intonational cues*
3. *e. holophrastic speech*
4. *h. referential style*
5. *a. vocal turn-taking*
6. *i. object scope constraint*
7. *d. telegraphic speech*
8. *b. syntactical bootstrapping*
9. *g. overextension*

Concept Check 10.3

1. *d. transformational grammar*
2. *c. metalinguistic awareness*
3. *f. morphological knowledge*
4. *a. referential communication skills*
5. *g. grammatical morphemes*
6. *b. overregularization*
7. *e. phonological awareness*

CHAPTER 11

Concept Check 11.1

1. *b. self-recognition*
2. *f. infant emotional expressions*
3. *e. emotional understanding*
4. *c. social referencing*
5. *d. disconfirmed expectancies*
6. *a. emotional self-regulation*

Concept Check 11.2

1. *e. Ainsworth's ethological viewpoint*
2. *c. learning perspective (Robert Sears)*
3. *f. cognitive-developmental perspective*
4. *a. Freud's psychoanalytic viewpoint*
5. *d. Bowlby's ethological viewpoint*
6. *b. Erikson's psychoanalytic viewpoint*

Concept Check 11.3

1. *c. Thomas and Chess's goodness-of-fit model*
2. *b. Kagan's temperament hypothesis*
3. *f. social stimulation hypothesis*
4. *a. Ainsworth's caregiving hypothesis*
5. *d. Bowlby/Bretherton "internal working models" hypothesis*
6. *e. maternal deprivation hypothesis*

CHAPTER 12

Concept Check 12.1

1. *c. self-esteem*
2. *h. private self*
3. *e. self-assertion*
4. *d. looking-glass self*
5. *a. delay of gratification*
6. *j. self-recognition*
7. *b. categorical self*
8. *g. belief-desire theory of mind*
9. *k. friendship quality*
10. *i. social comparison*

Concept Check 12.2

1. *f. identity foreclosure*
2. *b. negative peer influences*
3. *d. children with a mastery orientation*
4. *g. identity diffusion*
5. *e. children with a learned helplessness orientation*
6. *h. identity achievement*
7. *a. strong parental criticism of failures*
8. *c. stability of achievement attributions*

Concept Check 12.3

1. *c. psychological similarities*
2. *e. behavioral comparisons*
3. *a. loyalty/sharing of intimacies*
4. *f. psychological constructs*
5. *d. role-taking skills*
6. *b. common activities*
7. *h. social experiences with peers*
8. *g. psychological comparisons*

CHAPTER 13

Concept Check 13.1

1. *e. reading comprehension*
2. *b. gender identity*
3. *i. gender-role standard*
4. *f. self-fulfilling prophecy*
5. *h. visual/spatial ability*
6. *d. gender segregation*
7. *a. achievement motivation*
8. *c. gender intensification*
9. *g. gender-role stereotypes*

Concept Check 13.2

1. *h. gender consistency*
2. *a. Money and Erhardt's biosocial theory*
3. *c. Freud's psychoanalytic theory*
4. *g. basic gender identity*
5. *b. Halpern's psychobiosocial model*
6. *d. social-learning theory*
7. *f. Martin & Halverson's gender schema theory*
8. *e. Kohlberg's cognitive-developmental theory*

Concept Check 13.3

The program might target 3 to 6-year-olds whose gender stereotypes are just forming and are not entrenched. The program should encourage cross-sex as well as same-sex play activities, and its adult leaders should model both same- and cross-sex pursuits. Question and answer sessions about the gender stereotypes that children already hold should provide opportunities to point out that one's interests and willingness to learn, rather than one's gender, are the most important considerations in determining the activities that people should pursue (rule training). Giving children multiple classification tasks that require them to sort objects into more than one category (and illustrate that men and women often share similar interests and occupational goals) should also help children to break free of rigid gender stereotypes. Finally, at least part of the training might be conducted by an adult male, for it is males who normally make the stronger distinctions between what is "appropriate" for males and females and, thus, may be more noteworthy as agents of change.

CHAPTER 14

Concept Check 14.1

1. *d. relational aggression*
2. *h. proactive aggressors*
3. *g. negative reinforcement*
4. *a. deviant peer cliques*
5. *c. instrumental aggression*
6. *i. reactive aggressors*
7. *b. hostile aggression*
8. *f. peer rejection*
9. *e. coercive home environment*

Concept Check 14.2

1. *d. competitive orientation*
2. *e. self-oriented distress*
3. *a. altruistic norms*
4. *b. felt responsibility*
5. *c. role-taking skills*
6. *g. altruistic exhortations*
7. *f. sympathetic empathic arousal*

Concept Check 14.3

1. *e. moral rules*
2. *j. warm, responsive parenting*
3. *g. peer interactions*
4. *f. morality of care*
5. *h. power assertion*
6. *d. induction*
7. *i. secure attachment to parent* (alternative *j* might also be viewed as correct)
8. *b. formal operations*
9. *a. role-taking skills*
10. *c. disequilibrating social experiences*

CHAPTER 15

Concept Check 15.1

1. *g.* This finding illustrates that families are *embedded* in a larger societal context that influences parenting practices.
2. *e.* In this *direct effort,* the father's parenting influences the father–son relationship.
3. *d.* Such an arrangement is called a *blended family.*
4. *a. Traditional nuclear family*
5. *h.* Family dynamics change with the *development* of family members.
6. *c.* Due to divorce and out-of-wedlock deliveries, *single-parent* families are common today.
7. *b.* In communal societies, children in *extended families* seem to fare better.
8. *f.* In this *indirect effect,* the father–son relationship influences the husband–wife relationship.

Concept Check 15.2

1. *c. economic distress*
2. *e. increased academic aptitude* (younger sibs may share this benefit if older sibs teach them academic lessons).
3. *i. unwanted children*
4. *a. authoritarian parenting*
5. *g. only children*
6. *h. uninvolved parenting*
7. *d. emotional support*
8. *f. mastery motivation*
9. *b. authoritative parenting*

Concept Check 15.3

1. *d. delinquent conduct*
2. *b. girls*
3. *g. support* (both emotional and financial) *from the noncustodial parent*
4. *c. coercive parenting* by the custodial parent
5. *a. boys*
6. *h.* children of divorce are more likely than those from intact homes to experience an *unhappy marriage* themselves
7. *f. adoption*
8. *e. gay/lesbian parenting*

CHAPTER 16

Concept Check 16.1

1. *d. aggressive children*
2. *a. ethnic/gender stereotypes*
3. *h. ads for children*
4. *g. poor peer relations*
5. *e. disadvantaged children*
6. *i. metacognitive development*
7. *f. adult monitoring/encouragement*
8. *b. mean-world beliefs*
9. *c. television literacy*

Concept Check 16.2

1. *f. mainstreaming*
2. *i. peer support for academics*
3. *a. ability tracking*
4. *e. informal curriculum*
5. *g. monetary support*
6. *h. parental involvement*
7. *j. extracurricular activities*
8. *b. aptitude-treatment interaction*
9. *d. group differences in IQ*
10. *c. cooperative learning methods*

Concept Check 16.3

1. *g. authoritarian/uninvolved parenting*
2. *j. play complexity*
3. *d. crowd*
4. *b. rejected-aggressive children*
5. *a. neglected children*
6. *h. patterns of social behavior*
7. *f. deviant peer cliques*
8. *i. close friends*
9. *c. rejected-withdrawn children*
10. *e. same-sex clique*

Glossary

ability tracking: the educational practice of grouping students according to ability and then educating them in classes with students of comparable educational or intellectual standing.

acceptance/responsiveness: a dimension of parenting that describes the amount of responsiveness and affection that a parent displays toward a child.

accommodation: the process of modifying existing schemes in order to incorporate or adapt to new experiences.

accommodation: Piaget's term for the process by which children modify their existing schemes in order to incorporate or adapt to new experiences.

achievement attributions: causal explanations that one provides for his/her successes and failures.

achievement motivation: a willingness to strive to succeed at challenging tasks and to meet high standards of accomplishment.

acquired immune deficiency syndrome (AIDS): a viral disease that can be transmitted from a mother to her fetus or neonate and that results in a weakening of the body's immune system and, ultimately, death.

active genotype/environment correlations: the notion that our genotypes affect the types of environments that we prefer and seek out.

activity/passivity issue: a debate among developmental theorists about whether children are active contributors to their own development or passive recipients of environmental influence.

adaptation: an inborn tendency to adjust to the demands of the environment.

adolescent growth spurt: the rapid increase in physical growth that marks the beginning of adolescence.

adoption design: study in which adoptees are compared with their biological relatives and their adoptive relatives to estimate the heritability of an attribute.

age of viability: a point between the 22nd and 28th prenatal weeks when survival outside the uterus may be possible.

aging-ova hypothesis: the hypothesis that an older mother is more likely to have children with chromosomal abnormalities because her ova are degenerating as she nears the end of her reproductive years.

aggression: behavior performed with the intention of harming a living being who is motivated to avoid this treatment.

alleles: alternative forms of a gene that can appear at a particular site on a chromosome.

alternative birth center: a hospital birthing room or other independent facility that provides a homelike atmosphere for childbirth but still makes medical technology available.

altruism: a selfless concern for the welfare of others that is expressed through prosocial acts such as sharing, cooperating, and helping.

altruistic exhortations: verbal encouragements to help, comfort, share, or cooperate with others.

amniocentesis: a method of extracting amniotic fluid from a pregnant woman so that fetal body cells within the fluid can be tested for chromosomal abnormalities and other genetic defects.

amnion: a watertight membrane that surrounds the developing embryo, serving to regulate its temperature and to cushion it against injuries.

androgenized females: females who develop malelike external genitalia because of exposure to male sex hormones during the prenatal period.

androgyny: a gender-role orientation in which the individual has incorporated a large number of both masculine and feminine attributes into his or her personality.

animism: attributing life and lifelike qualities to inanimate objects.

anorexia nervosa: a life-threatening eating disorder characterized by self- starvation and a compulsive fear of getting fat.

A-not-B error: tendency of 8- to 12-month-olds to search for a hidden object where they previously found it even after they have seen it moved to a new location.

anoxia: a lack of sufficient oxygen to the brain; may result in neurological damage or death.

Apgar test: a quick assessment of the newborn's heart rate, respiration, color, muscle tone, and reflexes that is used to gauge perinatal stress and to determine whether a neonate requires immediate medical assistance.

appearance/reality distinction: ability to keep the true properties or characteristics of an object in mind despite the deceptive appearance that the object has assumed; notably lacking among young children during the preconceptual period.

aptitude-treatment interaction (ATI): phenomenon whereby characteristics of the student and of the school environment interact to affect student outcomes, such that any given educational practice may be effective with some students, but not with others.

asocial phase (of attachment): approximately the first 6 weeks of life, in which infants respond in an equally favorable way to interesting social and nonsocial stimuli.

assimilation: Piaget's term for the process by which children interpret new experiences by incorporating them into their existing schemes.

associative play: form of social discourse in which children pursue their own interests but will swap toys or comment on each other's activities.

attachment: a close emotional relationship between two persons, characterized by mutual affection and a desire to maintain proximity.

attachment Q-set: alternative method of assessing attachment security that is based on observations of the child's attachment-related behaviors at home, can be used with infants, toddlers, and preschool children.

attention deficit-hyperactivity disorder (ADHD): an attentional disorder involving distractibility, hyperactivity, and impulsive behavior that often leads to academic difficulties, poor self-esteem, and social/emotional problems.

attention span: capacity for sustaining attention to a particular stimulus or activity.

attribution retraining: therapeutic intervention in which helpless children are persuaded to attribute failures to their lack of effort rather than a lack of ability.

authoritarian parenting: a restrictive pattern of parenting in which adults set many rules for their children, expect strict obedience, and rely on power rather than reason to elicit compliance.

authoritative parenting: a flexible style of parenting in which adults allow their children autonomy, but are careful to explain the restrictions they impose and to ensure that their children follow these guidelines.

autiobiographical memory: memory for important experiences or events that have happened to us.

autonomous morality: Piaget's second stage of moral development, in which children realize that rules are arbitrary agreements that can be challenged and changed with the consent of the people they govern.

autonomy: the capacity to make decisions independently, to serve as one's own source of emotional strength, and to otherwise manage one's life tasks without depending on others for assistance; an important developmental task of adolescence.

autosomes: the 22 pairs of human chromosomes that are identical in males and females.

autostimulation theory: a theory proposing that REM sleep in infancy is a form of self-stimulation that helps the central nervous system to develop.

average-status children: children who receive a moderate number of nominations as a liked and/or a disliked individual from members of their peer group.

avoidant attachment: an insecure infant–caregiver bond, characterized by little separation protest and a tendency of the child to avoid or ignore the caregiver.

babbles: vowel–consonant combinations that infants begin to produce at about 4 to 6 months of age.

baby biography: a detailed record of an infant's growth and development over a period of time.

basic gender identity: the stage of gender identity in which the child first labels the self as a boy or a girl.

behavioral comparisons phase: the tendency to form impressions of others by comparing and contrasting their overt behaviors.

behavioral genetics: the scientific study of how genotype interacts with environment to determine behavioral attributes such as intelligence, personality, and mental health.

behavioral inhibition: a temperamental attribute reflecting one's tendency to withdraw from unfamiliar people or situations.
behavioral schemes: organized patterns of behavior that are used to represent and respond to objects and experiences.
behaviorism: a school of thinking in psychology that holds that conclusions about human development should be based on controlled observations of overt behavior rather than speculation about unconscious motives or other unobservable phenomena; the philosophical underpinning for the early theories of learning.
belief-desire theory: theory of mind that develops between ages 3 and 4; the child now realizes that both beliefs and desires may determine behavior and that people act on their beliefs, even if they are inaccurate.
benefits-to-risks ratio: a comparison of the possible benefits of a study for advancing knowledge and optimizing life conditions versus its costs to participants in terms of inconvenience and possible harm.
blended, or reconstituted, families: new families resulting from cohabitation or remarriage that include a parent, one or more children, and step-relations.
brain growth spurt: the period between the seventh prenatal month and 2 years of age when more than half of the child's eventual brain weight is added.
breech birth: a delivery in which the fetus emerges feet first or buttocks first rather than head first.
Broca's area: structure located in the frontal lobe of the left hemisphere of the cerebral cortex that controls language production.
bulimia: a life-threatening eating disorder characterized by recurrent eating binges followed by such purging activities as heavy use of laxatives or vomiting.
canalization: genetic restriction of phenotype to a small number of developmental outcomes; a highly canalized attribute is one for which genes channel development along predetermined pathways, so that the environment has little effect on the phenotype that emerges.
cardinality: principle specifying that the last number in a counting sequence specifies the number of items in a set.
caregiving hypothesis: Ainsworth's notion that the type of attachment that an infant develops with a particular caregiver depends primarily on the kind of caregiving he has received from that person.
carrier: a heterozygous individual who displays no sign of a recessive allele in his or her own phenotype but can pass this gene to offspring.
case study: a research method in which the investigator gathers extensive information about the life of an individual and then tests developmental hypotheses by analyzing the events of the person's life history.
catch-up growth: a period of accelerated growth in which children who have experienced growth deficits grow very rapidly to "catch up" to the growth trajectory that they are genetically programmed to follow.
castration anxiety: in Freud's theory, a young boy's fear that his father will castrate him as punishment for his rivalrous conduct.
categorical self: a person's classification of the self along socially significant dimensions such as age and sex.
centered thinking (or centration): in Piaget's theory, the tendency of preoperational children to attend to one aspect of a situation to the exclusion of others; in contrast with *decentration*.
cephalocaudal development: a sequence of physical maturation and growth that proceeds from the head (cephalic region) to the tail (or caudal region).
cerebral cortex: the outer layer of the brain's cerebrum that is involved in voluntary body movements, perception, and higher intellectual functions such as learning, thinking, and speaking.
cerebral lateralization: the specialization of brain functions in the left and right cerebral hemispheres.
cerebrum: the highest brain center; includes both hemispheres of the brain and the fibers that connect them.
cesarean section: surgical delivery of a baby through an incision made in the mother's abdomen and uterus.
child abuse: any extreme maltreatment of children, involving physical batterings, sexual molestations, psychological insults such as persistent ridicule, rejection, and terrorization, and physical or emotional neglect.
chorion: a membrane that becomes attached to the uterine tissues to gather nourishment for the embryo.
chorionic villus sampling (CVS): an alternative to amniocentesis in which fetal cells are extracted from the chorion for prenatal tests. CVS can be performed earlier in pregnancy than is possible with amniocentesis.
chromosome: a threadlike structure made up of genes; in humans, there are 46 chromosomes in the nucleus of each body cell.
chronosystem: in ecological systems theory, changes in the individual or the environment that occur over time and influence the direction of development.
class inclusion: the ability to compare a class of objects with its subclasses without confusing the two.
classical conditioning: a type of learning in which an initially neutral stimulus is repeatedly paired with a meaningful nonneutral stimulus so that the neutral stimulus comes to elicit the response originally made only to the nonneutral stimulus.
clinical method: a type of interview in which a participant's response to each successive question (or problem) determines what the investigator will ask next.
clique: a small group of friends that interacts frequently.
coaching: method of social-skills training in which an adult displays and explains various socially skilled behaviors, allows the child to practice them, and provides feedback aimed at improving the child's performances.
codominance: condition in which two heterozygous but equally powerful alleles produce a phenotype in which genes are both fully and equally expressed.
coercive home environment: a home in which family members often annoy one another and use aggressive or otherwise antisocial tactics as a method of coping with these aversive experiences.
cognition: the activity of knowing and the processes through which knowledge is acquired.
cognitive development: age-related changes that occur in mental activities such as attending, perceiving, learning, thinking, and remembering.
cognitive equilibrium: Piaget's term for the state of affairs in which there is a balanced, or harmonious, relationship between one's thought processes and the environment.
cognitive operation: an internal mental activity that one performs on objects of thought.
cognitive self-guidance system: in Vygotsky's theory, the use of private speech to guide problem-solving behavior.
cohort effect: age-related difference among cohorts that is attributable to cultural/historical differences in cohorts' growing-up experiences rather than to true developmental change.
committed compliance: compliance based on an eagerness or readiness to cooperate with a responsive parent who has been willing to cooperate with the child.
communication: the process by which one organism transmits information to and influences another.
compensatory interventions: special educational programs designed to further the cognitive growth and scholastic achievements of disadvantaged children.
compliance: the act of obeying the requests or commands of others.
computer-assisted instruction (CAI). use of computers to teach new concepts and practice academic skills.
conception: the moment of fertilization, when a sperm penetrates an ovum, forming a zygote.
concordance rate: the percentage of cases in which a particular attribute is present for one member of a twin pair if it is present for the other.
concrete operations: Piaget's third stage of cognitive development, lasting from about age 7 to age 11, when children acquire cognitive operations and think more logically about real objects and experiences.
conditioned response (CR): a learned response to a stimulus that was not originally capable of producing the response.
conditioned stimulus (CS): an initially neutral stimulus that comes to elicit a particular response after being paired with a UCS that always elicits the response.
confidentiality: the right of participants to concealment of their identity with respect to the data that they provide.
confluence hypothesis: Zajonc's notion that a child's intellectual development depends on the average intellectual level of all family members.
confounding variable: some factor other than the independent variable that if not controlled by the experimenter, could explain any differences across treatment conditions in participants' performance on the dependent variable.
congenital adrenal hyperplasia (CAH): a genetic anomaly that causes one's adrenal glands to produce unusually high levels of androgen from the prenatal period onward; often has masculinizing effects on female fetuses.
congenital defect: a problem that is present (though not necessarily apparent) at birth; such defects may stem from genetic and prenatal influences or from complications of the birth process.
conservation: the recognition that the properties of an object or substance do not change when its appearance is altered in some superficial way.
constructivist: one who gains knowledge by acting or otherwise operating on objects and events to discover their properties.
context-independent learning: learning that has no immediate relevance to the present context, as is done in modern schools; acquiring knowledge for knowledge's sake.
contextual model: view of children as active entities whose developmental paths represent a continuous, dynamic interplay between internal forces (nature) and external influences (nurture).
continuity/discontinuity issue: a debate among theorists about whether developmental changes are quantitative and continuous or qualitative and discontinuous (i.e., stage-like).
controversial children: children who receive many nominations by peers as a liked individual and many as a disliked individual.
convergent thinking: thinking that requires one to come up with a single correct answer to a problem; what IQ tests measure.

conventional morality: Kohlberg's term for the third and fourth stages of moral reasoning, in which moral judgments are based on a desire to gain approval (Stage 3) or to uphold laws that maintain social order (Stage 4).

cooperative learning methods: an educational practice whereby children of different races or ability levels are assigned to teams; each team member works on problems geared to his or her ability level, and all members are reinforced for "pulling together" and performing well as a team.

cooperative play: true social play in which children cooperate or assume reciprocal roles while pursuing shared goals.

coordination of secondary circular reactions: fourth substage of Piaget's sensorimotor stage; infants begin to coordinate two or more actions to achieve simple objectives.

coos: vowellike sounds that young infants repeat over and over during periods of contentment.

coparenting: circumstance in which parents mutually support each other and function as a cooperative parenting team.

corpus callosum: the bundle of neural fibers that connects the two hemispheres of the brain and transmits information from one hemisphere to the other.

correlation coefficient: a numerical index, ranging from −1.00 to +1.00, of the strength and direction of the relationship between two variables.

correlational design: a type of research design that indicates the strength of associations among variables; though correlated variables are systematically related, these relationships are not necessarily causal.

counterconditioning: a treatment based on classical conditioning in which the goal is to extinguish an undesirable response and replace it with a new and more adaptive one.

creativity: the ability to generate novel ideas or works that are useful and valued by others.

cross-cultural comparison: a study that compares the behavior and/or development of people from different cultural or subcultural backgrounds.

cross-generational problem: the fact that long-term changes in the environment may limit conclusions of a longitudinal project to that generation of children who were growing up while the study was in progress.

crossing over: a process in which genetic material is exchanged between pairs of chromosomes during meiosis.

cross-pressures: conflicts stemming from differences in the values and practices advocated by parents and those favored by peers.

cross-sectional design: a research design in which subjects from different age groups are studied at the same point in time.

crowd: a large, loosely organized peer group made up of several cliques that share similar norms, interests, and values.

crystallized intelligence: the ability to understand relations or solve problems that depend on knowledge acquired from schooling and other cultural influences.

cued recall: a recollection that is prompted by a cue associated with the setting in which the recalled event originally occurred.

cultural bias: the situation that arises when one cultural or subcultural group is more familiar with test items than another group and therefore has an unfair advantage.

cultural test bias hypothesis: the notion that IQ tests and testing procedures have a built-in, middle-class bias that explains the substandard performance of children from lower-class and minority subcultures.

culture-fair tests: intelligence tests constructed to minimize any irrelevant cultural biases in test content that could influence test performance.

cumulative-deficit hypothesis: the notion that impoverished environments inhibit intellectual growth and that these inhibiting effects accumulate over time.

decentration: in Piaget's theory, the ability of concrete operational children to consider multiple aspects of a stimulus or situation; in contrast with *centration.*

deferred imitation: the ability to reproduce a modeled activity that has been witnessed at some point in the past.

defiance: active resistance to others' requests or demands; noncompliant acts that are accompanied by anger and an intensification of ongoing behavior.

delay of gratification: a form of self-control that involves the capacity to inhibit impulses to seek small rewards available immediately in the interest of obtaining larger, delayed incentives.

demandingness/control: a dimension of parenting that describes how restrictive and demanding parents are.

deoxyribonucleic acid (DNA): long, double-stranded molecules that make up chromosomes.

dependent variable: the aspect of behavior that is measured in an experiment and assumed to be under the control of the independent variable.

deprivation dwarfism: a childhood growth disorder that is triggered by emotional deprivation and characterized by decreased production of GH, slow growth, and small stature.

desensitization hypothesis: the notion that people who watch a lot of media violence will become less aroused by aggression and more tolerant of violent and aggressive acts.

development: systematic continuities and changes in the individual over the course of life.

developmental continuities: ways in which we remain stable over time or continue to reflect our past.

developmental psychology: branch of psychology devoted to identifying and explaining the continuities and changes that individuals display over time.

developmental quotient (DQ): a numerical measure of an infant's performance on a developmental schedule relative to the performance of other infants of the same age.

developmental stage: a distinct phase within a larger sequence of development; a period characterized by a particular set of abilities, motives, behaviors, or emotions that occur together and form a coherent pattern.

diethylstilbestrol (DES): a synthetic hormone, formerly prescribed to prevent miscarriage, that can produce cervical cancer in adolescent female offspring and genital-tract abnormalities in males.

differentiation theory: a theory specifying that perception involves detecting distinctive features or cues that are contained in the sensory stimulation we receive.

difficult temperament: temperamental profile in which the child is irregular in daily routines and adapts slowly to new experiences, often responding negatively and intensely.

direct effect: instances in which any pair of family members affects and is affected by each other's behavior.

direct tuition: teaching young children how to behave by reinforcing "appropriate" behaviors and by punishing or otherwise discouraging inappropriate conduct.

disequilibriums: imbalances or contradictions between one's thought processes and environmental events. By contrast, *equilibrium* refers to a balanced, harmonious relationship between one's cognitive structures and the environment.

dishabituation: increase in responsiveness that occurs when stimulation changes.

disorganized/disoriented attachment: an insecure infant–caregiver bond, characterized by the infant's dazed appearance on reunion or a tendency to first seek and then abruptly avoid the caregiver.

distinctive features: characteristics of a stimulus that remain constant; dimensions on which two or more objects differ and can be discriminated (sometimes called invariances or invariant features).

divergent thinking: thinking that requires a variety of ideas or solutions to a problem when there is no one correct answer.

dizygotic (or fraternal) twins: twins that result when a mother releases two ova at roughly the same time and each is fertilized by a different sperm, producing two zygotes that are genetically different.

doctrine of specificity: a viewpoint shared by many social-learning theorists which holds that moral affect, reasoning, and behavior may depend as much or more on the situation that one faces than on an internalized set of moral principles.

dominant allele: a relatively powerful gene that is expressed phenotypically and masks the effect of a less powerful gene.

double standard: the view that sexual behavior that is appropriate for members of one gender is less appropriate for the other.

Down syndrome: a chromosomal abnormality (also known as trisomy-21) caused by the presence of an extra 21st chromosome; people with this syndrome have a distinctive physical appearance and are moderately to severely retarded.

dual representation (dual encoding; dual orientation): the ability to represent an object simultaneously as an object itself and as a representation of something else.

dynamic assessment: an approach to assessing intelligence that evaluates how well individuals learn new material when an examiner provides them with competent instruction.

dynamical systems theory: a theory that views motor skills as active reorganizations of previously mastered capabilities that are undertaken to find more effective ways of exploring the environment or satisfying other objectives.

easy temperament: temperamental profile in which the child quickly establishes regular routines, is generally good natured, and adapts easily to novelty.

eclectics: those who borrow from many theories in their attempts to predict and explain human development.

ecological systems theory: Bronfenbrenner's model emphasizing that the developing person is embedded in a series of environmental systems that interact with one another and with the person to influence development.

ecological validity: state of affairs in which the findings of one's research are an accurate representation of processes that occur in the natural environment.

effective schools: schools that are generally successful at achieving curricular and non curricular objectives, regardless of the racial, ethnic, or socioeconomic background of the student population.

ego: psychoanalytic term for the rational component of the personality.

egocentric speech: Piaget's term for the subset of a young child's utterances that are nonsocial—that is, neither directed to others nor expressed in ways that listeners might understand.

egocentrism: the tendency to view the world from one's own perspective while failing to recognize that others may have different points of view.

elaboration: a strategy for remembering that involves adding something to (or creating meaningful links between) the bits of information one is trying to retain.

Electra complex: female version of the Oedipus complex, in which a 3- to 6-year-old girl was thought to envy her father for possessing a penis and would choose him as a sex object in the hope that he to share with her this valuable organ that she lacked.

embryo: name given to the prenatal organism from the third through the eighth week after conception.

emotional bonding: term used to describe the strong affectionate ties that parents may feel toward their infant; some theorists believe that the strongest bonding occurs shortly after birth, during a sensitive period.

emotional display rules: culturally defined rules specifying which emotions should or should not be expressed under which circumstances.

emotional self-regulation: strategies for managing emotions or adjusting emotional arousal to a comfortable level of intensity.

empathic concern: a measure of the extent to which an individual recognizes the needs of others and is concerned about their welfare.

empathy: the ability to experience the same emotions that someone else is experiencing.

encoding: the process by which external stimulation is converted to a mental representation.

engrossment: paternal analogue of maternal emotional bonding; term used to describe fathers' fascination with their neonates, including their desire to touch, hold, caress, and talk to the newborn baby.

enrichment theory: a theory specifying that we must "add to" sensory stimulation by drawing on stored knowledge in order to perceive a meaningful world.

entity view of ability: belief that one's ability is a highly stable trait that is not influenced much by effort or practice.

environmental determinism: the notion that children are passive creatures who are molded by their environments.

environmental hypothesis: the notion that groups differ in IQ because the environments in which they are raised are not equally conducive to intellectual growth.

estrogen: female sex hormone, produced by the ovaries, that is responsible for female sexual maturation.

ethnography: method in which the researcher seeks to understand the unique values, traditions, and social processes of a culture or subculture by living with its members and making extensive observations and notes.

ethology: the study of the bioevolutionary bases of behavior and development.

event memory: long-term memory for events.

evocative genotype/environment correlations: the notion that our heritable attributes will affect others' behavior toward us and thus influence the social environment in which development takes place.

evoked potential: a change in patterning of the brain waves that indicates that an individual detects (senses) a stimulus.

executive control processes: the processes involved in regulating attention and determining what to do with information just gathered or retrieved from long-term memory.

exosystem: social systems that children and adolescents do not directly experience but that may nonetheless influence their development; the third of Bronfenbrenner's environmental layers or contexts.

expansions: responding to a child's ungrammatical utterance with a grammatically improved form of that statement.

experimental control: steps taken by an experimenter to ensure that all extraneous factors that could influence the dependent variable are roughly equivalent in each experimental condition; these precautions must be taken before an experimenter can be reasonably certain that observed changes in the dependent variable were caused by manipulation of the independent variable.

experimental design: a research design in which the investigator introduces some change in the participant's environment and then measures the effect of that change on the participant's behavior.

expressive role: a social prescription, usually directed toward females, that one should be cooperative, kind, nurturant, and sensitive to the needs of others.

expressive style: early linguistic style in which toddlers use language mainly to call attention to their own and others' feelings and to regulate social interactions.

extended family: a group of blood relatives from more than one nuclear family (for example, grandparents, aunts, uncles, nieces, and nephews) who live together, forming a household.

extinction: gradual weakening and disappearance of a learned response that occurs because the CS is no longer paired with the UCS (in classical conditioning) or the response is no longer reinforced (in operant conditioning).

extrafamilial influences: social agencies other than the family that influence a child's or an adolescent's cognitive, social, and emotional development.

factor analysis: a statistical procedure for identifying clusters of tests or test items (called factors) that are highly correlated with one another and unrelated to other test items.

false self behavior: acting in ways that do not reflect one's true self or the "true me."

falsifiability: a criterion for evaluating the scientific merit of theories. A theory is falsifiable when it is capable of generating predictions that could be disconfirmed.

family social system: the complex network of relationships, interactions, and patterns of influence that characterizes a family with three or more members.

fast mapping: process of linking a word with its referent after hearing the word a time or two.

"felt responsibility" hypothesis: the theory that empathy may promote altruism by causing one to reflect on altruistic norms and, thus, to feel some obligation to help distressed others.

fetal alcohol effects (FAE): a group of mild congenital problems that are sometimes observed in children of mothers who drink sparingly to moderately during pregnancy.

fetal alcohol syndrome (FAS): a group of serious congenital problems commonly observed in the offspring of mothers who abuse alcohol during pregnancy.

fetus: name given to the prenatal organism from the ninth week of pregnancy until birth.

field experiment: an experiment that takes place in a naturalistic setting such as home, school, or a playground.

first stage of labor: the period of the birth process lasting from the first regular uterine contractions until the cervix is fully dilated.

fixation: arrested development at a particular psychosexual stage which can prevent movement to higher stages.

fluid intelligence: the ability to perceive relationships and solve relational problems of the type that are not taught and are relatively free of cultural influences.

folic acid: B-complex vitamin that helps to prevent defects of the central nervous system.

foreclosure: identity status characterizing individuals who have prematurely committed themselves to occupations or ideologies without really thinking about these commitments.

formal operations: Piaget's fourth and final stage of cognitive development, from age 11 or 12 and beyond, when the individual begins to think more rationally and systematically about abstract concepts and hypothetical events.

fragile-X syndrome: abnormality of the X chromosome caused by a defective gene and associated with mild to severe mental retardation, particularly when the defective gene is passed from mother to child.

free recall: a recollection that is not prompted by specific cues or prompts.

friendship: a close and often enduring relationship between two individuals which may be characterized by loyalty and mutual affection.

fuzzy-trace theory: theory proposed by Brainerd & Reyna that postulates that people encode experiences on a continuum from literal, verbatim traces to fuzzy, gistlike traces.

g: Spearman's abbreviation for *neogenesis,* which, roughly translated, means one's ability to understand relations (or general mental ability).

gender consistency: the stage of gender identity in which the child recognizes that a person's gender is invariant despite changes in the person's activities or appearance (also known as *gender constancy).*

gender identity: one's awareness of one's gender and its implications.

gender intensification: a magnification of sex differences early in adolescence; associated with increased pressure to conform to traditional gender roles.

gender-role standard: a behavior, value, or motive that members of a society consider more typical or appropriate for members of one sex.

gender schemas: organized sets of beliefs and expectations about males and females that guide information processing.

gender segregation: children's tendency to associate with same-sex playmates and to think of the other sex as an out-group.

gender stability: the stage of gender identity in which the child recognizes that gender is stable over time.

gender typing: the process by which a child becomes aware of his or her gender and acquires motives, values, and behaviors considered appropriate for members of that sex.

genes: hereditary blueprints for development that are transmitted unchanged from generation to generation.

genetic counseling: a service designed to inform prospective parents about genetic diseases and to help them determine the likelihood that they would transmit such disorders to their children.

genetic epistemology: the experimental study of the development of knowledge, developed by Piaget.

genetic hypothesis: the notion that group differences in IQ are hereditary.

genetic imprinting: pattern of inheritance in which a pair of alleles is biochemically marked so that only one parent's allele is expressed, regardless of its composition.

genital herpes: a sexually transmitted disease that can infect infants at birth, causing blindness, brain damage, or even death.

genotype: the genetic endowment that an individual inherits.

germinal period: first phase of prenatal development, lasting from conception until the developing organism becomes firmly attached to the wall of the uterus (also called period of the zygote).

germline gene therapy: a procedure, not yet perfected or approved for use with humans, in which harmful genes would be repaired or replaced with healthy ones, thereby permanently correctly a genetic defect.

giftedness: the possession of unusually high intellectual potential or other special talents.

gist: a fuzzy representation of information that preserves the central content but few precise details.

glia: nerve cells that nourish neurons and encase them in insulating sheaths of myelin.

"goodness-of-fit" model: Thomas and Chess's notion that development is likely to be optimized when parents' child-rearing practices are sensitively adapted to the child's temperamental characteristics.

grammatical morphemes: prefixes, suffixes, prepositions, and auxiliary verbs that modify the meaning of words and sentences.

growth hormone (GH): the pituitary hormone that stimulates the rapid growth and development of body cells; primarily responsible for the adolescent growth spurt.

guided participation: adult–child interactions in which children's cognitions and modes of thinking are shaped as they participate with or observe adults engaged in culturally relevant activities.

habits: well-learned associations between stimuli and responses that represent the stable aspects of one's personality.

habituation: a decrease in one's response to a stimulus that has become familiar through repetition.

Head Start: a large-scale preschool educational program designed to provide children from low-income families with a variety of social and intellectual experiences that might better prepare them for school.

heritability: the amount of variability in a trait that is attributable to hereditary factors.

heritability coefficient: a numerical estimate, ranging from .00 to +1.00, of the amount of variation in an attribute that is due to hereditary factors.

heteronomous morality: Piaget's first stage of moral development, in which children view the rules of authority figures as sacred and unalterable.

heterozygous: having inherited two alleles for an attribute that have different effects.

heuristic value: a criterion for evaluating the scientific merit of theories. An heuristic theory is one that continues to stimulate new research and discoveries.

hierarchical model of intelligence: model of the structure of intelligence in which a broad, general ability factor is at the top of the hierarchy, with a number of specialized ability factors nested underneath.

high-amplitude sucking method: a method of assessing infants' perceptual capabilities that capitalizes on the ability of infants to make interesting events last by varying the rate at which they suck on a special pacifier.

high-risk neighborhood: a residential area in which the incidence of child abuse is much higher than in other neighborhoods with the same demographic characteristics.

holistic perspective: a unified view of the developmental process that emphasizes the important interrelationships among the physical, mental, social, and emotional aspects of human development.

holophrase: a single-word utterance that represents an entire sentence's worth of meaning.

holophrastic period: the period when the child's speech consists of one-word utterances, some of which are thought to be holophrases.

HOME inventory: a measure of the amount and type of intellectual stimulation provided by a child's home environment.

homozygous: having inherited two alleles for an attribute that are identical in their effects.

horizontal decalage: Piaget's term for a child's uneven cognitive performance; an inability to solve certain problems even though one can solve similar problems requiring the same mental operations.

hostile aggression: aggressive acts for which the perpetrator's major goal is to harm or injure a victim.

hostile attributional bias: tendency to view harm done under ambiguous circumstances as having stemmed from a hostile intent on the part of the harmdoer; characterizes reactive aggressors.

Huntington's disease: a genetic disease caused by a dominant allele that typically appears later in life and causes the nervous system to degenerate (see Box 3–1).

hypothesis: a theoretical prediction about some aspect of experience.

hypothetico-deductive reasoning: in Piaget's theory, a formal operational ability to think hypothetically.

id: psychoanalytic term for the inborn component of the personality that is driven by the instincts.

identification: Freud's term for the child's tendency to emulate another person, usually the same-sex parent.

identity: a mature self-definition; a sense of who one is, where one is going in life, and how one fits into society.

identity achievement: identity status characterizing individuals who have carefully considered identity issues and have made firm commitments to an occupation and ideologies.

identity crisis: Erikson's term for the uncertainty and discomfort that adolescents experience when they become confused about their present and future roles in life.

identity diffusion: identity status characterizing individuals who are not questioning who they are and have not yet committed themselves to an identity.

identity training: an attempt to promote conservation by teaching nonconservers to recognize that a transformed object or substance is the same object or substance, regardless of its new appearance.

ideographic development: individual variations in the rate, extent, or direction of development.

imaginary audience: allegedly a form of adolescent egocentrism that involves confusing one's own thoughts with those of a hypothesized audience and concluding that others share one's preoccupations.

immanent justice: the notion that unacceptable conduct will invariably be punished and that justice is ever present in the world.

implantation: the burrowing of the blastocyst into the lining of the uterus.

imprinting: an innate or instinctual form of learning in which the young of certain species follow and become attached to moving objects (usually their mothers).

incompatible-response technique: a nonpunitive method of behavior modification in which adults ignore undesirable conduct, while reinforcing acts that are incompatible with these responses.

incremental view of ability: belief that one's ability can be improved through increased effort and practice.

independent assortment: the principle stating that each pair of chromosomes segregates independently of all other chromosome pairs during meiosis.

independent variable: the aspect of the environment that an experimenter modifies or manipulates in order to measure its impact on behavior.

indirect, or third-party, effect: instances in which the relationship between two individuals in a family is modified by the behavior or attitudes of a third family member.

induction: a nonpunitive form of discipline in which an adult explains why a child's behavior is wrong and should be changed by emphasizing its effects on others.

infant states: levels of sleep and wakefulness that young infants display.

infantile amnesia: a lack of memory for the early years of one's life.

informal curriculum: non curricular objectives of schooling such as teaching children to cooperate, respect authority, obey rules, and become good citizens.

information-processing theory: a perspective that views the human mind as a continuously developing, symbol-manipulating system, similar to a computer, into which information flows, is operated on, and is converted to output (answers, inferences, and solutions to problems).

informed consent: the right of research participants to receive an explanation, in language they can understand, all aspects of research that may affect their willingness to participate.

in-group/out-group schema: one's general knowledge of the mannerisms, roles, activities, and behaviors that characterize males and females.

inhibition: the ability to prevent ourselves from executing some cognitive or behavioral response.

inhibitory control: an ability to display acceptable conduct by resisting the temptation to commit a forbidden act.

innate purity: the idea that infants are born with an intuitive sense of right and wrong that is often misdirected by the demands and restrictions of society.

inner experimentation: the sixth substage of Piaget's sensorimotor stage; the ability to solve simple problems on a mental, or symbolic, level without having to rely on trial-and-error experimentation.

instrumental aggression: aggressive acts for which the perpetrator's major goal is to gain access to objects, space, or privileges.

intelligence: in Piaget's theory, a basic life function that enables an organism to adapt to its environment.

intelligence quotient (IQ): a numerical measure of a person's performance on an intelligence test relative to the performance of other examinees.

internalization: the process of adopting the attributes or standards of other people, taking these standards as one's own.

internal working models: cognitive representations of self, others, and relationships that infants construct from their interactions with caregivers.

instinct: an inborn biological force that motivates a particular response or class of responses.

instrumental role: a social prescription, usually directed toward males, that one should be dominant, independent, assertive, competitive, and goal-oriented.

interactionist theory: the notion that biological factors and environmental influences interact to determine the course of language development.

intermodal perception: the ability to use one sensory modality to identify a stimulus or pattern of stimuli that is already familiar through another modality.

introversion–extroversion: the opposite poles of a personality dimension: Introverts are shy, anxious around others, and tend to withdraw from social situations; extroverts are highly sociable and enjoy being with others.

intuitive period: the later substage of preoperations, from age 4 to age 7, when the child's thinking about objects and events is dominated by salient perceptual features.

invariant developmental sequence: a series of developments that occur in one particular order because each development in the sequence is a prerequisite for the next.

investment theory of creativity: recent theory specifying that the ability to invest in innovative projects and to generate creative solutions depends on a convergence of creative resources, namely, background knowledge, intellectual abilities, personality characteristics, motivation, and environmental support/encouragement.

iron deficiency anemia: a listlessness caused by too little iron in the diet that makes children inattentive and may retard physical and intellectual development.

Kaufman Assessment Battery for Children (K-ABC): an individual intelligence test for children; grounded heavily in information-processing theory.

kewpie-doll effect: the notion that infantlike facial features are perceived as cute and lovable and elicit favorable responses from others.

kinetic cues: cues created by movements of objects or movements of the body; provide important information for the perception of forms and spatial relations.

kinship: the extent to which two individuals have genes in common.

knowledge base: one's existing information about a topic or content area.

kwashiorkor: a growth-retarding disease affecting children who receive enough calories, but little if any protein.

language: a small number of individually meaningless symbols (sounds, letters, gestures) that can be combined according to agreed-on rules to produce an infinite number of messages.

language acquisition device (LAD): Chomsky's term for the innate knowledge of grammar that humans were said to possess, which might enable young children to infer the rules governing others' speech and to use these rules to produce language.

language-making capacity (LMC): a hypothesized set of specialized linguistic processing skills that enable children to analyze speech and to detect phonological, semantic, and syntactical relationships.

lanugo: fine hair covering the fetus's body which helps vernix stick to the skin.

learned helplessness: the failure to learn how to respond appropriately in a situation because of previous exposures to uncontrollable events in the same or similar situations.

learned helplessness orientation: a tendency to give up or to stop trying after failing because these failures have been attributed to a lack of ability that one can do little about.

learning: a relatively permanent change in behavior (or behavioral potential) that results from one's experiences or practice.

learning goal: state of affairs in which one's primary objective in an achievement context is to increase one's skills or abilities.

Level I abilities: Jensen's term for lower-level intellectual abilities (such as attention and short-term memory) that are important for simple association learning.

Level II abilities: Jensen's term for higher-level cognitive skills that are involved in abstract reasoning and problem solving.

lexical contrast constraint: notion that young children make inferences about word meanings by contrasting new words with words they already know.

linguistic universal: an aspect of language development that all children share.

longitudinal design: a research design in which one group of subjects is studied repeatedly over a period of months or years.

long-term store (LTS): third information processing store, in which information that has been examined and interpreted is permanently stored for future use.

looking-glass self: the idea that a child's self-concept is largely determined by the ways that other people respond to him or her.

love withdrawal: a form of discipline in which an adult withholds attention, affection, or approval in order to modify or control a child's behavior.

macrosystem: the larger cultural or subcultural context in which development occurs; Bronfenbrenner's outermost environmental layer or context.

mainstreaming: the educational practice of integrating developmentally disabled students with special needs into regular classrooms rather than placing them in segregated special education classes.

manic depression: a psychotic disorder characterized by extreme fluctuations in mood.

marasmus: a growth-retarding disease affecting infants who receive insufficient protein and too few calories.

mastery motivation: an inborn motive to explore, understand, and control one's environment.

mastery orientation: a tendency to persist at challenging tasks because of a belief that one has high ability and/or that earlier failures can be overcome by trying harder.

maternal deprivation hypothesis: the notion that socially deprived infants develop abnormally because they have failed to establish attachments to a primary caregiver.

maturation: developmental changes in the body or behavior that result from the aging process rather than from learning, injury, illness, or some other life experience.

mean-world belief: a belief, fostered by televised violence, that the world is a more dangerous and frightening place than is actually the case.

mechanistic model: view of children as passive entities whose developmental paths are primarily determined by external (environmental) influences.

meiosis: the process in which a germ cell divides, producing gametes (sperm or ova) that each contain half of the parent cell's original complement of chromosomes; in humans, the products of meiosis contain 23 chromosomes.

memory span: a measure of the amount of information that can be held in the short-term store.

menarche: the first occurrence of menstruation.

mental age (MA): a measure of intellectual development that reflects the level of age-graded problems a child is able to solve.

mental retardation: significant subaverage intellectual functioning associated with impairments in adaptive behavior in everyday life.

mental seriation: a cognitive operation that allows one to mentally order a set of stimuli along a quantifiable dimension such as height or weight.

mesosystem: the interconnections among an individual's immediate settings or microsystems. The second of Bronfenbrenner's environmental layers or contexts.

metacognition: one's knowledge about cognition and about the regulation of cognitive activities.

metalinguistic awareness: a knowledge of language and its properties; an understanding that language can be used for purposes other than communicating.

metamemory: one's knowledge about memory and memory processes.

microsystem: the immediate settings (including role relationships and activities) that the person actually encounters; the innermost of Bronfenbrenner's environmental layers or contexts.

mitosis: the process in which a cell duplicates its chromosomes and then divides into two genetically identical daughter cells.

mnemonics (memory strategies): effortful techniques used to improve memory, including rehearsal, organization, and elaboration.

monozygotic (or identical) twins: twins that result when a single zygote divides into two separate but identical cells that each develop independently. As a result, each member of a monozygotic twin pair inherits exactly the same set of genes.

moral affect: the emotional component of morality, including feelings such as guilt, shame, and pride in ethical conduct.

moral behavior: the behavioral component of morality; actions that are consistent with one's moral standards in situations in which one is tempted to violate them.

morality: a set of principles or ideals that help the individual to distinguish right from wrong, to act on this distinction, and to feel pride in virtuous conduct and guilt (or shame) for conduct that violates one's standards.

morality of care: Gilligan's term for what she presumes to be the dominant moral orientation of females—an orientation focusing more on compassionate concerns for human welfare than on socially defined justice as administered through law.

morality of justice: Gilligan's term for what she presumes to be the dominant moral orientation of males, focusing more on socially defined justice as administered through law than on compassionate concerns for human welfare.

moral reasoning: the cognitive component of morality; the thinking that people demonstrate when deciding whether various acts are right or wrong.

moral rules: standards of acceptable and unacceptable conduct that focus on the rights and privileges of individuals.

moratorium: identity status characterizing individuals who are currently experiencing an identity crisis and are actively exploring occupational and ideological positions in which to invest themselves.

morphemes: the smallest meaningful units of language; these include words and grammatical markers such as prefixes, suffixes, and verb-tense modifiers (for example, -ed, -ing).

morphological knowledge: one's knowledge of the meaning of morphemes that make up words.

motherese: the short, simple, high-pitched (and often repetitive) sentences that adults use when talking with young children (also called *child-directed speech).*

"mother-only" monkeys: monkeys who are raised with their mothers and denied any contact with peers.

mutation: a change in the chemical structure or arrangement of one or more genes that has the effect of producing a new phenotype.

mutual exclusivity constraint: notion that young children assume that each object has only one label and that different words refer to separate and nonoverlapping categories.

myelinization: the process by which neurons are enclosed in waxy myelin sheaths that facilitate the transmission of neural impulses.

naming explosion: term used to describe the dramatic increase in the pace at which infants acquire new words in the latter half of the second year; so named because many of the new words acquired are the names of objects.

naturalistic observation: a method in which the scientist tests hypotheses by observing people as they engage in everyday activities in their natural habitats (for example, at home, at school, or on the playground).

natural, or prepared, childbirth: a delivery in which physical and psychological preparations for the birth are stressed and medical assistance is minimized.

natural (or quasi-) experiment: a study in which the investigator measures the impact of some naturally occurring event that is assumed to affect people's lives.

natural selection: an evolutionary process, proposed by Charles Darwin, stating that individuals with characteristics that promote adaptation to the environment will survive, reproduce, and pass these adaptive characteristics to offspring; those lacking these adaptive characteristics will eventually die out.

nature/nurture issue: the debate among developmental theorists about the relative importance of biological predispositions (nature) and environmental influences (nurture) as determinants of human development.

negative punishment: a punishing consequence that involves the removal of something pleasant following a behavior.

negative reinforcer: any stimulus whose removal or termination, as the consequence of an act, increases the probability that the act will recur.

neglected children: children who receive few nominations as either a liked or a disliked individual from members of their peer group.

Neonatal Behavior Assessment Scale (NBAS): a test that assesses a neonate's neurological integrity and responsiveness to environmental stimuli.

neonate: a newborn infant from birth to approximately 1 month of age.

neural tube: the primitive spinal cord that develops from the ectoderm and becomes the central nervous system.

neurons: nerve cells that receive and transmit neural impulses.

neurotic disorder: an irrational pattern of thinking or behavior that a person may use to contend with stress or to avoid anxiety.

nonorganic failure to thrive: an infant growth disorder, caused by lack of attention and affection, that causes growth to slow dramatically or stop.

nonrepresentative sample: a subgroup that differs in important ways from the larger group (or population) to which it belongs.

nonshared environmental influence (NSE): an environmental influence that people living together do not share which should make these individuals different from one another.

nonsocial activity: onlooker behavior and solitary play.

normal distribution: a symmetrical, bell-shaped curve that describes the variability of certain characteristics within a population; most people fall at or near the average score, with relatively few at the extremes of the distribution.

normative development: developmental changes that characterize most or all members of a species; typical patterns of development.

obese: a medical term describing individuals who are at least 20% above the ideal weight for their height, age, and sex.

object permanence: the realization that objects continue to exist when they are no longer visible or detectable through the other senses.

object scope constraint: the notion that young children assume that a new word applied to an object refers to the whole object rather than to parts of the object or to object attributes (for example, its color).

observer influence: tendency of participants to react to an observer's presence by behaving in unusual ways.

observational learning: learning that results from observing the behavior of others.

oedipal morality: Freud's theory that moral development occurs during the phallic period (ages 3 to 6) when children internalize the moral standards of the same-sex parent as they resolve their Oedipus or Electra conflicts.

Oedipus complex: Freud's term for the conflict that 3- to 6-year-old boys were said to experience when they develop an incestuous desire for their mothers and a jealous and hostile rivalry with their fathers.

open classroom: a less structured classroom arrangement in which there is a separate area for each educational activity and children distribute themselves around the room, working individually or in small groups.

operant learning: a form of learning in which voluntary acts (or operants) become either more or less probable, depending on the consequences they produce.

operating efficiency hypothesis: in Case's theory, the notion that operating space in working memory increases with age because we come to process information faster or more efficiently.

organismic model: view of children as active entities whose developmental paths are primarily determined by forces from within themselves.

organization: an inborn tendency to combine and integrate available schemes into coherent systems or bodies of knowledge.

original sin: the idea that children are inherently negative creatures who must be taught to rechannel their selfish interests into socially acceptable outlets.

otitis media: common bacterial infection of the middle ear that produces mild to moderate hearing loss.

overextension: the young child's tendency to use relatively specific words to refer to a broader set of objects, actions, or events than adults do (for example, using the word *car* to refer to all motor vehicles).

overregularization: the overgeneralization of grammatical rules to irregular cases where the rules do not apply (for example, saying *mouses* rather than *mice*).

own-sex schema: detailed knowledge or plans of action that enable a person to perform gender-consistent activities and to enact his or her gender role.

parallel play: largely noninteractive play in which players are in close proximity but do not often attempt to influence each other.

Parents Anonymous: an organization of reformed child abusers, (modeled after Alcoholics Anonymous).

parsimony: a criterion for evaluating the scientific merit of theories: a parsimonious theory is one that uses relatively few explanatory principles to explain a broad set of observations.

passive genotype/environment correlations: the notion that the rearing environments that biological parents provide are influenced by the parents' own genes, and hence are correlated with the child's own genotype.

peer acceptance: a measure of a person's likability (or dislikability) in the eyes of peers.

peer conformity: the tendency to go along with the wishes of peers or to yield to peer-group pressures.

peer group: a confederation of peers that interacts regularly, defines membership in the group, and formulates norms that specify how members are supposed to look, think, and act.

"peer-only" monkeys: monkeys who are separated from their mothers (and other adults) soon after birth and raised with peers.

peers: two or more persons who are operating at similar levels of behavioral complexity.

perception: the process by which we categorize and interpret sensory input.

perceptual learning: changes in one's ability to extract information from sensory stimulation that occur as a result of experience.

performance goal: state of affairs in which one's primary objective in an achievement context is to display one's competencies (or to avoid looking incompetent).

period of the embryo: second phase of prenatal development, lasting from the third through the eighth prenatal week, during which the major organs and anatomical structures take shape.

period of the fetus: third phase of prenatal development, lasting from the ninth prenatal week until birth; during this period, all major organ systems begin to function and the fetus grows rapidly.

permissive parenting: a pattern of parenting in which otherwise accepting adults make few demands of their children and rarely attempt to control their behavior.

personal fable: allegedly a form of adolescent egocentrism that involves thinking that oneself and one's thoughts and feelings are special or unique.

phallic stage: Freud's third stage of psychosexual development (from 3 to 6 years of age) in which children gratify the sex instinct by fondling their genitals and developing an incestuous desire for the parent of the other sex.

phase of indiscriminate attachments: period between 6 weeks and 6 to 7 months of age in which infants prefer social to nonsocial stimulation and are likely to protest whenever any adult puts them down or leaves them alone.

phase of multiple attachments: period when infants form attachments to companions other than their primary attachment object.

phase of specific attachment: period between 7 and 9 months of age when infants are attached to one close companion (usually the mother).

phenotype: the ways in which a person's genotype is expressed in observable or measurable characteristics.

phenylketonuria (PKU): a genetic disease in which the child is unable to metabolize phenylalanine; if left untreated, it soon causes hyperactivity and mental retardation.

phonemes: the basic units of sound that are used in a spoken language.

phonology: the sound system of a language and the rules for combining these sounds to produce meaningful units of speech.

pictorial (perspective) cues: depth and distance cues, including linear perspective, texture gradients, sizing, interposition, and shading, that are monocular—that is, detectable with only one eye.

pincer grasp: a grasp in which the thumb is used in opposition to the fingers, enabling an infant to become more dexterous at lifting and fondling objects.

pituitary: a "master gland" located at the base of the brain that regulates the endocrine glands and produces growth hormone.

placenta: an organ, formed from the lining of the uterus and the chorion, that provides for respiration and nourishment of the unborn child and the elimination of its metabolic wastes.

plasticity: capacity for change; a developmental state that has the potential to be shaped by experience.

polygenic trait: a characteristic that is influenced by the action of many genes rather than a single pair.

popular children: children who are liked by many members of their peer group and disliked by very few.

positive punishment: a punishing consequence that involves the presentation of something unpleasant following a behavior.
positive reinforcer: any stimulus whose presentation, as the consequence of an act, increases the probability that the act will recur.
postconventional morality: Kohlberg's term for the fifth and sixth stages of moral reasoning, in which moral judgments are based on social contracts and democratic law (Stage 5) or on universal principles of ethics and justice (Stage 6).
postpartum depression: strong feelings of sadness, resentment, and despair that may affect the mother shortly after childbirth and that can linger for months.
power assertion: a form of discipline in which an adult relies on his or her superior power (for example, by administering spankings or withholding privileges) to modify or control a child's behavior.
practice effect: changes in participants' natural responses as a result of repeated testing.
pragmatics: principles that underlie the effective and appropriate use of language in social contexts.
preadapted characteristic: an innate attribute that is a product of evolution and serves some function that increases the chances of survival for the individual and the species.
precausal, or transductive reasoning: reasoning from the particular to the particular, so that events that occur together are assumed to be causally related.
preconceptual period: the early substage of preoperations, from age 2 to age 4, characterized by the appearance of primitive ideas, concepts, and methods of reasoning.
preconventional morality: Kohlberg's term for the first two stages of moral reasoning, in which moral judgments are based on the tangible punitive consequences (Stage 1) or rewarding consequences (Stage 2) of an act for the actor rather than on the relationship of that act to society's rules and customs.
preference method: a method used to gain information about infants' perceptual abilities by presenting two (or more) stimuli and observing which stimulus the infant prefers.
prelinguistic phase: the period before children utter their first meaningful words.
premoral period: in Piaget's theory, the first 5 years of life, when children have little respect for or awareness of socially defined rules.
prenatal development: development that occurs between the moment of conception and the beginning of the birth process.
preoperational stage: Piaget's second stage of cognitive development, lasting from about age 2 to age 7, when children think at a symbolic level but do not yet use cognitive operations.
preterm babies: infants born more than 3 weeks before their normal due dates.
primary circular reactions: second substage of Piaget's sensorimotor stage; a pleasurable response, centered on the infant's own body, that is discovered by chance and performed over and over.
primary mental abilities: seven mental abilities, identified by factor analysis, that Thurstone believed to represent the structure of intelligence.
primary (or basic) emotions: the set of emotions present at birth or emerging early in the first year that some theorists believe to be biologically programmed.
primitive reflexes: reflexes controlled by subcortical areas of the brain that gradually disappear over the first year of life.
private self (or I): those inner, or subjective, aspects of self that are known only to the individual and are not available for public scrutiny.
private speech: Vygotsky's term for the subset of a child's verbal utterances that serve a self-communicative function and guide the child's thinking.
proactive aggressors: highly aggressive children who find aggressive acts easy to perform and who rely heavily on aggression as a means of solving social problems or achieving other personal objectives.
processing constraints: cognitive biases or tendencies that lead infants and toddlers to favor certain interpretations of the meaning of new words over other interpretations.
production deficiency: a failure to spontaneously generate and use known strategies that could improve learning and memory.
productive language: that which the individual is capable of expressing (producing) in his or her own speech.
proprioceptive information: sensory information from the muscles, tendons, and joints that help one to locate the position of one's body (or body parts) in space.
prosocial moral reasoning: the thinking that people demonstrate when deciding whether to help, share with, or comfort others when these actions could prove costly to themselves.
protection from harm: the right of research participants to be protected from physical or psychological harm.
proximodistal development: a sequence of physical maturation and growth that proceeds from the center of the body (the proximal region) to the extremities (distal regions).
psycholinguists: those who study the structure and development of children's language.
psychological comparisons phase: tendency to form impressions of others by comparing and contrasting these individuals on abstract psychological dimensions.
psychological constructs phase: tendency to base one's impressions of others on the stable traits that these individuals are presumed to have.
psychometric approach: a theoretical perspective that portrays intelligence as a trait (or set of traits) on which individuals differ; psychometric theorists are responsible for the development of standardized intelligence tests.
psychophysiological methods: methods that measure the relationships between physiological processes and aspects of children's physical, cognitive, or emotional behavior/development.
psychosexual theory: Freud's theory that states that maturation of the sex instinct underlies stages of personality development, and that the manner in which parents manage children's instinctual impulses determines the traits that children display.
psychosocial theory: Erikson's revision of Freud's theory that emphasizes sociocultural (rather than sexual) determinants of development and posits a series of eight psychosocial conflicts that people must resolve successfully to display healthy psychological adjustment.
puberty: the point at which a person reaches sexual maturity and is physically capable of fathering or conceiving a child.
public self (or me): those aspects of self that others can see or infer.
punisher: any consequence of an act that suppresses that act and/or decreases the probability that it will recur.
Pygmalion effect: the tendency of teacher expectancies to become self-fulfilling prophecies, causing students to perform better or worse depending on their teacher's estimation of their potential.

qualitative change: changes in kind that make individuals fundamentally different than they were before. The transformation of a prelinguistic infant into a language user is viewed by many as a qualitative change in communication skills.
quantitative change: incremental change in degree without sudden transformations; for example, some view the small yearly increases in height and weight that 2- to 11-year-olds display as quantitative developmental changes.

random assignment: a control technique in which participants are assigned to experimental conditions through an unbiased procedure so that the members of the groups are not systematically different from one another.
range-of-reaction principle: the idea that genotype sets limits on the range of possible phenotypes that a person might display in response to different environments.
reactive aggressors: children who display high levels of hostile, retaliatory aggression because they overattribute hostile intents to others and can't control their anger long enough to seek nonaggressive solutions to social problems.
reactive attachment disorder: inability to form *secure* attachment bonds with other people; characterizes many victims of early social deprivation and/or abuse.
recasts: responding to a child's ungrammatical utterance with a nonrepetitive statement that is grammatically correct.
receptive language: that which the individual comprehends when listening to others' speech.
recessive allele: a less powerful gene that is not expressed phenotypically when paired with a dominant allele.
reciprocal determinism: the notion that the flow of influence between children and their environments is a two-way street; the environment may affect the child, but the child's behavior also influences the environment.
referential communication skills: abilities to generate clear verbal messages, to recognize when others' messages are unclear, and to clarify any unclear messages one transmits or receives.
referential style: early linguistic style in which toddlers use language mainly to label objects.
reflex: an unlearned and automatic response to a stimulus or class of stimuli.
reflex activity: first substage of Piaget's sensorimotor stage; infants' actions are confined to exercising innate reflexes, assimilating new objects into these reflexive schemes, and accommodating their reflexes to these novel objects.
rehearsal: a strategy for remembering that involves repeating the items one is trying to retain.
reinforcer: any consequence of an act that increases the probability that the act will recur.
rejected-aggressive children: a subgroup of rejected children who display high levels of hostility and aggression in their interactions with peers.
rejected children: children who are disliked by many peers and liked by few.
rejected-withdrawn children: a subgroup of rejected children who are often passive, socially unskilled, and insensitive to peer-group expectations.
relational aggression: acts such as snubbing, exclusion, withdrawing acceptance, or spreading rumors that are aimed at damaging an adversary's self-esteem, friendships, or social status.
reliability: the extent to which a measuring instrument yields consistent results, both over time and across observers.
REM sleep: a state of active or irregular sleep in which the eyes move rapidly beneath the eyelids and brain-wave activity is similar to the pattern displayed when awake.
representational insight: the knowledge that an entity can stand for (represent) something other than itself.

repression: a type of motivated forgetting in which anxiety-provoking thoughts and conflicts are forced out of conscious awareness.
resistant attachment: an insecure infant–caregiver bond, characterized by strong separation protest and a tendency of the child to remain near but resist contact initiated by the caregiver, particularly after a separation.
respiratory distress syndrome: a serious condition in which a preterm infant breathes very irregularly and is at risk of dying (also called *hyaline membrane disease*).
retaliatory aggression: aggressive acts elicited by real or imagined provocations.
reticular formation: area of the brain that activates the organism and is thought to be important in regulating attention.
retrieval: class of strategies aimed at getting information out of the long-term store.
reversibility: the ability to reverse or negate an action by mentally performing the opposite action (negation).
RH factor: a blood protein that, when present in a fetus but not the mother, can cause the mother to produce antibodies. These antibodies may then attack the red blood cells of subsequent fetuses who have the protein in their blood.
rites of passage: rituals that signify the passage from one period of life to another (for example, puberty rites).
role taking: the ability to assume another person's perspective and understand his or her thoughts, feelings, and behaviors.
rubella (German measles): a disease that has little effect on a mother but may cause a number of serious birth defects in unborn children who are exposed in the first 3 to 4 months of pregnancy.

s: Spearman's term for mental abilities that are specific to particular tests.
scaffolding: process by which an expert, when instructing a novice, responds contingently to the novice's behavior in a learning situation, so that the novice gradually increases his or her understanding of a problem.
scheme: an organized pattern of thought or action that one constructs to interpret some aspect of one's experience (also called *cognitive structure*).
schizophrenia: a serious form of mental illness characterized by disturbances in logical thinking, emotional expression, and interpersonal behavior.
scientific method: an attitude or value about the pursuit of knowledge that dictates that investigators must be objective and allow their data to determine the merits of their theorizing.
script: a general representation of the typical sequencing of events (that is, what occurs and when) in some familiar context.
secondary circular reactions: third substage of Piaget's sensorimotor stage; a pleasurable response, centered on an external object, that is discovered by chance and performed over and over.
secondary (or complex) emotions: self-conscious or self-evaluative emotions that emerge in the second year and depend, in part, on cognitive development.
secondary reinforcer: an initially neutral stimulus that acquires reinforcement value by virtue of its repeated association with other reinforcing stimuli.
second stage of labor: the period of the birth process during which the fetus moves through the birth canal and emerges from the mother's body (also called *delivery*).
secular trend: a trend in industrialized societies toward earlier maturation and greater body size now than in the past.
secure attachment: an infant–caregiver bond in which the child welcomes contact with a close companion and uses this person as a secure base from which to explore the environment.
secure base: an infant's use of a caregiver as a base from which to explore the environment and to which to return for emotional support.
selective attention: capacity to focus on task-relevant aspects of experience while ignoring irrelevant or distracting information.
selective attrition: nonrandom loss of participants during a study which results in a nonrepresentative sample.
selective breeding experiment: a method of studying genetic influences by determining whether traits can be bred in animals through selective mating.
self: the combination of physical and psychological attributes that is unique to each individual.
self-assertion: noncompliant acts that are undertaken by children in the interest of doing things for themselves or otherwise establishing autonomy.
self-care, or latchkey, children: children who care for themselves after school or in the evenings while their parents are working.
self-concept: one's perceptions of one's unique attributes or traits.
self-control: ability to regulate one's conduct and to inhibit actions that are unacceptable or that conflict with a goal.
self-esteem: one's evaluation of one's worth as a person based on an assessment of the qualities that make up the self-concept.
self-fulfilling prophecy: phenomenon whereby people cause others to act in accordance with the expectations they have about those others.
self-oriented distress: feeling of *personal* discomfort or distress that may be elicited when we experience the emotions of (that is, empathize with) a distressed other; thought to inhibit altruism.
self-recognition: the ability to recognize oneself in a mirror or a photograph.
semantic organization: a strategy for remembering that involves grouping or classifying stimuli into meaningful (or manageable) clusters that are easier to retain.
semantics: the expressed meaning of words and sentences.
sensation: detection of stimuli by the sensory receptors and transmission of this information to the brain.
sensitive period: period of time that is optimal for the development of particular capacities or behaviors and in which the individual is particularly sensitive to environmental influences that would foster these attributes.
sensitive-period hypothesis (of language acquisition): the notion that human beings are most proficient at language learning before they reach puberty.
sensorimotor stage: Piaget's first intellectual stage, from birth to 2 years, when infants are relying on behavioral schemes as a means of exploring and understanding the environment.
sensory store (or sensory register): first information-processing store, in which stimuli are noticed and are briefly available for further processing.
separation anxiety: a wary or fretful reaction that infants and toddlers often display when separated from the person(s) to whom they are attached.
sequential design: a research design in which subjects from different age groups are studied repeatedly over a period of months or years.
sex-linked characteristic: an attribute determined by a recessive gene that appears on the X chromosome; more likely to characterize males.
sexuality: aspect of self referring to erotic thoughts, actions, and orientation.
shared environmental influence (SE): an environmental influence that people living together share which should make these individuals similar to one another.
short-term store (STS): second information-processing store, in which stimuli are retained for several seconds and operated upon (also called working memory).
sibling rivalry: the spirit of competition, jealousy, and resentment that may arise between two or more siblings.
sickle-cell anemia: a genetic blood disease that causes red blood cells to assume an unusual sickled shape and to become inefficient at distributing oxygen.
simple dominant-recessive inheritance: a pattern of inheritance in which one allele dominates another so that only its phenotype is expressed.
single-parent family: a family system consisting of one parent (either the mother or the father) and the parent's dependent child(ren).
size constancy: the tendency to perceive an object as the same size from different distances despite changes in the size of its retinal image.
situational compliance: compliance based primarily on the parent's power to control the child's conduct.
skeletal age: a measure of physical maturation based on the child's level of skeletal development.
slow-to-warm-up temperament: temperamental profile in which the child is inactive and moody and displays mild passive resistance to new routines and experiences.
small-for-date babies: infants whose birth weight is far below normal, even when born close to their normal due dates.
sociability: willingness to interact with others and to seek their attention or approval.
social cognition: thinking people display about the thoughts, feelings, motives, and behaviors of themselves and other people.
social comparison: the process of defining and evaluating the self by comparing oneself with other people.
social-conventional rules: standards of conduct determined by social consensus that indicate what is appropriate within a particular social context.
socialization: the process by which children acquire the beliefs, values, and behaviors considered desirable or appropriate by the society to which they belong.
social problem-solving training: method of social-skills training in which an adult helps children (through role playing or role-taking training) to make less hostile attributions about harmdoing and to generate nonaggressive solutions to conflict.
social referencing: the use of others' emotional expressions to infer the meaning of otherwise ambiguous situations.
social stimulation hypothesis: the notion that socially deprived infants develop abnormally because they have had little contact with companions who respond contingently to their social overtures.
social support: tangible and intangible resources provided by other people in times of uncertainty or stress.
sociocultural theory: Vygotsky's perspective on cognitive development, in which children acquire their culture's values, beliefs, and problem-solving strategies through collaborative dialogues with more knowledgeable members of society.
sociolinguistic knowledge: culturally specific rules specifying how language should be structured and used in particular social contexts.

sociometric techniques: procedures that ask children to identify those peers whom they like or dislike or to rate peers for their desirability as companions; used to measure children's peer acceptance (or nonacceptance).

spina bifida: a bulging of the spinal cord through a gap in the spinal column.

Stanford-Binet Intelligence Scale: modern descendent of the first successful intelligence test which measures general intelligence and four factors: verbal reasoning, quantitative reasoning, spatial reasoning, and short-term memory.

stereopis: fusion of two flat images to produce a single image that has depth.

stereotype threat: a fear that one will be judged to have traits associated with negative social stereotypes about his or her racial or ethnic group.

store model: information-processing model that depicts information as flowing through three processing units (or stores): the sensory store, the short-term store (STS), and the long-term store (LTS).

stranger anxiety: a wary or fretful reaction that infants and toddlers often display when approached by an unfamiliar person.

strange situation: a series of eight separation and reunion episodes to which infants are exposed in order to determine the quality of their attachments.

strategic memory: processes involved as one consciously attempts to retain or retrieve information.

strategies: goal-directed and deliberately implemented mental operations used to facilitate task performance.

strategy choice model: Siegler's model to describe how strategies change over time; the view that multiple strategies exist within a child's cognitive repertoire at any one time, with these strategies competing with one another for use.

structure-of-intellect model: Guilford's factor-analytic model of intelligence, which proposes that there are 180 distinct mental abilities.

structured interview or structured questionnaire: a technique in which all participants are asked the same questions in precisely the same order so that the responses of different participants can be compared.

structured observation: an observational method in which the investigator cues the behavior of interest and observes participants' responses in a laboratory.

sudden infant death syndrome (SIDS): the unexplained death of a sleeping infant who suddenly stops breathing (also called *crib death*).

superego: psychoanalytic term for the component of the personality that consists of one's internalized moral standards.

survival reflexes: inborn responses such as breathing, sucking, and swallowing that enable the newborn to adapt to the environment.

symbolic function: the ability to use symbols (for example, images and words) to represent objects and experiences.

symbolic schemes: internal mental symbols (such as images or verbal codes) that one uses to represent aspects of experience.

sympathetic empathic arousal: feelings of sympathy or compassion that may be elicited when one experiences the emotions of (that is, empathize with) a distressed other; thought to become an important mediator of altruism.

synapse: the connective space (juncture) between one nerve cell (neuron) and another.

synaptogenesis: formation of connections (synapses) among neurons.

synchronized routines: generally harmonious interactions between two persons in which participants adjust their behavior in response to the partner's actions.

syntactical bootstrapping: notion that young children make inferences about the meaning of words by analyzing the way words are used in sentences and inferring whether they refer to objects (nouns), actions (verbs), or attributes (adjectives).

syntax: the structure of a language; the rules specifying how words and grammatical markers are to be combined to produce meaningful sentences.

syphilis: a common sexually transmitted disease that may cross the placental barrier in the middle and later stages of pregnancy, causing miscarriage or serious birth defects.

tabula rasa: the idea that the mind of an infant is a "blank slate" and that all knowledge, abilities, behaviors, and motives are acquired through experience.

tacit (or practical) intelligence: ability to size up everyday problems and solve them; only modestly related to IQ.

telegraphic speech: early sentences that consist of content words and omit the less meaningful parts of speech, such as articles, prepositions, pronouns, and auxiliary verbs.

television literacy: one's ability to understand and interpret how information is conveyed in television programming.

temperament: a person's characteristic modes of responding emotionally and behaviorally to environmental events, including such attributes as activity level, irritability, fearfulness, and sociability.

temperament hypothesis: Kagan's view that the strange-situations test measures individual differences in infants' temperaments rather than the quality of their attachments.

teratogens: external agents such as viruses, drugs, chemicals, and radiation that can harm a developing embryo or fetus.

tertiary circular reactions: fifth substage of Piaget's sensorimotor stage; an exploratory scheme in which the infant devises a new method of acting on objects to reproduce interesting results.

testicular feminization syndrome (TFS): a genetic anomaly in which a male fetus is insensitive to the effects of male sex hormones and develops femalelike external genitalia.

test norms: standards of normal performance on psychometric instruments that are based on the average scores and the range of scores obtained by a large, representative sample of test takers.

testosterone: male sex hormone, produced by the testes, that is responsible for male sexual maturation.

thalidomide: a mild tranquilizer that, taken early in pregnancy, can produce a variety of malformations of the limbs, eyes, ears, and heart.

theory: a set of concepts and propositions designed to organize, describe, and explain an existing set of observations.

theory of multiple intelligences: Gardner's theory that humans display at least seven distinct kinds of intelligence, each linked to a particular area of the brain, several of which are not measured by IQ tests.

third stage of labor: expulsion of the placenta (afterbirth).

three-stratum theory of intelligence: Carroll's hierarchial model of intelligence with *g* at the top of the hierarchy, eight broad abilities at the second level, or stratum, and narrower domains of each second-stratum ability at the third stratum.

thyroxine: a hormone produced by the thyroid gland; essential for normal growth of the brain and the body.

time-out technique: a form of discipline in which children who misbehave are removed from the setting until they are prepared to act more appropriately.

timing-of-puberty effect: the finding that people who reach puberty late perform better on visual/spatial tasks than those who mature early.

tools of intellectual adaptation: Vygotsky's term for methods of thinking and problem-solving strategies that children internalize from their interactions with more competent members of society.

toxoplasmosis: disease caused by a parasite found in raw meat and cat feces; can cause birth defects if transmitted to an embryo in the first trimester and miscarriage later in pregnancy.

traditional classroom: a classroom arrangement in which all pupils sit facing an instructor, who normally teaches one subject at a time by lecturing or giving demonstrations.

traditional nuclear family: a family unit consisting of a wife/mother, a husband/father, and their dependent child(ren).

transactive interactions: verbal exchanges in which individuals perform mental operations on the reasoning of their discussion partners.

transformational grammar: rules of syntax that allow one to transform declarative statements into questions, negatives, imperatives, and other kinds of sentences.

transitivity: the ability to recognize relations among elements in a serial order (for example, if A > B and B > C, then A > C).

triarchic theory: a recent information-processing theory of intelligence that emphasizes three aspects of intelligent behavior not normally tapped by IQ tests: the *context* of the action; the person's *experience* with the task (or situation); and the *information-processing strategies* the person applies to the task (or situation).

twin design: study in which sets of twins that differ in zygosity (kinship) are compared to determine the heritability of an attribute.

two-generation intervention: interventions with goals to both stimulate children's intellectual development through preschool day-care/education and to assist parents to move out of poverty.

two-way bilingual education: programs in which English-speaking (or other majority-language) children and children who have limited proficiency in English are instructed half of the day in English and the other half in a second language.

ulnar grasp: an early manipulatory skill in which an infant grasps objects by pressing the fingers against the palm.

ultrasound: method of detecting gross physical abnormalities by scanning the womb with sound waves, thereby producing a visual outline of the fetus.

umbilical cord: a soft tube containing blood vessels that connects the embryo to the placenta.

unconditioned response (UCR): the unlearned response elicited by an unconditioned stimulus.

unconditioned stimulus (UCS): a stimulus that elicits a particular response without any prior learning.

unconscious motives: Freud's term for feelings, experiences, and conflicts that influence a person's thinking and behavior, but lie outside the person's awareness.

underextension: the young child's tendency to use general words to refer to a smaller set of objects, actions, or events than adults do (for example, using *candy* to refer only to mints).

uninvolved parenting: a pattern of parenting that is both aloof (or even hostile) and overpermissive, almost as if parents neither cared about their children nor about what they may become.

utilization deficiency: a failure to benefit from effective strategies that one has spontaneously produced; thought to occur in the early phases of strategy acquisition when executing the strategy requires much mental effort.

validity: the extent to which a measuring instrument accurately reflects what the researchers intended to measure.

vernix: white cheesy substance that covers the fetus to protect the skin from chapping.

visual acuity: a person's ability to see small objects and fine detail.

visual cliff: an elevated platform that creates an illusion of depth, used to test the depth perception of infants.

visual contrast: the amount of light/dark transition in a visual stimulus.

visual looming: the expansion of the image of an object to take up the entire visual field as it draws very close to the face.

visual/spatial abilities: the ability to mentally manipulate or otherwise draw inferences about pictorial information.

vitamin/mineral deficiency: a form of malnutrition in which the diet provides sufficient protein and calories but is lacking in one or more substances that promote normal growth.

vocables: unique patterns of sound that a prelinguistic infant uses to represent objects, actions, or events.

Wechsler Intelligence Scale for Children (WISC-III): widely used individual intelligence test that includes a measure of general intelligence and both verbal and performance intelligence.

Wernicke's area: structure located in the temporal lobe of the left hemisphere of the cerebral cortex that is responsible for interpreting speech.

working memory: the capacity to store and operate on information being held in the short-term store.

X chromosome: the longer of the two sex chromosomes; normal females have two X chromosomes, whereas normal males have but one.

Y chromosome: the shorter of the two sex chromosomes; normal males have one Y chromosome, whereas females have none.

zone of proximal development: Vygotsky's term for the range of tasks that are too complex to be mastered alone but can be accomplished with guidance and encouragement from a more skillful partner.

zygote: a single cell formed at conception from the union of a sperm and an ovum.

References

Abel, E. L. (1981). Behavioral teratology of alcohol. *Psychological Bulletin, 90,* 564–581.

Abma, J. C., & Mott, F. L. (1991). Substance use and prenatal care during pregnancy among young women. *Family Planning Perspectives, 23,* 117–122, 128.

Aboud, F. E. (1988). *Children and prejudice.* New York: Blackwell.

Abramovitch, R., Corter, C., & Pepler, D. J. (1980). Observations of mixed-sex sibling dyads. *Child Development, 51,* 1268–1271.

Abramovitch, R., Corter, C., Pepler, D. J., & Stanhope, L. (1986). Sibling and peer interaction: A final follow-up and a comparison. *Child Development, 57,* 217–229.

Abramovitch, R., Freedman, J. L., Henry, K., & Van Brunschot, M. (1995). Children's capacity to agree to psychological research: Knowledge of risks and benefits and voluntariness, *Ethics & Behavior, 5,* 25–48.

Abravanel, E., & Sigafoos, A. D. (1984). Exploring the presence of imitation during early infancy. *Child Development, 55,* 381–392.

Achenbach, T. M., Phares, V., Howell, C. T., Rauh, V. A., & Nurcombe, B. (1990). Seven-year outcome of the Vermont Intervention Program for low-birthweight infants. *Child Development, 61,* 1672–1681.

Ackerman, B. P. (1993). Children's understanding of the speaker's meaning in referential communication. *Journal of Experimental Child Psychology, 55,* 56–86.

Ackerman, B. P., Szymanski, J., & Silver, D. (1990). Children's use of common ground in interpreting ambiguous referential utterances. *Developmental Psychology, 26,* 234–245.

Ackermann-Liebrich, U., Voegeli, T., Gunter-Witt, K., Kunz, I., Zullig, M., Schlindler, C., & Maurer, M. (1996). Home versus hospital deliveries: Follow up study of matched pairs for procedures and outcome. *British Medical Journal, 313,* 1313–1318.

Ackil, J. K., & Zaragoza, M. S. (1995). Developmental differences in eyewitness suggestibility and memory for source. *Journal of Experimental Child Psychology, 60,* 57–83.

Acredolo, C. (1982). Conservation/nonconservation: Alternative explanations. In C. J. Brainerd (Ed.), *Progress in cognitive development* (Vol. 1). New York: Springer-Verlag.

Acredolo, L. P., & Goodwyn, S. W. (1990). Sign language in babies: The significance of symbolic gesturing for understanding language development. In R. Vasta (Ed.), *Annals of child development* (Vol. 7, pp. 1–42). Greenwich, CT: JAI Press.

Adams, G. R., Abraham, K. G., & Markstrom, C. A. (1987). The relations among identity development, self-consciousness, and self-focusing during middle and late adolescence. *Developmental Psychology, 23,* 292–297.

Adams, G. R., & Crane, P. (1980). An assessment of parents' and teachers' expectations of preschool children's social preference for attractive or unattractive children and adults. *Child Development, 51,* 224–231.

Adams, M. J. (1990). *Beginning to read: Learning and thinking about print.* Cambridge, MA: MIT Press.

Adey, P. S., & Shayer, M. (1992). Accelerating the development of formal thinking in middle and high school students: II. Postproject effects on science achievement. *Journal of Research in Science Teaching, 29,* 81–92.

Adler, A. (1964). *Problems of neurosis.* New York: Harper & Row. (Original work published 1929).

Adolph, K. E., Eppler, M. A., & Gibson, E. J. (1993). Crawling versus walking infants' perception of affordances for locomotion over sloping surfaces. *Child Development, 64,* 1158–1174.

Akhtar, N., Carpenter, M., & Tomasello, M. (1996). The role of discourse novelty in early word learning. *Child Development, 67,* 635–645.

Ainsworth, M. D. S. (1967). *Infancy in Uganda: Infant care and the growth of love.* Baltimore: Johns Hopkins University Press.

Ainsworth, M. D. S. (1979). Attachment as related to mother-infant interaction. In J. S. Rosenblatt, R. A. Hinde, C. Beer, & M. Busnel (Eds.), *Advances in the study of behavior* (Vol. 9). New York: Academic Press.

Ainsworth, M. D. S. (1989). Attachments beyond infancy. *American Psychologist, 44,* 709–716.

Ainsworth, M. D. S., Bell, S. M., & Stayton, D. J. (1972). Individual differences in the development of some attachment behaviors. *Merrill-Palmer Quarterly, 18,* 123–143.

Ainsworth, M. D. S., Blehar, M., Waters, E., & Wall, S. (1978). *Patterns of attachment.* Hillsdale, NJ: Erlbaum.

Al-Awad, A. M., & Sonuga-Barke, E. J. (1992). Childhood problems in a Sudanese city: A comparison of extended and nuclear families. *Child Development, 63,* 906–914.

Albert, R. S. (1994). The achievement of eminence: A longitudinal study of exceptionally gifted boys and their families. In R. F. Subotnik & K. D. Arnold (Eds.), *Beyond Terman: Contemporary studies of giftedness and talent* (pp. 282–315). Norwood, NJ: Ablex.

Aldridge, S. (1996). *The thread of life: The story of genes and genetic engineering.* Cambridge, England: Cambridge University Press.

Alessandri, S. M., & Lewis, M. (1996). Differences in pride and shame in maltreated and nonmaltreated toddlers. *Child Development, 67,* 1857–1869.

Alessandri, S. M., Sullivan, M. W., Imaizumi, S., & Lewis, M. (1993). Learning and emotional responsivity in cocaine-exposed infants. *Developmental Psychology, 29,* 989–997.

Alexander, B. K., & Harlow, H. F. (1965). Social behavior in juvenile rhesus monkeys subjected to different rearing conditions during the first 6 months of life. *Zoologische Jarbucher Physiologie, 60,* 167–174.

Alexander, G. M., & Hines, M. (1994). Gender labels and play styles: Their relative contribution to children's selection of playmates. *Child Development, 65,* 869–879.

Alexander, K. L., & Entwisle, D. R. (1988). Achievement in the first two years of school: Patterns and processes. *Monographs of the Society for Research in Child Development, 53* 2, Serial No. 218.

Alfieri, T., Ruble, D. N., & Higgins, E. T. (1996). Gender stereotypes during adolescence: Developmental changes and the transition to junior high school. *Developmental Psychology, 32,* 1129–1137.

Allen, J. P., Philliber, S., Herrling, S., & Kuperminc, G. P. (1997). Preventing teen pregnancy and academic failure: Experimental evaluation of a developmentally based approach. *Child Development, 68,* 729–742.

Allen, J. P., Weissberg, R. P., & Hawkins, J. A. (1989). The relation between values and social competence in early adolescence. *Developmental Psychology, 25,* 458–464.

Allen, M. C., & Capute, A. J. (1986). Assessment of early auditory and visual abilities of extremely premature infants. *Developmental Medicine and Child Neurology, 28,* 458–466.

Alley, T. R. (1981). Head shape and the perception of cuteness. *Developmental Psychology, 17,* 650–654.

Allgood-Merten, B., & Stockard, J. (1991). Sex role identity and self-esteem: A comparison of children and adolescents. *Sex Roles, 25,* 129–139.

Allison, P. D., & Furstenberg, F. F., Jr. (1989). How marital dissolution affects children: Variations by age and sex. *Developmental Psychology, 25,* 540–549.

Amabile, T. M. (1983). *The social psychology of creativity.* New York: Springer-Verlag.

Amato, P. R. (1993). Children's adjustment to divorce: Theories, hypotheses, and empirical support. *Journal of Marriage and the Family, 55,* 23–38.

Amato, P. R. (1996). Explaining the intergenerational transmission of divorce. *Journal of Marriage and the Family, 58,* 628–640.

Amato, P. R., & Booth, A. (1996). A prospective study of divorce and parent-child relationships. *Journal of Marriage and the Family, 58,* 356–365.

Ambert, A. (1992). *The effect of children on parents.* New York: Haworth.

Ambron, S. R., & Irwin, D. M. (1975). Roletaking and moral judgment in five- and seven-year-olds. *Developmental Psychology, 11,* 102.

American Academy of Pediatrics (1986). Sexuality, contraception, and the media. *Pediatrics, 71,* 535–536.

American Association of Mental Retardation (1992). *Mental retardation: Definition, classification, and systems of support* (9th ed.). Washington, DC: Author.

American Psychiatric Association (1994). *Diagnostic and statistical manual of mental disorders* (4th ed.). Washington, D.C.: American Psychiatric Association.

American Psychological Association (1992). Ethical principles of psychologists and code of conduct. *American Psychologist, 47,* 1597–1611. Washington, DC: American Psychological Association.

Ammerman, R. T., & Patz, R. J. (1996). Determinants of child abuse potential: Parent and child factors. *Journal of Clinical Child Psychology, 25,* 300–307.

Anderson, D. R., & Collins, P. A. (1988). *The impact on children's education: Television's influence on cognitive development.* Washington, DC: U.S. Department of Education.

Anderson, D. R., Lorch, E. P., Field, D. E., & Sanders, J. (1981). The effects of TV program comprehensibility on preschool children's visual attention to television. *Child Development, 52,* 151–157.

Anderson, J. (1996). Gynecological and obstetrical issues for HIV-infected women. In R. R. Faden & N. E. Kass (Eds.), *HIV, AIDS, and childbearing.* (pp. 31–62). New York: Oxford University Press.

Anderson, K. E., Lytton, H., & Romney, D. M. (1986). Mothers' interactions with normal and conduct-disordered boys: Who affects whom? *Developmental Psychology, 22,* 604–609.

Andersson, B. (1989). Effects of public day-care: A longitudinal study. *Child Development, 60,* 857–866.

Andersson, B. (1992). Effects of day-care on cognitive and socioemotional competence of thirteen-year-old Swedish schoolchildren. *Child Development, 63,* 20–36.

Anglin, J. M. (1993). Vocabulary development: a morphological analysis. *Monographs of the Society for Research in Child Development, 58*(10, Serial No. 238).

Apgar, V., & Beck, J. (1974). *Is my baby all right?* New York: Pocket Books.

Archer, J. (1991). The influence of testosterone on human aggression. *British Journal of Psychology, 82,* 1–28.

Archer, J. (1992a). Childhood gender roles: Social context and organization. In H. McGurk (Ed.), *Childhood social development: Contemporary perspectives.* Hove, England: Erlbaum.

Archer, J. (1992b). *Ethology and human development.* Hertfordshire, England: Harvester Wheatsheaf.

Archer, J. (1996). Sex differences in social behavior: Are the social role and evolutionary explanations compatible? *American Psychologist, 51,* 909–917.

Archer, S. L. (1982). The lower age boundaries of identity development. *Child Development, 53,* 1551–1556.

Archer, S. L. (1992c). A feminist's approach to identity research. In G. R. Adams, T. P. Gullotta, & R. Montemayor (Eds.), *Adolescent identity formation* (Advances in Adolescent Development, Vol. 4). Newbury Park, CA: Sage.

Archer, S. L. (1994). *Interventions for adolescent identity development.* Thousand Oaks, CA: Sage.

Aries, P. (1962). *Centuries of childhood.* New York: Knopf.

Arnett, J. (1990). Contraceptive use, sensation seeking, and adolescent egocentrism. *Journal of Youth and Adolescence, 19,* 171–180.

Arnett, J.J. (1995). Broad and narrow socialization: The family in the context of a cultural theory. *Journal of Marriage and the Family, 57,* 617–628.

Arnett, J., & Balle-Jensen, L. (1993). Cultural bases of risk behavior: Danish adolescents. *Child Development, 64,* 1842–1855.

Aro, H., & Taipale, V. (1987). The impact of timing of puberty on psychosomatic symptoms among fourteen- to sixteen-year-old Finnish girls. *Child Development, 58,* 261–268.

Aronson, E., Blaney, N., Stephan, C., Sikes, J., & Snapp, M. (1978). *The jigsaw classroom.* Beverly Hills, CA: Sage.

Aronson, E., & Rosenbloom, S. (1971). Space perception within a common auditory-visual space. *Science, 172,* 1161–1163.

Arsenio, W. F., & Kramer, R. (1992). Victimizers and their victims: Children's conceptions of mixed emotional consequences of moral transgressions. *Child Development, 63,* 915–927.

Arterberry, M., Yonas, A., & Bensen, A. S. (1989). Self-produced locomotion and the development of responsiveness to linear perspective and texture gradients. *Developmental Psychology, 25,* 976–982.

Aruffo, J. R., Coverdale, J. H., & Vallbona, C. (1991). AIDS knowledge in low-income and minority populations. *Public Health Reports, 106,* 115–119.

Asendorph, J. B., & Baudonniere, P. (1993) Self-awareness and other-awareness: Mirror self-recognition and synchronic imitation among unfamiliar peers. *Developmental Psychology, 29,* 88–95.

Asendorph, J. B., Warkentin, V., & Baudonniere, P. (1996). Self-awareness and other awareness. II: Mirror self-recognition, social contingency awareness, and synchronic imitation. *Developmental Psychology, 32,* 313–321.

Ashcraft M. H. (1990). Strategic processing in children's mental arithmetic: A review and proposal. In D. F. Bjorklund (Ed.), *Children's strategies: contemporary views of cognitive development* (pp. 185–211). Hillsdale, NJ: Erlbaum.

Ashcraft, M. H., & Fierman, B. A. (1982). Mental addition in third, fourth, and sixth grades. *Journal of Experimental Child Psychology, 33,* 216–234.

Asher, S. R., & Coie, J. D. (1990). *Peer rejection in childhood.* Cambridge, England: Cambridge University Press.

Asher, S. R., Renshaw, P. D., & Hymel, S. (1982). Peer relations and the development of social skills. In S. G. Moore (Ed.), *The young child: Reviews of research* (Vol. 3). Washington, DC: National Association for the Education of Young Children.

Aslin, R. N. (1987). Visual and auditory development in infancy. In J. D. Osofsky (Ed.), *Handbook of infant development* (2nd ed.). New York: Wiley.

Aslin, R. N., Pisoni, D. B., & Jusczyk, P. W. (1983). Auditory development and speech perception in infancy. In M. M. Haith & J. J. Campos (Eds.), *Handbook of child psychology* (Vol. 2). *Infancy and developmental psychobiology.* New York: Wiley.

Aslin, R. N., & Smith, L. B. (1988). Perceptual development. *Annual Review of Psychology, 39,* 435–473.

Associated Press (1994a, July 30). Science: A man's domain. *Atlanta Constitution,* p. A6.

Associated Press (1994b, August 24). Which practices work best in today's schools? *Atlanta Constitution,* p. A1, A14.

Associated Press (1994c, September 7). Study: TV ignores, maligns hispanics. *Fresno Bee,* F1, F4.

Associated Press (1996, December 30). Arizona to require divorcing parents to study impact on children. *Dallas Morning News,* p. 18a.

Astor, R. A. (1994). Children's moral reasoning about family and peer violence: The role of provocation and retribution. *Child Development, 65,* 1054–1067.

Atkin, C. (1978). Observation of parent-child interaction in supermarket decision-making. *Journal of Marketing, 42,* 41–45.

Atkinson, L., Scott, B., Chisholm, V., Blackwell, J., Dickens, S., Tam, F., & Goldberg, S. (1995). Cognitive coping, affective stress, and material sensitivity: Mothers of children with Down Syndrome. *Developmental Psychology, 31,* 668–676.

Atkinson, R. C., & Shiffrin, R. M. (1968). Human memory: A proposed system and its control processes. In K. W. Spence & J. T. Spence (Eds.), *The psychology of learning and motivation: Advances in research and theory* (Vol. 2, pp. 90–195). Orlando, FL: Academic Press.

Atwater, E. (1992). *Adolescence* (2nd ed.). Englewood Cliffs, NJ: Prentice-Hall.

Austin, R. J., & Moawad, A. H. (1993). The very low birth weight fetus. In C. Lin, M. S. Verp, & R. E. Sabbagha (Eds.), *The high-risk fetus: Pathophysiology, diagnosis, management.* New York: Springer-Verlag.

Azmitia, M. (1988). Peer interaction and problem-solving: When are two heads better than one? *Child Development, 59,* 87–96.

Azmitia, M. (1992). Expertise, private speech, and the development of self-regulation. In R. M. Diaz & L. E. Berk (Eds.), *Private speech: From social interaction to self-regulation.* Hillsdale, NJ: Erlbaum.

Azmitia, M., & Hesser, J. (1993). Why siblings are important agents of cognitive development: A comparison of siblings and peers. *Child Development, 64,* 430–444.

Backschneider, A. G., Shatz, M., & Gelman, S. A. (1993). Preschoolers' ability to distinguish living kinds as a function of regrowth. *Child Development, 64,* 1242–1257.

Baddeley, A. D. (1986). *Working memory.* Oxford: Clarendon Press.

Bagley, C. (1995). *Child sexual abuse and mental health in adolescents and adults.* Aldershot, England: Ashgate Publishing Company.

Bagwell, C. L., Newcomb, A. F., & Bukowski, W. M. (1998). Preadolescent friendship and peer rejection as predictors of adult adjustment. *Child Development, 69,* 140–153.

Bahrick, L. E. (1988). Intermodal learning in infancy: Learning on the basis of two kinds of invariant relations in audible and visible events. *Child Development, 59,* 197–209.

Bai, D. L., & Bertenthal, B. I. (1992). Locomotor status and the development of spatial search skills. *Child Development, 63,* 215–226.

Baier, J. L., Rosenzweig, M. G., & Whipple, E. (1991). Patterns of sexual behavior, coercion, and victimization of university students. *Journal of College Student Development, 32,* 310–322.

Bailey, J. M., Brobow, D., Wolfe, M., & Mikach, S. (1995). Sexual orientation of adult sons of gay fathers. *Developmental Psychology, 31,* 124–129.

Bailey, J. M., & Pillard, R. C. (1991). A genetic study of the male sexual orientation. *Archives of General Psychiatry, 48,* 1089–1096.

Bailey, J. M., Pillard, R. C., Neale, M. C., & Agyei, Y. (1993). Heritable factors influence sexual orientation in women. *Archives of General Psychiatry, 50,* 217–223.

Baillargeon, R. (1987). Object permanence in 3½- and 4½-month-old infants. *Developmental Psychology, 23,* 655–664.

Baillargeon, R., & De Vos, J. (1991). Object permanence in young infants: Further evidence. *Child Development, 62,* 1227–1246.

Baillargeon, R., & Graber, M. (1988). Evidence of location memory in 8-month-old infants in a nonsearch AB task. *Developmental Psychology, 24,* 502–511.

Baker, D. P., & Jones, D. P. (1992). Opportunity and performance: A sociological explanation for gender differences in academic mathematics. In J. Wrigley (Ed.), *Education and gender equality.* London: The Falmer Press.

Baker, L. A., & Daniels, D. (1990). Nonshared environmental influences and personality differences in adult twins. *Journal of Personality and Social Psychology, 58,* 103–110.

Baker, L. A., Mack, W., Moffitt, T. E., & Mednick, S. (1989). Sex differences in property crime in a Danish adoption cohort. *Behavior Genetics, 19,* 355–370.

Baker, R. L., & Mednick, B. R. (1984). *Influences on human development: A longitudinal perspective.* Boston: Kluwer Nijhoff.

Baker-Ward, L., Ornstein, P. A., & Holden, D. J. (1984). The expression of memorization in early childhood. *Journal of Experimental Child Psychology, 37,* 555–575.

Baldwin, D. A., Markman, E. M., Bill, B., Desjardins, R. N., Irwin, J. M., & Tidball, G. (1996). Infants' reliance on social criteria for establishing word-object relations. *Child Development, 67,* 3135–3153.

Baldwin, D. A., & Moses, L. J. (1996). The ontogeny of social information gathering. *Child Development, 67,* 1915–1939.

Baldwin, D. V., & Skinner, M. L. (1989). Structural model for antisocial behavior: Generalization to single-mother families. *Developmental Psychology, 25,* 45–50.

Ball, S., & Bogatz, C. (1970). *The first year of Sesame Street: An evaluation.* Princeton, NJ: Educational Testing Service.

Ball, S., & Bogatz, C. (1973). *Reading with television: An evaluation of The Electric Company.* Princeton, NJ: Educational Testing Service.

Bandura, A. (1965). Influence of models' reinforcement contingencies on the acquisition of imitative responses. *Journal of Personality and Social Psychology, 1,* 589–595.

Bandura, A. (1971). *Psychological modeling.* New York: Lieber-Atherton.

Bandura, A. (1977). *Social learning theory.* Englewood Cliffs, NJ: Prentice-Hall.

Bandura, A. (1986). *Social foundations of thought and action. A social cognitive theory.* Englewood Cliffs, NJ: Prentice-Hall.

Bandura, A. (1989). Social cognitive theory. In R. Vasta (Ed.), *Annals of child development;* (Vol. 6). *Theories of child development: Revised formulations and current issues* (pp. 1–60). Greenwich, CT: JAI Press.

Bandura, A. (1991). Social cognitive theory of moral thought and action. In Kurtines, W. M., & Gewirtz, J. L. (Eds.), *Handbook of moral behavior and development* (Vol 1, pp. 45–103). Hillsdale, NJ: Erlbaum.

Bandura, A. (1992). Perceived self-efficacy in cognitive development and functioning. *Educational Psychologist, 28,* 117–148.

Banks, J. A. (1993). Multicultural education: Historical development, dimensions,and practice. *Review of Educational Research, 19,* 3–49.

Banks, M. S., & Ginsburg, A. P. (1985). Infant visual preferences: A review and new theoretical treatment. In H. W. Reese (Ed.), *Advances in child development and behavior* (Vol. 19, pp. 207–246). Orlando, FL: Academic Press.

Banks, M. S., & Salapatek, P. (1983). Infant visual perception. In M. M. Haith & J. J. Campos (Eds.), *Handbook of child psychology.* (Vol. 2). *Infancy and developmental psychobiology* (pp. 436–571). New York: Wiley.

Barber, B. K., Olsen, J. E., & Shagle, S. C. (1994). Associations between parental psychological and behavioral control and youth internalized and externalized behaviors. *Child Development, 65,* 1120–1136.

Barber, B. L., & Eccles, J. S. (1992). Long-term influence of divorce and single parenting on adolescent family- and work-related values, behaviors, and aspirations. *Psychological Bulletin, 111,* 108–126.

Barden, R. C., Ford, M. E., Jensen, A. G., Rogers-Salyer, M., & Salyer, K. E. (1989). Effects of craniofacial deformity in infancy on the quality of mother-infant interactions. *Child Development, 60,* 819–824.

Barenboim, C. (1981). The development of person perception in childhood and adolescence: From behavioral comparisons to psychological constructs to psychological comparisons. *Child Development, 52,* 129–144.

Barker, D. J. P. (1994). *Mothers, babies, and disease in later life.* London: BMJ Publishing Group.

Barker, R. G., & Gump, P. V. (1964). *Big school, small school.* Stanford, CA: Stanford University Press.

Barnard, K. E., & Bee, H. L. (1983). The impact of temporally patterned stimulation on the development of preterm infants. *Child Development, 54,* 1156–1167.

Barnett, M. A. (1987). Empathy and related responses in children. In N. Eisenberg & J. Strayer (Eds.), *Empathy and its development.* Cambridge, England: Cambridge University Press.

Barnett, W. S. (1993). Benefit-cost analysis of preschool education: Findings from a 25-year follow-up. *American Journal of Orthopsychiatry, 63,* 500–508.

Baron, N. S. (1992). *Growing up with language: How children learn to talk.* Reading, MA: Addison-Wesley.

Baron, R. A., & Byrne, D. (1994). *Social psychology: Understanding human interaction* (7th ed.). Newton, MA: Allyn & Bacon.

Baroni, M. R., & Axia, G. (1989). Children's meta-pragmatic abilities and the identification of polite and impolite requests. *First Language, 9,* 285–297.

Barr, H. M., Streissguth, A. P., Darby, B. L., & Sampson, P. D. (1990). Prenatal exposure to alcohol, caffeine, tobacco, and aspirin: Effects on fine and gross motor performance in 4-year-old children. *Developmental Psychology, 26,* 339–348.

Barrera, M. E., & Maurer, D. (1981). Recognition of mother's photographed face by the three-month-old infant. *Child Development, 52,* 714–716.

Barrett, D. E., & Frank, D. A. (1987). *The effects of undernutrition on children's behavior.* New York: Gordon and Breach.

Barry, H., III, Bacon, M. K., & Child, I. L. (1957). A cross-cultural survey of some sex differences in socialization. *Journal of Abnormal and Social Psychology, 55,* 327–332.

Bar-Tal, D., Raviv, A., & Goldberg, M. (1982). Helping behavior among preschool children: An observational study. *Child Development, 53,* 396–402.

Bartholomew, K., & Horowitz, L. M. (1991). Attachment styles among young adults: A test of a four-category model. *Journal of Personality and Social Psychology, 61,* 226–244.

Barton, M. E., & Tomasello, M. (1991). Joint attention and conversation in mother-infant-sibling triads. *Child Development, 62,* 517–529.

Baskett, L. M. (1985). Sibling status effects: Adult expectations. *Developmental Psychology, 21,* 441–445.

Baskett, L. M., & Johnson, S. M. (1982). The young child's interaction with parents versus siblings: A behavioral analysis. *Child Development, 53,* 643–650.

Bates, E. (1993, March). *Nature, nurture, and language.* Invited address presented at the biennial meeting of the Society for Research in Child Development, New Orleans.

Bates, E., O'Connell, B., & Shore, C. (1987). Language and communication in infancy. In J. D. Osofsky (Ed.), *Handbook of infant development,* (2nd ed.). New York: Wiley.

Bates, E., Thal, D., Whitsell, K., Fenson, L., & Oakes, L. (1989). Integrating language and gesture in infancy. *Developmental Psychology, 25,* 1004–1019.

Batson, C. D. (1991). *The altruism question: Toward a social-psychological answer.* Hillsdale, NJ: Erlbaum.

Bauer, P. J. (1996). What do infants recall of their lives? Memory for specific events by one- to two-year-olds. *American Psychologist, 51,* 29–41.

Bauer, P. J. (1997). Development of memory in early childhood. In N. Cowan (Ed.), *The development of memory in childhood* (pp. 83–111). Hove East Essex, England: Psychology Press.

Bauer, P. J., & Mandler, J. M. (1989). One thing follows another: Effects of temporal structure on 1- to 2-year-olds' recall of events. *Developmental Psychology, 25,* 197–206.

Bauer, P. J., & Wewerka, S. S. (1995). One- and two-year-olds recall events: Factors facilitating immediate and long-term memory an 13.5 and 16.5-month-old children. *Child Development, 64,* 1204–1223.

Baumrind, D. (1967). Child care practices anteceding three patterns of preschool behavior. *Genetic Psychology Monographs, 75,* 43–88.

Baumrind, D. (1971). Current patterns of parental authority. *Developmental Psychology Monographs, 4,*1, 2.

Baumrind, D. (1973). The development of instrumental competence through socialization. In A. Pick (Ed.), *Minnesota symposium on child psychology* (Vol. 7). Minneapolis: University of Minnesota Press.

Baumrind, D. (1977, March). *Socialization determinants of personal agency.* Paper presented at the biennial meeting of the Society for Research in Child Development, New Orleans.

Baumrind, D. (1983). Rejoinder to Lewis's reinterpretation of parental firm control effects: Are authoritative families really harmonious? *Psychological Bulletin, 94,* 132–142.

Baumrind, D. (1991). Effective parenting during the early adolescent transition. In P. A. Cowan & M. Hetherington (Eds.), *Family transitions.* Hillsdale, NJ: Erlbaum.

Baumrind, D. (1993). The average expectable environment is not good enough: A response to Scarr. *Child Development, 64,* 1299–1317.

Baumrind, D. (1995). Commentary on sexual orientation: Research and social policy implications. *Developmental Psychology, 31,* 130–136.

Bayley, N. (1969). *Bayley Scales of Infant Development.* New York: The Psychological Corporation.

Bayley, N. (1993). *Bayley Scales of Infant Development* (2nd ed.). San Antonio, TX: Psychological Corporation.

Beach, F. A. (1965). *Sex and behavior.* New York: Wiley.

Beal, C. R. (1990). Development of knowledge about the role of inference in text comprehension. *Child Development, 61,* 1011–1023.

Beal, C. R. (1994). *Boys and girls: The development of gender roles.* New York: McGraw-Hill.

Beal, C. R., & Belgrad, S. L. (1990). The development of message evaluation skills in young children. *Child Development, 61,* 705–712.

Bear, G. G., & Rys, G. S. (1994). Moral reasoning, classroom behavior, and sociometric status among elementary school children. *Developmental Psychology, 30,* 633–638.

Beard, R., & Chapple, J. (1995). An evaluation of maternity services. In B. P. Sachs, R. Beard, E. Papiernik, & C. Russell (Eds.), *Reproductive health care for women and babies* (pp. 246–262). New York: Oxford University Press.

Beckwith, L., Rodning, C., & Cohen, S. (1992). Preterm children at early adolescence and continuity and discontinuity in maternal responsiveness from infancy. *Child Development, 63,* 1198–1208.

Behrend, D. A., Rosengren, K., & Perlmutter, M. (1989). A new look at children's private speech: The effects of age, task difficulty, and parent presence. *International Journal of Behavioral Development, 12,* 305–320.

Beidelman, T. O. (1971). *The Kaguru: A matrilineal people of East Africa.* New York: Holt, Rinehart & Winston.

Beilin, H. (1992). Piaget's enduring contribution to developmental psychology. *Developmental Psychology, 28,* 191–204.

Bell, A. P., Weinberg, M. S., & Hammersmith, S. K. (1981). *Sexual preference: Its development in men and women.* Bloomington, IN: Indiana University Press.

Bell, M. A., & Fox, N. A. (1992). The relations between frontal brain electrical activity and cognitive development during infancy. *Child Development, 63,* 1142–1163.

Bell, R. Q. (1979). Parent, child, and reciprocal influences. *American Psychologist, 34,* 821–826.

Bellugi, U. (1988). The acquisition of a spatial language. In F. S. Kessel (Ed.), *The development of language and language researchers: Essays in honor of Roger Brown.* Hillsdale, NJ: Erlbaum.

Belmont, L., & Marolla, F. A. (1973) Birth order, family size, and intelligence. *Science, 182,* 1096–1101.

Belsky, J. (1981). Early human experience: A family perspective. *Developmental Psychology, 17,* 3–23.

Belsky, J. (1985). Experimenting with the family in the newborn period. *Child Development, 56,* 407–414.

Belsky, J. (1993). Etiology of child maltreatment: A developmental ecological analysis, *Psychological Bulletin, 114,* 413–434.

Belsky, J. (1996). Parent, infant, and social-contextual antecedents of father-son attachment security. *Developmental Psychology, 32,* 905–913.

Belsky, J., Crnic, K., & Gable, S. (1995). The determinants of coparenting in families with toddler boys: Spousal differences and daily hassles. *Child Development, 66,* 629–642.

Belsky, J., Garduque, L., & Hrncir, E. (1984). Assessing performance, competence, and executive capacity in infant play: Relations to home environment and security of attachment. *Developmental Psychology, 20,* 406–417.

Belsky, J., Gilstrap, B., & Rovine, M. (1984). The Pennsylvania infant and family development project: I. Stability and change in mother-infant and father-infant interaction in a family setting at one, three, and nine months. *Child Development, 55,* 692–705.

Belsky, J., & Rovine, M. (1988). Nonmaternal care in the first year of life and the security of infant-parent attachment. *Child Development, 59,* 157–167.

Belsky, J., Rosenberger, K., & Crnic, K. (1995). Maternal personality, marital quality, social support, and infant temperament: Their significance for mother-infant attachment in human families. In C. Pryce, R. Martin, & D. Skuse (Eds.), *Motherhood in human and nonhuman primates* (pp. 115–124). Basel, Switzerland: Kruger.

Belsky, J., Rovine, M., & Taylor, D. G. (1984). The Pennsylvania Infant and Family Development Project III: The origins of individual differences in infant-mother attachment—maternal and infant contributions. *Child Development, 55,* 718–728.

Bem, S. L. (1974). The measurement of psychological androgyny. *Journal of Consulting and Clinical Psychology, 42,* 155–162.

Bem, S. L. (1975). Sex-role adaptability: One consequence of psychological androgyny. *Journal of Personality and Social Psychology, 31,* 634–643.

Bem, S. L. (1978). Beyond androgyny: Some presumptuous prescriptions for a liberated sexual identity. In J. A. Sherman & F. L. Denmark (Eds.), *The psychology of women: Future directions in research.* New York: Psychological Dimensions.

Bem, S. L. (1983). Gender schema theory and its implications for child development: Raising gender aschematic children in a gender-schematic society. *Signs: Journal of Women in Culture and Society, 8,* 598–616.

Bem, S. L. (1989). Genital knowledge and gender constancy in preschool children. *Child Development, 60,* 649–662.

Benasich, A. A., & Brooks-Gunn, J. (1996). Maternal attitudes and knowledge of child-rearing: Associations with family and child outcomes. *Child Development, 67,* 1186–1205.

Benbow, C. P., & Arjimand, O. (1990). Predictors of high academic achievement in mathematics and science by mathematically talented students: A longitudinal study. *Journal of Educational Psychology, 82,* 430–441.

Bendersky, M., & Lewis, M. (1994). Environmental risk, biological risk, and developmental outcome. *Developmental Psychology, 30,* 484–494.

Benedict, H. (1979). Early lexical development: Comprehension and production. *Journal of Child Language, 6,* 183–200.

Benenson, J. F., Apostoleris, N. H., & Parnass, J. (1997). Age and sex differences in dyadic and group interaction. *Developmental Psychology, 33,* 538–543.

Benoit, D., & Parker, K. C. H. (1994). Stability and transmission of attachment across three generations. *Child Development, 65,* 1444–1456.

Bentler, P. M. (1992). Etiologies and consequences of adolescent drug use: Implications for prevention. *Journal of Addictive Diseases, 11,* 47–61.

Berenbaum, S. A., & Snyder, E. (1995). Early hormonal influences on childhood sex-typed activity and playmate preferences: Implications for the development of sexual orientation. *Developmental Psychology, 31,* 31–42.

Berg, W. K., & Berg, K. M. (1987). Psychophysiologic development in infancy: State, startle, and attention. In J. Osofsky (Ed.), *Handbook of infant development* (2nd ed.). New York: Wiley.

Bergen, D. J., & Williams, J. E. (1991). Sex stereotypes in the United States revisited: 1972–1988. *Sex Roles, 24,* 413–424.

Berk, L. E. (1992). Children's private speech: An overview of theory and the status of research. In R. M. Diaz & L. E. Berk (Eds.), *Private speech: From social interaction to self-regulation.* Hillsdale, NJ: Erlbaum.

Berk, L. E., & Landau, S. (1993). Private speech of learning disabled and normally achieving children in classroom academic and laboratory contexts. *Child Development, 64,* 556–571.

Berk, L. E., & Spuhl, S. T. (1995). Maternal intervention, private speech, and task performance in preschool children. *Early Childhood Research Quarterly, 10,* 145–169.

Berkey, C. S., Wang, X., Dockery, D. W., & Ferris, B. G. (1994). Adolescent height growth of U.S. children. *Annals of Human Biology, 21,* 435–442.

Berko, J. (1958). The child's learning of English morphology. *Word, 14,* 150–177.

Berkowitz, M. W., & Gibbs, J. C. (1983). Measuring the developmental features of moral discussion. *Merrill-Palmer Quarterly, 29,* 399–410.

Berman, A. L., & Jobes, D. A. (1991). *Adolescent suicide: Assessment and intervention.* Washington, DC: American Psychological Association.

Berman, P. W., & Goodman, V. (1984). Age and sex differences in children's responses to babies: Effects of adults' caretaking requests and instructions. *Child Development, 55,* 1071–1077.

Bermejo, V. (1996). Cardinality development and counting. *Developmental Psychology, 22,* 263–268.

Bernal, M. E., & Knight, G. P. (1997). Ethnic identity of Latino children. In J. G. Garcia & M. C. Zea (Eds.), *Psychological intervention and research with Latino populations.* Boston: Allyn & Bacon.

Berndt, T. J. (1979). Developmental changes in conformity to peers and parents. *Developmental Psychology, 15,* 608–616.

Berndt, T. J. (1989). Friendships in childhood and adolescence. In W. Damon (Ed.), *Child development today and tomorrow.* San Francisco: Jossey-Bass.

Berndt, T. J., & Bulleit, T. N. (1985). Effects of sibling relationships on preschoolers' behavior at home and at school. *Developmental Psychology, 21,* 761–767.

Berndt, T. J., Hawkins, J. A., & Hoyle, S. G. (1986). Changes in friendship during a school year: Effects on children's and adolescents' impressions of friendship and sharing with friends. *Child Development, 57,* 1284–1297.

Berndt, T. J., & Hoyle, S. G. (1985). Stability and change in childhood and adolescent friendships. *Developmental Psychology, 21,* 1007–1015.

Berndt, T. J., & Keefe, K. (1995). Friends' influence on adolescents' adjustment to school. *Child Development, 66,* 1312–1329.

Berndt, T. J., & Perry, T. B. (1990). Distinctive features and effects of early adolescent friendships. In R. Montemayor, G. R. Adams, & T. P. Gulotta (Eds.), *From childhood to adolescence: A transitional period.* Newbury Park, CA: Sage.

Berrueta-Clement, J. R., Schweinhart, L. J., Barnett, S. W., Epstein, A. S., & Weikart, D. P. (1984). *Changed lives: The effects of the Perry Preschool Program on youths through age 19.* Ypsilanti, MI: High/Scope Press.

Berry, J. W. (1967). Independence and conformity in subsistence-level societies. *Journal of Personality and Social Psychology, 7,* 415–418.

Berry, J. W., Poortinga, Y. H., Segall, M., & Dasen, P. R. (1992). *Cross-cultural psychology: Research and applications.* Cambridge, England: Cambridge University Press.

Bertenthal, B. I. (1993, March). *Emerging trends in perceptual development.* Paper presented at the biennial meeting of the Society for Research in Child Development, New Orleans, LA.

Bertenthal, B. I., & Campos, J. J. (1987). New directions in the study of early experience. *Child Development, 58,* 560–567.

Bertenthal, B. I., Proffitt, D. R., & Cutting, J. E. (1984). Infant sensitivity to figural coherence in biomechanical motions. *Journal of Experimental Child Psychology, 37,* 213–230.

Bertenthal, B. I., Campos, J. J., Haith, M. M. (1980). Development of visual organization: The perception of Subjective contars. *Child Development, 51,* 1077–1080.

Bertenthal, B. I., Proffitt, D. R., Kramer, S. J., & Spetner, N. B. (1987). Infants' encoding of kinetic displays varying in relative coherence. *Developmental Psychology, 23,* 171–178.

Best, D. L. (1993). Inducing children to generate mnemonic organizational strategies: An examination of long-term retention and materials. *Developmental Psychology, 29,* 324–336.

Best, D. L., & Ornstein, P. A. (1986). Children's generation and communication of mnemonic organizational strategies. *Developmental Psychology, 22,* 845–853.

Best, D. L., Williams, J. E., Cloud, J. M., Davis, S. W., Robertson, L. S., Edwards, J. R., Giles, H., & Fowlkes, J. (1977). Development of sex-trait stereotypes among young children in the United States, England, and Ireland. *Child Development, 48,* 1375–1384.

Beyth-Marom, R., Austin, L., Fischoff, B., Palmgren, C., & Jacobs-Quadrel, M. (1993). Perceived consequences of risky behaviors: Adolescents and adults. *Developmental Psychology, 29,* 549–563.

Bialystok, E. (1986). Factors in the growth of linguistic awareness. *Child Development, 57,* 498–510.

Bialystok, E. (1988). Levels of bilingualism and levels of metalinguistic awareness. *Developmental Psychology, 24,* 560–567.

Bialystok, E. (1997). Effects of bilingualism and biliteracy on children's emerging concepts of print. *Developmental Psychology, 33,* 429–440.

Bickerton, D. (1983). Creole languages. *Scientific American, 249,* 116–122.

Bickerton, D. (1984). The language bioprogram hypothesis. *Behavioral and Brain Sciences, 7,* 173–221.

Bierman, K. L. (1986). Process of change during social skills training with preadolescents and its relation to treatment outcome. *Child Development, 57,* 230–240.

Bierman, K.L., & Furman, W. (1984). The effects of social skills training and peer involvement on the social adjustment of preadolescents. *Child Development, 55,* 157–162.

Biernat, M. (1991). Gender stereotypes and the relationship between masculinity and femininity: A developmental analysis. *Journal of Personality and Social Psychology, 61,* 351–365.

Bigler, R. S. (1995). The role of classification skill in moderating environmental influences on children's gender stereotyping: A study of the functional use of gender in the classroom. *Child Development, 66,* 1072–1087.

Bigler, R. S., & Liben, L. S. (1990). The role of attitudes and interventions in gender-schematic processing. *Child Development, 61,* 1440–1452.

Bigler, R. S., & Liben, L. S. (1992). Cognitive mechanisms in children's gender stereotyping: Theoretical and educational implications of a cognitive-based intervention. *Child Development, 63,* 1351–1363.

Bigler, R. S., & Liben, L. S. (1993). A cognitive-developmental approach to racial stereotyping and reconstructive memory in Euro-American children. *Child Development, 64,* 1507–1518.

Bigner, J. J., & Jacobsen, R. B. (1989). Parenting behaviors of homosexual and heterosexual fathers. *Journal of Homosexuality, 18,* 173–186.

Bijeljac-Babic, R., Bertoncini, J., & Mahler, J. (1993). How do 4-day-old infants categorize multisyllabic utterances? *Developmental Psychology, 29,* 711–721.

Biller, H. B. (1993). *Fathers and families: Paternal factors in child development.* Westport, CT: Auburn House.

Bingham, C. R., & Crockett, L. J. (1996). Longitudinal adjustment patterns of boys and girls experiencing early, middle, and later sexual intercourse. *Developmental Psychology, 32,* 647–658.

Birch, L. L. (1990). Development of food acceptance patterns. *Developmental Psychology, 26,* 515–519.

Birch, L. L., & Billman, J. (1986). Preschool children's food sharing with friends and acquaintances. *Child Development, 57,* 387–395.

Birch, L. L., Marlin, D. W., & Rotter, J. (1984). Eating as the "means" activity in a contingency: Effects on young children's food preference. *Child Development, 55,* 431–439.

Biringen, Z. (1990). Direct observation of maternal sensitivity and dyadic interactions in the home: Relations to maternal thinking. *Developmental Psychology, 26,* 278–284.

Biringen, Z., Emde, R. N., Campos, J. J., & Appelbaum, M. I. (1995). Affective reorganization in the infant, the mother, and the dyad: The role of upright locomotion and its timing. *Child Development, 66,* 499–514.

Bishop, D. (1988). Language development after focal brain damage. In D. Bishop & K. Mogford (Eds.), *Language development in exceptional circumstances.* Edinburgh: Churchill Livingstone.

Bivens, J. A., & Berk, L. E. (1990). A longitudinal study of the development of elementary school children's private speech. *Merrill-Palmer Quarterly, 36,* 443–463.

Bjorklund, D. F. (1987). How age changes in knowledge base contribute to the development of children's memory: An interpretive review. *Developmental Review, 7,* 93–130.

Bjorklund, D. F. (1995). *Children's thinking: Developmental function and individual differences* (2nd ed.). Pacific Grove, CA: Brooks/Cole.

Bjorklund, D. F. (1997). In search of a metatheory for cognitive development (or, Piaget's dead and I don't feel so good myself). *Child Development, 68,* 142–146.

Bjorklund, D. F., & Bjorklund, B. R. (1985). Organization versus item effects of an elaborated knowledge base on children's memory. *Developmental Psychology, 21,* 1120–1131.

Bjorklund, D. F., & Bjorklund, B. R. (1992). *Looking at children: An introduction to child development.* Pacific Grove, CA: Brooks/Cole.

Bjorklund, D. F., & Coyle, T. R. (1995). Utilization deficiencies in the development of memory strategies. In F. E. Weinert & W. Schneider (Eds.), *Memory performance and competencies: Issues in growth and development* (pp. 161–180). Hillsdale, NJ: Erlbaum.

Bjorklund, D. F., & Douglas, R N. (1997). The development of memory strategies. In N. Cowan (Ed.), *The development of memory in childhood* (pp. 201–246). London: London University College Press.

Bjorklund, D. F., & Harnishfeger, K. K. (1990). Children's strategies: Their definition and origins. In D. F. Bjorklund (Ed.), *Children's strategies: Contemporary views of cognitive development* (pp.309–323). Hillsdale, NJ: Erlbaum.

Bjorklund, D. F., Miller, P. H., Coyle, T. R., & Slawinski, J. L. (1997). Instructing children to use memory strategies: Evidence of utilization deficiencies in memory training studies. To appear in D. F. Bjorklund & P. H. Miller (Eds.), New themes in strategy development. Special Issue of *Developmental Review.*

Bjorklund, D. F., & Reubens, A. (1997). Collaborative learning of simple addition strategies between young children and their mothers in the context of a game. Unpublished data, Florida Atlantic University, Boca Raton, FL.

Bjorkqvist, K., Lagerspetz, K. M. J., & Kaukiainen, A. (1992). Do girls manipulate and boys fight? Developmental trends in regard to direct and indirect aggression. *Aggressive Behavior, 18,* 117–127.

Black-Gutman, D., & Hickson, F. (1996). The relationship between racial attitudes and social-cognitive development in children: An Australian study. *Developmental Psychology, 32,* 448–456.

Blake, J. & Boysson-Bardies, B. de (1992). Patterns in babbling: a cross-linguistic study. *Journal of Child Language, 19,* 51–74.

Blakemore, J. E. O., LaRue, A. A., & Olejnik, A. B. (1979). Sex-appropriate toy preference and the ability to conceptualize toys as sex-role related. *Developmental Psychology, 15,* 339–340.

Blasi, A. (1980). Bridging moral cognition and moral action: A critical review of the literature. *Psychological Bulletin, 88,* 1–45.

Blasi, A. (1990). Kohlberg's theory and moral motivation. In D. Schrader (Ed.), *New directions for child development* (No. 47, pp. 51–57). San Francisco: Jossey-Bass.

Blass, E. M., & Ciaramitaro, V. (1994). A new look at some old mechanisms in human newborns: Taste and tactile determinants of state, affect, and action. *Monographs of the Society for Research in Child Development, 59* (l, Serial No. 239).

Block, J. H. (1976). Issues, problems, and pitfalls in assessing sex differences: A critical review of *The psychology of sex differences. Merrill-Palmer Quarterly, 27,* 283–308.

Block, J. H., Block, J., & Gjerde, P. F. (1986). The personality of children prior to divorce: A prospective study. *Child Development, 57,* 827–840.

Block, J. H., Block, J., & Gjerde, P. F. (1988). Parental functioning and the home environment of families of divorce: Prospective and current analyses. *Journal of the American Academy of Child and Adolescent Psychiatry, 27,* 207–213.

Block, J., & Robins, R. W. (1993). A longitudinal study of consistency and change in self-esteem from early adolescence to early adulthood. *Child Development, 64,* 909–923.

Bloom, L. (1970). *Language development: Form and function in emerging grammars.* Cambridge, MA: M.I.T. Press.

Bloom, L. (1973). *One word at a time: The use of single word utterances before syntax.* The Hague: Mouton.

Bloom, L., Hood, L., & Lightbown, P. (1974). Imitation in language development: If, when and why. *Cognitive Psychology, 6,* 380–420.

Bloom, L., Margulis, C., Tinker, E., & Fujita, N. (1996). Early conversations and word learning: Contributions from child and adult. *Child Development, 67,* 3154–3175.

Bloom, L., Merkin, S., & Wootten, J. (1982). Wh- questions: Linguistic factors that contribute to the sequence of acquisition. *Child Development, 53,* 1084–1092.

Blount, R. (1986, May 4). "I'm about five years ahead of my age." *Atlanta Journal and Constitution,* C17-C20.

Bogatz, G. A., & Ball, S. (1972). *The second year of Sesame Street: A continuing evaluation.* Princeton, NJ: Educational Testing Service.

Boggiano, A. K., Klinger, C. A., & Main, D. S. (1986). Enhancing interest in peer interaction: A developmental analysis. *Child Development, 57,* 852–861.

Bohannon, J. N., III, & Bonvillian, J. D. (1997). Theoretical approaches to language acquisition. In J. K. Gleason (Ed.), *The development of language* (4th ed.). Boston: Allyn & Bacon.

Bohannon, J. N., MacWhinney, B., & Snow, C. (1990). No negative evidence revisited: Beyond learnability or who has to prove what to whom. *Developmental Psychology, 26,* 221–226.

Bohannon, J. N., III, Padgett, R. J., Nelson, K. E., & Mark, M. (1996). Useful evidence on negative evidence. *Developmental Psychology, 32,* 551–555.

Bohannon, J. N., & Stanowicz, L. (1988). The issue of negative evidence: Adult responses to children's language errors. *Developmental Psychology, 24,* 684–689.

Bohannon, J. N., & Warren-Leubecker, A. (1989). Theoretical approaches to language acquisition. In J. B. Gleason (Ed.), *The development of language.* Columbus, OH: Merrill.

Bohlin, G., & Hagekull, B. (1993). Stranger wariness and sociability in the early years. *Infant Behavior and Development, 16,* 53–67.

Bohman, M., & Sigvardsson S. (1990). Outcome in adoption: Lessons from longitudinal studies. In D. M. Brodzinsky (Ed.). *The psychology of adoption* (pp. 93–106). New York: Oxford University Press.

Boismier, J. D. (1977). Visual stimulation and the wake-sleep behavior in human neonates. *Developmental Psychobiology, 10,* 219–227.

Boivin, M., & Hymel, S. (1997). Peer experiences and social self-perceptions: A sequential model. *Developmental Psychology, 33,* 135–145.

Boldizar, J. P. (1991). Assessing sex-typing and androgyny in children: The children's sex-role inventory. *Developmental Psychology, 27,* 505–515.

Bolger, K. E., Patterson, C. J., Thompson, W. W., & Kupersmidt, J. B. (1995). Psychosocial adjustment among children experiencing persistent intermittent family economic hardship. *Child Development, 66,* 1107–1129.

Boloh, Y., & Champaud, C. (1993). The past conditional verb form in French children: The role of semantics in late grammatical development. *Journal of Child Language, 20,* 169–189.

Booth, A., & Amato, P. (1991). Divorce and psychological stress. *Journal of Health and Social Behavior, 32,* 396–407.

Booth, A., & Edwards, J. N. (1992). Starting over: Why remarriages are more unstable. *Journal of Family Issues, 13,* 179–194.

Bornstein, M. H. (1992). Perception across the life span. In M. H. Bornstein & M. E. Lamb (Eds.), *Developmental psychology: An advanced textbook* (pp. 155–209). Hillsdale, NJ: Erlbaum.

Bornstein, M. H. (1992). Perception across the lifespan. In M. H. Bornstein & M. E. Lamb (Eds.), *Developmental psychology. An advanced textbook* (3rd ed.). Hillsdale, NJ: Erlbaum.

Bornstein, M. H., Kessen, W., & Weiskopf, S. (1976). Color vision and hue categorization in young human infants. *Journal of Experimental Psychology: Human Perception and Performance, 2,* 115–129.

Borstelmann, L. J. (1983). Children before psychology: Ideas about children from antiquity to the late 1800s. In P. H. Mussen (Ed.), *Handbook of child psychology* (Vol. 1, pp. 1–40). New York: Wiley.

Bouchard, T. J., Jr., Lykken, D. T., McGue, M., Segal, N. L., & Tellegen, A. (1990). Sources of human psychological differences: The Minnesota study of twins reared apart. *Science, 250,* 223–228.

Bouchard, T. J., Jr., & McGue, M. (1981). Family studies of intelligence: A review. *Science, 212,* 1055–1059.

Bower, T. G. R. (1982). *Development in infancy.* New York: W. H. Freeman.

Bower, T. G. R., Broughton, J. M., & Moore, M. K. (1970). The coordination of vision and tactile input in infancy. *Perception and Psychophysics, 8,* 51–53.

Bowlby, J. (1969). *Attachment and loss* (Vol. 1). *Attachment.* New York: Basic Books.

Bowlby, J. (1973). *Attachment and loss* (Vol. 2). *Separation, anxiety and anger.* New York: Basic Books.

Bowlby, J. (1980). *Attachment and loss* (Vol. 3). *Loss, sadness, and depression.* New York: Basic Books.

Bowlby, J. (1988). *A secure base: Clinical applications of attachment theory.* London: Routledge.

Boyatzis, C. J., Matillo, G. M., & Nesbitt, K. M. (1995). Effects of the "Mighty Morphin Power Rangers" on children's aggression with peers. *Child Study Journal, 25,* 44–55.

Boyes, M. C., & Chandler, M. (1992). Cognitive development, epistemic doubt, and identity formation in adolescence. *Journal of Youth and Adolescence, 21,* 277–304.

Boykin, A. W. (1994). Harvesting talent and culture: African-American children and educational reform. In R. Rossi (Ed.), *Schools and students at risk* (pp. 116–138) New York: Teachers College Press.

Brabeck, M. (1983). Moral judgment: Theory and research on differences between males and females. *Developmental Review, 3,* 274–291.

Brackbill, Y. (1975). Continuous stimulation and arousal level in infancy: Effects of stimulus intensity and stress. *Child Development, 46,* 364–369.

Brackbill, Y., McManus, K., & Woodward, L. (1985). *Medication in maternity: Infant exposure and maternal information.* Ann Arbor: University of Michigan Press.

Bradbard, M. R., Martin, C. L., Endsley, R. C., & Halverson, C. F. (1986). Influence of sex stereotypes on children's exploration and memory: A competence versus performance distinction. *Developmental Psychology, 22,* 481–486.

Braddock, J. H. II, & McPartland, J. M. (1993). Education of early adolescents. *Review of Educational Research, 19,* 135–170.

Bradley, R. H., & Caldwell, B. M. (1982). The consistency of the home environment and its relationship to child development. *International Journal of Behavioral Development, 5,* 445–465.

Bradley, R. H., & Caldwell, B. M. (1984). 174 children: A study of the relationship between home environment and cognitive development during the first 5 years. In A. W. Gottfried (Ed.), *Home environment and early cognitive development: Longitudinal research.* Orlando, FL: Academic Press.

Bradley, R. H., Caldwell, B. M., & Rock, S. L. (1988). Home environment and school performance: A ten-year follow-up and examination of three models of environmental action. *Child Development, 59,* 852–867.

Bradley, R. H., Caldwell, B. M., Rock, S. L., Ramey, C. T., Barnard, K. E., Gray, C., Hammond, M. A., Mitchell, S., Gottfried, A. W., Siegel, L., & Johnson, D. L. (1989). Home environment and cognitive development in the first 3 years of life: A collaborative study involving six sites and three ethnic groups in North America. *Developmental Psychology, 25,* 217–235.

Bradley, R.H., Whiteside, L., Mundfrom, D.J., Casey, P.H., Kelleher, K.J. & Pope, S.K. (1994). Contribution of early intervention and early caregiving experiences to resilience of low-birthweight premature children living in poverty. *Journal of Clinical Child Psychology, 23,* 425–434.

Brainerd, C. J. (1974). Training and transfer of transitivity, conservation, and class inclusion of length. *Child Development, 45,* 324–334.

Brainerd, C. F. (1996). Piaget: A centennial celebration. *Psychological Science, 7,* 191–195.

Brainerd, C. J., & Gordon, L. L. (1994). Development of verbatim and gist memory for numbers. *Developmental Psychology, 30,* 163–177.

Brainerd, C. J., & Kingma, J. (1985). On the independence of short-term memory and working memory in cognitive development. *Cognitive Psychology, 17,* 210–247.

Brainerd, C. J., & Reyna, V. F. (1990). Gist is the grist: Fuzzy-trace theory and the new intuitionism. *Developmental Review, 10,* 3–47.

Brainerd, C. J., & Reyna, V. F. (1993). Domains of fuzzy trace theory. In M. L. Howe & R. Pasnak (Eds.), *Emerging themes in cognitive development, Vol. I.: Foundations* (pp. 50–93). New York: Springer-Verlag.

Brainerd, C. J., & Reyna, V. F. (1996). Mere memory testing creates false memories in children. *Developmental Psychology, 32,* 467–478.

Brainerd, C. J., Reyna, V. F., & Brandse, E. (1995). Are children's false memories more persistent than their true memories? *Psychological Science, 6,* 359–364.

Brand, E., Clingempeel, W. G., & Bowen-Woodward, K. (1988). Family relationships and children's psychological adjustment in stepmother and stepfather families: Findings and conclusions from the Philadelphia Stepfamily Research Project. In E. M. Hetherington & J. D. Arasteh (Eds.), *Impact of divorce, single-parenting, and stepparenting on children* (pp. 299–324). Hillsdale, NJ: Erlbaum.

Braungart, J. M., Fulker, D. W., & Plomin, R. (1992). Genetic mediation of the home environment during infancy: A sibling adoption study of the HOME. *Developmental Psychology, 28,* 1048–1055.

Braungart, J. M., Plomin, R., DeFries, J. C., & Fulker, D. W. (1992). Genetic influence on tester-rated infant temperament as assessed by Bayley's Infant Behavior Record: Nonadoptive and adoptive siblings and twins. *Developmental Psychology, 28,* 40–47.

Brazelton, T. B. (1979). Behavioral competence of the newborn infant. *Seminars in Perinatology, 3,* 35–44.

Bretherton, I. (1985). Attachment theory: Retrospect and prospect. In I. Bretherton & E. Waters (Eds.), Growing points of attachment theory and research. *Monographs of the Society for Research in Child Development, 50,* Nos. 1–2, Serial No. 209.

Bretherton, I. (1990). Open communication and internal working models: Their role in the development of attachment relationships. In R. A. Thompson (Ed.), Socioemotional development. *Nebraska Symposium on Motivation* (Vol. 36). Lincoln: University of Nebraska Press.

Bretherton, I., Stolberg, U., & Kreye, M. (1981). Engaging strangers in proximal interaction: Infants' social initiative. *Developmental Psychology, 17,* 746–755.

Britt, G. C., & Myers, B. J. (1994). The effects of the Brazelton intervention. *Infant Mental Health Journal, 15,* 278–292.

Broberg, A. G., Wessels, H., Lamb, M. E., & Hwang, C. P. (1997). Effects of day care on the cognitive development of 8-year-olds: A longitudinal study. *Developmental Psychology, 33,* 62–69.

Brockington, I. (1996). *Motherhood and mental health.* Oxford, England: Oxford University Press.

Brody, G. H., Graziano, W. G., & Musser, L. M. (1983). Familiarity and children's behavior in same-age and mixed-age peer groups. *Developmental Psychology, 19,* 568–576.

Brody, G. H., & Shaffer, D. R. (1982). Contributions of parents and peers to children's moral socialization. *Developmental Review, 2,* 31–75.

Brody, G. H., Stoneman, Z., & Flor, D. (1996). Parental religiosity, family processes, and youth competence in rural, two-parent African-American families. *Developmental Psychology, 32,* 696–706.

Brody, G. H., Stoneman, Z., & McCoy, J. K. (1994). Forecasting sibling relationships in early adolescence from child temperaments and family processes in middle childhood. *Child Development, 65,* 771–784.

Brody, N. (1997). Intelligence, schooling, and society. *American Psychologist, 52,* 1046–1050.

Brodzinsky, D. M., Radice, C. Huffman, L., & Merkler, K. (1987). Prevalence of clinically significant symptomatology in nonclinical samples of adopted and nonadopted children. *Journal of Clinical Child Psychology, 16,* 350–356.

Bronfenbrenner, U. (1970). *Two worlds of childhood: U.S. and U.S.S.R.* New York: Russell Sage Foundation.

Bronfenbrenner, U. (1977). Toward an experimental ecology of human development. *American Psychologist, 32,* 513–531.

Bronfenbrenner, U. (1979). *The ecology of human development.* Cambridge, MA: Harvard University Press.

Bronfenbrenner, U. (1986). Ecology of the family as a context for human development: Research perspectives. *Developmental Psychology, 22,* 723–742.

Bronfenbrenner, U. (1989). Ecological systems theory. In R. Vasta (Ed.) *Annals of child development: Theories of child development: Revised formulations and current issues* (Vol. 6, pp. 187–251). Greenwich, CT: JAI Press.

Bronfenbrenner, U. (1993). The ecology of cognitive development: Research models and fugitive findings. In R. H. Wozniak & K. W. Fischer (Eds)., *Development in context* (pp. 3–44). Hillsdale, NJ: Erlbaum.

Bronfenbrenner, U. (1995). The bioecological model from a life course perspective: Reflections of a participant observer. In P. Moen, G. H. Elder, Jr., & K. Luscher (Eds.), *Examining lives in context* (pp. 599–618). Washington, D.C.: American Psychological Association.

Bronfenbrenner, U., & Ceci, S.J. (1994). Nature-nurture reconceptualized in developmental perspective: A bioecological model. *Psychological Review, 101,* 568–586.

Bronfenbrenner, U., & Neville, P. R. (1995). America's children and families: An international perspective. In S. L. Kagan & B. Weissbourd (Eds.), *Putting families first* (pp. 3–27). San Francisco: Jossey-Bass.

Bronson, G. W. (1991). Infant differences in rate of visual encoding. *Child Development, 62,* 44–54.

Brookover, W., Beady, C., Flood, P., Schweitzer, J., & Wisenbaker, J. (1979). *School social systems and student achievement: Schools can make a difference.* New York: Praeger.

Brooks-Gunn, J. (1988). Antecedents and consequences of variation in girls' maturational timing. *Journal of Adolescent Health Care, 9,* 365–373.

Brooks-Gunn, J., & Furstenberg, F. F., Jr. (1989). Adolescent sexual behavior. *American Psychologist, 44,* 249–257.

Brooks-Gunn, J., Klebanov, P. K., & Duncan, G. J. (1996). Ethnic differences in children's intelligence test scores: Role of economic deprivation, home environment, and maternal characteristics. *Child Development, 67,* 396–408.

Brooks-Gunn, J., Klebanov, P. K., Liaw, F., & Spiker, D. (1993). Enhancing the development of low birthweight, premature infants: Changes in cognition and behavior over the first three years. *Child Development, 64,* 736–753.

Brooks-Gunn, J., & Warren, M. P. (1988). The psychological significance of secondary sexual characteristics in nine- to eleven-year-old girls. *Child Development, 59,* 1061–1069.

Broverman, I. K., Vogel, S. R., Clarkson, F. E., & Rosenkrantz, P. S. (1972). Sex-role stereotypes: A current appraisal. *Journal of Social Issues, 28,* 59–78.

Brown, A. L., Bransford, T. D., Ferrara, R. A., & Campione, J. C. (1983). Learning, remembering, and understanding. In J. H. Flavell & E. M. Markman (Eds.), *Handbook of child psychology:* (Vol. 3). *Cognitive development* (4th ed., pp. 77–166). New York: Wiley.

Brown, A. L., & Campione, J. C. (1990). Communities of learning and thinking, or a context by any other name. In D. Kuhn (Ed.), *Developmental perspectives on teaching, learning, and thinking skills.* Basel: Karger.

Brown, A. M. (1990). Development of visual sensitivity to light and color vision in human infants: A critical review. *Vision Research, 30,* 1159–1188.

Brown, B. B. (1990). Peer groups. In S. Feldman & G. Elliott (Eds.), *At the threshold: The developing adolescent.* Cambridge, MA: Cambridge University Press.

Brown, B. B., Clasen, D. R., & Eicher, S. A. (1986). Perceptions of peer pressure, peer conformity dispositions, and self-reported behavior among adolescents. *Developmental Psychology, 22,* 521–530.

Brown, B. B., & Lohr, M. J. (1987). Peer-group affiliation and adolescent self-esteem: An integration of ego-identity and symbolic-interaction theories. *Journal of Personality and Social Psychology, 52,* 47–55.

Brown, B. B., Mounts, N., Lamborn, S. D., & Steinberg, L. (1993). Parenting practices and peer group affiliation in adolescence. *Child Development, 64,* 467–482.

Brown, J. D. (1998). *The self.* New York: McGraw-Hill.

Brown, J. L. (1964). States in newborn infants. *Morrill-Palmer Quarterly, 10,* 313–327.

Brown, J. R., & Dunn, J. (1996). Continuities in emotion understanding from three to six years. *Child Development, 67,* 789–802.

Brown, P., & Elliot, R. (1965). Control of aggression in a nursery school class. *Journal of Experimental Child Psychology, 2,* 103–107.

Brown, R. (1973). *A first language: The early stages.* Cambridge, MA: Harvard University Press.

Brown, R., Cazden, C., & Bellugi, U. (1969). The child's grammar from I-III. In J. P. Hill (Ed.), *Minnesota Symposia on Child Psychology* (Vol. 2). Minneapolis: University of Minnesota Press.

Brown, S. S. (1988). *Prenatal care: Reaching mothers, reaching infants.* Washington, DC: National Academy Press.

Brownell, C. A. (1986). Convergent developments: Cognitive-developmental correlates of growth in infant/toddler peer skills. *Child Development, 57,* 275–286.

Brownell, C. A. (1990). Peer social skills in toddlers: Competencies and constraints illustrated by same-age and mixed-age interaction. *Child Development, 61,* 838–848.

Brownell, C. A., & Carriger, M. S. (1990). Changes in cooperation and self/other differentiation during the second year. *Child Development, 61,* 1164–1174.

Bruck, M., Ceci, S. J., Francoeur, E., & Barr, R. (1995b). "I hardly cried when I got my shot!" Influencing children's reports about a visit to their pediatrician. *Child Development, 66,* 193–208.

Bruck, M., Ceci, S. J., Francoeur, E., & Renick, A. (1995a). Anatomically detailed dolls do not facilitate preschoolers' reports of a pediatric examination involving genital touching. *Journal of Experimental Psychology: Applied, 1,* 95–109.

Bruck, M., Ceci, S. J., & Hembrooke, H. (1998). Reliability and credibility of young children's reports: From research to policy and practice. *American Psychologist, 53,* 136–151.

Bruggerman, E. L., & Hart, K. J. (1996). Cheating, lying, and moral reasoning by religious and secular high school students. *Journal of Educational Research, 89,* 340–344.

Bruner, J. S. (1983). *Child's talk: Learning to use language.* New York: Norton.

Buchanan, C. M., Eccles, J. S., & Becker, J. B. (1992). Are adolescents the victims of raging hormones: Evidence for activational effects of hormones on moods and behavior at adolescence. *Psychological Bulletin, 111,* 62–107.

Buchanan, C. M., Maccoby, E. E., & Dornbusch, S. M. (1991). Caught between parents: Adolescents' experiences in divorced homes. *Child Development, 62,* 1008–1029.

Bugental, D. B., Blue, J., & Cruzcosa, M. (1989). Perceived control over caregiving outcomes: Implications for child abuse. *Developmental Psychology, 25,* 532–539.

Buhrmester, D. (1990). Intimacy of friendship, interpersonal competence, and adjustment during preadolescence and adolescence. *Child Development, 61,* 1101–1111.

Buhrmester, D., & Furman, W. (1990). Perceptions of sibling relationships during middle childhood and adolescence. *Child Development, 61,* 1387–1398.

Bukowski, W. M., Gauze, C., Hoza, B., & Newcomb, A. F. (1993). Differences and consistency between same-sex and other-sex peer relationships during early adolescence. *Developmental Psychology, 29,* 253–263.

Bullock, M. (1985). Animism in childhood thinking: A new look at an old question. *Developmental Psychology, 21,* 217–225.

Bullock, M., & Lutkenhaus, P. (1990). Who am I? Self-understanding in toddlers. *Merrill-Palmer Quarterly, 36,* 217–238.

Bumpass, L. L. (1990). What's happening to the family? Interactions between demographic and institutional change. *Demography, 27,* 483–498.

Burchinal, M. R., Campbell, F. A., Bryant, D. M., Wasik, B. H., & Ramey, C. T. (1997). Early intervention and mediating processes in the cognitive performance of low-income African American families. *Child Development, 68,* 933–954.

Burchinal, M. R., Follmer, A., & Bryant, D. M. (1996). The relations of maternal social support and family structure with maternal responsiveness and child outcomes among African-American families. *Developmental Psychology, 32,* 1073–1083.

Burchinal, M. R., Roberts, J. E., Nabors, L. A., & Bryant, D. M. (1996). Quality of center child care and infant cognitive and language development. *Child Development, 67,* 606–620.

Burhans, K. K., & Dweck, C. S. (1995). Helplessness in early childhood: The role of contingent worth. *Child Development, 66,* 1719–1738.

Burkhardt, S. A., & Rotatori, A. F. (1995). *Treatment and prevention of childhood sexual abuse: A child-generated model.* Washington, D.C.: Taylor & Francis.

Burn, S., O'Neil, A. K., & Nederend, S. (1996). Childhood tomboyishness and adult androgeny. *Sex Roles, 34,* 419–428.

Burnette, E. (1997). Talking openly about race thwarts racism in children. *Monitor of the American Psychological Association, 28,* (6), 33.

Burnham, D. K., & Harris, M. B. (1992). Effects of real gender and labeled gender on adults' perceptions of infants. *Journal of Genetic Psychology, 153,* 165–183.

Burns, G. W., & Bottino, P. J. (1989). *The science of genetics* (6th ed.). New York: Macmillan.

Burns, L. H. (1990). An exploratory study of perceptions of parenting after infertility. *Family Systems Medicine, 8,* 177–189.

Bursik, K. (1991). Adaptation to divorce and ego development in adult women. *Journal of Personality and Social Psychology, 60,* 300–306.

Burton, L. M. (1990). Teenage childrearing as an alternative life-course strategy in multigenerational black families. *Human Nature, 1,* 123–143.

Burton, R. V. (1963). The generality of honesty reconsidered. *Psychological Review, 70,* 481–499.

Burton, R. V. (1976). Honesty and dishonesty. In T. Lickona (Ed.), *Moral development and behavior.* New York: Holt, Rinehart & Winston.

Bushnell, E. W., & Boudreau, J. P. (1993). Motor development and the mind: The potential role of motor abilities as a determinant of aspects of perceptual development. *Child Development, 64,* 1005–1021.

Buss, A. H., & Plomin, R. (1984). *Temperament: Early developing personality traits.* Hillsdale, NJ: Erlbaum.

Buss, D. M. (1995). Psychological sex differences: Origins through sexual selection. *American Psychologist, 50,* 164–168.

Bussey, K. (1992). Lying and truthfulness: Children's definitions, standards, and evaluative reactions. *Child Development, 63,* 129–137.

Bussey, K., & Bandura, A. (1992). Self-regulatory mechanisms governing gender development. *Child Development, 63,* 1236–1250.

Butler, R. (1990). The effects of mastery and competitive conditions on self-assessment at different ages. *Child Development, 61,* 201–210.

Butler, R., & Ruzany, N. (1993). Age and socialization effects on the development of social comparison motives and normative ability assessment in kibbutz and urban children. *Child Development, 64,* 532–543.

Butterfield, E. C., & Siperstein, G. N. (1972). Influence of contingent auditory stimulation on non-nutritional suckle. In J. F. Bosma (Ed.), *Third symposium on oral sensation and perception: The mouth of the infant.* Springfield, IL: Charles C. Thomas.

Buysse, V., & Bailey, D. B. (1993). Behavioral and developmental outcomes in young children with disabilities in integrated and segregated settings: A review of comparative studies. *Journal of Special Education, 26,* 434–461.

Bynner, J., O'Malley, P., & Bachman, J. (1981). Self-esteem and delinquency revisited. *Journal of Youth and Adolescence, 10,* 407–441.

Byrnes, J. P., & Takahira, S. (1993). Explaining gender differences on SAT-math items. *Developmental Psychology, 29,* 805–810.

Cabaniss, M. L. (1996). Amniocentesis. In J. A. Kuller, N. C. Cheschier, & R. C. Cefalo (Eds.), *Prenatal diagnosis and reproductive genetics* (pp. 136–144). St. Louis: Mosby.

Cahan, S., & Cohen, N. (1989). Age versus schooling effects on intelligence development. *Child Development, 60,* 1239–1249.

Cairns, R. B., Cairns, B. D., Neckerman, H. J., Ferguson, L. L., & Gariepy, J. (1989). Growth and aggression: 1. Childhood to early adolescence. *Developmental Psychology, 25,* 320–330.

Cairns, R. B., Cairns, B. D., Neckerman, H. J., Gest, S. D., & Gariepy, J. (1988). Social networks and aggressive behavior: Peer support or peer rejection. *Developmental Psychology, 24,* 815–823.

Cairns, R. B., Leung, M., Buchanan, L., & Cairns, B. D. (1995). Friendships and social networks in childhood and adolescence: Fluidity, reliability, and interrelations. *Child Development, 66,* 1330–1345.

Caldera, Y. M., Huston, A. C., & O'Brien, M. (1989). Social interactions and play patterns of parents and toddlers with feminine, masculine, and neutral toys. *Child Development, 60,* 70–76.

Caldwell, B. M., & Bradley, R. H. (1984). *Manual for the Home Observation for Measurement of the Environment.* Little Rock: University of Arkansas Press.

Calkins, S. D., Fox, N. A., & Marshall, T. R. (1996). Behavioral and physiological antecedents of inhibited and uninhibited behavior. *Child Development, 67,* 523–540.

Call, K. T., Mortimer, J. T., & Shanahan, M. (1995). Helpfulness and the development of competence in adolescence. *Child Development, 66,* 129–138.

Camara, K. A., & Resnick, G. (1988). Interparental conflict and cooperation: Factors moderating children's postdivorce adjustment. In E. M. Hetherington & J. D. Arasteh (Eds.), *Impact of divorce, single-parenting, and step-parenting on children.* Hillsdale, NJ: Erlbaum.

Campbell, F. A., & Ramey, C. T. (1994). Effects of early intervention on intellectual and academic achievement: A follow-up study of children from low-income families. *Child Development, 65,* 684–698.

Campbell, F. A., & Ramey, C. T. (1995). Cognitive and school outcomes for high-risk African-American students at middle adolescence: Positive effects of early intervention. *American Educational Research Journal, 32,* 743–772.

Campbell, R., & Sais, E. (1995). Accelerated metalinguistic (phonological) awareness in bilingual children. *British Journal of Developmental Psychology, 13,* 61–68.

Campbell, S. B., Cohn, J. F., Flanagan, C., Popper, S., & Meyers, T. (1992). Course and correlates of postpartum depression during the transition to parenthood. *Development and Psychopathology, 4,* 29–47.

Campbell, S. B., Cohn, J. F., & Myers, T. (1995). Depression in first-time mothers: Mother-infant interaction and depression chronicity. *Developmental Psychology, 31,* 349–357.

Campione, J. C., Brown, A. L., Ferrara, R. A., & Bryant, N. R. (1984). The zone of proximal development: Implications for individual differences and learning. In B. Rogoff & J. V. Wertsch (Eds.), *Children's learning in the "zone of proximal development"* (New Directions for Child Development, No. 23). San Francisco: Jossey-Bass.

Campos, J. J., Bertenthal, B. I., & Kermoian, R. (1992). Early experience and emotional development: The emergence of wariness of heights. *Psychological Science, 3,* 61–64.

Campos, J. J., Langer, A., & Krowitz, A. (1970). Cardiac responses on the visual cliff in prelocomotor human infants. *Science, 170,* 196–197.

Campos, R., Raffaelli, M., Ude, W., Greco, M., Ruff, A., Rolf, J., Antunes, C. M., Halsley, N., Greco, D., & Associates (1994). Social networks and daily activities of street youth in Belo Horizonte, Brazil. *Child Development, 65,* 319–330.

Campos, R. G. (1989). Soothing pain-elicited distress in infants with swaddling and pacifiers. *Child Development, 60,* 781–792.

Camras, L. A., Oster, H., Campos, J. J., Miyake, K., & Bradshaw, D. (1992). Japanese and American infants' responses to arm restraint. *Developmental Psychology, 28,* 578–583.

Canfield, R. L., & Smith, E. G. (1996). Number-based expectations and sequential enumeration by 5-month-old infants. *Developmental Psychology, 32,* 269–279.

Cantwell, D. P. (1996). Attention deficit disorder: A review of the past 10 years. *Journal of the American Academy of Child and Adolescent Psychiatry, 35,* 978–987.

Capaldi, D. M., Crosby, L., & Stoolmiller, M. (1996). Predicting the timing of first sexual intercourse for at-risk adolescent males. *Child Development, 67,* 344–359.

Capaldi, D. M., & Patterson, G. R. (1991). Relation of parental transitions to boys' adjustment problems: I. A linear hypothesis. II. Mothers at risk for transition and unskilled parenting. *Developmental Psychology, 27,* 489–504.

Caplan, M., Vespo, J., Pedersen, J., & Hay, D. F. (1991). Conflict and its resolution in small groups of one- and two-year-olds. *Child Development, 62,* 1513–1524.

Caputo, D. V., & Mandell, W. (1970). Consequences of low birth weight. *Developmental Psychology, 3,* 363–383.

Carlo, G. Koller, S. H., Eisenberg, N., Da Silva, M. S., & Frohlich, C. B. (1996). A cross-national study on the relations between prosocial moral reasoning, gender role orientations, and prosocial behaviors. *Developmental Psychology, 32,* 231–240.

Carlson, V., Cicchetti, D., Barnett, D., & Braunwald, K. (1989). Disorganized/disoriented attachment relationships in maltreated infants. *Developmental Psychology, 25,* 525–531.

Carnegie Council on Adolescent Development (1989). *Turning points: Preparing American youth for the 21st century.* Washington, DC: Carnegie Council on Adolescent Development.

Carpenter, T. P., & Moser, J. M. (1982). The development of addition and subtraction problem-solving skills. In T. P. Carpenter, J. M. Moser, & T. A. Romberg (Eds.), *Addition and substraction: A cognitive perspective.* Hillsdale, NJ: Erlbaum.

Carr, M., Kurtz, B. E., Schneider, W., Turner, L. A., & Borkowski, J. G. (1989). Strategy acquisition and transfer among American and German children: Environmental influences on metacognitive development. *Developmental Psychology, 25,* 765–771.

Carraher, T. N., Carraher, D., & Schliemann, A. D. (1985). Mathematics in the streets and in the schools. *British Journal of Developmental Psychology, 3,* 21–29.

Carrington, D. (1995). Infections. In M. J. Whittle & J. M. Connor (Eds.), *Prenatal diagnosis in obstetric practice* (2nd. ed., pp. 100–113). Oxford, England: Blackwell.

Carroll, J. B. (1993). *Human cognitive abilities: A survey of factor-analytic studies.* Cambridge, England: University of Cambridge Press.

Carroll, L. (1988). Concern with AIDS and the sexual behavior of college students. *Journal of Marriage and the Family, 50,* 405–411.

Carson, J. L., & Parke, R. D. (1996). Reciprocal negative affect on parent–child interactions and children's peer competency. *Child Development, 67,* 2217–2226.

Carson, S. A. (1993). Nongenetic causes of pregnancy loss. In C. Lin, M. S. Verp, & R. E. Sabbagha (Eds.), *The high-risk fetus: Pathophysiology, diagnosis, management.* New York: Springer-Verlag.

Case, R. (1985). *Intellectual development: Birth to adulthood.* Orlando, FL: Academic Press.

Case, R. (1992). *The mind's staircase: exploring the conceptual underpinnings of children's thought and knowledge.* Hillsdale, NJ: Erlbaum.

Case, R. (1997). The development of conceptual structures. In D. Kuhn & R. S. Siegler (Eds.), *Cognitive, language, and perceptual development* (Vol. 2). In B. Damon (General Editor), *Handbook of child psychology.* New York: Wiley.

Case, R., Kurland, M., & Goldberg, J. (1982). Operational efficiency and the growth of short-term memory span. *Journal of Experimental Child Psychology, 33,* 386–404.

Case, R., & Okamoto, Y. (1996). The role of central conceptual structures in the development of children's thought. *Monographs of the Society for Research in Child Development, 61,* Nos. 1–2, Serial No. 246.

Casey, M. B. (1996). Understanding individual differences in spatial ability within females: A nature/nurture interactions framework. *Developmental Review, 16,* 241–260.

Casey, M. B., Nuttall, R. L., & Pezaris, E. (1997). Mediators of gender differences in mathematics college entrance test scores: A comparison of spatial skills with internalized beliefs and anxieties. *Developmental Psychology, 33,* 669–680.

Casey, W. M., & Burton, R. V. (1982). Training children to be consistently honest through verbal self-instructions. *Child Development, 53,* 911–919.

Caspi, A., Elder, G. H., Jr., & Bem, D. J. (1988). Moving away from the world: Life-course patterns of shy children. *Developmental Psychology, 24,* 824–831.

Caspi, A., Lynam, D., Moffitt, T. E., & Silva, P. A. (1993). Unraveling girls' delinquency: Biological, dispositional, and contextual contributors to adolescent misbehavior. *Developmental Psychology, 29,* 19–30.

Caspi, A., & Silva, P. A. (1995). Temperamental qualities at age three predict personality traits in young adulthood: Longitudinal evidence from a birth cohort. *Child Development, 66,* 486–498.

Cassel, W. S., & Bjorklund, D. F. (1995). Developmental patterns of eyewitness memory and suggestibility: An ecologically based short-term longitudinal study. *Law & Human Behavior, 19,* 507–532.

Cassel, W. S., Roebers, C. E. M., & Bjorklund, D. F. (1996). Developmental patterns of eyewitness responses to increasingly suggestive questions. *Journal of Experimental Child Psychology, 61,* 116–133.

Cassidy, J., & Asher, S. R. (1992). Loneliness and peer relations in young children. *Child Development, 63,* 350–365.

Cassidy, J., & Berlin, L. J. (1994). The insecure/ambivalent pattern of attachment: Theory and research. *Child Development, 65,* 971–991.

Cassidy, J., Kirsh, S. J., Scolton, K. L., & Parke, R. D. (1996). Attachment and representations of peer relationships. *Developmental Psychology, 32,* 892–904.

Cassidy, J., Parke, R. D., Butkovsky, L., Braungart, J. M. (1992). Family-peer connections: The roles of emotional expressiveness within the family and children's understanding of emotions. *Child Development, 63,* 603–618.

Casteel, M. A. (1993). Effects of inference necessity and reading goal on children's inferential generation. *Developmental Psychology, 29,* 346–357.

Cates, W., Jr. (1995). Sexually transmitted diseases. In B. P. Sachs, R. Beard, E. Papiernik, & C. Russell (Eds.), *Reproductive health care for women and babies* (pp. 57–84). New York: Oxford University Press.

Catherwood, D., Crassini, B., & Freiberg, K. (1989). Infant response to stimuli of similar hue and dissimilar shape: Tracing the origins of the categorization of objects by hue. *Child Development, 60,* 752–762.

Cattell, R. B. (1963). Theory of fluid and crystallized intelligence: A critical experiment. *Journal of Educational Psychology, 54,* 1–22.

Cauffman, E., & Steinberg, L. (1996). Interactive effects of menarcheal status and dating on dieting and disordered eating among adolescent girls. *Developmental Psychology, 32,* 631–635.

Caughy, M. O. (1996). Health and environmental effects on the academic readiness of school-age children. *Developmental Psychology, 32,* 515–522.

Cavanaugh, J. C., & Perlmutter, M. (1982). Metamemory: A critical examination. *Child Development, 53,* 11–28.

Ceci, S. J. (1991). How much does schooling influence general intelligence and its cognitive components? A reassessment of the evidence. *Developmental Psychology, 27,* 703–722.

Ceci, S. J., & Bruck, M. (1993). Suggestibility of the child witness: A historical review and synthesis. *Psychological Bulletin, 113,* 403–439.

Ceci, S. J., & Bruck, M. (1995). *Jeopardy in the courtroom: A scientific analysis of children's testimony.* Washington, DC: American Psychological Association.

Ceci, S. J., Loftus, E. F., Leichtman, M., & Bruck, M. (1994). The role of source misattributions in the creation of false beliefs among preschoolers. *International Journal of Clinical and Experimental Hypnosis, 62,* 304–320.

Ceci, S. J., & Williams, W. W. (1997). Schooling, intelligence, and income. *American Psychologist, 52,* 1051–1058.

Cefalo, R. C. (1996). Prevention of neural tube defects. In J. A. Kuller, N. C. Cheschier, & R. C. Cefalo (Eds.), *Prenatal diagnosis and reproductive genetics* (pp. 2–9). St. Louis: Mosby.

Centers for Disease Control (1992). Sexual behavior among high-school students—United States, 1990. *Morbidity and Mortality Weekly Reports, 40,* 885–888.

Centers for Disease Control and Prevention (1994). *HIV/AIDS Surveillance Report, 6* (1). Washington, D. C.: U.S. Government Printing Office.

Cernoch, J. M., & Porter, R. H. (1985). Recognition of maternal axillary odors by infants. *Child Development, 56,* 1593–1598.

Cervantes, C. A., & Callanan, M. A. (1998). Labels and explanations in mother-child emotion talk: Age and gender differentiation. *Developmental Psychology, 34,* 88–98.

Chadwick, B. A., & Heaton, T. B. (1992). *Statistical handbook on the American family.* Phoenix, AZ: Onyx Press.

Chall, J. S. (1983). *Stages of reading development.* New York: McGraw-Hill.

Chalmers, J. B., & Townsend, M. A. R. (1990). The effects of training in social perspective taking on socially maladjusted girls. *Child Development, 61,* 178–190.

Chandler, M. J. (1973). Egocentrism and antisocial behavior: The assessment and training of social perspective taking skills. *Developmental Psychology, 9,* 326–332.

Chandler, S., & Field, P. A. (1997). Becoming a father: First-time fathers' experience of labor and delivery. *Journal of Nurse-Midwifery, 42,* 17–24.

Chao, R.K. (1994). Beyond parental control and authoritarian parenting style: Understanding Chinese parenting through the cultural notion of training. *Child Development, 65,* 1111–1119.

Chapman, M., & Lindenberger, U. (1988). Functions, operations, and decalage in the development of transitivity. *Developmental Psychology, 24,* 542–551.

Chapman, M., Zahn-Waxler, C., Cooperman, G., & Iannotti, R. J. (1987). Empathy and responsibility in the motivation of children's helping. *Developmental Psychology, 23,* 140–145.

Charlesworth, W. R. (1992). Darwin and developmental psychology: Past and present. *Developmental Psychology, 28,* 5–16.

Chase-Lansdale, P. L., Cherlin, A. J., & Kiernan, K. E. (1995). The long-term effects of parental divorce on the mental health of young adults: A developmental perspective. *Child Development, 66,* 1614–1634.

Chassin, L., Curran, P. J., Hussong, A. M., & Colder, C. R. (1996). The relation of parent alcoholism to adolescent substance use: A longitudinal follow-up study. *Journal of Abnormal Psychology, 105,* 70–80.

Chavkin, W. (1995). Substance abuse in pregnancy. In B. P. Sachs, R. Beard, E. Papiernik, & C. Russell (Eds.), *Reproductive health care for women and babies* (pp. 305–321). New York: Oxford University Press.

Chen, C., & Stevenson, H. W. (1988). Cross-linguistic differences in digit span of preschool children. *Journal of Experimental Child Psychology, 46,* 150–158.

Chen, C., & Stevenson, H. W. (1995). Motivation and mathematics achievement: a comparative study of Asian-American, Caucasian-American, and East Asian high school students. *Child Development, 66,* 1215–1234.

Chen, X., Rubin, K. H., & Li, D. (1997). Relation between academic achievement and social adjustment: Evidence from Chinese children. *Developmental Psychology, 33,* 518–525.

Chen, X., Rubin, K. H., & Li, Z. (1995). Social functioning and adjustment in Chinese children: A longitudinal study. *Developmental Psychology, 31,* 531–539.

Chen, X., Rubin, K. H., & Sun, Y. (1992). Social reputation in Chinese and Canadian children: A cross-cultural study. *Child Development, 63,* 1336-1343.

Cherlin, A. J., Furstenberg, F. F., Jr., Chase-Lansdale, P. L., Kiernan, K. E., Robins, P. K., Morrison, D. R., & Teitler, J. O. (1991). Longitudinal studies of effects of divorce on children in Great Britain and the United States. *Science, 252,* 1386–1389.

Cherlin, A. J., Kiernan, K. E., & Chase-Lansdale, P. L. (1995). Parental divorce in childhood and demographic outcomes in young adulthood. *Demography, 32,* 299–318.

Cheschier, N. C. (1996). Overview of obstetric sonography. In J. A. Kuller, N. C. Cheschier, & R. C. Cefalo (Eds.), *Prenatal diagnosis and reproductive genetics.* St. Louis: Mosby.

Chess, S., & Thomas, R. (1984). *Origins and evolution of behavior disorders.* New York: Brunner/Mazel.

Chi, M. H. T. (1978). Knowledge structures and memory development. In R. S. Siegler (Ed.), *Children's thinking: What develops*? (pp. 73–96). Hillsdale, NJ: Erlbaum.

Chomsky, N. (1959). A review of B. F. Skinner's *Verbal Behavior. Language, 35,* 26–129.

Chomsky, N. (1968). *Language and mind.* San Diego, CA: Harcourt Brace Jovanovich.

Christopherson, E. R. (1989). Injury control. *American Psychologist, 44,* 237–241.

Cillessen, A. H. N., van IJzendoorn, H. W., van Lieshout, C. F. M., & Hartup, W. W. (1992). Heterogeneity among peer-rejected boys: Subtypes and stabilities. *Child Development, 63,* 893–905.

Clarke, A. M., & Clarke, A. D. B. (1976). *Early experience: Myth and evidence.* New York: Free Press.

Clark, E. A., & Hanisee, J. (1982). Intellectual and adaptive performance of Asian children in adoptive American settings. *Developmental Psychology, 18,* 595–599.

Clark, E. V. (1973). What's in a word? On the child's acquisition of semantics in his first language. In T. E. Moore (Ed.), *Cognitive development and the acquisition of language.* Orlando, FL: Academic Press.

Clark, H. H., & Clark, E. V. (1977). *Psychology and language: An introduction to psycholinguistics.* San Diego, CA: Harcourt Brace Jovanovich.

Clark, R., Hyde, J. S., Essex, M. J., & Klein, M. H. (1997). Length of maternity leave and quality of mother-infant interactions. *Child Development, 68,* 364–383.

Clarke-Stewart, A. (1989). Infant day care: Maligned or malignant. *American Psychologist, 44,* 266–273.

Clarke-Stewart, A. (1993). *Daycare.* Cambridge, MA: Harvard University Press.

Clarke-Stewart, A., Thompson, W., & Lepore, S. (April, 1989). Manipulating children's testimony through interrogation. In G. S. Goodman (Chair), *Do children provide accurate eyewitness reports?: Social policy and research implications:* Symposium conducted at the Meetings of the Society for Research in Child Development, Kansas City, MO.

Clarkson, M. G., & Berg, W. K. (1983). Cardiac orienting and vowel discrimination in newborns: Crucial stimulus parameters. *Child Development, 54,* 162–171.

Clary, E. G., & Snyder, M. (1991). A functional analysis of altruism and prosocial behavior: The case of volunteerism. *Review of Personality and Social Psychology, 12,* 119–148.

Clausen, J. A. (1975). The social meaning of differential physical maturation. In D. E. Dragastin & G. H. Elder (Eds.), *Adolescence in the life cycle.* New York: Halsted Press.

Clements, D. H. (1990). Metacomponential development in a Logo programming environment. *Journal of Educational Psychology, 82,* 141–149.

Clements, D. H. (1991). Enhancement of creativity in computer environments. *American Educational Research Journal, 28,* 173–187.

Clements, D. H. (1995). Teaching creativity with computers. *Educational Psychology Review, 7,* 141–161.

Clements, D. H., & Nastasi, B. K. (1992). Computers and early childhood education. In M. Gettinger, S. N. Elliott, & T. R. Kratochwill (Eds.), *Advances in school psychology: Preschool and early childhood treatment directions.* Hillsdale, NJ: Erlbaum.

Clifton, R. K., Muir, D. W., Ashmead, D. H., & Clarkson, M. G. (1993). Is visually guided reaching in early infancy a myth? *Child Development, 64,* 1099–1110.

Clingempeel, W. G., Colyar, J. J., Brand, E., & Hetherington, E. M. (1992). Children's relationships with maternal grandparents: A longitudinal study of family structure and pubertal status effects. *Child Development, 63,* 1404–1422.

Clingempeel, W. G., & Segal, S. (1986). Stepparent-stepchild relationships and the psychological adjustment of children in stepmother and stepfather families. *Child Development, 57,* 474–484.

Coates, B., & Hartup, W. W. (1969). Age and verbalization in observational learning. *Developmental Psychology, 1,* 556–562.

Cohen, D., & Strayer, J. (1996). Empathy in conduct-disordered and comparison youth. *Developmental Psychology, 32,* 988–998.

Cohen, L. B., & Oakes, L. M. (1993). How infants perceive a simple causal event. *Developmental Psychology, 29,* 421–433.

Cohen, M. (1996) Preschooler's practical thinking and problem solving: The acquisition of an optimal solution. *Cognitive Development, 11,* 357–373.

Cohen, S., & Williamson, G. M. (1991). Stress and infectious disease in humans. *Psychological Bulletin, 109,* 5–24.

Coie, J. D., & Dodge, K. A. (1983). Continuities and changes in children's social status: A five-year longitudinal study. *Merrill-Palmer Quarterly, 19,* 261–282.

Coie, J. D., Dodge, K. A., & Coppotelli, H. (1982). Dimensions and types of social status: A cross-age perspective. *Developmental Psychology, 18,* 557–570.

Coie, J. D., Dodge, K. A., & Kupersmidt, J. B. (1990). Peer group behavior and social status. In S. R. Asher & J. D. Coie (Eds.), *Peer rejection in childhood.* Cambridge, England: Cambridge University Press.

Coie, J. D., Dodge, K. A., Terry, R., & Wright, V. (1991). The role of aggression in peer relations: An analysis of aggression episodes in boys' play groups. *Child Development, 62,* 812–826.

Coie, J. D., & Koeppl, G.K. (1990). Adapting intervention to the problems of aggressive and disruptive rejected children. In S. R. Asher & J. D. Coie (Eds.), *Peer rejection in childhood.* New York: Cambridge University Press.

Coie, J. D., & Krehbiel, G. (1984). Effects of academic tutoring on the social status of low-achieving, socially rejected children. *Child Development, 55,* 1465–1478.

Coie, J. D., & Kupersmidt, J. B. (1983). A behavioral analysis of emerging social status in boys' groups. *Child Development, 54,* 1400–1416.

Colburn, (1996; September 24). Fetal alcohol babies face life of problems. *Washington Post,* p. 5.

Colby, A., & Kohlberg, L. (1987). *The measurement of moral judgment.* (Vol. 1). *Theoretical foundations and research validation.* Cambridge: Cambridge University Press.

Colby, A., Kohlberg, L., Gibbs, J., & Lieberman, M. (1983). A longitudinal study of moral judgment. *Monographs of the Society for Research in Child Development, 48,* Nos. 1–2, Serial No. 200.

Cole, M. (1990). Cognitive development and formal schooling: The evidence from cross-cultural research. In L. C. Moll (Ed.), *Vygotsky and education* (pp. 89–110). New York: Cambridge University Press.

Cole, M., & Scribner, S. (1977). Cross-cultural studies of memory and cognition. In R. V. Kail & J. W. Hagen (Eds.), *Perspectives on the development of memory and cognition.* Hillsdale, NJ: Erlbaum.

Cole, P. M., Barrett, K. C., & Zahn-Waxler, C. (1992). Emotion displays in two-year-olds during mishaps. *Child Development, 63,* 314–324.

Cole, P. M., Michel, M. K., & Teti, L. O. (1994). The development of emotion regulation and dysregulation: A clinical perspective. In N. Fox (Ed.), The development of emotion regulation: Biological and behavioral considerations. *Monographs of the Society for Research in Child Development, 59,* Nos. 2–3, Serial No. 240.

Cole, P. M., & Putnam, F. W. (1992). Effect of incest on self and social functioning: A developmental psychopathology perspective. *Journal of Consulting and Clinical Psychology, 60,* 174–184.

Collis, B. A., (1996). *Children and computers at school.* Mahwah, NJ: Erlbaum.

Columbo, J. (1993). *Infant cognition: Predicting later intellectual functioning.* Newbury Park, CA: Sage.

Columbo, J., & Horowitz, F. D. (1987). Behavioral state as a lead variable in neonatal research. *Merrill-Palmer Quarterly, 33,* 423–437.

Committee on Adolescence Suicide (1996). *Adolescent suicide.* (Group for the Advancement of Psychiatry, Report No. 140). Washington, D. C.: American Psychiatric Press.

Comstock, G. A. (1993). The medium and society: The role of television in American life. In G. L. Berry & J. K. Asamen (Eds.), *Children and television: Images in a changing sociocultural world* (pp. 117–131). Newbury Park, CA: Sage.

Condry, J., & Condry, S. (1976). Sex differences: A study in the eye of the beholder. *Child Development, 47,* 812–819.

Conger, R. D., Conger, K. J., Elder, G. J., Jr., Lorenz, F. O., Simons, R. L., & Whitbeck, L. B. (1992). A family process model of economic hardship and adjustment of early adolescent boys. *Child Development, 63,* 527–541.

Conger, R. D., Ge, X., Elder, G. H., Jr., Lorenz, F. O., & Simons, R. L. (1994). Economic stress, coercive family processes, and developmental problems of adolescents. *Child Development, 65,* 541–561.

Conger, R. D., Patterson, G. R., & Ge, X. (1995). It takes two to replicate: A mediational model for the impact of parents' stress on adolescent adjustment. *Child Development, 66,* 80–97.

Connell, J. P., Spencer, M. B., & Aber, J. L. (1994). Educational risk and resilience in African-American youth: Context, self, action, and outcomes in school. *Child Development, 65,* 493–506.

Connolly, J. A., & Doyle, A. (1984). Relation of social fantasy play to social competence in preschoolers. *Developmental Psychology, 20,* 797–806.

Connor, J. M. (1995). Prenatal diagnosis of single-gene disorders by DNA analysis. In M. J. Whittle & J. M. Connor (Eds.), *Prenatal diagnosis in obstetric practice* (2nd ed., pp. 86–99). Oxford, England: Blackwell.

Coohey, C., & Braun, N. (1997). Toward an integrated framework for understanding child physical abuse. *Child Abuse and Neglect, 21,* 1081–1094.

Cook, T. D., Appleton, H., Conner, R. F., Shaffer, A., Tabkin, G., & Weber, J. S. (1975). *Sesame Street revisited.* New York: Russell Sage Foundation.

Cooke, T., & Apolloni, T. (1976). Developing positive social-emotional behaviors: A study of training and generalization effects. *Journal of Applied Behavior Analysis, 9,* 65–78.

Cooley, C. H. (1902). *Human nature and the social order.* New York: Scribner's.

Coon, H., Fulker, D. W., DeFries, J. C., & Plomin, R. (1990). Home environment and cognitive ability of 7-year-old children in the Colorado Adoption Project: Genetic and environmental etiologies. *Developmental Psychology, 26,* 459–468.

Cooper, H. M. (1979). Pygmalion grows up: A model for teacher expectation, communication, and performance influence. *Review of Educational Research, 49,* 389–410.

Cooper, H. M. (1989). Does reducing student-to-instructor ratios affect achievement? *Educational Psychologist, 24,* 79–98.

Cooper, R. P., & Aslin, R. N. (1990). Preference for infant-directed speech in the first month after birth. *Child Development, 61,* 1585–1595.

Coopersmith, S. (1967). *The antecedents of self-esteem.* New York: W. H. Freeman.

Corah, N. L., Anthony, E. J., Painter, P., Stern, J. A., & Thurston, D. (1965). Effects of perinatal anoxia after seven years. *Psychological Monographs, 79* (3, Whole No. 596).

Corbin, C. (1973). *A textbook of motor development.* Dubuque, IA: William C. Brown.

Coren, S., Porac, C., & Duncan, P. (1981). Lateral preference behaviors in preschool children and young adults. *Child Development, 52,* 443–450

Corteen, R. S., & Williams, T. (1986). Television and reading skills. In T. Williams (Ed.), *The impact of television: A natural experiment in three communities.* Orlando, FL: Academic Press.

Corter, C. M., Zucker, K. J., & Galligan, R. F. (1980). Patterns in the infant's search for mother during brief separation. *Developmental Psychology, 16,* 62–69.

Costin, S. E., & Jones, D. C. (1992). Friendship as a facilitator of emotional responsiveness and prosocial interventions among young children. *Developmental Psychology, 28,* 941–947.

Cote, J. E., & Levine, C. (1988). A critical examination of the ego identity status paradigm. *Developmental Review, 8,* 147–184.

Coulton, C. J., Korbin, J. E., Su, M., & Chow, J. (1995). Community level factors and child maltreatment rates. *Child Development, 66,* 1262–1276.

Cowan, P. A. (1978). *Piaget: With feeling.* New York: Holt, Rinehart and Winston.

Cowan, G., & Avants, S. K. (1988). Children's influence strategies: Structure, sex differences, and bilateral mother-child influences. *Child Development, 59,* 1303–1313.

Cox, C. M. (1926). *Genetic studies of genius.* (Vol. 2). *The early mental traits of three hundred geniuses.* Stanford, CA: Stanford University Press.

Cox, M. J., Owen, M. T., Henderson, V. K., & Margand, N. A. (1992). Prediction of infant-father and infant-mother attachment. *Developmental Psychology, 28,* 474–483.

Cox, M. J., Owen, M. T., Lewis, J. M., & Henderson, V. K. (1989). Marriage, adult adjustment, and early parenting. *Child Development, 60,* 1015–1024.

Coyle, T. R., & Bjorklund, D. F. (1996). The development of strategic memory: A modified microgenetic assessment of utilization deficiencies. *Cognitive Development, 11,* 295–314.

Coyle, T. R., & Bjorklund, D. F. (1997). Age differences in, and consequences of, multiple- and variable-strategy use on a multitrial sort-recall task. *Developmental Psychology, 33,* 372–380.

Crain-Thoreson, C., & Dale, P. S. (1992). Do early talkers become early readers? Linguistic precocity, preschool language, and emergent literacy. *Developmental Psychology, 28,* 421–429.

Craton, L. G. (1996). The development of perceptual completion abilities: Infants' perception of stationary partially occluded objects. *Child Development, 67,* pp. 890–904.

Craton, L. G., Elicker, J., Plumert, J. M., & Pick, H. L., Jr. (1990). Children's use of frames of reference in communication of spatial location. *Child Development, 61,* 1528–1543.

Craton, L. G., & Yonas, A. (1988). Infants' sensitivity to boundary flow information for depth at an edge. *Child Development, 59,* 1522–1529.

Crews, F. (1996). The verdict on Freud [Review of *Freud evaluated: The completed arc*]. *Psychological Science, 7,* 63–68.

Crick, N. R. (1996). The role of overt aggression, relational aggression, and prosocial behavior in the prediction of children's future social adjustment. *Child Development, 67,* 2317–2327.

Crick, N. R. (1997). Engagement in gender normative versus nonnormative forms of aggression: Links to social-psychological adjustment. *Developmental Psychology, 33,* 610–617.

Crick, N. R., Bigbee, M. A., & Howes, C. (1996). Gender differences in children's normative beliefs about aggression: How do I hurt thee? Let me count the ways. *Child Development, 67,* 1003–1014.

Crick, N. R., Casas, J. F., & Mosher, M. (1997). Relational and overt aggression in preschool. *Developmental Psychology, 33,* 579–588.

Crick, N. R., & Dodge, K. A. (1994). A review and reformulation of social information processing mechanisms in children's social adjustment. *Psychological Bulletin, 115,* 74–101.

Crick, N. R., & Dodge, K. A. (1996). Social information-processing mechanisms in reactive and proactive aggression. *Child Development, 67,* 993–1002.

Crick, N. R., & Grotpeter, J. K. (1995). Relational aggression, gender, and social-psychological adjustment. *Child Development, 66,* 710–722.

Crick, N. R., & Ladd, G. W. (1993). Children's perceptions of their peer experiences: Attributions, loneliness, social anxiety, and social avoidance. *Developmental Psychology, 29,* 244–254.

Crick, N. R., Wellman, N. E., Casas, J. F., O'Brien, K. M., Nelson, D. A., Grotpeter, J. K., & Markon, K. (1998). Childhood aggresson and gender: A new look at an old problem. In D. Bernstein (Ed.), *Nebraska Symposium on Motivation:* Vol. 44. Lincoln: University of Nebraska Press.

Crockenberg, S., & Litman, C. (1990). Autonomy as competence in 2-year-olds: Maternal correlates of child defiance, compliance, and self-assertion. *Developmental Psychology, 26,* 961–971.

Crockenberg, S., & Litman, C. (1991). Effects of maternal employment on maternal and two-year-old child behavior. *Child Development, 62,* 930–953.

Cronbach, L. J., & Snow, R. E. (1977). *Aptitude and instructional methods: A handbook for research on interactions.* New York: Irvington.

Crook, C. (1992). Cultural artefacts in social development: The case of computers. In H. McGurk (Ed.), *Childhood social development: Contemporary perspectives.* Hove, England: Erlbaum.

Crook, C. K. (1978). Taste perception in the newborn infant. *Infant Behavior and Development, 1,* 52–69.

Cross, W. E. (1985). Black identity: Rediscovering the distinction between personal identity and reference group orientation. In M. B. Spencer, G. K. Brookins, & W. R. Allen (Eds.), *Beginnings: The social and affective development of black children.* Hillsdale, NJ: Erlbaum.

Crouter, A. C., MacDermid, S. M., McHale, S. M., & Perry-Jenkins, M. (1990). Parental monitoring and perceptions of children's school performance and conduct in dual- and single-career families. *Developmental Psychology, 26,* 649–657.

Crouter, A. C., Manke, B. A., & McHale, S. M. (1995). The family context of gender intensification in early adolescence. *Child Development, 66,* 317–329.

Crowell, J. A., & Feldman, S. S. (1991). Mothers' working models of attachment relationships and mother and child behavior during separation and reunion. *Developmental Psychology, 27,* 597–605.

Crowley, K., & Siegler, R. S. (1993). Flexible strategy use in young children's tic-tac-toe. *Cognitive Science, 17,* 531–561.

Crowley, K., Shrager, J., & Siegler, R. S. (1997). Strategy discovery as a complete negotiation between metacognitive and associative mechanisms. *Developmental Review, 17,* 462–489.

Crystal, D. S., Chen, C., Fuligni, A. J., Stevenson, H. W., Hsu, C., Ko, H., Kitamura, S., & Kimura, S. (1994). Psychological maladjustment and academic achievement: A cross-cultural study of Japanese, Chinese, and American high school students. *Child Development, 65,* 738–753.

Culp, R. E., Little, V., Letts, D., & Lawrence, H. (1991). Maltreated children's self-concept: Effects of a comprehensive treatment program. *American Journal of Orthopsychiatry, 61,* 114–121.

Cummings, E. M., & Davies, P. T. (1994). *Children and marital conflict: The impact of family dispute and resolution.* New York: Guilford Press.

Cummings, E. M., Iannotti, R. J., & Zahn-Waxler, C. (1989). Aggression between peers in early childhood: Individual continuity and developmental change. *Child Development, 60,* 887–895.

Curtiss, S. (1977). *Genie: a psycholinguistic study of a modern-day "wild child."* New York: Academic Press.

Curtiss, S. (1988). *The case of Chelsea: a new test case of the critical period for language acquisition.* Unpublished manuscript. University of California, Los Angeles.

Czeizel, A. E. (1995). Folic acid in the prevention of neural tube defects. *Journal of Pediatric Nutrition, 20,* 4–16.

Dabbs, J. M., & Morris, R. (1990). Testosterone, social class, and antisocial behavior in a sample of 4,462 men. *Psychological Science, 1,* 209–211.

Dale, P. S. (1976). *Language development: Structure and function.* New York: Holt, Rinchart & Winston.

Damast, A. M., Tamis-LeMonda, C. S., & Bornstein, M. H. (1996). Mother-child play: Sequential interactions and the relation between maternal beliefs and behaviors. *Child Development, 67,* 1752–1766.

Damon, W. (1977). *The social world of the child.* San Francisco: Jossey-Bass.

Damon, W. (1988). *The moral child.* New York: Free Press.

Damon, W., & Hart, D. (1988). *Self-understanding in childhood and adolescence.* New York: Cambridge University Press.

Daniels, D. (1986). Differential experiences of siblings in the same family as predictors of adolescent sibling personality differences. *Journal of Personality and Social Psychology, 51,* 339–346.

Daniels, D., & Plomin, R. (1985). Differential experience of siblings in the same family. *Developmental Psychology, 21,* 747–760.

Dannemiller, J. L. (1989). A test of color constancy in 9- and 20-week-old human infants following simulated illuminant changes. *Developmental Psychology, 25,* 171–184.

Dannemiller, J. L., & Stephens, B. R. (1988). A critical test of infant pattern preference models. *Child Development, 59,* 210–216.

Darling, C. A., Davidson, J. K., & Passarello, L. C. (1992). The mystique of first intercourse among college youth: The role of partners, contraceptive practices, and psychological reactions. *Journal of Youth and Adolescence, 21,* 97–117.

Darlington, R. B. (1991). The long-term effects of model preschool programs. In L. Okagaki & R. J. Sternberg (Eds.), *Directors of development. Influences on the development of children's thinking.* Hillsdale, NJ: Erlbaum.

Darwin, C. A. (1877). A biographical sketch of an infant. *Mind, 2,* 285–294.

Das Eiden, R., Teti, D. M., & Corns, K. M. (1995). Maternal working models of attachment, marital adjustment, and the parent-child relationship. *Child Development, 66,* 1504–1518.

Dasen, P. R. (1977). *Piagetian psychology: Cross-cultural contributions.* New York: Gardner Press.

Daubman, K., Heatherington, L., & Ahn, A. (1992). Gender and the self-presentation of academic achievement. *Sex Roles, 27,* 187–204.

Davies, P. T., & Cummings, E. M. (1998). Exploring children's emotional security as a mediator of the link between marital relations and child adjustment. *Child Development, 69,* 124–139.

David, H. P. (1992). Born unwanted: Long-term developmental effects of denied abortion. *Journal of Social Issues, 48,* 163–181.

David, H. P. (1994). Reproductive rights and reproductive behavior: Clash or convergence of private values and public policies. *American Psychologist, 49,*343–349.

Davis, T. L. (1995). Gender differences in masking negative emotions: Ability or motivation. *Developmental Psychology, 31,* 660–667.

Day, R. H. (1987). Visual size constancy in infancy. In B. E. McKenzie & R. H. Day (Eds.), *Perceptual development in early infancy: Problems and issues.* Hillsdale, NJ: Erlbaum.

Day, R. H., & McKenzie, B. E. (1981). Infant perception of the invariant size of approaching and receding objects. *Developmental Psychology, 17,* 670–677.

DeAngelis, T. (1997). Chromosomes contain clues on schizophrenia. *Monitor of the American Psychological Association, 28,* (1) p. 26.

DeAngelis, T. (1997). When children don't bond with parents. *Monitor of the American Psychological Association, 28* (6), 10–12.

Deater-Deckard, K., Dodge, K. A., (1997). Externalizing behavior problems and discipline revisited: Nonlinear effects and variation by culture, context, and gender. *Psychological Inquiry, 8,* 161–175.

DeBerry, K. M., Scarr, S., & Weinberg, R. (1996). Family racial socialization and ecological competence: Longitudinal assessments of African-American transracial adoptees. *Child Development, 67,* 2375–2399.

DeCasper, A. J., & Fifer, W. P. (1980). Of human bonding: Newborns prefer their mother's voices. *Science, 208,* 1174–1176.

DeCasper, A. J., & Spence, M. J. (1986). Prenatal maternal speech influences newborns' perception of speech sounds. *Infant Behavior and Development, 9,* 133–150.

DeCasper, A. J., & Spence, M. J. (1991). Auditorially mediated behavior during the perinatal period: A cognitive view. In M. J. S. Weiss & P. R. Zelazo (Eds.), *Newborn attention: Biological constraints and the influence of experience.* Norwood, NJ: Ablex.

de Gaston, J. P., Jensen, L., & Weed, S. (1995). A closer look at adolescent sexual activity. *Journal of Youth and Adolescence, 24,* 465–479.

Dekovic, M., & Janssens, J. M. A. M. (1992). Parents' child-rearing style and children's sociometric status. *Developmental Psychology, 28,* 925–932.

Delcampo, D. S., & Delcampo, R. L. (1998). *Taking sides: Clashing views on controversial issues in childhood and society* (2nd ed.). Guilford, CT: Dushkin/McGraw-Hill.

De Lisi, R., & Staudt, J. (1980). Individual differences in college students' performance on formal operations tasks. *Journal of Applied Developmental Psychology, 1,* 163–174.

DeLoache, J. S. (1986). Memory in very young children: Exploitation of cues to the location of a hidden object. *Cognitive Development, 1,* 123–138

DeLoache, J. S. (1987). Rapid change in the symbolic functioning of very young children. *Science, 238,* 1556–1557.

DeLoache, J. S. (1991). Symbolic functioning in very young children: Understanding of pictures and models. *Child Development, 62,* 736–752.

DeLoache, J. S., Cassidy, D. J., & Brown, A. L. (1985). Precursors of mnemonic strategies in very young children's memory. *Child Development, 56,* 125–137.

DeLoache, J. S., Kolstad, V., & Anderson, K. N. (1991). Physical similarity and young children's understanding of scale models. *Child Development, 62,* 111–126.

DeLoache, J. S., & Marzolf, D. P. (1992). When a picture is not worth a thousand words: Young children's understanding of pictures and models. *Cognitive Development, 7,* 317–329.

DeMarie-Dreblow, D., & Miller, P. H. (1988). The development of children's strategies for selective attention: Evidence for a transitional period. *Child Development, 59,* 1504–1513.

deMause, L. (1974). The evolution of childhood. In L. deMause (Ed.), *The history of childhood.* New York: Harper & Row.

Dempster, F. N. (1981). Memory span: Sources of individual and developmental differences. *Psychological Bulletin, 89,* 63–100.

Dempster, F. N. (1985). Short-term memory development in childhood and adolescence. In C. J. Brainerd & M. Pressley (Eds.), *Basic processes in memory development. Progress in cognitive development research.* New York: Springer-Verlag.

Dempster, F. N. (1993). Resistance to interference: Developmental changes in a basic processing mechanism. In M. L. Howe & R. Pasnak (Eds.), *Emerging themes in cognitive development. Vol. 1: Foundations* (pp. 1–27). New York: Springer-Verlag.

Denham, S. A., McKinley, M., Couchoud, E. A., & Holt, R. (1990). Emotional and behavioral predictors of preschool peer ratings. *Child Development, 61,* 1145–1152.

Denham, S. A., Zoller, D., & Couchoud, E. A. (1994). Socialization of preschoolers' emotion understanding. *Developmental Psychology, 30,* 928–936.

Denning, C. R., Kagan, B. M., Mueller, D. H., & Neu, H. C. (1991). The CF gene—one year later. *Cystic Fibrosis Currents, 6,* 1–19.

Dennis, W. (1960). Causes of retardation among institutional children: Iran. *Journal of Genetic Psychology, 96,* 47–59.

Descartes, R. (1965). La dioptrique. In R. J. Herrnstein & E. G. Boring (Eds.), *A sourcebook in the history of psychology.* Cambridge, MA: Harvard University Press. (Original work published 1638).

Despert, J. L. (1965). *The emotionally disturbed child: Then and now.* New York: Brunner/Mazel.

de Villiers, J. G., & de Villiers, P. A. (1973). a cross-sectional study of the acquisition of grammatical morphemes in child speech. *Journal of Psycholinguistic Research, 2,* 267–278.

de Villiers, P. A., & de Villiers, J. G. (1979). *Early language.* Cambridge, MA: Harvard University Press.

de Villiers, P. A., & de Villiers, J. G. (1992). Language development. In M. H. Bornstein & M. E. Lamb (Eds.), *Developmental psychology: An advanced textbook* (3rd ed.). Hillsdale, NJ: Erlbaum.

DeVries, R. (1969). Constancy of generic identity in the years three to six. *Monographs of the Society for Research in Child Development, 34* (Serial No. 127).

De Wolff, M. S., & van IJzendoorn, M. H. (1997). Sensitivity and attachment: A meta-analysis on parental antecedents of infant attachment. *Child Development, 68,* 571–591.

Dews, S., Winner, E., Kaplan, J., Rosenblatt, E., Hunt, M., Lim, K., McGovern, A., Qualter, A., & Smarsh, B. (1996). Children's understanding of the meaning and functions of verbal irony. *Child Development, 67,* 3071–3085.

Dewsbury, D. A. (1992). Comparative psychology and ethology: A reassessment, *American Psychologist, 47,* 208–215.

Diamond, A. (1985). Development of the ability to use recall to guide action, as indicated by the infant's performance on AB. *Child Development, 56,* 868–883.

Diamond, A. (1991). Frontal lobe involvement in cognitive changes during the first year of life. In K. R. Gibson & A. C. Petersen (Eds.), *Brain maturation and cognitive development: Comparative and cross-cultural perspectives* (pp. 127–160). New York: Aldine de Gruyter.

Diamond, A. (1995). Evidence of robust recognition memory in early life even when assessed by reaching behavior. *Journal of Experimental Child Psychology, 59,* 419–456.

Diamond, M., & Sigmundson, H. K. (1997). Sex reassignment at birth: Long-term review and clinical implications. *Archives of Pediatric and Adolescent Medicine, 151,* 298–304.

Diaz, J. (1997). *How drugs influence behavior: A neuro-behavioral approach.* Upper Saddle, NJ: Prentice-Hall.

Diaz, R. M. (1983). Thought and two languages: The impact of bilingualism on cognitive development. In E. W. Gordon (Ed.), *Review of research in education* (Vol. 10). Washington, D.C.: American Educational Research Association.

Diaz, R. M. (1985). Bilingual cognitive development: Addressing three gaps in recent research. *Child Development, 56,* 1376–1388.

Diaz, R. M., Neal, C. J., & Vachio, A. (1991). Maternal teaching in the zone of proximal development: A comparison of low- and high-risk dyads. *Merrill-Palmer Quarterly, 37,* 83–108.

Dick-Read, G. (1972). *Childbirth without fear: The original approach to natural childbirth.* New York: Harper & Row. (Original work published 1933.)

Diener, E., Sandvik, E., & Larsen, R. J. (1985). Age and sex effects for emotional intensity. *Developmental Psychology, 21,* 542–546.

DiLalla, L. F., Kagan, J., & Reznick, J. S. (1994). Genetic etiology of behavioral inhibition among 2-year-old children. *Infant Behavior and Development, 17,* 405–412.

DiPietro, J. A., Hodgson, D. M., Costigan, K. A., Hilton, S. C., & Johnston, T. R. B. (1996). Fetal neurobehavioral development. *Child Development, 67,* 2553–2567.

Dishion, T. J. (1990). The family ecology of boys' peer relations in middle childhood. *Child Development, 61,* 874–892.

Dishion, T. J., Andrews, D. W., & Crosby, L. (1995). Antisocial boys and their friends in early adolescence: Relationship characteristics, quality, and interactional process. *Child Development, 66,* 139–151.

Dishion, T. J., Patterson, G. R., Stoolmiller, M., & Skinner, M. L. (1991). Family, school, and behavioral antecedents to early adolescent involvement with antisocial peers. *Developmental Psychology, 27,* 172–180.

Dittman, R. W., Kappes, M. E., & Kappes, M. H. (1992). Sexual behavior in adolescent and adult females with congenital adrenal hyperplasia. *Psychoneuroendocronology, 17,* 153–170.

Dodge, K. A. (1980). Social cognition and children's aggressive behavior. *Child Development, 51,* 162–170.

Dodge, K. A. (1983). Behavioral antecedents of peer social status. *Child Development, 54,* 1386–1399.

Dodge, K. A. (1986). A social information processing model of social competence in children. In M. Perlmutter (Ed.), *Minnesota symposia on child psychology* (Vol. 18). Hillsdale, NJ: Erlbaum.

Dodge, K. A. (1993). Social-cognitive mechanisms in the development of conduct disorder and depression. *Annual Review of Psychology, 44,* 559–584.

Dodge, K. A., Coie, J. D., Pettit, G. S., & Price, J. M. (1990). Peer status and aggression in boys' groups: Developmental and contextual analyses. *Child Development, 61,* 1289–1309.

Dodge, K. A., Pettit, G. S., & Bates, J. E. (1994). Socialization mediators of the relation between socioeconomic status and child conduct problems. *Child Development, 65,* 649–665.

Doherty, W. J., & Needle, R. H. (1991). Psychological adjustment and substance abuse among adolescents before and after a parental divorce. *Child Development, 62,* 328–337.

Dolgin, K. G., & Behrend, D. A. (1984). Children's knowledge about animates and inanimates. *Child Development, 55,* 1646–1650.

Domjan, M. (1993). *Principles of learning and behavior* (3rd ed.). Pacific Grove, CA: Brooks/Cole.

Dornbusch, S. M., Carlsmith, J. M., Bushwall, S. J., Ritter, P. L., Leiderman, P. H., Hastorf, A. H., & Gross, R. T. (1985). Single parents, extended households, and the control of adolescents. *Child Development, 56,* 326–341.

Dornbusch, S. M., Glasgow, K. L., & Lin, I. (1996). The social structure of schooling. *Annual Review of Psychology, 47,* 401–429.

Dossey, J. A., Mullis, I. V. S., Lindquist, M. M., & Chambers, D. L. (1988). *The Mathematics Report Card: Are we measuring up?* Princeton, NJ: Educational Testing Service.

Dougherty, T. M., & Haith, M. M. (1997). Infant expectations and reaction time as predictors of childhood speed of processing and IQ. *Developmental Psychology, 33,* 146–155.

Dow, G. A., & Pick, H. L. (1992). Young children's use of models and photographs as spatial representations. *Cognitive Development, 7,* 351–363.

Downing, L. L. (1998). *Fragile realities: Conversion and commitment in cults and other powerful groups:* State University of New York at Oneonta.

Doyle, A. B., & Aboud, F. E. (1993). A longitudinal study of white children's racial prejudice as a social-cognitive development. *Merrill-Palmer Quarterly, 41,* 209–228.

Doyle, A. B., Connolly, J., & Rivest, L. (1980). The effects of playmate familiarity on the social interaction of very young children. *Child Development, 51,* 217–223.

Doyle, A. B., Doehring, P., Tessier, O., de Lorimier, S., & Shapiro, S. (1992). Transitions in children's play: A sequential analysis of states preceding and following social pretense. *Developmental Psychology, 28,* 137–144.

Drabman, R. S., & Thomas, M. H. (1974). Does media violence increase children's toleration of real-life aggression? *Developmental Psychology, 10,* 418–421.

Dreyer, P. H. (1982). Sexuality during adolescence. In B. B. Wolman (Ed.), *Handbook of developmental psychology.* New York: Wiley.

Drillien, C. M. (1969). School disposal and performance for children of different birthweight born 1953–1960. *Archives of Diseases in Childhood, 44,* 562–570.

Droege, K. L., & Stipek, D. J. (1993). Children's use of dispositions to predict classmates' behavior. *Developmental Psychology, 29,* 646–654.

Drotar, D. (1992). Personality development, problem solving, and behavior problems among preschool children with early histories of nonorganic failure-to-thrive. *Developmental and Behavioral Pediatrics, 13,* 266–273.

Dubas, J. S., Graber, J. A., & Petersen, A. C. (1991). The effects of pubertal development on achievement during adolescence. *American Journal of Education, 99,* 444–460.

Dube, E. F. (1982). Literacy, cultural familiarity, and "intelligence" as determinants of story recall. In U. Neisser (Ed.), *Memory observed: Remembering in natural contexts.* San Francisco: W. H. Freeman.

Duke, P. M., Carlsmith, J. M., Jennings, D., Martin, J. A., Dornbusch, S. M., Gross, R. T., & Siegel-Gorelick, B. (1982). Educational correlates of early and late sexual maturation in adolescence. *Journal of Pediatrics, 100,* 633–637.

Duncan, G. J., & Brooks-Gunn, J. (1997). *Growing up poor: Consequences across the life span.* New York: Russell Sage Foundation.

Duncan, G. J., Brooks-Gunn, J., & Klebanov, P. K. (1994). Economic deprivation and early childhood development. *Child Development, 65,* 296–318.

Dunn, J. (1993). *Young children's close relationships. Beyond attachment.* Newbury Park, CA: Sage.

Dunn, J. (1994). Changing minds and changing relationships. In C. Lewis & P. Mitchel (Eds.), *Children's early understanding of mind: Origins and development* (pp. 297–310). Hove: Erlbaum.

Dunn, J., Brown, J., & Beardsall, L. (1991). Family talk about feeling states and children's later understanding of children's emotions. *Developmental Psychology, 27,* 448–455.

Dunn, J., Brown, J. R., & Maguire, M. (1995). The development of children's moral sensibility: Individual differences and emotional understanding. *Developmental Psychology, 31,* 649–659.

Dunn, J., & Kendrick, C. (1982). *Siblings: Love, envy, and understanding.* Cambridge, MA: Harvard University Press.

Dunn, J., & Plomin, R. (1990). *Separate lives: Why siblings are so different.* New York: Basic Books.

Dunn, J., Slomkowski, C., & Beardsall, L. (1994). Sibling relationships from the preschool period through middle childhood and early adolescence. *Developmental Psychology, 30,* 315–324.

Dunphy, D. C. (1963). The social structure of urban adolescent peer groups. *Sociometry, 26,* 230–246.

DuPaul, G. J., & Barkley, R. A. (1993). Behavioral contributions to pharmaco-therapy: The utility of behavioral methodology in medication treatment of children with Attention Deficit Hyperactivity Disorder. *Behavior Therapy, 24,* 47–65.

Dweck, C. S. (1975). The role of expectations and attributions in the alleviation of learned helplessness. *Journal of Personality and Social Psychology, 31,* 674–685.

Dweck, C. S. (1978). Achievement. In M. E. Lamb (Ed.), *Social and personality development* (pp. 114–130). New York: Holt, Rinehart, and Winston.

Dweck, C. S., Davidson, W., Nelson, S., & Enna, B. (1978). Sex differences in learned helplessness. II. The contingencies of evaluative feedback in the classroom. III. An experimental analysis. *Developmental Psychology, 14,* 268–276.

Dweck, C. S., & Elliott, E. S. (1983). Achievement motivation. In P. H. Mussen (Ed.), *Handbook of child psychology* (Vol. 4). *Socialization, personality, and social development.* New York: Wiley.

Dweck, C. S., & Leggett, E. L. (1988). A social-cognitive approach to motivation and personality. *Psychological Review, 95,* 256–273.

Dwyer, T., Ponsonby, A. L. B., Newman, N. M., & Gibbons, L. E. (1991). Prospective cohort study of prone sleeping position and sudden infant death syndrome. *Lancet, 337,* 1244–1247.

Dyer, K. F. (1977). The trend of male-female performance differential in athletics, swimming, and cycling 1948–1976. *Journal of Biosocial Science, 9,* 325–338.

Eagly, A. H. (1995). The science and politics of comparing men and women. *American Psychologist, 50,* 145–158.

East, P. L. (1996). The younger sisters of childbearing adolescents: Their attitudes, expectations, and behaviors. *Child Development, 67,* 267–282.

East, P. L., & Rook, K. S. (1992). Compensatory patterns of support among children's peer relationships: A test using school friends, nonschool friends, and siblings. *Developmental Psychology, 28,* 163–172.

Eaton, W. O., & Enns, L. R. (1986). Sex differences in human motor activity level. *Psychological Bulletin, 100,* 19–28.

Eaton, W. O., & Yu, A. P. (1989). Are sex differences in child motor activity level a function of sex differences in maturational status? *Child Development, 60,* 1005–1011.

Ebeling, K. S., & Gelman, S. A. (1988). Coordination of size standards by young children. *Child Development, 59,* 888–896.

Ebeling, K. S., & Gelman, S. A. (1994). Children's use of context in interpreting "big" and "little". *Child Development, 65,* 1178–1192.

Eccles, J. S., Flanagan, C., Lord, S., & Midgley, C. (1996). Schools, families, and early adolescents: What are we doing wrong and what can we do instead? *Journal of Developmental and Behavioral Pediatrics, 17,* 267–276.

Eccles, J. S., & Harold, R. D. (1993). Parent-school involvement during the early adolescent years. *Teachers College Record, 94,* 568–587.

Eccles, J. S., Jacobs, J. E., & Harold, R. D. (1990). Gender role stereotypes, expectancy effects, and parents' socialization of gender differences. *Journal of Social Issues, 46,* 183–201.

Eccles, J. S., Lord, S., & Midgley, C. (1991). What are we doing to early adolescents? The impact of educational contexts on early adolescents. *American Journal of Education, 99,* 521–542.

Eccles, J. S., Midgley, C., Wigfield, A., Buchanan, C. M., Reuman, D., Flanagan, C., & Mac Iver, D. (1993). Development during adolescence: The impact of stage-environment fit on young adolescents' experiences in schools and in families. *American Psychologist, 48,* 90–101.

Eckenrode, J., Laird, M., & Doris, J. (1993). School performance and disciplinary problems among abused and neglected children. *Developmental Psychology, 29,* 53–62.

Eckerman, C. O., & Didow, S. M. (1996). Nonverbal imitation and toddlers' mastery of verbal means of achieving coordinated action. *Developmental Psychology, 32,* 141–152.

Eckerman, C. O., & Stein, M. R. (1990). How imitation begets imitation and toddlers' generation of games. *Developmental Psychology, 26,* 370–378.

Eder, R. A. (1989). The emergent personalogist: The structure and content of 3½-, 5½-, and 7½-year olds' concepts of themselves and other persons. *Child Development, 60,* 1218–1228.

Eder, R. A. (1990). Uncovering young children's psychological selves: Individual and developmental differences. *Child Development, 61,* 849–863.

Egeland, B., Jacobvitz, D., & Sroufe, L. A. (1988). Breaking the cycle of abuse. *Child Development, 59,* 1080–1088.

Egerton, J. (1983). *Generations: An American Family.* Lexington, KY: University Press of Kentucky.

Eggebeen, D. J., & Lichter, D. T. (1991). Race, family structure, and changing poverty among American children. *American Sociological Review, 56,* 801–817.

Ehrhardt, A. A. (1985). The psychobiology of gender. In A. S. Rossi (Ed.), *Gender and the life course.* New York: Adline.

Ehrhardt, A. A., & Baker, S. W. (1974). Fetal androgens, human central nervous system differentiation, and behavioral sex differences. In R. C. Friedman, R. M. Rickard, & R. L. Van de Wiele (Eds.), *Sex differences in behavior.* New York: Wiley.

Eichorn, D. H. (1979). Physical development: Current foci of research. In J. D. Osofsky (Ed.), *Handbook of infant development.* New York: Wiley.

Eilers, R. E., & Oller, D. K. (1994). Infant vocalizations and the early diagnosis of severe hearing impairment. *Journal of Pediatrics, 124,* 199–203.

Eimas, P. D. (1975a). Auditory and phonetic cues for speech: Discrimination of the (r-l) distinction by young infants. *Perception and Psychophysics, 18,* 341–347.

Eimas, P. D. (1975b). Speech perception in early infancy. In L. B. Cohen & P. Salapatek (Eds.), *Infant perception: From sensation to cognition.* Orlando, FL: Academic Press.

Eimas, P. D. (1985). The perception of speech in early infancy. *Scientific American, 252,* 46–52.

Eisele, J., & Lust, B. (1996). Knowledge about pronouns: A developmental study using a truth-value judgment task. *Child Development, 67,* 3086–3100.

Eisenberg, N. (1983). Children's differentiations among potential recipients of aid. *Child Development, 54,* 594–602.

Eisenberg, N., Fabes, R. A., Carlo, G., Troyer, D., Speer, A. L., Karbon, M., & Switzer, G. (1992). The relations of maternal practices and characteristics to children's vicarious emotional responsiveness. *Child Development, 63,* 583–602.

Eisenberg, N., Fabes, R. A., Miller, P. A., Shell, R., Shea, C., & May-Plumlee, T. (1990). Preschoolers' vicarious emotional responding and their situational and dispositional prosocial behavior. *Merrill-Palmer Quarterly, 36,* 507–529.

Eisenberg, N., Fabes, R. A., Murphy, B., Maszk, P., Smith, M., & Karbon, M. (1995). The role of emotionality and regulation in children's social functioning: A longitudinal study. *Child Development, 66,* 1360–1384.

Eisenberg, N., Fabes, R. A., Schaller, M., Carlo, G., & Miller, P. A. (1991). The relations of parental characteristics and practices in children's vicarious emotional responding. *Child Development, 62,* 1393–1408.

Eisenberg, N., Guthrie, I. K., Fabes, R. A., Reiser, M., Murphy, B. C., Holgren, R., Maszk, P., & Losoya, S. (1997). The relations of regulation and emotionality to resiliency and competent social functioning in elementary school children. *Child Development, 68,* 295–311.

Eisenberg, N., Lennon, R., & Roth, K. (1983). Prosocial development: A longitudinal study. *Developmental Psychology, 19,* 846–855.

Eisenberg, N., Miller, P. A., Shell, R., McNalley, S., & Shea, C. (1991). Prosocial development in adolescence: A longitudinal study. *Developmental Psychology, 27,* 849–857.

Eisenberg, N., Murray, E., & Hite, T. (1982). Children's reasoning regarding sex-typed toy choices. *Child Development, 53,* 81–86.

Eisenberg, N., Schaller, M., Fabes, R. A., Bustamante, D., Mathy, R. M., Shell, R., & Rhodes, K. (1988). Differentiation of personal distress and sympathy in children and adolescents. *Developmental Psychology, 24,* 766–775.

Eisenberg, N., Shell, R., Pasternack, J., Lennon, R., Beller, R., & Mathy, R. M. (1987). Prosocial development in middle childhood: A longitudinal study. *Developmental Psychology, 23,* 712–718.

Eisenberg-Berg, N., & Hand, M. (1979). The relationship of preschoolers' reasoning about prosocial moral conflicts to prosocial behavior. *Child Development, 50,* 356–363.

Elder, G. H., Liker, J. K., & Cross, C. E. (1984). Parent-child behavior in the Great Depression: Life course and intergenerational influences. In P. B. Baltes & O. G. Brim (Eds.), *Life-span development and behavior* (Vol. 6). New York: Academic Press.

Eldred, L., & Chaisson, R. (1996). The clinical course of HIV infection in women. In R. R. Faden & N. E. Kass (Eds.), *HIV, AIDS, and childbearing.* (pp. 15–30). New York: Oxford University Press.

Elicker, J., Englund, M., & Sroufe, L. A. (1992). Predicting peer competence and peer relationships in childhood from early parent-child relationships. In R. D. Parke & G. W. Ladd (Eds.), *Family-peer relationships: Modes of linkage.* Hillsdale, NJ: Erlbaum.

Elkind, D. (1967). Egocentrism in adolescence. *Child Development, 38,* 1025–1033.

Elkind, D. (1977). Giant in the nursery—Jean Piaget. In E. M. Hetherington & R. D. Parke (Eds.), *Contemporary readings in child psychology.* New York: McGraw-Hill.

Elkind, D. (1981a). *Children and adolescents: Interactive essays on Jean Piaget* (3rd ed.). New York: McGraw-Hill.

Elkind, D. (1981b). *The hurried child: Growing up too fast too soon.* Reading, MA: Addison-Wesley.

Elkind, D. (1996), Inhelder and Piaget on Adolescence and adulthood: a postmodern appraisal. *Psychological Science, 7,* 216–220.

Ellis, N. C. & Hennelley, R. A. (1980). A bilingual word-length effect: Implications for intelligence testing and the relative ease of mental calculation in Welsh and English. *British Journal of Psychology, 71,* 43–52.

Ellis, S., Rogoff, B., & Cromer, C. C. (1981). Age segregation in children's social interactions. *Developmental Psychology, 17,* 399–407.

Ellsworth, C. P., Muir, D. W., & Hains, S. M. J. (1993). Social competence and person-object differentiation: An analysis of the still-face effect. *Developmental Psychology, 29,* 63–73.

Emde, R. N., Biringen, Z., Clyman, R. B., & Oppenheim, D. (1991). The moral self of infancy: Affective core and procedural knowledge. *Developmental Review, 11,* 251–270.

Emde, R. N., Plomin, R., Robinson, J., Corley, R., DeFries, J., Fulker, D. W., Reznick, J. S., Campos, J., Kagan, J., & Zahn-Waxler, C. (1992). Temperament, emotion, and cognition at fourteen months: The MacArthur longitudinal twin study. *Child Development, 63,* 1437–1455.

Emery, R. E. (1988). *Marriage, divorce, and children's adjustment.* Beverly Hills, CA: Sage.

Emery, R. E. (1989). Family violence. *American Psychologist, 44,* 321–328.

Emery, R. E., & Forehand, R. (1994). Parental divorce and children's well-being: A focus on resilience. In R. J. Haggerty, L. R. Sherrod, N. Garmezy, & M. Rutter (Eds.), *Stress, risk, and resilience in children and adolescents* (pp. 64–99). New York: Cambridge University Press.

Emery, R. E., & Laumann-Billings, L. (1998). An overview of the nature, causes, and consequences of abusive family relationships: Toward differentiating maltreatment and violence. *American Psychologist, 53,* 121–135.

Emery, R. E., & Tuer, M. (1993). Parenting and the marital relationship. In T. Luster & L. Okagaki (Eds.), *Parenting. An ecological perspective.* Hillsdale, NJ: Erlbaum.

Emery, R. E., & Wyer, M. M. (1987). Divorce mediation. *American Psychologist, 42,* 472–480.

Entwisle, D. R., & Alexander, K. L. (1990). Beginning school math competence: Minority and majority comparisons. *Child Development, 61,* 454–471.

Entwisle, D. R., & Baker, D. P. (1983). Gender and young children's expectations for performance in arithmetic. *Developmental Psychology, 19,* 200–209.

Epstein, L. H., McCurley, J., Wing, R. R., & Valoski, A. (1990). Five-year follow-up of family-based treatments for childhood obesity. *Journal of Consulting and Clinical Psychology, 58,* 661–664.

Epstein, L. H., Wing, R. R., Koeske, R., & Valoski, A. (1987). Long-term effects of family-based treatment of childhood obesity. *Journal of Consulting and Clinical Psychology, 55,* 91–95.

Erdley, C. A., Cain, K. M., Loomis, C. C., Dumas-Hines, F., & Dweck, C. S. (1997). Relations among children's social goals, implicit personality theories, and responses to social failure. *Developmental Psychology, 33,* 263–272.

Erel, O., & Burman, B. (1995). Interrelatedness of marital relations and parent-child relations: A meta-analytic review. *Psychological Bulletin, 118,* 108–132.

Erikson, E. H. (1963). *Childhood and society,* (2nd ed.). New York: Norton.

Erikson, E. H. (1982). *The life cycle completed. A review.* New York: Norton.

Eron, L. D. (1982). Parent-child interaction, television violence, and aggression of children. *American Psychologist, 37,* 197–211.

Etaugh, C., Levine, D., & Mennella, A. (1984). Development of sex biases in children: 40 years later. *Sex Roles, 10,* 911–922.

Etaugh, C., & Liss, M. B. (1992). Home, school, and playroom: Training grounds for adult gender roles. *Sex Roles, 26,* 129–147.

Eyer, D. E. (1992). *Mother-infant bonding. A scientific fiction.* New Haven, CT: Yale University Press.

Fabes, R. A., Eisenberg, N., Karbon, M., Bernzweig, J., Speer, A. L., & Carlo, G. (1994). Socialization of children's vicarious emotional responding and prosocial behavior: Relations with mothers' perceptions of children's emotional reactivity. *Developmental Psychology, 30,* 44–55.

Fabes, R. A., Eisenberg, N., & Miller, P. A. (1990). Maternal correlates of children's vicarious emotional responsiveness. *Developmental Psychology, 26,* 639–648.

Fabes, R. A., Eisenberg, N., Nyman, M., & Michealieu, Q. (1991). Young children's appraisals of others' spontaneous emotional reactions. *Developmental Psychology, 27,* 858–866.

Fabes, R. A., Fultz, J., Eisenberg, N., May-Plumlee, T., & Christopher, F. S. (1989). Effects of rewards on children's prosocial motivation: A socialization study. *Developmental Psychology, 25,* 509–515.

Fabricius, W. V., & Cavalier, L. (1989). The role of causal theories about memory in young children's memory strategy choice. *Child Development, 60,* 298–308.

Fabricius, W. V., & Steffe, L. (1989, April). *Considering all possible combinations: The early beginnings of a formal-operational skill.* Paper presented at the biennial meeting of the Society for Research in Child Development, Kansas City, MO.

Faden, R. R., & Kass, N. E. (1996). *HIV, AIDS, and childbearing.* New York: Oxford University Press.

Fagan, J. F., III. (1979). The origins of facial pattern recognition. In M. H. Bornstein & W. Kessen (Eds.), *Psychological development from infancy: Image to intention.* Hillsdale, NJ: Erlbaum.

Fagan, J. F., III (1984). Infant memory: History, current trends, and relations to cognitive psychology. In M. Moscovitch (Ed.), *Infant memory: Its relation to normal and pathological memory in humans and other animals.* New York: Plenum.

Fagot, B. I. (1978). The influence of sex of child on parental reactions to toddler children. *Child Development, 49,* 459–465.

Fagot, B. I. (1985a). Beyond the reinforcement principle: Another step toward understanding sex-role development. *Developmental Psychology, 21,* 1097–1104.

Fagot, B. I. (1985b). Changes in thinking about early sex-role development. *Developmental Review, 5,* 83–98.

Fagot, B. I. (1997). Attachment, parenting, and peer interactions of toddler children. *Developmental Psychology, 33,* 489–499.

Fagot, B. I., & Gauvain, M. (1997). Mother-child problem solving: Continuity through the early childhood years. *Developmental Psychology, 33,* 480–488.

Fagot, B. I., & Hagan, R. I. (1991). Observations of parent reactions to sex-stereotyped behaviors: Age and sex effects. *Child Development, 62,* 617–628.

Fagot, B. I., & Kavanagh, K. (1990). The prediction of antisocial behavior from avoidant attachment classifications. *Child Development, 61,* 864–873.

Fagot, B. I., & Kavanaugh, K. (1993). Parenting during the second year: Effects of children's age, sex, and attachment classification. *Child Development, 64,* 258–271.

Fagot, B. I., & Leinbach, M. D. (1989). The young child's gender schema: Environmental input, internal organization. *Child Development, 60,* 663–672.

Fagot, B. I., & Leinbach, M. D. (1993). Gender-role development in young children: From discrimination to labeling. *Developmental Review, 13,* 205–224.

Fagot, B. I., Leinbach, M. D., & Hagan, R. (1986). Gender labeling and the adoption of sex-typed behaviors. *Developmental Psychology, 22,* 440–443.

Fagot, B. I., Leinbach, M. D., & O'Boyle, C. (1992). Gender labeling, gender stereotyping, and parenting behaviors. *Developmental Psychology, 28,* 225–230.

Falbo, T. (1992). Social norms and the one-child family: Clinical and policy implications. In F. Boer & J. Dunn (Eds.), *Children's sibling relationships* (pp. 71–82). Hillsdale, NJ: Erlbaum.

Falbo, T., & Polit, D. F. (1986). Quantitative review of the only child literature: Research evidence and theory development. *Psychological Bulletin, 100,* 176–189.

Falbo, T., & Poston, D. L., Jr. (1993). The academic, personality, and physical outcomes of only children in China. *Child Development, 64,* 18–35.

Fantz, R. L. (1961). The origin of form perception. *Scientific American, 204,* 66–72.

Fantz, R. L. (1963). Pattern vision in newborn infants. *Science, 140,* 296–297.

Farber, S. L. (1981). *Identical twins reared apart: A reanalysis.* New York: Basic Books.

Farhl, P. (1998; January 10). "Educational" TV programs are flunking in viewership. Washington Post report as cited in the *Athens Banner-Herald,* p. A1, A14.

Farrar, M. J., & Goodman, G. S. (1992). Developmental changes in event memory. *Child Development, 63,* 173–187.

Farrington, D. P. (1987). Epidemology. In H. C. Quay (Ed.), *Handbook of juvenile delinquency.* New York: Wiley.

Farver, J. M., & Branstetter, W. H. (1994). Preschoolers' prosocial responses to their peers' distress. *Developmental Psychology, 30,* 334–341.

Faust, M. S. (1960). Developmental maturity as a determinant of prestige in adolescent girls. *Child Development, 31,* 173–184.

Feeney, J. A., & Noller, P. (1990). Attachment style as a predictor of adult romantic relationships. *Journal of Personality and Social Psychology, 58,* 281–291.

Fein, G. G. (1986). The affective psychology of play. In A. W. Gottfried & C. C. Brown (Eds.), *Play interactions. The contributions of play material and parental involvement to children's development.* Lexington, MA: Lexington Books.

Feingold, A. (1994). Gender differences in personality: A meta-analysis. *Psychological Bulletin, 116,* 429–456.

Feinman, S. (1992). *Social referencing and the social construction of reality in infancy.* New York: Plenum.

Feldhusen, J. F., & Goh, B. E. (1995). Assessing and accessing creativity: An interpretive review of theory, research, and development. *Creativity Research Journal, 8,* 231–247.

Feldman, D. H. (1982). A developmental framework for research with gifted children. In D. H. Feldman (Ed.), *New directions for child development: No. 17. Developmental approaches to giftedness and creativity.* San Francisco: Jossey-Bass.

Feldman, D. H., & Goldsmith, L. T. (1991). *Nature's gambit.* New York: Teacher's College Press.

Feldman, S. S., & Gehring, T. M. (1988). Changing perceptions of family cohesion and power across adolescence. *Child Development, 59,* 1034–1045.

Fentress, J. C. & McLeod, P. J. (1986). Motor patterns in development. In E. M. Blass (Ed.), *Handbook of behavioral neurobiology.* (Vol. 8). *Developmental psychology and developmental neurobiology.* New York: Plenum.

Ferguson, C. A. (1977). Learning to produce: The earliest stages of phonological development in the child. In F. D. Minifie & L. L. Lloyd (Eds.), *Communication and cognitive abilities: Early behavioral assessment.* Baltimore: University Park Press.

Fernald, A. (1989). Intonation and communicative intent in mothers' speech to infants: Is the melody the message? *Child Development, 60,* 1497–1510.

Fernald, A. (1993). Approval and disapproval: Infant responsiveness to vocal affect in familiar and unfamiliar languages. *Child Development, 64,* 657–674.

Fernald, A., & Morikawa, H. (1993). Common themes and cultural variations in Japanese and American mothers' speech to infants. *Child Development, 64,* 637–656.

Fernandez, E. (1997, June 3). The grim legacy of divorce. *The Atlanta Constitution,* p. F5.

Ferreira, F., & Morrison, F. J. (1994). Children's metalinguistic knowledge of syntactical constituents: Effects of age and schooling. *Developmental Psychology, 30,* 663–678.

Feshbach, S. (1956). The catharsis hypothesis and some consequences of interaction with aggressive and neutral play objects. *Journal of Personality, 24,* 449–461.

Feshbach, S. (1970). Aggression. In P. H. Mussen (Ed.), *Carmichael's manual of child psychology,* (Vol. 2). New York: Wiley.

Feuerstein, R., Feurstein, R., & Gross, S. (1997). The learning potential assessment device. In D. P. Flanagan, J. Genshaft, & P. L. Harrison (Eds.), *Contemporary intellectual assessment: Theories, tests, and issues.* New York: Guilford.

Field, D. (1981). Can preschool children really learn to conserve? *Child Development, 52,* 326–334.

Field, D. (1987). A review of preschool conservation training: An analysis of analyses. *Developmental Review, 7,* 210–251.

Field, T. M. (1987). Affective and interactive disturbances in infants. In J. D. Osofsky (Ed.), *Handbook of infant development* (2nd ed.). New York: Wiley.

Field, T. M, Greenwald, P., Morrow, C., Healy, B., Foster, T., Guthertz, M., & Frost, P. (1992). Behavior state matching during interactions of preadolescent friends versus acquaintances. *Developmental Psychology, 28,* 242–250.

Field, T. M., Healy, B., Goldstein, S., Perry, S., Bendell, D., Schanberg, S., Zimmerman, E. A., & Kuhn, C. (1988). Infants of depressed mothers show "depressed" behavior even with nondepressed adults. *Child Development, 59,* 1569–1579.

Field, T. M., Sandberg, D., Garcia, R., Nitza, V., Goldstein, S. & Guy, L. (1985). Pregnancy problems, postpartum depression, and early mother-infant interactions. *Developmental Psychology, 21,* 1152–1156.

Field, T. M., Schanberg, S. M., Scafidi, F., Bauer, C. R., Vega-Lahr, N., Garcia, R., Nystrom, J., & Kuhn, C. M. (1986). Effects of tactile/kinesthetic stimulation on preterm neonates. *Pediatrics, 77,* 654–658.

Field, T. M., Woodson, R., Greenberg, R., & Cohen, D. (1982). Discrimination and imitation of facial expressions by neonates. *Science, 218,* 179–181.

Finch, F. H. (1946). Enrollment increases and changes in the mental level of the high school population. *Applied Psychology Monographs,* No. 10.

Fincham, F. D., Hokoda, A., & Sanders, R., Jr. (1989). Learned helplessness, test anxiety, and academic achievement: A longitudinal analysis. *Child Development, 60,* 138–145.

Fine, M. A., & Kurdek, L. A. (1994). Parenting cognitions in stepfamilies: Differences between parents and stepparents and relations to parenting satisfaction. *Journal of Social and Personal Relationships, 11,* 95–112.

Finkelhor, D., & Dziuba-Leatherman, J. (1994). Victimization of children. *American Psychologist, 49,* 173–183.

Finkelhor, D., Hotaling, G. T., Lewis, I., & Smith, C. (1990). Sexual abuse in a national survey of adult men and women: Prevalence, characteristics, and risk factors. *Child Abuse & Neglect, 14,* 14–28.

Finkelstein, N. W., & Ramey, C. T. (1977). Learning to control the environment in infancy. *Child Development, 48,* 806–819.

Finn, J. D., & Achilles, C. M. (1990). Answers and questions about class size: A statewide experiment. *Educational Research Journal, 27,* 557–577.

Fischer, K. W. (1980). A theory of cognitive development: The control and construction of hierarchies of skills. *Psychological Review, 87,* 477–531.

Fischer, K. W., & Bidell, T. (1997). Dynamic development of psychological structures in action and thought. In R. M. Lerner (Ed.), *Theoretical models of human development* (Vol. 1). In W. Damon (Gen. ed.), *Handbook of child psychology* (pp. 467–561). New York: Wiley.

Fischer, K. W., & Hencke, R. W. (1996). Infants' construction of actions in context: Piaget's contribution to research on early development. *Psychological Science, 7,* 204–211.

Fischer, K. W., Kenny, S. L., & Pipp, S. L. (1990). How cognitive processes and environmental conditions organize discontinuities in the development of abstractions. In C. N. Alexander & E. J. Langer (Eds.), *Higher stages of human development. Perspectives on adult growth.* New York: Oxford University Press.

Fischer, K. W., & Rose, S. P. (1995, Fall). Concurrent cycles in the dynamic development of the brain and behavior. *SRCD Newsletter* pp. 3–4, 15–16.

Fischer, L., Ames, E. W., Chisholm, K., & Savoie, L. (1997). Problems reported by parents of Romanian orphans adopted to British Columbia. *International Journal of Behavioral Development, 20,* 67–82.

Fischer, M., Barkley, R. A., Edelbrock, C. S., & Smallish, L. (1990). The adolescent outcome of hyperactive children diagnosed by research criteria: II. Academic, attentional, and neuropsychological status. *Journal of Consulting and Clinical Psychology, 58,* 580–588.

Fischer, M., Barkley, R. A., Fletcher, K. E., & Smallish, L. (1993). The adolescent outcome of hyperactive children: Predictors of psychiatric, academic, social, and emotional adjustment. *Journal of the American Academy of Child and Adolescent Psychiatry, 32,* 324–332.

Fisher, C., & Tokura, H. (1996). Acoustic cues to grammatical structure in infant-directed speech: Cross-linguistic evidence. *Child Development, 67,* 3192–3218.

Fisher, C. B., Higgins-D'Alessandro, A., Rau, J. B., Kuther, T. L., & Belanger, S. (1996). Referring and reporting research participants at risk: Views from urban adolescents. *Child Development, 67,* 2086–2100.

Fisher, E. P. (1992). The impact of play on development: A meta-analysis. *Play and Culture, 5,* 159–181.

Fisher, J. A., & Birch, L. L. (1995). 3–5-year-old children's fat preferences and fat consumption are related to parental adiposity. *Journal of the American Dietetic Association, 95,* 759–764.

Fitch, M., Huston, A. C., & Wright, J. C. (1993). From television forms to gendre schemata: Children's perceptions of television reality. In G. L. Berry & J. K. Asamen (Eds.), *Children and television: Images in a changing sociocultural world* (pp. 38–52). Newbury Park, CA: Sage.

Fivush, R. (1997). Event memory in childhood. In N. Cowan (Ed.), *The development of memory in childhood* (pp. 139–161). Hove East Sussex: Psychology Press.

Fivush, R., Hayden, C., & Reese, E. (1996). Remembering, recounting, and reminiscing: The development of autobiographical memory in social context. In D. Rubin (Ed.), *Remembering our past: Studies in autobiographical memory* (pp. 341–359). New York: Cambridge University Press.

Fivush, R., & Hamond, N. R. (1990). Autobiographical memory across the preschool years: Toward reconceptualizing childhood amnesia. In R. Fivush & J. A. Hudson (Eds.), *Knowing and remembering in young children* (pp. 223–248). New York: Cambridge University Press.

Fivush, R., Kuebli, J., & Clubb, P. A. (1992). The structure of events and event representations: A developmental analysis. *Child Development, 63,* 188–201.

Flaks, D. K., Ficher, I., Masterpasqua, F., & Joseph, G. (1995). Lesbians choosing motherhood: A comparative study of lesbian and heterosexual parents and their children. *Developmental Psychology, 31,* 105–114.

Flanagan, C. A., & Eccles, J. S. (1993). Changes in parents' work status and adolescents' adjustment to school. *Child Development, 64,* 246–257.

Flavell, J. H. (1963). *The developmental psychology of Jean Piaget.* New York: Van Nostrand Reinhold.

Flavell, J. H. (1996). Piaget's legacy. *Psychological Science, 7,* 200–203.

Flavell, J. H., Beach, D. R., & Chinsky, J. H. (1966). Spontaneous verbal rehearsal in a memory task as a function of age. *Child Development, 37,* 283–299.

Flavell, J. H., Everett, B. H., Croft, K., & Flavell, E. R. (1981). Young children's knowledge about visual perception: Further evidence for the level 1-level 2 distinction. *Developmental Psychology, 17,* 99–103.

Flavell, J. H., Flavell, E. R., & Green, F. L. (1983). Development of the appearance-reality distinction. *Cognitive Psychology, 15,* 95–120.

Flavell, J. H., Flavell, E. R., & Green, F. L. (1987). Young children's knowledge about apparent-real and pretend-real distinctions. *Developmental Psychology, 23,* 816–822.

Flavell, J. H., Green, F. L., & Flavell, E. R. (1986). Development of knowledge about the appearance-reality distinction. *Monographs of the Society for Research in Child Development, 51,* (Serial No. 212).

Flavell, J. H., Green, F. L., & Flavell, E. R. (1989). Young children's ability to differentiate appearance-reality and level 2 perspectives in the tactile modality. *Child Development, 60,* 201–213.

Flavell, J. H., Green, F. L., & Flavell, E. R. (1995). Young chldren's knowledge about thinking. *Monographs of the Society for Research in Child Development, 60,* (1, Serial No. 243).

Flavell, J. H., Miller, P. H., & Miller, S. A. (1993). *Cognitive development* (3rd ed.). Englewood Cliffs, NJ: Prentice Hall.

Fletcher, A. C., Darling, N. E., Steinberg, L., & Dornbusch, S. M. (1995). The company they keep: Relation of adolescents' adjustment and behavior to their friends' perceptions of authoritative parenting in the social network. *Developmental Psychology, 31,* 300–310.

Fletcher-Flinn, C. M., & Gravatt, B. (1995). The efficacy of computer-assisted instruction (CAI): A meta-analysis. *Journal of Educational Computing Research, 12,* 219–242.

Fling, S., Smith, L., Rodriguez, T., Thornton, D., Atkins, E., & Nixon, K. (1992). Video games, aggression, and self-esteem: A survey. *Social Behavior and Personality, 20,* 39–46.

Flynn, J. R. (1991). *Asian-Americans: Achievement beyond IQ.* Hillsdale, NJ: Erlbaum.

Folds, T. H., Foote, M., Guttentag, R. E., & Ornstein, P. A. (1990). When children mean to remember: Issues of context specificity, strategy effectiveness, and intentionality in the development of memory. In D. F. Bjorklund (Ed.), *Children's Strategies: Contemporary views of cognitive development* (pp. 67–91). Hillsdale, NJ: Erlbaum.

Folven, R. J., & Bonvillian, J. D. (1991). The transition for nonreferential to referential language in children acquiring American Sign Language. *Developmental Psychology, 27,* 806–816.

Fonagy, P., Steele, H., & Steele, M. (1991). Maternal representations of attachment during pregnancy predict the organization of infant-mother attachment at one year of age. *Child Development, 62,* 891–905.

Fonzi, A., Schneider, B. H., Tani, F., & Tomada, G. (1997). Predicting children's friendship status from their dyadic interaction in structured situations of potential conflict. *Child Development, 68,* 496–506.

Ford, C. S., & Beach, F. A. (1951). *Patterns of sexual behavior.* New York: Harper & Row.

Ford, D. Y., & Harris, J. J., III (1996). Perceptions and attitudes of black students toward school, achievement, and other educational variables. *Child Development, 67,* 1141–1152.

Fordham, S., & Ogbu, J. (1986). Black students' school success: Coping with the "burden of 'acting white'". *Urban Review, 18,* 176–206.

Forrest, J. D., & Singh, S. (1990). The sexual and reproductive behavior of American women, 1982–1988. *Family Planning Perspectives, 22,* 206–214.

Fox, N. A., Bell, M. A., & Jones, N. A. (1992). Individual differences in response to stress and cerebral asymmetry. *Developmental Neuropsychology, 8,* 161–184.

Fox, N. A., & Fitzgerald, H. E. (1990). Autonomic function in infancy. *Merrill-Palmer Quarterly, 36,* 27–51.

Fox, N. A., Kimmerly, N. L., & Schafer, W. D. (1991). Attachment to mother/attachment to father: A meta-analysis. *Child Development, 62,* 210–225.

Fox, N. A., Rubin, K. H., Calkins, S. D., Marshall, T. R., Coplan, R. J., Porges, S. W., Long, J. M., & Stewart, S. (1995). Frontal activation asymmetry and social competence at four years of age. *Child Development, 66,* 1770–1784.

Frankel, K. A., & Bates, J. E. (1990). Mother-toddler problem-solving: Antecedents in attachment, home behavior, and temperament. *Child Development, 61,* 810–819.

Frankenberg, W. K., & Dodds, J. B. (1967). The Denver development screening test. *Journal of Pediatrics, 71,* 181–191.

Franklin, K. M., Janoff-Bulman, R., & Roberts, J. E. (1990). Long-term impact of parental divorce on optimism and trust: Changes in general assumptions or narrow beliefs? *Journal of Personality and Social Personality, 59,* 743–755.

Freedman, D. G. (1979). *Ethnic differences in babies.* Human Nature, *2,* 36–43.

French, L. A. (1989). Young children's responses to "when" questions: Issues of directionality. *Child Development, 60,* 225–236.

Freud, A., & Dann, S. (1951). An experiment in group upbringing. *The psychoanalytic study of the child, 6,* 127–168.

Freud, S. (1930). *Three contributions to the theory of sex.* New York: Nervous and Mental Disease Publishing Co. (Original work published 1905.)

Freud, S. (1933). *New introductory lectures in psychoanalysis.* New York: Norton.

Freud, S. (1960). *A general introduction to psychoanalysis.* New York: Washington Square Press. (Original work published 1935.)

Freud, S. (1961). The dissolution of the Oedipus complex. In J. Strachey (Ed. and Trans.), *The standard edition of the complete psychological works of Sigmund Freud* (Vol. 19). London: Hogarth Press. (Original work published 1924).

Freud, S. (1964). An outline of psychoanalysis. In J. Strachey (Ed. and Trans.), *The standard edition of the complete psychological works of Sigmund Freud* (Vol. 23). London: Hogarth Press. (Original work published 1940).

Freund, L. S. (1990). Maternal regulation of children's problem-solving behavior and its impact on children's performance. *Child Development, 61,* 113–126.

Frey, K. S., & Ruble, D. N. (1985). What children say when the teacher is not around: Conflicting goals in social comparison and performance assessment in the classroom. *Journal of Personality and Social Psychology, 48,* 550–562.

Frey, K. S., & Ruble, D. N. (1992). Gender constancy and the cost of sex-typed behavior: A test of the conflict hypothesis. *Developmental Psychology, 28,* 714–721.

Fried, P. A. (1993). Prenatal exposure to tobacco and marijuana: Effects during pregnancy, infancy, and early childhood. *Clinical Obstetrics and Gynecology, 36,* 319–337.

Fried, P. A., O'Connell, C. M., & Watkinson, B. (1992). 60- and 72-month followup of children prenatally exposed to marijuana, cigarettes, and alcohol: Cognitive and language assessment. *Developmental and Behavioral Pediatrics, 13,* 383–391.

Friedman, H. S., Tucker, J. S., Schwartz, J. E., Tomlinson-Keasey, C., Martin, L. R., Wingard, D. L., & Criqui, M. H. (1995). Psychosocial and behavioral predictors of longevity: The aging and death of the "termites." *American Psychologist, 50,* 69–78.

Friedman, J. M., & Polifka, J. E. (1996). *The effects of drugs on the fetus and nursing infant.* Baltimore: Johns Hopkins University Press.

Friedrich, L. K., & Stein, A. H. (1973). Aggressive and prosocial television programs and the natural behavior of preschool children. *Monographs of the Society for Research in Child Development, 38* (4, Serial No. 51).

Friedrich, L. K., & Stein, A. H. (1975). Prosocial television and young children: The effects of verbal labeling and role-playing on learning and behavior. *Child Development, 46,* 27–38.

Friedrich-Cofer, L. K., Huston-Stein, A., Kipnis, D. M., Susman, E. J., & Clewett, A. S. (1979). Environmental enhancement of prosocial television content: Effects on interpersonal behavior. *Developmental Psychology, 15,* 637–646.

Friel-Patti, S., & Finitzo, T. (1990). Language learning in a prospective study of otitis media with effusion in the first two years of life. *Journal of Speech and Hearing Research, 33,* 188–194.

Friend, M., & Davis, T. L. (1993). Appearance-reality distinction: Children's understanding of the physical and affective domains. *Developmental Psychology, 29,* 907–914.

Frodi, A. (1985). When empathy fails: Aversive infant crying and child abuse. In B. M. Lester & C. F. Z. Boukydis (Eds.), *Infant crying: Theoretical and research perspectives* (pp. 263–277), New York: Plenum.

Fuchs, D., & Thelen, M. H. (1988). Children's expected interpersonal consequences of communicating their affective state and reported likelihood of expression. *Child Development, 59,* 1314–1322.

Fuhrman, T., & Holmbeck, G. N. (1995). A contextual-moderator analysis of emotional anatomy and adjustment in adolescence. *Child Development, 66,* 793–811.

Fuligni, A. J. (1997). The academic achievement of adolescents from immigrant families: The roles of family background, attitudes, and behavior. *Child Development, 68,* 351–363.

Fuligni, A. J., & Eccles, J. S. (1993). Perceived parent-child relationships and early adolescents' orientation toward peers. *Developmental Psychology, 29,* 622–632.

Fuligni, A. J., Eccles, J. S., & Barber, B. K. (1995). The long-term effects of seventh-grade ability grouping in mathematics. *Journal of Early Adolescence, 15,* 58–69.

Fuligni, A. J., & Stevenson, H. W. (1995). Time use and mathematics achievement among American, Chinese, and Japanese high school students. *Child Development, 66,* 830–842.

Fuller, B., Holloway, S. D., & Liang, X. (1996). Family selection of child-care centers: The influence of household support, ethnicity, and parental practices. *Child Development, 67,* 3320–3337.

Fullerton, J. T., & Severino, R. (1992). In-hospital care for low-risk childbirth. Comparison with results from the National Birth Center Study. *Journal of Nurse Midwifery, 37,* 331–340.

Furman, W., & Buhrmester, D. (1985). Children's perceptions of the qualities of sibling relationships. *Child Development, 56,* 448–461.

Furman, W., & Buhrmester, D. (1992). Age and sex differences in perceptions of networks of personal relationships. *Child Development, 63,* 103–115.

Furstenberg, F. F., Jr. (1988). Child care after divorce and remarriage. In E. M. Hetherington & J. D. Arasteh (Eds.), *Impact of divorce, single-parenting, and stepparenting on children.* Hillsdale, NJ: Erlbaum.

Furstenberg, F. F., Jr., Brooks-Gunn, J., & Chase-Lansdale, L. (1989). Teenaged pregnancy and childbearing. *American Psychologist, 44,* 313–320.

Fuson, K. C. (1988). *Children's counting and concepts of number.* New York: Springer-Verlag.

Fuson, K. C. (1992). Research on learning and teaching addition and subtraction of whole numbers. In G. Leinhardt, R. T. Putnam, & R. A. Hattrup (Eds.). *The analysis of arithmetic for mathematics teaching* (pp. 53–187). Hillsdale, NJ: Erlbaum.

Fuson, K. C., & Kwon, Y. (1992). Korean children's understanding of multidigit addition and subtraction. *Child Development, 63,* 491–506.

Fyans, L. J., Jr., Salili, F., Maehr, M. L., & Desai, K. A. (1983). A cross-cultural exploration into the meaning of achievement. *Journal of Personality and Social Psychology, 44,* 1000–1013.

Gaddis, A., & Brooks-Gunn, J. (1985). The male experience of pubertal change. *Journal of Youth and Adolescence, 14,* 61–69.

Galambos, N. L., Almeida, D. M., & Petersen, A. C. (1990). Maculinity, femininity, and sex role attitudes in early adolescence: Exploring gender intensification. *Child Development, 61,* 1905–1914.

Galambos, N. L., & Maggs, J. L. (1991). Out-of-school care of young adolescents and self-reported behavior. *Developmental Psychology, 27,* 644–655.

Galambos, S. J., & Goldin-Meadow, S. (1990). The effects of learning two languages on levels of metalinguistic awareness. *Cognition, 34,* 1–56.

Galen, B. R., & Underwood, M. K. (1997). A developmental investigation of social aggression among children. *Developmental Psychology, 33,* 589–600.

Gallagher, J. M., & Easley, J. A., Jr. (1978). *Knowledge and development* (Vol. 2). *Piaget and education.* New York: Plenum.

Gallahue, D. L. (1989). *Understanding motor development* (2nd ed.). Carmel, ID: Benchmark Press.

Gallistel, C. R., & Gelman, R. (1992). Preverbal and verbal counting and computation. *Cognition, 44,* 43–74.

Gallup, G. G., Jr. (1979). Self-recognition in chimpanzees and man: A developmental and comparative perspective. In M. Lewis & L. A. Rosenblum (Eds.), *Genesis of behavior* (Vol. 2). *The child and its family.* New York: Plenum.

Galper, A., Wigfield, A., & Seefeldt, C. (1997). Head Start parents' beliefs about their children's abilities, task values, and performances on different activities. *Child Development, 68,* 897–907.

Galuska, D. A., Serdula, M., Pamuck, E., Siegel, P. Z., & Byers, T. (1996). Trends in overweight among U.S. adults from 1987 to 1993: A multistate telephone survey. *American Journal of Public Health, 86,* 1729–1735.

Ganchrow, J. R., Steiner, J. E., & Daher, M. (1983). Neonatal facial expressions to different qualities and intensities of gustatory stimuli. *Infant Behavior and Development, 6,* 189–200.

Gandelman, R. (1992). *Psychobiology of behavioral development.* New York: Oxford University Press.

Garbarino, J. (1992). *Children and families in the social environment* (2nd ed). New York: Aldine de Gruyter.

Garbarino, J., & Kostelny, K. (1992). Child maltreatment as a community problem. *Child Abuse & Neglect, 16,* 455–464.

Garbarino, J., & Sherman, D. (1980). High-risk neighborhoods and high-risk families: The human ecology of child maltreatment. *Child Development, 51,* 188–198.

Garcia, E. E. (1993). Language, culture, and education. *Review of Educational Research, 19,* 51–98.

Gardner, B. T., & Gardner, R. A. (1974). Comparing the early utterances of child and chimpanzee. In A. Pick (Ed.), *Minnesota Symposia on Child Psychology* (Vol. 8). Minneapolis: University of Minnesota Press.

Gardner, H. (1983). *Frames of mind: The theory of multiple intelligences.* New York: Basic Books.

Gardner, H. (1993). *Creating minds.* New York: Basic Books.

Gardner, H. (1998). Are there additional intelligences? The case for naturalist, spiritual, and existential intelligences. In J. Kane (Ed.), *Education, information, and transformation.* Englewood Cliffs, NJ: Prentice-Hall.

Gardner, L. J. (1972). Deprivation dwarfism. *Scientific American, 227,* 76–82.

Garland, A., & Zigler, E. (1993). Adolescent suicide prevention: Current research and social policy implications. *American Psychologist, 48,* 169–182.

Garner, P. W., Jones, D. C., & Miner, J. L. (1994). Social competence among low-income preschoolers: Emotion socialization practices and social cognitive correlates. *Child Development, 65,* 622–637.

Garner, P. W., Jones, D. C., & Palmer, D. J. (1994). Social-cognitive correlates of preschool children's sibling caregiving behavior. *Developmental Psychology, 30,* 905–911.

Garner, P. W., & Power, T. G. (1996). Preschoolers' emotional control in the disappointment paradigm and its relation to temperament, emotional knowledge, and family expressiveness. *Child Development, 67,* 1406–1419.

Garnets, L., & Kimmel, D. (1991). Lesbian and gay male dimensions of the psychological study of human diversity. In J. D. Goodchilds (Ed.), *Psychological perspectives on human diversity in America.* Washington, D.C.: American Psychological Association.

Garrett, P., Ng'andu, N., & Ferron, J. (1994). Poverty experiences of young children and the quality of their home environments. *Child Development, 65,* 331–345.

Garton, A. F., & Pratt, C. (1990). Children's pragmatic judgments of direct and indirect requests. *First Language, 10,* 51–59.

Gaultney, J. F. (1995). The effect of prior knowledge and metacognition on the acquisition of a reading comprehension strategy. *Journal of Experimental Child Psychology, 59,* 142–163.

Gauvain, M., & Rogoff, B. (1989). Collaborative problem solving and children's planning skills. *Developmental Psychology, 25,* 139–151.

Gauze, C., Bukowski, W. M., Aquan-Assee, J., & Sippola, L. K. (1996). Interactions between family environment and friendship and associations with well-being during early adolescence. *Child Development, 67,* 2201–2216.

Gavin, L. A., & Furman, W. (1989). Age differences in adolescents' perceptions of their peer groups. *Developmental Psychology, 25,* 827–834.

Gavin, L. A., & Furman, W. (1996). Adolescent girls' relationships with mothers and best friends. *Child Development, 67,* 375–386.

Gay, J., & Cole, M. (1967). *The new mathematics and an old culture.* New York: Holt, Rinehart & Winston.

Ge, X., Best, K. M., Conger, R. D., & Simons, R. L. (1996). Parenting behaviors and the occurrence and co-occurrence of adolescent depressive symptoms and conduct problems. *Developmental Psychology, 32,* 717–731.

Ge, X., Conger, R. D., & Elder, G. H., Jr. (1996). Coming of age too early: Pubertal influences on girls' vulnerability to psychological distress. *Child Development, 67,* 3386–3400.

Geary, D. C. (1995). Reflections on evolution and culture in children's cognition. *American Psychologist, 50,* 24–37.

Geary, D. C., Bow-Thomas, C. C., Fan, L., & Siegler, R. S. (1993). Even before formal instruction, Chinese children outperform American children in mental arithmetic. *Cognitive Development, 8,* 517–529.

Geary, D. C., Bow-Thomas, C. C., Liu, F., & Siegler, R. S. (1996). Development of arithmetical competencies in Chinese and American children: Influence of age, language, and schooling. *Child Development, 67,* 2022–2044.

Geary, D. C., & Burlingham-Dubre, M. (1989). External validation of the strategy choice model for addition. *Journal of Experimental Child Psychology, 47,* 175–192.

Geary, D. C., Fan, L., & Bow-Thomas, C. C. (1992). Numerical cognition: Loci of ability differences comparing children from China and the United States. *Psychological Science, 3,* 180–185.

Geary, D. C., Salthouse, T. A., Chen, P., & Fan, L. (1996). Are East Asian versus American differences in arithmetical ability a recent phenomenon? *Developmental Psychology, 32,* 254–262.

Geary, D. C. , & Widaman, K. F. (1992). Numerical cognition: On convergence of componential and psychometric models. *Intelligence 16,* 47–80.

Geiles, R. J. (1996). *The book of David: How preserving families can cost children's lives.* New York: Basic Books.

Gelman, R. (1969). Conservation acquisition: A problem of learning to attend to relevant attributes. *Journal of Experimental Child Psychology, 7,* 167–187.

Gelman, R. (1978). Cognitive development. *Annual Review of Psychology, 29,* 297–322.

Gelman, R., & Baillargeon, R. (1983). A review of Piagetian concepts. In P. H. Mussen (Ed.), *Handbook of child psychology. Cognitive development.* (Vol. 3). New York: Wiley.

Gelman, R., & Shatz, M. (1977). Appropriate speech adjustments: The operation of conversational constraints on talk to two-year-olds. In M. Lewis & L. A. Rosenblum (Eds.), *Interaction, conversation, and the development of language.* New York: Wiley.

Gelman, R., & Williams, E. M. (1997). Enabling constraints for cognitive development and learning: Domain-specificity and epigenesis. In D. Kuhn & R. S. Siegler (Eds.), *Cognition, perception, and language* (Vol. 2). of W. Damon (Gen. Ed.), *Handbook of child psychology.* New York: Wiley.

Gelman, S. A., & Ebeling, K. S. (1989). Children's use of nonegocentric standards in judgments of functional size. *Child Development, 60,* 920–932.

Gelman, S. A., & Gottfried, G. M. (1996). Children's causal explanations of animate and inanimate motion. *Child Development, 67,* 1970–1987.

George, T. P., & Hartmann, D. P. (1996). Friendship networks of unpopular, average, and popular children. *Child Development, 67,* 2301–2316.

Goals 2000: Educate America Act, Pub. L. No. 103–227 (1994).

Gerken, L., Landau, B., & Remez, R. E. (1990). Function morphemes in young children's speech perception and production. *Developmental Psychology, 26,* 204–216.

Gerken, L., & McIntosh, B. J. (1993). Interplay of function morphemes and prosody in early language. *Developmental Psychology, 24,* 448–457.

Gesell, A. (1933). Maturation and the patterning of behavior. In C. Murchison (ed.), *A handbook of child psychology.* Worcester, MA: Clark University Press.

Gesell, A., & Thompson, H. (1929). Learning and growth in identical twins: An experimental study by the method of co-twin control. *Genetic Psychology Monographs, 6,* 1–123.

Getzels, J. W., & Jackson, P. W. (1962). *Creativity and intelligence: Explorations with gifted children.* New York: Wiley.

Gewirtz, J. L., & Pelaez-Nogueras, M. (1992). Skinner, B. F.: Legacy to human infant behavior and development. *American Psychologist, 47,* 1411–1422.

Gewirtz, J. L., & Petrovich, S. B. (1982). Early social and attachment learning in the frame of organic and cultural evolution. In T. M. Field, A. Huston, H. C. Quay, L. Troll, & G. E. Finley (Eds.), *Review of human development.* New York: Wiley.

Ghatala, E. S., Levin, J. R., Pressley, M., Goodwin, D. (1986). A componential analysis of the effects of derived and supplied strategy-utility information on children's strategy selections. *Journal of Experimental Child Psychology, 41,* 76–92.

Ghim, H. (1990). Evidence for perceptual organization in infants: Perception of subjective contours by young infants. *Infant Behavior and Development, 13,* 221–248.

Gibbs, J. C., Potter, G. B., & Goldstein, A. P. (1995). *The EQUIP program: Teaching youth to think and act responsibly through a peer-helping approach.* Champaign, IL: Research Press.

Gibbs, J. C., & Schnell, S. V. (1985). Moral development "versus" socialization. A critique. *American Psychologist, 40,* 1071–1080.

Gibson, D., & Harris, A. (1988). Aggregated early information effects for Down's syndrome persons: Patterning and longevity of benefits. *Journal of Mental Deficiency Research, 32,* 1–7.

Gibson, E. J. (1969). *Principles of perceptual learning and development.* East Norwalk, CT: Appleton-Century-Crofts.

Gibson, E. J. (1987). Introductory essay: What does infant perception tell us about theories of perception? *Journal of Experimental Psychology: Human Perception and Performance, 13,* 515–523.

Gibson, E. J. (1992). How to think about perceptual learning: Twenty-five years later. In H. L. Pick, P. Van den Brock, & D. C. Knoll (Eds.), *Cognitive psychology: Conceptual and methodological issues.* Washington, DC.: American Psychological Association.

Gibson, E. J., Gibson, J. J., Pick, A. D., & Osser, H. A. (1962). A developmental study of the discrimination of letter like forms. *Journal of Comparative and Physiological Psychology, 55,* 897–906.

Gibson, E. J., & Levin, H. (1975). *The psychology of reading.* Cambridge, MA: M.I.T. Press.

Gibson, E. J., & Walk, R. D. (1960). The "visual cliff." *Scientific American, 202,* 64–71.

Gibson, E. J., & Walker, A. S. (1984). Development of knowledge of visual-tactile affordances of substance. *Child Development, 55,* 453–460.

Gil, D. G. (1970). *Violence against children.* Cambridge, MA: Harvard University Press.

Gilbert, N. (1997). *Combating child abuse: International perspectives and trends.* New York: Oxford University Press.

Gill, N. J., & Beazley, R. P. (1993). Grade 6 students benefit from learning about AIDS. *Canadian Journal of Public Health, 84,* (Suppl. 1), 524–527.

Gillberg, C., Melander, H., von Knorring, A-L., Janols, L-O., Thernlund, G., Hagglof, B., Eidevall-Wallin, L. Gustafsson, P., & Kopp, S. (1997). Long-term stimulant treatment of children with attention-deficit hyperactivity disorder symptoms: A randomized, double-blind, placebo-controlled trial. *Archives of General Psychiatry, 54,* 857–864.

Gilligan, C. (1982). *In a different voice: Psychological theory and women's development.* Cambridge, MA: Harvard University Press.

Gilligan, C. (1993). Adolescent development reconsidered. In A. Garrod (Ed.), *Approaches to moral development: New research and emerging themes.* New York: Teachers College Press.

Ginsburg, G. S., & Bronstein, P. (1993). Family factors related to children's intrinsic/extrinsic motivational orientation and academic performance. *Child Development, 64,* 1461–1474.

Ginsberg, H. J., & Opper, S. (1988). *Piaget's theory of intellectual development* (3rd ed.). Englewood Cliffs, NJ: Prentice-Hall.

Girard, C. (1993). Age, gender, and suicide: A cross-national analysis. *American Sociological Review, 58,* 553–574.

Glasgow, K. L., Dornbusch, S. M., Troyer, L., Steinberg, L., & Ritter, P. L. (1997). Parenting style, adolescents' attributions, and educational outcomes in nine heterogeneous high schools. *Child Development, 68,* 507–529.

Gleitman, H. (1991). *Psychology,* (3rd ed.). New York: Norton.

Gleitman, L. R. (1990). The structural sources of verb meanings. *Language Acquisition, 1,* 3–55.

Glick, P. C. (1989). Remarried families, stepfamilies, and stepchildren: A brief demographic profile. *Family Relations, 38,* 24–47.

Gnepp, J. (1989). Personalized inferences of emotions and appraisals: Component processes and correlates. *Developmental Psychology, 25,* 277–288.

Gnepp, J., & Klayman, J. (1992). Recognition of uncertainty in emotional inferences: Reasoning about emotionally equivocal situations. *Developmental Psychology, 28,* 145–158.

Golbus, M. S., & Fries, M. M. (1993). Surgical fetal therapy. In C. Lin, M. S. Verp, & R. E. Sabbagha (Eds.), *The high-risk fetus: Pathophysiology, diagnosis, management.* New York: Springer-Verlag.

Gold, D., & Andres, D. (1978). Developmental comparisons between 10-year-old children with employed and nonemployed mothers. *Child Development, 49,* 75–84.

Goldberg, G. R. & Prentice, A. M. (1994). Maternal and fetal determinants of adult diseases. *Nutrition Reviews, 52,* 191–200.

Goldberg, P. (1968). Are women prejudiced against women? *Trans/Action, 5,* 28–30.

Goldberg, S. (1983). Parent-infant bonding: Another look. *Child Development, 54,* 1355–1382.

Goldberg, S., Perrotta, M., Minde, K., & Corter, C. (1986). Maternal behavior and attachment in low-birth-weight twins and singletons. *Child Development, 57,* 34–46.

Goldberg, W. A., Greenberger, E., & Nagel, S. K. (1996). Employment and achievement: Mothers' work involvement in relation to children's achievement behaviors and mothers' parenting behaviors. *Child Development, 67,* 1512–1527.

Golden, M., Birns, B., Bridger, W., & Moss, A. (1971). Social class differentiation in cognitive development among black preschool children. *Child Development, 42,* 37–46.

Goldenberg, R. L. (1995). Small for gestational age infants. In B. P. Sachs, R. Beard, E. Papiernik, & C. Russell (Eds.), *Reproductive health care for women and babies* (pp. 391–399). New York: Oxford University Press.

Goldfarb, W. (1943). The effects of early institutional care on adolescent personality. *Journal of Experimental Education, 12,* 107–129.

Goldfarb, W. (1947). Variations in adolescent adjustment in institutionally reared children. *Journal of Orthopsychiatry, 17,* 449–457.

Goldfield, E. C. (1989). Transition from rocking to crawling: Postural constraints on infant movement. *Developmental Psychology, 25,* 913–919.

Goldin-Meadow, S., & Mylander, C. (1984). Gestural communication in deaf children: The effects and noneffects of parental input on early language development. *Monographs of the Society for Research in Child Development, 49* (Serial No. 207).

Goldsmith, H. H., & Alansky, J. A. (1987). Maternal and infant temperamental predictors of attachment: A meta-analytic review. *Journal of Consulting and Clinical Psychology, 55,* 805–816.

Goldsmith, H. H., Buss, A. H., Plomin, R., Rothbart, M. K., Thomas, A., Chess, S., Hinde, R. A., & McCall, R. B. (1987). Roundtable: What is temperament? Four approaches. *Child Development, 58,* 505–529.

Goldsmith, H. H., Buss, K. A., & Lemery, K. S. (1997). Toddler and childhood temperament: Expanded content, stronger genetic evidence, new evidence for the importance of environment. *Developmental Psychology, 33,* 891–905.

Golinkoff, R. M., Jacquet, R. C., Hirsh-Pasek, K., & Nandakumer, R. (1996). Lexical principles may underlie the learning of verbs. *Child Development, 67,* 3101–3119.

Golomb, C., & Galasso, L. (1995). Make believe and reality: Explorations of the imaginary realm. *Developmental Psychology, 31,* 800–810.

Golombok, S., Cook, R., Bish, A., & Murray, C. (1995). Families created by new reproductive technologies: Quality of parenting and social and emotional development of the children. *Child Development, 66,* 285–298.

Golombok, S., & Tasker, F. (1996). Do parents influence the sexual orientation of their children: Findings from a longitudinal study of lesbian families. *Developmental Psychology, 32,* 3–11.

Good, T. L. (1979). Teacher effectiveness in the elementary school: What do we know about it now? *Journal of Teacher Education, 30,* 52–64.

Good, T. L., & Brophy, J. E. (1994). *Looking in classrooms.* (6th ed.) New York: Harper Collins.

Goodall, J. (1986). *The chimpanzees of Gombe: Patterns of behavior.* Cambridge: Harvard University Press.

Goodenough, F. L. (1931). *Anger in young children.* Minneapolis: University of Minnesota Press.

Goodman, G. S., Aman, C. J., & Hirschman, J. (1987). Child sexual and physical abuse: Children's testimony. In S. J. Ceci, M. P. Toglia, & D. F. Ross (Eds.), *Children's eyewitness memory* (pp. 1–23). New York: Springer-Verlag.

Goodman, G. S., & Clarke-Stewart, A. (1991). Suggestibility in children's testimony: Implications for sexual abuse investigations. In J. Doris (Ed.), *The suggestibility of children's recollections: Implications for eyewitness testimony* (pp. 92–105). Washington, DC: American Psychological Association.

Goodman, G. S., Quas, J. A., Batterman-Faunce, J. M., Riddlesberger, & Kuhn, J. (1994). Predictors of accurate and inaccurate memories of traumatic events experiences in childhood. *Consciousness and Cognition, 3,* 269–294.

Goodwyn, S. W., & Acredolo, L. P. (1993). Symbolic gesture versus word: Is there a modality advantage for onset of symbol use. *Child Development, 64,* 688–701.

Goossens, F. A., & van IJzendoorn, M. H. (1990). Quality of infants' attachments to professional caregivers: Relation to infant-parent attachment and day-care characteristics. *Child Development, 61,* 832–837.

Gopnik, A. (1996). The post-Piaget era. *Psychological Science, 7,* 221–225.

Gopnik, A., & Choi, S. (1995). *Beyond names for things: Children's acquisition of verbs.* Hillsdale, NJ: Erlbaum.

Gopnik, A., & Meltzoff, A. N. (1987). Language and thought in the young child: Early semantic developments and their relationships to object permanence, means-ends understanding, and categorization. In K. Nelson & A. Van Kleeck (Eds.), *Children's language* (Vol. 6). Hillsdale, NJ: Erlbaum.

Gordon, P. (1990). Learnability and feedback. *Developmental Psychology, 26,* 217–220.

Goren, C. C., Sarty, M., & Wu, P. Y. K. (1975). Visual following and pattern discrimination of face-like stimuli by newborn infants. *Pediatrics, 56,* 544–549.

Gorer, G. (1968). Man has no "killer" instinct. In M. F. A. Montague (Ed.), *Man and aggression.* New York: Oxford University Press.

Gorn, G. J., Goldberg, M. E., & Kanungo, R. N. (1976). The role of educational television in changing the intergroup attitudes of children. *Child Development, 47,* 277–280.

Gosden, C., Nicolaides, K., & Whitting, V. (1994). *Is my baby all right?: A guide for expectant parents.* Oxford, England: Oxford University Press.

Gotlib, I. H., Whiffen, V. E., Wallace, P. M., & Mount, J. (1991). Prospective investigation of postpartum depression: Factors involved in onset and recovery. *Journal of Abnormal Psychology, 100,* 122–132.

Gottesman, I. I. (1963). Genetic aspects of intelligent behavior. In N. Ellis (Ed.), *Handbook of mental deficiency.* New York: McGraw-Hill.

Gottesman, I. I., & Shields, J. (1982). *Schizophrenia: The epigenetic puzzle.* Cambridge, England: Cambridge University Press.

Gottfredson, L. S. (1986). Societal consequences of the *g* factor in employment. *Journal of Vocational Behavior, 29,* 379–410.

Gottfried, A. E., Gottfried, A. W., & Bathurst, K. (1988). Maternal employment, family environment and children's development: Infancy through the school years. In A. E. Gottfried & A. W. Gottfried (Eds.), *Maternal employment and children's development: Longitudinal research* (pp. 11–58). New York: Plenum.

Gottfried, A. W. (1984). Home environment and early cognitive development: Integration, meta-analyses, and conclusions. In A. W. Gottfried (Ed.), *Home environment and early cognitive development: Longitudinal research.* Orlando, FL: Academic Press.

Gottfried, A. W., & Gottfried, A. E., Bathurst, K., & Guerin, D. W. (1994). *Gifted IQS: Early developmental aspects: The Fullerton Longitudinal Study.* New York: Plenum.

Gottlieb, D. (1966). Teaching and students: The views of Negro and white teachers. *Sociology of Education, 37,* 344–353.

Gottlieb, G. (1991a). Experiential canalization of behavioral development: Results. *Developmental Psychology, 27,* 35–39.

Gottlieb, G. (1991b). Experiential canalization of behavioral development. Theory and commentary. *Developmental Psychology, 27,* 4–13.

Gottlieb, G. (1996). Commentary: A systems view of psychobiological development. In D. Magnusson (Ed.), *The lifespan development of individuals: Behavioral, neurobiological, and psychosocial perspectives. A synthesis.* Cambridge, England: Cambridge University Press.

Graber, J. A., Brooks-Gunn, J. Paikoff, R. L., & Warren, M. P. (1994). Prediction of eating problems: An 8-year study of adolescent girls. *Developmental Psychology, 30,* 823–834.

Graham, S., Hudley, C., & Williams, E. (1992). Attributional and emotional determinants of aggression among African-American and Latino young adolescents. *Developmental Psychology, 28,* 731–740.

Granrud, C. E. (1987). Size constancy in newborn human infants. *Investigative Ophthalmology and Visual Science, 28,* 5.

Granrud, C. E., Yonas, A. (1984). Infants' perceptions of pictorally specified interposition. *Journal of Experimental Child Psychology, 37,* 500–511.

Grantham-McGregor, S. (1995). A review of studies of the effects of severe malnutrition on mental development. *Journal of Nutrition Supplement, 125,* 22335–22385.

Grantham-McGregor, S. , Powell, C., Walker, S., Chang, S., & Fletcher, P. (1994). The long-term follow-up of severely malnourished children who participated in an intervention program. *Child Development, 65,* 428–439.

Graves, S. B. (1975, April). *How to encourage positive racial attitudes.* Paper presented at the biennial meeting of the Society for Research in Child Develoment, Denver.

Graves, S. B. (1993). Television, the portrayal of African Americans, and the development of children's attitudes. In G. L. Berry & J. K. Asamen (Eds.), *Children and television: Images in a changing sociocultural world* (pp. 179–190).

Gray, S. W., & Klaus, R. A. (1970). The early training project: A seventh-year report. *Child Development, 41,* 909–924.

Gray, W. M., & Hudson, L. M. (1984). Formal operations and the imaginary audience. *Developmental Psychology, 20,* 619–627.

Graziano, W. G., French, D., Brownell, C. A., & Hartup, W. W. (1976). Peer interaction in same- and mixed-age triads in relation to chronological age and incentive condition. *Child Development, 47,* 707–714.

Green, R. (1987). *The "sissy boy syndrome" and the development of homosexuality,* New Haven, CT: Yale University Press.

Green, R. W., Biederman, J., Faraone, S. V., Sienna, M., & Garcia-Jetton, J. (1997). Adolescent outcome of boys with attention-deficity/hyperactivity disorder and social disability: Results from a 4-year longitudinal follow-up study. *Journal of Consulting and Clinical Psychology, 65,* 758–767.

Greenberg, M., & Morris, N. (1974). Engrossment: The newborn's impact upon the father. *American Journal of Orthopsychiatry, 44,* 520–531.

Greenberger, E., & Chen, C. (1996). Perceived family relationships and depressed mood in early and late adolescence: A comparison of European and Asian Americans. *Developmental Psychology, 32,* 707–716.

Greenberger, E., & Goldberg, W. A. (1989). Work, parenting, and the socialization of children. *Developmental Psychology, 25,* 22–35.

Greenberger, E., & O'Neil, R. (1993). Spouse, parent, worker: Role commitments and role-related experiences in the construction of adults' well-being. *Developmental Psychology, 29,* 181–197.

Greenberger, E., O'Neil, R., & Nagel, S. K. (1994). Linking workplace and homeplace: Relations between the nature of adult work and their parenting behavior. *Developmental Psychology, 30,* 990–1002.

Greenberger, E., & Steinberg, L. (1986). *When teenagers work: The psychological and social costs of adolescent employment.* New York: Basic Books.

Greenfield, P. M., & Smith, J. H. (1976). *The structure of communication in early language development.* New York: Academic.

Greenough, W. T., & Black, J. E. (1992). Induction of brain structure by experience: Substrates for cognitive development. In M. R. Gunnar & C. A. Nelson (Eds.), *Minnesota Symposia on Child Psychology* (pp. 155–200). Hillsdale, NJ: Erlbaum.

Greenough, W. T., Black, J. E., & Wallace, C. S. (1987). Experience and brain development. *Child Development, 58,* 539–559.

Greif, E. B., & Ulman, K. J. (1982). The psychological impact of menarche on early adolescent females: A review of the literature. *Child Development, 53,* 1413–1430.

Grolnick, W. S., Bridges, L. J., & Connell, J. P. (1996). Emotion regulation in two-year-olds: Strategies and emotional expression in four contexts. *Child Development, 67,* 928–941.

Grolnick, W. S., & Ryan, R. M. (1989). Parents' styles associated with children's self-regulation and competence in school. *Journal of Educational Psychology, 81,* 143–154.

Groome, L. J., Swiber, M. J., Atterbury, J. L., Bentz, L. S., & Holland, S. B. (1997). Similarities and differences in behavioral state organization during sleep periods in the perinatal infant before and after birth. *Child Development, 68,* 1–11.

Gross, A. L., & Ballif, B. (1991). Children's understanding of emotion from facial expressions and situations: A review. *Developmental Review, 11,* 368–398.

Grossman, F. K., Eichler, L. S., Winickoff, S. A., & Associates (1980). *Pregnancy, birth, and parenthood: Adaptations of mothers, fathers, and infants.* San Francisco: Jossey-Bass.

Grossmann, K., Grossmann, K. E., Spangler, S., Suess, G., & Unzner, L. (1985). Maternal sensitivity and newborn responses as related to quality of attachment in Northern Germany. In I. Bretherton & E. Waters, Growing points of attachment theory. *Monographs of the Society for Research in Child Development, 50,* (1–2, Serial No. 209).

Grotevant, H. D., & Cooper, C. R. (1986). Individuation in family relations: A perspective on individual differences in the development of identity and role-taking skills in adolescence. *Human Development, 29,* 82–100.

Gruber, H. (1982). On the hypothesized relation between giftedness and creativity. In D. H. Feldman (Ed.), *New directions for child development: No. 17. Developmental approaches to giftedness and creativity.* San Francisco: Jossey-Bass.

Grusec, J. E. (1991). Socializing concern for others in the home. *Developmental Psychology, 27,* 338–342.

Grusec, J. E. (1992). Social learning theory and developmental psychology: The legacies of Robert Sears and Albert Bandura. *Developmental Psychology, 28,* 776–786.

Grusec, J. E., & Goodnow, J. J. (1994). Impact of parental discipline methods on the child's internalization of values: A reconceptualization of current points of view. *Developmental Psychology, 30,* 4–19.

Grusec, J. E., Goodnow, J. J., & Cohen, L. (1996). Household work and the development of concern for others. *Developmental Psychology, 32,* 999–1007.

Grusec, J. E., Kuczynski, L., Rushton, J. P., & Simutis, Z. (1979). Learning resistance to temptation through observation. *Developmental Psychology, 15,* 233–240.

Grusec, J. E., & Walters, G. C. (1991). Psychological abuse and childrearing belief systems. In R. H. Starr, Jr., & D. A. Wolfe (Eds.), *The effects of child abuse and neglect* (pp. 186–202). New York: Guilford.

Grych, J. H., & Fincham, F. D. (1992). Interventions for children of divorce: Toward greater integration of research and action. *Psychological Bulletin, 111,* 434–454.

Guberman, S. R. (1996). The development of everyday mathematics in Brazilian children with limited formal education. *Child Development, 67,* 1609–1623.

Guerra, N. G., & Slaby, R. G. (1990). Cognitive mediators of aggression in adolescent offenders: 2. Intervention. *Developmental Psychology, 26,* 269–277.

Guilford, J. P. (1967). *The nature of human intelligence.* New York: McGraw-Hill.

Guilford, J. P. (1988). Some changes in the structure-of-the-intellect model. *Educational and Psychological Measurement, 40,* 1–4.

Gullota, T. P., Adams, G. R., & Alexander, S. J. (1986). *Today's marriages and families. A wellness approach.* Monterey, CA: Brooks/Cole.

Gunderson, V., & Sackett, G. P. (1982). Paternal effects on reproductive outcome and developmental risk. In M. E. Lamb & A. L. Brown (Eds.), *Advances in developmental psychology* (Vol. 2). Hillsdale, NJ: Erlbaum.

Gunnar, M. R., Brodersen, L., Krueger, K., & Rigatuso, J. (1996). Dampening of adrenocortical responses during infancy: Normative changes and individual differences. *Child Development, 67,* 877–889.

Gunnar, M. R., Malone, S., Vance, G., & Fisch, R. O. (1985). Coping with aversive stimulation in the neonatal period: Quiet sleep and plasma cortisol levels during recovery from circumcision. *Child Development, 56,* 824–834.

Guralnick, M. J., & Groom, J. M. (1988). Friendships of preschool children in mainstreamed playgroups. *Developmental Psychology, 24,* 595–604.

Gurucharri, C., & Selman, R. L. (1982). The development of interpersonal understanding during childhood, preadolescence, and adolescence: A longitudinal follow-up study. *Child Development, 53,* 924–927.

Gustafson, G. E., & Harris, K. L. (1990). Women's responses to young infants' cries. *Developmental Psychology, 26,* 144–152.

Guttentag, M., & Bray, H. (1976). *Undoing sex stereotypes. Research and resources for educators.* New York: McGraw-Hill.

Guttentag, R. E., Ornstein, P. A., & Seimans, L. (1987). Children's spontaneous rehearsal: Transitions in strategy acquisition. *Cognitive Development, 2,* 307–326.

Gzesh, S. M., & Surber, C. F. (1985). Visual perspective-taking skills in children. *Child Development, 56,* 1204–1213.

Haan, N., Aerts, E., & Cooper, B. A. B. (1985). *On moral grounds. The search for practical morality.* New York: New York University Press.

Hagerman, R. J. (1996). Biomedical advances in developmental psychology: The case of Fragile X syndrome. *Developmental Psychology, 32,* 416–424.

Hagerman, R. J., & Cronister, A. (1996). *Fragile X syndrome: Diagnosis, treatment, and research* (2nd ed.). Baltimore: Johns Hopkins University

Hakuta, K. (1988). Why bilinguals? In F. S. Kessel (Ed.), *The development of language and language researchers: Essays in honor of Roger Brown.* Hillsdale, NJ: Erlbaum.

Hakuta, K., & Garcia, E. E. (1989). Bilingualism and education. *American Psychologist, 44,* 374–379.

Hala, S., & Chandler, M. (1996). The role of strategic planning in accessing false-belief understanding. *Child Development, 67,* 2948–2966.

Hale, S., Fry, A., & Jessie, K. A. (1993). Effects of practice on speed of information processing in children and adults: Age sensitivity and age invariance. *Developmental Psychology, 29,* 880–892.

Hall, D. G., & Waxman, S. R. (1993). Assumptions about word meaning: Individuation and basic-level kinds. *Child Development, 64,* 1550–1570.

Hall, G. S. (1891). The contents of children's minds on entering school. *Pedagogical Seminary, 1,* 139–173.

Hall, G. S. (1904). *Adolescence.* New York: Appleton-Century-Crofts.

Halpern, D. F. (1997). Sex differences in intelligence: Implications for education. *American Psychologist, 52,* 1091–1102.

Halpern, L. F., MacLean, W. E., Jr., & Baumeister, A. A. (1995). Infant sleep-wake characteristics: Relation to neurological status and prediction of developmental outcome: *Developmental Review, 15,* 255–291.

Halverson, H. M. (1931). An experimental study of prehension in infants by means of systematic cinema records. *Genetic Psychology Monographs, 10,* 107–286.

Hamond, N. R., & Fivush, R. (1991). Memories of Mickey Mouse: Young children recount their trip to Disney world. *Cognitive Development, 6,* 433–448.

Hanna, E., & Meltzoff, A. N. (1993). Peer imitation by toddlers in the laboratory, home, and day-care contexts: Implications for social learning and memory. *Developmental Psychology, 29,* 701–710.

Hannah, J. S., & Kahn, S. E. (1989). The relationship of socioeconomic status and gender to the occupational choices of grade 12 students. *Journal of Vocational Behavior, 34,* 161–178.

Harkness, S., Edwards, C. P., & Super, C. M. (1981). Social roles and moral reasoning: A case study in a rural African community. *Developmental Psychology, 17,* 595–603.

Harlow, H. F., & Zimmerman, R. R. (1959). Affectional responses in the infant monkey. *Science, 130,* 421–432.

Harnishfeger, K. K. (1995). The development of cognitive inhibition: Theories, definitions, and research evidence. In F. Dempster & C. Brainerd (Eds.), *New perspectives on interference and inhibition in cognition* (pp. 176–204). New York: Academic Press.

Harnishfeger, K. K., & Bjorklund, D. F. (1990). Children's strategies: A brief history. In D. F. Bjorklund (Ed.), *Children's strategies: Contemporary views of cognitive development* (pp. 1–22). Hillsdale, NJ: Erlbaum.

Harnishfeger, K. K., & Bjorklund, D. F. (1994). The development of inhibition mechanisms and their relation to individual differences in children's cognitions. *Learning and Individual Differences, 6,* 331–355.

Harnishfeger, K. K., & Pope, S. (1996). Intending to forget: The development of cognitive inhibition in directed forgetting. *Journal of Experimental Child Psychology, 62,* 292–315.

Harold, G. T., Fincham, F. D., Osborne, L. M., & Conger, R. D. (1997). Mom and dad are at it again: Adolescent perceptions of marital conflict and adolescent psychological distress. *Developmental Psychology, 33,* 333–350.

Harper, L. V., & Huie, K. S. (1985). The effects of prior group experience, age, and familiarity on the quality and organization of preschoolers' social relationships. *Child Development, 56,* 704–717.

Harrington, D. M., Block, J. H., & Block, J. (1987). Testing aspects of Carl Rogers's theory of creative environments in young adolescents. *Journal of Personality and Social Psychology, 52,* 851–856.

Harris, L., & Associates (1986). *American teens speak: Sex, myths, TV, and birth control. The Planned Parenthood poll.* New York: Planned Parenthood Federation of America.

Harris, M. (1992). *Language experience and early language development: From input to uptake.* Hove, UK: Erlbaum.

Harris, M. J., & Rosenthal, R. (1986). Four factors in the mediation of teacher expectancy effects. In R. S. Feldman (Ed.), *The social psychology of education. Current research and theory.* Cambridge, England: Cambridge University Press.

Harris, N. B. (1992). Sex, race, and the experience of aggression. *Aggressive Behavior, 18,* 201–217.

Harris, P. L. (1989). Developmental changes in children's understanding of simple, multiple, and blended emotion concepts. In C. Saarni & P. Harris (Eds.), *Children's understanding of emotion.*

Harris, P. L., Kavanaugh, R. D., & Meredith, M. C. (1994). Young children's comprehension of pretend episodes: The integration of successive actions. *Child Development, 65,* 16–30.

Harrison, A. O., Wilson, M. N., Pine, C. J., Chan, S. Q., & Buriel, R. (1994). Family ecologies of ethnic minority children. In G. Handel & G. G. Whitchurch (Eds.), *The psychosocial interior of the family* (pp. 187–210). New York: Aldine De Gruyter.

Harrison, L. F., & Williams, T. (1986). Television and cognitive development. In T. Williams (Ed.), *The impact of television: A natural experiment in three communities.* Orlando, FL: Academic.

Harrist, A. W., Zaia, A. F., Bates, J. E., Dodge, K. A., & Pettit, G. S. (1997). Subtypes of social withdrawal in early childhood: Sociometric status and social-cognitive differences across four years. *Child Development, 68,* 278–294.

Hart, B., & Risley, T. R. (1995). *Meaningful differences in the everyday experiences of young American children.* Baltimore: Paul H. Brooks.

Hart, C. H., Burts, D. C., Durland, M. A., Charlesworth, R. DeWolf, M., & Fleege, P.O. (1998). Stress behaviors and activity type participation of preschoolers in more or less developmentally appropriate classroms: SES and sex differences. *Journal of Research in Childhood Education,* in press.

Hart, C. H., Ladd, G. W., & Burleson, B. R. (1990). Children's expectations of the outcomes of social strategies: Relations with socioeconomic status and maternal disciplinary styles. *Child Development, 61,* 127–137.

Hart, C. H., Nelson, D., Robinson, C. C., Olsen, S. F., & McNeilly-Choque, M. K. (1998). Overt and relational aggression in Russian nursery-school-age children: Parenting style and marital linkages. *Developmental Psychology,* in press.

Hart, C. H., Olsen, S. F., Robinson, C. C., & Mandleco, B. L. (1997). The development of social and communicative competence in childhood: Review and a model of personal, familial, and extrafamilial processes. *Communication Yearbook, 20,* 305–373.

Hart, D., & Chmiel, S. (1992). Influence of defense mechanisms on moral judgment development: A logitudinal study. *Developmental Psychology, 28,* 722–730.

Hart, D., Hofmann, V., Edelstein, W., & Keller, M. (1997). The relation of childhood personality types to adolescent behavior and development: A longitudinal study of Icelandic children. *Developmental Psychology, 33,* 195–205.

Hart, S. N. (1991). From property to person status: Historical perspective on children's rights. *American Psychologist, 46,* 53–59.

Hart, S. N., & Brassard, M. R. (1987). A major threat to children's mental health. Psychological maltreatment. *American Psychologist, 42,* 160–165.

Harter, S. (1982). The perceived competence scale for children. *Child Development, 53,* 87–97.

Harter, S. (1983). Developmental perspectives on the self-system. In P. H. Mussen (Ed.), *Handbook of child psychology.* (Vol. 4). *Socialization, personality, and social development.* New York: Wiley.

Harter, S. (1990). Issues in the assessment of the self-concept of children and adolescents. In A. M. LaGreca (Ed.), *Through the eyes of the child: Obtaining self-reports from children and adolescents.* Boston: Allyn & Bacon.

Harter, S., Marold, D. B., Whitesell, N. R., & Cobbs, G. (1996). A model of the effects of perceived parent and peer support on adolescent false self behavior. *Child Development, 67,* 360–374.

Harter, S., & Monsour, A. (1992). Developmental analysis of conflict caused by opposing attributes in the adolescent self-portrait. *Developmental Psychology, 28,* 251–260.

Harter, S., & Whitesell, N. (1989). Developmental changes in children's understanding of simple, multiple, and blended emotion concepts. In C. Saarni & P. Harris (Eds.), *Children's understanding of emotion.* Cambridge, England: Cambridge University Press.

Hartshorne, H., & May, M. S. (1928–1930). *Studies in the nature of character.* (Vol. 1). *Studies in deceit.* (Vol. 2). *Studies in self control.* (Vol. 3). *Studies in the organization of charachter.* New York: Macmillan.

Hartung, B., & Sweeney, K. (1991). Why adult children return home. *Social Science Journal, 28,* 467–480.

Hartup, W. W. (1974). Aggression in childhood: Developmental perspectives. *American Psychologist, 29,* 336–341.

Hartup, W. W. (1983). Peer relations. In P. H. Mussen (Ed.), *Handbook of Child psychology.* (Vol. 4). *Socialization, personality, and social development* (pp. 103–196). New York: Wiley.

Hartup, W. W. (1989). Social relationships and their developmental significance. *American Psychologist, 44,* 120–126.

Hartup, W. W. (1992). Friendships and their developmental significance. In H. McGurk (Ed.), *Childhood social development: Contemporary perspectives.* Hove, England: Erlbaum.

Hartup, W. W. (1996). The company they keep: Friendships and their developmental significance. *Child Development, 67,* 1–13.

Hartup, W. W., Laursen, B., Stewart, M. I., & Eastenson, A. (1988). Conflict and friendship relations of young children. *Child Development, 59,* 1590–1600.

Harvey, S., Jarrell, J., Brant, R., Stainton, C., & Rach, D. (1996). A randomized, controlled trial of nurse-midwifery care. *Birth, 23,* 128–135.

Harwood, R. L., Schoelmerich, A., Ventura-Cook, E., Schulze, P. A., & Wilson, S. P. (1996). Culture and class influences on Anglo and Puerto Rican mothers' beliefs regarding long-term socialization goals and child behavior. *Child Development, 67,* 2446–2461.

Hasher, L., & Zacks, R. T. (1979). Automatic and effortful processes in memory. *Journal of Experimental Psychology: General, 108,* 356–388.

Hashima, P. Y., & Amato, P. R. (1994). Poverty, social support, and parental behavior. *Child Development, 65,* 394–403.

Haskett, M. E., & Kistner, J. A. (1991). Social interactions and peer perceptions of young physically abused children. *Child Development, 62,* 979–990.

Hasselhorn, M. (1992). Task dependency and the role of category typicality and metamemory in the development of an organizational strategy. *Child Development, 63,* 202–214.

Hasselhorn, M. (1995). Beyond production deficiency and utilization inefficiency: Mechanisms of the emergence of strategic categorization in episodic memory tasks. In F. E. Weinert & W. Schneider (Eds.), *Memory performance and competencies: Issues in growth and development* (pp. 141–159). Hillsdale, NJ: Erlbaum.

Hatcher, P. J., Hulme, C., & Ellis, A. W. (1994). Ameliorating early reading failure by integrating the teaching of reading and phonological skills: The phonological linkage hypothesis. *Child Development, 65,* 41–57.

Hausen-Corn, P. (1995). Mastery motivation in toddlers with developmental disabilities. *Child Development, 66,* 236–248.

Hay, D. F., Caplan, M., Castle, J., & Stimson, C. A. (1991). Does sharing become increasingly "rational" in the second year of life? *Developmental Psychology, 27,* 987–993.

Hayden, C. A., Haine, R. R., & Fivush, R. (1997). Developing narrative structure in parent-child reminiscing across the preschool years. *Developmental Psychology, 33,* 295–307.

Hayne, H., & Rovee-Collier, C. (1995). The organization of reactivated memory in infancy. *Child Development, 66,* 893–906.

Hayward, C., Killen, J. D., Wilson, D. M., Hammer, L. D., Litt, I. F., Kraemer, H. C., Haydel, F., Varady, M., & Taylor, C. B. (1997). Psychiatric risk associated with puberty in adolescent girls. *Journal of the American Academy of Child and Adolescent Psychiatry, 36,* 255–262.

Hazan, C., & Shaver, P. (1987). Romantic love conceptualized as an attachment process. *Journal of Personality and Social Psychology, 52,* 511–524.

Hearold, S. (1986). A synthesis of 1043 effects of television on social behavior. In G. Comstock (Ed.), *Public communications and behavior: Volume I* (Vol. 1, pp. 65–133). New York: Academic Press.

Heath, S. B. (1989). Oral and literate traditions among black Americans living in poverty. *American Psychologist, 44,* 367–373.

Hebb, D. O. (1980). *Essay on mind.* Hillsdale, NJ: Erlbaum.

Hedges, L. V., & Nowell, A. (1995, July 7). Sex differences in mental test scores, variability,and numbers of high-scoring individuals. *Science, 269,* 41–45.

Heinonen, O. P., Slone, D., & Shapiro, S. (1977). *Birth defects and drugs in pregnancy.* Littleton, MA: Publishing Sciences Group.

Helms, J. E. (1992). Why is there no study of cultural equivalence in standardized cognitive-ability testing? *American Psychologist, 47,* 1083–1101.

Helms, J. E. (1997). The triple quandary of race, culture, and social class in standardized cognitive ability testing. In D. P. Flanagan, J. Genshaft, & P. L. Harrison (Eds.), *Contemporary intellectual assessment: Theories, tests, and issues.* New York: Guilford.

Hendler, M., & Weisberg, P. (1992). Conservation acquisition, maintenance, and generalization by mentally retarded children using equality-rule training. *Journal of Experimental Child Psychology, 54,* 258–276.

Hendrick, B. (1994, June 7). Teen sexual activity increases, as does kids' use of condoms. *Atlanta Constitution,* p. A1, A6.

Henker, B., & Whalen, C. K. (1989). Hyperactivity and attention deficits. *American Psychologist, 44,* 216–223.

Hennessey, B. A., & Amabile, T. M. (1988). The conditions of creativity. In R. J. Sternberg (Ed.), *The nature of creativity. Contemporary psychological perspectives.* Cambridge, England: Cambridge University Press.

Henry, B., Caspi, A., Moffitt, T.E., & Silva, P. A. (1996). Temperamental and familial predictors of violent and nonviolent criminal convictions: Age 3 to age 18. *Developmental Psychology, 32,* 614–623.

Herdt, G. H., & Davidson, J. (1988). The Sambia "turnim-man": Sociocultural and clinical aspects of gender formation in male pseudohermaphrodites with 5-alpha-reductase deficiency in Papua New Guinea. *Archives of Sexual Behavior, 17,* 33–56.

Herkowitz, J. (1978). Sex-role expectations and motor behavior of the young child. In M. V. Ridenour (Ed.), *Motor development: Issues and applications.* Princeton, NJ: Princeton Book Company.

Herman-Giddens, M. E., Slora, E. J., Wasserman, R. C., Bourdony, C. J., Bhapkar, M. V., Koch, G. G., & Hasemeier, C. M. (1997). Secondary sexual characteristics and menses in young girls seen in office practice: A study from the Pediatric Research in Office Settings Network. *Pediatrics, 99,* 505–512.

Hernandez, D. J. (1997). Child development and the social demography of childhood. *Child Development, 68,* 149–169.

Herrera, C., & Dunn, J. (1997). Early experiences with family conflict: Implications for arguments with a close friend. *Developmental Psychology, 33,* 869–881.

Herrnstein, R. J., & Murray, C. (1994). *The bell curve: Intelligence and class structure in American life.* New York: The Free Press.

Hershberger, S. L., & D'Augelli, A. R. (1995). The impact of victimization on the mental health and suicidality of lesbian, gay, and bisexual youths. *Developmental Psychology, 31,* 65–74.

Hertsgaard, L., Gunnar, M., Erickson, M. F., & Nachmias, M. (1995). Adrenocortical responses to the Strange Situation in infants with disorganized/disoriented attachment relationships. *Child Development, 66,* 1100–1106.

Hertzberger, S. D., & Hall, J. A. (1993). Consequences of retaliatory aggression against siblings and peers: Urban minority children's expectations. *Child Development, 64,* 1773–1785.

Hetherington, E. M. (1989). Coping with family transitions: Winners, losers, and survivors. *Child Development, 60,* 1–14.

Hetherington, E. M., Bridges, M., & Insabella, G. M. (1998). What matters? What does not?: Five perspectives on the association between marital transitions and children's adjustment. *American Psychologist, 53,* 167–184.

Hetherington, E. M., & Camara, K. A. (1984). Families in transition: The processes of dissolution and reconstitution. In R. D. Parke (Ed.), *Review of child development research.* Vol. 7: The family. Chicago: University of Chicago Press.

Hetherington, E. M. & Clingempeel, W. G. (1992). Coping with marital transitions. *Monographs of the Society for Research in Child Development, 57,* 2–3, Serial No. 227.

Hetherington, E. M., Cox, M., & Cox, R. (1982). Effects of divorce on parents and children. In M. E. Lamb (Ed.), *Nontraditional families* (pp. 233–288). Hillsdale, NJ: Erlbaum.

Hetherington, E. M., & Frankie, G. (1967). Effect of parental dominance, warmth, and conflict on imitation in children. *Journal of Personality and Social Psychology, 6,* 119–125.

Hetherington, E. M., & Jodl, K. M. (1994). Stepfamilies as settings for child development. In A. Booth & J. Dunn (Eds.), *Stepfamilies: Who benefits? Who does not?* (pp. 55–79). Hillsdale, NJ: Erlbaum.

Hetherington, E. M., & Parke, R. D. (1975). *Child psychology: A contemporary viewpoint.* New York: McGraw-Hill.

Heyman, G. D., Dweck, C. S., & Cain, K. M. (1992). Young children's vulnerability to self-blame and helplessness: Relationship to beliefs about goodness. *Child Development, 63,* 401–415.

Higgins, C. I., Campos, J. J., & Kermoian, R. (1996). Effect of self-produced locomotion on infant postural compensation to optic flow. *Developmental Psychology, 32,* 836–841.

Higgins, E. T., & Parsons, J. E. (1983). Stages as subcultures: Social-cognitive development and the social life of the child. In E. T. Higgins, W. W. Hartup, & D. N. Ruble (Eds.), *Social cognition and social development: A sociocultural perspective.* New York: Cambridge University Press.

Higley, J. D., Hopkins, W. D., Thompson, W. W., Byrne, E. A., Hirsh, R. M., & Suomi, S. J. (1992). Peers as primary attachment sources in yearling rhesus monkeys. *Developmental Psychology, 28,* 1163–1171.

Hill, A. E. (1997, May 13). Doctors debate circumcision for infants. *Atlanta Constitution,* B3.

Hill, J. P., & Lynch, M. E. (1983). The intensification of gender-related role expectations during early adolescence. In J. Brooks-Gunn & A. C. Petersen (Eds.), *Girls at puberty. Biological and psychosocial perspectives.* New York: Plenum.

Hill, P. T., Foster, G. E., & Gendler, T. (1990). *High schools with character: Alternatives to bureaucracy.* Santa Monica, CA: Rand Corporation.

Hill, S. D., & Tomlin, C. (1981). Self-recognition in retarded children. *Child Development, 53,* 1320–1329.

Hinde, R. A. (1989). Ethological and relationship approaches. In R. Vasta (Ed.), *Annals of child development.* (Vol. 6). *Theories of child development: Revised formulations and current issues.* Greenwich, CT: JAI Press.

Hines, M., & Kaufman, F. R. (1994). Androgen and the development of human sex-typical behavior: Rough-and-tumble play and sex of preferred playmates in children with congenital adrenal hyperplasia. *Child Development, 65,* 1042–1053.

Hinshaw, S. P., & Melnick, S. M. (1995). Peer relationships in boys with attention-deficit hyperactivity disorder with and without comorbid aggression. *Development and Psychopathology, 7,* 627–647.

Hinshaw, S. P., Zupan, B. A., Simmel, C., Nigg, J. T., & Melnick, S. (1997). Peer status in boys with attention-deficit hyperactivity disorder: Predictions from overt and covert antisocial behavior, social isolation, and authoritative parenting beliefs. *Child Development, 68,* 880–896.

Hirsh-Pasek, K., Kemler Nelson, D. G., Jusczyk, P. W., Cassidy, K. W., Druss, B., & Kennedy, L. (1987). Clauses are perceptual units for young infants. *Cognition, 26,* 269–286.

Hitch, G. J., & Halliday, M. S. (1983). Working memory in children. *Philosophical Transactions of the Royal Society, B302,* 324–340.

Hitch, G. J., & Towse, J. (1995). Working memory: What develops? In F. E. Weinert & W. Schneider (Eds.), *Research on memory development: State-of-the-art and future directions* (pp. 3–21). Hillsdale, NJ: Erlbaum.

Hobbes, T. (1904). *Leviathan.* Cambridge: Cambridge University Press. (Original work published 1651)

Hock, E., & DeMeis, D. K. (1990). Depression in mothers of infants: The role of maternal employment. *Developmental Psychology, 26,* 285–291.

Hodges, E. V. E., Malone, M. J., & Perry, D. G. (1997). Individual risk and social risk as interacting determinants of victimization in the peer group. *Developmental Psychology, 33,* 1032–1039.

Hodges, J., & Tizard, B. (1989). IQ and behavioral adjustment of ex-institutional adolescents. *Journal of Child Psychology and Psychiatry, 30,* 53–75.

Hoff-Ginsberg, E. (1997). *Language development.* Pacific Grove, CA: Brooks/Cole.

Hoffman, L. W. (1989). Effects of maternal employment in the two-parent family. *American Psychologist, 44,* 283–292.

Hoffman, L. W. (1991). The influence of family environment on personality: Accounting for sibling differences. *Psychological Bulletin, 108,* 187–203.

Hoffman, L. W. (1994). Commentary on Plomin, R. (1994): A proof and a disproof questioned. *Social Development, 3,* 60–63.

Hoffman, M. L. (1970). Moral development. In P. H. Mussen (Ed.), *Carmichael's manual of child psychology* (Vol. 2). New York: Wiley.

Hoffman, M. L. (1975). Moral internalization, parental power, and the nature of parent-child interaction. *Developmental Psychology, 11,* 228–239.

Hoffman, M. L. (1981). Is altruism part of human nature? *Journal of Personality and Social Psychology, 40,* 121–137.

Hoffman, M. L. (1988). Moral development. In M. H. Bornstein & M. E. Lamb (Eds.), *Developmental Psychology: An advanced textbook* (2nd ed., pp. 497–548). Hillsdale, NJ: Erlbaum.

Hoffman, M. L. (1993). Empathy, social cognition, and moral education. In A. Garrod (Ed.), *Approaches to moral development: New research and emerging themes.* New York: Teachers College Press.

Hoffner, C., & Badzinski, D. M. (1989). Children's integration of facial and situational cues to emotion. *Child Development, 60,* 411–422.

Hofsten, C. von (1984). Developmental changes in the organization of prereaching movements. *Developmental Psychology, 20,* 378–388.

Hofsten, C. von, & Spelke, E. S. (1985). Object perception and object-directed reaching in infancy. *Journal of Experimental Psychology: General, 114,* 198–212.

Holden, G. W. (1988). Adults' thinking about a child rearing problem: Effects of experience, parental status, and gender. *Child Development, 59,* 1623–1632.

Holmbeck, G. N., & Hill, J. P. (1991). Conflictive engagement, positive affect, and menarche in families with seventh-grade girls. *Child Development, 62,* 1030–1048.

Honzik, M. P. (1983). Measuring mental abilities in infancy. The value and limitations. In M. Lewis (Ed.), *Origins of intelligence. Infancy and early childhood* (2nd ed.). New York: Plenum.

Honzik, M. P., Macfarlane, J. W., & Allen, L. (1948). The stability of mental test performance between two and eighteen years. *Journal of Experimental Education, 17,* 309–324.

Hopkins, B. (1991). Facilitating early motor development: An intracultural study of West Indian mothers and their infants living in Britain. In J. K. Nugent, B. M. Lester, & T. B. Brazelton (Eds.), *The cultural context of infancy:* (Vol. 2). *Multicultural and interdisciplinary approaches to parent-infant relations.* Norwood, NJ: Ablex.

Hopwood, N. J., Kelch, R. P., Hale, P. M., Mendes, T. M., Foster, C. M., & Beitins, I. Z. (1990). The onset of human puberty: Biological and environmental factors. In J. Bancroft & J. M. Reinisch (Eds.), *Adolescence and puberty.* New York: Oxford University Press.

Horn, J. L., & Cattell, R. B. (1982). Whimsy and misunderstandings of G_f-G_c theory: A comment on Guilford. *Psychological Bulletin, 91,* 623–633.

Horn, J. L., & Noll, J. (1997). Human cognitive capabilities: G_f-G_c theory. In D. P. Flanagan, J. Genshaft, & P. L. Harrison (Eds.), *Contemporary intellectual assessment: Theories, tests, and issues.* New York: Guilford.

Horney, K. (1967). *Feminine psychology.* New York: Norton. (Original work published 1923–1937.)Horney, K. (1967). *Feminine psychology.* New York: Norton. (Original work published 1923–1937.)

Hornik, R., & Gunnar, M. R. (1988). A descriptive analysis of social referencing. *Child Development, 59,* 626–634.

Horowitz, F. D. (1992). John B. Watson's legacy: Learning and environment. *Developmental Psychology, 28,* 360–367.

Howard-Pitney, B., LaFramboise, T. D., Basil, M., September, B., & Johnson, M. (1992). Psychological and social indicators of suicide ideation and suicide attempts in Zuni adolescents. *Journal of Consulting and Clinical Psychology, 60,* 473–476.

Howe, M. L., & Courage, M. L. (1993). On resolving the enigma of infantile amnesia. *Psychological Bulletin, 113,* 305–326.

Howe, N., & Ross, H. S. (1990). Socialization, perspective-taking and the sibling relationship. *Developmental Psychology, 26,* 160–165.

Howes, C. (1988). Peer interaction of young children. *Monographs of the Society for Research in Child Development, 53*(1, Serial No. 217).

Howes, C. (1990). Can the age of entry into child care and the quality of child care predict adjustment in kindergarten? *Developmental Psychology, 26,* 292–303.

Howes, C., Droege, K., & Matheson, C. C. (1994). Play and communicative processes within long-term and short-term friendship dyads. *Journal of Social and Personal Relationships, 11,* 401–410.

Howes, C., Hamilton, C. E., & Matheson, C. C. (1994). Children's relationships with peers: Differential associations with aspects of the parent-child relationship. *Child Development, 65,* 253–263.

Howes, C., & Matheson, C. C. (1992). Sequences in the development of competent play with peers: Social and social pretend play. *Developmental Psychology,28,* 961–974.

Howes, C., Phillips, D. A., & Whitebrook, M. (1992). Thresholds of quality: Implications for the social development of children in center-based child care. *Child Development, 63,* 449–460.

Howes, P., & Markman, H. J. (1989). Marital quality and child functioning: A longitudinal investigation. *Child Development, 60,* 1044–1051.

Hsu, L. K. G. (1990). *Eating disorders.* New York: Guilford Press.

Hudson, J. A. (1990). Constructive processing in children's event memory. *Developmental Psychology, 26,* 180–187.

Huesmann, L. R. (1986). Psychological processes promoting the relation between exposure to media violence and aggressive behavior by the viewer. *Journal of Social Issues, 42,* 125–139.

Huesmann, L. R., Eron, L. D., Lefkowitz, M. M., & Walder, L. O. (1984). Stability of aggression over time and generations. *Developmental Psychology, 20,* 1120–1134.

Huesmann, L. R., Lagerspitz, K., & Eron, L. D. (1984). Intervening variables in the TV violence-aggression relation: Evidence from two countries. *Developmental Psychology, 20,* 746–775.

Hughes, R., Jr., Tingle, B. A., & Sawin, D. B. (1981). Development of empathic understanding in children. *Child Development, 52,* 122–128.

Hulme, C., Thompson, N., Muir, C., & Lawrence, A. (1984). Speech rate and the development of spoken words: The role of rehearsal and item identification processes. *Journal of Experimental Child Psychology, 38,* 241–253.

Humphrey, M., & Humphrey, H. (1988). *Families with a difference: Varieties of surrogate parenthood.* London: Routledge.

Humphreys, A. P., & Smith, P. K. (1987). Rough and tumble, friendship, and dominance in school children: Evidence for continuity and change with age. *Child Development, 58,* 201–212.

Humphreys, L. G., Rich, S. A., & Davey, T. C. (1985). A Piagetian test of general intelligence. *Developmental Psychology, 21,* 872–877.

Hunter, J. E., & Hunter, R. F. (1984). Validity and utility of alternative predictors of job performance. *Psychological Bulletin, 96,* 72–98.

Hunter, S. K., & Yankowitz, J. (1996). Medical fetal therapy. In J. A. Kuller, N. C. Cheschier, & R. C. Cefalo (Eds.), *Prenatal diagnosis and reproductive genetics.* St. Louis: Mosby.

Hura, S. L., & Echols, C. H. (1996). The role of stress and articulatory difficulty in childrens' early productions. *Developmental Psychology, 32,* 165–176.

Huston, A. C. (1983). Sex-typing. In P. H. Mussen (Ed.), *Handbook of child psychology* (4th ed.) (Vol. 4). *Socialization, personality, and social development.* (pp. 387–467). New York: Wiley.

Huston, A. C., Donnerstein, E., Fairchild, H., Feshbach, N. D., Katz, P. A., Murray, J. P., Rubinstein, E. A., Wilcox, B. L., & Zuckerman, D. (1992). *Big world, small screen.* Lincoln, NB: University of Nebraska Press.

Hutt, C. (1972). *Males and females.* Baltimore: Penguin Books.

Huttenlocher, P. R. (1994). Synaptogenesis, synapse elimination, and neural plasticity in the human cerebral cortex. In C. A. Nelson (Ed.), *Threats to optimal development: Integrating biological, psychological, and social risk factors: Minnesota symposia on child psychology* (Vol. 27, pp. 35–54). Hillsdale, NJ: Erlbaum.

Hutton, N. (1996). Health prospects for children born to HIV-infected women. In R. R. Faden & N. E. Kass (Eds.), *HIV, AIDS, and childbearing* (pp. 63–77). New York: Oxford University Press.

Hwang, C. P. (1986). Behavior of Swedish primary and secondary caretaking fathers in relation to mother's presence. *Developmental Psychology, 22,* 749–751.

Hyde, J. S. (1984). How large are sex differences in aggression? A developmental meta-analysis. *Developmental Psychology, 20,* 722–736.

Hyde, J. S., Fennema, E., & Lamon, S. J. (1990). Gender differences in mathematics performance: A meta-analysis. *Psychological Bulletin, 107,* 139–155.

Hyde, J. S., & Plant, E. A. (1995). Magnitude of psychological gender differences: Another side to the story. *American Psychologist, 50,* 159–161.

Hymel, S. (1983). Preschool children's peer relations: Issues in sociometric assessment. *Merrill-Palmer Quarterly, 19,* 237–260.

Hymel, S., Bowker, A., & Woody, E. (1993). Aggressive versus withdrawn unpopular children: Variations in peer and self-perceptions in multiple domains. *Child Development, 64,* 879–896.

Hymes, J. L. (1990). *The year in review: A look at 1989.* Washington D.C.: National Association for the Education of Young Children.

Hyson, M. C., Hirsch-Pasek, K., & Rescorla, L. (1989). *Academic environments in early childhood: Challenge or pressure?* Summary report to the Spencer Foundation.

Iannotti, R. J. (1978). Effect of role-taking experiences on role-taking, empathy, altruism, and aggression. *Developmental Psychology, 14,* 119–124.

Imperato-McGinley, J., Peterson, R. E., Gautier, T., & Sturla, E. (1979). Androgyns and the evolution of male gender identity among male pseudohermaphrodites with 5a-reducase deficiency. *New England Journal of Medicine, 300,* 1233–1237.

Ingram, D. (1986). Phonological development: Production. In P. Fletcher & M. Garman (Eds.), *Language acquisition* (2nd ed.). Cambridge: Cambridge University Press.

Ingram, D. (1989). *First language acquisition: Method, description, and explanation.* Cambridge: Cambridge University Press.

Inhelder, B., & Piaget, J. (1958). *The growth of logical thinking from childhood to adolescence.* New York: Basic Books.

Intons-Peterson, M. J. (1988). *Gender concepts of Swedish and American youth.* Hillsdale, NJ: Erlbaum.

Intons-Peterson, M. J., & Reddel, M. (1984). What do people ask about a neonate? *Developmental Psychology, 20,* 358–359.

Isabella, R. A. (1993). Origins of attachment: Maternal interactive behavior across the first year. *Child Development,* 605–621.

Isabella, R. A., & Belsky, J. (1991). Interactional synchrony and the origins of infant-mother attachment. *Child Development, 62,* 373–384.

Isberg, R. S., Hauser, S. T., Jacobson, A. M., Powers, S. I., Noam, G., Weiss-Perry, B., & Follansbee, D. (1989). Parental contexts of adolescent self-esteem: A developmental perspective. *Journal of Youth and Adolescence, 18,* 1–23.

Ismail, M. A. (1993). Maternal-fetal infections. In C. Lin, M. S. Verp, & R. E. Sabbagha (Eds.), *The high-risk fetus: Pathophysiology, diagnosis, management.* New York: Springer-Verlag.

Izard, C. E. (1982). *Measuring emotions in infants and children.* New York: Cambridge University Press.

Izard, C. E. (1993). Four systems for emotion activation: Cognitive and noncognitive processes. *Psychological Review, 100,* 68–90.

Izard, C. E., Fantauzzo, C. A., Castle, J. M., Haynes. O. M., Rayias, M. F., & Putnam, P. H. (1995). The ontogeny and significance of infants' facial expressions in the first 9 months of life. *Developmental Psychology, 31,* 997–1013.

Jacklin, C. N., & Maccoby, E. E. (1978). Social behavior at 33 months in same-sex and mixed-sex dyads. *Child Development, 49,* 557–569.

Jackson, J. F. (1993). Human behavioral genetics, Scarr's theory, and her views on interventions: A critical review and commentary on their implications for African-American children. *Child Development, 63,* 1318–1332.

Jacobs, J. E., & Eccles, J. S. (1992). The impact of mothers' gender-role stereotypic beliefs on mothers' and children's ability perceptions. *Journal of Personality and Social Psychology, 63,* 932–944.

Jacobsen, T., & Hofmann, V. (1997). Children's attachment representations: Longitudinal relations to school behavior and academic competency in middle childhood and adolescence. *Developmental Psychology, 33,* 703–710.

Jacobson, J. L., Jacobs, L. C., & Chase, C. I. (1989). Student participation in and attitudes toward high school activities. *The High School Journal, 22,* 175–181.

Jacobson, J. L., Jacobson, S. W. (1996). Methodological considerations in behavioral toxicology in infants and children. *Developmental Psychology, 32,* 390–403.

Jacobson, J. L., Jacobson, S. W., Fein, G. G., Schwartz, P. M., & Dowler, J. K. (1984). Prenatal exposure to an environmental toxin: A test of the multiple effects model. *Developmental Psychology, 20,* 523–532.

Jacobson, J. L., Jacobson, S. W., & Humphrey, H. E. (1990). Effects of in utero exposure to polychlorinated biphenyls and related contaminants on cognitive functioning in young children. *Journal of Pediatrics, 116,* 38–45.

Jacobson, J. L., Jacobson, S. W., Padgett, R., Brumitt, G. A., & Billings, R. L. (1992). Effects of PCB exposure and infant information processing ability. *Developmental Psychology, 28,* 297–306.

Jacobson, J. L., Jacobson, S. W., Sokol, R. J., Martier, S. S., Ager, J. W., & Kaplan-Estrin, M. G. (1993). Teratogenic effects of alcohol on infant development. *Alcoholism: Clinical and Experimental Research, 17,* 174–183.

Jacobson, J. L., & Wille, D. E. (1986). The influence of attachment pattern on developmental changes in peer interaction from the toddler to the preschool period. *Child Development, 57,* 338–347.

Jacobson, S. W. (1996). Methodological considerations in behavioral toxicology in infants and children. *Developmental Psychology, 32,* 390–403.

Jacobson, S. W., Fein, G. G., Jacobson, J. L., Schwartz, P. M., & Dowler, J. (1985). The effect of intrauterine PCB exposure on visual recognition memory, *Child Development, 56,* 853–860.

Jacobvitz, D., & Sroufe, L. A. (1987). The early caregiver-child relationship and attention-deficit disorder with hyperactivity in kindergarten: A prospective study. *Child Development, 58,* 1496–1504.

Jadack, R. A., Hyde, J. S., Moore, C. F., & Keller, M. L. (1995). Moral reasoning about sexually transmitted diseases. *Child Development, 66,* 167–177.

Jagers, R. J., Bingham, K., & Hans, S. L. (1996). Socialization and social judgments among inner-city African-American kindergarteners. *Child Development, 67,* 140–150.

Jaio, S., Ji, G., & Jing, Q. (1996). Cognitive development of Chinese urban only children and children with siblings. *Child Development, 67,* 387–395.

James, W. (1890). *Principles of psychology* (2 vols.). New York: Holt.

Janowsky, J. S., & Finlay, B. L. (1986). The outcome of perinatal brain damage: The role of normal neuron loss and axon retraction. *Developmental Medicine and Child Neurology, 28,* 375–389.

Jeffery, R., & Jeffery, P. M. (1993). Traditional birth attendants in rural northern India: The social organization of childbearing. In S. Lindenbaum & M. Lock (Eds.), *Knowledge, power, and practice: The anthropology of medicine and everyday life.* Berkeley, CA: University of California Press.

Jenkins, J. M., & Astington, J. W. (1996). Cognitive factors and family structure associated with theory of mind development in young children. *Developmental Psychology, 32,* 70–78.

Jensen, A. R. (1969). How much can we boost IQ and scholastic achievement? *Harvard Educational Review, 39,* 1–123.

Jensen, A. R. (1977). Cumulative deficit in the IQ of blacks in the rural South. *Developmental Psychology, 13,* 184–191.

Jensen, A. R. (1980). *Bias in mental testing.* New York: Free Press.

Jensen, A. R. (1985). The nature of black-white difference on various psychometric tests: Spearman's hypothesis. *Behavioral and Brain Sciences, 8,* 193–263.

Johnsen, E. P. (1991). Searching for the social and cognitive outcomes of children's play: A selective second look. *Play and Culture, 4,* 201–213.

Johnson, C. J., Pick, H. L., Siegel, G. M., Cicciarelli, A. W., & Garber, S. R. (1981). Effects of interpersonal distance on children's vocal intensity. *Child Development, 52,* 721–723.

Johnson, D. W., & Johnson, R. T. (1987). *Learning together and alone: Cooperative, competitive, and individualistic learning* (2nd ed.). Englewood Cliffs, NJ: Prentice Hall.

Johnson, D. W., & Johnson, R. T. (1989). *Cooperation and competition: Theory and research.* Edina, MN: Interaction.

Johnson, H., & Smith, L. B. (1981). Children's inferential abilities in the context of reading to understand. *Child Development, 52,* 1216–1223.

Johnson, J., & Newport, E. (1989). Critical period effects in second language learning: The influence of maturational state on the acquisition of English as a second language. *Cognitive Psychology, 21,* 60–99.

Johnson, M. H. (1997). *Developmental cognitive neuroscience: An introduction.* Cambridge, MA: Blackwell.

Johnson, M. H., Dziurawiec, S., Ellis, H., & Morton, J. (1991). Newborns' preferential tracking of face-like stimuli and its subsequent decline. *Cognition, 40,* 1–19.

Johnson, M. H., & Gilmore, R. O. (1996). Developmental cognitive neuroscience: A biological perspective on cognitive change. In R. Gelman & T. K. Au (Eds.), *Perceptual and cognitive development.* San Diego, CA: Academic Press.

Johnson, S. P., & Aslin, R. N. (1995). Perception of object unity in 2-month-old infants. *Developmental Psychology, 31,* 739–745.

Johnson, W. K., & Buskirk, E. R. (1974). *Science and Medicine of Exercise and Sport* (2nd ed.). New York: HarperCollins.

Johnson, W., Emde, R. N., Pannabecker, B., Stenberg, C., & Davis, M. (1982). Maternal perception of infant emotion from birth through 18 months. *Infant Behavior and Development, 5,* 313–322.

Johnston, J., & Ettema, J. S. (1982). *Positive images.* Newbury Park, CA: Sage.

Jones, D. S., Byers, R. H., Bush, T. J., Oxtoby, M. J., & Rogers, M. F. (1992). Epidemiology of transfusion-associated acquired immunodeficiency syndrome in children in the United States, 1981 through 1989. *Pediatrics, 89,* 123–127.

Jones, K. L., Smith, D. W., Ulleland, C. N., & Streissguth, A. P. (1973). Pattern of malformation in offspring of chronic alcoholic mothers. *Lancet, 1,* 1267–1271.

Jones, M. C. (1924). A laboratory study of fear: The case of Peter. *Pedagogical Seminary, 31,* 308–315.

Jones, M. C. (1965). Psychological correlates of somatic development. *Child Development, 36,* 899–911.

Jones, M. C., & Bayley, N. (1950). Physical maturing among boys as related to behavior. *Journal of Educational Psychology, 41,* 129–148.

Jones, S. S. (1996). Imitation or exploration: Young infant's matching of adults' oral gestures. *Child Development, 67,* 1952–1969.

Jonsen, A. R. (1996). The impact of mapping the human genome on the patient-physician relationship. In T. H. Murray, M. A. Rothstein, & R. F. Murray (Eds.). *The human genome project and the future of health care* (pp. 1–20). Bloomington, IN: University of Indiana Press.

Jonsson, J. O., & Gahler, M. (1997). Family dissolution, family reconstitution, and children's educational careers: Recent evidence for Sweden. *Demography, 34,* 277–293.

Jose, P. M. (1990). Just world reasoning in children's immanent justice arguments. *Child Development, 61,* 1024–1033.

Jouriles, E. N., Murphy, C. M., Farris, A. M., Smith, D. A., Richters, J. E., & Waters, E. (1991). Marital adjustment, parental disagreements about child rearing and behavior problems in boys: Increasing the specificity of the marital assessment. *Child Development, 62,* 1424–1433.

Jusczyk, P. W. (1995). Language acquisition: Speech sounds and phonological development. In J. L. Miller & P. D. Eimas (Eds.), *Handbook of perception and cognition* (Vol. 11). *Speech, language, and communication.* (pp. 263–301). Orlando, FL: Academic Press.

Jusczyk, P. W., Cutler, A., & Redanz, N. J. (1993). Infants' preference for the predominant stress patterns of English words. *Child Development, 64,* 675–687.

Jussim, L., & Eccles, J. S. (1992). Teacher expectations II: Construction and reflection of student achievement. *Journal of Personality and Social Psychology, 63,* 947–961.

Justice, E. M., Baker-Ward, L., Gupta, S., & Jannings, L. R. (1997). Means to the goal of remembering: Developmental changes in awareness of strategy use-performance relations. *Journal of Experimental Child Psychology, 65,* 293–314.

Kagan, J. (1972). Do infants think? *Scientific American, 226,* 74–82.

Kagan, J. (1976). Emergent themes in human development. *American Scientist, 64,* 186–196.

Kagan, J. (1984). *The nature of the child.* New York: Basic Books.

Kagan, J. (1989). *Unstable ideas: Temperament, cognition, and self.* Cambridge, MA: Cambridge University Press.

Kagan, J. (1991). Continuity and discontinuity. In S. E. Brauth, W. S. Hall, & R. J. Dooling (Eds.), *Plasticity of development.* Cambridge, MA: Bradford Books, MIT Press.

Kagan, J. (1992). Behavior, biology, and the meaning of temperamental constructs. *Pediatrics, 90,* 510–513.

Kagan, J., Kearsley, R. B., & Zelazo, P. R. (1978). *Infancy: Its place in human development.* Cambridge, MA: Harvard University Press.

Kagan, J., & Moss, H. A. (1962). *Birth to maturity.* New York: Wiley.

Kagan, J., & Snidman, N. (1991). Temperamental factors in human development. *American Psychologist, 46,* 856–862.

Kail, R. (1991). Processing time declines exponentially during childhood and adolescence. *Developmental Psychology, 27,* 259–266.

Kail, R. (1992). Processing speed, speech rate, and memory. *Developmental Psychology, 28,* 899–904.

Kail, R. (1997). Processing time, imagery, and spatial memory. *Journal of Experimental Child Psychology, 64,* 67–78.

Kail, R. V., & Salthouse, T. A. (1994). Processing speed as a mental capacity. *Acta Psychologica, 86,* 199–225.

Kaitz, M., Meschulach-Sarfaty, O., Auerbach, J., & Eidelman, A. (1988). A reexamination of newborns' ability to imitate facial expressions. *Developmental Psychology, 24,* 3–7.

Kaler, S. R., & Kopp, C. B. (1990). Compliance and comprehension in very young toddlers. *Child Development, 61,* 1997–2003.

Kandel, D. (1973). Adolescent marijuana use: Role of parents and peers. *Science, 181,* 1067–1070.

Kanfer, F. H., Stifter, E., & Morris, S. J. (1981). Self-control and altruism: Delay of gratification for another. *Child Development, 52,* 674–682.

Kant, I. (1958). *Critique of pure reason.* New York: Modern Library. (Original work published 1781.)

Kaplan, P. S., Jung, P. C., Ryther, J. S., & Zarlengo-Strouse, P. (1996). Infant-directed versus adult-directed speech as signals for faces, *Developmental Psychology, 32,* 880–891.

Karmiloff-Smith, A. (1992). *Beyond modularity: A developmental perspective on cognitive science.* Cambridge, MA: MIT Press.

Katcher, A. (1955). The discrimination of sex differences by young children. *Journal of Genetic Psychology, 87,* 131–143.

Katz, G. S., Cohn, J. F., & Moore, C. A. (1996). A combination of vocal, dynamic and summary features discriminates between three pragmatic categories of infant-directed speech. *Child Development, 67,* 205–217.

Katz, P. A. (1979). The development of female identity. *Sex Roles, 5,* 155–178.

Katz, P. A., & Walsh, P. V. (1991). Modification of children's gender-stereotyped behavior. *Child Development, 62,* 338–351.

Kaufman, A. S., Kamphaus, R. W., & Kaufman, N. L. (1985). New directions in intelligence testing: The Kaufman Assessment Battery for Children (K-ABC). In B. B. Wolman (Ed.), *Handbook of intelligence.* New York: Wiley.

Kaufman, A. S., & Kaufman, N. L. (1983). *Kaufman Assessment Battery for Children: Interpretive manual.* Circle Pines, MN: American Guidance Service.

Kaufman, J., & Zigler, E. (1989). The intergenerational transmission of child abuse. In D. Cicchetti & V. Carlson (Eds.), *Child maltreatment. Theory and research on the causes and consequences of child abuse and neglect* (pp. 129–150). New York: Cambridge University Press.

Kaye, K., & Marcus. (1981). Infant imitation: The sensory-motor agenda. *Developmental Psychology, 17,* 258–265.

Kazdin, A. E. (1995). *Conduct disorders in childhood and adolescence* (2nd ed.). Thousand Oaks, CA: Sage.

Kean, A. W. G. (1937). The history of the criminal liability of children. *Law Quarterly Review, 3,* 364–370.

Keane, S. P., Brown, K. P., & Crenshaw, T. M. (1990). Children's intention-cue detection as a function of maternal social behavior: Pathways to social rejection. *Developmental Psychology, 26,* 1004–1009.

Kearins, J. M. (1981). Visual-spatial memory in Australian aboriginal children of desert regions. *Cognitive Psychology, 13,* 434–460.

Keasey, C. B. (1971). Social participation as a factor in the moral development of preadolescents. *Developmental Psychology, 5,* 216–220.

Keating, D., & Clark, L. V. (1980). Development of physical and social reasoning in adolescence. *Developmental Psychology, 16,* 23–30.

Kee, D. W. (1986). Computer play. In A. W. Gottfried & C. C. Brown (Eds.), *Play interactions: The contribution of play materials and parental involvement to children's development.* Lexington, MA: Lexington Books.

Kee, D. W. (1994). Developmental differences in associative memory: Strategy use, mental effort, and knowledge-access interactions. In H. W. Reese (Ed.), *Advances in child development and behavior* (Vol. 25). New York: Academic Press.

Keith, J. (1985). Age in anthropological research. In R. H. Binstock & E. Shanus (Eds.), *Handbook of aging and the social sciences* (2nd ed.). New York: Van Nostrand Reinhold.

Keller, A., Ford, L. H., Jr., & Meachum, J. A. (1978). Dimensions of self-concept in preschool children. *Developmental Psychology, 14,* 483–489.

Keller, H., & Scholmerich, A. (1987). Infant vocalizations and parental reactions during the first four months of life. *Developmental Psychology, 23,* 62–67.

Kelley, M. L., Power, T. G., & Wimbush, D. D. (1992). Determinants of disciplinary practices in low-income Black mothers. *Child Development, 63,* 573–582.

Kelley-Buchanan, C. (1988). *Peace of mind during pregnancy: An A-Z guide to the substances that could affect your unborn baby.* New York: Facts on File Publications.

Kellman, P. J., & Spelke, E. S. (1983). Perception of partly occluded objects in infancy. *Cognitive Psychology, 15,* 483–524.

Kellman, P. J., Spelke, E. S., & Short, K. R. (1986). Infant perception of object unity from translatory motion in depth and vertical translation. *Child Development, 57,* 72–86.

Kempe, R. S., & Kempe, C. H. (1978). *Child abuse.* Cambridge, MA: Harvard University Press.

Kendall-Tackett, K. A., Williams, L. M., & Finkelhor, D. (1993). Impact of sexual abuse on children: A review and synthesis of recent empirical studies. *Psychological Bulletin, 113,* 164–180.

Kennell, J. H., Voos, D. K., & Klaus, M. H. (1979). Parent-infant bonding. In J. D. Osofsky (Ed.), *Handbook of infant development.* New York: Wiley.

Keough, J., & Sugden, D. (1985). *Movement skill development.* New York: MacMillan.

Kermoian, R., & Campos, J. J. (1988). Locomotor experience: A facilitator of spatial cognitive development. *Child Development, 59,* 908–917.

Kerns, K. A., & Berenbaum, S. A. (1991). Sex differences in spatial ability in children. *Behavior Genetics, 21,* 383–396.

Kerns, K. A., Klepec, L., & Cole, A. (1996). Peer relationships and preadolescents' perceptions of security in the child-mother relationship. *Developmental Psychology, 32,* 457–466.

Kerr, M., Lambert, W. W., & Bem, D. J. (1996). Life course sequelae of childhood shyness in Sweden: Comparison with the United States. *Developmental Psychology, 32,* 1100–1105.

Kerr, M., Lambert, W. W., Stattin, H., & Klackbengerg-Larsson, I. (1994). Stability of inhibition in a Swedish longitudinal sample. *Child Development, 65,* 138–146.

Kerwin, C., Ponterotto, J. G., Jackson, B. L., & Harris, A. (1993). Racial identity in biracial children: A qualitative investigation. *Journal of Counseling Psychology, 40,* 221–231.

Kessel, B. (1995). Reproductive cycles in women: Quality of life impact. In B. P. Sachs, R. Beard, E. Papiernik, & C. Russell (Eds.), *Reproductive health care for women and babies* (pp. 18–39). New York: Oxford University Press.

Kessen, W. (1965). *The child.* New York: Wiley.

Kessen, W. (1975). *Childhood in China.* New Haven, CT: Yale University Press.

Kessen, W. (1996). American psychology just before Piaget. *Psychological Science, 7,* 196–199.

Kessner, D. M. (1973). *Infant death: An analysis by maternal risk and health care.* Washington, D.C.: National Academy of Sciences.

Kett, J. F. (1977). *Rites of passage. Adolescence in America, 1790 to the present.* New York: Basic Books.

Khoury, M. S. and the Genetics Working Group (1996). From genes to public health: The applications of genetic technology in disease prevention. *American Journal of Public Health, 86,* 1717–1722.

Kilpatrick, A. (1992). *Long-range effects of child and adolescent sexual experiences: Myths, mores, and menaces.* Hillsdale, NJ: Erlbaum.

Kimura, D. (1992). Sex differences in the brain. *Scientific American, 267,* 119–125.

Kinney, D. A. (1993). From nerds to normals: The recovery of identity among adolescents from middle school to high school. *Sociology of Education, 44,* 21–40.

Kinsbourne, M. (1989). Mechanisms and development of hemisphere specialization in children. In C. R. Reynolds & E. Fletcher-Janzen (Eds.), *Handbook of clinical child neuropsychology.* New York: Plenum Press.

Kirchner, J. (1998, January 25). State making adoption process easier. Associated Press, as reported in the *Athens Banner Herald,* p. 4A.

Kisilevsky, B. S., & Muir, D. W. (1984). Neonatal habituation and dishabituation to tactile stimulation during sleep. *Developmental Psychology, 20,* 367–373.

Kitson, G. C., & Morgan, L. A. (1990). The multiple consequences of divorce: A decade review. *Journal of Marriage and the Family, 52,* 913–924.

Kitzinger, C., & Wilkinson, S. (1995). Transitions from heterosexuality to lesbianism: The discursive production of lesbian identities. *Developmental Psychology, 31,* 95–104.

Klahr, D. (1992). Information-processing approaches to cognitive development. In M. H. Bernstein & M. E. Lamb (Eds.), *Developmental psychology: An advanced textbook* (3rd ed., pp. 273–335). Hillsdale, NJ: Erlbaum.

Klahr, D., & MacWhinney, B. (1997). Information processing. In D. Kuhn & R. S. Siegler (Eds.), *Cognitive, language, and perceptual development* (Vol. 2). In B. Damon (General Editor), *Handbook of child psychology* (pp. 631–678). New York: Wiley.

Klaus, M. H., & Kennell, J. H. (1976). *Maternal-infant bonding.* St. Louis, MO: C. V. Mosby.

Klaus, M. H., & Kennell, J. H. (1982). *Parent-infant bonding.* St. Louis: Mosby.

Klein, D. M., & White, J. M. (1996). *Family theories: An introduction.* Thousand Oaks, CA: Sage.

Klimes-Dougan, B., & Kistner, J. (1990). Physically abused preschoolers' responses to peers' distress. *Developmental Psychology, 26,* 599–602.

Kline, M., Tschann, J. M., Johnston, J. R., & Wallerstein, J. S. (1989). Children's adjustment to joint and sole physical custody families. *Developmental Psychology, 25,* 430–438.

Klineberg, O. (1963). Negro-white differences in intelligence test performance: A new look at an old problem. *American Psychologist, 18,* 198–203.

Klinnert, M. D., Emde, R. N., Butterfield, P., & Campos, J. J. (1986). Social referencing: The infant's use of emotional signals from a friendly adult with mother present. *Developmental Psychology, 22,* 427–432.

Kobasigawa, A. (1974). Utilization of retrieval cues by children in recall. *Child Development, 45,* 127–134.

Kochanska, G. (1991). Socialization and temperament in the development of guilt and conscience. *Child Development, 62,* 1379–1392.

Kochanska, G. (1992). Children's interpersonal influence with mothers and peers. *Developmental Psychology, 28,* 491–499.

Kochanska, G. (1993). Toward a synthesis of parental socialization and child temperament in early development of conscience. *Child Development, 64,* 325–347.

Kochanska, G. (1995). Children's temperament, mother's discipline, and security of attachment: Multiple pathways to emerging internalization. *Child Development, 66,* 597–615.

Kochanska, G. (1997a). Multiple pathways to conscience for children with different temperaments: From toddlerhood to age 5. *Developmental Psychology, 33,* 228–240.

Kochanska, G. (1997b). Mutually responsive orientation between mothers and their young: Implications for early socialization. *Child Development, 68,* 94–112.

Kochanska, G., & Aksan, N. (1995). Mother-child mutually positive affect, the quality of child compliance to requests and prohibitions, and maternal control as correlates of early internalization. *Child Development, 66,* 236–254.

Kochanska, G., Casey, R. J., & Fukumoto, A. (1995). Toddlers' sensitivity to standard violations. *Child Development, 66,* 643–656.

Kochanska, G., Murray, K., Jacques, T. Y., Koenig, A. L., & Vandegeest, K. A. (1996). Inhibitory control in young children and its role in emerging internalization. *Child Development, 67,* 490–507.

Kochanska, G., Padavich, D. L., & Koenig, A. L. (1996). Children's narratives about hypothetical moral dilemmas and objective measures of their conscience: Mutual relations and socialization antecedents. *Child Development, 67,* 1420–1436.

Kochenderfer, B. J., & Ladd, G. W. (1996). Peer victimization: Cause or consequence of school maladjustment? *Child Development, 67,* 1305–1317.

Koff, E., & Rierdan, J. (1995). Early adolescent girls' understanding of menstruation. *Women and Health, 22,* 1–19.

Kohlberg, L. (1963). The development of children's orientations toward a moral order: I. Sequence in the development of moral thought. *Vita Humana, 6,* 11–33.

Kohlberg, L. (1966). A cognitive-developmental analysis of children's sex-role concepts and attitudes. In E. E. Maccoby (Ed.), *The development of sex differences.* Stanford, CA: Stanford University Press.

Kohlberg, L. (1975, June). The cognitive-developmental approach to moral education. *Phi Delta Kappan,* pp. 670–677.

Kohlberg, L. (1984). *Essays on moral development* (Vol. 2). *The psychology of moral development.* San Francisco: Harper & Row.

Kohlberg, L., Yaeger, J., & Hjertholm, E. (1968). Private speech: Four studies and a review of theories. *Child Development, 39,* 691–736.

Kohn, M. L. (1979). The effects of social class on parental values and practices. In D. Reiss & H. A. Hoffman (Eds.), *The American family: Dying or developing?* (pp. 49–68). New York: Plenum.

Kolata, G. B. (1986). Obese children: A growing problem. *Science, 232,* 20–21.

Kolb, B., & Fantie, B. (1989). Development of the child's brain and behavior. In C. R. Reynolds & E. Fletcher-Janzen (Eds.), *Handbook of clinical child neuropsychology.* New York: Plenum Press.

Kopp, C. B. (1983). Risk factors in development. In M. M. Haith & J. J. Campos (Eds.), *Handbook of child psychology.* (Vol. 2). *Infancy and developmental psychobiology.* New York: Wiley.

Kopp, C. B. (1987). The growth of self-regulation: Caregivers and children. In N. Eisenberg (Ed.), *Contemporary topics in developmental psychology.* New York: Wiley.

Kopp, C. B. (1989). Regulation of distress and negative emotions: A developmental view. *Developmental Psychology, 25,* 343–354.

Kopp, C. B., & Kaler, S. R. (1989). Risk in infancy. *American Psychologist, 44,* 224–230.

Korner, A. F. (1972). State as a variable, as obstacle and as mediator of stimulation in infant research. *Merrill-Palmer Quarterly, 18,* 77–94.

Korner, A. F. (1996). Reliable individual differences in preterm infants' excitation management. *Child Development, 67,* 1793–1805.

Kortenhaus, C. M., & Demarest, J. (1993). Gender role stereotyping in children's literature: An update. *Sex Roles, 28,* 219–232.

Kovacs, D. M., Parker, J. G., & Hoffman, L. W. (1996). Behavioral, affective, and social correlates of involvement in cross-sex friendships in elementary school. *Child Development, 67,* 2269–2286.

Kowal, A., & Kramer, L. (1997). Children's understanding of parental differential treatment. *Child Development, 68,* 113–126.

Krauss, R. M., & Glucksberg, S. (1977). Social and nonsocial speech. *Scientific American, 236,* 100–105.

Kreutzer, M. A., Leonard, C., & Flavell, J. H. (1975). An interview study of children's knowledge about memory. *Monographs of the Society for Research in Child Development, 40,* 1, Serial No. 159.

Krevans, J., & Gibbs, J. C. (1996). Parents' use of inductive discipline: Relations to children's empathy and prosocial behavior. *Child Development, 67,* 3263–3277.

Kroger, J. (1995). The differentiation of "firm" and "developmental" foreclosure identity statuses: A longitudinal study. *Journal of Adolescent Research, 10,* 317–337.

Kroger, J. (1996). Identity, regression, and development. *Journal of Adolescence, 19,* 203–222.

Kroll, J. (1977). The concept of childhood in the Middle Ages. *Journal of the History of the Behavioral Sciences, 13,* 384–393.

Kruger, A. C. (1992). The effect of peer and adult-child transductive discussions on moral reasoning. *Merrill-Palmer Quarterly, 38,* 191–211.

Kruger, A. C., & Tomasello, M. (1986). Transactive discussions with peers and adults. *Developmental Psychology, 22,* 681–685.

Kuczynski, L. (1983). Reasoning, prohibitions, and motivations for compliance. *Developmental Psychology, 19,* 126–134.

Kuczynski, L., & Kochanska, G. (1995). Function and content of maternal demands: Developmental significance of early demands for competent action. *Child Development, 66,* 616–628.

Kuczynski, L., Zahn-Waxler, C., & Radke-Yarrow, M. (1987). Development and content of imitation in the second and third years of life: A socialization perspective. *Developmental Psychology, 23,* 276–282.

Kuebli, J., Butler, S., & Fivush, R. (1995). Mother-child talk about past emotions: Relations of maternal language and child gender over time. *Cognition and Emotion, 9,* 265–283.

Kuhn, D. (1992). Cognitive development. In M. H. Bornstein & M. E. Lamb (Eds.), *Developmental psychology. An advanced textbook* (3rd ed.). Hillsdale, NJ: Erlbaum.

Kuhn, D., Kohlberg, L., Langer, J., & Haan, N. (1977). The development of formal operations in logical and moral judgment. *Genetic Psychology Monographs, 95,* 97–188.

Kuhn, D., Nash, S. C., & Brucken, L. (1978). Sex-role concepts of two- and three-year-olds. *Child Development, 49,* 445–451.

Kulik, J. A., & Kulik, C. C. (1992). Meta-analytic findings on grouping programs. *Gifted Child Quarterly, 36,* 73–77.

Kuller, J. A. (1996). Chorionic villus sampling. In J. A. Kuller, N. C. Cheschier, & R. C. Cefalo (Eds.), *Prenatal diagnosis and reproductive genetics,* (pp. 145–158). St. Louis: Mosby.

Kuller, J. A., Cheschier, N. C., & Cefalo, R. C. (1996). *Prenatal diagnosis and reproductive genetics.* St. Louis: Mosby.

Kunkel, D., & Roberts, D. (1991). Young minds and marketplace value: Issues in children's advertising. *Journal of Social Issues, 47*(1), 57–72.

Kurdek, L. A., & Fine, M. A. (1994). Family acceptance and family control as predictors of adjustment in young adolescents: Linear, curvilinear, or interactive effects? *Child Development, 65,* 1137–1146.

Kurdek, L. A., Fine, M. A., & Sinclair, R. J. (1995). School adjustment in sixth graders: Parenting transitions, peer climate, and peer norm effects. *Child Development, 66,* 430–445.

Kurtz, B. E. (1990). Cultural influences on children's cognitive and meta-cognitive development. In W. Schneider & F. E. Wienert (Eds.), *Interactions among aptitude, strategies, and knowledge in cognitive performance.* Hillsdale, NJ: Erlbaum.

Laboratory of Comparative Human Cognition (1983). Culture and cognitive development. In W. Kessen (Ed.), *Handbook of child psychology* (Vol. 1). *History, theory, and methods* (4th ed.). New York: Wiley.

Ladd, G. W. (1990). Having friends, keeping friends, making friends, and being liked by peers in the classroom: Predictors of children's early school adjustment. *Child Development, 61,* 1081–1100.

Ladd, G. W., & Golter, B. S. (1988). Parents' management of preschoolers' peer relations: Is it related to children's social competence? *Developmental Psychology, 24,* 109–117.

Ladd, G. W., & Hart, C. H. (1992). Creating informal play opportunities: Are parents' and preschoolers' initiations related to children's competence with peers? *Developmental Psychology, 28,* 1179–1187.

Ladd, G. W., Kochenderfer, B. J., & Coleman, C. C. (1996). Friendship quality as a predictor of young children's early school adjustment. *Child Development, 67,* 1103–1118.

Ladd, G. W., Kochenderfer, B. J., & Coleman, C. C. (1997). Classroom peer acceptance, friendship, and victimization: Distinct relational systems that contribute uniquely to children's school adjustment. *Child Development, 68,* 1181–1197.

Ladd, G. W., & Price, J. M. (1987). Predicting children's social and school adjustment following the transition from preschool to kindergarten. *Child Development, 58,* 1168–1189.

Ladd, G. W., Price, J. M., & Hart, C. H. (1988). Predicting preschoolers' play status from their playground behaviors. *Child Development, 59,* 986–992.

La Freniere, P., Strayer, F. F., & Gauthier, R. (1984). The emergence of same-sex affiliative preferences among preschool peers: A developmental ethological perspective. *Child Development, 55,* 1958–1965.

Lamaze, F. (1958). *Painless childbirth: Psychoprophylactic method.* London: Burke.

Lamb, M. E. (1975). Fathers: Forgotten contributors to child development. *Human Development, 18,* 245–266.

Lamb, M. E. (1981). *The role of the father in child development.* New York: Wiley.

Lamb, M. E., Easterbrooks, M. A., & Holden, G. W. (1980). Reinforcement and punishment among preschoolers: Characteristics, effects, and correlates. *Child Development, 51,* 1230–1236.

Lamb, M. E., & Oppenheim, D. (1989). Fatherhood and father-child relations. Five years of research. In S. H. Cath, A. Gurwitt, & L. Gunsberg (Eds.), *Fathers and their families.* Hillsdale, NJ: Erlbaum.

Lamborn, S. D., Mounts, N. S., Steinberg, L., & Dornbusch, S. M. (1991). Patterns of competence and adjustment among adolescents from authoritative, authoritarian, indulgent, and neglectful families. *Child Development, 62,* 1049–1065.

Lamborn, S. D., & Steinberg, L. (1993). Emotional autonomy redux: Revising Ryan and Lynch. *Child Development, 64,* 483–499.

Landau, S., Milich, S., & Lorch, E. P. (1992). Visual attention to and comprehension of television in attention-deficit hyperactivity disordered and normal boys. *Child Development, 63,* 928–937.

Langlois, J. H. (1986). From the eye of the beholder to behavioral reality: Development of social behaviors and social relations as a function of physical attractiveness. In C. P. Herman, M. P. Zanna, & E. T. Higgins (Eds.), *Physical appearance, stigma, and social behavior: The Ontario Symposium* (Vol. 3). Hillsdale, NJ: Erlbaum.

Langlois, J. H., & Downs, A. C. (1979). Peer relations as a function of physical attractiveness: The eye of the beholder or behavioral reality. *Child Development, 50,* 409–418.

Langlois, J. H., Ritter, J. M., Casey, R. J., & Sawin, D. B. (1995). Infant attractiveness predicts maternal behaviors and attitudes. *Developmental Psychology, 31,* 464–472.

Langlois, J. H., Ritter, J. M., Roggman, L. A., & Vaughn, L. S. (1991). Facial diversity and infant preferences for attractive faces. *Developmental Psychology, 27,* 79–84.

Langlois, J. H., Roggman, L. A., Casey, R. J., Ritter, J. M., Reiser-Danner, L. A., & Jenkins, V. Y. (1987). Infant preferences for attractive faces: Rudiments of a stereotype? *Developmental Psychology, 23,* 363–369.

Langlois, J. H., Roggman, L. A., & Rieser-Danner, L. A. (1990). Infants' differential social responses to attractive and unattractive faces. *Developmental Psychology, 26,* 153–159.

Lanza, E. (1992). Can bilingual 2-year-olds code-switch? *Journal of Child Language, 19,* 633–658.

Laosa, L. M. (1981). Maternal behavior: Sociocultural diversity in modes of family interaction. In R. W. Henderson (Ed.), *Parent-child interaction: Theory, research, and prospects* (pp. 125–167). Orlando, FL: Academic Press.

Lapsley, D. K. (1996). *Moral psychology.* Boulder, CO: Westview.

Lapsley, D. K., Milstead, M., Quintana, S. M., Flannery, D., & Buss, R. R. (1986). Adolescent egocentrism and formal operations: Tests of a theoretical assumption. *Developmental Psychology, 22,* 800–807.

Larroque, B., Kaminski, M., & Lelong, N. (1993). Effects on birth weight of alcohol and caffeine consumption during pregnancy. *American Journal of Epidemiology, 137,* 941–950.

Larson, R. W., & Ham, M. (1993). Stress and "storm and stress" in early adolescence: The relationship of negative events with dysphoric affect. *Developmental Psychology, 29,* 130–140.

Larson, R. W., & Richards, M. H. (1991). Daily companionship in late childhood and early adolescence: Changing developmental contexts. *Child Development, 62,* 284–300.

Larson, R. W., Richards, M. H., Moneta, G., Holmbeck, G., & Duckett, E. (1996). Changes in adolescents' daily interactions with their families from ages 10 to 18: Disengagement and transformation. *Developmental Psychology, 32,* 744–754.

Lazar, I., & Darlington, R. (1982). Lasting effects of early education: A report from the Consortium for Longitudinal Studies. *Monographs of the Society for Research in Child Development, 47,* 2–3, Serial No. 195.

Leal, L., Crays, N., & Moely, B. E. (1985). Training children to use a self-monitoring study strategy in preparation for recall: Maintenance and generalization effects. *Child Development, 56,* 643–653.

Leaper, C. (1994). *New directions for child development* (Vol. 65). *Childhood gender segregation: Causes and consequences.* San Francisco: Jossey-Bass.

Leaper, C., Anderson, K. J., & Sanders, P. (1998). Moderators of gender effects on parents' talk to their children. *Developmental Psychology, 34,* 3–27.

Leboyer, F. (1975). *Birth without violence.* New York: Knopf.

LeCapitaine, J. E. (1987). The relationship between emotional development and moral development and the differential impact of three psychological interventions on children. *Psychology in the Schools, 24,* 372–378.

Lefkowitz, M. M. (1981). Smoking during pregnancy: Long-term effects on offspring. *Developmental Psychology, 17,* 192–194.

Lehman, E. B., McKinley-Pace, M. J., Wilson, J. A., Savsky, M. D., & Woodson, M. E. (1997). Direct and indirect measures of intentional forgetting in children and adults: Evidence for retrieval inhibition and reinstatement. *Journal of Experimental Child Psychology, 64,* 295–316.

Leinbach, M. D., & Fagot, B. I. (1986). Acquisition of gender labeling: A test for toddlers. *Sex Roles, 15,* 655–666.

Leinbach, M. D., & Fagot, B. I. (1993). Categorical habituation to male and female faces: Gender schematic processing in infancy. *Infant Behavior and Development, 16,* 317–322.

LeMare, L. J., & Rubin, K. H. (1987). Perspective taking and peer interaction: Structural and developmental analyses. *Child Development, 58,* 306–315.

Lenneberg, E. H. (1967). *Biological foundations of language.* New York: Wiley.

Leon, M. (1984). Rules mothers and sons use to integrate intent and damage information in their moral judgments. *Child Development, 55,* 2106–2113.

Lepper, M. R. (1985). Microcomputers in education: Motivation and social issues. *American Psychologist, 40,* 1–18.

Lepper, M. R., & Gurtner, J. (1989). Children and computers: Approaching the twenty-first century. *American Psychologist, 44,* 170–178.

Lerner, R. M. (1991). Changing organism-context relations as the basic process of development: A developmental contextual perspective. *Developmental Psychology, 27,* 27–32.

Lerner, R. M. (1996). Relative plasticity, integration, temporality, and diversity in human development: A developmental contextual perspective about theory, process, and method. *Developmental Psychology, 32,* 781–786.

Lerner, R. M., & von Eye, A. (1992). Sociobiology and human development: Arguments and evidence. *Human Development, 35,* 12–33.

Lester, B. M. (1984). A biosocial model of infant crying. In L. P. Lipsitt (Eds.), *Advances in infancy research.* Norwood, NJ: Ablex.

Lester, B. M., Corwin, M. J., Sepkoski, C., Seifer, R., Peucker, M., McLaughlin, S., & Golub, H. L. (1991). Neurobehavioral syndromes in cocaine-exposed newborn infants. *Child Development, 62,* 694–705.

Lester, B. M., Hoffman, J., & Brazelton, T. B. (1985). The rhythmic structure of mother-infant interactions in term and preterm infants. *Child Development, 56,* 15–27.

Lester, B. M., Kotelchuck, M., Spelke, E., Sellers, M. J., & Klein, R. E. (1974). Separation protest in Guatemalan infants: Cross-cultural and cognitive findings. *Developmental Psychology, 10,* 79–85.

LeVay, S. (1996). *Queer science: The use and abuse of research into homosexuality.* Cambridge, MA: MIT Press.

Leve, L. D., & Fagot, B. I. (1997). Gender-role socialization and discipline processes in one- and two-point families. *Sex Roles, 36,* 1–21.

Levin, I., & Druyan, S. (1993). When sociocognitive transaction among peers fails: The case of misconceptions in science. *Child Development, 64,* 1571–1591.

LeVine, R. A., Dixon, S., LeVine, S., Richman, A., Liederman, P. H., Keefer, C. H., & Brazelton, T. B. (1994). *Child care and culture: Lessons from Africa.* New York: Cambridge University Press.

Levinson, D. (1989). *Family violence in cross-cultural perspective.* Newbury Park, CA: Sage.

Leviton, A. (1993). Coffee, caffeine, and reproductive hazards in humans. In S. Garattini (Ed.), *Monographs of the Mario Negri Institute for Pharmacological Research, Milan: Caffeine, Coffee, and Health* (pp. 348–358). New York: Raven Press.

Levitt, M. J., Weber, R. A., Clark, M. C., & McDonnell, P. (1985). Reciprocity of exchange in toddler sharing behavior. *Developmental Psychology, 21,* 122–123.

Levy, F., Hay, D. A., Mcstephen, M., Wood, C., & Waldman, I. (1997). Attention-deficit hyperactivity disorder: A category or a continuum? Genetic analysis of a large-scale twin study. *Journal of the American Academy of Child and Adolescent Psychiatry, 36,* 737–744.

Levy, G. D., Taylor, M. G., & Gelman, S. A. (1995). Traditional and evaluative aspects of flexibility in gender roles, social conventions, moral rules, and physical laws. *Child Development, 66,* 515–531.

Levy-Shiff, R. (1994). Individual and contextual correlates of marital change across the transition to parenthood. *Developmental Psychology, 30,* 591–601.

Levy-Shiff, R., Goldschmidt, I., & Har-Even, D. (1991). Transition to parenthood in adoptive families. *Developmental Psychology, 27,* 131–140.

Lewin, L. M., Hops, H., Davis, B., & Dishion, T. J. (1993). Multimethod comparison of similarity in school adjustment of siblings and unrelated children. *Developmental Psychology, 24,* 963–969.

Lewis, C. Freeman, N. H., Kyriakidou, C., Maridaki-Kassotaki, K., & Berridge, D. M. (1996). Social influences on false belief access: Specific sibling influences or general apprenticeship? *Child Development, 67,* 2930–2947.

Lewis, M., Alessandri, S. M., & Sullivan, M. W. (1990). Violation of expectancy, loss of control and anger expressions in young infants. *Developmental Psychology, 26,* 745–751.

Lewis, M., Alessandri, S. M., & Sullivan, M. W. (1992). Differences in shame and pride as a function of children's gender and task difficulty. *Child Development, 63,* 630–638.

Lewis, M., & Brooks-Gunn, J. (1979). *Social cognition and the acquisition of self.* New York: Plenum Press.

Lewis, M., & Rosenblum, M. A. (1975). *Friendship and peer relations.* New York: Wiley.

Lewis, M., Stanger, C., & Sullivan, M. W. (1989). Deception in 3-year-olds. *Developmental Psychology, 24,* 434–440.

Lewis, M., Sullivan, M. W., Stanger, C., & Weiss, M. (1989). Self-development and self-conscious emotions. *Child Development, 60,* 146–156.

Lewontin, R. C. (1976). Race and intelligence. In N. J. Block & G. Dworkin (Eds.), *The IQ Controversy.* New York: Pantheon.

Leyens, J. P., Parke, R. D., Camino, L., & Berkowitz, L. (1975). Effects of movie violence on aggression in a field setting as a function of group dominance and cohesion. *Journal of Personality and Social Psychology, 32,* 346–360.

Liben, L. S., & Signorella, M. L. (1993). Gender-schematic processing in children: The role of initial interrpretations of stimuli. *Developmental Psychology, 29,* 141–149.

Lidz, C. S., (1997). Dynamic assessment approaches. In D. P. Flanagan, J. Genshaft, & P. L. Harrison (Eds.), *Contemporary intellectual assessment: Theories, tests, and issues.* New York: Guilford.

Lieberman, P. (1984). *The biology and evolution of language.* Cambridge: Harvard University Press.

Liebert, R. M., & Baron, R. A. (1972). Some immediate effects of televised violence on children's behavior. *Developmental Psychology, 6,* 469–475.

Liebert, R. M., & Sprafkin, J. (1988). *The early window: Effects of television on children and youth* (3rd ed.). New York: Pergamon Press.

Lieven, E. V. M. (1994). Crosslinguistic and crosscultural aspects of language addressed to children. In C. Gallaway & B. J. Richards (Eds.), *Input and interaction in language acquisition.* Cambridge, England: Cambridge University Press.

Lillard, A. S. (1993). Pretend play skills and the child's theory of mind. *Child Development, 64,* 348–371.

Lin, C. (1993a). Breech presentation. In C. Lin, M. S. Verp, & R. E. Sabbagha (Eds.), *The high-risk fetus: pathophysiology, diagnosis, management.* New York: Springer-Verlag.

Lin, C. (1993b). Fetal growth retardation. In C. Lin, M. S. Verp, & R. E. Sabbagha (Eds.), *The high-risk fetus: Pathophysiology, diagnosis, management.* New York: Springer-Verlag.

Lin, C. C., & Fu, V. R. (1990). A comparison of child-rearing practices among Chinese, immigrant Chinese, and Caucasian-American parents. *Child Development, 61,* 429–433.

Linn, M. C., de Benedictis, T., & Delucchi, K. (1982). Adolescent reasoning about advertisements: Preliminary investigations. *Child Development, 53,* 1599–1613.

Linn, M. C., & Petersen, A. C. (1985). Emergence and characterization of sex differences in spatial ability: A meta-analysis. *Child Development, 56,* 1479–1498.

Lipsitt, L. P. (1979). Critical conditions in infancy: A psychological perspective. *American Psychologist, 34,* 973–980.

Lipsitt, L. P., & Kaye, H. (1964). Conditioned sucking in the human newborn. *Psychonomic Science, 1,* 29–30.

Liss, M. B. (1994). Child abuse: Is there a mandate for researchers to report. *Ethics & Behavior, 4,* 133–146.

Littenberg, R., Tulkin, S., & Kagan, J. (1971). Cognitive components of separation anxiety. *Developmental Psychology, 4,* 387–388.

Little, A. H., Lipsitt, L. P., & Rovee-Collier, C. K. (1984). Classical conditioning and retention of the infant's eyelid response: Effects of age and interstimulus interval. *Journal of Experimental Child Psychology, 37,* 512–524.

Littschwager, J. C., & Markman, E. M. (1994). Sixteen- and 24-month-olds' use of mutual exclusivity as a default assumption in second-label learning. *Developmental Psychology, 30,* 955–968.

Livesley, W. J., & Bromley, D. B. (1973). *Person perception in childhood and adolescence.* London: Wiley.

Livson, N., & Peskin, H. (1980). Perspectives on adolescence from longitudinal research. In J. Adelson (Ed.), *Handbook of adolescent psychology* (pp. 47–98). New York: Wiley.

Llamas, C. & Diamond, A. (April, 1991). *Development of frontal cortex abilities in children between 3–8 years of age.* Paper presented at meeting of the Society for Research in Child Development, Seattle, WA.

Lobel, M. (1994). Conceptualizations, measurement, and effects of prenatal maternal stress on birth outcomes. *Journal of Behavioral Medicine, 17,* 225–272.

Lobel, T. E., & Menashri, J. (1993). Relations of conceptions of gender-role transgressions and gender constancy to gender-typed toy preferences. *Developmental Psychology, 29,* 150–155.

Locke, J. (1913). *Some thoughts concerning education.* Sections 38 and 40. London: Cambridge University Press. (Original work published 1690).

Locke, J. L. (1997). A theory of neurolinguistic development. *Brain and Language, 58,* 265–326.

Loeber, R., & Stouthamer-Loeber, M. (1998). Development of juvenile aggression and violence: Some common misconceptions and controversies. *American Psychologist, 53,* 242–259.

Loehlin, J. C. (1985). Fitting heredity-environment models jointly to twin and adoption data from the California Psychological Inventory. *Behavior Genetics, 15,* 199–221.

Loehlin, J. C. (1992). *Genes and environment in personality development.* Newbury Park, CA: Sage.

Loehlin, J. C., Lindzey, G., & Spuhler, J. N. (1975). *Race differences in intelligence.* New York: W. H. Freeman.

Loehlin, J. C., & Nichols, R. C. (1976). *Heredity, environment, and personality.* Austin: University of Texas Press. Lerner, R. M. (1991).

Loftus, E. F., & Pickrell, J. E. (1995). The formation of false memories. *Psychiatric Annals, 25,* 720–725.

London, P. (1970). The rescuers: Motivational hypotheses about Christians who saved Jews from the Nazis. In J. Macaulay & L. Berkowitz (Eds.), *Altruism and helping behavior.* Orlando, FL: Academic Press.

Long, N., & Forehand, R. (1987). The effects of parental divorce and marital conflict on children: An overview. *Journal of Developmental and Behavioral Pediatrics, 8,* 292–296.

Longstreth, L., Davis, B., Carter, L., Flint, D., Owen, J., Rickert, M., & Taylor, E. (1981). Separation of home intellectual environment and maternal IQ as determinants of child IQ. *Developmental Psychology, 17,* 532–541.

Lorber, J. (1986). Dismantling Noah's ark. *Sex Roles, 14,* 567–580.

Lord, S. E., Eccles, J. S., & McCarthy, K. A. (1994). Surviving the junior high school transition: Family processes and self-perceptions as protective and risk factors. *Journal of Early Adolescence, 14,* 162–199.

Lorenz, K. Z. (1937). The companion in the bird's world. *Auk, 54,* 245–273.

Lorenz, K. Z. (1943). The innate forms of possible experience. *Zeitschrift fur Tierpsychologie, 5,* 233–409.

Lorsbach, T. C., & Reimer, J. F. (1997). Developmental changes in the inhibition of previously relevant information. *Journal of Experimental Child Psychology, 64,* 317–342.

Loupe, D. (1997, May 8). No consensus on best way to teach reading. *Atlanta Constitution,* C5.

Lozoff, B. (1989). Nutrition and behavior. *American Psychologist, 44,* 231–236.

Lubart, T.I. (1994). Creativity. In R. J. Sternberg (Eds.), *Thinking and problem solving* (pp. 289–322). San Diego: Academic Press.

Lubart, T. I., & Sternberg, R. J. (1995). An investment approach to creativity: Theory and data. In S. M. Smith, T. B. Ward, & R. A. Finke (Eds.), *The creative cognition approach* (pp. 269–302). Cambridge, MA: MIT Press.

Ludemann, P. M. (1991). Generalized discrimination of positive facial expressions by seven- and ten-month-old infants. *Child Development, 62,* 55–67.

Luecke-Aleksa, D., Anderson, D. R., Collins, P. A., & Schmitt, K. L. (1995). Gender constancy and television viewing. *Developmental Psychology, 31,* 773–780.

Lummis, M., & Stevenson, H. W. (1990). Gender differences in beliefs and achievement: A cross-cultural study. *Developmental Psychology, 26,* 254–263.

Luria, A. R. (1961). *The role of speech in the regulation of normal and abnormal behavior.* New York: Liveright Publishing.

Luster, T., & Dubow, E. (1992). Home environment and maternal intelligence as predictors of verbal intelligence: A comparison of preschool and school-age children. *Merrill-Palmer Quarterly, 38,* 151–175.

Luster, T., & McAdoo, H. (1996). Family and child influences on educational attainment: A secondary analysis of the High/Scope Perry preschool data. *Developmental Psychology, 32,* 26–39.

Lustig, J. L., Wolchik, S. A., & Braver, S. L. (1992). Social support in chumships and adjustment in children of divorce. *American Journal of Community Psychology, 20,* 393–399.

Lynch, M. P., Eilers, R. E., Oller, D. K., & Urbano, R. C. (1990). Innateness, experience, and music perception. *Psychological Science, 1,* 272–276.

Lynn, R. (1997). Direct evidence for a genetic basis for black-white differences in IQ. *American Psychologist, 52,* 73–74.

Lyon, T. D., & Flavell, J. H. (1993). Young children's understanding of forgetting over time. *Child Development, 64,* 789–800.

Lyons-Ruth, K., Alpern, L., & Repacholi, B. (1993). Disorganized infant attachment classification and maternal psychosocial problems as predictors of hostile-aggressive behavior in the preschool classroom. *Child Development, 64,* 572–585.

Lyons-Ruth, K., Connell, D. B., Grunebaum, H., & Botein, S. (1990). Infants at social risk: Maternal depression and family support services as mediators of infant development and security of attachment. *Child Development, 61,* 85–98.

Lyons-Ruth, K., Easterbrooks, M. A., & Cibelli, C. D. (1997). Infant attachment strategies, infant mental lag, and maternal depressive symptoms: Predictors of internalizing and externalizing problems at age 7. *Developmental Psychology, 33,* 681–692.

Lytton, H. (1990). Child and parent effects in boys' conduct disorder. A reinterpretation. *Developmental Psychology, 26,* 683–697.

Lytton, H., & Romney, D. M. (1991). Parents' differential socialization of boys and girls: A meta-analysis. *Psychological Bulletin, 109,* 267–296.

Maccoby, E. E. (1980). *Social development.* San Diego, CA: Harcourt Brace Jovanovich.

Maccoby, E. E. (1988). Gender as a social category. *Developmental Psychology, 24,* 755–765.

Maccoby, E. E. (1990). Gender and relationships: A developmental account. *American Psychologist, 45,* 513–520.

Maccoby, E. E. (1992). Family structure and children's adjustment: Is quality of parenting the major mediator? In E. M. Hetherington & W. G. Clingempeel. Coping with marital transitions. *Monographs of the Society for Research in Child Development, 57,* Nos. 2–3, Serial No. 227.

Maccoby, E. E., & Jacklin, C. N. (1974). *The psychology of sex differences.* Stanford, CA: Stanford University Press.

Maccoby, E. E., & Martin, J. A. (1983). Socialization in the context of the family: Parent-child interaction. In E. M. Hetherington (Ed.; P. H. Mussen, General Ed.), *Handbook of child psychology:* (Vol. 4). *Socialization, personality, and social development* (pp. 1–101). New York: Wiley.

MacDonald, K. (1992). Warmth as a developmental construct: An evolutionary analysis. *Child Development, 63,* 753–773.

McFarlane, A. (1977). *The psychology of childbirth.* Cambridge, MA: Harvard University Press.

MacGregor, S. N., & Chasnoff, I. J. (1993). Substance abuse in pregnancy. In C. Lin, M. S. Verp, & R. E. Sabbagha (Eds.), *The high-risk fetus: Pathophysiology, diagnosis, management.* New York: Springer-Verlag.

Mac Iver, D., & Reuman, D. A. (1988, April). *Decision-making in the classroom and early adolescents' valuing of mathematics.* Paper presented at the annual meeting of the American Educational Research Association, New Orleans, LA.

MacKinnon-Lewis, C., Starnes, R., Volling, B., & Johnson, S. (1997). Perceptions of parenting as predictors of boys' sibling and peer relations. *Developmental Psychology, 33,* 1024–1031.

MacKinnon-Lewis, C., Volling, B. L., Lamb, M. E., Dechman, K., Rabiner, D., & Curtner, M. E. (1994). A cross-contextual analysis of boys' social competence: From family to school. *Developmental Psychology, 30,* 325–333.

MacPhee, D., Fritz, J., & Miller-Heyl, J. (1996). Ethnic variations in personal social networks and parenting. *Child Development, 67,* 3278–3295.

MacPhee, D., Ramey, C. T., & Yeates, K. O. (1984). Home environment and early cognitive development: Implications for intervention. In A. W. Gottfried (Ed.), *Home environment and early cognition development. Longitudinal research.* Orlando, FL: Academic Press.

Mahoney, J. L., & Cairns, R. B. (1997). Do extracurricular activities protect against early school dropout? *Developmental Psychology, 33,* 241–253.

Madison, L. S., Madison, J. K., & Adubato, S. A. (1986). Infant behavior and development in relation to fetal movement and habituation. *Child Development, 57,* 1475–1482.

Magenis, R. E., Overton, K. M., Chamberlin, J., Brady, T., & Lorrien, E (1977). Parental origin of the extra chromosome in Down's syndrome. *Human Genetics, 37,* 7–16.

Magnusson, D. (1995). Individual development: A holistic, integrated model. In P. Moen, G. H. Elder, Jr., & K. Luscher (Eds.), *Examining lives in context: Perspectives on the ecology of human development.* Washington, D. C.: American Psychological Association.

Mahler, M. S., Pine, F., & Bergman, A. (1975). *The psychological birth of the infant.* New York: Basic Books.

Main, M., & Cassidy, J. (1988). Categories of response to reunion with the parent at age 6: Predictable from infant attachment classifications and stable over a 1-month period. *Developmental Psychology, 24,* 415–426.

Main, M., & George, C. (1985). Responses of abused and disadvantaged toddlers to distress in age mates: A study in the day-care setting. *Developmental Psychology, 21,* 407–412.

Main, M., & Goldwyn, R. (1994). *Interview-based adult attachment classifications: Related to infant-mother and infant-father attachment.* Unpublished manuscript. University of California, Berkeley.

Main, M., & Solomon, J. (1990). Procedures for identifying infants as disorganized/disoriented during the Ainsworth Strange Situation. In M. T. Greenberg, D. Cicchetti, & E. M. Cummings (Eds.), *Attachment in the preschool years: Theory, research, and intervention.* Chicago: University of Chicago Press.

Main, M., & Weston, D. R. (1981). The quality of the toddler's relationship to mother and to father: Related to conflict and the readiness to establish new relationships. *Child Development, 52,* 932–940.

Malatesta, C. Z., Culver, C., Tesman, J. R., & Shepard, B. (1989). The development of emotion expression during the first two years of life. *Monographs of the Society for Research in Child Development, 54,* 1–2, Serial No. 219.

Malatesta, C. Z., Grigoryev, P., Lamb, C., Albin, M., & Culver, C. (1986). Emotional socialization and expressive development in preterm and full-term infants. *Child Development, 57,* 316–330.

Malatesta, C. Z., & Haviland, J. M. (1982). Learning display rules: The socialization of emotion expression in infancy. *Child Development, 53,* 991–1003.

Malina, R. M. (1990). Physical growth and performance during the transitional years (9–16). In R. Montemayer, G. R. Adams, & T. P. Gullotta (Eds.), *From childhood to adolescence: A transitional period?* (pp. 41–62) Newbury Park, CA: Sage.

Malinosky-Rummell, R., & Hansen, D. J. (1993). Long-term consequences of childhood physical abuse. *Psychological Bulletin, 114,* 68–79.

Mandler, J. (1997). Representation. In D. Kuhn & R. S. Siegler (Eds.), *Cognition, perception, and language* (Vol. 2). In W. Damon (Gen. Ed.), *Handbook of child psychology.* New York: Wiley.

Mandler, J. & McDonough, L. (1995). Long-term recall of event sequences in infancy. *Journal of Experimental Child Psychology, 59,* 457–474.

Mangelsdorf, S. C. (1992). Developmental changes in infant-stranger interaction. *Infant Behavior and Development, 15,* 191–208.

Mangelsdorf, S., Gunnar, M., Kestenbaum, R., Lang, S., & Andreas, D. (1990). Infant proneness-to-distress temperament, maternal personality, and mother-infant attachment. Associations and goodness of fit. *Child Development, 61,* 820–831.

Mangelsdorf, S. C., Plunkett, J. W., Dedrick, C. F., Berlin, M., Meisels, S. J., McHale, J. L., & Dichtellmiller, M. (1996). Attachment security in very low birth weight infants. *Developmental Psychology, 32,* 914–920.

Mangelsdorf, S. C., Shapiro, J. R., & Marzolf, D. (1995). Developmental and temperamental differences in emotion regulation in infancy. *Child Development, 66,* 1817–1828.

Mannuzza, S., Klein, R. G., Bessler, A., Malloy, P., & LaPadula, M. (1993). Adult outcome of hyperactive boys: Educational achievement, occupational rank, and psychiatric status. *Archives of General Psychiatry, 50,* 565–576.

Marcia, J. E. (1980). Identity in adolescence. In J. Adelson (Ed.), *Handbook of adolescent psychology.* New York: Wiley.

Marcia, J. E., Waterman, A. S., Matteson, D., Archer, S. C., & Orlofsky, J. L. (1993). *Ego identity: A handbook for psychosocial research.* New York: Springer-Verlag.

Marcus, D. E., & Overton, W. F. (1978). The development of cognitive gender constancy and sex-role preferences. *Child Development, 49,* 434–444.

Marcus, G. F., Pinker, S., Ullman, M., Hollander, M., Rosen, T. J., & Xu, F. (1992). Overregularization in language acquisition. *Monographs of the Society for Research in Child Development, 57,* (4, Serial No. 228).

Marean, G. C., Werner, L. A., & Kuhl, P. K. (1992). Vowel categorization by very young infants. *Developmental Psychology, 28,* 396–405.

Marini, Z., & Case, R. (1994). The development of abstract reasoning about the physical and social world. *Child Development, 65,* 147–159.

Markus, G. B., & Zajonc, R. B. (1977). Family configuration and intellectual development: A simulation. *Behavioral Science, 22,* 137–142.

Markstrom-Adams, C. (1992). A consideration of intervening factors in adolescent identity formation. In G. R. Adams, T. P.. Gullotta, & R. Montemayer (Eds.), *Adolescent identity formation.* (Vol. 4). *Advances in Adolescent Development.* Newbury Park, CA: Sage.

Markstrom-Adams, C., & Adams, G. R. (1995). Gender, ethnic group, and grade differences in psychosocial functioning during middle adolescence? *Journal of Youth and Adolescence, 24,* 397–417.

Marsh, H. W. (1989). Age and sex effects in multiple dimensions of self-concept: Preadolescence to early adulthood. *Journal of Educational Psychology, 81,* 417–430.

Marshall, W. A. (1977). *Human growth and its disorders.* Orlando, FL: Academic Press.

Marshall, N. L., Coll, C. G., Marx, F., McCartney, K., Keefe, N., & Ruh, J. (1997). After-school time and children's behavioral adjustment. *Merrill-Palmer Quarterly, 43,* 497–514.

Martin, C. L. (1989). Children's use of gender-related information in making social judgments. *Developmental Psychology, 25,* 80–88.

Martin, C. L. (1990). Attitudes and expectations about children with non-traditional gender roles. *Sex Roles, 22,* 151–165.

Martin, C. L. (1994). Cognitive influences on the development and maintenance of gender segregation. *New directions for Child Development, 65,* 35–51.

Martin, C. L., Eisenbud, L., & Rose, H. (1995). Children's gender-based reasoning about toys. *Child Development, 66,* 1453–1471.

Martin, C. L., & Halverson, C. F., Jr. (1981). A schematic processing model of sex typing and stereotyping in children. *Child Development, 52,* 1119–1134.

Martin, C. L., & Halverson, C. F., Jr. (1983). The effects of sex-typing schemas on young children's memory. *Child Development, 54,* 563–574.

Martin, C. L., & Halverson, C. F., Jr. (1987). The roles of cognition in sex-roles and sex-typing. In D. B. Carter (Ed.), *Current conceptions of sex roles and sex-typing: Theory and Research.* New York: Praeger.

Martin, C. L., & Little, J. K. (1990). The relation of gender understanding to children's sex-typed preferences and gender stereotypes. *Child Development, 61,* 1429–1439.

Martin, G. B., & Clark, R. D., III. (1982). Distress crying in neonates: Species and peer specificity. *Developmental Psychology, 18,* 3–9.

Martin, N. G., & Jardine, R. (1986). Eysenck's contributions to behavior genetics. In S. Modgil & C. Modgil (Eds.), *Hans Eysenck: Consensus and controversy.* Philadelphia: Falmer.

Martorell, R. (1980). Interrelationships between diet, infectious disease, and nutritional status. In L. S. Green & F. E. Johnston (Eds.), *Social and biological predictors of nutritional status, physical growth, and neurological development.* New York: Academic Press.

Marx, M. H., & Henderson, B. B. (1996). A fuzzy trace analysis of categorical inferences and instantial associations as a function of retention interval. *Cognitive Development, 11,* 551–569.

Marzolf, D. P., & DeLoache, J. S. (1994). Transfer in young children's understanding of spatial representation. *Child Development, 65,* 7–15.

Masataka, N. (1992). Early ontogeny of vocal behavior of Japanese infants in response to maternal speech. *Child Development, 63,* 1177–1185.

Masataka, N. (1996). Perception of motherese in a signed language by 6-month-old deaf infants. *Developmental Psychology, 32,* 874–879.

Masden, A. S., Coatsworth, J. D., Neeman, J., Gest, J. D., Tellegen, A., & Garmezy, N. (1995). The structure and coherence of competence from childhood through adolescence. *Child Development, 66,* 1635–1659.

Mason, C. A., Cauce, A. M., Gonzales, N., & Hiraga, Y. (1996). Neither too sweet nor too sour: Problem peers, maternal control, and problem behavior in African-American adolescents. *Child Development, 67,* 2115–2130.

Mason, M. G., & Gibbs, J. C. (1993). Social perspective taking and moral judgment among college students. *Journal of Adolescent Research, 8,* 109–123.

Masters, J. C., Ford, M. E., Arend, R., Grotevant, H. D., & Clark, L. V. (1979). Modeling and labeling as integrated determinants of children's sex-typed imitative behavior. *Child Development, 50,* 364–371.

Matejcek, Z., Dytrych, Z., & Schuller, V. (1979). The Prague study of children born from unwanted pregnancies. *International Journal of Mental Health, 7,* 63–74.

Matias, R., & Cohn, J. F. (1993). Are Max-specified infant facial expressions during face-to-face interaction consistent with differential emotions theory? *Developmental Psychology, 29,* 524–531.

Matsumoto, D. (1990). Cultural similarities and differences in display rules. *Motivation and Emotion, 14,* 195–214.

Matthews, K. A., Batson, C. D., Horn, J., & Rosenman, R. H. (1981). "Principles in his nature which interest him in the fortune of others": The heritability of empathic concern for others. *Journal of Personality, 49,* 237–247.

Matula, K. E., Huston, T. L., Grotevant, H. D., & Zamutt, A. (1992). Identity and dating commitment among women and men in college. *Journal of Youth and Adolescence, 21,* 339–356.

Mayberry, R. I. (1994). The importance of childhood to language acquisition: Evidence from American Sign Language. In J. C. Goodman & H. C. Nusbalm (Eds.), *The development of speech perception: The transition from speech sounds to spoken words.* Cambridge, MA: MIT Press.

Mayes, L. C., & Zigler, E. (1992). An observational study of the affective concomitants of mastery in infants. *Journal of Psychology and Psychiatry, 4,* 659–667.

McBride-Chang, C. (1996). Models of speech perception and phonological processing in reading. *Child Development, 67,* 1836–1856.

McCabe, A., & Peterson, C. (1991). Getting the story: A longitudinal study of parental styles in eliciting narratives and developing narrative skill. In A. McCabe & C. Peterson (Eds.), *Developing narrative structure* (pp. 217–253). Hillsdale, NJ: Erlbaum.

McCall, R. B. (1977). Challenges to a science of developmental psychology. *Child Development, 48,* 333–344.

McCall, R. B. (1983). A conceptual approach to early mental development. In M. Lewis (Ed.), *Origins of intelligence. Infancy and early childhood* (2nd ed.). New York: Plenum.

McCall, R. B., Applebaum, M. I., & Hogarty, P. S. (1973). Developmental changes in mental test performance. *Monographs of the Society for Research in Child Development, 38,* (3, Serial No. 150).

McCall, R. B., & Carriger, M. S. (1993). A meta-analysis of infant habituation and recognition memory performance as predictors of later IQ. *Child Development, 64,* 57–79.

McCartney, K., Harris, M. J., & Bernieri, F. (1990). Growing up and growing apart: A developmental meta-analysis of twin studies. *Psychological Bulletin, 107,* 226–237.

McCarton, C. M., Brooks-Gunn, J., Wallace, I. F., Bauer, C. R., Bennett, F. C., Bernbaum, J. C., Broyles, S., Casey, P. H., McCormick, M. C., Scott, D. T., Tyson, J., Tonascia, J., & Meinhart, C. L. (1997). Results at age 8 years of early intervention for low-birth-weight premature infants. *Journal of the American Medical Association, 277,* 126–132.

McClelland, D. C., Atkinson, J. W., Clark, R. A., & Lowell, E. L. (1953). *The achievement motive.* East Norwalk, CT: Appleton-Century-Crofts.

McCloskey, L. A., Figueredo, A. J., & Koss, M. P. (1995). The effects of systematic family violence on children's mental health. *Child Development, 66,* 1239–1261.

McCubbin, J. A., Lawson, E. J., Cox, S., Shermin, J. J., Norton, J. A., & Read, J. A. (1996). Prenatal maternal blood pressure response to stress predicts birth weight and gestational age: A preliminary study. *American Journal of Obstetrics and Gynecology, 175,* 706–712.

McFadyen-Ketchum, S. A., Bates, J. E., Dodge, K. A., & Pettit, G. S. (1996). Patterns of change in early childhood aggressive-disruptive behavior: Gender differences in predictions from early coercive and affectionate mother-child interactions. *Child Development, 67,* 2417–2433.

McGhee, P. E., & Frueh, T. (1980). Television viewing and the learning of sex-role stereotypes. *Sex Roles, 6,* 179–188.

McGhee-Bidlack, B. (1991). The development of noun definitions: a metalinguistic analysis. *Journal of Child Languages, 18,* 417–434.

McGilly, K., & Siegler, R. S. (1990). The influence of encoding strategic knowledge on children's choices among serial recall strategies. *Developmental Psychology, 26,* 931–941.

McGraw, M. B. (1935). *Growth: A study of Johnny and Jimmy.* East Norwalk, CT: Appleton-Century-Crofts.

McGue, M., Sharma, A., & Benson, P. (1996). The effect of common rearing on adolescent adjustment: Evidence from a U.S. adoption cohort. *Developmental Psychology, 32,* 604–613.

McHale, J. P. (1995). Coparenting and triadic interactions during infancy: The roles of marital distress and child gender. *Developmental Psychology, 31,* 985–996.

McHale, S. M., Crouter, A. C., McGuire, S. A., & Updegraff, K. A. (1995). Congruence between mothers' and fathers' differential treatment of siblings: Links with family relations and children's well-being. *Child Development, 66,* 116–128.

McHale, S. M., & Gamble, W. C. (1989). Sibling relationships of children with disabled and nondisabled brothers and sisters. *Developmental Psychology, 25,* 421–429.

McKenna, M. A. J. (1997, May 2). U.S., Georgia get welcome news on teenagers and sex. *Atlanta Constitution,* D1.

McKusick, V. A. (1995). *Mendelian inheritance in Man* (10th Ed.). Baltimore: Johns Hopkins University Press.

McLoyd, V. C. (1989). Socialization and development in a changing economy: The effects of paternal job and income loss on children. *American Psychologist, 44,* 293–302.

McLoyd, V. C. (1990). The impact of economic hardship on Black families and children: Psychological distress, parenting, and socioemotional development. *Child Development, 61,* 311–346.

McLoyd, V. C. (1998). Socioeconomic disadvantage and child development. *American Psychologist, 53,* 185–204.

McLoyd, V. C., Jayaratne, T. E., Ceballo, R., & Borquez, J. (1994). Unemployment and work interruption among African-American single mothers. Effects on parenting and adolescent socioemotional functioning. *Child Development, 65,* 562–589.

McMahon, M. J., & Katz, V. L. (1996). Clinical teratology. In J. A. Kuller, N. C. Cheschier, & R. C. Cefalo (Eds.), *Prenatal diagnosis and reproductive genetics* (pp. 207–217). St. Louis: Mosby.

McNeill, D. (1970). *The acquisition of language.* New York: Harper & Row.

Meier, R. P. (1991). Language acquisition by deaf children. *American Scientist, 79,* 69–70.

McNeilly-Choque, M. K., Hart, C. H., Robinson, C. C., Nelson, L. J., & Olsen, S. F. (1996). Overt and relational aggression on the playground: Correspondence among different informants. *Journal of Research in Childhood Education, 11,* 47–67.

McNew, J., & Abell, N. (1995). Posttraumatic stress symptomatology: Similarities and differences between Vietnam veterans and adult survivors of childhood sexual abuse. *Social Work, 40,* 115–126.

Mead, G. H. (1934). *Mind, self, and society.* Chicago: University of Chicago Press.

Mead, M. (1935). *Sex and temperament in three primitive societies.* New York: William Morrow.

Mead, M., & Newton, N. (1967). Cultural patterning of perinatal behavior. In S. A. Richardson & A. F. Guttmacher (Eds.), *Childbearing: Its social and psychological aspects* (pp. 142–244). Baltimore: Williams & Wilkins.

Mediascope, Inc. (1996). *National Television Violence Study: Executive summary 1994–1995.* Studio City, CA: Author.

Meier, R. P. (1991). Language acquisition by deaf children. *American Scientist, 79,* 69–70.

Meilman, P. W. (1979). Cross-sectional age changes in ego identity status during adolescence. *Developmental Psychology, 15,* 230–231.

Mekos, D., Hetherington, E. M., & Reiss, D. (1996). Sibling differences in problem behavior and parental treatment in nondivorced and remarried families. *Child Development, 67,* 2148–2165.

Melson, G. F., Peet, S., & Sparks, C. (1991). Children's attachments to their pets: Links to socioemotional development. *Children's Environmental Quarterly, 8,* 55–65.

Meltzoff, A. N. (1988a). Imitation of televised models by infants. *Child Development, 59,* 1221–1229.

Meltzoff, A. N. (1988b). Infant imitation after a 1-week delay: Long-term memory for novel acts and multiple stimuli. *Developmental Psychology, 24,* 470–476.

Meltzoff, A. N. (1988c). Infant imitation and memory: Nine-month-olds in immediate and deferred tests. *Child Development, 59,* 217–225.

Meltzoff, A. N. (1990). Towards a developmental cognitive science. *Annuals of the New York Academy of Sciences, 608,* 1–37.

Meltzoff, A. N. (1995). Understanding the intentions of others: Re-enactment of intended acts by 18-month-old children. *Developmental Psychology, 31,* 838–850.

Meltzoff, A. N. (1995). What infant memory tells us about infantile amnesia: Long-term recall and deferred imitation. *Journal of Experimental Child Psychology, 59,* 497–515.

Meltzoff, A. N., & Moore, M. K. (1977). Imitation of facial and manual gestures by human neonates. *Science, 198,* 75–78.

Meltzoff, A. N., & Moore, M. K. (1989). Imitation in newborn infants: Exploring the range of gestures imitated and the underlying mechanisms. *Developmental Psychology, 25,* 954–962.

Meltzoff, A. N., & Moore, M. K. (1992). Early imitation within a functional framework: The importance of person, identity, movement, and development. *Infant Behavior and Development, 15,* 479–505.

Mervis, C. B., Golinkoff, R. M., & Bertrand, J. (1994). Two-year-olds readily learn multiple labels for the same basic-level category. *Child Development, 65,* 1163–1177.

Mervis, C. B., & Johnson, K. E. (1991). Acquisition of the plural morpheme: A case study. *Developmental Psychology, 27,* 222–235.

Meyer-Bahlberg, H. F. L., Ehrhardt, A. A., Rosen, L. R., Gruen, R. S., Veridiano, N. P., Vann, F. H., & Neuwalder, H. F. (1995). Prenatal estrogens and the development of homosexual orientation. *Developmental Psychology, 31,* 12–21.

Midgley, C., Feldlaufer, H., & Eccles, J. S. (1989). Student/teacher relations and attitudes toward mathematics before and after the transition to junior high school. *Child Development, 60,* 981–992.

Midlarsky, E., & Bryan, J. H. (1972). Affect expressions and children's imitative altruism. *Journal of Experimental Research in Personality, 6,* 195–203.

Miller, C. L. (1983). Developmental changes in male/female voice classification by infants. *Infant Behavior and Development, 6,* 313–330.

Miller, C. L., Miceli, P. J., Whitman, T. L., & Borkowski, J. G. (1996). Cognitive readiness to parent and intellectual-emotional development in children of adolescent mothers. *Developmental Psychology, 32,* 533–541.

Miller, G. V. (1995). *The gay male's odyssey in the corporate world.* Binghamton, NY: Haworth Press.

Miller, J. L., & Eimas, P. D. (1996). Internal structure of voicing categories in early infancy. *Perception and Psychophysics, 58,* 1157–1167.

Miller, L. T., & Vernon, P. A. (1997). Developmental changes in speed of information processing in young children. *Developmental Psychology, 33,* 549–554.

Miller, N. B., Cowan, P. A., Cowan, C. P., Hetherington, E. M., & Clingempeel, W. G. (1993). Externalizing in preschoolers and early adolescents: A cross-study replication of a family model. *Developmental Psychology, 29,* 3–18.

Miller, P. A., Eisenberg, N., Fabes, R. A., & Shell, R. (1996). Relations of moral reasoning and vicarious emotion to young children's prosocial behavior toward peers and adults. *Developmental Psychology, 32,* 210–219.

Miller, P. H. (1994). Individual differences in children's strategic behavior: Utilization deficiencies. *Learning and Individual Differences, 6,* 285–307.

Miller, P. H., & Aloise, P. A. (1989). Young children's understanding of the psychological causes of behavior: A review. *Child Development, 60,* 257–285.

Miller, P. H., & Harris, Y. R. (1988). Preschoolers' strategies of attention on a same-different task. *Developmental Psychology, 24,* 621–633.

Miller, P. H., & Seier, W. L. (1994). Strategy utilization deficiencies in children. In H. W. Reese (Ed.), *Advances in child development and behavior* (Vol. 25, pp. 107–156). New York: Academic Press.

Miller, P. H., & Weiss, M. G. (1981). Children's attention allocation, understanding of attention, and performance on the incidental learning task. *Child Development, 52,* 1183–1190.

Miller, P. H., & Weiss, M. G. (1982). Children's and adults' knowledge about what variables affect selective attention. *Child Development, 53,* 543–549.

Miller, P. H., Woody-Ramsey, J., & Aloise, P. A. (1991). The role of strategy effortfulness in strategy effectiveness. *Developmental Psychology, 27,* 738–745.

Miller, S. A. (1997). *Developmental research methods* (2nd ed.). Englewood Cliffs, NJ: Prentice-Hall.

Mills, R. S. L., & Rubin, K. H. (1990). Parental beliefs about problematic social behaviors in early childhood. *Child Development, 61,* 138–151.

Milunsky, A. (1992). *Genetic disorders and the fetus: Diagnosis, prevention, and treatment* (3rd ed.). Baltimore: Johns Hopkins University Press.

Minuchin, P. P. (1988). Relationships within the family: A systems perspective on development. In R. A. Hinde & J. Stevenson-Hinde (Eds.), *Relationships within families: Mutual influences* (pp. 7–26). New York: Oxford University Press.

Minuchin, P. P., & Shapiro, E. K. (1983). The school as a context for social development. In P. H. Mussen (Ed.), *Handbook of child psychology.* (Vol. 4). *Socialization, personality, and social development* (4th ed., pp. 197–274). New York: Wiley.

Minuchin, S., Rosman, B. L., & Baker, L. (1978). *Psychomatic families: Anorexia nervosa in context.* Cambridge, MA: Harvard University Press.

Mischel, H. N., & Mischel, W. (1983). The development of children's knowledge of self-control strategies. *Child Development, 53,* 603–619.

Mischel, W. (1970). Sex-typing and socialization. In P. H. Mussen (Ed.), *Carmichael's manual of child psychology.* (Vol. 2). New York: Wiley.

Mischel, W. (1974). Processes in the delay of gratification. In L. Berkowitz (Ed.), *Advances in experimental social psychology* (Vol. 7). New York: Academic.

Mischel, W. (1986). *Introduction to personality* (4th ed.). New York: Holt, Rinehart & Winston.

Mischel, W., & Baker, N. (1975). Cognitive appraisals and transformations in delay behavior. *Journal of Personality and Social Psychology, 31,* 254–261.

Mischel, W., & Ebbesen, E. B. (1970). Attention in delay of gratification. *Journal of Personality and Social Psychology, 16,* 329–337.

Mischel, W., & Patterson, C. J. (1976). Substantive and structural elements of effective plans for self-control. *Journal of Personality and Social Psychology, 34,* 942–950.

Mischel, W., Shoda, Y., & Peake, P. K. (1988). The nature of adolescent competencies predicted by preschool delay of gratification. *Journal of Personality and Social Psychology, 54,* 687–696.

Mistry, J. (1997). The development of remembering in cultural context. In N. Cowan (Ed.), *The development of memory in childhood* (pp. 343–368). Hove, East Sussex: Psychology Press.

Mitchell, J. E., Baker, L. A., & Jacklin, C. N. (1989). Masculinity and femininity in twin children: Genetic and environmental factors. *Child Development, 60,* 1475–1485.

Miyawaki, K., Strange, W., Verbrugge, R., Liberman, A. M., Jenkins, J. J., & Fujimura, D. (1975). An effect of linguistic experience: The discrimination of [r] and [l] by native speakers of Japanese and English. *Perception and Psychophysics, 18,* 331–340.

Mize, J., & Ladd, G. W. (1990). A cognitive-social learning approach to social skill training with low-status preschool children. *Developmental Psychology, 26,* 388–397.

Mize, J. & Pettit, G. S. (1997). Mother's social coaching, mother-child relationship style, and children's peer competence: Is the medium the message? *Child Development, 68,* 312–322.

Mize, J., Pettit, G. S., & Brown, E. G. (1995). Mothers' supervision of their children's peer play: Relations with beliefs, perceptions, and knowledge. *Developmental Psychology, 31,* 311–321.

Moely, B. E., Hart, S. S., Leal, L., Santulli, K. A., Rao, N., Johnson, T., & Hamilton, L. B. (1992). The teacher's role in facilitating memory and study strategy development in the elementary school classroom. *Child Development, 63,* 653–672.

Moely, B. E., Santulli, K. A., & Obach, M. S. (1995). Strategy instruction, metacognition, and motivation in the elementary school classroom. In F. E. Weinert & W. Schneider (Eds.), *Memory performance and competencies: Issues in growth and development.* Hillsdale, NJ: Erlbaum.

Moerk, E. L. (1989). The LAD was a lady and the tasks were ill-defined. *Developmental Review, 9,* 21–57.
Molfese, D. L. (1977). Infant cerebral asymmetry. In S. J. Segalowitz & F. A. Gruber (Eds.), *Language development and neurological theory.* Orlando, FL: Academic Press.
Molina, B. S. G., & Chassin, L. (1996). The parent-adolescent relationship at puberty: Hispanic ethnicity and parental alcoholism as moderators. *Developmental Psychology, 32,* 675–686.
Moller, L. C., & Serbin, L. A. (1996). Antecedents of toddler gender segregation: Cognitive consonance, gender-typed toy preferences and behavioral compatibility. *Sex Roles, 35,* 445–460.
Monass, J. A., & Engelhard, J. A., Jr. (1990). Home environment and the competitiveness of accomplished individuals in four talent fields. *Developmental Psychology, 26,* 264–268.
Money, J. (1965). Psychosexual differentiation. In J. Money (Ed.), *Sex research: New developments.* New York: Holt, Rinehart, and Winston.
Money, J. (1985). Pediatric sexology and hermaphrodism. *Journal of Sex and Marital Therapy, 11,* 139–156.
Money, J. (1988). *Gay, straight, and in-between: The sexology of erotic orientation.* New York: Oxford University Press.
Money, J., & Ehrhardt, A. (1972). *Man and woman, boy and girl.* Baltimore: Johns Hopkins University Press.
Money, J., & Tucker, P. (1975). *Sexual signatures: On being a man or a woman.* Boston: Little, Brown.
Montemayor, R., & Eisen, M. (1977). The development of self-conceptions from childhood to adolescence. *Developmental Psychology, 13,* 314–319.
Moon, C., Cooper, R. P., & Fifer, W. P. (1993). Two-day-olds prefer their native language. *Infant Behavior and Development, 16,* 495–500.
Moore, E. G. J. (1986). Family socialization and the IQ test performance of traditionally and transracially adopted black children. *Developmental Psychology, 22,* 317–326.
Moore, K. L., & Persaud, T. V. N. (1993). *Before we are born: Essentials of embryology and birth defects* (4th ed.). Philadelphia: Saunders.
Moore, S. M. (1995). Girls' understanding and social constructions of menarche. *Journal of Adolescence, 18,* 87–104.
Moorehouse, M. J. (1991). Linking maternal employment patterns to mother-child activities and children's school competence. *Developmental Psychology, 27,* 295–303.
Morgan, G. A., & Ricciuti, H. N. (1969). Infants' responses to strangers during the first year. In B. M. Foss (Ed.), *Determinants of infant behavior* (Vol. 4). London: Methuen.
Morgan, J. L., & Saffran, J. R. (1995). Emerging integration of sequential and suprasegmental information in preverbal speech segmentation. *Child Development, 66,* 911–936.
Morison, P., & Masten, A. S. (1991). Peer reputation in middle childhood as a predictor of adaptation in adolescence: A seven-year follow-up. *Child Development, 62,* 991–1007.
Morrison, F. J. (1984). Reading disability: A problem in rule learning and word decoding. *Developmental Review, 4,* 36–47.
Morrison, F. J., Griffith, E. M., & Alberts, D. M. (1997). Native-nurture in the classroom: Entrance age, school readiness, and learning in children. *Developmental Psychology, 33,* 254–262.
Morrison, F. J., Smith, L., & Dow-Ehrensberger, M. (1995). Education and cognitive development: A natural experiment. *Developmental Psychology, 31,* 789–799.
Mortimer, J. T., Finch, M. D., Ryu, S., Shanahan, M. J., & Call, K. T. (1996). The effects of work intensity on adolescent mental health, achievement, and behavioral adjustment: New evidence from a prospective study. *Child Development, 67,* 1243–1261.
Mounts, N. S., & Steinberg, L. (1995). An ecological analysis of peer influence on adolescent grade point average and drug use. *Developmental Psychology, 31,* 915–922.
Muir-Broaddus, J. E. (1995). Gifted underachievers: Insights from the characteristics of strategic functioning associated with giftedness and achievement. *Learning and Individual Differences, 7,* 189–206.
Mullis, A. K., Mullis, R. L., & Normandin, D. (1992). Cross-sectional and longitudinal comparisons of adolescent self-esteem. *Adolescence, 27,* 51–61.
Mumford, M. D., & Gustafson, S. B. (1988). Creativity syndrome: Integration, application, and innovation. *Psychological Bulletin, 103,* 27–43.
Mumme, D. L., Fernald, A., & Herrera, C. (1996). Infants' responses to facial and vocal emotional signals in a social referencing paradigm. *Child Development, 67,* 3219–3237.
Mundy, P., Sigman, M., Kasari, C., & Yirmiya, N. (1988). Nonverbal communication skills in Down syndrome children. *Child Development, 59,* 235–249.
Munro, G., & Adams, G. R. (1977). Ego-identity formation in college students and working youth. *Developmental Psychology, 13,* 523–524.
Munroe, R. H., Shimmin, H. S., & Munroe, R. L. (1984). Gender understanding and sex-role preferences in four cultures. *Developmental Psychology, 20,* 673–682.
Murphy, K., & Schneider, B. (1994). Coaching socially-rejected early adolescents regarding behaviors used by peers to infer liking: A dyad-specific intervention. *Journal of Early Adolescence, 14,* 82–94.
Murray, A. D., Dolby, R. M., Nation, R. L., & Thomas, D. B. (1981). Effects of epidural anesthesia on newborns and their mothers. *Child Development, 52,* 71–82.
Murray, B. (1997). Welfare reform spurs change in Head Start. *Monitor of the American Psychological Association, 28,* 42.
Murray, L., Fiori-Cowley, A., & Hooper, R. (1996). The impact of postnatal depression and associated adversity on early mother-infant interactions and later infant outcome. *Child Development, 67,* 2512–2526.
Mussen, P. H., & Rutherford, E. (1963). Parent-child relations and parental personality in relation to young children's sex-role preferences. *Child Development, 34,* 589–607.
Myers, B. J. (1982). Early intervention using Brazelton training with middle-class mothers and fathers of newborns. *Child Development, 53,* 462–471.
Nadler, A. (1986). Help-seeking as a cultural phenomenon: Differences between city and kibbutz dwellers. *Journal of Personality and Social Psychology, 51,* 976–982.
Nadler, A. (1991). Help-seeking behavior: Psychological costs and instrumental benefits. In M. S. Clark (Ed.), *Prosocial behavior.* Newbury Park, CA: Sage.
Naigles, L. G. (1990). Children use syntax to learn verb meanings. *Journal of Child Language, 17,* 357–374.
Naigles, L. G., & Gelman, S. A. (1995). Overextensions in comprehension and production revisited: Preferential looking in a study of dog, cat, and cow. *Journal of Child Language, 22,* 19–46.
Naigles, L. G., & Hoff-Ginsberg, E. (1995). Input to verb learning: Evidence for the plausibility of syntactic bootstrapping. *Developmental Psychology, 31,* 827–837.
Nanez, J. (1987). Perception of impending collision in 3- to 6-week-old infants. *Infant Behavior and Development, 11,* 447–463.
Nanez, J., & Yonas, A. (1994). Effects of luminance and texture motion on infant defensive reactions to optical collision. *Infant Behavior and Development, 17,* 165–174.
Nastasi, B. K., & Clements, D. H. (1993). Motivational and social outcomes of cooperative computer education environments. *Journal of Computing in Childhood Education, 4,* 15–43.
Nastasi, B. K., & Clements, D. H. (1994). Effectance motivation, perceived scholastic competence, and higher-order thinking in two cooperative computer environments. *Journal of Educational Computing Research, 10,* 249–275.
National Center for Health Statistics (1992). *Health, United States, 1991.* Hyattsville, MD: Public Health Service.
National Education Goals Panel (1992). *The National Education Goals Report, 1992.* Washington, DC: U.S. Department of Education.
Neimark, E. D. (1979). Current status of formal operations research. *Human Development, 22,* 60–67.
Neisser, U. (1997). Never a dull moment. *American Psychologist, 52,* 79–81.
Neisser, U., Boodoo, G., Bouchard, T. J., Jr., Boykin, A. W., Brody, N., Ceci, S. J., Halpern, D. F., Loehlin. J. C., Perloff, R., Sternberg, R. J., & Urbina, S. (1996). Intelligence: Knowns and unknowns. *American Psychologist, 51,* 77–101.
Nelson, C. A. (1987). The recognition of facial expressions in the first two years of life: Mechanisms of development. *Child Development, 58,* 889–909.
Nelson, C. A. (1995). The ontogeny of human memory: A cognitive neuroscience perspective. *Developmental Psychology, 31,* 723–738.
Nelson, C. A., & Bloom, F. E. (1997). Child development and neuroscience. *Child Development, 68,* 970–987.
Nelson, E. A., Grinder, R. E., & Biaggio, A. M. B. (1969). Relationships between behavioral, cognitive-developmental, and self-report measures of morality and personality. *Multivariate Behavioral Research, 4,* 483–500.
Nelson, J., & Aboud, F. E. (1985). The resolution of social conflict among friends. *Child Development, 56,* 1009–1017.
Nelson, K. (1973). Structure and strategy in learning to talk. *Monographs of the Society for Research in Child Development, 38* (Serial No. 149).
Nelson, K. (1981). Individual differences in language development: Implications for development and language. *Developmental Psychology, 17,* 170–187.
Nelson, K. (1993). The psychological and social origins of autobiographical memory. *Psychological Science, 4,* 1–8.
Nelson, K. (1996). *Language in cognitive development: The emergence of the mediated mind.* New York: Cambridge University Press.
Nelson, K. B. (1995). Cerebral palsy. In B. F. Sachs, R. Beard, E. Papiernik, & C. Russell (Eds.), *Reproductive health care for women and babies* (pp. 400–419). New York: Oxford University Press.
Nelson, K., Hampson, J., & Shaw, L. K. (1993). Nouns in early lexicons: Evidence, explanations, and implications. *Journal of Child Language, 20,* 61–64.
Nelson, S. A. (1980). Factors influencing young children's use of motives and outcomes as moral criteria. *Child Development, 51,* 823–829.
Neville, H. J., Coffey, S. A., Lawson, D. S., Fischer, A., Emmorey, K., & Bellugi, U. (1997). Neural systems mediating American Sign Language: Effects of sensory experience and age of acquisition. *Brain and Language, 57,* 285–308.

Newcomb, A. F., Bukowski, W. M., & Pattee, L. (1993). Children's peer relations: A meta-analytic review of popular, rejected, neglected, controversial, and average sociometric status. *Psychological Bulletin, 113,* 99–128.

Newcomb, M. D., & Bentler, P. M. (1989). Substance use and abuse among children and teenagers. *American Psychologist, 44,* 242–248.

Newcombe, N., & Dubas, J. S. (1987). Individual differences in cognitive ability: Are they related to timing of puberty? In R. M. Lerner & T. T. Foch (Eds.), *Biological-psychosocial interactions in early adolescence: A life-span perspective.* Hillsdale, NJ: Erlbaum.

Newcombe, N., & Dubas, J. S. (1992). A longitudinal study of predictors of spatial ability in adolescent females. *Child Development, 63,* 37–46.

Newcombe, N., & Fox, N. A. (1994). Infantile amnesia: Through a glass darkly. *Child Development, 65,* 31–40.

Newell, A., & Simon, H. A. (1961). Computer simulation of human thinking. *Science, 134,* 2011–2017.

Newman, D. L., Caspi, A., Moffitt, T. E., & Silva, P. A. (1997). Antecedents of adult interpersonal functioning: Effects of individual differences in age 3 temperament. *Developmental Psychology, 33,* 206–217.

Newport, E. L. (1991). Contrasting conceptions of the critical period for language. In S. Carey & R. Gelman (Eds.), *The epigenesis of mind: Essays on biology and cognition,* (pp. 111–130). Hillsdale, NJ: Erlbaum.

Newport, N., & Huttenlocher, J. (1992). Children's early ability to solve perspective-taking problems. *Developmental Psychology, 28,* 635–643.

NICHD Early Child Care Research Network (1997). The effects of infant child care on mother-infant attachment security: Results of the NICHD study of early child care. *Child Development, 68,* 860–879.

Nicholls, J. G., & Miller, A. T. (1984). Reasoning about the ability of self and others: A developmental study. *Child Development, 55,* 1990–1999.

Nichols, M. R. (1993). Parental perspectives on the childbirth experience. *Maternal-Child Nursing Journal, 21,* 99–108.

Ninio, A., & Rinott, N. (1988). Fathers' involvement in the care of their infants and their attributions of cognitive competence to infants. *Child Development, 59,* 652–663.

Norman-Jackson, J. (1982). Family interactions, language development, and primary reading achievement of Black children in families of low income. *Child Development, 53,* 349–358.

Nottlemann, E. D. (1987). Competence and self-esteem during transition from childhood to adolescence. *Developmental Psychology, 23,* 441–450.

Nucci, L., Camino, C., & Sapiro, C. M. (1996). Social class effects on northeastern Brazilian children's conceptions of areas of personal choice and social regulation. *Child Development, 67,* 1223–1242.

Nucci, L., & Smetana, J. G. (1996). Mothers' concepts of young children's areas of personal freedom. *Child Development, 67,* 1870–1886.

Nucci, L., & Turiel, E. (1993). God's word, religious rules, and their relation to Christian and Jewish children's concepts of morality. *Child Development, 64,* 1475–1491.

Nucci, L., & Weber, E.K. (1995). Social interactions in the home and the development of young children's conceptions within the personal domain. *Child Development, 66,* 1438–1452.

Nugent, J. K., Lester, B. M., & Brazelton, T. B. (1989). *Biology, culture, and development* (Vol. 1). Norwood, NJ: Eribaum.

Oates, R. K., & Bross, D. C. (1995). What have we learned about treating child physical abuse? A literature review of the last decade. *Child Abuse and Neglect, 19,* 463–473.

Ochs, E. (1982). Talking to children in western Samoa. *Language in Society, 11,* 77–104.

O'Connor, B. P. (1995). Identity development and perceived parental behavior as sources of adolescent egocentrism. *Journal of Youth and Adolescence, 24,* 205–227.

O'Connor, B. P., & Nikolic, J. (1990). Identity development and formal operations as sources of adolescent egocentrism. *Journal of Youth and Adolescence, 19,* 149–158.

O'Connor, N., & Hermelin, B. (1991). Talents and preoccupations in idiot-savants. *Psychological Medicine, 21,* 959–964.

Odden, A. (1990). Class size and student achievement: Research-based policy alternatives. *Educational Evaluation and Policy Analysis, 12,* 213–227.

O'Dempsey, T. J. D. (1988). Traditional belief and practice among the Pokot people of Kenya with particular reference to mother and child health: 2. Mother and child health. *Annals of Tropical Paediatrics, 8,* 125.

Oden, S., & Asher, S. R. (1977). Coaching children in social skills for friendship making. *Child Development, 48,* 495–506.

O'Donohue, W. T., & Elliott, A. N. (1992). Treatment of the sexually abused child: A review. *Journal of Clinical Child Psychology, 21,* 218–228.

Ogbu, J. U. (1981). Origins of human competence: A cultural-ethological perspective. *Child Development, 52,* 413–429.

Ogbu, J. U. (1988). Black education: A cultural-ecological perspective. In H. P. McAdoo (Ed.), *Black families.* Beverly Hills: Sage.

Ogbu, J. U. (1994). From cultural differences to differences in cultural frames of reference. In P. M. Greenfield & R. R. Cocking (Eds.), *Cross-cultural roots of minority child development* (pp. 365–391). Hillsdale, NJ: Erlbaum.

Ogletree, S. M., & Williams, S. W. (1990). Sex and sex-typing effects on computer attitudes and aptitude. *Sex Roles, 23,* 703–712.

O'Heron, C. A., & Orlofsky, J. L. (1990). Stereotypic and nonstereotypic sex role trait and behavior orientations, gender identity, and psychological adjustment. *Journal of Personality and Social Psychology, 58,* 134–143.

Oller, D. K., & Eilers, R. E. (1988). The role of audition in infant babbling. *Child Development, 59,* 441–449.

Olson, G. M., & Sherman, T. (1983). Attention, learning, and memory in infants. In P. H. Mussen (Ed.), *Handbook of child psychology* (Vol. 2). New York: Wiley.

Olvera-Ezzell, N., Power, T. G., & Cousins, J. H. (1990). Maternal socialization of children's eating habits: Strategies used by obese Mexican-American mothers. *Child Development, 61,* 395–400.

Olweus, D. (1984). Aggressors and their victims: Bullying at school. In H. Frude & H. Gault (Eds.), *Disruptive behaviors in schools* (pp. 57–76). New York: Wiley.

Olweus, D. (1993). *Bullying at school.* Oxford: Blackwell.

Olweus, D., Mattsson, A., Schalling, D., & Low, H. (1980). Testosterone, aggression, physical and personality dimensions in normal adolescent males. *Psychosomatic Medicine, 42,* 253–269.

O'Mahoney, J. F. (1989). Development of thinking about things and people: Social and nonsocial cognition during adolescence. *Journal of Genetic Psychology, 150,* 217–224.

O'Neill, D. K. (1996). Two-year-old children's sensitivity to a parent's knowledge state when making requests. *Child Development, 67,* 659–667.

Oppenheim, D., Nir, A., Warren, S., & Emde, R. N. (1997). Emotion regulation in mother-child narrative co-construction: Associations with children's narratives and adaptation. *Developmental Psychology, 33,* 284–294.

Oppenheim, D., Sagi, A., & Lamb, M. E. (1988). Infant-adult attachments on the kibbutz and their relation to socioemotional development 4 years later. *Developmental Psychology, 24,* 427–433.

O'Reilly, A. W., & Bornstein, M. H. (1993). Caregiver-child interaction in play. In M. H. Bornstein & A. W. O'Reilly (Eds.), *The role of play in the development of thought* (New Directions for Child Development, No. 59). San Francisco: Jossey-Bass.

Orlofsky, J. L. (1979). Parental antecedents of sex-role orientation in college men and women. *Sex Roles, 5,* 495–512.

Ornstein, P. A., Gordon, B. N., & Larus, D. M. (1992). Children's memory for a personally experienced event: Implications for testimony. *Applied Developmental Psychology, 6,* 49–60.

Ornstein, P. A., Medlin, R. G., Stone, B. P., & Naus, M. J. (1985). Retrieving for rehearsal: An analysis of active rehearsal in children's memory. *Developmental Psychology, 21,* 633–641.

Ornstein, P. A., Naus, M. J., & Liberty, C. (1975). Rehearsal and organizational processes in children's memory. *Child Development, 46,* 818–830.

Osborne, M. L., Kistner, J. A., & Helgemo, B. (1993). Developmental progression in children's knowledge of AIDS: Implications for educational and attitudinal change. *Journal of Pediatric Psychology, 18,* 177–192.

O'Sullivan, J. T. (1996). Children's metamemory about the influence of conceptual relations on recall. *Journal of Experimental Child Psychology, 62,* 1–29.

O'Sullivan, J. T. (1997). Effort, interest, & recall: Beliefs and behaviors of preschoolers. *Journal of Experimental Child Psychology, 65,* 43–67.

Overton, W. F. (1984). World views and their influence on psychological theory and research: Kuhn-Lakotes-Lunden. In H. W. Reese (Ed.), *Advances in child development and behavior* (Vol. 18). New York: Academic.

Overton, W. F., Ward, S. L., Noveck, I. A., Black, J., & O'Brien, D. P. (1987). Form and content in the development of deductive reasoning. *Developmental Psychology, 23,* 22–30.

Oviatt, S. L. (1980). The emerging ability to comprehend language: An experimental approach. *Child Development, 51,* 97–106.

Oyen, A-S., & Bebko, J. M. (1996). The effects of computer games and lesson context on children's mnemonic strategies. *Journal of Experimental Child Psychology, 62,* 173–189.

Paarlberg, K. M., Vingerhoets, Ad J. J. M., Passchier, J. Dekker, G. A., & van Geign, H. P. (1995). Psychosocial factors and pregnancy outcome: A review with emphasis on methodological issues. *Journal of Psychosomatic Research, 39,* 563–595.

Paikoff, R. L., & Brooks-Gunn, J. (1991). Do parent-child relationships change at puberty? *Psychological Bulletin, 110,* 47–66.

Palinscar, A. S., Brown, A. L., & Campione, J. C. (1993). First-grade dialogues for knowledge acquisition and use. In E. A. Forman, N. Minilk, & C. A. Stone (Eds.), *Contexts for learning* (pp. 43–57). New York: Oxford University Press.

Palkovitz, R. (1984). Parental attitudes and fathers' interactions with their 5-month-old infants. *Developmental Psychology, 20,* 1054–1060.

Palkovitz, R. (1985). Fathers' birth attendance, early contact, and extended contact with their newborns: A critical review. *Child Development, 56,* 392–406.

Palmer, C. F. (1989). The discriminating nature of infants' exploratory actions. *Developmental Psychology, 25,* 885–893.

Palmer, E. L. (1984). Providing quality television for America's children. In J. P. Murray & G. Salomon (Eds.), *The future of children's television.* Boys Town, NE: Boys Town Center.

Pan, B. A., & Gleason, J. K. (1997). Semantic development: Learning the meaning of words. In J. K. Gleason (Ed.). *The development of language* (4th ed.). Boston: Allyn & Bacon.

Papiernik, E. (1995). Prevention of preterm birth in France. In B. P. Sachs, R. Beard, E. Papiernik, & c. Russell (Eds.), *Reproductive health care for women and babies* (pp. 322–347). New York: Oxford University Press.

Papousek, H. (1967). Experimental studies of appetitional behavior in human newborns and infants. In H. W. Stevenson, E. H. Hess, & H. L. Rheingold (Eds.), *Early behavior: Comparative and developmental approaches.* New York: Wiley.

Paris, S. G. (1988).. Models and metaphors of learning strategies. In C. E. Weinstein, E. T. Goetz, & P. A. Alexander (Eds.), *Learning and study strategies: Issues in assessment, instruction, and evaluation.* Orlando, FL: Academic Press.

Park, S., Belsky, J., Putnam, S., & Cynic, K. (1997). Infant emotionality, parenting, and 3-year inhibition: Exploring stability and lawful discontinuity in a male sample. *Developmental Psychology, 33,* 218–227.

Parke, R. D. (1972). Some effects of punishment on children's behavior. In W. W. Hartup (Ed.), *The young child* (Vol. 2). Washington, DC: National Association for the Education of Young Children.

Parke, R. D. (1977). Some effects of punishment on children's behavior—revisited. In E. M. Hetherington & R. D. Parke (Eds.), *Contemporary readings in child psychology.* New York: McGraw-Hill.

Parke, R. D. (1995). Fathers and families. In M. Bornstein (Ed.), *Handbook of parenting* (Vol. 3, pp. 27–63). Hillsdale, NJ: Erlbaum.

Parke, R. D., & Kellum, S. G. (1994). *Exploring family relationships with other social contexts.* Hillsdale, NJ. Erlbaum.

Parke, R. D., & Slaby, R. G. (1983). The development of aggression. In P. H. Mussen (Ed.), *Handbook of child psychology.* (Vol. 4). *Socialization, personality, and social development* (pp. 547–641). New York: Wiley.

Parker, J. G., & Asher, S. R. (1987). Peer relations and later adjustment: Are low-accepted children "at risk"? *Psychological Bulletin, 102,* 357–389.

Parker, J. G., & Asher, S. R. (1993). Friendship and friendship quality in middle childhood: Links with peer group acceptance and feelings of loneliness and social dissatisfaction. *Developmental Psychology, 29,* 611–621.

Parker, J. G., Rubin, K. H., Price, J., & DeRosier, E. (1995). Peer relationships, child development, and adjustment. A developmental psychopathology perspective. In D. Cicchetti & E. Cohen (Eds.), *Developmental Psychopathology:* (Vol. 2). *Risk, disorder, and adaptation* (pp. 96–161). New York: Wiley.

Parker, J. G., & Seal, J. (1996). Forming, losing, renewing, and replacing friendships: Applying temporal parameters to the assessment of children's friendship experiences. *Child Development, 67,* 2248–2268.

Parkhurst, J. T., & Asher, S. R. (1992). Peer rejection in middle school: Subgroup differences in behavior, loneliness, and interpersonal concerns. *Developmental Psychology, 28,* 231–241.

Parsons, J. E., Adler, T. F., & Kaczala, C. M. (1982). Socialization of achievement attitudes and beliefs: Parental influences. *Child Development, 53,* 310–321.

Parsons, T. (1955). Family structure and the socialization of the child. In T. Parsons & R. F. Bales (Eds.), *Family socialization and interaction processes.* New York: Free Press.

Parten, M. (1932). Social participation among preschool children. *Journal of Abnormal and Social Psychology, 27,* 243–269.

Passingham, R. E. (1982). *The human primate.* Oxford: W. H. Freeman.

Pataki, S. P., Shapiro, C., & Clark, M. S. (1994). Children's acquisition of appropriate norms for friendships and acquaintances. *Journal of Social and Personal Relationships, 11,* 427–442.

Patel, N., Power, T. G., & Bhavnagri, N. P. (1996). Socialization values and practices of Indian immigrant parents: Correlates of modernity and acculturation. *Child Development, 67,* 303–313.

Patterson, C. J. (1994). Children of the lesbian baby boom: Behavioral adjustment, self-concepts, and sex-role identity. In B. Greene & G. Herek (Eds.), *Contemporary perspectives on gay and lesbian psychology: Theory, research, and applications* (pp. 156–175). Beverly Hills, CA: Sage.

Patterson, C. J. (1995a). Families of the lesbian baby boom: Parents' division of labor and children's adjustment. *Developmental Psychology, 31,* 115–123.

Patterson, C. J. (1995b). Sexual orientation and human development: An overview. *Developmental Psychology, 31,* 3–11.

Patterson, C. J., Kupersmidt, J. B., & Vaden, N. A. (1990). Income level, gender, ethnicity, and household compositions as predictors of children's school-based competence. *Child Development, 61,* 485–494.

Patterson, G. R. (1981). Mothers: The unacknowledged victims. *Monographs of the Society for Research in Child Development, 45,* 5, Serial No. 186.

Patterson, G. R. (1982). *Coercive family processes.* Eugene, OR: Castilia Press.

Patterson, G. R. (1993). Orderly change in a stable world: The antisocial trait as chimera. *Journal of Consulting and Clinical Psychology, 61,* 911–919.

Patterson, G. R., DeBaryshe, B. D., & Ramsey, E. (1989). A developmental perspective on antisocial behavior. *American Psychologist, 44,* 329–335.

Patterson, G. R., Littman, R. A., & Bricker, W. (1967). Assertive behavior in children: A step toward a theory of aggression. *Monographs of the Society for Research in Child Development, 32,* 5, Serial No. 113.

Patterson, G. R., Reid, J. B., & Dishion, T. (1992). *Antisocial boys.* Eugene, OR: Castalia Publishing.

Patterson, S. J., Sochting, I., & Marcia, J. E. (1992). The inner space and beyond: Women and identity. In G. R. Adams, T. P. Gullotta, & R. Montemayor (Eds.), *Adolescent identity formation.* (Vol. 4). *Advances in Adolescent Development.* Newbury Park, CA: Sage.

Paul, J. P. (1993). Childhood cross-gender behavior and adult homosexuality: The resurgence of biological models of sexuality. *Journal of Homosexuality, 24,* 41–54.

Paulhus, D., & Shaffer, D. R. (1981). Sex differences in the impact of number of older and number of younger siblings on scholastic aptitude. *Social Psychology Quarterly, 44,* 363–368.

Pearson, J. L., Hunter, A. G., Ensminger, M. E., & Kellam, S. G. (1990). Black grandmothers in multigenerational households: Diversity in family structure and parenting involvement in the Woodlawn community. *Child Development, 61,* 434–442.

Pederson, D. R., Moran, G. (1995). A categorical description of infant–mother relationships in the home and its relation to Q-sort measures of mother–infant interaction. In E. Waters, B. E. Vaughn, G. Posada, & K. Kondo-Ikemura (Eds.), Caregiving, cultural, and cognitive perspectives on secure-base behavior and working models: New growing points of attachment theory and research. *Monographs of the Society for Research in Child Development, 60,* 2–3, Serial No. 244.

Pederson, D. R., & Moran, G. (1996). Expressions of the attachment relationship outside of the Strange Situation. *Child Development, 67,* 915–929.

Pedlow, R., Sanson, A., Prior, M., & Oberklaid, F. (1993). Stability of maternally reported temperament from infancy to 8 years. *Developmental Psychology, 29,* 998–1007.

Pedro-Carroll, J. L., & Cowen, E. L. (1985). The children of divorce intervention program: An investigation of the efficacy of a school-based prevention program. *Journal of Consulting and Clinical Psychology, 53,* 603–611.

Pegg, J. E., Werker, J. F., & McLeod, P. J. (1992). Preference for infant-directed over adult-directed speech: Evidence from 7-week-old infants. *Infant Behavior and Development, 15,* 325–345.

Pelham, W. E., Jr., Carlson, C., Sams, S. E., Vallano, G., Dixon, M. J., & Hoza, B. (1993). Separate and combined effects of methylphenidate and behavior modification on boys with attention deficit-hyperactivity disorder in the classroom. *Journal of Consulting and Clinical Psychology, 61,* 506–515.

Pellegrini, D. S. (1985). Social cognition and competence in middle childhood. *Child Development, 56,* 253–264.

Penner, S. G. (1987). Parental responses to grammatical and ungrammatical child utterances. *Child Development, 58,* 376–384.

Pepler, D. J., & Craig, W. M. (1995). A peek behind the fence: Naturalistic observations of aggressive children with remote audiovisual recording. *Developmental Psychology, 31,* 548–553.

Perez-Granados, D. R., & Callanan, M. A. (1997). Conversations with mothers and siblings: Young children's semantic and conceptual development, *Developmental Psychology, 33,* 120–134.

Perlman, M., & Ross, H. S. (1997). The benefits of parent intervention in children's disputes: An examination of concurrent changes in children's fighting styles. *Child Development, 68,* 690–700.

Perner, J. Ruffman, T., & Leekam, S. R. (1994). Theory of mind is contagious: You can catch it from your sibs. *Child Development, 65,* 1228–1238.

Perry, D. G., Kusel, S. J., & Perry, L. C. (1988). Victims of peer aggression. *Developmental Psychology, 24,* 807–814.

Perry, D. G., Perry, L. C., Bussey, K., English, D., & Arnold, G. (1980). Processes of attribution and children's self-punishment following misbehavior. *Child Development, 51,* 545–551.

Perry, D. G., Perry, L. C., & Weiss, R. J. (1989). Sex differences in the consequences that children anticipate for aggression. *Developmental Psychology, 25,* 312–319.

Peskin, J. (1992). Ruse and representations: On children's ability to conceal information. *Developmental Psychology, 28,* 84–89.

Peterson, G. H., Mehl, L. E., & Liederman, P. H. (1979). The role of some birth-related variables in father attachment. *American Journal of Orthopsychiatry, 49,* 330–338.

Peterson, L., Ewigman, B., & Kivlahan, C. (1993). Judgments regarding appropriate child supervision to prevent injury: The role of environmental risk and child age. *Child Development, 64,* 934–950.

Pettit, G. S., Bates, J. E., & Dodge, K. A. (1997). Supportive parenting, ecological context, and children's adjustment: A seven-year longitudinal study. *Child Development, 68,* 908–923.

Pettit, G. S., Dodge, K. A., & Brown, M. M. (1988). Early family experience, social problem-solving patterns, and children's social competence. *Child Development, 59,* 107–120.

Pettit, G. S., Laird, R. D., Bates, J. E., & Dodge, K. A. (1997). Patterns of after-school care in middle childhood: Risk factors and developmental outcomes. *Merrill-Palmer Quarterly, 43,* 515–538.

Petitto, L. A., & Marentette, P. F. (1991). Babbling in the manual mode: Evidence for the ontogeny of language. *Science, 251,* 1493–1496.

Petretic, P. A., & Tweney, R. D. (1977). Does comprehension precede production? The development of children's responses to telegraphic sentences of varying grammatical adequacy. *Journal of Child Language, 4,* 201–209.

Pettersen, L., Yonas, A., & Fisch, R. O. (1980). The development of blinking in response to impending collision in preterm, full-term, and postterm infants. *Infant Behavior and Development, 3,* 155–165.

Phillips, D. (1984). The illusion of incompetence among academically competent children. *Child Development, 55,* 2000–2016.

Philpott, R. H. (1995). Maternal health care in the developing world. In B. P. Sachs, R. Beard, E. Papiernik, & C. Russell (Eds.), *Reproductive health care for women and babies* (pp. 226–245). New York: Oxford University Press.

Phinney, J. S. (1993). A three-stage model of ethnic identity development in adolescence. In M. E. Bernal & G. P. Knight (Eds.), *Ethnic identity: Formation and transmission among Hispanics and other minorities.* Albany, NY: State University of New York Press.

Phinney, J. S. (1996). When we talk about American ethnic groups, what do we mean? *American Psychologist, 51,* 918–927.

Phinney, J. S., & Rosenthal, D. A. (1992). Ethnic identity in adolescence: Process, context, and outcome. In G. R. Adams, T. P. Gullotta, & R. Montemayor (Eds.), *Adolescent identity formation.* (Vol. 4). *Advances in Adolescent Development.* Newbury Park, CA: Sage.

Piacentini, J., & Hynd, G. (1988). Language after dominant hemispherectomy: Are plasticity of function and equipotentiality viable concepts? *Clinical Psychology Review, 8,* 595–609.

Piaget, J. (1926). *The language and thought of the child.* New York: Harcourt, Bruce & World.

Piaget, J. (1950). *The psychology of intelligence.* San Diego, CA: Harcourt Brace Jovanovich.

Piaget, J. (1951). *Play, dreams, and imitation in childhood.* New York: Norton.

Piaget, J. (1952). *The origins of intelligence in children.* New York: International Universities Press.

Piaget, J. (1952). *The origins of intelligence in children.* New York: International Universities Press.

Piaget, J. (1954). *The construction of reality in the child.* New York: Basic Books.

Piaget, J. (1960). *Psychology of intelligence.* Paterson, NJ: Littlefield, Adams.

Piaget, J. (1965). *The moral judgment of the child.* New York: Free Press. (Original work published 1932)

Piaget, J. (1970a, May). A conversation with Jean Piaget. *Psychology Today,* pp. 25–32.

Piaget, J. (1970b). Piaget's theory. In P. H. Mussen (Ed.), *Carmichael's manual of child psychology* (Vol. 1). New York: Wiley.

Piaget, J. (1971). *Science of education and the psychology of the child.* New York: Viking Press.

Piaget, J. (1972). Intellectual evolution from adolescence to adulthood. *Human Development, 15,* 1–12.

Piaget, J. (1976). *To understand is to invent: The future of education.* New York: Penguin.

Piaget, J. (1977). The role of action in the development of thinking. In W. F. Overton & J. M. Gallagher (Eds.), *Knowledge and development* (Vol. 1). New York: Plenum.

Piaget, J., & Inhelder, B. (1956). *The child's conception of space.* New York: Norton.

Piaget, J., & Inhelder, B. (1969). *The psychology of the child.* New York: Basic Books.

Pickens, J. (1994). Perception of auditory-visual distance relations by 5-month-old infants. *Developmental Psychology, 30,* 537–544.

Pickens, J., & Field, T. (1993). Facial expressivity in infants of depressed mothers. *Developmental Psychology, 29,* 986–988.

Pike, A., McGuire, S., Hetherington, E. M., Reiss, D., & Plomin, R. (1996). Family environment and adolescent depressive symptoms and antisocial behavior: A multivariate genetic analysis. *Developmental Psychology, 32,* 590–603.

Pike, K. M., & Rodin, J. (1991). Mothers, daughters, and disordered eating. *Journal of Abnormal Psychology, 100,* 198–204.

Pillow, B. H. (1988). Young children's understanding of attentional limits. *Child Development, 59,* 31–46.

Pine, J. M. (1994). The language of primary caregivers. In C. Gallaway & B. J. Richards (Eds.), *Input and interaction in language acquisition.* Cambridge, England: Cambridge University Press.

Pine, J. M. (1995). Variation in vocabulary development as a function of birth order. *Child Development, 66,* 272–281.

Pinker, S. (1991). Rules of language. *Science, 253,* 530–535.

Pinon, M., Huston, A. C., & Wright, J. C. (1989). Family ecology and child characteristics that predict young children's educational television viewing. *Child Development, 60,* 846–856.

Pinto, A., Folkers, E., & Sines, J. O. (1991). Dimensions of behavior and home environment in school-age children: India and the United States. *Journal of Cross-Cultural Psychology, 22,* 491–508.

Pipp, S., Easterbrooks, M. A., & Harmon, R. J. (1992). The relation between attachment and knowledge of self and mother in one-year-old infants to three-year-old infants. *Child Development, 63,* 738–750.

Pipp-Siegel, S., & Foltz, C. (1997). Toddlers' acquisition of self/other knowledge: Ecological and interpersonal aspects of self and other. *Child Development, 68,* 69–79.

Plomin, R. (1986). *Development, genetics, and psychology.* Hillsdale, NJ: Erlbaum.

Plomin, R. (1990). *Nature and nurture: An introduction to behavior genetics.* Pacific Grove, CA: Brooks/Cole.

Plomin, R. (1994). *Genetics and experience: The interplay between nature and nurture,* Thousand Oaks, CA: Sage.

Plomin, R., DeFries, J. C., & Loehlin, J. C. (1977). Genotype-environment interaction and correlation in the analysis of human behavior. *Psychological Bulletin, 84,* 309–322.

Plomin, R., DeFries, J. C., McClearn, G. E., & Rutter, M. (1997). *Behavioral genetics: A primer* (3nd. ed.). New York: W. H. Freeman.

Plomin, R., Reiss, D., Hetherington, E. M., & Howe, G. W. (1994). Nature and nurture: Genetic contributions to measures of the family environment. *Developmental Psychology, 30,* 32–43.

Plomin, R., & Rende, R. (1991). Human behavioral genetics. *Annual Review of Psychology, 42,* 161–190.

Plumert, J. M. (1995). Relations between children's overestimation of their physical abilities and accident proneness. *Developmental Psychology, 31,* 866–876.

Plumert, J. M., Ewert, K., & Spear, S. J. (1995). The early development of children's communication about nested spatial relations. *Child Development, 66,* 959–969.

Pollack, R. H. (1997, March). *Personal communication.*

Pollitt, E. (1994). Poverty and child development: Relevance of research in developing countries to the United States. *Child Development, 65,* 283–295.

Pollitt, E., Golub, M., Gorman, K., Grantham-McGregor, S., Levitsky, D., Schurch, B. Strupp, B., & Wachs, T. (1996). A reconceptualization of the effects of undernutrition on children's biological, psychosocial, and behavioral development. *SRCD Social Policy Report* (Vol. 10, No. 5). Ann Arbor, MI: Society for Research in Child Development.

Pomerantz, E. M., & Ruble, D. N. (1997). Distinguishing multiple dimensions and conceptions of ability: Implications for self-evaluation. *Child Development, 68,* 1165–1180.

Pomerantz, E. M., Ruble, D. N., Frey, K. S., & Grenlich, F. (1995). Meeting goals and confronting conflict: Children's changing perceptions of social comparison. *Child Development, 66,* 723–738.

Pomerleau, A., Bolduc, D., Malcuit, G., & Cossette, L. (1990). Pink or blue: Environmental gender stereotypes in the first two years of life. *Sex Roles, 22,* 359–367.

Poole, D. A., & Lindsay, D. S. (1995). Interviewing preschoolers: Effects of nonsuggestive techniques, parental coaching and leading questions on reports of nonexperienced events. *Journal of Experimental Child Psychology, 60,* 129–154.

Poole, D., & White, L. (1995). Tell me again and again: Stability and change in the repeated testimonies of children and adults. In M. S. Zaragoza, J. R. Graham, C. N. Gordon, R. Hirschman, & Y. S. Ben Porath (Eds.), *Memory and testimony in the child witness* (pp. 24–43). Newbury Park, CA: Sage.

Pope, S., & Kipp, K. K. (1998). The development of efficient forgetting: Evidence from directed-forgetting tasks. *Developmental Review, 18,* 86–123.

Porter, F. L., Porges, S. W., & Marshall, R. E. (1988). Newborn pain cries and vagal tone: Parallel changes in response to circumcision. *Child Development, 59,* 495–505.

Porter, R. H., Makin, J. W., Davis, L. B., & Christensen, K. M. (1992). Breast-fed infants respond to olfactory clues from their own mother and unfamiliar lactating females. *Infant Behavior and Development, 15,* 85–93.

Posada, G., Gao, Y., Wu, F., Posada, R., Tascon, M., Schoelmerich, A., Sagi, A., Kondo-Ikemura, K., Haaland, W., & Synnevang, B. (1995). The secure base phenomenon across cultures: Children's behavior, mothers' preferences, and experts' concepts. In E. Waters, B. E. Vaughn, G. Posada, & K. Kondo-Ikemura (Eds.), Caregiving, cultural, and cognitive perspectives on secure-base behavior and working models: New growing points of attachment theory and research. *Monographs of the Society for Research in Child Development, 60,* 2–3, Serial No. 244.

Posner, J. K., & Vandell, D. L. (1994). Low-income children's after-school care: Are there beneficial effects of after-school programs? *Child Development, 65,* 440–456.

Poulin-Dubois, D., Serbin, L. A., Kenyon, B., & Derbyshire, A. (1994). Infants' intermodal knowledge about gender. *Developmental Psychology, 30,* 436–442.

Povinelli, D. J., Landau, K. R., & Perilloux, H. K. (1996). Self-recognition in young children using delayed versus live feedback: Evidence of a developmental asynchrony. *Child Development, 67,* 1540–1554.

Powlishta, K. K. (1995). Intergroup processes in childhood: Social categorization and sex role development. *Developmental Psychology, 31,* 781–788.

Pratt, K. C. (1954). The neonate. In L. Carmichael (Ed.), *Manual of child psychology.* New York: Wiley. Development: A review and reinterpretation. *Developmental Review.*

Pratt, M. W., Diessner, R., Hunsberger, B., Pancer, S. M., & Savoy, K. (1991). Four pathways in the analysis of adult development and aging: Comparing analyses of reasoning about personal life dilemmas. *Psychology and Aging, 4,* 666–675.

Pressley, M. (1982). Elaboration and memory development. *Child Development, 53,* 296–309.

Pressley, M., Cariglia-Bull, T., Deane, S., & Schneider, W. (1987). Short-term memory, verbal competence, and age as predictors of imagery instructional effectiveness. *Journal of Experimental Child Psychology, 43,* 194–211.

Previc, F. H. (1991). A general theory concerning the prenatal origins of cerebral lateralization in humans. *Psychological Review, 98,* 299–334.

Priel, B., & deSchonen, S. (1986). Self-recognition: A study of a population without mirrors. *Journal of Experimental Child Psychology, 41,* 237–250.

Provence, J., & Lipton, R. C. (1962). *Infants in institutions.* New York: International Universities Press.

Pungello, E. P., Kupersmidt, J. B., Burchinal, M. R., & Patterson, C.J. (1996). Environmental risk factors and children's achievement from middle childhood to early adolescence. *Developmental Psychology, 32,* 755–767.

Putallaz, M., & Heflin, A. H. (1990). Parent-child interactions. In S. R. Asher & J. D. Coie (Eds.), *Peer rejection in childhood* (pp. 189–216). Cambridge, England: Cambridge University Press.

Quay, L. C. (1971). Language dialect, reinforcement, and the intelligence-test performance of Negro children. *Child Development, 42,* 5–15.

Quiggle, N. L., Garber, J., Panak, W. F., & Dodge, K. A. (1992). Social information processing in aggressive and depressed children. *Child Development, 63,* 1305–1320.

Quinn, R. A., Houts, A. C., & Graesser, A. C. (1994). Naturalistic conceptions of morality: A question-answering approach. *Journal of Personality, 62,* 260–267.

Rabiner, D. L., Keane, S. P., & MacKinnon-Lewis, C. (1993). Children's beliefs about familiar and unfamiliar peers in relation to their sociometric status. *Developmental Psychology, 29,* 236–243.

Rabiner, D. L., Lenhart, L., & Lochman, J. E. (1990). Automatic versus reflective social problem solving in relation to children's sociometric status. *Developmental Psychology, 26,* 1010–1016.

Radke-Yarrow, M., Cummings, E. M., Kuczynski, L., & Chapman, M. (1985). Patterns of attachment in two- and three-year-olds in normal families and families with parental depression. *Child Development, 56,* 884–893.

Radke-Yarrow, M., Zahn-Waxler, C., & Chapman, M. (1983). Children's prosocial dispositions and behavior. In P. H. Mussen (Ed.), *Handbook of child psychology.* (Vol. 4). *Socialization, personality, and social development.* New York: Wiley.

Rakic, P. (1991). Plasticity of cortical development. In S. E. Brauth, W. S. Hall, & R. J. Dooling (Eds.), *Plasticity of development.* Cambridge, MA: Bradford/MIT Press.

Ramey, C. T., & Ramey, S. L. (1992). Effective early intervention. *Mental Retardation, 30,* 337–345.

Ramey, C. T., & Ramey, S. L. (1998). Early intervention and early experience. *American Psychologist, 53,* 296–309.

Ramos-Ford, V., & Gardner, H. (1997). Giftedness from a multiple intelligences perspective. In N. Conangelo & G. A. Davis (Eds.), *Handbook of gifted education* (2nd ed., pp. 54–66). Boston: Allyn & Bacon.

Ramsey, P. G. (1995). Changing social dynamics in early childhood classrooms. *Child Development, 66,* 764–773.

Ratcliffe, S. D., Byrd, J. E., & Sakornbut, E. L. (1996). *Handbook of pregnancy and perinatal care in family practice: Science and practice.* Philadelphia: Hanley & Belfus.

Ratner, H. H. (1984). Memory demands and the development of young children's memory. *Child Development, 55,* 2173–2191.

Raz, S., Goldstein, R., Hopkins, T. L., Lauterbach, M. D., Shah, F., Porter, C. L., Riggs, W. W., Magill, L. H., & Sander, C. J. (1994). Sex differences in early vulnerability to cerebral injury and their neurobehavioral implications. *Psychobiology, 22,* 244–253.

Raz, S., Lauterbach, M. D., Hopkins, T. L., Glogowski, B. K., Porter, C. L., Riggs, W. W., & Sander, C.J. (1995). A female advantage in cognitive recovery from early cerebral insult. *Developmental Psychology, 31,* 958–966.

Reed, T. E. (1997). "The genetic hypothesis": It was not tested but it could have been. *American Psychologist, 52,* 77–78.

Reeder, K. (1981). How young children learn to do things with words. In P. S. Dale & D. Ingram (Eds.), *Child language—an international perspective.* Baltimore: University Park Press.

Reese, E., & Fivush, R. (1993). Parental styles of talking about the past. *Developmental Psychology, 29,* 546–606.

Reese, E., Hayden, C., & Fivush, R. (1993). Mother-child conversations about the past: Relationships of style and memory over time. *Cognitive Development, 8,* 403–430.

Reese, H. A. (1963). Perceptual set in young children. *Child Development, 34,* 151–159.

Reich, P. A. (1986). *Language development.* Englewood Cliffs, NJ: Prentice-Hall.

Reikehof, L. (1963). *Talk to the deaf.* Springfield, MO: Gospel Publishing House.

Reinisch, J. M., Sanders, S. A., Hill, C. A., & Ziemba-Davis, M. (1992). High-risk sexual behavior among heterosexual undergraduates at a midwestern university. *Family Planning Perspectives, 24,* 116.

Reissland, N. (1988). Neonatal imitation in the first hour of life: Observations in rural Nepal. *Developmental Psychology, 24,* 464–469.

Remley, A. (1988, October). The great parental value shift: From obedience to independence. *Psychology Today,* pp. 56–59.

Repacholi, B. M., & Gopnik, A. (1997). Early reasoning about desires: Evidence from 14- and 18-month-olds. *Developmental Psychology, 33,* 12–21.

Resnick, S. M., Berenbaum, S. A., Gottesman, I. I., & Bouchard, T. J. (1986). Early hormonal influences on cognitive functioning in congenital adrenal hyperplasia. *Developmental Psychology, 22,* 191–198.

Rest, J. R., & Thoma, S. J. (1985). Relation of moral judgment development to formal education. *Developmental Psychology, 21,* 709–714.

Rest, J. R., Thoma, S. J., & Edwards, L. (1997). Designing and validating a measure of moral judgment: Stage preference and stage consistency approaches. *Journal of Educational Psychology, 89,* 5–28.

Revelle, G. L., Wellman, H. M., & Karabenick, J. D. (1985). Comprehension monitoring in preschool children. *Child Development, 56,* 654–663.

Reyna, V. F., & Brainerd, C. J. (1995). Fuzzy-trace theory: An interim synthesis. *Learning and Individual Differences, 7,* 1–75.

Reynolds, A. J., & Temple, J. A. (1998). Extended early childhood intervention and school achievement: Age thirteen findings from the Chicago Longitudinal Study. *Child Development, 69,* 231–246.

Reynolds, D. (1992). School effectiveness and school improvement: An updated review of the British literature. In D. Reynolds & P. Cuttance (Eds.), *School effectiveness: Research, policy, and practice.* London, England: Cassell.

Reznick, J. S., & Goldfield, B. A. (1992). Rapid change in lexical development in comprehension and production. *Developmental Psychology, 28,* 406–413.

Rheingold, H. L., & Adams, J. L. (1980). The significance of speech to newborns. *Developmental Psychology, 16,* 397–403.

Rheingold, H. L. (1982). Little children's participation in the work of adults, a nascent prosocial behavior. *Child Development, 53,* 114–125.

Rholes, W. S., & Ruble, D. N. (1984). Children's understanding of dispositional characteristics of others. *Child Development, 55,* 550–560.

Ribble, M. (1943). *The rights of infants.* New York: Columbia University Press.

Ricco, R. B. (1989). Operational thought and the acquisition of taxonomic relations involving figurative dissimilarity. *Developmental Psychology, 25,* 996–1003.

Rice, C., Koinis, D., Sullivan, K., Tager-Flusberg, & Winner, E. (1997). When 3-year olds pass the appearance-reality test. *Developmental Psychology, 33,* 54–61.

Rice, M. E., & Grusec, J. E. (1975). Saying and doing: Effects on observer performance. *Journal of Personality and Social Psychology, 32,* 584–593.

Rice, M. L. (1989). Children's language acquisition. *American Psychologist, 44,* 149–156.

Rice, M. L., Huston, A. C., Truglio, R., & Wright, J. (1990). Words from "Sesame Street": Learning vocabulary while viewing. *Developmental Psychology, 26,* 421–428.

Richards, J. E. (1997). Effects of attention on infant's preference for briefly exposed visual stimuli in the paired-comparison recognition-memory paradigm. *Developmental Psychology, 32,* 22–31.

Richards, M. H., Boxer, A. M., Petersen, A. C., & Albrecht, R. (1990). Relation of weight to body image in pubertal girls and boys from two communities. *Developmental Psychology, 26,* 313–321.

Richards, M. H., Crowe, P. A., Larson, R., & Swarr, A. (1998). Developmental patterns and gender differences in the experience of peer companionship during adolescence. *Child Development, 69,* 154–163.

Richards, M. H., & Duckett, E. (1994). The relationship of maternal employment to early adolescent daily experience with and without parents. *Child Development, 65,* 225–236.

Richardson, J. G., & Simpson, C. H. (1982). Children, gender, and social structure: An analysis of the contents of letters to Santa Claus. *Child Development, 53,* 429–436.

Richert, E. S. (1997). Excellence with equity in identification and programming. In N. Colangelo & G. A. Davis (Eds.), *Handbook of gifted education* (2nd ed., pp. 75–88). Boston: Allyn & Bacon.

Richman, E. (1997). *It's a whole 'nother ball game: Sports participation promotes women's self-esteem.* Unpublished Masters' thesis, University of Georgia.

Ridderinkhoff, K. R., & van der Molen, M. W. (1995). A psychophysiological analysis of developmental differences in the ability to resist interference. *Child Development, 66,* 1040–1056.

Riesen, A. H. (1947). The development of visual perception in man and chimpanzee. *Science, 106,* 107–108.

Riesen, A. H., Chow, K. L., Semmes, J., & Nissen, H. W. (1951). Chimpanzee vision after four conditions of light deprivation. *American Psychologist, 6,* 282.

Rieser, J., Yonas, A., & Wilkner, K. (1976). Radial localization of odors by human newborns. *Child Development, 47,* 856–859.

Roberts, K. (1988). Retrieval of a basic-level category in prelinguistic infants. *Developmental Psychology, 24,* 21–27.

Roberts, L. R., Sarigiani, P. A., Petersen, A. C., & Newman, J. L. (1990). Gender differences in the relationship between achievement and self-image during early adolescence. *Journal of Early Adolescence, 10,* 159–175.

Roberts, W., & Strayer, J. (1996). Empathy, emotional expressiveness, and prosocial behavior. *Child Development, 67,* 449–470.

Robertson, T. S., & Rossiter, J. R. (1974). Children and commercial persuasion: An attribution theory analysis. *Journal of Consumer Research, 1,* 13–20.

Robin, D. J., Berthier, N. E., & Clifton, R. K. (1996). Infants' predictive reaching for moving objects in the dark. *Developmental Psychology, 32,* 824–835.

Robinson, A., Bender, B. G., & Linden, M. G. (1992). Prenatal diagnosis of sex chromosome abnormalities. In A. Milunsky (Ed.), *Genetic disorders and the fetus: Diagnosis, prevention, and treatment.* Baltimore: Johns Hopkins University Press.

Robinson, C. C., & Morris, J. T. (1986). The gender-stereotyped nature of Christmas toys received by 36-, 48-, and 60-month-old children: A comparison between nonrequested vs. requested toys. *Sex Roles, 15,* 21–32.

Robinson, I., Ziss, K., Ganza, B., Katz, S., & Robinson, E. (1991). Twenty years of sexual revolution, 1965–1985: An update. *Journal of Marriage and the Family, 53,* 216–220.

Robinson, J. L., Kagan, J., Reznick, J. S., & Corley, R. (1992). The heritability of inhibited and uninhibited behavior. A twin study. *Developmental Psychology, 28,* 1030–1037.

Robinson, N. M., & Janos, P. M. (1986). Psychological adjustment in a college-level program of marked academic acceleration. *Journal of Youth and Adolescence, 15,* 51–60.

Rochat, P. (1989). Object manipulation and exploration in 2- to 5-month-old infants. *Developmental Psychology, 25,* 871–884.

Rochat, P., & Goubet, N. (1995). Development of sitting and reaching in 5- to 6-month-old infants. *Infant Behavior and Development, 18,* 53–68.

Rochat, P., & Morgan, R. (1995). Spatial determinants of the perception of self-produced leg movements by 3- to 5-month-old infants. *Developmental Psychology, 31,* 626–636.

Roche, A. F. (1981). The adipocyte-number hypothesis. *Child Development, 52,* 31–43.

Rocheleau, B. (1995). Computer use by school-age children: Trends, patterns, and predictors. *Journal of Educational Computing Research, 12,* 1–17.

Rodgers, J. L., & Rowe, D. C. (1988). Influence of siblings on adolescent sexual behavior. *Developmental Psychology, 24,* 722–728.

Rodning, C., Beckwith, L., & Howard, J. (1991). Quality of attachment and home environments in children prenatally exposed to PCP and cocaine. *Development and Psychopathology, 3,* 351–366.

Roeleveld, N., Zielhuis, G. A., & Gabreels, F. (1997). The prevalence of mental retardation: A critical review of present literature. *Developmental Medicine and Child Neurology, 39,* 125–132.

Roffwarg, H. P., Muzio, J. W., & Dement, W. C. (1966). Ontogenetic development of the human sleep-dream cycle. *Science, 152,* 604–619.

Rogoff, B. (1990). *Apprenticeship in thinking: Cognitive development in social context.* New York: Oxford University Press.

Rogoff, B. (1997). Cognition as a collaborative process. In D. Kuhn & R. S. Siegler (Eds.), *Cognition, language, and perceptual development* (Vol. 2). In B. Damon (Gen. Ed.), *Handbook of child psychology.* (pp. 679–744). New York: Wiley.

Rogoff, B., & Waddell, K. J. (1982). Memory for information organized in a scene by children from two cultures. *Child Development, 53,* 1224–1228.

Rogoff, B., Mistry, J., Goncu, A., & Mosier, C. (1993). Guided participation in cultural activity by toddlers and caregivers. *Monographs of the Society for Research in Child Development, 58,* 8, Serial No. 236.

Rogoff, B., Mistry, J., Goncu, A., & Mosier, C. (1993). Guided participation in cultural activity by toddlers and caregivers. *Monographs of the Society for Research in Child Development, 58* (8, Serial No. 236).

Roithmaier, A., Kiess, W., Kopecky, M., Fuhrmann, G., Butenandt, O. (1988). Psychosozialer Minderwuchs. *Monatschift fur Kinderheilkunde, 133,* 760–763.

Roland, M. G. M., Cole, T. J., & Whitehead, R. G. (1977). A quantitative study into the role of infection in determining nutritional status in Gambian village children. *British Journal of Nutrition, 37,* 441–450.

Roopnarine, J. L., Talukder, E., Jain, D., Joshi, P., & Srivastave, P. (1990). Characteristics of holding, patterns of play, and social behaviors between parents and infants in New Delhi, India. *Developmental Psychology, 26,* 667–673.

Rose, N. C. & Mennuti, M. T. (1994). Periconceptional folate supplementation and neural tube defects. *Clinical Obstetrics and Gynecology, 37,* 605–620.

Rose, R. M., Bernstein, I. S., & Gordon, T. P. (1975). Consequences of social conflict on plasma testosterone levels in rhesus monkeys. *Psychosomatic Medicine, 37,* 50–61.

Rose, S. A. (1988). Shape recognition in infancy: Visual integration of sequential information. *Child Development, 59,* 1161–1176.

Rose, S. A., & Feldman, J. F. (1995). Prediction of IQ and specific cognitive abilities from infancy measures. *Developmental Psychology, 31,* 685–696.

Rose, S. A., & Feldman, J. F. (1996). Memory and processing speed in preterm children at eleven years: A comparison with full-terms. *Child Development, 67,* 2005–2021.

Rose, S. A., Feldman, J. F., Wallace, I. F., & McCarton, C. (1989). Infant visual attention: Relation to birth status and developmental outcome during the first 5 years. *Developmental Psychology, 25,* 560–576.

Rose, S. A., Gottfried, A. W., & Bridger, W. H. (1981). Cross-modal transfer in 6-month-old infants. *Developmental Psychology, 17,* 661–669.

Rosen, B. C., & D'Andrade, R. (1959). The psychosocial origins of achievement motivation. *Sociometry, 22,* 185–218.

Rosen, J. C., Tracey, B., & Howell, D. (1990). Life stress, psychological symptoms, and weight reducing behavior in adolescent girls: A prospective analysis. *International Journal of Eating Disorders, 9,* 17–26.

Rosen, K. S., & Rothbaum, F. (1993). Quality of parental caregiving and security of attachment. *Developmental Psychology, 29,* 358–367.

Rosen, W. D., Adamson, L. B., & Bakeman, R. (1992). An experimental investigation of infant social referencing: Mothers' messages and gender differences. *Developmental Psychology, 28,* 1172–1178.

Rosenberg, M. (1979). *Conceiving the self.* New York: Basic Books.

Rosenhan, D. L. (1970). The natural socialization of altruistic autonomy. In J. L. Macaulay & L. Berkowitz (Eds.), *Altruism and helping behavior.* New York: Academic Press.

Rosenholtz, S. J., & Simpson, C. (1984). The formation of ability conceptions: Developmental trend or social construction? *Review of Educational Research, 54,* 31–63.

Rosenstein, D., & Oster, H. (1988). Differential facial responses to four basic tastes in newborns. *Child Development, 59,* 1555–1568.

Rosenthal, D. A., & Feldman, S. S. (1992). The relationship between parenting behavior and ethnic identity in Chinese-American and Chinese-Australian adolescents. *International Journal of Psychology, 27,* 19–31.

Rosenthal, M. K. (1982). Vocal dialogues in the neonatal period. *Developmental Psychology, 18,* 17–21.

Rosenthal, R., & Jacobson, L. (1968). *Pygmalion in the classroom.* New York: Holt, Rinehart and Winston.

Rosenthal, R., & Vandell, D. L. (1996). Quality of care at school-aged child-care programs: Regulatable features, observed experiences, child perspectives, and parent perspectives. *Child Development, 67,* 2434–2445.

Rosenwasser, S. M., Lingenfelter, M., & Harrington, A. F. (1989). Nontraditional gender role portrayals on television and children's gender role perceptions. *Journal of Applied Developmental Psychology, 10,* 97–105.

Rosenzweig, M. R. (1984). Experience, memory, and the brain. *American Psychologist, 39,* 365–376.

Ross, H. S., & Lollis, S. P. (1987). Communication within infant social games. *Developmental Psychology, 23,* 241–248.

Ross, R. T., Begab, M. J., Dondis, E. H., Giampiccolo, J. S., Jr., & Meyers, C. E. (1985). *Lives of the mentally retarded. A forty-year follow-up study.* Stanford, CA: Stanford University Press.

Rothbart, M. K. (1971). Birth order and mother-child interaction in an achievement situation. *Journal of Personality and Social Psychology, 17,* 113–120.

Rothbart, M. K. (1981). Measurement of temperament in infancy. *Child Development, 52,* 569–578.

Rothberg, A. D., & Lits, B. (1991). Psychosocial support for maternal stress during pregnancy: Effect on birth weight. *American Journal of Obstetrics and Gynecology, 165,* 403–407.

Rousseau, J. J. (1955). *Emile.* New York: Dutton. (Original work published 1762.)

Rovee-Collier, C. K. (1987). Learning and memory in infancy. In J. D. Osofsky (Ed.), *Handbook of infant development,* (2nd ed.). New York: Wiley.

Rovee-Collier, C. K. (1995). Time windows in cognitive development. *Developmental Psychology, 31,* 147–169.

Rovee-Collier, C. K. (1997). Dissociations in infant memory: Retention without remembering. In J. D. Osofsky (Ed.), *Handbook of infant development* (2nd ed.). New York: Wiley.

Rowe, D. C. (1994). *The limits of family influence: Genes, experience, and behavior.* New York: Guilford.

Rowe, D. C., & Plomin, R. (1981). The importance of nonshared (E_1) environmental influences in behavioral development. *Developmental Psychology, 17,* 517–531.

Rubenstein, J. L., Heeren, T., Housman, D., Rubin, C., & Stechler, G. (1989). Suicidal behavior in normal adolescents: Risks and protective factors. *American Journal of Orthopsychiatry, 59,* 59–71.

Rubin, K. H., Fein, G., & Vandenberg, B. (1983). Play. In E. M. Hetherington (Ed.), *Handbook of child psychology.* (Vol. 4). *Socialization, personality,and social development* (pp. 693–744). New York: Wiley.

Ruble, D. N., Balaban, T., & Cooper, J. (1981). Gender constancy and the effects of sex-typed televised toy commercials. *Child Development, 52,* 667–673.

Ruble, D. N., & Dweck, C. S. (1995). Self-conceptions, person conceptions, and their development. In N. Eisenberg (Ed.), *Social development.* Thousand Oaks, CA: Sage.

Ruble, T. L. (1983). Sex stereotypes: Issues of change in the 1970s. *Sex Roles, 9,* 397–402.

Rudin, M., Zalewski, C., & Bodmer-Turner, J. (1995). Characteristics of child sexual abusive victims according to perpetrator gender. *Child Abuse & Neglect, 19,* 963–973.

Rudolph, F. (1965). *Essays on early education in the republic.* Cambridge, MA: Harvard University Press.

Rudolph, K. D., Hammen, C., & Burge, D. (1995). Cognitive representations of self, family, and peers in school-age children: Links with social competence and sociometric status. *Child Development, 66,* 1385–1402.

Ruff, H. A., & Lawson, K. R. (1990). Development of sustained focused attention in young children during free play. *Developmental Psychology, 26,* 85–93.

Ruff, H. A., Lawson, K. R., Parrinello, R., & Weissberg, R. (1990). Long-term stability of individual differences in sustained attention in the early years. *Child Development, 61,* 60–75.

Ruffman, T. K., & Olson, D. R. (1989). Children's ascriptions of knowledge to others. *Developmental Psychology, 25,* 601–606.

Ruffman, T. K., Olson, D. R., Ash, T., & Keenan, T. (1993). The ABCs of deception: Do young children understand deception in the same way as adults? *Developmental Psychology, 29,* 74–87.

Runco, M. A. (1992). Children's divergent thinking and creative ideation. *Developmental Review, 12,* 233–264.

Rushton, J. P. (1980). *Altruism, socialization, and society.* Englewood Cliffs: NJ, Prentice Hall.

Rushton, J. P. (1997). Race, IQ, and the APA report on the Bell Curve. *American Psychologist, 52,* 69–70.

Rushton, J. P., Fulker, D. W., Neale, M. C., Nias, K. K. B., & Eysenck, H. J. (1986). Altruism and aggression. The heritability of individual differences. *Journal of Personality and Social Psychology, 50,* 1192–1198.

Russell, A., & Finnie, V. (1990). Preschool children's social status and maternal instructions to assist group entry. *Developmental Psychology, 26,* 600–611.

Russell, G. F. M., Szmukler, G. I., Dare, C., & Eisler, I. (1987). An evaluation of family therapy in anorexia nervosa and bulimia nervosa. *Archives of General Psychiatry, 44,* 1047–1056.

Rutter, D. R., & Durkin, K. (1987). Turn-taking in mother-infant interaction: An examination of vocalizations and gaze. *Developmental Psychology, 23,* 54–61.

Rutter, M. (1979). Protective factors in children's responses to stress and disadvantage. In M. W. Kent & J. E. Rolf (Eds .), *Primary prevention of psychopathology.* (Vol. 3). *Social competence in children.* Hanover, NH: University Press of New England.

Rutter, M. (1981). *Maternal deprivation revisited* (2nd ed.). New York: Penguin Books.

Rutter, M. (1983). School effects on pupil progress: Research findings and policy implications. *Child Development, 54,* 1–29.

Rutter, M., Maughan, B., Mortimore, P., Ouston, J., & Smith, A. (1979). *Fifteen thousand hours: Secondary schools and their effects on children.* Cambridge, MA: Harvard University Press.

Saarni, C. (1984). An observational study of children's attempts to monitor their expressive behavior. *Child Development, 55,* 1504–1513.

Saarni, C. (1990). Emotional competence: How emotions and relationships become integrated. In R. A. Thompson (Ed.), Socioemotional development. *Nebraska Symposium on Motivation* (Vol. 36). Lincoln: University of Nebraska Press.

Saarni, C. (1993). Socialization of emotion. In M. Lewis & J. M. Haviland (Eds.), *Handbook of emotions* (pp. 435–446). New York: Guilford.

Sadler, T. W. (1996). Embryology and experimental teratology. In J. A. Kuller, N. C. Cheschier, & R. C. Cefalo (Eds.), *Prenatal diagnosis and reproductive genetics* (pp. 218–226). St. Louis, MO: Mosby.

Sagi, A., & Hoffman, M. L. (1976). Empathic distress in newborns. *Developmental Psychology, 12,* 175–176.

Sagi, A., van IJzendoorn, M. H., Aviezer, O., Donnell, F., & Mayseless, O. (1994). Sleeping out of home in a kibbutz communal arrangement: It makes a difference for mother-infant attachment. *Child Development, 65,* 992–1004.

Sagotsky, G., & Lepper, M. R. (1982). Generalization of changes in children's preferences for easy or difficult goals induced through peer modeling. *Child Development, 53,* 372–375.

Sahni, R., Schulze, K. F., Stefanski, M., Myers, M. M., & Fifer, W. P. (1995). Methodological issues in coding sleep states in immature infants. *Developmental Psychobiology, 28,* 85–101.

Salapatek, P. (1975). Pattern perception in infancy. In L. B. Cohen & P. Salapatek (Eds.), *Infant perception: From sensation to cognition* (Vol. 1). Orlando, FL: Academic Press.

Salzinger, S., Feldman, R. S., Hammer, M., & Rosario, M. (1993). The effects of physical abuse on children's social relationships. *Child Development, 64,* 169–187.

Sameroff, A. J., & Chandler, M. J. (1975). Reproductive risk and the continuum of caretaking casualty. In F. D. Horowitz, M. Hetherington, S. Scarr-Salapatek, & G. Siegel (Eds.), *Review of child development research* (Vol. 4). Chicago: University of Chicago Press.

Sameroff, A. J., Seifer, R., Baldwin, A., & Baldwin, C. (1993). Stability of intelligence from preschool to adolescence: The influence of social and family risk factors. *Child Development, 64,* 80–97.

Samuels, C. (1986). Bases for the infant's development of self-awareness. *Human Development, 29,* 36–48.

Sansavini, A., Bertocini, J., & Giovanelli, G. (1997). Newborns discriminate the rhythm of multisyllabic stressed words. *Developmental Psychology, 33,* 3–11.

Santrock, J. W. (1975). Moral structure: The interrelations of moral behavior, moral judgment, and moral affect. *Journal of Genetic Psychology, 127,* 201–213.

Santrock, J. W., & Sitterle, K. A. (1987). Parent-child relationships in stepmother families. In K. Pasley & M. Ihinger-Tallman (Eds.), *Remarriage and stepparenting: Current research and theory.* New York: Guilford Press.

Sattler, J. M. (1992). *Assessment of children* (3rd rev. ed.). San Diego, CA: J. M. Sattler.

Savage, S. L., & Au, T. K. (1996). What word learners do when input contradicts the mutual exclusivity assumption. *Child Development, 67,* 3120–3134.

Savage-Rumbaugh, E. S., Murphy, J., Sevcik, R. A., Brakke, K. E., Williams, S. L., & Rumbaugh, D. M. (1993). Language comprehension in ape and child. *Monographs of the Society for Research in Child Development, 58,* 3–4, Serial No. 233.

Savage-Rumbaugh, E. S., Rumbaugh, D. M., & Boysen, S. (1978). Symbolic communication between two chimpanzees (Pan troglodytes). *Science, 201,* 641–644.

Savin-Williams, R. C. (1995). An exploratory study of pubertal maturation timing and self-esteem among gay and bisexual male youths. *Developmental Psychology, 31,* 1100–1110.

Savin-Williams, R. C., & Demo, D. H. (1984). Developmental change and stability in adolescent self-concept. *Developmental Psychology, 20,* 1100–1110.

Savin-Williams, R. C., & Small, S. A. (1986). The timing of puberty and its relationship to adolescent and parent perceptions of family interactions. *Developmental Psychology, 32,* 342–347.

Saxton, M. (1997). The contrast theory of negative input. *Journal of Child Language, 24,* 139–161.

Scafidi, F. A., Field, T. M., Schanberg, S. M., Bauer, C. R., Vega-Lahr, N., Garcia, R., Poirier, J., Nystrom, G., & Kuhn, C. M. (1986). Effects of tactile/kinesthetic stimulation on the clinical course and sleep/wake behavior pattern of preterm neonates. *Infant Behavior and Development, 9,* 91–105.

Scafidi, F. A., Field, T. M., Schanberg, S. M., Bauer, C. R., Vega-Lahr, N., Garcia, R., Poirer, J., Nystrom, G., & Kuhn, C. M. (1990). Massage stimulates growth in preterm infants: A replication. *Infant Behavior and Development, 13,* 167–188.

Scarr, S. (1992). Developmental theories for the 1990s: Development and individual differences. *Child Development, 63,* 1–19.

Scarr, S. (1998). American child care today. *American Psychologist, 53,* 95–108.

Scarr, S., & McCartney, K. (1983). How people make their own environments: A theory of genotype → environment effects. *Child Development, 54,* 424–435.

Scarr, S., Pakstis, A. J., Katz, S. H., & Barker, W. (1977) The absence of a relationship between degree of white ancestry and intellectual skills within a black population. *Human Genetics, 39,* 69–86.

Scarr, S., Phillips, D., McCartney, K., & Abbott-Shim, M. (1993). Quality of child care as an aspect of family and child care policy in the United States. *Pediatrics, 91,* 182–188.

Scarr, S., & Weinberg, R. A. (1978). The influence of family background on intellectual attainment. *American Sociological Review, 43,* 674–692.

Scarr, S., & Weinberg, R. A. (1983). The Minnesota adoption studies: Genetic differences and malleability. *Child Development, 54,* 260–267.

Schaefer, M., Hatcher, R. P., & Barglow, P. D. (1980). Prematurity and infant stimulation: A review of research. *Child Psychiatry and Human Development, 10,* 199–212.

Schaffer, H. R. (1971). *The growth of sociability.* Baltimore: Penguin Books.

Schaffer, H. R., & Emerson, P. E. (1964). The development of social attachments in infancy. *Monographs of the Society for Research in Child Development, 29,* 3, Serial No. 94.

Schaie, K. W. (1990). Intellectual development in adulthood. In E. J. Birren & K. W. Schaie (Eds.). *The handbook of the psychology of aging* (3rd ed.). San Diego, CA: Academic Press.

Schalock, R. L., Holl, C., Elliott, B., & Ross, I. (1992). A longitudinal follow-up of graduates from a rural special education program. *Learning Disability Quarterly, 15,* 29–38.

Schauble, L. (1990). Belief revision in children: The role of prior knowledge and strategies for generating evidence. *Journal of Experimental Child Psychology, 49,* 31–57.

Schieffelin, B. B. (1986). *How Kaluli children learn what to say, what to do, and how to feel.* New York: Cambridge University Press.

Schiff-Myers, N. (1988). Hearing children of deaf parents. In D. Bishop & K. Mogford (Eds.), *Language development in exceptional circumstances.* Edinburgh: Churchill Livingstone.

Schinke, S. P., Schilling, R. F. II, Barth, R. P., Gilchrist, L. D., & Maxwell, J. S. (1986). Stress-management intervention to prevent family violence. *Journal of Family Violence, 1,* 13–26.

Schlegel, A., & Barry, H., III. (1991). *Adolescence: An anthropological inquiry.* New York: Free Press.

Schliemann, A. D. (1992). Mathematical concepts in and out of school in Brazil: From developmental psychology to better teaching. *Newsletter of the International Society for the Study of Behavioral Development,* Serial No. 22, No. 2, 1–3.

Schmitz, S., Saudino, K. J., Plomin, R., Fulker, D. W., & DeFries, J. C. (1996). Genetic and environmental influences on temperament in middle childhood: Analyses of teacher and tester ratings. *Child Development, 67,* 409–422.

Schneider, B. H. (1992). Didactic methods for enhancing children's peer relations: A quantitative review. *Clinical Psychology Review, 12,* 363–382.

Schneider, W., & Bjorklund, D. F. (1992). Expertise, aptitude, and strategic remembering. *Child Development, 63,* 461–471.

Schneider, W., & Bjorklund, D. F. (1997). Memory. In D. Kuhn & R. S. Siegler (Eds.), *Cognitive, language, and perceptual development* (Vol. 2). In B. Damon (General Ed.), *Handbook of child psychology* (pp. 467–521). New York: Wiley.

Schneider, W., Bjorklund, D. F., & Maier-Bruckner, W. (1996). The effects of expertise and IQ on children's memory: When knowledge is, and when it is not enough. *International Journal of Behavioral Development, 19,* 773–796.

Schneider, W., Gruber, H., Gold, A., & Opwis, K. (1993). Chess expertise and memory for chess positions in children and adults. *Journal of Experimental Child Psychology, 56,* 328–349.

Schneider, W., Korkel, J., & Weinert, F. E. (1989). Domain-specific knowledge and memory performance: A comparison of high- and low-aptitude children. *Journal of Educational Psychology, 81,* 306–312.

Schneider, W., & Pressley, M. (1997). *Memory development between 2 and 20* (2nd. ed.). Mahwah, NJ: Erlbaum.

Scholl, T. O., Hediger, M. L., & Belsky, D. H. (1994). Prenatal care and maternal health during adolescent pregnancy: A review and meta-analysis. *Journal of Adolescent Health, 15,* 444–456.

Schulman, J. D., & Black, S. H. (1993). Genetics of some common inherited diseases. In R. G. Edwards (Ed.), *Preconception and preimplantation diagnosis of human genetic disease.* Cambridge, England: Cambridge University Press.

Schuster, D. T. (1990). Fulfillment of potential, life satisfaction, and competence: Comparing four cohorts of gifted women at midlife. *Journal of Educational Psychology, 82,* 471–478.

Schwartz, D., Dodge, K. A., Pettit, G. S., & Bates, J. E. (1997). The early socialization of aggressive victims of bullying. *Child Development, 68,* 665–675.

Scott, J. P. (1992). Aggression: Functions and control in social systems. *Aggressive Behavior, 18,* 1–20.

Scott, W. A., Scott, R., & McCabe, M. (1991). Family relationships and children's personality: A cross-cultural, cross-source comparison. *British Journal of Social Psychology, 30,* 1–20

Seabrook, C. (1997, February 12). Eating disorders can be overcome. *Atlanta Constitution,* C1.

Sears, R. R. (1963). Dependency motivation. In M. Jones (Ed.), *Nebraska Symposium on Motivation* (Vol. 11). Lincoln: University of Nebraska Press.

Sebald, H. (1986). Adolescents' shifting orientation toward parents and peers: A curvilinear trend over recent decades. *Journal of Marriage and the Family, 48,* 5–13.

Sedlak, A. J., & Kurtz, S. T. (1981). A review of children's use of causal inference principles. *Child Development, 52,* 759–784.

Segal, U. A. (1991). Cultural variables in Asian Indian families. *Families in society: The Journal of Contemporary Human Services, 72,* 233–242.

Seidman, E., Allen, L., Aber, J. L., Mitchell, C., & Feinman, J. (1994). The impact of school transitions in early adolescence on the self-system and perceived social context of poor urban youth. *Child Development, 65,* 507–522.

Seifer, R., Schiller, M., Sameroff, A. J., Resnick, S., & Riordan, K. (1996). Attachment, maternal sensitivity, and infant temperament during the first year of life. *Developmental Psychology, 32,* 12–25.

Seitz, V., & Apfel, N. H. (1994a). Effects of a school for pregnant students on the incidence of low-birthweight deliveries. *Child Development, 65,* 666–676.

Seitz, V., & Apfel, N. H. (1994b). Parent-focused intervention: Diffusion effects on siblings. *Child Development, 65,* 677–683.

Seitz, V., Rosenbaum, L. K., & Apfel, N. H. (1985). Effects of family support intervention: A ten-year follow-up. *Child Development, 56,* 376–391.

Selman, R. L. (1976). Social-cognitive understanding: A guide to educational and clinical practice. In T. Lickona (Ed.), *Moral development and behavior: Theory, research, and social issues.* New York: Holt, Rinehart and Winston.

Selman, R. L. (1980). *The growth of interpersonal understanding.* Orlando, FL: Academic Press.

Seppa, N. (1997a). Early intervention is key to mending reading problems. *Monitor of the American Psychological Association, 28,* 24–25.

Seppa, N. (1997b). Children's TV remains steeped in violence. *Monitor of the American Psychological Association, 28,* (6), 36.

Serbin, L. A., Powlishta, K. K., & Gulko, J. (1993). The development of sex typing in middle childhood. *Monographs of the Society for Research in Child Development, 58,* 2, Serial No. 232.

Shafer, H. H., & Kuller, J. A. (1996). Increased maternal age and prior anenploid conception. In J. A. Kuller, N. C. Cheschier, & R. C. Cefalo (Eds.), *Prenatal diagnosis and reproductive genetics* (pp. 23–28). St. Louis: Mosby.

Shaffer, D. R. (1973). *Children's responses to a hypothetical proposition.* Unpublished manuscript, Kent State University.

Shaffer, D. R. (1994a). Do naturalistic conceptions of morality provide any [novel] answers? *Journal of Personality, 62,* 263–268.

Shaffer, D. R. (1994b). *Social and personality development* (3rd ed.). Pacific Grove, CA: Brooks/Cole.

Shaffer, D. R., Pegalis, L. J., & Cornell, D. P. (1992). Gender and self-disclosure revisited: Personal and contextual variations in self-disclosure to same-sex acquaintances. *Journal of Social Psychology, 132,* 307–315.

Shanahan, M. J., Elder, G. H., Jr., Burchinal, M., & Conger, R. D. (1996). Adolescent paid labor and relationships with parents: Early work-family linkages. *Child Development, 67,* 2183–2200.

Shanahan, M. J., Finch, M. D., Mortimer, J. T., & Ryu, S. (1991). Adolescent work experience and depressive affect. *Social Psychology Quarterly, 54,* 299–317.

Shantz, C. U. (1983). Social cognition. In P. H. Mussen (Ed.), *Handbook of child psychology.* (Vol. 3). *Cognitive development.* New York: Wiley.

Shatz, M. (1994). Theory of mind and the development of sociolinguistic intelligence in early childhood. In C. Lewis & P. Mitchell (Eds.), *Children's early understanding of the mind* (pp. 311–329). Hillsdale, NJ: Erlbaum.

Shatz, M., & Gelman, R. (1973). The development of communication skills: Modifications in the speech of young children as a function of listener. *Monographs of the Society for Research in Child Development, 38,* Serial No. 152.

Shaw, D. S., Keenan, K., & Vondra, J. I. (1994). Developmental precursors of externalizing behavior: Ages 1 to 3. *Developmental Psychology, 30,* 355–364.

Shearer, L. (1994, April 2). U.Ga. symposium speaker raps "crack babies" research. *Athens Banner-Herald,* p. 1A, 10A.

Sheingold, K., & Tenney, Y. J. (1982). Memory for a salient childhood event. In U. Neisser (Ed.), *Memory observed: Remembering in natural contexts.* San Francisco: W. H. Freeman.

Shell, R. M., & Eisenberg, N. (1996). Children's reactions to the receipt of direct and indirect help. *Child Development, 67,* 1391–1405.

Sherif, M., Harvey, O. J., White, B. J., Hood, W. R., & Sherif, C. W. (1961). *Intergroup conflict and cooperation: The Robber's Cave experiment.* Norman: University of Oklahoma Press.

Sherman, S. (1996). Epidemiology. In R. J. Hagerman & A. Cronister (Eds.). *Fragile-x syndrome: Diagnosis, treatment, and research* (2nd ed., pp. 165–192). Baltimore: Johns Hopkins University Press.

Shiffrin, R. M., & Schneider, W. (1977). Controlled and automatic human information processing. II. Perceptual learning, automatic attending, and a general theory. *Psychological Review, 84,* 127–190.

Shigetomi, C. C., Hartmann, D. P., & Gelfand, D. M. (1981). Sex differences in children's altruistic behavior and reputations for helpfulness. *Developmental Psychology, 17,* 434–437.

Shirley, M. M. (1933). *The first two years: A study of 25 babies.* (Vol. 1). *Postural and locomotor development.* Minneapolis: University of Minnesota Press.

Shoda, Y., Mischel, W., & Peake, P.K. (1990). Predicting adolescent cognitive and self-regulatory competencies from preschool delay of gratification: Identifying diagnostic conditions. *Developmental Psychology, 26,* 978–986.

Short, R. J., & Talley, R. C. (1997). Rethinking psychology and the schools: Implications of recent national policy. *American Psychologist, 52,* 234–240.

Shulman, S., Elicker, J., & Sroufe, A. (1994). Stages of friendship growth in preadolescence as related to attachment history. *Journal of Social and Personal Relationships, 11,* 341–361.

Shure, M. B. (1989). Interpersonal competence training. In W. Damon (Ed.), *Child development today and tomorrow.* San Francisco: Jossey-Bass.

Shure, M. B., & Spivack, G. (1978). *Problem-solving techniques in childrearing.* San Francisco: Jossey-Bass.

Shurkin, J. N. (1992). *Terman's kids. The groundbreaking study of how the gifted grow up.* Boston: Little, Brown.

Shwe, H. I., & Markman, E. M. (1997). Young children's appreciation of the mental impact of their communicative signals. *Developmental Psychology, 33,* 630–636.

Shweder, R. A., Mahapatra, M., & Miller, J. G. (1990). Culture and moral development. In J. W. Stigler, R. A. Shweder, & G. Herdt (Eds.), *Cultural psychology. Essays on comparative human development.* Cambridge, England: Cambridge University Press.

Siegal, M., & Cowen, J. (1984). Appraisals of intervention: The mother's versus the culprit's behavior as determinants of children's evaluations of discipline techniques. *Child Development, 55,* 1760–1766.

Siegel, B. (1996). Was the emperor wearing clothes? Social policy and the empirical support for full inclusion of children with disabilities in the preschool and early elementary grades. *Social Policy Report, Society for Research in Child Development, 10,* 2–3, 2–17.

Siegel, L. S., & Ryan, E. B. (1989). The development of working memory in normally achieving and subtypes of learning disabled children. *Child Development, 60,* 973–980.

Siegler, R. S. (1976). Three aspects of cognitive development. *Cognitive Psychology, 8,* 481–520.

Siegler, R. S. (1987). The perils of averaging data over strategies: An example from children's addition. *Journal of Experimental Psychology: General, 116,* 250–264.

Siegler, R. S. (1991). *Children's thinking* (2nd ed.). Englewood Cliffs, NJ: Prentice Hall.

Siegler, R. S. (1996). A grand theory of development. In R. Case, Y. Okamoto & Associates, The role of central conceptual structures in the development of children's thought. *Monographs of the Society for Research in Child Development, 61,* (1–2, Serial No. 246).

Siegler, R. S. (1996). *Beyond the immaculate transition: Change processes in children's thinking.* New York: Oxford University Press.

Siegler, R. S. (1996). *Emerging minds: The process of change in children's thinking.* New York: Oxford University Press.

Siegler, R. S., & Crowley, K. (1992). Microgenetic methods revisited. *American Psychologist, 47,* 1241–1243.

Siegler, R. S., & Ellis, S. (1996). Piaget on childhood. *Psychological Science, 7,* 211–215.

Siegler, R. S., & Jenkins, E. (1989). *How children discover strategies.* Hillsdale, NJ: Erlbaum.

Siegler, R. S., & Munakata, Y. (1993, Winter). Beyond the immaculate transition: Advances in the understanding of change. *Newsletter of the Society for Research in Child Development.*

Sigelman, C. K., Carr, M. B., & Begley, N. L. (1986) Developmental changes in the influence of sex-role stereotypes on person perception. *Child Study Journal, 16,* 191–205.

Sigelman, C. K., Derenowski, E., Woods, T., Mukai, T., Alfred-Livo, L., Durazo, O., & Maddock, A. (1996). Mexican-American and Anglo-American children's responsiveness to a theory-centered AIDS education program. *Child Development, 67,* 253–266.

Sigelman, C. K., Miller, T. E., & Whitworth, L. A. (1986). The early development of stigmatizing reactions to physical differences. *Journal of Applied Developmental Psychology, 7,* 17–32.

Sigelman, C. K., & Shaffer, D. R. (1995). *Life-span human development* (2nd ed.), Pacific Grove, CA: Brooks/Cole.

Sigelman, C. K., & Waitzman, K. A. (1991). The development of distributive justice orientations: Contextual influences on children's resource allocations. *Child Development, 62,* 1367–1378.

Sigman, M., & Sena, R. (1993). Pretend play in high-risk and developmentally delayed children. In M. H. Bornstein & A. W. O'Reilly (Eds.), *The role of play in the development of thought* (New Directions for Child Development, No. 59). San Francisco: Jossey-Bass.

Signorella, M. L., Bigler, R. S., & Liben, L. S. (1993). Developmental differences in children's gender schemata about others: A meta-analytic review. *Developmental Review, 13,* 147–183.

Signorella, M. L., Jamison, W., & Krupa, M. H. (1989). Predicting spatial performance from gender stereotyping in activity preferences and in self-concept. *Developmental Psychology, 25,* 89–95.

Signorielli, N. (1991). *A sourcebook on children and television.* Westport, CT: Greenwood Press.

Signorielli, N., & Lears, M. (1992). Children, television, and conceptions about chores: Attitudes and behaviors. *Sex Roles, 27,* 157–170.

Silver, L. B. (1992). *Attention-deficit hyperactivity disorder: A clinical guide to diagnosis and treatment.* Washington, DC: American Psychiatric Press.

Simmons, R. G., & Blyth, D. A. (1987). *Moving into adolescence: The impact of pubertal change in school context.* New York: Aldine de Gruyter.

Simmons, R. G., Burgeson, R., Carlton-Ford, S., & Blyth, D. A. (1987). The impact of cumulative change in early adolescence. *Child Development, 58,* 1220–1234.

Simonoff, E., Bolton, P., & Rutter, M. (1996). Mental retardation: Genetic findings, clinical implications, and research agenda. *Journal of Child Psychology and Psychiatry and Allied Disciplines, 37,* 259–280.

Simons, R. L., Beaman, J. Conger, R. D., & Chao, W. (1993). Stress, support, and antisocial behavior trait as determinants of emotional well-being and parenting practices among single mothers. *Journal of Marriage and the Family, 55,* 385–398.

Simons, R. L., Whitbeck, L. B., Conger, R. D., & Wu, C. (1991). Intergenerational transmission of harsh parenting. *Developmental Psychology, 27,* 159–171.

Simonton, D. K. (1988). Age and outstanding achievement: What do we know after a century of research. *Psychological Bulletin, 104,* 251–267.

Simonton, D. K. (1994). Individual differences, developmental changes, and social context. *Behavioral and Brain Sciences, 17,* 552–553.

Simpson, J. L. (1993). Genetic causes of spontaneous abortion. In C. Lin, M. S. Verp, & R. E. Sabbagha (Eds.), *The high-risk fetus: Pathophysiology, diagnosis, management.* New York: Springer-Verlag.

Simpson, K. R., & Creehan, P. A. (1996). *Perinatal nursing.* Philadelphia: Lippincott-Raven.

Singer, D. G., & Singer, J. L. (1990). *The house of make-believe: Children's play and the developing imagination.* Cambridge, MA: Harvard University Press.

Singer, L. M., Brodzinsky, D. M., Ramsay, D., Steir, M., & Waters, E. (1985). Mother-infant attachments in adoptive families. *Child Development, 56,* 1543–1551.

Skinner, B. F. (1953). *Science and human behavior.* New York: Macmillan.

Skinner, B. F. (1957). *Verbal behavior.* East Norwalk, CT: Appleton-Century-Crofts.

Skodak,, & Skeels, H. M. (1949). A final follow-up study of children in adoptive homes. *Journal of Genetic Psychology, 75,* 85–125

Skouteris, H., McKenzie, B. E., & Day, R. H. (1992). Integration of sequential information for shape perception by infants: A developmental study. *Child Development, 63,* 1164–1176.

Slaby, R. G., & Crowley, C. G. (1977). Modification of cooperation and aggression through teacher attention to children's speech. *Journal of Experimental Child Psychology, 23,* 442–458.

Slaby, R. G., & Frey, K. S. (1975). Development of gender constancy and selective attention to same-sex models. *Child Development, 46,* 849–856.

Slaby, R. G., & Guerra, N. G. (1988). Cognitive mediators of aggression in adolescent offenders: 1. Assessment. *Developmental Psychology, 24,* 580–588.

Slaby, R. G., Roedell, W. C., Arezzo, D., & Hendrix, K. (1995). *Early violence prevention.* Washington, DC: National Association for the Education of Young Children.

Slade, A. (1987). A longitudinal study of maternal involvement and symbolic play during the toddler period. *Child Development, 58,* 367–375.

Slater, A., Mattock, A., & Brown, E. (1990a). Size constancy at birth: Newborn infants' responses to retinal and real size. *Journal of Experimental Child Psychology, 49,* 314–322.

Slater, A., Morrison, V., Somers, M., Mattock, A., Brown, E., & Taylor, D. (1990b). Newborn and older infants' perception of partly occluded objects. *Infant Behavior and Development, 13,* 33–49.

Slaughter-Defoe, D. T., Nakagawa, K., Takanishi, R., & Johnson, D. J. (1990). Toward cultural/ecological perspectives on schooling and achievement in African- and Asian-American children. *Child Development, 61,* 363–383.

Slavin, R. E. (1987). Ability grouping and student achievement in elementary schools: A best evidence synthesis. *Review of Educational Research, 57,* 293–336.

Slavin, R. E. (1989). Class size and student achievement: Small effects of small classes. *Educational Psychologist, 24,* 99–110.

Slavin, R. E. (1991). Cooperative learning and group contingencies. *Journal of Behavioral Education, 1,* 105–115.

Slavin, R. E. (1996). Research on cooperative learning and achievement: What we know, what we need to know. *Contemporary Educational Psychology, 21,* 43–69.

Sleek, S. (1994). Bilingualism enhances student growth. *Monitor of the American Psychological Association, 25*(4), 48–49.

Slobin, D. I. (1979). *Psycholinguistics.* Glenview, IL: Scott, Foresman.

Slobin, D. I. (1985). Crosslinguistic evidence for the language making capacity. In D. I. Slobin (Ed.), *The crosslinguistic study of language acquisition.* (Vol. 2). *Theoretical issues.* Hillsdale, NJ: Erlbaum.

Smetana, J. G. (1981). Preschool children's conceptions of moral and social rules. *Child Development, 52,* 1333–1336.

Smetana, J. G. (1985). Preschool children's conceptions of transgressions: Effects of varying moral and conventional domain-related attributes. *Developmental Psychology, 21,* 18–29.

Smetana, J. G., (1995). Parenting styles and conceptions of parental authority during adolescence. *Child Development, 66,* 299–316.

Smetana, J. G., & Bitz, B. (1996). Adolescents' conceptions of teachers' authority and their relations to rule violations at school. *Child Development, 67,* 1153–1172.

Smetana, J. G., Schlagman, N., & Adams, P. W. (1993). Preschool children's judgments about hypothetical and actual transgressions. *Child Development, 64,* 202–214.

Smith, B. A., & Blass, E. M. (1996). Taste-mediated calming in premature, preterm, and full-term human infants. *Developmental Psychology, 32,* 1084–1089.

Smith, F. (1977). Making sense of reading—and of reading instruction. *Harvard Educational Review, 47,* 386–395.

Smith, F. T. (1997). *Obesity in childhood.* New York: Basic Books.

Smith, L. B., & Katz, D. B. (1996). Activity-dependent processes in perceptual and cognitive development. In R. Gelman & T. K. Au (Eds.), *Perceptual and cognitive development.* San Diego, CA: Academic Press.

Smith, P. K., & Connolly, K. J. (1980). *The ecology of preschool behavior.* New York: Cambridge University Press.

Smith, P. K., & Daglish, L. (1977). Sex differences in parent and infant behavior in the home. *Child Development, 48,* 1250–1254.

Smith, S. (1942). Language and nonverbal test performance of racial groups in Honolulu before and after a 14-year interval. *Journal of General Psychology, 26,* 51–93.

Smith, T. W. (1990). Academic achievement and teaching younger siblings. *Social Psychology Quarterly, 53,* 352–363.

Smock, P. J. (1993). The economic costs of marital disruption for young women over the past two decades. *Demography, 30,* 353–371.

Smolak, L., & Levine, M. P. (1993). Separation-individuation difficulties and the distinction between bulimia nervosa and anorexia nervosa in college women. *International Journal of Eating Disorders, 14,* 33–41.

Smoll, F. L., & Schutz, R. W. (1990). Quantifying gender differences in physical performance: A developmental perspective. *Developmental Psychology, 26,* 360–369.

Snarey, J. R. (1985). Cross-cultural universality of social-moral development: A critical review of Kohlbergian research. *Psychological Bulletin, 97,* 202–232.

Snarey, J. R., & Keljo, K. (1991). In a gemeinschaft voice: The cross-cultural expansion of moral development theory. In W. M. Kurtines & J. L. Gewirtz (Eds.), *Handbook of moral behavior and development* (Vol. 1, pp. 395–424). Hillsdale, NJ: Erlbaum.

Snidman, N., Kagan, J., Riordan, L., & Shannon, D. C. (1995). Cardiac function and behavioral reactivity. *Psychophysiology, 32,* 199–207.

Snow, C. E., Arlman-Rupp, A., Hassing, Y., Jobse, J., Joosken, J., & Vorster, J. (1976). Mother's speech in three social classes. *Journal of Psycholinguistic Research, 5,* 1–20.

Snow, C. E., & Ferguson, C. A. (Eds.). (1977). *Talking to children.* Cambridge: Cambridge University Press.

Snow, M. E., Jacklin, C. N., & Maccoby, E. E. (1983). Sex-of-child differences in father-child interaction at one year of age. *Child Development, 54,* 227–232.

Sobesky, W. E. (1983). The effects of situational factors on moral judgments. *Child Development, 54,* 575–584.

Socha, T. J., & Socha, D, M. (1994). Children's task-group communication. In L. R. Frey (Ed.), *Group communication in context: Studies of natural groups.* Hillsdale, NJ: Erlbaum.

Society for Research in Child Development (1993). Ethical standards for reseach with children. In *Directory of members* (pp. 337–339). Ann Arbor, MI: Author.

Sodian, B., Taylor, C., Harris, P. L., & Perner, J. (1991). Early deception and the child's theory of mind: False trails and genuine markers. *Child Development, 62,* 468–483.

Sokolov, J. L. (1993). A local contingency analysis of the fine-tuning hypothesis. *Developmental Psychology, 29,* 1008–1023.

Sommer, K., Whitman, T. L., Borkowski, J. G., Schellenbach, C., Maxwell, S., & Kerugh, D. (1993). Cognitive readiness and adolescent parenting. *Developmental Psychology, 29,* 389–398.

Somsen, R. J. M., van't Klooster, B. J., van der Molen, M. W., van Leeuwen, H. M. P., & Licht, R. (1997). Growth spurts in brain maturation during middle childhood as indexed by EEG power spectra. *Biological Psychology, 44,* 187–209.

Sonnenschein, S. (1986). Development of referential communication skills: How familiarity with a listener affects a speaker's production of redundant messages. *Developmental Psychology, 22,* 549–555.

Sonnenschein, S. (1988). The development of referential communication: Speaking to different listeners. *Child Development, 59,* 694–702

Sorensen, A. B., & Hallinan, M. T. (1986). Effects of ability grouping on growth in academic achievement. *American Educational Research Journal, 23,* 519–542.

Sorensen, E. (1997). A national profile of nonresident fathers and their ability to pay child support. *Journal of Marriage and the Family, 59,* 785–797.

Spearman, C. (1927). *The abilities of man.* New York: Macmillan.

Speicher, B. (1994). Family patterns of moral judgment during adolescence and early adulthood. *Developmental Psychology, 30,* 624–632.

Spelke, E. S., & Newport, E. L. (1997). Nativism, empiricism, and the development of knowledge. In R. Lerner (Ed.), *Theories of development.* (Vol. 1). of W. Damon (Gen. Ed.), *Handbook of child psychology.* New York: Wiley.

Speltz, M. L., Endriga, M. C., Fisher, P. A., & Mason, C. A. (1997). Early predictors of attachment in infants with cleft lip/or palate. *Child Development, 68,* 12–25.

Spence, J. T. (1993). Gender-related traits and gender ideology: Evidence for a multifactorial theory. *Journal of Personality and Social Psychology, 64,* 624–635.

Spence, J. T., & Hall, S. K. (1996). Children's gender-related self-perceptions, activity preferences, and occupational stereotypes: A test of three models of gender constructs. *Sex Roles, 35,* 659–691.

Spence, J. T., & Helmreich, R. L. (1978). *Masculinity and femininity: Their psychological dimensions, correlates, and antecedents.* Austin: TX: University of Texas Press.

Spencer, M. B. (1988). Self-concept development. In D. T. Slaughter (Ed.), *Black children in poverty: Developmental perspectives.* San Francisco: Jossey-Bass.

Spencer, M. B., & Markstrom-Adams, C. (1990). Identity processes among racial and ethnic minority children in America. *Child Development, 61,* 290–310.

Spencer, P. E. (1996). The association between language and symbolic play at two years: Evidence from deaf toddlers. *Child Development, 67,* 867–876.

Spiker, D., Ferguson, J., & Brooks-Gunn, J. (1993). Enhancing maternal interactive behavior and child social competence in low birthweight, premature infants. *Child Development, 64,* 754–768.

Spitz, R. A. (1945). Hospitalism: An inquiry into the genesis of psychiatric conditions in early childhood. In A. Freud (Ed.), *The psychoanalytic study of the child* (Vol. 1). New York: International Universities Press.

Spitz, R. A. (1965). *The first year of life: A psychoanalytic study of normal and deviant object relations.* New York: International Universities Press.

Spitze, G. (1988). Women's employment and family relations: A review. *Journal of Marriage and the Family, 50,* 595–618.

Spreen, O., Risser, A. H., & Edgell, D. (1995). *Developmental neuropsychology.* New York: Oxford University Press.

Sprigle, J. E., & Schaefer, L. (1985). Longitudinal evaluation of the effects of two compensatory preschool programs on fourth- through sixth-grade students. *Developmental Psychology, 21,* 702–708.

Sroufe, L. A. (1977). Wariness of strangers and the study of infant development. *Child Development, 48,* 1184–1199.

Sroufe, L. A. (1985). Attachment classification from the perspective of infant-caregiver relationships and infant temperament. *Child Development, 56,* 1–14.

Sroufe, L. A. (1997). Psychopathology as an outcome of development. *Development of Psychopathology, 9,* 251–268.

Sroufe, L. A., Bennett, C., Englund, M., Urban, J., & Shulman, S. (1993). The significance of gender boundaries in preadolescence: Contemporary correlates and antecedents of boundary violation and maintenance. *Child Development, 64,* 455–466.

Sroufe, L. A., Egeland, B., & Kreutzer, T. (1990). The fate of early experience following developmental change: Longitudinal approaches to individual adaptation in childhood. *Child Development, 61,* 1363–1373.

Sroufe, L. A., Waters, E., & Matas, L. (1974). Contextual determinants of infant affectional response. In M. Lewis & L. A. Rosenblum (Eds.), *The origins of fear.* New York: Wiley.

Staats, A. (1975). *Social behaviorism.* Homewood, IL: Dorsey Press.

Stack, D. M., & Muir, D. W. (1992). Adult tactile stimulation during face-to-face interactions modulates five-month-olds' affect and attention. *Child Development, 63,* 1509–1525.

Staffieri, J. R. (1967). A study of social stereotype of body image in children. *Journal of Personality and Social Psychology, 7,* 101–104.

Stattin, H., & Magnusson, D. (1990). *Paths through life.* (Vol. 2). *Pubertal maturation in female development.* Hillsdale, NJ: Erlbaum.

Steele, B. F., & Pollack, C. B. (1974). A psychiatric study of parents who abuse infants and small children. In R. E. Helfer & C. H. Kempe (Eds.), *The battered child.* Chicago: University of Chicago Press.

Steele, C. M. (1997). A threat in the air: How stereotypes shape intellectual identity and performance. *American Psychologist, 52,* 613–629.

Steele, C. M., & Aronson, J. (1995). Stereotype threat and the intellectual test performance of African Americans. *Journal of Personality and Social Psychology, 69,* 797–811.

Steele, H., Steele, M., & Fonagy, P. (1996). Associations among attachment classifications of mothers, fathers, and their infants. *Child Development, 67,* 541–555.

Stein, J. H., & Reiser, L. W. (1994). A study of white middle-class adolescent boys' responses to "semenarche" (the first ejaculation). *Journal of Youth and Adolescence, 23,* 373–384.

Stein, Z. A., & Susser, M. W. (1976). Prenatal nutrition and mental competence. In J. D. Lloyd-Still (Ed.), *Malnutrition and intellectual development.* Littleton, MA: Publishing Sciences Group.

Steinberg, L. (1986). Latchkey children and susceptibility to peer pressure: An ecological analysis. *Developmental Psychology, 22,* 433–439.

Steinberg, L. (1987). Single parents, stepparents, and the susceptibility of adolescents to antisocial peer pressure. *Child Development, 58,* 269–275.

Steinberg, L. (1988). Reciprocal relation between parent-child distance and pubertal maturation. *Developmental Psychology, 24,* 122–128.

Steinberg, L. (1996). *Adolescence* (4th ed.). New York: McGraw-Hill.

Steinberg, L., & Dornbusch, S. M. (1991). Negative correlates of part-time employment during adolescence: Replication and elaboration. *Developmental Psychology, 27,* 304–313.

Steinberg, L., Dornbusch, S. M., & Brown, B. B. (1992). Ethnic differences in adolescent achievement: An ecological perspective. *American Psychologist, 47,* 723–729.

Steinberg, L., Elmen, J. D., & Mounts, N. S. (1989). Authoritative parenting, psychosocial maturity, and academic success among adolescents. *Child Development, 60,* 1424–1436.

Steinberg, L., Fegley, S., & Dornbusch, S. M. (1993). Negative impact of part-time work on adolescent adjustment: Evidence from a longitudinal study. *Developmental Psychology, 29,* 171–180.

Steinberg, L., Lamborn, S. D., Darling, N., Mounts, N. S., & Dornbusch, S. M. (1994). Over-time changes in adjustment and competence among adolescents from authoritative, authoritarian, indulgent, and neglectful families. *Child Development, 65,* 754–770.

Steinberg, L., & Silverberg, S. B. (1986). The vicissitudes of autonomy in early adolescence. *Child Development, 57,* 841–851.

Steinberg, S. (1996). Childbearing research: A transcultural review. *Social Science and Medicine, 43,* 1765–1784.

Steiner, J. E. (1979). Human facial expressions in response to taste and smell stimulation. In H. W. Reese & L. P. Lipsitt (Eds.), *Advances in child development and behavior* (Vol. 13). Orlando, FL: Academic Press.

Stern, D. (1977). *The first relationship: Infant and mother.* Cambridge, MA: Harvard University Press.

Stern, W. (1912). *Die psychologischen methoden der intelligenzprufung.* Liepzig: Barth.

Sternberg, K. J., Lamb, M. E., Greenbaum, C., Cicchetti, D., Dawud, S., Cortes, R. M., Krispin, O., & Lorey, F. (1993). Effects of domestic violence on children's behavior problems and depression. *Developmental Psychology, 29,* 44–52.

Sternberg, R. J. (1984). The Kaufman Assessment Battery for Children: An information-processing analysis and critique. *Journal of Special Education, 18,* 267–279.

Sternberg, R. J. (1985). *Beyond IQ. A triarchic theory of human intelligence.* Cambridge: Cambridge University Press.

Sternberg, R. J. (1991). Theory-based testing of intellectual abilities: Rationale for the triarchic abilities test. In H. A. H. Rowe (Ed.), *Intelligence: Reconceptualization and measurement.* Hillsdale, NJ: Erlbaum.

Sternberg, R. J. (1995). Investing in creativity: Many happy returns. *Educational Leadership, 53,* 80–84.

Sternberg, R. J. (1997). The concept of intelligence and its role in lifelong learning and success. *American Psychologist, 52,* 1030–1037.

Sternberg, R. J., & Lubart, T. I. (1996). Investing in creativity. *American Psychologist, 51,* 677–688.

Sternberg, R. J., Wagner, R. K., Williams, W. M., & Horvath, J. A. (1995). Testing common sense. *American Psychologist, 50,* 912–927.

Stevens, R. J., & Slavin, R. E. (1995a). Effects of a cooperative learning approach in reading and writing on academically handicapped and nonhandicapped students. *Elementary School Journal, 95,* 241–262.

Stevens, R. J., & Slavin, R. E., (1995b). The cooperative elementary school: Effects on students' achievement, attitudes, and social relations. *American Educational Research Journal, 32,* 321–351.

Stevenson, H. W., Chen, C., & Lee, S. (1993). Mathematics achievement of Chinese, Japanese, and American children: Ten years later. *Science, 259,* 53–58.

Stevenson, H. W., Chen, C., & Uttal, D. H. (1990). Beliefs and achievement: A study of Black, White, and Hispanic children. *Child Development, 61,* 508–523.

Stevenson, H. W., & Lee, S. Y. (1990). Contexts of achievement: A study of American, Chinese, and Japanese children. *Monographs of the Society for Research in Child Development, 55,* 1–2. Serial No. 221.

Stevenson, H. W., Lee, S. Y., & Stigler, J. W. (1986). Mathematics achievement of Chinese, Japanese, and American children. *Science, 231,* 693–699.

Stevenson, H. W., Stigler, J. W., Lee, S. Y., Lucker, G. W., Litamura, S., & Hsu, C. (1985). Cognitive performance and academic achievement of Japanese, Chinese, and American children. *Child Development, 56,* 718–734.

Stewart, R. B., & Marvin, R. S. (1984). Sibling relations: The role of conceptual perspective-taking in the ontogeny of sibling caregiving. *Child Development, 55,* 1322–1332.

Stice, E., & Barrera, M., Jr. (1995). A longitudinal examination of the reciprocal relations between perceived parenting and adolescents' substance use and externalizing behaviors. *Developmental Psychology, 31,* 322–334.

Stigler, J. W., Lee, S. , & Stevenson, H. W. (1986). Digit memory in Chinese and English: Evidence for a temporally limited store. *Cognition, 23,* 1–20.

Stigler, J. W., Lee, S. Y., & Stevenson, H. W. (1987). Mathematics classrooms in Japan, Taiwan, and the United States. *Child Development, 58,* 1272–1285.

Stipek, D., Feiler, R., Daniels, D., & Milbern, S. (1995). Effects of different instructional approaches on young children's achievement and motivation. *Child Development, 66,* 209–233.

Stipek, D., Gralinski, H., & Kopp, C. (1990). Self-concept development in the toddler years. *Developmental Psychology, 26,* 972–977.

Stipek, D., & Mac Iver, D. (1989). Developmental change in children's assessment of intellectual competence. *Child Development, 60,* 521–538.

Stipek, D. J., Recchia, S., & McClintic, S. (1992). Self-evaluation in young children. *Monographs of the Society for Research in Child Development, 57,* 1, Serial No. 226.

St. James-Roberts, I., & Plewis, I. (1996). Individual differences, daily fluctuations, and developmental changes in amounts of infant waking, fussing, crying, feeding, and sleeping. *Child Development, 67,* 2527–2540.

St. Lawrence, J. S., Jefferson, K. W., Alleyne, E., & Brasfield, T. L. (1995). Comparison of education versus behavioral skills training interventions in lowering sexual HIV risk behavior of substance dependent adolescents. *Journal of Consulting and Clinical Psychology, 63,* 221–237.

Stoddart, T., & Turiel, E. (1985). Children's concepts of cross-gender activities. *Child Development, 56,* 1241–1252.

Stone, R. (1992). Can a father's exposure lead to illness in his children? *Science, 258,* 31.

Stormshak, E. A., Bellanti, C. J., Bierman, K. L., and the Conduct Problems Prevention Research Group (1996). The quality of sibling relationships and the development of social competence and behavioral control in aggressive children. *Developmental Psychology, 32,* 79–89.

Strachan, T., & Read, A. P. (1996). *Human molecular genetics.* New York: Wiley.

Stratton, K., Howe, C., & Battaglia, F. (1996). *Fetal alcohol syndrome: Diagnosis, epidemiology, prevention, and treatment.* Washington, D.C.: National Academy Press.

Strassberg, Z. (1995). Social information processing in compliance situations by mothers of behavior-problem boys. *Child Development, 66,* 376–389.

Strauss, M. S., & Curtis, L. E. (1981). Infant perception of numerosity. *Child Development, 52,* 1146–1152.

Streissguth, A. P., Bookstein, F. L., Sampson, P. D., & Barr, H. M. (1993). *The enduring effects of prenatal alcohol exposure on child development.* Ann Arbor, MI: University of Michigan Press.

Streitmatter, J. (1993). Gender differences in identity development: An examination of longitudinal data. *Adolescence, 28,* 55–66.

Streri, A., & Spelke, E. S. (1988). Haptic perception of objects in infancy. *Cognitive Psychology, 20,* 1–23.

Strigini, P., Sanone, R., Carobbi, S., & Pierluigi, M. (1990). Radiation and Down's syndrome. *Nature, 347,* 717.

Strough, J., Berg, C. A., & Sansone, C. (1996). Goals for solving everyday problems across the life span: Age and gender differences in the salience of interpersonal concerns. *Developmental Psychology, 32,* 1106–1115.

Stuckey, M. R., McGhee, P. E., & Bell, N. J. (1982). Parent-child interaction: The influence of maternal employment. *Developmental Psychology, 18,* 635–644.

Stumpf, H., & Stanley, J. C. (1996). Gender-related differences on the College Board's Advanced Placement and Achievement Tests, 1982–1992. *Journal of Educational Psychology, 88,* 353–364.

Stumphauzer, J. S. (1972). Increased delay of gratification in young inmates through imitation of high-delay peer models. *Journal of Personality and Social Psychology, 21,* 10–17.

Stunkard, A. J., Harris, J. R., Pedersen, N., & McClearn, G. E. (1990). The body-mass index of twins who have been reared apart. *New England Journal of Medicine, 322,* 1483–1487.

Stuss, D. T. (1992). Biological and psychological development of executive functions. *Brain & Cognition, 20,* 8–23.

Subotnik. R. F., Karp, D. E., & Morgan, E. R. (1989). High IQ children at midlife: An investigation into the generalizability of Terman's genetic studies of genius. *Roeper Review, 11,* 139–144.

Sudhalter, V., & Braine, M. D. S. (1985). How does comprehension of passives develop? a comparison of actional and experiential verbs. *Journal of Child Language, 12,* 455–470.

Sue, S., & Okazaki, S. (1990). Asian-American educational achievements: A phenomenon in search of explanation. *American Psychologist, 45,* 913–920.

Sullivan, H. S. (1953). *The interpersonal theory of psychiatry.* New York: Norton.

Sullivan, M. L. (1993). Culture and class as determinants of out-of-wedlock childbearing and poverty during late adolescence. *Journal of Research on Adolescence, 3,* 295–316.

Sullivan, M. W., Lewis, M., & Alessandri, S. M. (1992). Cross-age stability in emotional expressions during learning and extinction. *Developmental Psychology, 28,* 58–63.

Suomi, S. J., & Harlow, H. F. (1978). Early experience and social development in rhesus monkeys. In M. E. Lamb (Ed.), *Social and personality development.* New York: Holt, Rinehart and Winston.

Super, C. M., Herrera, M. G., & Mora, J. O. (1990). Long-term effects of food supplementation and psychosocial intervention on the physical growth of Columbian infants at risk of malnutrition. *Child Development, 61,* 29–49.

Susser, M., & Stein, Z. (1994). Timing in prenatal nutrition: A reprise of the Dutch Famine Study. *Nutrition Reviews, 52,* 84–94.

Suzuki, L. A., & Valencia, R. R. (1997). Race-ethnicity and measured intelligence: Educational implications. *American Psychologist, 52,* 1103–1114.

Swarr, A. E., & Richards, M. H. (1996). Longitudinal effects of adolescent girls' pubertal development, perceptions of pubertal timing, and parental relations on eating problems. *Developmental Psychology, 32,* 636–646.

Tamis-LeMonda, C. S., & Bornstein, M. H. (1989). Habituation and maternal encouragement of attention as predictors of toddler language, play, and representational competence. *Child Development, 60,* 738–751.

Tanner, J. M. (1962). *Growth at adolescence* (2nd ed.). Oxford, England: Blackwell.

Tanner, J. M., (1978). *Education and physical growth* (2nd ed.). London: Hodder and Stroughton.

Tanner, J. M. (1981). Growth and maturation during adolescence. *Nutrition Review, 39,* 43–55.

Tanner, J. M. (1990). *Foetus into man: Physical growth from conception to maturity* (2nd Ed.). Cambridge, MA: Harvard University Press.

Tanner, J. M., Whithouse, R. H., & Takaishi, A. (1996). *Archives of Diseases in Childhood, 41,* 454–471.

Tardif, T. (1996). Nouns are not always learned before verbs: Evidence from Mandarin speakers' early vocabularies. *Developmental Psychology, 32,* 492–504.

Tarullo, L. B., DeMudler, E. K., Ronsaville, D. S., Brown, E., & Radke-Yarrow, M. (1995). Maternal depression and maternal treatment of siblings as predictors of child psychopathology. *Developmental Psychology, 31,* 395–405.

Taylor, A. R., Asher, S. R., & Williams, G. A. (1987). The social adaptation of mainstreamed mildly retarded children. *Child Development, 58,* 1321–1334.

Taylor, R. D. (1996). Adolescents' perceptions of kinship support and family management practices: Association with adolescent adjustment in African-American families. *Developmental Psychology, 32,* 687–695.

Taylor, R. D., & Roberts, D. (1995). Kinship support and maternal and adolescent well-being in economically disadvantaged African-American families. *Child Development, 66,* 1585–1597.

Taylor, M., & Carlson, S. M. (1997). The relation between individual differences in fantasy and theory of mind. *Child Development, 68,* 436–455.

Taylor, M., & Gelman, S. A. (1988). Adjectives and nouns: Children's strategies for learning new words. *Child Development, 59,* 411–419.

Taylor, M., & Gelman, S. A. (1989). Incorporating new words into the lexicon: Preliminary evidence for language hierarchies in two-year-old children. *Child Development, 60,* 625–636.

Taylor, M. G. (1996). The development of children's beliefs about social and biological aspects of gender differences. *Child Development, 67,* 1555–1571.

Taylor, R. E., & Richards, S. B. (1991). Patterns of intellectual differences of Black, Hispanic, and White children. *Psychology in the Schools, 28,* 5–9.

Teegartin, C. (1994, July 25). Never-marrieds soar among single parents. *Atlanta Constitution,* A1, A7.

Teele, D. W., Klein, J. O., Chase, C., et al., and the Greater Boston Otitis Media Study Group (1990). Otitis media in infancy and intellectual ability, school achievement, speech, and language at age 7 years. *Journal of Infectious Disease, 162,* 685–694.

Teeven, R. C., & McGhee, P. E. (1972). Childhood development of fear of failure motivation. *Journal of Personality and Social Psychology, 21,* 345–348.

Terman, L. M. (1954). The discovery and encouragement of exceptional talent. *American Psychologist, 9,* 221–238.

Terrace, H. S. (1979, November). How Nim Chimpsky changed my mind. *Psychology Today,* 65–76.

Terrace, H. S., Petitto, L. A., Sanders, R. J., & Bever, T. G. (1980). On the grammatical capacity of apes. In K. E. Nelson (Ed.), *Children's language.* New York: Gardner Press.

Terry, R., & Coie, J. D. (1991). A comparison of methods for defining sociometric status among children. *Developmental Psychology, 27,* 867–880.

Teti, D. M., & Ablard, K. E. (1989). Security of attachment and infant-sibling relationships: A laboratory study. *Child Development, 60,* 1519–1528.

Teti, D. M., & Gelfand, D. M., Messinger, D. S., & Isabella, R. (1995). Maternal depression and the quality of early attachment: An examination of infants, preschoolers, and their mothers. *Developmental Psychology, 31,* 364–376.

Teti, D. M., Sakin, J. W., Kucera, E., Corns, K. M., & Das Eiden, R. (1996). And baby makes four: Predictors of attachment security among preschool-age firstborns during the transition to siblinghood. *Child Development, 67,* 579–596.

Tharp, R. G. (1989). Psychocultural variables and constants: Effects on teaching and learning in schools. *American Psychologist, 44,* 349–359.

Tharp, R. G. (1994). Intergroup differences among Native Americans in socialization and child cognition: An ethnographic analysis. In P. M. Greenfield and R. Cocking (Eds.), *Cross-cultural roots of minority child development* (pp. 87–105). Hillsdale, NJ: Erlbaum.

Tharp, R. G., & Gallimore, R. (1988). *Rousing minds to life: Teaching, learning, and schooling in social context.* Cambridge, England: Cambridge University Press.

Thelen, E. (1984). Learning to walk: Ecological demands and phylogenetic constraints. In L. P. Lipsitt & C. Rovee-Collier (Eds.), *Advances in infancy research* (Vol. 3). Norwood, NJ: Ablex.

Thelen, E. (1986). Treadmill-elicited stepping in seven-month-old infants. *Child Development, 57,* 1498–1506.

Thelen, E. (1995). Motor development: a new synthesis. *American Psychologist, 50,* 79–95.

Thelen, E., Corbetta, D., Kamm, K., Spencer, J. P., Schneider, K., & Zernicke, R. F. (1993). The transition to reaching: Mapping intention and intrinsic dynamics. *Child Development, 64,* 1058–1098.

Thelen, E., & Fisher, D. M. (1982). Newborn stepping: An explanation for a disappearing reflex. *Developmental Psychology, 18,* 760–775.

Thoma, S. J., Rest, J. R., & Davison, M. L. (1991). Describing and testing a moderator of the moral judgment and action relationship. *Journal of Personality and Social Psychology, 61,* 659–669.

Thoman, E. B. (1990). Sleeping and waking states in infants: A functional perspective. *Neuroscience and Behavioral Review, 14,* 93–107.

Thoman, E. B., & Ingersoll, E. W. (1993). Learning in premature infants. *Developmental Psychology, 28,* 692–700.

Thoman, E. B., & Whitney, M. P. (1989). Sleep states of infants monitored in the home: Individual differences, developmental trends, and origins of diurnal cyclicity. *Infant Behavior and Development, 12,* 59–75.

Thomas, A., & Chess, S. (1977). *Temperament and development.* New York: Brunner/Mazel.

Thomas, A., & Chess, S. (1986). The New York longitudinal study: From infancy to early adult life. In R. Plomin & J. Dunn (Eds.). *The study of temperament: Changes, continuities, and challenges.* Hillsdale, NJ: Erlbaum.

Thomas, A., Chess, S., & Birch, H. G. (1970). The origin of personality. *Scientific American, 223,* 102–109.

Thomas, A., Chess, S., & Korn, S. (1982). The reality of difficult temperament. *Merrill-Palmer Quarterly, 28,* 1–20.

Thomas, D., Campos, J. J., Shucard, D. W., Ramsay, D. S., & Shucard, J. (1981). Semantic comprehension in infancy: a signal detection approach. *Child Development, 52,* 798–803.

Thomas, J. R., & French, K. E. (1985). Gender differences across age in motor performance: A meta-analysis. *Psychological Bulletin, 98,* 260–282.

Thomas, M. H., Horton, R. W., Lippincott, E. C., & Drabman, R. S. (1977). Desensitization to portrayals of real-life aggression as a function of exposure to television violence. *Journal of Personality and Social Psychology, 35,* 450–458.

Thompson, R. A. (1990). Vulnerability in research: A developmental perspective on research risk. *Child Development, 61,* 1–16.

Thompson, R. A. (1994). Emotion regulation: A theme in search of definition. In N. A. Fox (Ed.), The development of emotion regulation: Biological and behavioral considerations. *Monographs of the Society for Research in Child Development, 59,* Nos. 2–3, Serial No. 240.

Thompson, R. A. (1997). Early sociopersonality development. In N. Eisenberg (Ed.), W. Damon (Series Ed.), *Handbook of child psychology* (Vol. 3). *Social, emotional, and personality development* (5th ed.). New York: Wiley.

Thompson, R. A., Cicchetti, D., Lamb, M. E., & Malkin, C. (1985). Emotional responses of Down's syndrome and normal infants in the strange situation: The organization of affective behavior in infants. *Developmental Psychology, 21,* 828–841.

Thompson, R. A., Lamb, M. E., & Estes, D. (1982). Stability of infant-mother attachment and its relationship to changing life circumstances in an unselected middle-class sample. *Child Development, 53,* 144–148.

Thompson, R. F. (1993). *The brain: A neuroscience primer* (2nd ed.). New York: W.H. Freeman.

Thompson, S. K. (1975). Gender labels and early sex-role development. *Child Development, 46,* 339–347.

Thorndike, R. L., Hagen, E. P., & Sattler, J. M. (1986). *The Stanford-Binet Intelligence Scale* (4th Ed.). Chicago: Riverside Publishing.

Thorndike, R. M. (1997). The early history of intelligence testing. In D. P. Flanagan, J. L. Genshaft, & P. L. Morrison (Eds.), *Contemporary intellectual assessment: Theories, tests, and issues.* New York: Guilford.

Thorne, A., & Michaelieu, Q. (1996). Situating adolescent gender and self-esteem with personal memories. *Child Development, 67,* 1374–1390.

Thorne, B. (1993). *Gender play. Girls and boys in school.* New Brunswick, NJ: Rutgers University Press.

Thurber, C. A. (1995). The experience and expression of homesickness in preadolescent and adolescent boys. *Child Development, 66,* 1162–1178.

Thurstone, L. L. (1938). *Primary mental abilities.* Chicago: University of Chicago Press.

Tietjen, A. M. (1986). Prosocial reasoning among children and adults in a Papua New Guinea society. *Developmental Psychology, 22,* 861–868.

Tietjen, A. M., & Walker, L. J. (1985). Moral reasoning and leadership among men in a Papua New Guinea society. *Developmental Psychology, 21,* 982–992.

Tinsley, B. J. (1992). Multiple influences on the acquisition and socialization of children's health attitudes and behavior: An integrative review. *Child Development, 63,* 1043–1069.

Tirozzi, G. N., & Uro, G. (1997). Education reform in the United States: National policy in support of local efforts for school improvement. *American Psychologist, 52,* 241–249.

Tisak, M. S., & Tisak, J. (1990). Children's conceptions of parental authority, friendship, and sibling relations. *Merrill-Palmer Quarterly, 36,* 347–368.

Tolmie, J. L. (1995). Chromosome disorders. In M. J. Whittle & J. M. Connor (Eds.), *Prenatal diagnosis in obstetric practice* (2nd ed., pp. 34–57). Oxford, England: Blackwell.

Tomada, G., & Schneider, B. H. (1997). Relational aggression, gender, and peer acceptance: Invariance across culture, stability over time, and concordance among informants. *Developmental Psychology, 33,* 601–609.

Tomasello, M. (1995). Language is not an instinct. *Cognitive Development, 10,* 131–156.

Tomasello, M., & Camaioni, L. (1997). A comparison of the gestural communication of apes and human infants. *Human Development, 40,* 7–24.

Tomasello, M., Conti-Ramsden, G., & Ewert, B. (1990). Young children's conversations with their mothers and fathers: Differences in breakdown and repair. *Journal of Child Language, 17,* 115–130.

Tomlinson-Keasey, C., & Keasey, C. B. (1974). The mediating role of cognitive development in moral judgment. *Child Development, 45,* 291–298.

Tomlinson-Keasey, C., & Little, T. D. (1990). Predicting educational attainment, occupational achievement, intellectual skill, and personal adjustment among gifted men and women. *Journal of Educational Psychology, 82,* 442–455.

Toner, I. J. (1981). Role involvement and delay maintenance behavior in pre-school children. *Journal of Genetic Psychology, 138,* 245–251.

Toner, I. J., Moore, L. P., & Ashley, P. K. (1978). The effect of serving as a model of self-control on subsequent resistance to deviation in children. *Journal of Experimental Child Psychology, 26,* 85–91.

Toner, I. J., Moore, L. P., & Emmons, B. A. (1980). The effect of being labeled on subsequent self-control in children. *Child Development, 51,* 618–621.

Toner, I. J., & Potts, R. (1981). Effect of modeled rationales on moral behavior, moral choice, and level of moral judgment in children. *Journal of Psychology, 107,* 153–162.

Toner, M. (1991, Feb. 18). Worries mount as studies link birth defects to fathers' job perils. *Atlanta Journal,* p. A9.

Tooby, J., & Cosmides, L. (1992). The psychological foundations of culture. In J. H. Barkow, L. Cosmides, & J. Tooby (Eds.), *The adapted mind: Evolutionary psychology and the generation of culture* (pp. 19–136). New York: Oxford University Press.

Torrance, E. P. (1988). The nature of creativity as manifest in its testing. In R. J. Sternberg (Ed.), *The nature of creativity: Contemporary psychological perspectives.* Cambridge, England: Cambridge University Press.

Trabasso, T. (1975). Representation, memory, and reasoning: How do we make transitive inferences? In A. D. Pick (Ed.), *Minnesota symposia on child psychology* (Vol. 9). Minneapolis: University of Minnesota Press.

Trehub, S. E., Schneider, B. A., Thorpe, L. A., & Judge, P. (1991). Observational measures of auditory sensitivity in early infancy. *Developmental Psychology, 27,* 40–49.

Trickett, P. K., Aber, J. L., Carlson, V., & Cicchetti, D. (1991). Relationship of socioeconomic status to the etiology and developmental sequele of physical child abuse. *Developmental Psychology, 27,* 148–158.

Trickett, P. K., & McBride-Chang, C. (1995). The developmental impact of different forms of child abuse and neglect. *Developmental Review, 15,* 311–337.

Trickett, P. K., & Putnam, F. W. (1993). Impact of child sexual abuse on females: Toward a developmental, psychobiological integration. *Psychological Science, 4,* 81–87.

Trickett, P. K., & Susman, E. J. (1988). Parental perceptions of child-rearing practices in physically abusive and nonabusive families. *Developmental Psychology, 24,* 270–276.

Tronick, E. Z. (1989). Emotions and emotional communications in infants. *American Psychologist, 44,* 112–119.

Tronick, E. Z., Morelli, G. A., & Ivey, P. K. (1992). The Efe forager infant and toddler's pattern of social relationships: Multiple and simultaneous. *Developmental Psychology, 28,* 568–577.

Tronick, E. Z., Thomas, R. B., & Daltabuit, M. (1994). The Quecha Manta pouch: A caregiving practice for buffering the Peruvian infant against multiple stresses of high altitude. *Child Development, 65,* 1005–1013.

Tryon, R. C. (1940). Genetic differences in maze learning in rats. *Yearbook of the National Society for Studies in Education, 39,* 111–119.

Tubman, J. G., Windle, M., & Windle, R. C. (1996). The onset and cross-temporal patterning of sexual intercourse in middle adolescence: Prospective relations with behavioral and emotional problems. *Child Development, 67,* 327–343.

Tudge, J. R. H. (1992). Processes and consequences of peer collaboration: A Vygotskian analysis. *Child Development, 63,* 1364–1379.

Tulkin, S. R., & Konner, M. J. (1973). Alternative conceptions of intellectual functioning. *Human Development, 16,* 33–52.

Trachtenberg, S., & Viken, R. J. (1994). Aggressive boys in the classroom: Biased attributions or shared perceptions. *Child Development, 65,* 829–835.

Turiel, E. (1983). *The development of social knowledge: Morality and convention.* Cambridge, England: Cambridge University Press.

Turkheimer, E. (1991). Individual and group differences in adoption studies of IQ. *Psychological Bulletin, 110,* 392–405.

Turner, P. J., & Gervai, J. (1995). A multidimensional study of gender typing in preschool children and their parents: Personality, attitudes, preferences, behavior, and cultural differences. *Developmental Psychology, 31,* 759–772.

Turner-Bowker, D. M. (1996). Gender stereotyped descriptions in children's picture books: Does "curious Jane" exist in the literature? *Sex Roles, 35,* 461–488.

Twenge, J. M. (1997). Changes in masculine and feminine traits over time: A meta-analysis. *Sex Roles, 36,* 305–325.

Tyack, D., & Ingram, D. (1977). Children's production and comprehension of questions. *Journal of Child Language, 4,* 211–224.

Tyson, P., & Tyson, R. L. (1990). *Psychoanalytic theories of development: An integration.* New Haven, CT: Yale University Press.

Uba, L. (1994). *Asian Americans: Personality patterns, identity, and mental health.* New York: The Guilford Press.

Udry, J. R. (1990). Hormonal and social determinants of adolescent sexual initiation. In J. Bancroft & J. M. Reinisch (Eds.), *Adolescence and puberty* (pp. 70–87). New York: Oxford University Press.

Underwood, B., & Moore, B. (1982). Perspective-taking and altruism. *Psychological Bulletin, 91,* 143–173.

Underwood, M. K., Coie, J. D., & Herbsman, C. R. (1992). Display rules for anger and aggression in school-age children. *Child Development, 63,* 366–380.

Uniform Crime Reports for the United States, 1997. Federal Bureau of Investigation. Washington, D.C.: U. S. Government Printing Office. *University of Georgia Fact Book* (1997). Athens, GA: University of Georgia Press.

Urberg, K. A. (1979). Sex-role conceptualization in adolescents and adults. *Developmental Psychology, 15,* 90–92.

Urberg, K. A., Degirmencioglu, S. M., Tolson, J. M., & Halliday-Scher, K. (1995). The structure of adolescent peer networks. *Developmental Psychology, 31,* 540–547.

U.S. Bureau of the Census (1993). *Statistical abstract of the United States: 1993.* (113th ed.). Washington, DC: U.S. Government Printing Office.

U.S. Bureau of the Census (1996). *Statistical abstract of the United States: 1996* (116th ed.). Washington, DC: U.S. Government Printing Office.

U.S. Bureau of the Census (1997). *Statistical abstract of the United States* (117th ed.). Washington, D.C.: U.S. Government Printing Office.

U.S. Department of Education (1996). *Report to Congress: Goals 2000: Increasing student achievement through state and local initiatives.* Washington, DC: U.S. Government Printing Office.

U.S. Department of Health, Education and Welfare (1979). *Smoking and health: A report to the Surgeon General* (DHEW Pub. No. PHS 79–50066). Washington, DC: U.S. Government Printing Office.

U.S. Department of Justice (1995). *Crime in the United States.* Washington, D.C.: U.S. Government Printing Office.

Usher, J. A., & Neisser, U. (1993). Childhood amnesia and the beginnings of memory for four early life events. *Journal of Experimental Psychology: General, 122,* 155–165.

Uttal, D., Schreiber, J. C., & DeLoache, J. S. (1995). Waiting to use a symbol: The effects of delay on children's use of models. *Child Development, 66,* 1875–1889.

Valdez-Menchaca, M. C., & Whitehurst, G. J. (1992). Accelerating language development through picture book reading: a systematic extension to Mexican day care. *Developmental Psychology, 28,* 1106–1114.

Valenza, E., Simion, F., Cassia, V. M., & Umilta, C. (1996). Face perception at birth. *Journal of Experimental Psychology: Human Perception and Performance, 22,* 892–903.

Valenzuela, M. (1990). Attachment in chronically underweight young children. *Child Development, 61,* 1984–1996.

Valenzuela, M. (1997). Maternal sensitivity in a developing society: The context of urban poverty and infant chronic undernutrition. *Developmental Psychology, 33,* 845–855.

Valian, V., Hoeffner, J., & Aubry, S. (1996). Young children's imitation of sentence subjects: Evidence of processing limitations. *Developmental Psychology, 32,* 153–164.

Vandell, D. L., & Corasantini, M. A. (1988). The relation between third graders' after-school care and social, academic, and emotional functioning. *Child Development, 59,* 868–875.

Vandell, D. L., Henderson, V. K., & Wilson, K. S. (1988). A longitudinal study of children with day-care experiences of varying quality. *Child Development, 59,* 1286–1292.

Vandell, D. L., & Mueller, E. C. (1995). Peer play and friendships during the first two years. In H. C. Smith, A. J. Chapman, & J. R. Smith (Eds.), *Friendship and social relations in children* (pp. 181–208). New Brunswick, NJ: Transaction.

Vandell, D. L., & Ramanan, J. (1991). Children of the National Longitudinal Survey of Youth: Choices in after-school care and child development. *Developmental Psychology, 27,* 637–643.

Vandell, D. L., & Ramanan, J. (1992). Effects of early and recent maternal employment on children from low-income families. *Child Development, 63,* 938–949.

Vandell, D. L., Wilson, K. S., & Buchanan, N. R. (1980). Peer interaction in the first year of life: An examination of its structure, content, and sensitivity to toys. *Child Development, 51,* 481–488.

van den Boom, D. C. (1995). Do first-year intervention efforts endure? Follow-up during toddlerhood of a sample of Dutch irritable infants. *Child Development, 66,* 1798–1816.

van den Boom, D. C., (1997). Sensitivity and attachment: New steps for developmentalists. *Child Development, 68,* 592–594.

van den Broek, P. (1989). Causal reasoning and inference making in judging the importance of story statements. *Child Development, 60,* 286–297.

van den Broek, P. W. (1997). Discovering the element of the universe: The development of event comprehension from childhood to adulthood. In P. van den Broek, P. Bauer, & T. Bourg (Eds.), *Developmental spans in event comprehension: Bridging fictional and actual events* (pp. 321–342). Mahwah, NJ: Erlbaum.

van den Broek, P., Lorch, E. P., & Thurlow, R. (1996). Children's and adults' memory for television stories: The role of causal factors, story-grammar categories, and hierarchical level. *Child Development, 67,* 3010–3028.

van Doorninck, W. J., Caldwell, B. M., Wright, C., & Frankenberg, W. K. (1981). The relationship between twelve-month home stimulation and school achievement. *Child Development, 52,* 1080–1083.

van IJzendoorn, M. H. (1992). Intergenerational transmission of parenting: A review of studies in nonclinical populations. *Developmental Review, 12,* 76–99.

van IJzendoorn, M. H. (1995). Adult attachment representations, parental responsiveness, and infant attachment: A meta-analysis on the predictive validity of the Adult Attachment Interview. *Psychological Bulletin, 117,* 387–403.

van IJzendoorn, M. H., & De Wolff, M. S. (1997). In search of the absent father—meta-analysis of infant-father attachment: A rejoinder to our discussants. *Child Development, 68,* 604–609.

van IJzendoorn, M. H., Goldberg, S., Kroonenberg, P. M., & Frenkel, O. J. (1992). The relative effects of maternal and child problems on the quality of attachment: A meta-analysis of attachment in clinical samples. *Child Development, 63,* 840–858.

van IJzendoorn, M. H., & Kroonenberg, P. M. (1988). Cross-cultural patterns of attachment: A meta-analysis of the Strange Situation. *Child Development, 59,* 147–156.

Vannatta, R. A. (1996). Risk factors related to suicidal behavior among male and female adolescents. *Journal of Youth and Adolescence, 25,* 149–160.

Vartanian, L. R., & Powlishta, K. K. (1996). A longitudinal examination of the social-cognitive foundations of adolescent egocentrism. *Journal of Early Adolescence, 16,* 157–178.

Vasudev, J., & Hummel, R. C. (1987). Moral stage sequence and principled reasoning in an Indian sample. *Human Development, 30,* 105–118.

Vaughn, B., Block, J., & Block, J. (1988). Parental agreement on child rearing during early childhood and the psychological characteristics of adolescents. *Child Development, 59,* 1020–1033.

Vaughn, B. E., Bradley, C. F., Joffe, L. S., Seifer, R., & Barglow, P. (1987). Maternal characteristics measured prenatally are predictive of ratings of temperamental "difficulty" on the Carey Infant Temperament Questionnaire. *Developmental Psychology, 23,* 152–161.

Vaughn, B. E., Kopp, C. B., & Krakow, J. B. (1984). The emergence and consolidation of self-control from eighteen to thirty months of age: Normative trends and individual differences. *Child Development, 55,* 990–1004.

Vaughn, B. E., Stevenson-Hinde, J., Waters, E., Kotsaftis, A., Lefever, G. B., Shouldice, A., Trudel, M., & Belsky, J. (1992). Attachment security and temperament in infancy and early childhood: Some conceptual clarification. *Developmental Psychology, 28,* 463–473.

Vaughn, B. E., & Waters, E. (1990). Attachment behavior at home and in the lab: Q-sort observations and Strange Situation classifications of 1-year-olds. *Child Development, 61,* 1965–1973.

Vaughn, V. C., McKay, J. R., & Behrman, R. E. (1984). *Nelson textbook of pediatrics* (12th ed.). Philadelphia: W. B. Saunders.

Vellutino, F. (1991). Introduction to three studies on reading acquisition: Convergent findings on theoretical foundations of code-oriented versus whole language approaches to reading instruction. *Journal of Educational Psychology, 83,* 437–443.

Verhulst, F. C., & Versluis-Den Bieman, H. J. (1995). Developmental course of problem behaviors in adolescent adoptees. *Journal of the American Academy of Child and Adolescent Psychiatry, 34,* 151–159.

Vernon-Feagans, L., Manlove, E. E., & Volling, B. L. (1996). Otitis media and the social behavior of day-care-attending children. *Child Development, 67,* 1528–1539.

Verp, M. S. (1993). Environmental causes of pregnancy loss and malformations. In C. Lin, M. S. Verp, & R. E. Sabbagha (Eds.), *The high-risk fetus: Pathophysiology, diagnosis, management.* New York: Springer-Verlag.

Verp, M. S. (1993). Genetic counseling and screening. In C. Lin, M. S. Verp, & R. E. Sabbagha (Eds.), *The high-risk fetus: Pathophysiology, diagnosis,management.* New York: Springer-Verlag.

Verp, M. S., Simpson, J. L., & Ober, C. (1993). Prenatal diagnosis of genetic disorders. In C. Lin, M. S. Verp, & R. E. Sabbagha (Eds.), *The high-risk fetus: Pathophysiology, diagnosis, management.* New York: Springer-Verlag.

Verschueren, K., Marcoen, A., & Schoefs, V. (1996). The internal working model of self, attachment, and competence in five-year-olds. *Child Development, 67,* 2493–2511.

Vihman, M. M., Kay, E., Boysson-Bardies, B. de., Durand, C., & Sundberg, U. (1994). External sources of individual differences? a cross-linguistic analysis of the phonetics of mothers' speech to 1-year-old children. *Developmental Psychology, 30,* 651–662.

Vinden, P. G. (1996). Junin Quechua children's understanding of mind. *Child Development, 67,* 1707–1716.

Vinter, A. (1986). The role of movement in eliciting early imitation. *Child Development, 57,* 66–71.

Vitaro, F., Tremblay, R. E., Kerr, M., Pagani, L., & Bukowski, W. M. (1997). Disruptiveness, friends' characteristics, and delinquency in early adolescence: A test of two competing models of development. *Child Development, 68,* 676–689.

Vobejda, B. (1991, September 15). The future deferred. Longer road from adolescence to adulthood often leads back through parents' home. *The Washington Post,* pp. A1, A29.

Volling, B. L., & Belsky, J. (1992). The contribution of mother-child and father-child relationships to the quality of sibling interaction: A longitudinal study. *Child Development, 63,* 1209–1222.

Vondra, J., & Belsky, J. (1993). Developmental origins of parenting: Personality and relationship factors. In T. Luster & L. Okagaki (Eds.), *Parenting. An ecological perspective.* Hillsdale, NJ: Erlbaum.

Von Wright, M. R. (1989). Body image satisfaction in adolescent boys and girls: A longitudinal study. *Journal of Youth and Adolescence, 18,* 71–83.

Vorhees, C. V., & Mollnow, E. (1987). Behavioral teratogenesis: Long-term influences on behavior from early exposure to environmental agents. In J. D. Osofsky (Ed.), *Handbook of infant Development* (2nd ed., pp. 913–971). New York: Wiley.

Voyer, D., Voyer, S., & Bryden, M. P. (1995). Magnitude of sex differences in spatial abilities: a meta-analysis and consideration of critical variables. *Psychological Bulletin, 117,* 250–270.

Vuchinich, S., Bank, L., & Patterson, G. R. (1992). Parenting, peers, and the stability of antisocial behavior in preadolescent boys. *Developmental Psychology, 28,* 510–521.

Vuchinich, S., Hetherington, E. M., Vuchinich, R. A., & Clingempeel, W. G. (1991). Parent-child interaction and gender differences in early adolescents' adaptation to stepfamilies. *Developmental Psychology, 27,* 618–626.

Vurpillot, E. (1968). The development of scanning strategies and their relation to visual differentiation. *Journal of Experimental Child Psychology, 6,* 632–650.

Vurpillot, E. & Ball, W. A. (1979). The concept of identity and children's selective attention. In G. Hale and M. Lewis (Eds.), *Attention and cognitive development.* New York: Plenum.

Vygotsky, L. S. (1962). *Thought and language.* Cambridge, MA: MIT Press. (Original work published 1934.)

Vygotsky, L. S. (1978). *Mind in society: The development of higher mental processes.* M. Cole, V. John-Steiner, S. Scribner, & E. Souberman (Eds.). Cambridge, MA: Harvard University Press. (Original work published 1930, 1933, 1935.)

Wachs, T. D. (1992). *The nature of nurture.* Newbury Park, CA: Sage.

Waddington, C. H. (1966). *Principles of development and differentiation.* New York: Macmillan.

Wagner, B. M. (1997). Family risk factors for child and adolescent suicidal behavior. *Psychological Bulletin, 121,* 246–298.

Wagner, R. K., Torgesen, J. K., & Rashotte, C. A. (1994). Development of reading-related phonological processing abilities: New evidence of bidirectional causality from a latent variable longitudinal study. *Developmental Psychology, 30,* 73–87.

Wagner, R. K., Torgesen, J. K., & Rashotte, C. A., Hecht, S. A., Barker, T. A., Burgess, S. R., Donahue, J., & Garon, T. (1997). Changing relations between phonological processing abilities and word-level reading as children develop from beginning to skilled readers: A 5-year longitudinal study. *Developmental Psychology, 33,* 468–479.

Wainryb, C. (1993). The application of moral judgments to other cultures: Relativism and universality. *Child Development, 64,* 924–933.

Wainryb, C., & Turiel, E. (1994). Dominance, subordination, and concepts of personal entitlements in cultural contexts. *Child Development, 65,* 1701–1722.

Walden, T. A., & Baxter, A. (1989). The effect of context and age on social referencing. *Child Development, 60,* 1511–1518.

Waldman, I. D. (1996). Aggressive boys' hostile perceptual and response biases: The role of attention and impulsivity. *Child Development, 67,* 1015–1033.

Waldman, I. D., Weinberg, K. A., & Scarr, S. (1994). Racial-group differences in IQ in the Minnesota Transracial Adoption Study: A reply to Levin and Lynn. *Intelligence, 19,* 29–44.

Walker, D., Greenwood, C., Hart, B., & Carta, J. (1994). Prediction of school outcomes based on early language production and socioeconomic factors. *Child Development, 59,* 606–621.

Walker, L. J. (1980). Cognitive and perspective-taking prerequisites for moral development. *Child Development, 51,* 131–139.

Walker, L. J. (1995). Sexism in Kohlberg's moral psychology? In W. M. Kurtines & J. L. Gewirtz (Eds.), *Moral development: An introduction* (pp. 83–107). Boston: Allyn & Bacon.

Walker, L. J., & Taylor, J. H. (1991). Family interactions and the development of moral reasoning. *Child Development, 62,* 264–283.

Walker-Andrews, A. S., & Lennon, E. M. (1985). Auditory-visual perception of changing distance by human infants. *Child Development, 56,* 544–548.

Wallach, M. A. (1985). Creativity testing and giftedness. In F. D. Horowitz & M. O'Brien (Eds.), *The gifted and talented. Developmental perspectives.*

Wallach, M. A., & Kogan, N. (1965). *Modes of thinking in young children.* New York: Holt, Rinehart & Winston.

Wallen, K. (1996). Nature needs nurture: The interaction of hormonal and social influences on the development of behavioral sex differences in rhesus monkeys. *Hormones and Behavior, 30,* 364–378.

Wallerstein, J. S., & Blakeslee, S. (1989). *Second chances: Men, women, and children a decade after divorce.* New York: Ticknor and Fields.

Wallerstein, J. S., & Kelly, J. B. (1980). *Surviving the breakup: How children and parents cope with divorce.* New York: Basic Books.

Walters, A. S. (1997). *Survey of 500 adolescents' discoveries about the facts of life.* Unpublished data, University of Georgia.

Ward, M. J., & Carlson, E. A. (1995). Associations among adult attachment representations, maternal sensitivity, and infant-mother attachment in a sample of adolescent mothers. *Child Development, 66,* 69–79.

Ward, S. L., & Overton, W. F. (1990). Semantic familiarity, relevance, and the development of deductive reasoning. *Developmental Psychology, 26,* 488–493.

Wark, G. R., & Krebs, D. L. (1996). Gender and dilemma differences in real-life moral judgments. *Developmental Psychology, 32,* 220–230.

Warren-Leubecker, A., & Carter, B. W. (1988). Reading and growth in metalinguistic awareness: Relations to socioeconomic status and reading readiness skills. *Child Development, 59,* 728–742.

Wartner, U. G., Grossmann, K., Fremmer-Bombik, E., & Suess, G. (1994). Attachment patterns at age six in south Germany: Predictability from infancy and implications for preschool behavior. *Child Development, 65,* 1014–1027.

Waterman, A. S. (1982). Identity development from adolescence to adulthood: An extension of theory and a review of research. *Developmental Psychology, 18,* 341–358.

Waterman, A. S. (1992). Identity as an aspect of optimal psychological functioning. In G. R. Adams, T. P. Gullotta, & R. Montemayor (Eds.), *Adolescent identity formation.* (Vol. 4). *Advances in Adolescent Development.* Newbury Park, CA: Sage.

Waterman, A. S., & Archer, S. L. (1990). A life-span perspective on identity formation: Developments in form, function, and process. In P. B. Baltes, D. L. Featterman, & R. M. Lerner (Eds.), *Life-span development and behavior.* (Vol. 10). Hillsdale, NJ: Erlbaum.

Waters, E., Vaughn, B. E., & Egeland, B. R. (1980). Individual differences in mother-infant attachment relationships at age one: Antecedents in neonatal behavior in an urban, economically disadvantaged sample. *Child Development, 51,* 208–216.

Waters, E., Vaughn, B. E., Posada, G., & Kondo-Ikemura, K. (1995). Caregiving, cultural, and cognitive perspectives on secure-base behavior and working models: New growing points of attachment theory and research. *Monographs of the Society for Research in Child Development, 60,* 2–3, Serial No. 244.

Waters, E., Wippman, J., & Sroufe, L. A. (1979). Attachment, positive affect, and competence in the peer group: Two studies in construct validation. *Child Development, 50,* 821–829.

Watson, J. B. (1913). Psychology as the behaviorist views it. *Psychological Review, 20,* 158–177.

Watson, J. B. (1925). *Behaviorism.* New York: Norton.

Watson, J. B. (1928). *Psychological care of infant and child.* New York: Norton.

Watson, J. B., & Raynor, R. (1920). Conditioned emotional reactions. *Journal of Experimental Psychology, 3,* 1–14.

Watson, J. S., Hayes, L. A., Vietze, P., & Becker, J. (1979). Discriminative infant smiling to orientations of talking faces of mother and stranger. *Journal of Experimental Child Psychology, 28,* 92–99.

Watson, M. W., & Peng, Y. (1992). The relation between toy gun play and children's aggressive behavior. *Early Education and Development, 3,* 370–389.

Waxman, S. R., & Hatch, T. (1992). Beyond the basics: Preschool children label objects flexibly at multiple hierarchical levels. *Journal of Child Language, 19,* 153–166.

Waxman, S. R., & Senghas, A. (1992). Relations among word meanings in early lexical development. *Developmental Psychology, 28,* 862–873.

Weakliem, D., McQuillan, J., & Schauer, T. (1995). Toward meritocracy? Changing social-class differences in intellectual ability. *Sociology of Education, 68,* 271–286.

Wechsler, D. (1989). *Manual for the Wechsler Preschool and Primary Scale of Intelligence-Revised.* New York: Psychological Corporation.

Wechsler, D. (1991). *Manual, WISC-III: Wechsler Intelligence Scale for Children-Third Edition.* San Antonio, TX: Psychological Corporation.

Weinberg, R. A., Scarr, S., & Waldman, I. D. (1992). The Minnesota transracial adoption study: A follow-up of IQ test performance at adolescence. *Intelligence, 16,* 117–135.

Weiner, B. (1974). *Achievement and attribution theory.* Morristown, NJ: General Learning Press.

Weiner, B. (1986). *An attributional theory of motivation and emotion.* New York: Springer-Verlag.

Weinraub, M., Clemens, L. P., Sockloff, A., Ethridge, T., Gracely, E., & Myers, B. (1984). The development of sex-role stereotypes in the third year: Relationships to gender labeling, gender identity, sex-typed toy preferences, and family characteristics. *Child Development, 55,* 1493–1503.

Weinraub, M., & Lewis, M. (1977). The determinants of children's responses to separation. *Monographs of the Society for Research in Child Development, 42,* 4, Serial No. 172.

Weinstein, C. S. (1991). The classroom as a social context for learning. *Annual Review of Psychology, 42,* 493–525.

Weinstein, R. S., Marshall, H. H., Sharp, L., & Botkin, M. (1987). Pygmalion and the student: Age and classroom differences in children's awareness of teacher expectations. *Child Development, 58,* 1079–1093.

Weisberg, R. W. (1993). *Creativity: Beyond the myth of genius.* New York: Freeman.

Weisner, T. S., & Gallimore, R. (1977). My brother's keeper: Child and sibling caretaking. *Current Anthropology, 18,* 169–190.

Weisner, T. S., & Wilson-Mitchell, J. E. (1990). Nonconventional family lifestyles and sex typing in six-year-olds. *Child Development, 61,* 1915–1933.

Weiss, B., Dodge, K. A., Bates, J. E., & Pettit, G. S. (1992). Some consequences of early harsh discipline: Child aggression and a maladaptive social information processing style. *Child Development, 63,* 1321–1335.

Weiss, L. H., & Schwarz, J. C. (1996). The relationship between parenting types and older adolescents' personality, academic achievement, adjustment, and substance use. *Child Development, 67,* 2101–2114.

Weisz, J. R., Chaiyasit, W., Weiss, B., Eastman, K. L., & Jackson, E. W. (1995). A multimethod study of problem behavior among Thai and American children in school: Teacher reports versus direct observations. *Child Development, 66,* 402–415.

Welch-Ross, M. K., & Schmidt, C. R. (1996). Gender-schema development and children's constructive story memory: Evidence for a developmental model. *Child Development, 67,* 820–835.

Wellman, H. M. (1985). *Children's searching: The development of search skill and spatial representation.* Hillsdale, NJ: Erlbaum.

Wellman, H. M. (1990). *The child's theory of mind.* Cambridge, MA: MIT Press.

Wellman, H. M., Hollander, M., & Schult, C. A. (1996). Young children's understanding of thought bubbles and of thoughts. *Child Development, 67,* 768–788.

Wellman, H. M., & Lempers, J. D. (1977). The naturalistic communicative abilities of two-year-olds. *Child Development, 48,* 1052–1057.

Wellman, H. M., & Woolley, J. (1990). From simple desires to ordinary beliefs: The early development of everyday psychology. *Cognition, 35,* 245–275.

Wells, L. E. (1989). Self-enhancement through delinquency: A conditional test of self-derogation theory. *Journal of Research in Crime and Delinquency, 26,* 226–252.

Wender, P. H. (1995). *Attention-deficit hyperactivity disorder in adults.* New York: Oxford University, Press.

Wentzel, K. R., & Asher, S. R. (1995). The academic lives of neglected, rejected, popular, and controversial children. *Child Development, 66,* 754–763.

Werker, J. F., & Desjardins, R. N. (1995). Listening to speech in the first year of life: Experiential influences on phoneme perception. *Current Directions in Psychological Science, 4,* 76–81.

Werner, E. E., & Smith, R. S. (1992). *Overcoming the odds. High risk children from birth to adulthood.* Ithaca, NY: Cornell University Press.

Wertsch, J. V., & Tulviste, P. (1992). L. S. Vygotsky and contemporary developmental psychology. *Developmental Psychology, 28,* 548–557.

Whalen, C. K., & Henker, B. (1991). Therapies for hyperactive children: Comparisons, combinations, and compromises. *Journal of Consulting and Clinical Psychology, 59,* 126–137.

Whaley, K. L., & Rubenstein, T. S. (1994). How toddlers "do" friendship: A descriptive analysis of naturally occurring friendships in a group child care setting. *Journal of Social and Personal Relationships, 11,* 383–400.

Wheeler, L. R. (1932). The intelligence of East Tennessee children. *Journal of Educational Psychology, 23,* 351–370.

Wheeler, L. R. (1942). A comparative study of the intelligence of East Tennessee mountain children. *Journal of Educational Psychology, 33,* 321–334.

Whiffen, V. E. (1992). Is postpartum depression a distinct diagnosis? *Clinical Psychology Review, 12,* 485–508.

Whipp, B. J., & Ward, S. A. (1992). Will women soon outrun men? *Nature, 355,* 25.

Whipple, E. E., & Richey, C. A. (1997). Crossing the line between physical discipline and child abuse: How much is too much. *Child Abuse and Neglect, 21,* 431–444.

Whitall, J., & Getchell, N. (1995). From walking to running: Applying a dynamical systems approach to the development of locomotor skills. *Child Development, 66,* 1541–1553.

Whitbourne, S. K. (1986). *The me I know: A study of adult identity.* New York: Springer-Verlag.

White, K. J., & Kistner, J. (1992). The influence of teacher feedback on young children's peer preferences and perceptions. *Developmental Psychology, 28,* 933–940.

White, R. W. (1959). Motivation reconsidered: The concept of competence. *Psychological Review, 66,* 297–333.

White, S. H. (1992). G. Stanley Hall: From philosophy to developmental psychology. *Developmental Psychology, 28,* 25–34.

Whitehurst, G. J., & Valdez-Menchaca, M. C. (1988). What is the role of reinforcement in early language acquisition? *Child Development, 59,* 430–440.

Whitehurst, G. J., & Vasta, R. (1975). Is language acquired through imitation. *Journal of Psycholinguistic Research, 4,* 37–59.

Whiting, B. B., & Edwards, C. P. (1988). *Children of different worlds: The formation of social behavior.* Cambridge, MA: Harvard University Press.

Whiting, B. B., & Whiting, J. W. M. (1975). *Children of six cultures.* Cambridge, MA: Harvard University Press.
Whitley, B. E., Jr. (1983). Sex-role orientation and self-esteem: A critical meta-analytic review. *Journal of Personality and Social Psychology, 44,* 765–778.
Whittle, M. J., & Connor, J. M. (1995). *Prenatal diagnosis in obstetric practice* (2nd ed.). Oxford, England: Blackwell.
Widmayer, S., & Field, T. (1980). Effects of Brazelton demonstrations on early interactions of preterm infants and their teen-age mothers. *Infant Behavior and Development, 3,* 78–89.
Wiehe, V. R. (1996). *Working with child abuse and neglect.* Thousand Oaks, CA: Sage.
Wiggam, A. E. (1923). *The new decalogue of science.* Indianapolis: Bobbs-Merrill.
Wilcock, A., Kobayashi, L., & Murray, I. (1997). Twenty-five years of obstetric patient satisfaction in North America: A review of the literature. *Journal of Perinatal and Neonatal Nursing, 10,* 36–47.
Wilcox, A. J., Baird, D. D., Weinberg, C. R., & Associates (1995). Fertility in men exposed prenatally to diethylstilbestrol. *New England Journal of Medicine, 332,* 1411–1416.
Wilens, T. E., & Biederman, J. (1992). The stimulants. *Psychiatric Clinics of North America, 15,* 191–222.
Wilkinson, R. T., & Allison, S. (1989). Age and simple reaction time: Decade differences for 5,325 subjects. *Journal of Gerontology: Psychological Sciences, 44,* P29-P35.
Wille, D. (1991). Relation of preterm birth with quality of infant-mother attachment at one year. *Infant Behavior and Development, 14,* 227–240.
Willems, E. P., & Alexander, J. L. (1982). The naturalistic perspective in research. In B. B. Wolman (Ed.), *Handbook of developmental psychology.* Englewood Cliffs, NJ: Prentice Hall.
Williams, B. (1998; January 19). Stricter controls on internet access sorely needed, parents fear. *Atlanta Constitution,* pp. A1, A15.
Williams, C., & Bybee, J. (1994). What do children feel guilty about? Developmental and gender differences. *Developmental Psychology, 30,* 617–623.
Williams, E., & Radin, N. (1993). Parental involvement, maternal employment, and adolescents' academic achievement: An 11-year follow-up. *American Journal of Orthopsychiatry, 63,* 306–312.
Williams, J. E., Bennett, S. M., & Best, D. L. (1975). Awareness and expression of sex stereotypes in young children. *Developmental Psychology, 11,* 635–642.
Williams, J. E., & Best, D. L. (1990). *Measuring sex stereotypes: A multination study* (rev. ed.). Newbury Park, CA: Sage.
Wilson, M. N. (1989). Child development in the context of the Black extended family. *American Psychologist, 44,* 380–385.
Wilson, R. S. (1978). Synchronies in mental development: An epigenetic perspective. *Science, 202,* 939–948.
Wilson, R. S. (1983). The Louisville twin study: Developmental synchronies in behavior. *Child Development, 54,* 298–316.
Wilson, R. S. (1985). Risk and resilience in early mental development. *Developmental Psychology, 21,* 795–805.
Windle, R. C., & Windle, M. (1997). An investigation of adolescents' substance abuse behaviors, depressed affect, and suicidal behaviors. *Journal of Child Psychology and Psychiatry and Allied Disciplines, 38,* 921–929.
Winick, M. (1976). *Malnutrition and brain development.* New York: Oxford University Press.
Winner, E. (1997). Exceptionally high intelligence and schooling. *American Psychologist, 52,* 1070–1081.
Winterbottom, M. (1958). The relation of need for achievement to learning experiences in independence and mastery. In J. Atkinson (Ed.), *Motives in fantasy, action, and society.* Princeton, NJ: Van Nostrand.
Wise, P. H. (1995). Infant mortality: Confronting disciplinary fragmentation in research and policy. In B. R. Sachs, R. Beard, E. Papiernik, & C. Russell (Eds.), *Reproductive health care for women and babies* (pp. 375–390). New York: Oxford University Press.
Wissow, L., Hutton, N., & McGraw, D. C. (1996). Psychosocial issues for children born to HIV-infected mothers. In R. R. Faden & N. E. Kass (Eds.), *HIV, AIDS, and childbearing* (pp. 78–95). New York: Oxford University Press.
Witelson, S. F. (1987). Neurobiological aspects of language in children. *Child Development, 58,* 653–688.
Wolf, M., & Dickinson, D. (1985). From oral to written language: Transitions in the school years. In J. Berko Gleason (Ed.), *The development of language.* Westerville, OH: Merrill.
Wolff, M., Rutten, P., & Bayer, A. F., III (1992). *Where we stand: Can America make it in the race for health, wealth, and happiness?* New York: Bantam Books.
Wolff, P. H. (1966). The causes, controls, and organization of behavior in the neonate. *Psychological Issues, 5,* (1, Whole No. 17).
Wolff, P. H. (1969). The natural history of crying and other vocalizations in early infancy. In B. M. Foss (Ed.), *Determinants of infant behavior* (Vol. 4). London: Methuen.
Wolfner, G. D., & Gelles, R. J. (1993). A profile of violence toward children: A national study. *Child Abuse and Neglect, 17,* 197–212.
Woodward, A. L., Markman, E. M., & Fitzsimmons, C. M. (1994). Rapid word learning in 13- and 18-month-olds. *Developmental Psychology, 30,* 553–566.
Worobey, J. (1985). A review of Brazelton-based interventions to enhance parent-infant interaction. *Journal of Reproductive and Infant Psychology, 3,* 64–73.
Wright, J. C., & Huston, A. C. (1983). A matter of form: Potentials of television for young viewers. *American Psychologist, 38,* 835–843.
Wright, J. C., Huston, A. C., Reitz, A. L., & Piemyat, S. (1994). Young children's perception of television reality: Determinants and developmental differences. *Developmental Psychology, 30,* 229–239.
Wright, J. C., Huston, A. C., Truglio, R., Fitch, M. Smith, E., & Piemyat, S. (1995). Occupational portrayals on television: Children's role schemata, career aspirations, and perceptions of reality. *Child Development, 66,* 1706–1718.
Wrobel, G. M., Ayers-Lopez, S., Grotevant, H. D., McRoy, R. G., & Friedrick, M. (1996). Openness in adoption and level of child participation. *Child Development, 67,* 2358–2374.
Yang, B., Ollendick, T. H., Dong, Q., Xia, Y., & Lin, L. (1995). Only children and children with siblings in the People's Republic of China: Levels of fear, anxiety, and depression. *Child Development, 66,* 1301–1311.
Yankowitz, J. (1996). Surgical fetal therapy. In J. A. Kuller, N. C. Cheschier, & R. C. Cefalo (Eds.), *Prenatal diagnosis and reproductive genetics* (pp. 181–187). St. Louis: Mosby.
Yarrow, M. R., Scott, P. M., & Waxler, C. Z. (1973). Learning concern for others. *Developmental Psychology, 8,* 240–260.
Yau, J., & Smetana, J. G. (1996). Adolescent-parent conflict among Chinese adolescents in Hong Kong. *Child Development, 67,* 1262–1275.
Yazigi, R. A., Odem, R. R., & Polakoski, K. L. (1991). Demonstration of specific binding of cocaine to human spermatoza. *Journal of the American Medical Association, 266,* 1956–1959.
Yeates, K. O., MacPhee, D., Campbell, F. A., & Ramey, C. T. (1983). Maternal IQ and home environment as determinants of early childhood intellectual competence: A developmental analysis. *Developmental Psychology, 19,* 731–739.
Yeates, K. O., & Selman, R. L. (1989). Social competence in the schools: Toward an integrative developmental model for intervention. *Developmental Review, 9,* 64–100.
Yonas, A. (1981). Infants' responses to optical information for collision. In R. N. Aslin, J. R. Alberts, and M. R. Petersen (Eds.), *Development of perception: Psychobiological perspectives.* (Vol. 2.) *The visual system.* New York: Academic Press.
Yonas, A., Arterberry, M., & Granrud, C. E. (1987). Space perception in infancy. In R. A. Vasta (Ed.) *Annals of child development.* Greenwich, CT: JAI Press.
Yonas, A., Cleaves, W., & Pettersen, L. (1978). Development of sensitivity to pictorial depth. *Science, 200,* 77–79.
Yonas, A., & Hartman, B. (1993). Perceiving the affordance of contact in four- and five-month-old infants. *Child Development, 64,* 298–308.
Young, W. C., Goy, R. W., & Phoenix, C. H. (1964). Hormones and sexual behavior. *Science, 143,* 212–218.
Youngblade, L. M., & Belsky, J. (1992). Parent-child antecedents of 5-year-olds' close friendships: A longitudinal analysis. *Developmental Psychology, 28,* 700–713.
Youngblade, L. M., & Dunn, J. (1995). Individual differences in young children's pretend play with mother and sibling: Links to relationships and understanding other people's feelings and beliefs. *Child Development, 66,* 1472–1492.
Younger, A. J., & Daniels, T. M. (1992). Children's reasons for nominating their peers as withdrawn: Passive withdrawal versus active isolation. *Developmental Psychology, 28,* 955–960.
Younger, B. (1990). Infants' detection of correlations among feature categories. *Child Development, 61,* 614–620.
Younger, B. (1993). Understanding category members as "the same sort of thing": Explicit categorization in ten-month infants. *Child Development, 64,* 309–320.
Youniss, J., & Smollar, J. (1985). *Adolescent relations with mothers, fathers, and friends.* Chicago: University of Chicago Press.
Yussen, S. R., & Bird, J. E. (1979). The development of metacognitive awareness in memory, communication, and attention. *Journal of Experimental Child Psychology, 28,* 28, 300–313.
Zahavi, S., & Asher, S. R. (1978). The effect of verbal instructions on preschool children's aggressive behavior. *Journal of School Psychology, 16,* 146–153.
Zahn-Waxler, C., Friedman, R. J., Cole, P. M., Mizuta, I., & Himura, N. (1996). Japanese and United States preschool children's responses to conflict and distress. *Child Development, 67,* 2462–2477.
Zahn-Waxler, C., Radke-Yarrow, M., & King, R. A. (1979). Child rearing and children's prosocial initiations toward victims of distress. *Child Development, 50,* 319–330.
Zahn-Waxler, C., Radke-Yarrow, M., Wagner, E., & Chapman, M. (1992). Development of concern for others. *Developmental Psychology, 28,* 126–136.
Zahn-Waxler, C., Robinson, J. L., & Emde, R. N. (1992). The development of empathy in twins. *Developmental Psychology, 28,* 1038–1047.
Zajonc, R. B., & Markus, G. B. (1975). Birth order and intellectual development. *Psychological Review, 82,* 74–88.
Zajonc, R. B., & Mullally, P. R. (1997). Birth order: Reconciling conflicting effects. *American Psychologist, 52,* 685–699.

Zakriski, A. L., & Coie, J. D. (1996). A comparison of aggressive-rejected and nonaggressive-rejected children's interpretations of self-directed and other-directed rejection. *Child Development, 67,* 1048–1070.

Zani, B. (1991). Male and female patterns in the discovery of sexuality during adolescence. *Journal of Adolescence, 14,* 163–178.

Zarbatany, L., Brunschot, M. V., Meadows, K., & Pepper, S. (1996). Effects of friendship and gender on peer group entry. *Child Development, 67,* 2287–2300.

Zaslow, M. J. (1989). Sex differences in children's response to parental divorce: 2. Samples of variables, ages, and sources. *American Journal of Orthopsychiatry, 59,* 118–141.

Zelazo, N. A., Zelazo, P. R., Cohen, K. M., & Zelazo, P. D. (1993). Specificity of practice effects in elementary neuromotor patterns. *Developmental Psychology, 29,* 686–691.

Zelazo, P. D., Helwig, C. C., & Lau, A. (1996). Intention, act, and outcome in behavioral prediction and moral judgment. *Child Development, 67,* 2478–2492.

Zelazo, P. R., Zelazo, N. A., & Kolb, S. (1972). "Walking" in the newborn. *Science, 176,* 314–315.

Zeman, J., & Garber, J. (1996). Display rules for anger, sadness, and pain: It depends on who is watching. *Child Development, 67,* 957–973.

Zeman, J., & Shipman, K. (1997). Social-contextual influences on expectancies for managing anger and sadness: The transition from middle childhood to adolescence. *Developmental Psychology, 33,* 917–924.

Zerbe, K. J. (1993). *The body betrayed: Women, eating disorders, and treatment.* Washington, DC: American Psychiatric Press.

Zern, D. S. (1984). Relationships among selected child-rearing variables in a cross-cultural sample of 110 societies. *Developmental Psychology, 20,* 683–690.

Zeskind, P. S. (1980). Adult responses to the cries of low and high risk infants. *Infant Behavior and Development, 3,* 167–177.

Zeskind, P. S., Klein, L., & Marshall, T. R. (1992). Adults' perceptions of experimental modifications of durations of pauses and expiratory sounds in infant crying. *Developmental Psychology, 28,* 1153–1162.

Zeskind, P. S., & Ramey, C. T. (1981). Preventing intellectual and interactional sequelae of fetal malnutrition: A longitudinal, transactional, and synergistic approach to development. *Child Development, 52,* 213–218.

Zeskind, P. S., Sale, J., Maio, M. L., Huntington, L., & Weiseman, J. R. (1985). Adult perceptions of pain and hunger cries: A synchrony of arousal. *Child Development, 56,* 549–554.

Zigler, E. F. (1987). Formal schooling for four-year-olds? No. *American Psychologist, 42,* 254–260.

Zigler, E. F., Abelson, W. D., Trickett, P. K., & Seitz, V. (1982). Is an intervention program necessary to improve economically disadvantaged children's IQ scores? *Child Development, 53,* 340–348.

Zigler, E., & Finn-Stevenson, M. F. (1993). *Children in a changing world: Developmental and social issues.* Pacific Grove, CA: Brooks/Cole.

Zigler, E. F., & Gilman, E. (1993). Day care in America: What is needed? *Pediatrics, 91,* 175–178.

Zimiles, H., & Lee, V. E. (1991). Adolescent family structure and educational progress. *Developmental Psychology, 27,* 314–320.

Zimmerman, M. A., Salem, D. A., & Maton, K. I. (1995). Family structure and psychosocial correlates among urban African-American adolescent males. *Child Development, 66,* 1598–1613.

Zupan, B. A., Hammen, C., & Jaenicke, C. (1987). The effects of current mood and prior depressive history on self-schematic processing in children. *Journal of Experimental Child Psychology, 43,* 149–158.

Name Index

C

I

J

K

Y

Z

Subject Index

T

U

V

W X Y Z

Credits

These pages constitute an extension of the copyright page. We have made every effort to trace the ownership of all copyrighted material and to secure permission from copyright holders. In the event of any question arising as to the use of any material, we will be pleased to make the necessary corrections in future printings. Thanks are due to the following authors, publishers, and agents for permission to use the material indicated.

PHOTOGRAPHS

Chapter 1:

1: © PhotoDisc. **3:** © Corbis-Bettmann. **7:** © W.P.Wilstach Collection, Philadelphia Museum of Art. **9:** © The Image Works. **10:** © Corbis-Bettmann. **14:** © Mary Kate Denny/PhotoEdit. **15:** © Ann Clark. **17:** © David Austen/Stock Boston. **27a:** © Corbis-Bettmann. **27b:** © David Young-Wolff/PhotoEdit. **31:** © Jeffrey Aaronson/Network Aspen. **33:** © Pedrick/The Image Works.

Chapter 2:

37: © Lawrance Migdale/Stock Boston. **42:** © Corbis-Bettmann. **44:** © UPI/Corbis-Bettmann. **47:** © Corbis-Bettmann. **48:** © Archives of the History of American Psychology,University of Akron. **49:** © Courtesy of Albert Bandura. **53:** © Yves de Braine/Black Star. **54:** © Myrleen Ferguson/PhotoEdit. **60:** © Bob Daemmrich/Stock Boston. **63:** © Chris Hildreth/Cornell University. **66:** © Spencer Grant/Photo Researchers Inc.

Chapter 3:

72: © Francis Leroy/Photo Researchers, Inc. **77a:** © Ann Clark. **77b:** © Ann Clark. **77c:** © Biophoto Associates/Science Source/Photo Researchers Inc. **77d:** © Biophoto Associates/Science Source/Photo Researchers Inc. **81:** © Science Source/Photo Researchers Inc. **85:** © Jose Carrillo/Stock Boston. **99:** © Alan Carey/The Image Works. **104:** © Robert Burroughs.

Chapter 4:

110: © PhotoDisc. **112:** © Andy Walker/Midland Fertility Services/Photo Researchers Inc. **114:** © John Giannicchi/Science Photo Library/Photo Researchers Inc. **115:** © Keith/Custom Medical Stock. **116a:** © Lennart Nilsson/Albert Bonniers Forlag AB, A CHILD IS BORN. **116b:** © Lennart Nilsson/Albert Bonniers Forlag AB, A CHILD IS BORN. **122:** © Alistair Berg/FSP/Gamma-Liaison. **123:** © George Steinmetz. **132:** © David Sams/Stock Boston. **134:** © Anthro Photo. **135:** © Tom Tucker/Science Source/Photo Researchers Inc. **137:** © Jeff Persons/Stock Boston. **144a:** © Cunha/Petit Format/Photo Researchers Inc. **144b:** © Charles Gupton/Stock Boston. **148:** © Jean-Gerard Sidaner/Photo Researchers Inc.

Chapter 5:

151: © PhotoDisc. **153:** © Tony Freeman/PhotoEdit. **155:** © Novastock/PhotoEdit. **162:** © Elizabeth Crews/The Image Works. **163:** © H.Bruhat/Rapho/Gamma-Liaison. **164:** © B.Plotkin/The Image Works. **165:** © John Eastcott/The Image Works. **166:** © Bob Daemmrich/Stock Boston. **168:** © Bob Daemmrich/Stock Boston. **171:** © The Kansas City Star. **172:** © Bob Daemmrich/Stock Boston. **176:** © Bob Daemmrich/The Image Works. **180:** © Dorothy Littell Greco/Stock Boston. **183:** © Jean Michel Turpin/Gamma-Liaison.

Chapter 6:

189: © PhotoDisc. **192:** © David Linton. **194a:** © Sotographs/Gamma-Liaison. **194b:** © Sotographs/Gamma-Liaison. **195:** © Peter Chapman. **205:** © Mark Richards/PhotoEdit. **207:** © Bruce Plotkin/The Image Works. **209:** © Courtesy of Lorraine Bahrick,from Intermodel Learning in Infancy. **212:** © Mary Kate Denny/PhotoEdit. **214:** © Cathy Waterson/Gail Meese Photography. **216:** © D.Greco/The Image Works. **219:** © Courtesy of Carolyn Rovee-Collier/Rutgers University. **221:** © Ann Clark. **222:** © Courtesy of A.N.Meltzoff & A.K.Moore, University of Washington. **224:** © Peter Chapman.

Chapter 7:

228: © PhotoDisc. **231:** © Elizabeth Crews/The Image Works. **234:** © Myrleen Ferguson/PhotoEdit. **237:** © Jean-Claude Le Jeune/Stock Boston. **242:** © Jeff Greenberg/PhotoEdit. **244a:** © Courtesy of Rheta de Vries. **244b:** © Courtesy of Rheta de Vries. **252:** © Tony Freeman/PhotoEdit. **254:** © W.Hill/The Image Works. **259:** © Archives of the History of American Psychology, University of Akron. **261:** © Bob Daemmrich/Stock Boston. **266:** © Myrleen Ferguson/PhotoEdit.

Chapter 8:

270: © PhotoDisc. **282:** © Mary Kate Denny/PhotoEdit. **286:** © Ellen Senisi/The Image Works. **290:** © David Young-Wolff/PhotoEdit. **293:** © Cassy Cohen/PhotoEdit. **298:** © Elizabeth Crews/The Image Works. **300:** © Mark C.Burnett/Photo Researchers Inc. **302:** © Elizabeth Crews. **306:** © David Wells/The Image Works. **308:** © David Young-Wolff/PhotoEdit.

Chapter 9:

312: © Laura Dwight/PhotoEdit. **314:** © Corbis-Bettmann. **318:** © Cameramann/The Image Works. **326:** © Alan S.Weiner/Gamma-Liaison. **329:** © Ann Clark. **334:** © Bob Daemmrich/The Image Works. **344:** © Tony Freeman/PhotoEdit. **347:** © K.Cavanagh/Photo Researchers Inc. **348:** © Paul Conklin/Gail Meese Photography.

Chapter 10:

351: © PhotoDisc. **353:** © Sue Klemens/Stock Boston. **356:** © Corbis-Bettmann. **358a:** © Courtesy of Sue Savage-Rumbaugh. **358b:** © Courtesy of Sue Savage-Rumbaugh. **358c:** © Courtesy of Sue Savage-Rumbaugh. **358d:** © Courtesy of Sue Savage-Rumbaugh. **367:** © David M.Grossman/Photo Researchers Inc. **368:** © Tony Freeman/PhotoEdit. **369:** © Elizabeth Crews. **379:** © Lawrence Migdale/Stock Boston. **381:** © Myrleen Ferguson/PhotoEdit. **383:** © Joseph Nettis/Stock Boston. **387:** © Ann Clark.

Chapter 11:

391: © PhotoDisc. **393a:** © Courtesy of Carroll E.Izard, University of Delaware. **393b:** © Courtesy of Carroll E.Izard, University of Delaware. **393c:** © Courtesy of Carroll E.Izard, University of Delaware. **393d:** © Courtesy of Carroll E.Izard, University of Delaware. **393e:** © Courtesy of Carroll E.Izard, University of Delaware. **393f:** © Courtesy of Carroll E.Izard, University of Delaware. **395:** © Elizabeth Crews. **397:** © Amy Etra/PhotoEdit. **401:** © Bob Daemmrich/Stock Boston. **402:** © Ann Clark. **405:** © Robert Brenner/PhotoEdit. **406:** © Martin Rogers/Stock Boston. **408:** © Laura Dwight/PhotoEdit. **410:** © Steve Grand/Photo Researchers Inc. **414:** © Keren Su/Tony Stone Images. **417:** © Michael Newman/PhotoEdit. **424:** © H.Bradner/The Image Works. **428:** © Paul Conklin/PhotoEdit.

Chapter 12:

433: © PhotoDisc. **436:** © Jeff Greenberg/Photo Researchers Inc. **437a:** © Bob Daemmrich/Stock Boston. **437b:** © Jeffery W.Myers/Photo Network. **439:** © Myrleen Ferguson/PhotoEdit. **442:** © Jeff Greenberg/Photo Researchers Inc. **448:** © Chad Elders/Photo Network. **450:** © Elizabeth Crews. **451:** © Robert Reichert/Liaison International. **453:** © Tony Freeman/PhotoEdit. **462:** © Jonathan Nourok/PhotoEdit. **463:** © Bob Daemmrich/The Image Works. **469:** © Richard Hutchings/PhotoEdit.

Chapter 13:

472: © PhotoDisc. **473:** © Frank Pedrick/The Image Works. **477:** © Elizabeth Zuckerman/PhotoEdit. **483a:** © J.Kramer/The Image Works. **483b:** © Lawrence Migdale/Photo Researchers Inc. **491:** © Elizabeth Crews/The Image Works. **492:** © Rick Smolan/Stock Boston. **494:** © David Young-Wolff/PhotoEdit. **503:** © Cassy Cohen/PhotoEdit. **504:** © Roger Sandler/Gamma-Liaison.

Chapter 14:

508: © Bob Daemmrich/The Image Works. **510:** © Elizabeth Crews. **511:** © Catherine Ursillo/Photo Researchers Inc. **517:** © Dan Habib/Impact Visuals. **524:** © Mary Kate Denny/PhotoEdit. **527:** © David Young-Wolff/PhotoEdit. **529:** © Bob Daemmrich/Stock Boston. **531:** © Ann Clark. **543:** © Bob Daemmrich/Stock Boston. **547:** © Robert Brenner/PhotoEdit. **548:** © Mary Kate Denny/PhotoEdit.

Chapter 15:

557: © PhotoDisc. **559:** © Tom Raymond/Tony Stone Images. **561:** © David Young-Wolff/PhotoEdit. **563:** © Michelle Bridwell/PhotoEdit. **565:** © Brooks Dodge/Photo Network. **571:** © Michael Newman/PhotoEdit. **574:** © Elizabeth Crews. **575:** © Dennis MacDonald/PhotoEdit. **579:** © Michael Newman/PhotoEdit. **585:** © Elizabeth Crews. **587:** © Gail Meese/Gail Meese Photography. **589:** © Lionel Delevingne/Stock Boston. **590:** © Courtesy of the National Committee for Prevention of Child Abuse.

Chapter 16:

597: © PhotoDisc. **601:** © Dan Habib/Impact Visuals. **604:** © Big Bird © Jim Henson Productions. **606:** © Bob Daemmrich/Stock Boston. **613:** © Bob Daemmrich/The Image Works. **614:** © W.Hill,Jr./The Image Works. **617:** © David Young-Wolff/Tony Stone Images. **618:** © Fujifotos/The Image Works. **621:** © George Disario/The Stock Market. **622:** © Harlow Primate Laboratory, University of Wisconsin. **624:** © Laura Dwight/Peter Arnold Inc. **627:** © David Young-Wolff/PhotoEdit. **635:** © Frederik D.Bodin/Stock Boston. **639:** © Gail Meese/Gail Meese Photography.

ILLUSTRATIONS, TABLES, AND TEXT

Chapter 1

22: Figure in Box 1-2 adapted from "Effects of Movie Violence on Aggression in a Field Setting as a Function of Group Dominance and Cohesion," by J. P. Leyens, R. D. Parke, L. Camino, & L. Berkowitz, 1975, *Journal of Personality and Social Psychology, 1,* pp. 346–360. Copyright © 1975 by the American Psychological Association. Adapted by permission. **25:** Figure 1-3 adapted from "Age and Verbalization in Observational Learning," by B. Coates & W. W. Hartup, 1969, *Developmental Psychology, 1,* pp. 556–562. Copyright © 1969 by the American Psychological Association. Adapted by permission.

Chapter 2

50: Figure in Box 2-2 adapted from "Influence of Models' Reinforcement Contingencies on the Acquisition of Imitative Responses," by A. Bandura, 1965, *Journal of Personality and Social Psychology, 1,* pp. 589–595. Copyright © 1965 by the American Psychological Association. Adapted by permission. **51:** Figure 2-3 adapted from "The Self System in Reciprocal Determinism, by A. Bandura, 1978, *American Psychologist, 33,* p. 335. Copyright © 1978 by the American Psychological Association. Adapted by permission. **64:** Figure 2-4 based on *The Ecology of Human Development,* by U. Bronfenbrenner, 1979, Cambridge, MA: Harvard University Press.

Chapter 3

85: Table 3-2 adapted from "Increased Maternal Age and Prior Anenploid Conception," by H. H. Shafer & J. A. Kuller, 1996, in J. A. Kuller, N. C. Cheschier, & R. R. Cefalo (Eds.), *Prenatal Diagnosis and Reproductive Genetics,* pp. 23–28. St. Louis: CV Mosby Co. **89:** Figure 3-9 adapted from *Before We Are Born,* 4th Ed., by K. L. Moore & T. V. N. Persaud, 1993, p. 89. Philadelphia: Saunders. Adapted by permission of the author and publisher. **93:** Figure 3-10 from *Behaviorial Genetics: A Primer,* 3rd ed., by R. Plomin, J. C. DeFries, & G. E. McClearn, 1997. Copyright © W. H. Freeman and Company. **93:** Figure 3-11 based on "A Genetic Study of the Male Sexual Orientation," by J. M. Bailey & R.C. Pillard, 1991, *Archives of General Psychiatry, 48,* pp. 1089–1096. Copyright 1991 by the Archives of General Psychiatry. **94:** Table 3-4 based on "Family Studies of Intelligence: A Review," by T. J. Bouchard, Jr., & M. McGue, 1981, *Science, 212,* pp. 1055–1059. **97:** Figure 3-12 from "The Louisville Twin Study: Developmental Synchronies in Behavior," by R. S. Wilson, 1983, *Child Development, 54,* pp. 298–316. Copyright © 1983 by The Society for Research in Child Development, Inc. **102:** Figure 3-13 adapted from "Heritability of Personality: A Demonstration," by I. Gottesman, 1963, *Psychological Monographs, 11* (Whole No. 572). Copyright © 1963 by the American Psychological Association.

Chapter 4

115: Figure 4-4 adapted from *Before We Are Born,* 4th ed., by K. L. Moore & T. V. N. Persaud, 1993. Philadelphia: Saunders. Adapted by permission of the author and publisher. **119:** Figure 4-5 adapted from *Before We Are Born,* 4th ed., by K. L. Moore & T. V. N. Persaud, 1993, p. 130. Philadelphia: Saunders. Adapted by permission of the author and publisher. **129:** Figure 4-7 from *Infant Death: An Analysis by Maternal Risk and Health Care,* by D. Kessner, 1973, p. 100. Copyright © 1973 by the National Academy of Sciences, Washington, D. C. **139:** Data for Table 4-5 from "Fetal Growth Retardation," by C. Lin, 1993, in C. Lin, M. S. Verp, & R.E. Sabbagha (Eds.), *The High-Risk Fetus: Pathophysiology, Diagnosis, Management.* New York: Springer Verlag. **141:** Figure 4-9 adapted from "Risk and Resilience in Early Mental Development," by R. S. Wilson, 1985, *Developmental Psychology, 21,* pp.795–805. Copyright © 1985 by the American Psychological Association. **145:** Data for Table 4-7 from "The Causes, Controls, and Organization of Behavior in the Neonate," by P. H. Wolff, 1966, *Psychological Issues, 5* (1, Whole No. 17).

Chapter 5

153: Figure 5-1 based on a figure in *Archives of the Diseases in Childhood, 41,* by J. M. Tanner, R. H. Whithouse, & A. Takaishi, 1966, pp. 454–471. **155:** Figure 5-4 from *Growth at Adolescence,* 2nd ed., by J. M. Tanner, 1962. Oxford, England: Blackwell. Copyright © 1962 by Blackwell Scientific Publications, Inc. Reprinted by permission of Blackwell Science Ltd. **167:** Figure 5-7 from *Science and Medicine of Exercise and Sport,* 2nd ed., by Warren K. Johnson and Elsworth R. Buskirk, 1974. Copyright © 1974 by Warren K. Johnson and Ellsworth R. Buskirk. Reprinted by permission of Addison Wesley Educational Publishers, Inc. **169:** Figure 5-8 reprinted by permission of the publishers from *Foetus into Man: Physical Growth from Conception to Maturity,* 2nd ed., by J. M. Tanner, 1978. Cambridge, Mass.: Harvard University Press. Copyright © 1978, 1990 by J. M. Tanner. **183:** Figure 5-11 reprinted by permission of the publishers from *Foetus into Man: Physical Growth from Conception to Maturity,* 2nd ed., by J. M. Tanner, 1990. Cambridge, Mass.: Harvard University Press. Copyright © 1978, 1990 by J. M. Tanner. **185:** Figure 5-12 adapted from "Long-Term Effects of Family-Based Treatment of Childhood Obesity," by by L. H. Epstein, R. R. Wing, R. Koeske, & A. Valoski, 1987, *Journal of Consulting and Clinical Psychology, 55,* pp. 91–95. Copyright © 1987 by the American Psychological Association.

Chapter 6

191: Figure 6-1 adapted from "'Perceptual Set' in Young Children," by H. W. Reese, 1963, *Child Development, 34,* pp.151–159. **199:** Figure 6-3 adapted from "The Origin of Form Perception," by R. L. Fantz, May 1961, *Scientific American, 204,* p.72 (top). Copyright © 1961 by Scientific American, Inc. Adapted by permission of the artist, Alex Semenoick. **199:** Figure 6-4 adapted from "Infant Visual Perception," by M. S. Banks, in collaboration with P. Salapatek, 1983, in *Handbook of Child Psychology, Vol. 2: Infancy and Developmental Psychobiology,* by M. M. Haith & J. J. Campos (Eds.). Copyright © 1983 by John Wiley & Sons. Adapted by permission of John Wiley & Sons, Inc. **200:** Figure 6-5 adapted from "Pattern Perception in Infancy," by P. Salapatek, 1975, in *Infant Perception: From Sensation to Cognition,* by L. B. Cohen & P. Salapatek (Eds.). Copyright © 1975 by Academic Press, Inc. Adapted by permission. **200:** Figure 6-6 adapted from "Perception of Partly Occluded Objects in Infancy," by P. J. Kellman & E. S. Spelke, 1983, *Cognitive Psychology, 15,* 483–524. Copyright © 1983 by Academic Press, Inc. Adapted by permission. **201:** Figure 6-7 adapted from "Development of Visual Organization: The Perception of Subjective Contours," by B. I. Bertenthal, J. J. Campos, & M. M. Haith, 1980, *Child Development, 51,* pp. 1077–1080. Copyright © 1980 by The Society for Research in Child Development, Inc. Adapted by permission. **201:** Figure 6-8 from "Infant Sensitivity to Figural Coherence in Biomechanical Motions," by B. I. Bertenthal, D. R. Proffitt, & J. E. Cutting, 1984, *Journal of Experimental Child Psychology, 37,* pp. 213–230. Copyright © 1984 by Academic Press, Inc. **204:** Figure 6-9 adapted with permission from "Development of Sensitivity to Pictorial Depth," by A. Yonas, W. Cleaves, & L. Pettersen, 1978, *Science, 200,* pp. 77–79. Copyright © 1978 by the American Association for the Advancement of Science. **204:** Figure 6-10 from "Infants' Perceptions of Pictorially Specified Interposition," by C. E. Granrud & A. Yonas, 1984, *Journal of Experimental Child Psychology, 377,* pp. 500–511. Copyright © 1984 by Academic Press, Inc. Reprinted by permission. **205:** Figure 6-12 adapted from "Locomotor Status and the Development of Spatial Search Skills," by D. L. Bai & B. I. Bertenthal, 1992, *Child Development, 63,* pp. 215–226. Copyright © 1992 by The Society for Research in Child Development, Inc. **210:** Figure 6-14 Figure 6-14 adapted from "A Developmental Study of the Discrimination of Letter-Like Forms," by E. J. Gibson, J. J. Gibson, A. D. Pick, & H. A. Osser, 1962, *Journal of Comparative and Physiological Psychology, 55,* pp.897–906.

Chapter 7

238: Figure in Box 7-1 based on "Object Permanence in 3½- and 4½-month-old Infants," by R. Baillargeon, 1987, *Developmental Psychology, 23,* pp. 655–664. Copyright © 1987 by the American Psychological Association. Adapted by permission. **240:** Figure 7-2 from "Retrieval of Basic-Level Category in Prelinguistic Infants," by K. Roberts, 1988, *Developmental Psychology, 24,* p. 23. Copyright © 1988 by the American Psychological Association. Reprinted by permission. **241:** Figure 7-3 from "Rapid Change in the Symbolic Functioning of Very Young Children," by J. S. DeLoache, 1987, *Science, 238,* pp. 1556–1557. Copyright © 1987 by the American Association for the Advancement of Science. Reprinted by permission. **256:** Figure 7-8 adapted from "Individual Differences in College Students' Performance on Formal Operations Tasks," by R. De Lisi & J. Staudt, 1980, *Journal of Applied Developmental Psychology, 1,* pp. 163–174. Reprinted with the permission of Ablex Publishing Company. **263:** Examples of guided participation in Box 7-5 from "Guided Participation in Cultural Activity by Toddlers and Caregivers," by B. Rogoff, J. Minstry, A. Goncu, & C. Mosier, 1993, *Monographs of the Society for Research in Child Development, 58* (8, Serial No. 236). Copyright 1993 by The Society for Research in Child Development, Inc. Reprinted by permission.

Chapter 8

273: Figure 8-1 adapted from "Human Memory: A Proposed System and Its Control Processes," by R. C. Atkinson & R. M. Shiffrin, 1968, in K. W. Spence & J. T. Spence (Eds.), *The Psychology of Learning and Motivation: Advances in Research and Theory* (Vol. 2). Copyright © 1968 by Academic Press, Inc. Adapted by permission. **278:** Figure 8-2 adapted from "Memory Span: Sources of Individual and Developmental Differences," by F. N. Dempster, 1981, *Psychological Bulletin, 89,* pp. 63–100. Copyright © 1981 by the American Psychological Association. **278:** Figure 8-3 from "Knowledge Structures and Memory Development," by M. H. T. Chi, 1978, in R. S. Siegler (Ed.), *Children's Thinking: What Develops?* Copyright © 1978 by Lawrence Erlbaum Associates, Inc. Reprinted by permission. **280:** Figure 8-4 adapted from *Intellectual Development: Birth to Adulthood,* by R. Case, 1985. Copyright ©1985 by Academic Press, Inc. **285:** Figure 8-6 based on "The Development of Scanning Strategies and Their Relation to Visual Differentiation," by E. Vurpillot, 1968, *Journal of Experimental Child Psychology, 6,* pp. 632–650. **292:** Figure 8-8 from "Utilization of Retrieval Cues by Children in Recall," by A. Kobasigawa, 1974, *Child Development, 45,* pp. 127–134. Copyright 1974 by the Society for Research in Child Development, Inc. Reprinted by permission. **294:** Figure 8-9 adapted from data presented in "Domain-Specific Knowledge and Memory Performance: A Comparison of High- and Low-Aptitude Children," by W. Schneider, J. Korkel, & F. E. Weinert, 1989, *Journal of Educational Psychology, 81,* pp. 306–312. **297:** Figure in Box 8-3 from "Childhood Amnesia and the Beginnings of Memory for Four Early Life Events," by J. A. Usher & U. Neisser, 1993, *Journal of Experimental Psychology: General, 122,* p. 155–165. Copyright © 1993 by the American Psychological Association. Reprinted by permission. **306:** Figure 8-10 from "Contents of Achievement: A Study of American, Chinese, and Japanese Children," by H. W. Stevenson & S. Y. Lee, *Monographs of the Society for Research in Child Development, 55* (1–2, Serial No. 221). Copyright © 1990 by the Society for Research in Child Development, Inc. Reprinted by permission.

Chapter 9

316: Figure 9-2 adapted from a table in *The Nature of Human Intelligence,* by J. P. Guilford, 1967. Copyright © 1967 by McGraw-Hill, Inc. Adapted by permission. **317:** Figure 9-3 from *Human Cognitive Abilities: A Survey of Factor-Analytic Studies,* by J. B. Carroll, 1993. Copyright 1993 by Cambridge University Press. Reprinted by permission. **320:** Table 9-1 adapted from *Frames of Mind: The Theory of Multiple Intelligences,* by Howard Gardner, 1983. Copyright © 1983 by Howard Gardner. Reprinted by permission of BasicBooks, a division of Perseus Books Group, LLC. **323:** Figure 9-5 adapted from *Assessment of Children,* 3rd rev. ed., by J. M. Sattler, 1992, p.17. Copyright © 1992 by J. M. Sattler. Adapted by permission. **326:** Table 9-3 adapted from "The Stability of Mental Test Performance Between Two and Eighteen Years," by M. P. Honzik, J. W. MacFarlane, & L. Allen, 1948, *Journal of Experimental Education, 17,* pp. 309–324. **328:** Figure 9-6 from "Toward Meritocracy? Changing Social-Class Differences in Intellectual Ability," by D. Weakliem, J. McQuillan, & T. Schauer, 1995, *Sociology of Education, 68,* pp. 271–286 (Fig. 1, p. 276). Reprinted by permission. **330:** Table in Box 9-1 adapted from *Lives of the Mentally Retarded: A Forty-Year Follow-up,* by R. T. Ross, M. J. Begab, E. H. Dondis, J. S. Giampiccolo, Jr., & C. E. Meyers. Copyright © 1985 by Stanford University Press. Adapted by permission. **333:** Data and descriptions for Table 9-4 compiled from "Stability of Intelligence from Preschool to Adolescence: The Influence of Social and Family Risk Factors," by A. J. Sameroff, R. Seifer, A. Baldwin, & C. Baldwin, 1993, *Child Development, 64,* pp. 80–97. **334:** Table 9-5 adapted from the *Manual for the HOME Observation for Measurement of the Environment,* by B. M. Caldwell & R. H. Bradley, 1984, University of Arkansas. Copyright © 1984. Adapted by permission. **335:** Figure 9-7 adapted from "Birth Order and Intellectual Development," by R. B. Zajonc & G. B. Markus, 1975, *Psychological Review, 82,* pp.74–88. Copyright © 1975 by the American Psychological Association. Reprinted by permission. **338:** Figure 9-10 from "Stereotype Threat and the Intellectual Test Performance of African Americans," by C. M. Steele & J. Aronson, 1995, *Journal of Personality and Social Psychology, 69,* pp. 797–811 (Fig. 2, p. 802). Copyright © 1995 by the American Psychological Association. Adapted by permission.
339: Figure in Box 9-2 adapted from *Psychology,* 3rd ed., by Henry Gleitman, p. 699. Copyright © 1991, 1986, 1981 by W. W. Norton & Company, Inc. Reprinted by permission of W. W. Norton & Company, Inc. **345:** Figure 9-11 from *"Effects of Early Intervention on Intellectual and Academic Achievement,"* by F. A. Campbell & C. T. Ramey, 1994, *Child Development, 65,* pp. 684–698. Copyright © 1994 by the Society for Research in Child Development, Inc. Adapted by permission of the author. **346:** Figure 9-12 adapted from *Modes of Thinking in Young Children,* by Michael A. Wallach & Nathan Kogan. Copyright © 1965 by Holt, Rinehart and Winston, Inc. and renewed 1993 by Michael A. Wallach & Nathan Kogan. Adapted by permission of the publisher.

Chapter 10

357: Figure 10-2 adapted from "Critical Period Effects in Second Language Learning: The Influence of Maturational State on the Acquisition of English as a Second Language," by J. S. Johnson & E. L. Newport, 1989, *Cognitive Psychology, 21,* pp. 60–99. Copyright © 1989 by Academic Press, Inc. Adapted by permission. **368:** Table 10-1 adapted from "Structure and Strategy in Learning to Talk," by K. Nelson, 1973, *Monographs of the Society for Research in Child Development, 38,* (Whole No. 149). Copyright © 1973 by The Society for Research in Child Development, Inc. Adapted by permission. **373:** Table 10-3 adapted from *Psycholinguistics,* 2nd ed., by Dan Isaac Slobin, 1979, pp. 86–87. Copyright © 1979, 1974, 1971 by Scott, Foresman and Company. Adapted by permission of Addison Wesley Educational Publishers Inc. **374:** Data in Table 10-4 reprinted by permission of the publishers from *A First Language: The Early Stages,* by Roger Brown, Cambridge, Mass.: Harvard University Press. Copyright © 1973 by the President and Fellows of Harvard College. **375:** Figure in Box 10-3 from *Talk to the Deaf,* by Lottie Reikehof, 1963. Springfield, MO: Gospel Publishing House. Reprinted by permission. **377:** Table 10-5 adapted from *The Acquisition of Language: The Study of Developmental Psycholinguistics,* by D. McNeill, 1970. Harper & Row Publishers. Copyright © 1970 by HarperCollins, Inc. **378:** Table 10-6 adapted from *Psychology and Language: An Introduction to Psycholinguistics,* by H. H. Clark & E. V. Clark, p. 345. Copyright © 1977 by Harcourt Brace & Company; reproduced by permission of the publisher. **378:** Figure 10-4 from "The Child's Learning of English Morphology," by J. Berko, 1958, *Word, 14,* pp. 150-177.
384: Table 10-7 adapted from "Social and Non-Social Speech," by R. M. Krauss & S. Glucksberg, *Scientific American,* February 1977, 236, p. 104. Copyright © 1977 by Scientific American, Inc. Adapted by permission of the artist, Jerome Kuhl.

Chapter 11

396: Figure 11-2 adapted from "An Observational Study of Children's Attempts to Monitor Their Expressive Behavior," by C. Saarni, 1984, *Child Development, 55,* 1504–1513. Copyright © 1984 by The Society for Research in Child Development, Inc. Adapted by permission.
408: Figure 11-4 adapted from "The Innate Forms of Possible Experience," by K. Z. Lorenz, 1943, *Zeitschrift fur Tierpsychologie, 5,* pp. 233–409. **413:** Table 11-2 based on *Patterns of Attachment,* by M. D. S. Ainsworth, M. Blehar, E. Waters, & S. Wall, 1978. Copyright © 1978 by Lawrence Erlbaum Associates, Inc. **415:** Table 11-3 based on "Sensitivity and Attachment: A Meta-Analysis on Parental Antecedents of Infant Attachment," by M. S. De Wolff & M. H. van IJzendoorn, 1997, *Child Development, 68,* pp. 571–591. **419:** Table in Box 11-3 adapted from "The Quality of the Toddler's Relationship to Mother and to Father: Related to Conflict and the Readiness to Establish New Relationships," by M. Main & D. R. Weston, 1981, *Child Development, 52,* pp. 932–940. Copyright © 1981 by the Society for Research in Child Development, Inc.
420: Figure 11-5 based on "The Relative Effects of Maternal and Child Problems on the Quality of Attachment: A Meta-Analysis of Attachment in Clinical Samples," by M. H. van IJzendoorn, S. Goldberg, P. M. Kroonenberg, & O. J. Frenkel, 1992, *Child Development, 63,* pp. 840–858. Copyright © 1992 by the Society for Research in Child Development, Inc. **422:** Figure 11-6 adapted from "Attachment Styles among Young Adults: A Test of a Four-Category Model," by K. Bartholomew & L. M. Horowitz, 1991, *Journal of Personality and Social Psychology, 61,* pp. 226–244. Copyright © 1991 by the American Psychological Association. Adapted by permission.

Chapter 12

436 : Figure 12-1 based on "The Relation between Attachment and Knowledge of Self and Mother in One- to Three-Year-Old Infants," by S. Pipp, M. A. Easterbrooks, & R. J. Harmon, 1992, *Child Development, 63,* pp. 738–750. Copyright © 1992 by the Society for Research in Child Development, Inc. **441:** Figure 12-2 adapted from "Developmental Analysis of Conflict Caused by Opposing Attributes in the Adolescent Self-Portrait," by S. Harter & A. Monsour, 1992, *Developmental Psychology, 28,* pp. 251–260. Copyright © 1992 by the American Psychological Association. Adapted by permission. **444:** Data for figure in Box 12-1 from National Center for Health Statistics, reported in U. S. Bureau of the Census (1996), *Statistical Abstract of the United States,* 1996 (116th ed.). Washington, DC.: U. S. Government Printing Office. **446:** Figure 12-3 adapted from "The Emergence and Consolidation of Self-Control from Eighteen to Thirty Months of Age: Normative Trends and Individual Differences" by B. E. Vaughn, C. B. Kopp, & J. B. Krakow, 1984, *Child Development, 55,* pp. 990–1004. Copyright © 1984 by the Society for Research in Child Development, Inc. Adapted by permission. **452:** Table 12-1 adapted from "The Relationship Between Twelve-Month Home Stimulation and School Achievement," by W. J. van Doorninck, B. M. Caldwell, C. Wright, & W. K. Frankenberg, 1981, *Child Development, 52,* pp. 1080–1083. Copyright © 1981 by The Society for Research in Child Development, Inc. Adapted by permission. **459:** Figure 12-6 from "Cross-Sectional Age Changes in Ego Identity Status During Adolescence," by P. W. Meilman, 1979, *Developmental Psychology,* 15, pp. 230-231. Copyright © 1979 by the American Psychological Association. Reprinted by permission.
464: Figure 12-7 from "The Development of Person Perception in Childhood and Adolescence: From Behavioral Comparisons to Psychological Constructs to Psychological Comparisons," by C. Barenboim, 1981, *Child Development, 52,*

pp. 129–144. Copyright © 1981 by the Society for Research in Child Development, Inc. Reprinted by permission. **466:** Table 12-3 adapted from "Social Cognitive Understanding: A Guide to Educational and Clinical Experience," by R. L. Selman, 1976, in T. Lickona (Ed.), *Moral Development and Behavior: Theory, Research, and Social Issues*. Copyright © 1976 by Holt, Rinehart & Winston. Adapted by permission of the editor.

Chapter 13

474: Table 13-1 adapted from "A Cross-Cultural Survey of Some Sex Differences in Socialization," by H. Barry III, M. K. Bacon, & I. L. Child, 1957, *Journal of Abnormal and Social Psychology, 55*, pp. 327–332. **475:** List in Box 13-1 based on "Sex Stereotypes: Issues of Change in the 1970s," by T. L. Ruble, 1983, *Sex Roles, 9*, pp. 397–402. Copyright © 1983 by Plenum Publishing Company. Adapted by permission. **476:** Figure 13-1 from "Emergence and Characteristics of Sex Differences in Spatial Ability: A Meta-Analysis," by M. C. Linn & A. C. Petersen, 1985, *Child Development, 56*, pp. 1479–1498. Copyright © 1985 by the Society for Research in Child Development, Inc. Reprinted by permission. **477:** Figure 13-2 adapted from "Gender Differences in Mathematics Performance: A Meta-Analysis," by J. S. Hyde, E. Fennema, & S. J. Lamon, 1990, *Psychological Bulletin, 107*, pp. 139–155. Copyright © 1990 by the American Psychological Association. Adapted by permission. **479:** Table 13-2 adapted from *The Psychology of Sex Differences*, by E. E. Maccoby & C. N. Jacklin. Copyright © 1974 by Stanford University Press. Reprinted by permission of the Board of Trustees for the Leland Stanford Junior University. **484:** Figure 13-3 adapted from "Children's Concepts of Cross-Gender Activities," by T. Stoddart & E. Turiel, 1985, *Child Development, 59*, pp. 793–814. Copyright © 1985 by the Society for Research in Child Development, Inc. Adapted by permission. **486:** Figure 13-4 adapted from "Social Behavior at 33 Months in Same-Sex and Mixed-Sex Dyads," by C. N. Jacklin & E. E. Maccoby, 1978, Child Development, 49, pp. 557–569. Copyright © 1978 by the Society for Research in Child Development, Inc. Adapted by permission. **486:** Table 13-3 adapted from "Children, Gender and Social Structure: An Analysis of the Contents of Letters to Santa Claus," by J. G. Richardson & C. H. Simpson, 1982, *Child Development, 53*, 429–436. Copyright © 1982 by The Society for Research in Child Development, Inc. Adapted by permission. **490:** Figure 13-5 from *Man and Woman, Boy and Girl*, by J. Money & A. Ehrhardt, 1972. Copyright © 1972 by John Hopkins University Press. Reprinted by permission. **499:** Figure 13-6 adapted from "The Roles of Cognition in Sex Roles and Sex-Typing," 1987, in D. B. Carter (Ed.), *Current Conceptions of Sex Roles and Sex-Typing: Theory and Research*. Copyright ©1987 by Praeger Publishers. **502:** Table 13-6 adapted from "Assessing Sex-Typing and Androgyny in Children: The Children's Sex-Role Inventory," by J. P. Boldizar, 1991, *Developmental Psychology, 27*, pp. 505–515. Copyright © 1991 by the American Psychological Association.

Chapter 14

512: Figure in Box 14-1 adapted from "Relational Aggression, Gender, and Social-Psychological Adjustment," by N. A. Crick & J. K. Grotpeter, 1995, *Child Development, 66*, pp. 710–722. Copyright © 1995 by the Society for Research in Child Development, Inc.
513: Figure 14-1 from "Stability of Aggression over Time and Generations," by L. R. Huesmann, L. D. Eron, M. M. Lefkowitz, & L. O. Walder, 1984, *Developmental Psychology, 20*, p.1125. Copyright © 1984 by the American Psychological Association. Reprinted by permission. **514:** Figure 14-2 adapted from "A Review and Reformulation of Social Information Processing Mechanisms in Children's Social Adjustment," by N. R. Crick & K. A. Dodge, *Psychological Bulletin, 115*, pp. 74–101. Copyright © 1994 by the American Psychological Association. Adapted by permission. **520:** Figure 14-4 adapted from "A Developmental Perspective on Antisocial Behavior," by G. R. Patterson, B. D. DeBaryshe, & E. Ramsey, 1989, *American Psychologist, 44*, pp. 329–335. Copyright © 1989 by the American Psychological Association. Adapted by permission. **525:** Table 14-1 adapted from "Prosocial Development: A Longitudinal Study," by N. Eisenberg, R. Lennon, & K. Roth, 1983, *Developmental Psychology, 19*, pp. 846–855. Copyright © 1983 by the American Psychological Association. Adapted by permission. **528:** Table 14-2 based on data from *Children of Six Cultures*, by B. B. Whiting & J. W. M. Whiting. Cambridge, Mass: Harvard University Press. Copyright © 1975 by the President and Fellows of Harvard College. **535:** Figure 14-6 adapted from "Factors Influencing Young Children's Use of Motives and Outcomes as Moral Criteria," by S. A. Nelson, 1980, *Child Development, 51*, pp. 823–829. Copyright © 1980 by the Society for Research in Child Development, Inc. Adapted by permission.
536: Figure 14-7 adapted from "Factors Influencing Young Children's Use of Motives and Outcomes as Moral Criteria," by S. A. Nelson, 1980, *Child Development, 51*, pp. 823–829. Copyright © 1980 by the Society for Research in Child Development, Inc. Adapted by permission.
541: Figure 14-8 adapted from "A Longitudinal Study of Moral Judgment," by A. Colby, L. Kohlberg, J. Gibbs, & M. Lieberman, 1983, *Monographs of The Society for Research in Child Development, 48* (Nos. 1–2, Serial No. 200). Copyright © 1983 by the Society for Research in Child Development, Inc. Adapted by permission.
545: Figure in Box 14-3 adapted from "Culture and Moral Development," by R. Shweder, M. Mahapatra, & J. G. Miller, 1987, in J. Kagan & S. Lamb (Eds.), *The Emergence of Morality in Young Children*. Copyright © 1987 University of Chicago Press. Adapted by permission.
551: Table 14-3 adapted from "Contributions of Parents and Peers to Children's Moral Socialization," by G. H. Brody & D. R. Shaffer, 1982, *Developmental Review, 2*, pp. 31–75. Copyright © Academic Press, Inc. Adapted by permission.

Chapter 15

560: Figure 15-1 from "Early Human Experience: A Family Perspective," by J. Belsky, 1981, *Developmental Psychology, 17*, pp. 3–23. Copyright © 1981 by the American Psychological Association. Reprinted by permission. **562:** Figure 15-2 based on census data from "Never Marrieds Soar Among Single Parents," by C. Teegartin, 1994, *Atlanta Constitution*, July 25, pp. A1, A7.
565: Figure 15-3 based on data from "Socialization in the Context of the Family: Parent–Child Interaction," by E. E. Maccoby & J. A. Martin, 1983, in E. M. Hetherington (Ed.; P. H. Mussen, General Ed.), *Handbook of Child Psychology, Vol. 4: Socialization, Personality, and Social Development*, 4th ed. New York: John Wiley and Sons.
569: Figure 15-4 adapted from "A Family Process Model of Economic Hardship and Adjustment of Early Adolescent Boys," by R. D. Conger, K. J. Conger, G. H. Elder, Jr., F. O. Lorenz, R. L. Simons, & L. B. Whitbeck, 1992, *Child Development, 63*, pp. 526–541. Copyright © 1992 by the Society for research in Child Development, Inc.
573: Figure in Box 15-1 adapted from "The Effects of Work Intensity on Adolescent Mental Health, Achievement, and Behavioral Adjustment: New Evidence from a Prospective Study," by J. T. Mortimer, M. D. Finch, S. Ryu, M. J. Shanahan, & K. T. Call, 1996, *Child Development, 67*, pp. 1243–1261. Copyright © 1996 by the Society for Research in Child Developmen, Inc. Adapted by permission. **583:** Figure 15-6 from "Relation of Parental Transitions to Boys' Adjustment Problems: I. A Linear Hypothesis. II. Mothers at Risk for Transition and Unskilled Parenting," by D. M. Capaldi & G. R. Patterson, 1991, *Developmental Psychology, 27*, pp.489–504. Copyright © 1991 by the American Psychological Association. Reprinted by permission. **591:** Figure 15-7 adapted from "Responses of Abused and Disadvantaged Toddlers to Distress in Agemates: A Study in the Day-Care Setting," by M. Main & C. George, 1985, *Developmental Psychology, 21*, pp. 407–412. Copyright © 1985 by the American Psychological Association. Adapted by permission.

Chapter 16

598: Figure 16-1 from *The Early Window: Effects of Television on Children and Youth*, 3rd ed., by R. M. Liebert & J. Sprafkin, 1988. Copyright © 1988. Reprinted by permission of Allyn & Bacon. **600:** Figure 16-2 adapted from "Psychological Processes Promoting the Relation Between Exposure to Media Violence and Aggressive Behavior by the Viewer," by L. R. Huesmann, 1986, *Journal of Social Issues, 42*, No. 3, pp. 125–139. Copyright © 1986 by the Journal of Social Issues. Adapted by permission. **603:** Figure 16-3 from *The Early Window: Effects of Television on Children and Youth*, 3rd ed., by R. M. Liebert & J. Sprafkin, 1988. Copyright © 1988. Reprinted by permission of Allyn & Bacon. **609:** Figure 16-4 reprinted by permission of the publisher from *Fifteen Thousand Hours: Secondary Schools and Their Effects on Children*, by Michael Rutter, Barbara Maughan, Peter Mortimore, & Janet Ouston, Cambridge, Mass.: Harvard University Press. Copyright © 1979 by Michael Rutter, Barbara Maughan, Peter Mortimore, and Janet Ouston.
610: Figure 16-5 from "Do Extracurricular Activities Protect Against Early School Dropout?" by J. L. Mahoney & R. B. Cairns, 1997, *Developmental Psychology, 33*, pp. 241–252. Copyright © 1997 by the American Psychological Association. Reprinted by permission. **612:** Figure 16-6 adapted from *Rousing Minds to Life: Teaching, Learning, and Schooling in Social Context*, by R. G. Tharp & R. Gallimore, 1988, p. 116. Cambridge, England: Cambridge University Press. Adapted with the permission of Cambridge University Press. **619:** Figure 16-7 adapted from "Motivation and Mathematics Achievement: A Comparative Study of Asian-American, Caucasian-American, and East Asian high school students," by C. Chen & H. W. Stevenson, 1995, *Child Development, 66*, pp. 1215–1234. Copyright © 1995 by the Society for Research in Child Development, Inc. Adapted by permission.
620: This letter appears with the permission of its author and its recipient, Dr. Shirley G. Moore.
622: Figure 16-8 adapted from "Age Segregation in Children's Social Interactions," by S. Ellis, B. Rogoff, & C. C. Cromer, 1981. *Developmental Psychology, 17*, pp. 399–407. Copyright © 1981 by the American Psychological Association. Adapted by permission. **625:** Figure 16-9 adapted from "Social Participation among Preschool Children," by M. Parten, 1932, *Journal of Abnormal and Social Psychology, 27*, pp. 243–269.
626: Table 16-2 adapted from "Sequences in the Development of Competent Play with Peers: Social and Social Pretend Play," by C. Howes & C. C. Matheson, 1992, *Developmental Psychology, 28*, pp. 961–974. Copyright © 1992 the American Psychological Association. Adapted by permission. **628:** Figure 16-10 based on "Parents's Management for Preschoolers' Peer Relations: Is It Related to Children's Social Competence?" by G. W. Ladd & B. S. Golter, 1988, *Developmental Psychology, 24*, pp. 109–117. Copyright © 1988 by the American Psychological Association.
637: Figure 16-11 adapted from "Developmental Changes in Conformity to Peers and Parents," by T. J. Berndt, 1979, *Developmental Psychology, 15*, pp. 608–616. Copyright © 1979 by the American Psychological Association. Adapted by permission.

TO THE OWNER OF THIS BOOK:

I hope that you have found *Developmental Psychology: Childhood and Adolescence*, Fifth Edition, useful. So that this book can be improved in a future edition, would you take the time to complete this sheet and return it? Thank you.

School and address: ____

Department: ____

Instructor's name: ____

1. What I like most about this book is: ____

____

____

2. What I like least about this book is: ____

____

____

3. My general reaction to this book is: ____

____

4. The name of the course in which I used this book is: ______________________________

____

5. Were all of the chapters of the book assigned for you to read? ____________________

If not, which ones weren't? ____

6. In the space below, or on a separate sheet of paper, please write specific suggestions for improving this book and anything else you'd care to share about your experience in using the book.

____

____

____

____

____

____

Optional:

Your name: ______________________________ Date: ______________________________

May Brooks/Cole quote you, either in promotion for *Developmental Psychology: Childhood and Adolescence,* Fifth Edition, or in future publishing ventures?

Yes: __________ No: _________

Sincerely,

David R. Shaffer

FOLD HERE

NO POSTAGE NECESSARY IF MAILED IN THE UNITED STATES

BUSINESS REPLY MAIL

FIRST CLASS PERMIT NO. 358 PACIFIC GROVE, CA

POSTAGE WILL BE PAID BY ADDRESSEE

ATT: *David R. Shaffer*

Brooks/Cole Publishing Company
511 Forest Lodge Road
Pacific Grove, California 93950-5098

FOLD HERE